Contemporary Authors ®

NEW REVISION SERIES

ISSN 0275-7176

Contemporary Authors®

**A Bio-Bibliographical Guide to
Current Writers in Fiction, General Nonfiction,
Poetry, Journalism, Drama, Motion Pictures,
Television, and Other Fields**

NEW REVISION SERIES
volume 200

GALE
CENGAGE Learning

Detroit • New York • San Francisco • New Haven, Conn • Waterville, Maine • London

Contemporary Authors, New Revision Series, Vol. 200

Project Editor: Amy Elisabeth Fuller

Editorial: Mary Ruby

Composition and Electronic Capture: Gary Oudersluys

Manufacturing: Drew Kalasky

For product information and technology assistance, contact us at **Gale Customer Support, 1-800-877 4253.** For permission to use material from this text or product, submit all requests online at **www.cengage.com/permissions.** Further permissions questions can be emailed to **permissionrequest@cengage.com**

While every effort has been made to ensure the reliability of the information presented in this publication, Gale, a part of Cengage Learning, does not guarantee the accuracy of the data contained herein. Gale accepts no payment for listing; and inclusion in the publication of any organization, agency, institution, publication, service, or individual does not imply endorsement of the editors or publisher. Errors brought to the attention of the publisher and verified to the satisfaction of the publisher will be corrected in future editions.

EDITORIAL DATA PRIVACY POLICY. Does this publication contain information about you as an individual? If so, for more information about our editorial data privacy policies, please see our Privacy Statement at www.gale.cengage.com.

Gale
27500 Drake Rd.
Farmington Hills, MI, 48331-3535

LIBRARY OF CONGRESS CATALOG CARD NUMBER 81-640179

ISBN-13: 978-1-4144-4595-3
ISBN-10: 1-4144-4595-4

ISSN 0275-7176

This title is also available as an e-book.
ISBN-13: 978-1-4144-5681-2
ISBN-10: 1-4144-5681-6
Contact your Gale sales representative for ordering information.

Printed in the United States of America
1 2 3 4 5 6 7 14 13 12 11 10

Contents

Contents

Contents

Preface

Contemporary Authors (*CA*) provides information on approximately 135,000 writers in a wide range of media, including:

- Current writers of fiction, nonfiction, poetry, and drama whose works have been issued by commercial publishers, risk publishers, or university presses (authors whose books have been published only by known vanity or author-subsidized firms are ordinarily not included)

- Prominent print and broadcast journalists, editors, photojournalists, syndicated cartoonists, graphic novelists, screenwriters, television scriptwriters, and other media people

- Notable international authors

- Literary greats of the early twentieth century whose works are popular in today's high school and college curriculums and continue to elicit critical attention

A *CA* listing entails no charge or obligation. Authors are included on the basis of the above criteria and their interest to *CA* users. Sources of potential listees include trade periodicals, publishers' catalogs, librarians, and other users.

How to Get the Most out of *CA*: Use the Index

The key to locating an author's most recent entry is the *CA* cumulative index, which is published separately and distributed twice a year. It provides access to *all* entries in *CA* and *Contemporary Authors New Revision Series* (*CANR*). Always consult the latest index to find an author's most recent entry.

For the convenience of users, the *CA* cumulative index also includes references to all entries in these Gale Group literary series: *African-American Writers, African Writers, American Nature Writers, American Writers, American Writers: The Classics, American Writers Retrospective Supplement, American Writers Supplement, Ancient Writers, Asian American Literature, Authors and Artists for Young Adults, Authors in the News, Beacham's Encyclopedia of Popular Fiction: Analyses, Beacham's Encyclopedia of Popular Fiction: Biography and Resources, Beacham's Guide to Literature for Young Adults, Beat Generation: A Gale Critical Companion, Bestsellers, Black Literature Criticism, Black Literature Criticism Supplement, Black Writers, British Writers, British Writers: The Classics, British Writers Retrospective Supplement, British Writers Supplement, Children's Literature Review, Classical and Medieval Literature Criticism, Concise Dictionary of American Literary Biography, Concise Dictionary of American Literary Biography Supplement, Concise Dictionary of British Literary Biography, Concise Dictionary of World Literary Biography, Contemporary American Dramatists, Contemporary Authors Autobiography Series, Contemporary Authors Bibliographical Series, Contemporary British Dramatists, Contemporary Canadian Authors, Contemporary Dramatists, Contemporary Literary Criticism, Contemporary Novelists, Contemporary Poets, Contemporary Popular Writers, Contemporary Southern Writers, Contemporary Women Dramatists, Contemporary Women Poets, Contemporary World Writers, Dictionary of Literary Biography, Dictionary of Literary Biography Documentary Series, Dictionary of Literary Biography Yearbook, DISCovering Authors, DISCovering Authors 3.0, DISCovering Authors: British Edition, DISCovering Authors: Canadian Edition, DISCovering Authors Modules, Drama Criticism, Drama for Students, Encyclopedia of World Literature in the 20th Century, Epics for Students, European Writers, Exploring Novels, Exploring Poetry, Exploring Short Stories, Feminism in Literature, Feminist Writers, Gay & Lesbian Literature, Guide to French Literature, Harlem Renaissance: A Gale Critical Companion, Hispanic Literature Criticism, Hispanic Literature Criticism Supplement, Hispanic Writers, International Dictionary of Films and Filmmakers: Writers and Production Artists, International Dictionary of Theatre: Playwrights, Junior DISCovering Authors, Latin American Writers, Latin American Writers Supplement, Latino and Latina Writers, Literature and Its Times, Literature and Its Times Supplement, Literature Criticism from 1400-1820, Literature of Developing Nations for Students, Major Authors and Illustrators for Children and Young Adults, Major Authors and Illustrators for Children and Young Adults Supplement, Major 21st Century Writers* (eBook version), *Major 20th-Century Writers, Modern American Women Writers, Modern Arts Criticism, Modern Japanese Writers, Mystery and Suspense Writers, Native North American Literature, Nineteenth-Century Literature Criticism, Nonfiction Classics for Students, Novels for Students, Poetry Criticism, Poetry for Students, Poets: American and British, Reference Guide to American Literature, Reference Guide to English Literature, Reference Guide to Short Fiction, Reference Guide to World Literature, Science Fiction Writers, Shakespearean Criticism, Shakespeare for Students, Shakespeare's Characters for Students, Short Stories for Students, Short Story Criticism, Something About the Author, Something About the Author Autobiography Series, St. James Guide to Children's Writers, St. James Guide to Crime & Mystery Writers, St. James Guide to Fantasy Writers, St. James Guide to Horror, Ghost & Gothic Writers, St. James Guide to Science Fiction Writers, St. James Guide to Young Adult Writers, Supernatural Fiction*

Writers, Twayne Companion to Contemporary Literature in English, Twayne's English Authors, Twayne's United States Authors, Twayne's World Authors, Twentieth-Century Literary Criticism, Twentieth-Century Romance and Historical Writers, Twentieth-Century Western Writers, William Shakespeare, World Literature and Its Times, World Literature Criticism, World Literature Criticism Supplement, World Poets, World Writing in English, Writers for Children, Writers for Young Adults, and *Yesterday's Authors of Books for Children.*

A Sample Index Entry:

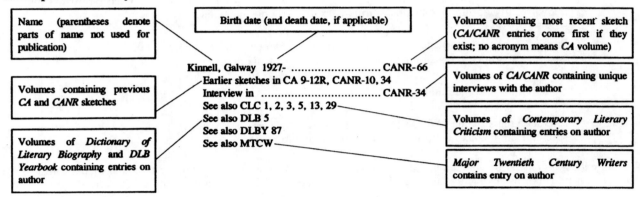

Name (parentheses denote parts of name not used for publication)

Birth date (and death date, if applicable)

Volume containing most recent sketch (*CA/CANR* entries come first if they exist; no acronym means *CA* volume)

Volumes containing previous *CA* and *CANR* sketches

Volumes of *Dictionary of Literary Biography* and *DLB Yearbook* containing entries on author

Kinnell, Galway 1927- CANR-66
Earlier sketches in CA 9-12R, CANR-10, 34
Interview in CANR-34
See also CLC 1, 2, 3, 5, 13, 29
See also DLB 5
See also DLBY 87
See also MTCW

Volumes of *CA/CANR* containing unique interviews with the author

Volumes of *Contemporary Literary Criticism* containing entries on author

Major Twentieth Century Writers contains entry on author

How Are Entries Compiled?

The editors make every effort to secure new information directly from the authors; listees' responses to our questionnaires and query letters provide most of the information featured in *CA*. For deceased writers, or those who fail to reply to requests for data, we consult other reliable biographical sources, such as those indexed in Gale's *Biography and Genealogy Master Index*, and bibliographical sources, including *National Union Catalog, LC MARC*, and *British National Bibliography*. Further details come from published interviews, feature stories, and book reviews, as well as information supplied by the authors' publishers and agents.

An asterisk (*) at the end of a sketch indicates that the listing has been compiled from secondary sources believed to be reliable but has not been personally verified for this edition by the author sketched.

What Kinds of Information Does An Entry Provide?

Sketches in *CA* contain the following biographical and bibliographical information:

- **Entry heading:** the most complete form of author's name, plus any pseudonyms or name variations used for writing

- **Personal information:** author's date and place of birth, family data, ethnicity, educational background, political and religious affiliations, and hobbies and leisure interests

- **Addresses:** author's home, office, or agent's addresses, plus e-mail and fax numbers, as available

- **Career summary:** name of employer, position, and dates held for each career post; resume of other vocational achievements; military service

- **Membership information:** professional, civic, and other association memberships and any official posts held

- **Awards and honors:** military and civic citations, major prizes and nominations, fellowships, grants, and honorary degrees

- **Writings:** a comprehensive, chronological list of titles, publishers, dates of original publication and revised editions, and production information for plays, television scripts, and screenplays

- **Adaptations:** a list of films, plays, and other media which have been adapted from the author's work

- **Sidelights:** a biographical portrait of the author's development; information about the critical reception of the author's works; revealing comments, often by the author, on personal interests, aspirations, motivations, and thoughts on writing

- **Interview:** a one-on-one discussion with authors conducted especially for *CA*, offering insight into authors' thoughts about their craft

- **Autobiographical essay:** an original essay written by noted authors for *CA*, a forum in which writers may present themselves, on their own terms, to their audience

- **Photographs:** portraits and personal photographs of notable authors

- **Biographical and critical sources:** a list of books and periodicals in which additional information on an author's life and/or writings appears

- **Obituary Notices** in *CA* provide date and place of birth as well as death information about authors whose full-length sketches appeared in the series before their deaths. The entries also summarize the authors' careers and writings and list other sources of biographical and death information.

Related Titles in the *CA* Series

Contemporary Authors Autobiography Series complements *CA* original and revised volumes with specially commissioned autobiographical essays by important current authors, illustrated with personal photographs they provide. Common topics include their motivations for writing, the people and experiences that shaped their careers, the rewards they derive from their work, and their impressions of the current literary scene.

Contemporary Authors Bibliographical Series surveys writings by and about important American authors since World War II. Each volume concentrates on a specific genre and features approximately ten writers; entries list works written by and about the author and contain a bibliographical essay discussing the merits and deficiencies of major critical and scholarly studies in detail.

Available in Electronic Formats

GaleNet. *CA* is available on a subscription basis through GaleNet, an online information resource that features an easy-to-use end-user interface, powerful search capabilities, and ease of access through the World-Wide Web. For more information, call 1-800-877-GALE.

Licensing. *CA* is available for licensing. The complete database is provided in a fielded format and is deliverable on such media as disk, CD-ROM, or tape. For more information, contact Gale's Business Development Group at 1-800-877-GALE, or visit us on our website at www.gale.com/bizdev.

Suggestions Are Welcome

The editors welcome comments and suggestions from users on any aspect of the *CA* series. If readers would like to recommend authors for inclusion in future volumes of the series, they are cordially invited to write the Editors at *Contemporary Authors*, Gale Cengage Learning, 27500 Drake Rd., Farmington Hills, MI 48331-3535; or call at 1-248-699-4253; or fax at 1-248-699-8054.

Indexing note: All *Contemporary Authors* entries are indexed in the *Contemporary Authors* cumulative index, which is published separately and distributed twice a year.

As always, the most recent Contemporary Authors cumulative index continues to be the user's guide to the location of an individual author's listing.

CA Numbering System and Volume Update Chart

Occasionally questions arise about the *CA* numbering system and which volumes, if any, can be discarded. Despite numbers like "29-32R," "97-100" and "292," the entire *CA* print series consists of 417 physical volumes with the publication of *CA* Volume 292. The following charts note changes in the numbering system and cover design, and indicate which volumes are essential for the most complete, up-to-date coverage.

CA **First Revision**	• 1-4R through 41-44R (11 books) *Cover:* Brown with black and gold trim. There will be no further First Revision volumes because revised entries are now being handled exclusively through the more efficient *New Revision Series* mentioned below.
CA **Original Volumes**	• 45-48 through 97-100 (14 books) *Cover:* Brown with black and gold trim. 101 through 292 (192 books) *Cover:* Blue and black with orange bands. The same as previous *CA* original volumes but with a new, simplified numbering system and new cover design.
CA **Permanent Series**	• *CAP*-1 and *CAP*-2 (2 books) *Cover:* Brown with red and gold trim. There will be no further Permanent Series volumes because revised entries are now being handled exclusively through the more efficient *New Revision Series* mentioned below.
CA **New Revision Series**	• CANR-1 through CANR-200 (200 books) *Cover:* Blue and black with green bands. Includes only sketches requiring significant changes; **sketches are taken from any previously published CA, CAP, or CANR volume.**

If You Have:	You May Discard:
CA First Revision Volumes 1-4R through 41-44R and *CA* Permanent Series Volumes 1 and 2	*CA* Original Volumes 1, 2, 3, 4 and Volumes 5-6 through 41-44
CA Original Volumes 45-48 through 97-100 and 101 through 292	**NONE:** These volumes will not be superseded by corresponding revised volumes. Individual entries from these and all other volumes appearing in the left column of this chart may be revised and included in the various volumes of the *New Revision Series*.
CA New Revision Series Volumes *CANR*-1 through *CANR*-200	**NONE:** The *New Revision Series* does not replace any single volume of *CA*. Instead, volumes of *CANR* include entries from many previous *CA* series volumes. All *New Revision Series* volumes must be retained for full coverage.

A Sampling of Authors and Media People
Featured in This Volume

Maria Arana

Arana's parents met in the 1940s when her father, Jorge Enrique Arana, was studying at the Massachusetts Institute of Technology. Her mother, Marie, was a violinist. After they married, they returned to her father's native country of Peru, where Arana was born and spent her early childhood until the family moved to the United States in 1959. Her father was working as an engineer for the multinational corporation W.R. Grace. Her mother was not welcomed into her husband's culture, and when the couple returned to the United States and settled in Summit, New Jersey, Arana would first feel the sting of those cultural differences. With a father who went back and forth between Peru and the United States and an awareness of the cultural gap between her parents, Arana realized early on that she would have to be adaptable, sometimes filling the role befitting her dark Peruvian features and sometimes the role of an American girl with an American heritage. Arana spent the first several decades of her career as a journalist, editor, and critic judging the writing of others. Her first book was *American Chica: Two Worlds, One Childhood,* a memoir which chronicles such struggles.

Diana Athill

As an editor at the London publishing company of André Deutsch, Athill worked with some of the most notable writers of the twentieth century. Her several volumes of memoirs detail her many relationships with literary figures and offer what critics have found to be a fascinating look behind the scenes of the publishing world. After working for the BBC during World War II, Athill met Hungarian émigré André Deutsch and accepted an editing job in his first publishing house, Allan Wingate. As recounted in *Stet: An Editor's Life,* she began a brief affair with Deutsch and was his partner in founding the company that bore his name. Though Athill admits she had no special qualifications for her job, she went on to work successfully with such major authors as V.S. Naipaul, Jack Kerouac, Molly Keane, Brian Moore, Mordecai Richler, Norman Mailer, Philip Roth, Jean Rhys, Margaret Atwood, and John Updike.

Jennifer Chiaverini

Chiaverini taught herself how to quilt in 1994. Her experiences with quilting led her to write her first novel, which revolves around the world of quilting and spurred the "Elm Creek Quilts" series. Chiaverini's first novel, *The Quilter's Apprentice,* is the story of two women, Sarah and Sylvia, one young and one old, coming together through quilting. Sarah agrees to work for Syl-

via on the condition that Sylvia will teach her to quilt. Through their instruction much of Sylvia's secret past is revealed and together they use Sylvia's inheritance to form the Elm Creek Quilting Camp. Chiaverini also wrote *Elm Creek Quilts: Projects Inspired by the Elm Creek Quilts Novels* with the help of quilt designer and teacher Nancy Odom, which is a pattern book for quilting projects based on and inspired by the characters and events of Chiaverini's novels.

Boze Hadleigh

Syrian-born Hadleigh began his career as a freelance journalist, eventually publishing in hundreds of periodicals in the United States and abroad on a wide variety of topics, from health and travel to history, pop culture, and Hollywood. As an author of books, however, he has focused mainly on the entertainment world, its impact and its behind-the-scenes workings. Several of Hadleigh's books have been firsts in their subject matter, including works that examine the homosexual and bisexual presence in and contributions to show business, particularly motion pictures. Nearly half of Hadleigh's books have been adapted for television or film in the United States and abroad, including the 2002 documentary film *The Bronze Screen: 100 Years of the Latino Image in American Cinema,* based on the book *Hispanic Hollywood: The Latins in Motion Pictures.*

Geoff Nicholson

Nicholson is a writer of both fiction and nonfiction works. His protagonists frequently take their interests to the point of obsession. The characters in *Hunters and Gatherers,* for instance, are consumed by collecting; a husband and wife collect cars and extramarital lovers, respectively, while another character, a writer, is obsessed with chronicling collectors. In one of his nonfiction works, Nicholson examines the common act of walking as part of humankind's intellectual and cultural history in his *The Lost Art of Walking: The History, Science, Philosophy, and Literature of Pedestrianism.* In the book he also notes how walking can be considered a mindless activity, as evidenced by an Oxford scholar's experiment of taking a dead cat, removing its brain, and finding a way to make it walk, a feat duplicated with aborted human fetuses many years later.

Steven Rinella

Outdoor enthusiast Steven Rinella is a frequent contributor to magazines such as *Outdoor* and *Field and Stream.* In his first book, *The Scavenger's Guide to Haute Cui-*

sine, Rinella tells the story of what happened when a friend gave him a copy of *Le Guide Culinaire,* a hundred-year-old cookbook originally published in 1903 by master chef Auguste Escoffier. The cookbook included a number of exotic recipes for wildlife-based dishes. As an avid hunter and sportsman, Rinella was experienced at hunting and cooking his own food. Inspired by the book, by his own outdoor skills, and by Escoffier's example, Rinella undertook a year-long project to gather the ingredients, hunt the wildlife, and stockpile the supplies for a massive three-day, forty-five course wild game and natural food banquet for himself and his friends.

Sister Souljah

Souljah, born Lisa Williamson, grew up in public housing projects and witnessed first-hand the effects that economic hardship and subtle discrimination had on her urban community. In *No Disrespect,* she writes of the unstable family life she experienced, and of her own determination to escape those circumstances. Souljah's mother encouraged her to read as a child, and her studiousness as a teen earned her scholarships that led to a university education. In her book, she discusses the environmental roadblocks that confront young African American women. After beginning her college career at Cornell University, Souljah transferred to New Jersey's Rutgers University to study history. During these years, she became a student activist. Souljah was also a member of the rap group Public Enemy.

Steve Watkins

Watkins's book *The Black O: Racism and Redemption in an American Corporate Empire* chronicles the employment discrimination case filed against the Shoney's Corporation (the parent company of Shoney's restaurants) on behalf of 20,909 claimants. After five years of litigation, the plaintiffs received a 132.5 million-dollar settlement and the Shoney's Corporation altered its hiring practices. The black "O" of Watkins's title refers to the common practice of blackening the letter "o" in the name Shoney's on any application submitted by an African American. The book describes how the attorney opposing the organization gathered support for his case by taking colleagues who had never been to a Shoney's restaurant to one of the restaurants for lunch. Before they arrived, Warren gave his lunch companions a preview of what they would encounter at the restaurant: the hostess, the manager at the cash register, and the waiters would be almost exclusively white. Kitchen workers (glimpsed from behind a swinging door), bus persons, and salad bar stockers would be almost exclusively black.

A

ADAMS, Nicholas
    See SMITH, Sherwood

*   *   *

ALMOND, David 1951-

PERSONAL: Born May 15, 1951, in Newcastle upon Tyne, England; son of James Arthur and Catherine Almond; married Sara Jane Palmer; children: Freya Grace Almond-Palmer. *Education:* University of East Anglia, B.A. (with honors). *Hobbies and other interests:* Walking, listening to music, traveling, spending time with family.

ADDRESSES: Home—Northumberland, England. *E-mail*—dalmond@lineone.net.

CAREER: Writer and educator. Teacher in primary, adult, and special-education schools in England; *Panurge* (fiction magazine), editor, 1987-93; creative writing tutor for Arvon Foundation, beginning 1987, and Open College of the Arts, 1995-99; Huntington School, York, England, visiting writer, 1996-98; Hartlepool Schools, writer-in-residence, spring, 1999; visiting speaker and course leader.

AWARDS, HONORS: Northern Arts Writers Award; Hawthornden fellowship, 1997; Whitbread Award, 1998, Lancashire Children's Book of the Year, Stockton Children's Book of the Year, *Guardian* Children's Fiction Prize shortlist, and Carnegie Medal, British Library Association, all 1999, Michael L. Printz Honor Book, American Library Association, 2000, and shortlist for Sheffield Children's Book of the Year, all for *Skellig;* British Arts Council Award for outstanding literature for young people, 1998, Smarties Silver Award, 1999, and Michael L. Printz Award, 2001, all for *Kit's Wilderness;* Smarties Gold Award, 2003, Carnegie Medal shortlist, 2003, Whitbread Award shortlist, 2003, and *Boston Globe/Horn Book* Award for fiction and poetry, 2004, all for *The Fire-eaters.*

WRITINGS:

JUVENILE FICTION

Skellig, Hodder Children's Books (London, England), 1998, Delacorte Press (New York, NY), 1999.
Kit's Wilderness, Hodder Children's Books (London, England), 1999, Delacorte Press (New York, NY), 2000.
Heaven Eyes, Hodder Children's Books (London, England), 2000, Delacorte Press (New York, NY), 2001.
Counting Stars (short stories), Hodder Children's Books (London, England), 2000, Delacorte Press (New York, NY), 2002.
Secret Heart, Hodder Children's Books (London, England), 2001, Delacorte Press (New York, NY), 2002.
The Fire-eaters, Hodder Children's Books (London, England), 2003, Delacorte Press (New York, NY), 2004.
Kate, the Cat, and the Moon (picture book), illustrated by Stephen Lambert, Random House (New York, NY), 2005.

Clay, Delacorte Press (New York, NY), 2006.

The Savage, illustrated by Dave McKean, Candlewick Press (Cambridge, MA), 2008.

My Dad's a Birdman (picture book), illustrated by Polly Dunbar, Candlewick Press (Cambridge, MA), 2008.

Jackdaw Summer, Hodder Children's Books (London, England), 2008, published in America as *Raven Summer,* Delacorte Press (New York, NY), 2009.

The Boy Who Climbed into the Moon, illustrated by Polly Dunbar, Candlewick Press (Somerville, MA), 2010.

OTHER

Mickey and the Emperor (play for children), produced at Washington Arts Center, 1984.

Sleepless Nights (short stories), Iron Press (North Shields, England), 1985.

A Kind of Heaven (short stories), Iron Press (North Shields, England), 1997.

Skellig: A Play (first produced on BBC Radio 4, 2000; also see below), Hodder Children's Books (London, England), 2002.

Wild Girl, Wild Boy: A Play (first produced in London, England, 2001; also see below), Hodder Children's Books (London, England), 2002.

Clay Boy (radio play), produced on BBC Radio 4, 2002.

Two Plays (contains *Wild Girl, Wild Boy* and *Skellig*), Delacorte Press (New York, NY), 2005.

My Dad's a Birdman (play), produced at the Edinburgh Fringe, 2005.

Also contributor to *Click: One Novel, Ten Authors,* Arthur A. Levine Books, 2007. Contributor to *London* and *Critical Quarterly.* Author's works have been published in twenty languages; short stories have been broadcast on BBC Radio 4.

ADAPTATIONS: Clay was adapted for film, British Broadcasting Corporation (BBC), 2008; *Skellig* was adapted for film, 2009.

SIDELIGHTS: British writer David Almond wrote for adults for a number of years before he achieved what amounted to overnight success with his first novel for young adults, *Skellig.* This 1998 tale of a young boy's discovery of a possibly supernatural creature in his own backyard was unanimously praised by reviewers, sold out its first printing in four days, and went on to win Britain's prestigious Whitbread Children's Book of the Year award and the Carnegie Medal. Almond has received numerous other honors for his work, including the Michael L. Printz Award for *Kit's Wilderness* and the *Boston Globe/Horn Book* Award for *The Fire-eaters.*

Like the hero in *Skellig,* Almond grew up on the fringes of a Northern English city, a landscape that offered great imaginative possibilities for him as a youth.

After earning a degree from the University of East Anglia, Almond became a teacher. In 1982, he quit a full-time job, sold his house, and moved to a commune in order to devote himself to writing. The result was a collection of stories, *Sleepless Nights,* published by a small press in 1985. As Almond once told CA: "I began to write properly after university, after five years of teaching. Short stories appeared in little magazines. A couple were broadcast on Radio 4. A small press collection, *Sleepless Nights,* appeared to a tiny amount of acclaim and a vast amount of silence. I ran a fiction magazine, *Panurge,* that excited and exhausted me for six years. I wrote The Great English Novel that took five years, went to thirty-three publishers and was rejected by them all. I went on writing. More stories, more publications, a few small prizes. Another novel, never finished. Another story collection was published, *A Kind of Heaven,* twelve years after the first. Then at last I started writing about growing up in our small, steep town: a whole sequence of stories, half-real, half-imaginary, that I called *Stories from the Middle of the World.* They took a year to write."

It was the act of finishing the Newcastle stories that inexplicably led Almond to the opening lines of *Skellig:* "I found him in the garage on Sunday afternoon," recalls the book's narrator, ten-year-old Michael—an opening line that, Almond said, simply came to him as he was walking down the street. As he explained in an interview with *Publishers Weekly:* "When I wrote the last of these stories, I stuck them into an envelope, and as soon as I'd posted away the book to my agent, the story of *Skellig* just flew into my head, as if it had just been waiting there." The Sunday on which *Skellig* begins, Michael and his family have just taken possession of an old, run-down house; also new to them is a newborn infant sister for Michael, who initially arrives home from the hospital but soon must return for heart surgery.

In the garage, behind a great deal of clutter, Michael discovers a man covered in dust and insects. At first he believes it is an old homeless man, but he finds that Skellig, who communicates with Michael but does not reveal much by way of explanation, has odd wing-like appendages. It seems Skellig has come there to die. As he begins his new school, while his mother is away with his sister at the hospital and his father is understandably preoccupied, Michael begins to bring Skellig food and medicine. He also befriends his new neighbor, a girl name Mina who is an intelligent, independent thinker. Mina explains to Michael a few of her interests, such as ornithology and the poetry of early nineteenth-century Romantic writer William Blake. She also shows him a nest of rare owls, which may have something to do with Skellig's presence.

As Perri Klass noted, writing about *Skellig* for the *New York Times Book Review,* the book's charm lies in its author's courage for allowing some things to remain a mystery. "In its simple but poetic language, its tender refusal to package its mysteries neatly or offer explanations for what happens in either world, it goes beyond adventure story or family-with-a-problem story to become a story about worlds enlarging and the hope of scattering death." As the story progresses, Michael shares the secret of Skellig with Mina, and as they both visit him in the garage, his health improves considerably. As a result, however, the mysterious occupant becomes even more secretive and mystical before he vanishes.

Michael feels his baby sister's heart beating one day, and realizes that love can achieve miracles that science cannot. Klass, in a *New York Times Book Review* critique, praised Almond's talent for weaving in the more prosaic details of life such as soccer practice and the daily school-bus ride with larger questions involving the metaphysical world. "Its strength as a novel is in its subtlety, its sideways angles," observed Klass. "It is a book about the business of everyday life proceeding on a canvas suddenly widened to include mystery and tragedy, although not everyone has eyes to see."

Other reviews were similarly positive. Cathryn M. Mercier, writing for *Five Owls,* called *Skellig* a "novel of faith and hope," and "a book of rare spirituality for young adults." *Reading Time* contributor Howard George described it as "a haunting story" whose impact lies in "the deep emotions evoked by the family crisis and the love given out to Skellig."

Almond had already completed his second young adult novel, *Kit's Wilderness,* before *Skellig* won several literary prizes in Britain, including the Whitbread and the Carnegie Medal. The focus of this second book is a game of pretend death that its characters play. "In my primary school—a spooky turreted place down by the river where the ancient coal mines had been—a bunch of kids used to play a fainting game in the long grass beyond the school yard wall," wrote Almond in *Carousel.* The story is far less insular than the secretive plot of *Skellig,* and Almond has noted that as a work of fiction it took him far longer to develop coherently. "At times I was scared stiff by what was happening in the tale," Almond admitted in *Carousel.* "Scared that it might all end dreadfully, scared that the darkness would gain the upper hand." But his next work, *Kit's Wilderness,* would prove equally successful. *Kit's Wilderness* is a tale that is "very linked to the scenery of my childhood and the stories and history of the place where I grew up," the author told *Booklist* interviewer Ilene Cooper.

In the novel, thirteen-year-old Kit Watson moves with his family to the old British coal-mining town of Stoneygate, where they will care for Kit's widowed grandfather. A troubled, enigmatic classmate named John Askew befriends Kit and introduces him to a bizarre game called "Death" that is played in the abandoned mines. Participants lie alone in the dark mines in an attempt to connect with the spirits of their ancestors, who died there as young boys in a terrible accident. Though several of the players treat the game as a lark, "Kit senses something far more profound and dangerous, and the connection he forges with the ancient past also circuitously seals a deeper bond with Askew," noted a critic writing for *Publishers Weekly.* When John disappears, Kit determines to locate his friend and reunite him with his family. At the same time, Kit discovers an artistic side to his personality through his relationship with his grandfather, a storyteller who inspires Kit to write his own tale, one that mirrors the events of Kit's life.

According to *School Library Journal* contributor Ellen Fader, the author "brings these complicated, interwoven plots to a satisfying conclusion as he explores the power of friendship and family, the importance of memory, and the role of magic in our lives." In her review of *Kit's Wilderness, Booklist* contributor Ilene Cooper remarked that "the story's ruminations about death and the healing power of love will strike children in unsuspected ways."

In 2000 Almond published his third novel for teens. *Heaven Eyes* blends everyday adventure with a dalliance in the netherworld; its characters are escapees of a juvenile home who flee on a raft to an old printing plant on the River Tyne. The autobiographical story collection *Counting Stars* followed, and in 2001 the author produced *Secret Heart*, "a thought-provoking allegory," wrote Daniel L. Darigan for *School Library Journal*. *Secret Heart* focuses on Joe Maloney, a lonely misfit who dreams of tigers and finds himself curiously drawn to a ragged traveling circus that arrives in his town. "Almond fans, who relish the author's skill at creating surreal landscapes and otherworldly images, will not be disappointed by this tale," remarked a *Publishers Weekly* contributor.

Almond's 2003 novel, *The Fire-eaters,* was shortlisted for both the Carnegie Medal and the Whitbread Award and received the Smarties Gold Award. Set in 1962 during the Cuban Missile Crisis, the book concerns twelve-year-old Bobby Burns, who lives with his family in a small English seaside village. Accepted into an elite private school, Bobby must deal with a cruel teacher who practices corporal punishment, his evolving relationships with a pair of old friends, and a strange illness that befalls his father. Overshadowing everything is the threat of nuclear war; according to a *Publishers Weekly* contributor: "Bobby's reflections . . . convey the young protagonist's uncertainties and a sense of the world itself being on the cusp of change." "The apocalyptic atmosphere is personified by the tragic character McNulty, a fire-eating exhibitionist whose torturous feats raise" another significant theme, observed *Horn Book* contributor Lauren Adams, "the human capacity for pain—giving it, accepting it, bearing it for another." A contributor to *Kirkus Reviews* deemed *The Fire-eaters* "breathtakingly and memorably up to Almond's best."

"I always knew that I wanted to be a writer," Almond stated on his Web site. "One of my uncles had a small printing works. My mum said that she used to take me there as a baby and I used to laugh and point at the printed pages coming off the rollers—so maybe I began to fall in love with print when I was just a few months old."

In his first picture book, *Kate, the Cat, and the Moon,* illustrated by Stephen Lambert, Almond features young Kate waking up in the middle of the night to the call of a meowing cat. She sees a cat in the moonlight sitting on a garden wall. Answering with a "Meow" to the cat, Kate proceeds to get out of bed and head down the stairs, all the while transforming into a cat. She goes out into the yard, and she and the other cat have an adventure roaming through the night. In the morning, her family all talk about their dreams and Kate's only comment when they ask about hers is to reply "Meow." Nicolette Jones, writing for the *Times Online,* commented that the author "takes the 'Was it all a dream?' formula and makes it into something new and imaginative." Noting that "this bedtime fantasy is sure to earn Almond new fans," *School Library Journal* contributor Maura Bresnahan also wrote in the same review: "This book will charm feline fanatics everywhere."

Set in Felling, England, in the 1960s, Almond's novel *Clay* features fourteen-year-old David, an altar boy at a Catholic church, who befriends the troubled Stephen Rose, who has been thrown out of the seminary. A gifted sculptor, Stephen also has the mystical power to bring his creations to life. Stephen recognizes that David also has the same power and convinces David, with the help of communion wafers, to bring to life a life-size figure the two have created. Clay is born innocent in nature but willing to obey the commands of his masters, and Stephen has destructive goals in mind for their creation. "This book will certainly fascinate readers, pulling them completely into the remarkable world Almond has created, leaving them reluctant to look up from this novel and force themselves back into the real world," wrote Jocelyn Pearce in a review for the *Curled Up with a Good Kid's Book* Web site. "David Almond shows, in this book, a rare gift for creating stories that literally will take your breath away." Hazel Rochman, writing for *Booklist,* commented that "this story will grab readers with its gripping action and its important ideas."

The Savage, illustrated by Dave McKean, features Blue Baker, who tries to come to terms with his father's death by writing a journal, as suggested by his counselor. Before long, Blue is making up a story about a savage who lives in the woods. As Blue continues to write, the line between reality and fantasy blur. Noting that "there has always been a fear on the part of humankind that words could carry this power" to become real, a *School Library Journal Online* contributor added: "Almond touches on this fear. If you could create a living breathing danger by simply writing about it, would you?" In Blue's case, he writes about the savage confronting the boy who keeps bullying him. The next day, the bully appears at school displaying prominent bruises. "The art ramps up the intensity of this provocative outing," wrote a *Kirkus Reviews* contributor of *The Savage.* Jonathan Hunt, writing for *Horn Book,* referred to *The Savage* as "a welcome addition to Almond's body of work."

Almond's short novel, *My Dad's a Birdman,* illustrated by Polly Dunbar, began as a play and was produced at the Edinburgh Fringe in 2005. "Afterwards, the script lay in my drawer," the author told a *Books for Keeps* Web site contributor. The author went on to note in the same interview: "I tried reducing it to a picture book text, but I couldn't get the story to fit." The author set aside the project but took it up again after the publication of his novel *Clay.* In his interview for the *Books for Keeps* Web site, the author commented that he wrote down the book's first line and "the whole thing burst into life. I couldn't stop. Within four days I had the first draft of a short novel."

The story revolves around young Lizzie's father, Jackie, who is trying to win Mr. Poop's Great Human Bird Competition. Intent on making wings that will help him win, Jackie, first eats bugs to try to grow wings. Before long, Lizzie joins her father in his quest as the two realize that they need faith and togetherness just as much as, if not more than, wings. As usual with works by Almond, the book includes dark undertones concerning the death of Lizzie's mother and her father's possible madness. "As always . . . Almond writes beautifully, and . . . this novel is a tribute to the human spirit," wrote Ilene Cooper in a review for *Booklist.*

Raven Summer, published in Europe as *Jackdaw Summer,* tells the story of Liam, who, along with his friend, Max, follows a jackdaw, or raven, into the country and eventually finds an abandoned baby in an old farmhouse. Along with the child is a jar filled with money and a note that reads "Please look after her rite. This is a childe of God." Initially, the discovery is a big news event but eventually the public forgets about the little girl as she is placed in foster care. When Liam and his family visit the girl, Liam ends up meeting two other foster children in the house. A young girl named Crystal is a troubled orphan who appears to want to harm herself. Oliver is a refugee from Liberia who witnessed his entire family get killed and then was forced to joint the soldiers when he is only ten years old. In the meantime, Liam's friendship with Max falls apart while Liam's self-absorbed father decries against the war in Iraq.

Noting that "all the ingredients are here for a worthy, socially conscious novel," *Independent Online* contributor Nicholas Tucker went on his review to write that the author also reveals "the darker side of his imagination," pointing out that the author's "good characters cannot escape the knowledge of their failings" and that the "villains have a way of saying . . . things containing a kernel of truth." A *Write Away* Web site contributor commented: "Credible, beautifully drawn characters and a sparse, exquisite prose which sparkles off the page take the reader into different territory."

BIOGRAPHICAL AND CRITICAL SOURCES:

BOOKS

Almond, David, *Skellig,* Hodder Children's Books (London, England), 1998.
Almond, David, *Raven Summer,* Delacorte Press (New York, NY), 2009.

PERIODICALS

Book, May, 2001, Kathleen Odean, review of *Kit's Wilderness,* p. 80.
Booklist, January 1, 2000, Ilene Cooper, "The Booklist Interview: David Almond," p. 898, and review of *Kit's Wilderness,* p. 899; April 1, 2001, Ilene Cooper, "The Booklist Interview," interview with Almond, p. 1464; February 1, 2002, Hazel Rochman, review of *Counting Stars,* p. 934; October 1, 2002, Michael Cart, review of *Secret Heart,* p. 322; March 15, 2004, Ilene Cooper, review of *The Fire-eaters,* pp. 1297-1298; July 1, 2005, Ilene Cooper, review of *Kate, the Cat, and the Moon,* p. 1929; October 1, 2005, Hazel Rochman, review of *Two Plays,* p. 51; June 1, 2006, Hazel Rochman, review of *Clay,* p. 74; September 15, 2007, Lynn Rutan, review of *Click: One Novel, Ten Authors,* p. 57; March 15, 2008, Ilene Cooper, review of *My Dad's a Birdman,* p. 54; September 15, 2008, Ian Chipman, review of *The Savage,* p. 49.
Bookseller, September 30, 2005, Benedicte Page, "Through Almond's Eyes: David Almond's New Book Brings the Frankenstein Myth to the Northeast. He Talks to Benedicte Page," p. 20; February 17, 2006, review of *Clay,* p. 42; May 9, 2008, "Watch the Birdie," p. 9; September 12, 2008, Caroline Horn, "Cracking Ahead: David Almond Talks to Caroline Horn about Being a Regional Writer and the Need for Constant Re-invention," p. 21.

Carousel, summer, 1999, David Almond, "Writing for Boys," p. 29.

Five Owls, May-June, 1999, Cathryn M. Mercier, review of *Skellig,* p. 110.

Horn Book, May, 1999, review of *Skellig,* p. 326; March-April, 2002, Gregory Maguire, review of *Counting Stars,* pp. 207-208; November-December, 2002, Christine M. Heppermann, review of *Secret Heart,* pp. 745-746; May-June, 2004, review of *The Fire-eaters,* p. 324; January-February, 2006, Deirdre F. Baker, review of *Two Plays,*; July-August, 2006, Vicky Smith, review of *Clay;* January-February, 2007, review of *Clay;* November-December, 2007, Vicky Smith, review of *Click;* May-June, 2008, Deirdre F. Baker, review of *My Dad's a Birdman;* September-October, 2008, Jonathan Hunt, review of *The Savage.*

Journal of Adolescent & Adult Literacy, October, 2007, James Blasingame, review of *Click,* p. 191.

Kirkus Reviews, March 15, 2002, review of *Counting Stars,* p. 404; September 1, 2002, review of *Secret Heart,* p. 1300; April 1, 2004, review of *The Fire-eaters,* p. 323; September 1, 2005, review of *Kate, the Cat, and the Moon,* p. 967; October 15, 2005, review of *Two Plays,* p. 1133; June 1, 2006, review of *Clay,* p. 567; September 15, 2007, review of *Click,*; March 15, 2008, review of *My Dad's a Birdman;* September 15, 2008, review of *The Savage.*

Kliatt, November, 2002, Paula Rohrlick, review of *Secret Heart,* p. 5; January, 2004, Nola Theiss, review of *Counting Stars,* p. 26; July, 2006, Paula Rohrlick, review of *Clay,* p. 7; May, 2008, Paula Rohrlick, review of *Clay,* p. 26.

Los Angeles Times, April 8, 2001, "Books for Kids," includes review of *Heaven Eyes,* p. 6.

New York Times Book Review, June 6, 1999, Perry Klass, review of *Skellig,* p. 49.

Publishers Weekly, June 28, 1999, Elizabeth Devereaux, "Flying Starts," discussion of author's debut children's novel, p. 25; January 3, 2000, review of *Kit's Wilderness,* p. 77; November 6, 2000, "Best Children's Books 2000," review of *Kit's Wilderness,* p. 43; April 1, 2002, review of *Counting Stars,* p. 85; July 1, 2002, "The British Invasion: PW Speaks to Five Authors Who Have Crossed the Atlantic and Found American Readers," pp. 26-29; August 19, 2002, review of *Secret Heart,* p. 90; May 3, 2004, review of *The Fire-eaters,* p. 192; September 5, 2005, review of *Kate, the Cat, and the Moon,* p. 61; May 29, 2006, review of *Clay,* p. 60.

Reading Time, May, 1999, Howard George, review of *Skellig,* p. 25.

Resource Links, December, 2007, Myra Junyk, review of *Click,* p. 37.

School Library Journal, March, 2000, Ellen Fader, review of *Kit's Wilderness,* p. 233; April, 2001, Kathleen Odean, review of *Mystic Man,* p. 48; March, 2002, William McLoughlin, review of *Counting Stars,* p. 225; May, 2004, Joel Shoemaker, review of *The Fire-eaters,* p. 140; September, 2005, Maura Bresnahan, review of *Kate, the Cat, and the Moon,* p. 164; December, 2005, Nancy Menaldi-Scanlan, review of *Two Plays,* p. 160; August, 2006, Joel Shoemaker, review of *Clay,* p. 113; October, 2006, review of *Two Plays,* p. 71; May, 2008, Margaret A. Chang, review of *My Dad's a Birdman,* p. 92; December, 2008, Johanna Lewis, review of *The Savage,* p. 118.

Voice of Youth Advocates, April, 2000, Bette Ammon, review of *Kit's Wilderness,* p. 42.

Washington Post, August 20, 2000, Linda Barrett Osbourne, "Children's Books; In These Two Suspenseful Young-Adult Novels, Resourceful Teenagers Come Face-to-Face with Death," p. X10.

ONLINE

Achuka Web site, http://www.achuka.co.uk/ (October 19, 2001), interview with Almond.

American Library Association Web site, http://www.ala.org/ (February 9, 2001), "David Almond Wins Printz Award."

Australian Online, http://www.theaustralian.news.com.au/ (March 28, 2009), review of *Jackdaw Summer.*

Birmingham Post Online, http://www.birminghampost.net/ (October 6, 2008), Terry Grimley, "Author David Almond Happy at Last with *Skellig* Success," interview with author.

BookLoons, http://www.bookloons.com/ (June 19, 2009), J.A. Kaszuba Locke, reviews of *Clay, Two Plays,* and *Kate, the Cat, and the Moon.*

Books for Keeps, http://www.booksforkeeps.co.uk/ (June 19, 2009), David Almond, "*My Dad's a Birdman* David Almond on His New Novel."

Columbus Dispatch Online, http://www.dispatch.com/ (June 11, 2008), Nancy Gilson, "Father-Daughter Story a Tender, Funny Tale," review of *My Dad's a Birdman.*

Contemporary Writers, http://www.contemporarywriters.com/ (June 19, 2009), biography of author.

Curled Up with a Good Kid's Book, http://www.curledupkids.com/ (June 19, 2009), Jocelyn Pearce, review of *Clay.*

David Almond Home Page, http://www.davidalmond. com (June 19, 2009).

East Sussex County Council Web site, http://www. eastsussex.gov.uk/ (June 19, 2009), review of *The Savage.*

Evansville Courier & Press Online, http://www.courier press.com/ (December 21, 2008), Charles Sutton, "Tales of Graphic Novels Paint Pictures for All Ages," review of *The Savage.*

Excelsior File, http://excelsiorfile.blogspot.com/ (August 24, 2008), David Elzey, review of *My Dad's a Birdman.*

Female First, http://www.femalefirst.co.uk/ (April 20, 2009), "David Almond Interview."

Fortean Times Online, http://www.forteantimes.com/ (June 19, 2009), Gordon Rutter, "A Fortean at the Fringe— Part I," review of *Clay.*

Hack Writers, http://www.hackwriters.com/ (June 19, 2009), Michael Phillip Webb, review of *Jackdaw Summer.*

Independent.ie, http://www.independent.ie/ (December 7, 2008), Celia Keenan, "Tales of Love and Death with a Little Bit of Gore," brief review of *The Savage.*

Independent Online, http://www.independent.co.uk/ (November 6, 2005), Benedicte Page, "David Almond: Frankenstein Goes to Tyneside," review of *Clay;* (November 17, 2008) Nicholas Tucker, review of *Jackdaw Summer.*

JournalLive, http://www.journallive.co.uk/ (October 3, 2008), Barbara Hodgson "Author David Almond Shares His Secrets."

Jubilee Books Web site, http://www.jubileebooks.co.uk/ (October 19, 2001), interview with Almond.

Long Long Time Ago, http://www.longlongtimeago.com (June 19, 2009), biography of author.

Metro Online, http://www.metro.co.uk/ (march 26, 2002), Fiona MacDonald, "David Almond," interview with author.

School Library Journal Online, http://www.school libraryjournal.com/ (July 13, 2007), Elizabeth Bird, review of *Click;* (December 6, 2008) review of *The Savage.*

Scotland on Sunday Online, http://scotlandonsunday. scotsman.com/ (March 16, 2008), Janet Christie, "Round-Up: Children's Books," includes review of *The Savage.*

Scottish Book Trust, http://www.scottishbooktrust.com/ (June 19, 2009), "David Almond & Sara Grady," interview with author.

Seattle Post-Intelligencer Online, http://www.seattlepi. com/ (June 19, 2006), Cecelia Goodnow, "Wade into Summer Reading Fun," review of *Clay.*

Star Online, http://www.thestar.com/ (November 26, 2006), Deirdre Baker, "Just the Right Read for Every Single Kid," review of *Clay.*

Teen Reads Web site, http://www.teenreads.com/ (October 19, 2001), interview with Almond.

Telegraph Online, http://www.telegraph.co.uk/ (October 24, 2008), Nicolette Jones, "David Almond: 'Story Is a Kind of Redemption,'" interview with author.

Time Out London, http://www.timeout.com/ (April 11, 2008), review of *The Savage;* (December 2, 2008) review of *Jackdaw Summer.*

Times Online, http://www.timesonline.co.uk/ (October 24, 2004), Nicolette Jones, review of *Kate, the Cat, and the Moon;* (October 21, 2007) Nicolette Jones, review of *My Dad's a Birdman.*

Write Away, http://www.writeaway.org.uk/ (March 14, 2008), review of *My Dad's a Birdman;* (September 28, 2008) review of *Jackdaw Summer.**

*   *   *

ANDERSON, Kevin J. 1962-
(Kevin James Anderson)

PERSONAL: Born March 27, 1962, in Racine, WI; son of Andrew James (a banker) and Dorothy Arloah (a homemaker) Anderson; married Mary Franco Nijhuis, November 17, 1983 (divorced, June, 1987); married Rebecca Moesta (a technical editor and writer), September 14, 1991; children: Jonathan Macgregor Cowan (stepson). *Education:* University of Wisconsin— Madison, B.S. (with honors), 1982. *Hobbies and other interests:* Hiking, camping, reading, astronomy.

ADDRESSES: Home—CO.

CAREER: Writer. Lawrence Livermore National Laboratory, Livermore, CA, technical writer/editor, 1983-95; Materials Research Society, Pittsburgh, PA, columnist, 1988—; International Society for Respiratory Protection, Salem, OR, copy editor, 1989-95.

MEMBER: Science Fiction Writers of America, Horror Writers of America, International Association of Media Tie-In Writers.

AWARDS, HONORS: Dale Donaldson Memorial Award for lifetime service to the small-press field, 1987; Bram Stoker Award nomination for best first novel, Horror

Writers of America, 1988, for *Resurrection, Inc.;* Nebula award nomination for best science fiction novel, 1993, for *Assemblers of Infinity; Locus* magazine award for best science-fiction paperback novel of 1995, for *Climbing Olympus;* readers' choice award, *SFX,* 1995, for *Ground Zero;* readers's choice award, Science Fiction Book Club, and notable book citation, *New York Times,* 2000, both for *Dune: House Atreides.*

WRITINGS:

NOVELS; WITH DOUG BEASON

Lifeline, Bantam (New York, NY), 1991.
The Trinity Paradox, Bantam (New York, NY), 1991.
Assemblers of Infinity, Bantam (New York, NY), 1993.
Ill Wind, Forge (New York, NY), 1995.
Virtual Destruction, Ace Books (New York, NY), 1996.
Ignition, Forge (New York, NY), 1997.
Fallout, Ace Books (New York, NY), 1997.
Lethal Exposure, Ace Books (New York, NY), 1998.

NOVELS; WITH KRISTINE KATHRYN RUSCH

Afterimage, Roc (New York, NY), 1992.
Afterimage/ Aftershock, Meisha Merlin (Decatur, GA), 1998.

"X-FILES" SERIES

Ground Zero, HarperPrism (New York, NY), 1995.
Ruins, HarperPrism (New York, NY), 1996.
Antibodies, HarperPrism (New York, NY), 1997.

SCIENCE FICTION

Resurrection, Inc., Signet (New York, NY), 1988, tenth anniversary limited edition, Overlook Connection Press (Woodstock, GA), 1998.
Climbing Olympus, Warner (New York, NY), 1994.
Blindfold, Warner (New York, NY), 1995.
(With John Gregory Betancourt) *Born of Elven Blood* (young adult), Atheneum (New York, NY), 1995.
Darksaber ("Star Wars" Series), Bantam (New York, NY), 1995.
(Editor) *War of the Worlds: Global Dispatches* (anthology), Bantam (New York, NY), 1996.

Dogged Persistence (short stories), Golden Gryphon Press (Urbana, IL), 2001.
Hopscotch, Bantam (New York, NY), 2002.
Artifact, Forge (New York, NY), 2003.
Landscapes (short stories), introduction by Neil Peart, Five Star (Waterville, ME), 2006.
(With A.E. Van Vogt) *Slan Hunter,* Tor (New York, NY), 2007.
The Last Days of Krypton, HarperEntertainment (New York, NY), 2007.
Enemies & Allies, William Morrow (New York, NY), 2009.
Edge of the World, Orbit (New York, NY), 2009.

"SAGA OF SEVEN SUNS" SERIES

Hidden Empire, Aspect (New York, NY), 2002.
Forest of Stars, Aspect (New York, NY), 2003.
Horizon Storms, Aspect (New York, NY), 2004.
Scattered Suns, Aspect (New York, NY), 2005.
Of Fire and Night, Warner Books (New York, NY), 2006.
Metal Swarm, Orbit (New York, NY), 2007.
The Ashes of Worlds, Orbit (New York, NY), 2008.

"GAMEARTH" SERIES

Gamearth, Signet (New York, NY), 1989.
Gameplay, Signet (New York, NY), 1989.
Game's End, Roc (New York, NY), 1990.

GRAPHIC NOVELS

Veiled Alliances, DC Comics (New York, NY), 2004.
(With wife, Rebecca Moesta) *Grumpy Old Monsters,* IDW Publishing (San Diego, CA), 2004.
Orc's Treasure, Ibooks, 2005.

"CRYSTAL DOORS" SERIES; WRITTEN WITH REBECCA MOESTA

Crystal Doors #1: Island Realm, Little, Brown Young Readers (New York, NY), 2007.
Crystal Doors #2: Ocean Realm, Little, Brown Young Readers (New York, NY), 2007.
Crystal Doors #3: Sky Realm, Little, Brown Young Readers (New York, NY), 2008.

"STAR WARS: JEDI ACADEMY" TRILOGY

Jedi Search (also see below), Bantam (New York, NY), 1994.

Dark Apprentice (also see below), Bantam (New York, NY), 1994.

Champions of the Force (also see below), Bantam (New York, NY), 1994.

Jedi Academy Trilogy (includes *Jedi Search, Dark Apprentice*, and *Champions of the Force*), Doubleday (New York, NY), 1994.

"STAR WARS: YOUNG JEDI KNIGHTS" SERIES; WITH REBECCA MOESTA

Heirs of the Force, Boulevard (New York, NY), 1995.

Shadow Academy, Boulevard (New York, NY), 1995.

The Lost Ones, Boulevard (New York, NY), 1995.

Lightsabers, Boulevard (New York, NY), 1996.

Darkest Knight, Boulevard (New York, NY), 1996.

Jedi Under Siege, Boulevard (New York, NY), 1996.

Shards of Alderaan, Boulevard (New York, NY), 1997.

Delusions of Grandeur, Boulevard (New York, NY), 1997.

Diversity Alliance, Boulevard (New York, NY), 1997.

Jedi Bounty, Boulevard (New York, NY), 1997.

Crisis at Crystal Reef, Boulevard (New York, NY), 1998.

Trouble on Cloud City, Boulevard (New York, NY), 1998.

Return to Ord Mantell, Boulevard (New York, NY), 1998.

The Emperor's Plague, Boulevard (New York, NY), 1998.

"STAR WARS" ANTHOLOGIES; EDITOR

Star Wars: Tales from the Mos Eisley Cantina, Bantam (New York, NY), 1995.

Star Wars: Tales from Jabba's Palace, Bantam (New York, NY), 1995.

Star Wars: Tales of the Bounty Hunters, Bantam (New York, NY), 1995.

"STAR WARS: TALES OF THE JEDI" SERIES

Dark Lords of the Sith, Dark Horse Comics (Milwaukie, OR), 1996.

The Sith War, Dark Horse Comics (Milwaukie, OR), 1996.

Golden Age of Sith, Dark Horse Comics (Milwaukie, OR), 1997.

Fall of the Sith Empire, Dark Horse Comics (Milwaukie, OR), 1998.

Redemption, Titan Books (New York, NY), 2000.

"DUNE" SERIES; WITH BRIAN HERBERT

Dune: House Atreides, Bantam (New York, NY), 1999.

Dune: House Harkonnen, Bantam (New York, NY), 2000.

Dune: House Corrino, Bantam (New York, NY), 2001.

(With Frank Herbert) *The Road to Dune,* Tor (New York, NY), 2005.

Hunters of Dune, Tor (New York, NY), 2006.

Sandworms of Dune, Tor (New York, NY), 2007.

Paul of Dune, Tor (New York, NY), 2008.

Wind of Dune, Tor (New York, NY), 2009.

WITH BRIAN HERBERT

Butlerian Jihad, Tor Books (New York, NY), 2002.

Machine Crusade, Tor Books (New York, NY), 2003.

Battle of Corrin, Tor Books (New York, NY), 2004.

NONFICTION

The Illustrated Star Wars Universe, illustrated by Ralph McQuarrie, with additional art by Michael Butkus and others, Bantam (New York, NY), 1995.

(With Rebecca Moesta) *Star Wars: The Mos Eisley Cantina Pop-up Book,* illustrated by Ralph McQuarrie, Little, Brown (Boston, MA), 1995.

(With Rebecca Moesta) *Jabba's Palace Pop-up Book,* illustrated by Ralph McQuarrie, Little, Brown (Boston, MA), 1996.

(With Alice Bows and Paul Upham) *Aviation and Climate Change: Lessons for European Policy,* Routledge (New York, NY), 2008.

OTHER

(With L. Ron Hubbard) *Ai! Pedrito! When Intelligence Goes Wrong,* Bridge Publications (Los Angeles, CA), 1998.

(With Harlan Ellison) *The Outer Limits: Armageddon Dreams,* Quadrillion Media (Scottsdale, AZ), 2000.

(With Gregory Benford and Marc Scott Zicree) *Science Fiction Theater,* edited by Brian Forbes, Quadrillion Media (Scottsdale, AZ), 2000.

(With Rebecca Moesta) *Supernova,* Quadrillion Media (Scottsdale, AZ), 2000.

(With Rebecca Moesta) *Star Trek—The Next Generation: The Gorn Crisis* (comic book), painted by Igor Kordey, WildStorm/DC Comics (La Jolla, CA), 2001.

League of Extraordinary Gentlemen (adapted from film screenplay), Pocket Books (New York, NY), 2003.

Sky Captain and the World of Tomorrow (adapted from film screenplay), Onyx Books (New York, NY), 2004.

Prodigal Son ("*Dean Koontz's Frankenstein*" series), Bantam (New York, NY), 2005.

(Editor) *The Horror Writers Association Presents Blood Lite: An Anthology of Humorous Horror Stories,* Pocket Books (New York, NY), 2008.

Work represented in anthologies, including *Full Spectrum,* volumes I, III, and IV; *The Ultimate Dracula;* and *The Ultimate Werewolf.* Contributor of short stories, articles, and reviews to periodicals, including *Analog, Amazing,* and *Magazine of Fantasy and Science Fiction.* Also author of several comic book series. Over two dozen of Anderson's books have been translated for foreign publication.

ADAPTATIONS: The X-Files: Ground Zero was recorded as an audiocassette, read by Gillian Anderson, Harper Audio, 1995; *The Road to Dune* was adapted for audio, Books on Tape, 2005.

SIDELIGHTS: Kevin J. Anderson, the author of a daunting array of science fiction books for young adults, has emerged as one of the most successful writers in the genre's history. Over ten million copies of books by Anderson were in print by the late 1990s, and in 1998 he set a world record for the largest single-author book signing while promoting his spoof-filled spy thriller *Ai! Pedrito! When Intelligence Goes Wrong* in Los Angeles. In addition to creating original novels with themes of space exploration and new frontiers, Anderson has written many books in the "Star Wars" series for teen readers under the auspices of Lucasfilm. For a 1999 prequel to the science fiction classic *Dune,* Anderson set another record when he was signed to the most lucrative book publishing contract yet drawn up for a science fiction author.

Anderson was born in 1962, and grew up in a small town in Wisconsin. He recalled in a biography published on his Web site that a television movie of the H.G. Wells classic *War of the Worlds* made a tremendous impression on his five-year-old mind. Originally a radio play, *War of the Worlds* caused a stir when first broadcast in the late 1930s, sending many Americans into a panic after convincing them that the Earth was being attacked by Martians. The television movie, based on the radio play, made such an impression on Anderson that, still too young to read or write well, he began drawing pictures of the movie scenes the next day.

Anderson wrote his first short story at the age of eight, and two years later he bought a typewriter with savings from his allowance. The year he entered high school, he began submitting short stories to science fiction magazines, but received nothing but peremptory rejection letters. By the time he entered the University of Wisconsin—Madison, he had begun to enjoy minor success with his fiction. After he graduated from college with an honors degree in 1982, he began working for the Lawrence Livermore National Laboratories in Livermore, California. As a technical writer at the important defense-industry complex, Anderson was exposed to ideas and technologies that fired his imagination. He also met his future wife and coauthor, Rebecca Moesta, and another future collaborator, physicist Doug Beason.

Anderson's first published book was *Resurrection, Inc.,* which appeared in 1988. Its protagonist is François Nathans, founder of a company that recycles human corpses. Nathans owns technology that can animate the cadavers with a microchip, and, since their human memory has been erased, these "Servants" are used to free the living from difficult, drudge-like, or dangerous labor. When some of the Servants begin to recover their memories, they rebel. One of them possesses inside knowledge about the company because his father, once the greedy Nathans's partner, had been ousted from the partnership. "Although familiar in outline, this first effort is well plotted and lively in the telling," wrote Barbara Bannon in *Publishers Weekly.* As testament to its appeal, *Resurrection, Inc.* was published in a tenth-anniversary edition in 1998.

Anderson's next project was a series of novels based on the fantasy role-playing games popular with teenagers and young adults in the late 1980s. *Gamearth* introduced Melanie, David, Tyrone, and Scott, a quartet of students deeply involved in a Dungeons-and-Dragons-style fantasy game. David begins to think that the others are taking the plotted movements and created characters too seriously, and he wants to quit. To extricate himself, he creates a monstrous character that will destroy the other players' characters. His strategy backfires, however, and the book's ending is a cliffhanger. A *Locus* contributor wrote that "the characters within the game are rather humorously limited by their dice-given powers."

In the sequel, *Gameplay,* the four teens and their two-year-long role-playing game continues. Baffled by some occurrences, they come to realize that some of the created characters have begun to make their own moves. The forces of good and evil meet in battle, aided by a new character who speaks only in advertising and pop culture platitudes. "Anderson adds a delightfully fresh sense of humor in his character of Journeyman, the clay golem Melanie sends to save the day," noted a contributor to *Kliatt.*

Beginning in the early 1990s, Anderson found success with several titles coauthored with his Livermore colleague, Doug Beason. The first of these books, 1991's *Lifeline,* posits a futuristic scenario of an American base on the Moon, a corporate satellite called Orbitech, and a Soviet counterpart that is viewed with some suspicion. At the beginning of the story, the U.S. government has agreed to a deal with the Philippines: in order to extend the leases for their military bases on the Pacific archipelago, the government has provided the Philippines with a space station, called Aguinaldo. There, scientist Luis Sandovaal and his team of 1,500 researchers are creating groundbreaking new scientific products, including wall-kelp, a quick-growing edible that provides all necessary nutrients for humans. Aguinaldo is also home to experimental prototypes of fantastic flying creatures that can be transformed into sails for the satellites.

Lifeline's action starts with the space settlers observing nuclear mushroom clouds on Earth. The United States and the Soviet Union have attacked one another, and all space stations are stranded. The Russians on Kibalchick put themselves into suspended animation, while the Americans on Orbitech attempt to find a more immediate solution. When Brahms, the director of Orbitech, turns tyrannical and ejects 150 "under-performing" personnel, Duncan McLaris flees to the moon base Clavius. Then the Soviets unexpectedly awaken, and tensions mount. "The posing and solving of apparently

insuperable problems keeps the reader involved in that classic way," stated Tom Easton in *Analog Science Fiction and Fact,* who nonetheless faulted Anderson's pacing and his rapid introduction of technological innovations that come to the rescue. "At the same time, the characters are real enough to engage the reader's sympathy," Easton wrote, adding that "at the end there is a very real sense of resolution and satisfaction."

Anderson and Beason's second collaboration, *The Trinity Paradox,* "demonstrates their collaborative storytelling powers . . . effectively," wrote Dan Chow in *Locus.* This time the protagonist is Elizabeth Devane, a radical anti-nuclear activist. She and her boyfriend plan to disable a nuclear weapon sitting unguarded in the desert of the American Southwest, but a mishap occurs. Her boyfriend dies, and she is catapulted back in time to Los Alamos, New Mexico, during World War II, when that locale was the primary research site for U.S. nuclear weapons technology. Finding herself in the midst of a feverish race to master nuclear technology at the top-secret national laboratory, Devane realizes that through her actions she might be able to change history and sabotage the invention of the atomic bomb.

Instead of stopping the future Cold War, however, Devane's actions set in motion a new version of Cold War history: the outcome of World War II is affected, and nuclear technology heads in an entirely new direction. Realizing that she possesses the power to change the world, she becomes as dangerous as the scientists she considers traitors to humankind. "Hers is the most chilling of revolutionary beliefs, that with a constituency of one," noted Chow in *Locus. The Trinity Paradox* includes several real scientists in its plot, such as Robert Oppenheimer and Edward Teller, and the "Trinity" of the title takes its name from the site of the first successful test explosion.

Anderson and Beason continued their successful collaboration in *Assemblers of Infinity.* Set in the early decades of the twenty-first century, the plot centers around a group of scientists who believe an alien invasion is imminent. A team of investigators is sent to a suspicious site at the Earth's base on the moon, but they mysteriously die shortly after landing. Back on Earth, other researchers are positing that the relatively new field of nano-technology—machines run by microprocessors—may have something to do both the deaths and the threat of invasion. Erika Trace, one of the Earth's leading nano scientists, is enlisted to help.

Assemblers of Infinity won praise from reviewers. *Kliatt* contributor Bette D. Ammon noted: "The premise is riveting and the technology is fascinating." Ammon added that Anderson and Beason create a situation "utterly plausible and frightening—the stuff of which good SF is made." In a review for *Voice of Youth Advocates,* Rosie Peasley praised its "sophisticated science fiction concepts," declaring that "the plot hums along at high speed." In a *Booklist* critique, Roland Green compared it to "the techno-thriller, sort of a Tom-Clancy-meets-space-advocacy effort."

Ill Wind was Anderson's fourth collaboration with Beason, an eco-thriller involving a massive oil spill in San Francisco Bay. The large corporation responsible for this disaster, eager to clean up both the spill and its corporate image as quickly as possible, unleashes an untried new microbe to do the job. Soon the uncontrollable organism begins eating everything made from petroleum products, such as gasoline and plastic. When martial law is declared and the electricity fails, a scientist and two pilots try to save the world.

In *Virtual Destruction,* Anderson and Beason move the action closer to home: the story is set at the Livermore Labs and shows how large national defense labs were forced to refocus their missions after the end of Cold War tensions. After decades of relying heavily on federal funding to develop new weapons technology, Livermore and other facilities were challenged to find consumer and private-sector applications for their patents. The conflicts presented by this new era—specifically between profit-minded management and the more altruistic scientists—is the focus of *Virtual Destruction.* The plots revolves around a virtual reality chamber that produces devastatingly real effects; Livermore executive Hal Michaelson is discussing with the government possible uses for this chamber in the dangerous realm of nuclear-weapons surveillance. One of Michaelson's researchers, Gary Lesserec, who has been involved with the Virtual Reality Lab from its conception, knows that this is not feasible, that even sound recordings can trick entrants. Lesserec is about to be fired when Michaelson is found dead inside the chamber. FBI agent Craig Kreident investigates and uncovers nefarious industrial espionage links to the computer-gaming industry. The introduction of Kreident changes the novel's genre from sci-fi thriller to detective fiction, but as Tom Easton noted in *Analog Science Fiction and Fact:* "There's not much detecting going on here. The tale exists to give us a tour of Livermore, explicate some interesting technology, and discuss the problems the end of the Cold War has given the national labs."

For help with the details in his next book with Beason, Anderson was able to make an insider's visit to Kennedy Space Center in Florida. *Ignition* chronicles the planning and sabotage of a joint U.S.-Soviet mission on the space shuttle *Atlantis.* The first commodore, Colonel Adam "Iceberg" Friese, suffers an accident that cancels his participation. He becomes vitally involved, nevertheless, when a band of terrorists, organized by a famous Wall Street criminal, takes the crew hostage. The pilot's former paramour, Nicole Hunter, an astronaut-turned-launch controller, is also held hostage, but manages to help Friese battle the gang, some of whom have unusual personal quirks. The realistic details pertaining to the launch pad and pre-launch tensions, somewhat altered for security reasons, make *Ignition* "a nail biter" of a book, according to *Library Journal* contributor Grant A. Frederickson.

Intrepid FBI agent Kreident reappears in Anderson and Beason's next thriller, *Lethal Exposure.* This work is set at another government-funded research facility, the Fermi National Accelerator Laboratory in Illinois. Kreident arrives to investigate the mysterious radiation death of renowned physicist Georg Dumenco. A contributor to *Publishers Weekly* observed that the authors' familiarity with the subject matter and lab environment "gives their latest [book] plenty of scientific authenticity."

Anderson is also the author of several books in the "Star Wars" series. The plots, aimed at young-adult readers but popular with "Star Wars" fans of all ages, help provide panoramic details of the factions, clans, and worlds in this classic saga of good and evil. The first series is set at the Jedi Academy and begins with *Jedi Search.* Heroic Han Solo is married to Princess Leia, and they have three small children. Other characters from the original 1977 film make appearances, including Luke Skywalker and Chewbacca, and a new one is introduced, the teenager Kyp Durron. Spice mines and a space battle lead to a "rollicking SF adventure," reported Ingrid von Hausen in a review for *Kliatt.* Together with the Anderson-penned sequels *Dark Apprentice* and *Champions of the Force,* the books were published under the collective title *Jedi Academy Trilogy.*

Anderson has written several other "Star Wars" books that are not part of a definitive series. In *Darksaber* the Empire is again attempting to resurrect its former glory, aided by a new leader of the Hutt group named Durga.

Luke Skywalker is in love with a Jedi named Callista, whose special powers have vanished. Many other successful science-fiction writers have authored titles for various "Star Wars" series, but "Anderson leads the pack in both overall popularity and sheer storytelling power," opined Carl Hays in *Booklist.* Hays further remarked that Anderson's well-developed characters add greatly to their appeal, giving readers a far more in-depth treatment than is possible in the film plots.

Anderson has coauthored most of the books for the "Young Jedi Knights" series with his wife, Rebecca Moesta. In this series, the heroes are teen twins Jacen and Jaina, the offspring of Han Solo and Princess Leia. Series debut *Heirs of the Force* finds the two at the fabled Jedi Academy founded by their uncle, Luke Skywalker. When the teens are captured by a fighter pilot from the evil Empire, they are threatened with being stranded on a jungle moon. In *The Lost Ones,* Anderson and Moesta again place Jacen and Jaina in danger. As expected, the fourteen-year-olds ably extricate from danger both themselves and a friend who has been lured astray by the malevolent Dark Jedi Master, Brakiss. The Dark Jedi Force is attempting to revive the empire, creating a Second Imperium that will rule the galaxy. Hugh M. Flick, reviewing *The Lost Ones* in *Kliatt,* called it, along with its two series predecessors, "well written and . . . interesting for *Star Wars* fans of all ages."

Lightsabers, another book in the series, features the maimed Tenel Ka, a friend of Jacen and Jaina. Tenel Ka's arm was destroyed when her lightsaber misfired, and out of shame she has exiled herself to the planet Hapes, where she is now the crown princess. Jacen and Jaina help her attempt to maintain political stability on her home planet, and convince her to return to the Jedi Academy despite her accident. In the fifth book in the "Young Jedi Knights" series, *Darkest Knight,* Jacen and Jaina travel to Kashyyk, home of Lowbacca and the Wookies. The Dark Jedis of the Shadow Academy steal vital computer technology to help build the Second Imperium, But Jacen and Jaina save the galaxy once again.

Anderson has authored several solo titles outside the young adult market that have garnered him definitive praise. Among these is the short story collection *Dogged Persistence,* which includes eighteen stories that range from "Scientific Romance," a tale of H.G. Wells as an earnest young student, to "Final Performance," wherein lumber from the demolished Globe Theatre brings with

it the ghosts of long-dead actors when it is used to construct a new stage. Praising the collection, a *Publishers Weekly* contributor noted that the collection "provide[s] solid entertainment, and reveal[s] depths not evident in Anderson's more commercial fiction," while *Booklist* reviewer Roland Green dubbed *Dogged Persistence* "pretty good reading."

Climbing Olympus is set on a planet Mars inhabited by three types of humans. Rachel Dycek, the United Nations commissioner there, is in charge of Lowell Base. She is the famous surgeon who created *adins* (Russian for "first"), surgically modified prisoners from Soviet labor camps whose physiology was altered to enable them to survive on Mars and construct a colony.

After the adins rebelled and fled to another part of the planet, Dycek created the *dva* (Russian for "two"), much less monstrously engineered and in possession of a higher degree of intelligence. The dvas were sent to Mars to prepare an infrastructure that would allow average, non-modified humans to survive there. As their work nears completion, both the dvas and Dycek are being phased out. When a landslide kills a large number of dvas, Dycek learns that, although adins and dvas were sterilized, the partner of an escaped adin named Boris is now expecting a child. On the mountain Pavonis Mons, Dycek finds the unbalanced Boris ruling over the remaining adins and she attempts to right her past wrongs and direct the planet toward a more harmonious future. Reviewers praised Anderson's vividly drawn portrayals, and Russell Letson in *Locus* called Dycek and Boris "characters as compelling as the technological widgetry of survival augmentation or the extremities of the Martian landscape and climate."

Anderson's rank as a leading American science fiction writer was reinforced by his selection as coauthor in creating companion works to Frank Herbert's classic sci-fi novel, *Dune,* and its five sequels. Anderson first teamed with Herbert's son, Brian Herbert, to write *Dune: House Atreides,* and received for it the most lucrative contract ever signed by a science fiction author. The novel has since been followed by several other "Dune" novels.

Dune: House Atreides and the subsequent *Dune: House Harkonnen* and *Dune: House Corrino* serve as a "prequel" trilogy to *Dune.* As such, the coauthors' first task was to explain some of the relationships and feuds behind the extremely intricate plot of the original book.

Central to all characters and subplots is the vast wasteland of Dune, where nothing except "Spice" lives. Authors Anderson and Herbert won praise from a *Publishers Weekly* contributor for their creation of a complex groundwork for lovers of the original *Dune*. The critic wrote: "The attendant excitement and myriad revelations not only make this novel a terrific read in its own right but will inspire readers to turn, or return, to its great predecessor." *New York Times Book Review* contributor Gerald Jonas thought Anderson and Herbert "fall far short of their model when describing action," but allowed that "the new work captures the sense of seriousness that distinguished the earlier works." Jonas added that *Dune* enthusiasts "will rejoice in this chance to return to one of science fiction's most appealing futures."

Of *Dune: House Harkonnen,* a *Publishers Weekly* contributor stated: "Although myriad plot lines abound and plans are afoot in every Great House to bring down the Kwisatz's enemies, very little actually happens for much of the book." However, Jackie Cassada in *Library Journal* highly recommended the novel, stating that it offers "strong characterizations, consistent plotting, and rich detail" that allow for "the same evocative power of the original novels." Jonas remarked that *Dune: House Harkonnen* "succeeds admirably in setting the stage for the epic conflicts recounted" in Herbert's original "Dune" volumes.

In the concluding volume of the trilogy, *Dune: House Corrino,* a weak-willed emperor, head of the ruling House Corrino, is threatened by the devious Count Fenring, who learns of the location of a synthetic spice operation. In a *Booklist* review of the work, Roberta Johnson noted that the coauthors "draw emotional power from every character to fuel the complex political tale they tell."

Sandworms of Dune, which Anderson wrote with Brian Herbert, provides readers with yet another installment in the "Dune" series, one designed to wrap up the world and close the saga. At this point in the series, humankind and the planets they live on face potential annihilation. In an effort to defeat the machines, Sheanna has put the ghola cloning effort to work recreating the greatest minds of the history of the series, including Paul, Jessica, both the first and second Leto, Chani, Stilgar, Wellington Yueh, and Baron Harkonnen. The natural result of such a cast in a certain amount of disagreement and internal bickering over the plan. The opposi-

tion is led by the thinking machines Omnius and Erasmus, who seek to locate the no-ship which houses the human leaders. Anderson and Herbert based the book on notes left by Frank Herbert, and the plot itself is somewhat uneven, with many of the characters left undeveloped and the action sparse if exciting. *Booklist* reviewer Freida Murray commented that the book "should fascinate Dune fans." A reviewer for *Publishers Weekly,* however, noted that "others will be underwhelmed." *Library Journal* contributor Jackie Cassada found the book "complex in structure though never hard to follow."

In his 2006 collection of short stories titled *Landscapes,* Anderson presents twenty-two science fiction and fantasy stories, including some collaborative efforts with his wife and others. The book also includes two essays by Anderson. "A generous variety of themes and settings should please existing Anderson devotees while also providing a warm welcome for new fans," wrote Carl Hays in *Booklist.* Harriet Klausner, writing on the *Harriet Klausner's Book Review* Web site, noted the author's "ability to paint seemingly realistic backgrounds regardless of genre."

Anderson has also continued to contribute to his "Saga of Seven Suns" series, which began with *Hidden Empire.* The fifth book in the series, *Of Fire and Night,* is a novel about the ruler of earth, Basil Wenceslas, slowly going insane and alienating both humans and nonhumans throughout space as he continues to maintain a stranglehold on his power. Ultimately, nonhumans may decide to destroy Earth in order to get rid of the mad leader. Roland Green, writing in *Booklist,* noted that the book is part of "a large canvas being filled with notable skill, sure to please lovers of action." A *Publishers Weekly* contributor wrote that the author "combines glitzy space-opera flash with witty, character-driven action."

In the *Crystal Doors #1: Island Realm,* Anderson and coauthor Moesta tell the story of cousins Gwen and Vic, children of archaeologists and two strange women that the archaeologists met while on a dig. After Gwen's parents are killed and Vic's mother goes missing, they find Vic's father in a room full of crystals, leading them to be transported to the world of Elantya, a type of way station for travelers from different worlds. Although the many visitors offer to help the two teens get home, Gwen and Vic end up involved in a war with monsters called "merlons." Saleena L. Davidson, writing in the

School Library Journal, noted that "the protagonists are realistically drawn and the adventures exciting." A *Kirkus Reviews* contributor referred to *Crystal Doors #1* as a "tension-filled work . . . with . . . likable teen characters and exciting plot."

Anderson also completed an unfinished draft of a book by the late A.E. Van Vogt to produce the novel *Slan Hunter,* a follow-up to Van Vogt's 1940 novel *Slan.* The novel features an invasion of earth by Martians. A *Publishers Weekly* contributor noted that "the fast pacing, melodramatic situations and snappy . . . dialogue all match the original seamlessly."

In *The Last Days of Krypton,* Anderson goes back to the home planet of Superman in an effort to provide comic fans and other readers with a clear picture of that world and the various steps that led to its eventual destruction. Anderson was motivated to write the book by the general lack of an overall history of the planet that is so frequently referred to in the Superman comic books, as well as the radio shows, films, books, and various television programs that were spun off from the original comic concept. Given that Krypton and its death served as the impetus for Superman's arrival on Earth, Anderson felt that it was a vital piece of the back story that needed to be addressed. The book begins with Jor-El and Lara, Superman's parents, as they meet and court each other before eventually marrying. Jor-El is a brilliant scientist, and in Anderson's story he spends much of his time and energy stressing the need for the planet to reach out across the galaxies and to endorse space travel as a means of expanding their own knowledge. He comes up with a number of inventions designed to aid in this project, but all are rejected by the committee led by General Zod, who later becomes his nemesis and Superman's as well, stalling Jor-El's efforts. Though Jor-El's inventions are banned from use, that does not stop Zod from putting them to work on his own behalf. Carl Hays, reviewing for *Booklist,* remarked that "in providing a rich overview of Kryptonian civilization, Anderson turns in another solid sf performance."

BIOGRAPHICAL AND CRITICAL SOURCES:

BOOKS

St. James Guide to Science-Fiction Writers, 4th edition, St. James Press (Detroit, MI), 1996.

PERIODICALS

Analog Science Fiction and Fact, May, 1991, Tom Easton, review of *Lifeline,* pp. 178-180; August, 1996, Tom Easton, review of *Virtual Destruction,* p. 146.

Booklist, February 15, 1993, Roland Green, review of *Assemblers of Infinity,* p. 1041; September 15, 1995, Carl Hays, review of *Darksaber,* p. 144; May 15, 2001, Roland Green, review of *Dogged Persistence,* p. 1738; August, 2001, Roberta Johnson, review of *Dune: House Corrino,* p. 2051; February 15, 2006, Carl Hays, review of *Landscapes,* p. 54; June 1, 2006, Roland Green, review of *Of Fire and Night,* p. 49; June 1, 2007, Frieda Murray, review of *Sandworms of Dune,* p. 6; October 1, 2007, Carl Hays, review of *The Last Days of Krypton,* p. 41.

Kirkus Reviews, June 1, 2006, review of *Crystal Doors #1: Island Realm,* p. 577.

Kliatt, January, 1990, review of *Gameplay,* p. 16; May, 1993, Bette D. Ammon, review of *Assemblers of Infinity,* p. 12; May, 1994, Ingrid Von Hausen, review of *Jedi Search,* p. 13; May, 1996, Hugh M. Flick, review of *The Lost Ones,* p. 12.

Library Journal, January, 1997, Grant A. Frederickson, review of *Ignition,* p. 141; October 15, 1999, Jackie Cassada, review of *Dune: House Atreides,* p. 109; September 15, 2000, Jackie Cassada, review of *Dune: House Harkonnen,* p. 118; February 15, 2006, Jackie Cassada, review of *Landscapes,* p. 110; July 1, 2007, Jackie Cassada, review of *Sandworms of Dune,* p. 80.

Locus, February, 1989, review of *Gamearth,* p. 21; November, 1989, review of *Gamearth,* p. 53; December, 1991, Dan Chow, review of *The Trinity Paradox,* p. 31; August, 1994, Russell Letson, review of *Climbing Olympus,* p. 27.

New York Times Book Review, November 28, 1999, Gerald Jonas, review of *Dune: House Atreides;* October 1, 2000, review of *Dune: House Harkonnen.*

Publishers Weekly, June 3, 1988, Barbara Bannon, review of *Resurrection, Inc.,* p. 83; June 15, 1998, review of *Lethal Exposure,* p. 57; August 30, 1999, review of *Dune: House Atreides,* p. 57; October 2, 2000, review of *Dune: House Harkonnen,* p. 63; May 21, 2001, review of *Dogged Persistence,* p. 86; December 19, 2005, review of *Landscapes,* p. 46; May 22, 2006, review of *Of Fire and Night,* p. 34; April 9, 2007, review of *Slan Hunter,* p. 36; July 23, 2007, review of *Sandworms of Dune,* p. 48.

School Library Journal, September, 2006, Saleena L. Davidson, review of *Crystal Doors #1: Island Realm,* p. 212.

Voice of Youth Advocates, August, 1993, Rosie Peasley, review of *Assemblers of Infinity,* p. 159.

ONLINE

Harriet Klausner's Book Reviews, http://harrietklausner. wwwi.com/ (July 30, 2007), review of *Landscapes.*

Kevin J. Anderson Home Page, http://www.wordfire. com (July 30, 2007).*

*　　　*　　　*

ANDERSON, Kevin James
　　See ANDERSON, Kevin J.

*　　　*　　　*

ANDREISSEN, David
　　See POYER, David

*　　　*　　　*

ARANA, Marie 1949-

PERSONAL: Born September 15, 1949, in Lima, Peru; immigrated to the United States, 1959; daughter of Jorge Enrique (an engineer) and Marie Elverine Arana; married Wendell B. Ward, Jr., December 18, 1972 (divorced, 1998); married Jonathan Yardley, March 21, 1999; children: Hilary Walsh, Adam Williamson Ward. *Education:* Northwestern University, B.A., 1971; Yale University in China, certificate of scholarship, 1976; British University, M.A., 1977.

ADDRESSES: Home—Washington, DC, and Lima, Peru. *Office*—Washington Post, 1150 15th St., NW, Washington, DC 20071-0002. *E-mail*—aranam@washpost.com.

CAREER: Writer, journalist, critic, editor, novelist. British University, Hong Kong, lecturer in linguistics, 1978-79; Harcourt, Brace, Jovanovich, New York, NY, senior editor, 1980-89; Simon & Schuster, New York, NY, senior editor and vice president, 1989-92; *Washington*

Post, writer and editor, 1992-99, *Book World,* editor-in-chief, 1999-2008. Director and member of board of Center for Policy Research, Washington, DC, 1994-99.

MEMBER: National Association of Hispanic Journalists (member of board of directors, 1996-99), National Book Critics Circle (member of board of directors, 1996-2000).

AWARDS, HONORS: Award for excellence in editing, ABA, 1985; Christopher Award for excellence in editing, 1986; finalist, National Book Award and PEN Memoir Award, for *American Chica.*

WRITINGS:

American Chica: Two Worlds, One Childhood (memoir), Dial Press (New York, NY), 2001.

(Editor and author of introduction) *The Writing Life: Writers on How They Think and Work: A Collection from the Washington Post Book World,* Public Affairs (New York, NY), 2003.

Cellophane (novel), Dial Press (New York, NY), 2006.

(Author of introduction) *Off the Page: Writers Talk about Beginnings, Endings, and Everything in Between,* edited by Carole Burns, W.W. Norton (New York, NY), 2008.

Lima Nights (novel), Dial Press (New York, NY), 2009.

Editor of *Studies in Bilingualism,* 1978.

SIDELIGHTS: Marie Arana spent the first several decades of her career as a journalist, editor, and critic judging the writing of others. When her own work, a memoir titled *American Chica: Two Worlds, One Childhood,* was published by Dial Press in 2001, Arana decided that it would not be reviewed in *Book World,* the respected weekly book review section she oversees for the *Washington Post.*

Arana's parents met in the 1940s when her father, Jorge Enrique Arana, was studying at the Massachusetts Institute of Technology. Her mother, Marie, was a violinist. After they married, they returned to her father's native country of Peru, where Arana was born and spent her early childhood until the family moved to the United States in 1959. As Arana describes it in *American Chica,* it was a childhood "rooted to the Andean dust" in the family's hacienda in Cartavio, Peru.

Her father was working as an engineer for the multi-national corporation W.R. Grace. Her mother was not welcomed into her husband's culture, and when the couple returned to the United States and settled in Summit, New Jersey, Arana would first feel the sting of those cultural differences. She relates in her memoir that on a train ride west to visit her mother's family in Wyoming, another passenger looked at her and remarked: "Well, I'll be. She's a little foreigner." In New Jersey the Aranas were the only Hispanic family. One black girl told her: "You oughta go back where you belong." With a father who went back and forth between Peru and the United States and an awareness of the cultural gap between her parents, Arana realized early on that she would have to be adaptable, sometimes filling the role befitting her dark Peruvian features and sometimes the role of an American girl with an American heritage.

Arana studied Russian language and literature at Northwestern University, where she received her degree in 1971. Her early marriage in 1972 to Wendell Ward took her to Hong Kong, where she received a certificate of scholarship in the Mandarin language through Yale University in China and a master's degree in linguistics from the British University there in 1977, while she also taught linguistics. When she returned to the United States, she worked as an editor at Harcourt, Brace, Jovanovich and at Simon & Schuster, dividing her time between New York and Washington, DC, Focusing on nonfiction, she worked with such authors as Eugene McCarthy and Pat Moynihan, both former U.S. senators. She also enjoyed working on fiction and edited the works of such novelists as Stanley Elkin and Manuel Puig. By 1992 Arana had joined the *Post* as deputy book editor, and eventually she rose to editor of its weekly book review supplement, *Book World*.

Arana revealed in a *Publishers Weekly* interview with Joseph Barbato that it was a comment made on her first day on the job that marked a new beginning for her—thinking of herself as a member of a minority group. She told Barbato: "My first day on the job, the head of recruitment stopped when she saw on my forms that I was born in Lima. 'Oh, are you a minority hire?' she asked me, wondering how to put me down. 'Well, I guess you could say so,' I told her." Arana realized she was a member of a growing group of Americans, that of a minority, and she began to serve on various committees on diversity, working to get more coverage of the Hispanic population into the newspaper. As a panel moderator for the National Association of Hispanic

Journalists, she realized that her sense of her own Latina identity was not easy to define. "When I was in either place, Peru or the U.S., I felt one parent was a blip," Arana told Barbato. "My own experience was of blipping in and out; of belonging and not belonging." It was a fellow panelist, the poet Judith Ortiz Cofer, who afterward encouraged her to write a memoir.

For Arana, writing *American Chica* represented more than the publication of her first book. "I had done a good job of burying the child I was. As I wrote, I found there was something very rigid and false about the armor I had built around myself. I was always the professional businesswoman who was a certain way—who would never want to have anything but a perfect life revealed," she told Barbato. Writing the book not only transformed her emotions but brought about the end of her marriage when she realized she was in love with a fellow *Post* staffer, the book critic Jonathan Yardley, who was reading each chapter as she finished it. Yardley came to realize that he was in love with her as well. Their lives changed dramatically as they left their respective families and eventually married. All of this dramatic change was the result of writing a book she had not set out to write.

In 1996 Arana was on a one-month media fellowship at Stanford University. When she completed her project, she researched the story of Julio Cesar Arana, an infamous Peruvian rubber baron known in the early 1900s as the "Devil of Putumayo." He imposed cruel and unusual punishments on his workers, the thousands of indigenous peoples working the rubber plantations. His scandalous behavior was eventually exposed to international scrutiny by an Irish patriot named Roger Casement. Although Arana was told repeatedly by her family that he was not a relative, she nonetheless maintained the suspicion that he was. While sifting through the stacks of information she found at Stanford on this vicious man, Arana became absorbed in wondering what it might mean if he were a relative. Then she began to think about her childhood, caught between two different worlds.

When an enthusiastic book agent responded positively to sample pages of the book Arana had begun to write, she decided to take an eight-month leave of absence from her job at the *Post* in order to finish it. During that time she returned to the Peru of her early childhood to explore more fully the story of the possible ancestor. Not only did she find out that she was indeed related to

Julio Cesar Arana, but she had the unsettling experience of being told by a local historian that she "had his face." It was then that she decided the book would be the story of her parents.

In her review for the *New York Times Book Review,* Wendy Gimbel characterized *American Chica* as a work that sometimes reads like "a collaboration between John Cheever and Isabel Allende. Arana's mother and father constantly lose their balance as they stumble over cultural minefields. Of free-spirited pioneer stock, the young wife feels shackled, the prisoner of Peru's demanding traditions. But her husband doesn't understand her need to turn her back on the past." Barbara Wallraff noted in her review for the *Atlantic* that "a person of a metaphorical turn of mind can read into this book the history of U.S.-Latin American relations, and if that's what you feel like doing, you'll suspect that Arana is abetting you. But the book also reads like a novel—almost. A fiction writer aiming for verisimilitude would have toned some of this material down. Surely no novelist would have had the narrator's mother marry so many times. And no one but Gabriel García Marquez would have dared to invent an adventurer uncle who lends the household a monkey and an anteater. *American Chica* tells a fantastical, spellbinding tale."

Arana noted that during the first four years of her life in Peru, a total of eighteen earthquakes shook the country. She saw those tremors, according to Donna Seaman, writing for *Booklist,* as "emblematic of the forces that jeopardized her family's attempt to span the vast divide between North and South America."

Arana became a novelist in 2006 with publication of *Cellophane,* a blend of magical realism and realistic fiction, set in the Amazon at the height of the Great Depression. Arana's protagonist is the successful engineer and paper producer Don Victor Sobrevilla, who has carved out a fabulous estate, Floralinda, in the Amazon region of Peru. There he lives with his extended family, on the cusp of a changing world. His great desire has always been to create cellophane, not paper, and when he decides to redirect his mills to that production, "his life and those of the people around him change in unexpected ways, both humorous and tragic," according to *BookPage* Web site contributor Harvey Freedenberg. As with the transparent product at the heart of this novel, Don Victor's decision spawns an avalanche of honesty among his family: he confesses an earlier love affair to his wife, who, in turn, tells him of her own first affair at the same time Don Victor was courting her. Characters discover honesty and transparency are not always the best policies.

Cellophane, with its butterflies appearing out of a doffed hat and strange growths on the bodies of some of the characters, invited obvious comparisons to the work of other Latin American writers of magical realism such as Isabel Allende and Gabriel Garcia Marquez. For Clark Collis, writing for *Entertainment Weekly,* however, despite the book's "richly descriptive and, at times, darkly comic tone," *Cellophane* did not live up to such a lofty comparison. Other reviewers had a more positive assessment of this debut novel. Pope Brock, writing in *People,* noted that even those readers who did not like magical realism "may fall under its spell when it's this well done." Brock went on to call Arana's novel a "great book." *Booklist* contributor Donna Seaman termed the same work a "bewitching story shaped by a profound understanding of the oneness of life," while a *Kirkus Reviews* contributor found it a "pleasure to read." Further praise came from a *Publishers Weekly* reviewer who described *Cellophane* as "a tale as bawdy, raucous and dense as the jungle whose presence encroaches on every page," and from *Miami Herald* writer Fabiola Santiago, who thought it was "exquisitely written." Santiago also noted: "Arana is a finely tuned writer who knows how to harvest her worlds and bring them to the main stage, an intellectual who delivers insight and story in any genre." Liesl Schillinger, writing for the *New York Times,* was also impressed with *Cellophane,* commenting that Arana "has flown above her own history to construct a surreal but orderly pattern: a fiction that's stranger than her truth but shares its bones."

Arana is also editor of *The Writing Life: Writers on How They Think and Work: A Collection from the Washington Post Book World.* Published in 2003, the book features contributions from more than fifty writers discussing various aspects of being a writer. The entries were previously published in the *Washington Post* column titled "The Writing Life." Arana is also author of the book's introduction and of the brief biographies of the writers that accompany each of their essays, which are arranged thematically in six sections titled: "On Becoming a Writer," "Raw Material," "Hunkering Down," "Old Bottle, New Wine," "Facing the Facts," and "Looking Back."

The book's contributors are primarily professional writers, including novelists, E.L. Doctorow, Nadine Gordiner, Julia Alvarez, Alice McDermott, Scott Turow,

John Edgar Wideman, Anita Desai, and Joyce Carol Oates. Nonfiction writers featured in the book include David Halberstam, Bill McKibben, and Tracy Kidder. In addition to these professional writers, other contributors include people who have specialized in other careers but who have also written books. They include E.O. Wilson and former U.S. President Jimmy Carter. "This vividly enlightening and entertaining collection is highly recommended," wrote Angela Weiler in a review for *Library Journal.* A *Kirkus Reviews* contributor commented that the book "meanders through everything from practical advice to thoughts of childhood to vague but entertaining musings on a career." Several reviewers also commented on Arana's contributions to the book. "In her introduction, Arana emphasizes the obvious but still necessary point that although there is much to learn from professional authors, there is no one way to write a great novel or nonfiction book," wrote Steve Weinberg in a review for the *Writer.* Hazel Rochman, writing for *Booklist,* noted that the author's "lively, highly readable, fairly lengthy bios capture each subject's essence."

Arana's second novel, *Lima Nights,* was published in 2009. Calling the book "an ambitious set of narrative ingredients" in a review for the *Rocky Mountain News Online* Web site, A.H. Goldstein added: "Questions of race, class, colonialism and love pervade Arana's latest novel." The novel revolves around Carlos Bluhm and Maria Fernandez. Carlos maintains a hold on the upper-class world of Lima despite the fact that the fortunes of his prominent German Peruvian family have fallen as Peru is terrorized by rebels in 1986, when the beginning of the novel takes place. Nevertheless, Carlos has an elegant wife, and his occasional trysts with other women are brief and mean little to him. However, when he meets the fifteen-year-old Maria at a tango bar in a seedy part of town, Carlos becomes intoxicated with the young girl, who is a dark, indigenous Peruvian from the dangerous part of town.

Maria's father was murdered and her mother and brothers have largely succumbed to a failed life living in the poorest part of Lima. Maria, however, works hard at a grocery story and dancing in the evenings at the Lima Nights club, where she meets Carlos. "Bluhm is shocked to learn that she is only fifteen, but he can't keep away," wrote Donna Seaman in a review for the *Los Angeles Times Online.* "He finds Maria wild and joyous, the opposite of his restrained, increasingly severe wife. Determined Maria sees her golden admirer as the key to a better life."

The first half of the novel follows Carlos and Maria as their relationship intensifies and Carlos becomes more and more focused on pleasing Maria in every way he can, much of it materially. "Skillfully blending Bluhm's growing obsession with Maria and the demands of wife and children, the author sets the stage for tragedy," noted *Curled Up with a Good Book* Web site contributor Luan Gaines. Eventually, Carlos decides to leave his wife, Sophie, and children, Fritz and Rudy, to live with Maria despite the fact that it means the loss not only of his family but also of his friends and his way of life. The second half of the novel takes place twenty years later in 2006. Carlos and Maria are still together but their relationship has disintegrated as each sees the other in far different light than when they met. Eventually, violent emotions that have remained beneath the surface of their relationship erupt.

In a review of *Lima Nights* for the *San Francisco Chronicle Online,* Joseph Olshan noted that "the final outcome is a true, cinematic cliff-hanger that seems both poignant and right," adding: "It is a testimony to this author's finesse that despite a certain pull of inevitability, we are kept in suspense until the last word." Noting that the author "explores with psychological awareness and sympathy" the intricate reasons why the relationship between Carlos and Maria finally ends badly, a *Kirkus Reviews* contributor went on in the same review to call the novel "brooding and elegant, much against the grain of lighthearted South American love stories."

Arana is also the author of the introduction to *Off the Page: Writers Talk about Beginnings, Endings, and Everything in Between.* Edited by Carole Burns, the book is a collection of interviews drawn from an online chat program conducted by the *Washington Post.* The book includes a wide range of writers, including Richard Ford, A.S. Byatt, Doreen Baingana, and Martin Amis. A contributor to the *Publishers Weekly Online* called the book a "treat for avid readers and writers."

BIOGRAPHICAL AND CRITICAL SOURCES:

BOOKS

Arana, Marie, *American Chica: Two Worlds, One Childhood,* Dial Press (New York, NY), 2001.

PERIODICALS

Atlantic, June, 2001, Barbara Wallraff, review of *American Chica,* p. 104.

Booklist, April 15, 2001, Donna Seaman, review of *American Chica,* p. 1511; March 15, 2003, Hazel Rochman, review of *The Writing Life: Writers on How They Think and Work: A Collection from the Washington Post Book World,* p. 1269; November 15, 2005, Molly McQuade, "Marie Arana, Book Critic Turned First Novelist," p. 19; May 15, 2006, Donna Seaman, review of *Cellophane,* p. 21; December 1, 2008, Donna Seaman, review of *Lima Nights,* p. 24.

Christian Science Monitor, January 9, 2009, Yvonne Zipp, review of *Lima Nights,* p. 25.

Entertainment Weekly, May 11, 2001, review of *American Chica,* p. 74; June 30, 2006, Clark Collis, review of *Cellophane,* p. 166.

Fort Worth Star-Telegram (Ft. Worth, TX), August 7, 2001, Rebecca Rodriguez, "Visiting the Compelling World of an 'American Chica.'"

Hispanic Magazine, September, 2001, Gigi Anders, "Marie Arana: American Chica," interview with author, p. 102.

Houston Chronicle (Houston, TX), August 22, 2001, Malinda Nash, "Life from Both Sides: Marie Arana Memoir Probes Her Family's Biculturalism."

Kirkus Reviews, May 15, 2006, review of *Cellophane,* p. 475; February 15, 2003, review of *The Writing Life,* p. 280; October 15, 2008, review of *Lima Nights.*

Library Journal, April 15, 2001, Adriana Lopez, review of *American Chica,* p. 106, and Rebecca Miller, "Bridging a Bicultural Divide," interview with author, p. 112; April 1, 2003, Angela Weiler, review of *The Writing Life,* p. 111; June 15, 2006, Jennifer Stidham, review of *Cellophane,* p. 54; November 15, 2008, Jenn B. Stidham, review of *Lima Nights,* p. 59.

Miami Herald (Miami, FL), July 5, 2006, Fabiola Santiago, review of *Cellophane.*

New York Times, July 16, 2006, Liesl Schillinger, "A Wilderness of Mud," review of *Cellophane.*

New York Times Book Review, May 13, 2001, Wendy Gimbel, "Bilingual Education: Born to a Peruvian Father and an American Mother, Author Examines Her Hyphenated Life," p. 7; February 8, 2009, Jan Stuart, "Obsession," review of *Lima Nights,* p. 19.

People, July 3, 2006, Pope Brock, review of *Cellophane,* p. 47.

Publishers Weekly, April 2, 2001, review of *American Chica,* p. 48; June 4, 2001, Joseph Barbato, "Uniting Worlds Through Language," interview with author, p. 51; April 24, 2006, review of *Cellophane,* p. 37; October 20, 2008, review of *Lima Nights,* p. 34.

Writer, September, 2003, Steve Weinberg, "New Collections on Writing Are Meant to Be Savored.," review of *The Writing Life,* p. 45.

ONLINE

Beattie's Book Blog, http://beattiesbookblog.blogspot.com/ (December 31, 2008), "Marie Arana Leaves the Washington Post's Book World."

BookPage, http://www.bookpage.com/ (December 18, 2006), Harvey Freedenberg, review of *Cellophane.*

Boston Globe Online, http://www.boston.com/ (January 11, 2009), Amanda Heller, "Short Takes," review of *Lima Nights.*

Chicago Tribune Online, http://www.chicagotribune.com/ (January 17, 2009), Beth Kephart, review of *Lima Nights.*

Curled Up with a Good Book, http://www.curledup.com/ (June 19, 2009), Luan Gaines, review of *Lima Nights.*

Emprise Review, http://muttsbane.com/ (June 19, 2009), Karen Rigby, "Tango Between Two Worlds: Marie Arana," review of *Lima Nights.*

Literary Kicks, http://www.litkicks.com/ (February 8, 2009), Levi Asher, "Reviewing the Review."

Los Angeles Times Online, http://www.latimes.com/ (January 4, 2009), Donna Seaman, review of *Lima Nights.*

Publishers Weekly Online, http://www.publishersweekly.com/ (January 7, 2008), review of *Off the Page: Writers Talk about Beginnings, Endings, and Everything In Between,*

Rocky Mountain News Online, http://m.rockymountainnews.com/ (January 8, 2009), A.H. Goldstein, review of *Lima Nights.*

Salon.com, http://www.salon.com/ (July 15, 1999), Craig Offman, "Washington Post Book World Editor Steps Down."

San Francisco Chronicle Online, http://www.sfgate.com/ (December 28, 2008), Joseph Olshan, review of *Lima Nights.*

Spanish Journal Online, http://www.spanishjournal.com/ (June 19, 2009), review of *Lima Nights.*

Washington Independent Writers, http://www.washwriter.org/ (December 18, 2006), "Marie Arana."

Washington Post Online, http://www.washpost.com/ (September 13, 2001), "Testimonials: Marie Arana"; (December 10, 2007) Carole Burns, "Off the Page: Marie Arana and Richard Bausch," interview with author.*

ATHILL, Diana 1917-

PERSONAL: Born December 21, 1917, in London, England; daughter of Lawrence Francis Imbert and Katharine Carr Athill. *Education:* Lady Margaret Hall, Oxford, B.A., 1939.

ADDRESSES: Home—London, England.

CAREER: British Broadcasting Corp. (BBC), London, England, researcher, 1941-46; Allan Wingate Publishers Ltd., London, England, editor, 1946-51; André Deutsch Publishers Ltd., London, England, director, 1952-92.

AWARDS, HONORS: Short story prize, London *Observer,* 1958; Costa Prize for biography, Booksellers Association of Great Britain and Ireland, 2008, for *Somewhere towards the End;* decorated officer, Order of the British Empire, 2009.

WRITINGS:

An Unavoidable Delay, and Other Stories, Doubleday (New York, NY), 1962.
Don't Look at Me like That (fiction), Chatto & Windus (London, England), 1967, Viking (New York, NY), 1967.

MEMOIRS

Instead of a Letter, Chatto and Windus (London, England), 1962, Doubleday (New York, NY), 1962.
After a Funeral, Jonathan Cape (London, England), 1986, Ticknor & Fields (New York, NY), 1986.
Make Believe: A True Story, Sinclair-Stevenson (London, England), 1993, Steerforth Press (Royalton, VT), 1993.
Stet: An Editor's Life, Granta Books (London, England), 2000, Grove Press (New York, NY), 2001.
Yesterday Morning, Granta Books (London, England), 2002.
Somewhere towards the End, Granta Books (London, England), 2008, W.W. Norton (New York, NY), 2009.

TRANSLATOR

Berthe Grimault, *Beau Clown,* André Deutsch (London, England), 1957.

Christine Arnothy, *Women of Japan,* André Deutsch (London, England), 1959.
Jacques Valentin, *The Monks of Mount Athos,* André Deutsch (London, England), 1960.
Christine Rivoyre, *The Sultans,* André Deutsch (London, England), 1967.
Pia Paoli, *Atoms at Tea-time: The Story of a Cure,* André Deutsch (London, England), 1968.
Liane de Pougy, *My Blue Notebooks,* Andre Deutsch (London, England), 1979, Harper (New York, NY), 1979.

Contributor to *Short Story One,* Hutchinson, 1961. Also contributor of short stories to periodicals, including *London Magazine, Evergreen Review, Harper's, Harper's Bazaar, Glamour,* and *Gentleman's Quarterly.*

SIDELIGHTS: As an editor at the London publishing company of André Deutsch, Diana Athill worked with some of the most notable writers of the twentieth century. Her several volumes of memoirs detail her many relationships with literary figures and offer what critics have found to be a fascinating look behind the scenes of the publishing world.

After working for the BBC during World War II, Athill met Hungarian émigré André Deutsch and accepted an editing job in his first publishing house, Allan Wingate. As recounted in *Stet: An Editor's Life,* she began a brief affair with Deutsch and was his partner in founding the company that bore his name. Though Athill admits she had no special qualifications for her job, she went on to work successfully with such major authors as V.S. Naipaul, Jack Kerouac, Molly Keane, Brian Moore, Mordecai Richler, Norman Mailer, Philip Roth, Jean Rhys, Margaret Atwood, and John Updike. "She had near impeccable editorial judgment," observed Evelyn Toynton in the *New York Times Book Review.*

In the opinion of many critics, she also had considerable literary talent of her own. Noel Perrin, in a *Washington Post Book World* assessment of her first memoir, *Instead of a Letter,* called her a "gifted writer" capable of the rare achievement of writing about oneself without any egotistical illusions. The book, written when Athill was forty-three, chronicles her privileged childhood and her adolescent love affair with Paul, an Oxford student who was her brother's tutor. After Paul rejected her, Athill began her career, but, according to Perrin, "led a kind of half-life" devoid of real joy. At age forty-one, however, her life reached a turning point when she began to write fiction and entered into a new and more rewarding romantic relationship. Noting that the book contains "the plot of many a romance novel," Perrin singled it out for its exceptional honesty and "overwhelming sense of female life," which he linked to Athill's talent for observation and detail. "I sighed with pleasure at how well this woman writes," he wrote.

Perrin expressed similar enthusiasm for Athill's second memoir, *After a Funeral,* an account of her five-year relationship with "Didi" (Waguih Ghali), a penniless Egyptian aristocrat living in London and ten years Athill's junior. In the book, which Perrin describes as "completely uncensored," Athill describes Didi as a reckless, brilliant romantic with whom she fell in love, who finally killed himself in her apartment. Didi was reluctant to make their relationship anything more than intellectual; though he lived with her for three years, he didn't want anyone to consider him Athill's lover. Perrin marveled at the author's ability to admit this embarrassing truth with such honesty. He also admired her insight. "Here a subtle woman is depicting the gradual self-destruction of an equally subtle man," he wrote. "The book reads like a first-rate psychoanalysis without the jargon and without the theories."

Another tumultuous relationship is at the heart of *Make Believe: A True Story.* In 1969 Athill met a radical African American writer, Hakim Jamal, fourteen years her junior. In *Make Believe,* Athill writes that when Jamal approached her with the idea for a book project about his relationship with Malcolm X, she and Jamal were immediately attracted to each other. Jamal, who grew up in Boston, had struggled with alcoholism and drug addiction and had been in prison for attempted murder. He was also notorious for the brutal treatment of his wife and children, lovers, and friends; he allowed his British companion, Gail Benson, to be murdered by the followers of Trinidadian racial extremist Michael X. A year after Benson's death, Jamal was murdered in an unrelated incident in the United States.

Critical response to *Make Believe* was mixed. Sean French, in *New Statesman & Society,* discerned an "elusive racism" in its theme of "attraction by whites to blackness and black culture, to its supposed air of primitive vitality, danger and primal sexuality." Finding a large element of "escape, experimentation and fantasy" in the relationship, French observed that Athill "writes honestly and painfully" about its ambiguities but in the end has written "a deeply disturbing book . . . that

. . . vividly enacts a racist fantasy." A reviewer for *Publishers Weekly,* however, found the book "occasionally compelling," while *Booklist* contributor Mary Ellen Sullivan appreciated its depiction of a "life-altering" relationship that is "ultimately less about political upheaval than about how personal histories shape personal futures."

Stet met with more consistent praise. Critics enjoyed its mix of gossip and insight and its candid detail. "Athill's own forte is describing people," commented Gabriele Annan in the *Times Literary Supplement,* finding the author's insights often "wickedly comical . . . but not unkind." Some of Athill's portraits, Annan observed, are "so perceptive as to be almost shocking." Critics particularly noted her insights on American writer Alfred Chester and on Jean Rhys, whose chapter Toynton considered "a miniature masterpiece." In the *Boston Globe,* Jules Verdone wrote that "What's exceptional [about *Stet*] is the way in which Athill tells stories, in utterly personal terms, about tantrums and trysts and drug use and poor judgment and unseemly behavior, presenting them with a matter-of-factness that can camouflage what they often are: gossip. It's a rare individual who can dish that kind of dish without suggesting that what she knows makes her special, without melodrama or apparent malice. Her tone says that she is merely passing along a bit of history."

In 2002 Athill published *Yesterday Morning.* The recollections here address Athill's memories from her childhood in the English countryside and how she found herself to be more similar to her mother than she once thought. Janice P. Nimura, writing in the *New York Times Book Review,* observed that the book "isn't all elegy. Athill strays from the rhapsodic mode to deliver bracingly candid opinions." Nimura added that "the book feels at times like a grab bag, a collection of all the odds and ends Athill traces to her early years. It is best enjoyed as a coda, since she refers back to her previous memoirs rather than describe a particular event over again." In an article in *Sydney Morning Herald,* Gaby Naher stated that "Athill is not the slightest bit coy in portraying her family's innate sense of superiority during her childhood years. But, instead of coming across as distant, she is earthy and refreshingly frank." Naher found the story relayed to be both "elegantly" and "evocatively" told.

Kate Kellaway, reviewing the book in the London *Observer,* described the book as "an inward book and memory—subversive, unpredictable—is her editor. She writes beautifully about the way children make up parables. I loved the saga of the cherry stains she and her cousin try to rinse out." Clare Colvin, reviewing the book in the London *Independent,* commented that "Athill's honesty in describing her feelings as a young girl and old woman makes her memoir universal. The humiliations of being young, the fear of looking silly, will strike a chord with anyone who remembers growing up. Nostalgia for the past is balanced by her clear-sighted view of exactly how it was."

Athill published another memoir, *Somewhere towards the End,* in 2008. The account won the Costa Prize for biography, making Athill the eldest recipient of the award at age ninety-one. The account describes what Athill considers to be the final chapters of her life, where she confronts her mortality, her physical abilities, and what she will leave behind.

Sarah Birke, reviewing the memoir in *New Statesman,* commented that "her memoirs display a vivacious appreciation of the life she has lived and what is still to come." *Lancette Arts Journal* contributor Alidë Kohlhaas thought that the account "felt empty," explaining that "it seemed to me that Athill has given us far too rational a book, one that avoids the real subject, namely The End. After reading her book I contemplated that I might have missed something in her writing; I am now convinced that I did not. After learning of the impending end of that someone related to me I can see that she, like him, has played the game of avoidance all her life, if this book is any indication." Leslie Cauley, reviewing the memoir in *USA Today,* warned that "beautiful prose goes only so far when the outlook is so dreary."

In an article in the *Boston Globe,* Barbara Fisher noted that "as an editor of many great writers, Athill writes on this potentially grim subject with clarity, calm, and common sense." A contributor to *Culturazzi* quoted one of the judges of the Costa Award committee as calling the memoir "candid, detailed, charming, totally lacking in self-pity or sentimentality and above all, beautifully, beautifully written." Martin Levin wrote in the Toronto *Globe & Mail* that "certainly not everyone possesses the same generosity of spirit that is a clear hallmark of the still remarkable and fearless Diana Athill. Instead of raging at the dying of the light, she continues to bask in its remaining rays."

Reviewing the book on *Salon.com,* Laura Miller summarized that "the best sort of inspiration to be had from those who've aged gracefully, it seems, comes in the examples they set. Diana Athill, a woman who worked for 50 years in the British publishing industry before making a late-life career as a memoirist, offers an excellent illustration of this principle with *Somewhere towards the End,* an account of how life looks to someone in her late 80s." Miller revealed that "while searching through *Somewhere towards the End* for pithy quotes that could convey the pervasive sense of wisdom I received from it, I came up almost empty-handed, despite the fact that the book is beautifully written. Athill's wisdom is more ambient than aphoristic; to read her memoir is to feel as if you are sitting in the company of someone who has really got things sorted out, even if you can't always discern the overarching system."

Karen Brady, reviewing the book in the *Buffalo News,* observed that "this is clearly a no-holds-barred book, one in which Athill shares information and interior thoughts that may not be every reader's cup of tea. She makes no bones about being selfish, judgmental and given to intellectual arrogance. She lets us know she has had at least one abortion and one miscarriage, was sexually active well into her 70s." Susan Salter Reynolds, reviewing the memoir in the *Los Angeles Times,* found that Athill "generously describes her mistakes with no trace of bitterness—this alone makes the book a great gift to us," labeling the memoir as "a warm, inspiring book." In an article in the *Washington Post Book World,* Michael Dirda concluded that "a refusal to sugar-coat and a commitment to utter frankness, coupled with an engaging style, make Diana Athill's *Somewhere towards the End* unusually appealing, despite its inherently cheerless subject. Certainly no amount of mendacity or whining will change the facts: The end of life is hard. With luck and adequate health, you might be able to enjoy a few simple pleasures for a while longer. But that's about it. And be grateful for even the smallest of such favors. Time is not on your side."

BIOGRAPHICAL AND CRITICAL SOURCES:

BOOKS

Athill, Diana, *Instead of a Letter,* Doubleday (New York, NY), 1962.

Athill, Diana, *After a Funeral,* Ticknor & Fields (New York, NY), 1986.

Athill, Diana, *Make Believe: a True Story,* Steerforth Press (Royalton, VT), 1993.

Athill, Diana, *Stet: An Editor's Life,* Granta Books (London, England), 2000, Grove Press (New York, NY), 2001.

Athill, Diana, *Yesterday Morning,* Granta Books (London, England), 2002.

Athill, Diana, *Somewhere towards the End,* Granta Books (London, England), 2008.

PERIODICALS

Antioch Review, winter, 1987, review of *After a Funeral,* p. 114.

Atlantic, January 1, 2003, review of *Yesterday Morning,* p. 168.

Best Sellers, November 15, 1967, review of *Don't Look at Me like That,* p. 329.

Booklist, November 15, 1967, review of *Don't Look at Me like That,* p. 375; March 15, 1994, Mary Ellen Sullivan, review of *Make Believe: A True Story,* p. 1323; March 1, 2001, Donna Seaman, review of *Stet: An Editor's Life,* p. 1207; December 1, 2008, Deborah Donovan, review of *Somewhere towards the End,* p. 13.

Books & Bookman, February, 1977, review of *Instead of a Letter,* p. 66; February, 1986, review of *After a Funeral,* p. 15.

Boston Globe, March 26, 2001, Jules Verdone, review of *Stet,* p. D18; January 18, 2009, Barbara Fisher, review of *Somewhere towards the End.*

British Book News, May, 1986, review of *After a Funeral,* p. 315.

Buffalo News (Buffalo, NY), March 22, 2009, Karen Brady, review of *Somewhere towards the End.*

Contemporary Review, September 1, 2002, review of *Yesterday Morning,* p. 191.

Economist, September 9, 2000, review of *Stet.*

First Post (London, England), January 9, 2009, "Diana Athill Wins Costa Award at 91."

Globe & Mail (Toronto, Ontario, Canada), November 25, 2000, review of *Stet,* p. D9; August 3, 2002, review of *Yesterday Morning,* p. D12; March 6, 2009, Martin Levin, review of *Somewhere towards the End.*

Guardian (London, England), January 5, 2008, "Getting Things Right"; February 28, 2009, John Mullan, review of *Somewhere towards the End,* p. 19; March 14, 2009, review of *Somewhere towards the End,* p. 6.

Harper's, November, 1967, review of *Don't Look at Me like That,* p. 130.

Houston Chronicle, February 8, 2009, Dwight Garner, "A Candid Look at Growing Old, Warts and All," p. 15.

Independent (London, England), January 12, 2002, Clare Colvin, review of *Yesterday Morning;* January 9, 2009, Katy Guest, "Rising Star"; January 11, 2009, Clare Colvin, review of *Somewhere towards the End;* January 13, 2009, D.J. Taylor, review of *Somewhere towards the End;* February 1, 2009, Brandon Robshaw, review of *Somewhere towards the End.*

Intelligent Life, summer, 2008, Maureen Cleave, author interview.

Kirkus Reviews, September 1, 1967, review of *Don't Look at Me like That,* p. 1069; January 1, 1994, review of *Make Believe,* p. 26; September 1, 2002, review of *Yesterday Morning,* p. 1274; October 1, 2008, review of *Somewhere towards the End.*

Lancette Arts Journal, April, 2008, Alidë Kohlhaas, review of *Somewhere towards the End,* p. 9.

Library Journal, November 1, 1967, review of *Don't Look at Me like That,* p. 4025; March 15, 1994, Wilda Williams, review of *Make Believe,* p. 78; January 1, 2001, Ellen Sullivan, review of *Stet,* p. 106.

Listener, October 26, 1967, review of *Don't Look at Me like That,* p. 546; March 6, 1986, review of *After a Funeral,* p. 26.

London Review of Books, July 3, 1986, review of *After a Funeral,* p. 11.

Los Angeles Times, January 4, 2009, Susan Salter Reynolds, review of *Somewhere towards the End.*

M2 Best Books, June 4, 2003, review of *Yesterday Morning.*

Mature Times, January 12, 2009, "'Retired' Author Shortlisted for Prestigious Costa Book of The Year."

Ms., June, 1985, Carolyn Heilbrun, review of *Instead of a Letter,* p. 58.

New Statesman, December 17, 1982, review of *Instead of a Letter,* p. 29; March 21, 1986, Gillian Wilce, review of *After a Funeral,* p. 29; January 22, 1988, Paul Hallam, review of *After a Funeral,* p. 32; January 24, 2008, Sarah Birke, review of *Somewhere towards the End,* p. 58.

New Statesman & Society, January 15, 1993, Sean French, review of *Make Believe,* p. 39.

New Yorker, November 25, 1967, review of *Don't Look at Me like That,* p. 244; December 10, 1984, Whitney Balliett, review of *Instead of a Letter,* p. 184; February 23, 2009, review of *Somewhere towards the End,* p. 70.

New York Times Book Review, November 5, 1967, review of *Don't Look at Me like That,* p. 59; January 6, 1980, review of *My Blue Notebooks,* p. 12; September 25, 1994, Bruce Allen, review of *Make*

Believe, p. 24; April 1, 2001, Evelyn Toynton, review of *Stet*, p. 22; November 24, 2002, Janice P. Nimura, review of *Yesterday Morning;* January 14, 2009, Dwight Garner, review of *Somewhere towards the End*, p. C1; February 8, 2009, Erica Jong, review of *Somewhere towards the End*, p. 13.

New Zealand Herald, January 10, 2009, Arifa Akbar, "Old Age Comes at Little Costa."

Observer (London, England), October 29, 1967, review of *Don't Look at Me like That*, p. 27; February 23, 1986, review of *After a Funeral*, p. 29; January 17, 1993, review of *Make Believe*, p. 49; November 26, 2000, review of *Stet*, p. 2; January 13, 2002, Kate Kellaway, review of *Yesterday Morning*, p. 9; January 18, 2009, review of *Somewhere towards the End*, p. 25.

Palm Beach Post (West Palm Beach, FL), January 25, 2009, Scott Eyman, review of *Somewhere towards the End.*

People, February 2, 2009, Kim Hubbard, K.C. Baker, and Josh Emmons, review of *Somewhere towards the End*, p. 47.

Publishers Weekly, September 4, 1967, review of *Don't Look at Me like That*, p. 51; January 17, 1994, review of *Make Believe*, p. 386; December 18, 2000, review of *Stet*, p. 63; September 22, 2008, review of *Somewhere towards the End*, p. 46.

Punch, December 27, 1967, review of *Don't Look at Me like That*, p. 985; May 14, 1986, review of *After a Funeral*, p. 60.

Rapport, January, 1994, review of *Make Believe*, p. 35.

San Francisco Chronicle, January 4, 2009, Heller McAlpin, review of *Somewhere towards the End*, p. M7.

Scotsman (Edinburgh, Scotland), January 6, 2009, David Robinson, "Age No Barrier as Writer, 91, Wins Book Prize."

Small Press, spring, 1994, review of *Make Believe*, p. 76.

Spectator, November 10, 1967, review of *Don't Look at Me like That*, p. 579; March 1, 1986, review of *After a Funeral*, p. 26; January 9, 1993, review of *Make Believe*, p. 21; October 7, 2000, review of *Yesterday Morning*, p. 52; January 26, 2002, Clayre Percy, review of *Yesterday Morning*, p. 50; January 2, 2009, Anne Chisholm, review of *Somewhere towards the End.*

Sydney Morning Herald, February 15, 2003, Gaby Naher, review of *Yesterday Morning;* February 29, 2008, Helen Elliott, review of *Somewhere towards the End.*

Telegraph (London, England), January 11, 2008, Carmen Callil, "How Diana Athill's Hockey-Sticks Stayed Jolly"; February 5, 2009, Sameer Rahim, "Appreciation of Diana Athill's *Somewhere towards the End.*"

Times (London, England), January 6, 2009, Kaya Burgess, "Editor Diana Athill Wins Award for 'Perfect Memoir of Old Age';" January 6, 2009, Jenny Diski, review of *Somewhere towards the End.*

Times Educational Supplement, February 28, 1986, review of *After a Funeral*, p. 22; February 22, 2002, review of *Yesterday Morning*, p. 20.

Times Higher Educational Supplement, November 17, 2000, Mary Tomlinson, review of *Stet*, p. 37.

Times Literary Supplement, November 23, 1967, review of *Don't Look at Me like That*, p. 1101; February 28, 1986, review of *After a Funeral*, p. 212; January 15, 1993, review of *Make Believe*, p. 27; August 11, 2000, Gabriele Annan, review of *Stet*, p. 36; November 8, 2000, Gabriele Annan, review of *Stet;* September 6, 2002, review of *Yesterday Morning*, p. 30; January 23, 2009, Lindsay Duguid, review of *Somewhere towards the End*, p. 28.

USA Today, January 21, 2009, Leslie Cauley, review of *Somewhere towards the End.*

Vogue, November, 1986, Susan Bolotin, review of *After a Funeral*, p. 240.

Washington Post Book World, January 27, 1985, Noel Perrin, review of *Instead of a Letter*, p. 9; February 1, 1987, Noel Perrin, review of *After a Funeral*, p. 8; June 10, 2001, review of *Stet*, p. 9; January 4, 2009, Michael Dirda, review of *Somewhere towards the End*, p. 10.

ONLINE

BBC Online, http://www.bbc.co.uk/ (January 5, 2009), "Costa Book Award Winners Revealed."

Culturazzi, http://culturazzi.org/ (January 9, 2009), review of *Somewhere towards the End.*

Encompass Culture, http://www.encompassculture.com/ (June 8, 2009), Susan Tranter, review of *Somewhere towards the End.*

Ralph, http://www.ralphmag.org/ (June 8, 2009), review of *Somewhere towards the End.*

Salon.com, http://www.salon.com/ (January 23, 2009), Laura Miller, review of *Somewhere towards the End.*

B

BAINES, Lew
See RANDISI, Robert J.

*   *   *

BARLOW, John 1967-
(John Stephen Barlow)

PERSONAL: Born September 13, 1967, in Gomersal, England; married; wife's name Susana; children: Nico. Education: Attended Cambridge University and University of Hull; earned Ph.D.

ADDRESSES: Home—La Coruña, Spain. Agent—Liz Darhansoff, Darhansoff, Verill, Feldman Literary Agents, 236 W. 26th St., New York, NY 10001. E-mail—johnstephenbarlow@hotmail.com; mail@johnbarlow.net.

CAREER: Writer and educator. English instructor in Santiago de Compostela, Spain; University of La Coruña, La Coruña, Spain, English instructor; University of York, Norwegian Study Centre, Heslington, England, English instructor; writer, 2003—. Also worked as a piano player.

AWARDS, HONORS: Discovery Prize, Paris Review, 2002, for the novella "Eating Mammals"; editor's choice selection, Historical Novel Society, and Book-Sense notable title selection, American Booksellers Association, both 2006, for Intoxicated.

WRITINGS:

Eating Mammals (contains the novellas "Eating Mammals," "The Possession of Thomas-Bessie," and "The Donkey Wedding at Gomersal"), Fourth Estate (London, England), 2004, Perennial (New York, NY), 2004.
Intoxicated: A Novel of Money, Madness, and the Invention of the World's Favorite Soft Drink, Morrow (New York, NY), 2006.
Everything but the Squeal: Eating the Whole Hog in Northern Spain, Farrar, Straus & Giroux (New York, NY), 2008.

Eating Mammals was also published in Italian.

SIDELIGHTS: John Barlow, a former university professor, gave up teaching in 2003 to focus on his writing. His first offering was Eating Mammals. The book is a collection of three novellas supposedly based on true events from Victorian England: the title work plus "The Possession of Thomas-Bessie" and "The Donkey Wedding at Gomersal." The first novella tells the story of Michael Mulligan, who will eat anything for money—be it animal, vegetable, or mineral—and the chef who both prepares his food and aspires to be like Mulligan. "The Possession of Thomas-Bessie" follows the life of a winged cat and the people who own him and use him to better their lives. In the last tale, romance grows between a middle-aged couple in nineteenth-century England. The whimsy of Barlow's tales was viewed favorably by critics, such as School Library Journal contributor Matthew L. Moffett, who found Eating Mammals to be "wildly imaginative" and noted that the novellas "successfully walk a . . . line between the magical and the ridiculously probable." Suzy Hansen, writing in the New York Times Book Review, noted Barlow's "dry wit" and suggested that the author's "imagination appears unlimited." Booklist reviewer Jennifer Baker called Eating Mammals "hilarious" and "wonderfully innovative." Additionally, a *Publishers Weekly* critic observed that the tales are "delightfully gothic, witty and sometimes macabre," and summed up the book as "idiosyncratic and memorable."

Barlow returned to the Victorian setting of *Eating Mammals* for his first novel, *Intoxicated: A Novel of Money, Madness, and the Invention of the World's Favorite Soft Drink.* The book tells the mythical story of the beginnings of carbonated sodas. A chance meeting between Rodrigo Vermilion, a deformed midget, and Isaac Brookes, a wealthy businessman, leads to a professional relationship between the two. Rodrigo presents Isaac with an investment idea—a cool, refreshing, nonalcoholic, fizzy soft drink to capitalize on the recent temperance movement. The men become partners, create a beverage complete with a secret ingredient—rhubarb and coca leaves—and *Intoxicated* follows the ups and downs of their business venture. Called "part fable and part vaudeville" by a *Publishers Weekly* reviewer, the book was widely favored by critics. A *Kirkus Reviews* contributor noted the "risk-taking" that stems from Barlow's "lively imagination." Marika Zemke, writing in the *Library Journal*, predicted that Barlow's work will "intoxicate readers" with its "irreverent humor," a sentiment similar to that of *Booklist* contributor Steve Powers; Powers found the book "odd and entrancing," noting that the personality combinations in this "whimsical, farcical novel" make for "a madcap read."

Everything but the Squeal: Eating the Whole Hog in Northern Spain is a food travelogue of the remote, mountainous area of Galicia, in northwestern Spain, of which Barlow's wife is a native. In this depopulated and poor area, pork is a mainstay, and Barlow began his trip vowing to eat every part of a pig's body, as the locals would. Along his journey to devour an entire pig, Barlow provides commentary on the land, the people, and, its cuisine. Barlow samples stews made from obscure pig parts, pig-bladder pudding, cocida, and pig head.

Gilbert Cruz, reviewing the book in *Time*, observed that "as Barlow writes it, Galicia is a misty, mysterious place full of cagey old coots and rustic food fanatics. What better place, then, to embark on a semi-ridiculous, typically male journey. With good humor and shameless enthusiasm, he has written a delicious meat mash note." Barbara Fisher, reviewing the book in the *Boston Globe*, commented that Barlow "has revealed himself to be an amiable, curious, and uncomplaining guide." John

Greenya, writing in the *Washington Times*, revealed that "*Everything but the Squeal* is as much a travel book, though certainly a rather bizarre one—far more Anthony Bourdain than Alice Waters—as it is a book about food." Greenya explained that "Bourdain is a fairly apt comparison, because John Barlow is also your basic smart aleck, and his observations about people and places are often as funny, if a tad mean, as they are informative, and therefore even more entertaining." Greenya also added that "he has such a good eye for describing both people and places."

Irene Wanner, reviewing the book in the *Los Angeles Times*, commented that the author "is so unabashedly in love with almost all things porcine (though maybe not trotters, feet or botelo, 'smashed-up vertebrae and other stuff' boiled in a bag of intestines) that rambling the countryside with him is a mouthwatering adventure." Ben Schmerler, reviewing the book in the *New York Post*, reported that "perhaps even more satisfying than his madcap extreme eating and cooking experiences are Barlow's quotable observations about Galicians." A contributor to *Kirkus Reviews* called the book "a savory travelogue with insights that go beyond taste and texture." Another contributor, writing in the *Midwest Book Review*, noted that Barlow's book "makes for a powerful presentation indeed."

Booklist contributor Mark Knoblauch observed that "Barlow knows Galicians intimately and finds them warm but contrarian." A contributor to *Publishers Weekly* mentioned that the author "doesn't scrimp on either culinary or cultural delights in this charmingly informative and witty narrative." A reviewer in the *Economist* said that "no answer is ever a straightforward yes or no. No bureaucratic process is ever simple. No bit of history is without its compelling trivia," adding that "Barlow pokes his nose in everywhere, and almost without exception people are kind and hospitable." Dwight Garner, writing in the *New York Times*, noted that "there have been plenty of macho, red-blooded books written about pork and barbecue, and Mr. Barlow's squeamishness about being near the killing ground is refreshingly honest in its way. But it also threatens to warp the meaning of his book's title." Garner wrote: "OK, we get it—he can eat almost everything but the squeal. But if Mr. Barlow can barely cope with the final, primal squeals themselves, it's possible he should have written about herring or polenta instead."

In a statement posted on Barlow's home page, he commented on his writing process: "Each day starts off slowly. If it picks up, I more or less enjoy that. If it doesn't, I stop writing." Barlow continued: "But I do enjoy revising a lot. I do too much revising, because I enjoy it, and because it means I don't have to write more and can hide behind the idea that I am working."

BIOGRAPHICAL AND CRITICAL SOURCES:

PERIODICALS

Booklist, August, 2004, Jennifer Baker, review of *Eating Mammals,* p. 1895; January 1, 2006, Steve Powers, review of *Intoxicated: A Novel of Money, Madness, and the Invention of the World's Favorite Soft Drink,* p. 52; September 15, 2008, Mark Knoblauch, review of *Everything but the Squeal: Eating the Whole Hog in Northern Spain,* p. 19.
Boston Globe, December 21, 2008, Barbara Fisher, review of *Everything but the Squeal.*
California Bookwatch, January 1, 2009, review of *Everything but the Squeal.*
Economist, U.S. edition, November 1, 2008, review of *Everything but the Squeal,* p. 85EU.
Kirkus Reviews, July 1, 2004, review of *Eating Mammals,* p. 588; December 15, 2005, review of *Intoxicated,* p. 1287; October 1, 2008, review of *Everything but the Squeal.*
Library Journal, February 15, 2006, Marika Zemke, review of *Intoxicated,* p. 106.
Los Angeles Times, December 30, 2008, Irene Wanner, review of *Everything but the Squeal.*
New York Post, November 2, 2008, Ben Schmerler, review of *Everything but the Squeal.*
New York Times, November 26, 2008, Dwight Garner, review of *Everything but the Squeal,* p. C1.
New York Times Book Review, September 26, 2004, Suzy Hansen, review of *Eating Mammals,* p. 24.
Publishers Weekly, July 12, 2004, review of *Eating Mammals,* p. 41; January 30, 2006, review of *Intoxicated,* p. 43; September 22, 2008, review of *Everything but the Squeal,* p. 49.
School Library Journal, January, 2005, Matthew L. Moffett, review of *Eating Mammals,* p. 158.
Time, November 10, 2008, Gilbert Cruz, review of *Everything but the Squeal.*
Toronto Star, January 8, 2009, Shaun Smith, "Galician Gastronomes Savour Every Part of the Pig."
Washington Times, March 29, 2009, John Greenya, review of *Everything but the Squeal.*

ONLINE

John Barlow Home Page, http://www.johnbarlow.net (June 6, 2009).*

BARLOW, John Stephen
    See BARLOW, John

*   *   *

BASS, Bill 1928-
    (Jefferson Bass, a joint pseudonym, William M. Bass)

PERSONAL: Born 1928; married twice (widowed). *Education:* University of Virginia, B.S.; University of Kentucky, M.S.; University of Pennsylvania, Ph.D., 1961.

ADDRESSES: Home—TN.

CAREER: Educator, archaeologist, forensic anthropologist, writer. Smithsonian Institution, Washington, DC, anthropologist; University of Kansas, Lawrence, former instructor; Kansas Bureau of Investigation, forensic consultant; University of Tennessee, Knoxville, forensic anthropology department, former professor; forensic consultant. Founder of Anthropology Research Center, "The Body Farm," University of Tennessee. *Military service:* Served in the U.S. Army.

AWARDS, HONORS: National Professor of the Year, Council for Advancement and Support of Education.

WRITINGS:

NONFICTION

(With Jon Jefferson) *Death's Acre: Inside the Legendary Forensic Lab the Body Farm Where the Dead Do Tell Tales,* Putnam (New York, NY), 2003.
(With Jon Jefferson) *Beyond the Body Farm: A Legendary Bone Detective Explores Murders, Mysteries, and the Revolution in Forensic Science,* William Morrow (New York, NY), 2007.

FICTION; AS JEFFERSON BASS

Carved in Bone: A Body Farm Novel, William Morrow (New York, NY), 2006.

Flesh and Bone: A Body Farm Novel, William Morrow (New York, NY), 2007.

The Devil's Bones, William Morrow (New York, NY), 2008.

NONFICTION; AS WILLIAM M. BASS

Human Osteology: A Laboratory and Field Manual of the Human Skeleton, Missouri Archaeological Society (Columbia, MO), 1971, 5th edition published as *Human Osteology: A Laboratory and Field Manual,* 2005.

(With David R. Evans and Richard L. Jantz) *The Leavenworth Site Cemetery: Archaeology and Physical Anthropology,* University of Kansas (Lawrence, KS), 1971.

(Author of appendix) Robert W. Neuman, *The Sonota Complex and Associated Sites on the Northern Great Plains,* Nebraska State Historical Society (Lincoln, NE), 1975.

(Editor) *Fay Tolton and the Initial Middle Missouri Variant,* College of Arts and Science, University of Missouri—Columbia (Columbia, MO), 1976.

(With Larry Miller and Ramona Miller) *Human Evidence in Criminal Justice,* Pilgrimage (Cincinnati, OH), 1983, 2nd edition, 1985.

Author or coauthor of over two hundred articles in professional journals.

ADAPTATIONS: *Death's Acre* was adapted for audio cassette, Simon & Schuster Audio, 2003.

SIDELIGHTS: Writing under his own name and also under the joint pseudonym of Jefferson Bass, renowned forensic anthropologist Bill Bass has collaborated with writer and filmmaker Jon Jefferson on several works of nonfiction and fiction. In the 2003 *Death's Acre: Inside the Legendary Forensic Lab the Body Farm Where the Dead Do Tell Tales,* Bass and Jefferson tell the story of the University of Tennessee's Anthropology Research Facility (a.k.a. the "Body Farm"), which Bass founded in 1981 and about which Jefferson wrote and directed two documentary films for the National Geographic Channel. The Body Farm is a research facility that allows forensic scientists to study and document the decomposition of human bodies in different environments. Bass's credentials as a forensic anthropologist include the standard textbook *Human Osteology: A Laboratory and Field Manual of the Human Skeleton,*

as well as consultancy on dozens of homicide cases. *Death's Acre* begins with a summary of Bass's more difficult cases and his ensuing decision to create a facility dedicated to the trickier aspects of forensic science. Subsequent chapters deal with the actual analysis of decomposing corpses on the Body Farm and how this knowledge has helped to solve numerous high-profile criminal cases. Reviewing *Death's Acre,* a *Publishers Weekly* contributor found Bass, with the aid of Jefferson, to be a "witty storyteller with a welcome sense of humor." The same reviewer went on to note: "Bass may deal with the dead, but he has a lust for life that comes across in his writing." Similarly, *Entertainment Weekly* writer Alynda Wheat thought the writing team "uses . . . folksy humor and extensive knowledge to share the gory details." Theodore Dalrymple, writing in the *Spectator,* also had praise for the book, observing: "To his credit, . . . Professor Bass reveals his embarrassments as well as his triumphs." *Booklist* contributor David Pitt found *Death's Acre* an "informative book," but not one for the "queasy."

Bass and Jefferson have also collaborated on mystery novels, again writing as Jefferson Bass. Their 2006 *Carved in Bone: A Body Farm Novel* is the first in a series of forensic mysteries featuring Dr. Bill Brockton in the guise of Bass himself. Brockton works at the University of Tennessee, where Bass himself long worked, and in this first outing he attempts to solve the case of a body found in a cave. Brockton and his team at the Body Farm attempt to identify the remains of a young pregnant woman whose body was long ago left in the cave and subsequently mummified naturally. Once the body is identified, friends and family of the young woman are all involved in the hunt for dark secrets from the past. *Carved in Bone* earned critical praise from many sources. Writing for *Bookreporter.com,* Rachel Egelman noted: "The forensic details are the heart of this novel. The science is fascinating and written in a way easy for readers to understand." High praise also came from *Houston Chronicle Online* critic Steve Weinberg, who called *Carved in Bone* a "superb mystery." Weinberg further noted that the novel was "well-plotted, filled with memorable characters, based on accurate forensic science and written with more flair and literary sensibility than anything by John Grisham." *USA Today* contributor Carol Memmott had positive words for the same work, observing that it "has a unique corpse, solid science, quirky humor and a lovable protagonist." A *Kirkus Reviews* critic thought *Carved in Bone* was "a neatly-done mystery," while a *Publishers Weekly* reviewer concluded: "The pacing and action bode well for this crime series."

Bass and Jefferson continued the series in their 2007 title, *Flesh and Bone: A Body Farm Novel,* in which Brockton himself becomes a suspect in a killing. Investigating the mutilation-death of a transvestite in a Tennessee state park, Brockton recreates the scene of the crime at the Body Farm, aided by the female medical examiner of Knoxville, Dr. Jess Carter. Brockton and Carter are soon more than mere colleagues, attracted physically to one another. When Carter's nude corpse is found at Brockton's recreated crime scene, the police ban him from the Body Farm and begin investigating him as the perpetrator. Brockton's subsequent private investigation to clear his name ultimately puts him in harm's way.

As with the first fictional collaboration between Bass and Jefferson, *Flesh and Bone* also earned critical praise. Writing in *Author's Den,* Christy Tillery French termed the novel "a good whodunit" as well as "an edifying look into the fascinating world of forensic anthropology." Harriet Klausner called the same work a "tense crime thriller" on *Bookreview.com.* A *Kirkus Reviews* critic, however, complained that "the book bores with its ham-handed focus on Brockton." The same critic called it a "sophomore slump." Similarly, a *Publishers Weekly* contributor felt that "the story veers wildly from fascinating forensics with a high yuck factor to sophomoric and corny romantic byplay." *Booklist* contributor David Pitt had a more positive assessment: "The story is razor sharp . . . with a nice mixture of mystery and horror."

The author's reprise Brockton in the third novel in the series, *The Devil's Bones,* in which the killer of Dr. Carter from *Flesh and Bone* escapes custody before his trial begins, but is thought to later die in a cabin fire. Brockton continues other investigations, among which is the debunking of a crematorium that discards bodies and provides false ashes to relatives. Writing in the *Library Journal,* A.J. Wright commented: "The authors juggle several quickly moving narratives until the final confrontation between Brockton and his nemesis." Such juggling bothered a *Publishers Weekly* critic, who thought that "a more focused look at a single case might have made the novel a better read." *Booklist* contributor Pitt was less critical of this supposed lack of focus, however, terming *The Devil's Bones* "the best of a steadily improving series, but it's doubtful we've seen the finest moments yet." Klausner, in a *Bookcrossing. com* review, called the novel "a fascinating look at how forensic anthropology helps the police solves crimes."

Bass also teamed up with Jefferson for *Beyond the Body Farm: A Legendary Bone Detective Explores Murders,* *Mysteries, and the Revolution in Forensic Science,* the nonfiction companion to their *Death's Acre.* A *Publishers Weekly* contributor dubbed this an "unnervingly cheerful collection . . . of case studies and anecdotes from the field of corpse identification." The same reviewer praised the authors' "attention to detail and the occasional darkly humorous aside" as they recount investigations from the identification of bodies blown apart in a fireworks factory to the use of sonar in forensic science. A *Kirkus Reviews* critic was unimpressed with this sequel, terming it "a cut-and-paste string of individual cases written up in prosaic prose." Writing for *Bookpage,* Pat H. Broeske was more positive about *Beyond the Body Farm,* writing: "This book is scientifically authoritative, as well as accessible to mainstream crime buffs—though not for the squeamish."

BIOGRAPHICAL AND CRITICAL SOURCES:

BOOKS

Bass, Bill, and Jon Jefferson, *Death's Acre: Inside the Legendary Forensic Lab the Body Farm Where the Dead Do Tell Tales,* Putnam (New York, NY), 2003.

PERIODICALS

Booklist, October 15, 2003, David Pitt, review of *Death's Acre: Inside the Legendary Forensic Lab the Body Farm Where the Dead Do Tell Tales,* p. 366; December 15, 2006, David Pitt, review of *Flesh and Bone: A Body Farm Novel,* p. 24; February 1, 2008, David Pitt, review of *The Devil's Bones,* p. 30.

Chronicle of Higher Education, October 27, 2006, Peter Monaghan, "The Truths That Bodies Yield."

Entertainment Weekly, December 5, 2003, Alynda Wheat, review of *Death's Acre,* p. 104.

Kirkus Reviews, January 15, 2006, review of *Carved in Bone: A Body Farm Novel,* p. 53; December 1, 2006, review of *Flesh and Bone,* p. 1184; July 15, 2007, review of *Beyond the Body Farm: A Legendary Bone Detective Explores Murders, Mysteries, and the Revolution in Forensic Science.*

Library Journal, February 15, 2008, A.J. Wright, review of *The Devil's Bones,* p. 89.

Public Libraries, September 1, 2006, review of *Death's Acre.*

Publishers Weekly, October 13, 2003, review of *Death's Acre,* p. 69; November 21, 2005, review of *Carved in Bone,* p. 26; December 11, 2006, review of *Flesh and Bone,* p. 47; July 16, 2007, review of *Beyond the Body Farm,* p. 159; December 24, 2007, review of *The Devil's Bones,* p. 30.

School Library Journal, March, 2004, Peggy Bercher, review of *Death's Acre,* p. 252.

Science & Justice, October 1, 2004, Tim Thompson, review of *Death's Acre.*

Spectator, January 31, 2004, Theodore Dalrymple, "Pioneer in a Peculiar Science," review of *Death's Acre,* p. 54.

USA Today, February 28, 2006, Carol Memmott, review of *Carved in Bone,* p. D4.

ONLINE

AllReaders.com, http://www.allreaders.com/ (September 12, 2006), review of *Death's Acre.*

Author's Den, http://authrosden.com/ (March 5, 2008), Christy Tillery French, review of *Flesh and Bone.*

Blogcritics Magazine, http://blogcritics.org/ (April 25, 2008), review of *The Devil's Bones.*

Bookcrossing.com, http://www.bookcrossing.com/ (June 18, 2008), Harriet Klausner, review of *The Devil's Bones.*

Bookpage, http://www.bookpage.com/ (June 18, 2008), Pat H. Broeske, review of *Beyond the Body Farm.*

Bookreporter.com, http://www.bookreporter.com/ (September 12, 2006), Rachel Egelman, review of *Carved in Bone.*

Bookreview.com, http://www.bookreview.com/ (June 18, 2008), Harriet Klausner, review of *Flesh and Bone.*

CourtTV Crime Library Web site, http://www.crime library.com/ (September 12, 2006), Katherine Ramsland, "The Body Farm."

CrimeSpreeMag.com, http://www.crimespreemag.com/ (September 12, 2006), review of *Carved in Bone.*

Daily News-Record Online, http://www.dnronline.com/ (February 23, 2006), Lucy Bednar, "Too Much Fat and Not Enough Meat on This Bone," review of *Carved in Bone.*

Death's Acre Web site, http://www.deathsacre.com (September 12, 2006).

Houston Chronicle Online, http://www.houstonchronicle .com/ (February 3, 2006), Steve Weinberg, "Down on the Body Farm," review of *Carved in Bone.*

Jefferson Bass Home Page, http://www.jeffersonbass. com (August 21, 2008).

Not Enough Books, http://notenoughbooks.blogspot. com/ (April 16, 2008), review of *The Devil's Bones.*

Smithsonian Resident Associates Web site, http:// residentassociates.org/ (February 23, 2006), Elizabeth A. Davis, "'Body Farm' Founder Tries Hand at Fiction."*

* * *

BASS, Jefferson
See BASS, Bill

* * *

BASS, William M.
See BASS, Bill

* * *

BAUSCH, Richard 1945-
(Richard Carl Bausch)

PERSONAL: Born April 18, 1945, in Fort Benning, GA; son of Robert Carl and Helen Bausch; married Karen Miller (a photographer), May 3, 1969; children: Wesley, Emily, Paul, Maggie, Amanda. *Education:* George Mason University, B.A., 1973; University of Iowa, M.F. A., 1975; also attended Northern Virginia Community College. *Hobbies and other interests:* Singing and songwriting.

ADDRESSES: Office—Department of English, University of Memphis, Memphis, TN 38152. *Agent*—Harriet Wasserman, Russell & Volkening, Inc., 551 Fifth Ave., New York, NY 10017. *E-mail*—rbausch@memphis.edu.

CAREER: Educator, writer. Worked as singer-songwriter and comedian. George Mason University, Fairfax, VA, former professor of English and Heritage Chair of Creative Writing, beginning 1980; University of Memphis, TN, professor of English and Lillian and Morrie A. Moss Chair of Excellence. Visiting professor at University of Virginia—Charlottesville, 1985, 1988, and Wesleyan University, 1986, 1990, 1992, and 1993. *Military service:* U.S. Air Force, survival instructor, 1966-69.

MEMBER: Associated Writing Programs.

AWARDS, HONORS: PEN/Faulkner Award nominations, 1982, for *Take Me Back,* and 1988, for *Spirits and Other Stories;* National Endowment for the Arts grant, 1982; Guggenheim fellowship, 1984; Lila Wallace-*Reader's Digest* Best Writer's Award, Lila Wallace Fund, 1992; American Academy of Arts and Letters, Academy Award in Literature, 1993; PEN/Malamud Award for *The Stories of Richard Bausch,* 2004.

WRITINGS:

NOVELS

Real Presence, Dial (New York, NY), 1980.
Take Me Back, Dial (New York, NY), 1981.
The Last Good Time, Dial (New York, NY), 1984.
Mr. Field's Daughter, Linden Press/Simon & Schuster (New York, NY), 1989.
Violence, Houghton Mifflin/Seymour Lawrence (Boston, MA), 1992.
Rebel Powers, Houghton Mifflin/Seymour Lawrence (Boston, MA), 1993.
Good Evening Mr. and Mrs. America, and All the Ships at Sea, HarperCollins (New York, NY), 1996.
In the Night Season: A Novel, HarperFlamingo (New York, NY), 1998.
Hello to the Cannibals, HarperCollins (New York, NY), 2002.
Wives and Lovers: Three Short Novels, Perennial (New York, NY), 2004.
Thanksgiving Night: A Novel, HarperCollins (New York, NY), 2006.
Peace, Knopf (New York, NY), 2008.

SHORT STORY COLLECTIONS

Spirits and Other Stories, Linden Press/Simon & Schuster (New York, NY), 1987.
The Fireman's Wife and Other Stories, Linden Press (New York, NY), 1990.
Rare & Endangered Species (novella and stories), Houghton Mifflin/Seymour Lawrence (Boston, MA), 1994.
The Selected Stories of Richard Bausch, Random House (New York, NY), 1996.
Someone to Watch Over Me: Stories, HarperFlamingo (New York, NY), 1999.
The Stories of Richard Bausch, HarperCollins (New York, NY), 2004.

OTHER

(Editor) *The Cry of an Occasion: Fiction from the Fellowship of Southern Writers,* Louisiana State University Press (Baton Rouge, LA), 2001.
(Editor, with R.V. Cassill) *The Norton Anthology of Short Fiction,* 7th edition, W.W. Norton (New York, NY), 2007.
(Guest editor and author of foreword) *Best New American Voices 2008,* edited by John Kulka and Natalie Danford, Harvest Books (New York, NY), 2007.

Work represented in anthologies, including *O'Henry Prize Stories* and *Best American Short Stories.* Contributor of short stories to various periodicals, including *Harper's, Ploughshares, Esquire, Atlantic,* and the *New Yorker.*

ADAPTATIONS: The Last Good Time was adapted for a feature film, 1994; "The Man Who Knew Belle Star" was adapted for a movie short, 2001; "Two Altercations" was adapted for a film, 2002.

SIDELIGHTS: "My vital subjects are family, fear, love, and anything that is irrecoverable and *missed,*" Richard Bausch once told *CA,* "but I'll dispense with all of that for a good story. . . . I grew up listening to my father tell stories—he is a great story-teller, and all the Bauschs can do it." Bausch added that he has no literary creed: "My only criterion is that fiction make feeling, that it deepen feeling. If it doesn't do that it's not fiction." Bausch's works are true to his self-description: dealing with the ordinary tragedies of American family life in our time, they spring from feeling and, at their best, create it.

Bausch's first novel, *Real Presence,* examines the crisis of faith of an aging priest, Monsignor Vincent Shepherd. Bitter, withdrawn, recovering from a heart attack, Shepherd is assigned to a West Virginia parish whose beloved previous priest is a hard act to follow. He is shaken from his doldrums by the arrival of a down-and-out family, the Bexleys, which includes the terminally ill war veteran and ex-convict, Duck, and his wife, Elizabeth, who is pregnant with her sixth child. The Bexleys test Shepherd's ability to live up to his symbolic surname, and Elizabeth succeeds in reaching him. After Duck is killed, and while Elizabeth is in labor, Shepherd declares his desire to leave the priesthood and replace

Duck as the surviving Bexleys' father figure. In an *America* review, Thomas M. Gannon criticized the novel's ending, saying: "The abrupt disregard for the emotional and physical limitations the author has previously imposed on this character is a serious defect in Bausch's otherwise careful effort." Scott Spencer, however, reviewing the novel for the *New York Times Book Review,* called the ending "moving and even satisfying" but also "a foregone conclusion." Other reviewers praised Bausch's first effort, including *Washington Post Book World*'s Doris Grumbach, who found *Real Presence* distinguished by "its distance from the customary first novel subjects." A *Critic* reviewer called it "excellently crafted," and *Los Angeles Times Book Review* critic Dick Roraback found it an "exquisite, excruciating novel" and concluded: "Bausch has written a book that disturbs; sometimes it is good to be disturbed."

Bausch wrote his second novel, *Take Me Back,* in four months of fifteen-hour days. Set in a low-rent area of Virginia, the novel dissects the lives of Gordon Brinhart, an unsuccessful and hard-drinking insurance salesman, his wife Katherine, a former rock musician, and Katherine's illegitimate son Alex, as well as a neighboring family which includes Amy, a thirteen-year-old who is dying of leukemia. Gordon goes on a binge, loses his job, and sleeps with a seventeen-year-old neighbor; in response Katherine attempts suicide, and Alex witnesses it all. "Telling the story skillfully from the alternating points of view of the three members of the [Brinhart] family, Bausch has us suffer through the whole ordeal right along with them," wrote Bruce Cook in the *Washington Post Book World.* Cook added: "*Take Me Back* isn't pretty. It is, however, as well written as any novel I have read in a while. . . . Richard Bausch has captured something essential in the quality of American life today in these pages." *New York Times Book Review* contributor Richard P. Brickner gave a nod to the novel's "uncanny skillfulness in dialogue and atmosphere" but objected to its "smallness of vision," finding in it "no evident conviction beyond the glum one that life stinks."

Bausch's third novel, *The Last Good Time,* was again the product of mere months of work. It is about two men, seventy-five-year-old Edward Cakes and eighty-nine-year-old Arthur Hagood, into whose lives the twenty-four-year-old Mary Virginia Bellini arrives by chance. Mary makes love to Edward in exchange for friendship and material support; meanwhile Arthur, bedridden in a hospital and learning of the events

through Edward's visits, is jealous. On Mary's departure, Edward takes up with Ida Warren, the elderly woman upstairs whose phonograph records have been keeping him awake. "Bausch makes them all believable," wrote Art Seidenbaum in the *Los Angeles Times.* "These are little people at work here . . . what stamps them as human is the novelist's gift of character." In the *Washington Post Book World,* Stephen Dobyns had high praise for Bausch's style, and despite "shortcomings" of plot, structure, and character believability, called *The Last Good Time* "quite a good novel." *New York Times Book Review* critic Nancy Forbes called particular attention to the way Bausch's narrative relates the elderly's experience of time, and remarked that the book "has a way of being superlatively funny and disturbing by turns, but the experience that emerges most strongly is that of spending an interesting time getting to know the sort of people whose lives we take for granted."

While strengthening his reputation as a novelist, Bausch has also written numerous short stories. His 1987 collection, *Spirits and Other Stories,* won considerable critical praise. Michael Dorris, in the *Washington Post Book World,* called Bausch "a master of the short story," while Madison Smartt Bell, in the *New York Times Book Review,* termed the book a "thoughtful, honest collection" and remarked upon the absence of "superfluous stylistic flash." Thomas Cahill, writing in *Commonweal,* praised the stories' narrative magnetism and the author's ability to imagine his characters in all their details, and asserted: "It is my deep, perverse suspicion that, when I am an old man . . . all of Bausch . . . will be in print, and names like Updike, Roth, Bellow will have faded from view."

In *Mr. Field's Daughter,* Bausch's next novel, James Field, a sixty-something widower and loan officer, leads a household that includes his widowed sister Ellen, his daughter Annie, and Annie's daughter Linda. Linda's father, the cocaine-snorting Cole Gilbertson, soon arrives, wielding a .22 pistol. Opting for realistic drama rather than melodrama, Bausch fashioned from these familiar narrative ingredients and from the conventional thoughts of his characters a work that Jonathan Yardley, writing in the *Washington Post Book World,* called "exceptionally mature and satisfying" as well as "original and immensely affecting." "Strong characters sustain a family story line as a gifted novelist mines the universal in a pit of the mundane," summarized *Los Angeles Times Book Review* contributor Seidenbaum. Gene Lyons in the *New York Times Book Review* called

Bausch "an author of rare and penetrating gifts, working at the height of his powers."

Bausch published a second short-story collection, *The Fireman's Wife and Other Stories,* in 1990. Bette Pesetsky noted in the *New York Times Book Review* that the stories "are all about relationships; they are all about redemption through understanding," and asserted: "We are fortunate to have [*The Fireman's Wife and Other Stories*] with which to explore and search for the meaning of how we live today." *Los Angeles Times* critic Richard Eder found "Consolation," in which a young widow takes her baby to visit her dead husband's parents, the best story in *The Fireman's Wife and Other Stories,* and called it "subtle and moving—with a fine comic turn by the widow's bossy and self-centered sister—even if the warmth at the end is a shade overinsistent."

Violence, Bausch's 1992 novel, continued the author's tradition of dealing realistically with the troubles of ordinary Americans. Charles Connally, in the grip of an emotional crisis, wanders into a Chicago convenience store where a robbery is taking place, saves the life of a woman, and is treated as a hero by the press. In the aftermath, he succumbs to depression, dropping out of college and questioning his marriage to dental hygienist Carol. "This is a sad and daring book," Carolyn See commented in the *Washington Post Book World. New York Times Book Review* contributor Susan Kenney called the novel "masterly" for Bausch's realistic exploration of "both the public and private manifestations of violence with persistence as well as sensitivity. And he does so with a redeeming grace of language and detail that goes beyond mere witnessing, straight to the heart."

Rebel Powers, drew mixed comments from reviewers. *Tribune Books* contributor Joseph Coates started his assessment of the novel by calling Bausch "one of our most talented writers," yet went on to say that this book "never engages its subject and amounts to one long denouement that fizzles out in anticlimax," because it is wholly concerned with a woman's refusal to face her emotions. That main character, Connie, defies her father by marrying Daniel Boudreaux, an Air Force daredevil who dreams of getting rich from Alaskan oil. His tour of duty in Vietnam robs him of the reckless bravery that attracted Connie to him, however, and their marriage deteriorates into violent fighting. Their son, Thomas, narrates the tale. Although Coates rated the book a

failed effort, Elizabeth Tallent was much more positive in her assessment, writing in the *New York Times Book Review:* "As a narrator, Thomas is willing to qualify his perceptions, to admit incomprehension, to examine and even reverse his judgments. Indeed, the originality of Mr. Bausch's novel lies in its unapologetic devotion to the process of perception. Obsession usually censors the peripheral, but Thomas's intense concentration on the unraveling of his family is richly generous and accommodating. There are savage rages here, and great loss, but grievance, irritation, foolishness and the range of little daily miseries occupy psychic space in a way that is common in real life but rare in fiction."

In *Good Evening Mr. and Mrs. America, and All the Ships at Sea,* Bausch treats the details of daily life with his usual style and also explores the socio-political issues of the early 1960s. The story revolves around Walter, who is nineteen years old in 1964. Sweet, devoutly Catholic, and idealistic, Walter is devastated by the assassination of John F. Kennedy, participates in civil rights sit-ins, and generally has his consciousness raised throughout the course of the book. According to *Publishers Weekly* critic Sybil S. Steinberg, "Bausch is a wily and subtle writer," and "Walter's slide from idealism to disillusionment is revealed through brilliant passages of mundane (but revealing) conversations, hilarious comic moments and characters' poignant attempts to communicate with one another." "Mr. Busch spins this intricate and delicious story with a wondrously tender touch," reported Richard Bernstein in the *New York Times.* "There is an intermingling of the comic and the dangerous in the qualities and foibles of his characters, well-formed, resistant to simplification, stubbornly individualistic. . . . Walter exists on that narrow patch of ground in American history between reverence and disillusionment." *Booklist* contributor Donna Seaman stated of *Good Evening Mr. and Mrs. America, and All the Ships at Sea:* "Bausch's brilliant dialogue, quicksilver comedy, and perception into the nature of innocence give this vivacious novel a George Cukor-like dazzle, and you can't get much better than that."

Seaman also applauded the collection *The Selected Stories of Richard Bausch,* declaring that in it, the "ever-inventive" author "presents fresh takes on his favorite theme, the failure to communicate. His complex and troubled characters talk at cross-purposes and misinterpret one another, often to rather painful or violent ends." *Dictionary of Literary Biography* contributor Paul R. Lilly, Jr., summarized Bausch's themes in this way: "Bausch's concerns are moral; his subject matter is the self in conflict with the need to discover or invent a better version of itself and a need to hold on to a haunted, often unhappy past. Bausch's stories probe this tension between self and selfishness in the form of tormented sons whose fathers have been alcoholic or violent, wives who repress their anger at husbands who fail to do the right thing, and daughters who are crippled by the memory of their parents' silent combats of will."

Bausch's *In the Night Season: A Novel* is the story of Nora Michaelson, who is left destitute with her son Jason after her husband Jack is killed in a bus accident. Her African American neighbor Edward Bishop helps Nora each afternoon by checking in on Jason but he later receives a series of threatening hate letters warning him to stay away from the white Michaelsons. Bishop is later murdered and slowly Jack Michaelson's secret past is revealed. Bausch's "subject this time is not disillusionment," argued A.O. Scott in the *New York Times Book Review,* "but terror, not the loss of innocence but its harassment by gratuitous and unchecked evil." Critical reaction to the novel was mixed. Scott felt that there was nothing in the novel that a "competent committee of screenwriters couldn't have come up with. From a novelist as skilled, as insightful and as original as Richard Bausch we are entitled to expect more." Other reviewers offered a different reaction. A *Publishers Weekly* reviewer called Bausch "a writer who thrills and moves us at once." "With his powerful style and penetrating sense of character, Bausch keeps us hooked even through stretches of almost excruciating tension and sporadic violence that some readers may find excessive," said Pam Lambert in *People.*

"Confused relations and the panic of loss suffuse the tales in Bausch's stunning fifth collection of short fiction," wrote a *Publishers Weekly* reviewer of *Someone to Watch Over Me: Stories.* The collection is "primarily concerned with communication between loved ones, when it works and especially when it fails," summarized Donna Seaman in *Booklist.* Critics received the collection enthusiastically. David W. Henderson, reviewing the work in *Library Journal,* called it a "rewarding read for those who appreciate good as opposed to flamboyant writing." "Bausch has a keen ear for the back-and-forthness of the dialogues of love and he brings as much compassion as talent to his shining stories," argued Seaman.

Bausch charted new literary ground for himself with the 2002 novel, *Hello to the Cannibals,* a work featuring two independent-minded women separated by a century

in time. The modern-day protagonist, Lily, is beset by familial and marital woes; she has also become fascinated with the life of the nineteenth-century British explorer and writer Mary Kingsley, about whom she begins to write a play. The novel is then told from both viewpoints via the dramatic piece Lily fashions. For *Booklist* contributor Seaman, *Hello to the Cannibals* was both "radiant and transporting," and Bausch's "most ambitious, compulsively readable, and deeply pleasurable novel to date." Other reviewers also had praise for the work. A *Kirkus Reviews* critic called it "expansive," and Bausch's "most interesting [novel] thus far." Similarly, *New York Times* contributor Janet Burroway found the same work "ambitious not only in its historical and geographical sweep but also in its author's choice to confine himself, with admirable conviction and credibility, to the consciousness of two women."

With his 2004 comprehensive collection, *The Stories of Richard Bausch,* the author won the prestigious PEN/Malamud Award. This gathering of "42 indelible tales" as *Booklist* writer Seaman termed the book, presents Bausch at his best, in "electrifying" stories that are "notable for their structural perfection, convincing physicality, and psychological depth." Similar praise came from *Entertainment Weekly* contributor Emily Mead, who felt the collection "solidifies Bausch's rep as a master of compact, closely observed vignettes." A *Kirkus Reviews* critic joined the chorus of acclaim, concluding: "This is the book for which Bausch will be remembered."

Another publication from 2004 bridges the gap between short story and novel. *Wives and Lovers: Three Short Novels,* like Bausch's novels and short stories, "probes the tensions that seethe in families and marriages," according to a *Kirkus Reviews* critic. Two of the novellas, "Spirits" and "Rare & Endangered Species," were previously published as the title pieces of story collections, while "Requisite Kindness," previously unpublished, features a man who is taking care of his dying mother and looks back on the domestic failures of his life. The *Kirkus Reviews* critic felt the novellas displayed "a bleak vision, tempered by sensitive affection for human beings in all their frailty." Nicholas Fonseca, reviewing the collection in *Entertainment Weekly,* was also impressed, terming the tales "fascinating" and "undeniably moving." A *Publishers Weekly* contributor also had praise for the volume, noting, "Bausch strikes another blow against sloppy, maudlin sentimentality with this slim gathering of three razor-sharp novellas." Annette

Gallagher Weisman, writing in *People,* found the novellas to be "haunting and beautifully crafted."

Bausch's 2006 work, *Thanksgiving Night: A Novel,* is set in a small Virginia town on the last Thanksgiving of the twentieth century. The book features "several incomplete and varyingly dysfunctional . . . families," a *Kirkus Reviews* contributor noted, whose varying interactions "produce both sparks of contention and seeds of potential growth and change." The same reviewer called the novel "amiable." Melissa Rose Bernardo, writing in *Entertainment Weekly,* felt that Bausch, with plots involving "kooky relatives, drunken antics, and near-death experiences," had enough material for several volumes. A *Publishers Weekly* critic had a mixed assessment of *Thanksgiving Night,* observing that the author "engages stock characters and a predictable theme of holiday forgiveness this time out, but he injects some crackle into the heartwarming elements." Higher praise came from *Library Journal* contributor Beth E. Andersen, who concluded: "Bausch elevates familial squabbling to an art form."

Speaking with Art Taylor of the *Carolina Quarterly,* Bausch delineated the overall perspective and thematic direction of his work: "I'm the crying on the inside kind of clown, I guess. Actually, I write about individual people—and to do so with any truthfulness, it seems to me, is always going to lead to some sort of element of the remorseless facts of individual fate. I think Chekhov, along with being far better than I, is also quite consistently 'dark' in his best stories. To me, it isn't a question of darkness so much as it's a matter of faithfulness to the felt life. Fiction is about trouble, and I suppose my interest is in how people contend with troubles that don't go away or dissolve very easily."

Bausch's 2008 novel, *Peace,* deals with troubles brought on in wartime. He sets three Americans into the cauldron of World War II in Italy in this "slim and nervewracking novel that does justice to its mighty era by setting its focus on one harrowing sliver of time within it," as Sam Sacks noted on the *Open Letters* Web site. In the novel, set near Monte Cassino in 1944, the Germans are retreating from Naples after the American landings at Salerno, attempting to establish a new defensive line. In the opening scenes of the novel, a company of American soldiers surprises a German officer and his girlfriend under some hay in a cart. The German shoots and kills two of the Americans who in turn kill the German and the woman. Corporal Marson, who shot the officer, is to head up a party including the soldiers Asch and Joyner to follow the German retreat. An old Italian, Angelo, is pressed into service the next day as their guide up a slippery hillside. The action takes place as these soldiers scramble up the side of the steep incline, and soon come under sniper fire. Each of the men wonders thereafter if Angelo is actually a Fascist who led them into the ambush, and they try to determine what to do while also trying to deal with the moral dimensions of the shooting of the woman earlier. Marson, who is in civilian life a semi-pro baseball player, is the ethical witness of the action in this relatively short work. Art Winslow, writing for *Tribune Books,* found *Peace* "a morally inquisitive novel that refrains from moralizing in a strict sense." Winslow further noted that "the emotional vacillations and complexity of responses to mortal stress are evoked by Bausch in ways that render them resistant to traditional labels."

"This riveting new novel by Richard Bausch is a terrible but true reminder in a season of war," wrote John Freeman in the *Milwaukee Journal Sentinel.* Not all reviewers were impressed with *Peace.* Writing in the *Rocky Mountain News,* Jennie Camp commented, "While smoothly written and readable, Bausch's novel doesn't succeed in breaking new literary ground." David Ignatius, reviewing *Peace* for the *Washington Post Book World,* felt that the work was too short to encompass the character development and moral questioning it sets out to do. "It's a powerful tale, well told by one of America's gifted writers, but it reads like a prologue to the larger story that would encompass the world of war he sketches here," Ignatius wrote. However, Damian Kelleher, writing for *Curled Up with a Good Book,* was less critical of the book's length. Kelleher noted that the novel "could be read over a quiet evening." The same critic noted, "The impact of it, however, should stay for much longer. The questions [Bausch] has posed in *Peace* are questions that need to be answered by each generation of young men and women and, when answered, need to be examined and studied in case we have made the wrong decision." A *Kirkus Reviews* critic also had praise for the novel and its author, noting: "Bausch admirably turns a familiar story into something genuinely new." Similarly, *Booklist* contributor Seaman felt that *Peace* was "razor-sharp, sorrowfully poetic, and steeped in the wretched absurdity of war, the dream of peace," while a *Publishers Weekly* contributor called it "a dark war story of unyielding sorrow." *New York Times Book Review* writer Ben Macintyre found the same work "a short, bleakly brilliant one-act drama depicting the futility and moral complexity of combat."

Speaking on a forum for the *Washington Post Online,* Bausch confessed to no grand purpose in his chosen profession: "I write because it's fun, and I can do it. It's something I can do." He also noted that writer's block is not a problem for him: "I stopped trying to hit a homerun with every line. I'm just a story teller. I'm just telling a story."

BIOGRAPHICAL AND CRITICAL SOURCES:

BOOKS

Contemporary Authors Autobiography Series, Volume 14, Gale (Detroit, MI), 1992.

Contemporary Literary Criticism, Volume 51, Gale (Detroit, MI), 1989.

Dictionary of Literary Biography, Volume 130: *American Short-Story Writers since World War II,* Gale (Detroit, MI), 1993.

PERIODICALS

America, August 23, 1980, Thomas M. Gannon, review of *Real Presence,* pp. 77-78.

Booklist, August, 1996, Donna Seaman, reviews of *Good Evening Mr. and Mrs. America, and All the Ships at Sea* and *The Selected Stories of Richard Bausch,* p. 1880; May 15, 1999, Donna Seaman, review of *Someone to Watch Over Me: Stories,* p. 1666; October 1, 2002, Donna Seaman, review of *Hello to the Cannibals,* p. 300; November 15, 2003, Donna Seaman, review of *The Stories of Richard Bausch,* p. 547; October 1, 2007, Katherin Boyle, review of *Best New American Voices 2008,* p. 29; April 15, 2008, Donna Seaman, review of *Peace,* p. 32.

Carolina Quarterly, winter, 2005, Art Taylor, "An Interview with Richard Bausch," p. 69.

Commonweal, October 9, 1987, Thomas Cahill, review of *Spirits and Other Stories,* pp. 568-569.

Critic, September, 1980, review of *Real Presence,* p. 8.

Entertainment Weekly, October 31, 2003, Emily Mead, review of *The Stories of Richard Bausch,* p. 77; July 16, 2004, Nicholas Fonseca, review of *Wives and Lovers: Three Short Novels,* p. 83; October 6, 2006, Melissa Rose Bernardo, review of *Thanksgiving Night: A Novel,* p. 74.

Houston Chronicle (Houston, TX), May 11, 2008, Charles Matthews, review of *Peace,* p. 15.

Kirkus Reviews, September 15, 2002, review of *Hello to the Cannibals,* p. 1331; September 15, 2003, review of *The Stories of Richard Bausch,* p. 1138; May 1, 2004, review of *Wives and Lovers,* p. 407; August 1, 2006, review of *Thanksgiving Night,* p. 736; August 15, 2007, review of *Best New American Voices 2008;* March 15, 2008, review of *Peace.*

Library Journal, June 1, 1999, David W. Henderson, review of *Someone to Watch Over Me,* p. 180; August 1, 2006, Beth E. Andersen, review of *Thanksgiving Night,* p. 66; March 15, 2008, Edward B. St. John, review of *Peace,* p. 56.

Los Angeles Times, August 20, 1980, review of *Real Presence;* November 9, 1984, Art Seidenbaum, review of *The Last Good Time;* August 16, 1990, Richard Eder, review of *The Fireman's Wife and Other Stories.*

Los Angeles Times Book Review, August 20, 1980, Dick Roraback, review of *Real Presence;* May 7, 1989, Art Seidenbaum, review of *Mr. Field's Daughter.*

Milwaukee Journal-Sentinel (Milwaukee, WI), October 26, 2006, Carol Deptolla, review of *Thanksgiving Night;* April 19, 2008. John Freeman, review of *Peace.*

New York Times, September 25, 1996, Richard Bernstein, review of *Good Evening Mr. and Mrs. America, and All the Ships at Sea,* p. C15; September 8, 2002, Janet Burroway, "In Mary's Footsteps," review of *Hello to the Cannibals.*

New York Times Book Review, September 7, 1980, Scott Spencer, review of *Real Presence,* pp. 13, 38; April 26, 1981, Richard P. Brickner, review of *Take Me Back,* p. 14; December 23, 1984, Nancy Forbes, review of *The Last Good Time,* p. 25; April 26, 1987, Madison Smartt Bell, review of *Spirits and Other Stories,* p. 16; August 27, 1989, Gene Lyons, review of *Mr. Field's Daughter,* p. 14; August 19, 1990, Bette Pesetsky, review of *The Fireman's Wife and Other Stories,* p. 9; January 26, 1992, Susan Kenney, review of *Violence,* p. 7; May 16, 1993, Elizabeth Tallent, review of *Rebel Powers,* p. 9; June 7, 1998, A.O. Scott, review of *In the Night Season: A Novel;* May 11, 2008, Ben Macintyre, "Three Soldiers," review of *Peace,* p. 8.

People, June 1, 1998, Pam Lambert, review of *In the Night Season,* p. 41; August 16, 2004, Annette Gallagher Weisman, review of *Wives and Lovers,* p. 52.

Pittsburgh Post-Gazette (Pittsburgh, PA), October 27, 2002, Sharon Dilworth, review of *Hello to the Cannibals.*

Publishers Weekly, July 15, 1996, Sybil S. Steinberg, review of *Good Evening Mr. and Mrs. America, and All the Ships at Sea,* pp. 52-53; March 23, 1998, review of *In the Night Season,* p. 75; April 19, 1999, review of *Someone to Watch Over Me,* p. 57; May 24, 2004, review of *Wives and Lovers,* p. 41; August 7, 2006, review of *Thanksgiving Night,* p. 29; February 25, 2008, review of *Peace,* p. 50.

Rocky Mountain News (Denver, CO), April 24, 2008, Jennie Camp, review of *Peace.*

Seattle Times, May 16, 2008, Michael Upchurch, review of *Peace.*

Star Tribune (Minneapolis, MN), May 18, 2008, John Freeman, review of *Peace,* p. F16.

Time, September 22, 1980, review of *Real Presence,* p. E4.

Tribune Books (Chicago, IL), April 11, 1993, Joseph Coates, review of *Rebel Powers,* p. 6; April 19, 2008, Art Winslow, review of *Peace.*

Washington Post Book World, June 15, 1980, Doris Grumbach, review of *Real Presence,* p. 4; May 3, 1981, Bruce Cook, review of *Take Me Back,* p. 5; December 11, 1984, Stephen Dobyns, review of *The Last Good Time;* June 28, 1987, Michael Dorris, review of *Spirits and Other Stories,* p. 6; April 30, 1989, Jonathan Yardley, review of *Mr. Field's Daughter,* p. 3; December 29, 1991, Carolyn See, review of *Violence;* November 5, 2006, "Our Town: A Wise Tragicomedy about the Eccentric Citizens of a Virginia Village," p. 5; May 4, 2008, David Ignatius, review of *Peace,* p. 6.

ONLINE

Annotico Report, http://www.annoticoreport.com/ (April 21, 2008), review of *Peace.*

Curled Up with a Good Book, http://www.curledup.com/ (December 18, 2006), review of *The Stories of Richard Bausch;* June 18, 2008, Damian Kelleher, review of *Peace.*

Internet Movie Database, http://www.imdb.com/ (December 18, 2006), "Richard Bausch."

Open Letters, http://www.openlettersmonthly.com/ (May 26, 2008), Sam Sacks, review of *Peace.*

Perpetual Folly, http://www.perpetualfolly.blogspot.com/ (May 17, 2008), Clifford Garstang, review of *Peace.*

University of Memphis, Department of English Web site, http://english.memphis.edu/ (December 18, 2006), "Richard Bausch."

Washington Post Online, http://www.washingtonpost.com/ (November 20, 2003), "Off the Page: Richard Bausch"; (December 10, 2007) "Off the Page: Marie Arana and Richard Bausch."*

BAUSCH, Richard Carl
   See BAUSCH, Richard

     *   *   *

BEAHRS, Andrew 1973-

PERSONAL: Born 1973, in CT; married; wife's name Eli (a teacher); children: Erik. *Education:* University of California, Berkeley, B.A.; University of Virginia, M.S.; Spalding University, M.F.A. *Hobbies and other interests:* SCUBA diving, capoeira, playing the cello, bluegrass music.

ADDRESSES: Home—Berkeley, CA. *E-mail*—apbeahrs@mac.com; andrew@andrewbeahrs.com.

CAREER: Writer.

WRITINGS:

Strange Saint (novel), Toby Press (Danbury, CT), 2005.
The Sin Eaters (novel), Toby Press (Danbury, CT), 2008.

Contributor to periodicals and journals, including *Gastronomica, Food History News, Ocean, Virginia Quarterly Review, Alligator Juniper,* and the *Writer's Chronicle.*

SIDELIGHTS: An archaeologist by training, Andrew Beahrs endeavored to write a first novel that uses some of his educational background, adding realism to his tale about the Pilgrims. Melode, the main character in *Strange Saint,* is enduring a life of servitude in England when she joins Adam, the son of a minister of the Saints—or Pilgrims—on a boat to the New World. Although she is falling in love with Adam, in his increasing religious fervor he soon rejects her. Melode subsequently has an affair with another man and becomes pregnant. Disgraced, she is thrown off the ship and left in Newfoundland, where she and her child face a new struggle just to survive. In a mixed blessing, she is rescued and makes her way to the new colony, where she finds herself a social reject among the pious Pilgrims. Although Mark Andre Singer commented in a *Library Journal* review that the heroine's views on sex were a bit hard to believe, the exciting plot in *Strange*

Saint "smoothes out the occasional stylistic wrinkle." A *Publishers Weekly* contributor praised this "moving" story for its "sumptuous description and . . . period's language."

Beahrs published his second novel, *The Sin Eaters,* in 2008. Elder herbalist and healer Sarah flees her town in the midst of social upheaval. Along the road she meets Bill, a sin-eater, who is forced to eat foods that have been laid out upon the body of a corpse to symbolically remove them of their sins. Sarah tries to help Bill relieve his burdens, but they are both pursued by Sam Ridley.

Eileen Charbonneau, reviewing the novel in the *Historical Novels Review* Web site, described the language used in the novel as being "dense, intimate, and beautiful." Charbonneau further commented that "Beahrs's richly imagined novel travels though meadow, forest, plague-flagged town, and ruined monastery. It is peopled by characters brimming with life." A contributor writing in *Kirkus Reviews* concluded: "Sensitive work—sometimes fusty, finally affecting." A contributor writing in *Publishers Weekly* claimed that the outcome of the final confrontation with Ridley "will surprise few readers." However, the same contributor noted that Beahrs "convincingly presents the main characters' inner lives in a manner" similar to that of Iain Pears' *An Instance of the Fingerposts.* Amy Ford, reviewing the novel in *Library Journal,* worried that readers unfamiliar with Jacobean-era England and its slang would find the text "slowgoing." Ford also lamented that "the prolog is so confusing that readers may be tempted to skip it." On the other hand, Ford took note of the characters that populate the novel, describing them as being "complex." Ford also recorded that Beahrs' combination of Jacobean England's socio-economic conditions were "beautifully portrayed."

BIOGRAPHICAL AND CRITICAL SOURCES:

PERIODICALS

Kirkus Reviews, September 15, 2008, review of *The Sin Eaters.*
Library Journal, September 1, 2005, Mark Andre Singer, review of *Strange Saint,* p. 127; September 15, 2008, Amy Ford, review of *The Sin Eaters,* p. 43.
Publishers Weekly, September 5, 2005, review of *Strange Saint,* p. 36; September 8, 2008, review of *The Sin Eaters,* p. 35.

ONLINE

Andrew Beahrs Home Page, http://www.andrewbeahrs. com (February 1, 2006), author biography.
Historical Novels Review, http://www.historicalnovel society.org/ (November 30, 2008), Eileen Charbonneau, review of *The Sin Eaters.*
Word Museum, http://www.wordmuseum.com/ (February 1, 2006), Julie Failla Earhart, review of *Strange Saint.**

* * *

BEASLEY, Bruce 1958-

PERSONAL: Born January 20, 1958, in Thomaston, GA; son of Harold and Dorothy Leming Beasley; married Suzanne Paola (a poet), August 7, 1982; children: Jin. *Education:* Oberlin College, B.A., 1980; Columbia University, M.F.A., 1982; University of Virginia, Ph.D., 1993.

ADDRESSES: Home—Bellingham, WA. *Office*—Department of English, Western Washington University, Bellingham, WA 98225. *E-mail*—info@brucebeasley. net.

CAREER: Poet, c. 1988—. Western Washington University, Bellingham, WA, professor of English, 1992—.

AWARDS, HONORS: Ohio State University Press/*The Journal* Award, 1994, for *The Creation;* Colorado Prize, 1996, for *Summer Mystagogia;* National Endowment for the Arts fellowship, 1992; Artist Trust fellowship, 1999; Pushcart Prize, 1999.

WRITINGS:

Spirituals, Wesleyan University Press (Middletown, CT), 1988.
The Creation, Ohio State University Press (Columbus, OH), 1994.
Summer Mystagogia, University Press of Colorado (Niwot, CO), 1996.
Signs and Abominations, University Press of New England (Hanover, NH), 2000.

Lord Brain: Poems, University of Georgia Press (Athens, GA), 2005.

The Corpse Flower: New and Selected Poems, University of Washington Press (Seattle, WA), 2007.

Also contributor of poems to periodicals, including *Poetry, Yale Review, Kenyon Review, Southern Review, New American Writing, Field, Ploughshares, Iowa Review, Fence,* and *Gettysburg Review.*

SIDELIGHTS: Poet Bruce Beasley, who grew up in Georgia, has penned several volumes of poetry and won awards for his verse. His first book, *Spirituals,* saw print in 1988 and established his frequently used theme of Christianity. Beasley is also known for his poems concerning grief and loss—some of which describe his childhood with alcoholic parents—as well as his use of tales from classical mythology. In addition to his book-length collections, his poetry has appeared in such periodicals as *America, Poetry,* and the *Yale Review.*

Spirituals was well received by critics. Staige Blackford in the *Virginia Quarterly Review* hailed it as "a beautiful first book" in which "one can see the potential for genius." The strength of Beasley's narrative poems, Blackford observed, "is in their lyricality." Mark Jarman in the *Hudson Review* praised the poet's "original imagination and style in the way he retells Biblical stories" and cited "Death of Lazarus" as a "particularly effective" example. The volume also includes poems such as "Novice," "From Grace"—a retelling of the Genesis story of the fall of man—and "Elegy," an account of Christ's Last Supper that Jarman lauded for its "fresh portrait" of a well-known biblical scene.

Beasley's second volume, 1994's *The Creation,* garnered him the Ohio State University Press/*The Journal* Award. In addition to religious poems such as "Tracing the Angel," *The Creation* includes "Going Home to Georgia," a personal tribute to Beasley's childhood home. The collection also features the classically themed "Eurydice in Hades" and "Zeta Hercules." B. Wallenstein, reviewing *The Creation* in *Choice,* singled out "The Instrument and Proper Corps of the Soule" for particular attention, applauding it as "a free-wheeling, five-part meditation on the brain." Though Beasley does not quite measure up to the standards of T.S. Eliot and W.H. Auden, Wallenstein asserted, his poems can be compared with the works of these great metaphysical and religious poets. Molly McQuade in *Publishers*

Weekly also lauded *The Creation,* proclaiming it "a gracefully lush reverie on matters of earth and spirit." She further noted that Beasley "shares what he knows as our fellow traveler, and not as a guide who would like to find acolytes." Blackford, in a *Virginia Quarterly Review* assessment, described Beasley's approach as "always measured, yet sure," and finished with the declaration that *The Creation* "is filled with thoughtful and serious poems."

Beasley was awarded the Colorado Prize for *Summer Mystagogia.* The poet defines the last word in his title as "the period immediately following the initiation into a mystery." Assessing the book for the *Boston Review,* Daniel Tobin cited the title poem and "The Monologue of the Signified" as noteworthy examples of Beasley's work. Overall, Tobin found the collection "brilliant," and he stated that the poems, which are "often both mythic and demotic," serve as a powerful initiation into a world that is flawed yet suffused with grace. Tobin noted Beasley's persistent return to his childhood memories, which are shadowed by his parents' problems with alcoholism. Those memories, the evocation of a marred but beautiful world, and the desire to give things their proper names combine to form what Tobin called "a wonderfully resilient and hard-won poetry of witness"—poetry that is at once "emotionally present and intellectually supple."

In *Signs and Abominations,* Beasley ponders the relationship between art and religion in the late twentieth century. His images range from that of mankind as a damaged likeness of God to that of a crucifix submerged in urine. His poems demonstrate the intertwined nature of the spiritual and profane, and of religion and art. Mark Jarman stated in *Poetry Daily* that Beasley's verse is "as close to the bone of meaning" as any poet's, and that *Signs and Abominations* is a "passionate, difficult book." Ethan Paquin, a reviewer in *Contemporary Poetry Review,* stated: "Bruce Beasley has written a piece of supreme symmetry." Paquin noted that *Signs and Abominations* is "a book of intersections, of vantages, of careful dovetails that complement and reflect those around them." A *Publishers Weekly* reviewer compared Beasley to Flannery O'Connor and Annie Dillard in his belief that "in ugliness and in the profane an affirmation rather than repudiation of the idea of God" can be found. According to that reviewer, Beasley's best poems have "a density of language and observed detail that capture, in their vertiginous forms, the qualities of modern life."

In 2005 Beasley published *Lord Brain: Poems.* The collection of poetry takes as its theme the allied health industry, particularly that of neuroscience. The poems explore the quirkiness of the human mind, and frequently mix in quotes by noted scholars and great minds.

Sarah Law, reviewing the book in *Stride* Magazine, observed that "spirituality has a real presence in this collection; not at all as a doctrinal certainty, but as an elusive, sometimes ludic presence running through the interstices of poetic awareness." Law summarized that "Beasley can write in a number of different styles: the dislocated and experimental as well as the simply lyrical—I like those poems which strike a middle ground. *Lord Brain* is in no way a technical manual, but I had a satisfactory sense of learning a lot . . . as well as being taken on a poetic journey which made my thoughts, on occasion, soar." Sheila Farr, writing in the *Seattle Times,* concluded that the book "isn't the kind of poetry to be read lightly. But for those who appreciate the challenge of intellectual puzzles and don't mind learning the language of neuroscience through a set of endnotes worthy of T.S. Eliot . . . *Lord Brain* offers plenty of rewards."

BIOGRAPHICAL AND CRITICAL SOURCES:

PERIODICALS

Books and Religion, summer, 1990, review of *Spirituals,* p. 6.
Boston Review, February-March, 1997, Daniel Tobin, review of *Summer Mystagogia.*
Chelsea, 1997, review of *Summer Mystagogia,* p. 193.
Choice, October, 1994, B. Wallenstein, review of *The Creation,* p. 278.
Christianity and Literature, autumn, 1997, Donald Platt, review of *Summer Mystagogia,* p. 114.
Cresset, April, 1989, review of *Spirituals,* p. 24.
Hudson Review, winter, 1989, Mark Jarman, review of *Spirituals,* pp. 734-735.
Publishers Weekly, April 25, 1994, review of *The Creation,* p. 65; November 6, 2000, review of *Signs and Abominations,* p. 85.
Seattle Times, October 21, 2005, Sheila Farr, review of *Lord Brain: Poems.*
Stride Magazine, November, 2005, Sarah Law, review of *Lord Brain.*
Virginia Quarterly Review, summer, 1988, Staige Blackford, review of *Spirituals,* pp. 99-100; autumn, 1994, Staige Blackford, review of *The Creation,* p. 136; summer, 2001, review of *Signs and Abominations,* p. 106.

ONLINE

Bruce Beasley Home Page, http://www.brucebeasley.net (June 6, 2009), author biography.
Contemporary Poetry Review, http://www.cprw.com/ (January 4, 2002), review of *Signs and Abominations.*
Poetry Daily, http://www.poems.com/ (February 17, 2001), Mark Jarman, review of *Signs and Abominations.*
PoetryNet, http://www.poetrynet.org/ (May 31, 2007), author profile.*

*   *   *

BERGER, John 1926-
(John Peter Berger)

PERSONAL: Born November 5, 1926, in London, England; son of S.J.D. and Miriam Berger; divorced; children: two sons and one daughter. *Education:* Attended Central School of Art and Chelsea School of Art, London, England. *Politics:* Marxist.

ADDRESSES: Office—Quincy, Mieussy, 74440 Taninges, France. *Agent*—Anna Arthur PR, Ground Flr., 3 Charlotte Mews, London W1T 4DZ, England.

CAREER: Writer, editor, translator, painter, art critic, art historian, actor, and educator. Painter and teacher of drawing; actor in films, including *Walk Me Home.* *Exhibitions:* Has exhibited work at the Wildenstein, Redfern, and Leicester Galleries, London, England. *Military service:* British Army, 1944-46, served in the Oxford and Buckinghamshire Infantry.

AWARDS, HONORS: Booker Prize, 1972, and James Tait Black Memorial Prize, 1973, both for *G;* New York Critics Prize for the Best Scenario of the Year, 1976, for *Jonah Who Will Be Twenty-five in the Year 2000;* Prize for Best Reportage, Union of Journalists and Writers, Paris, 1977, for *A Seventh Man: A Book of Images and Words about the Experience of Migrant Workers in Europe.*

WRITINGS:

FICTION

A Painter of Our Time, Secker & Warburg (London, England), 1958, expanded edition, Pantheon (New York, NY), 1989.

The Foot of Clive, Methuen (London, England), 1962.

Corker's Freedom, Methuen (London, England), 1964.

G, Viking (New York, NY), 1972.

Pig Earth (part one of trilogy; also see below), Writers and Readers Publishing Cooperative (London, England), 1979, Vintage (New York, NY), 1992.

Once in Europa (part two of trilogy; also see below), Pantheon (New York, NY), 1987.

Lilac and Flag: An Old Wives' Tale of a City (part three of trilogy; also see below), Pantheon (New York, NY), 1990.

Into Their Labours (trilogy; contains *Pig Earth, Once in Europa,* and *Lilac and Flag: An Old Wives' Tale of a City*), Pantheon (New York, NY), 1991.

To the Wedding (novel), Pantheon (New York, NY), 1995.

(With Nella Bielski) *Isabelle: A Story in Shots,* Dufour (Chester Springs, PA), 1998.

(With Timothy O'Grady and Steve Pyke) *I Could Read the Sky,* Harvill Press (London, England), 1998.

King: A Street Story, Random House (New York, NY), 1999.

(With Nella Bielski) *Oranges for the Son of Alexander Levy/Isabelle,* Arcadia Books Ltd. (London, England), 2001.

Here Is Where We Meet, Pantheon Books (New York, NY), 2005.

NONFICTION

Permanent Red: Essays in Seeing, Methuen (London, England), 1960, published as *Toward Reality: Essays in Seeing,* Knopf (New York, NY), 1962.

The Success and Failure of Picasso, Penguin (London, England), 1965, Vintage (New York, NY), 1993.

A Fortunate Man: The Story of a Country Doctor, photographs by Jean Mohr, Holt (New York, NY), 1967.

Art and Revolution: Ernst Neizvestny and the Role of the Artist in the U.S.S.R., Pantheon (New York, NY), 1969.

The Moment of Cubism, and Other Essays, Pantheon (New York, NY), 1969.

Selected Essays and Articles: The Look of Things, edited by Nikos Stangos, Penguin (London, England), 1972, published as *The Look of Things: Essays,* Viking (New York, NY), 1974.

Ways of Seeing (based on a television series), Penguin (London, England), 1972, Viking (New York, NY), 1973.

A Seventh Man: A Book of Images and Words about the Experience of Migrant Workers in Europe, photographs by Jean Mohr, Penguin (London, England), 1975, published as *A Seventh Man: Migrant Workers in Europe,* Viking (New York, NY), 1975.

About Looking (essays), Pantheon (New York, NY), 1980.

Une autre facon de raconter, photographs by Jean Mohr, F. Maspero (Paris, France), 1981, published as *Another Way of Telling,* Pantheon (New York, NY), 1982.

And Our Faces, My Heart, Brief as Photos, Pantheon (New York, NY), 1984.

The Sense of Sight: Writings (essays), edited by Lloyd Spencer, Pantheon (New York, NY), 1985, published as *The White Bird: Writings,* Chatto & Windus (London, England), 1985.

Keeping a Rendezvous (essays), Pantheon (New York, NY), 1991.

Photocopies, Pantheon (New York, NY), 1995.

Titian: Nymph and Shepherd, Te Neues Publishing (New York, NY), 1996.

(With Jean Mohr) *At the Edge of the World,* Reaktion (London, England), 1999.

Selected Essays, Pantheon (New York, NY), 2001.

The Shape of a Pocket (essays), Pantheon (New York, NY), 2001.

(With Michael Hofmann and Christopher Lloyd) *Arturo di Stefano,* Merrell (London, England), 2002.

TRANSLATOR

Wolfgang Martini, *Renato Guttuso,* Verlag der Kunst (Dresden, Germany), 1957.

(With Anya Bostock) Bertolt Brecht, *Poems on the Theatre,* Scorpion (Buckhurst, England), 1961, published as *The Great Art of Living Together: Poems on the Theatre,* Granville Press (London, England), 1972.

(With Anya Bostock) Bertolt Brecht, *Helene Weigel, Actress,* Veb Edition (Leipzig, Germany), 1961.

(With Anya Bostock) Aime Cesaire, *Return to My Native Land,* Penguin (London, England), 1969.

(With Jonathan Steffen) Nella Bielski, *After Arkadia,* Penguin (London, England), 1992.

(With Lisa Appignanesi) Nella Bielski, *The Year Is '42,* Pantheon Books (New York, NY), 2004.

SCREENPLAYS

Marcel Frishman, New Yorker Films (New York, NY), 1958.

City at Chandigarh (documentary), New Yorker Films (New York, NY), 1966.

(With Alain Tanner) *La Salamandre* (title means "The Salamander"), New Yorker Films (New York, NY), 1971.

(With Alain Tanner) *Le Metier du Monde* (title means "The Middle of the World"), New Yorker Films (New York, NY), 1974.

(With Alain Tanner) *Jonas qui aura 25 ans en l'an 2000*, translation by Michael Palmer, published as *Jonah Who Will Be Twenty-five in the Year 2000*, North Atlantic Books (Berkeley, CA), 1983.

(With Timothy Neat) *Play Me Something*, British Film Institute (London, England), 1989.

OTHER

Poems in Voix, Maspero (Paris, France), 1977.

(With Nella Bielski) *Question de geographie* (play; produced at Theatre National de Marseille, 1984), J. Laffitte (Marseilles, France), 1984, published as *A Question of Geography*, Faber (London, England), 1987.

(With Nella Bielski) *Le dernier portrait de Francisco Goya: le peintre joue aujourd'hui* (play), Champ Vallon (Seyssel, France), 1989.

Géo Chavez: der erste Flug ueber die Alpen = Géo Chavez: The First Flight Across the Alps, idee und gestaltung by Heidi und Peter Wenger, Rotten (Visp, Switzerland), 2001.

Forest, Steidl (Göttingen, Germany), 2005.

Hold Everything Dear: Dispatches on Survival and Resistance, Pantheon Books (New York, NY), 2007.

From A to X, Pantheon Books (New York, NY), 2008.

Contributor to books, including *Artists and Writers: Ways of Seeing Art in Small Countries*, Duncan of Jordanstone College of Art (Dundee, Scotland), 1981; and *About Time* (based on a television series directed by Michael Dibb and Christopher Rawlence), edited by Rawlence, J. Cape, Channel 4 Television Co. (London, England), 1985. Author of introduction, *Prison Paintings*, by Michael Quanne, J. Murray (London, England), 1985; and *Between the Eyes: Essays on Photography and Politics*, by David Levi Strauss, Aperture (New York, NY), 2003. Also contributor to periodicals, including *Nation* and *New Statesman*.

SIDELIGHTS: "John Berger is perhaps the most challenging British writer of his generation," declared a *Dictionary of Literary Biography* contributor. Berger, known primarily as an author of art criticism and fiction, is also a poet, essayist, translator, playwright and screenwriter. The *Dictionary of Literary Biography* contributor further commented that Berger's "writings in a wide variety of genres and his way of life have constituted a distinctive artistic statement." Assessing the writer's achievements in the *New York Times Book Review*, Robert Boyers proclaimed that in all his work, Berger has shown "great vividness of imagination and extraordinary clarity of intention." Boyers went on to write: "To read Mr. Berger over the last thirty years has been to feel oneself in the presence of an intelligence utterly unmoved by literary or political fashion and unfailingly committed to its own clear vision of what is decent and important, in art and in life."

Berger began his working life as an artist and teacher, exhibiting his work at galleries in London, including Wildenstein, Redfern, and Leichester. During this period, he also served as art critic for such prominent periodicals as *New Statesman*, *New Society*, *Punch* and the *Sunday Times*. Some of his early essays were collected and published in *Permanent Red: Essays in Seeing*, the title of which reflects the author's dedication to Marxist philosophies. According to a *Dictionary of Literary Biography* contributor, Berger's criticism is unique in that it avoids "the given historical categories of art criticism in favor of an existential engagement with the historical moment of the artist and the work of art." Berger's interest in the relationship between art and politics is further illustrated in *The Moment of Cubism, and Other Essays*. Berger contends that the revolutionary art form of cubism presaged the political and economic revolution in Russia. The "moment of cubism," according to Berger, was that brief period in which artists reached an understanding of the changes occurring in the outside world and reflected this understanding in their paintings. Adapted from a 1972 television series, his *Ways of Seeing* has become regarded as something of a modern masterpiece on art appreciation and is a perennial favorite for introduction to art classes.

Berger's nonfiction began to take on a more mixed-media appearance, including essays, criticism, poetry, and prose commentary. In 1982 he collaborated with photographer Jean Mohr (and was aided by Nicholas Philibert) on *Une autre facon de raconter*, which was also published as *Another Way of Telling*. Suzanne Muchnic in the *Los Angeles Times Book Review* called *Another Way of Telling* the "most original photography book to appear in recent months." Edward W. Said in

Nation argued that the photographs are "extraordinary both as pictures and as accompaniment to the text." Said commented that the book's basic premise is "an argument *against* linear sequence—that is, sequence construed by Berger as the symbol of dehumanizing political processes . . . engaged in the extinction of privacy, subjectivity, free choice." A *Newsweek* contributor noted that *Another Way of Telling* would "certainly be widely read and hotly debated."

And Our Faces, My Heart, Brief as Photos, noted Peter Schjeldahl in the *New York Times Book Review,* is "a series of prose meditations and poems on themes of loss and love, both individual and historical." Containing some passages of art criticism as well, *And Our Faces, My Heart, Brief as Photos* reflects the eclectic nature of Berger's work. "Modern history, as Berger sees it, no longer guarantees the present's incorporation into the past, but hastens the present towards a future which never comes," argued *Observer* contributor Peter Conrad. For Conrad, Berger's "reflection on the twin determinants of our fate, time and space" is "high-minded rather than inspired," but also "noble and moving." Michael Ignatieff in the *Times Literary Supplement* noted that "Time and Death are grand and risky themes," but concluded that *And Our Faces, My Heart, Brief as Photos* is "among the most finished of Berger's works because it is the most serene, the one least troubled by the impulse to instruct or convert."

As his career progressed, Berger's essays drifted away from pure art criticism and became increasingly involved with the processes of seeing and thinking. In *The Sense of Sight: Writings,* for example, he includes his impressions of some of the world's great cities, peasant art, and the work of such artists as Goya, Rembrandt, and Amedeo Modigliani. Reviewing the book in *Time,* Otto Friedrich called it the work of "a resourceful mind passionately at work." He praised Berger for his "vivid prose" and his avoidance of "windy academic generalities." Friedrich summarized: "He not only sees more than most people do but seizes what he sees, twisting and probing until it yields up its meaning."

Berger's 1991 collection, *Keeping a Rendezvous,* includes essays, poems and meditations, most of which concern visual art. As John Barrell noted in the *London Review of Books,* "none of them is about art alone: they place the paintings, the sculptures, the films, the photographs they discuss in the context of geography, sexuality, the nature of time, the rise of multinationals,

the collapse of totalitarian Communism." Barrell argued that Berger values the visual arts "for their ability, as he believes, to put us in touch with the pre-verbal" but concluded that the author is not clear upon how this is accomplished or why "that should be a particularly good thing for art to do." *Times Literary Supplement* contributor Roger Moss commented that *Keeping a Rendezvous,* like *Into Their Labours,* is "a consistent meditation on what might save us, on the possibility of paradise. This alone makes them a welcome antidote to the infectious cynicism that has come to characterize so much English left-wing writing." Geoff Dyer in *Guardian Weekly* noted that, although "Berger's answers are becoming increasingly spiritual, they are still rooted in a visceral sense of the needs and hopes of the oppressed." Dyer added: "It is exactly this recognition and quality that gives Berger's own books their gravity and grace."

Berger's *Photocopies,* which was published in 1996, is a collection of vignettes drawn from memorable moments in his life over the past several decades. Hailed as a work "that brings nonfiction writing close to drawing" by *New Statesman* contributor Michele Roberts, *Photocopies* contains ephemeral moments, remembered fragments of larger incidents. Many of these short vignettes involve meetings with Berger's neighbors from the village of Haute-Savoie, people now long since dead but "intensely alive a second time in Berger's memory, and immortalised in his crisp, terse, completely unsentimental prose," according to Roberts. "Each is a 'verbal photocopy,'" explained Amy Edith Johnson in the *New York Times Book Review.* "Neither life nor art, these impressions embody a wish that—as in the frugal, meticulous lives of Mr. Berger's rural neighbors in the French Alps—nothing should be lost or wasted." While noting that not all of the vignettes are successful, Johnson praised the volume as a hybrid of fiction and nonfiction: "Mr. Berger's artists, peasants, revolutionaries are united . . . in the human economy they share, [where] no labor is spared and all is worthy."

In 2001 two works rounding out Berger's nonfiction oeuvre were published: *The Shape of a Pocket* and *Selected Essays.* The former title is a collection of essays, many of which have been published in foreign language publications. The twenty-four pieces collected in *The Shape of a Pocket* deal with artists from Rembrandt to Degas to Frieda Kahlo. A critic writing for *Kirkus Reviews* noted that "in his essays on great artists, Berger always offers up something like an epiphany." Additionally, a large chunk of the book is taken up with a dialogue with Mexico's Subcomandante

Marcos, and there are also "familiar barnyard observations from Berger as the rural dweller in the French Alps," according to a *Publishers Weekly* contributor, who added that "most of the present book, integrating the author's own aging and physical decay, rings as true as the rest of his much-appreciated work." Kenneth Baker, reviewing *The Shape of a Pocket* in the *San Francisco Chronicle*, praised in particular "an ingenious piece about Hieronymus Bosch as a prophetic artist," as well as the "pleasant surprise" of a 1996 radio piece, "Will It Be a Likeness?," the "most puzzling and involving thing Berger has published in years."

Berger's *Selected Essays*, on the other hand, gathers the work of decades, including pieces from earlier collections of essays which allow the reader "to trace the arc of Berger's writing toward ever more direct expressions of the ways historical circumstances shape and color individual experience," according to Baker. The same reviewer also commented that *Selected Essays* "makes a wonderful introduction to Berger's critical work," reprinting outstanding essays on Picasso, Goya, and Turner, among others. Baker commented: "Even if Berger had never written stirring fiction and first-hand accounts of people living out their fates in such books as *A Fortunate Man: The Story of a Country Doctor* and *A Seventh Man*, the *Selected Essays* would establish him as an indispensable late 20th century voice." A critic for *Publishers Weekly*, also reviewing *Selected Essays*, commented that "in the tradition of energetic British eccentrics, Berger has contributed much to writing on modern art, often speaking sense and doing it more entertainingly than most salaried newspaper specialists."

Berger's fiction has also attracted a great deal of critical attention and debate. *Corker's Freedom*, his 1964 novel, was praised in England upon its initial publication. When released in the United States nearly twenty years later, it was again acclaimed as a "contemporary masterwork," in the words of Douglas Glover, contributor to the *Washington Post Book World*. *Corker's Freedom* describes one day in the life of a sixty-four-year-old man who decides to strike out on his own, leaving the home he has shared for years with his invalid sister. This adventure, the greatest ever to occur in the man's life, quickly comes to a miserable end. Glover called *Corker's Freedom* "an exhilarating achievement, wise, unsettling, and alive with a sense of humanity that is flawed, doomed, yet oddly indomitable." Joyce Reiser Kornblatt, in a retrospective review of *Corker's Freedom* in the *New York Times Book Review*, referred to

the book as "a valuable antecedent to the greater novels that followed it," and concluded that Berger is "one of the most intelligent writers alive."

Berger followed *Corker's Freedom* with *G*—the tale of a modern Don Juan, presented in what Gerald Marzorati described in the *New York Times* as a "brilliant, late-modernist" style. Berger's fascination with the impact that social structures have on the individual is reflected in the character G, the protagonist of the novel, who is essentially apolitical though profoundly affected by the historical events of his time. Duncan Fallowell in *Books and Bookmen* called *G* "terribly good" and also "terribly pretentious." Fallowell concluded that Berger's "undoubted power to move the reader is too frequently undersold by the author himself." Leo Baudy in the *New York Times Book Review* argued that *G* "belongs to that other tradition of the novel, the tradition of George Eliot, [Leo] Tolstoy, D.H. Lawrence and Norman Mailer, the tradition of fallible wisdom, rich, nagging and unfinished. To read [*G*] is to find again a rich commitment to the resources and possibilities of the genre." Arnold Kettle in the *New Republic* commented that although *G* "isn't an easy book to deal with," it is a "fine, humane and challenging book." Though not embraced by all critics, *G* nevertheless won the prestigious Booker Prize in 1972 and secured Berger's reputation as a novelist of the first order.

In the early 1970s Berger moved to the Giffre River valley in France to make his home in a peasant village, where he began work on what some commentators consider his greatest work, the trilogy *Into Their Labours*. In the first volume of this trilogy, *Pig Earth*, Berger created a portrait of the ancient lifestyle of the French peasant class. "Fiction or anthropology? The publisher's catalogue heading lists both, but it is difficult to categorize this rich melange of story, fable, and social document—with poems interspersed between the chapters," reported William Wiser in the *New York Times Book Review*. Wiser noted that as Berger "faithfully records the seasons of the pig earth and searches for the French peasant in himself, he reveals something elemental in us all." A *Washington Post Book World* contributor claimed that Berger "evokes with remarkable economy a peasant world as resilient to history, as sensual and as unpredictable as the village of Macondo built so lavishly by [Gabriel] Garcia Marquez."

Once in Europa, the second part of Berger's *Into Their Labours* trilogy, shows the intrusion of the modern world into the old ways, and the swift crumbling of centuries-old traditions that follows. *Progressive* reviewer Saul Landau found the stories "beautiful and painful" and credited Berger with painting "the characters and landscapes like a Goya with words, conjuring up horrifying yet real images of devastating change." Richard Critchfield in the *New York Times Book Review* argued that a "sense of loss—both of loved people and a whole way of life . . . haunts this second volume" of Berger's trilogy. Critchfield hoped Berger would gain a wider readership in America with this volume, and called him "one of the most gifted and imaginative [of] contemporary writers."

In *Lilac and Flag: An Old Wives' Tale of a City,* the author focuses on the final degradation of the village people who have attempted to start new lives in the city. This culminating novel of Berger's trilogy received mixed reviews. Guy Mannes-Abbott in the *New Statesman* argued that throughout the trilogy, "the stories get longer as they approach the challenge of the modern, until they fracture into the complexity of [*Lilac and Flag*]." Mannes-Abbott commented that the "simple, but not simplistic, life [Berger] records slides into idealisation," but concluded that *Lilac and Flag* is "a unique piece of fiction." Robert Boyers in the *New York Times Book Review* noted that although Berger's "characteristic eye for telling physical detail and his feeling for the poetry of everyday life" are evident in *Lilac and Flag,* the book is burdened by its "fragmentariness and dreaminess." Boyers concluded: "One wonders how a writer of his experience and sophistication can have gone so wrong."

To the Wedding, Berger's 1995 work, depicts two young lovers whose relationship continues even after the woman, Ninon, reveals that she is HIV-positive. The story culminates with the couple's wedding. A writer for *Kirkus Reviews* commented: "While the tragedy of AIDS has spawned many poignant works in the last decade, few have achieved the level of emotional, psychological, and physical harmony found here." Donna Seaman in *Booklist* noted that Berger avoids "melodrama and overanalysis . . . [and] has gone straight to the heart of the matter." Joanna M. Burkhardt in *Library Journal* wrote that royalties from *To the Wedding* will be donated to aid those with HIV and AIDS, and called the novel "bittersweet."

In his 1999 novel, *King: A Street Story,* Berger turns the convention of the animal story on its head. Whereas most such tales tell of man's cruelties to the beasts of the world, Berger's tells of cruelty to humans. Using the voice of a dog, the "King" of the title, the author spins a story of homelessness. King's masters are Vico and Vica, old people who live rough in temporary shelters near the coast on a stretch of land called Saint Valery. King is able to talk with all the people of this homeless community, "stray dogs," as *Booklist* reviewer Ray Olson describes them, seen thus in the eyes of those with their own homes. The book chronicles one day in the life of these poor people, one that ends with their violent eviction by police and bulldozers. Writing in the *New York Times,* Brigitte Frase noted that Berger "has been paring down his style." With *King,* Frase felt the author is "sparer than ever, and less successful" than in novels such as *To The Wedding.* Frase also complained that it is "just too hard to believe in a poetic dog." Other reviewers sharply differed from this judgment, however. Olson called Berger a "brilliant, experimental fiction writer" whose *King* "immerses readers so artfully, beautifully, and humanely in the experiences of homelessness." A *Publishers Weekly* contributor noted the difficulty of Berger's task in telling a "serious story" in the voice of a dog, but felt that the author "accomplished an impressive technical feat" by bringing the reader "so believably inside the head of an animal to elucidate the vagaries of human nature." Chris Searle, writing in *Race and Class,* thought that Berger "has pitched his own bivouac of truth and written a profound novel of our times." Searle also noted that "prophetic and teeming with insight about our times, *King* is an epochal novel."

Berger's eclectic approach has led some reviewers to consider him a difficult, albeit intelligent and original, author. Summarizing Berger's career, Edward W. Said in *Nation* wrote: "Berger is not easy to digest partly because he has a great deal to say in his stream of essays, books of criticism, film scripts and novels, and partly because he says it in unusual ways." Said added: "His knowledge of art history, philosophy and literature, like his acute political sense, is sophisticated without being heavy or obtrusive. The best thing about him, though, is his relentless striving for accessible truths about the visual arts—their ambiguity, memorial enchainments, half-conscious projections and irreducibly subjective force."

A *Dictionary of Literary Biography* contributor noted that the "lasting value of his work consists precisely in the intellectual restlessness that makes it necessary for him to cross frontiers between established cultural and social institutions in his pursuit of a synthetic critique of contemporary civilization." Paul Bonaventura concluded in a *New Statesman* interview with the author with the following summation: "At its best, Berger's work has changed the way we think about the world, about creativity and intellectual reach and what the linkages might be between them. In his fiction and nonfiction, Berger has irrevocably transformed the relationship between reader and subject."

An octogenarian in 2006, Berger continued to write. In his collection titled *Here Is Where We Meet,* the author presents a book that crosses genres, from autobiographical fiction to nonfiction. He writes about his journeys, including times spent in Lisbon, Geneva, Krakow, Madrid, and London. On one trip he talks with his dead mother while shopping, just one of many people out of Berger's past that reappear in his mind during his travels. In another vignette, Berger comes across Cro-Magnons in a cave in Chauvet, France, known for its ancient rock paintings. The author also writes about the living, and presents a touching story about an old friend taking his wife home to meet his family in Poland. In a review of *Here Is Where We Meet* in *Publishers Weekly,* a contributor noted that it may become difficult to tell who is real and who exists only in Berger's imagination. The reviewer also wrote: "With its clarity and beautifully proportioned contours of fictive memory, this book makes the perfect site to encounter Berger." A *Kirkus Reviews* contributor noted that the author "has the appropriate historical consciousness and breadth of vision" to write about all of Europe. "The effect of these encounters is not whimsical or fantastical," declared David Horspool in the *Sunday Times*. "The tone of Berger's writing is so generally imbued with a calm awe that meeting and talking to the dead merely becomes another way of seeing and thinking about the world with rapt attention to detail." In each and "every line he draws—his beloved ghosts, a Polish wedding that exceeds its proverbial joy, a newly discovered cave of paintings 30,000 years old—the essential point is the dignity of work and of workers," explained Michael Alec Rose in his *BookPage* Web site review. "Berger seasons his . . . tales with observations about the ubiquity of pain, the importance of human frailty and the sharpness of expectancy—all childhood hunches that he later found borne out by his adult experience," wrote Heller McAlpin in the *San Francisco Chronicle*. "One observation is so important he sets it, somewhat curiously, on a page by itself: 'The number of lives that enter our own is incalculable.' With a potent mix of memory and imagination, Berger successfully resuscitates several lives that have stayed deep within him for decades." "In letting the dead speak plainly and simply,

in showing how we can travel back into our own history, in informing us how looking and listening matter so much," concluded *Seattle Times* contributor Richard Wallace. "Berger once again is our guide to being truly present in life." John Leonard, writing in *Harper's,* referred to *Here Is Where We Meet* as a "hybrid of breviary, consecration, and ancestor worship." Leonard went on to call the book "quite brilliant."

Berger's *Hold Everything Dear: Dispatches on Survival and Resistance* is "a series of reflections written between 2001 and 2006 that arise from contemporary political moments; London in the aftermath of the July 7 bombings, New Orleans after its destruction by Hurricane Katrina, New York after 9/11, and the Middle Eastern troubles, from Baghdad to Gaza," declared Ramona Koval in an interview for the Australian National Broadcasting Corporation's radio program *Book Show.* The book, Mark Espiner stated in the *New Statesman,* "is consistent with his hitherto strident stance. Yet evident on almost every page of these sixteen essays—subtitled *Dispatches on Survival and Resistance*—is his compassion, his sympathy for struggle, his passion for language, his contempt for political lies and his belief in the power of art." Reviews of the volume were mixed; many reviewers objected to Berger's politics while admiring his writing. "Concluding, in good Marxist manner, that the pursuit of profit is a pitiless business," wrote a *Kirkus Reviews* contributor, Berger "paints himself into a distant corner of irrelevance, even if he does get off a few good zingers." "This unflinching internalization of the bigger picture . . . makes this kind of writing different," declared Horatio Morpurgo in the *New Internationalist*. "Read Berger attentively for how much more words can do." "Compassionate and tender in his vision of our endangered world," Donna Seaman wrote in her *Booklist* review, "Berger has seen much and felt more."

Berger's *From A to X* is a book of letters that crosses years of the communication from A'ida, to her lover, Xavier, a political prisoner. In the story, the letters have been discovered after Xavier's imprisonment in the abandoned prison inside the cell that once housed him. Berger presents no responses from Xavier to A'ida, but scribblings on the back of A'dia's do exist to give readers an idea of Xavier's position on the issues presented by his lover. A reviewer stated in *New Nationalist* that *From A to X* "is a beautiful, poetic hymn to the human spirit that will live long in the minds of all who read it." Seaman, writing in *Booklist,* commented that Berger tells a "beautifully sorrowful story of love, conviction, and defiance in a time of brutal indifference." A *Kirkus Reviews* contributor wrote: "Berger's writing comes off as equal parts somber and exalted."

BIOGRAPHICAL AND CRITICAL SOURCES:

BOOKS

Contemporary Literary Criticism, Gale (Detroit, MI), Volume 2, 1974, Volume 19, 1981.

Dictionary of Literary Biography, Gale (Detroit, MI), Volume 14: *British Novelists since 1960,* 1983, Volume 207: *British Novelists since 1960, Third Series,* 1999, pp. 34-44.

Dyer, Geoff, *Ways of Telling: The Work of John Berger,* Pluto Press (London, England), 1986.

Modern British Literature, 2nd edition, St. James Press (Detroit, MI), 2000.

Papastergiadis, Nikos, *Modernity as Exile: The Stranger in John Berger's Writing,* Manchester University Press (Manchester, England), 1993.

Weibel, Paul, *Reconstructing the Past: G and The White Hotel, Two Contemporary "Historical" Novels,* P. Lang (Bern, Switzerland), 1989.

PERIODICALS

American Book Review, May 1, 2006, "The Self the Night Knows."

American Library Association, September 15, 2008, Donna Seaman, review of *From A to X.*

Book, January-February, 2002, Sean McCann, review of *The Shape of a Pocket,* p. 65.

Booklist, May 1, 1995, Donna Seaman, review of *To the Wedding;* May 1, 1999, Ray Olson, review of *King: A Street Story,* p. 1576; September 1, 2007, Donna Seaman, review of *Hold Everything Dear: Dispatches on Survival and Resistance,* p. 28; August 1, 2008, Donna Seaman, review of *From A to X.*

Books and Bookmen, September, 1972, Duncan Fallowell, review of *G.*

Books in Canada, January 1, 2006, "Documenting Old Europe."

Financial Times, July 21, 2007, Ed Holland, review of *Hold Everything Dear,* p. 40.

Guardian Weekly, February 16, 1992, Geoff Dyer, review of *Keeping a Rendezvous.*

Harper's, August, 2005, John Leonard, review of *Here Is Where We Meet,* p. 81.

Kirkus Reviews, March 1, 1995, review of *To the Wedding,* pp. 246-247; November 15, 2001, review of *The Shape of a Pocket,* p. 1589; May 15, 2005, review of *Here Is Where We Meet,* p. 554; August 1, 2007, review of *Hold Everything Dear;* August 1, 2008, review of *From A to X.*

Library Journal, May 1, 1995, Joanna M. Burkhardt, review of *To the Wedding;* December 1, 2004, Edward Cone, review of *The Year Is '42,* p. 97; September 15, 2007, Shedrick Pitman-Hassett, review of *Hold Everything Dear,* p. 74; September 1, 2008, Evelyn Beck, review of *From A to X.*

London Observer, April 3, 2005, Sean O'Hagan, "A Radical Returns," profile of author.

London Review of Books, April 9, 1992, John Barrell, review of *Keeping a Rendezvous,* p. 3; January 26, 2006, "Berger on Drawing," p. 25.

Los Angeles Times Book Review, March 13, 1983, Suzanne Muchnic, review of *Another Way of Telling,* p. 6.

Nation, December 4, 1982, Edward W. Said, review of *Another Way of Telling,* pp. 595-597.

New Internationalist, November 1, 2007, Horatio Morpurgo, review of *Hold Everything Dear,* p. 31; October 1, 2008, review of *From A to X.*

New Republic, October 7, 1972, Arnold Kettle, review of *G,* p. 31.

New Statesman, February 1, 1991, Guy Mannes-Abbott, review of *Lilac and Flag: An Old Wives' Tale of a City,* p. 36; June 28, 1996, Michele Roberts, review of *Photocopies,* pp. 47-48; November 12, 2001, Paul Bonaventura, "Master of Diversity," p. 38; July 9, 2007, "Reclaiming Language," p. 58; October 20, 2008, review of *From A to X.*

Newsweek, September 6, 1982, review of *Another Way of Telling,* pp. 76-77.

New York Times, June 13, 1999, Brigitte Frase, review of *King,* section 7, p. 21; January 13, 2002, David Thomson, "What Are You Looking At?," section 7, p. 16.

New York Times Book Review, September 10, 1972, Leo Baudy, review of *G,* pp. 5, 18; September 21, 1980, William Wiser, review of *Pig Earth,* pp. 14, 39; May 13, 1984, Peter Schjeldahl, review of *And Our Faces, My Heart, Brief as Photos,* p. 18; April 5, 1987, Richard Critchfield, review of *Once in Europa,* pp. 9-10; August 19, 1990, Robert Boyers, review of *Lilac and Flag,* p. 20; January 6, 1993; November 7, 1993, Joyce Reiser Kornblatt, review of *Corker's Freedom,* p. 15; April 14, 1996, Amy Edith Johnson, review of *Photocopies,* p. 32; June 13, 1999, review of *King,* p. 21; January 20, 2002, review of *Selected Essays,* p. 18.

New York Times Magazine, November 29, 1987, Gerald Marzorati, review of *G,* pp. 39, 46, 50, 54.

Observer (London, England), December 16, 1984, Peter Conrad, review of *And Our Faces, My Heart, Brief as Photos,* p. 19.

Parachute: Contemporary Art Magazine, June, 2002, Ana Honigman, review of *The Shape of a Pocket,* p. 134.

Progressive, June, 1988, Saul Landau, review of *Once in Europa,* pp. 30-31.

Publishers Weekly, March 15, 1999, review of *King,* p. 45; October 29, 2001, reviews of *Selected Essays* and *The Shape of a Pocket,* pp. 45-47; October 4, 2004, review of *The Year Is '42,* p. 66; July 11, 2005, review of *Here Is Where We Meet,* p. 62; August 11, 2008, review of *From A to X.*

Race and Class, January-March, 2000, Chris Searle, review of *King,* p. 101.

San Francisco Chronicle, January 6, 2002, Kenneth Baker, "Berger's Pockets of Resistance," p. 2; August 7, 2005, Heller McAlpin, "Such a Tender Nostalgia After Visits with the Dead."

Seattle Times, September 9, 2005, Richard Wallace, review of *Here Is Where We Meet.*

Sunday Times, May 15, 2005, David Horspool, review of *Here Is Where We Meet.*

Time, July 21, 1986, Otto Friedrich, review of *The Sense of Sight: Writings,* p. 73.

Times Literary Supplement, January 4, 1985, Michael Ignatieff, review of *And Our Faces, My Heart, Brief as Photos,* p. 7; May 22, 1992, Roger Moss, review of *Keeping a Rendezvous;* February 12, 1999, review of *King,* p. 23; June 8, 2007, Alex Danchev, review of *Hold Everything Dear,* p. 33.

Washington Post, February 10, 2002, "Dissenting Views," p. T13.

Washington Post Book World, October 12, 1980, review of *Pig Earth,* p. 7; February 27, 1994, Douglas Glover, review of *Corker's Freedom,* p. 6.

ONLINE

Bookreporter.com, http://www.bookreporter.com/ (August 28, 2008), Alexis Burling and Michael Alec Rose, reviews of *Here Is Where We Meet.*

Book Show, http://www.abc.net.au/ (August 28, 2008), Ramona Koval, "John Berger's Political Way of Seeing."

John Berger Home Page, http://www.johnberger.org (August 28, 2008), author profile.

OpenDemocracy.net, http://www.opendemocracy.net/ (August 28, 2008), author profile.

Random House Web site, http://www.randomhouse.com/ (August 28, 2008), author profile.*

*   *   *

BERGER, John Peter
  See BERGER, John

*   *   *

BERNIÈRES, Louis de
  See DE BERNIERES, Louis

*   *   *

BOUILLIER, Grégoire 1960-

PERSONAL: Born 1960, in Tizi-Ouzou, Great Kabylia, Algeria.

ADDRESSES: Home—Paris, France.

CAREER: Painter and writer.

AWARDS, HONORS: Prix de Flore, 2002, for *Rapport sur moi.*

WRITINGS:

MEMOIRS

Rapport sur moi, Allia (Paris, France), 2002, translation by Bruce Benderson published as *Report on Myself,* Houghton Mifflin Company (Boston, MA), 2009.

L'invité mystère, Allia (Paris, France), 2004, translation by Lorin Stein published as *The Mystery Guest: An Account,* Farrar, Straus & Giroux (New York, NY), 2006.

Contributor to *L'Infini, NRV,* and *New York Times Magazine.*

SIDELIGHTS: Paris-based writer Grégoire Bouillier is the author of *Rapport sur moi,* an award-winning memoir, and *The Mystery Guest: An Account,* "an ostensibly autobiographical novella that is charmingly absurd, gently metafictional, and gloriously French," noted *Booklist* critic Brendan Driscoll. In *The Mystery Guest,* Bouillier receives a phone call from the woman who left him, without explanation, years before. Instead of discussing her abrupt departure, she invites him to serve as the "mystery guest" at a birthday party for her husband's best friend, the artist Sophie Calle. The bewildered narrator accepts the invitation but is overwhelmed by suspicion and self-doubt as he deliberates endlessly on the caller's motivations. "Anyone whose anxieties tend to buzz in the ear, creating a din that makes it impossible to act unself-consciously, will enjoy this slim volume," noted Emily Bobrow in the *New York Observer.* "Mr. Bouillier is looking back and poking fun at himself, but the events are captured with a raw immediacy, making his parade of humiliations feel fresh and profound."

The Mystery Guest received strong critical acclaim. Bouillier's "text is brilliantly entertaining and at times hilarious," Regan McMahon stated in the *San Francisco Chronicle.* "His biting observations have the ring of truth, whether he's berating himself in his gloomy apartment, where for the longest time he refuses to change the lightbulb (a metaphor for the extinguished relationship) or mocking the celebrity artistic and literary elite he finds at the party." According to Erica Wagner, writing in the *New York Times Book Review,* "This memoir—which is shot through with references to the literature that Bouillier loves, to Ulysses and to 'Ulysses' and to Virginia Woolf—gives shape to the question of 'meaning,' whether it's illusory, whether that matters at all." "We're always hearing that truth is stranger than fiction, and yet it's amazing how many books act as if nothing happened and keep telling stories that can't hold a candle to reality," Bouillier told Yann Nicol in the *Brooklyn Rail.* "When it's this continual tendency of truth—to keep being stranger than fiction—that is the very essence of the novelistic. And in everything I've written I've tried to capture this novelistic effect."

Bruce Benderson's English translation of *Rapport sur moi* was published as *Report on Myself* in 2009. Bouillier covers his life through his many loves and losses, ranging from a staph infection he caught as a child that left him unable to smell, through odd relationships with his family members, to his infatuation with a local prostitute. Elizabeth Bachner, writing on the *Bookslut* Web site, remarked that the memoir "is filled with the kind of strange, private, utterly unique revelations that

each of us has in life, but that are almost impossible to write about. It's the kind of book you'll want to roll around on your tongue." Bachner found that "like *The Mystery Guest,* it's hilarious, and like *The Mystery Guest,* it's curative, medicinal somehow, something you administer to yourself in a time of need. With this one, though, I can't figure out the exact details of the medicine." In an article in the *Baltimore Sun,* Dave Rosenthal thought that the book seemed longer than it was, likening that "much of the prose is delivered in long stretches that twist, turn and loop back on themselves. I didn't mind that. In fact, the translation was so well done that even such complex sentences were clear." A contributor to the *National Public Radio* Web site commented that "the book—content to be minor, determined to avoid uplift—is an affair of offbeat charisma. Its fragments add up to a frank attempt to capture the weirder mysteries of life's truths." Janday Wilson, writing in *Two.One.Five* magazine, mentioned that "for the most part, *Report [on Myself]* is a charmingly dizzying piece of work." Susan Salter Reynolds, reviewing the memoir in the *Los Angeles Times,* claimed that it is undoubtedly "Bouillier's failure, in this and in *The Mystery Guest,* to locate himself concretely in the world, no matter how hard he tries, that makes him at once delightful and important to read." In an article in *Time Out New York,* Michael Miller recorded that the author's "writing is so euphoric that it would be a drag to stop and wonder how he acquires his energy—just be thankful he possesses it." A contributor writing in *Kirkus Reviews* labeled Bouillier and this book as "an author who vaunts his 'likable kookiness' finds fresh invention in the sum lessons of his life." A contributor writing in *Publishers Weekly* opined that "while his first book was a lyrical self-exploration, Bouillier here comes across as little more than self-indulgent." Caroline Weber, writing in an article in the *New York Times Book Review,* fondly recalled the author's mother's explanation of his conception. However, Weber noted that "less enjoyable is Bouillier's predilection for wordplay, as when he notes that the name 'Laurence' can, in French, be broken down into l'eau rance: rancid water. ('Her name was Laurence, I guess because "Low Rinse," a kind of dirty water, isn't a first name.') Puns like this are distracting, partly because they sound so clunky in English, and partly because Bouillier seems to want them to carry more meaning than they actually do." Weber conceded that "luckily, however, such false notes are few and far between." Weber concluded her review by claiming that the memoir is "an excruciating yet exquisite account of the manifold ways in which—to borrow a famous, non-French expression—love hurts."

BIOGRAPHICAL AND CRITICAL SOURCES:

BOOKS

Bouillier, Grégoire, *Rapport sur moi,* Allia (Paris, France), 2002, translation by Bruce Benderson published as *Report on Myself,* Houghton Mifflin Company (Boston, MA), 2009.

Bouillier, Grégoire, *L'invité mystère,* Allia (Paris, France), 2004, translation by Lorin Stein published as *The Mystery Guest: An Account,* Farrar, Straus & Giroux (New York, NY), 2006.

PERIODICALS

Baltimore Sun, March, 2009, Dave Rosenthal, review of *Report on Myself.*

Booklist, October 15, 2006, Brendan Driscoll, review of *The Mystery Guest,* p. 27.

Kirkus Reviews, June 15, 2006, review of *The Mystery Guest,* p. 609; October 15, 2008, review of *Report on Myself.*

Library Journal, October 15, 2006, Ali Houissa, review of *The Mystery Guest,* p. 59.

Los Angeles Times, January 4, 2009, Susan Salter Reynolds, review of *Report on Myself.*

New York Observer, August 28, 2006, Emily Bobrow, review of *The Mystery Guest,* p. 13; November 6, 2006, Sheelah Kolhatkar, "Who's *Le Plus Chaud?* French Emo-Memoirist Grégoire Bouillier," p. 1.

New York Times Book Review, September 17, 2006, Erica Wagner, review of *The Mystery Guest,* p. 8; February 15, 2009, Caroline Weber, review of *Report on Myself,* p. 11.

New York Times Magazine, October 15, 2006, Grégoire Bouillier, "Meanings of Origin," p. 88.

Publishers Weekly, July 17, 2006, review of *The Mystery Guest,* p. 149; October 13, 2008, review of *Report on Myself,* p. 46.

San Francisco Chronicle, September 10, 2006, Regan McMahon, review of *The Mystery Guest,* p. M1.

Time Out New York, August 24-30, 2006, Michael Miller, review of *The Mystery Guest;* January 22-28, 2009, Michael Miller, review of *Report on Myself.*

ONLINE

Bookslut, http://www.bookslut.com/ (December 31, 2008), Elizabeth Bachner, review of *Report on Myself.*

Brooklyn Rail Online, http://brooklynrail.org/ (September, 2006), Yann Nicol, "Experiential Lit: Grégoire Bouillier with Yann Nicol, translated by Violaine Huisman and Lorin Stein."

National Public Radio, http://www.npr.org/ (April 7, 2009), Troy Patterson, review of *Report on Myself.**

Two.One.Five magazine, http://www.twoonefive magazine.com/ (June 8, 2009), Janday Wilson, review of *Report on Myself.*

*   *   *

BRANDS, Henry William
See BRANDS, H.W.

*   *   *

BRANDS, Henry William, Jr.
See BRANDS, H.W.

*   *   *

BRANDS, H.W. 1953-
(Henry William Brands, Henry William Brands, Jr.)

PERSONAL: Born August 7, 1953, in Portland, OR; son of Henry William Brands; married; wife's name Ginger; children: five. *Education:* Stanford University, B.A., 1975; Reed College, M.A., 1978; Portland State University, M.S., 1981; University of Texas at Austin, Ph.D., 1985.

ADDRESSES: Home—Austin, TX. *Office*—Department of History, University of Texas at Austin, 1 University Station, Austin, TX 78712. *E-mail*—hwbrands@ hwbrands.com.

CAREER: Writer, historian, and educator. Austin Community College, Austin, TX, instructor, 1981-86; Vanderbilt University, Nashville, TN, visiting assistant professor, 1986-87; Texas A&M University, College Station, assistant professor, 1987-89, associate professor, 1990-92, professor, 1992-98, Ralph R. Thomas '21 Professor of Liberal Arts, 1998-2001, distinguished professor, 2000-04, Melbern G. Glasscock Professor of

American History, 2001-04, coordinator of History of the Americas Research Program, 1998-2001; University of Texas at Austin, Dickson Allen Anderson Centennial Professor of History and Professor of Government, 2005—. University of Texas at Austin, visiting assistant professor, 1990; Society for Historians of American Foreign Relations, Bernath Lecturer, 1992; public speaker; frequent guest on television and radio programs.

MEMBER: Society of American Historians, Institute of Texas Letters, Philosophical Society of Texas.

AWARDS, HONORS: National Endowment for the Humanities fellow, 1985; citation for outstanding academic book, *Choice,* 1995, for *The Wages of Globalism: Lyndon Johnson and the Limits of American Power;* Pulitzer Prize nomination, 1999, for *What America Owes the World: The Struggle for the Soul of Foreign Policy;* Bancroft Award nomination, 1999, for *What America Owes the World;* named South Central regional scholar of the triennium, Phi Kappa Phi, 1998-2001; Pulitzer Prize nominations, 2001, for *The First American: The Life and Times of Benjamin Franklin,* and 2009, for *Traitor to His Class: The Privileged Life and Radical Presidency of Franklin Delano Roosevelt; Washington Post* Best Book Award, 2002, for *Age of Gold: The California Gold Rush and the New American Dream;* Deolece Parmelee Award, Texas Historical Foundation, 2005, for *Lone Star Nation: How a Ragged Army of Volunteers Won the Battle for Texas Independence and Changed America.*

WRITINGS:

Cold Warriors: Eisenhower's Generation and American Foreign Policy, Columbia University Press (New York, NY), 1988.
The Specter of Neutralism: The United States and the Emergence of the Third World, 1947-1960, Columbia University Press (New York, NY), 1989.
India and the United States: The Cold Peace, Twayne (New York, NY), 1990.
Inside the Cold War: Loy Henderson and the Rise of the American Empire, 1918-1961, Oxford University Press (New York, NY), 1991.
Bound to Empire: The United States and the Philippines, Oxford University Press (New York, NY), 1992.
The Devil We Knew: Americans and the Cold War, Oxford University Press (New York, NY), 1993.

Into the Labyrinth: The United States and the Middle East, 1945-1993, McGraw (New York, NY), 1994.
The United States in the World: A History of American Foreign Relations, Houghton Mifflin (Boston, MA), 1994.
The Wages of Globalism: Lyndon Johnson and the Limits of American Power, Oxford University Press (New York, NY), 1995.
The Reckless Decade: America in the 1890s, St. Martin's Press (New York, NY), 1995.
Since Vietnam: The United States in World Affairs, 1973-1995, McGraw Hill (New York, NY), 1995.
T.R.: The Last Romantic, HarperCollins (New York, NY), 1997.
What America Owes the World: The Struggle for the Soul of Foreign Policy, Cambridge University Press (New York, NY), 1998.
Masters of Enterprise: Giants of American Business from John Jacob Astor and J.P. Morgan to Bill Gates and Oprah Winfrey, Free Press (New York, NY), 1999.
The First American: The Life and Times of Benjamin Franklin, Doubleday (New York, NY), 2000.
The Strange Death of American Liberalism, Yale University Press (New Haven, CT), 2001.
The Age of Gold: The California Gold Rush and the New American Dream, Doubleday (New York, NY), 2002.
Woodrow Wilson, Times Books/Henry Holt (New York, NY), 2003.
Lone Star Nation: How a Ragged Army of Volunteers Won the Battle for Texas Independence and Changed America, Doubleday (New York, NY), 2004.
(With Robert A. Divine and others) *America Past and Present,* 7th edition, Longman (New York, NY), 2004.
(With Robert A. Divine and others) *The American Story,* Pearson Longman (New York, NY), 2005.
Andrew Jackson: A Life and Times, Doubleday (New York, NY), 2005.
The Money Men: Capitalism, Democracy, and the Hundred Years' War over the American Dollar, W.W. Norton and Co. (New York, NY), 2006.
(With Kathleen Dalton, Lewis L. Gould and Natalie A. Naylor) *Theodore Roosevelt and His Sagamore Hill Home: Historic Resource Study, Sagamore Hill National Historic Site,* National Park Service (Boston, MA), 2007.
Traitor to His Class: The Privileged Life and Radical Presidency of Franklin Delano Roosevelt, Doubleday (New York, NY), 2008.

American Stories: A History of the United States, two volumes, Pearson Longman (New York, NY), 2009.

EDITOR

The Foreign Policies of Lyndon Johnson: Beyond Vietnam, Texas A&M Press (College Station, TX), 1999.

The Use of Force after the Cold War, Texas A&M Press (College Station, TX), 2000.

(With Martin J. Medhurst) *Critical Reflections on the Cold War: Linking Rhetoric and History,* Texas A&M Press (College Station, TX), 2000.

The Selected Letters of Theodore Roosevelt, Cooper Square Press (Lanham, MD), 2001.

Contributor of scholarly articles to professional journals, as well as articles to periodicals, including *Atlantic Monthly, Wall Street Journal, New York Times, Washington Post, Boston Globe,* and *International Herald Tribune.*

Brands's writings have been translated into Spanish, French, German, Russian, Chinese, Japanese, and Korean.

ADAPTATIONS: *The First American* and *Masters of Enterprise* were both adapted as audio books by Modern Scholar/Recorded Books, 2003; *Lone Star Nation* was adapted as an audio book by Random House Audio, 2004.

SIDELIGHTS: H.W. Brands is the author of a score of nonfiction titles dealing with topics from revisionist examinations of the Cold War era to American involvement with India to Texas independence to biographies of famous American presidents. Brands, who holds advanced degrees in both mathematics and history, is the Dickson Allen Anderson Centennial Professor of History at the University of Texas at Austin.

In *The Reckless Decade: America in the 1890s* and *T.R.: The Last Romantic,* Brands focuses on American society of the turn of the twentieth century and its adventurous president, Theodore Roosevelt. *The Reckless Decade* examines the widespread sense of doom that the end of the nineteenth century brought to many countries around the world, including the United States. Brands notes that the end of a century "sets people to thinking about

their collective prospects and ultimate destiny." Melissa Knox wrote in *New Leader,* at a time when America was "becoming the wealthiest nation on Earth," there was a general feeling of malaise brought about by the perceived end of an era. Some worried that with the end of the frontier, a vital impetus to American life had vanished. While Brands describes the many technological innovations seen in the 1890s, the political conflicts, and the economic growth, he notes the effects these changes had upon the ordinary American of the time. Knox concluded: "That the country overcame the gloom afflicting the final decade of the last century is, says Brands, a reflection of its resilience."

In the book *T.R.* Brands looks at an American president at the turn of the twentieth century, Theodore Roosevelt, who was inaugurated in 1901. In a narrative that a contributor to *Publishers Weekly* found to be "lucid, fast-moving and unblinded by hero worship," Brands details Roosevelt's remarkable career and argues that both the president and the nation were romantic in outlook. "Brands uses Roosevelt's many personal letters to tell his story in a firsthand manner," wrote Boyd Childress in the *Library Journal,* "resulting in the most comprehensive Roosevelt biography yet." Writing in the *American Spectator,* Philip Terzian observed: "Brands has allowed us to see Roosevelt as he was, and perhaps more important, as he saw himself. The times are bound to alter our retrospective view, but the careful historian has performed his basic task with elegance, insight, sympathy, and style."

Brands examines the evolution of American business in his book *Masters of Enterprise: Giants of American Business from John Jacob Astor and J.P. Morgan to Bill Gates and Oprah Winfrey.* Through the lives of twenty-five prominent business leaders, he illustrates the course of American business history. Brands also demonstrates the qualities that members of this disparate group of people have in common: good health, abundant energy, a clear and burning creative vision, and a powerful hunger for success. A reviewer in *Publishers Weekly* commented that, although John Astor and Cornelius Vanderbilt "would have difficulty understanding the technology behind the companies" established by entrepreneurs such as Andy Grove and Bill Gates, "they would have completely understood their business models." David Rouse noted in *Booklist* that, while the life stories of most of Brands's subjects are familiar, the author's "storytelling skills animate the details of how each got started." His writing style was also mentioned by a contributor to *Kirkus Reviews,* who commented: "The freshness of the narrative is well suited to the positive message imparted by the contents. It serves as an invigorating justification of the business of business."

The First American: The Life and Times of Benjamin Franklin provides a new look at one of America's most famous citizens. Although Franklin's autobiography was once required reading for almost every American high school student, during the last half of the twentieth century he began losing popularity. Brands was quoted as saying in a 2000 interview with Thomas J. Brady for the *Knight-Ridder/Tribune News Service* that "dead white guys were falling out of fashion, and people were looking in other directions. . . . They focused on some of the other Founding Fathers and Founding Mothers and various minorities and people who hadn't been written about. . . . That's the best that I can explain for the fact that there really hasn't been that much interest in Franklin for quite a long time." Brands's book recounts Franklin's early life, his many business enterprises and inventions, his transformation from British loyalist to one of America's first patriots, and his successes as ambassador to France. The author notes that the breadth of Franklin's achievements is almost incredible. "To some degree, I suppose, one of the reasons that people lost interest in him is that he was just too good to be true. And, actually, he almost is," mused Brands in the interview with Brady.

From early American history, Brands turned to more recent developments in *The Strange Death of American Liberalism*. In this work, he argues, as noted by Daniel Jacobson in *American Studies International,* "that foreign threats, not domestic comforts, propelled forward postwar liberalism in the United States." In other words, programs such as Franklin Roosevelt's New Deal and the Great Society of Lyndon Johnson were not what brought Americans around to liberalism for a time; rather, it was the imminent threat of World War II and the Cold War. With the end of the Cold War, Americans, in Brands's analysis, went back to their traditional distrust of big government. Jacobson went on to call the author's thesis "provocative," but also suggested that it "frustrates more than it explains." Jon Schaff, writing in *Perspectives on Political Science,* expressed similar concerns, noting that Brands's book "makes interesting reading, but ultimately his argument is thin and unconvincing."

In *The Age of Gold: The California Gold Rush and the New American Dream,* Brands focuses on another major theme in American history—with an emphasis not on the gold fields themselves, but on how the entire enterprise shaped American society. Not only did the discovery of gold lead to the accession of California as a state, but it also tipped the balance in the ongoing debate over slavery, eventually leading to the Civil War. Bob Trimble wrote in the *Dallas Morning News:* "Few historians can tell a better tale than H.W. Brands."

Continuing speculation about the manner in which history influenced the formation of the American polity and character emerges in *Lone Star Nation: How a Ragged Army of Volunteers Won the Battle for Texas Independence and Changed America.* Brands recounts the usual particulars of the story of Tennessee farmers inspired to break new farmland in Texas and the subsequent Battle of the Alamo, focusing on major characters such as Stephen Austin and Sam Houston. He also turns a critical eye on Mexicans such as Antonio López de Santa Anna, who, as a contributor to *Kirkus Reviews* noted, "earns points for bravery." Brands thus tells the story from both the American and Mexican points of view but reportedly remains objective in the telling. The *Kirkus Reviews* contributor called Brands "one of the most fluent of narrative historians," and further noted that he "spins a good yarn, strong on colorful characters and situations." *Booklist* contributor Gilbert Taylor considered the book to be not only an "excellent, fair-minded chronicle," but also an "impressive integrative account" that demonstrates "trenchant psychological insights."

Brands returns to biography for two additional books on U.S. presidents. *Woodrow Wilson* is, at under 200 pages, a "digestible precis," according to Taylor, again writing in *Booklist.* Brands recounts the major achievements of this president and proposes that it was not the initiation of the income tax or establishment of the Federal Reserve that were Wilson's real and lasting achievements, but rather his leadership and rhetoric that brought the United States onto the world stage by taking the nation into World War I. Gilbert made note of the author's "proven success in popular-history writing over the past decade." Thomas J. Baldino, writing in the *Library Journal,* deemed *Woodrow Wilson* a "balanced, well-written treatment."

An earlier president is featured in *Andrew Jackson: A Life and Times.* This time, the treatment—at over 700 pages—is anything but brief. According to a *Kirkus Reviews* contributor, "Brands's biography is more action-packed than bookish, suiting its subject." Brands traces Jackson's Scots-Irish roots, who was called Old Hickory by admirers and detractors alike. Jackson grew from an adolescent fan of the American Revolution to military commander to presidential candidate who, after winning the popular vote, lost the election when the House of Representatives voted instead for John Quincy Adams. This outraged many people and led eventually to election reform. Four years later, in 1828, Jackson was voted into office and served for two terms. The *Kirkus Reviews* contributor noted that the book *Andrew Jackson* would be a "pleasure for history buffs." Noting that Brands displays both Jackson's accomplishments as well as his flaws, such as his roles in Indian massacres, a reviewer for *Publishers Weekly* called the resulting work "a bracing, human portrait of both a remarkable man and of American democracy."

Brands returns to money matters in *The Money Men: Capitalism, Democracy, and the Hundred Years' War over the American Dollar*. Here, according to *EH.net: Economic History Services* reviewer David J. Cowen, "Brands combines his skill sets of biography and history to render a flowing work about early American finance, a period covering roughly the beginning of the finance system under the stewardship of Alexander Hamilton to the 1907 financial panic and its aftermath." Opening the work with a profile of Hamilton, Brands demonstrates the man's emphasis on economics as the lynchpin of world power. As the first appointed Secretary of the Treasury, Hamilton oversaw bank legislation and the creation of government funding. Cowen noted one apparent oversight in this first part of the book, commenting that brands "omitted any mention of the creation of the Mint, which defined the dollar as the measure of money." Brands then chronicles what historians call the Bank War of 1832. Nicholas Biddle, president of the Second Bank of the United States, attempted to renew the charter of this bank before it had expired, and found himself in a battle against Andrew Jackson, who did not trust banks that were not "properly" funded by gold. Jackson, representing the democratic side of the equation in this fight, prevailed over the autocratic Biddle, the capitalist. Next, Brands focuses on financier Jay Cooke who helped the Union finance the Civil War by selling war bonds. Later Cooke also took part in another major episode in Brands's account, teaming with Jay Gould and Jim Fisk, Jr., to try, in 1869, to corner the market in gold. Government intervention was able to thwart this scheme. Legendary financier J.P. Morgan figures in the concluding section of the book, playing the role of "financier, amasser of capital, savior of the financial system, and enigmatic greedy capitalist all rolled into one," accord-

ing to Cowen. In this section Brands deals with the battle between the gold standard and the silver standard, which pitted Morgan against William Jennings Bryan, the populist, as well as Theodore Roosevelt. These battles ultimately led, according to Brands's account, to the creation of the Federal Reserve System in 1913.

Reviewing *The Money Men* in *Booklist*, Mary Whaley observed that Brands "identifies five Americans who played critical roles in America's formation of a monetary system." A *Kirkus Reviews* contributor called the book "a lively and accessible history of a once-dominant issue in American life." According to a *Publishers Weekly* reviewer, the author "delivers a competent but schematic general history." *Wilson Quarterly* contributor Robert E. Wright offered a more favorable opinion: "Overall, Brands's account of American history as a series of monetary struggles is a fruitful interpretation well worth a reader's dollars."

In *Traitor to His Class: The Privileged Life and Radical Presidency of Franklin Delano Roosevelt*, Brands returns to presidential biography. He presents, according to *Library Journal* contributor William D. Pederson, "a broad yet nuanced overview" of the man many argue is the greatest president. In Brands's view, the man affectionately known as "FDR" plotted a course in politics highly influenced by the mistakes and accomplishments of both his cousin Theodore Roosevelt and Woodrow Wilson. Brands follows the full course of Franklin Roosevelt's career, from his stint in the Wilson administration to the polio that changed his life both physically and mentally, to his ascendancy as president. A full two-thirds of the biography is devoted to Roosevelt's time in the presidency. Here Brands documents achievements of the Roosevelt administration in pulling the country out of the Great Depression with its New Deal programs such as the Works Progress Administration and the creation of social safety nets such as Social Security. These great social engineering projects did make Roosevelt, as the title of the book suggests, something of a traitor to his upper-class ancestors. For Brands, the low point of Roosevelt's presidency was his attempt in 1937 to pack the Supreme Court with judges favorable to his New Deal policies. However, Brands writes, by 1942, with the nation at war, Roosevelt had become one of the most powerful presidents of all time.

Reviewing *Traitor to His Class*, a contributor to *Publishers Weekly* noted that it appeared along with other biographies of Roosevelt, but observed that it is "an entirely adequate narrative detailing the well-known facts of Roosevelt's life." *Booklist* reviewer Brad Hooper described the work as "a finely balanced biography certain to garner much critical attention." A reviewer for the *Economist* felt that Brands "copes skilfully with [Roosevelt's] complexity," while *Christian Science Monitor* contributor Terry Hartle observed: "More than other biographers, Brands convincingly shows that Roosevelt was a careful student of executive leadership." Writing for the *San Diego Union-Tribune*, Charles A. Zappia suggested that "Brands does a good job in reminding us that government can effectively promote economic and social justice." Acknowledging that the biography appeared just as Barack Obama was elected president during another severe financial crisis, Zappia concluded: "The timing of such a reminder could not be more propitious." Similarly, a reviewer for *Texas Monthly* noted that Brands's book "makes abundantly clear [that] a capitalist democracy can't survive without a sensible and compassionate public policy: Social Security, fair financial market regulation, even massive government spending in times of crisis. These are the kinds of things we all depend on but which delusional free-market puritans see only as 'socialism.'" The same reviewer also noted that "Brands reminds us just how center-seeking FDR actually was and how integral his achievement has been to American freedom and prosperity ever since," and commented that this "magisterial volume could hardly be more useful or timely."

BIOGRAPHICAL AND CRITICAL SOURCES:

PERIODICALS

American Political Science Review, June, 1989, Michael Schaller, review of *Cold Warriors: Eisenhower's Generation and American Foreign Policy,* p. 680.

American Spectator, March, 1998, Philip Terzian, review of *T.R.: The Last Romantic,* pp. 76-78.

American Studies International, February, 2003, Daniel Jacobson, review of *The Strange Death of American Liberalism,* p. 242.

Argumentation and Advocacy, summer, 2001, Davis W. Houck, review of *Critical Reflections on the Cold War: Linking Rhetoric and History,* p. 51.

Booklist, May 1, 1992, Steve Weingartner, review of *Bound to Empire: The United States and the Philippines,* p. 1566; October 15, 1997, review of *T.R.,* p. 381; June 1, 1999, David Rouse, review of *Masters of Enterprise: Giants of American Busi-*

ness *from John Jacob Astor and J.P. Morgan to Bill Gates and Oprah Winfrey,* p. 1755; March 15, 2003, Gilbert Taylor, review of *Woodrow Wilson,* 127; January 1, 2004, Gilbert Taylor, review of *Lone Star Nation: How a Ragged Army of Volunteers Won the Battle for Texas Independence and Changed America,* p. 813; September 1, 2006, Mary Whaley, review of *The Money Men: Capitalism, Democracy, and the Hundred Years' War over the American Dollar,* p. 29; October 15, 2008, Brad Hooper, review of *Traitor to His Class: The Privileged Life and Radical Presidency of Franklin Delano Roosevelt,* p. 16.

Boston Globe, February 15, 2009, David M. Shribman, review of *Traitor to His Class.*

California Bookwatch, November 1, 2006, review of *The Money Men.*

Choice: Current Reviews for Academic Libraries, May, 1998, review of *T.R.,* p. 1589; April, 1993, M.P. Onorato, review of *Bound to Empire,* p. 1365; May, 1998, R.M. Hyser, review of *T.R.,* p. 1589; June, 1999, review of *What America Owes the World: The Struggle for the Soul of Foreign Policy,* p. 1865; January, 2000, R.H. Immerman, review of *The Foreign Policies of Lyndon Johnson: Beyond Vietnam,* p. 1010.

Current, September, 1999, Christopher M. Gray, "The Struggle for the Soul of American Foreign Policy," p. 35.

Dallas Morning News, October 29, 2002, Bob Trimble, review of *The Age of Gold: The California Gold Rush and the New American Dream;* November 16, 2008, Philip Seib, review of *Traitor to His Class.*

Economist, April 18, 1998, review of *T.R.,* p. 6; May 15, 1999, review of *Masters of Enterprise,* p. 7; November 1, 2008, review of *Traitor to His Class,* p. 83.

Foreign Affairs, fall, 1988, Gladys Smith, review of *Cold Warriors,* p. 187; fall, 1991, Gaddis Smith, *Inside the Cold War: Loy Henderson and the Rise of the American Empire, 1918-1961,* p. 174; March-April, 1994, Stephen E. Ambrose, review of *The Devil We Knew: Americans and the Cold War,* p. 152; January-February, 1995, David Fromkin, review of *The Wages of Globalism: Lyndon Johnson and the Limits of American Power,* p. 161; September, 1998, review of *What America Owes the World,* p. 153.

Fort Worth Star-Telegram, Scott Nishimura, review of *The Age of Gold.*

Journal of American History, June, 1991, Arlene Lazarowitz, review of *India and the United States: The Cold Peace,* p. 383; June, 1991, Robert J. McMahon, review of *Inside the Cold War,* p. 314; September, 1992, Diane B. Kuntz, review of *The Specter of Neutralism: The United States and the Emergence of the Third World, 1947-1960,* p. 728; September, 1994, Michael S. Sherry, review of *The Devil We Knew,* p. 794; March, 2000, Robert D. Schulzinger, review of *What America Owes the World,* p. 1791.

Journal of Economic History, December, 1999, review of *What America Owes the World,* p. 1126.

Kirkus Reviews, July 1, 1993, review of *The Devil We Knew;* October 1, 1997, review of *T.R.,* p. 1498; May 1, 1999, review of *Masters of Enterprise,* p. 686; December 15, 2003, review of *Lone Star Nation,* p. 1432; July 15, 2005, review of *Andrew Jackson: A Life and Times,* p. 772; July 15, 2006, review of *The Money Men,* p. 708.

Knight-Ridder/Tribune News Service, October 4, 2000, Thomas J. Brady, author interview.

Library Journal, October 15, 1997, Boyd Childress, review of *T.R.,* p. 68; May 1, 1999, review of *Masters of Enterprise,* p. 90; September 15, 2000, Robert C. Jones, "The Life and Times of Benjamin Franklin," p. 85; June 15, 2001, Thomas J. Baldino, review of *The Selected Letters of Theodore Roosevelt,* p. 95; May 1, 2003, Thomas J. Baldino, review of *Woodrow Wilson,* p. 128; October 1, 2008, William D. Pederson, review of *Traitor to His Class,* p. 77.

Nation, April 27, 2009, Thomas J. Sugrue, review of *Traitor to His Class.*

National Review, December 15, 2008, Conrad Black, review of *Traitor to His Class,* p. 50.

New Leader, January 29, 1996, Melissa Knox, review of *The Reckless Decade: America in the 1890s,* p. 18.

New Republic, August 15, 1994, Jacob Heilbrun, review of *The Devil We Knew,* p. 31.

News & Observer (Raleigh, NC), November 9, 2008, Steve Weinberg, review of *Traitor to His Class.*

Newsweek, December 1, 2008, John Sparks, review of *Traitor to His Class.*

New Yorker, February 16, 1998, review of *T.R.,* p. 81.

New York Review of Books, February 12, 2009, Russell Baker, review of *Traitor to His Class.*

New York Times, October 10, 2000, Michiko Kakutani, review of *The First American: The Life and Times of Benjamin Franklin,* p. B8.

New York Times Book Review, Adam Garfinkle, September 13, 1998, review of *What America Owes the World,* p. 43.

Perspectives on Political Science, fall, 1999, Gordon Mace, review of *What America Owes the World,*

p. 225; spring, 2002, Jon Schaff, review of *The Strange Death of American Liberalism,* p. 102.

Political Science Quarterly, fall, 1999, review of *What America Owes the World,* p. 517.

Presidential Studies Quarterly, June, 2001, David A. Crockett, review of *Critical Reflections on the Cold War,* p. 370.

Providence Journal, November 30, 2008, Luther Spoehr, review of *Traitor to His Class.*

Publishers Weekly, March 1, 1991, Genevieve Stuttaford, review of *Inside the Cold War,* p. 65; July 12, 1993, review of *The Devil We Knew,* p. 63; October 13, 1997, review of *T.R.,* p. 61; April 12, 1999, review of *Masters of Enterprise,* p. 61; September 4, 2000, review of *The First American,* p. 98; September 3, 2001, review of *The Selected Letters of Theodore Roosevelt,* p. 76; December 15, 2003, review of *Lone Star Nation,* p. 61; July 11, 2005, review of *Andrew Jackson,* p. 69; August 21, 2006, review of *The Money Men,* p. 60; August 18, 2008, review of *Traitor to His Class,* p. 52.

Reference & Research Book News, August, 1998, review of *T.R.,* p. 46; February 1, 2007, review of *The Money Men.*

Teaching History, fall, 2004, Mark Davis, review of *The Reckless Decade,* p. 102.

Times Literary Supplement, May 22, 1998, review of *T.R.,* p. 27; September 24, 1999, review of *What America Owes the World,* p. 8.

Wall Street Journal Central edition, September 20, 2000, review of *The First American,* p. A24.

Washington Post Book World, January 18, 1998, review of *T.R.,* p. 1.

Washington Times, December 28, 2008, John M. Taylor and Priscilla S. Taylor, review of *Traitor to His Class.*

Wilson Quarterly, January 1, 2007, Robert E. Wright, review of *The Money Men,* p. 98.

ONLINE

Blogcritics, http://blogcritics.org/ (November 3, 2008), Gordon Hauptfleisch, review of *Traitor to His Class.*

Christian Science Monitor Online, http://features.csmonitor.com/ (November 13, 2008), Terry Hartle, review of *Traitor to His Class.*

EH.net: Economic History Services, http://eh.net/ (May 17, 2009), David J. Cowen, review of *The Money Men.*

H.W. Brands Home Page, http://www.hwbrands.com (May 17, 2009).

National Endowment for the Humanities Web site, http://www.neh.fed.us/ (November 17, 2005), "How the Century Began: A Conversation with H.W. Brands."

NJ.com, http://www.nj.com/ (November 15, 2008), Tom Mackin, review of *Traitor to His Class.*

Oregonian Online, http://blog.oregonlive.com/ (October 28, 2008), Jeff Baker, "Portland Native, Historian H.W. Brands at Wordstock."

San Diego Union-Tribune Online, http://www.signonsandiego.com/ (November 2, 2008), Charles A. Zappia, review of *Traitor to His Class.*

Texas Monthly Online, http://www.texasmonthly.com/ (January 1, 2009), "The New New Deal," review of *Traitor to His Class.*

Texas Observer Online, http://www.texasobserver.org/ (May 18, 2007), Matthew Stevenson, review of *The Money Men.*

University of Texas Web Site, http://www.utexas.edu/ (April 22, 2009), "H.W. Brands Named as Pulitzer Prize Finalist For His Book *Traitor to His Class*"; (May 17, 2009) author profile.*

*   *   *

BROWNING, Don S. 1934-
(Don Spencer Browning)

PERSONAL: Born January 13, 1934, in Trenton, MO; son of R.W. (a physician) and Nell Juanita Browning; married Carol Kohl; children: Elizabeth, Christopher. *Education:* Central Methodist College, A.B., 1956; University of Chicago, B.D., 1959, M.A., 1962, Ph.D., 1964.

ADDRESSES: Office—Divinity School, University of Chicago, 1025 E. 58th St., Chicago, IL 60637. *E-mail*—dbrowni@emory.edu; dsbrowni@midway.uchicago.edu.

CAREER: Writer, educator, theologian. Minister of Christian church in Kearney, MO, 1952-56; University Church of Disciples of Christ, Chicago, IL, minister of students, 1957-60; Illinois Children's Hospital School, Chicago, chaplain, 1960-61; William Healy School, Chicago, IL, counselor, 1962-63; Phillips University, Enid, OK, assistant professor of theology and pastoral care, 1963-65; University of Chicago, Divinity School, Chicago, IL, instructor, 1965-66, assistant professor, 1967-68, associate professor of religion and personality, 1968-78, professor of religion and psychological stud-

ies, 1978-80, Alexander Campbell Professor of Religion and Psychological Studies, 1980-2002, Alexander Campbell Professor of Religion and Psychological Studies Emeritus, 2002—. Robert W. Woodruff Visiting Professor of Interdisciplinary Religious Studies, Emory University Law School, Atlanta, GA, 2001-02.

MEMBER: American Association of Pastoral Counselors (fellow), American Academy of Religion, Society for the Scientific Study of Religion.

AWARDS, HONORS: National Book Award nomination in philosophy and religion, 1974, for *Generative Man;* Guggenheim Fellowship, 1974-75; Honorary Doctor of Divinity, Central College, 1984; fellow, Center of Theological Inquiry, 1990; Honorary Doctor of Divinity, University of Glasgow, 1998; Oskar Pfister Award Lecture, American Psychiatry Association. 1999.

WRITINGS:

Atonement and Psychotherapy, Westminster (Louisville, KY), 1966.

(Contributor) Peter Homans, editor, *Essays in Divinity,* University of Chicago Press (Chicago, IL), 1968.

William Oglesby, editor, *Essays in Honor of Seward Hiltner,* Abingdon (Nashville, TN), 1969.

Ralph James, editor, *Process Theology Reader,* Bobbs-Merrill (Indianapolis, IN), 1971.

Howard Clinebell, editor, *Mental Health and the Church,* Abingdon (Nashville, TN), 1971.

Generative Man: Psychoanalytic Perspectives, Westminster (Louisville, KY), 1973.

(Contributor) Peter Homans, editor, *Erik Erikson and His Impact on Religious Studies,* University of Chicago Press (Chicago, IL), 1975.

The Moral Context of Pastoral Care, Westminster (Louisville, KY), 1976.

Pluralism and Personality: William James and Some Contemporary Cultures of Psychology, Bucknell University Press (Lewisburg, PA), 1980.

Religious Ethics and Pastoral Care, Fortress Press (Philadelphia, PA), 1983.

Religious Thought and the Modern Psychologies: A Critical Conversation in the Theology of Culture, Fortress Press (Philadelphia, PA), 1987, second edition, with Terry D. Cooper, published as *Religious Thought and the Modern Psychologies,* Fortress Press (Minneapolis, MN), 2004.

A Fundamental Practical Theology: Descriptive and Strategic Proposals, Fortress Press (Minneapolis, MN), 1991.

(With others) *From Culture Wars to Common Ground: Religion and the American Family Debate,* Westminster John Knox Press (Louisville, KY), 1997.

(With Gloria Rodriguez) *Reweaving the Social Tapestry: Toward a Public Philosophy and Policy for Families,* Norton (New York, NY), 2002.

Marriage and Modernization: How Globalization Threatens Marriage and What to Do about It, William B. Eerdmans Pub. (Grand Rapids, MI), 2003.

Christian Ethics and the Moral Psychologies, William B. Eerdmans Pub. Co. (Grand Rapids, MI), 2006.

Equality and the Family: A Fundamental, Practical Theology of Children, Mothers, and Fathers in Modern Societies, William B. Eerdmans Pub. (Grand Rapids, MI), 2007.

EDITOR

(With Donald Capps) *Life Cycle Theory and Pastoral Care,* Fortress Press (Philadelphia, PA), 1983.

(Also author of introduction) *Practical Theology: The Emerging Field in Theology, Church, and World,* Harper & Row (San Francisco, CA), 1983.

Donald Capp, *Pastoral Care and Hermeneutics,* Fortress Press (Philadelphia, PA), 1984.

Thomas C. Oden, *Care of Souls in the Classic Tradition,* Fortress Press (Philadelphia, PA), 1984.

(With Herbert Anderson) *The Family and Pastoral Care,* Fortress Press (Philadelphia, PA), 1984.

Alastair Campbell, *Professionalism and Pastoral Care,* Fortress Press (Philadelphia, PA), 1985.

K. Brynolf Lyon, *Toward a Practical Theology of Aging,* Fortress Press (Philadelphia, PA), 1985.

Nelson S.T. Thayer, *Spirituality and Pastoral Care,* Fortress Press (Philadelphia, PA), 1985.

Robert L. Katz, *Pastoral Care and the Jewish Tradition: Empathic Process and Religious Counseling,* Fortress Press (Philadelphia, PA), 1985.

Elaine Ramshaw, *Ritual and Pastoral Care,* Fortress Press (Philadelphia, PA), 1987.

(With David Polk and Ian S. Evison) *The Education of the Practical Theologian: Responses to Joseph Hough and John Cobb's Christian Identity and Theological Education,* Scholars Press (Atlanta, GA), 1989.

(With Thomas Jobe and Ian S. Evison) *Religious and Ethical Factors in Psychiatric Practice,* Nelson-Hall in association with the Park Ridge Center for the Study of Health, Faith, and Ethics (Chicago, IL), 1990.

(With Ian S. Evison) *Does Psychiatry Need a Public Philosophy?,* Nelson-Hall Publishers in association with the Park Ridge Center for the Study of Health, Faith, and Ethics (Chicago, IL), 1991.

(With Francis Schussler Fiorenza) *Habermas, Modernity, and Public Theology,* Crossroad (New York, NY), 1992.

(With Max L. Stackhouse) *God and Globalization,* Volume 2, Trinity Press (Harrisburg, PA), 2000.

(With others) *Marriage: Just a Piece of Paper?,* Eerdmans (Grand Rapids, MI), 2002.

(With David Blankenhorn and Mary Stewart Van Leeuwen) *Does Christianity Teach Male Headship? The Equal-regard Marriage and Its Critics,* William B. Eerdmans Pub. Co. (Grand Rapids, MI), 2004.

Universalism Vs. Relativism: Making Moral Judgments in a Changing, Pluralistic, and Threatening World, Rowman and Littlefield (Lanham, MD), 2006.

(With M. Christian Green and John Witte, Jr.) *Sex, Marriage, and Family in World Religions,* Columbia University Press (New York, NY), 2006.

(With David A. Clairmont) *American Religions and the Family: How Faith Traditions Cope with Modernization and Democracy,* Columbia University Press (New York, NY), 2007.

(With Marcia J. Bunge) *Children and Childhood in World Religions: Primary Sources and Texts,* Rutgers University Press (New Brunswick, NJ), 2009.

(With Bonnie J. Miller-McLemore) *Children and Childhood in American Religions,* Rutgers University Press (New Brunswick, NJ), 2009.

Contributor of articles and reviews to theology journals, including *Criterion, Dialogue, Christian Century, Pastoral Psychology, Journal of Religion, Theology Today, Interpretation, Encounter,* and *Christian Medical Society Journal.* Editor, *Pastoral Psychology,* March, 1968, and November, 1969.

ADAPTATIONS: Marriage: Just a Piece of Paper? was adapted as a documentary by PBS in 2002.

SIDELIGHTS: In a *Christian Century* review of *Atonement and Psychotherapy,* Daniel Day Williams commented: "Don S. Browning has written an admirable book on the atonement to show how Christian doctrine can be analyzed and illuminated on the basis of the insights offered by psychotherapy. . . . Browning's critique of traditional theological doctrine is sharp and constructive. He shows not only that theology can learn from psychology but that theology brings an integrity and insight to life which can illuminate man's condition and his hope." Clark M. Williamson of *Encounter* called the book "one of the most significant theological works yet to have been produced by any writer in the area of pastoral care and counseling." He continued: "This is an important, creative and constructive work and will undoubtedly serve the helpful purpose of enabling many pastors and counselors to see their ministry in its relation to the atoning work of Jesus Christ as theologically interpreted; at the same time, it will help many theologians to comprehend the ministerial and therapeutic significance of their theological work. It should help us all to see the work of the ministry in more holistic and adequate terms."

In 1999, Browning's Religion, Culture and Family Project at the University of Chicago produced a book, titled *From Culture Wars to Common Ground: Religion and the American Family Debate.* "It is rare for a just-published book to be immediately considered a potential classic in Christian theology and thought," wrote Stephen Post of the *Journal of Religion,* but *Culture Wars* is one such book, he added. In this work the authors "defend the Christian normative model of 'the committed, intact, equal-regard, public-private family,'" according to Post. "Though media and church debates suggest that the most pressing sex-related issues today are homosexuality, sexual violence and abortion," noted Garrett Paul in a *Christian Century* review, the authors "argue that there is something more urgent: the crisis of the family. And mainline churches have been extraordinarily slow to respond to that crisis." *Culture Wars* identifies what it calls four "massive social and cultural trends" that have had an effect on the American family. They are: "heightened individualism," "the increased role of market forces and government bureaucracies in family life," the "powerful psychological shifts caused by these forces," and the "lingering influence" of patriarchy. Combined, according to Paul, "these forces greatly weaken the essential commitments that allow families to survive, let alone thrive."

In the view of *Theological Studies* contributor John Coleman, "the metaphor of 'common ground' in the title refers to the fact that the authors see great wisdom in contemporary pro-family voices. Pro-family conservatives refuse to privatize marriage; they see its public role. They also see what the authors call 'the make problematic.'" But, Coleman continued, the authors' sympathies do not extend to "single-parent families or to gays and lesbians. They fail to champion full equality, or what feminists would call 'family justice.' They

fail to see the public need for government support and policy, e.g., for child care." Nonetheless, Coleman recommended *Culture Wars* to pastors, clergy members, theologians and ethicists who the critic said "would profit from this eminently sensible and compelling book." Paul noted that each author was a theologian, though they represented diverse backgrounds. "This helps account for one of the book's most impressive achievements." He said. "That it goes beyond the gridlock and one-sidedness that characterize most debates about sexuality and families."

In 2002 Browning and Gloria Rodriguez produced *Reweaving the Social Tapestry: Toward a Public Philosophy and Policy for Families.* The book is based on the platform that out-of-wedlock births and rising divorce rates have transformed the American family. While some conservative pundits would cry moral degeneracy, while more liberal thinkers would testify to diversity and progress, the authors "[reject] the oversimplifications of both the Right and the Left," said *Booklist*'s Bryce Christiansen. Instead, Browning and Rodriguez "interpret widespread family disruption as the consequence of a complex network" of cultural and sociological developments. While the book takes a mostly conservative standpoint—advocating government-mandated ways to foster "traditional" heterosexual marriages to the exclusion of other categories—Christiansen concluded that the arguments are well-prepared and stated "with a rational civility intended to advance not stifle debate."

In his 2003 study, *Marriage and Modernization: How Globalization Threatens Marriage and What to Do About It,* Browning examines the deleterious effects socially, economically, morally, and religiously that globalization has had on the institution of marriage. He employs research from around the globe to demonstrate that globalization itself is influencing a gradual drift of males away from their familial responsibilities. Browning also details strategies, both practical and intellectual, to counteract this tendency. Among these are reduced working hours for two-parent families as well as a global call for strengthening marriage. Writing in the *Christian Century,* Victoria Barnett noted: "One of Browning's central arguments is that . . . modernization and its changes are pushing men to the periphery, detaching them from traditional, religiously grounded commitments." Barnett further explained: "One of Browning's most intriguing suggestions is that all world religions can help address these questions." *Interpretation* contributor Gloria H. Albrecht observed: "Browning's faith in the power of human ideas and beliefs to reconstruct a pro-marriage culture assumes that rightly enculturated people can resist and reshape the globalized appetite of capitalism." For Barnett, *Marriage and Modernization* was a "thoughtful, provocative book." *Theological Studies* reviewer Judith A. Merkle also had praise for the work, concluding that Browning "provides a valuable direction to the revitalization of marriage and a helpful method for addressing the issue's complexity." Writing for *Theology Today,* Julie Hanlon Rubio had a similar assessment: "Browning clearly shows that it is possible both to construct a serious theological ethic and to join effectively in more pragmatic discussions about how to improve people's lives. The worldwide marriage movement he seeks to promote will be enriched by his work."

Browning furthers this discussion with his 2007 work, *Equality and the Family: A Fundamental, Practical Theology of Children, Mothers, and Fathers in Modern Societies.* Here he gathers a score of his previously published essays that place the author's "deliberations about modern families within the context of his commitment to practical theology as the most fruitful theological method for considering urgent questions of our time," according to *Theological Studies* contributor Mary M. Doyle Roche. Browning also continues to address the problems arising in families as a result of absent males and fathers, pointing to a new family model which he terms the "equal-regard family" as a counterbalance. Reviewing the work in *Interpretation,* Joretta L. Marshall wrote: "This book is essential for practical theologians who desire a provocative conversation about method and family." Marshall further commented: "In particular, the book is exquisite in noting that it is not only the method one brings to the discourse that is important, but also the interpretation of resources (history, tradition, reason, experience, and Scripture) that determine the outcome of any normative vision of the family."

Editors Browning, David Blankenhorn, and Mary Stewart examine aspects of the equal-regard family in *Does Christianity Teach Male Headship? The Equal-regard Marriage and Its Critics* The collected essays look at various aspects of a renewed male presence in marriage. Browning, as opposed to some of his fellow editors, continues to contend that male participation in a marriage does not mean male dominance. Instead, it implies equal regard of wife and husband for one another. Thus, mates treat themselves as equals in marriage. "This relational framework means that the equal-

regard advocates in this book do not come across as ideologues committed to an abstract ideal, but as scholars concerned for healthy marriages," noted David Neff in a *Christianity Today* review of *Does Christianity Teach Male Headship?*

Browning turns to more general issues of ethical behavior in his *Christian Ethics and the Moral Psychologies.* Here he surveys the work of psychologists such as Erik Erikson and his stages of psychological development; Lawrence Kohlberg and his stages of moral development; Carol Gilligan and her moral development theory; and Johannes A. Van der Ven and his moral education theory, among others. Browning argues in this work that morality is more than a psychological formula. As Pamela Cooper-White noted in *Interpretation,* "Morality, for Browning, is grounded in the Christian ethic of love." Robin Lovin, writing in the *Christian Century,* termed *Christian Ethics and the Moral Psychologies* a "masterful survey of the interaction of psychology and ethics."

BIOGRAPHICAL AND CRITICAL SOURCES:

PERIODICALS

America, September 15, 1984, Paul Roy, review of *Religious Ethics and Pastoral Care,* p. 133.

Booklist, January 1, 2002, Bryce Christensen, review of *Reweaving the Social Tapestry: Toward a Public Philosophy and Policy for Families,* p. 782.

Christian Century, June 14, 1967, Daniel Day Williams, review of *Atonement and Psychotherapy;* December 19, 1973, review of *Generative Man: Psychoanalytic Perspectives,* p. 1255; May 18, 1977, review of *Generative Man,* p. 487; November 9, 1977, review of *The Moral Context of Pastoral Care,* p. 1036; May 6, 1981, Clyde Holbrook, review of *Pluralism and Personality: William James and Some Contemporary Cultures of Psychology,* p. 522; August 31, 1983, Lee Snook, review of *Practical Theology: The Emerging Field in Theology, Church, and World,* p. 782; May 23, 1984, John Rosenberg, review of *Religious Ethics and Pastoral Care,* p. 555; March 20, 1991, John Patton, review of *Religious and Ethical Factors in Psychiatric Practice,* p. 341; October 14, 1992, Thomas Ogletree, review of *A Fundamental Practical Theology: Descriptive and Strategic Proposals,* p. 904; May 9, 2001, Garrett Paul, review of *From*

Culture Wars to Common Ground: Religion and the American Family Debate, p. 18; December 12, 2001, Douglas Hicks, review of *God and Globalization,* p. 14; June 15, 2004, Victoria Barnett, review of *Marriage and Modernization: How Globalization Threatens Marriage and What to Do about It,* p. 39; May 1, 2007, Robin Lovin, review of *Christian Ethics and the Moral Psychologies,* p. 24.

Christianity Today, September 8, 1989, Gary Furr, review of *Religious Thought and the Modern Psychologies: A Critical Conversation in the Theology of Culture,* p. 33; August, 2004, David Neff, review of *Does Christianity Teach Male Headship? The Equal-regard Marriage and Its Critics.*

Commonweal, September 11, 1987, Eugene Fontinell, review of *Religious Thought and the Modern Psychologies,* p. 505; December 21, 2007, Robert K. Vischer, review of *Equality and the Family: A Fundamental, Practical Theology of Children, Mothers, and Fathers in Modern Societies,* p. 18.

Encounter, summer, 1967, Clark M. Williamson, review of *Atonement and Psychotherapy.*

Ethics, April, 1988, Gordon Marino, review of *Religious Thought and the Modern Psychologies,* p. 641; July, 1992, Rem Edwards, review of *Does Psychiatry Need a Public Philosophy?,* pp. 894-895.

First Things: A Monthly Journal of Religion and Public Life, March 1, 2004, review of *Marriage and Modernization,* p. 54.

Interpretation, July, 1993, C. Ellis Nelson, review of *A Fundamental Practical Theology,* p. 307.

Journal of Ecumenical Studies, spring, 1990, Roger Timm, review of *Religious Thought and the Modern Psychologies,* p. 393; April, 2004, Gloria H. Albrecht, review of *Marriage and Modernization,* p. 200; January, 2008, Pamela Cooper-White, review of *Christian Ethics and the Moral Psychologies,* p. 106; April, 2008, Joretta L. Marshall, review of *Equality and the Family,* p. 217.

Journal of Religion, October, 1992, review of *Does Psychiatry Need a Public Philosophy?* and *Religious and Ethical Factors in Psychiatric Practice,* pp. 639-640; July, 1992, Thomas Parker, review of *A Fundamental Practical Theology,* p. 430; July, 1994, Paul Lakeland, review of *Habermas, Modernity, and Public Theology,* p. 408; October, 1999, Stephen Post, review of *From Culture Wars to Common Ground,* p. 641.

Journal of the American Academy of Religion, winter, 1998, Christine Gundorf, review of *From Culture Wars to Common Ground,* p. 930.

Kirkus Reviews, July 15, 1976, review of *The Moral Context of Pastoral Care,* p. 838.

Library Journal, December, 1997, Leroy Hommerding, review of *From Culture Wars to Common Ground,* p. 111.

Modern Theology, January, 1994, Richard Lischer, review of *A Fundamental Practical Theology,* p. 119, John McCarthy, review of *Habermas, Modernity, and Public Theology,* p. 127.

Psychology Today, May, 1974, review of *Generative Man,* p. 17.

Social Service Review, June, 1993, Mary Brabeck, review of *Religious and Ethical Factors in Psychiatric Practice,* p. 302.

Sociological Analysis, summer, 1989, A. Javier Trevino, review of *Religious Thought and the Modern Psychologies,* p. 204.

Theological Studies, December, 1992, Michael McGinniss, review of *A Fundamental Practical Theology,* p. 772; March, 1999, John Coleman, review of *From Culture Wars to Common Ground,* p. 181; December, 2004, Judith A. Merkle, review of *Marriage and Modernization,* p. 883; June, 2008, Mary M. Doyle Roche, review of *Equality and the Family,* p. 462.

Theology Today, April, 1975, Sara Little, review of *Generative Man,* p. 106; April, 1977, James N. Lapsley, review of *The Moral Context of Pastoral Care,* p. 134; January, 1985, Robert L. Kinast, review of *Religious Ethics and Pastoral Care;* July, 2001, Arthur Holmes, review of *From Culture Wars to Common Ground,* p. 229; October, 2004, Julie Hanlon Rubio, review of *Marriage and Modernization.*

Zygon, June, 1994, Kenneth Vaux and Glenn Brichacek, review of *Religious and Ethical Factors in Psychiatric Practice,* p. 233; December, 1994, Kyle Pasewark, review of *A Fundamental Practical Theology,* p. 661.*

ONLINE

Center for the Study of Law and Religion, Emory University School of Law Web Site, http://www.law.emory.edu/ (May 18, 2009), "Don S. Browning."

Divinity School, University of Chicago Web site, http://divinity.uchicago.edu/ (May 18, 2009), "Don S. Browning."

H-Net: Humanities and Social Sciences Online, http://www.h-net.org/ (May 18, 2009), Michael LeFlem, review of *American Religions and the Family: How Faith Traditions Cope with Modernization and Democracy.*

New York Times, http://www.nytimes.com/ (June 21, 2003), Peter Steinfels, "Beliefs: Efforts to Redefine Marriage Stumble over Same-Sex Unions."*

* * *

BROWNING, Don Spencer
See BROWNING, Don S.

* * *

BUCKNER, M.M.

PERSONAL: Married. *Education:* Memphis State University, B.A.; attended Harvard University; Boston University, M.A. *Hobbies and other interests:* Environmental activism, kayaking, biking, scuba diving, hiking, and snow skiing.

ADDRESSES: Home—Nashville, TN. *E-mail*—hyperthought@mmbuckner.com.

CAREER: Novelist and editor. Former vice president of marketing for a financial firm.

AWARDS, HONORS: Southeastern Science Fiction Achievement Award for best novel and finalist for Philip K. Dick award, Philadelphia Science Fiction Society, 2004, for *Hyperthought;* Philip K. Dick award, Philadelphia Science Fiction Society, 2006, for *War Surf.*

WRITINGS:

"GREENHOUSE EARTH" SERIES

Hyperthought, Ace Books (New York, NY), 2003.
Neurolink, Ace Books (New York, NY), 2004.
War Surf, Ace Books (New York, NY), 2005.
Watermind, Tor (New York, NY), 2008.

Ensign Literary Review, member of editorial board.

SIDELIGHTS: M.M. Buckner appeared on the science fiction scene in 2003 with her debut novel, *Hyperthought.* The novel was the first in Buckner's "Greenhouse Earth" series, which takes place in a not-so-distant future in which Earth has been greatly affected by global warming. *Hyperthought* revolves around the activities of Jolie Sauvage, a tour guide to the wealthy owners of the dot-com businesses that now rule the earth, while *Neurolink,* the second novel in the series, tells the story of Dominic Jedes, the cloned son of one of the ruling elite, who has a neural profile of his father piggybacked into his own brain.

Buckner's novels garnered praise from several critics, including *Booklist* contributor Regina Schroeder, who described *Hyperthought* as "one successful adventure story" and a "neatly packaged allegory." On the Web site *SciFiDimensions,* John C. Snider praised the novels, describing *Hyperthought* as "a hip, fast-moving action adventure with a cyberpunk feel" and *Neurolink* as "cyberpunk with an old-fashioned social conscience." "A nicely constructed, mildly satirical dystopian future" were the terms *Chronicle* reviewer Don D'Ammassa used to describe *Neurolink.* A number of reviewers have pointed to the cyberpunk style of Buckner's novels, and although the author does not see herself in the dark world of cyberpunk, she has acknowledged similarities. "I generally call my work 'post-cyberpunk' because neither my vision nor my writing style is as dark as those of the cyberpunk masters," she wrote in an interview on *SciFiDimensions.* "Like them, I extrapolate a near future from present trends, so it's not surprising that our outlooks are similar."

Buckner continues her series with the 2005 title, *War Surf,* winner of the 2006 Philip K. Dick Award. Here she posits a world run by corporations. Executives bored with their money, power, and longevity turn to war surfing—an extreme "sport," involving deadly battles—for thrills. When two-hundred-year-old Nasir Deepra, leader of the Agonists, becomes captivated by Sheeba, his twenty-year-old masseuse, the resulting rift among the Agonists leads to a miserable loss in war surfing. To get back on top, the Agonists plan to do battle with the orbiting factory, Heaven, where workers, or plebes, once staged a revolution and of which Nasir continues to be a CEO. Since the revolt, the orbiting factory has been declared off limits. When Nasir and Sheeba arrive on Heaven they discover something that will change them and also alter the future for the plebes there. Reviewing the novel for the online *SF Site,* Georges T. Dodds found it "well worth the read." *Booklist* reviewer Schroeder had higher praise for this third novel, calling it a "thrilling, entertaining romp through a corporate-ruled world." Schroeder went on to note that the book also examines "immortality, boredom, and the changes necessary for continued vitality." In an interview with Byron Merritt for the *SFF World* Web site, Buckner acknowledged that *War Surf* provided a rather bleak view of corporate greed in the future, and went on to explain part of her inspiration for the novel: "Greed is intrinsic to human experience. Today's corporate criminals didn't invent it, they're simply carrying on a time-honored tradition. Greed is a good subject to write about because we all carry this dirty little secret of our own personal greed. That's why we love to read about outlaws."

The fourth installment in the "Greenhouse Earth" series, *Watermind,* deals more directly with environmental degradation. Here the idea of waste is expanded to include nanotechnology and the detritus of other forms of communications technology. Speaking with Lesley L. Smith of the *Electric Spec* Web site, Buckner explained the basic plot concept: "*Watermind* is set in present-day Louisiana. It's about a liquid artificial intelligence, spontaneously self-assembled from trash in the Mississippi River." Buckner continued: "Every day, the Mississippi carries up to 400,000 tons of rubbish from forty-one U.S. states and three Canadian provinces. All of North America's most advanced technology flows into the river—microchips, nano-devices, pharmaceuticals, genetically modified seed. Now in the Louisiana Delta, a radically new primordial soup gives birth to an elusive entity. Drifting in the water, it's more alien than anything that might come from outer space—because it springs from the waste-stream of our own civilization." In the novel, a Massachusetts Institute of Technology graduate school dropout, C.J. Reilly, discovers the existence of this ice-like stuff and also that it has the power to purify water. C.J. wants to become an eco-warrior and use the substance to save a polluted world. She discovers that it responds to music and is convinced that it can think. But when the substance kills a man, C.J.'s plans for salvation are threatened by those who want to destroy this emerging life form. A reviewer for *SciFi.com* termed *Watermind* an "ambitious SF thriller." Similarly, *Booklist* contributor Schroeder called the same work "a fast-paced, amusing thriller."

On *SciFiDimensions,* Buckner also reflects on her aspirations and writing career: "Writing has always been my dream. But it took a while to arrange my life to have enough time to write novels." By the 1990s, she was able to focus on her writing instead of her business career. She makes extensive working notes that include maps, histories, timelines, sketches of economic and social structures, and descriptions of religions and musical styles of her fictional world and its characters. She does not overwhelm her novels with such information, however, preferring instead to include only the telling details that lend verisimilitude to her future world and its action-packed plots. "I began sending material to Ace [publishers] in the late 1990s," she recalls, "and by an immense piece of good fortune, one of the editors noticed and liked my work. Even though he rejected the first two novels I sent, he encouraged me to keep trying."

Buckner told *CA:* "I grew up in the country, reading and daydreaming. I began my first novel in the third grade. From then on, I've filled notebooks with poems, essays, stories, and travel journals. For me, writing is like breathing, only more fun.

"Reading is my primary influence. I am a compulsive reader of fiction, especially literary fiction and literary science fiction. Also, I enjoy nonfiction about science, economics, political news, and world cultures.

"Before I wrote my first novel, the idea of completing such a long work seemed impossible. Now every time I start a new one, it still seems impossible, and yet it happens. I finish. Wow, I'm always amazed."

Buckner further expanded on her writing process: "Wandering, getting lost, exploring unknown territory, feeling my way by intuition. My physical process is pretty chaotic. I often draw story maps and do outlines, but I just as often abandon them half-way through the journey.

"First, I hope my books entertain readers. That's mandatory. Second, I hope readers find things in my stories that mean something personal to them on a deeper level and that make their lives a little bit richer."

BIOGRAPHICAL AND CRITICAL SOURCES:

PERIODICALS

Booklist, January 1, 2003, Regina Schroeder, review of *Hyperthought,* p. 860; September 1, 2005, Schroeder, review of *War Surf,* p. 74; October 1, 2008, Schroeder, review of *Watermind,* p. 33.

Chronicle, November, 2004, Don D'Ammassa, review of *Neurolink,* p. 46.

Entertainment Weekly, September 10, 2004, Noah Robischon, review of *Neurolink,* p. 167.

Kirkus Reviews, October 1, 2008, review of *Watermind.*

Library Journal, August 1, 2008, Jackie Cassada, review of *Watermind,* p. 74.

Publishers Weekly, September 15, 2008, review of *Watermind,* p. 50.

ONLINE

Apex Book Company, http://www.apexbookcompany. com/ (May 19, 2008), Jason Sizemore, "Interview: M.M. Buckner."

Electric Spec, http://www.electricspec.com/ (October 31, 2008), Lesley L. Smith, "Interview with Award-Winning Author M.M. Buckner."

M.M. Buckner Home Page, http://www.mmbuckner.com (May 19, 2009).

SciFi.com, http://www.scifi.com/ (October 29, 2008), Cynthia Ward, review of *Watermind.*

SciFiDimensions, http://www.scifidimensions.com/ (March, 2004), John C. Snider, review of *Hyperthought;* (September, 2004) review of *Neurolink* and interview with Buckner.

SFF World, http://www.sffworld.com/ (October 14, 2006), Byron Merritt, "Interview with M.M. Buckner."

SF Site, http://www.sfsite.com/ (May 19, 2009), Georges T. Dodds, review of *War Surf.*

Strange Horizons, http://www.strangehorizons.com/ (January 19, 2009), Timmel Duchamp, review of *Watermind.*

*   *   *

BURNES, Caroline
See HAINES, Carolyn

C

CARTER, Nick
  See RANDISI, Robert J.

*   *   *

CHASE, Robert David
  See GORMAN, Ed

*   *   *

CHIAVERINI, Jennifer

PERSONAL: Married; children: two sons. *Education:* Graduated from the University of Notre Dame and the University of Chicago. *Hobbies and other interests:* Quilting.

ADDRESSES: Home—Madison, WI. *Office*—P.O. Box 620824, Middleton, WI 53562.

CAREER: Writer and designer. Designer of the Elm Creek Quilts fabric lines from Red Rooster Fabrics. Former writing instructor at the Pennsylvania State University, State College, PA, and Edgewood College, Madison, WI.

WRITINGS:

"ELM CREEK QUILTS" SERIES

The Quilter's Apprentice, Simon & Schuster (New York, NY), 1999.

Round Robin, Simon & Schuster (New York, NY), 2000.

The Cross Country Quilters, Simon & Schuster (New York, NY), 2001.

The Runaway Quilt (also see below), Simon & Schuster (New York, NY), 2002.

The Quilter's Legacy (also see below), Simon & Schuster (New York, NY), 2003.

The Master Quilter (also see below), Simon & Schuster (New York, NY), 2004.

The Sugar Camp Quilt, Simon & Schuster (New York, NY), 2005.

The Christmas Quilt, Simon & Schuster (New York, NY), 2005.

Circle of Quilters, Simon & Schuster (New York, NY), 2006.

An Elm Creek Quilts Album: Three Novels in the Popular Series (contains *The Runaway Quilt, The Quilter's Legacy,* and *The Master Quilter*), Simon & Schuster (New York, NY), 2006.

The Quilter's Homecoming, Simon & Schuster (New York, NY), 2007.

The New Year's Quilt, Simon & Schuster (New York, NY), 2007.

The Winding Ways Quilt, Simon & Schuster (New York, NY), 2008.

The Quilter's Kitchen, Simon & Schuster (New York, NY), 2008.

The Lost Quilter, Simon & Schuster (New York, NY), 2008.

A Quilter's Holiday, Simon & Schuster (New York, NY), 2009.

OTHER

(With Nancy Odom) *Elm Creek Quilts: Projects Inspired by the Elm Creek Quilts Novels,* C & T Publishing (Lafayette, CA), 2002.

Return to Elm Creek: More Quilt Projects Inspired by the Elm Creek Quilts Novels, C & T Publishing (Lafayette, CA), 2004.

More Elm Creek Quilts: 30+ Traditional Blocks, Eleven Projects, Favorite Character Sketches, C & T Publishing (Lafayette, CA), 2008.

Sylvia's Bridal Sampler from Elm Creek Quilts, C & T (Lafayette, CA), 2009.

Author of foreword, *The Quilt: A History and Celebration of an American Art Form,* by Elise Schebler Roberts, Voyageur Press (St. Paul, MN), 2007.

ADAPTATIONS: Several books have been adapted for audio, including *The Quilter's Apprentice, The Quilter's Legacy, The Master Quilter, The Sugar Camp Quilt, Circle of Quilters, The Quilter's Homecoming,* and *The New Year's Quilt,* Recorded Books.

SIDELIGHTS: Jennifer Chiaverini taught herself how to quilt in 1994. Her experiences with quilting led her to write her first novel, which revolves around the world of quilting and spurred a whole series of novels about a quilting community in Pennsylvania.

Chiaverini's first novel, *The Quilter's Apprentice,* is the story of two women, Sarah and Sylvia, one young and one old, coming together through quilting. Sarah agrees to work for Sylvia on the condition that Sylvia will teach her to quilt. Through their instruction much of Sylvia's secret past is revealed and together they use Sylvia's inheritance to form the Elm Creek Quilting Camp. *Booklist* critic Vanessa Bush wrote: "There's plenty of folklore about quilting and how these artistic endeavors bring women together in circles of quilting and friendship." A contributor to *Kirkus Reviews* observed: "Nicely stitched together (and fun for quilters)." Ellen R. Cohen, writing in the *Library Journal,* remarked: "Chiaverini . . . has pieced together a beautiful story in this first novel."

The second novel in what has come to be called the "Elm Creek Quilts" series is titled *Round Robin.* The story picks up where the last left off, still focusing on Sarah and Sylvia, only now expanding to include other quilters who visit the camp. The women come together to make a round robin quilt, and through the process learn more about themselves, each other, and friendship. A reviewer writing in *Publishers Weekly* called it a "sugary story" that "is neatly concluded on a tender if sentimental note." A *Kirkus Reviews* contributor wrote: "It's all very predictable, and every problem is resolved with a maximum of sentiment. But Chiaverini spins a bunch of compelling yarns and expertly weaves them together." Cohen commented in the *Library Journal:* "Women readers in particular will be touched and charmed."

For the third installment of the series, Chiaverini brings together a new group of women in *The Cross Country Quilters.* A group of diverse women, each with their own problems, meet at the Elm Creek quilt camp and agree to make a Challenge Quilt together. Each participant must overcome one of their own personal challenges before they can begin their section of the quilt. They agree to meet back at the camp a year later. A *Publishers Weekly* contributor noted: "Endearing characters and pleasant vignettes render this series as charming and cozy as a favorite blanket."

The Runaway Quilt is the fourth book and focuses on Sylvia and her family history. It documents the story of Elm Creek Manor, Sylvia's family home and site of the Elm Creek quilting camp. When a mysterious quilt is discovered, Sylvia is left with many questions about what she thought she knew of her family. A reviewer writing in *Publishers Weekly* observed: "Chiaverini manages to impart a healthy dollop of history in a folksy style, while raising moral questions in a suspenseful narrative."

Published the same year as *The Runaway Quilt* was *Elm Creek Quilts: Projects Inspired by the Elm Creek Quilts Novels.* Chiaverini wrote this text with the help of quilt designer and teacher Nancy Odom. It is a pattern book for quilting projects based on and inspired by the characters and events of Chiaverini's novels. A contributor to the *Library Journal* commented: "Reading the novels is not a prerequisite for making the quilts pictured, but they will take on deeper meaning for those familiar with the books."

The fifth book in the series appeared as *The Quilter's Legacy.* The book focuses again on Sylvia, this time chronicling her search for five quilts her mother made before she died. A reviewer writing in *Publishers Weekly* called it the best of the "Elm Creek Quilts" novels, and noted: "Chiaverini's storytelling skills have noticeably improved. She approaches but never succumbs to sentimentality and keeps her account of hunts for antique quilts from becoming too predictable." Vanessa Bush, writing in *Booklist,* noted: "Series fans will enjoy this latest installment."

In *The Master Quilter,* each of Sylvia's friends who help her run Elm Creek Manor are given a chapter to tell a story, with each story covering the same events. The quilting project this time is a wedding gift for Sylvia and her new husband, Andrew. As the quilt is made, each friend must deal with a crisis in their own lives, including one quilter who must tell her mother she is moving in with her boyfriend, another who is ignored for appointment as the head of her academic department, and another whose husband is leaving her and trying to take all of their money in the process. "Long-buried secrets, animosities, and yearnings rise to the surface," noted Vanessa Bush in *Booklist.* A reviewer writing in *Publishers Weekly* commented that the author "intensifies the story's texture by retelling key scenes from multiple points of view." A *Kirkus Reviews* contributor wrote: "Fans will love the further development of the Elm Creek characters."

The seventh book in the series, *The Sugar Camp Quilt,* is a historical novel that takes place before the Civil War in Creeks Crossing, Pennsylvania. The story revolves around the Granger family, caught up in the issue of runaway slaves and the Underground Railroad. When teenaged Dorothea Granger is asked by her uncle to make a special quilt with a specific pattern, she has no idea that the quilt, like others, will be used as a marker for the Underground Railroad. When the uncle dies, Dorothea and her parents Robert and Lorena Granger decide to take up his cause by helping runaway slaves. When confronted by slave catchers, Dorothea turns to the unlikable Thomas Nelson for help. Her dislike for Thomas, however, soon fades and turns into love. An *MBR Bookwatch* contributor noted: "Dorothea is a brave and realistic heroine who along with her family needs to star in future historicals." Beth E. Andersen, writing in *Library Journal,* commented that the book "captures the courage of the Underground Railroad supporters and the runaways who risked everything to find freedom."

In *The Christmas Quilt,* the author takes the reader back to a time between *The Quilter's Apprentice* and *The Master Quilter.* The story revolves around family problems and regrets, with the then widowed Sylvia advising Sarah to make amends with her mother. When Sylvia finds an old, unfinished Christmas quilt in the attic, she thinks back to her own family Christmases as a girl and to a tragic Christmas she spent at Elk Creek Manor, where she has returned to celebrate her first Christmas in fifty years. A *Publishers Weekly* contributor commented that "there's no saccharine in this sweet story." Rebecca Vnuk, writing in the *Library Journal,* noted that "readers . . . will enjoy this charming story of love and family."

Circle of Quilters finds Sylvia and her friends at Elm Creek Quilt Camp looking for a new instructor. The various candidates must tell what quilting has meant to them, from women such as Anna, a superb quilter with a relationship that is falling apart, to Russell, who completed a cancer quilt his wife began before she died. "Diehard fans may want more than mere cameos from their favorite characters, but overall, a pleasant addition to the series," wrote a *Kirkus Reviews* contributor. In a review for *Bookreporter.com,* Judy Gigstad noted that "a glimpse into the popular activity of quilting offers an education to the art."

The protagonist of *The Quilter's Homecoming* is Elizabeth, cousin of Sylvia. Set in 1925, Elizabeth marries Henry Nelson at Elm Creek Manor and moves with him to Southern California to live on his newly purchased cattle ranch. They discover, however, that the deed is invalid and worthless and that he has been swindled. The actual owners of the ranch, the Jorgensen's, offer them jobs on the ranch—Henry as a hand, and Elizabeth as a housemaid—and being too proud to ask for the return fare from the folks back home, they accept. Their hardships cause Henry to lose his spirit, resulting in Elizabeth's reexamination of her marriage to him. They meet the original owners of the land, the Rodriquez family, who lost it in the 1880s. The wife, Rosa, is trying to escape a bad marriage and is in a relationship with Lars Jorgensen. A *Kirkus Reviews* critic called the plot involving the struggles of Elizabeth and Henry "lackluster" but added that the "strangely discordant plot lines merge in the guns-blazing finale that serves to rescue all involved." *Booklist* contributor Michele Leber concluded: "A reliably pleasant addition to the series, this should please its fans."

The New Year's Quilt is set immediately following *The Christmas Quilt,* in which Sylvia married Andrew on Christmas Eve. They are driving to Hartford, Connecticut, to break the news to his daughter Amy, who considers them too old to marry. As they drive, Sylvia works on a New Year's resolution quilt for Amy and recalls family estrangements and the highs and lows of her own life, as well as how her community of quilters has always been there to give her strength. They make a side trip to New York, where Sylvia visits her mother's childhood home. This book offers a more thorough understanding of Sylvia's history. Bush wrote in *Booklist*: "Fans of the "Elm Creek Quilts" series will love this latest installment." A *Publishers Weekly* reviewer concluded: "Chiaverini's stitching is sound."

The Winding Ways Quilt provides considerable backstory as it reveals that Judy and her husband Steve are about to move to Philadelphia for new jobs and a new life. Sarah discovers that she is going to have twins, and Bonnie is faced with the decision of whether she should or should not invest in correcting damage done to the quilt shop by vandals. New characters include Anna Del Maso and Gretchen Hartley, who join the quilting camp staff. That part of the story concerned with Gwen searching for the person responsible for a quilt found in a church lost and found was deemed "the most powerful and poignant in Chiaverini's latest patchwork confection" by a *Publishers Weekly* reviewer.

BIOGRAPHICAL AND CRITICAL SOURCES:

PERIODICALS

Booklist, March 1, 1999, Vanessa Bush, review of *The Quilter's Apprentice*, p. 1151; April 15, 2003, Vanessa Bush, review of *The Quilter's Legacy*, p. 1447; February 1, 2004, Vanessa Bush, review of *The Master Quilter*, p. 948; March 15, 2005, Vanessa Bush, review of *The Sugar Camp Quilt*, p. 1263; April 1, 2006, Vanessa Bush, review of *Circle of Quilters*, p. 18; March 1, 2007, Michele Leber, review of *The Quilter's Homecoming*, p. 59; November 15, 2007, Vanessa Bush, review of *The New Year's Quilt*, p. 19.

Kirkus Reviews, February 1, 1999, review of *The Quilter's Apprentice*, p. 162; March 15, 2000, review of *Round Robin*, p. 332; February 1, 2004, review of *The Master Quilter*, p. 97; August 15, 2005, review of *The Christmas Quilt*, p. 868; February 15, 2006, review of *Circle of Quilters*, p. 144; January 15, 2007, review of *The Quilter's Homecoming*, p. 39; September 1, 2007, review of *The New Year's Quilt*.

Library Journal, February 15, 1999, Ellen R. Cohen, review of *The Quilter's Apprentice*, p. 182; February 15, 2000, Ellen R. Cohen, review of *Round Robin*, p. 194; April 15, 2003, review of *Elm Creek Quilts: Projects Inspired by the Elm Creek Quilts Novels*, p. 84; December 1, 2004, Barbara Hoffert, review of *The Sugar Camp Quilt*, p. 86; March 1,

2005, Beth E. Andersen, review of *The Sugar Camp Quilt*, p. 76; March 15, 2005, Barbara Hoffert, "Q&A: Jennifer Chiaverini," p. 76; October 15, 2005, Rebecca Vnuk, review of *The Christmas Quilt*, p. 46.

MBR Bookwatch, April, 2005, review of *The Sugar Camp Quilt*.

Publishers Weekly, January 18, 1999, review of *The Quilter's Apprentice*, p. 324; February 14, 2000, review of *Round Robin*, p. 173; March 5, 2001, review of *The Cross Country Quilters*, p. 63; February 25, 2002, review of *The Runaway Quilt*, p. 39; April 7, 2003, review of *The Quilter's Legacy*, p. 47; February 16, 2004, review of *The Master Quilter*, p. 149; August 29, 2005, review of *The Christmas Quilt*, p. 33; January 22, 2007, review of *The Quilter's Homecoming*, p. 156; August 13, 2007, review of *The New Year's Quilt*, p. 44; December 10, 2007, review of *The Winding Ways Quilt*, p. 31.

ONLINE

AEI Speakers Bureau Web site, http://www.aeispeakers. com/ (February 1, 2007), brief profile of author.

BestReviews.com, http://thebestreviews.com/ (October 15, 2005), Harriet Klausner, reviews of *The Master Quilter*, *The Sugar Camp Quilt*, and *The Christmas Quilt*.

Bookreporter.com, http://www.bookreporter.com/ (February 1, 2007), Melissa A. Palmer, reviews of *The Master Quilter* and *The Master Quilter*; Judy Gigstad, reviews of *Circle of Quilters* and *The Sugar Camp Quilt*; Carole Turner, review of *The Christmas Quilt*.

Jennifer Chiaverini Home Page, http://www.elmcreek. net/ (July 14, 2008).*

*   *   *

CHOYCE, Lesley 1951-
(Lesley Willis Choyce)

PERSONAL: Born March 21, 1951, in Riverside, NJ; immigrated to Canada; son of George (a mechanic) and Norma (a homemaker) Choyce; children: Sunyata, Pamela. *Education:* Rutgers University, B.A., 1972; Montclair State College, M.A. (American literature), 1974; City University of New York, M.A. (English literature), 1983. *Hobbies and other interests:* Surfing, "transcendental wood-splitting."

ADDRESSES: Home—East Lawrencetown, Nova Scotia, Canada. *Office*—Pottersfield Press, 83 Leslie Rd., East Lawrencetown, Nova Scotia B2Z 1PG, Canada. *E-mail*—lesley@lesleychoyce.com.

CAREER: Writer, publisher, educator, musician, filmmaker, and television host. Referrals Workshop, Denville, NJ, rehabilitation counselor, 1973-74; Bloomfield College, Bloomfield, NJ, coordinator of writing tutorial program, 1974; Montclair State College, Upper Montclair, NJ, instructor in English, 1974-78; Alternate Energy Consultants, Halifax, Nova Scotia, Canada, writer and consultant to Energy, Mines and Resources Canada, 1979-80; Dalhousie University, Halifax, 1981—, began as instructor, became professor of English. Pottersfield Press, founder; Canadian Writers' Foundation, board member. City of Halifax, creative writing teacher in continuing education program, 1978-83; instructor at St. Mary's University, 1978-82, Nova Scotia College of Art and Design, 1981, and Mount St. Vincent University, 1982; participant in creative writing workshops; public reader and lecturer. Freelance broadcaster, beginning 1972; host of the nationally syndicated television talk show *Choyce Words,* beginning 1985; Surf Poets, musician-poet. Creator of the animal film *Skunk Whisperer,* 2002; creator of numerous music videos. Formerly worked as a freight hauler, corn farmer, janitor, journalist, newspaper delivery person, and well digger.

MEMBER: International PEN, Atlantic Publishers Association, Association of Canadian Publishers, Literary Press Group, Canadian Poetry Association, Writers' Union of Canada, Writers Federation of Nova Scotia.

AWARDS, HONORS: Award of Merit, Order of St. John, 1986; Dartmouth Book Award, 1990, and 1995, for *The Republic of Nothing;* creative nonfiction prize, *Event* magazine, 1990; Ann Connor Brimer Award for Children's Literature, 1994, and 2003, for *Shoulder the Sky;* co-recipient of Authors Award, Foundation for the Advancement of Canadian Letters, 1995; first place award, Canadian Surfing Championships, 1995; Landmark East Literacy Award, 2000; poet laureate, Peter Gzowski Invitational Golf Tournament, 2000.

WRITINGS:

FOR CHILDREN AND YOUNG ADULTS

Skateboard Shakedown, Formac Publishing (Halifax, Nova Scotia, Canada), 1989.

Hungry Lizards, Collier-Macmillan (Toronto, Ontario, Canada), 1990.

Wave Watch, Formac Publishing (Halifax, Nova Scotia, Canada), 1990.

Some Kind of Hero, Maxwell-Macmillan (Toronto, Ontario, Canada), 1991.

Wrong Time, Wrong Place, Formac Publishing (Halifax, Nova Scotia, Canada), 1991.

Clearcut Danger, Formac Publishing (Halifax, Nova Scotia, Canada), 1992.

Full Tilt, Maxwell-Macmillan (Toronto, Ontario, Canada), 1993.

Good Idea Gone Bad, Formac Publishing (Halifax, Nova Scotia, Canada), 1993.

Dark End of Dream Street, Formac Publishing (Halifax, Nova Scotia, Canada), 1994.

Big Burn, Thistledown (Saskatoon, Saskatchewan, Canada), 1995.

Falling through the Cracks, Formac Publishing (Halifax, Nova Scotia, Canada), 1996.

Go for It, Carrie (chapter book), Formac Publishing (Halifax, Nova Scotia, Canada), 1997.

Famous at Last, illustrated by Jill Quinn, Pottersfield Press (East Lawrencetown, Nova Scotia, Canada), 1998.

Carrie's Crowd (chapter book), illustrated by Mark Thurman, Formac Publishing (Halifax, Nova Scotia, Canada), 1998.

Roid Rage, Harbour Publishing (Madeira Park, British Columbia, Canada), 1999.

The Summer of Apartment X, Goose Lane Editions (Fredericton, New Brunswick, Canada), 1999.

Far Enough Island, illustrated by Jill Quinn, Pottersfield Press (Lawrencetown Beach, Nova Scotia, Canada), 2000.

Carrie's Camping Adventure (chapter book), illustrated by Mark Thurman, Formac Publishing (Halifax, Nova Scotia, Canada), 2001.

Shoulder the Sky, Dundurn Press (Toronto, Ontario, Canada), 2002.

Refuge Cove, Orca Book (Victoria, British Columbia, Canada), 2002.

Smoke and Mirrors, Boardwalk Books (Toronto, Ontario, Canada), 2004.

Thunderbowl, Orca Soundings (Victoria, British Columbia, Canada), 2004.

Sudden Impact, Orca Soundings (Victoria, British Columbia, Canada), 2005.

Deconstructing Dylan, Dundurn Group (Toronto, Ontario, Canada), 2006.

Skunks for Breakfast: Based on a True Story, illustrated by Brenda Jones, Nimbus Publishing (Halifax, Nova Scotia, Canada), 2006.

The End of the World as We Know It, Red Deer Press (Markham, Ontario, Canada), 2007.

Couleurs troubles, Red Deer Press (Markham, Ontario, Canada), 2007.

Wave Warrior, Orca Book (Victoria, British Columbia, Canada), 2007.

The Book of Michael, Red Deer Press (Markham, Ontario, Canada), 2008.

Skate Freak, Orca Book (Victoria, British Columbia, Canada), 2008.

FICTION; FOR ADULTS

Eastern Sure, Nimbus Publishing (Halifax, Nova Scotia, Canada), 1981.

Billy Botzweiler's Last Dance (short stories), Blewointment Press (Vancouver, British Columbia, Canada), 1984.

Downwind, Creative Publishers (St. John's, Newfoundland, Canada), 1984.

Conventional Emotions (short stories), Creative Publishers (St. John's, Newfoundland, Canada), 1985.

The Dream Auditor (science fiction), Ragweed Press (Charlottetown, Prince Edward Island, Canada), 1986.

Coming Up for Air, Creative Publishers (St. John's, Newfoundland, Canada), 1988.

The Second Season of Jonas MacPherson, Thistledown Press (Saskatoon, Saskatchewan, Canada), 1989.

Magnificent Obsessions (photo-novel), Quarry Press (Kingston, Ontario, Canada), 1991.

The Ecstasy Conspiracy, Nuage Editions (Montreal, Quebec, Canada), 1992.

Margin of Error (short stories), Borealis Press (Ottawa, Ontario, Canada), 1992.

The Republic of Nothing, Goose Lane Editions (Fredericton, New Brunswick, Canada), 1994.

The Trap Door to Heaven (science fiction), Quarry Press (Kingston, Ontario, Canada), 1996.

Dance the Rocks Ashore, Goose Lane Editions (Fredericton, New Brunswick, Canada), 1997.

World Enough, Goose Lane Editions (Fredericton, New Brunswick, Canada), 1998.

Cold Clear Morning, Porcepic Books (Vancouver, British Columbia, Canada), 2002.

Sea of Tranquility, Simon & Pierre (Tonawanda, NY), 2003.

NONFICTION

Edible Wild Plants of the Maritimes, Wooden Anchor Press (Halifax, Nova Scotia, Canada), 1977.

An Avalanche of Ocean (autobiography), Goose Lane Editions (Fredericton, New Brunswick, Canada), 1987.

December Six/The Halifax Solution, Pottersfield Press (East Lawrencetown, Nova Scotia, Canada), 1988.

Transcendental Anarchy: Confessions of a Metaphysical Tourist (autobiography), Quarry Press (Kingston, Ontario, Canada), 1993.

Nova Scotia: Shaped by the Sea, Penguin (Toronto, Ontario, Canada), 1996, revised edition, Pottersfield Press (East Lawrencetown, Nova Scotia, Canada), 2007.

The Coasts of Canada: A History, Goose Lane Editions (Fredericton, New Brunswick, Canada), 2002.

Driving Minnie's Piano: Memoirs of a Surfing Life in Nova Scotia, Pottersfield Press (East Lawrencetown, Nova Scotia, Canada), 2006.

The Discipline of Ice, Ekstasis Editions (Victoria, British Columbia, Canada), 2008.

Peggy's Cove: The Amazing History of a Coastal Village, Pottersfield Press (East Lawrencetown, Nova Scotia, Canada), 2008.

POETRY

Reinventing the Wheel, Fiddle Head Poetry Books (Fredericton, New Brunswick, Canada), 1980.

Fast Living, Fiddle Head Poetry Books (Fredericton, New Brunswick, Canada), 1982.

The End of Ice, Fiddle Head Poetry Books (Fredericton, New Brunswick, Canada), 1982.

The Top of the Heart, Thistledown Press (Saskatoon, Saskatchewan, Canada), 1986.

The Man Who Borrowed the Bay of Fundy, Brandon University (Brandon, Manitoba, Canada), 1988.

The Coastline of Forgetting, Pottersfield Press (East Lawrencetown, Nova Scotia, Canada), 1995.

Beautiful Sadness, Ekstasis Editions (Victoria, British Columbia, Canada), 1998.

Caution to the Wind, Ekstasis Editions (Victoria, British Columbia, Canada), 2000.

Typographical Eras, Gaspereau Press (Kentville, Nova Scotia, Canada), 2003.

Revenge of the Optimist, Ekstasis Editions (Victoria, British Columbia, Canada), 2004.

EDITOR

The Pottersfield Portfolio, seven volumes, Pottersfield Press (East Lawrencetown, Nova Scotia, Canada), 1971–85.

Alternating Current: Renewable Energy for Atlantic Canada, Wooden Anchor Press (Halifax, Nova Scotia, Canada), 1977.

Chezzetocook (fiction and poetry), Wooden Anchor Press (Halifax, Nova Scotia, Canada), 1977.

(With Phil Thompson) *ACCESS,* Pottersfield Press (East Lawrencetown, Nova Scotia, Canada), 1979.

(With John Bell) *Visions from the Edge,* Pottersfield Press (East Lawrencetown, Nova Scotia, Canada), 1981.

The Cape Breton Collection, two volumes, Pottersfield Press (East Lawrencetown, Nova Scotia, Canada), 1984–89.

(With Andy Wainwright) Charles Bruce, *The Mulgrave Road,* Pottersfield Press (East Lawrencetown, Nova Scotia, Canada), 1985.

Ark of Ice: Canadian Futurefiction, Pottersfield Press (East Lawrencetown, Nova Scotia, Canada), 1985.

(With Rita Joe) *The Mi'kmaq Anthology,* Pottersfield Press (East Lawrencetown, Nova Scotia, Canada), 1997.

(And contributor) *Atlantica: Stories from the Maritimes and Newfoundland,* Goose Lane Editions (Fredericton, New Brunswick, Canada), 2001.

Pottersfield Nation: East of Canada, Pottersfield Press (East Lawrencetown, Nova Scotia, Canada), 2004.

Nova Scotia: A Traveller's Companion: Over 300 Years of Travel Writing, Pottersfield Press (East Lawrencetown, Nova Scotia, Canada), 2005.

Contributor to more than one hundred magazines and anthologies.

Contributor of lyrics and music to poetry-music recordings, including *Sea Level,* Pottersfield Press, 1999, and *Long Lost Planet,* 1999.

Author of the blog *Lesley Choyce.*

ADAPTATIONS: *Republic of Nothing* was optioned for film.

SIDELIGHTS: American-born Canadian author Lesley Choyce has written numerous works of fiction for both adults and young adults, as well as nonfiction, science fiction, and poetry. He works some of his many interests—including nature and the environment, surfing, skateboarding, and music—into his novels for young adults, which include *Hungry Lizards, Wrong Time, Wrong Place, Roid Rage,* and *Smoke and Mir-* *rors.* Choyce's teen novels feature high-interest story lines and accessible vocabulary, making them popular among reluctant readers. "Choyce's talent for portraying quirky, if troubled, idealists" as lead characters has also made him popular with teens, according to *Resource Links* contributor Nadine d'Entremont in a review of *Smoke and Mirrors.*

In Choyce's first book, *Skateboard Shakedown,* a skateboarder, his girlfriend, and a group of friends take on a corrupt mayor who wants to turn their favorite skateboard site into a shopping mall. Skateboarding is also the focus of *Smoke and Mirrors,* which focuses on a sixteen-year-old boy whose skateboarding injury caused the brain damage that he suspects is causing him to see and speak with a strange classmate who seems too good—and too mysterious—to be real. Reviewing *Skateboard Shakedown* for *Quill & Quire,* Norene Smiley noted that Choyce's "fast-paced novel marks the entrance of a new and refreshing voice for young readers." Further skating adventures are presented in *Skate Freak,* a novel about teenager Quinn Dorfman, who has just moved after his mother has deserted the family. Quinn tries to win a place in his new school with his skateboarding skills. Writing in *Booklist,* John Peters observed: "Though thin on skateboard action and lingo, the book's . . . brief chapters may draw reluctant readers." In *Wave Watch* Choyce brings forward a sport in which he has won some local renown, surfing. In this novel sixteen-year-old Randy lives and surfs year-round, like the author, at Lawrencetown Beach on the outskirts of Halifax, Nova Scotia. Randy and his friends face challenges to their surfing from the local park commission, which is about to change the designation of certain beaches, and also from surfers from Halifax who want to use their surf territory but do not respect nature. To make matters worse, Randy develops a crush on the girlfriend of the rival surf group. Reviewing this work for *Canadian Review of Materials,* Floyd Spracklin called it "a compelling book for just about any teenager." More surfing is served up in *Wave Warrior.* Again the setting is Lawrencetown Beach, a Nova Scotia surfing mecca, and the protagonist is another male teen, Ben. Unlike Randy, however, Ben is no surfer; he is even a poor swimmer. But one summer he determines to learn the sport and perhaps win the heart of the lovely surfer Tara. He tries out surfing and nearly drowns. With the help of Ray, an elderly surfer from the United States who has come to this unspoiled surfing center to die, Ben is eventually able to hold his own on the water. *Canadian Review of Materials* contributor Carole Marion wrote of *Wave Warrior:* "This coming-of-age story is condensed into a brief, engaging tale of a 16-year-old boy who challenges himself and comes out a winner." *Resource Links* contributor Emily Springer observed that "cancer, death, the elderly, teen life and conflicts are all handled very well in this short novel."

A sport of another sort is central to *Roid Rage,* which focuses on the use of steroids in athletic competition. Ray's use of performance-enhancing drugs is of growing concern to best buddy Craig, who watches Ray's skills on the football field increase as his well-being declines. In *Quill & Quire,* Paul Challen noted the book's "snappy junior-jock dialogue and realistic game-action description," adding that *Roid Rage* portrays "the kind of teen peer pressure" that causes teen steroid use. Adolescent "pressure to perform above expectations is enormous," wrote a *Resource Links* reviewer, "and Choyce develops this theme in fine style." *Sudden Impact* is another sports story with an edge. Soccer player Kurt collapses on the field during a match, and his girlfriend, Tina, fears that something serious has happened. She is right; Kurt is diagnosed with a liver condition that necessitates a transplant. While Kurt's parents are too stunned by the news to take appropriate action, Tina begins looking for a liver donor and finds one in the least expected place. Kurt's main rival on the soccer team, Jason, is killed in a motorcycle accident and proves to be a match for Kurt's blood type. Tina must convince Jason's parents to allow the harvesting of his liver. Intended for reluctant readers, the novel provides "a hard hitting story that will stay with you long after you close the book," according to *Canadian Review of Materials* contributor Liz Greenaway. Similar comments came from *Resource Links* reviewer Rachel Steen, who observed: "Choyce successfully raises several points about selflessness and friendship, while creating a powerful story that will hook readers and keep them reading until the satisfying conclusion."

Rock music takes center stage in several of Choyce's novels, including *Hungry Lizards* and *Thunderbowl.* In *Hungry Lizards,* a sixteen-year-old rock band leader learns that the advantages of winning a performing contract at a local club are outweighed by the realities of the entertainment business, the conflicting time demands of school and work, and the temptations of a questionable lifestyle. In *Thunderbowl,* talented teen guitarist Jeremy wins a band playoff; the prize is a chance to perform at a popular bar called the Dungeon. The opportunity forces the teen to weigh the importance of his obligations to his family and educational commitments against his dream of becoming a professional

musician, and his ultimate choice is prompted by some harsh lessons about the life he has chosen. Commenting on *Hungry Lizards,* Kenneth Oppel concluded in *Quill & Quire* that Choyce's "tempered view of teenage street life and the rock n' roll underworld should appeal to young readers." Reviewing *Thunderbowl* in *Resource Links,* Maria Forte noted that the voice of Choyce's young protagonist "rings true" and that Jeremy's story "deals with teenage angst without being corny or superficial."

Wrong Time, Wrong Place explores racial tensions and social injustice through the story of Corey, a young man with one parent who is black and one who is white. Corey first becomes aware of the disadvantages of being biracial when he is branded as a troublemaker and rebel and begins to notice how both students and faculty treat lighter-skinned students differently. Through his uncle Larry's positive example and the man's stories of a black community in Halifax called Africville, Corey begins to identify with his black forebears. *Canadian Children's Literature* reviewer Heidi Petersen noted that Corey "realises that he must face injustices himself, and embraces a form of social activism which begins by keeping the past, the truth, alive."

Coping with the loss of a parent and the many feelings that can result is the subject of *Shoulder the Sky,* Choyce's award-winning novel. Seemingly untroubled and thus encouraged by his father to explore his emotions by writing, sixteen-year-old Martin Emerson divides himself into three different personas: the average, everyday, school-going teen; the outgoing, egocentric Emerson, who comes into being on Martin's personal Web site; and the nameless guy who sometimes blacks out and cannot remember things that have just happened. Between the precocious Internet rants of Emerson, Martin details his day-to-day life before and after his mother's death, including his efforts at rebellion, his unrequited love for a classmate, and his friendship with a boy named Darrell. A family road trip to Alaska causes the teen to confront his mother's death and begin the process of reworking his fractured self into whole cloth. Praising the colorful secondary characters introduced in the novel, *Canadian Review of Materials* contributor Dave Jenkinson predicted that Choyce's protagonist will be "quite interesting to the adolescent reader" despite the fact that Martin's character "unfolds slowly." Dubbing Martin "a sweet funny kid," *Quill & Quire* contributor Teresa Toten added that in *Shoulder the Sky* the author "expertly infuses his characters with an engaging combination of muscle and poetry" and creates a lead character that young readers will "root for."

Choyce has also written other "problem" novels for teenage readers, including *The Book of Michael, Deconstructing Dylan,* and *The End of the World as We Know It*. In *The Book of Michael* Choyce features a youth who was, at sixteen, wrongly convicted for murdering his girlfriend. Though the real killer confessed and Michael was released from prison after serving six months, he is still regarded as a criminal by neighbors and kids at school. Michael now relives the experiences that led up to the death of his girlfriend—his experimenting with drugs and sex—in a "thought-provoking young adult novel [that] deals with a variety of current issues such as capital punishment, troubled youth and our justice system," according to *Canadian Review of Materials* contributor Ann Ketcheson. *School Library Journal* reviewer Jennifer Barnes called the novel "a compelling read with a well-rounded cast of characters." A *Kirkus Reviews* writer commended the work for "examining redemption and re-assimilation."

Deconstructing Dylan is set in the near future and features the sixteen-year-old Dylan Gibson, who has always felt there was something wrong with him, as if there was a part of him missing that everyone else has. Partly, this feeling of difference is the result of being raised by scientist parents, who have been involved in genetic engineering for many years. Finally, with the aid of new friend Robyn, Dylan discovers the secret of his past: he is actually a clone of his dead brother who died of cancer as a nine-year-old. The grieving parents wanted to re-create their much-loved son and Dylan is the result. Responding with feelings that go beyond rage, Dylan begins to counsel other clones. Reviewing *Deconstructing Dylan* in *Canadian Review of Materials,* Darleen Golke noted that "Choyce raises ethical questions about cloning that scientists, philosophers, the religious community, and others have long debated."

In *The End of the World as We Know It,* Choyce presents an unlikable protagonist in seventeen-year-old Carlson, whose chronic bad behavior is actually the result of undiagnosed depression. In his final year of high school he makes friends with Christine, a girl worse off than he is: she self-mutilates as a response to her parents abandoning her. Together these teens forge an unlikely relationship that allows both to gain some degree of mental health. *Canadian Review of Materials* writer Joan Marshall reported, apparently with relief, that Choyce did not end his book with some sort of miraculous breakthrough for the pair: "Fortunately, Choyce ends the book realistically, although for the intended audience, that may be a let-down."

In addition to fiction for older readers, Choyce has produced several chapter books for early elementary-graders, many published by his own Pottersfield Press. As part of Pottersfield's illustrated series of readers, Choyce penned *Famous at Last;* a story about a nine-year-old who turns a role in a local television commercial for beans into a chance at superstardom—even though he really hates beans. "When his career path takes him from beans to Brussels sprouts to stewed tomatoes, Fred draws the line," explained *Quill & Quire* reviewer Maureen Garvie, noting the boy's late-dawning conscience. In *Resource Links,* Ann Abel described *Famous at Last* as "fast-paced" and "hilarious."

Other beginning readers written by Choyce include several volumes in Formac's "First Novel" series, all of which feature a high-spirited and likeable ten-year-old named Carrie. In *Go for It, Carrie,* the desire to learn how to roller skate prompts the girl to find a creative way to find skates she can afford and overcome her frustration while working to master the sport. A camping trip with friends introduces the city girl to more wildlife than she wants to experience in *Carrie's Camping Adventure*. In *Carrie's Crowd,* which a *Resource Links* reviewer called a "brisk story," Carrie plans her strategy to become part of the popular clique until she realizes that the loss of her old friends will be too high a cost to pay. In each of the "Carrie" books Choyce highlights the young girl's resourcefulness. Gillian Richardson noted in a review of *Carrie's Camping Adventure* for *Canadian Review of Materials* that elementary-aged girls in particular will likely "enjoy the obvious superiority in competence" of the girls featured in the story.

Additionally, Choyce is the author of a number of novels for adults, the best known of which may be *The Republic of Nothing,* first published in 1994. According to Mary Somers, writing for the Web site of Dalhousie University, where Choyce has long taught writing classes, that novel is "a Canadian classic, made popular largely by word of mouth among lovers of fiction." Optioned for a film, the novel has not been out of print since its original publication. For the novel, Choyce invents an island, Whalebone, off the eastern coast of Nova Scotia. In an effort to keep the problems of the world out of their tranquil lives, the islanders declare independence from it. However, as the protagonist Ian McQuade—born in 1951 and coming to age during the turbulent sixties—discovers, it is not always possible to avoid the world. Somers observed: "Mr. Choyce deliberately set the story on an island, idealizing a way of life in Nova Scotia. It reflects the place that he found when he left the United States in the 1970s for Canada and made his home at Lawrencetown Beach." An *Internet Bookwatch* reviewer called the novel "a quirky yet compelling drama where anything and everything can happen."

Describing his growth as a writer, Choyce once commented: "As a kid, I had a fairly minute ego; no one within earshot was ready to persuade me that my opinions and insights were of much value in the world I lived in. So later, when I grew into my skin as a writer, I pretended for awhile that *what I had to say* really was of importance. After a time, I started believing in the myth, and this convinced me to abandon fiction for awhile and get autobiographical.

"Since my life story would be exceedingly boring, I was forced to edit my personal history ruthlessly until there was something left worth sharing. My first fragmented history of the self came out as *An Avalanche of Ocean,* and I almost thought that I was done with autobiography. What more could I possibly say once I'd written about winter surfing, transcendental wood-splitting, and getting strip-searched for cod tongues in a Labrador airport?

"But then something happened to me that I can't quite explain. *Avalanche* set off something in me: a kind of manic, magical couple of years where I felt like I was living on the edge of some important breakthrough. It was a time of greater compressed euphoria and despair than I'd ever felt before. Stuff was happening to me, images of the past were flooding through the doors, and I needed to get it all down. Some of it was funny, some of it was not. Dead writers were hovering over my shoulder, saying, 'Dig deep; follow it through. Don't let any of it go.' And I didn't.

"So again I have the audacity to say that these things that happened to me are worth your attention. Like Wordsworth, I am a man 'pleased with my own volitions.' Like Whitman, I find myself saying to readers, 'to you, endless announcements.'

"Write about what makes you feel the most uncomfortable, a voice in my head told me. So I tackled fear and my own male anger and my biggest failures. And, even more dangerous, I tried writing about the most ordinary of things: a morning in Woolco, an unexceptional day, the thread of things that keeps a life together.

"Throughout it all, there is, I hope, a record of a search for love and meaning fraught with failure and recovery. Maybe I've developed a basic mistrust of the rational, logical conclusions. I've only had the briefest glimpses beyond the surface, but I've seen enough to know that sometimes facts are not enough. There are times to make the leap, to get metaphysical, and suppose that we all live larger lives than appearances would suggest."

BIOGRAPHICAL AND CRITICAL SOURCES:

BOOKS

Choyce, Lesley, *An Avalanche of Ocean,* Goose Lane Editions (Fredericton, New Brunswick, Canada), 1987.
Choyce, Lesley, *Transcendental Anarchy: Confessions of a Metaphysical Tourist,* Quarry Press (Kingston, Ontario, Canada), 1993.
Choyce, Lesley, *Driving Minnie's Piano: Memoirs of a Surfing Life in Nova Scotia,* Pottersfield Press (East Lawrencetown, Nova Scotia, Canada), 2006.

PERIODICALS

Booklist, September 15, 2008, John Peters, review of *Skate Freak,* p. 51.
Books in Canada, October, 1995, review of *Big Burn,* p. 49.
Canadian Book Review Annual, 1998, review of *Carrie's Crowd,* p. 497; 1999, review of *World Enough,* p. 162, review of *Roid Rage,* p. 488; 2000, review of *The Summer of Apartment X,* p. 140.
Canadian Children's Literature (annual), 1994, Heidi Petersen, review of *Wrong Time, Wrong Place,* pp. 72-76.
Canadian Review of Materials, January 1, 1989, Lillian M. Turner, review of *December Six/The Halifax Solution;* November 1, 1989, Katheryn Broughton, "The Second Season of Jonas MacPherson"; March 1, 1991, Floyd Spracklin, review of *Wave Watch;* May 1, 1992, Margaret Mackey, review of *Some Kind of Hero;* February 2, 1996, Pat Bolger, review of *The Coastline of Forgetting;* October 18, 1996, Jennifer Sullivan, review of *Big Burn;* January 31, 1997, Irene Gordon, review of *Falling through the Cracks;* September 19, 1997, Irene Gordon, review of *Go for It, Carrie;* November 2, 2001, Gillian Richardson, review of *Carrie's Camping Adventure;* November 29, 2002, Dave Jenkinson, review

of *Shoulder the Sky;* January 6, 2006, Liz Green-away, review of *Sudden Impact;* June 9, 2006, Darleen Golke, review of *Deconstructing Dylan;* April 27, 2007, Robert Groberman, review of *Skunks for Breakfast: Based on a True Story;* June 8, 2007, Carole Marion, review of *Wave Warrior;* September 28, 2007, Joan Marshall, review of *The End of the World as We Know It;* August 29, 2008, Maha Kumaran, review of *Skate Freak;* September 26, 2008, Ann Ketcheson, review of *The Book of Michael.*

Kirkus Reviews, September 15, 2008, review of *The Book of Michael.*

Kliatt, January, 2003, review of *Refuge Cove,* p. 18; May 1, 2006, Lisa M. Carlson, review of *Sudden Impact,* p. 18.

Maclean's, August 15, 1994, review of *The Republic of Nothing,* p. 44.

Publishers Weekly, June 28, 1999, review of *World Enough,* p. 56.

Quill & Quire, March, 1990, Norene Smiley, review of *Skateboard Shakedown,* p. 22; August, 1990, Kenneth Oppel, review of *Hungry Lizards,* p. 15; May, 1993, Patty Lawlor, review of *Clearcut Danger,* pp. 33-34; March, 1995, Fred Boer, review of *Dark End of Dream Street,* p. 79; May, 1995, Maureen Garvie, review of *Big Burn,* pp. 46-47; September 1, 1996, Janet McNaughton, review of *The Trap Door to Heaven;* May, 1998, Maureen Garvie, review of *Famous at Last,* p. 35; July, 1999, review of *The Summer of Apartment X,* p. 42; August, 1999, Paul Challen, review of *Roid Rage,* p. 39; February, 2003, Teresa Toten, review of *Shoulder the Sky.*

Resource Links, April, 1999, Ann Abel, review of *Famous at Last,* p. 9; June, 1999, review of *Carrie's Crowd,* p. 10; October, 1999, review of *Roid Rage,* p. 25; October, 2001, Mavis Holder, review of *Carrie's Camping Adventure,* p. 12; June, 2004, Maria Forte, review of *Thunderbowl,* p. 24; April, 2005, Nadine d'Entremont, review of *Smoke and Mirrors,* p. 29; February 1, 2006, Rachel Steen, review of *Sudden Impact,* p. 43; June 1, 2007, Emily Springer, review of *Wave Warrior,* p. 26.

School Library Journal, August, 1999, Cheryl Cufari, review of *Carrie's Crowd,* p. 124; January 1, 2009, Jennifer Barnes, review of *The Book of Michael,* p. 99.

ONLINE

Books in Canada Online, http://www.booksincanada. com/ (May 19, 2009), M. Wayne Cunningham, review of *Deconstructing Dylan.*

Dalhousie University Web site, http://dalnews.dal.ca/ (June 29, 2007), Mary Somers, *How to Write a Canadian Classic.*

Danforth Review, http://www.danforthreview.com/ (May 19, 2009), Mark Sampson, review of *Atlantica: Stories from the Maritimes and Newfoundland.*

Internet Bookwatch, http://www.midwestbookreview. com/ibw/ (October 1, 2007), review of *The Republic of Nothing.*

Lesley Choyce Home Page, http://www.lesleychoyce. com (May 19, 2009).

Reader Views Kids, http://readerviewskids.com/ (May 19, 2009), Neha Kashmiri, review of *The Book of Michael.*

Stellar Award, http://www.stellaraward.ca/ (May 19, 2009), "Lesley Choyce."

University of Toronto Library Online, http://www. library.utoronto.ca/ (May 19, 2009), author profile.

Writers' Federation of Nova Scotia Web site, http:// www.writers.ns.ca/ (August 15, 2005), author profile.

Writers Union of Canada Web site, http://www.writers union.ca/ (October 20, 2005), author profile.*

*   *   *

CHOYCE, Lesley Willis
    See CHOYCE, Lesley

*   *   *

COONEY, Caroline B. 1947-

PERSONAL: Born May 10, 1947, in Geneva, NY; daughter of Dexter Mitchell (a purchasing agent) and Martha (a teacher) Bruce; married (divorced); children: Louisa, Sayre, Harold. *Education:* Attended Indiana University, 1965-66, Massachusetts General Hospital School of Nursing, 1966-67, and University of Connecticut, 1968. *Hobbies and other interests:* Playing the piano and organ, singing.

ADDRESSES: Home—Westbrook, CT. *Agent*—Curtis Brown Ltd., 10 Astor Pl., New York, NY 10003.

CAREER: Writer and author, 1978—.

MEMBER: Authors Guild, Authors League of America, Mystery Writers of America.

AWARDS, HONORS: Award for Juvenile Literature, American Association of University Women, North Carolina chapter, 1980, for *Safe as the Grave;* Romantic Book Award, Teen Romance category, 1985, for body of work; International Reading Association/Children's Book Centre Choice designation, Pacific States Award, and Iowa Teen Award, all for *The Face on the Milk Carton;* Best Young-Adult Fiction Books citation, *Booklist,* 1993, for *Flight Number 116 Is Down;* American Library Association (ALA) Notable Children's Book designation, 1990, for *The Face on the Milk Carton,* 2001, for *The Ransom of Mercy Carter,* and 2002, for *Goddess of Yesterday.*

WRITINGS:

YOUNG-ADULT FICTION

Safe as the Grave, illustrated by Gail Owens, Coward, McCann (New York, NY), 1979.

The Paper Caper, illustrated by Gail Owens, Coward, McCann (New York, NY), 1981.

An April Love Story, Scholastic (New York, NY), 1981.

Nancy and Nick, Scholastic (New York, NY), 1982.

He Loves Me Not, Scholastic (New York, NY), 1982.

A Stage Set for Love, Archway (New York, NY), 1983.

Holly in Love, Scholastic (New York, NY), 1983.

I'm Not Your Other Half, Putnam (New York, NY), 1984.

Sun, Sea, and Boys, Archway (New York, NY), 1984.

Nice Girls Don't, Scholastic (New York, NY), 1984.

Rumors, Scholastic (New York, NY), 1985.

Trying Out, Scholastic (New York, NY), 1985.

Suntanned Days, Simon & Schuster (New York, NY), 1985.

Racing to Love, Archway (New York, NY), 1985.

The Bad and the Beautiful, Scholastic (New York, NY), 1985.

The Morning After, Scholastic (New York, NY), 1985.

All the Way, Scholastic (New York, NY), 1985.

Saturday Night, Scholastic (New York, NY), 1986.

Don't Blame the Music, Putnam (New York, NY), 1986.

Saying Yes, Scholastic (New York, NY), 1987.

Last Dance, Scholastic (New York, NY), 1987.

The Rah Rah Girl, Scholastic (New York, NY), 1987.

Among Friends, Bantam (New York, NY), 1987.

Camp Boy-meets-Girl, Bantam (New York, NY), 1988.

New Year's Eve, Scholastic (New York, NY), 1988.

Summer Nights, Scholastic (New York, NY), 1988.

The Girl Who Invented Romance, Bantam (New York, NY), 1988, reprinted, Delacorte (New York, NY), 2006.

Camp Reunion, Bantam (New York, NY), 1988.

Family Reunion, Bantam (New York, NY), 1989, reprinted, Delacorte (New York, NY), 2004.

The Fog, Scholastic (New York, NY), 1989.

The Face on the Milk Carton, Bantam (New York, NY), 1990.

Summer Love, Mammoth (London, England), 1990.

The Snow, Scholastic (New York, NY), 1990.

The Fire, Scholastic (New York, NY), 1990.

The Party's Over, Scholastic (New York, NY), 1991.

The Cheerleader, Scholastic (New York, NY), 1991.

Twenty Pageants Later, Bantam (New York, NY), 1991.

The Perfume, Scholastic (New York, NY), 1992.

Operation: Homefront, Bantam (New York, NY), 1992.

Freeze Tag, Scholastic (New York, NY), 1992.

The Return of the Vampire (sequel to *The Cheerleader*), Scholastic (New York, NY), 1992.

Flight Number 116 Is Down, Scholastic (New York, NY), 1992.

The Vampire's Promise (sequel to *The Return of the Vampire*), Scholastic (New York, NY), 1993.

Whatever Happened to Janie? (sequel to *The Face on the Milk Carton*), Scholastic (New York, NY), 1993.

Forbidden, Scholastic (New York, NY), 1993.

The Stranger, Scholastic (New York, NY), 1993.

Twins, Scholastic (New York, NY), 1994.

Emergency Room, Scholastic (New York, NY), 1994.

Driver's Ed, Bantam (New York, NY), 1994.

Unforgettable, Point (New York, NY), 1994.

Flash Fire, Scholastic (New York, NY), 1995.

Night School, Scholastic (New York, NY), 1995.

The Voice on the Radio (sequel to *What Ever Happened to Janie?*), Delacorte Press (New York, NY), 1996.

The Terrorist, Scholastic (New York, NY), 1997.

Wanted!, Scholastic (New York, NY), 1997.

What Child Is This? A Christmas Story, Delacorte Press (New York, NY), 1997.

Burning Up, Delacorte Press (New York, NY), 1999.

Tune in Anytime, Delacorte Press (New York, NY), 1999.

Hush Little Baby, Scholastic Paperbacks (New York, NY), 1999.

What Janie Found (sequel to *The Voice on the Radio*), Delacorte Press (New York, NY), 2000.

Mummy, Scholastic (New York, NY), 2000.

The Ransom of Mercy Carter, Delacorte Press (New York, NY), 2001.

Fatality, Scholastic (New York, NY), 2001.

Goddess of Yesterday, Delacorte (New York, NY), 2002.

Mercy, Macmillan Children's Books (London, England), 2002.

On the Seas to Troy, Macmillan Children's Books (London, England), 2004.

Code Orange, Delacorte (New York, NY), 2005.

Hit the Road, Delacorte (New York, NY), 2005.

A Friend at Midnight, Delacorte (New York, NY), 2006.

Enter Three Witches: A Story of Macbeth, Scholastic (New York, NY), 2007.

Diamonds in the Shadows, Delacorte (New York, NY), 2007.

It the Witness Lied, Delacorte (New York, NY), 2009.

"VAMPIRE'S PROMISE" SERIES; FOR YOUNG ADULTS

Evil Returns, Topeka Bindery (Topeka, KS), 2003.

The Fatal Bargain, Topeka Bindery (Topeka, KS), 2003.

Deadly Offer, Topeka Bindery (Topeka, KS), 2003.

"TIME-TRAVEL" NOVEL SERIES; FOR YOUNG ADULTS

Both Sides of Time (also see below), Delacorte Press (New York, NY), 1995.

Out of Time (also see below), Delacorte Press (New York, NY), 1996.

Prisoner of Time (also see below), Delacorte (New York, NY), 1998.

For All Time (also see below), Delacorte Press (New York, NY), 2001.

Time Travelers, Volume One (contains *Both Sides of Time* and *Out of Time*), Laurel Leaf (New York, NY), 2006.

Time Travelers, Volume Two (contains *Prisoner of Time* and *For All Time*), Laurel Leaf (New York, NY), 2006.

NOVELS

Rear View Mirror (adult), Random House (New York, NY), 1980.

Sand Trap (adult), Berkley (New York, NY), 1983.

Personal Touch, Silhouette (New York, NY), 1983.

Contributor of stories to periodicals, including *Seventeen, American Girl, Jack and Jill, Humpty Dumpty,* and *Young World.*

ADAPTATIONS: Rear View Mirror was adapted as a television movie starring Lee Remick, Warner Bros., 1984; *The Face on the Milk Carton* and *Whatever Happened to Janie?* were adapted as a television movie broadcast by CBS in 1995. Many of Cooney's books have been adapted as audiobooks.

SIDELIGHTS: A prolific author for young adults, Caroline B. Cooney has become known for her teen romances, as well as for writing more edgy novels that explore the ways that the horrors of the world at large can infiltrate even the most mundane life of the average American adolescent. While she began her writing career focusing on adult readers, Cooney quickly learned that she had a gift for connecting with young adults, and this led her to "the type of writing that I could both be successful at and enjoy," as she once recalled. In addition to winning the respect of critics for their likeable protagonists, fast-moving plots, and relevant topical focus, her novels *The Face on the Milk Carton, The Ransom of Mercy Carter,* and *The Girl Who Invented Romance* are also considered must-reads by many teens.

Cooney began writing when she was a young homemaker raising three children. "Sitting home with the babies," the writer once commented, "I had to find a way to entertain myself. So I started writing with a pencil, between the children's naps—baby in one arm, notebook in the other." She had difficulty marketing her novel-length historical novels for adults, but found that the short stories she wrote for a young-adult readership were quickly accepted by magazines such as *Seventeen.* "Having already written eight books with no luck," Cooney once recalled, "I wasn't interested in wasting my time writing another unpublishable novel. So instead I wrote an outline [of a teen mystery novel] and mailed it along with my short story-resumé to a number of publishers, saying: 'Would you be interested in seeing this'—knowing, of course, that they wouldn't. Naturally, when they all said 'yes,' I was stunned; the only thing to do was to quick write the book." That book was published in 1979 as *Safe as the Grave.*

Safe as the Grave, in which a young girl encounters a secret in the family cemetery, was followed up by Cooney with the adult suspense novel *Rear View Mirror,* the story of a young woman who is kidnapped and forced to drive two killers in her car. Michele Slung, reviewing Cooney's second novel for the *Washington Post,* called *Rear View Mirror* "so tightly written, so fast-moving, that it's easy not to realize until the last paragraph is over that one hasn't been breathing all the while." In 1984 *Rear View Mirror* was made into a television movie starring Lee Remick as the kidnapped woman.

Cooney returned to young-adult writing with *An April Love Story,* a romance novel published in 1981. Except for one more adult novel—1983's *Sand Trap*—her focus is now exclusively on a young-adult readership, and her original story ideas have been supplemented by plot suggestions from her editor as well as by her contribution to the "Cheerleader" and "Chrystal Falls" novel series. "It is exciting 'to write to order,'" Cooney once explained. "It often involves an idea or characters I've never thought about before, and I have to tackle it cold like any other assignment. Editors have such good ideas! I also continue to write my own ideas, like *The Girl Who Invented Romance.* 'Romance' is a board game that Kelly designs and the board game [is] part of the book."

Though Cooney enjoys penning teen romances and stories of strong friendships such as the 2006 cross-generational novel *Hit the Road,* many of her books deal with serious topical issues that affect teens directly. In *Operation: Homefront,* a wife and mother with three children is called up for National Guard duty and shipped off to Saudi Arabia during the Gulf War, while *Family Reunion* focuses on a teen dealing with her parents' separation and divorce, as well as with her dad's remarriage. In *A Friend at Midnight* a teen must decide whether to betray a confidence when her older sister insists on inviting their abusive father to her wedding, while *Burning Up* finds an affluent Connecticut adolescent coming face to face with prejudice after the inner-city church where she volunteers is torched by an arsonist. As Stephanie Zvirin noted in her *Booklist* review of *Burning Up,* Cooney excels at portraying both "the tentative boy-girl relationship between" her teen protagonists, and the "questioning and fervor that propels some teens to look beyond themselves and their families to larger issues."

While teens encounter divorce, prejudice, and separation within their own families and personal interactions, other more abstract issues are made equally personal in several of Cooney's timely works of fiction. In *The Terrorist,* for example, she deals with the sobering subject of international terrorism, and, in the opinion of a *Publishers Weekly* contributor, "combines heartpound-

ing suspense with some sobering reflections on the insular attitude characteristic of many Americans both at home and abroad." Terrorism of a different kind is the focus of *Code Orange,* a novel written in response to the nation's state of heightened vigilance following the September 11, 2001 terrorist attacks. While conducting research for a school paper on smallpox, slacker prep-school student Mitty Blake discovers an old envelope tucked into a book that contains hundred-year-old smallpox scabs. As the Manhattan teen researches the highly contagious infectious disease, he realizes that he may have infected himself; in fact, he may be a danger to everyone he has contacted since first opening the envelope. Panic turns into a bumbling attempt to solve the problem as Mitty contacts both Federal authorities and inadvertently attracts the notice of a terrorist group that has far darker motives. Praising *Code Orange* in *Horn Book,* Jeannine M. Chapman noted that Mitty's growing resourcefulness "is believably conveyed," as the "lighthearted tone" at the beginning of the novel builds to a "thrilling climax (with a twist)." A *Publishers Weekly* wrote that the author's "rat-a-tat delivery and hairpin turns keep the pages turning," and *Booklist* contributor John Peters cited the novel's "profoundly disturbing premise" and "its likable, ultimately heroic slacker protagonist."

Perhaps Cooney's most widely read novel, the critically acclaimed *The Face on the Milk Carton,* deals with the topic of child abduction. Janie Johnson is kidnapped when she is three years old by Hannah, a teenaged cult member; unaware of her past, she is raised by Hannah's parents. Janie's picture, displayed on a milk carton as that of a missing child, leads her to uncover her past. Cooney continues Janie's story in the novels *Whatever Happened to Janie?, The Voice on the Radio,* and *What Janie Found,* which follow the efforts of Cooney's determined young heroine to discover the truth about her family and her true identity. Citing Cooney's "skilled writing," a *Publishers Weekly* contributor noted of *The Face on the Milk Carton* that the book's likeable protagonist and "suspenseful, impeccably-paced action add to this novel's appeal" among teen readers. "Cooney seems to have a special radar for adolescent longings and insecurities," noted another critic in the same periodical during a review of *The Voice on the Radio.* While the *Publishers Weekly* contributor also noted the plot's lack of believability, this quality is more than outweighed by the novel's "psychological accuracy and well-aimed, gossipy views of teens," according to the reviewer.

Somewhat of a departure from her other books, Cooney's novel *Among Friends* features a unique structure.

Six students have been given an assignment to write in journals during a three-month period. The entries from those journals, providing a variety of points of view, make up the novel. This approach, stated Mitzi Myers in the *Los Angeles Times,* provides "a more rounded interpretation than any single character could supply." Myers concluded: "It is a pleasure to find a book for young readers that not only individualizes characters through their writing but also has wise words to say about how writing offers very real help in coping with the problems of growing up."

Cooney mixes romance with science fiction with her "Time-Travel" novel series, which includes *Both Sides of Time, Out of Time, Prisoner of Time,* and *For All Time.* In *Both Sides of Time* readers meet high school graduate Annie Lockwood, whose romantic perspective would have made her better suited for life in the past. When Annie gets her wish and winds up in 1895, however, her twenty-first-century attitudes and expectations make her realize that living in the past means dealing with far more than long gowns, lavish balls, and dapper, respectful young gentlemen. However, when she falls in love with Strat, her link with the past is forever cemented, and she must learn to balance both her worlds. After revealing Annie's secret to his father in *Out of Time,* Strat is dismissed as insane and sent to a mental asylum. Despite the family problems in her modern life, Annie must now risk everything to return through time and bring her beloved to safety in her (for him) futuristic world. The series takes a new twist in *Prisoner of Time,* as Strat's sister Devonny finds herself betrothed to an unpleasant English noble and requires her brother's help in breaking the engagement. Surprise turns to romance when Annie's brother Tod Lockwood answers the call back through time. The series concludes in *For All Time,* as Annie's effort to control her travel through time misfires and she winds up at the right place but the wrong time. Transported back into ancient times, Annie finds herself trapped in an Egyptian city. Meanwhile, her beloved Strat awaits her in the same city, three thousand years in the future, unaware of his time-traveling girlfriend's fate. In a review of *Both Sides of Time* for *Horn Book,* Sarah Guille deemed Cooney's story "suspenseful and poignant," noting that her heroine matures while learning an important lesson: "That real love has consequences and obligations that fantasies don't." Dubbing the series "a breathlessly romantic whirl through the centuries," a *Publishers Weekly* contributor noted that readers will be carried along by Cooney's "characteristically breezily, intimate style."

In *The Ransom of Mercy Carter,* Cooney offers readers another departure from her contemporary-theme novels: a historical fiction based on the 1704 raid on the English settlement at Deerfield, Massachusetts, when Kahnawake Mohawks destroyed the village and took more than one hundred captives back to Canada. The novel focuses on young Mercy, a captive whose growing respect for the Native American culture into which she is forced must ultimately cause her to question her loyalty to her own family. Calling *The Ransom of Mercy Carter* a "gripping and thought-provoking account," a *Publishers Weekly* contributor added that, though Cooney oversimplifies some historical elements, "the immediacy of Mercy's dilemma comes through." In her *Kliatt* review, Sally M. Tibbetts praised the author's detailed research, calling the novel "a great story about a young girl who learns to adapt and survive." Noting that Cooney raises "excellent questions" about how different cultures view what it means to be civilized or savage, *Booklist* contributor Gillian Engberg deemed *The Ransom of Mercy Carter* a "vivid, dramatic novel."

Another travel back through time is offered to readers of *Goddess of Yesterday,* which transports readers back to the classical world and the years leading up to the Trojan War. When readers meet Anaxandra, the six year old is living on an island in the Aegean sea until she is sent as a hostage to the King of Siphnos. Six years later, her life is again thrown into turmoil when the king's palace is attacked and all are killed. By assuming the identity of the king's daughter, Callisto, Anaxandra is accepted at the palace of Sparta's King Menelaus, whose young wife is destined to become the fabled Helen of Troy. Charged with caring for the king's two-year-old son, Callisto/Anaxandra soon learns of the clandestine romantic affair between the boy's mother and Paris, prince of Troy. As the political tensions between Sparta and Troy mount, Helen's jealousy of her grows, forcing Callisto/Anaxandra to navigate the shifting allegiances in order to survive. Her destiny alters once again when she is ordered to accompany Helen and her young son on the deceitful queen's pivotal journey to Troy. There, in the company of her lover, the ill-fated Trojan prince Paris, one of the most dramatic battles of the ancient world will play out. Reviewing the novel for *Horn Book,* Kristi Elle Jemtegaard described *Goddess of Yesterday* as "by turns gruesome, dramatic, and tenderly domestic." In *Booklist,* Frances Bradburn praised Cooney for the "fresh perspective" from which she spins her "exciting, complex adventure story," although the critic added that the plot might confuse teens unfamiliar with the history of the Trojan War. In the opinion of *Kliatt* contributor Claire Rosser, *Goddess of Yesterday* stands as one of Cooney's "most ambitious" books for teen readers.

Through the book's likeable fictional heroine, the novel "will make the ancient Greek world" come alive for teens, Rosser added, especially the actual men and women who figure in the tragedies preserved through the literary works of "Homer and the Greek dramatists." Noting that Cooney refashions the classic tale as a "grand adventure with a heroic girl at the center," Angela J. Reynolds predicted in *School Library Journal* that her "fine-tuned adventure . . . may leave middle-schoolers asking to read Homer."

History again mixes with literature in *Enter Three Witches: A Story of Macbeth,* which a *Publishers Weekly* contributor dubbed a "compulsively readable, behind-the-scenes peek into the rise and fall of Lord and Lady Macbeth." In bringing the Shakespearean drama to life for teens—revealing portions of the bard's text begin each chapter—Cooney mixes the play's characters with fictional ones such as Lady Mary, the fourteen-year-old ward of Lady Macbeth, until her father falls from grace and she is promised in marriage to a ruthless friend of the Scottish king. In her "engaging" retelling of the tragic story of how the lust for power can destroy lives and torment the soul, Cooney crafts prose with what *School Library Journal* contributor Nancy Menaldi-Scanlan described as an "elevated tone." "While it may be difficult at first," the critic hastened to add, Cooney's text is "interesting and appropriate" enough to sustain reader interest. Although noting that fans of the original drama can most fully appreciate Cooney's "fascinating, humanizing" insight into each familiar character, Phelan added in *Booklist* that the likeable teen at the center of *Enter Three Witches* will engage fans of historical fiction and even inspire some to track out *Macbeth* in the original.

As noted earlier, in *Hit the Road* the author features another a complex topical issue, namely the problems associated with growing old. Brittany is sent to stay with her grandmother, Nannie Scott, while her parents go on vacation. Before long, she is caught up in an adventure featuring Nannie and three friends driving off to their college reunion despite the fact that they no longer have drivers' licenses. To make matters worse, another friend has been sent to a nursing home against her will. Janis Flint-Ferguson, writing for *Kliatt,* noted that the author "delivers with humor the poignant interaction between young and old."

A Friend at Midnight finds Lily living with her mother while her eight-year-old brother, Michael, goes to live with her father following their parents divorce. Before

long, Lily realizes that her father has abandoned her brother. Lily, who turned all her inner anger towards her father, finds the renewed feelings becoming too much to bear. Kate E. Schmelzer, writing in *Campus Life's Ignite Your Faith,* commented that the author does not "offer easy answers and simple solutions to complex problems."

In *Diamonds in the Shadows,* published in 2007, Cooney once again takes on a topical issue as she tells the story of the Finch family agreeing to take in a refugee family from Liberia, which has undergone a Civil War. "This tense thriller has more heart, and depth, than some of Cooney's others," wrote Paula Rohrlick in a review for *Kliatt.* Jared Finch, a teenager, is not happy that he will have to share his room with the young son in the African family while his ten-year-old sister Mopsy will have to make room for their daughter. When they pick the family up at the airport, they find that Andre Amabo, the father, has lost his arms in the war. Along with him are his wife Celestine and his children. Although the refugee family has a harrowing story to tell, Jared is mostly unsympathetic and growing increasingly discontent with his new roommate, Mattue, as well as the Amabo family in general. Mopsy, on the other hand, seems to enjoy rooming with young Alake, even if the refugee seems to be suffering terribly from her past and doesn't talk. Jared, however, is suspicious of the family's story and begins to look into things, thinking that the Amabos may not be a family at all. When he snoops into the cremated remains the Amabos brought with them, he finds a stash of diamonds. His discovery soon puts both his family and the refugee family in danger, and the culprit may be the fifth refugee who arrived with the Amabo family at the airport. The book includes an afterword in which the author writes about the time she hosted an African family of refugees and provides statistical information on Darfu, which has undergone a civil war and refugee crisis. "*Diamonds in the Shadows* is an interesting Christian thriller in which good intentions and deeds may pave the road to hell," wrote Harriet Klausner for the *Harriet Klausner's Book Reviews* Web site. *Horn Book* contributor Lauren Adams noted: "The satisfying thriller introduces the complex issues of African civil war and violence with compassion."

Cooney is also the author of a series of vampire books sometimes referred to as "The Vampire's Promise" series. The books typically feature an evil vampire and a young person or persons who must face a moral choice. For example, in *Evil Returns,* young Devenee wants to be pretty and popular. A vampire offers her both, but in exchange for a price that may be too high. *The Fatal Bargain* features a group of teens having to choose who to leave behind in an old house so that the vampire who lives there will let the others leave. In *Deadly Offer,* Althea must agree to an evil deal to gain the popularity in school that a vampire guarantees to provide.

When Cooney started her writing career, she wrote in a spontaneous fashion. "I never used to know what was going to happen in the story until I wrote it," she once observed. "Then I began doing paperbacks for Scholastic and they required outlines, largely just to ensure that two writers didn't waste time and effort on similar ideas. Before, I'd always allowed the story to develop out of the characters, but the outlines demanded that the plot and characters evolve together at the same time. Now I wouldn't do it any other way."

Cooney's decision to create novels with compelling, high-energy stories, interesting protagonists, and strong, upbeat resolutions has been prompted by her observation that young people want stories that end on an upbeat note and a future that looks positive. "They want hope," she explained, "want things to work out, want reassurance that even were they to do something rotten, they and the people around them would still be all right. No matter what it is that they're doing, I don't think they want to have to read about it. Teenagers looking for books to read don't say, 'Oh, good, another depressing story.'"

BIOGRAPHICAL AND CRITICAL SOURCES:

BOOKS

Beacham's Guide to Literature for Young Adults, Gale (Detroit, MI), Volume 10, 2000, Volume 11, 2000.

Carroll, Pamela Sissi, *Caroline Cooney: Faith and Fiction* ("Scarecrow Studies in Young-Adult Literature" series), Scarecrow Press (Metuchen, NJ), 2002.

Drew, Bernard A., *The One Hundred Most Popular Young Adult Authors,* Libraries Unlimited (Englewood, CO), 1996.

St. James Guide to Young-Adult Writers, 2nd edition, St. James Press (Detroit, MI), 1999.

PERIODICALS

Booklist, March 15, 1993, review of *Flight Number 116 Is Down,* p. 89; June 1, 1994, Stephanie Zvirin, review of *Driver's Ed,* p. 1809; November 1, 1995, Susan Dove Lempke, review of *Flash Fire,* p. 464; February 15, 1996, Sally Estes, review of *Out of Time,* p. 1004; July, 1997, Anne O'Malley, review of *The Terrorist,* p. 1810; June 1, 1998, Sally Estes, review of *Prisoner of Time,* p. 1745; December 1, 1998, Stephanie Zvirin, review of *Burning Up,* p. 661; April 1, 2001, Gillian Engberg, review of *The Ransom of Mercy Carter,* p. 1481; September 15, 2001, Debbie Carton, review of *For All Time,* p. 215; June 1, 2002, Frances Bradburn, review of *Goddess of Yesterday,* p. 1704; September 1, 2005, John Peters, review of *Code Orange,* p. 124; March 15, 2006, review of *Hit the Road,* p. 46; December 15, 2006, Jennifer Mattson, review of *A Friend at Midnight,* p. 44; March 1, 2007, Carolyn Phelan, review of *Enter Three Witches: A Story of Macbeth,* p. 73; September 1, 2007, Hazel Rochman, review of *Diamonds in the Shadows,* p. 104.

Books, November 10, 2007, Mary Harris Russell, review of *Diamonds in the Shadows.*

Bulletin of the Center for Children's Books, July-August, 1986, review of *Don't Blame the Music,* p. 205; April, 1991, review of *The Party's Over,* p. 187; December, 1992, review of *Operation: Homefront,* p. 108; September, 1994, review of *Driver's Ed,* p. 10; October, 1995, review of *Both Sides of Time,* p. 50; May, 1996, review of *Out of Time,* p. 296; November, 1999, review of *Tune in Anytime,* p. 87; March, 2000, review of *What Janie Found,* p. 241; November, 2001, review of *For All Time,* p. 97; July, 2002, review of *Goddess of Yesterday,* p. 397; June, 2006, Deborah Stevenson, review of *Hit the Road,* p. 448; September, 2007, Deborah Stevenson, review of *Diamonds in the Shadows,* p. 3.

Campus Life's Ignite Your Faith, June-July, 2007, Kate E. Schmelzer, review of *A Friend at Midnight.*

Horn Book, November-December, 1995, Sarah Guille, review of *Both Sides of Time,* p. 745; November-December, 2003, Kristi Elle Jemtegaard, review of *Goddess of Yesterday,* p. 774; September-October, 2005, Jeannine M. Chapman, review of *Code Orange,* p. 574; November-December, 2007, Lauren Adams, review of *Diamonds in the Shadows.*

Kirkus Reviews, September 1, 2005, review of *Code Orange,* p. 970; March 1, 2007, review of *Enter Three Witches,* p. 218; September 1, 2007, review of *Diamonds in the Shadows.*

Kliatt, March, 2003, Sally M. Tibbetts, review of *The Ransom of Mercy Carter,* p. 21; September, 2003, Barbara McKee, review of *For All Time,* p. 24; January, 2004, Claire Rosser, review of *Goddess of Yesterday,* p. 16; September, 2005, Paula Rohrlick, review of *Code Orange,* p. 6; September, 2007, Paula Rohrlick, review of *Diamonds in the Shadows,* p. 8; March, 2008, Francine Levitov, review of *Enter Three Witches,* p. 44; March, 2008, Janis Flint-Ferguson, review of *Hit the Road,* p. 23.

Los Angeles Times, February 6, 1988, Mitzi Myers, "High Schoolers Learn about the Meaning of Friendship."

Publishers Weekly, August 25, 1989, review of *The Fog,* p. 65; January 12, 1990, review of *The Face on the Milk Carton,* p. 62; March 23, 1992, review of *Flight Number 116 Is Down,* p. 73; June 14, 1993, review of *Whatever Happened to Janie?,* p. 72; July 4, 1994, review of *Unforgettable,* p. 65; July 10, 1995, review of *Both Sides of Time,* p. 59; July 22, 1996, review of *The Voice on the Radio,* p. 242; July 28, 1997, review of *The Terrorist,* p. 75; October 6, 1997, review of *What Child Is This? A Christmas Story,* p. 57; December 7, 1998, review of *Burning Up,* p. 61; July 26, 1999, review of *Tune in Anytime,* p. 92; January 3, 2000, review of *What Janie Found,* p. 77; February 12, 2001, review of *The Ransom of Mercy Carter,* p. 213; October 22, 2001, review of *For All Time,* p. 77; July 8, 2002, review of *Goddess of Yesterday,* p. 50; September 5, 2005, review of *Code Orange,* p. 63; May 22, 2006, review of *Hit the Road,* p. 54; November 6, 2006, review of *A Friend at Midnight,* p. 62; April 2, 2007, review of *Enter Three Witches,* p. 58; September 17, 2007, review of *Diamonds in the Shadows,* p. 55.

St. Petersburg Times, March 24, 2008, "Code Orange Red Hot among Middle School Readers," p. 3.

School Library Journal, February, 1990, Tatiana Castleton, review of *The Face on the Milk Carton,* p. 109; February, 1992, review of *Flight Number 116 Is Down,* p. 107; November, 1992, Kenneth E. Kowen, review of *Operation,* p. 88; June, 1993, Jacqueline Rose, review of *Whatever Happened to Janie?,* p. 126; August, 1994, Susan R. Farber, review of *Driver's Ed,* p. 168; July, 1995, Connie Tyrrell Burns, review of *Both Sides of Time,* p. 168; February, 1999, Claudia Moore, review of *The Voice on the Radio,* p. 69; August, 2001, Renee Steinberg, review of *The Ransom of Mercy Carter,* p. 213; June, 2002, Angela J. Reynolds, review of *Goddess of Yesterday,* p. 134; August, 2005, Blair Christolin, review of *The Ransom of Mercy Carter,* p. 48; October, 2005, Courtney Lewis, review of *Code Orange,* p. 156; November, 2006, Marie Orlando, review of *A Friend at Midnight,* p. 132; May, 2007, Nancy Menaldi-Scanlan, review of *Enter Three Witches,* p. 130; September, 2007, Lillian Hecker, review of *Diamonds in the Shadows,* p. 194.

Social Education, May-June, 2008, review of *Diamonds in the Shadows.*

Times Literary Supplement, May 20, 1988, review of *The Girl Who Invented Romance.*

Voice of Youth Advocates, February, 1990, review of *The Face on the Milk Carton,* p. 341; October, 1992, review of *Operation,* p. 222; December, 1992, review of *The Return of the Vampire,* p. 291; April, 1993, review of *The Perfume,* pp. 20-21, 38; August, 1993, Samantha Hunt, review of *The Vampire's Promise,* p. 162; April, 1994, review of *The Stranger,* p. 36; August, 1994, review of *Emergency Room,* pp. 143-144; August, 1995, review of *Both Sides of Time,* p. 168; October, 1997, review of *The Terrorist,* p. 242; June, 1998, review of *What Child Is This?,* p. 128; February, 1999, review of *Burning Up,* p. 431; April, 2000, review of *What Janie Found,* p. 33; April 1, 2001, review of *The Ransom of Mercy Carter,* p. 36; June, 2001, review of *The Voice on the Radio,* p. 97; August, 2002, review of *Goddess of Yesterday,* p. 200; October, 2005, review of *Code Orange,* p. 298; December, 2006, review of *A Friend at Midnight,* p. 421; June, 2007, Laura Panter, review of *Enter Three Witches,* p. 158.

Washington Post, June 1, 1980, Michele Slung, review of *Rear View Mirror.*

ONLINE

Harriet Klausner's Book Reviews, http://harrietklausner. wwwi.com/ (August 4, 2008), Harriet Klausner, review of *Diamonds in the Shadows.**

*   *   *

CUTTER, Tom
See RANDISI, Robert J.

D

DAVIDSON, Diane Mott 1949-

PERSONAL: Born March 22, 1949, in Honolulu, HI; married Jim Davidson (an electrical engineer), 1969; children: Jeffrey, Jonathan, Joe. *Education:* Attended Wellesley College; Stanford University, B.A., 1970; Johns Hopkins University, M.A., 1976; studied at the Bishop's School of Theology and the Ilif School of Theology. *Hobbies and other interests:* Cooking.

ADDRESSES: Home—Evergreen, CO. *Agent*—Taryn Fagerness, Sandra Dijkstra Literary Agency, PMB 515, 1155 Camino del Mar, Del Mar, CA 92014-3115.

CAREER: Writer and novelist. Worked as a teacher and as a volunteer Sunday School teacher with the Episcopal Church, volunteer rape counselor, volunteer tutor at a juvenile correctional facility, and a political party caucus chair. Licensed lay preacher in the Episcopal Church. Served on the Episcopal Church's Diocesan Board of Examining Chaplains for ten years.

MEMBER: Rocky Mountain Fiction Writers.

AWARDS, HONORS: Named Writer of the Year, Rocky Mountain Fiction Writers, 1990; Anthony Award for best short story, 1992.

WRITINGS:

"GOLDY BEAR SCHULZ" SERIES

Catering to Nobody, St. Martin's Press (New York, NY), 1990.

Dying for Chocolate, Bantam Books (New York, NY), 1992.

The Cereal Murders, Bantam Books (New York, NY), 1993.

The Last Suppers, Bantam Books (New York, NY), 1994.

Killer Pancake, Bantam Books (New York, NY), 1995.

The Main Corpse, Bantam Books (New York, NY), 1996.

The Grilling Season, Bantam Books (New York, NY), 1997.

Prime Cut, Bantam Books (New York, NY), 1998.

Tough Cookie, Bantam Books (New York, NY), 2000.

Sticks and Scones, Bantam Books (New York, NY), 2001.

Chopping Spree, Bantam Books (New York, NY), 2002.

Double Shot, William Morrow (New York, NY), 2004.

Dark Tort, HarperCollins (New York, NY), 2006.

Sweet Revenge, William Morrow (New York, NY), 2007.

Fatally Flaky, William Morrow (New York, NY), 2009.

ADAPTATIONS: Novels adapted for audio include *Catering to Nobody,* 1997; *Dying for Chocolate,* 1997; *The Cereal Murders,* 1997; *The Grilling Season,* Recorded Books, 1997; *Prime Cut,* BDD, 1998; *Tough Cookie,* BDD, 2000; and *Sticks and Scones,* BDD, 2001.

SIDELIGHTS: Diane Mott Davidson had been writing for years when she and her husband settled in Evergreen, Colorado, but it was only after her youngest son was in preschool that she began to focus her work. She wrote in a café that also did catering, and Davidson's interest in the business gave her the idea for her successful series of culinary mystery novels starring Goldy Bear, a small-town caterer and the mother of a young son named Arch. Goldy is divorced from an abusive husband, and by the fourth book, she has married Tom Schulz, an investigator with the Aspen Meadows sheriff's office.

Davidson calls on her husband, her sons, their friends, and even the United Parcel Service deliveryman to try out new recipes for her stories. Since she lives at a high altitude, over eight thousand feet, her sisters on the East Coast test them at sea level for her, and Davidson adds notations for high-altitude cooking to the recipes that require them.

In the series opener, *Catering to Nobody,* Goldy's former father-in-law nearly dies when someone adds poison to the lemonade prepared by Goldilocks Catering for the wake of her son's former teacher. Goldy's business is shut down while Tom looks for the killer, but Goldy begins an investigation of her own. A *Kirkus Reviews* contributor called the novel "a genial debut . . . chatty, sort of sexy, amusingly improbable."

A *Publishers Weekly* reviewer described *Dying for Chocolate* as a "perky mystery complete with toothsome hi-cal recipes." Goldy is being stalked by her physician ex-husband and takes a job with a retired general and former Pentagon terrorism expert for the summer while a security system is installed in the house she shares with her son. Arch finds a new swimming coach and mentor in Julian, the family's handyman, while Goldy enjoys the company of two men, Tom and psychiatrist Philip Miller. When Philip dies after his car plunges from a cliff, Goldy is left to solve his death and unravel the plot connections. A *Kirkus Reviews* writer called the character of Arch "true and likable." A *Publishers Weekly* contributor commented that Davidson "makes sure that all enigmas wind up in solutions that will surprise and please."

The class valedictorian at a pricey prep school is murdered in *The Cereal Murders,* strangled with Goldy's extension cord. Tom helps get her out of the jam, then is kidnapped in the next story, *The Last Suppers,* just as he and Goldy are about to marry. In addition, the priest who was to marry them is killed. A *Kirkus Reviews* contributor wrote that Davidson "deftly dovetails Episcopal intrigue and more formulaic genre mayhem, though the conflict between the old guard and those huggy-feely charismatics wears a little thin."

In *Killer Pancake,* Goldy and Julian—now her assistant—have a catering gig preparing a low-fat luncheon for Mignon Cosmetics, which is introducing a new line of makeup. The company is picketed by animal rights activists, and Claire, a sales associate and Julian's girlfriend, is killed in a hit-and-run in the parking lot. While trying to comfort Julian, Goldy juggles two jobs and consoles friend Marla Korman, who suffers a heart attack. As she gets into her investigation and learns about Claire's past, her own life is threatened. *Armchair Detective* reviewer Liz Currie wrote that "as always, Davidson keeps readers guessing up until the last second. . . . All Davidson's books feature mouthwatering recipes from Goldy's catering menus, and the recipes in *Killer Pancake* continue that tradition."

BookBrowser reviewer Harriet Klausner called *The Main Corpse* "emotionally gratifying while simultaneously fun to read." Goldy's business is down, and Julian has left for school. Goldy investigates a catering client, Prospect Financial Partners, when Marla becomes a murder suspect. Marla, who invested in the gold mine the company is promoting, has learned that the mine is a fake, and her boyfriend, a partner, is missing. Currie called *The Main Corpse* "a strong entry in this enjoyable series."

In *The Grilling Season* Suz Craig, girlfriend of Goldy's former husband, is murdered, and Goldy is sure he is capable of the crime. However, Arch asks her to help his father, and she agrees for her son's sake. Susan Scribner, who reviewed the novel for the *Mystery Reader* Web site, noted that the series "takes a darker turn in this installment."

A new caterer is underbidding Goldy in *Prime Cut,* and she has also been abandoned by a contractor who has left her business in shambles. Goldy later finds the body of the missing contractor, and an old friend is arrested on circumstantial evidence. *Booklist* reviewer Stuart Miller wrote that "good characterizations and a zippy style make this another enjoyable installment in this appealing series."

In *Tough Cookie* Goldy's kitchen is closed by the health inspector, and she does a live spot on the local PBS cooking show. Everything that can go wrong does, and after the show she finds the friend she was to meet dead in the snow. She becomes a suspect and a target when her catering van is demolished and she is threatened via telephone. Miller noted that the best recipe in this outing is Davidson's chocolate coma cookies.

Goldy is preparing Elizabethan food at a castle that was shipped from England and reassembled in Colorado in *Sticks and Scones.* The owners, who intend to turn the castle into a conference center, invite Goldy, her son, and her dog to stay with them after a rock is thrown through Goldy's window. As the story progresses, Tom is shot and Goldy attacked. Her ex, just out of prison, may have ties to a murder victim. "Goldy's an engaging companion and her recipes are divine," wrote GraceAnne A. DeCandido in *Booklist,* and added: "Wait till you try the scones."

Julian, once again Goldy's assistant, is arrested in *Chopping Spree* for the murder of Goldy's old school friend. In another *BookBrowser* review, Klausner commented that "readers will have a hard time deciding what is better: the mouth-watering descriptions of various recipes or the fast-paced, compelling story line."

In *Double Shot,* a brazen attacker is out to disrupt Goldy's latest project, a memorial luncheon for prominent local physician Dr. Albert Kerr, a former colleague of her noxious ex-husband, John Korman. Her kitchen is severely vandalized, and on the way to the luncheon she is attacked and beaten by an unknown assailant. During the luncheon itself, Korman, recently released from jail, arrives and starts a vicious argument with Goldy over visitation rights with Arch. When Goldy takes Arch to his father's home for the visit, she finds Korman shot to death; worse, it looks as if he was shot with Goldy's own missing .38 pistol. She is immediately suspected in Korman's death. Goldy's best friend, Marla Korman, John's other ex-wife, hires powerhouse attorney Brewster Motley to represent her while Goldy's husband Tom applies his own skills as a policeman and detective to help ferret out the guilty parties. Despite the efforts of friends and family, Goldy's situation looks grim, but suspects soon turn up and it becomes clear that John Korman had more enemies than aggrieved ex-wives. "*Double Shot* represents an upturn for the series. The relationships are sharper and more realistic and Goldy's work is a bit more believable," commented Shannon Bloomstran on the *Mostly Fiction* Web site. Further, a *Publishers Weekly* critic observed that the book "marks a turning point for Davidson, as the elimination of Korman provides a much needed jolt to the series." Readers who have enjoyed previous outings with the "chatty, hard-working Goldy will be pleasantly energized" by this novel, commented Janice Nimura in *People.*

At the beginning of *Dark Tort,* Goldy arrives at the offices of Hanrahan & Jule, an upscale law firm that hires her to provide food services for staff and clients. To her surprise, she discovers the body of Dusty Routt, a twenty-year-old paralegal whose hard work and dedication were just beginning to help her overcome a tragic and impoverished past. Dusty's death is traumatic for her mother and grandmother, who are still in shock from her brother's death while in police custody. Soon, Goldy is asked by Dusty's mother to investigate the young woman's death. Unable to refuse, Goldy's search brings her uncomfortably close to suspects within Hanrahan & Jule, and draws unexpected connections between the case and the firm's collection of high-concept food paintings by artist Charlie Barker. In this installment of the series, "Davidson delivers another entertaining whodunit with delectable recipes," remarked a *Publishers Weekly* reviewer. "Goldy and her coterie always provide some enjoyable moments," mused a contributor to *Kirkus Reviews. Booklist* reviewer Stephanie Zvirin concluded: "In the subgenre of foodie mysteries, Davidson remains the master chef."

Sweet Revenge finds Goldy juggling several big jobs during the beginning of the holiday season. In addition to catering a breakfast at the library, she will handle two parties for Hermie and Smithfield MacArthur, wealthy Southerners who have moved to Aspen Meadow. As Goldy heads to their home on the Friday after Thanksgiving to plan their events, she sees Sandee Brisbane, the woman who killed Goldy's former husband, and who supposedly died in a forest fire after throwing herself from a cliff. Former District Attorney Drew Wellington was to attend one of the parties, but he is found dead in the library, and Goldy learns that he had been receiving threatening e-mails sent through the library network. Meanwhile, Goldy herself is the target of Larry Craddock, a map dealer who is also murdered.

Davidson includes ten recipes that are intended for the library's 'What the Dickens Breakfast," with names like Great Expectations Grapefruit, Tale of Two Cities French Toast, Bleak House Bars, and Hard Times Ham. "Readers will happily sink their teeth into Goldy's latest case and come away hungry for more," concluded a *Publishers Weekly* contributor. Marge Fletcher reviewed *Sweet Revenge* for *Bookreporter.com,* writing: "Reminiscent of a new age Miss Marple with a good business mind, sense of humor and great cooking skills, Goldy is sure to please. Bon appetit!"

BIOGRAPHICAL AND CRITICAL SOURCES:

PERIODICALS

Armchair Detective, spring, 1996, Liz Currie, review of *Killer Pancake,* p. 234; winter, 1997, Liz Currie, review of *The Main Corpse,* p. 96.

Asia Africa Intelligence Wire, December 5, 2004, Mary Kennard, "Davidson Serves 12th Deadly Course," review of *Double Shot.*

Belles Lettres, winter, 1991, review of *Catering to Nobody,* p. 41.

Booklist, August, 1990, Stuart Miller, review of *Catering to Nobody,* p. 2158; August, 1992, Mary Carroll, review of *Dying for Chocolate,* p. 1998; October 15, 1993, Stuart Miller, review of *The Cereal Murders,* p. 420; October 1, 1994, Caroline Andrew, review of *The Last Suppers,* p. 241; September 1, 1996, Stuart Miller, review of *The Main Corpse,* p. 66; August, 1997, Stuart Miller, review of *The Grilling Season,* p. 1884; September 1, 1998, Stuart Miller, review of *Prime Cut,* p. 69; March 1, 2000, Stuart Miller, review of *Tough Cookie,* p. 1198; March 15, 2001, GraceAnne A. DeCandido, review of *Sticks and Scones,* p. 1357; November 15, 2004, GraceAnne A. DeCandido, review of *Double Shot,* p. 564; March 15, 2006, Stephanie Zvirin, review of *Dark Tort,* p. 30; September 15, 2007, Mark Knoblauch, review of *Sweet Revenge,* p. 40.

Gazette (Colorado Springs, CO), October 17, 2007, Teresa J. Farney, review of *Sweet Revenge.*

Kirkus Reviews, July, 1990, review of *Catering to Nobody,* p. 968; June 15, 1992, review of *Dying for Chocolate,* p. 748; August 15, 1994, review of *The Last Suppers,* p. 1086; September 15, 1995, review of *Killer Pancake,* p. 1310; August 1, 1996, review of *The Main Corpse,* p. 1098; August 15, 1997, review of *The Grilling Season,* p. 1261; February 1, 2000, review of *Tough Cookie,* p. 151; October 1, 2004, review of *Double Shot,* p. 941; February 15, 2006, review of *Dark Tort,* p. 163; August 1, 2007, review of *Sweet Revenge.*

Library Journal, May 15, 1998, Juleigh Muirhead Clark, review of *The Grilling Season,* p. 132; October 1, 2004, Jennifer Burek Pierce, review of *Double Shot,* p. 65.

New York Times Book Review, November 7, 2004, Dwight Garner, review of *Double Shot,* p. 28.

People, September 30, 1996, Cynthia Sanz, "Murder on the Menu," p. 34; November 8, 2004, Janice Nimura, review of *Double Shot,* p. 59.

Publishers Weekly, June 29, 1990, Sybil Steinberg, review of *Catering to Nobody,* p. 89; June 22, 1992, review of *Dying for Chocolate,* p. 48; September 20, 1993, review of *The Cereal Murders,* p. 64; September 5, 1994, review of *The Last Suppers,* p. 96; August 28, 1995, review of *Killer Pancake,* p. 105; July 22, 1996, review of *The Main Corpse,* p. 228; July 7, 1997, review of *The Grilling Season,* p. 53; August 17, 1998, review of *Prime Cut,* p. 51; February 21, 2000, review of *Tough Cookie,* p. 69; March 12, 2001, review of *Sticks and Scones,* p. 66; September 13, 2004, Melissa Mia Hall, "Cold (and Bloody) Catering," interview with Diane Mott Davidson, p. 61, and review of *Double Shot,* p. 61; March 6, 2006, review of *Dark Tort,* p. 47; July 30, 2007, review of *Sweet Revenge,* p. 54.

School Library Journal, March, 1994, Pam Spencer, review of *The Cereal Murders,* p. 246.

Washington Post Book World, March 26, 2000, Maureen Corrigan, review of *Tough Cookie,* p. 13.

ONLINE

BookBrowser, http://www.bookbrowser.com/ (January 24, 1998), Harriet Klausner, review of *The Grilling Season;* (March 8, 1998) Harriet Klausner, reviews of *Killer Pancake* and *The Main Corpse;* (January 1, 2000) Harriet Klausner, review of *Tough Cookie;* (May 4, 2002) Harriet Klausner, review of *Chopping Spree.*

Bookreporter.com, http://www.bookreporter.com/ (June 4, 2007), Roz Shea, review of *Tough Cookie;* Debbie Ann Weiner, review of *Sticks and Scones;* (August 25, 2008) Marge Fletcher, review of *Sweet Revenge.*

Diane Mott Davidson Home Page, http://www.diane mottdavidson.com (August 25, 2008).

Mostly Fiction, http://www.mostlyfiction.com/ (January 16, 2005), Shannon Bloomstran, review of *Double Shot.*

Mystery Reader, http://www.themysteryreader.com/ (June 4, 2007), Susan Scribner, review of *The Grilling Season;* Eleanor Mikucki, review of *Sticks and Scones.**

* * *

de BERNIERES, Louis 1954-
(Louis de Bernières)

PERSONAL: Born December 8, 1954, in London, England; son of Reginald Piers Alexander (a charity director) and Jean (a homemaker) de Berniere-Smart. *Education:* Victoria University of Manchester, B.A. (with honors), 1977; Leicester Polytechnic, postgraduate certificate in education, 1981; University of London, M.A. (with distinction), 1985. *Hobbies and other interests:* Playing classical and flamenco guitar.

ADDRESSES: Home—South Norfolk, England.

CAREER: Writer. Landscape gardener in Surrey, England, 1972-73; schoolteacher and cowboy in Colombia, 1974; mechanic, 1980; former teacher in London, England, beginning 1981. *Military service:* British Army, officer cadet at Sandhurst, 1973-74.

AWARDS, HONORS: Commonwealth Writers prize, 1991 and 1992; Lannan Literary Award, 1995; *Captain Corelli's Mandolin* was voted one of Britain's twenty-one best-loved novels by the British public as part of the BBC's The Big Read, 2003; shortlist, Whitebread Novel Award and Commonwealth Writers Prize, 2005, both for *Birds without Wings;* shortlist, Costa Novel Award, 2008, for *A Partisan's Daughter.*

WRITINGS:

NOVELS; EXCEPT AS NOTED

Corelli's Mandolin, Pantheon Books (New York, NY), 1994, published in England as *Captain Corelli's Mandolin,* Secker & Warburg (London, England), 1994.
Sunday Morning at the Centre of the World: A Play for Voices, Vintage (London, England), 2001.
Birds without Wings, Knopf (New York, NY), 2004.
A Partisan's Daughter, Knopf (New York, NY), 2008.

SHORT STORIES

Labels, illustrated by Christopher Wormell, One Horse Press (London, England), 1993.
A Day Out for Mehmet Erbil, Tatler Publications (London, England), 1999.
Gunter Weber's Confession, Tartarus Press (North Yorkshire, England), 2001.
Red Dog, illustrated by Alan Baker, Pantheon Books (New York, NY), 2001.
Notwithstanding: English Village Stories, Harvill Secker (London, England), 2009.

"LATIN AMERICAN TRILOGY"

The War of Don Emmanuel's Nether Parts, Secker & Warburg (London, England), 1990, Morrow (New York, NY), 1991.

Señor Vivo and the Coca Lord, Morrow (New York, NY), 1991.
The Troublesome Offspring of Cardinal Guzman, Morrow (New York, NY), 1994.

ADAPTATIONS: Captain Corelli's Mandolin was adapted for film by Shawn Slovo, 2001, and featured Nicolas Cage and Penelope Cruz in the lead roles; *Birds without Wings* was adapted as an audio book for Books on Tape, 2004.

SIDELIGHTS: In his novels, English writer Louis de Bernieres has developed his own brand of magical realism featuring little-known historical incidents and locations far from the mainstream. He told *CA* that he seeks to explore "issues of freedom, power, and ideology" through his writings. His magical realism moves "between vividly rendered incidents that stay within the confines of credibility, pastiches of anthropological and travel writing, and evocations of preternatural events and entities," observed Nicolas Tredell in *Contemporary Novelists.* The people of villages that do not appear on any maps of South America or of Greek islands overrun by World War II Axis powers—wealthy landowners, peasants, members of the military, guerrillas, drug lords, priests and defrocked priests, saints and sinners—mingle with ghosts, resurrected conquistadors, and frolicking dolphins. This approach enables de Bernieres "to engage with major issues of the 20th century—in particular, political and religious corruption and oppression—while retaining a keen perception of the pleasures of life, a sense of humor, a tempered anger, and a graceful utopianism," Tredell noted. Although the magical realistic style is not typically associated with mainstream English literature, de Bernieres's version is not a pale imitation. Tredell wrote: "His actual knowledge of the area whose literature, in its magical-realistic incarnation, he was colonizing . . . prevented this work from ever quite becoming cheap."

The War of Don Emmanuel's Nether Parts tells of a conflict in an unnamed South American country between wealthy Dona Constanza Evans and some villagers, represented by British landowner Don Emmanuel, that becomes a minor revolution. Dona Constanza Evans wants to divert a river critical to the villagers, one which Don Emmanuel uses to wash his nether parts, so that she can keep her swimming pool filled. "The novel's pace is brisk," wrote Susan Lowell in the *New York Times Book Review,* adding: "Farcical incidents alternate with graphic descriptions of torture, ribald sex scenes with tender love stories, political satire with supernatural events." These strong farcical elements set de Bernieres apart from others writing in the same genre. As Lowell suggested: "He is funnier than most magical realists, and more hopeful—perhaps too optimistic, in spite of the grimness of his political and military satire."

De Bernieres continues what has become known as his "Latin American Trilogy" with the 1991 *Señor Vivo and the Coca Lord,* an "audacious story of drug trafficking, corruption, love and murder," according to a *Publishers Weekly* reviewer. The author sets his tale in an unnamed South American country very much resembling Colombia, where de Bernieres lived and worked for a time. The novel features Dionisio Vivo, a professor of philosophy who manages to make public the wrongdoings of the country's coca cartel via a series of letters to the editor, while also avoiding assassination attempts. The policeman Ramon, a friend of Vivo's, is not so fortunate, however, nor is the professor's sweetheart who is brutally raped by the drug lord El Jerarca's minions. But Vivo, another of de Bernieres's magical realist characters (he walks in the company of two jaguars and is able to talk to animals), gets his revenge in a series of incidents that are, according to the *Publishers Weekly* contributor "by turns ribald, surreal, horrific, uproarious and tragic." Reviewing the novel in the *New York Times Book Review,* Anne Whitehouse noted de Bernieres's debt to the magical realist author Gabriel Garcia Marquez, but added that "this is a wholly original book, with a richly developed narrative, eccentric characters and vivid descriptions spiked with thought-provoking epigrams." Whitehouse went on to term *Señor Vivo and the Coca Lord* "amusing, terrifying and ultimately sobering."

In *The Troublesome Offspring of Cardinal Guzman,* a self-absorbed president and a laissez-faire military have left a power vacuum in de Bernieres's unnamed South American country. The vacuum is filled by Cardinal Guzman. Guzman "is a once-decent man corrupted my money and power, whose uncharacteristic attempt to reform national morality produces a crusade led by a pious fanatic and conducted by loot-happy brutes," explained Phoebe-Lou Adams in the *Atlantic Monthly.* "As in its predecessors . . . the improbable characters populating *The Troublesome Offspring of Cardinal Guzman* interact in ways that are never predictable and are often truly weird," James Polk observed in the *New York Times Book Review.* Adams pointed out that while "the details of the action are wildly fanciful, comically

grotesque, mercilessly savage, and altogether unpredictable," she believed that "the author's satirical commentary hits targets well beyond the confines of South America." In Polk's estimation, de Bernieres's unusual story just takes on a classic theme in a new way. "What we have here is the age-old fight between good and evil. . . . Taking more than a page from Gabriel Garcia Marquez (who has obviously taught him a great deal)," commented the reviewer, "Mr. de Bernieres . . . comes down hard on the side of good times and fornication." According to a reviewer for *Publishers Weekly:* "As the novel works to a dramatic climax, readers will join the author in rooting for the life affirming joyousness of [the village of] Cochadebajo, which is skillfully contrasted with the Cardinal's evil nature."

"Eccentric and larger-than-life characters, scenes of bloody horror and grotesque comedy" also characterize *Corelli's Mandolin,* according to Adams in another *Atlantic Monthly* review. In this case, however, de Bernieres sets his novel in a real place in the midst of an actual historical event. During World War II, the Greek island of Cephallonia was occupied by Benito Mussolini's Italians and Adolf Hitler's Nazis. The occupation and the tragic events that took place because of it have had lasting effects on the people of Cephallonia. The author explores these effects through the lives of Dr. Iannis, his daughter Pelagia, her fisherman fiancé, and the Italian captain, Antonio Corelli, with whom she has an affair. Tredell wrote in *Contemporary Novelists:* "De Bernieres dramatizes both the cruelties of the conflict and the possibilities of transcending them through love." In what *New York Times Book Review* contributor W.S. Di Piero called "a high-spirited historical romance," de Bernieres demonstrates that he "understands that history is not only a set of actions but also a style of reporting actions." Di Piero explained: "He builds *Corelli's Mandolin* out of different kinds of reports, composing entire chapters from letters, monologues, memoirs, speeches, excerpts from Dr. Iannis's history, imaginary dialogues, bits of mythography and, in one instance, a propaganda pamphlet." The love story unfolds against a backdrop of reports of an Italian occupation giving way to brutal Nazi domination, that includes a German massacre of its Italian allies.

Corelli's Mandolin continues the story of the island and the lovers long after the war has ended, but according to Di Piero, after the World War II years, "the novel loses its momentum. . . . The set pieces can be stunning, but the narrative tissue binding them becomes increasingly lumpy or thinned out." A *Publishers Weekly* contributor commented: "Swinging between antic ribaldry and criminal horror, between corrosive satire and infinite sorrow, this soaring novel glows with a wise humanity that is rare in contemporary fiction."

De Bernieres followed *Corelli's Mandolin* with *Red Dog,* a book of fifteen related tales focusing on an Australian sheepdog. The dog's name is Tally Ho, but he is referred to as Red Dog by the locals who work in the iron and salt mines of the stories. The tales related by de Bernieres are based on the legends surrounding the real-life Tally Ho, who was memorialized with a bronze statue in Australia. In his fictionalized account, the author presents a dog known for farting and roaming around the outback making friends. Eventually being adopted by a bus driver for the mineworkers, the dog becomes a fixture on the bus with his own seat. When Red Dog is shot, the locals band together to raise the veterinarian fees needed to bring him back to health. Writing in the *Spectator,* Sandra Howard noted that the "story is presented in a fictional form and designed, it would seem from its youthfully doggy style, to captivate all ages, even preteens." In a review in *Booklist,* Benjamin Segedin called the stories a "delightful collection."

The author's next book, *Sunday Morning at the Centre of the World: A Play for Voices,* was originally a radio play and focuses on the author's neighbors in the Earlsfield area of London. The narrator provides profiles of the locals and they, in turn, provide their own input on the neighborhood and each other in the form of a dialogue. Howard, once again writing in the *Spectator,* noted: "All the voices spoke to me. . . . I found this little play for voices beautifully readable, tender and poetic."

De Bernieres returns to the theme of war and its impact on peoples' lives in his novel *Birds without Wings.* This time the author focuses on the ways in which World War I led to the dissolution of the Ottoman Empire and the effects of the war on the people living in a small Turkish village. Although the people are of different religions and backgrounds, they live together relatively peacefully until 1914, when the war breaks out. The conflict leads to various discriminations as the empire crumbles in the late teens through the 1920s: Greek Orthodox Christians are exiled, and the Turks launch the brutal but little-known Armenian genocide. Writing in *Time International,* James Inverne commented: "The main plot, such as it is, is the violent sundering of these people, who had considered themselves simply Ot-

tomans, into two fiercely nationalistic camps." In a review in the *Library Journal,* Mark Andre Singer wrote: "This novel emphasizes the brutalities and stupidities of modern warfare." Singer went on to note that the book includes "vivid characterization, wry humor, believable bawdiness, pathos, and trenchant observations."

In his 2008 novel, *A Partisan's Daughter,* de Bernieres tells an unlikely love story. The novel is set in London during the winter of 1978 to 1979, the period the English call the "winter of discontent," a time of unrest with England's labor unions as a result of government efforts to impose a wage freeze to battle inflation. Numerous unions brought their members out on strike during these months, including the garbage or refuse collectors, which resulted in smelly chaos in urban centers such as London. The book features two main characters: Chris, middle aged and lonely, disliking his job as a pharmaceutical salesman as much as he does his largely loveless marriage, and Roza, a young refugee from Serbia and one of hundreds of squatters in condemned buildings in the city. Chris initially mistakes Roza for a prostitute, though she is not. It is unclear, but she may indeed have once been a prostitute. The book is told in retrospect by Chris, long after the fact when he is in old age and wondering about the events of that winter.

The two meet one day when Chris spots her from his car and, thinking she is a prostitute, stops and propositions her. She is amused by the suggestion, it seems, and accepts a lift from him to her squat in the basement of an old house. There, nursing cups of black coffee, the couple initiates one of numerous times together, the chain-smoking Roza entertaining him Scheherazade-like, with stories from her life in Yugoslavia. Chris learns that she is the daughter of a savage partisan who fought with Tito, who, in 1978, was still the head of the shaky alliance of Balkan countries called Yugoslavia. But the seams are beginning to show in this increasingly unwilling alliance of nations. A mathematics student at Zagreb University, Roza seemed, as she relates to Chris, to be on the road to academic success. But she wanted none of the safe life. Out of curiosity and perhaps spite, she seduced her own father and then left him guilt-ridden and miserable. She managed to get to England, lived for a time with a man she refused to marry, and then became a hostess in a Soho club. She was kidnapped for four days by a mobster, raped repeatedly and tortured. Suddenly her decision to flee her homeland did not seem so smart to her. All the while

Chris sits in her kitchen, listening to her tales throughout that winter, trying to forget his own wife whom he terms the "Great White Loaf." Chris tells the reader at the outset that he is not the type to go to prostitutes, but that is exactly what he hopes is happening; and that he will soon be able to have a sampling of all that Roza is telling him about her sexual life. He even saves up money surreptitiously to pay her. As if dreading the fact that Chris might grow bored with her tales, Roza fabricates ever more fanciful stories of sexual exploits. As a *Kirkus Reviews* contributor noted, Roza "is a gifted liar, and the sexually stunning life force of Chris's wildest dreams." "The solace the characters seek in one another slowly blurs into something deeper, obscuring the lines between lust and love," noted William Lee Adams in a *Time International* review of *A Partisan's Daughter*. Adams further observed: "It's made clear from the start that Chris and Roza's relationship will not last—and their separation resonates with the sorrow of what could have been." Writing in the *New York Times Book Review,* Liesl Schillinger provided a key to the ultimate tragedy: "Blinded by his fantasy of her exoticism, clueless as a schoolboy, Chris fails to notice their commonality, fails to consider that he might represent a fantasy to [Roza]."

This sixth novel from de Bernieres earned both critical approbation and acclaim. Those who had a negative evaluation of the work pointed to such aspects as unlikable protagonists, incredible plot, and a story that goes nowhere. Thus, the *Kirkus Reviews* contributor felt that de Bernieres "tests his devoted readership's patience again" with this "malodorous turkey." Writing for London's *Daily Telegraph,* David Robson called *A Partisan's Daughter* a "sour, charmless book," as well as "still-born." Chitra Ramaswamy, writing for *Scotland on Sunday,* complained of the "unbelievably" unlikely way in which the story begins and of the baseness of Chris. Noting that Chris's attention to Roza's storytelling is supposed to be "touching, sweet even," Ramaswamy went on to comment: "I spent most of my time willing her to get away from him."

Other reviewers found much more to like in this sad and cautionary tale. Reviewing the book in the *Spectator,* Digby Durrant noted: "It's a sad tale and although I found my original disbelief difficult to suspend, by the end I was impressed, moved and touched." Similarly, a *Publishers Weekly* reviewer opined: "The conclusion is crushing, and Chris's scorching regret burns brightly to the last line." *Booklist* contributor Carol Haggas thought that de Bernieres "vividly celebrates the tantalizing

strength of stories to transform individual lives through their eternal and universal appeal." For *New Statesman* reviewer Natasha Tripney the same work was "a striking and wise novel, deceptively slight yet emotionally profound," while London *Times* writer Hugo Barnacle felt that "this sad, strange fable still has a resonance." London *Independent* contributor Christian House added further praise: "By the time I'd finished this sleek little novel I'd laughed out loud numerous times and, eventually, cried. That's as true a testimony to a book's loveliness as I know."

BIOGRAPHICAL AND CRITICAL SOURCES:

BOOKS

Contemporary Novelists, 6th edition, St. James Press (Detroit, MI), 1996.

PERIODICALS

Atlantic Monthly, March, 1994, Phoebe-Lou Adams, review of *The Troublesome Offspring of Cardinal Guzman,* p. 128; October, 1994, Phoebe-Lou Adams, review of *Corelli's Mandolin,* p. 132.

Booklist, January 1, 1994, Tom Gaughan, review of *The Troublesome Offspring of Cardinal Guzman,* p. 804; September 15, 1994, Greg Burkman, review of *Corelli's Mandolin,* p. 110; September 15, 2001, Benjamin Segedin, review of *Red Dog,* p. 191; September 15, 2008, Carol Haggas, review of *A Partisan's Daughter,* p. 26.

Bookseller, November 16, 2007, review of *A Partisan's Daughter,* p. 25; March 21, 2008, "Partisan Reviews: Another from de Bernieres Grabs the Critics," p. 36; April 11, 2008, Rose Williams, review of *A Partisan's Daughter,* p. 17.

Daily Mirror (London, England), July 3, 2008, Henry Sutton, review of *A Partisan's Daughter.*

Daily Telegraph (London, England), March 15, 2008, Toby Clements, review of *A Partisan's Daughter;* March 15, 2008, David Robson, review of *A Partisan's Daughter.*

Independent (London, England), June 25, 2004, Boyd Tonkin, "Louis de Bernieres: An accidental Hero Returns"; March 16, 2008, Christian House, review of *A Partisan's Daughter.*

Kirkus Reviews, August 1, 2001, review of *Red Dog,* p. 1046; August 15, 2008, review of *A Partisan's Daughter.*

Library Journal, January, 1994, Harold Augenbraum, review of *The Troublesome Offspring of Cardinal Guzman,* p. 158; July, 1994, Olivia Opello, review of *Corelli's Mandolin,* p. 125; September 15, 2004, Mark Andre Singer, review of *Birds without Wings,* p. 48; September 1, 2008, Christine Perkins, review of *A Partisan's Daughter,* p. 116.

Los Angeles Times, November 9, 2008, Nick Owchar, review of *A Partisan's Daughter.*

New Statesman, April 22, 1994, Roz Kaveney, review of *Corelli's Mandolin,* p. 45; April 7, 2008, Natasha Tripney, review of *A Partisan's Daughter,* p. 60.

New York Times Book Review, March 1, 1992, Susan Lowell, review of *The War of Don Emmanuel's Nether Parts;* September 13, 1992, Anne Whitehouse, review of *Señor Vivo and the Coca Lord;* May 8, 1994, James Polk, review of *The Troublesome Offspring of Cardinal Guzman,* p. 6; June 5, 1994, review of *The Troublesome Offspring of Cardinal Guzman,* p. 29; November 13, 1994, W.S. Di Piero, review of *Corelli's Mandolin,* p. 7; December 4, 1994, review of *Corelli's Mandolin,* p. 70; November 2, 2008, Liesl Schillinger, review of *A Partisan's Daughter,* p. 16.

Publishers Weekly, May 25, 1992, review of *Señor Vivo and the Coca Lord,* p. 36; December 20, 1993, review of *The Troublesome Offspring of Cardinal Guzman,* p. 51; June 27, 1994, review of *Corelli's Mandolin,* p. 54; November 7, 1994, review of *Captain Corelli's Mandolin,* p. 39; August 4, 2008, review of *A Partisan's Daughter,* p. 43.

Scotland on Sunday (Edinburgh, Scotland), March 2, 2008, Chitra Ramaswamy, review of *A Partisan's Daughter,* p. 1.

Spectator, April 16, 1994, Cressida Connolly, review of *Corelli's Mandolin,* p. 37; October 13, 2001, Sandra Howard, review of *Red Dog* and *Sunday Morning at the Centre of the World: A Play for Voices,* p. 59; March 15, 2008, Digby Durrant, review of *A Partisan's Daughter,* p. 52.

Times (London, England), March 7, 2008, Sarah Vine, review of *A Partisan's Daughter;* March 9, 2008, Hugo Barnacle, review of *A Partisan's Daughter.*

Time International, July 19, 2004, James Inverne, review of *Birds without Wings,* p. 55; April 21, 2008, William Lee Adams, review of *A Partisan's Daughter,* p. 6.

Times Literary Supplement, April 8, 1994, David Horspool, review of *Captain Corelli's Mandolin,* p. 21.

ONLINE

Blogcritics, http://blogcritics.org/ (March 21, 2009), Maggie Ball, review of *A Partisan's Daughter.*

Louis de Bernieres Home Page, http://www.louisde bernieres.co.uk (May 19, 2009).

Morning News, http://themorningnews.org/ (May 19, 2009), Kate Schlegel, review of *A Partisan's Daughter.*

New Zealand Listener Online, http://www.listener.co.nz/ (April 5, 2008), Elspeth Sandys, review of *A Partisan's Daughter.*

Seattle Times Online, http://seattletimes.nwsource.com/ (May 19, 2009), Valerie Ryan, review of *A Partisan's Daughter.**

*   *   *

DENT, Grace 1973-

PERSONAL: Born 1973, in Carlisle, England; married. *Education:* Stirling University, B.A.

ADDRESSES: Home—London, England. *E-mail*—worldoflather@hotmail.com.

CAREER: Author and journalist. *Marie Claire* (magazine), London, England, worked as editorial assistant; freelance writer and journalist. *Culture Show* (television program aired by British Broadcasting Corp.), presenter; guest on other British television programs.

WRITINGS:

Curse of the Mega-boobed Bimbos (young adult novel), Puffin (London, England), 2006.
Diary of a Snob (young adult novel), Hodder Children's Books (London, England), 2009.

"LBD" YOUNG ADULT NOVEL SERIES

LBD: It's a Girl Thing, Putnam (New York, NY), 2003.
LBD: The Great Escape, Puffin (New York, NY), 2004.
LBD: Live and Fabulous!, Putnam (New York, NY), 2006.

LBD: Friends Forever!, Putnam (New York, NY), 2006.

"DIARY OF A CHAV" YOUNG ADULT NOVELS

Trainers v. Tiaras, Hodder Children's Books (London, England), 2007, published as *Diary of a Chav: A Novel*, Little, Brown and Co. (New York, NY), 2008, published as *Diva without a Cause*, Little, Brown and Co. (New York, NY), 2009.

Slinging the Bling, Hodder Children's Books (London, England), 2007, published as *Posh and Prejudice*, Little, Brown and Co. (New York, NY), 2009.

Too Cool for School, Hodder Children's Books (London, England), 2008.

Shiraz BW: Lost in Ibiza; The Ibiza Diaries, Hodder Children's Books (London, England), 2008.

Shiraz BW: Fame and Fortune; The Fame Diaries, Hodder Children's Books (London, England), 2008.

Shiraz BW: Keeping It Real; The Real Diaries, Hodder Children's Books (London, England), 2009.

Author of *"World of Lather,"* a soap opera column for *Guardian TV Guide* (London, England), and *"Big Brother,"* a column in *Radio Times*. Television scripts include an episode of the British television series *Screenwipe*, March 2, 2006. Contributor of articles and columns to periodicals, including *CosmoGirl, More!, Glamour, Cosmopolitan, Marie Claire*, and London *Daily Mirror*.

SIDELIGHTS: Grace Dent is a British journalist, columnist, and critic whose work has appeared in periodicals ranging from the London *Guardian* to *Cosmopolitan* and *Glamour* to popular teen magazines. Her career as a roving reporter has enabled her to engage in unusual activities ranging from driving a Formula One race car and taking hunting and taxidermy lessons to lacing up her skates and auditioning for a British touring show on ice.

While she was growing up, Dent wanted to be a novelist, and this dream finally came true in 2003 with the publication of *LBD: It's a Girl Thing*. The first installment in the "LBD" series, *It's a Girl Thing* focuses on flirtatious Claude, overachieving Fleur, and "totally hip" Ronnie, Les Bambinos Dangereuses (the "LBD" of the title). As readers meet them, the girls are fourteen years old going on twenty-one, dealing with typical teen frustrations. When their "totally unreasonable" respec-

tive parents refuse to allow them to attend the upcoming Astlebury Music Festival, the three friends decide to do the next best thing: stage their own music festival at their school. With the permission of the Blackwell School headmaster and armed with cell phones and computers, Claude, Fleur, and Ronnie begin to organize the Blackwell Live, while romance, heartbreak, and temperamental but appealing boy musicians fuel their efforts. As narrated by Ronnie, *LBD: It's a Girl Thing* was cited for its similarity to novels by Louise Rennison and Ann Brashares. Ilene Cooper wrote in *Booklist* that Dent serves up "a fun, if derivative" reading experiences. The first "LBD" novel "is a delightful read," concluded *School Library Journal* contributor Janet Hilbun, adding that the novel "easily makes the transition from England to America."

The adventures of the three LBD's continue in *LBD: Live and Fabulous!*, in which the trio has grown a year older but remains as entertaining as before. Now fifteen, Claude, Fleur, and Ronnie have finally made it to Astlebury, with Fleur's older sister as their chaperone. In *LBD: Friends Forever!* the girls have aged yet another year, and now they seem to be somewhat out of step with one another. In the hope that they can repair their friendship, Ronnie, Claude, and Fleur decided to find summer jobs as waitresses at a fancy resort hotel that will plant them within striking range of a popular beach party. "Lovers of guilty-pleasure reading will hit the jackpot," Anita L. Burkham wrote in her *Horn Book* review of *LBD: Live and Fabulous!*, as Dent shares "the adventures, misadventures, and complete-and-utter-wish-fulfillment-fantasies-come-true" of her likable heroines. In *School Library Journal*, Catherine Ensley noted Dent's "wildly sarcastic wit," adding that *LBD: Friends Forever!* is a "fast-paced, plot-driven page-turner."

Dent initiated another young adult series with "Diary of a Chav." The series features teenager Shiraz Bailey Wood of Essex in England, who is a self-proclaimed "chav:" charming, hilarious, articulate and vibrant. To most people, *chav* is a British slang term that denigrates working-class people for aping American street fashions (in Shiraz's case, for example, her usual uniform of tracksuit and hoop earrings), but Shiraz has turned the insult into something positive. The series debuted in 2007 with *Trainers v. Tiaras* (published in the United States, somewhat confusingly, as *Diary of a Chav* in hardback and as *Diva without a Cause* in paperback). In this novel Shiraz, the daughter of a working-class family, has developed a crush on Wesley Barrington

Baines II, but is otherwise quite bored with life. She wanted an iPod for Christmas but only received a diary, so she begins recording her thoughts about life within its pages. Shiraz longs to leave Essex, her pregnant sister, her dysfunctional family, and her overweight dog, and move to London. Then a new English teacher comes to Mayflower Academy. Miss Brackett pulls Shiraz out of her torpor and prompts her to begin thinking of her future. Shiraz also begins to see that, if some of her supposed "chav" qualities could be left behind, she might be able to improve her relationships with the people around her. In her *School Library Journal* review of this volume, Heather E. Miller observed that "Shiraz is a witty and amusing narrator, and there are some laugh-out-loud moments." A *Kirkus Reviews* writer called the novel "Hilarious and unflinching"

In the second book of the series, *Slinging the Bling* (published as *Posh and Prejudice* in the United States), Shiraz is surprised by her end-of-term test results and decides that maybe she has some brainpower after all. Instead of being satisfied with a miserable job at the local "greasy spoon" restaurant, she hopes for a place in college. She decides to sign up for the Center for Excellence at Mayflower Academy, otherwise known as Superchav Academy because of its mostly working-class student population. Thus, she and best friend Carrie enter the Center the following term and make some interesting new friends, most of whom expect to attend college. The series has added new volumes on a regular basis, growing in size as Shiraz herself grows up.

BIOGRAPHICAL AND CRITICAL SOURCES:

PERIODICALS

Booklist, November 15, 2003, Ilene Cooper, review of *LBD: It's a Girl Thing,* p. 606.

Bulletin of the Center for Children's Books, November, 2003, Karen Coats, review of *LBD: It's a Girl Thing,* p. 98.

Horn Book, March-April, 2005, Anita L. Burkham, review of *LBD: Live and Fabulous!,* p. 199.

Kirkus Reviews, August 15, 2003, review of *LBD: It's a Girl Thing,* p. 107; February 1, 2005, review of *LBD: Live and Fabulous!,* p. 176; September 15, 2008, review of *Trainers v. Tiaras.*

Kliatt, March, 2005, Myrna Marler, review of *LBD: Live and Fabulous!,* p. 10; September, 2003, Claire Rosser, review of *LBD: It's a Girl Thing,* p. 7.

Observer (London, England), May 25, 2003, review of *LBD: It's a Girl Thing,* p. 17.

Publishers Weekly, September 22, 2003, review of *LBD: It's a Girl Thing,* p. 105.

School Librarian, winter, 2003, review of *LBD: It's a Girl Thing,* p. 210; spring, 2008, Eileen Armstrong, review of *Slinging the Bling,* p. 50.

School Library Journal, December, 2003, Janet Hilbun, review of *LBD: It's a Girl Thing,* p. 148; March, 2005, Kelly Czarnecki, review of *LBD: Live and Fabulous!,* p. 210; October, 2006, Catherine Ensley, review of *LBD: Friends Forever!,* p. 150; December 1, 2008, Heather E. Miller, review of *Trainers v. Tiaras,* p. 122.

Voice of Youth Advocates, October, 2003, review of *LBD: It's a Girl Thing,* p. 303; April, 2005, Caitlin Augusta, review of *LBD: Live and Fabulous!,* p. 37; December, 2008, Geri Diorio and Lucy Freeman, review of *Trainers v. Tiaras,* p. 432.

Washington Post Book World, July 9, 2006, Elizabeth Ward, review of *LBD: Friends Forever!,* p. 11.

ONLINE

LBD Web site, http://www.lbditsagirlthing.com (June 5, 2009).

Pop Syndicate, http://www.popsyndicate.com/ (November 13, 2008), Bella Phen, review of *Trainers v. Tiaras.*

Trashionista, http://www.trashionista.com/ (July 2, 2008), author interview.*

* * *

DOUGLAS, Carole Nelson 1944-

PERSONAL: Born November 5, 1944, in Everett, WA; daughter of Arnold Peter (a fisherman) and Agnes Olga (a teacher) Nelson; married Sam Douglas (an artist), November 25, 1967. *Education:* College of St. Catherine, B.A., 1966. *Hobbies and other interests:* Graphic design, designing and making silversmithed and strung jewelry, collecting fashion prints.

ADDRESSES: Home—TX. *Agent*—Howard Morhaim, 30 Pierrepont St., Brooklyn, NY 11201. *E-mail*—cdouglas@catwriter.com.

CAREER: Writer, novelist, editor, and journalist. *St. Paul Pioneer Press & Dispatch* (now *St. Paul Pioneer Press*), St. Paul, MN, reporter and feature writer, 1967-

83, copy and layout editor and occasional editorialist for opinion pages, 1983-84; full-time writer, 1984—. Member of board of directors, Twin Cities Local of the Newspaper Guild, 1970-72; first woman chair of annual Gridiron show, 1971; honorary member of board of directors, St. Paul Public Library Centennial, 1981.

MEMBER: Novelists, Inc., International Thriller Writers, Cat Writers' Association, Science Fiction and Fantasy Writers of America, Romance Writers of America, Sisters in Crime.

AWARDS, HONORS: Finalist in *Vogue* Prix de Paris writing competition for college seniors, 1966; Page One Award from the Newspaper Guild of the Twin Cities, 1969, 1971, 1972, 1973, 1974, 1975 and 1984; Catherine L. O'Brien Award honorable mention from Stanley Home Products, Inc., for outstanding achievement in women's interest newspaper reporting, and second place newswriting award from the Minnesota Associated Press, both 1975, both for an article on destitute elderly; president's citation from the American Society of Interior Designers (Minnesota chapter), 1980, for design and home furnishing reporting; Silver Medal, Sixth Annual West Coast Review of Books, 1982, for *Fair Wind, Fiery Star;* Golden Medallion Award finalist citation from Romance Writers of America for *Fair Wind, Fiery Star,* 1982, *In Her Prime,* 1983, *Lady Rogue,* 1984, and *The Exclusive,* 1987; Science Fiction/Fantasy Award from *Romantic Times Online,* 1984; Science Fiction Award from *Romantic Times Online* and Nebula Award nomination from Science Fiction Writers of America, both 1986, both for *Probe;* Popular Fiction Award, 1987, and Lifetime Achievement Award for Versatility, 1991, both from *Romantic Times Online;* Best Novel of Romantic Suspense citation from American Mystery Awards, 1990, and *New York Times Book Review* notable book citation, 1991, both for *Good Night, Mr. Holmes;* Cat Writers' Association Best Novel, 1995, for *Cat in a Crimson Haze,* and 2005, for *Cat in an Orange Twist,* Best Short Story, 1995, for "Coyote Peyote," 2004, for "License to Koi," and 2006, for "The Riches That There Lie"; Pioneer of the Industry Award, *Romantic Times Online,* 2008.

WRITINGS:

In Her Prime, Ballantine Books (New York, NY), 1982.
Her Own Person, Ballantine Books (New York, NY), 1982.

"SWORD AND CIRCLET" FANTASY SERIES

Six of Swords, Del Rey Books (New York, NY), 1982.
Exiles of the Rynth, Del Rey Books (New York, NY), 1984.
Keepers of Edanvant, Tor Books (New York, NY), 1987.
Heir of Rengarth, Tor Books (New York, NY), 1988.
Seven of Swords, Tor Books (New York, NY), 1989.

"PROBE" SERIES

Probe, Tor Books (New York, NY), 1985.
Counterprobe, Tor Books (New York, NY), 1988.

"IRENE ADLER" SERIES

Good Night, Mr. Holmes, Tor Books (New York, NY), 1990.
Good Morning, Irene, Tor Books (New York, NY), 1991.
Irene at Large, Tor Books (New York, NY), 1992.
Irene's Last Waltz, Forge (New York, NY), 1994.
Chapel Noir, Forge (New York, NY), 2001.
Castle Rouge, Forge (New York, NY), 2002.
Femme Fatale, Forge (New York, NY), 2003.
Spider Dance, Forge (New York, NY), 2004.

"TALISWOMAN" FANTASY SERIES

Cup of Clay, Tor Books (New York, NY), 1991.
Seed upon the Wind, Tor Books (New York, NY), 1992.

"MIDNIGHT LOUIE" MYSTERY SERIES

Catnap, Tor Books (New York, NY), 1992.
Pussyfoot, Tor Books (New York, NY), 1993.
Cat on a Blue Monday, Forge (New York, NY), 1994.
Cat in a Crimson Haze, Forge (New York, NY), 1995.
Cat in a Diamond Dazzle, Forge (New York, NY), 1996.
Cat with an Emerald Eye, Forge (New York, NY), 1996.
Cat in a Flamingo Fedora, Forge (New York, NY), 1997.
Cat in a Golden Garland, Forge (New York, NY), 1997.

Cat on a Hyacinth Hunt, Forge (New York, NY), 1998.

Cat in an Indigo Mood, Forge (New York, NY), 1999.

Cat in a Jeweled Jumpsuit, Forge (New York, NY), 1999.

Cat in a Kiwi Con, Forge (New York, NY), 2000.

Cat in a Leopard Spot, Forge (New York, NY), 2001.

Cat in a Midnight Choir, Forge (New York, NY), 2002.

Cat in a Neon Nightmare, Forge (New York, NY), 2003.

Cat in an Orange Twist, Forge (New York, NY), 2004.

Cat in a Hot Pink Pursuit, Forge (New York, NY), 2005.

Cat in a Quicksilver Caper, Forge (New York, NY), 2006.

Cat in a Red Hot Rage, Forge (New York, NY), 2007.

Cat in a Sapphire Slipper, Forge (New York, NY), 2008.

Cat in a Topaz Tango, Forge (New York, NY), 2009.

"DELILAH STREET, PARANORMAL INVESTIGATOR" SERIES

Dancing with Werewolves, Juno Books (Rockville, MD), 2007.

Brimstone Kiss, Juno Books (Rockville, MD), 2008.

"CAT AND A PLAYING CARD" SERIES

The Cat and the King of Clubs, Five Star (Unity, ME), 1999.

The Cat and the Queen of Hearts, Five Star (Unity, ME), 1999.

The Cat and the Jack of Spades, Five Star (Unity, ME), 2000.

The Cat and the Jill of Diamonds, Five Star (Unity, ME), 2000.

OTHER

Amberleigh, Jove (New York, NY), 1980.

Fair Wind, Fiery Star, Jove (New York, NY), 1981.

The Best Man, Ballantine (New York, NY), 1983.

Lady Rogue, Ballantine (New York, NY), 1983.

Azure Days and Quicksilver Nights, Bantam (New York, NY), 1985.

The Exclusive, Ballantine (New York, NY), 1986.

Crystal Days and Crystal Nights, two volumes, Bantam (New York, NY), 1990.

(Editor) *Marilyn: Shades of Blonde*, Forge (New York, NY), 1997.

(Editor) *Midnight Louie's Pet Detectives*, Forge (New York, NY), 1998.

(Editor) *White House Pet Detectives: Tales of Crime and Mystery at the White House from a Pet's-eye View*, Cumberland House (Nashville, TN), 2002.

Contributor to anthologies, including *Felonious Felines*, edited by Carol Gorman and Ed Gorman, Five Star (Unity, ME), 2000. *Fort Worth Star-Telegram*, Op Ed contributor, 1985—; author of column, *Mystery Scene* magazine, 1992-97.

SIDELIGHTS: Carole Nelson Douglas is, as she declares on her Home Page, "a literary chameleon." With dozens of books to her credit (her first novel was published in 1980), she is both a prolific and well-respected novelist and editor. As she further notes on her Home Page, Douglas writes "mainstream, mystery, thriller, high fantasy, science fiction, and romance/women's fiction," and has won and been nominated for numerous writing awards. A journalist-turned-author, Douglas is perhaps best known for her mysteries, writing popular series featuring protagonists from a feline detective to a female rival to Sherlock Holmes and a paranormal PI, among others. Though she has also written stand-alone titles, Douglas has had most success in such series which combine whimsy with detection. In all her books Douglas features strong female characters. As Douglas notes on her Home Page, she began writing her first novel, a Gothic, while still in college, because "I was fed up with the wimpy heroines of then-popular Gothics. . . . Since then, I've merrily reformed the fiction genres, reinventing women as realistic protagonists."

"An only child who often had to amuse myself, I used to think that everybody made up poems and descriptive sentences when lying on the grass and looking up at the clouds," she once explained. Spurred by her childhood creativity, Douglas studied creative writing in college. After a career as a newspaper journalist, she yearned to try her hand at fiction. In 1980, Douglas's first novel was published. "*Amberleigh,* " she once told *CA*, "was my Victorian-set update of what has been a model for so-called women's fiction since *Jane Eyre*—the Gothic. I call mine a 'post-feminist' Gothic. Submitting *Amberleigh* to publishers unsolicited resulted in getting it returned unread (because it was considered 'off market'—no sex) until playwright-author Garson Kanin volunteered to take it to his publisher." Douglas and Kanin continued their friendship and it turned out to be a nurturing one for Douglas. "I interviewed Garson on two separate occasions," she explained to *CA*, "and it was his enduring enthusiasm for my writing style that was the key to opening the door to publishing for me."

Douglas's second novel, *Fair Wind, Fiery Star*, was also an historical novel. After writing these two works, Douglas decided to try a different genre. She told *CA* that, "although fiction directed at a woman's audience is extremely lucrative to publishers right now, this very popularity, I discovered, hampers writers who want to expand on the publishers' current limitations of formula. Frustrated by the fact that 'transcending a genre,' as my books do, is considered a handicap rather than an advantage, I turned to applying my same themes in a more veiled and symbolic manner with *Six of Swords*, a fantasy that showed up on national science fiction/ fantasy top-ten-bestseller lists its first week out and is now in its thirteenth printing. . . . I find [that] both fantasy and science fiction encourage originality and imagination."

The "Sword and Circlet" fantasy series began with the publication of *Six of Swords*. Douglas once explained that these books "document the [protagonists'] magical adventures, a means of exploring relationships and the search for self. I describe the series as a 'domestic epic,' because it examines how men and women can form lasting alliances without losing their individuality and independence. By the fifth book, Irissa and Kendric's children are teenagers confronting the same relationship quandaries as their parents. One child is magically gifted; the other not. Each has a special bond with the opposite parent. Fantasy novels offer a writer a subtle means of dealing with contemporary issues like gender role reversal, animal rights, and ecology without getting on a soapbox."

With the publication of *Probe* in 1985 and *Counterprobe* in 1988, Douglas entered the science fiction market. "I want my books to appeal to a wide variety of readers on different levels, and to contain enough levels that they bear re-reading," she once remarked. "Although labeled as science fiction novels, *Probe* and *Counterprobe* are contemporary-set suspense/psychological adventure stories with a strong feminist sub-text, the kind that husbands recommend to wives, and vice versa; teenagers to parents, and vice versa. To write books that cross common ground between the sexes and span the generation gap is rewarding, especially in this pigeonholed publishing world."

With *Good Night, Mr. Holmes*, published in 1990, Douglas launched a new series of books. In this novel she expands upon the character Irene Adler, the only woman to outwit Sherlock Holmes, an event that took place in Arthur Conan Doyle's story "A Scandal in Bohemia." "This book evolved the way most of my ideas come to me: I realized that all the recent novels set in the Sherlock Holmes world were written by men," Douglas once pointed out. "Yet I had loved the stories as a youngster. My years as a newspaper reporter taught me that when men monopolize anything it's time for women to examine it from a female point of view."

Douglas wrote more novels in this series, including *Good Morning, Irene, Irene at Large,* and *Irene's Last Waltz.* "My Irene Adler is as intelligent, self-sufficient and serious about her professional and personal integrity as Sherlock Holmes, and far too independent to be anyone's mistress but her own," Douglas explained. "She also moonlights as an inquiry agent while building her performing career, so she is a professional rival of Holmes's rather than a romantic interest. Her adventures intertwine with Holmes's, but she is definitely her own woman in these novels."

Good Night, Mr. Holmes takes place a short time after Irene bests Holmes. Irene finds herself becoming romantically interested in the king of Bohemia. But all is not well with that union and, in the end, she has to outwit him as well as Holmes. By her side, Irene has assistant Nell Huxleigh, who is as steady and stable as Holmes's friend Watson.

In *Irene at Large,* Irene and Nell find themselves exiled in Paris when they happen upon an acquaintance who has been poisoned. Nell falls in love with the man, and they spend the rest of the book trying to untangle the intrigue around the attempt to murder him. Writing in the *New York Times Book Review*, Marilyn Stasio noted that in *Irene at Large* "the action never loses its jaunty, high-heeled pace."

In *Irene's Last Waltz,* Irene ventures to Prague to check on strange happenings there, as well as to meet up with her former suitor, the king of Bohemia. The pair investigate the murder of a young girl that seems to be connected to other strange happenings, including the haunting of the city by the Golem, a mythical monster. A *Kirkus Reviews* contributor called the book "the best . . . of Irene's adventures to date."

After a seven-year absence from the bookshelves, Irene returns in *Chapel Noir.* In the shadow of the newly constructed Eiffel Tower, Irene and her colleague Nell

Huxley investigate a series of brutal mutilation killings of Parisian prostitutes and women in the sewers and catacombs beneath the Paris streets. Close behind, Irene's rival, the inimitable Sherlock Holmes, conducts his own search for clues and answers. The slayings have characteristics of the notorious Jack the Ripper's handiwork, and are certainly the work of a sexual psychopath who hates women. Meanwhile, Irene's husband, barrister Godfrey Norton, comes up missing in Transylvania, and Nell is influenced by apparently supernatural forces she can't resist or understand. Rex E. Klett, writing in *Library Journal,* called the book a "vastly entertaining tale." "Douglas cleverly balances tragedy and farce in a gentle mockery of period adventure and a ruthless depiction of all-too-contemporary hatreds," commented a *Kirkus Reviews* contributor.

Irene takes up an enduring mystery for mystery buffs and investigators around the world when she tackles the subject of Jack the Ripper in *Castle Rouge.* All of Europe is on edge as it appears that the Ripper's vicious killing spree has spread across the continent. Worse, the new murders appear to be connected with a mysterious cult that performs violent sexual rituals. Irene's husband, Godfrey Norton, has disappeared, and her closest friend and secretary, Penelop Huxleigh, has been abducted, adding additional impetus to Irene's quest to solve the case. Holmes and Irene both search for clues and try to find the most likely suspect, deranged upholsterer James Kelly. Other suspects emerge, including Bram Stoker, the author of *Dracula.* The story culminates in a dank Transylvanian castle, where Holmes's old foe, Colonel Moran, along with a young Rasputin and other unsavory characters, conduct their foul rituals and hold Stoker and others hostage. Readers "who relish lots of action, including chases and close calls, will feel amply rewarded," commented a *Publishers Weekly* reviewer.

In *Spider Dance,* reported to be the final book in the "Irene Adler" series, Irene delves into her own past and seeks to uncover the identities and history of her unknown parents. At Holmes's urging, Irene investigates the background of Eliza Gilbert, a woman who died thirty years earlier but whose own past might contain a clue to the mysterious black-clad woman who abandoned Irene with a group of actors when she was a very young child. Gilbert, it turns out, was actually a notorious dancer, entertainer, and woman of loose morals, named Lola Montez. Her deathbed conversion was witnessed by an Episcopalian priest, Father Hawks, who

has recently turned up dead himself. As Irene and Nell continue to look into Gilbert's background, Holmes looks into Father Hawks's suspicious demise. In the background, Nell appears to have found a suitor in British secret agent Quentin Stanhope, and reporter Nellie Bly uncovers a scandalous baby-buying ring. The novel, like the other books in the series, stands as a "paean to women's audacity, pugnacity, and street smarts, told with frisky good humor and nicely integrated historical asides," commented a *Kirkus Reviews* critic. A *Publishers Weekly* contributor concluded: "If indeed this is the last of the series, as the author has indicated, it closes on a definite high note."

In the "Taliswoman" series, Douglas again turned to fantasy. The first novel in the series, *Cup of Clay,* focuses on Alison Carver, a journalist who lives in Minnesota. Needing a break after working on a scandalous child-abuse trial, Carver goes to her own island in a mountain lake. Her vacation takes a strange twist as she finds herself transported into another world, where she wins the Cup of Earth. She becomes the Taliswoman, empowered with skills to save the world—if she decides such a depraved world deserves to be saved. Laura Staley commented in the *Voice of Youth Advocates* that "the more serious themes of this book seem to have produced an even better story than usual."

The second book of the series, *Seed upon the Wind,* finds Carver back in the world called Veil. Her friend Rowan Firemayne blames Carver for the mysterious blight that has come over Veil. The two begin to work out their differences, and form a deeper relationship as they set out to make a powerful talisman from the ashes of Rowan's brother. They confront the danger to the world of Veil, and Alison finds that it is too similar to the evils in our own world. A *Publishers Weekly* reviewer commented that "Douglas's increasingly intricate fantasy raises disturbing issues about environmental depredations."

Douglas once wrote: "Another favorite character of mine is Midnight Louie, an eighteen-pound, crime-solving black tomcat who is the part-time narrator of a new mystery series. . . . Like many of my creations, Louie goes way back. He was a real if somewhat larger-than-life stray cat I wrote a feature story about for my newspaper in 1973." Beginning with *Catnap,* published in 1992, the "Midnight Louie" mysteries have become one of Douglas's most popular series. She refers to them as "cozy-noirs." According to Douglas's Home Page:

"Midnight Louie's turf is the sizzling asphalt-and-neon jungle of the country's hottest gambling mecca, Las Vegas—a 90's version of Damon Runyon's 1920's Broadway of gold-hearted showgirls and not-so-cold-hearted bookies. The novels contrast Midnight Louie's back-alley first-person twang with the third-person adventures of a quartet of human mystery-solvers." Chief among Louie's cohorts is Temple Barr, "a petite public relations woman . . . with a penchant for high heels." Also joining Louie in his sleuthing are C.R. Molina, a "flat-footed female police lieutenant; Matt Devine, a model-handsome crisis-hotline counselor . . . and Temple's ex-live-in-lover, the Mystifying Max, a stage magician."

Catnap follows the adventures of Temple Barr at an American Booksellers Association meeting held in Las Vegas. Midnight Louie is able to assist Barr in finding out more information about the murder of Chester Royal, a big-time publisher. A *Publishers Weekly* contributor related that "Douglas's fine-tuned sense of humor gives her tame plot enough of a spin to keep readers entertained."

In *Pussyfoot,* the second "Midnight Louie" mystery, Temple Barr finds herself once again in a murder investigation. This time she has been employed to do publicity for a competition of exotic dancers. When one of the contestants is killed, Barr goes into action, and Louie helps her find the unsavory characters involved in the scheme. A *Kirkus Reviews* contributor criticized the story, saying "dog lovers, and lovers of well-made plots and prose, need not apply." A *Publishers Weekly* reviewer, however, praised the characterization of Barr, noting that she is "a reasonably modern and liberated female."

In *Cat on a Blue Monday* not only the detective but the mystery is decidedly feline. Midnight Louie receives a warning from a psychic cat named Karma that danger threatens a group of cats. The target may be either the Las Vegas Cat Show or the many strays adopted by the elderly cat-lover Blandina Tyler. In the course of the action, a nun is pushed down a staircase to her death while a convent cat narrowly escapes crucifixion. *Cat on a Blue Monday* also introduces the hostile kitten, Midnight Louise, who is later revealed as Midnight Louie's offspring. "Louie sniffs though plenty of plausible red herrings," stated a *Publishers Weekly* reviewer, "and avoids getting himself tacked up on the church door before pointing a claw at the killer in this brisk tail [sic] that even mystery readers who don't love cats will relish."

In the award-winning *Cat in a Crimson Haze* Temple Barr is hired to make over the organized-crime-tainted image of the Crystal Phoenix Hotel to that of a family entertainment center. The subsequent shenanigans involve Temple, Midnight Louise, Matt Devine, and Lieutenant Molina in the murder of Devine's stepfather, a search for missing treasure, and the investigation of an unsolved murder from Las Vegas's past. The seafaring black cat, Three O'Clock Louie, also makes an appearance. According to a *Publishers Weekly* contributor: "This is the best Louie adventure yet, full of intricate plotting and sharp characterization. And Louie? Nine lives wouldn't be nearly enough for this dude."

Publishers Weekly reviewers have found few faults with the Midnight Louie mysteries. Commenting on *Cat in a Diamond Dazzle,* one reviewer noted that Douglas's "prose and plotting are sometimes overwrought," but added that she "tells her tale with such good humor that readers are likely to forgive her occasional excess." A reviewer of *Cat on a Hyacinth Hunt,* the ninth "Midnight Louie" novel, felt that Temple's "vacillation between her two admirers," Matt Devine and Magical Max, has become "increasingly tiresome." Rex E. Klett of *Library Journal* characterized the series as "[p]roven fare for cat fans and others."

Cat in a Midnight Choir finds Temple working to clear her magician boyfriend Mystifying Max Kinsella of suspicion in a series of vicious murders of strippers and prostitutes on the Las Vegas strip. Temple's other romantic interest, ex-priest and radio show host Matt Devine, is dodging Kitty the Cutter, a licentious sort who seeks to claim the virginity of unsullied but delectable Devine. Police detective C.R. Molina, also known as the jazz singer Carmen, struggles to nail her ex-husband—and father of a daughter he does not know he has—Rafi Nadir in the stripper murders. In the background, The Synth, an ominous cult of rogue magicians, dispenses its own brand of lethal justice to prestidigitators who reveal the ancient secrets of magic to the public at large. Meanwhile, Midnight Louie has entered into a partnership with his daughter, Midnight Louise, and the other alley cats on Twenty-Fourth Street to create feline detective agency Midnight, Inc. With this "Midnight Louie" installment, Douglas "just keeps getting better at juggling mystery, humor, and romance," observed a *Publishers Weekly* contributor. A contributor to *Kirkus Reviews* commented favorably on the "terrific cliffhanger" that ends the book, and complimented Douglas's signature wordplay as "great fun."

Cat in an Orange Twist takes Temple and Louie into the high-intensity world of high-strung designers, interior decorators, and upscale home furnishing. In her role as a public relations consultant, Temple is in charge of the opening of a trendy furniture store, Maylords, featuring the stylish modern design work of Amelia Wong. A violent, terrorist-style shooting disrupts the opening, after which Temple discovers that Amelia had received several death threats. When a body is discovered in the SUV slated to be given away as part of the opening festivities, Temple considers the possibility that the murder and mayhem might be connected to hatred and bigotry directed against homosexuals. The dead man is stellar designer Simon Foster, the life partner of her friend, choreographer Danny Dove. The series does not take itself "too seriously," observed a *Publishers Weekly* critic, who noted this "wickedly witty cozy series continues to build sexy suspense while providing liberal doses of swaggering feline whimsy."

Cat in a Hot Pink Pursuit opens with a confrontation between Temple and her sometime nemesis, detective Carmen Molina. Carmen has come to ask Temple to go undercover as a contestant on a teen reality show, *Teen Idol,* in order to help protect Carmen's thirteen-year-old daughter Mariah, also a contestant, from a stalker. In return, Carmen agrees to lay off Temple's boyfriend, Mystifying Max. Temple agrees, and creates the flamboyant punk-rock character of Xoe Chloe Ozone as cover for her presence on the show. As Temple zeroes in on the stalker menacing the teenage contestants and Midnight Louie prowls around in his unique fashion, the inevitable murders pile up, and the stakes intensify. While the investigation is underway, a complicated relationship looms between Carmen and her ex, Mariah's father, and Temple's relationship with her other suitor, Matt Devine, escalates to another level. The "indefatigable Midnight Louie series never seems to run out of steam," commented Margaret Flanagan, writing in *Booklist.* A *Publishers Weekly* reviewer called the novel "one of the stronger, leaner entries in this crime-solving cat series."

With *Cat in a Quicksilver Caper,* Louie and Temple find themselves investigating a death at a high-wire act in a new Las Vegas hotel and casino. The Russians are involved in this mystery that also involves the disappearance of a priceless heirloom from the same hotel, the Czar Alexander Scepter. In his nineteenth outing, *Cat in a Red Hot Rage,* Midnight Louie and Temple Barr again team up to prove the innocence of their landlady, Electra Lark, in a charge of murder. The victim was a member of the Red Hat Sisterhood, a group of women of a certain age who sponsor events to

show that they have not lost their energy for life. The victim happened to be an ex-wife of Electra's third husband and Electra was seen tying a purple scarf around the woman's neck; the same scarf was the murder weapon in the strangling death. Louie and Temple, with a little help from some of the Sisterhood, must work hard to find the guilty party and save Electra. A contributor for *Publishers Weekly* noted of this series addition: "Douglas's humor and keen plot twists keep this long-running series purring." Similarly, *Booklist* contributor Mary Frances Wilkens wrote: "Leave it to Louie to solve this mystery in his usual cunning manner." A *Kirkus Reviews* contributor called the book "catnip for Louie's devoted fans."

Midnight Louie returns in the 2008 *Cat in a Sapphire Slipper,* "another crazy crime-and-cat-filled romp," according to *Booklist* reviewer Jessica Moyer. Here Louie is keeping eye on Matt, Temple's newest boyfriend, at a bachelor party. Matt, as it turns out, needs the help, for the party ends up at a Nevada brothel, or "chicken ranch," as they are called, and then Matt and the others are kidnapped. Meanwhile, a dead body at the brothel complicates matters for the men, especially Matt, and in a subplot it is discovered that Temple's former lover, Mystifying Max Kinsella, is confined in a European hospital, suffering from amnesia, and not dead as she believed. Meanwhile, in his struggle to save Matt, Louie finds help from Satin, a feline lover and possible mother of his daughter, Midnight Louise, in this novel with "a fast-moving plot and lively narration," as Moyer noted. A *Publishers Weekly* reviewer commented, "Douglas explores the campy, lighter side of 'chicken ranches' at the same time she exposes their seamier aspects." And a *Kirkus Reviews* contributor concluded: "As always, Louie outshines the human cast." Matt is once again in need of saving in the 2009 series installment, *Cat in a Topaz Tango.* Temple and Matt are now engaged, and she encourages him to be part of a charity event dance contest. However, a murderer is following the tangoing celebrities, and Temple and Louie come to the rescue.

Douglas has also published a quartet of books featuring Midnight Louie, the "Cat and the Playing Card" books, which form a prequel to her "Midnight Louie" series. Beginning in 1996, Douglas's book signings for the Midnight Louie mysteries have been linked to cat adoption programs sponsored by humane societies and the American Society for the Prevention of Cruelty to Animals. Orphaned cats are available for adoption right in the bookstore, and those who take one home receive a free Midnight Louie paperback.

In 2007 Douglas initiated a new series featuring a paranormal investigator named Delilah Street. The series opener, *Dancing with Werewolves,* is set in the new millennium a decade after the world discovers that such supernatural creatures as vampires, witches, and werewolves are in fact all too real. Delilah, formerly a paranormal investigative reporter for a sleepy Kansas television, has quit her job and found a new one on *CSI Las Vegas.* In Sin City she falls for an ex-FBI agent, Ric Montoya, who is able to discover dead bodies with a dowsing stick. Las Vegas is a town basically run by a werewolf combine and chock full of undead as well as formerly dead stars resurrected through magic. A reviewer for *Internet Bookwatch* termed *Dancing with Werewolves* "a smartly written, plot driven, original novel that deftly combines the elements of fantasy, mystery, and romance." Further praise for this debut came from a *Publishers Weekly* reviewer who called the same novel a "fantastic first of a new paranormal series," and further commented: "Readers will eagerly await the sequel."

The sequel, *Brimstone Kiss,* was published in 2008. A *Publishers Weekly* reviewer declared that this second novel featuring Delilah Street is "filled with kisses and kick-ass action." Here Delilah takes on her first case, with a little help from Ric, who has found some half-century-old murder victims. One of the victims, a young girl, returns as a ghost to accuser her own father, a werewolf mobster, of her murder. Howard Hughes is a vastly wealthy vampire and hires Delilah to get to the bottom of the murders. "Douglas's dishy style compliments the twisty plot," concluded the *Publishers Weekly* reviewer. Likewise, Kimberly Swan, writing for *Darque Reviews* Web site, felt that *Brimstone Kiss* "has all of the dark, dangerous, and unique paranormal elements readers seek, along with the passion, love and exciting temptations that add spice to the mix."

Reflecting on her work, Douglas once told *CA:* "Because of my undergraduate major in theater, I'm especially interested in fiction that captures and affects an audience with the immediacy of a stage play. For this reason, I prefer working in 'popular' fiction forms and find nothing unusual in the idea of fiction being 'entertaining' as well as enlightening. . . . I like to say that what I write is principally entertainment, but that the best entertainment always has principles." She went on to point out that "in effect, I write on a fine line between 'serious' fiction on one hand and sneered-at 'popular' fiction on the other. It is not a particularly comfortable position, but somebody has to do it;

otherwise we will have nothing but serious writers that nobody knows how to read and popular writers that nobody ought to read."

BIOGRAPHICAL AND CRITICAL SOURCES:

BOOKS

St. James Guide to Crime and Mystery Writers, 4th edition, St. James Press (Detroit, MI), 1996.
St. James Guide to Fantasy Writers, St. James Press (Detroit, MI), 1996.

PERIODICALS

Booklist, September 15, 1998, Barbara Duree, review of *Midnight Louie's Pet Detectives,* p. 203; July, 2000, Jenny McLarin, review of *Felonious Felines,* p. 2012; April 1, 2003, Ilene Cooper, review of *Cat in a Neon Nightmare,* p. 1382; September 1, 2003, review of *Femme Fatale,* p. 68; December 15, 2004, Margaret Flanagan, review of *Spider Dance,* p. 710; May 1, 2005, Margaret Flanagan, review of *Cat in a Hot Pink Pursuit,* p. 1520; June 1, 2007, Mary Frances Wilkens, review of *Cat in a Red Hot Rage,* p. 46; July 1, 2008, Jessica Moyer, review of *Cat in a Sapphire Slipper,* p. 41.
Internet Bookwatch, November 1, 2007, review of *Dancing with Werewolves.*
Kirkus Reviews, February 1, 1993, review of *Pussyfoot,* p. 101; December 15, 1993, review of *Irene's Last Waltz,* p. 1553; September 1, 2001, review of *Chapel Noir,* p. 1247; April 1, 2002, review of *Cat in a Midnight Choir,* p. 455; October 15, 2002, review of *Castle Rouge,* p. 1506; March 1, 2003, review of *Cat in a Neon Nightmare,* p. 348; December 1, 2004, review of *Spider Dance,* p. 1119; May 1, 2006, review of *Cat in a Quicksilver Caper,* p. 439; March 1, 2007, review of *Cat in a Red Hot Rage,* p. 196; July 15, 2008, review of *Cat in a Sapphire Slipper.*
Library Journal, November 1, 1997, Rex E. Klett, review of *Cat in a Golden Garland,* p. 120; February 1, 1999, review of *Cat on a Hyacinth Hunt,* p. 148; March 1, 1999, Rex E. Klett, review of *Cat in an Indigo Mood,* p. 114, and Sally Estes, review of *Cat in a Golden Garland,* p. 161; May 1, 2000, Rex E. Klett, review of *Cat in a Kiwi Con,* p. 158; October 1, 2001, Rex E. Klett, review of *Chapel Noir,* p. 146; May 1, 2002, Rex E. Klett, review of *Cat in a Midnight Choir,* p. 138.

New York Times Book Review, December 16, 1990, Marilyn Stasio, review of *Good Night, Mr. Holmes,* p. 33; August 9, 1992, Marilyn Stasio, review of *Irene at Large,* p. 20.

Publishers Weekly, January 20, 1992, review of *Catnap,* p. 49; October 19, 1992, review of *Seed upon the Wind,* p. 62; January 25, 1993, review of *Pussyfoot,* p. 81; January 17, 1994, review of *Irene's Last Waltz,* p. 412; April 11, 1994, review of *Cat on a Blue Monday,* p. 58; April 10, 1995, review of *Cat in a Crimson Haze,* p. 57; April 8, 1996, review of *Cat in a Diamond Dazzle,* p. 59; September 16, 1996, review of *Cat with an Emerald Eye,* p. 74; April 21, 1997, review of *Cat in a Flamingo Fedora,* p. 64; October 20, 1997, Robert Dahlin, "This Promotion Is the Cat's Meow," p. 46; October 27, 1997, review of *Cat in a Golden Garland,* p. 55; June 15, 1998, review of *Cat on a Hyacinth Hunt,* p. 46; March 15, 1999, review of *Cat in an Indigo Mood,* p. 50; November 1, 1999, review of *Cat in a Jeweled Jumpsuit,* p. 76; April 24, 2000, review of *Cat in a Kiwi Con,* p. 65; March 26, 2001, review of *Cat in a Leopard Spot,* p. 66; September 24, 2001, review of *Chapel Noir,* p. 72; April 22, 2002, review of *Cat in a Midnight Choir,* p. 53; April 22, 2002, M.M. Hall, "PW Talks with Carole Nelson Douglas," p. 53; October 28, 2002, review of *Castle Rouge,* p. 55; April 7, 2003, review of *Cat in a Neon Nightmare,* p. 49; August 11, 2003, review of *Femme Fatale,* p. 260; July 26, 2004, review of *Cat in an Orange Twist,* p. 42; November 29, 2004, review of *Spider Dance,* p. 27; April 4, 2005, review of *Cat in a Hot Pink Pursuit,* p. 46; May 1, 2006, review of *Cat in a Quicksilver Caper,* p. 41; March 12, 2007, review of *Cat in a Red Hot Rage,* p. 41; October 22, 2007, review of *Dancing with Werewolves,* p. 41; July 7, 2008, review of *Cat in a Sapphire Slipper,* p. 41; October 20, 2008, review of *Brimstone Kiss,* p. 40.

Voice of Youth Advocates, February, 1992, review of *Cup of Clay,* p. 380.

ONLINE

Blog Critics, http://blogcritics.org/ (December 1, 2007), Katie Trattner, review of *Dancing with Werewolves.*

Carole Nelson Douglas Home Page, http://www.carolenelsondougles.com (April 15, 2009).

CatWriter.com, http://cdouglas2.home.mindspring.com/ (December 5, 2006), profile of Carole Nelson Douglas.

Crescent Blues, http://www.crescentblues.com/ (December 5, 2006), "The Nine+ Lives of Carole Nelson Douglas," interview with Carole Nelson Douglas.

Curled Up with a Good Book, http://www.curledup.com/ (April 15, 2009), Helen Hancox, review of *Dancing with Werewolves.*

Darque Reviews, http://darquereviews.blogspot.com/ (October 1, 2008), Kimberly Swan, review of *Brimstone Kiss.*

Dear Author, http://dearauthor.com/ (November 20, 2007), review of *Dancing with Werewolves.*

SciFiGuy, http://www.scifiguy.ca/ (November 7, 2008), review of *Brimstone Kiss.*

Scooper Peaks, http://scooper.wordpress.com/ (September 24, 2007), review of *Dancing with Werewolves.**

*   *   *

DOYLE, Roddy 1958-

PERSONAL: Born May 8, 1958 in Dublin, Ireland; son of Rory (a printer) and Ida (a secretary) Doyle; married; wife's name Belinda; children: Rory, Jack. *Education:* Attended University College, Dublin.

CAREER: Playwright, screenwriter, educator, and novelist. Greendale Community School, Kilbarrack, Dublin, English and geography teacher, 1980-93; full-time writer, 1993—.

AWARDS, HONORS: The Van was shortlisted for the Booker Prize, British Book Trust, 1991; Booker Prize, 1993, for *Paddy Clarke Ha Ha Ha;* W.H. Smith Children's Book of the Year Award shortlist, 2001, for *The Giggler Treatment;* honorary doctorate from Dublin City University.

WRITINGS:

NOVELS

The Commitments, Heinemann (London, England), 1988, Random House (New York, NY), 1989.

The Snapper, Secker & Warburg (London, England), 1990, Penguin (New York, NY), 1992.

The Van, Viking (New York, NY), 1991.

The Barrytown Trilogy, Secker & Warburg (London, England), 1992.

Paddy Clarke Ha Ha Ha, Secker & Warburg (London, England), 1993.

The Woman Who Walked into Doors, Viking (New York, NY), 1996.

A Star Called Henry, Viking (New York, NY), 1999.

Oh, Play That Thing, Viking (New York, NY), 2004.

Paula Spencer, Viking (New York, NY), 2006.

Mad Weekend, New Island (Dublin, Ireland), 2006.

SCREENPLAYS

(With Dick Clement and Ian La Frenais) *The Commitments* (based on the novel by Doyle), Twentieth Century-Fox, 1991.

The Snapper (based on the novel by Doyle), Miramax Films, 1993.

The Van (based on the novel by Doyle), British Broadcasting Corp. (BBC), 1996.

Famine, Crom Films, 1998.

When Brendan Met Trudy, Collins Avenue, 2000.

PLAYS

Brownbread (produced in Dublin, Ireland; also see below), Secker & Warburg (London, England), 1987.

Brownbread and War, Minerva (London, England), 1993, Penguin Books (New York, NY), 1994.

War (produced in Dublin, Ireland; also see below), Passion Machine (Dublin, Ireland), 1989.

No Messin' with the Monkeys! (play for children), produced by The Ark (Dublin, Ireland), 2005.

(With Bisi Adigun) *The Playboy of the Western World* (two-act play; based on the play by John Millington Synge), produced in Dublin, Ireland, 2007.

CHILDREN'S BOOKS

Not Just for Christmas, New Island Books (Dublin, Ireland), 1999.

The Giggler Treatment, illustrated by Brian Ajhar, Arthur A. Levine Books (New York, NY), 2000.

Rover Saves Christmas, illustrated by Brian Ajhar, Arthur A. Levine Books (New York, NY), 2001.

The Meanwhile Adventures, illustrated by Brian Ajhar, Scholastic (New York, NY), 2004.

Her Mother's Face, illustrated by Freya Blackwood, Arthur A. Levine Books (New York, NY), 2008.

OTHER

Family (television script), BBC, 1994.

Rory & Ita, Viking (New York, NY), 2002.

Wilderness (young adult), Arthur A. Levine Books (New York, NY), 2007.

The Deportees: And Other Stories, Viking (New York, NY), 2008.

Also author of screenplay *When Brendan Met Trudy,* 2001. Contributor to anthologies, including *My Favorite Year,* Witherby (London, England), 1993; *Yeats Is Dead! A Mystery by Fifteen Irish Writers,* edited by Joseph O'Connor, Knopf (New York, NY), 2001; and *Click* (for children), Arthur A. Levine Books (New York, NY), 2007.

SIDELIGHTS: Roddy Doyle's trilogy of novels about the Irish Rabbitte family, known informally as the "Barrytown trilogy," has been internationally acclaimed for wit, originality, and powerful dialogue. Each of the three books—*The Commitments, The Snapper,* and *The Van*—focuses on a single character of the large Rabbitte family who live in Barrytown, Dublin. They are "a likeable, rough, sharp-witted clan," observed Lawrence Dugan in the *Chicago Tribune.* Typical workingclass citizens, the Rabbittes are a vivacious and resilient household, lustily displaying an often ribald sense of humor. "These books are funny all the way down to their syntax," claimed Guy Mannes-Abbott in the *New Statesman & Society,* "enabling Doyle to sustain my laughter over two or three pages."

The Commitments is, perhaps, Doyle's most well-recognized work. The successful novel was adapted in 1991 into a very popular screenplay by Doyle, Dick Clement, and Ian La Frenais, and directed by award-winning filmmaker Alan Parker. In both the novel and the film, Doyle's wit and originality are evident. The main character, Jimmy Rabbitte, inspired by the rhythm and blues music of James Brown, B.B. King, and Marvin Gaye, resolves to form an Irish soul band in Dublin. He places a musicians-wanted ad in the paper: "Have you got Soul? If yes, . . . contact J. Rabbitte." And so is born the "Commitments," with Jimmy as the manager of a group which includes Imelda, a singer, and Joey "The Lips" Fagan, a musician who claims to have "jammed with the man" James Brown. "The rehearsals, as Mr. Doyle chronicles them," wrote Kinky Friedman in the *New York Times Book Review,* "are authentic, joyous, excruciating and funny as hell." Dugan, in the *Chicago Tribune,* described *The Commitments* as "a beautifully told story about the culture that absorbed the Vikings, Normans, Scots, and British now trying its luck with black America." The film version stars an all-Irish cast, including Robert Arkins, Andrew Strong, and singer Maria Doyle performing such 1960s hits as "Mustang Sally" and "In the Midnight Hour." A *People* critic reviewed the film and concluded: "The cathartic power of music has never been more graphically demonstrated."

Doyle's second novel, *The Snapper,* focuses on Sharon Rabbitte, Jimmy's older sister, who is young, unmarried, and pregnant. As Sharon refuses to reveal the identity of the father of her "snapper," her predicament has the Rabbitte household in a tizzy, and she becomes the target of humorous speculations by the Barrytown citizens. As a result of Sharon's pregnancy, relationships within the family undergo various transformations ranging from the compassionate (dad Jimmy, Sr.) to the murderous (mom Veronica), while Sharon herself tries to understand the changes within her own body. A *Los Angeles Times Book Review* critic noted that "few novels depict parent-child relationships—healthy relationships, no less—better than this one, and few men could write more sensitively about pregnancy."

Like *The Commitments, The Snapper* is written in the Irish vernacular, with little descriptive intrusion, and with an enormous sense of humor. John Nicholson in the London *Times* pointed out Doyle's "astonishing talent for turning the humdrum into high comedy" in the novel. He also singled out the characters' vernacular banter for critical praise—"the dialogue of *The Snapper* crackles with wit and authenticity." *Times Literary Supplement* critic Stephen Leslie asserted: "*The Snapper* is a worthy successor to *The Commitments.*"

Shortlisted for Britain's prestigious Booker Prize, Roddy Doyle's third Rabbitte novel, *The Van,* changes the focus to Jimmy, Sr., the Rabbitte family's ribald, fun-loving father, who has been recently laid off of work. Jimmy and his best friend, Bimbo, open a portable fast-food restaurant—Bimbo's Burgers—housed in a greasy van that is a health inspector's nightmare. The antics of the two friends running the business provide much of the hilarity of the book; for

example, they mistakenly deep-fry a diaper, serve it up to a customer like cod, and then flee—restaurant and all—from his wrath, hurling frozen fish at their victim from the back of the van. Jimmy and his friends are Irish laborers "whose idea of wit and repartee is putting on fake Mexican accents and 'burstin' their shite' at jokes about farting," wrote Anne-Marie Conway in the *Times Literary Supplement.* "*The Van* is not just a very funny book," insisted Mannes-Abbott, "it is also faultless comic writing."

Critical response toward *The Van* was enthusiastic, with many reviewers finding a special appeal in what a *Publishers Weekly* commentator called Doyle's "brash originality and humor that are both uniquely Irish and shrewdly universal." Reviewer Tim Appelo in the *Los Angeles Times Book Review* maintained that "Doyle has perfect pitch from the get-go. He can write pages of lifelike, impeccably profane dialogue without a false note or a dull fill, economically evoking every lark and emotional plunge in the life of an entire Irish family."

Doyle's next book, *Paddy Clarke Ha Ha Ha,* was awarded the prestigious Booker Prize in 1993. The novel is written from the point of view of Paddy Clarke, a ten-year-old Irish boy, whose often humorous escapades become gradually more violent and disturbing as the story progresses. John Gallagher in the *Detroit News and Free Press* commented on Doyle's effective use of a stream-of-consciousness narrative, and noted a "theme of undeserved suffering. . . . *Paddy Clarke Ha Ha Ha* matures into an unforgettable portrait of troubled youth."

In the *New York Times,* Mary Gordon established her admiration for Doyle by stating that "perhaps no one has done so much to create a new set of images for the Ireland of the late twentieth century as Roddy Doyle." Doyle's book *The Woman Who Walked into Doors* is about an abused, beaten wife who continually goes to the hospital emergency room and is never questioned by the staff, who merely "chalk [her repeat visits] up to her drinking or clumsiness or bad luck." Paula came from a family with loving, affectionate parents and three sisters, and her marriage started out with a "blissful honeymoon at the seaside." Gordon ruminates about Doyle's description of "what it's like to be beaten by your lover, the father of your children," and feels that it "is a masterpiece of virtuoso moves. Nothing is blinked; nothing is simplified." Paula finally comes to her senses when she sees her husband "looking at their daughter, not with desire . . . but with hate and a wish to annihilate. She stops being a battered wife when she becomes a protective mother."

In *A Star Called Henry,* Doyle delves into Irish history and nationalism as experienced by the book's title character, Henry Smart. "Henry is the dark horse of Irish history, Forrest Gump with a brain, and an attitude—the man cropped out of the official photographs, the boy soldier not credited for even his dirtiest work," wrote Robert Cremins in the *Houston Chronicle.* Born into poverty in the early 1900s, Henry is streetwise by the age of three, wandering the lanes and alleys with his year-old brother Victor, stealing what the pair needs to survive. His mother is weary with a bleak outlook, and his father is a one-legged bouncer at a brothel, a sometime murderer, and drop-of-the-hat brawler. Henry's single day of formal education ends with him being ousted by the head nun, but he cements a relationship with his teacher, Miss O'Shea, that will be taken up again in earnest later in life. Victor dies, his father abandons them, and he loses contact with his mother. Despite his disadvantages, Henry is clever and cunning, strikingly handsome, and able to use the brains that nature gave him. He inherits his father's wooden leg, and uses it both as a weapon and as a talisman to remind him where he came from and where he wants to go.

While still a teen, Henry joins the Irish Republican Army (IRA), doing so "because of his resentment of the squalor he grew up in, rather than any passion for nationhood," wrote Anthony Wilson-Smith in *Maclean's.* In his first combat against the British, Henry is more interested in shooting out store windows—symbols of the wealth and life he never had—than at British soldiers. At age fourteen, Henry finds himself fighting along legendary Irish revolutionaries Michael Collins, James Connolly, and Padraig Pearce in the Easter Uprising of 1916 and the occupation of the General Post Office. "The account of the 1916 Easter Uprising, the occupation of the GPO, and the bloodshed that follows must be one of the boldest and vivid descriptions of civil strife in a familiar city ever penned," observed a *Publishers Weekly* reviewer. Henry meets up again with Miss O'Shea, and the two consummate their relationship on stacks of unused stamps in the basement of the post office. They are separated after the fierce battle of Easter, 1916; Henry barely escapes with his life, and continues to rise in the ranks of the IRA. Henry and Miss O'Shea meet again—and marry—three years later, with Henry deliberately avoiding knowledge of her given name. Henry emerges from the

story as larger-than-life, a prodigy and a kind of home-grown superhero of the stature of Finn McCool. "Fact and fiction aside, historians and non-historians alike will find little not to like about Henry Smart—his confidence, his humor, his pride," wrote Clare Bose in *Europe.* "He is a myth and not a legend, more Butch and Sundance than Bonnie and Clyde, but a very well-created myth at that." David Kirby, writing in *Atlanta Journal-Constitution,* also found Henry to be an engaging character: "He's an impetuous, lucky fellow who always manages to find a way out of the fire and back into the frying pan, saved again and again either by some gooey-eyed damsel or his pop's prosthesis, surely the oddest good luck charm in all literature." James Hopkin, writing in *New Statesman,* observed: "There are enough fine moments in *A Star Called Henry* to remind us that Doyle is an accomplished writer; his dialogue is earthy and effective, he can render a scene as well as anyone, and a simple poetry plays around the edges of his prose." Still, for Hopkin, "stylistic flaws and heavy doses of sentiment" mar the story. Other critics, including Grace Fill in *Booklist,* remarked that "Doyle expertly weaves his well-known wit into even the most violent and most tender passages of the tale." Colleen Kelly-Warren, writing in the *St. Louis Post-Dispatch,* commented that "Doyle's writing combines rhythmic, cadenced prose, rich description, and dialogue that's real enough to feel overheard." Critic William Hutchings, in a *World Literature Today* review, remarked that the novel's "psychological insights into an adolescent gunman are remarkable, and its portrait of childhood homelessness in the streets and slums of turn-of-the-century Dublin, where rat-catching for profit provides a means of subsistence, is unforgettable, heartrending, and harrowingly real."

Doyle has also turned his keen observations and wit to good use in a pair of children's books. In *The Giggler Treatment* adults who are mean to children are given the signature treatment of the Gigglers: a smear of dog excrement on their shoes. The furry little Gigglers have placed their smelly payload directly in the path of Mister Mack, a cookie taster who is thought to have transgressed against his children. The action and suspense of the book—whether Mister Mack will step in the dog poo or not—takes less than a minute, but throughout Doyle digresses and diverges into such material as a history of gigglers, secrets about dogs, and a dictionary of Irish terms. However, it emerges that Mister Mack is innocent of any wrongdoing, and his entire family, including a Giggler and dog Rover, rush to ensure his shoes remain clean. A *Publishers Weekly* reviewer called the book a "bracingly rude dose of fun," while Steven Engelfried, writing in *School Library Journal,* observed that "the imaginative narrative and clever plotting make this more than just another silly read."

Rover Saves Christmas finds the usually steadfast and resolute Rudolph suffering from a cold and a possible mid-life crisis. Santa asks talking-dog Rover to take over for the incapacitated reindeer. The Mack children (from *The Giggler Treatment*), their friend Victoria, and lizards Hans and Heidi join Santa and Rover on the worldwide journey on Christmas Eve. The non-linear text constantly veers from the main story to other features, including glossaries of Irish words, warnings to children, funny commercials, descriptions, and even the rebellion of the surly Chapter Six. "Such digressions have a joyous, vigorous lunacy, absolutely in tune with a child's way of thinking," commented Sarah Crompton in the *Daily Telegraph.* A *Publishers Weekly* critic called the book "enormously entertaining," and Regan McMahon, writing in *San Francisco Chronicle,* remarked that *Rover Saves Christmas* "may not be the first story of how Christmas gets saved just in the nick of time, but it may be the funniest."

Doyle's *Rory & Ita* is the nonfiction biography of his parents. "It's Roddy's job to take his parents' oral history of their times and relationship and transform it into something interesting," wrote Steven E. Alford in the *Houston Chronicle.* "And in *Rory & Ita,* his first nonfiction work, he largely succeeds." Ita was born in 1925, and "so surrounded was she by poverty that she didn't recognize deprivation and hardship for what it was," Alford wrote. After a dubious first meeting at a local dance—Rory was inebriated and unappealing—their courtship thrived, and they were married in 1951. "Doyle's art consists in taking these disjointed memories and, through discreet stitching, turning them into a smooth narrative fabric," Alford observed. "This is a charming story of two ordinary people whose lives were beset by routine struggles, most of them occasioned by the lack of money," Alford further remarked. "Now and then, the account offers insight into the lifestyle changes over a single generation," wrote a *Publishers Weekly* reviewer. Some poignant moments, such as the death of the Doyles' third baby, are recounted. Rory's past as a member of the IRA is hinted at. But mostly, the book emerges as "a study in ordinariness," wrote Charlotte Moore in the *Spectator.* "Either you like this kind of thing or you don't," Moore observed. "I love it. I relished every word of *Rory & Ita.*" Some critics remarked that because of their ordinary lives, the Doyles may not merit a full-blown biography. However, "all

personal testimony is of historical interest," Moore declared. "This book is Doyle's very personal endeavor at capturing his family's history, and his parents come across as lovely, genuine people," wrote Elsa Gaztambide in *Booklist.* "It's a pity we can't all have our memories handled with such dignity and care," Moore concluded.

In *Oh, Play That Thing,* Doyle returned to the protagonist of his earlier *A Star Called Henry.* In this installment, Henry Smart leaves Dublin, as well as his wife and daughter, to start a new life in New York, one step ahead of a death warrant issued for him by the IRA. In New York he gains fitful employment as a sandwich-board street advertiser, selling bootleg whiskey on the side. Soon, however, Henry runs afoul of his employers, and is on the run again, this time to Chicago. There he becomes involved in the jazz scene, becoming the assistant to Louis Armstrong, and returning to New York and Harlem where jazz is king. Still, Henry misses his old life in Ireland, and his wife, Miss O'Shea. *Booklist* contributor Allison Block had praise for this work, noting: "Doyle displays his trademark sensitivity and wit in a tale full of adventure, passion, and prose as punchy as a Satchmo riff." *Entertainment Weekly* reviewer Troy Patterson was less impressed by the novel, however, complaining that, "in the absence of a genuine story, phony history must suffice." Similarly, a *Kirkus Reviews* contributor called the novel "an uncharacteristic misstep in a brilliant writer's estimable career." *People* reviewer Vick Boughton had a higher assessment of *Oh, Play That Thing,* commenting that "in prose that echoes the syncopated beat of the Jazz Age itself, Doyle brings Henry as well as Armstrong and his music to vibrant life."

With *Paula Spencer,* Doyle presents another sequel, this to his 1996 novel, *The Woman Who Walked into Doors.* Here Paula is attempting to build a new life for herself after the death of her husband. She has mostly given up drinking, but must still get by on meager cleaning woman wages, and is determined to get her part of the new wealth entering Ireland as the so-called "Celtic Tiger." Writing in *Library Journal,* Starr E. Smith felt "the story captures the lower levels of North Dublin's working-class populace." Higher praise came from a *Kirkus Reviews* critic who concluded: "Profound, subtle and unsentimental—the latest from a master back in top form." Likewise, Benjamin Segedin, writing in *Booklist,* termed *Paula Spencer* "grand," while *Entertainment Weekly* contributor Rebecca Ascher-Walsh called the novel "a tale of triumph and great humor." Daniel Trilling, writing in the *New Statesman,* noted: "Doyle tells this tale of redemption with insight and respect."

Wilderness is a young adult novel featuring parallel narratives. Two brothers, Johnny, twelve, and Tom, ten, embark on a dogsled tour in Finland with their mother, while their eighteen-year-old half sister, Grainne, stays at home in Dublin. The boys love the dogs, the hard work, and the experience of traveling over the frozen landscape—until their mother disappears. The trip was arranged so that Grainne could more easily reunite with her birth mother, Rosemary, who abandoned her husband and child years earlier, and who is now coming to see her.

Doyle proposed a collaborative effort to support Amnesty International to editor Arthur A. Levine, who then passed on the concept to ten authors. Other contributors signing on to the project included Nick Hornby, Tim Wynne-Jones, Ruith Ozeki, David Almond, Deborah Ellis, Margo Lanagan, Gregory Maguire, Eoin Colfer, and Linda Sue Park, whose original story was the basis for the connected stories that became *Click.* Maggie, who is in junior high, and her brother Jason, a senior in high school, lose their much-loved grandfather George "Gee" Keane, a world-famous journalist. Gee leaves Jason a number of autographed photographs of famous people and he leaves Maggie a box of sea shells. The stories reveal the life of Gee and follow those of Jason and Maggie through old age. *Resource Links* contributor Myra Junyk wrote: "This book is an amazing accomplishment! The title *Click* unites this beautiful tapestry of stories which are woven about the life of a photographer and his impact on his family and the world. Not only have ten writers been able to work together to tell a beautiful story, but they have done it for a good cause."

The Deportees: And Other Stories is a collection of eight hundred-word installments written for *Metro Eireann,* a newspaper founded by two Nigerian journalists living in Dublin. The weekly, that began as a monthly, is devoted to the "new Irish," most of whom immigrated to Ireland from many countries during the 1990s. Some of the stories have also been published in the *New Yorker* and *McSweeney's.*

Jimmy Rabbitte, Jr. returns in the title story, now married to Aoife and the father of three with another on the way. Jimmy decides to form another band, this time made up of immigrant members of the underclass. He posts an ad that reads "White Irish need not apply" for his band "The Deportees," named for a 1930s Woody Guthrie song about migrant Mexicans who were brought north to pick fruit in California orchards, then deported when they finished the job. Although Jimmy's band is made up of very talented multi-ethnic musicians who do great justice to the Guthrie songs, their only hit is a spoof of a World cup song, which they title "You Might Well Beat the Irish but We Won't Give a Shite." Some of the stories are darker, including "The Pram," in which Polish nanny Alina tells a frightening tale to two little girls. *Star Tribune* contributor Peter Moore wrote that "it's in the dialogue that these stories truly and vividly come to life. These stories are perfect showcases for Doyle's much-praised sharp wit and acute ear; there is the clear ring of authenticity in every line, and you will no doubt find yourself laughing out loud and often."

BIOGRAPHICAL AND CRITICAL SOURCES:

BOOKS

Contemporary Literary Criticism, Volume 81, Gale (Detroit, MI), 1994.

Dictionary of Literary Biography, Volume 194: *British Novelists since 1960, Second Series,* Gale (Detroit, MI), 1998.

Drabble, Margaret, editor, *Oxford Companion to English Literature,* 6th edition, Oxford University Press (New York, NY), 2000.

Modern British Literature, 2nd edition, St. James Press (Detroit, MI), 2000.

Stade, George, and Sarah Hanna Goldstein, editors, *British Writers,* Scribner (New York, NY), 1999.

PERIODICALS

America, February 19, 2000, James Martin, James S. Torrens, and John Breslin, review of *A Star Called Henry,* p. 25; March 17, 2008, Tom Deignan, review of *The Deportees: And Other Stories,* p. 35.

Atlanta Journal-Constitution, October 10, 1999, David Kirby, "Doyle's *Star* Casts a Pall of Darkness on Irish Life," review of *A Star Called Henry,* p. L10.

Book, September, 1999, review of *A Star Called Henry,* p. 69.

Booklist, June 1, 1999, Grace Fill, review of *A Star Called Henry,* p. 1741; June 1, 1999, review of *The Woman Who Walked into Doors,* p. 1797; March 15, 2000, review of *A Star Called Henry,* p. 1337;

February 1, 2002, Joanne Wilkinson, review of *A Star Called Henry,* p. 925; November 15, 2002, Elsa Gaztambide, review of *Rory & Ita,* p. 562; September 1, 2004, Allison Block, review of *Oh, Play That Thing,* p. 4; November 1, 2004, Todd Morning, review of *The Meanwhile Adventures,* p. 484; October 15, 2006, Benjamin Segedin, review of *Paula Spencer,* p. 5; September 15, 2007, Lynn Rutan, review of *Click,* p. 57; October 1, 2007, Jerry Eberle, review of *The Deportees,* p. 4; November 15, 2007, Jennifer Mattson, review of *Wilderness,* p. 44.

Boston Globe, December 19, 1993, review of *Paddy Clarke Ha Ha Ha.*

Chicago Tribune, August 9, 1992, Lawrence Dugan, review of *The Commitments,* p. 5.

Christian Science Monitor, September 16, 1999, review of *A Star Called Henry,* p. 16; November 18, 1999, review of *A Star Called Henry,* p. 12; January 15, 2008, Heller McAplin, review of *The Deportees,* p. 15.

Commonweal, November 19, 1999, review of *A Star Called Henry,* p. 56.

Daily Telegraph (London, England), December 1, 2002, Sarah Crompton, review of *Rover Saves Christmas.*

Detroit News and Free Press, December 12, 1993, John Gallagher, review of *Paddy Clarke Ha Ha Ha.*

Entertainment Weekly, September 17, 1999, review of *A Star Called Henry,* p. 74; December 24, 1999, review of *A Star Called Henry,* p. 144; November 19, 2004, Troy Patterson, review of *Oh, Play That Thing,* p. 89; January 12, 2007, Rebecca Ascher-Walsh, review of *Paula Spencer,* p. 85.

Europe, March, 2000, Claire Bose, review of *A Star Called Henry,* p. 34.

Financial Times, September 8, 2007, Mark Ford, review of *The Deportees,* p. 36; September 22, 2007, James Lovegrove, review of *Wilderness,* p. 41; October 12, 2007, John Murray Brown, review of *The Playboy of the Western World,* p. 19.

Fort Worth Star-Telegram, December 1, 2004, "Disjointed *Oh, Play That Thing* Takes Immigrant on American Adventures."

Globe and Mail (Toronto, Ontario, Canada), September 11, 1999, review of *A Star Called Henry,* p. D18; November 27, 1999, review of *A Star Called Henry,* p. D50; December 1, 2001, review of *Rover Saves Christmas,* p. D16.

Guardian (London, England), September 2, 2000, review of *A Star Called Henry,* p. 11.

Hartford Courant, January 20, 2008, Carole Goldberg, review of *The Deportees.*

Horn Book, January-February, 2008, Jennifer M. Brabander, review of *Wilderness,* p. 85.

Houston Chronicle, October 10, 1999, Robert Cremins, review of *A Star Called Henry,* p. 15; December 15, 2002, Steven E. Alford, review of *Rory & Ita,* p. 23; February 4, 2007, Robert Cremins, review of *Paula Spencer,* p. 19.

Independent (London, England), April 14, 1996, review of *The Woman Who Walked into Doors,* p. 32.

Journal of Adolescent & Adult Literacy, October, 2007, James Blasingame, review of *Click,* p. 191.

Kirkus Reviews, June 15, 1999, review of *A Star Called Henry,* p. 901; November 1, 2001, review of *Rover Saves Christmas,* p. 1548; September 15, 2002, review of *Rory & Ita,* p. 1363; September 1, 2004, review of *Oh, Play That Thing,* p. 823; October 15, 2004, review of *The Meanwhile Adventures,* p. 1004; November 1, 2006, review of *Paula Spencer,* p. 1091; August 15, 2007, review of *Wilderness;* October 1, 2007, review of *The Deportees.*

Knight Ridder/Tribune News Service, Dave Ferman, review of *Rory & Ita,* p. K6369.

Library Journal, August, 1999, Heather McCormack, review of *A Star Called Henry,* p. 137; November 15, 2006, Starr E. Smith, review of *Paula Spencer,* p. 55; November 1, 2007, Starr E. Smith, review of *The Deportees,* p. 62.

Literary Review, summer, 1999, Karen Sbrockey, "Something of a Hero: An Interview with Roddy Doyle," p. 537.

Los Angeles Times Book Review, July 19, 1992, review of *The Snapper,* p. 6; September 20, 1992, Tim Appelo, review of *The Van,* p. 3; October 3, 1999, review of *A Star Called Henry,* p. 2.

Maclean's, August 30, 1993, review of *Paddy Clarke Ha Ha Ha,* p. 50; October 25, 1999, Anthony Wilson-Smith, review of *A Star Called Henry,* p. 93.

Miami Herald, January 20, 2008, Connie Ogle, review of *The Deportees.*

Nation, April 16, 2001, Tim Appelo, review of *When Brendan Met Trudy,* p. 35.

New Republic, September 16, 1991, review of *The Snapper,* p. 30.

New Statesman, September 6, 1999, James Hopkin, review of *A Star Called Henry,* p. 54; September 11, 2006, Daniel Trilling, review of *Paula Spencer,* p. 59.

New Statesman & Society, August 23, 1991, Guy Mannes-Abbott, review of *The Van,* pp. 35-36; June 18, 1993, review of *Paddy Clarke Ha Ha Ha,* p. 39.

New Straits Times, August 7, 1996, review of *The Woman Who Walked into Doors.*

Newsweek, December 27, 1993, review of *Paddy Clarke Ha Ha Ha,* p. 48.

Newsweek International, September 20, 1999, Carla Power, "The Myths of Rebellion: A New Novel Takes on Freedom Fighters," review of *A Star Called Henry,* p. 35.

New Yorker, January 24, 1994, review of *Paddy Clarke Ha Ha Ha,* p. 91; February 5, 1996, review of *The Woman Who Walked into Doors,* p. 56; October 4, 1999, Daphne Merkin, review of *A Star Called Henry,* pp. 110-117.

New York Review of Books, February 3, 1994, review of *Paddy Clarke Ha Ha Ha,* p. 3.

New York Times, July 23, 1989, review of *The Commitments,* p. 11; December 13, 1993, Christopher Lehmann-Haupt, review of *Paddy Clarke Ha Ha Ha,* p. B2; May 16, 1997, Mary Gordon, review of *The Woman Who Walked into Doors,* p. B12; September 10, 1999, Richard Bernstein and Eric Asimov, review of *A Star Called Henry,* p. B42; September 10, 1999, review of *A Star Called Henry,* p. E44.

New York Times Book Review, July 23, 1989, Kinky Friedman, review of *The Commitments,* p. 11; October 11, 1992, Bruce Allen, review of *The Van,* p. 15; July 18, 1993, review of *The Van,* p. 24; January 2, 1994, Mary Flanagan, review of *Paddy Clarke Ha Ha Ha,* pp. 1, 21; April 28, 1996, review of *The Woman Who Walked into Doors,* p. 7; May 2, 1999, Katharine Weber, "Finbar's Hotel," p. 19; September 12, 1999, Richard Eder, review of *A Star Called Henry,* p. 7; December 5, 1999, review of *A Star Called Henry,* p. 106; September 17, 2000, "So Watch Your Step," p. 33; December 16, 2001, review of *Rover Saves Christmas,* p. 20; January 20, 2008, Erica Wagner, review of *The Deportees,* p. 6.

Observer (London, England), October 31, 1993, review of *Paddy Clarke Ha Ha Ha,* p. 18; August 29, 1999, review of *A Star Called Henry,* p. 11; September 12, 1999, review of *A Star Called Henry,* p. 7; October 28, 2001, review of *Rover Saves Christmas,* p. 16.

People, August 26, 1991, review of *The Commitments,* pp. 13-14; November 29, 2004, Vick Boughton, review of *Oh, Play That Thing,* p. 58.

Philadelphia Inquirer, January 20, 1994, review of *Paddy Clarke Ha Ha Ha,* pp. E1, E7.

Publishers Weekly, May 25, 1992, review of *The Van,* p. 36; June 22, 1992, review of *The Snapper,* p. 55; March 25, 1996, review of *The Woman Who Walked into Doors,* pp. 55-56; July 12, 1999, review of *A Star Called Henry,* p. 70; October 4, 1999, review of *A Star Called Henry,* p. 36; November 1, 1999, review of *A Star Called Henry,* p. 45; July 24, 2000, review of *The Giggler Treat-*

ment, p. 94; September 24, 2001, review of *Rover Saves Christmas,* p. 54; September 24, 2001, review of *The Giggler Treatment,* p. 95; September 23, 2002, review of *Rory & Ita,* p. 59; September 20, 2004, review of *Oh, Play That Thing,* p. 43; October 16, 2006, review of *Paula Spencer,* p. 29; August 13, 2007, review of *Wilderness,* p. 68; September 24, 2007, review of *The Deportees,* p. 41.

Reading Teacher, May, 2001, review of *The Giggler Treatment,* p. 827.

Resource Links, December, 2007, Myra Junyk, review of *Click,* p. 37.

Rolling Stone, September 21, 1989, review of *The Commitments,* p. 27.

St. Louis Post-Dispatch, September 19, 1999, Colleen Kelly-Warren, "Doyle's Exuberant, Bleak Story Introduces Henry Smart, an IRA Assassin Born to the Job," review of *A Star Called Henry,* p. F10.

St. Petersburg Times, January 27, 2008, Colette Bancroft, review of *The Deportees,* p. 11.

San Francisco Chronicle, October 2, 1999, Sam Whiting, "A Star Called Roddy Doyle: Irish Novelist's Latest Best-seller Delves into History, Both Personal and National," profile of Roddy Doyle, p. B1; December 16, 2001, Regan McMahon, review of *Rover Saves Christmas,* p. 4.

School Library Journal, November, 2000, Steven Engelfried, review of *The Giggler Treatment,* p. 119; October, 2001, review of *Rover Saves Christmas,* p. 64; November, 2007, Connie Tyrrell Burns, review of *Wilderness,* p. 120.

Sewanee Review, fall, 1999, Floyd Skloot, review of *A Star Called Henry,* p. C3.

Spectator, September 4, 1999, Kevin Myers, review of *A Star Called Henry,* pp. 32-33; November 30, 2002, Charlotte Moore, "In Their Own Words," review of *Rory & Ita,* p. 54; September 30, 2006, "Mother Courage on the Wagon"; September 15, 2007, Cressida Connelly, review of *The Deportees,* p. 51.

Star-Telegram (Fort Worth, TX), February 5, 2003, Dave Ferman, review of *Rory & Ita.*

Star Tribune (Minneapolis, MN), January 20, 2008, Peter Moore, review of *The Deportees,* p. 12.

Time, December 6, 1993, review of *Paddy Clarke Ha Ha Ha,* p. 82; September 6, 1999, review of *A Star Called Henry,* p. 76; October 4, 1999, Walter Kirn, "The Best of the Boyos: Roddy Doyle Vividly Portrays the Wild Passions of an Irish Everyman in *A Star Called Henry,*" p. 102.

Times (London, England), August 16, 1990, John Nicholson, review of *The Snapper;* October 5, 1991, review of *The Van,* p. 51.

Times Educational Supplement, July 2, 1993, review of *Paddy Clarke Ha Ha Ha,* p. 18.

Times Literary Supplement, December 21, 1990, Stephen Leslie, review of *The Snapper,* p. 1381; August 16, 1991, Anne-Marie Conway, review of *The Van,* p. 22; June 11, 1993, review of *Paddy Clarke Ha Ha Ha,* p. 21; September 3, 1999, review of *A Star Called Henry,* p. 8.

Wall Street Journal, September 10, 1999, Allen Barra, review of *A Star Called Henry,* p. W7; March 9, 2001, Joe Morgenstern, review of *When Brendan Met Trudy,* p. W4.

Washington Post Book World, August 10, 1992, review of *The Snapper,* p. B2; September 5, 1999, review of *A Star Called Henry,* p. 3; October 31, 1999, review of *A Star Called Henry,* p. 4.

World Literature Today, summer, 2000, William Hutchings, review of *A Star Called Henry,* p. 594.

World of Hibernia, winter, 1999, John Boland, review of *A Star Called Henry,* p. 155.

ONLINE

Booklit, http://www.booklit.com/ (September 23, 2007), review of *The Deportees.*

Emory University English Department Web site, http://www.english.emory.edu/ (August 18, 2008), profile.

Guardian Online, http://guardian.co.uk/ (January 14, 2003), "Roddy Doyle."

Internet Movie Database, http://www.imdb.com/ (June 6, 2007), *Roddy Doyle.*

Irish Writers Online, http://www.irishwriters-online.com/ (August 18, 2008), profile.

New York State Writers Institute Web site, http://www.albany.edu/ (June 6, 2007), "Roddy Doyle."

Powells.com. http://www.powells.com/ (October 4, 1999), Dave Weich, "Roddy Doyle, Unleashed."

Salon.com, http://www.salon.com/ (October 28, 1999), Charles Taylor, interview with Doyle.*

*   *   *

DRISCOLL, Richard
   See GORMAN, Ed

*   *   *

DRUETT, Joan 1939-
   (Jo Friday)

PERSONAL: Born April 11, 1939, in Nelson, New Zealand; daughter of Ralph Totten Griffin and Colleen Butcher; married Ronald John Druett (a maritime art-

ist), February 11, 1966; children: Lindsay John, Alastair Ronald. *Education:* Victoria University of Wellington, B.A., 1960.

ADDRESSES: Home—Wellington, New Zealand. *Agent*—Laura J. Langlie, 275 President St., No. 3, Brooklyn, NY 11231.

CAREER: Teacher of biology and English literature until 1983; writer, 1983—.

MEMBER: Authors Guild, Martha's Vineyard Historical Society (Edgartown, MA), Mystic Seaport Museum, New Bedford Whaling Museum, Wellington Museum of City & Sea, Friends of the Turnbull Library (New Zealand), Friends of Te Papa (National Museum of New Zealand), Friends of the International Arts Festival (New Zealand), Friends of the New Zealand Symphony Orchestra.

AWARDS, HONORS: Best first prose book, International PEN, 1984, for *Exotic Intruders: The Introduction of Plants and Animals to New Zealand;* Fulbright Writer's Cultural Award, 1986; John Lyman Award for best book of American maritime history, 1992, for *"She Was a Sister Sailor": The Whaling Journals of Mary Brewster, 1845-1851;* Oysterponds Historical Society Scholar-in-residence Award, 1993; New York Public Library Award, 1998, for *Hen Frigates: Wives of Merchant Captains Under Sail;* L. Byrne Waterman Award for outstanding contributions to history and women's history, 1999; John David Stout Research Fellowship Award, University of Wellington, 2001.

WRITINGS:

NONFICTION

Exotic Intruders: The Introduction of Plants and Animals to New Zealand, Heinemann (Auckland, New Zealand), 1983.

Fulbright in New Zealand, New Zealand-U.S. Educational Foundation (Wellington, New Zealand), 1988.

Petticoat Whalers: Whaling Wives at Sea, 1820-1920, illustrated by husband, Ron Druett, HarperCollins (Auckland, New Zealand), 1991, HarperCollins (New York, NY), 1992.

(Editor) *"She Was a Sister Sailor": The Whaling Journals of Mary Brewster, 1845-1851,* Mystic Seaport Museum (Mystic, CT), 1991.

(With Mary Anne Wallace) *The Sailing Circle: Nineteenth-century Seafaring Women from New York,* introduction by Lisa Norling, Three Village Historical Society (East Setauket, NY), and Cold Spring Harbor Whaling Museum (Cold Spring Harbor, NY), 1995.

Captain's Daughter, Coasterman's Wife: Carrie Hubbard Davis of Orient, Oysterponds Historical Society (Orient, NY), 1995.

Hen Frigates: Wives of Merchant Captains under Sail, Simon & Schuster (New York, NY), 1998.

Rough Medicine: Surgeons at Sea in the Age of Sail, Routledge (New York, NY), 2000.

She Captains: Heroines and Hellions of the Sea, Simon & Schuster (New York, NY), 2000.

In the Wake of Madness: The Murderous Voyage of the Whaleship Sharon, Algonquin Books (Chapel Hill, NC), 2003.

Island of the Lost: Shipwrecked at the Edge of the World, Algonquin Books (Chapel Hill, NC), 2007.

NOVELS

Abigail, Random House (New York, NY), 1988.
A Promise of Gold, Bantam (New York, NY), 1990.
Murder at the Brian Boru, HarperCollins (Auckland, New Zealand), 1992.

"WIKI COFFIN" MYSTERY SERIES

A Watery Grave, St. Martin's Minotaur (New York, NY), 2004.
Shark Island, St. Martin's Minotaur (New York, NY), 2005.
Run Afoul, St. Martin's Minotaur (New York, NY), 2006.
Deadly Shoals, St. Martin's Minotaur (New York, NY), 2007.

Contributor to periodicals, including *Log of Mystic Seaport, Newport History, Sea History, Dukes County Intelligencer, Mains'l Haul,* and *No Quarter Given.* Author of science fiction stories published under pseudonym Jo Friday in magazine *Te Ao Hou.*

SIDELIGHTS: Joan Druett is a former teacher whose interest in maritime history prompted her to conduct extensive research that has taken her across several continents and resulted in a collection of books about seafaring women. Among Druett's titles are *The Sailing Circle: Nineteenth-century Seafaring Women from New York, Hen Frigates: Wives of Merchant Captains Under Sail,* and *In the Wake of Madness: The Murderous Voyage of the Whaleship Sharon.*

Druett studied at Victoria University of Wellington and went on to become a teacher of both biology and English literature. In 1983, however, she decided to concentrate on a writing career. That year she published her first book, *Exotic Intruders: The Introduction of Plants and Animals to New Zealand,* which won an award from International PEN. Five years later, Druett completed two more projects, *Fulbright in New Zealand* and the novel *Abigail,* and in 1990 she issued *A Promise of Gold.*

Petticoat Whalers: Whaling Wives at Sea, 1820-1920, Druett's first nonfiction book about maritime history, was inspired by her discovery of a buried headstone. "My engrossing interest in the history of women in whaling began in May, 1984, when I came across a young Maori scraping at a patch of waste ground on the tiny South Pacific island of Rarotonga," she once explained to *CA.* "I was told that he had a dream in which an ancestor came to him and told him to clear the land because it was a lost graveyard. Three days later the young man had gone, so I investigated the heaps of weeds and broken stones and ended up falling into a hole where a great tree had been uprooted during a recent storm. At the bottom of that hole, I found a coral rock grave with a headstone set into it like a door. The inscription was a memorial to a twenty-four-year-old American girl, Mary Ann Sherman, the wife of the captain of the American whaling ship *Harrison,* who had died January 5, 1850. A girl on a whaling ship? It seemed impossible! How had she lived . . . and died? This was the beginning of my quest." The book is illustrated with paintings by Druett's husband, maritime artist Ron Druett.

After producing *Petticoat Whalers,* Druett served as editor of *"She Was a Sister Sailor": The Whaling Journals of Mary Brewster, 1845-1851,* which provides what a *Publishers Weekly* contributor described as "detail concerning shipboard life and the whaling industry, as well as a portrait of missionary life on the island of Maui." She then wrote *Murder at the Brian Boru* and, three years later, *Captain's Daughter, Coasterman's Wife: Carrie Hubbard Davis of Orient.* In addition, she collaborated with Mary Anne Wallace in writing *The Sailing Circle.*

Druett's *Hen Frigates* relates the experiences of women on shipping expeditions. Among the notable women in this volume is a teenager who replaced her dead father as commander and subsequently repelled a sexually aggressive sailor, quashed a mutiny, and even convinced her crew to dump the ship's alcohol overboard. Other women in Druett's study bear children, combat illnesses such as malaria and plague, and endure dangerous storms.

Hen Frigates won praise for its exploration of a little-known topic. An *Atlantic* contributor wrote that the book "casts light on an odd corner of nineteenth-century life," and *Library Journal* contributor Roseanne Castellino called it "informative and entertaining reading." Margaret Flanagan declared in *Booklist* that Druett's volume constituted "an intimate glimpse" back in time and noted that *Hen Frigates* "provides the reader with an intriguing entrée into an exotic lifestyle." Holly Morris wrote in the *New York Times Book Review* that Druett's work serves as "a valuable collective portrait of intrepid seafaring women."

Druett's other books include *Rough Medicine: Surgeons at Sea in the Age of Sail* and *She Captains: Heroines and Hellions of the Sea.* In *Rough Medicine* Druett describes the adventures of English physicians who put to sea in the early nineteenth century in the wake of John Woodall, considered "the father of sea surgery." Based on primary documents, Druett notes that the doctors were driven to dangerous positions on shipboard mainly for the sake of adventure. The latter volume relates the exploits of seafaring women from the time of Ancient Egypt to the twentieth century. Among the various figures in the book are Tomyris, a Massegetae queen who triumphed in battle against Persian forces, and Lucy Brewer, who posed as a man and obtained assignment as a sailor aboard the U.S.S. *Constitution.*

Upon its publication in 2000, *She Captains* received recognition as a provocative chronicle. *Booklist* contributor Donna Seaman wrote: "Maritime lore has always been rich in romance and suffering; Druett's revelations increase its fascination tenfold." A *Publishers Weekly* contributor was likewise impressed, describing *She Captains* as an "entertaining work . . . filled with fascinating characters." *Library Journal* reviewer Roseanne Castellino remarked: "The stories are lively, the characters vivid and eccentric," while Louise Jarvis noted in the *New York Times Book Review* that *She Captains* presents "wild tales of women's bravery and

bloodlust from antiquity to the twentieth century." Jarvis added: "Druett descends on the gory tidbits and operatic tableaus with a cheeky tone that seems to acknowledge our own perverse fascination—delight even—with atrocities and hardships that would make Melville's or Hemingway's sea dogs buckle."

Having exhausted research documentation on seafaring women in her previous books, Druett's next work, *In the Wake of Madness,* concentrates on a specific incident in maritime lore. In 1841 the whaler *Sharon,* led by Captain Howes Norris, "a seagoing psychopath of the classic mold," according to Peter Nichols, writing in the *New York Times Book Review,* left Fairhaven, Massachusetts, for the South Pacific. When the ship returned three years later, only four of the original twenty-nine crew members were aboard, and Captain Norris was not among them. He had been murdered in the South Pacific by Kanaka tribesmen taken aboard as crew members. Based on the journals of Benjamin Clough, the third mate who recaptured the ship from the Pacific islanders who killed Norris, and Andrew White, the ship's cooper, Druett's book is the account to analyze Norris's behavior and shows it to have been instrumental in his demise.

According to the records Druett uncovered, Norris was a racist and a drunkard who repeatedly beat and tortured his crew members and eventually killed his steward. In return, many men deserted the ship, which forced Norris to hire locals to flesh out the crew during the long voyage. The Kanaka tribesmen had no reason to remain loyal to the captain, so when the rest of the crew was offboard searching for whales, three of them hacked Norris in half with a sharp spade used for cutting whale blubber. For the remainder of their days, the surviving crew members largely skirted the truth about what happened during the voyage. Druett asserts they were ashamed by their lack of courage in standing up to a captain who did not have a firm grip on reality.

A reviewer for *Publishers Weekly* called *In the Wake of Madness* "a terrific account of an unusually eventful voyage," adding that it "manages a perfect balance between telling the story in an unfussy yet dramatic manner and honoring its complexity." *Library Journal* contributor Robert C. Jones characterized the book as "a murder investigation mixed with equal parts whaling lore, mystery, retribution, and history" that is "informative and vividly re-created." Nichols wrote that Druett "draws a fine picture of the floating community of whalers and deserters scattered across the Pacific." Other critics also appreciated Druett's ability to evoke a detailed portrait of a bygone era. *In the Wake of Madness* provides an "excellent insight into the whaling life and human nature," wrote *Kliatt* reviewer Sunnie Grant, and a writer for *Kirkus Reviews* called the book a "swift, absorbing saga of the sea [that] invokes malice, mayhem, murder, and, hovering over it all, Herman Melville."

Druett turns to mystery writing with *A Watery Grave,* published in 2004. The author introduces as her hero and sleuth William "Wiki" Coffin, who is half Maori with an American sea-captain father. Wiki joins the United States South Seas Exploring Expedition of 1838 as a "linguister," or translator. Before the expedition can leave, however, Wiki is arrested for the murder of Mrs. Tristram T. Stanton, who is married to the expedition's civilian astronomer. When Wiki clears himself, the sheriff, who has found a connection between the murder and the expedition, asks Wiki to help continue the investigation as Wiki accompanies the explorers. A *Publishers Weekly* contributor called *A Watery Grave* "a fine start to a series sure to appeal to lovers of historical mysteries and fans of sea adventures." Lesley Dunlap, writing on *MysteryReader.com,* noted that the author's "familiarity with naval matters is evident," adding: "The whodunit is satisfyingly complex, but the real pleasure in reading *A Watery Grave* is the glimpse into the past and the world it portrays." A *Kirkus Reviews* contributor wrote: "The debut of a smart, appealing hero whose tale unfolds amid lots of interesting cross-cultural, historical, and nautical detail."

In the sequel to *A Watery Grave,* titled *Shark Island,* readers find Wiki still part of the South Seas expedition and investigating the foundering of the *Anawan* at Shark Island. Once Wiki and his crewmates board the ship, they meet Captain Ezekiel Reed and his beautiful bride Annabelle, who had previously had an affair with Wiki. When Captain Reed is murdered and the unlikable Captain Forsythe is accused of the crime, Wiki thinks someone else is guilty and investigates, leading him to discover that the murder may have to do with some missing cargo. A *Publishers Weekly* contributor noted that the author "should win plaudits from both mystery fans and aficionados of naval adventures." A *Kirkus Reviews* contributor wrote that Druett "describes with contagious conviction floggings, cramped quarters, pettifogging officers and rum rations."

Wiki returns in *Run Afoul,* this time investigating the illness and, according to Dr. Olliver, the possible poisoning of the South Seas expedition's astronomer Grimes. When Grimes dies, the crew believes that the cook Festin killed him because he had been tried for poisoning on a previous voyage but found innocent. Although an inquest rules it an accidental death, Wiki suspects a villain, a suspicion supported when Dr. Olliver is killed. The novel also features Wiki's reunion with his adventuresome father, Captain William Coffin, who is later charged with murder. "Comic complications and unsettling racist views bubble up" during the course of the story, noted a *Kirkus Reviews* contributor. A *Publishers Weekly* reviewer commented that the author "makes the vanished world she depicts come alive."

Deadly Shoals is based on a real adventure. In 1838, six ships of the U.S. Exploring Expedition sailed from Norfolk Virginia bound for the Pacific. In these pre-Panama Canal days, it was necessary to travel along the coast of South America in order to do so. Of the 346 men, twenty-eight died, and two ships were lost. Lieutenant Charles Wilkes was a tyrannical leader whose men suffered under his command.

Druett adds a seventh fictional ship, the *Swallow.* It is on this ship that Wiki sails, and as the story opens, his ship is off the coast of Patagonia, "with the shoal-ridden estuary of the Rio Negro on the western horizon." The *Trojan,* a whaling ship from New England, appears, and her captain, Stackpole, asks Wiki to assist him. Stackpole had paid Caleb Adams to outfit a schooner for him so that he could hunt seal, as the whale hunting was not going well, but, he tells Wiki, Caleb has disappeared with his money. Stackpole would rather have an American law enforcement agent assist him than the locals, and Wiki goes ashore to investigate. What he discovers is the murder of a store keeper, raising suspicion that Caleb may have committed more serious crimes than thievery. Other characters include Wiki's father, naturalist Titian Peale, and philologist Horatio Hale.

"Gauchos, Indians, revolutionaries and adventurers flock across the beautifully rendered landscape," commented a *Publishers Weekly* reviewer. Kirstin Merrihew reviewed the novel for *Mostly Fiction* online, noting that "Druett has chosen her source material brilliantly; she can mine tons more from documented history for future volumes." A *Kirkus Reviews* contributor concluded: "Fascinating tidbits come left and right, and Druett's prose gains vigor with every volume."

Island of the Lost: Shipwrecked at the Edge of the World is Druett's history of two shipwrecked crews of men who, in 1864, became castaways on opposite sides of the Auckland Islands, off the coast of New Zealand. The *Grafton,* which was headed toward Campbell Island to retrieve silver-laden tin, was returning to Sydney, Australia, because of poor weather and illness when a storm descended upon them. Druett draws on the journals of the ship's captain, Thomas Musgrave, and Francois Raynal, a prospector and the ship's navigator, who documented how the five men survived for eighteen months while planning their escape. Druett notes the plants that were eaten and that prevented scurvy, the meat eaten from animals that included sea lion and birds, and other survival techniques employed by the men. "The amount of detail Druett has amassed is truly impressive," wrote George Cohen in *Booklist.* They suffered from biting flies as they built a forge and a cabin from wood recovered from the ship's hull, and the resourceful men then constructed a small boat and sailed to New Zealand

The Scottish *Invercauld,* headed for South America, ran aground some months later, but the crew had no knowledge of the men on the other side, and could not, because of an impassable mountain range. The nineteen desperate surviving members of the twenty-five-man crew ate their dead mates, and only three ultimately managed to stay alive, and that because of the resourcefulness of a young sailor, Robert Holding. They were eventually rescued by a passing Spanish vessel.

A *Kirkus Reviews* contributor described this volume: "Swashbuckling maritime history reanimated by a noted naval enthusiast."

In a phone interview with Denis Welch for *New Zealand Listener Online,* Druett described the contrast between these two groups of men as being like *Robinson Crusoe* and *Lord of the Flies.* She said the film rights were purchased by South Pacific Pictures, producers of *Whale Rider.*

Welch noted that Druett goes on voyages to "ensure authenticity." "'A ship under sail is a marvelous thing—grab it if you ever have the chance,' she says memorably. 'Because it has lift: it's light in the water. There's this silence—just the ripple of the water and the crack of the canvas—and the lift, the feeling of lightness, of weightlessness. Even with a big ship, which is really quite miraculous. They are like birds: you almost expect them to take off.'"

BIOGRAPHICAL AND CRITICAL SOURCES:

PERIODICALS

American History Illustrated, July-August, 1993, review of *"She Was a Sister Sailor": The Whaling Journals of Mary Brewster, 1845-1851,* p. 17.

Atlantic, August 1, 1998, review of *Hen Frigates: Wives of Merchant Captains Under Sail,* p. 104.

Biography, September 22, 2007, review of *Island of the Lost,* p. 719.

Booklist, May 15, 1998, Margaret Flanagan, review of *Hen Frigates,* p. 1570; February 15, 2000, Donna Seaman, review of *She Captains: Heroines and Hellions of the Sea;* September 15, 2000, William Beatty, review of *Rough Medicine: Surgeons at Sea in the Age of Sail,* p. 197; February 1, 2007, George Cohen, review of *Island of the Lost: Shipwrecked at the Edge of the World,* p. 18; September 1, 2007, Margaret Flanagan, review of *Deadly Shoals,* p. 60.

Choice, April, 2001, review of *Rough Medicine.*

Entertainment Weekly, June 8, 2007, Wook Kim, review of *Island of the Lost,* p. 84.

Journal of the American Medical Association, April 11, 2000, Hans A. Brings, "Nautical Medicine," p. 1894.

Journal of the Early Republic, winter, 1993, Mary Zwiep, review of *"She Was a Sister Sailor,"* p. 582.

Kirkus Reviews, March 1, 2003, review of *In the Wake of Madness: The Murderous Voyage of the Whaleship Sharon,* p. 359; August 1, 2004, review of *A Watery Grave,* p. 715; August 15, 2005, review of *Shark Island,* pp. 883-884; September 1, 2006, review of *Run Afoul,* pp. 876-877; April 1, 2007, review of *Island of the Lost;* September 1, 2007, review of *Deadly Shoals.*

Kliatt, September, 2003, Sunnie Grant, review of *In the Wake of Madness,* p. 60.

Library Journal, July, 1998, Roseanne Castellino, review of *Hen Frigates,* p. 108; March 15, 2000, Roseanne Castellino, review of *She Captains,* p. 104; March 15, 2003, Robert C. Jones, review of *In the Wake of Madness,* p. 96; August 15, 2004, Rex E. Klett, review of *A Watery Grave,* p. 59.

New York Times Book Review, July 26, 1998, Holly Morris, "First Helpmates"; March 26, 2000, Louise Jarvis, "Dames at Sea," p. 15; May 4, 2003, Peter Nichols, "Psycho at Sea," p. 16; July 15, 2007, Florence Williams, review of *Island of the Lost,* p. 26.

Publishers Weekly, November 16, 1992, review of *"She Was a Sister Sailor,"* p. 55; January 31, 2000, review of *She Captains;* December 18, 2000, review of *Rough Medicine,* p. 70; April 28, 2003, review of *In the Wake of Madness,* p. 61; July 26, 2004, review of *A Watery Grave,* p. 41; August 8, 2005, review of *Shark Island,* p. 216; September 18, 2006, review of *Run Afoul,* p. 39; March 12, 2007, review of *Island of the Lost,* p. 44; October 15, 2007, review of *Deadly Shoals,* p. 45.

School Library Journal, April 1, 2007, Joanne Ligamari, review of *Island of the Lost,* p. 172.

ONLINE

A.V. Club, http://www.avclub.com/ (July 26, 2007), Noel Murray, review of *Island of the Lost.*

Joan Druett Home Page, http://members.authorsguild.net/druettjo (March 7, 2007).

Mostly Fiction, http://mostlyfiction.com/ (December 27, 2007), Kirstin Merrihew, review of *Deadly Shoals.*

MysteryReader.com, http://www.themysteryreader.com/ (March 6, 2007), Lesley Dunlap, review of *A Watery Grave.*

New Zealand Listener Online, http://www.listener.co.nz/ (May 10, 2008), Denis Welch, "The Seafarer" (interview).

Paste Online, http://www.pastemagazine.com/ (July 3, 2007), H.M. Starkey, review of *Island of the Lost.*

*　　　*　　　*

DUBOIS, Brendan

PERSONAL: Married; wife's name Mona Pinette. *Education:* Graduated from University of New Hampshire. *Hobbies and other interests:* Astronomy and the space program.

ADDRESSES: *Home*—Exeter, NH. *E-mail*—brendan@brendandubois.com.

CAREER: Novelist and short story writer, newspaper reporter.

AWARDS, HONORS: Shamus Award for Best Short Story of the Year, Private Eye Writers of America, for "The Necessary Brother," 1995, and "The Road's End,"

2001; Al Blanchard Crime Fiction Award for Best Short Crime Fiction Story at the fourth annual New England Crime Bake, for "The Road's End," 2005.

WRITINGS:

"LEWIS COLE MYSTERY" SERIES

Dead Sand, Otto Penzler Books (New York, NY), 1994.

Black Tide, Otto Penzler Books (New York, NY), 1995.

Shattered Shell, St. Martin's Press (New York, NY), 1999.

Killer Waves, Thomas Dunne Books (New York, NY), 2002.

Buried Dreams, Thomas Dunne Books (New York, NY), 2004.

Primary Storm, Thomas Dunne Books (New York, NY), 2006.

OTHER FICTION

Resurrection Day (novel), G.P. Putnam's Sons (New York, NY), 1999.

Six Days, Little, Brown (London, England), 2001.

The Dark Snow and Other Mysteries (short stories), Crippen & Landru Publishers (Norfolk, VA), 2002.

Tales From the Dark Woods (short stories), Five Star (Waterville, ME), 2002.

Betrayed (novel), Thomas Dunne Books (New York, NY), 2003.

Final Winter (novel), Time Warner UK (London, England), 2005, Five Star (Detroit, MI), 2008.

Dead of Night, Sphere (London, England), 2007, published as *Twilight,* St. Martin's Minotaur (New York, NY), 2007.

Contributor of short fiction to numerous periodicals, including *Playboy, Ellery Queen's Mystery, Mary Higgins Clark Mystery* magazine, and *Alfred Hitchcock's Mystery;* contributor to various anthologies, including *The Year's Best Mystery & Suspense Stories,* Walker Books (New York, NY), 1988, 1990, 1992, 1995, *Year's 25 Best Mystery Short Stories,* 1995, 1997, *Best American Mystery Stories,* Houghton Mifflin (Boston, MA), 1997, 1999, 2001, 2003, *Best American Mystery Stories of the Century,* edited by Otto Penzler and Tony Hillerman, Houghton Mifflin (Boston, MA), 2000, and *The World's Finest Mystery and Crime Stories,* Forge (New York, NY), 2001-04.

SIDELIGHTS: Brendan DuBois, a life-long resident of New Hampshire, has set his mystery novels in the area in which he lives. He is best known as the author of the "Lewis Cole" series, but has also written numerous short stories and an alternative history novel titled *Resurrection Day.* At one point in his life, DuBois seriously considered a career with the National Security Agency, going so far as to complete the testing process and interview for three jobs. He has also worked as a journalist. He has taken this experience and made journalism and a murky entanglement with espionage a part of fictional sleuth Lewis Cole's profile. These two elements play large roles in the plot development and help to define the atmosphere of suspense in DuBois's novels. His deep knowledge of New Hampshire and its people is also an asset to the stories. DuBois's work has been favorably compared to the mystery novels of Robert Parker, whose sleuth, Spencer, is also an intelligent, tough, and erudite man.

Through the "Lewis Cole" novels, DuBois has created not only a group of well-plotted mysteries, but also an interesting community. The action of the books is set in a fictional town in coastal New Hampshire. As the stories unfold, readers become well acquainted with the local people and develop an appreciation of their nuanced relationships. *Dead Sand,* the first title in the "Lewis Cole" series, finds the hero living in New Hampshire as a magazine writer. He is drawn into the investigation of some suspicious deaths after a friend, the only detective on the local police force, asks his help. Cole's unearthing of secrets lead to attempts on his life. The discovery of the truth becomes imperative as the danger escalates.

In DuBois' second "Lewis Cole" novel, *Black Tide,* the hero is drawn into the puzzling circumstances surrounding an oil spill on the New Hampshire coast. To complicate matters, a mutilated corpse has washed ashore. Cole's friend and sometime sidekick, Felix Tinios adds another level of complexity by his involvement in a major art theft and the criminal underworld. Critics noted that DuBois reveals the connecting elements between the separate mysteries in a suspenseful ending.

The desolation of winter on the New Hampshire coast sets the tone for the third novel in the series, *Shattered Shell.* Cole's town has been plagued by arson and he takes an unofficial interest in the investigation. When a local woman, the lover of the police department's detective, is raped and beaten, the usually dormant winter atmosphere becomes tense. Complications ensue when Cole realizes that the woman's description of the crime does not match the physical evidence. Discovering the connections between the two crimes keeps Cole busy and in danger until the very end. In *Killer Waves,* Cole investigates the mysterious death of a man in a parking lot near his home. The matter quickly comes to the attention of some people with phony DEA identification, and Cole is soon embroiled in something more menacing than he could ever have imagined.

DuBois continues his series with *Buried Dreams,* in which Cole makes the acquaintance of Jon Ericson when he appears on Cole's doorstep, claiming that his Viking ancestors had landed on the beachfront property hundreds of years earlier and he is intent on searching for historic proof with the aid of his metal detector. However, Ericson is later murdered, and Cole investigates who killed him. In a review for *Booklist,* David Pitt remarked that "this fifth entry will have readers hoping there are many more to follow." A *Kirkus Reviews* contributor wrote: "So much geography you'll want a road map, but briskly paced, with a neatly sprung ending." In *Primary Storm,* the next volume in the series, a Secret Service agent tracks Cole down despite all of his efforts to hide himself away in the country. When the agent turns out to be a fake, and ends up murdered, Cole is more than a little annoyed. A *Kirkus Reviews* contributor wrote: "DuBois keeps everything deft and literate until the ending, as wild and wooly as you'd expect from the premise."

Resurrection Day is something of a departure for DuBois. In this book he enters the realm of alternative history with a novel formed around the Cuban missile crisis. The story takes place ten years after the crisis, but in this telling, the Russians have destroyed the major U.S. cities and the U.S. military has destroyed Russia. Great Britain takes a humanitarian role, and saves what remains of the United States from starvation and complete destruction. Newspaper reporter Carl Landry becomes involved in the investigation of a murder and soon finds himself enmeshed in a complex plot that would return the United States to the status of a British colony. As he learns more, his life, like the life of the country, becomes endangered. The book's premise, according to *Library Journal* reviewer Kent Rasmussen, is "intriguing," but "its development is unsatisfactory." A writer for *Publishers Weekly,* however, commented that *Resurrection Day* "deserves to be as popular as Robert Harris's *Fatherland.*" Reviewer David Pitt expressed similar praise in *Booklist,* calling the book a "feast for the mind" and a "first-rate novel."

DuBois continues to intersperse stand-alone thrillers between his "Lewis Cole" novels. With *Betrayed,* he offers readers a thriller about Vietnam soldier Roy Harper, who was reported missing in action, yet suddenly appears on his brother's doorstep thirty years later. Roy has a twisted story of torture and abuse, and it appears that, while he might have come home, he is far from free of his experiences. A contributor for *Kirkus Reviews* found the novel "not always plausible, but the story grabs, and the pages turn, testimony to the power of the narrative." A reviewer for *Publishers Weekly* noted: "DuBois has a way of taking stock characters . . . and surprising us with fresh insights into their behavior."

Final Winter tells the story of a group of law enforcement officers drawn together after the 9-11 attacks to counter the next series of terrorist assaults on the United States. When the CIA discovers that an anthrax attack is planned, the groups—called Tiger Teams—go into action. The novel's "execution is inventive," declared a *Publishers Weekly* contributor, "with plot twists good enough to keep readers whipping through the pages." *Final Winter* is "solid thriller fare," concluded David Pitt, writing in *Booklist,* "from an author on the edge of a breakthrough."

Twilight focuses on the attempts of a team led by Canadian journalist Samuel Simpson to document a war-crimes site for the United Nations: a place where the bodies of hundreds of civilians massacred by a local militia are buried. The twist is in the location: upstate New York. The United States has broken up, with civil war raging between red and blue states. The cause of the breakup is a series of small nuclear bombs delivered by weather balloons—one of which has devastated lower Manhattan. The UN has had to intervene to keep peace between the different factions until some form of order can be restored to the country. "DuBois," wrote a contributor to *Kirkus Reviews,* "does . . . a razor-sharp job of detailing the surreal perils of the war-torn American landscape." "The balance between action and introspection is superb," stated a *Publishers Weekly* reviewer, "and DuBois . . . avoid[s] a pat, upbeat ending." *Twilight,* concluded Thomas Gaughan in *Booklist,* is a "gut-wrenching, heartrending plausibility of a frightened, angry, post-Katrina America riven by bad government and the politics of division."

BIOGRAPHICAL AND CRITICAL SOURCES:

PERIODICALS

Booklist, May 15, 1994, Emily Melton, review of *Dead Sand,* p. 1666; February 15, 1995, Emily Melton,

review of *Black Tide,* p. 1061; February 15, 1999, John Rowen, review of *Shattered Shell,* p. 1044; April 15, 1999, David Pitt, review of *Resurrection Day,* p. 1476; May 15, 2004, Bratt Pitt, review of *Buried Dreams,* p. 1600; October 15, 2007, Thomas Gaughan, review of *Twilight,* p. 38; December 1, 2007, David Pitt, review of *Final Winter,* p. 25.

Kirkus Review, January, 1995, review of *Black Tide,* p. 28; January 15, 1999, review of *Shattered Shell,* p. 106; April 1, 2002, review of *Killer Waves,* p. 456; May 1, 2003, review of *Betrayed,* p. 625; May 15, 2004, review of *Buried Dreams,* p. 474; August 1, 2006, review of *Primary Storm,* p. 755; October 1, 2007, review of *Twilight.*

Library Journal, June 1, 1999, Barbara Conaty, review of *Resurrection Day,* p. 173; November 1, 2000, Kent Rasmussen, review of *Resurrection Day,* p. 158.

Publishers Weekly, April 11, 1994, review of *Dead Sand,* p. 58; January 9, 1995, review of *Black Tide,* p. 58; February 15, 1999, review of *Shattered Shell,* p. 90; May 17, 1999, review of *Resurrection Day,* p. 57; May 20, 2002, review of *Killer Waves,* p. 49; May 26, 2003, review of *Betrayed,* p. 52; October 1, 2007, review of *Twilight,* p. 41; November 5, 2007, review of *Final Winter,* p. 45.

School Library Journal, December, 1999, Anita Short, review of *Resurrection Day,* p. 163.

Washington Post Book World, February 27, 1999, Joan Richter, review of *Shattered Shell,* p. 8.

ONLINE

Brendan DuBois Web site, http://brendandubois.com (September 2, 2008), author profile.*

*   *   *

DUFFY, Margaret 1942-

PERSONAL: Born March 3, 1942, in Woodford, England; daughter of Leslie Oscar (a hairdresser and author) and Ethel Margaret (a court dressmaker) Zenker; married Gordon Frederick Duffy (a consultant engineer), April 9, 1966; children: Hayley Ann Ball. *Education:* Attended Worthing Technical College. *Politics:* "Conservative." *Hobbies and other interests:* Gardening, cookery, nature, birds, archaeology (especially shipwrecks).

ADDRESSES: Home—Dousland, England. *Agent*— Vanessa Holt, 59 Crescent Rd., Leigh-on-Sea, Essex SS9 2PF, England.

CAREER: Writer. Clerical officer in Worthing, England, 1958-66, and for Ministry of Defense, Avon, England, 1969-74.

WRITINGS:

MYSTERIES

Man of Blood, St. Martin's Press (New York, NY), 1992.
Corpse-candle, Piatkus Books (London, England), 1995.

"PATRICK GILLARD AND INGRID LANGLEY MYSTERY" SERIES

A Murder of Crows, St. Martin's Press (New York, NY), 1987.
Death of a Raven, St. Martin's Press (New York, NY), 1988.
Brass Eagle, St. Martin's Press (New York, NY), 1988.
Who Killed Cock Robin?, St. Martin's Press (New York, NY), 1990.
Rook-shoot, Piatkus Books (London, England), 1990.
Gallows-bird, Piatkus Books (London, England), 1993.
A Hanging Matter, Allison & Busby (London, England), 2002.
So Horrible a Place, Allison & Busby (London, England), 2004.
Dead Trouble, Allison & Busby (London, England), 2004.
Tainted Ground, Severn House (Sutton, England), 2006.
Cobweb, Severn House (Sutton, England), 2007.
Blood Substitute, Severn House (Sutton, England), 2008.
Souvenirs of Murder, Severn House (Sutton, England), 2009.

"JOANNA MCKENZIE AND JAMES CARRICK MYSTERY" SERIES

Dressed to Kill, Piatkus Books (London, England), 1994.
Prospect of Death, St. Martin's Press (New York, NY), 1996.

Music in the Blood, Piatkus Books (London, England), 1997.
A Fine Target, Piatkus Books (London, England), 1998.

SIDELIGHTS: Many of Margaret Duffy's mysteries feature the husband-and-wife detecting team of Ingrid Langley and Patrick Gillard. Langley is a novelist and Gillard is an army officer, but both are members of D-12, a super-secret division of British intelligence. In the fourth title in the series, *Who Killed Cock Robin?,* Langley and Gillard are in mourning for a colleague blown up in a car bomb incident. Code-named Robin, this operative is replaced by an agent not easy to adapt to. Langley and Gillard have little time to worry about this, though, as they are sent to a picturesque village to investigate the murder of a senior MI5 official, Sir John Westfield. There they must deal with uncooperative villagers, seeming supernatural occurrences, and racketeers from the capital in a story with a "many-layered plot [that] delivers plenty of satisfying action," according to *Publishers Weekly* contributor Sybil Steinberg. In *Rook-shoot,* Langley and Gillard are planning a vacation when Gillard's brother Larry petitions them for help. The Outward-Bound type survival courses he leads are being sabotaged by an unknown enemy. When Langley and Gillard try to intervene, they are captured by an old nemesis, Lyndberne, who runs a school for terrorists. The couple find themselves part of a demonstration on how to torture and interrogate subjects. A *Kirkus Reviews* writer found the book's scenes of torture "appalling," but praised the depiction of the couple's relationship.

In *Man of Blood,* Duffy introduces undercover policeman Rolt and his sidekick Piers Ashley, who infiltrate a crime mob so thoroughly that Ashley spends six months in prison. The action moves from the city to a country castle and involves run-ins with the police and the underworld. According to another *Kirkus Reviews* contributor, *Man of Blood* "combines derring-do with a cozy, upper-crust charm—somewhat reminiscent of Golden Age detective fiction. . . . The steely Rolt and the dashing Piers will wow devoted Anglophiles."

Duffy creates another crime-solving couple in *Dressed to Kill.* James Carrick is a detective chief inspector with the police force in Bath, England; Joanna MacKenzie is a member of the force, but she becomes a private investigator when she is fired because of her affair with Carrick. In *Prospect of Death,* Carrick and MacKenzie join forces with Patrick Gillard to solve the brutal murder of a movie producer. *Prospect of Death* was criticized in *Kirkus Reviews* for having "too many plot lines, corpses, beatings, and detectives in an overrich brew," but the reviewer added that it was all "made readable . . . by the author's graceful style and command of local color."

Duffy returns to the detecting couple of Langley and Gillard with the 2006 installment, *Tainted Ground,* which finds them newly retired from the secret service, with Langley taking up script writing. However, Gillard is having trouble finding a vocation for himself until an opportunity comes along to join the police. His old friend, DCI James Carrick, whom he has teamed up with before, recommends him for the position. Uncomfortably for them both, Gillard is quickly promoted above Carrick, which causes tension between the two. However, Gillard has no time for turf battles. He is no sooner on the job than he is presented with a troubling case: three bodies are discovered in a barn, and the clues lead nowhere. A *Kirkus Reviews* critic complained that there were "few clues, no suspense and not the slightest interest in any of the suspects" in this procedural. *Booklist* contributor Emily Melton, though, found this a "competently written, creatively plotted British mystery."

Langley and Gillard continue their investigations in *Cobweb,* which finds Gillard a new recruit for the Serious Organized Crime Agency (SOCA) battling crimes that have a distinct Mafia flavor to them. His first case is a challenge: two policemen investigating the murder of a member of Parliament have themselves died under mysterious circumstances. Gillard and Langley do not think these deaths are mere coincidence. *Booklist* reviewer Melton termed this a "suspenseful adventure," and further praised the "solid action-adventure plotting." In the 2008 series addition, *Blood Substitute,* Gillard and Langley take on another SOCA case, tracking down a killer who was assumed to be dead. Now it appears, however, that the assassin, who carves his initials in his victims, is alive and well and responsible for a series of gang hits. However, as they pick up the trail of this man, Gillard and Langley wonder if the killer himself is not the intended victim. On the domestic front, Langley is now pregnant yet still game for adventure. A *Kirkus Reviews* contributor had a mixed assessment of this installment, concluding: "Lashings of Bond-style derring-do cover up nicely for some slapdash plotting." However, a *Publishers Weekly* reviewer had a higher opinion of the same work, noting that "Duffy injects this crisp if sometimes too chatty police procedural with some great action scenes."

Duffy once told *CA:* "I started by writing science fiction, which at that time—in the days before fantasy really became a cult genre in the early eighties—was in the doldrums. *Chimera* was followed by *Barefoot upon Thorns* and *Brittle Star.* Publishers and agents liked my writing style but shook their heads over the subject matter. I could not stop writing—I had too worthwhile of a central character, someone by that time who was too much a part of my life to forget and shove into a drawer. So I brought Patrick Gillard back into the twentieth century and turned him into a Falklands War veteran, trying to pick up the pieces of his life after serious injury. It seemed logical that a major in a special operations unit might be asked to work for MI5 and that as socializing was part of the job be expected to find a female partner. Gillard's choice was his ex-wife, Ingrid, and he prayed that she would agree. When a man has suffered injuries of the worst possible kind, he is not looking for sexual challenges and after the acrimonious divorce, he knew Ingrid would be the last woman on earth to want to go to bed with him. As it happened, he was wrong about quite a few things on this subject, but it only served to make life more interesting for both of them.

"I enjoy writing about people who, with courage and determination, triumph over the setbacks that life throws at them. There has to be humor of course, there can be no real life without it.

"I have branched out from thrillers into whodunits. I suppose writers on such subjects hope their work will be dramatized for television and film, and I am no exception. One day, perhaps, I will also see the one remaining science fiction story in print, the one that escaped the wastepaper basket—*Mindspinner,* the light of my life."

Duffy later added: "My father wrote and had a novel published called *Many Bridges.* I suppose writing is in my blood.

"Reading Dorothy Dunnett's historical novels made me burn to want to write—they are wonderful.

"I write when the house can be described as reasonably straight. I can't work if my house is a mess.

"The most surprising thing I learned as a writer is about myself—I am much more tenacious and thick-skinned than I thought. You have to be to or you give up at the first rejection [letter]."

"My favorite book is *A Fine Target,* but I'm not sure why."

BIOGRAPHICAL AND CRITICAL SOURCES:

PERIODICALS

Booklist, September 1, 2006, Emily Melton, review of *Tainted Ground,* p. 61; September 1, 2007, Emily Melton, review of *Cobweb,* p. 60.

Kirkus Reviews, October 15, 1991, review of *Rookshoot,* p. 1312; August 15, 1992, review of *Man of Blood,* p. 1019; October 15, 1994, review of *Dressed to Kill,* p. 1372; May 1, 1996, review of *Prospect of Death,* p. 642; September 1, 2006, review of *Tainted Ground,* p. 877; October 1, 2008, review of *Blood Substitute.*

Publishers Weekly, August 10, 1990, Sybil Steinberg, review of *Who Killed Cock Robin?,* p. 436; October 6, 2008, review of *Blood Substitute,* p. 38.

F

FERGUSON, Niall 1964-

PERSONAL: Born April 18, 1964, in Glasgow, Scotland; son of James Campbell (a consultant physician) and Molly Archibald (a physicist) Ferguson; married Susan Margaret Douglas (a consultant editor), July 25, 1994; children: Felix, Freya, Lachlan. *Education:* Magdalen College, Oxford, B.A. (first class honors), 1985, D.Phil., 1989; attended University of Hamburg.

ADDRESSES: Office—Center for European Studies, Harvard University, 27 Kirkland St., Cambridge, MA 02138. *Agent*—The Wylie Agency, 250 W. 57th St., Ste. 2114, New York, NY 10107. *E-mail*—nfergus@fas. harvard.edu.

CAREER: Christ's College, Cambridge, England, research fellow, 1989-90; Peterhouse, Cambridge, official fellow and lecturer, 1990-92; Jesus College, Oxford University, fellow and tutor in modern history, 1992-2000, professor of political and financial history, 2000-02; Stern Business School, New York University, Herzog Chair in Financial History, 2002-04; Harvard University, Cambridge, MA, Laurence A. Tisch Professor of History, and William Ziegler Professor of Business Administration, 2004—.

AWARDS, HONORS: Wadsworth Prize for Business History, 1998, for *The World's Banker;* Houblon-Norman Fellowship, Bank of England, 1998-99.

WRITINGS:

Paper and Iron: Hamburg Business and German Politics in the Era of Inflation, 1897-1927, Cambridge University Press (New York, NY), 1995.

(Editor) *Virtual History: Alternatives and Counterfactuals,* Macmillan (London, England), 1997, Basic Books (New York, NY), 1999.

The World's Banker, Weidenfeld & Nicolson (London, England), 1998, published in two volumes as *The House of Rothschild: Money's Prophets, 1798-1848,* Viking (New York, NY), 1998, and *The House of Rothschild: The World's Banker, 1849-1999,* Viking (New York, NY), 1999.

The Pity of War: Explaining World War I, Allen Lane/Penguin Press (London, England), 1998, Basic Books (New York, NY), 1999.

The Cash Nexus: Money and Power in the Modern World, 1700-2000, Allen Lane/Penguin Press (London, England), 2001.

Empire: The Rise and Demise of the British World Order and the Lessons for Global Power (companion book to television documentary series), Basic Books (New York, NY), 2003, published as *Empire: How Britain Made the Modern World,* Allen Lane (London, England), 2003.

Colossus: The Price of America's Empire (companion book to television documentary series), Penguin Press (New York, NY), 2004, reprinted as *The Rise and Fall of the American Empire,* 2005.

The War of the World: Twentieth-century Conflict and the Descent of the West (companion book to television documentary series), Penguin Press (New York, NY), 2006, published as *The War of the World: History's Age of Hatred,* Allen Lane (London, England), 2006.

The Ascent of Money: A Financial History of the World (companion book to television documentary series), Penguin Press (New York, NY), 2008.

Author of radio series *Days that Shook the World,* BBC Radio 4. Contributor to periodicals, including the *Times,*

Sunday Times, Financial Times, Daily Telegraph, New York Times, Independent, Guardian, Spectator, New Republic, Wall Street Journal, Washington Post, Die Welt (Germany), *Past & Present, English Historical Review, Economic History Review, Foreign Affairs,* and the *Journal of Economic History;* contributor to books, including *Secrets of the Press: Journalists on Journalism,* edited by Stephen Glover, Penguin, 1999; *Progress and Emancipation in the age of Metternich: Jews and Modernisation in Austria and Germany, 1815-1848,* edited by Andrea Hamel and Edward Timms, Edwin Mellen Press, 1999; *The Short Oxford History of Europe: The Nineteenth Century,* edited by T.C.W. Blanning, Oxford University Press, 2000; and *Great War, Total War: Combat and Mobilization on the Western Front,* edited by Roger Chickering and Stig Förster, Cambridge University Press, 2000. Also author of e-lecture, "Why the World Wars Were Won." Ferguson's works have been published in Spain, Germany, Poland, Italy, and Japan.

SIDELIGHTS: Professor Niall Ferguson, an Oxford University historian, has published several works on the political and financial histories of Europe in the nineteenth and twentieth centuries. A regular contributor to periodicals, Ferguson has also appeared on BBC2's *Midnight Hour, Newsnight,* and BBC1's *Question Time.* Ferguson told *CA:* "I regard engagement with the media as an integral part of my role as an historian." Ferguson won the Wadsworth Prize for Business History in 1998.

Ferguson's first book, *Paper and Iron: Hamburg Business and German Politics in the Era of Inflation, 1897-1927,* is an expanded version of his Ph.D. thesis. Ferguson drew on Hamburg's archives and other sources in Germany, Great Britain, and the United States in writing this study of the economic and political history of Germany from World War I until the mid-1920s. Ferguson focuses on the Port of Hamburg throughout the book as he describes the effects of the war, unemployment, and inflation. He examines the roles of many of the influential figures of the time, including Hamburg bankers and industrialists such as Max Warburg, Carl Melchior, and others, during the period from the Paris peace conference until the final days of Wilhelm Cuno's term as Reich chancellor.

Many historians minimize the negative effects of Germany's postwar inflation, making the case that it helped to create investment, cut debt, and raise wages

for the German worker. Ferguson takes a different position. Stefan Berger wrote in *History Today* that he "draws up a negative balance sheet by stressing that inflationary policies neither stopped political and social unrest on a hitherto unprecedented level, nor, for a variety of reasons, made sense in economic terms. All it achieved in the end was the complete alienation of the German middle classes from the republic." Sidney Pollard of *Business History* wrote: "Ferguson differs from most other historians by believing that hyperinflation could have been prevented, that it was due largely to the fear of revolution which might follow deflation, to the continued weakness of the German central authorities, and to the underlying policy of wishing to sabotage the reparations payments." "The author postulates that currency stabilization constituted an option in 1920 that was not followed," wrote Elisabeth Glaser in *Business History Review.* "Skillfully shifting perspectives back and forth from Hamburg to the Reich, Ferguson emphasizes that even during the temporary halt in the mark's fall from June to September 1920, the Wirth government took no serious fiscal or political steps toward stabilization." Glaser concluded that *Paper and Iron* "offers a multifold perspective on the causes and effects of inflation in wartime and postwar Hamburg and Germany as a whole."

Virtual History: Alternatives and Counterfactuals is a collection of nine "what if" essays edited by Ferguson, including one by Diane Kunz that speculates on what might have happened if President Kennedy had not been assassinated. Jonathan Clarke, in another essay, considers whether the American Revolution would have been avoided if Britain had pursued a different policy of taxation, whether a later war might have occurred over the slavery issue, and if continued British colonization would have avoided the U.S. Civil War. Of the essays, Conrad Russell commented in *New Statesman:* "The counterfactual hypothesis is the nearest historians can manage to a controlled experiment of the sort that scientists carry out. But it is not, all the same, a proper scientific experiment: the rerun without the variable has no existence outside the historian's mind." Peter Clarke of *London Review of Books,* however, stated that in *Virtual History* "Ferguson shows himself both erudite and cogent in staking out the ground. While building on the insights of predecessors like Bury, Popper, or W.B. Gallie, Ferguson reformulates the essential arguments with characteristically late twentieth-century appeal to chaos theory in reconciling causation and contingency."

Ferguson titled the afterword "A Virtual History, 1646-1996." Clarke wrote that in it Ferguson "is on one long tease: stitching together some of the counterfactuals proposed by his contributors. . . . Cheek never tongue-less, Ferguson projects and extends his counterfactuals along a single line of increasingly attenuated plausibil-ity, and increasingly tedious whimsy—exactly like those earlier authors whom he reprimands for cheapening and weakening an intellectually serious exercise."

Ferguson's lengthy history of the Rothschild family was first published in Great Britain as *The World's Banker* and covered the period from 1798 until 1915. It was then reissued in the United States in two volumes as *The House of Rothschild: Money's Prophets, 1798-1848* and *The House of Rothschild: The World's Banker, 1849-1999*. Ferguson added an epilogue to the second volume in order to extend the saga until 1999. In reviewing the first volume in *Time,* Lance Morrow noted that Ferguson "finds enough great material for a dozen mini-series." The one-time wealthiest family on earth was comprised largely of prolific letter writers, and Fer-guson was able to gain access to 135 boxes of cor-respondence and business documents, much of it from the family's London archives, in compiling his history. As Geoffrey Wheatcroft wrote of the volumes in the *New York Times Book Review,* the Rothschilds' "enthral-ling story has been told before, but never in such authoritative detail."

Nathan Rothschild, born in 1777, is the central figure in the book and key to the family's success. He began as a textile merchant and sometime smuggler in Manchester, England. He moved to London in 1810 to begin his career as a banker. At Napoleon's defeat in 1815, the Rothschilds had established themselves as the preemi-nent European banking house. In 1818 Nathan issued bonds for Prussia, with dividends payable in London, the first step in the family's control of the foreign bond market until the end of the nineteenth century. In 1825, Nathan helped the Bank of England meet its obliga-tions. Wheatcroft noted that the Rothschilds "never became big American players. They liked to lend to the government of a country before they did commercial business there, but this was difficult when the United States was a genuinely loose federation, some of whose states were 'among the least reliable' of all borrowers in the nineteenth century, and especially when Andrew Jackson was conducting his war against the Bank of the United States." When Nathan died in 1836, he was the most powerful Rothschild and the richest man in England. "The Rothschilds were renowned for their intelligence, in every sense of the word," wrote Fritz Stern in the *New Republic.* He continued: "Ferguson is

right: they were more like royalty than aristocracy. They knew their worth, and also that it was unprecedented." Stern said that Ferguson "writes impeccably, and with empathy. . . . This is a major achievement of historical scholarship and historical imagination. Ferguson's work reaffirms one's faith in the possibility of great historical writing." *Booklist* reviewer David Rouse described the family's saga as "exhaustively detailed and well-crafted."

The Pity of War: Explaining World War I is Ferguson's revisionist account of the war that left nearly ten mil-lion dead and fifteen million wounded in the years from 1914 to 1918. A *Kirkus Reviews* writer called the book "moving, penetrating, eye-opening, and lucidly rea-soned. An important work of historical analysis." Fergu-son writes that Germany went to war not because it was militarily the strongest but because it feared it was los-ing the arms race to Britain, Russia, and France. He argues that Great Britain escalated the war upon joining it, supposedly to defend Belgian neutrality, prompted by the fear of a German conquest of France. He writes that if Britain had sacrificed Belgium to Germany, there would not have been a Bolshevik Revolution. Germany would have formed a European state, and Britain would have remained powerful. Ferguson feels a quick Ger-man victory could have spared millions of lives and that Germany was actually winning the war before its leadership collapsed in 1918. He wrote that "with the Kaiser triumphant, Adolph Hitler could have eked out his life as a mediocre postcard painter . . . in a German-dominated Central Europe about which he could have found little to complain. And Lenin could have carried on his splenetic scribbling in Zurich, forever waiting for capitalism to collapse—and forever be disap-pointed."

Ferguson cites the economics of casualties, noting that the German cost for each Allied death was just over five thousand dollars, while the Allies paid over sixteen thousand dollars for each German death. A *Publishers Weekly* reviewer called Ferguson's war "simply an economic problem. . . . Ultimately, it is hard to feel satisfied with Ferguson's narrow analysis of what is surely a far more complex equation." Other reviewers found unique insights in Ferguson's work. V.R. Berghahn reviewed *The Pity of War* in the *New York Times Book Review* and referred to the chapter titled "The Myth of War Enthusiasm," writing that Ferguson "investigates why men continued to fight long after it had dawned on them that this was not a conventional nineteenth-century war to be won in three months." An

Economist reviewer felt the book "is heavily concentrated on the Anglo-German relationship. France and Russia are by comparison neglected, not to speak of Austro-Hungary and Italy." But in spite of these flaws, the reviewer concluded that Ferguson "argues trenchantly and marshals evidence fluently, on a wide front. . . . *The Pity of War* is also a work of grace and feeling."

Ferguson, who joined the faculty of Harvard University in 2004, next wrote *The Cash Nexus: Money and Power in the Modern World, 1700-2000.* Here he combines history and economics in studying the national debts of countries over three centuries and in noting the ways in which states have raised money to wage war. *Red Herring* reviewer Mark Williams wrote: "Mr. Ferguson's understanding of international finance and its development is encyclopedic."

Ferguson suggests that France should have prevailed over Britain in the wars of the eighteenth century but did not because it lacked what Ferguson calls the "square of power." Britain did have the four institutions that made it a strong state: a legislature that represented taxpayers, a tax-gathering system, a national debt that funded wars, and a central bank. Ferguson also contends that if Britain had mobilized a large standing army and opposed German aggression leading to the two world wars, it could have remained a world power and changed the course of history.

Ferguson's next several volumes are companion books to television documentary series. In *Empire: The Rise and Demise of the British World Order and the Lessons for Global Power,* Ferguson disputes the idea that the golden age of British imperialism, with its racism, slavery, and plundering of countries and peoples, was a low point in human history. Instead, he argues, imperialism can and did result in good, and writes that the British were chiefly responsible for progressivism around the world during the nineteenth and twentieth centuries. Ferguson acknowledges that atrocities were committed, but he contends that the British tried to prevent racism in its colonized lands, knowing that it would be easier to rule if it were lessened or did not exist. He notes that the businessmen who gained from colonization often promoted racist policies in spite of the best efforts of the central government. Such policies eventually resulted in the Indian nationalist movement that forced the British from that country. In reviewing *Empire,* a *Kirkus Reviews* contributor concluded: "Lively and thoughtful: provocative both as history and forecast." *America* reviewer Victor Ferkiss wrote: "Whether one agrees with Ferguson or not, anyone seriously concerned with America's rapidly changing role in the world should read this richly informative and thought-provoking book."

In *Colossus: The Price of America's Empire,* Ferguson continues a theme found in the final pages of *Empire,* that the United States has the ability for imperial superiority, but that it has neither the foresight nor the courage to seize it. Ferguson also writes that the United States, while a fearsome military combatant, would be lacking as a long-term global administrator. He suggests that if it were to follow in the footsteps of the British, the United States could secure global peace and order. Ferguson writes that "many parts of the world would benefit from a period of American rule." He sees the United States as an "empire in denial," adding that empires in denial, in intervening in the affairs of lesser states, make two mistakes. They "allocate insufficient resources to the non-military aspects of the project" and they "attempt economic and political transformation in an unrealistically short time frame." Writing for *Salon. com,* Ted Widmer wrote: "There is much to admire in *Colossus:* reasoned historical analysis (showing more knowledge of obscure bits of U.S. imperial history than most Americans possess), firm command of economic statistics, pleasing literary cadences. The English, God bless 'em, can still turn out writers along with would-be colonial administrators. Ferguson's central point is important and indisputable—that the United States resembles a global empire far more than most Americans, still living in L. Frank Baum's prelapsarian Kansas, take the time to understand."

Ferguson contends that the ability of the United States to effectively perform as a world power will soon be compromised, in great measure because of the costs of Social Security and Medicare for its aging population, as well as because of a lack of manpower.

Ferguson studies the period from before World War I to the end of the Korean War in *The War of the World: Twentieth-century Conflict and the Descent of the West.* He notes that this is one of the bloodiest periods in history; one during which countries slaughtered their own people as well as the populations of other countries. A *Kirkus Reviews* critic concluded: "A lucid, blood-soaked study that will give no comfort to those pining for peace in our time."

In reviewing Ferguson's next book, *The Ascent of Money: A Financial History of the World*, New York Times reviewer Michael Hirsh wrote that he is "like the brightest kid in the debating club, the one who pulls all-nighters in the library and ferrets out facts no one thought to uncover. And in his latest book, *The Ascent of Money*—humbly subtitled *A Financial History of the World*—Ferguson takes us on an often enlightening and enjoyable spelunking tour through the underside of great events, a lesson in how the most successful great powers have always been underpinned by smart money." Published during the worst financial crisis since the Great Depression, Ferguson, who had previously accused the United States of "imperial understretch," now chastises it for becoming deeply indebted to the rest of the world, particularly China. He refers to the two countries as "Chimerica," and he blames the increase in bank lending, derivative contracts, and bond issuance that began in 2000 on the availability of that easy money. An *Economist* contributor wrote: "The world needs a book that puts today's crisis into context. It is too late now to warn investors about expensive houses and financiers about cheap credit. But perhaps the past can help make sense of the wreckage of banks, brokers and hedge funds that litters the markets. Looking back may help suggest what to do next. And when the crisis is over and it is time for the great reckoning, the lessons of history should inform the arguments about what must change."

BIOGRAPHICAL AND CRITICAL SOURCES:

PERIODICALS

African Business, January, 2009, review of *The Ascent of Money: A Financial History of the World,* p. 64.

Air & Space Power Journal, summer, 2008, Thomas A. Henwood, review of *The War of the World: Twentieth-century Conflict and the Descent of the West,* p. 121.

America, May 28, 2001, Victor Ferkiss, review of *The Cash Nexus: Money and Power in the Modern World, 1700-2000,* p. 26; August 4, 2003, Victor Ferkiss, review of *Empire: The Rise and Demise of the British World Order and the Lessons for Global Power,* p. 26; August 30, 2004, William J. Byron, review of *Colossus: The Price of America's Empire,* p. 23.

American Scholar, spring, 2001, Deirdre McCloskey, review of *The Cash Nexus,* p. 142; winter, 2007, Charles Trueheart, review of *The War of the World,* p. 141.

Booklist, October 1, 1999, David Rouse, review of *The House of Rothschild;* March 1, 2001, David Rouse, review of *The Cash Nexus,* p. 1213; April 15, 2003, Brad Hooper, review of *Empire,* p. 1444; March 1, 2004, Brendan Driscoll, review of *Colossus,* p. 1115; September 1, 2006, Brendan Driscoll, review of *The War of the World,* p. 40; October 15, 2008, Brad Hooper, review of *The Ascent of Money,* p. 17.

Boston Review, February-March, 2005, Vivek Chibber, review of *Colossus.*

Business History, April, 1996, Sidney Pollard, review of *Paper and Iron: Hamburg Business and German Politics in the Era of Inflation, 1897-1927,* p. 116.

Business History Review, spring, 1997, Elisabeth Glaser, review of *Paper and Iron,* p. 140.

Business Week, December 22, 2008, Hardy Green, review of *The Ascent of Money,* p. 75.

Cato Journal, fall, 2004, Christopher Preble, review of *Colossus,* p. 386.

Christian Science Monitor, January 7, 2009, Randy Dotinga, review of *The Ascent of Money,* p. 25.

Commentary, September, 2004, Sean McMeekin, review of *Colossus,* p. 95; March, 2007, Edward N. Luttwak, review of *The War of the World,* p. 74.

Contemporary Review, January, 2005, Ian Jackson, review of *Colossus,* p. 47.

Economist, June 21, 1997, review of *Virtual History: Alternatives and Counterfactuals,* p. R9; November 14, 1998, review of *The Pity of War: Explaining World War I,* p. 1; February 10, 2001, review of *The Cash Nexus,* p. 3; June 3, 2006, review of *The War of the World,* p. 81; October 11, 2008, review of *The Ascent of Money.*

Finance & Development, September, 2002, Michael Taylor, review of *The Cash Nexus,* p. 52.

Foreign Affairs, September-October, 2003, Stanley Hoffman, review of *Empire;* November-December, 2006, John Ikenberry, review of *The War of the World;* March-April, 2009, Richard N. Cooper, review of *The Ascent of Money,* p. 144.

Harvard, May-June, 2007, Janet Tassel, "The Global Empire of Niall Ferguson: Doing History on a Sweeping Scale."

Harvard Law Review, January, 2007, John Fabian Witt, review of *Empire.*

Historian, spring, 2008, Gerhard L. Weinberg, review of *The War of the World,* p. 188.

History Today, July, 1996, Stefan Berger, review of *Paper and Iron,* p. 54; May, 2001, Martin Daunton, review of *The Cash Nexus,* p. 54; February, 2009, Peter Jay, review of *The Ascent of Money,* p. 63.

Institutional Investor, May, 2001, Andrew Capon, review of *The Cash Nexus,* p. 148.

International Socialist Review, November-December, 2003, Paul D'Amato, review of *Empire.*

Kirkus Reviews, March 19, 1999, review of *The Pity of War;* February 15, 2003, review of *Empire,* p. 284; February 1, 2004, review of *Colossus,* p. 117; July 15, 2006, review of *The War of the World,* p. 710; October 1, 2008, review of *The Ascent of Money.*

Library Journal, March 15, 2001, Dale Farris, review of *The Cash Nexus,* p. 92; April 15, 2003, Thomas A. Karel, review of *Empire,* p. 106; April 15, 2004, Marcia L. Sprules, review of *Colossus,* p. 104; July 1, 2006, Patti C. McCall, review of *The War of the World,* p. 89; November 1, 2008, Lawrence Maxted, review of *The Ascent of Money,* p. 87.

London Review of Books, November 13, 1997, Peter Clarke, review of *Virtual History,* pp. 16-17.

Management Today, September 1, 2004, Mark Lasswell, review of *Colossus,* p. 35.

National Review, April 30, 2001, David Pryce-Jones, review of *The Cash Nexus;* May 5, 2003, David Harsanyi, review of *Empire;* June 14, 2004, David Frum, review of *Colossus,* p. 46; September 25, 2006, Paul Johnson, review of *The War of the World,* p. 48; December 15, 2008, Allan H. Meltzer, review of *The Ascent of Money,* p. 53.

New Republic, February 8, 1999, Fritz Stern, review of *The House of Rothschild.*

New Statesman, June 6, 1997, Conrad Russell, review of *Virtual History,* p. 45; February 5, 2001, John Gray, review of *The Cash Nexus,* p. 54; January 27, 2003, Richard Gott, review of *Empire,* p. 52; May 31, 2004, Michael Lind, review of *Colossus,* p. 52; August 23, 2004, Justin Cartwright, review of *Empire,* p. 39; June 19, 2006, Joanna Bourke, review of *The War of the World.*

New York Times, April 18, 2003, Michiko Kakutani, review of *Empire;* December 2, 2008, Michiko Kakutani, review of *The Ascent of Money,* p. C1.

New York Times Book Review, December 20, 1998, Geoffrey Wheatcroft, review of *The House of Rothschild,* p. 12; May 9, 1999, V.R. Berghahn, review of *The Pity of War,* p. 12; March 25, 2001, David P. Calleo, review of *The Cash Nexus,* p. 9; April 20, 2003, Margaret MacMillan, review of *Empire,* p. 12; July 25, 2004, John Lewis Gladdis, review of *Colossus,* p. 11; November 12, 2006, Simon Sebag Montefiore, review of *The War of the World,* p. 14.

Parameters, spring, 2006, William J. Gregor, review of *Colossus,* p. 133.

Publishers Weekly, March 8, 1999, review of *The Pity of War,* p. 56; February 12, 2001, review of *The Cash Nexus,* p. 194; February 24, 2003, review of *Empire,* p. 61; January 26, 2004, review of *Colossus,* p. 238; July 17, 2006, review of *The War of the World,* p. 149.

Reason, January, 2005, Michael Young, review of *Colossus.*

Red Herring, September 15, 2001, Mark Williams, review of *The Cash Nexus,* p. 41.

Spectator, May 1, 2004, Sam Leith, review of *Colossus,* p. 33; May 27, 2006, Sam Leith, review of *The War of the World;* November 15, 2008, Christopher Fildes, review of *The Ascent of Money,* p. 49.

Time, December 7, 1998, Lance Morrow, review of *The House of Rothschild,* p. 222.

Time International, January 20, 2003, Michael Brunton, review of *Empire,* p. 54.

ONLINE

Age Online, http://www.theage.com.au/ (September 4, 2004), Michael Gawenda, review of *Colossus.*

American Spectator Online, http://spectator.org/ (March 11, 2009), Brandon Crocker, review of *The Ascent of Money.*

Asian Review of Books, http://www.asianreviewofbooks. com/ (July 14, 2006), Michael Hsu, review of *The War of the World.*

Atlantic Online, http://www.theatlantic.com/ (May 25, 2004), Frank Bures, "Niall Ferguson, the author of *Colossus,* Laments the Emasculation of American Imperialism" (interview).

Boston Globe Online, http://www.boston.com/ (September 24, 2006), Harvey Blume, "Q&A with Niall Ferguson"; (December 14, 2008) James Grant, review of *The Ascent of Money.*

California Literary Review, http://calitreview.com/ (April 24, 2007), David Loftus, review of *The War of the World.*

Harry Walker Agency Web site, http://www.harrywalker. com/ (June 28, 2009), profile.

Harvard University Department of History Web site, http://history.fas.harvard.edu/ (June 28, 2009), profile.

History News Network, http://hnn.us/ (February 18, 2005), Richard B. Speed, review of *Colossus.*

Independent Online (London, England), http://www. independent.co.uk/ (February 17, 2001), Frank McLynn, review of *The Cash Nexus;* (January 11, 2003) Piers Brendon, review of *Empire;* (May 16, 2004) Cal McCrystal, review of *Colossus;* (October 31, 2008) Hamish McRae, review of *The Ascent of Money.*

National Review Online, http://www.nationalreview. com/ (June 18, 2004), Rich Lowry, review of *Colossus.*

Niall Ferguson Home Page, http://www.niallferguson. com (June 28, 2009).

Political Affairs, http://www.politicalaffairs.net/ (July 26, 2005), Norman Markowitz, review of *Empire.*

Salon.com, http://salon.com/ (April 17, 2004), Farhad Manjoo, review of *Empire;* (May 20, 2004) Ted Widner, review of *Colossus.*

Scotsman Online, http://living.scotsman.com/ (May 16, 2004), Alex Massie, review of *Colossus.*

Spectator Online, http://www.spectator.co.uk/ (November 12, 2008), Andro Linklater, review of *The Ascent of Money.*

Telegraph Online, http://www.telegraph.co.uk/ (November 6, 2008), review of *The Ascent of Money.*

Times Online, http://entertainment.timesonline.co.uk/ (January 12, 2003), Felipe Fernandez-Armesto, review of *Empire;* (October 26, 2008) Edward Chancellor, review of *The Ascent of Money;* (October 31, 2008) Robert Cole, review of *The Ascent of Money.*

Tribune Online (Chandigarh, India), http://www. tribuneindia.com/ (August 14, 2005), M. Rajiv-lochan, review of *Colossus.*

Weekly Standard Online, http://www.weeklystandard. com/ (March 24, 2003), review of *Empire.*

Yale Global Online, http://yaleglobal.yale.edu/ (June 28, 2009), Immanuel Wallerstein, review of *Empire.**

*   *   *

FERRIS, Monica 1943-

[A pseudonym]

(Margaret Frazer, a joint pseudonym, Mary Kuhfeld, Mary Pulver Kuhfeld, Mary Monica Pulver)

PERSONAL: Born October 15, 1943, in Terre Haute, IN; daughter of Harry Gene (an electrician) and Marie Therese (a homemaker) Pulver; married Albert W. Kuhfeld (a museum curator). *Education:* Attended the University of Wisconsin—Madison.

ADDRESSES: Home and office—St. Louis Park, MN. *Agent*—Lowenstein-Yost Associates, 121 W. 27th St., Ste. 601, New York, NY 10001. *E-mail*—marypulver@ aol.com.

CAREER: Secretary in Milwaukee and Madison, WI, and in Minneapolis—St. Paul, MN, beginning 1968; volunteer teacher of medieval living and mystery writing at local elementary schools. Member of Minneapolis Third Precinct Advisory Committee; Cathedral Church of St. Mark, Minneapolis, MN, Lay Eucharistic Visitor, lector, and usher. *Military service:* U.S. Navy, journalist, 1962-68.

MEMBER: Society for Creative Anachronism, Sisters in Crime.

AWARDS, HONORS: Anthony Award nomination, Best First Novel, for *Murder at the War;* Edgar Award nomination, Best Original Paperback, 1993, for *The Servant's Tale.*

WRITINGS:

"PETER BRICHTER" SERIES; AS MARY MONICA PULVER

Murder at the War, St. Martin's Press (New York, NY), 1987.

The Unforgiving Minutes, St. Martin's Press (New York, NY), 1988.

Ashes to Ashes, St. Martin's Press (New York, NY), 1988.

Original Sin, Walker (New York, NY), 1991.

Show Stopper, Diamond Books (New York, NY), 1992.

"SISTER FREVISSE MEDIEVAL MYSTERY" SERIES; WITH GAIL FRAZER UNDER JOINT PSEUDONYM MARGARET FRAZER

The Novice's Tale, Jove Books (New York, NY), 1993.

The Servant's Tale, Jove Books (New York, NY), 1993.

The Outlaw's Tale, Jove Books (New York, NY), 1994.

The Bishop's Tale, Jove Books (New York, NY), 1994.

The Boy's Tale, Jove Books (New York, NY), 1995.

The Murderer's Tale, Jove Books (New York, NY), 1996.

"NEEDLECRAFT MYSTERY" SERIES; UNDER PSEUDONYM MONICA FERRIS

Crewel World, Berkley Prime Crime (New York, NY), 1999.

Framed in Lace, Berkley Prime Crime (New York, NY), 1999.

A Stitch in Time, Berkley Prime Crime (New York, NY), 2000.

Unraveled Sleeve, Berkley Prime Crime (New York, NY), 2001.

A Murderous Yarn, Berkley Prime Crime (New York, NY), 2002.

Hanging by a Thread, Berkley Prime Crime (New York, NY), 2003.

Cutwork, Berkley Prime Crime (New York, NY), 2004.

Crewel Yule, Berkley Prime Crime (New York, NY), 2004.

Embroidered Truths, Berkley Prime Crime (New York, NY), 2005.

Patterns of Murder, Berkley Prime Crime (New York, NY), 2005.

Sins and Needles, Berkley Prime Crime (New York, NY), 2006.

Knitting Bones, Berkley Prime Crime (New York, NY), 2007.

Thai Die, Berkley Prime Crime (New York, NY), 2008.

Blackwork, Berkley Prime Crime (New York, NY), 2009.

Contributor to anthologies, including *The Mammoth Book of Historical Detectives, The Mammoth Book of Historical Whodunnits, Shakespearean Mysteries, Royal Whodunnits, Unholy Orders, Murder Most Crafty,* and *Silence of the Loons.* Contributor of stories to magazines, including *Alfred Hitchcock's Mystery Magazine.* Author's works have been translated into German, Italian, and French.

SIDELIGHTS: A mystery novelist under several different names, Monica Ferris is the author of series that include the "Peter Brichter" police series. Books include various themes, including one set at a medieval recreationist event. She collaborated with coauthor Gail Frazer, under the joint pseudonym Margaret Frazer, to produce the first six books of the "Sister Frevisse Medieval Mystery" series. Ferris also writes the "Needlecraft" mystery series, each of which concentrates on amateur detective Betsy Devonshire and themes related to knitting, needleworking, and related handcrafts.

Betsy is a needleworker and amateur sleuth based in Excelsior, Minnesota. The proprietor of a craft and yarn shop, Crewel World, Betsy hones her knitting skills while finding herself involved in mysteries related to needlework and stitchery. As an added attraction to stitch-minded readers, the books also include considerable information on needlework as well as patterns for interested handcrafters.

The series begins with *Crewel World,* in which Betsy's sister Margot is found dead in her shop. *Framed in Lace* finds Betsy identifying the clue, a piece of lace, to the murder of a woman whose body is discovered when a ferry that sank in 1949 is reclaimed from the bottom of a lake. Dawn Dowdle, writing for *Best Reviews* online, concluded: "Even though I am not a big crafts person, this book was enjoyable and held my full attention. I look forward to reading the rest of this series." A piece of damaged tapestry found in a church closet is the clue in *A Stitch in Time.*

Betsy inherits Margot's estate, including her shop Crewel World, and remains in Excelsior. In *Unraveled Sleeve* she is overwhelmed by requests for money. She is also haunted by nightmares of a murder that hasn't been committed. She seeks relief by attending a stitch-in convention on Lake Superior with police officer Jill Cross and meets a woman who is having marital problems. When she later discovers the woman's dead body, they approach her husband, who insists that he is alone and that they are estranged.

Jill's boyfriend Lars, also a police officer, buys a 1911 Stanley Steamer automobile and restores it in *A Murderous Yarn.* Betsy and Crewel World sponsor the car in an antique car race. During a preliminary run, while Betsy and Charlotte Birmingham wait together at the finish, Charlotte's husband Bill is found dead under his burning car. Betsy investigates at the request of Charlotte and Bill's daughter, although his son would prefer that she not. Harriet Klausner reviewed this title for the *Best Reviews* Web site, calling it "a delightful cozy that entertains as well as educates the audience."

Betsy needs roofing work done, and in *Hanging by a Thread,* she hires Foster Johns, a general contractor she is later told is suspected of killing his lover, Angela, and her husband, Paul. Foster tells Betsy he is innocent and asks her to help him clear his name. Betsy soon discovers that Paul was abusing Angela, and could very well have been her killer. Klausner, again for the *Best Reviews* Web site, wrote: "The heroine has shown tremendous growth as a character and the support cast makes the story line both colorful and humorous."

Jill, recently promoted, has talked to Betsy about official police business and has been chastised for it. Consequently, when a murder occurs, Betsy leans toward steering clear of the investigation, but at the urging of friends, she looks for the killer of woodworking artist Robert McFey, whose throat is slashed with one of his own tools during the annual art festival. She agrees to help because although the evidence points to sixteen-year-old Mickey Sinclair, townspeople don't believe he would commit such a crime. Vickie Gilpin reviewed *Cutwork* for *Best Reviews,* writing: "New readers should have no trouble falling immediately into the fast-paced, riveting storyline.

The first seven titles in the series were published in paperback, but with *Crewel Yule,* the eighth novel in the series, Betsy made her first appearance hardcover. In this story, Betsy is attending a national needlework convention in Nashville, Tennessee, along with Jill, and store manager and friend Godwin du Lac. A heavy snowstorm hits the area during the convention, stranding everyone inside the hotel. The bad weather cannot keep out murder, however, as Belle Hammermill, a shop owner from Milwaukee, Wisconsin, falls nine stories to her gruesome death in the hotel atrium. At first the attendees assume the woman's fall to be an accident, but as Betsy and friends begin to ask questions of the other convention goers, they discover that Hammermill was a selfish, unpleasant person with no shortage of enemies who might wish her dead, and most of them are snowbound inside the convention hotel and could have killed her. "Ferris's characterizations are topnotch, and the action moves along at a crisp pace," commented *Booklist* reviewer Ilene Cooper.

Embroidered Truths finds Godwin accused of murder. Tossed out by his lover, attorney John Nye, when the two returned from a Mexico City trip, Godwin has found temporary respite at Betsy's house. However, Betsy and Godwin later find Nye dead, and some valuables missing from his body. During the police investigation, two wills are discovered; the second, unsigned one cuts Godwin out of a considerable inheritance. Godwin is summarily arrested and accused of Nye's murder. Betsy knows her trusted friend is incapable of murder. She begins her own investigation into the case, while an assortment of friends and colleagues pitch in to keep Crewel World open and running. As the investigation develops, Nye's brother John discovers that the attorney maintained a false identity and had accumulated a great deal of money. Another resource, Susan Lavery, a Crewel World customer who worked for Nye's firm, offers to search for possible suspects in the legal world, but is later attacked and stuffed in a car trunk. Ultimately, Betsy ties the divergent threads together to solve the case and rescue Godwin from false accusation. A *Kirkus Reviews*

contributor called the story "a lighthearted tale with no real sense of danger."

Sins and Needles places Betsy in the midst of an adoptee's search for her birth mother. When Lucille Jones visits from Texas, Betsy sees a strong resemblance between her and a local customer, nurse Jan Henderson. Lucille, eager to locate her birth mother, also noticed the resemblance when she met Henderson at a medical conference. In fact, she deliberately stole Jan's hairbrush with the intent of running DNA tests. The case is complicated by the fact that Jan and her mother, Susan McConnell, are in line to inherit a large sum of money from Susan's Aunt Edyth, a cranky, eccentric old woman whose hatred of men is so keen that she removed Susan's brother Stewart and the rest of the family from her will. When Aunt Edyth is found dead with a knitting needle stabbed into her head, Jan turns to Betsy for help in finding the killer. A chance for Edyth's relatives to choose a keepsake from the woman's mansion finds Stewart's daughters all selecting valuable antiques, but Stewart himself opting for a beat-up old motorboat. An old knitted cushion on the boat is apparently a genuine treasure map that points the way to the solution to the murder and the mystery. "Betsy, who's growing as a character, gets an especially interesting case this time," mused a *Kirkus Reviews* critic. A *Publishers Weekly* reviewer observed that the "brisk plot and well-developed characters make this complex novel" a strong entry in the series.

The next title in the series is *Patterns of Murder,* followed by *Knitting Bones,* in which Betsy suffers a broken leg. She calls on Godwin for help with the next crime, which is the disappearance of Bob Germaine of the National Heart Coalition, along with the check he was given to benefit his organization at a convention of the Embroiderers' Guild. Bob's wife is certain that he is in danger, but the gay Godwin suspects that Bob has decided to come out of the closet to start a new life. They both prove to be wrong, however, when Bob's naked body is discovered in the trunk of a car. Assisting them is con-man Tony Milan, who had planned to steal the check, but who suffered a concussion and woke up three days later wearing Bob's clothes and watch. In the meantime, Betsy oversees the investigation from home while caring for an injured crow. *Booklist* reviewer Sue O'Brien wrote: "Cozy fans will respond to Ferris's cast of appealing, folksy characters."

Thai Dai, Ferris's twelfth "Needlecraft Mystery," was called "one of the strongest entries in the series" by *Booklist* contributor Judy Coon.

Mary Pulver Kuhfeld once told *CA:* "'Write what you know' sounds far more simple than it is. A writer should never stop expanding his or her field of knowledge, if only to discover a new angle for a story or a new area of research needed to complete one.

"My books are mysteries—murder mysteries. I like the mystery genre because there is a strong element of morality in it. Good triumphs and wickedness is punished and all (or much) is well at the end. Both in writing and reading them one comes away with a feeling of something having been accomplished.'

BIOGRAPHICAL AND CRITICAL SOURCES:

PERIODICALS

AudioFile, April 1, 2009, Judy B. Gummere, review of *Thai Die.*

Booklist, October 15, 2004, Ilene Cooper, review of *Crewel Yule,* p. 393; December 15, 2007, Sue O'Brien, review of *Knitting Bones,* p. 29; December 1, 2008, Judy Coon, review of *Thai Die,* p. 33.

Kirkus Reviews, April 15, 2005, review of *Embroidered Truths,* p. 453; May 1, 2006, review of *Sins and Needles,* p. 440; October 15, 2007, review of *Knitting Bones;* November 1, 2008, review of *Thai Die.*

Library Journal, June 1, 2004, Ann Kim, review of *Crewel Yule,* p. 109.

Publishers Weekly, September 27, 2004, "October Publications," review of *Crewel Yule,* p. 41; May 9, 2005, "June Publications," review of *Embroidered Truths,* p. 59; April 24, 2006, review of *Sins and Needles,* p. 42; October 8, 2007, review of *Knitting Bones,* p. 40; October 20, 2008, review of *Thai Die,* p. 39.

Star Tribune (Minneapolis, MN), January 31, 2007, David Gustafson, "Curious Writer Makes Living Off Curious Subjects" (interview), p. 6W.

ONLINE

Associated Content, http://www.associatedcontent.com/ (July 31, 2008), "An Exclusive Interview with Author Monica Ferris."

Best Reviews, http://thebestreviews.com/ (February 7, 2002), Harriet Klausner, review of *A Murderous Yarn;* (October 10, 2002) Dawn Dowdle, reviews of *Framed in Lace* and *A Murderous Yarn;* (December 15, 2002) Harriet Klausner, review of *Hanging by a Thread;* (December 20, 2003) Harriet Klausner, review of *Cutwork;* (December 26, 2003) Vicky Gilpin, review of *Cutwork;* (November 2, 2007) Harriet Klausner, review of *Knitting Bones.*

BookReview.com, http://www.bookreview.com/ (July 31, 2008), Harriet Klausner, review of *Unraveled Sleeve.*

Monica Ferris Home Page, http://www.monica-ferris.com (July 31, 2008).*

*   *   *

FORD, Michael Thomas 1968-

PERSONAL: Born 1968; partner with Patrick Crowe, beginning c. 2001. *Hobbies and other interests:* SCUBA diving.

ADDRESSES: Home—San Francisco, CA. *Agent*—Mitchell Waters, Curtis Brown Ltd., 10 Astor Place, New York, NY 10003. *E-mail*—writemtf@michaelthomasford.com.

CAREER: Writer, novelist, columnist, and radio commentator.

AWARDS, HONORS: American Library Association (ALA) best book for young adults, 1992, for *One Hundred Questions and Answers about AIDS;* ALA best book for young adults, *Booklist* editor's choice, and National Science Teachers Association/ Children's Book Council (CBC) outstanding science trade book designation, all 1995, all for *The Voices of AIDS;* National Council of Social Studies/CBC Notable Children's Book, 1998, for *Outspoken;* Lambda Literary Award for best humor book, 1999, for *Alec Baldwin Doesn't Love Me, and Other Trials of My Queer Life,* 2000, for *That's Mr. Faggot to You: Further Trials from My Queer Life,* 2001, for *It's Not Mean If It's True,* and 2002, for *The Little Book of Neuroses;* New York Public Library Best Books for the Teen Age designation, 2000, for *Paths of Faith: Conversations about Religion and Spirituality;* Lambda Literary Award for best romance novel, 2004, for *Last Summer.*

WRITINGS:

NONFICTION

One Hundred Questions and Answers about AIDS: A Guide for Young People, New Discovery Books

(New York, NY), 1992, published as *One Hundred Questions and Answers about AIDS: What You Need to Know Now,* Beech Tree Books (New York, NY), 1993.

The Voices of AIDS: Twelve Unforgettable People Talk about How AIDS Has Changed Their Lives, Morrow Junior Books (New York, NY), 1995.

The World out There: Becoming Part of the Lesbian and Gay Community, New Press (New York, NY), 1996.

Alec Baldwin Doesn't Love Me, and Other Trials of My Queer Life, Alyson Books (Los Angeles, CA), 1998.

Outspoken: Role Models from the Lesbian and Gay Community, Morrow Junior Books (New York, NY), 1998.

That's Mr. Faggot to You: Further Trials from My Queer Life, Alyson Books (Los Angeles, CA), 1999.

It's Not Mean If It's True: More Trials from My Queer Life, Alyson Books (Los Angeles, CA), 2000.

Paths of Faith: Conversations about Religion and Spirituality, Simon & Schuster Books for Young Readers (New York, NY), 2000.

The Little Book of Neuroses: Ongoing Trials from My Queer Life, Alyson Books (Los Angeles, CA), 2001.

My Big Fat Queer Life: The Best of Michael Thomas Ford, Alyson Books (Los Angeles, CA), 2003.

Ultimate Gay Sex, DK Publishers (New York, NY), 2004.

The Path of the Green Man: Gay Men, Wicca and Living a Magical Life, Citadel (New York, NY), 2005.

FICTION

(With others) *Masters of Midnight,* Kensington Books (New York, NY), 2003.

Last Summer, Kensington Books (New York, NY), 2003.

Looking for It, Kensington Books (New York, NY), 2004.

(With others) *Midnight Thirsts,* Kensington Books (New York, NY), 2004.

Tangled Sheets: Tales of Erotica, Kensington Books (New York, NY), 2005.

Full Circle, Kensington Books (New York, NY), 2005.

Changing Tides, Kensington Books (New York, NY), 2007.

Suicide Notes, HarperTeen (New York, NY), 2008.

Author of *"My Queer Life"* (syndicated newspaper column), beginning 1996; contributor to *Instinct* magazine and to Web sites.

Author of young adult fiction under various pseudonyms. Also author of musical *Alec Baldwin Doesn't Love Me.* Contributor of a novella to the anthology *Midnight Thirsts: Erotic Tales of the Vampire,* Kennsington Books, 2005.

ADAPTATIONS: Selections from Ford's columns have been recorded as *My Queer Life,* Fluid Word, 2000.

SIDELIGHTS: As the author of "My Queer Life," a syndicated column that touches on everything from life after Viagra to the legal troubles of oft-reviled and equally admired business tycoon Martha Stewart, Michael Thomas Ford has been compared to writers such as James Thurber and been called everything from the "gay Erma Bombeck" to the "gay Everyman." Ford has been widely applauded throughout the gay community for his dry humor, which is reflected in the titles of several anthologies of his columns: *Alec Baldwin Doesn't Love Me, and Other Trials of My Queer Life; That's Mr. Faggot to You: Further Trials from My Queer Life,* and *The Little Book of Neuroses: Ongoing Trials from My Queer Life.* The last book, in particular, showcases what a *Publishers Weekly* contributor dubbed Ford's "delightfully inventive wit" in its tackling of such compelling subjects as "how *Tiger Beat* magazine made him gay" as well as providing "relationship tips for the neurotically inclined and mus[ing] . . . on how eBay allows us to relive our childhood by buying back our past." However, he also has a more serious side that has also been expressed in his award-winning books for young adults, such as *One Hundred Questions and Answers about AIDS: A Guide for Young People* and *Outspoken: Role Models from the Lesbian and Gay Community.*

Interviews are an important component of all of Ford's books for teen readers; they have been particularly important in making his nonfiction books on coming-of-age issues popular among a readership for whom peer identification is important. In *One Hundred Questions and Answers about AIDS* he talks to four teens who are HIV positive, supplementing those discussions with what a *Publishers Weekly* contributor noted are "concise, very candid explanations" of the symptoms and effects of the disease. Ford's 1995 book *The Voices of AIDS: Twelve Unforgettable People Talk about How*

AIDS Has Changed Their Lives continues to address the concerns of teens, particularly those in the gay community, by introducing a range of men and women who either have the disease, are involved with an infected lover or family member, or are educators or AIDS activists. "Ford's careful, pointed questions bring out issues related to self-esteem, stereotyping, and discrimination that make the people he's talking to seem very real," noted Stephanie Zvirin in a review for *Booklist,* reflecting the view of other appreciative critics.

From books addressing the most important issue facing young gay Americans—AIDS—Ford has also addressed the social issues that, to many adolescents dealing with their own homosexuality, can often feel as devastating. *Outspoken* does more than just present interviews with eleven gay and lesbian Americans: it allows readers the opportunity to meet eleven men and women who have allowed their differences to make them stronger individuals. Praising Ford's skill in posing "good, interesting questions" to his subjects—which include boxer Mark Leduc, actor Dan Butler, Rabbi Lisa Edwards, and artist Alison Bechdel—Christine Heppermann added in a review for *Horn Book* that *Outspoken* "illustrates that there are as many different ways of coming to and participating in the gay community as there are people in it." In *Booklist,* Zvirin praised the book as "accessible, informative, and sensitive" to its intended audience.

Continuing his focus on teens, Ford has also gone beyond issues of sexuality to address another aspect of personal identity in *Paths of Faith: Conversations about Religion and Spirituality.* Again centering his book on interviews, he talks with Wiccan writer Starhawk, Catholic Archbishop John Cardinal O'Connor, and representatives of Shaker, Islamic, Episcopal, Quaker, Hindu, Jewish Reform, and Buddhist spiritual communities. "Just as good biography can bring to life an historical era, these individuals' stories provide intriguing introductions to a variety of religious faiths," noted a *Horn Book* contributor, while a *School Library Journal* contributor dubbed *Paths of Faith* "a thoughtful look at contemporary religious practice in the United States." Although some critics noted that the individuals interviewed reflect predominately liberal religious views, as a *Publishers Weekly* contributor maintained: "Ford does an expert job of balancing discussions about the particulars of a religion with the overarching concerns common to most faiths."

From his stance as a commentator on gay culture, Ford continues to strike a balance between entertainment and education in his writing. While continuing his column, he has also branched out into fiction, and his novels of gay life and love have been praised for their likeable characters and insights into romantic relationships even as they have gained a following for their sexual content. Ford also remains outspoken on serious issues within the gay community at large, particularly racial issues, drug and alcohol abuse, and depression. As he commented during an interview with Paul J. Willis for the *Lambda Book Report:* "What we call the queer 'community' is really an extremely diverse group of people united by one commonality—our sexuality." Ford went on to note: "Because of that one commonality, we've been brought together as a family that has to learn how to support one another and look out for one another. Until we do that, then gay rights laws and marriage initiatives and all of those things will mean very little. If the individual members of a community are not working together, then there is no community."

My Big Fat Queer Life: The Best of Michael Thomas Ford features previously published writings of the author as well as five new essays. Ford also continues to write novels and is a contributor of a novella to *Midnight Thirsts: Erotic Tales of the Vampire.* Writing for the *Lambda Book Report,* Michael G. Cornelius called Ford's entry, "Carnival," "the best of the four novellas by far." The story takes place during the Great Depression and features a carnival freak show and a mechanical genius.

Full Circle, Ford's 2005 novel, finds Ned Brummel, a history professor, learning from his estranged friend, Jack, that their mutual friend, Andy, is sick and possibly dying. Ned takes a plane to Chicago to visit Andy and begins to recall these two friends from his past. Ned grew up with Jack in Philadelphia in the 1950's, where, as teenagers, they came to recognize their homosexuality but, in the stifling society of the times, kept their sexual orientation a secret. The two eventually go off to college together where they meet Andy. Despite the fact that Andy is a heterosexual, both Ned and Jack are attracted to him, leading to a number of liaisons and betrayals as the three men come together and part several times over the years.

"Author Michael Thomas Ford charts a formidable course as he skillfully integrates this fated trio with the convergence of world events, their lives shattered by the conflict in Vietnam, the Seventies gay liberation movement, and the AIDS epidemic of the eighties," wrote Michael Leonard in a review for the *Curled Up with a Good Book* Web site. Also commenting on the historical aspects of the novel, *Lambda Book Report* contributor Scott Whittier noted that the author "emphasizes an element of history that makes it so much more personal and more interesting—the individual." In the same review, Whittier wrote that the various historical events in the novel—from the war in Vietnam to the Kent State shooting of students by the Ohio National Guard to the appearance of AIDS and its effects on the gay community—are incorporated into the story effectively by the author. Whitter wrote that, "no matter how deeply these events touch the narrator, they are simply and inevitably the backdrop to his everyday life. And this is what makes the story so impactful, so real."

In his 2007 novel, *Changing Tides,* the author tells the story of Ben Ransome, a marine biologist; his sixteen-year-old daughter, Caddie; and Hudson Jones, an ambitious graduate student. Caddie is coming to live with Ben in Monterey, California, for the summer, and Ben is shocked to find that the child he always thought of as being happy has morphed into an angry teenager who resents her father. Hudson has also come to Monterey seeking to prove that he has found a lost novel by John Steinbeck called *Changing Tides* and that the novel indicates that Steinbeck was in love with his best friend, Ed "Doc" Ricketts. As Caddie acts out and makes some dangerous decisions, Hudson seeks help from Ben in conducting his local research. Ben and Hudson spend more and more time together and began to discover that there is more between them than friendship.

In interview with Ford for the *Curled Up with a Good Book* Web site, Michael Leonard noted the symbolism contained in the book and wrote: "The symbolic power of the ocean seems to have the capacity to change lives, and throughout the course of the novel it allows Ben, Caddie and Hudson to grow and transform." When asked by Leonard why he chose this theme, the author replied: "I've long had a love affair with the ocean, which was deepened when I started diving and saw what a magnificent world there is beneath the surface. What's most interesting about the ocean is how it itself is a living thing apart from the creatures that live in it, and how different people react to it in different ways, often based on their approaches to life." The author later added: "I've often found that these reactions relate directly to how a person reacts to situations in his or her own life."

Reviewers generally had high praise for *Changing Tides.* Whitney Scott, writing for *Booklist,* noted that the author provides "beautifully detailed descriptions of watery depths—clearly heartfelt labors of love." *Lambda Book Report* contributor Cecelia Martin commented that the author's "novel doesn't disappoint," adding: "Well-rounded characters, great writing and a strong theme make *Changing Tides* one of his best novels to date."

The novel *Suicide Notes,* published in 2008, finds fifteen-year-old Jeff waking up on the psychiatric ward of a hospital. Jeff does not believe he is crazy, even though he has bandages on his wrists. Forced to spend forty-five days on the ward, the sarcastic Jeff at first sees himself as being quite different from the other teens there. As time passes, however, he starts to identify with his fellow ward detainees, seeing them as real people and not that different from himself. In the process, Jeff comes to terms with the own realities of his life and why he tried to kill himself. "Jeff's journey is wittily unique, balancing a fresh voice and a uniquely realistic character with comedy and seriousness," wrote Ashleigh Larsen in a review for *Kliatt. School Library Journal* contributor Kat Redniss wrote: "Readers will relate to Jeff['s] . . . horrible embarrassment and . . . shame . . ., and they will be inspired by his eventual integrity and grace."

BIOGRAPHICAL AND CRITICAL SOURCES:

PERIODICALS

Advocate, September 26, 2000, Edward Guthmann, "Seriously Funny," review of *It's Not Mean If It's True: More Trials from My Queer Life,* p. 73.

Booklist, August, 1995, Stephanie Zvirin, review of *The Voices of AIDS: Twelve Unforgettable People Talk about How AIDS Has Changed Their Lives,* p. 1948; July, 1996, Ray Olson, review of *The World out There: Becoming Part of the Lesbian and Gay Community,* p. 1783; May 1, 1998, Stephanie Zvirin, review of *Outspoken: Role Models from the Lesbian and Gay Community,* p. 1516; October 1, 2000, Ilene Cooper, review of *Paths of Faith: Conversations about Religion and Spirituality,* p. 353; November 1, 2001, Michael Spinella, review of *The Little Book of Neuroses: Ongoing Trials from My Queer Life,* p. 456; August, 2003, review of *Last Summer,* p. 1952; August, 2004, Whitney Scott, review of *Looking for It,* p. 1908; September 1, 2007, Whitney Scott, review of *Changing Tides,* p. 50; October 1, 2008, Hazel Rochman, review of *Suicide Notes,* p. 39.

Entertainment Weekly, September 23, 2003, review of *Last Summer,* p. 158; June 16, 2006, Tim Stack, review of *Full Circle,* p. 81.

Horn Book, May-June, 1998, Christine Heppermann, review of *Outspoken,* p. 358; January, 2001, review of *Paths of Faith,* p. 108.

Kirkus Reviews, September 15, 2008, review of *Suicide Notes.*

Kliatt, November, 2008, Ashleigh Larsen, review of *Suicide Notes,* p. 11.

Lambda Book Report, July-August, 1999, Louis Bayard, review of *That's Mr. Faggot to You: Further Trials from My Queer Life,* p. 24; September, 2000, Paul J. Willis, "Michael Thomas Ford Tells the Awful Truth," interview with author, p. 8; April, 2001, Nancy Garden, review of *Paths of Faith,* p. 24; May, 2004, Jonathan Harper, review of *Ultimate Gay Sex,* p. 29; January-March, 2005, Michael G. Cornelius, review of *Queer Vamps Times Four;* summer, 2006, Scott Whittier, review of *Full Circle,* p. 30; fall, 2007, Cecelia Martin, review of *Changing Tides,* p. 25.

Publishers Weekly, October 12, 1992, review of *One Hundred Questions and Answers about AIDS: A Guide for Young People,* p. 81; November 13, 1995, review of *The Voices of AIDS,* p. 63; April 5, 1999, review of *That's Mr. Faggot to You,* p. 226; August 14, 2000, review of *It's Not Mean If It's True: More Trials from My Queer Life,* p. 339; January 29, 2001, review of *Paths of Faith,* p. 87; October 8, 2001, review of *The Little Book of Neuroses,* p. 58; August 4, 2003, review of *Last Summer,* p. 56; April 5, 2004, review of *Ultimate Gay Sex,* p. 58; July 19, 2004, review of *Looking for It,* p. 145; July 30, 2007, review of *Changing Tides,* p. 55; September 1, 2008, review of *Suicide Notes,* p. 55.

San Francisco Chronicle, July 11, 2006, David Wiegand, "To Michael Thomas Ford, It's All about Capturing the Essence of today, Not Just the Pretty Prose Gay-Themed Essays Filled a Void, Looking at Everyday Guys and Life," interview with author.

School Library Journal, January, 2001, Elaine Fort Weischedel, review of *Paths of Faith,* p. 144; February, 2009, Kat Redniss, review of *Suicide Notes,* p. 98.

ONLINE

Chicago Pride, http://www.chicagopride.com/ (September 13, 2007), PJ Gray, "Interview: Michael Thomas Ford."

Curled Up with a Good Book, http://www.curledup.com/ (June 22, 2009), Michael Leonard, reviews of *Changing Tides, Full Circle,* and interview with author.

Edge, http://www.edgeboston.com/ (May 14, 2009), Kilian Melloy, "Michael Thomas Ford on 'What We Remember,'" interview with author.

Entertainment Weekly Online, http://www.ew.com/ (August 31, 2007), Adam B. Vary, review of *Changing Tides.*

GMax, http://www.gmax.co.za/ (August 5, 2008), Neil Plakcy, "Changing Tides," interview with author.

Metro Weekly, http://www.metroweekly.com/ (July 27, 2006), Randy Shulman, "What Comes Around," review of *Full Circle.*

Michael Thomas Ford Home Page, http://www.michaelthomasford.com (June 22, 2009).

Ralph, http://www.ralphmag.org/ (June 22, 2009), Ignacio Schwartz, review of *My Big Fat Queer Life: The Best of Michael Thomas Ford.**

*   *   *

FOSTER, Jake
See GORMAN, Ed

*   *   *

FOX, Paula 1923-

PERSONAL: Born April 22, 1923, in New York, NY; daughter of Paul Hervey (a writer) and Elsie Fox; briefly married Howard Bird (divorced); married Richard Sigerson, 1948 (divorced, 1954); married Martin Greenberg, June 9, 1962; children: (first marriage) Linda (put for adoption); (second marriage) Adam, Gabriel. *Education:* Attended Columbia University, 1955-58.

ADDRESSES: Home—New York, NY. *Agent*—Robert Lescher, 155 East 71st St., New York, NY 10021.

CAREER: Writer and educator. Has worked in numerous occupations, including model, saleswoman, public relations worker, machinist, staff member for the British publisher Victor Gollancz, reader for a film studio, reporter in Paris, France, and Warsaw, Poland, for the British wire service Telepress, English-as-a-second-language instructor, and teacher at the Ethical Culture

School in New York, NY and for emotionally disturbed children in Dobbs Ferry, NY; University of Pennsylvania, Philadelphia, professor of English literature, beginning 1963.

MEMBER: PEN, Authors League of America, Authors Guild.

AWARDS, HONORS: Finalist in National Book Award children's book category, 1971, for *Blowfish Live in the Sea;* National Institute of Arts and Letters Award, 1972; Guggenheim fellowship, 1972; National Endowment for the Arts grant, 1974; Newbery Medal, American Library Association, 1974, for *The Slave Dancer;* Hans Christian Andersen Medal, 1978; National Book Award nomination, 1979, for *The Little Swineherd and Other Tales; A Place Apart* was selected one of *New York Times*'s Outstanding Books, 1980, and received the American Book Award, 1983; Child Study Children's Book Award from the Bank Street College of Education and one of *New York Times*'s Notable Books, both 1984, Christopher Award and Newbery Honor Book, both 1985, and International Board on Books for Young People Honor List for Writing, 1986, all for *One-eyed Cat;* Brandeis Fiction citation, 1984; Rockefeller Foundation grant, 1984; *The Moonlight Man* was selected one of the *New York Times*'s Notable Books, 1986, and one of the Child Study Association of America's Children's Books of the Year, 1987; Silver Medallion, University of Southern Mississippi, 1987; *Boston Globe/Horn Book* Award for fiction and Newbery Honor Book, 1989, for *The Village by the Sea;* Empire State Award for children's literature, 1994; nominee for National Book Critics Circle Award in category for biography/autobiography, 2001, for *Borrowed Finery: A Memoir;* O. Henry Prize, 2005, for the short story "Grace."

WRITINGS:

FOR CHILDREN

Maurice's Room, illustrated by Ingrid Fetz, Macmillan (New York, NY), 1966.

A Likely Place, illustrated by Edward Ardizzone, Macmillan (New York, NY), 1967.

How Many Miles to Babylon?, illustrated by Paul Giovanopoulos, David White (New York, NY), 1967.

The Stone-faced Boy, illustrated by Donald A. Mackay, Bradbury (New York, NY), 1968, reprinted, Front Street (Asheville, NC), 2005.

Dear Prosper, illustrated by Steve McLachlin, David White (New York, NY), 1968.

Portrait of Ivan, illustrated by Saul Lambert, Bradbury (New York, NY), 1969, reprinted, Aladdin (New York, NY), 2004.

The King's Falcon, illustrated by Eros Keith, Bradbury (New York, NY), 1969.

Hungry Fred, illustrated by Rosemary Wells, Bradbury (New York, NY), 1969.

Blowfish Live in the Sea, Bradbury (New York, NY), 1970.

Good Ethan, illustrated by Arnold Lobel, Bradbury (New York, NY), 1973.

The Slave Dancer, illustrated by Keith, Bradbury (New York, NY), 1973.

The Little Swineherd and Other Tales, Dutton (New York, NY), 1978.

A Place Apart, Farrar, Straus (New York, NY), 1980.

One-eyed Cat, Bradbury (New York, NY), 1984.

(Author of introduction) Marjorie Kellogg, *Tell Me That You Love Me, Junie Moon,* Farrar, Straus (New York, NY), 1984.

The Moonlight Man, Bradbury (New York, NY), 1986, reprinted, Aladdin (New York, NY), 2003.

Lily and the Lost Boy, Orchard Books (New York, NY), 1987, published as *The Lost Boy,* Dent (London, England), 1988.

The Village by the Sea, Orchard Books (New York, NY), 1988.

In a Place of Danger, Orchard Books (New York, NY), 1989.

Monkey Island, Orchard Books (New York, NY), 1991.

(With Floriano Vecchi) *Amzat and His Brothers: Three Italian Tales,* illustrated by Emily Arnold McCully, Orchard Books (New York, NY), 1993.

Western Wind, Orchard Books (New York, NY), 1993.

The Eagle Kite, Orchard Books (New York, NY), 1995.

Radiance Descending, D.K. Inc. (New York, NY), 1997.

Traces, illustrated by Karla Kuskin, Front Street (Asheville, NC), 2008.

NOVELS FOR ADULTS

Poor George, Harcourt (New York, NY), 1967, published with introduction by Jonathan Lethem, W.W. Norton (New York, NY), 2001.

Desperate Characters, Harcourt (New York, NY), 1970, with an afterword by Irving Howe, Nonpareil, 1980.

The Western Coast, Harcourt (New York, NY), 1972, published with introduction by Frederick Busch, W.W. Norton (New York, NY), 2001.

The Widow's Children, Dutton (New York, NY), 1976.

A Servant's Tale, North Point Press (New York, NY), 1984, published with introduction by Melanie Rehak, W.W. Norton (New York, NY), 2001.

The God of Nightmares, North Point Press (New York, NY), 1990, published with an introduction by Rosellen Brown, W.W. Norton (New York, NY), 2002.

OTHER

"*Rain in the Morning,*" *Matinee Theatre* (television script), National Broadcasting Company (NBC), 1957.

"*The Virtues of Madame Douvay,*" *Naked City* (television script), Shelle Productions, 1962.

Borrowed Finery: A Memoir, Henry Holt (New York, NY), 2001.

The Coldest Winter: A Stringer in Liberated Europe (memoir), Henry Holt (New York, NY), 2005.

Contributor to periodicals, including *Harper's.*

ADAPTATIONS: Desperate Characters was adapted as a motion picture by Paramount, 1970; a cassette and a film strip accompanied by cassette have been produced of *One-eyed Cat* by Random House.

SIDELIGHTS: Paula Fox is best known for her children's books, which have won numerous awards, including the prestigious Hans Christian Andersen Medal, the Newbery Medal, and the American Book Award for Children's Fiction Paperback. She is also the author of novels for adults, and has been described by *Nation* contributor Blair T. Birmelin as "one of our most intelligent (and least appreciated) contemporary novelists." Fox, however, does not feel the need to distinguish between these two types of writing. She commented in John Rowe Townsend's *A Sense of Story: Essays on Contemporary Writers for Children:* "I never think I'm writing for children, when I work. A story does not start *for* anyone, nor an idea, nor a feeling of an idea; but starts more for oneself." "At the core of everything I write," she explained to *Publishers Weekly* contributor Sybil S. Steinberg, "is the feeling that the denial of the truth imprisons us even further in ourselves. Of course there's no one 'truth.' The great things, the insights that happen to you, come to you in some internal way."

Fox spent her childhood moving from place to place and school to school. Her father was a writer who worked in New York City, he earned a living by rewriting plays by other authors, as well as writing several of his own, and later he went to Hollywood and England to work for film studios. While her parents were traveling, Fox was sent to live with a minister and his invalid mother in New York's Hudson valley. An avid reader, poet, and history buff, the minister had a profound influence on Fox. He taught her to read and to appreciate the works of authors like Rudyard Kipling, Eugene Field, Mark Twain, Washington Irving, and Walt Whitman; and he also told her tales of the Revolutionary War and other events in history. All these stories inevitably rubbed off on the young Fox.

When Fox was six years old, she left the minister's home to live in California for two years, and in 1931 she moved again, this time to live with her grandmother on a sugar plantation in Cuba. Here, Fox quickly picked up Spanish from her fellow students while attending classes in a one-room schoolhouse. Three years after her arrival, the revolution led by Batista y Zaldivar forced Fox to return to New York City. By this time, Fox had attended nine schools and had hardly ever seen her parents. However, she found some solace and stability in her life by visiting public libraries. "Reading was everything to me," Fox revealed to Steinberg. "Wherever I went—except in Cuba—there was a library. Even though my schools changed, I'd always find a library."

Fox worked several different jobs after finishing high school, ranging from machinist to publishing company employee. Her desire to travel led her to a position with a leftist British news service which assigned her to cover Poland after World War II. Later, she returned to the United States, married, and had children, but the marriage ended in divorce. Afterwards, Fox resolved to finish her education, attending Columbia University for four years, until she could no longer afford the expense and had to leave before receiving her degree. Nevertheless, Fox's knowledge of Spanish helped her find a job as an English teacher for Spanish-speaking children. She also found other teaching positions, including one as a teacher for the emotionally disturbed. In 1962, Fox married an English professor and moved to Greece for six months while her husband wrote on a Guggenheim fellowship. During this period, she harbored hopes of one day becoming a writer.

For Fox, the same reason for reading books applies to her desire to write them: books help both reader and writer to experience and understand—if not necessarily sympathize with—the lives of other people. In her acceptance speech for the Newbery award, reprinted in *Newbery and Caldecott Medal Winners, 1966-1975,* she declared that writing helps us "to connect ourselves with the reality of our own lives. It is painful; but if we are to become human, we cannot abandon it."

Fox's juvenile novels have a complexity and sincerity that make them popular with readers and critics alike. These books cover a wide range of subjects, including parental conflict, alcoholism, and death. Frequently her young protagonists are emotionally withdrawn children who undertake a journey that is symbolic of their emotional development. In *Blowfish Live in the Sea,* for example, nineteen-year-old Ben travels from New York to Boston to see his estranged, alcoholic father after a twelve-year absence. Because of a past trauma involving a lie his father told him, Ben has withdrawn into himself to the point where he no longer speaks to anyone. His sister Carrie is the only family member who tries to reach out to Ben. The importance of Ben and Carrie's journey to Boston, explained a *Horn Book* contributor, is that "each step . . . relays something further in their tenuous gropings towards an understanding of themselves and of others."

Other award-winning children's novels by Fox, such as *A Place Apart, One-eyed Cat,* and *The Village by the Sea,* are similarly concerned with relationships, strong characterization, and emotionally troubled protagonists. *A Place Apart* concerns Victoria Finch, a thirteen-year-old girl whose comfort and security are shaken when her father dies suddenly. Victoria's grief, wrote *Washington Post Book World* contributor Katherine Paterson, "is the bass accompaniment to the story. Sometimes it swells, taking over the narrative, the rest of the time it subsides into a dark, rhythmic background against which the main story is played." Victoria must also come to terms with her infatuation with Hugh, a manipulative boy who "exerts . . . a power over her spirit," according to Paterson. This relationship compels Victoria "to explore the difficult terrain between the desire for closeness and the tendency to 'make ourselves a place apart,'" observed Jean Strouse in a review for *Newsweek.*

One-eyed Cat, according to a *Dictionary of Literary Biography* contributor, "is one of Fox's finest literary achievements." The title refers to a stray cat which the main character Ned accidentally injures with an air rifle. The guilt Ned feels afterwards plagues him through most of the rest of the book, even making him physically ill at one point, until at last he confesses his thoughtless act to his mother, who in turn confesses that she had once deserted Ned and his father when he was younger. Recognizing these flaws leads Ned to a reconciliation with his parents and himself.

A typical Fox device is to put a main character in an unfamiliar and hostile setting. In *The Village by the Sea,* for example, Emma is sent to live with her uncle and her neurotic, alcoholic aunt for two weeks when her father has to go to the hospital for heart surgery. Unable to cope with her hateful aunt and troubled about her father's health, Emma finds some solace in creating a make-believe village on the beach. However, as Rosellen Brown related in *New York Times Book Review:* "Emma's miniature haven is ultimately beyond her protection. She can only cherish the building of it, and then the memory."

Of all her books, Fox is most often associated with her controversial yet highly acclaimed work, *The Slave Dancer,* which won the 1974 Newbery Medal. It is the story of a New Orleans boy who is kidnapped and placed on a slave ship bound for West Africa. The boy, Jessie Bollier, is chosen for his ability to play the fife; his task aboard ship is to "dance" the slaves so they can exercise their cramped limbs. Eventually, Jessie escapes when the ship's crew is drowned in a storm, but he is forever scarred by his experience. Despite the praise *The Slave Dancer* has received, a number of critics complained that Fox's portrayal of the slaves made them appear to be merely dispirited cattle, and that she appeared to excuse the slave drivers as being victims of circumstance. Binnie Tate, for one, commented in *Interracial Books for Children:* "Through the characters' words, [Fox] excuses the captors and places the blame for the slaves' captivity on Africans themselves. The author slowly and systematically excuses almost all the whites in the story for their participation in the slave venture and by innuendo places the blame elsewhere." Other reviewers, however, viewed *The Slave Dancer* as a fair and humane treatment of a sensitive subject. Writing for *Horn Book,* Alice Bach called the book "one of the finest examples of a writer's control over her material." Bach went on to write in the same article: "With an underplayed but implicit sense of rage, Paula Fox exposes the men who dealt in selling human beings." The selection of *The Slave Dancer* for the Newbery caused a number of protests, including demonstrations during the awards ceremony.

Continuing her practice of placing her young protagonists in difficult circumstances, Fox, in *Monkey Island,* examines the issue of homelessness and explores the more general childhood fear of abandonment. The story concerns an eleven-year-old middle-class boy named Clay Garrity, whose father loses his job as a magazine art director and abandons his family. Because his mother is eight months pregnant and can't work, Clay fears the social services department will take him away and put him in a foster home. "The novel individualizes the problems of homeless people and puts faces on those whom society has made faceless," remarked Ellen Fader, writing for *Horn Book*. Fader commented that "readers' perceptions will be changed after reading the masterfully crafted *Monkey Island.*" Writing for the *New York Times Book Review*, Dinitia Smith called the novel "delicate and moving," and a "relentless story that succeeds in conveying the bitter facts" of homelessness.

In *Western Wind*, Fox was praised for taking a rather well-worn premise in children's literature—a lonely young girl is sent by her parents to live with an elderly relative who proves to be quite wise—and making it original and interesting. This is achieved mainly by Fox's depiction of the young heroine's grandmother, an eccentric painter who lives on a remote island off the coast of Maine in a house without indoor plumbing. Though *Booklist* contributor reviewer Ilene Cooper found Fox's "delicate craftsmanship" overdone, others praised the author's descriptive skills and emotional insights. Patricia J. Wagner in the *Bloomsbury Review* noted that both "adult and junior fiction writers should study her work with care," and Betsy Hearne, in *Bulletin of the Center for Children's Books*, observed that "Fox's style especially suits this taut narrative."

Homosexuality and AIDS are the issues that Liam Cormac and his family must confront in *The Eagle Kite*, a novel that *Horn Book* contributor Nancy Vasilakis hailed for its "painstaking honesty." Young Liam's father is dying from AIDS. His imminent death and the circumstances under which he contracted the disease cause the family almost unbearable grief; they also provide the narrative struggles through which some memorable characters are defined. Writing for *Voice of Youth Advocates*, W. Keith McCoy described the book as "a brief, but intense, portion of one young boy's life," and further noted that "Fox's spare prose enhances the emotions that are buffeting the Cormacs."

Such emotional honesty is also displayed in *Radiance Descending*, the story of an adolescent boy struggling with his resentment toward his younger brother, who

has Down syndrome. Having just moved to Long Island from New York City, Paul is eager to avoid Jacob, who nevertheless idealizes him. Paul is also frustrated at how Jacob monopolizes all their parents' attention. Slowly, however, Paul comes to realize that the mere fact of avoiding Jacob is still focusing on him, and that there may be a middle ground. "Older readers will find many layers of meaning in this novel," noted a contributor to *Publishers Weekly*. "Younger readers may be put off by a few esoteric allusions . . . but will still be able to recognize the gradual blossoming of Paul's compassion." Edward Sullivan, writing for *Voice of Youth Advocates*, called *Radiance Descending* "a quiet, introspective novel told with great eloquence."

Although Fox has not received as much recognition for her adult novels as she has for her children's books, she has nevertheless been widely praised for works like *Desperate Characters*. Her adult novels are "concerned with the cataclysmic moments of private lives, and the quiet desperation of ordinary people," wrote Linda Simon in *Commonweal*. *Desperate Characters* explores the lives of Sophie and Otto Bentwood, a childless couple in their mid-forties. The Bentwoods live in a renovated Brooklyn townhouse amid the squalor of a slum. While the Bentwoods' marriage is troubled, they are content with their orderly, comfortable lives. As the novel progresses, however, their security is gradually encroached upon.

In both Fox's children's and adult novels, her characters suffer through tragic situations for which there are no simple solutions, and this has led some critics to categorize her as an author of serious and depressing works. Fox has at times been frustrated by this label.

A number of critics have defended Fox's approach to fiction, and have praised her ability to address her younger audience frankly. "What sets [Fox] above the gaudy blooms—the social workers and fortunetellers—who are knocking out books as fast as kids can swallow them," wrote *Horn Book* contributor Alice Bach, "is her uncompromising integrity. Fox is nobody's mouthpiece. Her unique vision admits to the child what he already suspects: Life is part grit, part disappointment, part nonsense, and occasionally victory." Bach also added: "And by offering children no more than the humanness we all share—child, adult, reader, writer—she acknowledges them as equals."

Fox's reputation as an novelist for adults underwent a revival when noted author Jonathan Franzen rediscovered her first novel, *Desperate Characters* in a library and became outraged when he found it was out of print. Since then, the author's adult novels have been published in new editions for a modern audience. Writing a review of *Desperate Characters* and *The Widow's Children* for the London *Times Online* Web site, Alex Clark called *Desperate Characters* "a small-scale masterpiece: in 154 pages, it captures perfectly a moment in American social life; it draws on and amplifies both European and American novelistic traditions; it provides a compelling, disquieting portrait of a marriage; and it is a brilliantly sustained tale of menace." Commenting on Fox's first novel, *Poor George*— about a Manhattan English teacher who moves to the country and loses his sense of identity and becomes bored with his life and wife—*Boston Review* Web site contributor Randall Curb wrote "that there's not an off-key passage in the book," adding: "This early in her career Fox was already a master of cadence and elegant syntax. Every line is lucid, and no paragraph goes on too long."

Fox is also the author to two memoirs, *Borrowed Finery: A Memoir,* published in 2001, and *The Coldest Winter: A Stringer in Liberated Europe,* published in 2005. *Borrowed Finery* covers the first twenty years of Fox's life. In an interview for the *New Yorker Online,* Mary Hawthorne asked Fox why she decided to write a memoir at this stage in her life. Fox replied: "I really don't know. It just occurred to me that I wanted very much to write about the minister, Mr. Corning, who took care of me when I was a child. I had written about him indirectly, in *One-eyed Cat,* which is a children's book, but I wanted to write about him directly."

Borrowed Finery follows the author from her traumatic childhood on through her very short first marriage. Fox unflinchingly describes her parents, who often abandon her, first to care in an orphanage and then often with friends. The author describes her mother as a woman who seemed to have absolutely no maternal feelings for her daughter. At one point in her memoir, Fox writes: "I sensed that if she could have hidden the act she would have killed me." At the same time, her father could be both loving and harsh. The author writes: "What I was sure of was that fate had determined that her presence [Fox's mother] was the price I had to pay in order to see my father. But when I did see him, his behaviour with me—playful, sometimes cruel, a voice of utterly inconsistent and capricious authority—confirmed my uneasiness, my ever growing sense of being an impostor outside life's laws."

In her memoir the author also reveals that she gave her baby daughter up for adoption. Years later, Fox's daughter Linda finally tracks down her mother. (Linda is the mother of musician and actor Courtney Love.) Fox also writes lovingly of Elwood Corning, a minister who helped care for her and was the first real father figure in her life. Writing for the London *Guardian,* Aida Edemariam called the memoir "a tale of startling neglect, told with a combination of directness and reticence unusual for the form. As with her fiction, the impression is of distanced, though not unfeeling, control."

Fox's second memoir, *The Coldest Winter,* begins in 1946 as Fox leaves for Europe, where she ends up working as a model and as a reader for the film company 20th-Century Fox and publisher Victor Gollancz Ltd. Eventually, she becomes a "stringer" for a news agency in Great Britain and ends up in Poland reporting on the city of Warsaw's reconstruction following the end of World War II. The author details the hardships suffered by the Polish people and their indomitable spirit. Comparing the author's writing style in this memoir to the author's first memoir, *Boston Globe* contributor Dan Cryer commented that *The Coldest Winter* "shares a penchant for austere, unadorned sentences that keep emotion on a short leash. Likewise, the scenes amount to quick descriptive snapshots, with explanation and interpretation kept to a minimum."

During her travels in Europe, the author encounters many survivors of the Nazi holocaust, such as a man who had both of his twin daughters die at the hands of Josef Mengele, a Nazi doctor who conducted experiments on Jewish prisoners. Another encounter recalled by the author is her meeting an American Midwestern Jewish homemaker on a bus tour of Silesia. The woman is on a mission to help the sparse Jewish population still left in Poland emigrate to Palestine. Fox's memoir also features several famous people she meets during her time in Europe, such as noted singer, actor, and activist Paul Robeson and the philosopher Jean-Paul Sartre.

Although focused primarily on others, the author also details her own experiences and confesses to an affair with a hero in the Resistance during the war. The man was married, and his wife sacrificed much to protect him from the Gestapo. Writing for the *Washington Post Book World,* Jonathan Yardley commented that the author's description of the affair "takes only four paragraphs, every word of them precise, painful and—I have no doubt—true. Every page of this short, intense book is like that. It is self-revelatory but never self-absorbed, beautifully written but never showily so."

Several other reviewers also commented on the author's ability to write a memoir that is not self-absorbed but focuses on the plight of others. Noting that "what rings strong and true throughout this book is the need to get outside one's own self and one's own grief if one has any hope of growing," Juliet Waters, writing for the *Montreal Mirror Online* Web site, went on to suggest that this memoir should perhaps be among the first, if not the first, book that new readers of Fox should read. Waters noted that the author's "commitment to detaching from her past, and to immersing herself in situations that forced her to empathize with others' grief explains far more about her writing than her actual past," adding that *The Coldest Winter* "is . . . beautiful . . ., full of both pain and transcendence." In a review for the *Chicago Tribune*, Heller McAlpin wrote that the author "reassesses her past and extracts indelible insights" and added in an assessment similar to that of Waters: "Fox's minimalist prose evokes for the reader something other than ourselves—and the effect is deeply moving."

BIOGRAPHICAL AND CRITICAL SOURCES:

BOOKS

Beacham's Guide to Literature for Young Adults, Beacham Publishing (Osprey, FL), Volume 3, 1990, Volume 8, 1994.

Benbow-Pfalzgraf, Taryn, editor, *American Women Writers,* 2nd edition, St. James Press (Detroit, MI), 2000.

Carpenter, Humphrey, and Mari Prichard, editors, *The Oxford Companion to Children's Literature,* Oxford University Press (Oxford, England), 1984.

Children's Literature Review, Volume 1, Gale (Detroit, MI), 1976, Volume 44, 1997.

Contemporary Literary Criticism, Gale (Detroit, MI), Volume 2, 1974, Volume 8, 1978, Volume 121, 2000.

Dictionary of Literary Biography, Volume 52: *American Writers for Children since 1960: Fiction,* Gale (Detroit, MI), 1986.

Drew, Bernard A., *The One Hundred Most Popular Young Adult Authors,* Libraries Unlimited (Englewood, CO), 1996.

Fox, Paula, *Borrowed Finery: A Memoir,* Henry Holt (New York, NY), 2001.

Fox, Paula, *The Coldest Winter: A Stringer in Liberated Europe,* Henry Holt (New York, NY), 2005.

Kingman, Lee, editor, *Newbery and Caldecott Medal Winners, 1966-1975,* Horn Book, 1975.

Major Twentieth-Century Writers, Gale (Detroit, MI), 1991.

Ousby, Ian, editor, *The Cambridge Guide to Literature in English,* Cambridge University Press (London, England), 1988.

St. James Guide to Young Adult Writers, 2nd edition, St. James Press (Detroit, MI), 1999.

Silvey, Anita, editor, *Children's Books and Their Creators,* Houghton Mifflin (Boston, MA), 1995.

Tate, Binnie, *Interracial Books for Children,* Volume 5, number 5, 1974.

Townsend, John Rowe, *A Sense of Story: Essays on Contemporary Writers for Children,* revised edition, Lippincott, 1979.

Ward, Martha E., and others, editors, *Authors of Books for Young People,* 3rd edition, Scarecrow Press, 1990.

PERIODICALS

Bloomsbury Review, March-April, 1994, Patricia J. Wagner, review of *Western Wind.*

Booklist, March 15, 1993, Ilene Cooper, *Amzat and His Brothers: Three Italian Tales,* p. 64; October 15, 1993, Ilene Cooper, review of *Western Wind,* p. 432; February 1, 1995, Hazel Rochman, review of *The Eagle Kite,* p. 1003; September 1, 1997, Hazel Rochman, review of *Radiance Descending,* p. 124; September 1, 2005, Hazel Rochman, review of *The Coldest Winter: A Stringer in Liberated Europe,* p. 41; March 1, 2008, John Peters, review of *Traces,* p. 74.

Boston Globe, January 1, 2006, Dan Cryer, "Educated by a War-Weary Europe," review of *The Coldest Winter.*

Boston Review, December, 2001-January, 2002, Randall Curb, review of *Poor George, Desperate Characters,* and *The Widow's Children.*

Bulletin of the Center for Children's Books, November, 1980, Zena Sutherland, review of *A Place Apart,* p. 52; September, 1993, Betsy Hearne, review of *Western Wind,* pp. 9-10.

Chicago Tribune, December 25, 2005, Heller McAlpin, "A Memoir of a Young Woman's Experience in War's Aftermath," review of *The Coldest Winter.*

Columbus Dispatch, January 15, 2006, "Postwar Europe Shocks Young Writer."

Commonweal, January 11, 1985, Linda Simon, review of *A Servant's Tale.*

Guardian (London, England), June 21, 2003, Aida Edemariam, "A Qualified Optimist," profile of author.

Harper's, November, 2005, John Leonard, review of *The Coldest Winter,* p. 90.

Harper's Bazaar, February, 2001, Melanie Rehak, "Fox Tale," review of *Poor George,* p. 168.

Horn Book, September-October, 1967, Ruth Hill Viguers, review of *How Many Miles to Babylon?;* August, 1969, review of *The King's Falcon,* p. 410; November-December, 1970, review of *Blowfish Live in the Sea;* December, 1973, review of *The Slave Dancer,* p. 596; September-October, 1977, Alice Bach, "Cracking Open the Geode: The Fiction of Paula Fox," pp. 514-521; April, 1984, Christine McDonnell, review of *The Stone-faced Boy,* p. 219; January-February, 1985, Ethel L. Heins, review of *One-eyed Cat,* pp. 57-58; September-October, 1991, Ellen Fader, review of *Monkey Island,* pp. 596-597; July-August, 1993, Nancy Vasilakis, review of *Amzat and His Brothers,* p. 468; March-April, 1994, Maeve Visser Knoth, review of *Western Wind,* p. 198; September-October, 1995, Nancy Vasilakis, review of *The Eagle Kite,* pp. 608-609; September-October, 1997, Joanna Rudge Long, review of *Radiance Descending,* p. 569.

Interracial Books for Children, Volume 5, number 5, 1974, Albert V. Schwartz and Binnie Tate, review of *The Slave Dancer.*

Kirkus Reviews, April 1, 1968, review of *Dear Prosper,* p. 393; September 1, 1997, review of *Radiance Descending,* p. 1389; September 15, 2005, review of *The Coldest Winter,* p. 1011; March 1, 2008, review of *Traces.*

Library Journal, October 1, 2005, Jan Brue Enright, review of *The Coldest Winter,* p. 88.

Los Angeles Times, November 20, 2005, Lynne Tillman, "The Lingering Chill of War," review of *The Coldest Winter.*

Ms., October, 1984, Diane Cole, review of *A Servant's Tale,* p. 144.

Nation, November 3, 1984, Blair T. Birmelin, review of *A Servant's Tale.*

Newsweek, December 1, 1980, Jean Strouse, review of *A Place Apart,* p. 104.

New York Times, March 4, 2001, Melanie Rehak, "The Life and Death And Life of Paula Fox."

New York Times Book Review, July 21, 1968, Margaret F. O'Connell, review of *Dear Prosper,* p. 22; January 20, 1974, Julius Lester, review of *The Slave Dancer;* October 3, 1976; November 9, 1980, Anne Tyler, "Staking out Her Own Territory," review of *A Place Apart,* p. 55; November 11, 1984, Anne Tyler, "Trying to Be Perfect," review of *One-eyed Cat,* p. 48; November 18, 1984, Paula Giddings, review of *A Servant's Tale,* p. 9; March 23, 1986, Hazel Rochman, "Children's Books," includes review of *The Moonlight Man;* February 5, 1989, Rosellen Brown, review of *The Village by the Sea,* p. 37; July 8, 1990, Jill Mccorkle, "Post-Poughkeepskie," review of *The God of Nightmares,* p. 18; November 10, 1991, Dinitia Smith, "No Place to Call Home," review of *Monkey Island,* p. 52; April 10, 1994, Cyrisse Jaffee, review of *Western Wind,* p. 35; December 17, 2006, Ishan Taylor, "Paperback Row," includes review of *The Coldest Winter.*

O: The Oprah Magazine, November, 2005, Pam Houston, "An Innocent Abroad: An Intensely Felt Memoir of a Young Woman Wading through the Bright Shards of 1946 Europe," review of *The Coldest Winter,* p. 182.

Publishers Weekly, April 6, 1990, Sybil S. Steinberg, "Paula Fox: Writing for Two Genres, She Has Earned a Reputation for High Quality Novels and Books for Young People," interview with author, pp. 99-100; February 2, 1990, Sybil Steinberg, review of *The God of Nightmares,* p. 76; April 12, 1993, review of *Amzat and His Brothers,* p. 64; August 23, 1993, review of *Western Wind,* p. 73; February 20, 1995, review of *The Eagle Kite,* p. 207; January 13, 1997, review of *The Slave Dancer,* p. 36; July 27, 1997, review of *Radiance Descending,* p. 202; July 9, 2001, review of *Borrowed Finery,* p. 54; September 5, 2005, review of *The Coldest Winter,* p. 45; September 5, 2005, Jenny Brown, "A Barge of Folly," interview with author, p. 44; April 14, 2008, Jon J. Muth, review of *Traces,* p. 54.

San Diego Reader, November 3, 2005, interview with author.

San Francisco Chronicle, December 4, 2005, Darrell Hartman, "Memories of a War Just Ended," review of *The Coldest Winter.*

School Library Journal, August, 1988, Amy Kellerman, review of *The Village by the Sea,* p. 93; April, 2008, Heidi Estrin, review of *Traces,* p. 106.

Seattle Times, January 1, 2006, "Author's Trauma Enhances Her Story," p. 7.

Vogue, November, 2005, Melanie Rehak, "Continental Divide; Paula Fox's New Memoir Recounts Her Adventures as a Young Reporter in Postwar Europe," review of *The Coldest Winter,* p. 242.

Voice of Youth Advocates, December, 1993, review of *Western Wind,* p. 290; June, 1995, W. Keith McCoy, review of *The Eagle Kite,* pp. 93-94; October,

1995, review of *The Eagle Kite,* p. 210; February, 1998, Edward Sullivan, review of *Radiance Descending,* p. 383.

Washington Post Book World, February 8, 1981, Katherine Paterson, review of *A Place Apart;* May 7, 1995, Elizabeth Hand, review of *The Eagle Kite,* p. 14; November 15, 2005, Jonathan Yardley, "A Writer Is Born," review of *The Coldest Winter,* p. C2.

ONLINE

Australian Broadcasting Corporation Radio National Web site, http://www.abc.net.au/rn/ (June 22, 2009), "Paula Fox," interview with author.

Bomb, http://www.bombsite.com/ (June 22, 2009), Lynne Tillman, "Paula Fox," interview with author.

BookPage, http://www.bookpage.com/ (June 22, 2009), Michelle Jones, review of *The Coldest Winter.*

City University of New York Web site, http://www1.cuny.edu/ (February 27, 2006), "Author Paula Fox Reads from Her Newest Work, *The Coldest Winter: A Stringer in Liberated Europe,* at Brooklyn College, March 13."

Montreal Mirror Online, http://www.montrealmirror.com/ (June 22, 2009), Juliet Waters, "Fox on the Run," review of *The Coldest Winter.*

New Yorker Online, http://www.newyorker.com/ (July 2, 2001), Mary Hawthorne, "Advancing the Water," interview with author.

New York Observer Online, http://www.observer.com/ (December 18, 2005), Jessica Joffe, "Paula Fox," profile of author.

Times Online, http://entertainment.timesonline.co.uk/ (July 27, 2003), Alex Clark, review of *Desperate Characters* and *The Widow's Children.*

Village Voice Online, http://www.villagevoice.com/ (November 1, 2005), Rebecca Tuhus-Dubrow, "European Mutilation," review of *The Coldest Winter.**

*   *   *

FRAZER, Margaret
See FERRIS, Monica

*   *   *

FRIDAY, Jo
See DRUETT, Joan

FULTON, Alice 1952-

PERSONAL: Born January 25, 1952, in Troy, NY; daughter of John R. (a businessman) and Mary (a nurse) Fulton; married Hank De Leo (an artist), June, 1980. *Education:* State University of New York Empire State College, B.A., 1979; Cornell University, M.F.A., 1982.

ADDRESSES: Office—Department of English, 250 Goldwin Smith Hall, Cornell University, Ithaca, NY 14853-3201. *E-mail*—af89@cornell.edu.

CAREER: Poet, writer, and educator. University of Michigan, Ann Arbor, assistant professor, 1983-86, William Wilhartz Professor, 1986-89, associate professor, 1990-92, professor of English, 1992-2001; Cornell University, Ithaca, NY, Ann S. Bowers Professor of English, 2002—. Visiting professor at Vermont College, 1987, University of California, Los Angeles, 1991, Ohio State University, 1995, University of North Carolina, 1997, and University of California, Berkeley, 2004. Member of American Delegation at Chinese/American Writers' Conference, 1988.

AWARDS, HONORS: MacDowell Colony fellowship, 1978, 1979; Millay colony fellowship, 1980; Emily Dickinson Award, Poetry Society of America, 1980; award from Associated Writing Programs, 1982, for *Dance Script with Electric Ballerina;* Academy of American Poets prize, 1982; fellowship from the Michigan Society of Fellows, 1983-86; Consuelo Ford Award from Poetry Society of America, 1984, for "Terrestrial Magnetism"; Rainer Maria Rilke award, 1984; National Poetry Series award, 1985, and Society of Midland Authors Award, 1987, for *Palladium;* Michigan Council for the Arts grant, 1986, 1991; Yaddo Colony fellowship, 1987; John Simon Guggenheim Memorial Foundation fellowship, 1986-87; Bess Hokin award, *Poetry,* 1989; Ingram Merril Foundation award, 1990; Henry Russel Award for promise of distinction in writing and excellence in teaching, University of Michigan, 1990; John D. and Catherine T. MacArthur Foundation fellow, 1991-96; Elizabeth Matchett Stover award, *Southwest Review,* 1994; honorary D.Litt., State University of New York, 1994; Editor's Prize in Fiction, *Missouri Review,* 1997; Pushcart Prizes for poetry and fiction; Elizabeth Matchett Stover Award, *Southwest Review;* Rebekah Johnson Bobbitt National Prize for Poetry, Library of Congress, 2002, for *Felt;* 2004 Holloway Poet at University of California, Berkeley; fellowships from Michigan Society of Fellows, Provincetown Fine Arts Work Center, and the National Endowment for the Arts.

WRITINGS:

POETRY

Anchors of Light, Swamp Press (Oneonta, NY), 1979.

Dance Script with Electric Ballerina, University of Pennsylvania Press (Philadelphia, PA), 1983.

Palladium, University of Illinois Press (Urbana, IL), 1986.

Powers of Congress, David Godine (Boston, MA), 1990.

Sensual Math, W.W. Norton (New York, NY), 1995.

Felt, W.W. Norton (New York, NY), 2001.

Cascade Experiment: Selected Poems, W.W. Norton (New York, NY), 2004.

OTHER

Feeling as a Foreign Language: The Good Strangeness of Poetry, Graywolf Press (St. Paul, MN), 1999.

The Nightingales of Troy: Stories of One Family's Century, W.W. Norton and Co. (New York, NY), 2008.

Poetry and writings included in anthologies, including *The Best American Poetry* series, the tenth anniversary edition *The Best of the Best American Poetry, 1988-1997, Best American Short Stories, 1993, Cabbage and Bones,* and the *Pushcart Prize XXVIII* and *Pushcart Prize XXIX* anthologies. Contributor to magazines, including *Tin House, Parnassus, Paris Review, New Republic, Atlantic Monthly, New Yorker, Poetry,* and *Georgia Review.* Author of short stories, song lyrics, and critical essays. Also contributor to *Turbulence: A Romance,* a song cycle with music by William Bolcom and words by Alice Fulton, performed by Marsha Hunter and Brian Kent at the Walker Art Center, Minneapolis, 1997.

ADAPTATIONS: Poetry has been adapted for music and stage, including the poem "Mail" by Enid Sutherland for mezzo-soprano Deanna Relyea, Rackham Auditorium, University of Michigan, 2000; *Give: A Sequence Reimaginging Daphne & Apollo* by Enid Sutherland, Lydia Mendelssohn Theater, Ann Arbor, MI, 2003; . . .

turns and turns into the night, by Anthony Cornicello, a setting of four poems from *Sensual Math,* Guggenheim Museum, New York, NY, 2001; computer music adaptation of three poems, Joseph Klein, University of North Texas Center for Experimental Music & Intermedia Concert Series, 2005; *The Etiquette of Ice,* settings of three poems sung by soprano Heidi Klein and conducted by Joseph Klein; *I Will Breathe A Mountain: A Cycle from American Women Poets,* William Bolcom, performed by Marilyn Horne at Carnegie Hall's Centennial Celebration, New York, NY.

SIDELIGHTS: Alice Fulton's poetry explores the human mind, faith, science, and technology. "Her poems are at once deeply personal and defiantly abstract," asserted Sergei Lobanov-Rostovsky in *Dictionary of Literary Biography.* The essayist found that Fulton's work gives insight into "the workings of the poetic imagination, the way poetry emerges from the mind's web of associations, stimulated by memory, experience, and the seductions of popular culture." Lobanov-Rostovsky characterized Fulton's work as challenging but rewarding: "Her poems demand from her readers nothing less than immersion, a process in which they share the creation of meaning by allowing the poem to shape—but not dictate—their own consciousness. Her meanings are multiple, fluid, and provisional; reading her work reveals our minds to be the same."

Commenting on Fulton's vivid imagery in poetry collections such as *Palladium* and *Sensual Math,* Julie Miller, writing in *Contemporary Women Poets,* counted "faith" as one of the major concerns of Fulton's poetry, and noted that when the poet turned to science and technology, that faith increased rather than diminished.

Fulton's 1990 collection, *Powers of Congress,* also includes pyrotechnics in the wordplay of poems such as "Romance in the Dark" and "Point of Purchase." However, *Publishers Weekly* reviewer Penny Kaganoff faulted the poet for "incoherent or heavy-handed" imagery, despite "a keen sense of the pliability of language." Kaganoff felt that the narrative poems of the collection, such as "A Union House," which relates her own father's connection to an old hotel, or "Overlord," about the experiences of a paratrooper in World War II, were more successful.

Reviewing Fulton's fourth collection of poems, *Sensual Math,* a *Publishers Weekly* contributor noted: "In a complex metaphorical alchemy," the poet mixes classical with modern themes using "controlled language and . . . mastery of the lyric." The same reviewer called the collection "brilliant." In a tour de force, Fulton combines elements of television commercials and Darwinian theory in "My Last TV Campaign: A Sequence," she examines gender transformations in "Give: A Sequence Reimagining Daphne and Apollo," and she further explores myth and visions of contemporary life in other poems of the collection. In the *Los Angeles Times,* poet Amy Gerstler lauded the *Sensual Math,* noting: "Fulton's voice in readers' ears asserts itself immediately, confidently." Gerstler went on to comment: "In these poems '90s-minded concerns are tartly and smartly articulated from word one, and readers will quickly be able to calculate whether the book's taut dialectics and language play, erudite wisecracking and finger-popping, with occasional detonations of overt emotionality, are for them."

Fulton offered readers a collection of prose essays with *Feeling as a Foreign Language: The Good Strangeness of Poetry.* Using scientific theories to comment on poetry, Fulton suggests a "less stable world view" with "a less predictable aesthetics, and aesthetics of playfulness and irregularity," commented Scott Hightower in *Library Journal.* "These essays . . . address the deepest inner insistencies of style and our humanity. The result is a provocative ride." A *Publishers Weekly* contributor also commented favorably on the "wit and verve" in *Feeling as a Foreign Language,* further noting that Fulton "wants her readers to share her beliefs—in the worth of disjunction, in the value of physics for poets, and in the need to work for women's equality. In several of these essays, they'll find the exemplary verve to do so."

Fulton's collection *Felt,* received the 2002 Rebekah Johnson Bobbitt National Prize for Poetry, which is a biennial poetry prize awarded by the Library of Congress in recognition of the most distinguished book of poetry written by an American and published during the preceding two years. *Felt* features free-verse poems that cover a wide spectrum of human emotions, from the extreme highs and lows of adolescence to grief, suicide, and obsession. For example, in the poem "Maidenhead," Fulton writes an autobiographical reflection on her youth and growing awareness of the realities of life around and beyond her. Writing in *Poetry,* Bill Christophersen commented on the author's style, noting her use of "cobbled-together words; the alternation of long lines with lines made up of one word; the deployment of mixed metaphors, neologisms, and non

sequiturs; the interweaving of scientific language and street slang; the forcing of nouns to serve as verbs, and adjectives to serve as nouns." Christophersen went on to call these stylistic traits as "the rough equivalent of an abstract expressionist painter's palette knife, spray gun, and drip can." Jane Satterfield, writing in the *Antioch Review,* commented that in this collection "the poet's gaze ricochets between surface and depth, proximity and distance, revealing the way these forces determine the intricate and baffling processes of art and human relations." Satterfield called the poems "texturally rich." A *Publishers Weekly* contributor wrote that the Fulton "composes multi-page poems out of ever-expanding sentences, stretching her phrases like tightropes over the vast reaches of information." The reviewer went on to note that "this may be Fulton's best book."

Fulton's next collection of poetry, titled *Cascade Experiment: Selected Poems,* features selected poems from nearly two decades and includes poems from all of her previous books of poetry, from *Dance Script with Electric Ballerina,* first published in 1983, on up through *Felt.* Writing in the *Harvard Review,* Kathleen Rooney commented that "there's so much to absorb that you're unlikely to glean everything there is to learn and appreciate from the collection the first time through." Rooney added: "Essentially, *Cascade Experiment* is a book that invites repeat attention, even study—a book to which you can go back and back and discover something new each time." Rooney also called Fulton "an experimental genius" who focuses on "making sure [her poems] proceed with the correct degree of innovation and inevitability." In a review in *Kliatt,* Beth Lizardo noted that *Cascade Experiment* "serves as a good introduction to the work of a tremendously insightful poet whose work is sure to leave its mark on American poetry." A *Publishers Weekly* contributor commented that the collection "cements her reputation as a quirky, increasingly challenging assembler of a pleasantly cluttered, pluralistic, kaleidoscopic world."

With her 2008 work *The Nightingales of Troy: Stories of One Family's Century,* Fulton turns to fiction for a debut collection of ten interlinked tales featuring four generations in the family of the Garrahan sisters and their female descendants. Set in Fulton's hometown of Troy, New York, the tales follow the female line of an Irish Catholic family through the twentieth century. In the first story in the collection, "Happy Dust," Mamie Flynn Garrahan, a farming woman dealing with the effects of tuberculosis and pregnant with her fifth child, takes center stage. Other tales relate humorous and deadly serious events in the lives of the Garrahan women. Peg Flynn in "Queen Wintergreen" wonders about a marriage proposal now that she is sixty-five. Other stories evoke the 1920s or Depression-age Troy. The Beatles even make an appearance in "The Real Eleanor Rigby."

Speaking with a contributor for the online *L Magazine,* Fulton remarked on this change in literary direction: "I wanted to write fiction as soon as I began reading it, as a child. I advise students to write the kind of book they love to read. I love to read both poetry and fiction, so the thought of writing fiction was very appealing. I messed around with a narrative in the early 1980s, but I wasn't really trying. Years later, I decided to give fiction my best shot. I spent some time trying to figure out what made a story a story as opposed to fifteen pages of meandering." The first story she wrote for the eventual collection, "Queen Wintergreen," was inspired by Louise Erdrich's *Love Medicine.* Published in the magazine *TriQuarterly,* it was also included in an edition of *Best American Short Stories.* However, it was still many years before Fulton developed all the tales for *The Nightingales of Troy.* In an interview with *Boston Globe* contributor Anna Mundow, Fulton expounded on the differences between writing poetry and fiction: "It is entirely different, very refreshing. I think what I bring from poetry is the interest in language and in compression. But the difference is character, psychology; the external world is much more important to fiction. It allows me to create a world and think more deeply about other people."

The Nightingales of Troy earned wide critical acclaim. Mundow noted that in "her outstanding first fiction collection, poet Alice Fulton reveals herself to be triumphantly at home in the short story." Writing for the *Winston-Salem Journal,* Tracy V. Wilson felt that "the collection reflects Fulton's skill as a poet." Wilson went on to observe: "The stories are equally well crafted, playing off and enhancing the meaning of one another." Similarly *L Magazine* reviewer Thea Brown noted, "Fulton's prose thrives on the tactile, and, as in her poetry, the language is brilliantly precise." For a *Kirkus Reviews* contributor, the same work provided "emotionally satisfying and extremely well-crafted short fiction." *Booklist* reviewer Donna Seaman offered higher praise, remarking: "Every element in this collection of scintillating linked short stories is surprising, pleasurable, and stealthily affecting." Likewise, a *Publishers Weekly* contributor called *The Nightingales of Troy* "a book

that's rich with feeling for its characters yet willing to expose their faults." *Seattle Times* reviewer Richard Wallace wrote, "Alice Fulton is a writer who can provide the complicated pleasures of accomplished fiction." *New York Times Book Review* writer Sarah Fay concluded: "If this collection is any indication, Fulton may be firmly establishing herself in a different genre. . . . It's exciting to watch Fulton as she finds the right threads with which to create nuanced fiction, firmly bound."

BIOGRAPHICAL AND CRITICAL SOURCES:

BOOKS

Contemporary Women Poets, St. James Press (Detroit, MI), 1998.

Dictionary of Literary Biography, Gale (Detroit, MI), Volume 139: *American Poets since World War II, Sixth Series,* 1994.

Frost, Elisabeth A., and Cynthia Hogue, editors, *Innovative Women Poets: An Anthology of Contemporary Poetry and Interviews,* University of Iowa Press (Iowa City, IO), 2006, pp. 121-123.

Gioia, Dana, David Mason, and Meg Schoerke, editors, *Twentieth-Century American Poetics: Poets on the Art of Poetry,* McGraw-Hill (New York, NY), 2004, p. 469.

Keller, Lynn, and Cristanne Miller, editors, *Feminist Measures: Soundings in Poetry and Theory,* University of Michigan Press (Ann Arbor, MI), 1994.

St. John, David, and Cole Swenson, editors, *American Hybrid: A Norton Anthology of Contemporary Poetry,* W.W. Norton (New York, NY), 2009.

PERIODICALS

Antioch Review, spring, 2002, Jane Satterfield, review of *Felt,* p. 348.

Booklist, July 1, 2008, Donna Seaman, review of *The Nightingales of Troy: Stories of One Family's Century,* p. 35.

Harvard Review, December, 2004, Kathleen Rooney, review of *Cascade Experiment: Selected Poems,* p. 176.

Irish Times (Dublin, Ireland), July 12, 2008, "Legends of Troy," review of *The Nightingales of Troy.*

Kliatt, March, 2006, Beth Lizardo, review of *Cascade Experiment,* p. 34.

Kirkus Reviews, June 1, 2008, review of *The Nightingales of Troy.*

Library Journal, December 15, 1983, Rochelle Ratner, review of *Dance Script with Electric Ballerina,* p. 2334; September 1, 1986, review of *Palladium,* p. 204; February 1, 1991, Kathleen Norris, review of *Powers of Congress,* p. 80; April 1, 1995, Doris Lynch, review of *Sensual Math,* p. 98; March 15, 1999, Scott Hightower, review of *Feeling as a Foreign Language: The Good Strangeness of Poetry,* p. 78. May 1, 2008, Donna Bettencourt, review of *The Nightingales of Troy,* p. 55.

Los Angeles Times, July 23, 1995, Amy Gerstler, review of *Sensual Math,* p. 15.

Los Angeles Times Book Review, July 6, 2008, Susan Salter Reynolds, review of *The Nightingales of Troy.*

New York Times Book Review, December 10, 1995, William Logan, review of *Sensual Math,* p. 37; September 5, 1999, Emily Barton, review of *Feeling as a Foreign Language,* p. 17; September 7, 2008, Sarah Fay, review of *The Nightingales of Troy,* p. 15.

Poetry, November, 1984, William Logan, review of *Dance Script with Electric Ballerina,* p. 102; October, 1986, J.D. McClatchy, review of *Palladium,* p. 43; June, 1991, David Baker, review of *Powers of Congress,* p. 172; August, 1996, Sandra M. Gilbert, review of *Sensual Math,* p. 281; January, 2002, Bill Christophersen, review of *Felt,* p. 217.

Publishers Weekly, October 21, 1983, review of *Dance Script with Electric Ballerina,* p. 55; July 4, 1986, review of *Palladium,* p. 65; October 5, 1990, Penny Kaganoff, review of *Powers of Congress,* p. 94; February 27, 1995, review of *Sensual Math,* p. 97; February 22, 1999, review of *Feeling as a Foreign Language,* p. 90; November 20, 2000, review of *Felt,* p. 64; April 26, 2004, review of *Cascade Experiment,* p. 56; March 24, 2008, review of *The Nightingales of Troy,* p. 49.

Seattle Times, August 3, 2008, Richard Wallace, review of *The Nightingales of Troy,* p. 6.

Times Union, November 9, 2008, C.J. Lais, Jr., "Alice Fulton Discusses Tales of Troy: Alice Fulton Continues to Be Inspired by Her Hometown."

Winston-Salem Journal (Winston-Salem, NC), October 5, 2008, Tracy V. Wilson, review of *The Nightingales of Troy.*

ONLINE

Alice Fulton Home Page, http://alicefulton.com (May 26, 2009).

Boston Globe Online, http://www.boston.com/ (June 29, 2009), Anna Mundow, "Distilling Decades into Fiction," author interview.

Cornell University Chronicle Online, http://www.news. cornell.edu/ (September 5, 2008), Daniel Aloi, "Alice Fulton Explores Family-Based Fiction in New Book," review of *The Nightingales of Troy.*

L Magazine, http://www.thelmagazine.com/ (June 18, 2008), Thea Brown, review of *The Nightingales of Troy;* (September 17, 2008) "Author Interview: Alice Fulton."

New York State Writers Institute, State University of New York Web site, http://www.albany.edu/writersinst/ (May 26, 2009), author profile.

St. Rose Chronicle, http://media.www.strosechronicle. com/ (November 19, 2008), Kali Zigrino and Danielle O'Malley, "Frequency North Continues with Fulton."

G

GELARDI, Julia P.

PERSONAL: Born in Manila, Philippines; married; children: two daughters. *Education:* Simon Fraser University, M.A., 1998.

ADDRESSES: Home—Plymouth, MN. *Agent*—Julie Castiglia, Castiglia Literary Agency, 1155 Camino del Mar, Ste. 510, Del Mar, CA 92014. *E-mail*—juliap gelardi@yahoo.com.

CAREER: Independent historian.

WRITINGS:

Born to Rule: Five Reigning Consorts, Granddaughters of Queen Victoria, St. Martin's Press (New York, NY), 2005.
In Triumph's Wake: Royal Mothers, Tragic Daughters, and the Price They Paid for Glory, St. Martin's Press (New York, NY), 2008.

Contributor to a number of scholarly journals, including *Royalty Digest, Atlantis: In the Courts of Memory, European Crown, Imperial Russian Journal, Habsburg Quarterly,* and *European Royal History Journal.*

SIDELIGHTS: Julia P. Gelardi, an independent historian, specializes in European royal history from the Victorian era to the present. She is also a prolific writer, contributing essays and articles to a number of scholarly journals related to European royal history. In 2005 Gelardi published her first book, *Born to Rule: Five Reigning*

Consorts, Granddaughters of Queen Victoria. The book outlines the lives of five of Queen Victoria's granddaughters—Alexandra of Russia, Marie of Romania, Victoria Eugenie of Spain, Sophie of Greece, and Maud of Norway—who reigned across Europe during the early part of the twentieth century. The princesses' personal and political lives are detailed, as well as the women's respective roles and effects on the countries they governed. Gelardi drew much of her information from primary sources and private correspondence, and she also includes a genealogical chart.

Many critics offered positive assessments of *Born to Rule,* particularly appreciating Gelardi's detailed exploration of the lives of the lesser-known princesses. The book is "sometimes solemn, sometimes frisky, but always captivating," observed a *Kirkus Reviews* contributor. Others thought Gelardi's book fills a niche in the study of royal history. *Born to Rule* is "highly recommended for public, academic, and libraries specializing in European history," asserted Gail Benjafield in the *Library Journal.*

Gelardi published her second book, *In Triumph's Wake: Royal Mothers, Tragic Daughters, and the Price They Paid for Glory,* in 2008. The account examines the daughters of three renowned monarchs in Europe, Queen Isabella of Castile's Catherine of Aragon, Empress Maria Theresa of Austria's Queen Marie Antoinette of France, and Queen Victoria of England's Empress Frederick of Germany. The lives of these three women, though positioned for greatness, failed to measure up to the reputations held by their mothers and ended tragically.

Faye Jones, reviewing the account in *BookPage,* observed that "despite their tragic ends, Gelardi shows there is much to admire in the lives of these women." Holly Tucker, writing in the *San Francisco Chronicle,* found that the book "makes a convincing argument for the stunning similarities among these women. It also weaves together their stories so tightly—in time, place and various cultural geographies—that mothers, daughters and chapters seem nearly interchangeable." To this extent, however, Tucker proposed that "perhaps the real story of these fascinating women is less in their similarities and more in their differences."

A contributor writing in *Kirkus Reviews* remarked: "Bending over backward to make a sympathetic case for the underachieving offspring, Gelardi . . . delivers substantial, accessible European history." A contributor reviewing the book in *Publishers Weekly* commented that with this book Gelardi "produces an excellent, comprehensive study of six fascinating women and the troubled times that shaped their lives." Tessa L.H. Minchew, writing in *Library Journal,* said of the women covered that "Gelardi seeks to humanize them as she tells these doubly sad stories."

Gelardi once told *CA:* "I have always had a strong affinity for books and the written word. This, coupled with a keen interest in history and researching has led me to write about historical figures, particularly European royalty from the Victorian era to the present. This interest stemmed in large part from reading numerous biographies and historical works starting in my teenage years, a habit which happily, has not abated. A particular favorite book has been Robert K. Massie's *Nicholas and Alexandra,* which highlights the lives of Tsar Nicholas II of Russia and his wife, Tsarina Alexandra. Though first published nearly forty years ago, Massie's dramatic tale of imperial tragedy still resonates thanks to his impeccable writing which makes for compelling reading.

"Writing compelling books that resonate with readers is the goal of nearly every author, and it is certainly something that I strive for in my works. Writing is a demanding craft; history and biography more so as the author is constrained by actual events and sources connected to a book's protagonists. Central to honing the skill and craft of writing is reading and to that end, I try to read as many books and articles as I can, both older works and current ones.

"Being essentially a solitary craft, writing also requires self-discipline. My writing routine varies, though it mainly consists of researching and writing for hours at a stretch, mainly in the mornings and afternoons. The research involved in my works varies, depending upon the topic and sources at hand. This can range from examining personal letters, diaries, and diplomatic documents to tracking down and reading out-of-print newspapers and books, and conducting interviews. Much time is spent studying a multitude of material for hours on end, often in libraries and archives. Then comes the task of analyzing and synthesizing the material, leading to the process of writing and revising, which eventually progresses to the finished article or book. The kind of research involved in my book, *Born to Rule,* involved a wide variety of sources that inevitably led to my visiting several countries to access some of the material. I also owe a debt of gratitude to numerous individuals who helped me gain access to sources and who shared their own knowledge, which contributed to the stories told in the book. In *Born to Rule,* I hope that readers can come to appreciate a special group of individuals, most of whom are long forgotten, but whose moving lives, both on a personal and public level, are such that their stories remain timeless and compelling."

BIOGRAPHICAL AND CRITICAL SOURCES:

PERIODICALS

Historian, fall, 2006, John Plunkett, review of *Born to Rule: Five Reigning Consorts, Granddaughters of Queen Victoria,* p. 628.
History: Review of New Books, fall, 2005, Patricia Kollander, review of *Born to Rule,* p. 22.
Kirkus Reviews, December 15, 2004, review of *Born to Rule,* p. 1181; October 1, 2008, review of *In Triumph's Wake: Royal Mothers, Tragic Daughters, and the Price They Paid for Glory.*
Library Journal, December 1, 2004, Gail Benjafield, review of *Born to Rule,* p. 135; October 15, 2008, Tessa L.H. Minchew, review of *In Triumph's Wake,* p. 79.
Publishers Weekly, October 6, 2008, review of *In Triumph's Wake,* p. 49.
San Francisco Chronicle, December 9, 2008, Holly Tucker, review of *In Triumph's Wake,* p. E-8.
Washington Post Book World, March 19, 2006, Rachel Hartigan Shea, review of *Born to Rule,* p. 11.

ONLINE

BookPage, http://www.bookpage.com/ (June 8, 2009), Faye Jones, review of *In Triumph's Wake.*

Julia P. Gelardi Home Page, http://www.juliapgelardi. com (August 13, 2005), author biography.

* * *

GEORGE, Sally
See ORR, Wendy

* * *

GILSON, Jamie 1933-

PERSONAL: Born July 4, 1933, in Beardstown, IL; daughter of James Noyce (a flour miller) and Sallie (an educator) Chisam; married Jerome Gilson (a lawyer), June 19, 1955; children: Tom, Matthew, Anne. *Education:* Attended University of Missouri, 1951-52; Northwestern University, B.S., 1955.

ADDRESSES: Home—Wilmette, IL. *E-mail*—jamie@ jamiegilson.com.

CAREER: Educator and writer. Thacker Junior High School, Des Plaines, IL, speech and English teacher, 1955-56; writer and producer for radio and television division of public school system in Chicago, IL, 1956-59; WFMT-Radio, Chicago, continuity director, 1959-63; Encyclopaedia Britannica, Chicago, writer in film division, 1963-65. Lecturer and writing-workshop teacher, Wilmette Public Schools, 1974-90.

MEMBER: Society of Children's Book Writers and Illustrators, Society of Midland Authors, PEN American Center, Authors Guild.

AWARDS, HONORS: Merit Award, Friends of American Writers, 1979, for *Harvey, the Beer Can King;* Carl Sandburg Award, Friends of the Chicago Public Library, 1981, and Charlie May Simon Award, Arkansas Elementary School Council, 1983, both for *Do Bananas Chew Gum?;* Dallas Market Center Gift Editorial Award, 1983, for column "The Goods"; Sequoyah Award and Pacific Northwest Young Readers Choice Award, both 1985, Land of Enchantment Award, 1986, and Buckeye Award, and Sunshine Award, both 1987, all for *Thirteen Ways to Sink a Sub;* Children's Reading Round Table Award, 1992; Society of Midland Authors Award for Children's Fiction, 2002, for *Stink Alley;* Illinois Reading Council Prairie State Award for Excellence in Writing for Children.

WRITINGS:

FOR CHILDREN

Harvey, the Beer Can King, illustrated by John Wallner, Lothrop (New York, NY), 1978.
Dial Leroi Rupert, DJ, illustrated by John Wallner, Lothrop (New York, NY), 1979.
Do Bananas Chew Gum?, Lothrop (New York, NY), 1980.
Can't Catch Me, I'm the Gingerbread Man, Lothrop (New York, NY), 1981.
Thirteen Ways to Sink a Sub, illustrated by Linda Straus Edwards, Lothrop (New York, NY), 1982, Marshall Cavendish (Tarrytown, NY), 2009.
4-B Goes Wild, illustrated by Linda Straus Edwards, Lothrop (New York, NY), 1983.
Hello, My Name Is Scrambled Eggs, illustrated by John Wallner, Lothrop (New York, NY), 1985.
Hobie Hanson, You're Weird, illustrated by Elise Primavera, Lothrop (New York, NY), 1987.
Double Dog Dare, illustrated by Elise Primavera, Lothrop (New York, NY), 1988.
Hobie Hanson: Greatest Hero of the Mall, illustrated by Anita Riggio, Lothrop (New York, NY), 1989.
Itchy Richard, illustrated by Diane de Groat, Clarion (New York, NY), 1991.
Sticks and Stones and Skeleton Bones, illustrated by Dee DeRosa, Lothrop (New York, NY), 1991.
You Cheat!, illustrated by Maxine Chambliss, Bradbury Press (New York, NY), 1992.
Soccer Circus, illustrated by Dee DeRosa, Lothrop (New York, NY), 1993.
It Goes Eeeeeeeeeeeee!, illustrated by Diane de Groat, Clarion (New York, NY), 1994.
Wagon Train 911, Lothrop (New York, NY), 1996.
Bug in a Rug, Clarion (New York, NY), 1998.
Stink Alley, HarperCollins (New York, NY), 2002.
Gotcha!, illustrated by Amy Wummer, Clarion (New York, NY), 2006.
Chess! I Love It, I Love It, I Love It!, illustrated by Amy Wummer, Clarion Books (New York, NY), 2008.

Author of *Chicago Magazine* column "The Goods," 1977-87. Contributor of articles to *WFMT Guide* and *Perspective* magazine.

SIDELIGHTS: Since the 1980s, Jamie Gilson's humorous books for middle-grade and elementary-grade readers have won fans through their humor and likeable characters. In her stories for young teens, all written in first-person from the perspective of an adolescent, Gilson demonstrates her keen understanding of the priorities and concerns of younger teens, while her chapter books, such as *You Cheat!* and *Gotcha!*, mix an engaging story with interesting facts and useful vocabulary. "Before writing books for children, all of my professional writing had been for the voice—radio, TV, films—so that my books, too, are *told,* as a child would tell them," Gilson once explained. "To keep that voice genuine, I work with children a good deal, speaking to them about my writing, teaching writing to sixth graders, sitting in with classes, going with a fifth-grade class on a nature study overnight. . . . My research is a joy."

One of the first books to grow out of Gilson's experience with children is *Do Bananas Chew Gum?*, published in 1980. Gilson got the idea for the story from an assignment she had as a reporter for *Chicago Magazine* to cover an archaeological dig in southern Illinois. "I discovered the real excitement that comes from finding broken arrowheads and shards of once-used clay pots," she recalled. "Sam Mott in *Do Bananas Chew Gum?* shares that enthusiasm." Sam is a sixth grader who has become the subject of his classmates' unkind jokes because he reads at a second-grade level. His reading difficulties make him feel stupid, so he tries to hide them from his family and friends. As the story progresses, Sam receives encouragement and motivation to overcome his problem from a young archaeologist who shares her love of history with him, as well as from both the kind woman for whom he baby sits and one of his classmates. He agrees to a series of tests and learns that he is not stupid after all: instead, he has a learning disability. By working with an understanding teacher, Sam is not only able to read better, but also improves his confidence and outlook on life. "Told with humor and subtle compassion, this is a story that leaves you feeling good," reviewer Jane VanWiemokly commented in *Voice of Youth Advocates.* "I hope that children will not only find *Bananas* fun to read, but also revealing of the difficulties that a learning-disabled child faces," Gilson explained.

Gilson introduces one of her most popular characters, Hobie Hanson, in *Thirteen Ways to Sink a Sub,* published in 1982. In this story, Hobie and his fourth-grade classmates are surprised to find a substitute teacher, Miss Svetlana Ivanovich, taking over their lessons for the day. The boys and the girls quickly face off to see which team can be the first to "sink the sub," or upset her to the point of tears. Some of their antics include switching names, pretending not to speak the English language, and faking the loss of a contact lens. Miss Ivanovich remains pleasant and good-natured throughout the contest, which eventually makes the class like her too much to continue trying to "sink" her. Barbara Elleman, reviewing the story for *Booklist,* praised Gilson's tale for its "crisp, inventive plot that is top drawer in the contemporary fiction genre for this age group."

Gilson rejoins Hobie and his friends in several other books, including *Hobie Hanson, You're Weird, Hobie Hanson: Greatest Hero of the Mall,* and *Soccer Circus.* When Hobie's best friend, Nick Rossi, goes away to computer camp for the summer, Hobie is left on his own in *Hobie Hanson, You're Weird.* At first the boy is annoyed when his classroom rival, Molly Bosco, begins following him around, but before long the two fourth graders discover how much they have in common and share some entertaining adventures. Writing in *School Library Journal,* Julie Cummins noted that, "with dialogue right on target for the age, Gilson writes with humor and appeal for kids." A *Booklist* reviewer praised Gilson's "bulls-eye wit and ease with the written word" and predicted that "kids will be attracted to this like steel to a magnet."

Hobie has a harrowing adventure in *Hobie Hanson.* In this story, heavy rains cause the nearby Hawk River to overflow its banks and flood much of Hobie's hometown. Although Hobie tries to act the hero, instead Molly Bosco floats by on an inflatable giraffe and rescues him as well as the little boy he is baby-sitting. Since their elementary school has been damaged in the flood, Hobie and his friends learn that school will be held temporarily in an empty department store at the local mall. In this unusual educational setting, the class finds a variety of new ways to make hilarious mischief. Hobie finally does become a hero by finding some diamond earrings that were lost in the flood and returning them to their owner, and he is only slightly less pleased with himself when he learns that the diamonds are fake. Denise Wilms, writing in *Booklist,* stated that Gilson's story "has action, humor, and a protagonist familiar enough to be the boy next door," and predicted that "Hobie's fans will be quick to line up for this one."

Hobie Hanson and friends are again featured at their temporary school in the mall in *Sticks and Stones and Skeleton Bones.* In this tale, Hobie and classmates Nick

Rossi and Molly Bosco become embroiled in an accelerating cycle of practical jokes, misunderstandings, and retaliation, until all three end up in the school's new conflict management program, where they—and readers—learn that there are two sides to every story. Reviewing *Sticks and Stones and Skeleton Bones* for *Booklist*, Deborah Abbott maintained that Gilson "paints her characters with a refined brush, showing in an uncanny fashion the intricacies and nuances of the world of fifth-graders."

Stink Alley marks a thematic departure from Gilson's other stories for older readers. Set in Leiden in 1614, the novel follows the adventures of a fictitious Puritan girl named Lizzy who escapes the harsh conditions in the Brewster household by taking a servant's job with a wealthy family. There she meets a precocious boy who loves to draw, and together they embark upon a series of pranks that are both amusing and hair-raising. When the young boy finally reveals his name, he is seen to be Rembrandt, the famous Dutch painter. Jeanette Larson, writing in *School Library Journal*, praised *Stink Alley* as a novel that "provides a glimpse of life in a time and place [about] . . . which not much else is available," while *Booklist* contributor Lauren Peterson noted that Gilson "does a nice job of weaving pleasant, fictional Lizzy into a cast of historical characters to give a sense of the past." In *Horn Book*, Margaret A. Bush concluded that the coming-of-age story presented in *Stink Alley* is "a deftly woven mix of adventure, youthful ingenuity, and overcoming the odds."

Gilson explores the relationship between two young brothers in *You Cheat!*, one of several books she has penned for younger readers. Active six-year-old Nathan longs to show up his video-game-loving older brother, Hank. When he cannot beat Hank at cards, Nathan challenges his brother to go fishing with him and see who can land the biggest fish. Since Hank thinks worms are gross and fishing is boring, Nathan convinces him to accept the challenge by promising to kiss every fish Hank catches on the mouth. Deciding that the prospect of watching Nathan kiss a fish is too good an opportunity to pass up, Hank agrees to the contest and makes Nathan deliver on his promise. In a review for *School Library Journal*, Maggie McEwen called *You Cheat!* "an excellent beginning chapter book" and noted that the "simple adventure will appeal to early readers."

Other books geared for young, beginning readers deal with subjects that range from head lice—*Itchy Richard*—and bats—*It Goes Eeeeeeeeeeeee!*—to bullying—

Gotcha! In *Itchy Richard* someone in Mrs. Zookey's second-grade class has head lice, and rumors begin to fly among the children when the head nurse comes in to check each of their scalps. As the students exchange exaggerated ideas about these bugs and what they do, central protagonist Richard begins to feel kind of itchy himself. Mrs. Zookey settles everyone down with a simple explanation of head lice and how they are treated. Noting that the book is "loaded with kid-appealing humor and personalities straight out of a grade-school classroom," Stephanie Zvirin added in her *Booklist* review that "Gilson's sensitive story takes a fairly common elementary school problem and makes it seem . . . less scary." A reviewer for *Publishers Weekly* added that in *Itchy Richard* "Gilson displays the same snappy dialogue and brisk humor that have made her Hobie Hanson novels so popular with youngsters."

Richard and his friends from Mrs. Zookey's class return in *It Goes Eeeeeeeeeeeee!*, a story supplying a palatable dose of information about bats to again clear up young students' misconceptions and fears. In her review of this tale for *Booklist*, Zvirin noted that Gilson "feeds the facts smoothly and memorably into the fictional format." Other commentators cited the author's trademark warmth, humor, and first-person narration, while appreciatively underscoring her remarkable understanding of the world of grade-school students. In *Gotcha!* Richard is paired up with Patrick, the class bully, during Mrs. Zookey's class field trip to a nature area to study spiders. While Patrick manages to cause all manner of mischief, he ultimately learns the price of breaking the rules in a story that *School Library Journal* contributor Debbie Whitbeck called "fast paced and engaging."

In 2008 Gilson published *Chess! I Love It, I Love It, I Love It!* With illustrations by Amy Wummer, the children's book finds second-grader Richard having to work together with classmate Patrick as they are on the same chess team. Even though Patrick annoys Richard, he worries that neither of them will be able to focus enough to win their inter-school chess tournament.

Rick Kennedy, writing in *Chessville*, opined that "the exuberance of the front cover of *Chess! I Love It, I Love It, I Love It!* is a grabber," noting the way that the children displayed are happy and excited to play the game. Kennedy concluded that the book "is great fun, as she has captured her young characters perfectly. The resilient Mrs. Zookey and the effervescent chess coach

Mr. E are adults who would be welcome in any student's classroom." *Booklist* contributor Carolyn Phelan thought that "Gilson shows a sound knowledge of grade-school psychology," adding that the book is "entertaining." Reviewing the book in *School Library Journal,* Sarah O'Holla noted that "humorous, full-page illustrations appear throughout." O'Holla cautioned, however, that the book is "more demanding" than other books by Gilson. A contributor writing in *Kirkus Reviews* concluded that "though the emotions are genuine, the characters are stiff."

On her home page, Gilson explained that, although she did a great deal of writing during her career as a journalist, she never considered writing for young readers until she had children of her own. Then, by listening to them and reading with them, she learned what her children and their friends found humorous, and she uses their experiences in her own stories. Because her children are now grown, Gilson now tries her out ideas on schoolchildren during visits to area schools.

BIOGRAPHICAL AND CRITICAL SOURCES:

PERIODICALS

Booklist, May 1, 1978, review of *Harvey, the Beer Can King,* p. 1430; June 1, 1979, review of *Dial Leroi Rupert, DJ,* p. 1491; November 1, 1980, review of *Do Bananas Chew Gum?,* p. 404; May 1, 1981, review of *Can't Catch Me, I'm the Gingerbread Man,* p. 1196; October 1, 1982, review of *Thirteen Ways to Sink a Sub,* p. 244; September 1, 1983, review of *4-B Goes Wild,* p. 85; April 15, 1985, review of *Hello, My Name Is Scrambled Eggs,* p. 1191; June 15, 1987, review of *Hobie Hanson, You're Weird,* p. 1601; September 1, 1988, review of *Double Dog Dare,* p. 76; September 1, 1989, review of *Hobie Hanson: Greatest Hero of the Mall,* p. 71; September 15, 1991, review of *Itchy Richard,* p. 150; November 15, 1991, review of *Sticks and Stones and Skeleton Bones,* p. 632; August, 1992, review of *You Cheat!,* p. 2011; April 1, 1993, review of *Thirteen Ways to Sink a Sub,* p. 1431; April 1, 1994, review of *Soccer Circus,* p. 1446; April 1, 1994, review of *It Goes Eeeeeeeeeeeee!,* p. 1446; September 1, 1996, Michael Cart, review of *Wagon Train 911,* p. 130; April 15, 1998, GraceAnne A. DeCandido, review of *Bug in a Rug,* p. 1444; April 15, 2002, Lauren

Peterson, review of *Stink Alley,* p. 1400; April 15, 2006, Nancy Kim, review of *Gotcha!,* p. 48; March 1, 2008, Carolyn Phelan, review of *Chess! I Love It, I Love It, I Love It!,* p. 70.

Bulletin of the Center for Children's Books, November, 1978, review of *Harvey, the Beer Can King,* p. 43; August, 1979, review of *Dial Leroi Rupert, DJ,* p. 137; March, 1981, review of *Do Bananas Chew Gum?,* p. 133; May, 1981, review of *Can't Catch Me, I'm the Gingerbread Man,* p. 171; December, 1982, review of *Thirteen Ways to Sink a Sub,* p. 67; October, 1983, review of *4-B Goes Wild,* p. 27; September, 1988, review of *Double Dog Dare,* p. 8; April, 1991, review of *Sticks and Stones and Skeleton Bones,* p. 192; May, 1994, review of *It Goes Eeeeeeeeeeeee!,* p. 286; January, 1997, review of *Wagon Train 911,* p. 170; September, 2002, review of *Stink Alley,* p. 17; April, 2006, Loretta Gaffney, review of *Gotcha!,* p. 353.

Chicago Tribune Books, June 16, 2002, review of *Stink Alley,* p. 5.

Childhood Education, March, 1982, review of *Can't Catch Me, I'm the Gingerbread Man,* p. 257; January, 1986, review of *Hello, My Name Is Scrambled Eggs,* p. 221; spring, 1992, review of *Sticks and Stones and Skeleton Bones,* p. 179.

Children's Book Review Service, September, 1982, review of *Thirteen Ways to Sink a Sub,* p. 8; September, 1983, review of *4-B Goes Wild,* p. 8; August, 1985, review of *Hello, My Name Is Scrambled Eggs,* p. 130.

Children's Literature Association Quarterly, summer, 1991, review of *Hello, My Name Is Scrambled Eggs,* p. 52; summer, 1991, review of *Harvey, the Beer Can King,* p. 58.

Curriculum Review, December, 1996, review of *Wagon Train 911,* p. 12.

English Journal, September, 1993, review of *Hello, My Name Is Scrambled Eggs,* p. 43.

Horn Book, July, 1989, review of *Hobie Hanson,* p. 74; fall, 1991, review of *Sticks and Stones and Skeleton Bones,* p. 268; spring, 1992, review of *Itchy Richard,* p. 58; spring, 1993, review of *You Cheat!,* p. 57; fall, 1993, review of *Soccer Circus,* p. 298; fall, 1994, review of *It Goes Eeeeeeeeeeeee!,* p. 300; spring, 1997, review of *Wagon Train 911,* p. 67; fall, 1998, review of *Bug in a Rug,* p. 103; September-October, 2002, Margaret A. Bush, review of *Stink Alley,* p. 572; spring, 2003, review of *Stinky Alley,* p. 80.

Interracial Books for Children Bulletin, June, 1982, review of *Do Bananas Chew Gum?,* p. 8.

Kirkus Reviews, May 1, 1978, review of *Harvey, the Beer Can King,* p. 497; June 15, 1979, review of

Dial Leroi Rupert, DJ, p. 686; December 15, 1980, review of *Do Bananas Chew Gum?,* p. 1570; July 15, 1981, review of *Can't Catch Me, I'm the Gingerbread Man,* p. 872; September 1, 1983, review of *4-B Goes Wild,* p. 161; March 1, 1985, review of *Hello, My Name Is Scrambled Eggs,* p. 11; July 1, 1988, review of *Double Dog Dare,* p. 972; September 15, 1989, review of *Hobie Hanson,* p. 1402; April 1, 1991, review of *Sticks and Stones and Skeleton Bones,* p. 470; October 15, 1991, review of *Itchy Richard,* p. 1353; August 15, 1992, review of *You Cheat!,* p. 1061; February 15, 1993, review of *Soccer Circus,* p. 226; May 1, 1994, review of *It Goes Eeeeeeeeeeeee!,* p. 629; July 1, 1996, review of *Wagon Train 911,* p. 967; April 15, 1998, review of *Bug in a Rug,* p. 579; May 1, 2002, review of *Stinky Alley,* p. 654; February 15, 2006, review of *Gotcha!,* p. 182; February 15, 2008, review of *Chess! I Love It, I Love It, I Love It!*

Kliatt, winter, 1983, review of *Can't Catch Me, I'm the Gingerbread Man,* p. 8.

Publishers Weekly, December 3, 1982, review of *Can't Catch Me, I'm the Gingerbread Man,* p. 60; May 8, 1987, review of *Hobie Hanson, You're Weird,* p. 70; June 24, 1988, review of *Double Dog Dare,* p. 114; July 28, 1989, review of *Hobie Hanson,* p. 222; January 18, 1991, review of *Sticks and Stones and Skeleton Bones,* p. 58; September 20, 1991, review of *Itchy Richard,* p. 134; March 8, 1993, review of *Soccer Circus,* pp. 79-80; June 24, 1996, review of *Wagon Train 911,* p. 61; September 1, 1997, review of *Can't Catch Me, I'm the Gingerbread Man,* p. 67; May 24, 1999, review of *Dial Leroi Rupert, DJ,* p. 81.

School Library Journal, May, 1978, review of *Harvey, the Beer Can King,* p. 66; September, 1979, review of *Dial Leroi Rupert, DJ,* p. 138; August, 1980, Marjorie Lewis, review of *Do Bananas Chew Gum?,* p. 64; September, 1981, Steve Matthews, review of *Can't Catch Me, I'm the Gingerbread Man,* p. 124; January, 1983, review of *Thirteen Ways to Sink a Sub,* p. 75; December, 1983, review of *4-B Goes Wild,* p. 66; August, 1985, review of *Hello, My Name Is Scrambled Eggs,* p. 64; June-July, 1987, review of *Hobie Hanson, You're Weird,* p. 95; September, 1988, Susannah Price, review of *Double Dog Dare,* p. 183; October, 1989, Phyllis Graves, review of *Hobie Hanson,* p. 118; March, 1991, Pamela K. Bomboy, review of *Sticks and Stones and Skeleton Bones,* p. 193; December, 1991, review of *Itchy Richard,* p. 90; September, 1992, review of *You Cheat!,* p. 203; June, 1993,

George Delais, review of *Soccer Circus,* p. 106; June, 1994, review of *It Goes Eeeeeeeeeeeee!,* p. 100; September, 1996, review of *Wagon Train 911,* p. 201; June, 1998, Anne Knickerbocker, review of *Bug in a Rug,* p. 103; July, 2002, Jeanette Larson, review of *Stink Alley,* p. 120; April, 2006, Debbie Whitbeck, review of *Gotcha!,* p. 106; May 1, 2008, Sarah O'Holla, review of *Chess! I Love It, I Love It, I Love It!,* p. 98.

Voice of Youth Advocates, April, 1981, review of *Do Bananas Chew Gum?,* p. 34; April, 1981, review of *Can't Catch Me, I'm the Gingerbread Man,* p. 34.

ONLINE

Chessville, http://www.chessville.com/ (June 16, 2009), Rick Kennedy, review of *Chess! I Love It, I Love It, I Love It!*

Jamie Gilson Home Page, http://www.jamiegilson.com (June 16, 2009).

*   *   *

GOODWIN, Jason 1964-

PERSONAL: Born 1964; married; wife's name Kate; children: four, including two sons. *Education:* Attended Cambridge University.

ADDRESSES: Home—West Sussex, England.

CAREER: Journalist, writer, and historian.

AWARDS, HONORS: John Llewellyn Rhys Prize for *On Foot to the Golden Horn.*

WRITINGS:

NONFICTION

The Gunpowder Gardens: Travels through India and China in Search of Tea, Chatto & Windus (London, England), 1990, also published as *A Time for Tea: Travels through China and India in Search of Tea,* Knopf (New York, NY), 1991.

On Foot to the Golden Horn: A Walk to Istanbul, Chatto & Windus (London, England), 1993, Henry Holt (New York, NY), 1995.

Lords of the Horizons: A History of the Ottoman Empire, Henry Holt (New York, NY), 1999.

Otis: Giving Rise to the Modern City, Ivan R. Dee (Chicago, IL), 2001.

Greenback: The Almighty Dollar and the Invention of America, Henry Holt (New York, NY), 2003.

"YASHIM THE EUNUCH" SERIES

The Janissary Tree (mystery novel), Farrar, Straus and Giroux (New York, NY), 2006.

The Snake Stone, Sarah Crichton Books/Farrar (New York, NY), 2007.

The Bellini Card, Faber & Faber (London, England), 2008.

Contributor to periodicals, including *Conde Nast Traveler* and the *New York Times.*

SIDELIGHTS: English journalist, historian and travel writer Jason Goodwin has focused much of his writing on areas where East meets West. From the history of the Ottoman Empire, to the history of tea in Asia and Europe, his travels and studies are interesting for their investigation of the two worlds' exchanges. Goodwin's first book, *The Gunpowder Gardens: Travels through India and China in Search of Tea,* is both history book and travelogue. Inspired by his grandmothers' teapots (which reside on his mantle), he traveled through China and India to unravel the history of tea. He narrates tea's incarnations and culture in the East and throughout the West, especially in England: from the Chinese folk tale of its origins, to 1,000-year-old tea bushes, to the development of packaged tea bags by American millionaire Tommy Lipton, to the Mad Hatter's Tea party. Molly Mortimer, in *Contemporary Review,* noted that Goodwin does not include the tea histories of Japan, Tibet, or Africa: "Perhaps his lively imagination will find some interesting facets of British Colonials on the vast Brook Bond estates in Kenya." Christopher Lehmann-Haupt, writing in the *New York Times Books Review* called the book "funny" and "evocative," writing: "Mr. Goodwin's imagination stays vibrant. It has summoned up all the tea in China and India. And made one thirst for a spicy cup of the brew."

The same year Goodwin's tea book was published in England, he embarked with two traveling companions on a walking tour of Eastern Europe. He describes his travels in his second book, *On Foot to the Golden Horn: A Walk to Istanbul.* The early 1990s marked a time of transition for the former Soviet Bloc countries, and Goodwin notes this in his descriptions of the towns and people he encounters. The journey covers some two thousand miles, mostly through the countryside. Philip Glazebrook wrote in his review in *Spectator:* "Goodwin's book, . . . contains many an interesting page, and a good many remarks which show insight and intelligence." Jonathan Sunley, in the *Times Literary Supplement,* commented that the author "is to be congratulated on producing one of the truest portraits of present-day Central Europe available." *On Foot to the Golden Horn* won the John Llewellyn Rhys Prize.

Lords of the Horizons: A History of the Ottoman Empire covers the history of the area, from the Byzantine empire's collapse in the fourteenth century to the Ottoman's own demise at the end of World War I. For 600 years the Ottoman Empire stretched from the border of Iran to the waters of the Danube. It encompassed over three dozen nations and hundreds of ethnic groups, including Spanish Jews, Albanian tribesmen, Venetian merchants, Orthodox Greeks, and Arab Bedouins. Under tolerant Sunni Muslim rule, Ottoman Turks created a culture that "was such a prodigy of pep, such a miracle of human ingenuity, that contemporaries felt it was helped into being by powers not quite human—diabolical or divine, depending on their point of view," as Goodwin writes. However, the Turks neglected to keep up with the industrial revolution in Europe, and military, civilian, and royal turbulence weakened the once-mighty empire. Fouad Ajami praised Goodwin's style in his review in the *New York Times Book Review:* "He does it in a beguiling way, the pace of his narrative catching, at times, the speed and swiftness of those Ottoman horsemen of the frontier in their days of glory, and then the ponderous style of a decaying empire that answered the calls for reform with pretense and show and outright cruelty as well as with a frenzy of palace building that could not lift the gloom, as the unhappy sultans 'dragged the terrible burden of their line from one palace to the next.'" Ajami added: "He has . . . stripped that Ottoman past of its 'otherness,' the alienness that has been its lot in this age of unyielding nationalism."

In *Otis: Giving Rise to the Modern City,* Goodwin traces the history of the elevator company founded by Elisha

Otis in the 1850s. According to Goodwin, Otis made the elevator a dependable part of life in the big cities. Due to the invention and refinement of the elevator, the building of skyscrapers was made possible. The book also touches on the less-than-ethical business practices within the elevator industry. A *Publishers Weekly* contributor called *Otis* "a well-paced book, which weaves business, technological and social history into a seamless and entertaining narrative," and "a thumbnail history of American business, with its mistakes, sins and undeniable triumphs."

In his next book, *Greenback: The Almighty Dollar and the Invention of America,* Goodwin focuses on the American dollar and the role it has played in American history. The author traces the history of "paper money," which was created in Boston in the late seventeenth century, and many of the key figures who played a dominant role in the history of the United States, eventually leading the American dollar to become the number one currency in the world. In an interview in *Business Week Online,* the author noted that he "tried to write a book about the dollar and American money as if it were something beyond finance." The author went on to explain his fascination with the American one-dollar bill: "The one dollar bill, in particular, has this character: It sells, it's worth more than the [face] value of the bill itself, and it's a historical artifact rich with legends and conspiracy." Goodwin also noted: "Nothing else compares to the beauty and mystery of the dollar."

"Goodwin's narrative, which elegantly recounts the difficulties preceding its arrival as an instrument of global hegemony, establishes that from the beginning the dollar was symbolic of—and a receptacle for—the aspirations of the American people," wrote Archie Cotterell in the *Spectator.* A *Publishers Weekly* contributor commented that Goodwin has a "flair for a colorful tale [that] makes for rich reading," adding that the author "makes some excellent points about the role of paper money in early U.S. history." Lucy Heckman remarked in the *Library Journal* that Goodwin "takes readers on an intriguing journey" and called the book an "informative and often entertaining account." *Wilson Quarterly* contributor Louis B. Jones wrote that Goodwin "makes a persuasive case that paper money is a specifically American innovation, one that has helped to establish the nation's global caliphate."

Goodwin turns from fact to fiction in his first mystery, *The Janissary Tree.* The story takes place during the final days of the Ottoman Empire in 1836 and features a eunuch, Yashim Togalu, who begins investigating a series of murders that take place in the court of the sultan. As he looks into the matter, Yashim discovers that an elite band of soldiers known as the Janissaries, who were once a special protectorate for the sultans but have been ousted by the current sultan, may have a connection to the crimes as part of their effort to stage a coup. Yashim is aided in his investigation by a Polish ambassador named Palieski and a transvestite dancer named Preen. A *Publishers Weekly* contributor commented that the author "makes a welcome shift to fiction with this impressive first." Margaret Flanagan, writing in *Booklist,* referred to *The Janissary Tree* as a "promising new mystery series," adding that "the reader is treated to an appropriately exotic tour." Natasha Tripney remarked in the *New Statesman* that "the historical detail can't be faulted." Marilyn Stasio, writing in the *New York Times Book Review,* called *The Janissary Tree* a "perfect escapist mystery, with its . . . dynamic scenes of the cosmopolitan city beyond the palace walls."

Goodwin continued the adventures of Yashim in another mystery, *The Snake Stone.* In this story, Yashim becomes involved with investigating the murder of Lefevre, a French archaeologist who was researching an ancient text that could hold clues to a great Byzantium treasure, said to have been hidden in the face of the Ottoman invasion. Yashim the eunuch was the last person to have seen Lefevre alive, and as such, he is suspected of being involved in the murder. The archaeologist's case is of interest to the sultana, who is herself French, and who is Yashim's patroness. Yashim, highly cultured, moves easily through the many levels of Istanbul's social structure as he attempts to clear his name. That complex world is a large part of the book's appeal, according to Janet Maslin, a reviewer for the *New York Times Book Review Online.* Maslin described Yashim as "debonair" and called the Istanbul setting "extremely fertile ground, not only as a place full of mysteries but as a place where Yashim can be treated to a thumbnail sketch of some marauding culture every time he engages in conversation." Maslin also commented: "Although Mr. Goodwin has a tendency to overcomplicate, he is able to link even the smallest-seeming developments to matters of major resonance." The depth of the story was also noted by Vikram Johri, who commented in *California Literary Review:* "The mystery morphs into an historical inquiry: of the presence of secret societies that have defied the inexorable march of time. The nostalgia for a bygone age seeps through the pages as the book combines literary acuity and mystical exoticism with formidable skill." A *Publishers Weekly* reviewer also recommended *The Snake Stone,* calling it "as intricate and delightful as the first" mystery featuring Yashim.

Goodwin's *The Bellini Card,* also features Yashim. A *Publishers Weekly* contributor commented that Goodwin "skillfully blends deduction, action sequences and period color."

BIOGRAPHICAL AND CRITICAL SOURCES:

BOOKS

Goodwin, Jason, *Lords of the Horizons: A History of the Ottoman Empire,* Henry Holt (New York, NY), 1999.

PERIODICALS

Booklist, December 15, 2002, Mary Whaley, review of *Greenback: The Almighty Dollar and the Invention of America,* p. 714; March 15, 2006, Margaret Flanagan, review of *The Janissary Tree,* p. 31; September 15, 2007, Allison Block, review of *The Snake Stone,* p. 40; January 1, 2009, Jen Baker, review of *The Bellini Card,* p. 51.

Bookseller, June 27, 2008, review of *The Bellini Card,* p. 14.

Choice, February, 2002, F. Potter, review of *Otis: Giving Rise to the Modern City,* p. 1067.

Contemporary Review, September, 1990, Molly Mortimer, review of *The Gunpowder Gardens: Travels through India and China in Search of Tea,* pp. 167-168; October, 2003, review of *Greenback,* p. 252.

Financial Times, May 24, 2008, James Urduhat, review of *The Snake Stone,* p. 17.

Independent (London, England), June 18, 2006, Julian Fleming, review of *The Janissary Tree.*

Kirkus Reviews, November 1, 2002, review of *Greenback,* p. 1588; March 1, 2006, review of *The Janissary Tree,* p. 210; August 15, 2007, review of *The Snake Stone.*

Library Journal, January, 2003, Lucy Heckman, review of *Greenback,* p. 128; April 1, 2006, Jo Ann Vicarel, review of *The Janissary Tree,* p. 68.

London Review of Books, July 26, 1990, review of *The Gunpowder Gardens,* pp. 18-19.

New Statesman, July 24, 2006, Natasha Tripney, review of *The Janissary Tree,* p. 59.

New York Times Book Review, September 9, 1991, Christopher Lehmann-Haupt, review of *A Time for Tea: Travels through India and China in Search of Tea,* p. B2; May 2, 1999, Fouad Ajami, review of *Lords of the Horizons,* p. 7; January 12, 2003, review of *The Janissary Tree,* p. 18; June 4, 2006, Marilyn Stasio, review of *The Janissary Tree,* p. 20; October 29, 2007, Janet Maslin, review of *The Snake Stone.*

Publishers Weekly, August 13, 2001, review of *Otis,* p. 304; November 18, 2002, review of *Greenback,* p. 50; February 6, 2006, review of *The Janissary Tree,* p. 46; August 27, 2007, review of *The Snake Stone,* p. 64; December 8, 2008, review of *The Bellini Card,* p. 46.

Spectator, July 17, 1993, Philip Glazebrook, review of *On Foot to the Golden Horn: A Walk to Istanbul,* p. 27; March 8, 2003, Archie Cotterell, review of *Greenback,* p. 37; August 27, 2007, review of *The Snake Stone,* p. 64.

Technology and Culture, April, 2002, Robert M. Vogel, review of *Otis,* p. 431.

Times Literary Supplement, August 6, 1993, Jonathan Sunley, review of *On Foot to the Golden Horn,* p. 12.

Wall Street Journal, October 9, 2001, Daniel Akst, "Going Up," p. A20.

Wilson Quarterly, summer, 2003, Louis B. Jones, review of *Greenback,* p. 121.

ONLINE

Business Week Online, http://pda.businessweek.com/ (October 1, 2007), "The Buck Started Here; Jason Goodwin, Author of *Greenback: The Almighty Dollar and the Invention of America,* on the History and Mystique of U.S. Currency."

California Literary Review, http://calitreview.com/ (July 28, 2008), Vikram Johri, review of *The Snake Stone.*

Euro Crime, http://www.eurocrime.co.uk/ (July 28, 2008), Norman Price, review of *The Snake Stone.*

Jason Goodwin Home Page, http://www.jasongoodwin. net (July 28, 2008).

London Independent, http://www.independent.co.uk/ (July 31, 2007), Jane Jakeman, review of *The Snake Stone.*

Metro Active, http://www.metroactive.com/ (January 2, 2008), Michael S. Gant, review of *The Snake Stone.*

New York Times Book Review Online, http://www.nytimes.com/ (October 29, 2007), Janet Maslin, review of *The Snake Stone.**

* * *

GORMAN, Ed 1941-

(Robert David Chase, Richard Driscoll, Jake Foster, E.J. Gorman, Edward Gorman, Edward Joseph Gorman, Christopher Keegan, Chris Shea McCarrick, Chris North, Daniel Ransom)

PERSONAL: Born November 29, 1941, in Cedar Rapids, IA; son of Edward and Bernadine Gorman; married Kathleen Stevens (divorced, 1968); married Carol Maxwell (a novelist), 1982; children: Joseph Wyndham, Ben. *Education:* Coe College, Cedar Rapids, IA, graduated, 1968.

CAREER: Writer and editor. Worked in advertising as a writer and director of television commercials, 1968-87; publisher of *Mystery Scene,* 1985—.

AWARDS, HONORS: Bram Stoker Award Best Collection nominee, 1996, for *Cages,* and 2002, for *The Dark Fantastic.*

WRITINGS:

"LEO GUILD" SERIES; WESTERN NOVELS

Guild, M. Evans (New York, NY), 1987.
Death Ground, M. Evans (New York, NY), 1988.
Blood Game, M. Evans (New York, NY), 1989.
Dark Trail, M. Evans (New York, NY), 1990.

"JACK DWYER MYSTERY" SERIES

New, Improved Murder, St. Martin's Press (New York, NY), 1985.
Murder Straight Up, St. Martin's Press (New York, NY), 1986.
Murder in the Wings, St. Martin's Press (New York, NY), 1986.

The Autumn Dead, St. Martin's Press (New York, NY), 1987.
A Cry of Shadows, St. Martin's Press (New York, NY), 1990.
The Night Remembers, St. Martin's Press (New York, NY), 1991.

"ROBERT PAYNE" SERIES

Blood Moon, St. Martin's Press (New York, NY), 1994.
Hawk Moon, St. Martin's Press (New York, NY), 1996.
Harlot's Moon, St. Martin's Press (New York, NY), 1998.
Voodoo Moon, St. Martin's Press (New York, NY), 2000.

"TOBIN MYSTERY" SERIES

Murder on the Aisle, St. Martin's Press (New York, NY), 1987.
Several Deaths Later, St. Martin's Press (New York, NY), 1988.

"SAM MCCAIN" MYSTERY SERIES

The Day the Music Died, Carroll & Graf (New York, NY), 1999.
Wake Up Little Susie, Carroll & Graf (New York, NY), 2000.
Will You Still Love Me Tomorrow?, Carroll & Graf (New York, NY), 2001.
Everybody's Somebody's Fool, Carroll & Graf (New York, NY), 2002.
Save the Last Dance for Me, Worldwide (New York, NY), 2003.
Breaking Up Is Hard to Do, Carroll & Graf (New York, NY), 2004.
Fools Rush In, Pegasus Books (Waltham, MA), 2006.

"CALVARY MAN" SERIES

Cavalry Man: The Killing Machine, HarperTorch (New York, NY), 2005.
Calvary Man: Powder Keg, HarperTorch (New York, NY), 2006.
Cavalry Man: Doom Weapon LP, HarperLuxe (New York, NY), 2007.

SHORT STORIES

Cages, Deadline Press (Apache Junction, AZ), 1989.

Prisoners: And Other Stories, C.D. Publications (Baltimore, MD), 1992.

Dark Whispers: And Other Stories, Pulphouse Publications (Eugene, OR), 1992.

The Best Western Stories of Ed Gorman, edited by Bill Pronzini and Martin H. Greenberg, Swallow Press/ Ohio University Press (Athens, OH), 1992.

Moonchasers and Other Stories, Forge (New York, NY), 1996.

Famous Blue Raincoat: Mystery Stories, Crippen & Landru (Norfolk, VA), 1999.

The Dark Fantastic, Leisure Books (New York, NY), 2001.

Such A Good Girl and Other Crime Stories, introduction by Richard Laymon, Five Star (Waterville, ME), 2001.

(With Susan Slater, Irene Marcuse, and Michael Jahn) *Crooks, Crimes, and Christmas,* Harlequin Enterprises Limited (Toronto, Ontario, Canada), 2003.

Branded (western stories), Berkley (New York, NY), 2004.

The Long Ride Back, Leisure Books (New York, NY), 2004.

Different Kinds of Dead and Other Tales, Five Star (Waterville, ME), 2005.

The Collected Ed Gorman: Out There in Darkness v. 1, PS Publishing (London, England), 2007.

The Collected Ed Gorman: Moving Coffin v. 2, PS Publishing (London, England), 2007.

The Collected Ed Gorman: Out There in Darkness v. 1 and Moving Coffin v. 2, PS Publishing (London, England), 2007.

FICTION

(With Max Allan Collins) *Jim Thompson: The Killers inside Him,* Fedora Press (Cedar Rapids, IA), 1983.

Rough Cut, St. Martin's Press (New York, NY), 1985.

Grave's Retreat (historical novel), Doubleday (New York, NY), 1989.

Cold Blue Midnight, St. Martin's Press (New York, NY), 1996.

Cage of Night, Trafalgar Square (North Pomfret, VT), 2000.

The Poker Club, Leisure Books (New York, NY), 2000.

Lawless, Berkley (New York, NY), 2000.

Ghost Town, Berkley (New York, NY), 2001.

Blood Game, Forge (New York, NY), 2001.

Rituals, DAW Books (New York, NY), 2002.

Vendetta (western), Berkley (New York, NY), 2002.

Lynched (western), Berkley (New York, NY), 2003.

Relentless (western), Berkley (New York, NY), 2003.

Gun Truth (western), Dorchester Publishing (New York, NY), 2003.

(Author of introduction) Russell Davis, *Waltzing with the Dead,* Wildside (Rockville, MD), 2004.

Bad Money, Berkley (New York, NY), 2005.

(With Dean Koontz) *Dean Koontz's Frankenstein: Book Two, City of Night,* Bantam Books (New York, NY), 2005.

Shoot First, Berkley (New York, NY), 2006.

Fast Track, Berkley (New York, NY), 2006.

Dean Koontz's Frankenstein: Dead and Alive, Harper-Collins (London, England), 2007.

A Knock at the Door, Borderlands Press (Falston, MD), 2007.

Sleeping Dogs, Thomas Dunne Books/St. Martin's Minotaur (New York, NY), 2008.

EDITOR

(And author of introduction) *The Second Black Lizard Anthology of Crime Fiction,* Black Lizard (Berkeley, CA), 1989.

(With Martin H. Greenberg) *Stalkers: All New Tales of Terror and Suspense,* Dark Harvest (Arlington Heights, IL), 1989.

(With Bob Randisi) *Under the Gun* (anthology of mystery stories), NAL Books (New York, NY), 1990.

Night Kills, Ballantine (New York, NY), 1990.

Dark Crimes: Great Noir Fiction from the '50s to the '90s, Carroll & Graf (New York, NY), 1991.

Solved, Carroll & Graf (New York, NY), 1991.

(With Martin H. Greenberg) *Cat Crimes,* Donald I. Fine (New York, NY), 1991.

(With Martin H. Greenberg) *Cat Crimes II,* Donald I. Fine (New York, NY), 1992.

(With Martin H. Greenberg) *Cat Crimes III,* Donald I. Fine (New York, NY), 1992.

I, Werewolf, illustrated by Angelo Torres, Little, Brown (Boston, MA), 1992.

Wolf Moon, Fawcett Gold Medal (New York, NY), 1993.

(With Martin H. Greenberg) *Cat Crimes: A Large Print Anthology,* G.K. Hall (Boston, MA), 1993.

(With Martin H. Greenberg) *Danger in DC: Cat Crimes in the Nation's Capital,* Donald I. Fine (New York, NY), 1993.

(With Martin H. Greenberg, Larry Segriff, and Jon L. Breen) *The Fine Art of Murder: The Mystery Reader's Indispensable Companion,* Carroll & Graf (New York, NY), 1993.

(With Martin H. Greenberg) *Predators,* ROC (New York, NY), 1993.

(With Martin H. Greenberg) *Feline and Famous: Cat Crimes Goes Hollywood,* Donald I. Fine (New York, NY), 1994.

(With Martin H. Greenberg and Bill Munster) *The Dean Koontz Companion,* Berkeley (New York, NY), 1994.

(With Martin H. Greenberg) *Woman on the Beat: Stories of Women Police Officers,* Gramercy Books (New York, NY), 1995.

(With Martin H. Greenberg) *Cat Crimes Takes a Vacation,* Donald I. Fine (New York, NY), 1995.

(With Martin H. Greenberg and Bill Pronzini) *Gunslinger, and Nine Other Action-packed Stories of the Wild West,* Barricade Books (New York, NY), 1995.

(With Larry Segriff and Martin H. Greenberg) *An Anthology of Angels,* Glorya Hale Books (New York, NY), 1996.

(With Martin H. Greenberg) *Love Kills,* Carroll & Graf (New York, NY), 1997.

(With Martin H. Greenberg) *The Fatal Frontier,* Carroll & Graf (New York, NY), 1997.

(With Bill Pronzini and Martin H. Greenberg) *American Pulp,* Carroll & Graf (New York, NY), 1997.

A Modern Treasury of Great Detective and Murder Mysteries, Carroll & Graf (New York, NY), 1997.

(With Martin H. Greenberg and Larry Segriff) *Cat Crimes for the Holidays,* Donald I. Fine (New York, NY), 1997.

(With Martin H. Greenberg) *Once Upon a Crime: Fairy Tales for Mystery Lovers,* Berkley Prime Crime (New York, NY), 1998.

(With Martin H. Greenberg) *Speaking of Murder: Interviews with the Masters of Mystery and Suspense* (two volumes), Berkley (New York, NY), 1998–1999.

(With Kevin McCarthy) *"They're Here—": Invasion of the Body Snatchers,* Berkley (New York, NY), 1999.

(With Kirby McCauley and Martin H. Greenberg) Dashiell Hammett, *Nightmare Town: Stories,* Knopf (New York, NY), 1999.

(With Jon L. Breen and Martin H. Greenberg) *Sleuths of the Century,* Carroll & Graf (New York, NY), 2000.

(With wife, Carol Gorman) *Felonious Felines,* Five Star (Unity, ME), 2000.

(With Martin H. Greenberg) *The World's Finest Mystery and Crime Stories* (annual; four volumes), Forge (New York, NY), 2000–03.

(With Martin H. Greenberg) *Desperadoes,* Berkley (New York, NY), 2001.

(With Martin H. Greenberg) *Pulp Masters,* Carroll & Graf (New York, NY), 2001.

(With Martin H. Greenberg and Larry Segriff) *Murder Most Feline: Cunning Tales of Cats and Crime,* Cumberland House (Nashville, TN), 2001.

(And contributor) *The Blue and the Gray Undercover,* Forge (New York, NY), 2001.

(With Martin H. Greenberg) *Guns of the West,* Berkley (New York, NY), 2002.

Kittens, Cats, and Crime, Five Star (Waterville, ME), 2003.

(With Martin H. Greenberg and Larry Segriff) *Murder Most Feline: Cunning Tales of Cats and Crime,* Gramercy Books (New York, NY), 2003.

Stagecoach, Berkley (New York, NY), 2003.

(With Martin H. Greenberg) *The Adventure of the Missing Detective: And 19 of the Year's Finest Crime and Mystery Stories!,* Carroll & Graf (New York, NY), 2005.

(With Martin H. Greenberg) *The Deadly Bride: And 19 of the Year's Finest Crime and Mystery Stories,* Carroll & Graf (New York, NY), 2006.

(With Martin H. Greenberg) *The Widow of Slane: And Six More of the Best Crime and Mystery Novellas of the Year,* Carroll & Graf (New York, NY), 2006.

FICTION; UNDER NAME ROBERT DAVID CHASE

(With Ed and Lorraine Warren) *Ghost Hunters: True Stories from the World's Most Famous Demonologists,* St. Martin's Press (New York, NY), 1989.

(With Ed and Lorraine Warren and Bill Ramsey) *Werewolf: A Story of Demonic Possession,* St. Martin's Press (New York, NY), 1991.

(With Ed and Lorraine Warren) *Graveyard: True Hauntings from an Old New England Cemetery,* St. Martin's Press (New York, NY), 1992.

FICTION; UNDER NAME DANIEL RANSOM

Daddy's Little Girl, Zebra (New York, NY), 1985.

Toys in the Attic, Zebra (New York, NY), 1986.

Night Caller, Zebra (New York, NY), 1987.

The Forsaken, Zebra (New York, NY), 1988.

The Babysitter, St. Martin's Press (New York, NY), 1989.

Nightmare Child, St. Martin's Press (New York, NY), 1990.

The Long Midnight, Dell (New York, NY), 1992.

The Serpents Kiss, Dell (New York, NY), 1992.

The Fugitive Stars, Forge (New York, NY), 1995.

Zone Soldiers, DAW (New York, NY), 1996.

Night Screams (young adult), Avon (New York, NY), 1996.

Blackmail and Lace (western), Foggy Windows Books (Scarborough, ME), 2001.

FICTION; UNDER NAME JAKE FOSTER

Two Guns to Yuma, Kensington Publishing (New York, NY), 1989, reprinted, Thorndike Press (Waterville, ME), 2005.

Three Rode South, Kensington Publishing (New York, NY), 1990.

Texas Noose, Kensington Publishing (New York, NY), 1990.

Hell-for-Leather Rider, Kensington Publishing (New York, NY), 1991.

Ramrod Revenge, Kensington Publishing (New York, NY), 1991.

FICTION; UNDER NAME E.J. GORMAN

The First Lady, Forge (New York, NY), 1995.

The Marilyn Tapes, Forge (New York, NY), 1995.

Senatorial Privilege, Forge (New York, NY), 1997.

"STAR PRECINCT" SERIES; UNDER NAME RICHARD DRISCOLL

(With Kevin Randle) *Star Precinct,* Berkley (New York, NY), 1992.

(With Kevin Randle) *Mind Slayer,* Berkley (New York, NY), 1992.

(With Kevin Randle) *Inside Job,* Berkley (New York, NY), 1992.

OTHER FICTION

(Editor, contributor, and author of introduction) *Black Lizard Anthology of Crime Fiction,* Black Lizard (Berkeley, CA), 1987.

(Editor) *Westeryear: Stories about the West, Past and Present,* M. Evans (New York, NY), 1988.

Night of Shadows (historical novel), Doubleday (New York, NY), 1990.

What the Dead Men Say (historical novel), M. Evans (New York, NY), 1990.

(Under name Christopher Keegan) *Ride into Yesterday,* Walker (New York, NY), 1992.

(Under name Chris Shea McCarrick) *Run to Midnight,* Ace (New York, NY), 1992.

(Under name Chris Shea McCarrick) *Now You See Her,* Berkley (New York, NY), 1993.

(Editor) *A Modern Treasury of Great Detective and Murder Mysteries,* Carroll & Graf (New York, NY), 1994.

(Under name Chris North) *Killer,* William Morrow (New York, NY), 1995.

(Editor, with Martin H. Greenberg) *The Fatal Frontier,* Carroll & Graf (New York, NY), 1997.

Under name Robert David Chase, contributor to books, including *Murder for Father,* edited by Martin H. Greenberg, Signet (New York, NY), 1994; and *Monster Brigade 3000,* edited by Martin H. Greenberg and Charles G. Waugh, Ace (New York, NY), 1996.

Contributor of short stories to anthologies, including *Criminal Elements,* Fawcett (New York, NY), 1988; *Felonious Assaults,* Fawcett (New York, NY), 1989; and *New Crimes,* Robinson, 1990.

Also author of the novella *Stalker,* 2006; coauthor with Dean Koontz of the graphic novel *Trapped,* 1993; author of the chapbooks *Out There in the Darkness,* 1995, and *Cast in Dark Waters,* with Tom Piccirilli, 2002.

ADAPTATIONS: Relentless was made into an audiobook, Recorded Books, 2004.

SIDELIGHTS: Author and editor Ed Gorman spent twenty years in the advertising industry before finally breaking into freelance writing in the mid-1980s. Since embarking on his new career as a novelist and editor of mystery and western short-story anthologies, Gorman has become well known for his wit, his gritty prose, and the unique characters he creates. A *Twentieth-Century Crime and Mystery Writers* contributor noted that Gorman's novels are "an amalgam of pure entertainment, social commentary, symbolic statement, and in-depth studies of what he terms 'outsiders trying to make their peace with the world.'"

Gorman used his knowledge of the advertising business to write his first mystery, *Rough Cut,* in which disillusioned advertising executive Jack Ketchum must search through various layers of sleaze to find his former partner's killer. Gorman once remarked to *CA:* "One advertising magazine called the novel 'a hate letter' to the advertising industry." Gorman went on to create the character Jack Dwyer, a security cop who moonlights as an actor, in a series of popular crime novels. In *New, Improved Murder* Dwyer's ex-girlfriend is found, gun in hand, near the body of her account-executive boyfriend in a whodunit that Jean M. White described as "a tangle of strange obsessions and relationships," in her review for the *Washington Post Book World.* Other Jack Dwyer mysteries include *Murder Straight Up, Murder in the Wings,* and *The Autumn Dead,* in which Dwyer investigates the death of his high-school sweetheart only to uncover a blackmail plot and other strange goings-on amidst an untimely class reunion.

Murder on the Aisle and *Several Deaths Later* both feature another of Gorman's popular off-beat detectives. Tobin, an alcoholic movie critic, makes guest appearances on television shows that provide him with plenty of opportunities for inadvertently staggering into compromising situations involving murder. Because of the popularity of his fictional detectives, Gorman's work is sought out by readers who enjoy his energetic plots and unpredictable endings. His books have also received consistently high marks from reviewers.

Gorman set his "Sam McCain" mystery series in Iowa during the 1950s. The protagonist is a lawyer, music enthusiast, and sometime private investigator. In *The Day the Music Died,* McCain mourns the deaths of Buddy Holly, Richie Valens, and the Big Bopper, whose fatal plane crash occurred nearby, while he looks into the murders of a pregnant teen and a wealthy married couple. *The Day the Music Died* prompted Wes Lukowsky to write in *Booklist* that "Gorman is one of the genre's best craftsmen."

Gorman then wrote a "prequel" to *The Day the Music Died* titled *Wake Up Little Susie.* Set in 1957, the mystery begins when a young woman's dead body is discovered in a new Ford Edsel during a parade in McCain's town, Black River Falls. The victim is Susan Squires, the abused wife of an ambitious district attorney. The D.A. is the prime suspect until he is murdered soon after his wife. As McCain hunts for the killer, a *Publishers Weekly* contributor felt the author spent too much time discussing the "town's social intrigues and recounting Sam's love life" instead of getting to the center of the story. Nevertheless, the critic praised "Gorman's assured prose" and felt the "depiction of the town's rivalries keeps the tension strong."

Continuing his "Sam McCain" series, Gorman tackles the Communist "Red Scare" of the 1950s with *Will You Still Love Me Tomorrow?* After attending an appearance by Nikita Khruschev, a liberal lawyer tells McCain that he would like to hire him. The next day, the lawyer is beaten and killed, but before he dies, he refuses to tell McCain who attacked him. McCain's investigation turns up more dead bodies; right-wing activists and anti-Communists. Rex Klett, writing in *Library Journal,* found *Will You Still Love Me Tomorrow?* "exciting and intense," while a *Publishers Weekly* reviewer wrote, "Gorman adds plenty of apt references to the music, movies and personalities of the late '50s to make this trip a real blast from the past." Wes Lukowsky, writing in *Booklist,* called Gorman "an underappreciated master of the genre."

As well as achieving renown as a mystery writer, Gorman has gained a strong reputation as an author of western novels. As with his detective fiction, his western protagonists are unique in their tendency to exist outside the boundaries of normal society. Bounty hunter Leo Guild, one of Gorman's most popular western characters, is featured in *Guild, Blood Game,* and *Death Ground,* all of which take place in the late 1800s. "The 'Guild' novels have a haunting, almost mystical quality that lifts them to the brink of allegory," noted a *Twentieth-Century Crime and Mystery Writers* contributor. Gorman does the unexpected in featuring a female protagonist in the western detective novel *Night of Shadows.* This work was inspired by the real-life story of the first uniformed policewoman in Cedar Rapids, Iowa, in the late 1800s.

Gorman's involvement in detective and western fiction has included editing several well-received short story collections. Anthologies in the areas of suspense, western, and crime fiction include *Black Lizard Anthology of Crime Fiction, Westeryear: Stories about the West, Past and Present,* and *Dark Crimes: Great Noir*

Fiction from the '50s to the '90s, all of which have been highly praised by critics. In 2000, Gorman started an annual anthology, titled *The World's Finest Mystery and Crime Stories.* Gorman's writing is inspired by the works of authors who he feels have broadened the various genres within which they worked. "My literary heroes, in addition to Fitzgerald, Hemingway, Faulkner, and Graham Greene, are people who made of popular fiction more than the skeptics thought it could be," Gorman once told *CA.* "I have in mind Raymond Chandler, Ray Bradbury, John D. MacDonald, Ross McDonald, and Margaret Millar—writers who worked with the givens of their respective forms but imbued them with their own spiritual poetry."

Gorman has continued to write a wide range of fiction, including short stories and novels that encompass the genres of science fiction, mystery, historical thrillers, ghost stories, and westerns. Gorman's novel *Save the Last Dance for Me* is another entry in the "Sam McCain" mystery series. It takes place in the 1960's and finds McCain trying to find out who wants to kill the Reverend John Muldaur, a religious zealot with plenty of enemies. Unfortunately, McCain is barely started on the case when Muldaur dies on the pulpit from strychnine poisoning. A *Kirkus Reviews* contributor noted the story's "affectionate period detail."

In *Fools Rush In,* a double murder in Black River Falls, Iowa, takes place against the backdrop of the civil rights era. One of the men murdered is a Peeping Tom with a penchant for taking pictures, while the other is David Leeds, a young black man popular with the ladies and who just happened to be dating Lucy, a white girl and the daughter of a Republican senator. Sam McCain dusts off his detective hat and attempts to get to the bottom of the mystery. Unsurprisingly, he finds plenty of people with motives for murder. In the case of David Leeds, the local bikers were less than happy with his romantic relationship with the daughter of the senator, a young woman whose white ex-boyfriend has a violent nature. The senator himself appears to have been having an affair. As for the photographer, he was using his skills as a blackmailer. Wes Lukowsky, in a review for *Booklist,* remarked that "readers unfamiliar with this fine series should hop onboard now." A reviewer for *Publishers Weekly* remarked that the book "realistically portrays the small town's mixed response to the exploding national demand for long overdue justice." A contributor for *Kirkus Reviews* called this installment in the "Sam McCain" mystery series "another picture postcard from middle America at a time when things seemed simpler but weren't."

Sleeping Dogs begins with the suicide of Phil Wylie, political consultant to Illinois Senator Warren Nichols, just as Nichols is in the midst of his campaign for re-election. Nichols swiftly replaces Wylie, hiring on Dev Conrad. He is just in the nick of time, as when Nichols goes to debate his opponent in a nationally televised event, someone decides to sabotage the program. Nichols initially suspects his opponent, Jim Lake, of having his political trickster R.D. Greaves do his dirty work for him. However, while Greaves plans on attempting to bury Nichols's campaign, that was not his method of choice, which turns out to be a blackmail video that proves just how frequently, and with what enthusiasm, Senator Nichols finds someone new to share his bed. The price for Greaves's silence is one million dollars, far more than Nichols can pull together in a short time frame. Dev Conrad is planning a way to bring Greaves's price down when someone murders him and saves both Dev and Nichols the effort. The timing might have been fortuitous, but Nichols isn't safe quite yet, as no one seems to know what happened to the blackmail video. A contributor for *Kirkus Reviews* commented that "veteran Gorman . . . provides rewardingly dry-eyed political savvy without the bloat of most novelists who patrol this turf." A reviewer for *Publishers Weekly* found Dev Conrad likeable, and remarked that "readers will hope his appealing hero will return in future outings."

In his collection of fifteen stories titled *Different Kinds of Dead and Other Tales,* Gorman presents a variety of strange tales written over a twenty-five-year period, including ghost stories, science fiction, and horror. Jackie Cassada, writing in *Library Journal,* referred to them as "superb storytelling." In the western genre, Gorman's novel *What the Dead Men Say* takes place in 1901 and combines a tale of revenge and a coming-of-age story when a man takes his nephew with him as he seeks to find and kill the men who murdered his daughter.

Gorman also continues to serve as editor of numerous story collections, such as *The Blue and the Gray Undercover,* a collection of Civil War stories about spying and espionage. A *Kirkus Reviews* contributor referred to the stories as "a diverting curio for Civil War buffs, as well as mystery and western fans." Another reviewer writing in *Publishers Weekly* commented on Gorman's own story contribution, noting that it has "a surprise ending to what is perhaps the saddest tale in the collection." Gorman has coedited several books with Martin H. Greenberg, including *The Adventure of the Missing*

Detective: And 19 of the Year's Finest Crime and Mystery Stories! A *Publishers Weekly* contributor called the tales "superior stories augmented by various 'state of the mystery' reports." Another reviewer writing in *Kirkus Reviews* commented that "all [the stories] are worth the time."

BIOGRAPHICAL AND CRITICAL SOURCES:

BOOKS

Twentieth-Century Crime and Mystery Writers, 3rd edition, St. James Press (Detroit, MI), 1991.

PERIODICALS

Booklist, May 15, 1992, Barbara Dupree, review of *Cat Crimes II,* p. 1664; September 1, 1992, Wes Lukowsky, review of *Prisoners: And Other Stories,* p. 36; April 1, 1996, Emily Melton, review of *Hawk Moon,* p. 1346; November 1, 1996, Wes Lukowsky, review of *Cold Blue Midnight,* p. 483; January 1, 1997, Wes Lukowsky, review of *The Fatal Frontier,* p. 824; May 1, 1997, Emily Melton, review of *Love Kills,* p. 1482; February 15, 1998, Wes Lukowsky, review of *Harlot's Moon,* p. 988; June 1, 1998, Bill Ott, review of *Speaking of Murder: Interviews with the Masters of Mystery and Suspense,* p. 1707; January 1, 1999, Ray Olson, review of *"They're Here—": Invasion of the Body Snatchers,* p. 817, and Wes Lukowsky, review of *The Day the Music Died,* p. 837; April 15, 1999, Richard Bleiler, review of *The Fine Art of Murder: The Mystery Reader's Indispensable Companion,* p. 1464; November 15, 1999, David Pitt, review of *The Poker Club,* p. 607; January 1, 2000, Wes Lukowsky, review of *Wake Up Little Susie,* p. 884; November 15, 2000, Wes Lukowsky, review of *Will You Still Love Me Tomorrow?,* p. 623; May 1, 2007, Wes Lukowsky, review of *Fools Rush In,* p. 26.

Kirkus Reviews, December 1, 2001, review of *The Blue and the Gray Undercover,* p. 1631, and review of *Save the Last Dance for Me,* p. 1648; January 1, 2006, review of *The Adventure of the Missing Detective: And 19 of the Year's Finest Crime and Mystery Stories!,* p. 18; April 1, 2007, review of *Fools Rush In;* February 1, 2008, review of *Sleeping Dogs.*

Library Journal, October 1, 1993, Rex E. Klett, review of *Danger in DC: Cat Crimes in the Nation's Capital;* November 15, 1993, Denise Johnson, review of *The Fine Art of Murder,* p. 70; July, 1994, Rex E. Klett, review of *Blood Moon,* p. 133; July, 1995, Rex E. Klett, review of *Cat Crimes Takes a Vacation,* p. 127; May 1, 1997, Rex E. Klett, review of *Love Kills,* p. 144; February 1, 1998, Rex E. Klett, review of *Harlot's Moon,* p. 116; January, 1999, Rex E. Klett, review of *The Day the Music Died,* p. 164; January, 2000, Rex E. Klett, review of *Wake Up Little Susie,* p. 166; January 1, 2001, Rex Klett, review of *Will You Still Love Me Tomorrow?,* p. 162; July 1, 2005, Jackie Cassada, *Different Kinds of Dead and Other Tales,* p. 73.

New York Times Book Review, April 30, 1989, Marilyn Stasio, review of *The Second Black Lizard Anthology of Crime Fiction,* p. 45; March 21, 1999, Marilyn Stasio, review of *The Day the Music Died,* p. 26; September 19, 1999, Terry Teachout, review of *Nightmare Town: Stories,* p. 21.

Publishers Weekly, June 5, 1987, Sybil Steinberg, review of *Murder on the Aisle,* p. 72; September 23, 1988, Sybil Steinberg, review of *Several Deaths Later,* p. 65; December 9, 1988, review of *The Second Black Lizard Anthology of Crime Fiction,* p. 58; October 27, 1989, Sybil Steinberg, review of *Stalkers: All New Tales of Terror and Suspense,* p. 56; May 18, 1990, Sybil Steinberg, review of *A Cry of Shadows,* p. 72; June 15, 1990, Sybil Steinberg, review of *What the Dead Men Say,* p. 57; February 1, 1991, Sybil Steinberg, review of *The Night Remembers,* p. 69; May 31, 1991, review of *Cat Crimes,* p. 62; July 25, 1991, review of *Dark Crimes: Great Noir Fiction from the '50s to the '90s,* p. 40; September 20, 1991, review of *Solved,* p. 122; May 25, 1992, review of *Cat Crimes II,* p. 42; November 2, 1992, review of *Cat Crimes III,* p. 54; September 20, 1993, review of *Danger in DC,* p. 65; June 27, 1994, review of *Blood Moon,* p. 60; September 19, 1994, review of *Feline and Famous: Cat Crimes Goes Hollywood,* p. 54; November 25, 1996, review of *The Fatal Frontier,* p. 59; October 27, 1997, review of *Cat Crimes for the Holidays,* p. 56; January 5, 1998, review of *Harlot's Moon,* p. 61; November 23, 1998, review of *The Day the Music Died,* p. 62; August 9, 1999, review of *Wake Up Little Susie,* p. 343; October 4, 1999, review of *Wake Up Little Susie,* p. 68; December 20, 1999, review of *Wake Up Little Susie,* p. 59; October 30, 2000, review of *Will You Still Love Me Tomorrow?,* p. 49;

November 5, 2001, review of *The Blue and the Gray Undercover*, p. 41; December 5, 2005, review of *The Adventure of the Missing Detective*, p. 35; March 19, 2007, review of *Fools Rush In*, p. 46; February 4, 2008, review of *Sleeping Dogs*, p. 41.

Washington Post Book World, January 19, 1986, Jean M. White, review of *New, Improved Murder*, p. 10.

Wilson Library Bulletin, February, 1984, Kathleen Maio, review of *Jim Thompson: The Killers inside Him*, p. 400; May, 1991, Kathleen Maio, review of *The Night Remembers*, p. 133; February, 1994, review of *The Fine Art of Murder*, p. 66.

ONLINE

Coe College Web site, http://www.coe.edu/ (October 19, 2006), brief faculty profile of author.

Fantastic Fiction, http://www.fantasticfiction.co.uk/ (October 26, 2003).

Locus, http://www.locusmag.com/ (October 26, 2003).*

*   *   *

GORMAN, Edward
    See GORMAN, Ed

*   *   *

GORMAN, Edward Joseph
    See GORMAN, Ed

*   *   *

GORMAN, E.J.
    See GORMAN, Ed

*   *   *

GREEN, Norman 1954-

PERSONAL: Born 1954, in MA; married.

ADDRESSES: Home—Emerson, NJ.

CAREER: Writer.

WRITINGS:

NOVELS

Shooting Dr. Jack, HarperCollins (New York, NY), 2001.

The Angel of Montague Street, HarperCollins (New York, NY), 2003.

Way Past Legal, HarperCollins (New York, NY), 2004.

Dead Cat Bounce (sequel to *Shooting Dr. Jack*), HarperCollins (New York, NY), 2006.

The Last Gig, Minotaur Books (New York, NY), 2008.

SIDELIGHTS: Although Norman Green didn't become a writer until he was forty-three, he produced several noir thrillers in quick succession. Green's books are known for their likeable yet credible heroes. In a *New York Times Book Review* assessment of Green's first novel, *Shooting Dr. Jack*, Dana Kennedy found "such indelible portraits . . . that the reader is drawn into their world and starts to care about them more than the plot."

In *Shooting Dr. Jack*, quirky characters Fat Tommy Rosselli and his partner, Stoney, run a Brooklyn junkyard that doubles as a chop-shop; they find dead bodies in the junkyard and befriend prostitutes. According to a contributor in *Kirkus Reviews*, Green neglects the story's plot in order to paint "a group portrait of despair so deep that getting killed just doesn't seem like that much of a risk." Green's second noir thriller, *The Angel of Montague Street*, follows a similar pattern. Silvano Iurata, the book's protagonist, is a Buddhist Vietnam veteran who returns to Brooklyn to find his missing brother. A *Publishers Weekly* reviewer stated that Silvano "may seem like the usual noir hero at war with himself, but Green taps into something larger with his subtle pronouncements about family curses, bad choices, lost souls, mindless violence and redemption."

In *Way Past Legal*, Manny joins a group of criminals to pull off a million-dollar heist. When one of his partners starts to kill the other burglars, Manny takes the money, as well as his five-year-old son, and runs for it. When Manny's car breaks down in a small town in Maine, strangers take them in. While he is in Maine, remarked a contributor in *Kirkus Reviews*, "what catches Manny off guard, transforming him forever, is how willing he is in the end to exchange kindness for kindness." A *Publishers Weekly* reviewer reported, however, that "the story takes an unusual detour," and while Green's change in "format is refreshing, [it] might not satisfy his usual audience."

Green's next novel, *Dead Cat Bounce,* continues the adventures of Fat Tommy Rosselli and Stoney, which kick off when Stoney sets out to trail Mr. Prior, the creepy man his daughter Marisa informs him is now dating Stoney's ex-wife. Stoney learns more than he bargained for when he discovers that Mr. Prior is actually following Marisa, who is working at a strip club, unbeknown to her parents. The more he digs into Prior's past, the more dead bodies he finds, until Stoney decides to set up a sting to put Prior out of business. A reviewer for *Publishers Weekly* wrote that "Green's well-drawn characters and nimble plot lift this above the common run of mysteries." Allison Block remarked in a *Booklist* review that Green "delivers crisp prose and a collection of flawed characters navigating the rocky road to redemption."

Green introduces a female protagonist in *The Last Gig.* Alessandra "Al" Martillo is a smart, sexy, tough assistant to private investigator Marty Stiles. Al's mother committed suicide when Al was twelve, and her father's only contribution to her upbringing was his instruction in the self-preservation skills she needed to survive as a homeless child on the streets of Brooklyn. She was then taken in by her gay Uncle Tio and his partner. Uncle Tio is now dying, which "provides the catalyst for Al to put aside her tough-Puerto-Rican-chick persona and find the revelation and redemption all of Green's best main characters seek," noted Barbara Tom in a review for the *Oregonian Online.* Much of Marty's work is repossessions, but a bigger job comes along in the person of Daniel "Mickey" Caughlan, a mobster who has discovered that his legitimate trucking company is being used to move drugs. Mickey's twenty-year-old son died six months earlier, supposedly from an overdose. When Willy died, he was filling in for the lead guitarist of an up-and-coming thrash band, who at the time was in rehab. A subplot involves the music

business. A *Kirkus Reviews* contributor wrote that Al is "just about the freshest heroine to enhance genre fiction in forever. Don't miss her."

BIOGRAPHICAL AND CRITICAL SOURCES:

PERIODICALS

Booklist, May 1, 2004, Connie Fletcher, review of *Way Past Legal,* p. 1503; August 1, 2006, Allison Block, review of *Dead Cat Bounce,* p. 50; November 15, 2008, Thomas Gaughan, review of *The Last Gig,* p. 20.

Kirkus Reviews, July 15, 2001, review of *Shooting Dr. Jack,* p. 965; April 1, 2003, review of *The Angel of Montague Street,* p. 495; April 1, 2004, review of *Way Past Legal,* p. 301; October 15, 2008, review of *The Last Gig.*

New York Times Book Review, October 21, 2001, Dana Kennedy, review of *Shooting Dr. Jack,* p. 28; May 18, 2003, Marilyn Stasio, review of *The Angel of Montague Street,* p. 33.

Publishers Weekly, August 6, 2001, review of *Shooting Dr. Jack,* p. 59; May 19, 2003, review of *The Angel of Montague Street,* p. 54; April 12, 2004, review of *Way Past Legal,* p. 36; June 26, 2006, review of *Dead Cat Bounce,* p. 36; November 3, 2008, review of *The Last Gig,* p. 41.

St. Louis Post-Dispatch, May 21, 2003, Jeremy C. Shea, review of *The Angel of Montague Street,* p. E3.

ONLINE

Books 'n' Bytes, http://www.booksnbytes.com/ (June 11, 2009), John Jordan, interview.

Houston Chronicle Online, http://www.chron.com/ (February 8, 2009), P.G. Koch, review of *The Last Gig.*

Oregonian Online, http://www.oregonlive.com/books/ (March 16, 2009), Barbara Tom, "Murder By the Book Review: *The Last Gig.*"*

H

HADLEIGH, Boze 1954-
(George Hadley-Garcia, George Hadley)

PERSONAL: Born May 15, 1954, in Syria; name originally George Hadley; son of a professor; married October 5, 1975. *Education:* University of California, Santa Barbara, B.A., 1975; San Jose State University, M.S., 1976. *Hobbies and other interests:* International travel (more than seventy countries), languages (speaks five).

ADDRESSES: Home—Beverly Hills, CA; Sydney, New South Wales, Australia.

CAREER: Author.

WRITINGS:

NONFICTION

(Under pseudonym George Hadley-Garcia) *The Films of Jane Fonda,* Citadel Press (Secaucus, NJ), 1981.
Conversations with My Elders, St. Martin's Press (New York, NY), 1986, reprinted with new foreword as *Celluloid Gaze,* Limelight Editions (New York, NY), 2002.
(Under pseudonym George Hadley-Garcia) *Hispanic Hollywood: The Latins in Motion Pictures,* Citadel Press (Secaucus, NJ), 1990.
The Vinyl Closet: Gays in the Music World, Los Hombres Press (San Diego, CA), 1991, updated edition published as *Sing Out! Gays and Lesbians in the Music World,* Barricade Books (New York, NY), 1997.

Leading Ladies, Robson Books (London, England), 1992.
The Lavender Screen: Gay and Lesbian Films, Citadel Press (Secaucus, NJ), 1993, updated edition, Kensington Publishing (New York, NY), 2001.
(Compiler) *Hollywood Babble On,* Birch Lane Press (Secaucus, NJ), 1994.
Hollywood Lesbians: Conversations with Barbara Stanwyck, Agnes Moorehead, Marjorie Main, Nancy Kulp, Patsy Kelly, Edith Head, Sandy Dennis, Capucine, Dorothy Arzner, Dame Judith Anderson, Barricade Books (New York, NY), 1994.
Bette Davis Speaks, Barricade Books (New York, NY), 1996.
Hollywood Gays: Conversations with Cary Grant, Liberace, Tony Perkins, Paul Lynde, Cesar Romero, Brad Davis, Randolph Scott, James Coco, William Haines, David Lewis, Barricade Books (New York, NY), 1996.
(Compiler) *Hollywood and Whine,* Birch Lane Press (Secaucus, NJ), 1998, revised edition, Kensington Publishing (New York, NY), 2001.
Celebrity Feuds!, Taylor Publishing (Dallas, TX), 1999.
(Compiler) *In or Out: Gay and Straight Celebrities Talk about Themselves and Each Other,* Barricade Books (New York, NY), 2000.
Celebrity Lies: Stars, Fibs, Fabrications, Myths and Little White Lies, Barricade Books (New York, NY), 2003.
Holy Matrimony! Better Halves and Bitter Halves, Andrews McMeel (Kansas City, MO), 2003.
Celebrity Diss and Tell, Andrews McMeel (Kansas City, MO), 2005.
The Damned Don't Cry: The Crawford Formula—Real and Reel (documentary film), 2005.
Broadway Babylon: Glamour, Glitz, and Gossip on the Great White Way, Back Stage Books (New York, NY), 2007.

Mexico's Most Wanted, Potomac Books (Dulles, VA), 2007.

Contributor to periodicals.

Hadleigh's books have been translated in more than a dozen languages.

ADAPTATIONS: Nearly half of Hadleigh's books have been adapted for television or film in the United States and abroad; these include the 2002 documentary film *The Bronze Screen: 100 Years of the Latino Image in American Cinema,* based on the book *Hispanic Hollywood: The Latins in Motion Pictures.*

SIDELIGHTS: Boze Hadleigh began his career as a freelance journalist, eventually publishing in hundreds of periodicals in the United States and abroad on a wide variety of topics, from health and travel to history, pop culture, and Hollywood. As an author of books, however, he has focused mainly on the entertainment world, its impact and its behind-the-scenes workings. Several of Hadleigh's books have been firsts in their subject matter, including works that examine the homosexual and bisexual presence in and contributions to show business, particularly motion pictures.

Hadleigh, a "smart, resourceful, and daring conversationalist," to quote a *Film Quarterly* contributor, wrote four question-and-answer interview books, commencing with *Conversations with My Elders.* The subjects were gay men of cinema: designer Sir Cecil Beaton, actors Rock Hudson and Sal Mineo, and directors George Cukor, Luchino Visconti, and Rainer Werner Fassbinder. *Hollywood Gays: Conversations with Cary Grant, Liberace, Tony Perkins, Paul Lynde, Cesar Romero, Brad Davis, Randolph Scott, James Coco, William Haines, David Lewis* and *Hollywood Lesbians: Conversations with Barbara Stanwyck, Agnes Moorehead, Marjorie Main, Nancy Kulp, Patsy Kelly, Edith Head, Sandy Dennis, Capucine, Dorothy Arzner, Dame Judith Anderson* are also collections of interviews. Columnist Liz Smith of *Newsday* called Hadleigh's interviews in *Hollywood Lesbians* "fascinating." A reviewer for *Publishers Weekly* noted: "An enlightening picture emerges of Tinseltown, different from that presented by the Fanzines."

Bette Davis Speaks is based on numerous interviews taped over the years with the screen legend, as well as briefer interviews with Davis's associates and intimates.

Booklist contributor Charles Harmon predicted that the actress's fans would "purr with delight" while reading this book by a "world-class interviewer." *Leading Ladies* is a non-question-and-answer collection of profiles of British stage and screen stars, from Dames Edith Evans and Sybil Thorndike to Elsa Lanchester, Joan Greenwood, and Estelle Winwood. "The main pleasure comes from the leading ladies' own words," observed *Sight and Sound* reviewer Geoffrey Macnab, who found "Hadleigh's enthusiasm" to be "infectious, if wearing."

Two of Hadleigh's books, *The Films of Jane Fonda* and *Hispanic Hollywood: The Latins in Motion Pictures* were published under the pseudonym George Hadley-Garcia. *The Lavender Screen: Gay and Lesbian Films*—an illustrated genre overview, like *Hispanic Hollywood*—was called a "clever, entertaining, and shameless compendium" by *Films in Review* correspondent John Nangle. In *The Lavender Screen,* Hadleigh showcases approximately fifty films featuring major gay, lesbian, or bisexual characters, also describing the behind-the-scenes conflicts, "closetings," and censorship involved in their production. *Sing Out! Gays and Lesbians in the Music World,* originally published as *The Vinyl Closet: Gays in the Music World,* was, according to Hadleigh, the first overview of gay men in music, from Tchaikovsky to Cole Porter, to Johnny Mathis, Boy George, George Michael, and Leonard Bernstein, who penned the foreword. One of the chapters spotlights the many lesbian and bisexual women singers who predated K.D. Lang and Melissa Etheridge.

Behind-the-scenes stories of sexual escapades on Broadway are the subject of Hadleigh's book *Broadway Babylon: Glamour, Glitz, and Gossip on the Great White Way,* published in 2007. The title is a reference to Kenneth Anger's classic book about Hollywood's hidden stories, *Hollywood Babylon.* According to Erik Haagensen in *Back Stage West,* however, Hadleigh's book has few real similarities to Anger's in-depth portrait of Hollywood's hidden side. A *Kirkus Reviews* writer commented that the author is primarily focused on "who slept with whom and who was/is bi-, gay or straight." Some of the celebrities discussed in the pages of *Broadway Babylon* include Lucille Ball, Ethel Merman, Carol Channing, Mary Martin, and Bob Fosse. Hadleigh comments on the ways that homophobia may have had an impact on the lives and careers of playwrights such as Tennessee Williams and William Inge, but throughout the book, he touches on such subjects without going into them deeply. The author "has looked at the subtext of celebrity more piercingly" in his earlier books, such as *Hollywood Gays* and *Hollywood Lesbians,* said Haagensen. By contrast, *Broadway Babylon* is made up mainly of anecdotes, quotations, and gossip, rather than original interviews with celebrities. Still, some new facts do surface in the book, and even well-known stories "remain entertaining and even enlightening," noted Haagensen.

Hadleigh, who once won 16,400 dollars on the game show *Jeopardy,* and donated a portion of it to a library in Australia damaged by fire, is also the compiler of celebrity quotations books, including the lesbian, bisexual, and gay collection *In or Out: Gay and Straight Celebrities Talk about Themselves and Each Other.* His first such book, *Hollywood Babble On,* contained only "star vs. star" quotations and led *People* contributor Alex Tresnowski to comment that Hollywood celebrities are "major-league trash talkers." In the same combative vein, the non-quotes book *Celebrity Feuds!* chronicles over two dozen feuds, from David Letterman versus Jay Leno to Sonny versus Cher. *Celebrity Feuds!* also contains a section on family feuds, including that of siblings Eric and Julia Roberts. Ilene Cooper described the work in *Booklist* as a "quick, funny read," and a *Publishers Weekly* reviewer called it a "sassy compendium of fights, feuds, and flying fur." Hadleigh noted that the book is as much about relationships— "why they sometimes sour and stay soured, even within families"—as about celebrities. "Hopefully, my books enlighten as well as entertain," Hadleigh once told *CA.* He added: "You can't always judge a book by its title!"

More recently Hadleigh added: "I *imagine* that most fiction writers write to escape into another world. I *know* that most nonfiction writers, including myself, write to delve deeper into this one. After nearly twenty published books, I've not yet explored fiction, except as a reader. As such, I can enjoy a novel—contemporary or historical (whose research makes it a cousin to nonfiction)— as much as a nonfiction book. It depends on the subject and how interestingly it's done.

"I've been fortunate not to have to write for the money, have enjoyed all my chosen subjects. But although I'm not a huge fan of Hollywood-themed books, several of mine have focused on the entertainment world; less, however, on the stars and glitz than the behind-the-scenes workings of popular culture: of how films, topics, trends, personalities and, yes, propaganda are marketed to an often gullible public. In every nation, including this one, still striving for actual equality of all its citizens and above-board government (for the measure of democracy isn't just voting, it's how the votes are counted), it's important to question and to seek the truth, to recognize the machinations behind entertainment, politics, religion, et cetera. What is more important—or more fascinating—than knowing how our world really works?

"All my books have sought to entertain and enlighten, necessarily in that order. To me, growing up in different cultures and languages, surrounded by books—some by my father and grandfather—the act of reading was always entertaining. Books were accessible and dependable friends and teachers; still are. There were always so many books and so much time that it didn't matter if you spent a week reading a purely escapist novel; the month still held three other weeks for more substantial fare. The main thing was to read (but not fiction only; when a rare person tells me that he or she reads only novels—let alone just one genre of novels—I have to wonder while inwardly shaking my head).

"The real world is too intriguing—in both senses of the word!—and too important to keep escaping it via novels, chemicals, indifference, et cetera. To me, the more one reads—and learns and questions—the more one wishes to write, to express oneself, to communicate. Communication is the key to human existence and well being. I was pleasantly quite surprised when, months after earning my master's degree in journalism, I stared at the document for the first time and discovered that it wasn't actually in journalism, but in mass communications, and it was an M.S., not an M.A. You live and learn—hopefully in both senses of that excellent word."

BIOGRAPHICAL AND CRITICAL SOURCES:

PERIODICALS

Back Stage East, October 4, 2007, Erik Haagensen, review of *Broadway Babylon: Glamour, Glitz, and Gossip on the Great White Way,* p. 42.

Back Stage West, October 4, 2007, Erik Haagensen, review of *Broadway Babylon,* p. 19.

Booklist, October 15, 1992, Charles Harmon, review of *The Lavender Screen: Gay and Lesbian Films,* p. 391; November 1, 1994, Ilene Cooper, review of *Hollywood Lesbians: Conversations with Barbara Stanwyck, Agnes Moorehead, Marjorie Main,*

Nancy Kulp, Patsy Kelly, Edith Head, Sandy Dennis, Capucine, Dorothy Arzner, Dame Judith Anderson, p. 470; April 15, 1996, Charles Harmon, review of *Bette Davis Speaks,* p. 1406; October 15, 1999, Ilene Cooper, review of *Celebrity Feuds!,* p. 407.

Film Quarterly, fall, 1988, review of *Conversations with My Elders,* p. 64.

Films in Review, December, 1993, John Nangle, review of *The Lavender Screen,* p. 425; March-April, 1995, John Nangle, review of *Hollywood Lesbians,* p. 69.

Kirkus Reviews, July 15, 2007, review of *Broadway Babylon.*

Library Journal, October 1, 1996, Ed Halter, review of *Hollywood Gays: Conversations with Cary Grant, Liberace, Tony Perkins, Paul Lynde, Cesar Romero, Brad Davis, Randolph Scott, James Coco, William Haines, David Lewis,* p. 79.

Newsday, November 8, 1994, column by Liz Smith.

Observer (London, England), June 21, 1992, Peter Matthews, review of *Leading Ladies,* p. 59.

People, August 1, 1994, Alex Tresnowski, review of *Hollywood Babble On,* p. 26.

Publishers Weekly, October 17, 1994, review of *Hollywood Lesbians,* p. 73; September 9, 1996, review of *Hollywood Gays,* p. 73; October 4, 1999, review of *Celebrity Feuds!,* p. 56.

Sight and Sound, October, 1992, Geoffrey Macnab, "Preserved for Posterity," p. 41.

ONLINE

Internet Movie Database, http://www.imdb.com/ (July 28, 2008), biographical information about Boze Hadleigh.

OTHER

Double Take: A Conversation with Boze Hadleigh (film), 2004.

* * *

HADLEY, George
    See HADLEIGH, Boze

* * *

HADLEY-GARCIA, George
    See HADLEIGH, Boze

HAILEY, J.P.
    See HALL, Parnell

* * *

HAINES, Carolyn 1953-
    (Caroline Burnes, Lizzie Hart)

PERSONAL: Born May 12, 1953, in Hattiesburg, MS; daughter of Roy (a journalist) and Hilda (a journalist) Haines. *Education:* University of Southern Mississippi, B.S., 1974; University of Southern Alabama, M.A., 1985. *Hobbies and other interests:* Horseback riding.

ADDRESSES: E-mail—cehaines@mindspring.com.

CAREER: Writer. Formerly worked as a journalist for the *George County Times, Mobile Register, Hattiesburg America,* and *Mississippi Press;* University of Southern Alabama, Mobile, AL, Public Relations Office, staff member.

WRITINGS:

NOVELS

Summer of Fear, Windsor (New York, NY), 1993.

Summer of the Redeemers, Dutton (New York, NY), 1994, published in England as *Season of Innocents,* Headline (London, England), 1994.

Touched, Dutton (New York, NY), 1996.

Judas Burning, River City (Montgomery, AL), 2005.

Penumbra, St. Martin's Minotaur (New York, NY), 2006.

Fever Moon, St. Martin's Minotaur (New York, NY), 2007.

Revenant, Mira Books (New York, NY), 2007.

"BONES" SERIES

Them Bones, Bantam (New York, NY), 1999.

Buried Bones, Bantam (New York, NY), 2000.

Splintered Bones, Delacorte (New York, NY), 2002.

Crossed Bones, Delacorte (New York, NY), 2003.

Hallowed Bones, Delacorte (New York, NY), 2004.

Bones to Pick, Kensington Books (New York, NY), 2006.

Ham Bones, Kensington Books (New York, NY), 2007.

Wishbones, St. Martin's Minotaur (New York, NY), 2008.

Greedy Bones, St. Martin's Minotaur (New York, NY), 2009.

ROMANCE NOVELS; UNDER PSEUDONYM CAROLINE BURNES

A Deadly Breed, Harlequin Intrigue (New York, NY), 1988.

Measure of Deceit, Harlequin Intrigue (New York, NY), 1988.

Phantom Filly, Harlequin Intrigue (New York, NY), 1989.

The Jaguar's Eye, Harlequin Intrigue (New York, NY), 1991.

Deadly Currents, Harlequin Intrigue (New York, NY), 1992.

Fatal Ingredients, Harlequin Intrigue (New York, NY), 1992.

Hoodwinked, Harlequin Intrigue (New York, NY), 1993.

Flesh and Blood, Harlequin Intrigue (New York, NY), 1993.

Cutting Edge, Harlequin Intrigue (New York, NY), 1994.

A Christmas Kiss, Harlequin Intrigue (New York, NY), 1996.

Midnight Prey, Harlequin Intrigue (New York, NY), 1997.

Remember Me, Cowboy, Harlequin (New York, NY), 1998.

(With Rebecca York) *After Dark: Counterfeit Wife,* Harlequin (New York, NY), 1999.

Texas Midnight, Harlequin (New York, NY), 2000.

Midnight Burning, Harlequin (New York, NY), 2001.

(With Anne Stuart and Joanna Wayne) *What Lies Beneath* (contains *"Primal Fear"*), Harlequin (New York, NY), 2002.

Babe in the Woods, Harlequin (New York, NY), 2003.

Rider in the Mist, Harlequin (New York, NY), 2003.

"CAT FAMILIAR" SERIES; UNDER PSEUDONYM CAROLINE BURNES

Fear Familiar, Harlequin (New York, NY), 1990.

Too Familiar, Harlequin (New York, NY), 1993.

Thrice Familiar, Harlequin (New York, NY), 1993.

Shades of Familiar, Harlequin (New York, NY), 1994.

Familiar Remedy, Harlequin (New York, NY), 1994.

Familiar Tale, Harlequin (New York, NY), 1995.

Bewitching Familiar, Harlequin (New York, NY), 1995.

Familiar Heart, Harlequin (New York, NY), 1997.

Familiar Fire, Harlequin (New York, NY), 1998.

Familiar Valentine, Harlequin (New York, NY), 1999.

Familiar Christmas, Harlequin (New York, NY), 1999.

Familiar Obsession, Harlequin (New York, NY), 2000.

Familiar Lullaby, Harlequin (New York, NY), 2001.

Familiar Mirage, Harlequin (New York, NY), 2002.

Familiar Oasis, Harlequin (New York, NY), 2002.

Familiar Double, Harlequin (New York, NY), 2003.

Familiar Texas, Harlequin (New York, NY), 2005.

Familiar Escape, Harlequin (New York, NY), 2006.

Familiar Vows, Harlequin (New York, NY), 2009.

OTHER

(Under pseudonym Lizzie Hart) *Shop Talk,* Kalioka Press (Semmes, AL), 1998.

(Editor, with Rebecca Barrett) *Moments with Eugene: A Collection of Memories,* Kalioka Press (Semmes, AL), 2000.

My Mother's Witness: The Peggy Morgan Story, River City (Montgomery, AL), 2003.

ADAPTATIONS: Books have been adapted for audio format, including *Crossed Bones,* Recorded Books, c. 2003.

SIDELIGHTS: Carolyn Haines has produced numerous mystery and romance novels as well as general fiction, and her stories are often set in the Mississippi Delta. Haines, who comes from a different section of Mississippi, writes on her Home Page that she found the delta a "land of stark contrasts and strange beauty" and was determined to write about it. Her "Bones" mystery series is set in the fictional delta town of Zinnia. She has often won critical praise for her novels' detailed southern atmosphere.

Haines's early novels are not mysteries per se, but they have "strong mystery elements," as she notes on her Home Page. *Summer of the Redeemers* centers on thirteen-year-old Rebekkah Rich and her experiences in rural Mississippi in the summer of 1963, as the civil rights movement is gaining strength. Her parents are liberal intellectuals surrounded by reactionary people largely opposed to black civil rights. Her life is further complicated by the odd behavior of a sophisticated, attractive neighbor as well as the fact that a bizarre religious cult has moved in just down the road. Rebek-kah becomes curious and soon discovers that horrible things are going on in the usually peaceful countryside, including child-selling and murder.

Some reviewers found Haines's setting vividly rendered and her story compelling. Though *Kirkus Reviews* contributor thought *Summer of the Redeemers* "severely hindered" by having an adolescent protagonist, the critic added that the author's "evocation of a particular place and time are certainly masterful." A *Publishers Weekly* praised the novel as "harrowing, richly atmospheric and sharp-edged," saying it "maintains suspense until its final pages." Pat Dole, writing in *Kliatt,* noted: "The sense of setting is outstanding, the plot gripping, and the pace brisk."

For *Touched,* Haines uses roughly the same setting, four decades earlier. In the book, sixteen-year-old Mattie arrives during the 1920s as a mail-order bride to the cruel and abusive Elikah Mills, who serves as the barber to the small town of Jexville, Mississippi. Mattie's only real friends in Jexville are the McVays, a couple with a young daughter, Duncan, who come from a more sophisticated place. When Duncan survives being struck by lightning and subsequently develops the ability of prophecy, the residents of Jexville, including Elikah, begin to suspect that she has been touched by Satan. Mrs. McVay rightly begins to fear for her family's safety, and she convinces Mattie and some of the community's other outcasts to attempt escape together. First, however, she and Mattie must rescue some of their small group, who have been captured by irate towns-people. Finally, the readers are given a report of Mattie's final revenge on Elikah, twenty years later. This novel received scattered praise from critics. Katherine Alberg, writing in the *New York Times Book Review,* cited the novel's "undeniable intensity" and noted that "it's impossible to shake its brooding atmosphere." A reviewer for *Publishers Weekly* also enjoyed *Touched,* praising its "languid sensuality" and "quirky, fully developed characters involved in an unpredictable story."

Haines's "Bones" books followed *Touched.* The mystery series stars Southern belle Sarah Booth Delaney, who runs a detective agency in Zinnia, Mississippi, while keeping up acquaintances with a resident ghost nick-named Jitty. In the third entry, *Splintered Bones,* Sarah investigates the demise of a horse breeder who was stomped to death—allegedly—by his prize stallion.

Sarah's sleuthing brings her into contact with a sexy stable hand, a trio of gangsters, and a would-be country-music diva. Reviewers commented on the story's eccentricities, with a *Kirkus Reviews* contributor remarking that *Splintered Bones* has "something for everyone—spandex-wearing ghosts, horses and more horses, southern-fried dysfunctional families." A *Publishers Weekly* critic found the novel "long on accent if short on clues that help elucidate the mystery," but added that Haines's sense of humor saves the day, "holding the reader's attention and internal laugh track right down to the last snicker." Rex E. Klett, writing in *Library Journal,* noted that *Splintered Bones,* "certainly offers welcome escape."

The next book in the series, *Crossed Bones,* finds Sarah and her partner, Tinkie, who exemplifies the "southern" woman, trying to clear the name of white blues guitarist Scott Hampton, who has been arrested for the murder of her husband. The two have numerous suspects to consider, including a black supremacist, racist bikers, and a blues collector. With the help of their dogs Sweetie Pie and Chablis and the resident ghost in Sarah's house, the partners discover that the murder may have something to do with recordings of the blues duo Elvis and Ivory that have never been released and are worth a fortune. Some critics praised the novel's atmosphere, among other things. "This cozy read is the next best thing to curling up with a mint julep on the porch swing on a lazy afternoon," wrote a *Publishers Weekly* reviewer. A *Kirkus Reviews* contributor called *Crossed Bones* "a down-home valentine . . . that couldn't be more southern if it were packaged with grits." Sue O'Brien, writing in *Booklist,* referred to Sarah as "a charming, likable hero."

Hallowed Bones features the murder of a handicapped infant girl, as Sarah and Tinkie set out to clear the girl's mother, a supposed miracle worker named Doreen Mallory, of the crime. There are three men who could have fathered the baby, and Sarah and Tinkie set their sights on them as the primary suspects while Sarah deals with her love for a local married sheriff and the possibility that Tinkie has breast cancer. Sue O'Brien, writing in *Booklist,* noted that Sarah's "first-person narration draws readers close to her." A *Publishers Weekly* contributor wrote that "the conclusion is both clever and impressive."

In *Bones to Pick,* Sarah investigates the murder of Quentin McGee after McGee's life partner, Allison Tatum, is arrested for the crime. With Tinkie's assistance, Sarah soon learns that the Quentin and Allison, both graduates of the Carrington School for Well-Bred Ladies, have made plenty of local enemies by ruining reputations. However, as the investigation goes on, Sarah and Tinkie come to realize they are pursuing a serial killer focusing on Carrington School alums. "Non-southerners will find the madcap adventure an informative peek into an alien culture," related a *Kirkus Reviews* critic.

Another entry in the series, *Ham Bones,* has a theatrical setting. A touring production of *Cat on a Hot Tin Roof* comes to Zinnia, and its stars are Graf Milieu, a onetime boyfriend of Sarah's, and Renata Trovaioli, an egotistical actress whom Sarah dislikes. At Graf's urging, Sarah, a former actress, becomes Renata's understudy, and then becomes both star and murder suspect when Renata is poisoned in her dressing room. Further distressed because her married lover, Sheriff Coleman Peters, seems to think her guilty, Sarah endeavors to prove her innocence, with help from Tinkie and the ghost Jitty. Again, several critics found Haines's work entertaining. "The humorous romp through the pages is well worth taking," observed a *Publishers Weekly* reviewer, who described the novel as "outrageous" and the series as "delightful." Sue O'Brien, writing in *Booklist,* called *Ham Bones* a "charming southern cozy."

Later novels outside the series include *Judas Burning,* which retains the Mississippi Delta setting. Journalist Dixon Sinclair has just returned to Jexville to live in the family home, and she buys the local newspaper. Dixon, who has a drinking problem and numerous other emotional troubles, is soon delving into the disappearance of two teenage girls and the desecration of a statue of the Virgin Mary. The mutilated body of one of the missing girls is found in a local swamp, along with a mysterious religious shrine. Some reviewers had praise for this nonseries novel. Jenny McLarin, a contributor to *Booklist,* noted that the author "crafts a story as rich as a thick slice of Mississippi mud pie." A *Kirkus Reviews* critic remarked: "Sympathetic characters and an unblinking look at the banality and breathtaking evil below Jexville's surface make this a must-read."

Haines's novel *Fever Moon,* set in Louisiana at the end of World War II, features Deputy Raymond Thibodeaux on the trail of the killer of wealthy Henri Bastion. Thibodeaux does not pay much attention to the fact that a local woman, Adele Hebert, who believes she is possessed, has confessed to the crime. Meanwhile, the superstitious locals think Adele may be a werewolf. A *Publishers Weekly* contributor commented on the author's "powerful sense of place" and called *Fever Moon* "an engaging, memorable story."

Haines is also author of the nonfiction *My Mother's Witness: The Peggy Morgan Story,* which tells the story of Peggy Morgan, her mother Inez, and the role they played in helping bring to justice the murderer of civil rights leader Medgar Evers in 1963. A *Publishers Weekly* critic noted Haines's "powerful storytelling." In addition to the books published under her own name, Haines has produced numerous romance and intrigue novels under the pseudonym Caroline Burnes. One of her series has a cat-detective as protagonist. That feline, Familiar, is based on one of the author's pets, a black cat named E.A. Poe.

BIOGRAPHICAL AND CRITICAL SOURCES:

PERIODICALS

Booklist, June 1, 1996, Nancy Pearl, review of *Touched,* pp. 1674, 1676; February 1, 2003, Sue O'Brien, review of *Crossed Bones,* p. 975; February 15, 2004, Sue O'Brien, review of *Hallowed Bones,* p. 1042; September 15, 2005, Jenny McLarin, review of *Judas Burning,* p. 35; June 1, 2007, Sue O'Brien, review of *Ham Bones,* p. 44.

Kirkus Reviews, April 1, 1994, review of *Summer of the Redeemers,* p. 419; December 15, 2001, review of *Splintered Bones,* p. 1724; February 1, 2003, review of *Crossed Bones,* p. 187; January 15, 2004, review of *Hallowed Bones,* p. 63; August 1, 2005, review of *Judas Burning,* p. 818; May 15, 2006, review of *Bones to Pick,* p. 497.

Kliatt, September, 1995, Pat Dole, review of *Summer of the Redeemers,* p. 10.

Library Journal, February 1, 2002, Rex E. Klett, review of *Splintered Bones,* p. 135; March 1, 2003, Rex Klett, review of *Crossed Bones,* p. 122; April 1, 2004, Rex Klett, review of *Hallowed Bones,* p. 126; February 1, 2006, Jo Ann Vicarel, review of *Penumbra,* p. 56.

New York Times Book Review, September 22, 1996, Katherine Alberg, review of *Touched,* p. 25.

Publishers Weekly, April 18, 1994, review of *Summer of the Redeemers,* p. 45; June 3, 1996, review of *Touched,* p. 62; February 11, 2002, review of *Splintered Bones,* p. 164; March 3, 2003, review of

Crossed Bones, p. 57; September 22, 2003, review of *My Mother's Witness: The Peggy Morgan Story,* p. 100; March 1, 2004, review of *Hallowed Bones,* p. 53; August 15, 2005, review of *Judas Burning,* p. 28; February 27, 2006, review of *Penumbra,* p. 35; December 4, 2006, review of *Fever Moon,* p. 37; May 7, 2007, review of *Ham Bones,* p. 45.

ONLINE

Alabama Bound, http://www.alabamabound.org/ (April 18, 2002), "Carolyn Haines," profile of author.

Carolyn Haines Home Page, http://www.carolynhaines.com (May 26, 2008).

Crescent Blues, http://www.crescentblues.com/ (March 9, 2007), Dawn Goldsmith, review of *Hallowed Bones.*

Mystical Unicorn Bookstore, http://www.myunicorn.com/ (March 29, 2007), bibliography of Haines.

Romantic Times Online, http://www.romantictimes.com/ (May 26, 2008), Cindy Whitesel, review of *Familiar Double;* Catherine Witmer, review of *Revenant.* *

*   *   *

HALL, Parnell 1944-
(J.P. Hailey)

PERSONAL: Born October 31, 1944, in Culver City, CA; son of James and Frances Hall; married Lynn Mandel, 1975; children: Justin, Toby. *Education:* Marlboro College, B.A., 1968.

ADDRESSES: *Home*—New York, NY. *Agent*—Donald Maass, Donald Maass Literary Agency, 160 W. 95th St., Ste. 1B, New York, NY 10025. *E-mail*—parnellh@pipeline.com.

CAREER: Writer, screenwriter, educator, and actor. Marlboro Theater Company, actor, 1968, 1970-74; Windsor Mountain School, Lenox, MA, teacher, 1974-75; Berkshire Community College, Pittsfield, MA, teacher, 1975; Stockbridge School, Stockbridge, MA, teacher, 1975-76; screenwriter, 1977-84; Claims Investigation Bureau, Mount Vernon, NY, private detective, 1985-87; novelist, 1987—. Appeared in the films *Hercules in New York,* 1969, and *A New Leaf.*

MEMBER: International Association of Crime Writers, Private Eye Writers of America (vice president, 1993-94; president, 1995-96), Mystery Writers of America, American Crime Writers, Sisters in Crime.

AWARDS, HONORS: Edgar Award nomination for best first novel, Mystery Writers of America, 1988, for *Detective;* Shamus Award nomination for best first private eye novel, Private Eye Writers of America, 1988, for *Detective;* Shamus Award nomination for best private eye novel, Private Eye Writers of America, 1996, for *Movie.*

WRITINGS:

C.H.U.D. (screenplay), C.H.U.D. Productions, 1984.

"STANLEY HASTINGS" MYSTERY SERIES

Detective, Donald I. Fine (New York, NY), 1987.
Murder, Donald I. Fine (New York, NY), 1988.
Favor, Donald I. Fine (New York, NY), 1988.
Strangler, Donald I. Fine (New York, NY), 1989.
Client, Donald I. Fine (New York, NY), 1990.
Juror, Donald I. Fine (New York, NY), 1990.
Shot, Donald I. Fine (New York, NY), 1991.
Actor, Mysterious Press (New York, NY), 1993.
Blackmail, Mysterious Press (New York, NY), 1994.
Movie, Mysterious Press (New York, NY), 1995.
Trial, Mysterious Press (New York, NY), 1996.
Scam, Mysterious Press (New York, NY), 1997.
Suspense, Mysterious Press (New York, NY), 1998.
Cozy, Carroll & Graf (New York, NY), 2001.
Manslaughter: A Stanley Hastings Mystery, Carroll & Graf (New York, NY), 2003.
Hitman: A Stanley Hastings Mystery, Pegasus Books (New York, NY), 2007.

"PUZZLE LADY" MYSTERY SERIES

A Clue for the Puzzle Lady, Bantam (New York, NY), 1999.
Last Puzzle and Testament, Bantam (New York, NY), 2000.
Puzzled to Death, Bantam (New York, NY), 2001.
A Puzzle in a Pear Tree, Bantam (New York, NY), 2002.

With This Puzzle, I Thee Kill, Bantam (New York, NY), 2003.

And a Puzzle to Die On: A Puzzle Lady Mystery, Bantam (New York, NY), 2004.

Stalking the Puzzle Lady, Bantam (New York, NY), 2005.

You Have the Right to Remain Puzzled: A Puzzle Lady Mystery, Bantam (New York, NY), 2006.

The Sudoku Puzzle Murders, Thomas Dunne Books/St. Martin's Press (New York, NY), 2008.

Dead Man's Puzzle, St. Martin's Press Minotaur (New York, NY), 2009.

"STEVE WINSLOW" MYSTERY SERIES; UNDER PSEUDONYM J.P. HAILEY

The Baxter Trust, Donald I. Fine (New York, NY), 1988.

The Anonymous Client, Donald I. Fine (New York, NY), 1989.

The Underground Man, Donald I. Fine (New York, NY), 1990.

The Naked Typist, Donald I. Fine (New York, NY), 1990.

The Wrong Gun, Donald I. Fine (New York, NY), 1992.

SIDELIGHTS: Perhaps best known for his mystery novels featuring Manhattan private detective Stanley Hastings, Parnell Hall also authors the "Steve Winslow" series of novels, about an iconoclastic lawyer, under the pseudonym J.P. Hailey, and a series focusing on a hard-drinking, middle-aged sleuth known as the Puzzle Lady. Hastings, as reviewers have frequently pointed out, is one of the more likable and less hard-boiled private eyes in fiction. Although a licensed detective, this frustrated playwright and happily married family man makes his living as an "ambulance chaser" for a personal-injury lawyer, signing up clients and taking their statements. The criminal cases that come his way, often accidentally, cause him to rely on his "street smarts," his wit, and the overcoming of his realistic fears as he fumbles his way toward solutions. Hall, according to reviewer Marvin Lachman in the *Armchair Detective,* based Hastings's character on some of his own experiences as an aspiring writer and New York City dweller.

In Hall's debut novel, *Detective,* Hastings finds his first client murdered and tracks down the killer at his own expense. Lachman found the puzzle element of the novel to be "rather ordinary," although its writing makes it "an often amusing, fast-paced first novel with considerable suspense." In a review of Hall's second novel, *Murder,* a *Publishers Weekly* writer looked back on *Detective* as a "notable debut." *Murder* involves a neighbor of Hastings who has been blackmailed into working as a prostitute; when she is killed, Hastings comes under suspicion and solves the crime to clear his own name. As in *Detective,* Hastings collaborates with Police Sergeant MacAuliff, whom author Hall uses as a foil for his protagonist and a source of witty observations on police procedure.

In his third published adventure, *Favor,* Hastings is sent to Atlantic City to investigate MacAuliff's sleazy son-in-law as a favor for the police sergeant. He infiltrates the mob using what a *Publishers Weekly* contributor called "a hilarious, albeit unbelievable, modus operandi" and plunges into "a web of intrigue that is pure entertainment for the reader." For a *Booklist* contributor, *Favor* is a "spirited, well-made" entry in "a very funny, very smart mystery series." A *Library Journal* contributor wrote that after a slow beginning, the novel moves along in a way that is both enjoyably comical and believable.

Hastings's fourth volume, *Strangler,* finds the detective accused by an unpleasant police sergeant (not MacAuliff) of committing a series of murders by strangulation. His clearing of his own name results in what *Library Journal* contributor Rex E. Klett called "a great addition to the series." A *Booklist* contributor wrote: "It's great fun to meet a sleuth with very few answers." Hastings, the reviewer explained, "reaffirms one's belief in the power of relentless mediocrity."

With his next assignment, in *Client,* Hastings follows a client's wife to a motel, falls asleep on his stakeout, and finds himself framed for her murder. This prompted *Booklist*'s Stuart Miller to call Hastings "delightfully inept," and the case "yet another highly readable mystery starring one of the most unusual private eyes ever to take on a case." For *Library Journal* contributor Rex E. Klett, *Client* represents "continued high quality" in the series, marked by a swift, humorous style.

Juror finds Hastings performing jury duty on a case he finds boring. Soon a fellow juror is murdered, a woman Hastings had been driving to the courtroom each morning. The novel provides an occasion for observations on jury trials and on murder investigations, which a *Publishers Weekly* contributor found to be the book's strong points. *Kliatt* contributor Rita M. Fontinha found *Juror* "suspenseful to the end, and great fun too," and *Armchair Detective* contributor Jon L. Breen declared it "hugely enjoyable" for its "terrific stunt payoff" and its observations on the jury system.

Hall's next Hastings title, *Shot,* finds Hastings working for a wealthy woman to investigate her own boyfriend; the boyfriend is then found dead, and once again, Hastings is a suspect. The plot, a *Publishers Weekly* contributor warned, contains an "all-encompassing red herring" but is enlivened by two climaxes—one comic and one serious—and "vivid looks at Manhattan's seamier side." In Chicago's *Tribune Books,* reviewer Kevin Moore commented that Hastings's ordinariness and the other characters' believability, although well rendered, make the tale less exciting. For *New York Times Book Review* contributor Marilyn Stasio, however, *Shot* provided evidence that Hall's series is "forever fresh."

In *Actor,* Hastings accepts a friend's invitation to perform in a Connecticut theater group; the stabbing death of the stage manager provides the crime, and the setting affords an opportunity for observations about the denizens of the theatrical profession. Writing in the *New York Times Book Review,* Marilyn Stasio noted: "Mr. Hall knows the theatrical drill to which he hilariously subjects Stanley." The protagonist, Stasio asserted, "wins our vote for Best Performance by an Actor on the Verge of a Nervous Breakdown." A *Publishers Weekly* critic noted that despite a slow start, the novel deserves a "standing ovation."

Blackmail concerns an attractive female client who hires Hastings to pay off a blackmailer for pornographic pictures in which the client does not even appear. The client then turns up dead, as does another individual, and an elaborate sting is gradually uncovered by Hastings with the aid of his wife, Alice. *Booklist* contributor Wes Lukowsky found this "an intelligent, unusual spin on the tough-guy detective" and called the dialogue "the best this side of George V. Higgins." A *Kirkus Reviews* contributor, claiming that Hall's novels often start with great ideas, found this one to be a winner from beginning to end, noting: "Every page quivers with comic frustration, and the result is an absolute joy."

Hastings's tenth published adventure, *Movie,* gives him the opportunity to observe the world of filmmaking, as a screenplay of his is accepted by a producer. Murder enters when a homeless man is killed near the set, and then a sound technician is found dead. A *Kirkus Reviews* contributor felt the plot does not meet the level of the witty banter in the book, but that "anyone who can relax and ignore the mystery is guaranteed a good time." Writing in *Booklist,* Wes Lukowsky called this book "an entertaining entry in an underappreciated series."

Hastings's next book appearance, in *Trial,* finds him once again on his professional turf as an ambulance-chaser for a lawyer. His employer is defending a man accused of murdering his wife; the defendant has an apparently good alibi concerning a poker game, but Hastings has doubts, and then one of the poker players is killed. The novel ends with a surprise, and *Booklist* contributor George Needham called it "lots of fun." For a *Publishers Weekly* reviewer, the novel was well paced and balanced, containing a complex alibi with "a lot of very sharp turns in the courtroom." A *Kirkus Reviews* contributor remarked that the novel's climactic scene is "memorable, though far-fetched," and that the series itself is "rollicking."

Hastings moves on to an "intricate and fiendishly funny case," in the words of a *Publishers Weekly* contributor, in his next book, *Scam.* In this installment of the series an investment banker hires the private detective to collect information about a woman he met in a singles bar. A series of dead bodies impinge on the investigation, and once again Hastings is framed for murder. A *Publishers Weekly* reviewer wrote that "smart dialogue, clever plotting and a perfectly executed reverse scam . . . result in sparkling entertainment." The novel also won plaudits from a *Kirkus Reviews* contributor, who commended Hall for taking "slender material" and weaving it into "a gossamer web of riddles by turns puzzling, suspenseful, and hilarious." According to Marilyn Stasio, writing in the *New York Times Book Review,* *Scam* showed that "what Mr. Hall does to the private-eye formula is very funny, but it isn't frivolous. His puzzles, for all their manic nonsense, are fiendish constructions of sound logic."

Hastings's thirteenth outing, *Suspense,* brings him good luck as well, in the opinion of a *Publishers Weekly* contributor. Here, a best-selling suspense novelist's wife hires Hastings to uncover the source of harassing phone calls, and the calls lead to murder. The case gives Hastings an opening to offer comically wise observations on the publishing industry and its agents, editors, and would-be writers. David Pitt, writing in *Booklist,* pointed out the self-referential nature of this comedy in this "very clever" novel about the suspense genre; for example, the characters frequently state that the case on which Hastings is working would make a bad novel. For Pitt, this experiment worked, because *Suspense* is "first-class fun from start to finish."

Hastings reappears in *Cozy*. In this adventure, Hastings is vacationing at a New England B & B when one of the other guests is murdered. When the local police chief misinterprets the clues and places the blame for the murder on Hastings and his wife, Alice, Hastings has little choice but to find the real killer. Writing in *Booklist,* Ilene Cooper noted that the mystery itself "takes a backseat to the delicious style with which the tale is told." A *Publishers Weekly* contributor commented: "The book's real strength is its plot, which has a certain crazed logic that will keep most readers turning the pages."

In *Manslaughter: A Stanley Hastings Mystery,* Hastings finds himself working for an ex-con, Joe Balfour, who is being blackmailed. As the case progresses, Hastings, aided by his cop friend, MacAuliff, soon learns that Joe Balfour the criminal does not exist. The case becomes further complicated by the murder of the blackmailer. "As usual, Hall has crafted a mystery that's both funny and genuinely mysterious," wrote David Pitt in *Booklist.* A *Publishers Weekly* contributor commented: "Whodunit fans with a taste for the unconventional will find this just what the doctor ordered."

In *Hitman: A Stanley Hastings Mystery,* Hastings finds himself in truly deep water with a case he probably had no business taking. The client is Martin Kessler, a high school English teacher who approaches Hastings because he has a problem with his second job: Kessler apparently moonlights as a hit man. Hastings knows better than to put himself in a precarious position with such a person, and so attempts to avoid the real issue by using every stalling tactic in his arsenal, talking about hypothetical circumstances until Kessler finally presses the matter and blurts out his problem. Kessler has been offered a hit job, but he does not actually want to go through with the job. In fact, Kessler is looking to get out of the business, but he is well aware that it is not one from which people typically retire gracefully, or even alive. He wants Hastings to follow him to make sure he does not carry out his new assignment, as well as to be sure that no one else is watching him. Unfortunately, while trailing Kessler, Hastings sees him

talking to another hit man for the Mob, a man who later turns up dead himself. It appears that the Kessler who hired Hastings is not the real Kessler after all, though the real Kessler's life is still in danger. To make matters more complicated, someone is now trying to kill Hastings as well. A reviewer for *Publishers Weekly* was relatively unimpressed by the mystery but remarked that "it's good to see Stanley returning to the lists, even in such a humble offering." A contributor for *Kirkus Reviews* opined that the novel "begins with an idiotic premise and then gradually works its way through an endless filigree of Q-and-A to a surprisingly logical solution."

Hall introduced a new mystery series and a new leading character, Cora Felton, in *A Clue for the Puzzle Lady.* Cora, the "Puzzle Lady," lives in Bakerhaven, a charming suburban town in Connecticut, where her neighbors frown on her heavy drinking but bask in her fame as a creator of nationally syndicated crossword puzzles without realizing that her niece Sherry ghostwrites the puzzles. Cora gets to work on a different kind of puzzle, though, when crossword-puzzle clues start turning up on dead bodies. A *Publishers Weekly* contributor welcomed the character of Cora, describing her as "a true original" and "Miss Marple as a promiscuous lush." The reviewer also commended the supporting characters, the dialogue, and the plot. *Booklist* contributor GraceAnne A. DeCandido noted that some of the book's elements seemed overly familiar but added that "Hall works with them in such deft ways, with such spiffy dialogue, that we are immediately seduced."

Cora and Sherry return in *Last Puzzle and Testament,* in which a strange woman named Emma Hurley dies and leaves a will granting her substantial wealth to whichever one of her heirs can solve a complicated puzzle—with Cora in charge of the judging. Someone starts killing the players, and Cora and her niece must shift into crime-solving mode. "The second puzzle for Cora Felton . . . is even better than her clever debut," noted a *Publishers Weekly* contributor. GraceAnne A. DeCandido, once again reviewing for *Booklist,* predicted that "this novel's puzzles within puzzles will charm and so will its attractive cast."

Cora and her editor are hosting a puzzle tournament when people begin turning up dead in *Puzzled to Death.* Although the murders initially seem unrelated, Cora soon finds a strange connection. "Cruciverbalists will get a bang out of working out the three crossword puzzles critical to solving the mystery," wrote Cathy Burke in *People.* GraceAnne A. DeCandido, writing in *Booklist,* noted that "the crosswordiana remains engaging."

A Puzzle in a Pear Tree finds Cora rehearsing as one of the maids-a-milking for a theatrical presentation of "The Twelve Days of Christmas," which is part of the Baker-haven Christmas Pageant. Meanwhile, Sherry is the Virgin Mary in a recreation of the Nativity scene. Before long, someone poisons a pear tree given to Becky Baldwin, who is the star of the pageant. Cora sets out to find the culprit along with the help of Jonathon Doddsworth, a Scotland yard detective visiting his daughter. Things go awry, however, when Sherry is arrested for the murder of another actor. A *Kirkus Reviews* writer called the novel "less abrasive and more amusing than [Hall's] previous outings." Ilene Cooper, writing in *Booklist,* noted: "Here, the puzzles are acrostics . . . [and] their presence adds freshness to the problem solving."

In *With This Puzzle, I Thee Kill,* Cora sets out to solve murders via the solution of cryptograms. All this takes place within the context of Cora's ex-husband showing up with his new bride-to-be and asking that their daughter Sherry be in his wedding. "Hall's trademark word play and gift for creating eccentric characters remain as sharp as ever," wrote a *Publishers Weekly* contributor.

Stalking the Puzzle Lady features Cora selling cereal on a media junket and being stalked by a former high-school classmate. When another young woman on the media tour is murdered, Cora sets out to solve the mystery. Stephanie Zvirin, writing in *Booklist,* noted that "feisty, contentious Cora has plenty of quirky charm." A *Kirkus Reviews* critic wrote: "Hall juggles facile satire and suspense in an entertaining effort."

You Have the Right to Remain Puzzled: A Puzzle Lady Mystery finds Cora accused of plagiarism and then of murder when her accuser is found dead. The problem Cora faces is to solve the murder without revealing that it is really Sherry and not Cora who creates the puzzles. In *Booklist,* David Pitt noted the novel's "suspenseful mystery, engaging characters, [and] dialogue that sparkles." A *Kirkus Reviews* contributor wrote that "Cora . . ., one tough cookie, provides amusing fodder for crossword fans."

The next installment in the "Puzzle Lady" mystery series is *The Sudoku Puzzle Murders.* In this book Hall gives readers a slight twist on the previous entries. With the introduction of sudoku, the Japanese numeric puzzles in which a series of numbers are placed into a grid so that each of the sides add up to the same total, Cora discovers a brand-new talent. In this particular type of puzzle, she soon proves to be a master constructor, and the new skill results in her being offered a Japanese publishing contract. In fact, Cora's talents are so impressive that she soon has two different publishers, Aoki Yoshiaki and Hideki Takiyama, in competition over who will ultimately land her book deal. Sherry acts as Cora's agent, negotiating the deal. Unfortunately, Sherry inadvertently signs the contract with the wrong publisher, and the other man, who was the first of the pair to approach Cora about the potential for a book, becomes very angry. Cora finds herself with more to worry about when two different private investigators are murdered. One of them is found with copies of her puzzles on him, implicating one of the two Japanese gentlemen and making both of them suspects, along with one of their wives. Sherry's former husband also comes on the scene, and he too is thrown under suspicion. As with previous books in the series, Hall provides readers with not just the mystery but also a number of crossword puzzles, along with four sudoku puzzles created by *New York Times* puzzle scribe Will Shortz, that they can solve. Sue O'Brien, in a review for *Booklist,* called Cora "a full-bodied character with an insatiable taste for mystery." However, a contributor for *Kirkus Reviews* commented that "the included batch of crosswords and sudoku puzzles may give readers less of a headache than the meandering mystery." A reviewer for *Publishers Weekly* opined that the "quirky characters and humorous dialogue help lighten the somewhat tedious [plot] details."

Hall once told *CA:* "I began writing my first novel, *Detective,* in 1985, when I was working as a private investigator in New York City. The firm I worked for serviced negligence lawyers, the type who advertised for clients on TV. I interviewed the accident victims, usually those who had fallen on the city sidewalk, and photographed the casts on their arms and legs, and the cracks in the pavement that had tripped them. While this was real detective work, it was not the type I was used to reading about in mystery novels, and it occurred to me how ill equipped I would be if I had to solve a murder. So that's how I began my novel. The detective is in his office, and the client is telling him, 'You have to help me, someone's trying to kill me.' This is where the P.I. says, 'There, there, citizen,' straps on his gun, and goes out to fight the bad guys. Stanley Hastings says, 'Are you kidding? I don't have a gun, I have a camera. I take pictures of cracks in the sidewalk.' When the man is killed, Stanley is devastated, and he spends the rest of the book trying to make up for the fact he could not help him because he was not 'a real detective.'"

BIOGRAPHICAL AND CRITICAL SOURCES:

PERIODICALS

Armchair Detective, winter, 1992, Jon L. Breen, review of *Juror,* pp. 58-59; spring, 1996, Marvin Lachman, review of *Detective,* pp. 174-175.

Booklist, January 15, 1988, review of *Murder,* p. 830; September 15, 1988, review of *Favor,* p. 123; July, 1989, review of *Strangler,* p. 1871; March 15, 1990, Stuart Miller, review of *Client,* p. 1418; March 15, 1994, Wes Lukowsky, review of *Blackmail,* p. 1330; March 15, 1995, Wes Lukowsky, review of *Movie,* p. 1311; January 1, 1996, George Needham, review of *Trial,* pp. 795-796; December 1, 1997, David Pitt, review of *Suspense,* p. 611; October 1, 1999, GraceAnne A. DeCandido, review of *A Clue for the Puzzle Lady,* p. 346; July, 2000, GraceAnne A. DeCandido, review of *Last Puzzle and Testament,* p. 2013; May 1, 2001, Ilene Cooper, review of *Cozy,* p. 1632; May 21, 2001, review of *Cozy,* p. 83; September 15, 2001, GraceAnne A. DeCandido, review of *Puzzled to Death,* p. 198; November 15, 2002, Ilene Cooper, review of *A Puzzle in a Pear Tree,* p. 580; February 15, 2003, David Pitt, review of *Manslaughter: A Stanley Hastings Mystery,* p. 1053; November 15, 2003, Ilene Cooper, review of *With This Puzzle, I Thee Kill,* p. 585; November 1, 2004, Ilene Cooper, review of *And a Puzzle to Die On: A Puzzle Lady Mystery,* p. 466; September 1, 2005, Stephanie Zvirin, review of *Stalking the Puzzle Lady,* p. 69; September 1, 2006, David Pitt, review of *You Have the Right to Remain Puzzled: A Puzzle Lady Mystery,* p. 61; March 1, 2008, Sue O'Brien, review of *The Sudoku Puzzle Murders,* p. 54.

Decatur Daily, June 18, 2006, Jane Davis, "Puzzle Lady Series Unappealing, Lame."

Kirkus Reviews, December 15, 1987, review of *Murder,* p. 1701; March 1, 1993, review of *Actor,* p. 262; January 1, 1994, p. 20; February 1, 1995, review of *Movie,* p. 109; December 1, 1995, review of *Trial,* p. 1670; February 15, 1997, review of *Scam,* p. 258; November 1, 1997, review of *Suspense,* p. 1608; October 1, 1999, review of *A Clue for the*

Puzzle Lady, p. 1527; August 15, 2001, review of *Puzzled to Death,* p. 1166; October 1, 2002, review of *A Puzzle in a Pear Tree,* p. 1429; December 15, 2002, review of *Manslaughter,* p. 1807; September 1, 2005, review of *Stalking the Puzzle Lady,* p. 944; August 15, 2006, review of *You Have the Right to Remain Puzzled,* p. 811; September 15, 2008, review of *Hitman: A Stanley Hastings Mystery;* February 15, 2008, review of *The Sudoku Puzzle Murders.*

Kliatt, September, 1993, Rita M. Fontinha, review of *Juror,* p. 10.

Library Journal, September 1, 1988, Rex E. Klett, review of *Favor,* pp. 185-186; May 1, 1989, Rex E. Klett, review of *Strangler,* p. 101; April 1, 1990, Rex E. Klett, review of *Client,* p. 140; November 1, 1999, review of *A Clue for the Puzzle Lady,* p. 128; July, 2001, Rex E. Klett, review of *Cozy,* p. 130; November 1, 2002, Rex E. Klett, review of *A Puzzle in a Pear Tree,* p. 132.

New York Times Book Review, July 15, 1990, Marilyn Stasio, review of *Client,* p. 26; February 7, 1993, Marilyn Stasio, review of *Shot,* p. 28; May 30, 1993, Marilyn Stasio, review of *Actor,* p. 13; April 27, 1997, Marilyn Stasio, review of *Scam,* p. 36; December 12, 1999, review of *A Clue for the Puzzle Lady,* p. 41; July 22, 2001, Marilyn Stasio, review of *Cozy,* p. 22; March 9, 2003, Marilyn Stasio, review of *Manslaughter,* p. 21; November 27, 2005, Marilyn Stasio, review of *Stalking the Puzzle Lady,* p. 30.

People, January 28, 2002, Cathy Burke, review of *Puzzled to Death,* p. 43.

Publishers Weekly, December 18, 1987, review of *Murder,* p. 57; August 19, 1988, Sybil Steinberg, review of *Favor,* pp. 60-61; October 5, 1990, Sybil Steinberg, review of *Juror,* p. 92; April 26, 1991, Sybil Steinberg, review of *Shot,* p. 49; March 8, 1993, review of *Actor,* p. 70; January 10, 1994, review of *Blackmail,* p. 47; January 30, 1995, review of *Movie,* p. 88; December 11, 1995, review of *Trial,* p. 59; January 27, 1997, review of *Scam,* p. 80; October 20, 1997, review of *Suspense,* p. 57; October 25, 1999, review of *A Clue for the Puzzle Lady,* p. 54; August 14, 2000, review of *Last Puzzle and Testament,* p. 332; May 21, 2001, review of *Cozy,* p. 83; November 25, 2002, review of *A Puzzle in a Pear Tree,* p. 47; January 27, 2003, review of *Manslaughter,* p. 239; October 27, 2003, reviews of *Puzzled to Death* and *With This Puzzle, I Thee Kill,* p. 46; October 25, 2004, review of *And a Puzzle to Die On,* p. 32; September 5, 2005, review of *Stalking the Puzzle Lady,* p. 39;

September 11, 2006, review of *You Have the Right to Remain Puzzled,* p. 38; September 10, 2007, review of *Hitman,* p. 43; February 11, 2008, review of *The Sudoku Puzzle Murders,* p. 54.

Reviewer's Bookwatch, November, 2004, Debra Hamel, review of *A Puzzle in a Pear Tree.*

Tribune Books (Chicago, IL), July 2, 1989, review of *Strangler,* pp. 4-5; July 7, 1991, Kevin Moore, review of *Shot,* p. 6.

Wall Street Journal, December 10, 2002, review of *A Puzzle in a Pear Tree,* p. D6.

ONLINE

Internet Movie Database, http://www.imdb.com/ (May 2, 2007), information on author's film work.

MysteryNet.com, http://www.mysterynet.com/ (May 2, 2007), brief profile of author.

Parnell Hall Home Page, http://www.parnellhall.com (May 2, 2007).*

* * *

HAMPL, Patricia 1946-

PERSONAL: Born March 12, 1946, in St. Paul, MN; daughter of Stanley R. (a florist) and Mary (a librarian) Hampl. *Education:* University of Minnesota, B.A., 1968; University of Iowa, M.F.A., 1970.

ADDRESSES: Home—St. Paul, MN. *Office*—Department of English, University of Minnesota, 207 Lind Hall, Minneapolis, MN 55455. *Agent*—Marly Rusoff & Associates, Inc., P.O. Box 524, Bronxville, NY 10708. *E-mail*—hampl@umn.edu.

CAREER: Writer, educator, lecturer, memoirist, and poet. Formerly worked as a sales clerk and telephone operator; KSJN-Radio, St. Paul, MN, editor of *Minnesota Monthly,* 1973-75; freelance editor and writer, 1975-79; University of Minnesota, Minneapolis, visiting assistant professor, 1979-84, associate professor, 1984-89, professor of English, 1989-96, McKnight Distinguished Professor, 1996-97, Regents' Professor, 1997—. Carleton College, Benedict Distinguished Visiting Professor of Literature, 1987; Ball State University, Emens Distinguished Professor, 1989; University of Iowa, Distinguished Visiting Professor of Writing, 1994; West Virginia University, Strum Distinguished Visiting

Writer, 1995; Breadloaf Writers Conference, faculty member, 1995 and 1996; Prague Summer Seminars, permanent faculty member. Founding member of The Loft Literary Center. Lecturer and presenter at universities and professional conferences.

AWARDS, HONORS: Guggenheim Foundation fellowship; National Endowment for the Arts grant, 1976, one other; Bush Foundation fellowship, 1979, one other; Houghton Mifflin literary fellowship, 1981, for *A Romantic Education;* named Distinguished Teacher of the Year, University of Minnesota College of Liberal Arts, 1985; Ingram-Merrill fellowship, 1986; Bellagio resident fellow, Bellagio Study Center of the Rockefeller Foundation, Bellagio, Italy, 1991; MacArthur fellowship, 1990-95; Fulbright fellowship, 1995; McKnight Distinguished University Professorship, 1996; Pushcart Prize, 1999, for short story "The Bill Collector's Vacation"; Minnesota Book Award, 2000, for "The Summer House"; National Book Critics Circle Award finalist in General Nonfiction, 2000, for *I Could Tell You Stories;* Distinguished Achievement Award, Western Literature Association, 2001; Ruth Christie Award for Outstanding Undergraduate Teaching of English, University of Minnesota, 2002; American Academy of Arts and Science, 2007; Minnesota Book Award, 2008, for *The Florist's Daughter;* Camargo Foundation fellow, Cassis, France, 2001; Notable Book of the Year designation, *New York Times Book Review,* for *Virgin Time,* and *Spillville;* Djerassi Foundation fellowship. Recipient of honorary degrees from the College of St. Catherine, the University of St. Thomas, and Luther College.

WRITINGS:

In a Winter Garden (printed piano-vocal score), music by Libby Larsen, E.C. Schirmer (Boston, MA), 1982.

Steven Sorman (essay), Dolan/Maxwell Gallery (Philadelphia, PA), 1986.

(With Steven Sorman) *Spillville,* Milkweed Editions (Minneapolis, MN), 1987.

I Could Tell You Stories: Sojourns in the Land of Memory, Norton (New York, NY), 1999.

(Editor, with Dave Page) F. Scott Fitzgerald, *The St. Paul Stories of F. Scott Fitzgerald,* Borealis Books (St. Paul, MN), 2004.

(Author of foreword) Mary Luddington, *The Nature of Dogs,* Simon & Schuster (New York, NY), 2007.

(Editor, with Elaine Tyler May) *Tell Me True: Memoir, History, and Writing a Life,* Borealis Books (St. Paul, MN), 2008.

MEMOIRS

A Romantic Education, Houghton Mifflin (Boston, MA), 1981, 10th anniversary edition, Norton (New York, NY), 1999.

Virgin Time: In Search of the Contemplative Life, Farrar, Straus, and Giroux (New York, NY), 1992.

Blue Arabesque: A Search for the Sublime, Harcourt (Orlando, FL), 2006.

The Florist's Daughter: A Memoir, Harcourt (Orlando, FL), 2007.

POETRY

Woman Before an Aquarium, University of Pittsburgh Press (Pittsburgh, PA), 1978.

Resort: A Poem, Bookslinger Editions (St. Paul, MN), 1982, revised edition edited by Gerald Costanzo, Carnegie Mellon University Press (Pittsburgh, PA), 2001.

Resort and Other Poems, Houghton Mifflin (Boston, MA), 1983.

(Editor) *Burning Bright: An Anthology of Sacred Poetry,* Ballantine (New York, NY), 1995.

(With Michael Dennis Browne) *2 for 5* (chapbook), Minnesota Center for Book Arts (Minneapolis, MN), 1999.

Contributor to books, including *Best American Short Stories 1977,* edited by Martha Foley, Houghton Mifflin (Boston, MA), 1977; *Walt Whitman: The Measure of His Song,* edited by Jim Perlman, Ed Folsom, and Dan Campion, Holy Cow! Press (Minneapolis, MN), 1981; *Best American Essays 1999;* and *Best American Spiritual Writing,* 2005.

Contributor to periodicals, including *American Poetry Review, New Yorker, Paris Review, New York Times Book Review, Ploughshares, Antaeus, Granta, Iowa Review, Ms., Los Angeles Times, Kenyon Review, Ironwood,* and *Sophisticated Traveler.*

Lamp in the Spine, coeditor, 1971-74; *Houghton Mifflin Anthology of Short Fiction,* contributing editor, Houghton Mifflin, (Boston, MA), 1989; *Iowa Non-Fiction Series,* editor, with Carl Klaus.

Author of screenplay for *Spillville,* 1987.

SIDELIGHTS: Patricia Hampl is best known for her memoirs *A Romantic Education* and *Virgin Time: In Search of the Contemplative Life.* In these books, she reflects on her Roman Catholic upbringing and her adult travels to numerous sites of Catholic history and practice. *A Romantic Education,* in which Hampl relates her journey to Prague to explore her Czech heritage, is generally considered a classic of the memoir genre. Besides being a uniquely personal story, it was also hailed by many commentators as a brilliant portrait of life in Communist Europe in the days of the Iron Curtain.

This dual nature of many memoirs is part of the genre's appeal, according to Hampl. In a *Touchstone* interview she stated: "We like the personal essay not just because it tells us about a person's life, but because it allows an individual, the poor, unarmed, unguarded, individual self an opportunity to investigate something much larger." In addition, Hampl concluded, "What we're interested in is not just the story but the ability of that self to contend with something that's bigger, more difficult, and in some ways maybe requiring expert information to understand."

In *Virgin Time,* Hampl gives an account of her pilgrimage to Assisi—home of Saints Francis and Clare—and to a Franciscan monastery in northern California. She recalls the richness of her early Catholic education, her eventual disillusionment with Roman Catholicism, and her midlife reexamination of it. "Hampl writes with real insight about the intimacies of faith, and at the same time employs language beautifully," wrote Mary Ann Donovan in *America.*

The author blended her own memories with a study of the memoir form in the essay collection *I Could Tell You Stories: Sojourns in the Land of Memory.* It is an "erudite narrative about her life of the mind," according to a *Publishers Weekly* reviewer, who continued: "The passions, concerns and ethical wranglings of this reader, reviewer, poet, historian, family scribe, and theorist . . . converge here as flashes of memoir. . . . Hampl's writing displays many of the tantalizing elements that have distinguished her previous work." *Booklist* critic Donna Seaman termed *I Could Tell You Stories* a "remarkable volume of essays. . . . Lucid and questing, Hampl ponders the spirituality inherent in the work of poets and memoirists, impassioned witnesses to the inner life."

Hampl is also a poet, and in both her prose and poetry she exhibits an elegiac tone and temper. Reviewing *A Romantic Education* in the *New York Times Book Re-*

view, Paul Zweig detected in the book's mixture of personal and cultural history a "mourning" on Hampl's behalf for what he called "the 'greened' America of her adolescence: the failed communes, the moral fervor of the anti-war movement." Though he took exception to Hampl's repetitiveness and "penchant for orotund generality," Zweig described her prose as "strong, at times even brilliant" and praised in particular Hampl's fusion of reality and fantasy. "At its best," he said, *A Romantic Education* "is a quarry of richly imaged lines."

Alfred Corn, also writing in the *New York Times Book Review,* offered a similar commendation for *Resort: A Poem,* Hampl's second volume of poetry. Concerned with what occurs when a love has come to an end, the first half of these poems are, in Corn's words, "a solemn notation of visual particulars and elusive emotions." Corn went on to praise Hampl not only for her "rapturous" descriptions and humor, but especially for her skillful use of metaphor in the unfolding of her somewhat wistful themes.

Blue Arabesque: A Search for the Sublime serves as something of a continuation of the memoir Hampl left off with in *Virgin Time.* As part of her ongoing search for the more sublime experiences in life, Hampl paid a visit to the Art Institute of Chicago, where she was enamored by the works of Matisse. Her examination of Matisse's works, particularly those containing women in exotic or erotic poses, extends to a study of Delacroix, and then beyond painting to the works of other great masters in their fields, such as writers Katherine Mansfield and F. Scott Fitzgerald, filmmaker Jerome Hill, and teacher Doris Derman. She looks not only at their work but also at the lives they led and how life and craft intertwined and nourished each other, even in those artists with self-destructive or depressive tendencies. A reviewer for *Publishers Weekly* wrote: "Hampl proves to be an authoritative and beguiling guide to the joys of leisure and the intellect." Donna Seaman, in a review for *Booklist,* remarked that "Hampl does with words what Matisse does with line and color, that is, reaches to the essence of perception." The *New York Times Book Review* declared *Blue Arabesque* one of the one hundred notable books of the year.

Hampl's work touches on a lighter theme with her contribution to the photography book, *The Nature of Dogs.* Photographer Mary Luddington collects several of her favorite pictures of dogs, taken over a period of

some twenty years, and assembles them with essays from a number of writers and fellow dog lovers. Photographs and essays explore the distinct characteristics and personalities of dogs, the variations between breeds, and the pleasures of having canine companions. *Booklist* reviewer Nancy Bent called the volume "a truly lovely book."

Hampl again turns to the heartfelt memoir in *The Florist's Daughter.* Hampl's "exquisite prose and her knack for memoir writing" are evident in this book about her sometimes restless and troubled life in St. Paul, Minnesota, as the dutiful daughter of her Czech father Stan, the florist of the title, and her Irish mother, Mary, noted Frederic and Mary Ann Brussat on the Web site *Spirituality and Practice.*

As the memoir opens, Hampl is at her dying mother's bedside. With one hand, she holds her mother's own frail hand; with her other, she begins composing her mother's obituary. These two acts symbolize the strong underlying theme of the rest of the memoir: reconciling the tricky balancing act of obligations with a desire to hold on to the past, retaining a firm grip on the people, things, and environments she knows best. She clearly and precisely describes her parents. Her father is cheerful and trusting, an artistic florist whose arrangements were coveted by the St. Paul elite but whose flaws as a businessman led to frequent financial struggle. Hampl portrays her mother, a former librarian, as worldly and keenly intelligent, shrewd in business, cautious if not distrustful, and a natural storyteller with a love for smoking. Between the dramatic opposites of her parents, Hampl developed her own tastes and sense of self, inclining toward literature and the writing that her mother assiduously saved, even on sticky-notes.

Throughout this personal history and memoir, Hampl "speaks to a generation of American women who struggle with responsibility and regrets" as they become the primary caregivers for their elderly parents, *BustedHalo.com* reviewer Christine B. Whelan observed. Hampl reflects on her decision to remain in St. Paul rather than act on the desires of her younger self to seek a more exciting life in a bustling metropolis such as New York or Paris.

Danielle Trussoni, writing in the *New York Times Book Review,* remarked that *The Florist's Daughter* is Hampl's "finest, most powerful book yet." Trussoni, though, commented that the title does not represent the book's brilliant content. A *Kirkus Reviews* critic deemed *The Florist's Daughter* "a memoir for memoirists to admire—with language that pierces."

Hampl herself is conscious of her preoccupation with the past. She once told *CA:* "I suppose I write about all the things I intended to leave behind, to grow out of, or deny: being a Midwesterner, a Catholic, a woman."

BIOGRAPHICAL AND CRITICAL SOURCES:

BOOKS

Hampl, Patricia, *Virgin Time: In Search of the Contemplative Life,* Farrar, Straus (New York, NY), 1992.

Hampl, Patricia, *A Romantic Education,* 10th anniversary edition, Norton (New York, NY), 1999.

Hampl, Patricia, *Blue Arabesque: A Search for the Sublime,* Harcourt (Orlando, FL), 2006.

Hampl, Patricia, *The Florist's Daughter: A Memoir,* Harcourt (Orlando, FL), 2007.

PERIODICALS

America, January 2, 1993, Mary Ann Donovan, review of *Virgin Time: In Search of the Contemplative Life;* October 1, 2007, Sally Cunneen, "Going Home Again," review of *The Florist's Daughter,* p. 30.

Baltimore Sun, April 6, 2008, Susan Reimer, "Poet Plucks at Petals of Her Life."

Booklist, May 1, 1999, Donna Seaman, review of *I Could Tell You Stories: Sojourns in the Land of Memory,* p. 1572; September 15, 2006, Donna Seaman, review of *Blue Arabesque,* p. 16; September 1, 2007, Donna Seaman, review of *The Florist's Daughter,* p. 38; September 15, 2007, Nancy Bent, review of *The Nature of Dogs,* p. 11.

Christian Science Monitor, October 16, 2007, Marjorie Kehe, "Patricia Hampl: A True Daughter of the Midwest," review of *The Florist's Daughter,* p. 13.

Commonweal, February 23, 2007, A.G. Harmon, "Still Life & Matisse," review of *Blue Arabesque: A Search for the Sublime,* p. 20.

Entertainment Weekly, October 27, 2006, Jennifer Reese, review of *Blue Arabesque,* p. 75; October 5, 2007, Jennifer Reese, review of *The Florist's Daughter,* p. 74.

Kirkus Reviews, August 15, 2006, review of *Blue Arabesque,* p. 821; July 1, 2007, review of *The Florist's Daughter.*

Library Journal, September 1, 2007, Rebecca Bollen Manalac, review of *The Florist's Daughter,* p. 144.

MPLS, October 1, 2007, Tad Simons, review of *The Nature of Dogs,* p. 234.

New York Times Book Review, March 29, 1981, Paul Zweig, review of *A Romantic Education;* March 11, 1984, Alfred Corn, review of *Resort: A Poem;* October 7, 2007, Danielle Trussoni, "The Hopelessness of Escape," review of *The Florist's Daughter,* p. 16.

Publishers Weekly, May 3, 1999, review of *I Could Tell You Stories,* p. 57; September 11, 2006, review of *Blue Arabesque,* p. 44; July 9, 2007, review of *The Florist's Daughter,* p. 42.

Reviewer's Bookwatch, February 1, 2007, Molly Beer, review of *Blue Arabesque.*

Star Tribune (Minneapolis-St. Paul, MN), September 28, 2007, Brigitte Frase, review of *The Florist's Daughter.*

Touchstone, Volume 33, 2001, "'We Were Such a Generation'—Memoir, Truthfulness, and History: An Interview with Patricia Hampl," p. 90.

ONLINE

Beth Kephart Books Web log, http://beth-kephart.blog spot.com/ (March 28, 2008), Beth Kephart, review of *The Florist's Daughter.*

Bookreporter.com, http://www.bookreporter.com/ (May 25, 2008), Norah Piehl, review of *The Florist's Daughter.*

BustedHalo.com, http://www.bustedhalo.com/ (May 25, 2008), Christine B. Whelan, "Pure Sex, Pure Love," review of *The Florist's Daughter.*

Catholic Book Journal, http://www.catholicbookjournal. com/ (January 28, 2008), Dan Pierson, review of *The Florist's Daughter;* (January 30, 2008) Kate Budzynski, review of *The Florist's Daughter.*

Compulsive Reader, http://www.compulsivereader.com/ (May 25, 2008), Bob Williams, review of *The Florist's Daughter.*

Marly Rusoff Agency Web site, http://www.rusoffagency. com/ (May 25, 2008), biography of Patricia Hampl.

Patricia Hampl Home Page, http://www.patriciahampl. com (May 25, 2008).

Spirituality and Practice, http://www.spiritualityand practice.com/ (May 25, 2008), Frederic and Mary Ann Brussat, review of *The Florist's Daughter.*

Story Circle Book Reviews, http://www.storycirclebook
reviews.org/ (November 2, 2007), Donna Van Stra-
ten Remmert, review of *The Florist's Daughter.*

Time Out New York, http://www.timeout.com/newyork/
(October 25, 2007), Kelly McMasters, review of
The Florist's Daughter.

Twin Cities Daily Planet, http://www.tcdailyplanet.net/
(April 12, 2008), Anne Nicolai, review of *The
Florist's Daughter.*

*University of Minnesota College of Liberal Arts Web
site,* http://english.cla.umn.edu/ (June 22, 2007),
"Patricia Hampl."

Writing Cabin Web log, http://writingcabin.blogspot.
com/ (October 21, 2007), review of *The Florist's
Daughter.**

*   *   *

HART, Lizzie
See HAINES, Carolyn

*   *   *

HENBEST, Nigel 1951-

PERSONAL: Born May 6, 1951, in Manchester,
Lancashire, England; son of Harold Bernard (a professor) and Rosalind Eve Skone (a psychiatrist) Henbest.
Education: University of Leicester, B.S. (with first class
honors), 1972; Cambridge University, M.S., 1975. *Hobbies and other interests:* Travel, good and homemade
wine, vegetarian food, music.

ADDRESSES: Home and office—Buckinghamshire,
England. *E-mail*—nigel@hencoup.com.

CAREER: Writer, consultant, film producer, and radio
broadcaster. University of Leicester, Leicester, England,
research assistant at Mount Etna, Sicily, 1976-77; *New
Scientist,* London, England, astronomy consultant, 1980-
92; Hencoup Enterprises (consultants), Loosley Row,
Buckinghamshire, England, founder and director.
Pioneer Productions (film production company), founder
and director, productions include *Body Atlas,* a thirteen-
part series, TLC; documentaries *On Jupiter,* Discovery,
and *Black Holes,* C4/Discovery/ABC; *Universe, Edge
of the Universe* and *The Day the Earth was Born,* all
for BBC Channel 4, left company in 2008; and *Chal-*

lenger, C4/National Geographic, 2006. Also British
Broadcasting Corp. (BBC), presenter of the program
Seeing Stars, broadcast by BBC-Radio; chaired the science quiz *The Litmus Test,* BBC Radio 4. Worked as
media consultant to Science and Engineering Research
Council and consultant to Royal Greenwich Observa-
tory.

MEMBER: British Astronomical Association (past
public relations officer), Royal Astronomical Society,
Association of British Science Writers.

AWARDS, HONORS: Special award, outstanding series
on engineering and technology, New York Academy of
Sciences, 1978, for *Space Frontiers;* Gold Medal for
Science and Technology, New York Television Awards,
1994 and 1996; Banff Rockie Award, 1995, for popular
science programs; Glaxo-Wellcome-Science Writers'
Award, Association of British Science Writers, 1999,
for the television series *Universe;* Children's Science
Book Award, New York Academy of Sciences; Senior
Information Book Award, *Times Educational Supple-
ment;* asteroid 3795 "Nigel" in honor of author,
International Astronomical Union, 2006.

WRITINGS:

The Exploding Universe, Macmillan (New York, NY),
1979.

Spotter's Guide to the Night Sky (juvenile), illustrated
by Michael Roffe, Mayflower (London, England),
1979, updated edition published as *The Night Sky,*
Usborne (London, England), 2006.

Mysteries of the Universe, Van Nostrand (New York,
NY), 1981, published as *The Mysterious Universe,*
Ebury Press (London, England), 1981.

(With Michael Marten) *The New Astronomy,* Cambridge
University Press (New York, NY), 1983, revised
edition, 1996.

(Editor) *Observing the Universe,* Blackwell/New
Scientist (Oxford, England), 1984.

Comets, Stars, Planets, Admiral (Lancashire, England),
1985.

(Editor) *Halley's Comet,* New Science Publications
(London, England), 1985.

(With Michael Bennett) *It's All in the Stars!* (play),
Molecule Theater of Science, 1989.

The Universe, Weidenfeld & Nicolson (London,
England), 1992.

Universe: A Computer-generated Voyage Through Time and Space, Macmillan (New York, NY), 1992.

The Planets: A Guided Tour of Our Solar System Through the Eyes of America's Space Probes, Viking (New York, NY), 1992.

The Planets (juvenile), Ladybird (New York, NY), 1996.

Space Hopping (juvenile), Hamlyn (London, England), 1999.

WITH HEATHER COUPER

Space Frontiers (juvenile), edited by Christopher Cooper, Viking (New York, NY), 1978.

All about Space (juvenile), edited by Christopher Cooper, Marshall Cavendish (Freeport, NY), 1981.

The Restless Universe, Philip and Son (London, England), 1982.

Astronomy (juvenile), F. Watts (New York, NY), 1983.

Physics (juvenile), F. Watts (New York, NY), 1983.

The Planets (also see below), Pan Books (London, England), 1985, published as *New Worlds: In Search of Planets,* Addison-Wesley (Reading, MA), 1986.

The Sun, F. Watts (New York, NY), 1986.

The Moon, F. Watts (New York, NY), 1986.

Galaxies and Quasars, F. Watts (New York, NY), 1986.

Telescopes and Observatories, F. Watts (New York, NY), 1987.

Spaceprobes and Satellites, F. Watts (New York, NY), 1987.

Guide to the Galaxy, Cambridge University Press (New York, NY), 1988.

The Stars, Pan Books (London, England), 1988.

The Space Atlas, Dorling Kindersley (New York, NY), 1992.

The Guide to the Galaxy, Cambridge University Press (New York, NY), 1994.

How the Universe Works, Dorling Kindersley (New York, NY), 1994.

Black Holes, Dorling Kindersley (New York, NY), 1996.

Big Bang, DK Publishing (New York, NY), 1996.

Is Anybody out There?, DK Publishing (New York, NY), 1998.

To the Ends of the Universe, Dorling Kindersley (New York, NY), 1998.

Universe, Channel 4 Books (London, England), 1999.

DK Space Encyclopedia, DK Publishing (New York, NY), 1999.

Mars: The Inside Story of the Red Planet, Headline (London, England), 2001.

Extreme Universe, Channel 4 Books (London, England), 2001.

The History of Astronomy, foreword by Arthur C. Clarke, Firefly Books (Buffalo, NY), 2007.

Philip's Stargazing (revised edition), Philip's (London, England), 2007.

TELEVISION SCRIPTS

(With G. Jones) *IRAS: The Infrared Eye,* BBC-TV, 1985.

(With Heather Couper) *The Planets* (based on Couper and Henbest's book of the same title), Moving Picture Co., 1986.

Space Shuttle Discovery, Channel 4 (London, England), 1993.

Universe (series), The Learning Channel, 1999.

Edge of the Universe (series), Channel 4 (London, England), 2002.

Planets from Hell, The Learning Channel, 2002.

Columnist for *Independent;* former columnist, *European* and *Focus.* Contributor to encyclopedias. Contributor to periodicals, including *Sunday Times, Guardian, Popular Astronomy, Astronomy, Christian Science Monitor, Newton, Journal of Vulcanology, Geothermal Research, Journal of Physics,* and *British Archaeological Reports.* Editor, *Journal of the British Astronomical Association,* 1985-87.

Author's books and articles have been translated into twenty-seven languages.

SIDELIGHTS: Considered clear and understandable by critics, Nigel Henbest's books fill a literary black hole by guiding the reader through many of the most important achievements in astronomy and science in the past twenty-five years. In *The Exploding Universe,* Henbest provides a synopsis of the most outstanding developments in the sciences, from cosmology to physics, in the 1970s. Henbest and coauthor Heather Couper, in *New Worlds: In Search of Planets,* provide new information about the planets gathered by the fleet of interplanetary space probes sent out during the 1980s and update current information in language understandable to the general reading public.

The New Astronomy concentrates on observational techniques and provides depictions of new findings gathered by radio, infrared, ultraviolet, X-ray, and gamma ray exploration of space. Colin Ronan, writing for the *Times Literary Supplement*, claimed that Henbest's *The New Astronomy* is "the first [book] to present and explain 'new astronomy' to a wide public—[and] deserves every success."

Henbest once told *CA:* "Astronomy is one of the few areas of science that the average person finds fascinating. By writing about the sky, its beauty and its mysteries, an author can not only grip his audience, but also impart—in a most gentle way—an understanding of how science and scientists work.

"When I began my career as an author, I was doing research at Cambridge, under the then Astronomer Royal. As a research scientist, I was learning more and more—about less and less! In my case, that meant the exploding gases from a supernova that went off over 400 years ago.

"At the same time, there were very few people with a professional background who could—or who wanted to—explain astronomy to the public. So I moved into the field, and (somewhat to my surprise) found a virtually unlimited market for astronomy titles."

Henbest more recently added: "*Mars: The Inside Story of the Red Planet,* written with Couper, is a no-holds-barred investigation of the mysteries of Mars, including behind-the-scenes revelations about the supposed 'Martian fossils' and the very real possibility that the Viking probes of the National Aeronautic and Space Administration (NASA) did detect Martian life in 1976. In our research we traveled to meet over fifty leading Mars experts, both inside and outside NASA, including British and Russian researchers, as well as Americans. Much of what they told us has never been published in book form before."

In books such as *The Planets: A Guided Tour of Our Solar System Through the Eyes of America's Space Probes* and *Universe: A Computer-Generated Voyage Through Time and Space,* the author employs modern technology to provide a more comprehensive view of his topics. A *Publishers Weekly* contributor called *The Planets* "a fine . . . tour from a veteran guide to the solar system."

Henbest also continues his collaboration with Couper, producing numerous books explaining complex astronomical and scientific ideas, discoveries, and theories to

a young audience. For example, *How the Universe Works* provides an education in astronomy through various activities, from the simple project of obtaining a core sample from a bar of ice cream to building a model of a space probe. Writing for *Booklist,* Carolyn Phelan commented that the book's "format will make this an attractive choice."

In *Big Bang,* the authors discuss the big bang theory of the origin of the universe. The book includes double-page spreads of paintings and smaller illustrations that the authors use to enhance their explanation of what the theory is and its implications for understanding the universe. Carolyn Phelan, writing for *Booklist,* called *Big Bang* "enthusiastic and visually dynamic . . . offering on a complex topic."

Black Holes was called "a wonderfully readable introduction to a complicated subject" by *Booklist* contributor Chris Sherman. Henbest and Couper examine scientific luminaries who played a role in the eventual discovery of black holes, including Albert Einstein and Stephen Hawking. They also delve into some of the theories and issues associated with these galactic phenomena, including the idea that our universe may be a black hole. A *Publishers Weekly* contributor remarked that the authors "tackle a mystifying phenomenon."

In *DK Space Encyclopedia,* Henbest and Couper arrange their topics thematically as they discuss astronomical discoveries, equipment, and concepts. The book includes an index, time line, glossary, brief biographies, and astronomical names. The book also features "Find Out More" references, via which the authors connect concepts throughout the book, and the *Eyewitness Encyclopedia of Space and the Universe* CD-ROM. "Both adults and children will appreciate the nice overview," wrote a contributor to *Booklist.*

Mary Romano Marks, writing for *Booklist,* called *Is Anybody out There?* a "visually exciting examination [that] looks at both the myth and the science" concerning ponderings about extraterrestrial life. Among the topics discussed by Henbest and Couper are what aliens could look like and potential ways to communicate with them. The book includes a fold-out board game.

The History of Astronomy, also written by Henbest and Couper, provides and in-depth look at how the science of astronomy was born and developed into an ultramodern science with the help of advanced telescope technology. With the help of numerous pictures and illustrations, the authors examine the various eras of astronomy, "from the earliest archaeo-astronomical efforts by cultures around the world to the very latest efforts of 21st century astronomy to push back the frontiers of our understanding of the universe," as noted by William Nedblake in a review for the *Science Books Reviewed* Web site. The authors examine the major figures in the history of astronomy, dating back to the ancient Egyptians and Greeks. In addition to Galileo, the authors' include discussions of Nicolaus Copernicus, Tyco Brahe, Asaph Halley, and Isaac Newton. Among the modern-era contributors discussed by the authors are Percival Lowell, Albert Einstein, Edwin Hubble, and Frank Drake. Henbest and Couper also examine many of the early devices used for astronomical studies, such as Antikythera Mechanism. First discovered in 1900, this ancient device is believed to be a simple type of computer that ancients used to calculate the positions of the stars and planets. In terms of past astronomy, the authors also pay special attention to the important contributions made by the Arabic and Asian cultures. *Sky & Telescope* contributor Jeff Kanipe noted that, "if you've never been a big fan of astronomy history . . . chances are you'll want to read this book cover to cover." In his review for *Booklist,* Gilbert Taylor commented that "the authors' enthusiasm should excite readers new to the subject."

BIOGRAPHICAL AND CRITICAL SOURCES:

PERIODICALS

Astronomy, December, 1994, John Shibley, review of *The Guide to the Galaxy,* p. 114; January, 1997, review of *The New Astronomy,* p. 102.

Booklist, June 1, 1994, Carolyn Phelan, review of *How the Universe Works,* p. 1806; August, 1996, Chris Sherman, review of *Black Holes,* p. 1892; June 1, 1997, Carolyn Phelan, review of *Big Bang,* p. 1690; July 1, 1998, Mary Romano Marks, review of *Is Anybody out There?,* p. 1874; February 1, 2000, review of *DK Space Encyclopedia,* p. 1040; December 1, 2007, Gilbert Taylor, review of *The History of Astronomy,* p. 16.

Publishers Weekly, March 23, 1992, review of *Universe: A Computer-generated Voyage Through Time and Space,* p. 52; December 14, 1992, review of *The Planets: A Guided Tour of Our Solar System Through the Eyes of America's Space Probes,* p. 51; May 20, 1996, review of *Black Holes,* p. 259.

Science News, January 26, 2008, review of *The History of Astronomy,* p. 63.

Sky & Telescope, July, 2008, Jeff Kanipe, "Astronomy's Storied Past," review of *The History of Astronomy,* p. 44.

Statesman, March 4, 2009, "Stargazing."

Teacher Librarian, December, 1999, Jessica Higgs, review of *Big Bang,* p. 54; December, 1999, Jessica Higgs, review of *Black Holes,* p. 54.

Times Literary Supplement, February 17, 1984, Colin Ronan, review of *The New Astronomy.*

ONLINE

British Rocketry Oral History Programme Web site, http://www.brohp.org.uk/ (June 23, 2009), biography of author.

David Higham Associates Web site, http://www.david higham.co.uk/ (June 24, 2009), profile of author.

Nigel Henbest Home Page, http://www.hencoup.com (June 23, 2009).

Science Books Reviewed, http://sciencebooksreviewed. blogspot.com/ (April 11, 2008), William Nedblake, review of *The History of Astronomy.*

Why Is Space Important?, http://whyscience.co.uk/ (April 21, 2009), "Nigel Henbest: Moving on from Gods and Demons," short profile of author and brief interview.*

*   *   *

HOSPITAL, Janette Turner 1942-
(Alex Juniper)

PERSONAL: Born November 12, 1942, in Melbourne, Victoria, Australia; daughter of Adrian C. (a painter) and Elsie Turner; married Clifford G. Hospital (a professor), February 5, 1965; children: Geoffrey, Cressida. *Education:* University of Queensland, St. Lucia, Brisbane, Australia, B.A., 1966, D.Litt, 2003; Queen's University, Kingston, Ontario, Canada, M.A., 1973; Griffith University, Australia, D.Univ., 1996.

ADDRESSES: Home—Boston, MA; Brisbane, Queensland, Australia; and Kingston, Ontario, Canada. *E-mail*—hospitjt@mailbox.sc.edu.

CAREER: Writer and educator. High school teacher of English in Brisbane, Australia, 1963-66; Harvard University, Cambridge, MA, librarian, 1967-71;

Queen's University, Kingston, Ontario, Canada, teaching fellow, 1971-74; teacher of English at several institutions, including St. Lawrence College 1973-82; lecturer in English literature at federal penitentiaries, Kingston, 1975-76; writer in residence at various institutions, including Massachusetts Institute of Technology, Boston, MA, 1985-86, 1987, 1989; University of Ottawa, Canada, 1987; University of Sydney, Australia, 1989; La Trobe University, Melbourne, 1989; and Boston University, Boston, fall, 1991; La Trobe University, adjunct professor of English, 1991-93; University of South Carolina, Columbia, Carolina Distinguished Professor of English, c. 2003.

AWARDS, HONORS: Ontario graduate fellow, 1972-73; Canadian Council doctoral fellow, 1974-75; Atlantic First Citation, *Atlantic Monthly,* 1978; gold medal, Canadian National Magazine Awards, 1980, for travel writing; citation from *Atlantic Monthly,* 1982, for story "Waiting"; Seal First Novel Award, Seal Books, 1982, for *The Ivory Swing;* CBC Literary Prize, 1986, for short story; Fellowship of Australian Writers award, 1988, for *Dislocations;* Torgi award, Canadian Association for the Blind, 1988; Australian National Book Council award, 1989; Queensland Premier's Literary Award, 2003, and Davitt Award from Sisters in Crime for "best crime novel of the year by an Australian woman," both for *Due Preparations for the Plague;* Patrick White Award, 2003, for lifetime literary achievement; Doctor of Letters honoris causa, University of Queensland, 2003; Russell Research Award for Humanities and Social Sciences, University of South Carolina, 2003.

WRITINGS:

NOVELS

The Ivory Swing, McClelland & Stewart (Toronto, Ontario, Canada), 1982, Dutton (New York, NY), 1983.
The Tiger in the Tiger Pit, Dutton (New York, NY), 1983.
Borderline, Dutton (New York, NY), 1985.
Charades, Bantam (New York, NY), 1989.
(As Alex Juniper) *A Very Proper Death,* Penguin (Melbourne, Victoria, Australia), 1990, Scribner (New York, NY), 1991.
The Last Magician, Holt (New York, NY), 1992.
Oyster, W.W. Norton & Company (New York, NY), 1998.

Due Preparations for the Plague, Norton (New York, NY), 2003.
Orpheus Lost (novel), W.W. Norton (New York, NY), 2007.

SHORT STORIES

Dislocations, Norton (New York, NY), 1986.
Isobars, University of Queensland Press (New York, NY), 1990.
Collected Stories, 1970-1995, University of Queensland Press (Brisbane, Queensland, Australia), 1995.
North of Nowhere, South of Loss, University of Queensland Press (Lucia, Queensland, Australia), 2003, W.W. Norton (New York, NY), 2004.

Work represented in anthologies, including *CBC Anthology.* Contributor of stories to magazines in Canada, the United States, England, and Australia, including the periodicals *Atlantic Monthly, Canadian Forum, Commonweal, North American Review, Queen's Quarterly, Saturday Night,* and *Yale Review.*

SIDELIGHTS: Janette Turner Hospital once told *CA:* "I have lived for extended periods in Australia, the United States, Canada, England, and India, and I am very conscious of being at ease in many countries but belonging nowhere. All my writing reflects this. My characters are always caught between worlds or between cultures or between subcultures."

"All my writing," she commented in *Contemporary Novelists,* "in a sense, revolves around the mediation of one culture (or subculture) to another." It is, an essayist observed in the same source, "intellectually sophisticated writing which spirals through mysteries and indeterminacies but never loosens its tug on the senses. Much of [Hospital's] work is about the borderlines of things, of art and self, of time and space." The writer went on to note: "Intellectually compelling yet fiery and dynamic, her work is baroque, elegant yet with a sensuous energy and immediacy."

Hospital's first novel, *The Ivory Swing,* tells the story of a university professor's wife who goes with her husband and children to India for a year and wrestles during that time with the questions of love and marriage, and of freedom—both her own and what the concept means in another culture. Christopher Schemering, writing in *Washington Post Book World,* described it as "a disturbing meditation on the clash of cultures and the rebellion and feminine rage in each." Gail Pearce, writing for *Quill and Quire*, called *The Ivory Swing* "compelling and enjoyable reading" and reported that "the plot is well constructed [and] the characters are plausible and sympathetic."

The Tiger in the Tiger Pit, Hospital's second novel, derives its name from T.S. Eliot's "Lines for an Old Man," the author told *CA.* The story centers on the members of the unhappy, patriarchal Carpenter family, who, as Judith Fitzgerald noted in *Books in Canada,* "display a perverse tendency for chaos." Clare Colvin, in a review for *Books and Bookmen,* remarked that Hospital "portrays the claustrophobic web of family relationships with perception."

Hospital's fascination with borders is obvious not only in the title of her third novel, *Borderline,* but in its plot as well, in which a couple help an injured South American woman who is attempting to cross the border between the United States and Canada. In the *New York Times Book Review,* Cheri Fein labeled Hospital's third novel "by far her most complex and disturbing." M.G. Vassanji observed in *Books in Canada* that *Borderline* contains "echoes . . . of Conrad, parallels in theme and form with Renaissance art, allusions to Indian mythology" and interpreted the borderline of the title as "a metaphor for other barriers," particularly in interpersonal relationships. Writing in *Saturday Night,* Elspeth Cameron called *Borderline* "a coup" in which Hospital "brings to the fore political issues that seemed slight and redundant in her first two novels (though not in some of her stories), and through symbolic parallels integrates their startling relevance with her almost existentialist musings on the nature of reality, perception, and art."

Hospital's novel *Charades,* in the words of *New York Times Book Review* writer Ron Loewinsohn, "manages to combine images from our Judeo-Christian myth of origin—the Garden of Eden story—with metaphors and concepts from quantum physics and cosmology" in the tale of a young Australian graduate student who seeks to piece together her sketchy past during an affair she initiates with a professor of cosmology. She does this by entertaining her lover, a la Scheherazade, with nightly stories—her guesses about her past, her parents, her life—and by the end has woven together an incomplete but acceptable truth for herself. Linda Barrett Osborne, writing in *Washington Post Book*

World, described Hospital's prose in *Charades* as "clever and lyrical, and her characterization superb," and Alan Cheuse, writing for the Chicago *Tribune,* praised the novel's "mixture of intelligence and sensuality, idea and deeply felt drama."

The Last Magician begins with strong Dantean allusions that foreshadow the hellish Sydney catacombs that house the Quarry, an area of destitution and depravity. This is where the "last magician," photographer and filmmaker Charlie Chang, and other characters go in search of Cat, the lost figure around whom the story revolves. The first of Hospital's novels to be set wholly in Australia, where the author has tended to spend more and more of her time through the years, garnered praise from major review journals. In the opinion of Aamer Hussein in *Times Literary Supplement, The Last Magician* surpassed "even the excellent *Borderline,* and should establish [Hospital] as one of the most powerful and innovative writers in English today."

Hussein found the book "unashamedly dense with ideas: reflections on the art of photography collide with meditations on science; Taoist citations . . . intertwine with a critique of contemporary literary norms (many of which Hospital challenges and brilliantly contravenes)." Writing in the *New York Times Book Review,* Edward Hower lauded Hospital for knowing "how to cast a spell that makes us as eager as her narrator to uncover the truth," and added that Hospital "fills her novel with evocative settings, characters we care deeply about and language that is entrancingly lyrical." In *Washington Post Book World,* Carol Anshaw criticized Hospital's lapses into overwrought writing but acknowledged that risk as inherent in "trying to pull off a highwire act." Anshaw added: "The up-side of the author's full-tilt style is that, when the prose and ideas of this book resonate against each other, the result is passages of stunning clarity and beauty."

Comparing Hospital's novels with the short stories in her second collection, *Isobars,* Hussein noted that the latter "collide with, and diverge from, her novels, finishing incomplete phrases, casting light on distant corners, indicating new projects." In the *New York Times Book Review,* Richard Burgin found the prose in these stories "too feverish and preachy" at times and the irony "too heavy-handed." He concluded, however, that "much more often [Hospital is] able to fuse her disparate talents and concerns to create an original, convincing vision of our struggles with ourselves and others, and with our memories and dreams."

Hospital took on the pseudonym of Alex Juniper for her mystery-thriller *A Very Proper Death*. Working as a real estate broker in Boston, Marni Verstak has a complicated life. She is hiding the existence of her son Matthew from his homosexual father, Anderson Thorpe, III, who is dying of AIDS. However, Marni receives a mysterious phone call saying that Matthew is dead, a statement that almost comes true when Matthew is nearly killed later in a mysterious car wreck. In the meantime, the renovator of a house that Marni owns in a drug-infested neighborhood is killed on the job. When Anderson is also found murdered, Marni is the main suspect after police discover that she was hiding Matthew. A *Publishers Weekly* contributor noted that the author "embroils her heroine in a suspenseful and complex plot."

In her novel *Oyster*, Hospital tells the story of Outer Maroo, a remote town in the Australian outback, and a charlatan named Oyster. When Oyster arrives in Outer Maroo, the town is largely populated by opal miners and religious fanatics, and he establishes an apocalyptic-driven cult and even sways the rough miners in his favor by offering to tell them where they can find a large amount of precious opals. However, when two parents looking for their missing children also come to town, the townspeople are unaware that their presence will lead toward their own personal Armageddon. The story is told after-the-fact by a young girl who got caught up in the cult. Bill Ott, writing in *Booklist,* called *Oyster* "a genuinely hypnotic novel." This critique was generally upheld by numerous other critics. A contributor to the *Economist* referred to the novel as "highly readable." In her review in *People*, Emily Mitchell commented that the author "writes with brilliance and originality." Several reviewers also noted the author's ability to produce a good mystery with literary overtones. Carolyn Bliss, writing in *World Literature Today,* referred to the novel as "an old-fashioned page-turner which offers up an intriguing mystery."

Due Preparations for the Plague revolves around a 1987 terrorist hijacking of an Air France plane that results in the death of the young Lowell Hawthorne's mother. As an adult, Lowell has never gotten over his mother's death, and this has led to his failed marriage and his being the single father of two young children. Eventually, Samantha, the child of another person who died in the hijacking, convinces Lowell that the true story of the hijacking has been classified by the government. When Lowell uncovers evidence that Samantha may be right the two set out to discover what the government is hiding. As noted by most reviewers, the novel is not a typical thriller but instead focuses on the horrors of terrorism and how people must confront their fears about it. "Much of this novel is excruciatingly painful . . . but the pain is never gratuitous or sensationalistic," Ott wrote in *Booklist.*

Due Preparations for the Plague generally received widespread praise from critics, especially for the author's literary approach to the thriller genre. For example, a *Kirkus Reviews* contributor referred to the novel as "strong stuff: an accomplished fusion of doomsday thriller and mordant morality play." Another reviewer writing in *Publishers Weekly* noted that the author's "sophisticated psychological thriller offers a thought-provoking glimpse of the sociopolitical intricacies of the individuals and organizations that track terrorism, as well as of the enduring personal struggles of those left behind after an attack."

Hospital's short-story collection *North of Nowhere, South of Loss* presents a wide range of characters in various circumstances that reveal how their interior lives are bound together by their memories and, more often than not, confused remembrances. For example, in the story "For Mr Voss or Occupant," a woman renting a house receives mysterious mail and is eventually confused with the house's former tenant, a case of mistaken identity that has deadly consequences. Many of the stories, however, focus on Philippa and Brian, whose long-distance friendship is followed until Brian eventually succumbs to mental illness and death in the final story about the two friends titled "Night Train."

Misha Stone, writing in *Booklist,* referred to the short-story collection as "riveting," and also noted that the author's "characters are continually in search of a homeland they may never return to" again. Other critics also praised the collection, including Kellie Gillespie, who wrote in the *Library Journal* that the author has "set a new standard for the short story genre that will be hard to surpass." A *Kirkus Reviews* contributor summed up a review by noting: "Stylistically demanding, sometimes overly so, but unforgettable. This woman can write."

The inspiration for *Orpheus Lost* came to Hospital in 2003 when she was visiting Boston. In the Harvard Square subway station she was watching and listening to a young violinist perform, when she suddenly realized that he was "the perfect contemporary image of Orpheus in the Underworld," as she explained to *Curled*

Up with a Good Book Web site interviewer Luan Gaines. This image prompted Hospital to write a retelling of the Orpheus myth, but with a feminist perspective. In the myth, Orpheus is a gifted musician who falls in love with Eurydice. When she dies, Orpheus bargains with the god of the underworld to give her back. The god agrees, but insists that Orpheus must not look back as he leads Eurydice back up to the world of the living. At the last minute, however, Orpheus cannot help glancing back to make sure Eurydice is following him—and at that instant, loses her forever. In retelling this story, Hospital wanted to make Eurydice more than just a passive figure, waiting to be rescued. In an interview with *Critique* contributor Donald J. Greiner, Hospital said that "in the myth, she's simply a lovely young woman gathering flowers when the snake bites her and she dies, but obviously a modern Eurydice would have to be more than a flower gatherer. She must have some interest in music, or why would [she and Orpheus] be attracted?"

Hospital decided to make her Eurydice figure, Leela, a mathematics student at MIT. Her Orpheus figure, Mishka, is in a Ph.D. program in music at Harvard. What begins as a simple love story between them quickly darkens when a suicide bomber attacks Boston's Prudential tower; more attacks follow. Mishka, who plays Middle Eastern music at a local cafe and visits a local mosque, becomes a suspect. Cobb Slaughter, the chief investigator on the case, grew up with Leela and now subjects her to harsh interrogation about her lover. Is Mishka really the innocent man he purports to be? Or has Leela been duped?

As Hospital told Greiner: "I've always been interested in how people negotiate the rest of their lives in the wake of catastrophic events. . . . It has simply been the nature of life in the last decade that those catastrophes are now more likely to arise from political upheaval and terrorism than from familial issues. I absorb what is around me in the air. There's also the fact that I've had a couple of close brushes with political cataclysm myself. That gives a novelist visceral input."

Reviewers appreciated the novel's suspenseful plot as well as its evocation of a dystopian America and its exploration of serious moral themes. Claudia Smith Brinson, writing in the Columbia, South Carolina *State*, described the book as "beautifully written and disturbing." *Critique* contributor Peter Craven also lavished

praise on the book, noting its "pitch perfect" exposure of counterterrorism being another form of terror. *Orpheus Lost*, wrote Craven, is "a book not only about the reality of terrorism but also a novel in which terrorism is the engulfing fog through which the characters wander as if in a dark wood enclosing hell, from which they strike with a sadism born of the warping of love." A writer for *Publishers Weekly* acknowledged the book's "timely, provocative premise," but found the novel marred by "florid" prose. Valerie Miner, writing in the *Boston Globe*, also identified some weaknesses in the novel, noting that "coincidences and premonitions are [occasionally] too easy. And the metaphors become labored." But Miner praised the book's timely and insightful exploration of difficult issues, concluding that *Orpheus Lost* is "a rich, wise, alarming novel" that "poses provocative challenges about individual agency in public and private spheres. Hospital understands that we each write the headlines. She leaves readers feeling hope and grief and a terrible sense of urgency about our lives at this fragile moment in history."

BIOGRAPHICAL AND CRITICAL SOURCES:

BOOKS

Contemporary Literary Criticism, Volume 42, Gale (Detroit, MI), 1987.
Contemporary Novelists, St. James Press (Detroit, MI), 6th edition, 1996.

PERIODICALS

American Libraries, September 1, 2007, "Janette Turner Hospital and Me," p. 84.
Antigonish Review, September 22, 2006, Melinda Price Wiltshire, review of *Due Preparations for the Plague,* p. 101.
Antipodes, May 15, 2003, "Patrick White Award," p. 1618; June, 2004, Richard Carr, "'Just Enough Religion to Make Us Hate': The Case of Tourmaline and Oyster," p. 9, and Nathanael O'Reilly, review of *Due Preparations for the Plague,* p. 88.
Australian, May 19, 2007, reader review of *Orpheus Lost.*
Booklist, March 15, 1998, Bill Ott, review of *Oyster,* p. 1203; May 15, 2003, review of *Due Preparations for the Plague,* p. 1618; January 1, 2004, review of *Due Preparations for the Plague,* p. 776;

August, 2004, Misha Stone, review of *North of Nowhere, South of Loss,* p. 1899; August 1, 2004, Misha Stone, review of *North of Nowhere, South of Loss,* p. 1899; September 15, 2007, Bill Ott, review of *Orpheus Lost,* p. 34.

Books and Bookmen, August, 1984, Clare Colvin, review of *The Tiger in the Tiger Pit,* pp. 33-34.

Books in Canada, November 9, 1983, Judith Fitzgerald, review of *The Tiger in the Tiger Pit,* p. 33; January-February, 1986, M.G. Vassanji, review of *Borderline,* p. 27.

Boston Globe, December 16, 2007, Valerie Miner, review of *Orpheus Lost.*

Bulletin with Newsweek, May 22, 2007, "A Fine Rendition," p. 64.

Chicago Tribune, March 13, 1989, Alan Cheuse, review of *Charades.*

CRITIQUE: Studies in Contemporary Fiction, June 22, 2007, Peter Craven, "Beauty in Terror: Janette Turner Hospital's *Orpheus Lost,*" p. 355; June 22, 2007, Donald J. Greiner, "Ideas of Order in Janette Turner Hospital's *Oyster,*" p. 381, David Callahan, "Particles, Waves, and Stories: Janette Turner Hospital's *Charades,*" p. 363, and Donald J. Greiner, "The 'God Itch': An Interview with Janette Turner Hospital," p. 331.

Economist, July 11, 1998, review of *Oyster,* p. S17.

Entertainment Weekly, July 18, 2003, Rebecca Ascher-Walsh, review of *Due Preparations for the Plague,* p. 81; October 29, 2004, Jennifer Reese, review of *North of Nowhere, South of Loss,* p. 72.

Kirkus Reviews, May 1, 2003, review of *Due Preparations for the Plague,* p. 629; August 1, 2004, review of *North of Nowhere, South of Loss,* p. 705; August 1, 2004, review of *North of Nowhere, South of Loss,* p. 705; August 1, 2007, review of *Orpheus Lost.*

Library Journal, June 1, 2003, Lawrence Rungren, review of *Due Preparations for the Plague,* p. 166; August, 2004, Kellie Gillespie, review of *North of Nowhere, South of Loss,* p. 72; August 1, 2004, Kellie Gillespie, review of *North of Nowhere, South of Loss,* p. 72; August 1, 2007, Barbara Hoffert, review of *Orpheus Lost,* p. 68.

New Yorker, December 10, 2007, review of *Orpheus Lost,* p. 113.

New York Times Book Review, April 15, 1984, Mona Simpson, review of *The Tiger in the Tiger Pit,* p. 22; September 1, 1985, Cheri Fein, review of *Borderline,* p. 8; March 12, 1989, Ron Loewinsohn, review of *Charades,* p. 14; September 29, 1991, Richard Burgin, review of *Isobars,* p. 18; September 13, 1992, Edward Hower, review of *The*

Last Magician, p. 15; September 7, 2003, Richard Eder, review of *Due Preparations for the Plague,* p. 29.

People, March 30, 1998, Emily Mitchell, review of *Oyster,* p. 31.

Publishers Weekly, May 17, 1991, review of *A Very Proper Death,* p. 57; January 12, 1998, review of *Oyster,* p. 44; June 2, 2003, review of *Due Preparations for the Plague,* p. 32; October 18, 2004, review of *North of Nowhere, South of Loss,* p. 49; October 18, 2004, review of *North of Nowhere, South of Loss,* p. 49; August 20, 2007, review of *Orpheus Lost,* p. 43.

Quill and Quire, October, 1982, Gail Pearce, review of *The Ivory Swing,* p. 31.

Saturday Night, April, 1986, Elspeth Cameron, review of *Borderline,* pp. 57-59.

State (Columbia, SC), October 10, 2007, Claudia Smith Brinson, review of *Orpheus Lost.*

Time, April 6, 1998, John Skow, review of *Oyster,* p. 77.

Times Literary Supplement, July 3, 1992, Aamer Hussein, review of *The Last Magician,* p. 25; October 29, 1993, review of *The Ivory Swing,* p. 22.

Washington Post Book World, June 5, 1983, Christopher Schemering, review of *The Ivory Swing,* p. 10; February 26, 1989, Linda Barrett Osborne, review of *Charades,* p. 8; August 30, 1992, Carol Anshaw, review of *The Last Magician,* p. 8.

World Literature Today, autumn, 1997, Carolyn Bliss, review of *Oyster,* p. 861; May-August, 2004, Carolyn Bliss, review of *Due Preparations for the Plague,* p. 78.

ONLINE

Blogcritics.org, http://blogcritics.org/ (January 23, 2006), Gordon Hauptfleisch, review of *Due Preparations for the Plague.*

Curled Up with a Good Book, http://www.curledup.com/ (July 30, 2008), Luan Gaines, interview with Hospital, and review of *Orpheus Lost.*

Janette Turner Hospital Home Page, http://www.janetteturnerhospital.com (July 30, 2008).

Mostly Fiction, http://www.mostlyfiction.com/ (July 30, 2008), Mary Whipple, review of *Orpheus Lost.*

PopMatters, http://www.popmatters.com/ (June 10, 2003), Nikki Tranter, review of *Due Preparations for the Plague.*

University of Queensland Alumni Web site, http://www.alumni.uq.edu.au/ (April 4, 2007), "Dr. Janette Turner Hospital, Acclaimed Author."*

HUMPHREYS, Susan L.
   See LOWELL, Susan

*   *   *

HURWITZ, Gregg 1973-
   (Gregg Andrew Hurwitz)

PERSONAL: Born August 12, 1973. *Education:* Harvard University, B.A., 1995; Trinity College, Oxford University, M.A., 1996.

ADDRESSES: Agent—Aaron Priest Literary Agency, 708 3rd Ave., 23rd Fl., New York, NY 10017. *E-mail*—gregghurwitzbooks@gmail.com.

CAREER: Writer and educator. Creator of television show for Warner Brothers Studios. University of Southern California, instructor in fiction writing; Harvard University, guest lecturer; University of California, Los Angeles, guest lecturer.

AWARDS, HONORS: Knox Fellow.

WRITINGS:

NOVELS

The Tower, Simon & Schuster (New York, NY), 1999.
Minutes to Burn, Cliff Street Books (New York, NY), 2001.
Do No Harm, Morrow (New York, NY), 2002.
The Kill Clause, Morrow (New York, NY), 2003.
The Program, Morrow (New York, NY), 2004.
Troubleshooter, Morrow (New York, NY), 2005.
Last Shot, Morrow (New York, NY), 2006.
The Crime Writer, Viking (New York, NY), 2007.
I See You, Sphere (London, England), 2007.
We Know, Sphere (London, England), 2008.
Foolkiller: Fool's Paradise, illustrated by Lan Medina, Marvel Comics (New York, NY), 2008.
Trust No One, St. Martin's Press (New York, NY), 2009.

Contributor to books, including *Show Business Is Murder,* Berkeley Crime Press, 2004; *Meeting across the River,* Bloomsbury, 2005; and *Thriller,* Mira Books, 2006.

Contributor to academic journals, including *Word & Image, Upstart Crow,* and *Sexuality and Culture.*

Author of screenplays for Jerry Bruckheimer Films, Paramount Studios, Metro-Goldwyn Mayer, and the Entertainment and Sports Programming Network. Developer of television series for Warner Brothers Studios.

Also author of the *Gregg Hurwitz* Web log. Contributor to *MAX Sampler,* Marvel Comics, 2006; writer for *Wolverine,* 2007, and *Foolkiller,* 2008.

Author's books have been translated into fourteen languages.

SIDELIGHTS: Gregg Hurwitz grew up in the San Francisco Bay area of California, and he wrote his first novel, *The Tower,* while completing his education. The story is a psychological thriller set in the Bay area where, in an offshore maximum security prison, maniac Allander Atlasia kills everyone except for one other inmate and then escapes. The U.S. Federal Bureau of Investigation calls in Jade Marlow, a former agent turned bounty hunter who is known for his extraordinary tracking ability. In pursuing Allander, Marlow deals with the criminal's demons, as well as a few of his own. *Booklist* reviewer David Pitt commented that Hurwitz's characters "aren't likable, but they are vividly rendered, the narration is sharp, and the dialogue jumps off the page." A *Kirkus Reviews* contributor called *The Tower* a "sucker-punching, tongue-in-cheek debut psychokiller tale that spoofs, and tops, the hyperviolent Hollywood genre films that have inspired it."

In the environmental thriller *Minutes to Burn,* Hurwitz places the action in a *Jurassic Park*-like Galapagos Islands setting. The year is 2007, the ozone layer is gone, and earthquakes are shaking the world. A deadly virus develops, and a swarm of nine-foot praying mantis-like creatures threatens scientists studying the earthquakes and the U.S. Navy SEALS brought in to assist them. The navy crew includes the leader, Derek; a husband and wife team; and an immense operative named Tank. "Most enjoyable is the fiftyish knife-wielding Nam vet, Savage, who practically steals the book," wrote a *Publishers Weekly* reviewer.

Hurwitz was inspired to write the novel while performing research in the Galapagos, where he encountered the strange amphibians, reptiles, and insects that are specific to the region. When he returned, he enlisted the aid of scientific experts in order to flesh out his story. "I was amazed how believable this story is, especially considering its somewhat outlandish plot," commented Marc Ruby for *Mystery Reader* online. Ruby also mentioned: "Hurwitz has taken the time to fill in all the interesting details of ozone depletion as well as biological and tectonic information. The science is fascinating." A *Kirkus Reviews* writer who thought the book is also reminiscent of *Lord of the Flies, The Dirty Dozen,* "and maybe even *Beowulf,*" noted the book's "vivid cast" and "engrossing story. Hurwitz demonstrates once again that he's a thriller writer to be reckoned with."

Hurwitz dedicates *Do No Harm* to his physician father, "who taught [him] that ethics are never timid, rarely convenient, and always vital." The story is set in Los Angeles, California, and the University of California, Los Angeles Medical Center, where Clyde, a man who had been included in a psychological experiment as a boy, throws corrosive lye into the face of an emergency-room nurse and then attacks a female doctor in a similar fashion. The brother of the nurse is with the police department, whose full force and fury are directed at finding the perpetrator. When he is caught, Clyde is beaten by the police and scarred by the substance. Afterwards, he is brought to the emergency room, where the staff, with the exception of chief of emergency services David Spier, refuses to treat him. Clyde escapes the hospital, and David risks his own life in order to recapture him.

Reviewing *Do No Harm,* Jabari Asim wrote in the *Washington Post Book World* that David Spier "is fully realized," and added that "another supporting player is the most intriguing character in the book . . . and is one with whom Hurwitz has a great deal of fun. A shadowy operative named Ed Pinkerton—who seems to know everything and demonstrates a convenient mastery of covert surveillance, computer science, and disguise—steps in from time to time and offers David lifesaving assistance," Asim noted. "The pair's banter is believable and funny, and Ed is a character worth seeing again." *Booklist* critic William Beatty wrote that David's application of medical ethics in his practice is just one of the threads "in a smoothly written, gripping fabric of believable incidents, ethical questions, and changing relationships." *Library Journal* reviewer Jo Ann Vicarel called Hurwitz "a brilliant storyteller." Harriet Klausner reviewed *Do No Harm* for *BookBrowser,* saying that Hurwitz "is the heir apparent to Robin Cook if this medical thriller is an indicator of the chill level

that leaves readers reconsidering any visit to an emergency room." Klausner called the novel "a compelling read."

Hurwitz explores themes of honor and vengeance in his fourth novel, *The Kill Clause.* Tim Rackley, a U.S. deputy marshal, and his wife, Dray, a Los Angeles County sheriff, receive news that their daughter has been savagely murdered on her seventh birthday. Though the perpetrator is quickly arrested, the prosecution bungles the case and the killer is set free on a technicality. Tim is then contacted by the Commission, a vigilante group dedicated to correcting miscarriages of justice, and he is offered membership into the organization as its executioner. *The Kill Clause* received mixed reviews. A critic in *Kirkus Reviews* observed: "Hurwitz, . . . wanting to write a novel of ideas that's also a fast-paced thriller, gets hung up between the two," and *Entertainment Weekly* contributor Scott Brown remarked that the author "comes alive only when he's describing men locked in mortal struggle: The violence is so detailed, so mercilessly, excruciatingly storyboarded, it's almost erotic." Joe Hartlaub, in a review for *Bookreporter.com,* stated that "the ultimate aim of this fine novel is not simply to entertain but to get the reader thinking about the consequences of stepping outside the system in order to obtain a measure of justice that otherwise is denied."

Tim Rackley enters a cult to save a film producer's child in *The Program.* Having lost his job due to his involvement with the Commission, Tim accepts a proposition from Hollywood mogul Will Henning: rescue Will's teenage daughter, Leah, from "The Program," and Will will use his influence to help Rackley rejoin the U.S. marshal's service. After adopting a new identity, Tim goes undercover in "The Program," where he matches wits with cult founder T.D. Betters. "Grounded in character and believable detail, Hurwitz's thriller engages on every level," wrote a *Publishers Weekly* contributor. Wes Lukowsky, writing in *Booklist,* called the novel "a gripping read from start to finish."

In *Troubleshooter,* Tim Rackley has rejoined the U.S. marshals and tangles with an outlaw motorcycle gang called the Laughing Sinners. Having learned that their president, Den Laurey, is being escorted to a federal penitentiary, members of the Sinners stage an ambush to free him, killing two marshals in the process. When Dray Rackley, now eight months pregnant, attempts to recapture Laurey, she is seriously wounded, and her husband is determined to track down the gang leader. "Hurwitz is a rock-solid writer, researcher, and plotter," observed a critic in *Publishers Weekly*. A *Kirkus Reviews* stated: "It's the righteously resolute Rackley you pay your money for, and he doesn't disappoint."

A former marine breaks out of prison and goes on a murderous rampage in *Last Shot*, another work featuring U.S. marshal Tim Rackley. The marshal must follow the trail of Walker Jameson, a Desert Storm veteran who masterminds his escape from Terminal Island Penitentiary and begins targeting officers of a pharmaceutical company. Hurwitz "moves easily between the gritty scenes of violence and the more subtle abuses of power in corporate boardrooms," noted a reviewer in *Publishers Weekly*.

Hurwitz taps into his professional experiences as a novelist to produce *The Crime Writer*. Protagonist Drew Danner is a successful crime novelist whose books all bear the hallmarks of his careful research into methods of murder and techniques of forensic detection. When he wakes up in a hospital bed after brain tumor surgery, he cannot remember how or why he got there. Any relief Drew feels soon turns to horror when he finds out that he is suspected of brutally murdering his ex-fiancée, Genevieve Bertrand. Police tell him that he was found beside her body with a bloody knife in his hand. Drew has no memory of harming Genevieve and cannot think of any reason why he would kill her. He knows, however, that the pernicious effects of the tumor could have caused him to do something drastic and out of character and then block the memory from his mind.

When Drew is later acquitted of murder by reason of temporary insanity caused by the brain tumor, he investigates Genevieve's death and whether he was really capable of viciously killing a loved one. After a second similar murder occurs, Drew's blood is found on the scene, and he believes someone is trying to frame him for murder. Preston, Drew's book editor, urges him to write down what is happening and approach the case analytically as he would a crime novel. He is assisted by friends in his search, including a police forensic specialist and a juvenile delinquent. A *Kirkus Reviews* critic remarked that Hurwitz's "carefully interwoven plot lines and taut writing . . . make for a deeply satisfying read." The story's "fast pace and ingenious setup provide considerable tension," observed a *Publishers Weekly* critic. Hurwitz "has written a nice puzzler," commented Jane Jorgenson, writing in *Library Journal*.

Trust No One is another foray into the mystery-thriller genre. The novel opens with protagonist Nick Horrigan being kidnapped by the U.S. Secret Service. Secret Service agents explain that a terrorist has taken control of a nuclear power plant and will blow it up unless he can speak with Nick. A conspiracy then unfolds encompassing all known levels of the government, including the president of the United States. Joel W. Tscherne, writing for *Library Journal*, remarked that the tale that unfolds "keeps the reader guessing about the motives of nearly every character." Thomas Gaughan, a contributor to *Booklist*, called *Trust No One* a "page-to-page suspense" with "breakneck pacing" that "will please Hurwitz's growing audience."

BIOGRAPHICAL AND CRITICAL SOURCES:

PERIODICALS

Booklist, March 1, 1999, David Pitt, review of *The Tower,* p. 1158; July, 2001, Roland Green, review of *Minutes to Burn,* p. 1980; August, 2002, William Beatty, review of *Do No Harm,* p. 1931; June 1, 2004, Wes Lukowsky, review of *The Program,* p. 1708; March 1, 2009, Thomas Gaughan, review of *Trust No One,* p. 30.
Entertainment Weekly, August 15, 2003, Scott Brown, review of *The Kill Clause,* p. 79; August 6, 2007, Adam Markovitz, review of *The Crime Writer.*
Kirkus Reviews, February 15, 1999, review of *The Tower,* p. 245; June 1, 2001, review of *Minutes to Burn,* p. 761; June 15, 2003, review of *The Kill Clause,* p. 825; July 15, 2004, review of *The Program,* p. 649; July 15, 2005, review of *Troubleshooter,* p. 756; May 15, 2007, review of *The Crime Writer.*
Library Journal, March 15, 1999, Jo Ann Vicarel, review of *The Tower,* p. 109; June 15, 2002, Jo Ann Vicarel, review of *Do No Harm,* p. 93; September 15, 2006, Patrick Wall, review of *Last Shot,* p. 48; June 1, 2007, Jane Jorgenson, review of *The Crime Writer,* p. 114; June 15, 2009, Joel W. Tscherne, review of *Trust No One,* p. 60.
Publishers Weekly, February 1, 1999, review of *The Tower,* p. 73; July 2, 2001, review of *Minutes to Burn,* p. 49; July 15, 2002, review of *Do No Harm,* p. 56; May 26, 2003, review of *The Kill Clause,* p. 43, and Adam Dunn, interview with Gregg Hurwitz, p. 44; July 12, 2004, review of *The Program,* p. 44; July 25, 2005, review of *Troubleshooter,* p. 45; July 24, 2006, review of *Last Shot,* p. 36; May 14, 2007, review of *The Crime Writer,* p. 32; April 20, 2009, review of *Trust No One,* p. 28.

School Library Journal, June 1, 2009, Angela Carstensen, review of *Trust No One,* p. 150.

Washington Post Book World, August 13, 2002, Jabari Asim, review of *Do No Harm,* p. C3.

ONLINE

BookBrowser Web site, http://www.bookbrowser.com/ (February 15, 1999), Harriet Klausner, review of *The Tower;* (June 14, 2002) Harriet Klausner, review of *Do No Harm.*

BookLoons, http://www.bookloons.com/ (May 25, 2008), Hilary Williamson, review of *The Crime Writer.*

Bookreporter.com, http://www.bookreporter.com/ (May 25, 2008), Joe Hartlaub, reviews of *Do No Harm, The Kill Clause, The Program, Troubleshooter,* and *Last Shot.*

Curled Up with a Good Book Web site, http://www.curledup.com/ (May 25, 2008), Phillip Tomasso III, review of *The Kill Clause.*

Gregg Andrew Hurwitz Home Page, http://www.gregghurwitz.net (May 25, 2008).

Mercury News Web site, http://www.bayarea.com/ (August 1, 2002), Mark Johnson, review of *Do No Harm.*

Mystery Ink Web site, http://www.mysteryinkonline.com/ (May 25, 2008), David J. Montgomery, review of *Last Shot.*

Mystery Reader, http://www.themysteryreader.com/ (October 18, 2002), Marc Ruby, review of *Minutes to Burn;* (February 25, 2007) Lesley Dunlap, review of *The Program.*

Pop Matters, http://www.popmatters.com/ (July 31, 2002), Celia S. McClinton, review of *Do No Harm.**

*   *   *

HURWITZ, Gregg Andrew
See HURWITZ, Gregg

J

JOHANSEN, Iris 1938-

PERSONAL: Born 1938. Children: Roy, Tamara.

ADDRESSES: Home—Atlanta, GA. *E-mail*—mail@ irisjohansen.com.

CAREER: Writer. Romance and romantic suspense novelist. Previously worked for a major airline.

WRITINGS:

"SHAMROCK" SERIES

York the Renegade, Bantam Books (New York, NY), 1986.

"RELUCTANT LARK" SERIES

The Reluctant Lark, Bantam Books (New York, NY), 1983.
The Bronzed Hawk, Bantam Books (New York, NY), 1983.

"CLANAD" SERIES

The Lady and the Unicorn, Bantam Books (New York, NY), 1984.
Across the River of Yesterday, Bantam Books (New York, NY), 1987.

Last Bridge Home, Bantam Books (New York, NY), 1987.
Magnificent Folly, Bantam Books (New York, NY), 1987.
A Tough Man to Tame, Bantam Books (New York, NY), 1991.

"DONOVAN ENTERPRISES" SERIES

Stormy Vows (also see below), Bantam Books (New York, NY), 1983.
Tempest at Sea (also see below), Bantam Books (New York, NY), 1983.
Stormy Vows [and] *Tempest at Sea* (omnibus), Bantam Books (New York, NY), 2007.

"SEDIKHAN" SERIES

Capture the Rainbow, Bantam Books (New York, NY), 1984.
The Golden Valkyrie, Bantam Books (New York, NY), 1984.
Touch the Horizon, Bantam Books (New York, NY), 1984.
The Trustworthy Redhead, Bantam Books (New York, NY), 1984.
A Summer Smile, Bantam Books (New York, NY), 1985.
Everlasting, Bantam Books (New York, NY), 1986.
'Til the End of Time, Bantam Books (New York, NY), 1987.
Star Light, Star Bright, Bantam Books (New York, NY), 1988.

Blue Skies and Shining Promises, Bantam Books (New York, NY), 1988.

Man from Half Moon Bay, Bantam Books (New York, NY), 1988.

Strong, Hot Winds, Bantam Books (New York, NY), 1988.

Notorious, Doubleday Loveswept Hardcover (New York, NY), 1990.

The Golden Barbarian, Doubleday Loveswept (New York, NY), 1990, Bantam Books (New York, NY), 1992.

"SANTA FLORES" SERIES

Return to Santa Flores, Bantam Books (New York, NY), 1984.

No Red Roses, Bantam Books (New York, NY), 1984.

"WHITE SATIN" SERIES

White Satin, Bantam Books (New York, NY), 1985.

Blue Velvet, Bantam Books (New York, NY), 1985.

And the Desert Blooms, Bantam Books (New York, NY), 1986.

"DELANEYS OF KILLAROO" SERIES

(With Kay Hooper) *Golden Flames,* Bantam Books (New York, NY), 1988.

Wild Silver, Bantam Books (New York, NY), 1988.

Satin Ice, Bantam Books (New York, NY), 1988.

Matilda the Adventuress, Bantam Books (New York, NY), 1997.

"WIND DANCER" TRILOGY

The Wind Dancer, Bantam Books (New York, NY), 1991.

Storm Winds, Bantam Books (New York, NY), 1991.

Reap the Wind, Bantam Books (New York, NY), 1991.

"EVE DUNCAN" SERIES

The Face of Deception, Bantam Books (New York, NY), 1998.

The Killing Game, Bantam Books (New York, NY), 1999.

Body of Lies, Bantam Books (New York, NY), 2002.

Blind Alley, Bantam Books (New York, NY), 2004.

Countdown, Bantam Books (New York, NY), 2005.

Stalemate, Bantam Books (New York, NY), 2006.

Quicksand, St. Martin's Press (New York, NY), 2008.

Blood Game, St. Martin's Press (New York, NY), 2009.

OTHER NOVELS

The Forever Dream, Bantam Books (New York, NY), 1985.

Always, Bantam Books (New York, NY), 1986.

Last Bridge Home, Bantam Books (New York, NY), 1987.

Across the River of Yesterday, Bantam Books (New York, NY), 1987.

The Spellbinder, Bantam Books (New York, NY), 1987.

One Touch of Topaz, Bantam Books (New York, NY), 1988.

This Fierce Splendor, Bantam Books (New York, NY), 1988.

Wicked Jake Darcy, Bantam Books (New York, NY), 1990.

Tender Savage, Bantam Books (New York, NY), 1991.

The Tiger Prince, Bantam Books (New York, NY), 1993.

Star Spangled Bride, Bantam Books (New York, NY), 1993.

The Magnificent Rogue, Bantam Books (New York, NY), 1993.

The Beloved Scoundrel, Bantam Books (New York, NY), 1994.

Midnight Warrior, Bantam Books (New York, NY), 1994.

Dark Rider, Bantam Books (New York, NY), 1995.

Lion's Bride, Bantam Books (New York, NY), 1995.

The Ugly Duckling, Bantam Books (New York, NY), 1996.

Long After Midnight, Bantam Books (New York, NY), 1996.

And Then You Die, Bantam Books (New York, NY), 1998.

The Search, Bantam Books (New York, NY), 2000.

Final Target, Bantam Books (New York, NY), 2001.

No One to Trust, Bantam Books (New York, NY), 2002.

Dead Aim, Bantam Books (New York, NY), 2003.

Fatal Tide, Bantam Books (New York, NY), 2003.

Firestorm, Bantam Books (New York, NY), 2004.

On the Run, Bantam Books (New York, NY), 2006.

Killer Dreams, Bantam Books (New York, NY), 2006.

An Unexpected Song, Bantam Books (New York, NY), 2006.

Pandora's Daughter, St. Martin's Press (New York, NY), 2007.

The Treasure, Bantam Books (New York, NY), 2008.

(With Roy Johansen) *Silent Thunder,* St. Martin's Press (New York, NY), 2008.

Dark Summer, St. Martin's Press (New York, NY), 2008.

Deadlock, St. Martin's Press (New York, NY), 2009.

(With Roy Johansen) *Storm Cycle,* St. Martin's Press (New York, NY), 2009.

Contributor to anthologies.

Also author of the novella *"Christmas Past,"* published in *The Delaney Christmas Carol,* with novellas by Kay Hooper and Fayrene Preston, Doubleday (New York, NY), 1992.

ADAPTATIONS: Many of the author's books have been made into audio recordings, including *Stalemate,* available from Books on Tape, 2006.

SIDELIGHTS: Iris Johansen is a popular and prolific author of romance and suspense novels. She has published more than one novel per year since 1983, and has published as many as eight novels in one year. Quantity of output, however, has not stopped her from being an innovator, in the view of a contributor to *Twentieth-Century Romance and Historical Writers,* who wrote: "She has stretched the boundaries of the standard formulas in the category romance field and has written some of the best historical romance novels." Johansen writes category romances set in several historical eras, and has become known for the conviction with which she describes bygone places and people. Her characterizations are considered among the more complex in the genre. As for sex, a *Twentieth-Century Romance and Historical Writers* contributor pointed out that the presence of one or more long seduction scenes is a hallmark of Johansen's work, and that, although the seduction often contains "an element of punishment," it is always made clear that the heroine is not in real physical danger. Commented a *Twentieth-Century Romance and Historical Writers* contributor: "The uncertainty of remaining safely on the edge of possible pain adds sexual tension to the stories."

Several of Johansen's novels have belonged to Bantam/Doubleday's Loveswept line of romances, beginning with *Stormy Vows,* Johansen's first novel, published in 1983. With her historical novels, she has taken her readers to far corners of the earth. In particular, Johansen has made two imaginary countries of her own: the Middle Eastern kingdom of Sedikhan and the Balkan state of Tamrovia. Characters recur from book to book, and the two nations are linked by marriage; thus, Johansen's loyal readers can follow the fortunes of favorite characters such as recovering drug addict David Bradford (who originally appeared in *The Trustworthy Redhead*), who finds love and contentment in *Touch the Horizon* with a woman, Billie Callahan, herself a star of *Capture the Rainbow.*

Johansen's novels are sometimes included in established series which feature novels written by several authors. For example, in the "Shamrock" Trilogy, a series about the Delaney brothers of Ireland, Johansen wrote *York the Renegade* while the two other novels were written by Kay Hooper and Fayrene Preston. The "Delaneys of Killaroo" series is a spin-off of the Shamrock tales, focusing on three sisters in the Australian branch of the Delaney family. Although not officially part of the Delaney series, the novel *This Fierce Splendor* deals with a male character who is a Delaney. The trio of authors contributing to the trilogy also wrote a Christmas book, *The Delaney Christmas Carol,* in which each writer contributed a novella.

As an individual, Johansen wrote the novels comprising the "Wind Dancer" trilogy of 1991, the first two volumes of which received considerable acclaim from romance reviewers. The novels, spanning much of European history, deal with the Andreas family's quest for a legendary golden statue called the Wind Dancer. The first novel, *The Wind Dancer,* is set in sixteenth-century Italy, and the second, *Storm Winds,* is set in France during the Reign of Terror near the end of the eighteenth century. *The Wind Dancer,* which had a first printing of 700,000 copies, is "a lively and imaginative blend of romance and adventure," according to a *Publishers Weekly* contributor. That reviewer also applauded the character of Lorenzo Vasaro, the hero's friend, who is "an unlikely but likable character . . . a worldly-wise and intriguing blend of ruthlessness and charm." *Publishers Weekly* contributor Peggy Kaganoff called *Storm Winds* "a diverting romance" with "plot twists worthy of a mystery novel."

Another series follows Eve Duncan, a successful forensics sculptor, who was raised in poverty by a single, cocaine-addicted mother. In *The Killing Game,* readers learn that Eve's daughter Bonnie was murdered, and though her body was never found, her alleged murderer was executed. Duncan moved away to a Tahitian island where her friend Joe Quinn finds her and tells her that he has found a mass grave with a body that might be Bonnie's. Eve returns to the States, but before the body can be identified, a stalker begins to pursue Eve, insisting that he was Bonnie's actual killer. He threatens to kill Eve as well as a ten-year-old girl, Jane MacGuire, whom she has befriended. Eve is terrified but vows to catch the killer, even if she must be the bait. Emily Melton, writing in *Booklist,* called it "a cross between King's nightmarish chillers and Cornwell's forensic thrillers" and observed that the book is a "certain winner." *The Killing Game* received many positive reviews. According to a *Publishers Weekly* reviewer, "Johansen maintains perfect pacing." The same reviewer observed: "Aided by smart and realistic dialogue, the suspense holds until the very end."

Jane MacGuire shows up again in *Countdown,* in which she is a twenty-year-old archeology major at Harvard. On a dig in Herculaneum, MacGuire learns that her face is identical to that of Cira, a Roman courtesan who has been dead for 2,000 years. Cira is the link to riches, and when MacGuire's close friend is murdered, she fears for her safety. Mark Trevor, another friend who lusts after MacGuire, flies her to Aberdeen. Much of the book occurs at MacDuff's Run, a fictional castle in Scotland. MacGuire's foster mother, Eve Duncan, flies her back to the States where MacGuire and Trevor plan to stop suicide bombers who are on a countdown to blow up a nuclear plant. Like most of Johansen's books, *Countdown* received positive reviews. A *Publishers Weekly* reviewer noted: "Action, romance, castles, bomb plots and a booby-trapped hideaway in snowbound Idaho—what more could Johansen fans want?"

Johansen produced other well-received romance novels in the 1990s. Commenting on *The Magnificent Rogue,* published in 1993, a *Booklist* contributor commented: "Passion and suspense abound in [this] . . . robust romance. . . . Spellbinding romantic fiction from a master of the genre." The same year, Johansen produced *Midnight Warrior,* a tale of England and Wales set in 1066. Kristin Ramsdell, writing in *Library Journal* commented on the book and wrote: "Believable, thoughtfully constructed characters, complex plotting, and lively dialog characterize this sensual historical."

Johansen achieved a personal milestone in 1996 with the publication of *The Ugly Duckling.* It was her most prestigious publication to date, although not the "hardcover debut" that a *Kirkus Reviews* contributor termed it (at least two of her previous novels had been placed between hardcovers, but in the Loveswept line rather than as solo creations). In *The Ugly Duckling,* commented the *Kirkus Reviews* contributor, "megaseller Johansen abandons the lush historical romances that have made her reputation and stakes out the proven market of Nora Roberts and Sidney Sheldon." The heroine, Nell, is the plain wife of a rich man who, along with their daughter, is murdered before her eyes; Nell herself is thrown off a cliff and survives but is disfigured. Hero Nicholas, pursuing the drug dealers who killed Nell's family, takes her under his wing and sees that she receives state-of-the-art plastic surgery that turns her into a beauty. He also teaches her martial arts. Nell and Nicholas set out to destroy the villains and do so with the help of what the *Kirkus Reviews* contributor called "inventive surprises." A *Publishers Weekly* reviewer called *The Ugly Duckling* "spectacular" and elaborated: "The romance here is suspenseful, and the suspense is romantic; for fans of each, this is a keeper." *Booklist* contributor Brad Hooper announced that, in *The Ugly Duckling,* "the romantic suspense genre is done a good turn."

Having achieved this new level of success, Johansen went on to create another successful thriller with her next book, *Long After Midnight,* a tale of scientific breakthroughs and corrupt corporations. The heroine, Kate, is a high-level working mother doing important research for top scientist Noah Smith and trying to give her nine-year-old son a good life at the same time. When Noah's lab blows up and attempts are made on Kate's life, Kate and Noah go into hiding to escape from the psychopathic hit man who is stalking them. Kate has two love interests, Noah and his solder-of-fortune friend Seth. Noting that the plot premise contains some familiar, conventional elements, a *Publishers Weekly* contributor added that "Johansen knows how to take the formula and run with it," appealing to readers with her believable characters, effective dialogue, and interesting plotting. The review also noted that a plot strand involving the heroine's father, an Alzheimer's patient, gives "the deft but somewhat protracted finish a moving, unexpected touch."

Elena Kyler is the central character in *No One to Trust.* Trained to survive the Columbian jungles by her mercenary parents, Elena flirts with danger and gets too close. Drug lord Rico Chavez rapes her, which results in her having a child. For most of the story, Elena and her now five-year-old son are being pursued by Chavez, who wants to find Elena and take their son. Sean Galen, a CIA operative who also appeared in Johansen's novel *Body of Lies,* plans to protect Elena and her son by bringing them to the United States. When Chavez follows her, Galen plans to capture him. However, Chavez sends his thugs instead, and the situation spins out of control. As Elena and Galen flee across the country, they also fall in love. Patty Engelmann, writing in *Booklist,* commented: "With its taut plot and complex characters, this is vintage, fan-pleasing Johansen." A *Publishers Weekly* contributor acknowledged that in light of terrorism and national security, "the threat of drug cartels feels dated and Chavez is so over-the-top nasty that he's downright silly." Of the novel as a whole, the same reviewer observed: "Johansen has delivered better in the past." A *Kirkus Reviews* contributor summed up the novel: "Fast-moving plot, elementary prose: another zippy read from megaselling Johansen."

Final Target revolves around the escape, rescue, and psychological recovery of Cassie, the U.S. president's seven-year-old daughter. Cassie was rescued from a kidnapping attempt in France by international thief Michael Travis, who turns up at the home of Cassie's psychiatrist, Dr. Jessica Riley. Although told by the president to keep Michael away from his daughter, Jessica instead enlists his help in Cassie's treatment, leading to Cassie, Jessica, and Michael being pursued not only by the Secret Service but also by some of Michael's nefarious associates. In a review in *Booklist,* Patty Engelmann called *Final Target* "a winning page-turner that will please old and new fans alike."

In *Dead Aim,* photojournalist Alex Graham, emotionally scarred after the terrorist attacks of 9/11, is covering the collapse of the Arapahoe Dam and discovers that there are villains who actually caused the dam to collapse and who may be part of a Central American terrorist group. When she is pursued by the bad guys, Alex is helped by ex-CIA agent Judd Morgan. After coming to her rescue, Judd teams up with Alex and the two go after the terrorists who may be planning to assassinate the president. In an interview with Adam Dunn in *Publishers Weekly,* the author commented on the involvement of 9/11 in Alex's life. "I had already started *Dead Aim* before 9/11. After it happened, I redid the first two chapters. There was just no way I could ignore it." A *Kirkus Reviews* contributor referred to *Dead Aim* as a "smoothly written, tightly plotted, turbocharged thriller." Another reviewer, writing in *Publishers Weekly,* noted that "Johansen's latest fast-moving thriller offers lots of cinematic action" and later added that "the nonstop action and slick plotting won't disappoint."

Fatal Tide focuses on Melis, a woman who was sold into white slavery at the age of eleven. When Melis's foster dad, a scientist who researches mysteries of the deep sea, is blown up in his boat, Melis and ex-Navy SEAL Jed Kelby set out to solve the case, which may involve a lethal new weapon that is wanted by a Middle Eastern dictator. In the process, they end up in the Canary Islands, hoping that a group of dolphins can lead them to the hidden weapon. In a review of *Fatal Tide* in *Publishers Weekly,* a contributor wrote that "the exotic locals, lusty sex and capering dolphins provide easy-reading entertainment." *Booklist* contributor Patty Engelmann commented that the author "is in fine form here as she presents a truly deranged villain, a reluctant heroine, and a less-than-perfect hero."

Kerry Murphy is a fire investigator with psychic abilities in Johansen's novel *Firestorm.* Emotionally traumatized from a house fire in her youth, Kerry and her dog Sam team up with fellow psychic Brad Silver to investigate a secret plot to incinerate the earth. The two have more in common than psychic abilities, however, as both have lost loved ones in fires. A *Publishers Weekly* contributor commented that the author "ably captures the smell, the smoke and the terror of fire."

Blind Alley once again features forensic sculptor Eve Duncan. This time, when Eve reconstructs the face of a murder victim, she is startled to find that it looks just like her adopted daughter, Jane. The victim is just one murder committed by a serial killer who is the reincarnation of a Roman slave. The novel also continues to explore Duncan's battle with the unsolved death of her daughter Bonnie. A *Publishers Weekly* contributor referred to *Blind Alley* as a "far-fetched but expertly plotted, eminently entertaining novel." Patty Engelmann, writing in *Booklist,* commented: "Solid suspense, a vicious killer, and the heroine's rough transition to adulthood will keep teens involved."

Johansen continued her prolific output with four more novels published in 2006. In her thriller *Killer Dreams,* Johansen tells the story of Sophie Dunston, a sleep researcher who has developed a drug for insomnia. Sophie's former boss is using the drug to alter people's minds, however. He targets Sophie's father, who ends up killing his wife. Sophie seeks revenge and teams up with Matt Royd, a troubled man who also suffers from the drug experiments. Maria Hatton, writing in *Booklist,* called *Killer Dreams* a "suspenseful tale of nightmarish evil." *Entertainment Weekly*'s Eric Kohn commented: "*Dreams* is no snooze."

Grace Archer and her daughter Frankie are under protective custody thanks to the CIA in *On the Run.* The goal is to trap Marvot, a French underworld figure who is after Grace because of her involvement in a CIA plot involving Marvot and two dangerous horses. Rogue CIA agent Jake Kilmer is on hand to help protect Grace but also has ulterior motives as he seeks the valuable horses for himself. "Johansen gives her readers what they have come to expect from the queen of suspense," wrote Patty Engelmann in *Booklist.* A *Publishers Weekly* contributor commented: "The Johansen formula works so well in this novel that readers may expect a sequel."

In *Stalemate,* Eve Duncan returns and finds herself in Colombia helping a weapons dealer in exchange for finding out what really happened to her murdered daughter. In a review of *Stalemate* in *Library Journal,* Sheri Melnick called the novel "a first-rate suspense thriller complete with expertly developed characters." Maria Hatton wrote in *Booklist:* "Johansen strikes again, creating both a nonstop thriller and a character study."

In her novel *Pandora's Daughter,* Johansen told the story of Megan Blair, a doctor who possesses incredibly powerful psychic abilities. Megan was orphaned as a teenager, and since then, she has lived an uneventful life with her Uncle Phillip. One night, Megan's world is torn apart. While driving, she finds herself menaced and eventually forced off the road. Phillip contacts Neal Grady, a government agent, to tell him about the incident. Neal had known Megan's mother, and had spent time with the two of them in the summer before Megan's mother died. Grady reveals the incredible truth to Megan: her mother was a "Pandora," a person with strong psychic gifts. Neal also has some of these psychic powers, and Megan herself is what is called a "Listener," someone capable of hearing the echo of terrible things that have taken place in the past. Megan's mother did not really die an accidental death, and Phillip is not her uncle; he has been employed by Neal for all these years to protect Megan. She is now the target of Molino, the man responsible for her mother's death. Molino's henchmen end up injuring Phillip when they make an attempt on Megan's life. As Neal and Megan work on an important mission to find an ancient ledger

related to a family with powerful psychic abilities, they find themselves falling in love with each other. Megan must "hear" the echoes of past horrors along the way, and according to Terry Miller Shannon, a contributor to *Bookreporter,* the author "delivers some interesting plot twists and ideas, and she keeps the surprises coming until the very last page." *Booklist* reviewer Patty Engelmann recommended *Pandora's Daughter* as "an exhilarating thriller" with well-drawn characters. Another reviewer, Sheri Melnick, noted in her *Library Journal* review that the psychic aspect of the story is made "eerily believable" by Johansen, who "captivates readers" with her story.

The character of Megan appeared again in the Eve Duncan thriller *Quicksand,* published in 2007. In this story, Eve's lover, Joe Quinn, works to hunt down Henry Kistle, a man suspected of at least partial responsibility for the murder of Eve's daughter, Bonnie, years before. Quinn is certain that Eve will not have real peace until her daughter's body is located and identified. What he doesn't know is that Eve frequently sees and converses with the ghost of her daughter. When Eve sees a demonstration of Megan's ability to hear past traumas, Eve is convinced that she may be able to help solve the case of her daughter's murder. Eventually, Eve and Megan are drawn to a remote area deep in the Okefenokee swamp, where they may either find out the truth of what happened to Bonnie, or become a killer's latest victims. Shannon, in another review for *Bookreporter,* called *Quicksand* "a fast-paced read that is nearly impossible to put down." Weaving together the stories of Eve and Megan "intensifies both," according to the reviewer for *Publishers Weekly,* who predicted that readers would "eagerly" follow the narrative.

Johansen teamed with her son, Roy Johansen, to write another thriller, *Silent Thunder.* The story concerns Hannah Bryson, a marine architect, whose brother Connor was killed by an explosion that occurred on a Russian submarine being prepared for a museum. Connor's death is passed off as an accident by government officials, but Hannah thinks there was more to it than that. She knows that Connor had discovered some mysterious symbols deep inside the sub, and she is convinced his death is tied to these symbols. The book features some elements so common to the thriller genre that they could have seemed trite, but according to Carol Haggas in *Booklist,* the "muscular characters" and a well-paced narrative keep this story "gripping and relevant." A *Publishers Weekly* writer also praised the book, noting in particular its "exciting finale."

BIOGRAPHICAL AND CRITICAL SOURCES:

BOOKS

Twentieth-Century Romance and Historical Writers, 3rd edition, St. James Press (Detroit, MI), 1994.

PERIODICALS

Book, September, 2003, review of *Fatal Tide,* p. 928.

Booklist, September 1, 1993, Margaret Flanagan, review of *The Magnificent Rogue,* p. 34; March 1, 1996, Brad Hooper, review of *The Ugly Duckling,* p. 1076; November 1, 1997, Kathleen Hughes, review of *And Then You Die,* p. 435; August 1, 1998, Diana Tixier Herald, review of *The Face of Deception,* p. 1923; August, 1999, Emily Melton, review of *The Killing Game,* p. 1987; September 15, 2000, Nina Davis, review of *Dark Rider,* p. 224; March 15, 2001, Patty Engelmann, review of *Final Target,* p. 1333; May 1, 2001, Nancy Spillman, review of *The Search,* p. 1615; October 1, 2001, Joyce Saricks, review of *Final Target,* p. 342; September 1, 2002, Patty Engelmann, review of *No One to Trust,* pp. 5-6; February 1, 2003, Patty Engelmann, review of *Dead Aim,* p. 955; July 1, 2003, Patty Engelmann, review of *Fatal Tide,* p. 1845; August 1, 2004, Patty Engelmann, review of *Blind Alley,* p. 1871; November 1, 2005, Patty Engelmann, review of *On the Run,* p. 4; May 1, 2006, Maria Hatton, review of *Killer Dreams,* p. 34; May 1, 2006, Jeanette Larson, review of *On the Run,* p. 52; October 15, 2006, Maria Hatton, review of *Stalemate,* p. 5; March 15, 2007, Mary Frances Wilkens, review of *Stalemate,* p. 71; July 1, 2007, Patty Engelmann, review of *Pandora's Daughter,* p. 8; December 15, 2007, Patty Engelmann, review of *Quicksand,* p. 5; March 1, 2008, Carol Haggas, review of *Silent Thunder,* p. 30.

Detroit Free Press, March 10, 2002, review of *Body of Lies,* p. 4G.

Entertainment Weekly, September 17, 2004, Nancy Miller, review of *Blind Alley,* p. 84; June 9, 2006, Eric Kohn, review of *Killer Dreams,* p. 142.

Globe & Mail (Toronto, Ontario, Canada), September 25, 1999, review of *The Killing Game,* p. D15; June 9, 2001, review of *Final Target,* p. 342; March 23, 2002, review of *Body of Lies,* p. D22; October 19, 2002, review of *No One to Trust,* p. D22; April 26, 2003, review of *Dead Aim,* p. D39.

Kirkus Reviews, February 15, 1996, review of *The Ugly Duckling,* p. 249; November 15, 1997, review of *And Then You Die,* p. 1664; September 1, 1998, review of *The Face of Deception,* p. 1218; August 1, 1999, review of *The Killing Game,* p. 1155; July 15, 2002, review of *No One to Trust,* p. 981; February 1, 2003, review of *Dead Aim,* p. 165; July 15, 2003, review of *Fatal Tide,* p. 928; February 15, 2004, review of *Firestorm,* p. 155; August 15, 2004, review of *Blind Alley,* p. 766; May 1, 2005, review of *Countdown,* p. 497; November 1, 2006, review of *Stalemate,* p. 1094; August 15, 2007, review of *Pandora's Daughter.*

Kliatt, May, 2003, Nola Theiss, review of *No One to Trust,* pp. 48-49; November 1, 2004, Bette Ammon, review of *Firestorm,* p. 46.

Library Journal, December, 1993, review of *The Beloved Scoundrel,* pp. 174-175; May 15, 1994, Kristin Ramsdell, review of *Midnight Warrior,* p. 66; January 1, 1998, Jo Ann Vicarel, review of *And Then You Die,* p. 142; March 1, 2000, review of *The Search,* p. S1; April 15, 2000, Jane Jorgenson, review of *The Search,* p. 123; May 1, 2001, Adrienne Furness, review of *The Search,* p. 145; December 1, 2004, Barbara Hoffert, review of *Countdown,* p. 88; December 1, 2006, Sheri Melnick, review of *Stalemate,* p. 111; August 1, 2007, Sheri Melnick, review of *Pandora's Daughter,* p. 69; December 1, 2007, Amanda Scott, review of *Quicksand,* p. 100.

Mystery Reader, July 10, 2000, review of *The Search.*

People Weekly, February 9, 1998, Cynthia Sanz, review of *And Then You Die,* pp. 34-35; August 7, 2000, review of *The Search,* p. 51; December 16, 2003, review of *No One to Trust,* p. 63.

Publishers Weekly, January 4, 1991, review of *The Wind Dancer,* p. 68; April 26, 1991, Peggy Kaganoff, review of *Storm Winds,* p. 55; September 13, 1991, review of *Reap the Wind,* pp. 73-74; November 30, 1992, review of *The Tiger Prince,* p. 49; July 26, 1993, review of *The Magnificent Rogue,* p. 63; January 3, 1994, review of *The Beloved Scoundrel,* p. 78; July 4, 1994, review of *Midnight Warrior,* p. 57; March 13, 1995, review of *Dark Rider,* p. 65; December 4, 1995, review of *Lion's Bride,* p. 58; February 26, 1996, review of *The Ugly Duckling,* p. 84; December 30, 1996, review of *Long After Midnight,* p. 54; November 10, 1997, review of *And Then You Die,* p. 54; August 17, 1998, review of *The Face of Deception,* p. 45; July 12, 1999, review of *The Killing Game,* p. 75; May 1, 2000, review of *The Search,* p. 49; April 30, 2001, review of *Final Target,* p. 55;

August 12, 2002, review of *No One to Trust*, p. 274; March 24, 2003, review of *Dead Aim*, p. 955; May 5, 2003, Adam Dunn, "Taking Dead Aim: Iris Johansen," review of *Dead Aim*, p. 192; July 14, 2003, review of *Fatal Tide*, p. 53; February 9, 2004, review of *Firestorm*, p. 56; August 23, 2004, review of *Blind Alley*, p. 37; April 25, 2005, review of *Countdown*, p. 39; October 24, 2005, review of *On the Run*, p. 36; April 17, 2006, review of *Killer Dreams*, p. 165; October 9, 2006, review of *Stalemate*, p. 37; August 27, 2007, review of *Pandora's Daughter*, p. 60; February 11, 2008, review of *Quicksand*, p. 50; May 12, 2008, review of *Silent Thunder*, p. 38.

Reviewer's Bookwatch, February 1, 2007, Theodore Feit, review of *Stalemate*.

Romance Reader, November 5, 1998, review of *The Face of Deception*, p. 1218; June 29, 2000, review of *The Search*.

School Library Journal, July, 2002, Pam Johnson, review of *Body of Lies*, p. 143.

ONLINE

Associated Content, http://www.associatedcontent.com/ (May 29, 2008), Todd Michael Greene, review of *Pandora's Daughter*.

Bookreporter.com, http://www.bookreporter.com/ (May 27, 2005), interview with Iris Johansen; (July 23, 2008) Terry Miller Shannon, reviews of *Pandora's Daughter* and *Quicksand*.

Iris Johansen's Home Page, http://www.irisjohansen. com (July 23, 2008).

Random House Web site, http://www.randomhouse.com (January 29, 1999).*

*   *   *

JOHNSON, Steven 1968-

PERSONAL: Born June 6, 1968; married; children: three sons. *Education:* Brown University, B.A.; Columbia University, M.A.

ADDRESSES: Home—New York, NY. *E-mail*— sbj6668@earthlink.net.

CAREER: Writer, editor, educator, cultural critic, and computer expert. *Feed* (online magazine), founder and editor-in-chief; New York University, New York, NY, Distinguished Writer-in-Residence; lecturer to corporate and educational institutions.

WRITINGS:

NONFICTION

Interface Culture: How New Technology Transforms the Way We Create and Communicate, HarperEdge (San Francisco, CA), 1997.

Emergence: The Connected Lives of Ants, Brains, Cities, and Software, Scribner (New York, NY), 2001.

Mind Wide Open: Your Brain and the Neuroscience of Everyday Life, Scribner (New York, NY), 2004.

Everything Bad Is Good for You: How Today's Popular Culture Is Actually Making Us Smarter, Riverhead Books (New York, NY), 2005, with a new afterword by the author, Riverhead Books (New York, NY), 2006.

The Ghost Map: The Story of London's Most Terrifying Epidemic—and How It Changed Science, Cities, and the Modern World, Riverhead Hardcover (New York, NY), 2006.

Invention of Air: A Story of Science, Faith, Revolution, and the Birth of America, Riverhead Books (New York, NY), 2009.

(Editor) *The Best of Technology Writing, 2009*, Yale University Press (New Haven, CT), 2009.

Contributor to periodicals, including the *Guardian* (London, England), *Lingua Franca, Harper's, Brill's Content*, the *New Yorker*, the *Wall Street Journal*, and the *New York Times*. Contributing editor, *Wired*; monthly columnist, *Discover* magazine.

SIDELIGHTS: Steven Johnson is a writer, media expert, and science maven whose books confront the complexities of the zones where science and culture meet. In 1995, Johnson founded the now defunct online journal *Feed*, which examined the front lines of Web life and the development of computers and interconnectivity as a normal part of everyday existence.

In *Interface Culture: How New Technology Transforms the Way We Create and Communicate*, Johnson explores in-depth how digital information technology, particularly the Internet, interacts with and changes the commonplace acts of communication. As much as prior innovations such as the printing press and television, computer-based means of interacting with the world are creating fundamental changes in the most basic cultural interactions. "*Interface Culture* is one of the first books to analytically critique and explore the forces unleashed by this new media and their broad cultural consequences," wrote Deborah A. Salazar in a review for the *Journal of Cultural Geography.*

The "information space" where general users spend time "creating and exploring environments that reflect cultural values and aesthetics"—particularly the online world—is influenced not only by cultural preferences but by the tools and interfaces used to explore that world, Salazar wrote. Johnson's theory is that Web browsers, computer desktops, online chat rooms, hyperlinks, Windows, Web sites, search engines—all of these interfaces between humans and technology serve to help users understand and utilize the technical advances going on around them, much the same way that novels helped readers in Victorian times make sense of their own society and surroundings. The design of the interface itself affects what type of information is available, how that information is retrieved, and what kind of material cannot be retrieved through that particular interface. "The interface serves as a kind of translator, mediating between the two parties, making one sensible to the other," Johnson maintains.

A *Publishers Weekly* contributor remarked that readers familiar with *Feed* might be "disappointed" by Johnson's "engaging but superficial analysis of the way personal computers are changing our lives." However, Salazar found *Interface Culture* to be "an excellent introduction to a culturally based critique of what is happening in information space both from a design perspective, but more fundamentally, from a human cultural orientation as well." Harvey Blume, writing in the *American Prospect,* called the book "probably the single most memorable volume to come out of the Internet explosion of the 1990s. It was an intellectually bold, often exhilarating read, full of unexpected perspectives on culture and digital media."

Johnson's 2001 book, *Emergence: The Connected Lives of Ants, Brains, Cities, and Software,* expands on arguments in *Interface Culture* and ties them into the concept of emergence. Johnson defines emergence as "the movement from low-level rules to high-level sophistication." Emergent systems do not derive their organization and structure from a king, manager, dictator, or any type of centralized authority. Instead, the emergent system organizes itself, independent of any overall knowledge of the whole, into a fully functioning unit made up of the individual actions of its components. These individual actions naturally contribute to the

function and well-being of the entire system without being directed by any sort of centralized manager or system of laws. The complex behavior of an entire emergent system is brought about by the simple, seemingly insignificant actions of the individuals in the system. "This delightful book introduces readers to the subject of complex adaptive systems (such as ant colonies), and discusses how large-scale order emerges from a series of small-scale interactions," wrote Peter Merholz in *New Architect.*

The prime example of an emergent system in Johnson's book is that of an ant colony. Individually, a single ant may forage for food, build tunnels, or defend the colony. These actions are driven by instinct, and can be altered by chemical signals from other members of the colony; a forager can stop looking for food and take up another activity if the communication it receives from other individuals indicates that food is plentiful and other work is necessary. This type of message, however, does not come down as orders from the colony's queen; instead, the message to adapt behavior comes from other individual components of the system. The emergent system of the ant colony regulates itself, changing almost immediately to adapt to different conditions. No command from a monarch is necessary; the system polices itself, and the individual components alter their behavior to best benefit the society as a whole.

Johnson also provides other examples of emergent systems. Under conditions of abundant food, slime mold cells swarm and move about, consuming vegetation; but when conditions worsen, the cells disband into individual units. *Slashdot,* a popular online community, is not governed by an editor or moderator, but is instead controlled by the participants who constantly review content, assign it ratings, and encourage the proliferation of content that meets overall approval while discouraging objectionable material. Programmer Danny Hillis created a "genetic algorithm" that evolved thousands of individual data-sorting programs into a single functional and efficient sorting program—one that Hillis himself could not understand.

Even cities can display emergent behavior in development of business districts, suburbs, slums, and population centers. "Cities seem to have emergent lives of their own, governed by the usually unwitting actions of their inhabitants over many generations," wrote a contributor to the *Guardian.* "We are the ants, in other words, and cities are our colonies."

A *Publishers Weekly* contributor remarked that the "wide scope of the book may leave some readers wanting greater detail, but it does an excellent job of putting the Web into historical and biological context, with no dotcom diminishment." A *Guardian* contributor called *Emergence* "a fascinating book, full of surprises and insights, and written in an easy, engaging style." In *Emergence*, Blume observed in *American Prospect*, "Johnson has put some powerful ideas through a literary feedback loop that will, in all likelihood, accelerate and magnify their effect on our culture."

For Johnson's third book, *Mind Wide Open: Your Brain and the Neuroscience of Everyday Life,* he turns his attentions to matters of the mind. Johnson subjected himself to a series of tests ranging from brain imaging techniques to neurochemical analysis to get at the heart of the mind-brain connection. "Johnson is an engaging and intelligent guide," remarked *Discover* contributor Robert Wilson. "One follows him eagerly when he explores the neurophysiology of laughter or allows himself to be inserted into a magnetic resonance imaging machine," Wilson continued. Through his various self-experiments, Johnson formed conclusions on how the brain influences how we think, feel, and act. "Johnson weaves disparate strands of brain research and theory smoothly into the narrative," observed a contributor to *Publishers Weekly*. "Only a concluding section on Freud's modern legacy feels like a tangent," added the reviewer. *Top Producer* reviewer John Phipps pointed out that "while the working of the mind is not simple or easily described, Johnson's accounts of current research do offer realistic ideas that may well be confirmed by later, more rigorous studies." "Johnson very capably reduces the hard science of mind research into readable and even usable tools for all of us," noted Phipps.

Johnson's fourth book, *Everything Bad Is Good for You: How Today's Popular Culture Is Actually Making Us Smarter,* delivers his controversial contrarian standpoint that video games, television, and the Internet are actually making us smarter. David Eaves in his review of the book on *eaves.ca* pointed out that "Johnson is not applauding or even condoning the content of pop culture, what he is celebrating is how the increasing complexity of TV shows, video games and internet content is forcing us to work harder to explore, understand, engage and even guide, the content." Johnson uses the collective rise in IQ points (at three points per decade) over the past thirty years as proof that Americans are getting smarter, and connects it to

the advent of more sophisticated television shows and video games. "But how direct is this link, if it exists at all? And how would someone whose cultural diet has not changed at all over the same period measure up? Without a control group to make such comparisons, Johnson wisely turns his focus to various cultural genres and the specific skills they inspire," maintained *San Francisco Chronicle* contributor Peter Hyman. "When he compares contemporary hit crime dramas like *The Sopranos* and *24*—with their elaborate, multilevel plotlines, teeming casts of characters and open-ended narrative structures—with popular numbskull clunkers of yore like *Starsky and Hutch* . . . it's almost impossible not to agree with him that television drama has grown up and perhaps even achieved a kind of brilliance that probably rubs off on its viewers," observed *New York Times* contributor Walter Kirn. Johnson, however, does "see risks, for example, if children watch too much television or play too many video games. And some cultural works 'are more rewarding than others,' he writes, acknowledging that good literature ought to command people's attention, too," stated *Boston Globe* contributor Joseph Rosenbloom.

Johnson's 2006 study, *The Ghost Map: The Story of London's Most Terrifying Epidemic—and How It Changed Science, Cities, and the Modern World,* deals with the cholera epidemic in London's Soho district in 1854 that killed nearly seven hundred people in two weeks, and was one of the worst cholera outbreaks in London's history. In this book, "Johnson adds a new and welcome element—old-fashioned storytelling flair, another form of street knowledge—to his fractal, multifaceted method of unraveling the scientific mysteries of everyday life," commended *Los Angeles Times* contributor Mark Coleman. Conventional wisdom of the period regarded miasma (smelly air in dirty spaces) as the culprit for the outbreak. However, physician John Snow believed that cholera was spread through water, no thanks to London's horrifically unsanitary methods of dealing with waste. Along with clergyman Henry Whitehead (who initially set out to prove Snow wrong), Snow was able to successfully back up his theory. His map (referred to as a "ghost map"), depicting where people died in relation to their water source finally convinced city leaders to take action. Kevin Crowley, reviewing for *inthenews.co.uk,* believed that Johnson's "narration of the intertwining tales of Snow and Whitehead is undermined by explaining their findings within the first fifty pages thus quashing any sense of tension." The book does more than tell their story though: "Johnson shows the reader a vast, interconnected picture about urban and bacterial life: how information and illness spreads, how ideas and sewage flow; in short, the whole ecosystem of what a city 'means,'" noted Stuart Kelly, reviewer for *Scotland on Sunday*. "*The Ghost Map* is not just a remarkable story, but a remarkable study in what we might learn from that story," added Kelley.

In his next book, *The Invention of Air: A Story of Science, Faith, Revolution, and the Birth of America,* Johnson presents a portrait of Joseph Priestly (1733-1804), a scientist and theologian. The author evaluates Preistly's friendship with the founding fathers of the United States, including Thomas Jefferson, John Adams, and Benjamin Franklin, and examines Priestly's role in the nation's development intellectually. As Johnson points out, Priestly was held in high regards by the founding fathers. As evidence, the author notes that the historical correspondence between John Adams and Thomas Jefferson later in their lives included fifty-two references to Priestly, who was British but spent the last ten years of his life in the United States, while only mentioning Benjamin Franklin five times and George Washington three times.

In an interview with Blake Wilson for the *New York Times,* Johnson noted that he was supposed to write another book first "about how important ideas emerge and spread through society." However, Johnson commented that "I came across the story of Joseph Priestley when I was researching the ideas book, and got so enthralled that I decided to write about Priestley first."

The author examines numerous ideas that changed the world as he provides a narrative of Priestly's life and accomplishments, which include seminal contributions to the discovery of oxygen and the founding of the Unitarian Church. However, as noted by Johnson, Priestly was also a radical thinker who, even though he was British, was a strong supporter of the American Revolution. While Johnson pays due attention to Priestly's role in the discovery of oxygen and his contributions to the Unitarian faith and the United States, the author is much more interested in another contribution by Priestly that has important implications in the modern world.

"Johnson's book throws a certain amount of cold water on the oxygen claim, but more important, Johnson sees all of that as secondary to Priestley's greatest accomplishment, a paradigm-changing discovery that neither he nor anyone else in the 18th century was entirely equipped to understand," wrote Andrew

O'Hehir in a review for *Salon.com*. As Johnson points out in his book, among the group of scientists from various places who played a role in discovering the existence of oxygen, Priestly probably understood the discovery and its implications less than the others involved. He never understood that oxygen was important for combustion and continued to proffer a notion that rose up around medieval times that burning objects let out something called phlogiston into the air, making it poisonous.

According to Johnson, however, Priestly should be highly revered for making another discovery. Priestly was conducting an experiment that included having mint and mice together in a jar. He observed that the mint sprigs could keep mice alive, which was the beginning of science's ability to isolate a gaseous element. However, according to Johnson, Priestly's discovery was even more important in that it was leading to "a whole new way of thinking about the planet itself, and its capacity for sustaining life." Essentially, according to Johnson, Priestly's experiment represented "a microcosm of a vast system that had been evolving on Earth for two billion years."

Priestly wrote to Franklin about his experiment, leading Franklin to ponder it and, according to *Salon.com* contributor O'Hehir: "Franklin came eerily close, in his 18th-century language, to nailing the entire concept of ecosystem science in one shot." O'Hehir went on to note that Franklin's description of the earth's "ecosystem" does not accurately represent in detail what scientists today know about the ecosystem. Nevertheless, O'Hehir observed that "it's a remarkable insight" for Priestly and Franklin to have made at the time, adding: "At least momentarily, Franklin and Priestley seemed to glimpse a branch of scientific inquiry that would not reach the mainstream until the mid-20th century: the study of all planetary life as a single interlocking system, a complex web of energy flows and chemical interactions that extended from the smallest microorganism to giant redwoods and blue whales."

Several reviewers commented that *The Invention of Air* defies easy classification. Noting that the book is not a "straightforward biography" or a simple recounting of Priestly's achievements in science or in other areas, a *PhiloBiblos* Web site contributor added: "Nor is it a history of the Enlightenment processes which contributed to Priestley's worldview, or an exploration of how that worldview shaped and was shaped by the times, or a treatise on the interstices of science, government and religion." Nevertheless, the reviewer commented: "Each of those elements plays a role in Johnson's story."

Throughout the book, Johnson also takes readers on various intellectual sidetracks. For example, at one point, according to *New York Times Book Review* contributor Russell Shorto, the author "offers a brilliant 'Intermezzo' set in 300 million B.C., which roots Priestley's work on oxygen, and the whole advent of life on earth as we know it, in the Carboniferous era, when supersize plant-life—130-foot-high mosses, trees with three-foot leaves—led to a rise in the oxygen content of the atmosphere." Shorto noted that another aside examines how the discovery and early widespread use of coffee might have impacted the Enlightenment.

A *Kirkus Reviews* contributor called *The Invention of Air* "another rich, readable examination of the intersections where culture and science meet from a scrupulous historian who never offers easy answers to troubling, perhaps intractable questions." In a review for the *Seattle Times*, Bruce Ramsey compared *The Invention of Air* to Johnson's earlier book *The Ghost Map*, noting: "Both are about a moment in science that illuminates how science comes about and what it means for human society."

BIOGRAPHICAL AND CRITICAL SOURCES:

BOOKS

Johnson, Steven, *Interface Culture: How New Technology Transforms the Way We Create and Communicate*, HarperEdge (San Francisco, CA), 1997.
Johnson, Steven, *The Invention of Air: A Story of Science, Faith, Revolution, and the Birth of America*, Riverhead Books (New York, NY), 2009.

PERIODICALS

American Prospect, November 19, 2001, Harvey Blume, review of *Emergence: The Connected Lives of Ants, Brains, Cities, and Software*, pp. 42-45.
American Scholar, autumn, 2001, Alex Soojung-Kim Pang, review of *Emergence*, pp. 138-142.
Booklist, July, 2001, review of *Emergence*, p. 1953; December 1, 2008, Ray Olson, review of *The Invention of Air*, p. 20.

Boston Globe, May 1, 2005, Joseph Rosenbloom, review of *Everything Bad Is Good for You: How Today's Popular Culture Is Actually Making Us Smarter*.
Discover, July 1, 2004, Robert Wilson, review of *Mind Wide Open: Your Brain and the Neuroscience of Everyday Life*, p. 82.
Economist, October 27, 2001, review of *Emergence*.
Guardian (London, England), November 24, 2001, review of *Emergence*, p. 10; August 24, 2002, review of *Emergence*, p. 25.
Humanities, November/December, 2006, Bruce Cole, "A Conversation with Steven Johnson," interview.
Independent (London, England), October 9, 2001, Roz Kaveny, review of *Emergence*, p. 5.
Journal of Cultural Geography, fall-winter, 2001, Deborah A. Salazar, review of *Interface Culture*, pp. 140-142.
Kirkus Reviews, December 1, 2003, review of *Mind Wide Open*, p. 1393; October 15, 2008, review of *The Invention of Air*.
Library Journal, December 1, 2008, Eric D. Albright, review of *The Invention of Air*, p. 155.
Los Angeles Times, October 15, 2006, Mark Coleman, review of *The Ghost Map: The Story of London's Most Terrifying Epidemic—and How It Changed Science, Cities, and the Modern World*.
New Architect, March, 2002, Peter Merholz, review of *Emergence*, p. 56.
New Statesman, April 26, 2004, Bryan Appleyard, review of *Mind Wide Open*, p. 53.
New Yorker, February 2, 2009, review of *The Invention of Air*, p. 67.
New York Times, December 9, 2001, Steven Johnson, "Populist Editing," p. 90; April 6, 2002, Steven Johnson, "Games People Play on Computers," p. A15; May 22, 2005, Walter Kirn, review of *Everything Bad Is Good for You*; May 26, 2005, Janet Maslin, review of *Everything Bad Is Good for You*; February 6, 2009, Blake Wilson, "Stray Questions for: Steven Johnson."
New York Times Book Review, January 25, 2009, Russell Shorto, "Breath of Thought," review of *The Invention of Air*.
Pittsburgh Post-Gazette, January 18, 2009, Glenn C. Altschuler, "When Science and Politics Worked Hand in Hand," review of *The Invention of Air*.
Plain Dealer (Cleveland, OH), November 4, 2001, Dan Tranberg, "Straightforward Writing Makes the Complex Simple; An Easy Look at the Concept of Emergence," p. 112.
Publishers Weekly, October 27, 1997, review of *Interface Culture*, p. 60; July 23, 2001, review of

Emergence, p. 61; December 1, 2003, review of *Mind Wide Open*, p. 50; November 10, 2008, Simon Winchester, review of *The Invention of Air*, p. 40.

St. Petersburg Times (St. Petersburg, FL), February 19, 2009, David L. Beck, "Science, Politics and a Young U.S.," review of *The Invention of Air*.

San Francisco Chronicle, May 22, 2005, Peter Hyman, review of *Everything Bad Is Good for You*, p. F3; January 9, 2009, Troy Jollimore, review of *The Invention of Air*.

School Library Journal, October 1, 2005, Catherine Gilbride, review of *Everything Bad Is Good for You*, p. 201.

Scotland on Sunday, November 19, 2006, Stuart Kelly, review of *The Ghost Map*.

Seattle Times, January 11, 2009, Bruce Ramsey, "*The Invention of Air* Captures a Moment in Scientific Time; Books and Authors," p. 4.

Spectator, December 29, 2001, Hugh Lawson-Tancred, review of *Emergence*, p. 38.

Time, May 9, 2005, James Poniewozik, review of *Everything Bad Is Good for You*, p. 67.

Time International, December 18, 2006, Michael Brunton, review of *The Ghost Map*, p. 6.

Top Producer, December 4, 2005, John Phipps, review of *Mind Wide Open*.

WorldLink, January-February, 2002, Lance Knobel, review of *Emergence*, pp. 186-187.

ONLINE

Ape Culture, http://www.apeculture.com/ (February 6, 2006), Mary E. Ladd, review of *Everything Bad Is Good for You*.

Arrow through the Sun, http://arrowthroughthesun.blogspot.com/ (May 27, 2009), review of *The Invention of Air*.

Atlantic Unbound, http://www.theatlantic.com/ (September 17, 2002), Harvey Blume, interview with Johnson.

Best Reviews, http://thebestreviews.com/ (June 25, 2009), Viviane Crystal, "The Building Innovation," review of *The Invention of Air*.

Bookslut, http://www.bookslut.com/ (June, 2005), Liz Miller, review of *Everything Bad Is Good for You*.

Dallas News Online, http://www.dallasnews.com/ (January 4, 2009), Alexandra Witze, review of *The Invention of Air*.

eaves.ca, http://eaves.ca/ (February 27, 2007), David Eaves, review of *Everything Bad Is Good for You*.

Fiddle and Burn, http://www.fiddleandburn.com/ (January 23, 2009), Jason Pomerantz, review of *The Invention of Air*.

Frontline Web site, http://www.pbs.org/wgbh/pages/frontline/ (January 24, 2002), Wen Stephenson, "Beyond the Bubble," interview with Johnson.

inthenews.co.uk, http://www.inthenews.co.uk/ (December 12, 2006), review of *The Ghost Map*.

Oregonian, http://blog.oregonlive.com/ (January 9, 2009), Paul Collins, review of *The Invention of Air*.

O'Reilly Network Web site, http://www.oreillynet.com/ (September 17, 2002), David Sims and Rael Dornfest, interview with Johnson.

Peterme.com, http://www.peterme.com/ (December 30, 2008), review of *The Invention of Air*.

PhiloBiblos, http://philobiblos.blogspot.com/ (January 28, 2009), review of *The Invention of Air*.

PopMatters, http://www.popmatters.com/ (April 6, 2007), Jason B. Jones, "Long Zoom: Interview with Steven Johnson"; (January 19, 2009) Michael Patrick Brady, review of *The Invention of Air*.

Salon.com, http://www.salon.com/ (September 17, 2002), Scott Rosenberg, review of *Interface Culture*; (January 9, 2009) Andrew O'Hehir, "Father of the Ecosystem," review of *The Invention of Air*.

Stating the Obvious, http://www.theobvious.com/ (January 21, 1998), Michael Sippey, "Just One Question for Steven Johnson" (interview).

Steven Johnson Home Page, http://www.stevenberlinjohnson.com (June 25, 2009).*

*   *   *

JONES, Victoria Mary
See JONES, V.M.

*   *   *

JONES, V.M. 1958-
(Victoria Mary Jones)

PERSONAL: Born August 23, 1958, in Luanshya, Northern Rhodesia (now Zambia); married; children: two sons. *Education:* University of Cape Town, B.A.

ADDRESSES: Home—Lunnon, Swansea, West Glamorgan, New Zealand.

CAREER: Writer, novelist, and marketing consultant. Worked previously as a desktop publishing and promotions manager for McGraw-Hill in South Africa. Certified gemologist. Active in the New Zealand Book Council's Writers in School program.

AWARDS, HONORS: Esther Glen Medal shortlist, Library Information Association of New Zealand, 2003, for *Buddy;* *New Zealand Post* book awards for junior fiction and best first book, both 2003, both for *Buddy; New Zealand Post* book award for Junior Fiction, 2004, for *Jugglilng with Mandarins.*

WRITINGS:

Buddy, HarperCollins New Zealand (Auckland, New Zealand), 2002.
Juggling with Mandarins, HarperCollins New Zealand (Auckland, New Zealand), 2003, published as *Out of Reach,* Marshall Cavendish (Tarrytown, NY), 2008.
Shooting the Moon, HarperCollins New Zealand (Auckland, New Zealand), 2006.
Shooting the Moon, illustrated by Scott Tulloch, HarperCollins New Zealand (Auckland, New Zealand), 2008.
Echo and Hush, illustrated by Scott Tulloch, HarperCollins New Zealand (Auckland, New Zealand), 2008.

"KARAZAN QUARTET"

The Serpents of Arakesh, HarperCollins New Zealand (Auckland, New Zealand), 2003.
Beyond the Shroud, HarperCollins New Zealand (Auckland, New Zealand), 2004.
Prince of the Wind, HarperCollins (Auckland, New Zealand), 2004, also published as *The Lost Prince,* Puffin (London, England), 2006.
Quest for the Sun, HarperCollins New Zealand (Auckland, New Zealand), 2006.

SIDELIGHTS: Born in Zambia, educated in Zimbabwe, and currently living in New Zealand, V.M. Jones has seen and lived in many exotic and beautiful places in the world. She was born in Luanshya, a tiny mining town in what was then Northern Rhodesia, now known as Zambia. As a child, she lived in Pietermaritzburg, Durban, and Welkom in South Africa and Redcliff in Zimbabwe. "Many people have commented that my books seem to lack a sense of 'place'—perhaps the amount we moved round when I was a child is partly responsible for this!," Jones said in an interview in *Magpies.*

Jones attended the University of Cape Town, in South Africa, where she completed a bachelor's degree in English, anthropology, and social anthropology. A certified gemologist, Jones worked in this field while she was in South Africa as well as in the publishing industry, as a desktop publishing and promotions manager at McGraw-Hill.

A highly imaginative and literate child, Jones spent most of her childhood "secretly pretending to be someone else—not one particular person, but an endless succession of alter egos," she said in the *Magpies* interview. "That was far more interesting than being an ordinary little girl growing up in a small mining town!" It was this trait, she believes, that helped her develop her early writing skills and her ability to imagine how her characters think, act, and feel. She also read frequently, but noted that "I'm not a particularly fast reader. I tend to wallow in books, rather than devour them, reveling in the rhythm and flow of the language," she noted in *Magpies.*

Whether done quickly or slowly, reading widely and constantly is one of the best pieces of advice she gives to aspiring writers. "Read heaps—and write heaps, too," Jones said in an interview for the *Christchurch City Libraries* Web site. "It's like any exercise—it gets easier the more you do it." She also advises hopeful writers: "Listen to your internal voice, and believe what it tells you—what's real to you will be real to other people, too." To develop a writer's inquisitive mind, Jones advises beginners to: "Keep asking two questions: Why, and What next?"

Jones's novel *Buddy* demonstrates the results of her advice. In the book, teenagers Josh Cranford and Shane Hunter enjoy a fierce rivalry in athletics. The two thirteen-year-olds are both good students, popular with the other kids in school, and extremely good at a variety of sports. But behind the friendly rivalry, Josh's life is not as happy as it seems at school and on the playing field. His parents have divorced, and he does not approve of the new, younger woman that his father has invited into their home. She is no replacement for his mother, and there is little about her that he likes at all. Josh has a great deal of difficulty adjusting to the presence of this new woman in his life and in his house.

The announcement of an underage triathlon at school appears to offer Josh a distraction and a way to again challenge Shane to see who is the superior athlete. But a deeper family secret threatens to disrupt Josh's plans to compete. Years earlier, his twin brother, Buddy, was seriously injured in an accident on the beach. Josh subconsciously blamed himself for the accident, and because of that, he developed a terrible fear of the water and never learned to swim. To compete in the triathlon, however, requires a swimming phase, and Josh must overcome his fear if he hopes to beat Shane in the competition. Calling Jones's first effort "an extraordinary book," Neville Barnard wrote in a review for *Magpies* that the author delivers the theme "you don't have to come first to win. . . . It's a powerful message told in an easy, fluent style that will snare young, fully independent readers—and hold the attention of older ones, too." The novel "deserves to be widely read—books this good are rare and should be shared and enjoyed by as many readers as possible," Barnard also noted.

In *Out of Reach,* first published in New Zealand as *Juggling with Mandarins,* Jones tells the story of thirteen-year-old Phillip (Pip) McLeod. The novel focuses on Pip as he struggles in his relations with his father, a former fire fighter who is now disabled and runs a milk delivery route that is failing. Pip is embarrassed by the fact that his father is very vocal, always making comments heard by everyone during Pip's soccer games. As a result of his father and because he doesn't feel like he can compete with his older, very athletic brother, Pip doesn't want to play soccer anymore. Eventually, Pip discovers the community's new sporting complex and that he is a natural at indoor rock climbing. His friend Kate starts hanging out with Jordan, an egotistical rock climber, leaving Pip behind. During an indoor climbing competition, however, Pip, who now has new friends and is called Phil, beats all the competitors, including Jordan. "A heart-warming story about finding one's strengths and confronting problems," wrote Joel Shoemaker in a review for *School Library Journal.* Noting that "So much life was packed into 264 pages," a contributor to the Web blog *SherMeree's Musing* went on to write in the same review: "The wonderful characters are so realistic they jump out at you."

Jones is also author of the "Karazan Quartet" fantasy series. *The Serpents of Arakesh* begins the series and introduces readers to Adam Equinox, an orphan who suddenly finds that he can enter the adventurous and dangerous parallel world of Karazan. The next book in

the series, *Beyond the Shroud,* finds Adam back in the orphanage, having left Karazan behind. Adam is invited to Quested Court for the holidays. However, once he's there, he discovers that Quentin Quested's daughter Hannah is missing. Adam and his friends set out to find her and discover that she is in Karazan, held captive by the evil King Karazeel.

The next book in the series, *Prince of the Wind,* was also published in England as *The Lost Prince.* Adam finds himself the only child left in the orphanage as all the other children have been adopted. He is going to be sent to another orphanage, and it appears he may never enter the computer-simulated world of Karazan again. The creator of this world, Q, has a secretary, Ms. Usherwood, who adopts Adam, reuniting him with his friends and a new adventure in Karazan as Q comes out with a new video game and Pip and his friends set out to find a lost prince. With *Quest for the Sun,* Jones concludes the series. Adam discovers his true identity and has one last adventure searching for Zenith, Prince of the Sun, who is the brother of Zephyr, Prince of the Wind.

BIOGRAPHICAL AND CRITICAL SOURCES:

PERIODICALS

Bulletin of the Center for Children's Books, December, 2008, Deborah Stevenson, review of *Out of Reach,* p. 158.

Magpies, July, 2002, Neville Barnard, review of *Buddy,* p. 48; July, 2003, Trevor Agnew, interview with V.M. Jones; July, 2003, Neville Barnard, review of *Juggling with Mandarins,* p. 7; July, 2008, Lorraine Orman, review of *Echo and Hush,* p. 4.

New Zealand Listener (Auckland, New Zealand), May 14-20, 2007, David Larsen, "Planet Karazan," interview with author.

School Library Journal, January, 2009, Joel Shoemaker, review of *Out of Reach,* p. 106.

Voice of Youth Advocates, December, 2008, Kim Carter, review of *Out of Reach,* p. 435.

ONLINE

Christchurch City Libraries Web site, http://www. library.christchurch.org.nz/ (October 1, 2003), interview with V.M. Jones.

Flamingnet Young Adult Book, http://flamingnet. blogspot.com/ (December 26, 2008), review of *Out of Reach.*

HarperCollins New Zealand Web site, http://www. harpercollins.co.nz/ (June 25, 2009), overview of *Prince of the Wind.*

Inside a Dog, http://www.insideadog.com.au/ (June 25, 2009), review of *Juggling with Mandarins.*

KIWIreviews.co.nz, http://www.kiwireviews.co.nz/ (June 25, 2009), overview of *Beyond the Shroud.*

New Zealand Book Council Web site, http://www. bookcouncil.org.nz/ (October 1, 2003), profile of V.M. Jones.

Penguin Books Web site, http://www.penguin.co.uk/ (June 25, 2009), overview of *Quest for the Sun.*

SherMeree's Musing, http://shermereem94.blogspot. com/ (March 2, 2009), review of *Out of Reach.*

Wheelers Books, http://www.wheelers.co.nz/ (June 25, 2009), overview of *Serpent's of Arakesh.**

*   *   *

JUNIPER, Alex
See HOSPITAL, Janette Turner

K

KALLOS, Stephanie

PERSONAL: Born in Mountainhome, ID; daughter of Greg and Dorie Kallos; married Bill Johns; children: two sons.

ADDRESSES: Home—Seattle, WA. *Agent*—Writers House, 21 West 26th St., New York, NY 10010. *E-mail*—stevie@stephaniekallos.com.

CAREER: Writer. Previously worked as an actor and teacher.

AWARDS, HONORS: Pushcart Prize nomination, for short story "The Failure of Therapy"; Raymond Carver Short Story Award finalist, for short story "FSBO"; *The Today Show* book club selection, 2004, Pacific Northwest Booksellers Association Award, 2005, and Washington State Book Award, 2005, all for *Broken for You.*

WRITINGS:

Broken for You (fiction), Grove Press (New York, NY), 2004.
Sing Them Home, Grove Press (New York, NY), 2009.

Contributor to periodicals, including *Iconoclast, Chelsea 73,* and *Carve. Broken For You* has been translated into ten languages.

SIDELIGHTS: Stephanie Kallos is an actress-turned-novelist who impressed many critics with her first novel, *Broken for You.* The story centers around two women living with loss. The first, Margaret, has lived in virtual isolation in a Seattle mansion since the death of her son and her divorce from her husband. In her seventies, Margaret discovers she has a brain tumor and decides that she must do something different with her life as the end is apparently near. She opens her mansion to borders, among them Wanda, a maniacally organized stage manager who was abandoned by her parents and is in town looking for a recent boyfriend who did the same. The novel essentially follows Margaret and Wanda as they interact with each other and come to terms with the ghosts of their respective pasts. Bronwyn Miller, in a review for *Bookreporter.com,* noted that as the book is "told in alternating chapters that illuminate the characters as they are now, we also are privy to their back-stories of how they came to be 'broken.' With such insight into these people, *Broken for You* ends up being a life-affirming read rather than a depressing one." Writing for *Booklist,* Jennifer Baker commented: "Well-crafted plotting and crackling wit make this debut novel . . . a delight to read and a memory to savor." *Library Journal* contributor Jenn B. Stidham wrote that the author "has given us a compelling, richly layered story," and a *Publishers Weekly* contributor commented: "Though it takes a while to get started, this haunting and memorable debut is . . . peopled by lovably imperfect and eccentric characters."

The author's second novel, *Sing Them Home,* tells the story of three siblings who continue to grapple with their grief following their mother's disappearance years earlier when a tornado swept through their small town in 1978. "The initial idea for *Sing Them Home* arose from a photo from the March 1974 *National Geographic*—and from my family's personal connection to that photo," the author noted in an interview for the *Midwest Booksellers Association* Web site.

The author goes on in the interview to explain that at the age of five her family lived in Wymore, Nebraska, and were friends with a family that lived outside of town in a restored nineteenth-century farmhouse. The author and her family moved in 1960 and, in 1974, a freak tornado landed on the old farmhouse. "*The National Geographic* photo was taken a few miles away, near Blue Springs, Nebraska," the author recounted. "It shows a vast, flattened, muddied milo field with a farmer leaning over the remains of [our friend's] baby grand piano. It was the only thing that came down in any kind of recognizable form." Kallos also recalled that her mother asked how everything could just disappear and wondered where the house's contents went. "These questions—and their implications—have haunted me ever since," revealed Kallos.

In *Sing Them Home*, Aneira Hope Jones has disappeared from the tiny fictional town of Emlyn Springs, Nebraska, during a tornado, and her three children, now grown, continue to deal with the loss of their mother. Larken, the oldest child, is a history professor who finds solace in food. Bonnie, the middle child, is an amateur archivist who continues to search for clues to her mother's legacy. Meanwhile, the youngest son, Gaelan, is a television weatherman who is dedicated to predicting the area's largely unpredictable weather. When their distant father, Llewellyn Jones, dies in a strange way, the three children return home and are face-to-face once again with their family's tragic past and their father's longtime lover, Viney Closs, who was their mother's best friend and ended up helping to raise her kids.

A contributor to the *Book Chick* Web site remarked that "I found myself reading with increasing desperation to find out the secrets of Emlyn Springs." Kallos tells the story via various characters' points of view, including Hope's missing diaries. As the story progresses, readers, as well as the three siblings in the novel, learn about the past of Hope and Llewellyn, including the fact that Hope had several miscarriages and was diagnosed with multiple sclerosis just before she was taken.

The town of Emlyn Springs and its inhabitants also play a major role in the novel. Each year, the townspeople's Welsh heritage leads them to honor their dead in a strange way featuring a week of silence and song meant to help the newly dead pass on into the afterlife. "With its Welsh heritage especially—reflected and really outlined here in language, rituals and traditions—as well as characters far richer than small town clichés,

the town becomes actually not a backdrop at all, but is as much of a character in the story as its residents," noted a contributor to the *Pickle Me This* Web site. The novel fluctuates between the story of Hope and Llewellyn from the past and the yearlong story of three siblings finally coming to resolutions in their own lives of personal pain, all through love and the formation of a new family.

"The author, who has roots in Nebraska, is working in a vast landscape here, both emotional and physical," wrote Shawna Seed in a review for the *Dallas News Online*. "She handles it all with grace, giving each character and plot line a satisfying finish, like chords resolving themselves." Heather Paulson, writing for *Booklist*, commented that the author "stitches together a colorful patchwork of memories and images, creating a rich narrative fabric."

BIOGRAPHICAL AND CRITICAL SOURCES:

PERIODICALS

Booklist, August, 2004, Jennifer Baker, review of *Broken for You*, p. 1900; November 1, 2008, Heather Paulson, review of *Sing Them Home*, p. 25.
Entertainment Weekly, January 16, 2009, Karen Valby, review of *Sing Them Home*, p. 69.
Kirkus Reviews, July 15, 2004, review of *Broken for You*, p. 650; October 15, 2008, review of *Sing Them Home*.
Library Journal, August, 2004, Jenn B. Stidham, review of *Broken for You*, p. 68; September 1, 2008, Barbara Hoffert, review of *Sing Them Home*, p. 118.
Marie Claire, January, 2009, Lori Fradkin, review of *Sing Them Home*, p. 43.
Publishers Weekly, July 12, 2004, review of *Broken for You*, p. 41; September 1, 2008, review of *Sing Them Home*, p. 33.
Seattle Times, January 11, 2009, "A Family's Fate Is in the Wind; Books and Authors," p. 4.
Star Tribune (Minneapolis, MN), January 4, 2009, Katherine Bailey, "Implausibility Casts Specter over Melodrama; FICTION: Three Siblings Reunite for the Funeral of Their Welsh Father," p. 12.

ONLINE

Book Chick, http://book-chic.blogspot.com/ (February 25, 2009), review of *Sing Them Home*.

BookPage, http://www.bookpage.com/ (June 25, 2009), Deborah Donovan, review of *Sing Them Home.*

Bookreporter.com, http://www.bookreporter.com/ (May 30, 2005), Bronwyn Miller, review of *Broken for You;* (June 25, 2009) Norah Piehl, review of *Sing Them Home.*

Dallas News Online, http://www.dallasnews.com/ (January 12, 2009), Shawna Sees, *"Sing Them Home* by Stephanie Kallos: Plot Twister Sets Sprawling Novel in Motion."

Ezine Articles, http://ezinearticles.com/ (June 25, 2009), Karen Haney, review of *Sing Them Home.*

Hedgebrook, http://www.hedgebrook.org/ (June 25, 2009), short biography and list of books and awards.

Midwest Booksellers Association Web site, http://www.midwestbooksellers.org/ (June 25, 2009), "Q & A with Stephanie Kallos."

Oregonian, http://blog.oregonlive.com/ (January 16, 2009), Alexis Nelson, review of *Sing Them Home.*

Pickle Me This, http://picklemethis.blogspot.com/ (February 27, 2009), review of *Sing Them Home.*

Seattlepi.com, http://blog.seattlepi.com/ (June 25, 2009), "A Conversation with Seattle Author Stephanie Kallos."

Stephanie Kallos Home Page, http://stephaniekallos. com (June 25, 2009).

*　*　*

KAMEN, Paula 1967-

PERSONAL: Born April 9, 1967, in Chicago, IL; daughter of Joseph and Beatrice Kamen. *Education:* University of Illinois at Urbana-Champaign, B.S., 1989.

ADDRESSES: Home—Chicago, IL. *Office*—PMB 274, 5315 N. Clark St., Chicago, IL 60640-2113. *Agent*—Daniel Greenberg, Levine Greenberg Literary Agency, 307 7th Ave., Ste. 2407, New York, NY 10001. *E-mail*—paulak2289@aol.com.

CAREER: Writer, playwright, journalist, public speaker, and educator. Star Publications, Chicago Heights, IL, reporting intern, 1987; Whittle Communications, Knoxville, TN, editorial intern, 1988; *Daily Herald,* Du Page County, IL, stringer, 1989; *Kenosha News,* reporter, 1990; visiting research scholar at Northwestern University, 1994—. Aunt Martha's Social Service Agency, big sister to foster children, 1991.

AWARDS, HONORS: Certificate of Merit, feature writing, Hearst National Writing Competition, 1988; *Chicago Tribune* favorite books of 2007 citation, and 2007 *Booksense* pick, both for *Finding Iris Chang: Friendship, Ambition and the Loss of an Extraordinary Mind.*

WRITINGS:

Feminist Fatale: Voices from the Twentysomething Generation Explore the Future of the Women's Movement, Donald I. Fine (New York, NY), 1991.

Seven Dates with Seven Writers (play), first produced at the Factory Theater Comedy Festival, 1998.

Jane: Abortion and the Underground (play), first produced by the Green Highway Theater Company in Chicago, IL, 1999.

A Cure for AIDS (play), first produced by SNAP! Productions in Omaha, NE, July, 2000.

Her Way: Young Women Remake the Sexual Revolution, New York University (New York, NY), 2001.

All in My Head: An Epic Quest to Cure an Unrelenting, Totally Unreasonable, and Only Slightly Enlightening Headache (memoir), Da Capo (Cambridge, MA), 2005.

Finding Iris Chang: Friendship, Ambition and the Loss of an Extraordinary Mind (memoir and biography), Da Capo (Cambridge, MA), 2007.

Contributor to anthologies, including *Next: Young American writers on the New Generation,* Norton, 1994; *"Bad Girls/ Good Girls": Women, Sex and Power in the Nineties,* Rutgers University Press, 1996; *Shiny Adidas Track Suits and the Death of Camp: The Best of Might Magazine,* Berkley Boulevard, 1998; and *Appeal to Reason: The First Twenty-five Years of In These Times,* 2002. Guest columnist, *New York Times Online,* spring, 2008. Contributor to periodicals, including *New York Times, Washington Post, Chicago Tribune, Might, Seventeen,* and *Ms.* Kamen's research papers are housed at the Special Collections Department of the Northwestern University Library and at the Sallie Bingham Center for Women's History and Culture at Duke University.

SIDELIGHTS: Paula Kamen told *CA:* "I specialize in writing on feminist and health issues and the post-boomer generation, with an accessible, humorous style." Kamen's *Feminist Fatale: Voices from the Twentysomething Generation Explore the Future of the Women's Movement* discusses feminist topics from the perspective of younger women. *Los Angeles Times Book Review* contributor Jacqueline Austin found the book filled with "interesting, surprising assertions" and hailed it as a "broad portrait of today's women's movement" written from a "singularly intelligent point of view." Based on 236 interviews, the book covers such issues as women's health, the effects of Republican agendas on the women's movement, and problems faced by women of color. Throughout, Kamen argues that the feminist cause has been hurt by its past successes, that established feminist organizations do not actively welcome the contributions of younger women, and that younger women are generally less politicized than earlier generations—unless a negative experience radicalizes them. Austin praised Kamen for asking readers some difficult questions, and commended *Feminist Fatale* as a "thoughtful book by a promising, provocative writer."

In *Her Way: Young Women Remake the Sexual Revolution,* Kamen offers a survey of young women's attitudes toward sex at the end of the 1990s. Based on more than one hundred interviews, the book shows that young women expect more autonomy and choice in their sexual lives—to the extent that college-age women reveal attitudes and behaviors similar to those of college-age men. Seeing these new mores as evidence of confidence, Kamen finds that young women exhibit a high degree of comfort with their own sexuality. Many reviewers welcomed *Her Way* as an intelligent and informative book. In the *New York Times Book Review,* Courtney Weaver called it an "exhaustive and complex survey of what women want," and praised Kamen's ability to highlight her data's more startling and amusing material. Though Weaver noted that the book is "sometimes spread too thin," the critic went on to write that "reading it is an education." *National Review* contributor Maggie Gallagher wrote that "Kamen is . . . a good journalist who asks key questions and lets her subjects speak for themselves."

In her memoir *All in My Head: An Epic Quest to Cure an Unrelenting, Totally Unreasonable, and Only Slightly Enlightening Headache,* Kamen recounts her long battle with chronic headaches. Her headaches began at the age of twenty-four. The book follows Kamen's experience over the next ten years as she tries various remedies, from standard drugs with their annoying and sometimes dangerous side effects to alternative medicines, which proved to be ineffective in the author's case. Through a series of interviews, the author also probes the problems of chronic pain sufferers in general. Kamen includes numerous sidebars throughout the book in which the latest scientific research concerning chronic

pain problems and new treatments are discussed. Although several critics noted that a book about a ten-year constant headache might not sound like a fun read, most agreed that Kamen's handling of the topic manages to overcome that obstacle. A *Publishers Weekly* contributor, for example, noted that the author's "irreverent sense of humor about her pain and herself makes the book a delight to read." Eris Weaver, writing in the *Library Journal,* called *All in My Head* "engaging, informative, and at times humorous." A *Kirkus Reviews* contributor referred to the memoir as "sharp, entertaining, informative, and blessedly free of poor-me-see-how-I-suffered-ism."

Kamen's *Finding Iris Chang: Friendship, Ambition and the Loss of an Extraordinary Mind* tells the story of journalist Iris Chang, the Chinese American author of the worldwide best seller *The Rape of Nanking.* Chang and Kamen were friends from the time they were in school together, and Kamen was one of the last people Chang spoke to before she committed suicide by shooting herself in the head on a lonely California road in November of 2004. "The news of [Chang's] death was so startling," declared Stephanie Losee in *Salon.com,* "that many concluded she had been murdered by political or government organizations, angered by her unflinching exposure of the rape, torture and murder of more than 300,000 Chinese civilians and soldiers by the Japanese army during a weeks-long siege of Nanking in 1937. When the *San Francisco Chronicle* published excerpts of Chang's three suicide notes, along with details of her breakdown, the mystery only deepened." "Chang was 36 and had much to live for—fame, fortune, beauty, a loving husband, caring parents, and a beautiful new baby," explained Andrew Lam in *New American Media.* "Seeking to reconcile Chang's seemingly perfect life with her mysterious suicide, Kamen scoured correspondences, diaries, archival material as well as her own memories. The result is *Finding Iris Chang,* a suspenseful investigation into a writer's journey and mental illness." "As exuberant and zealous as Chang may have seemed to many people, Kamen discovered Chang strived hard to outwit the public and even those close to her," *Beijing Review* reporter Wu Yiqing stated. "To her surprise, Kamen learned that Chang suffered miscarriages and in the end resorted to use a surrogate mother to conceive her only child. Chang stayed at home till the baby was born—to purport the idea that she was pregnant." "Kamen concludes," wrote *San Francisco Chronicle* contributor Mary D'Ambrosio, "that bipolar disorder drove Chang to kill herself." "Kamen dutifully delves into the larger issues of suicide and mental illness in Asian-American communities," a *Kirkus Reviews* contributor stated, "and into the peculiar immigrant drive to succeed that seized Chang so forcefully at such a young age."

"*Finding Iris Chang* also examines the link between madness and genius, reminding that mood disorders aren't required for great accomplishment (and that you can be sick without accomplishing any particular greatness)," Jeff Wenger declared in the *Asian Reporter,* "but 'that the creative are disproportionately affected by these conditions.'" "She notes," reported D'Ambrosio, "that some 50 percent of those with bipolar disorder attempt suicide and that Asian American women ages 15 to 34 are twice as likely as their white counterparts to kill themselves." "Kamen also explains the forensic evidence concerning Chang's death," Wenger continued, "and is satisfied that it was, in fact, a suicide, and that she was not assassinated by extremist elements and that, while we're at it, the U.S. government was not out to get her." "Through her discoveries," Wu concluded, "Kamen ruled out rumors of a Japanese right-wing's assassination plot and concluded that Chang was her own worst enemy." *Finding Iris Chang* explores "the unique genius and creativity of Chang, the far-reaching effects of her persistent social activism and compassion," Allison Hood wrote on *BookPage,* "and, sadly, the relentless escalation of the bipolar disorder that impelled her to suicide."

BIOGRAPHICAL AND CRITICAL SOURCES:

BOOKS

Kamen, Paula, *All in My Head: An Epic Quest to Cure an Unrelenting, Totally Unreasonable, and Only Slightly Enlightening Headache,* Da Capo (Cambridge, MA), 2005.

Kamen, Paula, *Finding Iris Chang: Friendship, Ambition and the Loss of an Extraordinary Mind,* Da Capo (Cambridge, MA), 2007.

PERIODICALS

American Scientist, May-June, 2005, Amos Esty, review of *All in My Head: An Epic Quest to Cure an Unrelenting, Totally Unreasonable, and Only Slightly Enlightening Headache,* p. 269.

Beijing Review, December 1, 2007, Wu Yiqing, "Connecting the Threads of Tragedy."

Booklist, December 15, 2000, Vanessa Bush, review of *Her Way: Young Women Remake the Sexual Revolution,* p. 766.

Books, November 17, 2007, "A Short, Passionate Life: Paula Kamen Seeks Answers about the Death of Her Friend, Author Iris Chang," p. 4.

California Bookwatch, January 1, 2008, review of *Finding Iris Chang.*

Chicago, January, 2001, Robert Kurson, "Virgin Territory," author interview, p. 18.

Chicago Reader, November 1, 2007, Kerry Reid, "What Happened to Iris Chang?"

Deseret News, November 18, 2007, Dennis Lythgoe, "'Finding Iris Chang' Is Friend's Take on Troubled Author."

Internet Bookwatch, September, 2006, review of *All in My Head.*

Kirkus Reviews, January 1, 2005, review of *All in My Head,* p. 35; September 15, 2007, review of *Finding Iris Chang.*

Library Journal, September 15, 1991, Beverly Miller, review of *Feminist Fatale: Voices from the Twenty-something Generation Explore the Future of the Women's Movement,* p. 104; February 15, 2005, Eris Weaver, review of *All in My Head,* p. 150; December 1, 2007, Kathryn R. Bartelt, review of *Finding Iris Chang,* p. 128.

Los Angeles Times Book Review, October 20, 1991, Jacqueline Austin, review of *Feminist Fatale.*

Ms., December, 2000, Sanaz Mozafarian, review of *Her Way,* p. 88.

National Review, July 9, 2001, Maggie Gallagher, review of *Her Way.*

New Directions for Women, May, 1992, review of *Feminist Fatale,* p. 19.

New York Times Book Review, January 28, 2001, Courtney Weaver, review of *Her Way,* p. 20.

Publishers Weekly, September 13, 1991, review of *Feminist Fatale,* p. 74; November 20, 2000, review of *Her Way,* p. 57; January 17, 2005, review of *All in My Head,* p. 44; September 10, 2007, review of *Finding Iris Chang,* p. 51.

St. Louis Post-Dispatch, December 9, 2007, Repps Hudson, "Finding Iris Chang: Friendship, Ambition, and the Loss of an Extraordinary Mind."

San Francisco Chronicle, November 11, 2007, Mary D'Ambrosio, "Paula Kamen Investigates Friend's Suicide in 'Finding Iris Chang.'"

School Library Journal, April, 1992, Christine C. Menefee, review of *Feminist Fatale,* p. 165.

Women's Review of Books, June, 2001, Rebecca L. Walkowitz, review of *Her Way,* p. 20; May-June, 2006, Debra Spark, review of *All in My Head,* p. 11.

ONLINE

Asian Reporter, http://www.asianreporter.com/ (August 28, 2008), Jeff Wenger, review of *Finding Iris Chang.*

BookPage, http://www.bookpage.com/ (August 28, 2008), Alison Hood, review of *Finding Iris Chang.*

ChronicBabe.com, http://www.chronicbabe.com/ (August 28, 2008), Jenni Prokopy, review of *All in My Head.*

Dancing with Pain, http://dancingwithpain.com/ (August 28, 2008), Loolwa Khazzoom, "Paula Kamen Talks Shop about Writing a Book on Chronic Daily Headache."

New American Media, http://news.newamericamedia. org/ (August 28, 2008), Andrew Lam, review of *Finding Iris Chang.*

Paula Kamen Home Page, http://www.paulakamen.com (August 28, 2008).

Reading Archives, http://readingarchives.blogspot.com/ (August 28, 2008), review of *Finding Iris Chang.*

Salon.com, http://www.salon.com/ (August 28, 2008), Stephanie Losee, "The Demons You Know."

SFist, http://www.sfist.com/ (August 28, 2008), "Interview: Paula Kamen."*

*   *   *

KANFER, Stefan 1933-

PERSONAL: Born May 17, 1933; son of Allen (a teacher) and Violet (a scriptwriter) Kanfer; married May Markey (a teacher), 1956; children: Lilian, Ethan. *Education:* New York University, B.A., 1953, graduate study, 1955-57.

ADDRESSES: Home—New York, NY. *Agent*—Kathy Robbins, The Robbins Office, 405 Park Ave., New York, NY 10020. *E-mail*—kanfer1@aol.com.

CAREER: Writer, journalist, editor, critic, television screenwriter, and educator. *New York Herald Tribune,* New York, NY, copy boy, 1951-53; television writer for *The Patty Duke Show* in the early 1960s and for Victor Borge and Allen Funt, 1964-65; *Time,* New York, NY, show business writer, cinema critic, essay anchor man, and book review editor, 1967-75, senior editor, 1975-88; *New Leader,* theatre critic and columnist, beginning 1990. Member of Distinguished Writer program,

Southampton College, Long Island University; has been a writer in residence at the City University of New York, (CUNY), and a visiting professor at State University of New York at Purchase and Wesleyan University. Served on the President's Commission on the Holocaust. *Military service:* U.S. Army, 1953-55.

MEMBER: Writers Guild of America, Dramatists Guild.

AWARDS, HONORS: J.C. Penney-University of Missouri Journalism Award, 1975; named Literary Lion of the New York Public Library, 1988; Westchester Writers Prize, 1995, 2000.

WRITINGS:

NONFICTION

A Journal of the Plague Years, Atheneum (New York, NY), 1973.

A Summer World: The Attempt to Build a Jewish Eden in the Catskills from the Days of the Ghetto to the Rise of the Borscht Belt, Farrar, Straus (New York, NY), 1989.

The Last Empire: De Beers, Diamonds, and the World, Farrar, Straus (New York, NY), 1993.

Serious Business: The Art and Commerce of Animation in America from Betty Boop to Toy Story, Scribner (New York, NY), 1997.

Groucho: The Life and Times of Julius Henry Marx, Knopf (New York, NY), 2000.

(Editor and author of introduction) *The Essential Groucho: Writings by and for Groucho Marx,* Vintage (New York, NY), 2000.

Ball of Fire: The Tumultuous Life and Comic Art of Lucille Ball, Knopf (New York, NY), 2003.

Stardust Lost: The Triumph, Tragedy, and Mishugas of the Yiddish Theater in America, Knopf (New York, NY), 2006.

The Voodoo That They Did so Well: The Wizards Who Invented the New York Stage, Ivan R. Dee (Chicago, IL), 2007.

Somebody: The Reckless Life and Remarkable Career of Marlon Brando, Alfred A. Knopf (New York, NY), 2008.

NOVELS

The Eighth Sin, Random House (New York, NY), 1978.
Fear Itself, Putnam (New York, NY), 1981.

The International Garage Sale, Norton (New York, NY), 1985.

PLAYS

I Want You (two-act musical), first produced Off-Broadway at Maidman Playhouse, 1958.
The Coffee Lover (two-act comedy), first produced in Eastern United States at summer stock theaters, 1964.

Author of short stories. Contributor of articles and reviews to periodicals, including *Atlantic, New York Times, Harper's,* and *New Republic.* Contributing editor, *City Journal.*

ADAPTATIONS: *Groucho: The Life and Times of Julius Henry Marx,* has been purchased by Stephen Spielberg for a film on Marx.

SIDELIGHTS: Stefan Kanfer has produced a diverse selection of books, encompassing satirical and serious novels as well as chronicles of diamond mining in South Africa and the life of famed comedian Groucho Marx. His first book, *A Journal of the Plague Years,* is an account of the "blacklisting and persecution" in the entertainment industry during the McCarthy era. Convinced that such a plague could again afflict the United States, Kanfer warns that complacency in such matters "is extremely ill-advised." The author offers another admonition in his second book, a novel, *The Eighth Sin,* where the sin of the title refers to forgetting about the Nazi Holocaust.

The Eighth Sin tells the story of Benoit, a gypsy survivor of the Auschwitz prison camp where the rest of his family has died. He is adopted by an American and his wife in England and then moves with his new family to New York City. His talent for painting is obscured by a penchant for shoplifting, a term in prison, and later a troubled marriage and alcoholism. In addition to his personal problems, Benoit carries with him the haunting memory of prison camp life. As Richard Freedman pointed out in the *New York Times Book Review,* "Benoit cannot and will not forget; the memory of the horror blights his life . . . Ultimately Benoit must seek revenge on Elezar Jassy, a gypsy who collaborated with the Nazis while protecting the boy when he was in Auschwitz." Freedman, however, objected to the "factual 'Items'" that "obstruct the fictional flow,

suggesting cool authorial research rather than genuine remembrance of nightmares past. This only slightly mars an absorbing narrative otherwise compounded of hot rage and ribald humor."

A subsequent novel, *The International Garage Sale,* is lighter in tone but still has serious points to make. Its protagonist is Alex Lessing, a television journalist covering the World Body, an organization resembling the United Nations. He finds a surreal environment where lies, bribery, and even murder are accepted means of managing world affairs. He is "the sane, principled character in a world lacking a common moral denominator," explained Eugene J. McCarthy in the *New Republic.* McCarthy had high praise for the novel: "The book is very close to what Evelyn Waugh might have written were he living and observing, as Kanfer does, the United Nations, network television, and today's sexual, social, and family mores." *People* contributor Campbell Geeslin also applauded the work, calling it "an elaborate, carefully crafted book that has too much truth in its outrageous plot."

The Last Empire: De Beers, Diamonds, and the World is a study of the Oppenheimer family, controllers of two huge South African companies, De Beers and Anglo American, involved in diamond and gold mining and many other enterprises. The Oppenheimers have been not only successful capitalists but strong voices of opposition to South Africa's apartheid system, which was finally dismantled in the 1990s. "They have also been inevitably accused of hypocrisy for criticizing the repressive policies of South African governments while continuing to exploit cheap black labor," reported Peter Foster in a review of Kanfer's book for *Canadian Business.* "Nevertheless, one of the first people Nelson Mandela wanted to see on his release from prison . . . was Harry Oppenheimer, son of Ernest, the founder of the De Beers/Anglo American empire." Foster thought highly of *The Last Empire*'s telling of the Oppenheimer saga, noting: "Kanfer deals well with the enormous complexities of South African history in particular with the evolution of the frequently testy relationship between commercial adventurers such as [Cecil] Rhodes and [Ernest] Oppenheimer and the local farmers of Dutch origin, the Boers." A *Publishers Weekly* contributor, however, commented that Kanfer "focuses more clearly on history than on analysis" and lamented the absence of information about the role of De Beers and Anglo in constructing a post-apartheid South Africa and what reforms in the nation would mean for the companies.

In other works, Kanfer has dealt with various aspects of show business, and one of its icons is the subject of *Groucho: The Life and Times of Julius Henry Marx.* Kanfer chronicles the launching of the Marx Brothers' career by their ambitious mother, Minnie; their success in vaudeville, on Broadway, and in films; Groucho's development into the most famous member of the act, with his wisecracking, mustachioed, cigar-chomping persona; and his personal failings, including mistreatment of his wives and children. *New York Times Book Review* commentator Gary Giddins described the book as "a vivid, cleanly written biography," and he observed that Kanfer "stays away from facile psychology and moves his story along at a clip." However, he found that Kanfer had made several factual errors, something that "undermines his authority," and he deplored the dearth of primary research on Kanfer's part. Groucho's grandson, Andy Marx, reviewing the book for *Variety,* noted that "there's very little that hasn't appeared somewhere else," but "Kanfer has managed the Herculean task of synthesizing the material into a thorough, all-encompassing, though sometimes heavy-handed" account of Groucho and his brothers. Still, Marx found the book lacking in drama: "While Groucho's career was certainly fascinating, he didn't lead a life teeming with explosive secrets." Marx went on to note: "Sure, he was married three times, a modest number by Hollywood standards. And, yes, he was abusive to the people around him, including his wives and children, and was a narcissistic parent. But these traits aren't exactly rare in the entertainment industry. And the profile of the comedian with the dark, sad persona is as old as the history of clowns."

Kanfer further explores the legend and talent of the most famous Marx brother in *The Essential Groucho: Writings by and for Groucho Marx.* In the volume, Kanfer presents a variety of works from the comic's lengthy and irreverent career, including scripts of the numerous movies in which he appeared, transcripts from the Groucho-headed quiz show *You Bet Your Life,* and much more. Kanfer also includes several essays by Marx himself, pieces that reveal the depth of Groucho's own talent as a writer, comic, and thinker. "Groucho was the most verbal Marx, gifted from the beginning with a wit capable of hilariously reducing, in mere seconds, any conversation, however rational and civilized, to free-associating, anarchic drivel," observed Ray Olsen, writing for *Booklist.* Other essays by Marx address the early years of the Marx Brothers' career, including their lean times while developing their comedic talents, the decline of vaudeville, and the burgeoning of their widespread fame in the infancy of Hollywood. "Grou-

cho's iconoclastic wit has certainly left a stamp on Western humor and certainly his style and image have passed into 20th-century mythology as much as Elvis Presley (who died the same week Groucho did), Marilyn Monroe, or Albert Einstein," noted reviewer Claude Lalumière for the *January* magazine Web site. A *Publishers Weekly* contributor called the book "a delicious distillation of the comic's verve."

Serious Business: The Art and Commerce of Animation in America from Betty Boop to Toy Story contains a detailed study of movie cartoons, biographical information on the pioneering animators and creators who made them, and consideration of their position and importance within the wider world of politics, popular culture, and entertainment. Kanfer looks carefully at the numerous studios that made cartoons and animated features, including Warner Brothers, UPA, Fleischer Brothers, and, largest of them all, Walt Disney Studios. He uncovers biographical and professional highlights of prominent creators, including pioneer Ub Iwerks, Otto Messmer (who created Felix the Cat), Tex Avery, Ralph Bakshi, and many others. He notes how the technologies of the time, from the painstaking hand-drawing of each frame in the early days to the streamlined computer animation of today, influenced the tone and content of animated works. *Booklist* contributor Mike Tribby remarked that Kanfer's book stands as an "essential resource for students of animation and entertaining fun for all its fans." Kanfer's book "should certainly join the ranks of important literature in the field," commented Carol J. Binkowski in *Library Journal.* The narrative's "quick pace and juicy anecdotes" constitute a "fascinating look at a largely neglected part of Hollywood history," noted Alex Abramovich, writing for *Entertainment Weekly.*

In *Ball of Fire: The Tumultuous Life and Comic Art of Lucille Ball* Kanfer presents a detailed biography of one of the icons of television comedy. Kanfer profiles Ball in depth, covering her early and often neglected years as a glamorous Hollywood beauty, her entry into comedy, and the evolution of her style as a redheaded purveyor of slapstick for a thoroughly appreciative television audience who tuned in throughout the medium's infancy. Approximately a third of Kanfer's biography focuses on Ball's nine years playing Lucy Ricardo opposite her then-husband, Desi Arnaz. Her work during these years constitutes her "claim to immortality; nothing she did before or after, in six decades of performing, would get her into comedy's hall of fame on the first ballot," commented Terrence Rafferty in a review for the *New York Times*. Kanfer also considers Ball's personal life and her stormy marriage to Arnaz, who remained perpetually smitten by her even though he was prone to philandering. Through it all, Ball remained a pioneer who pushed the boundaries of comedy as well as women's place in Hollywood. "Lucy took great chances, wanted many of the things we all want, and got everything she'd wanted and then some, all at once and late. She was in her forties by the time they got their TV show on the air, had their two children, and became rich and famous," noted Mona Simpson in the *Atlantic*. Yet her comedy would become, and remain, a defining force in television, powerfully influential in its day and with repercussions still felt in modern programming. "As Kanfer tells it, Ball was a hot-tempered star, and she wasn't much of a mom. But, as a TV producer who helped establish an important studio, she forged new territory for women in Hollywood," noted reviewer Pat Broeske for the *BookPage* Web site. Ball's tenure at Desilu Studios not only resulted in the various incarnations of the *Lucy Show*, but in other television programming that has reached iconic status. It was through Ball's influence, for example, that a maverick science fiction program called *Star Trek* was produced and aired, as was legendary spy program *Mission: Impossible*. In the book's final chapters, Kanfer looks at Ball's declining years and ultimate death. "The final third of the book is pure Hollywood tragedy, as Ball confronts old age and a declining career," noted Robert Ito in a review for *Los Angeles*.

In general, critics and reviewers responded well to *Ball of Fire*. *Library Journal* contributor Rosellen Brewer called it an "important book" and the "first study to examine all aspects of Ball's life, work, and business acumen." A writer for the *Hollywood Reporter* named it a "fine portrait that honors its complex subject," while a *Publishers Weekly* contributor named it an "excellent, compulsively readable biography." *Time* magazine contributor James Poniewozik noted: "Ball's many fans . . . will enjoy how vividly Kanfer captures Ball in her prime—brave, pioneering and, above all, ravenous for applause."

Stardust Lost: The Triumph, Tragedy, and Mishugas of the Yiddish Theater in America traces the formation and development of Yiddish theater from its origins in Eastern Europe during the Crimean War to its successful expression and profound influence a half-century later in London and New York. In its early days, Yiddish theater was a form of escape for war-weary viewers. While crude, it was well appreciated, and flourished wherever writers, directors, performers, and viewers were passionate enough to support it. Later, early performers such as Jacob Adler and writers such as Sholem Aliechem "transformed it into highly literate entertainment" and helped propel Yiddish theater to world-class stature, noted Jack Helbig, writing for *Booklist*. *Library Journal* contributor Larry Schwartz called the book a "vibrant and painful recapitulation of a world that is nearly gone forever." As Kanfer points out, however, the influence of the Yiddish theater can still be seen in the works of actors such as Marlon Brando and Al Pacino and in the works of directors such as Sidney Lumet. "Kanfer's book solidly conveys the excitement and impact of Yiddish theater, not to mention its long shadow," commented Joseph Dorman in the *New York Times*.

In his next book, *The Voodoo That They Did so Well: The Wizards Who Invented the New York Stage*, Kanfer provides a history of modern theater in New York City via biographies of some of Broadway's most famous contributors. Focusing primarily on musical theatre, the author profiles luminaries such as Irving Berlin, Stephen Sondheim, Richard Rodgers, Cole Porter, and George and Ira Gershwin. Kanfer also provides accounts of major contributors to Yiddish theater and vaudeville. In addition, he includes the story of Lorenzo Da Ponte, a librettist for Mozart who wrote the libretti to *Così Fan Tutte, Don Giovanni,* and *The Marriage of Figaro*. Kanfer recounts how Ponte dazzles audiences in Europe before coming to America, where he falls onto hard times and ends up selling groceries and teaching Italian at Columbia University. An *Internet Bookwatch* contributor called *The Voodoo That They Did so Well* "an outstanding, lively history."

Kanfer turns his focus to one of film's most lauded and most troubled actors with *Somebody: The Reckless Life and Remarkable Career of Marlon Brando*. Siobhan Synnot, writing for the *Scotland on Sunday* Web site, described Brando this way: "Movies often posed moral questions for men to resolve, but Brando was one of the first actors to wrestle with them. Heart-stoppingly handsome . . ., he brought new emotional tools to male screen acting, such as improvisatory passion, vulnerability, self-loathing and cool. Even now, seeing the Hamlet of Hollywood pick up Eva Marie Saint's glove and put it on his big paw in *On The Waterfront* is one of the smallest but most expressive character gestures on film."

The author begins with Brando's early life in Nebraska, where he was born in 1924. Kanfer writes of Brando growing up in the depression but focuses primarily on his relationship with his distant and sometimes brutal father and his alcoholic mother. Eventually Brando escaped from his repressive life in Nebraska and headed to New York City. As noted by *New York Times* contributor Claudia Roth Pierpont, Brando made an immediate impact on the Broadway stage. Playing an ex-G.I. in the short-lived *Truckline Café,* Brando only had a secondary role. However his five-minute soliloquy, during which he confesses to murdering his wife after finding out that she was unfaithful to him during the war, held audiences spellbound. Pierpont noted: "Karl Malden, who played another minor role, reported that the rest of the cast sometimes had to wait for nearly two minutes after Brando's exit while the audience screamed and stamped its feet."

Kanfer goes on to describe how Brando's big break came when John Garfield, an established Hollywood star set to play the anti-hero Stanley Kowaslki in Tennessee Williams's play *A Streetcar Named Desire,* was replaced by the still relatively unknown Brando after Garfield made too many demands on the play's producer. It became apparent even in rehearsals that Brando's character was taking over the play, which was written to revolve around the character of Blanche DuBois, played by Jessica Tandy. "'Streetcar' was an enormous hit and Tandy received excellent notices, but it was Brando the audiences loved," noted Pierpont in her book review for the *New York Times.*

The author then follows Brando to Hollywood in 1949, where he impressed audiences in his first film, *The Men,* about a paralyzed World War II veteran. However, it was Brando's next project, the film version of *A Streetcar Named Desire,* for which he received an academy award nomination, that projected him to the top echelon of film actors in terms of talent. It was during this time as well, that the American public began to learn more about Brando's outrageous personality as the tabloids began reporting on the actor's personal life.

Although the author chronicles Brando's career in depth, he also closely examines Brando the man, from all of his personal peccadilloes to the many tragedies that he would face later in his personal life. Writing for *Booklist,* Joanne Wilkinson commented that the author attributes Brando's "compulsive womanizing and overeating, deep ambivalence about acting, and general self-destructiveness . . . to his treatment at the hands of a belittling, authoritarian father." Kanfer points out

that Brando's father had told him from a young age that he would not accomplish much in life and, even after Brando became a successful actor, condemned his son's profession as meaningless. In relation to his career, Kanfer writes that Brando never did reach the great heights that many people predicted for his career as he began picking mediocre projects in which, according to a *New York Times Book Review* contributor, Brando "gave indifferent performances, however speckled they might be with astonishing flashes." However, as chronicled by Kanfer, Brando did make a comeback in the seventies with films such as *The Godfather.*

Kanfer goes on to examine Brando's later life, during which he became excessively overweight and endured such tragedies as the suicide of one of his daughters and a son being convicted of murder. He also writes of Brando's later troubles with money and his support of various radical causes, such as the Black Panthers and issues concerning Native Americans. The book includes a list of all of Brando's Broadway and film credits.

"Over nearly 400 pages of insightful text . . . Kanfer . . . tracks Brando's bizarre life effectively, delivering a portrait that, while critical, is also appropriately respectful," wrote Carlo Wolff in a review for he *Denver Post.* Calling the biography "a thoughtful and well-balanced look at the man who changed film acting forever," *Straight.com* contributor John Lekich went on in the same review to call *Somebody* "a valuable portrait of a man who paid a high price for . . . working without a mask."

Kanfer told *CA:* "I became interested in writing at an early age when I read the published books of my maternal grandparents, as well as the poetry of my father, which appeared in various quarterlies, *Harpers,* etc. Literature, in fact, is a family tradition.

"The influences on my work are too numerous to list. Writers are the beneficiaries of all who went before. In the last decade or so I have specialized in biography, but the poetry of Wallace Stevens and the satires of Evelyn Waugh are just as influential as the biographical works of Lytton Strachey and David McCullough.

"In general, I take about a year and a half to do the detective work necessary for biography or social history. During that time I steep like a tea bag in various libraries, ranging from the Sterling Library at Yale to the 42nd Street and Lincoln Center libraries in New York City. At the same time I conduct interviews with the people relevant to the narrative. After that (and sometimes during it), the writing process begins. I start to work at about 8:00 a.m., break for lunch, and resume in the afternoon or evening. I write every day, including weekends, just to keep the instrument sharp.

"Perhaps the most surprising thing I learned as a writer is how much the Internet has affected research—in detrimental as well as positive ways. A journalism professor in Florida put it well. When it came time to discuss research, he asked his class to buy newsstand copies of the *New York Times* every day. They complained: 'Why can't we just get it on the Net?' Replied the Prof: 'Because then you'll only find what you're looking for.' Just so. The best research often happens by accident. One comes across a long out-of-print book wedged in a library shelf, an old yellowed newspaper, a forgotten letter. No computer can furnish these accidental discoveries.

"I have no particular preference among the books I have published. My greatest enthusiasm is usually for the book on which I'm currently working. But once that is published, a new manuscript becomes the favored child.

"If my biographies have any effect, it will probably be to create new interest in old icons. Popular culture moves very fast these days, and it's important to slow down the process, allowing the young to understand the rapidly receding past.

"My social histories are another matter; the Holocaust novel, *The Eighth Sin*, is sometimes used as a college text, and serves as a severe reminder of the greatest crime of the twentieth century. *The Last Empire*, about the creation of South Africa, has also received academic attention, as has *A Journal of the Plague Years*, about the show business blacklist of the 1940s and 50s, and *Stardust Lost*, the story of the Yiddish Theater in New York. Again, it's important for new generations to understand the institutions and people that have preceded them."

BIOGRAPHICAL AND CRITICAL SOURCES:

BOOKS

Kanfer, Stefan, *A Journal of the Plague Years*, Atheneum (New York, NY), 1973.

PERIODICALS

Atlantic, September 1, 2003, Mona Simpson, "'Loosie!' The Rise and Fall of a Great Collaboration," review of *Ball of Fire: The Tumultuous Life and Comic Art of Lucille Ball*, p. 151.

Back Stage West, December 6, 2007, David Finkle, review of *The Voodoo That They Did So Well: The Wizards Who Invented the New York Stage*, p. 15.

Book, July-August, 2003, Elaine Szewczyk, "Big Red," review of *Ball of Fire*, p. 26.

Booklist, April 1, 1997, Mike Tribby, review of *Serious Business: The Art and Commerce of Animation in America from Betty Boop to Toy Story*, p. 1275; May 1, 2000, Ray Olson, review of *The Essential Groucho: Writings by and for Groucho Marx*, p. 1586; June 1, 2003, Brad Hooper, review of *Ball of Fire*, p. 1708; October 1, 2006, Jack Helbig, review of *Stardust Lost: The Triumph, Tragedy, and Mishugas of the Yiddish Theater in America*, p. 16; September 15, 2008, Joanne Wilkinson, review of *Somebody: The Reckless Life and Remarkable Career of Marion Brando*, p. 4.

Canadian Business, April, 1994, Peter Foster, review of *The Last Empire: De Beers, Diamonds, and the World*, p. 94.

Denver Post, November 30, 2008, "Brando at Full Throttle Bio Captures the Contender's Enormous Talent, Magical Performances, Bizarre Life," review of *Somebody*, p. 13.

Entertainment Weekly, April 18, 1997, Alex Abramovich, review of *Serious Business*, p. 62; August 15, 2003, Michael Sauter, review of *Ball of Fire*, p. 81; November 28, 2008, Gregory Kirschling, review of *Somebody*, p. 79.

Hollywood Reporter, December 4, 2003, review of *Ball of Fire*, p. 23.

Internet Bookwatch, September, 2007, review of *The Voodoo That They Did So Well*.

Kirkus Reviews, June 15, 2003, review of *Ball of Fire*, p. 846; July 15, 2006, review of *Stardust Lost*, p. 712; October 1, 2008, review of *Somebody*.

Library Journal, May 15, 1997, Carol J. Binkowski, review of *Serious Business*, p. 78; August 1, 2003, Rosellen Brewer, review of *Ball of Fire*, p. 86; September 1, 2006, Larry Schwartz, review of *Stardust Lost*, p. 148; November 1, 2008, Rosalind Dayen, review of *Somebody*, p. 68.

Los Angeles, August 1, 2003, Robert Ito, "Red Snapper," review of *Ball of Fire*, p. 150; November 1, 2008, Tom Carson, "The Brando Myth: In Stefan Kanfer's Biography, the Actor Was Doomed to

Throw It All Away from the Start," review of *Somebody,* p. 104.

New Leader, July-August, 2003, "Between Issues," review of *Ball of Fire,* p. 2.

New Republic, February 17, 1986, Eugene J. McCarthy, review of *The International Garage Sale,* p. 40.

New Yorker, October 27, 2008, Claudia Roth Pierpont, "Method Man," review of *Somebody,* p. 66.

New York Times, August 10, 2003, Terrence Rafferty, "Seeing Red," review of *Ball of Fire,* p. 11; December 3, 2006, Joseph Dorman, "East Side Story," review of *Stardust Lost,* p. 46; December 9, 2008, Michiko Kakutani, "The Lion of the Screen, and What Made Him Roar," review of *Somebody,* p. 1.

New York Times Book Review, April 30, 1978, Richard Freedman, review of *The Eighth Sin;* June 18, 2000, Gary Giddins, review of *Groucho;* January 4, 2009, "Method and Madness," review of *Somebody,* p. 12.

People, September 16, 1985, Campbell Geeslin, review of *The International Garage Sale,* p. 23; August 25, 2003, Tom Gliatto, review of *Ball of Fire,* p. 43.

Publishers Weekly, July 5, 1993, review of *The Last Empire,* p. 54; March 3, 1997, review of *Serious Business,* p. 56; June 12, 2000, review of *The Essential Groucho,* p. 66; June 2, 2003, review of *Ball of Fire,* p. 42; August 7, 2006, review of *Stardust Lost,* p. 47.

Reference & Research Book News, February, 2007, review of *Stardust Lost;* August, 2007, review of *The Voodoo That They Did So Well.*

San Francisco Chronicle, December 7, 2008, Walter Addiego, review of *Somebody.*

Time, September 1, 2003, James Poniewozik, "Playing Fast and Lucy: A Dish-Filled Biography of the Insecure B-Movie Actress Who Became the Undisputed Queen of TV," review of *Ball of Fire,* p. 63.

USA Today, August 19, 2003, Deirdre Donahue, "*Ball of Fire* illuminates Lucy's Brilliant, Betrayed Life," p. 1.

Variety, May 1, 2000, Andy Marx, review of *Groucho,* p. 39.

ONLINE

BookPage, http://www.bookpage.com/ (May 7, 2007), Pat Broeske, "Everybody's Favorite Redhead," review of *Ball of Fire.*

CNN Online, http://www.cnn.com/ (August 28, 2003), Anderson Cooper, "Live from the Headlines," interview with Stefan Kanfer.

Culture Kiosque, http://www.culturekiosque.com/ (November 10, 2003), Joel Kasow, "I Love Lucy, You Love Lucy, We All Love Lucy," review of *Ball of Fire.*

Daily Express Online, http://weather.dailyexpress.co.uk/ (November 14, 2008), Peter Burton, "Tough Guy: The Wild Times of a Flawed Idol," review of *Somebody.*

Fredericksburg.com, http://fredericksburg.com/ (November 30, 2008), Kurt Rabin, "Somebody Could Be a Contender," review of *Somebody.*

January, http://januarymagazine.com (May 7, 2007), Claude Lalumière, "Groucho Speaks," review of *The Essential Groucho.*

KGBBar, http://www.kgbbar.com/ (May 7, 2007), Jonathan Lachance, review of *Stardust Lost.*

Los Angeles Times Online, http://articles.latimes.com/ (November 27, 2008), Jonathan Shapiro, review of *Somebody.*

Manhattan Institute Web site, http://www.manhattan-institute.org/ (June 26, 2009), profile of author.

Scotland on Sunday Online, http://scotlandonsunday.scotsman.com/ (October 27, 2008), Siobhan Synnot, "Book Review: *Somebody.*"

Straight.com, http://www.straight.com/ (December 4, 2008), John Lekich, "Stefan Kanfer's *Somebody* a Valuable portrait of Marlon Brando."

Telegraph Online, http://www.telegraph.co.uk/ (December 12, 2008), Christopher Bray, "Marlon Brando: 'You Get Paid for Nothing,'" review of *Somebody.*

Vancouver Sun Online, http://www2.canada.com/vancouversun/ (November 5, 2008), Jay Stone, "*Somebody*—The Weird and Wacky Life of Marlon Brando."

Variety Online, http://www.variety.com/ (June 26, 2009), Diane Garrett, review of *Somebody.*

*   *   *

KASISCHKE, Laura 1961-

PERSONAL: Born December 5, 1961, in Lake Charles, LA; daughter of Edward (a postal worker) and Suzanne (a teacher) Kasischke; married William Abernethy, August, 1994; children: John Sullivan Abernethy. *Education:* University of Michigan, B.A. (with high honors), 1984, M.F.A., 1987; graduate study at Columbia University.

ADDRESSES: Home—Chelsea, MI. *Agent*—Lisa Bankoff, International Creative Management, 40 W. 57th St., New York, NY 10019. *E-mail*—laurakk@umich.edu.

CAREER: Writer, novelist, poet, and educator. South Plains College, Levelland, TX, writing instructor, 1987-88; Eastern Michigan University, visiting lecturer in creative writing and literature, 1989-90; Washtenaw Community College, Ann Arbor, MI, instructor of creative writing and literature, beginning 1990; University of Nevada, Las Vegas, associate professor, 1994-95; University of Michigan, Ann Arbor, associate professor.

AWARDS, HONORS: Hopwood Awards, for poetry, 1982, for fiction, 1982, for essay, 1984, and for drama; Cowden fellowships, 1982-83; Michael Gutterman Poetry Award, 1983; Arts Foundation of Michigan grants, 1983-84; Warner Communications fellowship, Columbia University, 1985; Marjorie Rapaport Poetry Award, 1986; Michigan Council for the Arts Individual Artist grant, 1990; Ragdale Foundation fellowships, 1990-92; Elmer Holmes Bobst Award for Emerging Writers, 1991, for *Wild Brides;* MacDowell Colony fellow, 1992; Bread Loaf fellow in poetry, 1992; Alice Fay DiCastagnola Award, 1993; Pushcart Prize, 1993; Creative Artists Award, Arts Foundation of Michigan, 1993; National Endowment for the Arts fellowship (two), including one in 1994; Barbara Deming Memorial Award, 1994; Poets & Writers Exchange fellowship, 1994; Juniper Prize, 2002, for *Dance and Disappear;* Beatrice Hawley Award; Guggenheim Fellowship, 2009.

WRITINGS:

POETRY

Brides, Wives, and Widows, American Studies Press (Tampa, FL), 1990.
Wild Brides, New York University Press (New York, NY), 1992.
Housekeeping in a Dream, Carnegie Mellon University Press (Pittsburgh, PA), 1995.
Fire & Flower: Poems, Alice James Books (Farmington, ME), 1998.
What It Wasn't: Poems, Carnegie Mellon University Press (Pittsburgh, PA), 2002.
Gardening in the Dark, Ausable Press (Keene, NY), 2004.

Lilies Without, Ausable Press (Port Townsend, WA), 2007.

NOVELS

Suspicious River, Houghton Mifflin (Boston, MA), 1996.
White Bird in a Blizzard, Hyperion (New York, NY), 1999.
The Life before Her Eyes, Harcourt (New York, NY), 2002.
Boy Heaven (young adult novel), HarperTempest (New York, NY), 2006.
Be Mine, Harcourt (Orlando, FL), 2007.
Feathered (young adult novel), HarperTeen (New York, NY), 2008.
In a Perfect World, Perennial (New York, NY), 2009.

OTHER

Woman in a Circle, Carnegie Mellon University Press (Pittsburgh, PA), 1999.
Dance and Disappear, University of Massachusetts Press (Amherst, MA), 2002.

Contributor of poems to periodicals, including *American Poetry Review, Antioch Review, Beloit Poetry Journal, Chelsea, Epoch, Georgia Review, Graham House Review, Green Mountains Review, Harper's, Indiana Review, Kenyon Review, Michigan Quarterly Review, Missouri Review, New England Review, New Republic, Ploughshares, Plum Review, Poetry, Prairie Schooner, Seneca Review,* and *Witness.*

ADAPTATIONS: Novels have been adapted for film: *Suspicious River,* 2000, and *The Life Before Her Eyes,* 2007.

SIDELIGHTS: Laura Kasischke is an award-winning poet and novelist whose verses have been widely published in literary journals and gathered in numerous collections. In addition, when her first novel, the dark and violent *Suspicious River,* was published in 1996, it introduced Kasischke to an even wider readership. *Suspicious River,* narrated in the first person, tells the lurid tale of Leila Murray, a twenty-year-old married woman who works behind the desk of the Swan Motel in the small town of Suspicious River in western Michigan. For some unstated reason, Leila decides to become a prostitute and offers her favors to the motel's clients whenever her husband is out of town on business. The night she provides her services to Gary Jensen, a charismatic stranger in town, marks the beginning of Leila's obsession with the brutal stranger and the spiral that could lead to her death. As the story unfolds, Leila suffers flashbacks from her childhood, when her mother, a prostitute, was stabbed to death by a client, who happened to be Leila's uncle. Leila appears to be reliving her mother's past, moving to embrace an identical fate in a reading experience that George Stade, writing for the *New York Times Book Review,* likened to "driving too fast on the Pacific Coast Highway."

Suspicious River elicited much praise from reviewers. *Boston Globe* contributor Diane White called it "an extremely intelligent novel, intricately constructed, beautifully written," and Erika Taylor, writing for the *Los Angeles Times,* labeled it an "impressive first novel" and "a story that is profoundly disturbing but also resonant with hope and rebirth." Moreover, in a review for the *Seattle Times,* Johanna Stoberock declared that Kasischke has written "a work of such eerie beauty, such immediate and vibrant imagery, that it will haunt readers for years." In the words of Stade, *Suspicious River* "is written with the skill of an old hand, though not with skill only. The novel's past and present spiral around and condition each other like the strands of a double helix. Chains of imagery, visual, olfactory and tactile, link up scenes in unexpected ways. The peripheral characters, the physical setting, the claustrophobic horrors of American small-town life are evoked with austere precision." Stade noted that "Lila's case got to me in spite of my resistance to all it reveals of what I don't want to face in human nature, for Ms. Kasischke's characters are all too convincing." He noted: "I truly and immensely admire this novel, but I am not sure I like it."

As would be expected of a poet's work, Kasischke's use of language in *Suspicious River* attracted the attention of reviewers. The author's style is to follow a plain short statement with several poetic sentence fragments. According to Molly E. Rauch, in the *Nation:* "Luscious, disjointed images pile upon one another until the novel is teeming with phrases—looping, frenzied words, breathlessly pounding toward a frozen white winter and the story's inexorable conclusion." "Her fine sense of the nuance of language is obvious on just about every page," White wrote. "The images she chooses are original, unexpected, unclichéd. In less skillful hands Leila's would be just a depressing story about a very

troubled young woman. Kasischke's writing endows it with universality and elevates it to tragedy. It's an amazing first novel." Stoberock remarked: " *Suspicious River* tells a difficult story, one borne by painful images that give Leila's journey no easy ending. It is also a novel of depth, beauty and insight, hauntingly told by a powerful writer."

Kasischke once told *CA:* "The narrative of *Suspicious River* grew out of the writing of a poem, and the image which suggested the novel to me simply mushroomed until it could no longer be contained by that poem—an image of a young woman buried in red raked leaves at the side of a road. As cars blew past, the leaves rose briefly around her nude body like bloody baby-hands, then settled over her again, a grave. That was everything I needed to know in the beginning about Leila—the public violence of her life, a glimpse of her naked shame, and the season that contained her.

"The first draft of the novel did come very quickly, and I attribute this to the season. I began writing in mid-September, and ended in October—a very dramatic time in Michigan. Color, death, fury. As I wrote, it seemed to me that Leila's voice was part of that frantic change. An end or a beginning was approaching for her almost too quickly to record, and the trees, the gardens, the sky, the air seemed to be taking part in—or were victims of—the same violation and disorder Leila was experiencing. Every morning before work and every night after, I felt I had to hurry to write about that experience, had to get the season into the novel before it was over, and had to reach the end of Leila's story before she did."

In her second novel, *White Bird in a Blizzard,* Kasischke tells the story of sixteen-year-old Katrina Connors. Teetering on the edge of womanhood, Katrina struggles with aspects of her life in an Ohio suburb. Overweight and socially awkward, Katrina is an outcast among her peers. Still, she is as preoccupied with sex, dating, and other rites of adulthood as any other teenager, and she strains against the oppressive home atmosphere in which her brusque, demanding, and insulting mother makes daily life miserable for her and her father. While struggling with the physical and emotional turmoil of her late adolescence, Katrina suddenly faces the abrupt disappearance of her mother on a cold day in January. At first bucking up stoically and calmly, Katrina comes to realize that she feels a new sense of freedom, and even some relief, in the absence of her frequently unpleasant mother. Even so, many questions remain unanswered, such as why her mother would suddenly vanish without a word or trace; where she went; and if she would ever be back. Dreams and strong emotions begin to trouble Katrina, and over time the difficult truth about her mother's disappearance emerges. Finally, Katrina must not only face the circumstances of her mother's departure but must also take the final steps that overcome her circumstances and transform her into an adult. "Kasischke's heroine is a fully rounded, distinctively portrayed character—a self-centered, typically hormone-crazed teenager who painstakingly develops into a self-aware young woman," observed a contributor to *Publishers Weekly.* Other reviewers commented favorably on the quality of writing and language in the novel. The "soft, almost ethereal language makes the horrifying reality at the core of the book shockingly powerful," noted Eleanor J. Bader in *Library Journal.* Grace Fill, writing for *Booklist,* remarked that "Kasischke's writing is so seductively rich in sensory imagery that reading is pure pleasure."

A terrible, irreversible choice lies at the center of *The Life before Her Eyes.* Maureen and Diana, both good friends, are two teenage girls who encounter random, life-changing violence in their school. In the school washroom, they hear the distant sounds of gunshots; soon, the shooter storms into the room, where he threatens the two girls. He gives the two an agonizing choice: he will kill only one of them, and asks the two to decide which it will be. In that moment, Maureen offers herself to be killed in order to save her friend; at the same time, Diana hears herself ask the killer to slay Maureen instead of her. At this pivotal point in the narrative, the story travels backward in time to the beginnings of the girls' friendship, then shimmers forward twenty years to Diana's happy suburban life as the wife of a professor, mother of a delightful daughter, and owner of a charming house. Gradually, darkness creeps into this idyllic life as Diana begins to see her life slowly crack and fall apart. As the story continues to unfold, the reader has the opportunity to consider whether Diana's diminished circumstances are the result of long-held guilt, the inevitable effects of entropy, or something more sinister. Lisa Shea, writing in *O,* called the novel a "tour de force by Kasischke." Kasischke's story "plays teenage Diana's youthful illusions of immortality and beauty against the shifting, uneasy reality of middle age," commented Reba Leiding in *Library Journal.* "This song of innocence and of experience reads like a fairy tale gone drastically wrong, the sensibility heightened by Kasischke's emphasis on language," observed a *Publishers Weekly* contributor.

Writing for *Booklist,* Joanne Wilkinson noted: "There's no denying that Kasischke is a fearless writer."

Boy Heaven, Kasischke's first novel for young adults, embroils protagonist Kristy Sweetland, a seventeen-year-old cheerleader, in the eerie circumstances of a local legend. While attending a cheerleading camp, Kristy, her friend Desiree, and new girl Kristi sneak away to go skinny dipping in local Lost Lake. On the way, they flirt daringly with two young local men in an adjacent car, giving them a quick flash of their breasts. The event seems to be little more than an instance of youthful sexual bravado until the girls realize that the creepy yokels have been seen lurking around their cabins at night, whispering in the dark and mounting an ominous presence. Circumstances worsen when Kristi begins to fall apart psychologically, refusing to eat, sleep, or take a bath. Kristi also mutters forbidding warnings about troubles to come. Soon, the girls realize that their taunting game with the two locals has led to problems and potentially deadly consequences. "Kasischke's writing imbues the book with such an eerie sense of apprehension that the pages keep turning," commented Susan Riley in *School Library Journal.*

Sherry Seymour, the protagonist of *Be Mine,* is an English teacher at a community college in Michigan. She is reasonably happy in her relationship with her husband, but she is struggling with empty-nest syndrome after her son Chad's recent departure for college. When she receives an anonymous valentine in her school mail box, she is intrigued and flattered, as well as pleased by the possibility of having a secret admirer. Soon, she receives more admiring notes, each more explicit than the last. She tells her husband, Jon, about the notes, and he finds them stimulating, resulting in an increase in the couple's sex life. Soon, Sherry believes she has identified the writer of the notes and, with the encouragement of her husband, embarks on an affair with the man. However, she comes to realize that the man she thought was the note-writer was not. Too late to back out, she becomes embroiled with her controlling lover even as her relationship with Jon sours—he did not think she was actually having an affair, believing instead that her stories were simply a tactic to add spice to their love life. Death looms menacingly in the narrative as Sherry, Jon, and the other characters struggle to break the grip of obsession, bad judgment, and irreversible actions. With this novel, "Kasischke has proven herself again to be a bold chronicler of dark obsession," commented a *Publishers Weekly* contributor. Kasischke "aims toward tragedy, using delicate, elegant prose to expose the psychological and moral rot that can lie beneath the most normal facade," observed a contributor to *Kirkus Reviews.*

Kasischke's seventh collection of poems, *Lilies Without,* published in 2007, were described as "confessional" poems by *Boston Reviews* contributor Stephen Burt. A reviewer for *Poetry* magazine referred to them as "atmospheric." The author's themes in this collection include the relationship between past and present and consumer culture's influence on society's expectations of women. Many of the poems deal with aspects of parenthood, such as how parents sometimes have unrealistically high expectations for their teenagers and, conversely, how grown children often realize later in life how their parents have influenced them negatively.

Commenting that the author uses a wide variety of techniques in the poems, the *Poetry* contributor went on to note that most of these techniques appear in the author's very first poem in the collection, "New Dress." According to the reviewer this poem contains "the use of deep-image nouns . . . mythological and fairy-tale tropes . . . and formulae." *Boston Review* contributor Burt noted of the poems: "If Kasischke's poems get half the attention they deserve, they will be praised . . ., not just for their music, but for their demographically representative qualities: for the way they capture the excitements and the anxieties of a generation just after that generation realizes that it, too, has entered adulthood, that its teens are a memory and its mortgage a burden."

Kasischke's 2008 young adult novel, *Feathered,* focuses on two senior girls in high school during spring break. Terri, Anne, and Michelle decide to go to Cancun to party and meet boys. However, after accepting an offer from a middle-aged stranger named Ander to tour the Mayan ruins with him, Anne and Michelle start to become uneasy. They then decide to take up the offer of two middle-class suburban boys to drive them back to where they are staying. It turns out that the boys are the ones they should have feared as the boys drug and rape the girls, leaving Michelle naked in the jungle while Anne escapes. Several months pass and Ander finally helps rescuers find Michelle, who has been living with natives in the jungle. Michelle has no memory or voice, but it is Anne who finally gets through to her friend. The story is told in alternating chapters that feature Michelle in a third-person and Anne in a first-person narrative.

"The prose is beautiful and the mystery seductive," wrote Myrna Marler in a review for *Booklist.* A *Kirkus Reviews* contributor noted: "Bright flashes of horror, exaltation and folklore draw teens into the . . . story." While some reviewers saw the book as a cautionary tale, others had a different view of the novel. "Lest you think Feathered a run-of-the-mill cautionary tale, it's not," wrote a contributor to the *Slayground* Web site. Noting that "this book does not promote anxiety or xenophobia," the reviewer went on to add later in the same article that the author's "lyrical writing shines."

BIOGRAPHICAL AND CRITICAL SOURCES:

PERIODICALS

Booklist, December 1, 1998, Grace Fill, review of *White Bird in a Blizzard,* p. 651; December 1, 2001, Joanne Wilkinson, review of *The Life before Her Eyes,* p. 628; November 15, 2006, Maria Hatton, review of *Be Mine,* p. 34; July 1, 2008, Kathleen Isaacs, review of *Feathered,* p. 54.

Boston Globe, July 4, 1996, Diane White, review of *Suspicious River,* p. 63.

Boston Review, March-April, 2008, Stephen Burt, "The Speed of Life," review of *Lilies Without.*

Kirkus Reviews, November 21, 2001, review of *The Life before Her Eyes,* p. 1570; October 15, 2006, review of *Be Mine,* p. 1036; March 1, 2008, review of *Feathered.*

Kliatt, May, 2003, Francisca Goldsmith, review of *The Life before Her Eyes,* p. 18; March, 2008, Myrna Marler, review of *Feathered,* p. 16.

Library Journal, December, 1998, Eleanor J. Bader, review of *White Bird in a Blizzard,* p. 156; December, 2001, Reba Leiding, review of *The Life before Her Eyes,* p. 173; December, 2006, Karen Kleckner, review of *Be Mine,* p. 111.

Los Angeles Times, August 4, 1996, Erika Taylor, review of *Suspicious River,* p. 6.

Nation, April 22, 1996, Molly E. Rauch, review of *Suspicious River,* p. 35.

New York Times Book Review, May 5, 1996, George Stade, review of *Suspicious River,* p. 11.

O, The Oprah Magazine, February, 2002, Lisa Shea, review of *The Life before Her Eyes,* p. 115.

Poetry, March, 2008, review of *Lilies Without,* p. 520.

Prairie Schooner, summer, 2001, Jenny Factor, review of *Fire & Flower: Poems,* p. 183.

Publishers Weekly, October 19, 1998, review of *White Bird in a Blizzard,* p. 52; January 14, 2002, review of *The Life before Her Eyes,* p. 39; May 27, 2002, review of *Dance and Disappear,* p. 51; October 2, 2006, review of *Be Mine,* p. 39.

School Library Journal, September, 2006, Susan Riley, review of *Boy Heaven,* p. 209; June, 2008, Marie C. Hansen, review of *Feathered,* p. 144.

Seattle Times, July 14, 1996, Johanna Stoberock, review of *Suspicious River.*

Time, May 9, 2005, Lev Grossman, review of *Gardening in the Dark,* p. 70.

ONLINE

Arborweb, http://www.arborweb.com/ (May 7, 2007), Keith Taylor, review of *The Life before Her Eyes.*

Ausable Press Web site, http://www.ausablepress.org/ (May 7, 2007), biography of Laura Kasischke.

Boston Review Online, http://www.bostonreview.net/ (May 7, 2007), Joanna Klink, review of *Fire & Flower.*

Curled Up with a Good Book, http://www.curledup. com/ (May 7, 2007), Luan Gaines, review of *Be Mine.*

Five Chapters, http://www.fivechapters.com/ (June 26, 2009), brief biography of author.

Harcourt Trade Publishers Web site, http://www. harcourtbooks.com/ (May 7, 2007), interview with Laura Kasischke.

Internet Movie Database, http://www.imdb.com/ (June 26, 2009), filmography.

January, http://www.januarymagazine.com/ (May 7, 2007), Tony Buchsbaum, "Be Better," review of *Be Mine.*

John Simon Guggenheim Memorial Foundation Web site, http://www.gf.org/ (June 26, 2009), biography of author.

Not Acting My Age, http://blog.goldschp.net/ (February 10, 2009), review of *Feathered.*

Reader's Corner, http://read.blee.net/ (May 11, 2009), "New & Upcoming Books," review of *In a Perfect World.*

Slayground, http://slayground.livejournal.com/ (April 8, 2008), review of *Feathered.*

University of Michigan Department of English Web site, http://www.lsa.umich.edu/english/ (June 26, 2009), faculty profile of author.

Whistling Shade, http://www.whistlingshade.com/ (May 7, 2007), Joel Van Valin, review of *The Life before Her Eyes.*

*　　*　　*

KEEGAN, Christopher
See GORMAN, Ed

KETTL, Donald F. 1952-
(Donald Francis Kettl)

PERSONAL: Born February 9, 1952, in Philadelphia, PA; son of Raymond P. and Mary Louise Kettl; married Susan Carmela Amato. *Education:* Yale University, B.A. (summa cum laude), 1974, M.A. and M.Phil., 1976, Ph.D., 1978.

ADDRESSES: Office—Fels Institute of Government, University of Pennsylvania, 3814 Walnut St., Philadelphia, PA 19104-6197. *E-mail*—dkettl@sas.upenn.edu.

CAREER: Political scientist, educator, and writer. Yale University, New Haven, CT, lecturer in political science, 1976; Columbia University, New York, NY, assistant professor of political science, 1978-79; University of Virginia, Charlottesville, assistant professor, 1979-85, associate professor of government, 1985-89; Vanderbilt University, Nashville, TN, associate professor of political science, 1989-90; University of Wisconsin—Madison, Madison, professor of political science and affiliate of La Follette Institute of Public Affairs, 1990-2004; University of Pennsylvania, Philadelphia, professor of political science and holder of Stanley I. Sheerr Endowed Term Professor of Social Sciences, 2004-08, Robert A. Fox Professor of Leadership, 2008—, director of Fels Institute of Government, 2005—. Brookings Institution, nonresident senior fellow, 1994—, director of Center for Public Management, 1997-99; Century Foundation, executive director of Project on Federalism and Homeland Security, 2002—; also testified before U.S. Congress; consultant to World Bank, Organization for Economic Cooperation and Development, and several U.S. federal agencies and commissions. Federal Executive Institute, adjunct faculty, 1988; Virginia Polytechnic Institute and State University, guest lecturer, 1997; Carroll College, Daniel Halloran Memorial Lecturer, 1997; New York City Bar Association, Goldman Memorial Lecturer, 1998; University of Alabama, Boyne Lecturer in Public Administration, 1999; Park University, Jerzy Hauptmann Distinguished Guest Lecturer, 2000; conference participant; guest on numerous media programs. Wisconsin Governor's Blue-Ribbon Commission on Campaign Finance Reform, chair, 1996-97, and member of other state commissions; National Academy of Public Administration, chair of New Source Review for Panel on the Environmental Protection Agency, 2001-02; U.S. Office of Management and Budget, member of performance measurement advisory committee, 2002-03; Pew

Charitable Trusts, academic coordinator of Governor Performance Project, 2003—; member of editorial boards of scholarly publications, including *International Public Management Journal, Administration and Society, Public Administration Review, Journal of Public Administration Research and Theory, American Review of Public Administration,* and *Journal of Policy Analysis and Management;* board member of Meriter Health Services and Meriter Hospital.

MEMBER: American Political Science Association, American Society for Public Administration, National Academy of Public Administration (fellow), Academy of Political Science, Phi Beta Kappa.

AWARDS, HONORS: American Society for Public Administration, Marshall E. Dimock Award, 1990, for "The Perils—and Prospects—of Public Administration" in *Public Administration Review,* Charles H. Levine Memorial Award, 1998, for contributions to the field, and Donald C. Stone Award, 2005; Louis Brownlow Book Award, National Academy of Public Administration, 2003, for *The Transformation of Governance;* Warner W. Stockberger Achievement Award, International Public Management Association for Human Resources, 2007; John Gaus Award, American Political Science Association, 2008.

WRITINGS:

Managing Community Development in the New Federalism, Praeger (New York, NY), 1980.
The Regulation of American Federalism, Louisiana State University Press (Baton Rouge, LA), 1983.
Leadership at the Fed, Yale University Press (New Haven, CT), 1986.
Government by Proxy: Mis(?)Managing Federal Programs, Congressional Quarterly (Washington, DC), 1988.
Public Administration: Theory and Practice, Chatham House (Chatham, NJ), 1991.
(With James W. Fesler) *The Politics of the Administrative Process,* Chatham House (Chatham, NJ), 1991, 4th edition, CQ Press (Washington, DC), 2009.
Deficit Politics: Public Budgeting in Its Institutional and Historical Context, Macmillan (New York, NY), 1992, reprinted as *Deficit Politics: The Search for Balance in American Politics,* foreword by Ross K. Baker, Longman (New York, NY), 2003.
(With John J. DiIulio, Jr. and Gerald Garvey) *Improving Government Performance: An Owner's Manual,* Brookings Institution (Washington, DC), 1993.

Sharing Power: Public Governance and Private Markets, Brookings Institution (Washington, DC), 1993.
Reinventing Government? Appraising the National Performance Review, Brookings Institution (Washington, DC), 1994.
(With John J. DiIulio, Jr.) *Fine Print: The Contract with America, Devolution, and the Administrative Realities of American Federalism,* Brookings Institution (Washington, DC), 1995.
(With John J. DiIulio, Jr.) *Cutting Government,* Brookings Institution (Washington, DC), 1995.
The Global Public Management Revolution: A Report on the Transformation of Governance, Brookings Institution (Washington, DC), 2000, 2nd edition, 2005.
The Transformation of Governance: Public Administration for Twenty-first Century America, Johns Hopkins University Press (Baltimore, MD), 2002.
Team Bush: Leadership Lessons from the Bush White House, McGraw-Hill (New York, NY), 2003.
System under Stress: Homeland Security and American Politics, CQ Press (Washington, DC), 2004, 2nd edition, 2007.
(With Steven Kelman) *Reflections on 21st Century Government Management,* IBM Center for the Business of Government (Washington, DC), 2007.
The Next Government of the United States: Why Our Institutions Fail Us and How to Fix Them, W.W. Norton and Co. (New York, NY), 2009.

EDITOR

(With Patricia W. Ingrahm, and contributor) *Issues for the American Public Service,* Chatham House (Chatham, NJ), 1991.
(With Patricia W. Ingrahm) *Agenda for Excellence: Public Service in America,* Chatham House (Chatham, NJ), 1992.
(With John J. DiIulio, Jr., and contributor) *Inside the Reinvention Machine: Appraising Governmental Reform,* Brookings Institution (Washington, DC), 1995.
(With H. Brinton Milward, and author of introduction) *The State of Public Management,* Johns Hopkins University Press (Baltimore, MD), 1996.
Environmental Governance: A Report on the Next Generation of Environmental Policy, Brookings Institution (Washington, DC), 2002.
(And author of introduction) *The Department of Homeland Security's First Year: A Report Card,* Century Foundation (New York, NY), 2004.

(With Ronald J. Daniels and Howard Kunreuther, and contributor) *On Risk and Disaster: Lessons from Hurricane Katrina,* University of Pennsylvania Press (Philadelphia, PA), 2006.

(With Stephen Goldsmith) *Unlocking the Power of Networks: Keys to High-performance Government,* Ash Institute for Democratic Governance and Innovation (Cambridge, MA), 2009.

Contributor to books, including *Civil Service Reform: Building a Government that Works,* Brookings Institution (Washington, DC), 1996; *Understanding the Presidency,* edited by James Pfiffner and Roger H. Davidson, Longman (New York, NY), 2000; and *The Tools of Government: A Public Management Handbook for the Era of Third-party Government,* edited by Lester M. Salamon, Oxford University Press (New York, NY), 2002. Author of "Poromac Chronicle," a regular column in the magazine *Governing.* Contributor to scholarly publications, including *Renewable Resource Journal, Environmental Forum, Journal of Public Affairs Education, Public Administration Review, Journal of Public Administration Research and Theory,* and *Journal of Policy Analysis and Management.*

Kettl's books have been translated into Japanese, Chinese, Arabic, and Indonesian.

SIDELIGHTS: Donald F. Kettl is an expert in public policy and public administration. He has written and edited numerous books on these topics, many in association with the Brookings Institution. In *Leadership at the Fed,* for example, the author examines the Federal Reserve. Writing in *Business History Review,* James Livingston noted that "the question Kettl raises is not whether an independent agency [a central bank] is compatible with American democracy, but whether capitalism is. That his book equips us to answer this question is one measure of its importance."

Kettl and coeditor Patricia W. Ingrahm present a collection of papers that offer a mostly favorable view of the federal government in the book *Agenda for Excellence: Public Service in America.* "These finely crafted, carefully researched, and well-reasoned essays examine the theory and practice of managing the federal executive work force," wrote Carol W. Lewis in the *American Review of Public Administration.* Lewis continued: "These studies challenge popular myths about frozen stability and excessive uniformity of the federal bureaucracy; in fact, they belie monolithic generaliza-

tions." Writing in *Public Administration Review,* Eugene B. McGregor, Jr., noted: "The collected essays remind us that the American public service is a dynamic institution that, contrary to some popular belief, resounds with examples of excellence."

Kettl collaborated with John J. DiIulio, Jr. and Gerald Garvey to write *Improving Government Performance: An Owner's Manual.* "For those who like things made simple, *Improving Government Performance* provides a brief overview of past and current efforts to reform the federal bureaucracy," wrote Gerald E. Caiden in *Public Administration Review.* In *Sharing Power: Public Governance and Private Markets,* Kettl focuses on the relationship between public governments and private markets in relation to public services. "Through a description and analysis of five 'case studies,' Kettl identifies some of the fundamental forces in government and in the market that make the sharing of power complex and difficult," wrote Gerald W. Johnson in the *American Political Science Review.* Johnson observed: "At its core, this is a book about democratic theory—about what governments and markets can and cannot do." Timothy H. Riordan, writing in the *Government Finance Review,* commented: "The book does a good job of talking about the realities of managing in today's environment without dwelling on the platitudes of private-sector mythology."

Kettl and DiIulio edited *Inside the Reinvention Machine: Appraising Governmental Reform,* a series of scholarly essays focusing on various government reform theories and actions. James D. Carroll, writing in the *American Review of Public Administration,* called the book "part of the historical record, as well as sources of insight into how reform has been defined and pursued in the 1990s."

Kettl and DiIulio wrote *Fine Print: The Contract with America, Devolution, and the Administrative Realities of American Federalism.* In this work the authors examine the Republican-created "Contract with America" of the mid-1990s. The "agreement" promised the American people that its elected Republican representatives in the federal government would work toward smaller federal government while placing increasing responsibility and authority on the state level. Writing in *Public Manager: The New Bureaucrat,* Hyong Yi pointed out that the authors "address the issue of how these promises will be implemented administratively."

The State of Public Management, which Kettl edited with H. Brinton Milward, contains essays from a conference on public management. Norman Gill, writing in *Perspectives on Political Science,* noted that the book highlights "important milestones in the new discipline of public management. They [the essays] not only explore how public programs can be managed to work better, but they also chart the maturation of thinking about how it ought to be done."

In *The Global Public Management Revolution: A Report on the Transformation of Governance,* Kettl addresses the movement to make governments work better in terms of greater efficiency and performance coupled with lower costs. In the process, the author analyzes various localized movements, such as the "new public management" movement in Australia. Writing in the *Review of Policy Research,* Jeremy F. Plant commented: "Kettl has earned a reputation as one of the finest writers in public policy and administration. His work is characterized by clarity, precision in terms, and a remarkable economy of argument to convey his ideas. This book only reinforces his skills in condensing a great deal of information into its essentials."

Kettl turns his eye to the leadership style of President George W. Bush in *Team Bush: Leadership Lessons from the Bush White House.* Although Kettl describes a president of average intelligence, he relates how Bush has used his M.B.A. and his background in business to assemble an effective management team to help him make decisions. A *Publishers Weekly* contributor noted that the book has "stimulating ideas" about leadership. In *The Transformation of Governance: Public Administration for Twenty-first Century America,* Kettl writes about how governance has changed in the United States. Writing in the *Public Manager,* A.C. Hyde noted that the "historical overview bridges past and present nicely in explaining what's different about governance now and why it's so significant for public administration." Kettl is also the editor of a collection of papers titled *Environmental Governance: A Report on the Next Generation of Environmental Policy. American Journal of Agricultural Economics* contributor Darrell J. Bosch commented: "This book will be helpful, accessible reference for professional practitioners and citizens who are concerned with adapting environmental policymaking and management to meet future challenges.

It was the parallels between his mother-in-law's experience with Medicare and the inadequate government response to Hurricane Katrina that prompted Kettl to write *The Next Government of the United States: Why Our Institutions Fail Us and How to Fix Them.* Observing that his mother-in-law received satisfactory treatment through Medicare but never actually dealt with a federal employee, Kettl examines the nature of federal bureaucracies and finds that the programs they administer have become too large and complex to allow real hands-on oversight. For relatively mundane procedures, such as issuing checks, the system works adequately, but when a crisis occurs that requires emergency action, as happened when the city of New Orleans was inundated by floodwaters during Hurricane Katrina, the system cannot function effectively. "The lack of centralized control of the system," writes Kettl, "frustrated angry residents searching for someone to blame. [But] there was no single cause of the levee failure, no smoking gun pointing to a target at which to aim the anger of New Orleanians." As the federal government has grown and assumed greater and more numerous responsibilities, he continues, it has created "a system in which no one is fully accountable for anything government does." When responsibilities are shared among various federal organizations and agencies, there is confusion about who is ultimately responsible for decision-making and execution of policy. Much of the blame for this state of affairs, says Kettl, rests with Congress, which—in a disastrous example of the inability of the legislature to abandon outdated models of accountability—refused to allow the separate jurisdictions of the newly-formed Department of Homeland Security to be overseen by one Congressional committee. As a result, according to Kettl, the department must report to eighty-eight separate committees and subcommittees, virtually ensuring its inefficiency and ineffectiveness. Though Kettl does not focus on concrete solutions to this dilemma, he argues in favor of increased involvement of the private sector in emergency responses, pointing out that public-private partnerships can act with the kind of flexibility that is needed in crises. A contributor to *Kirkus Reviews* considered *The Next Government of the United States* to be a "well-reasoned" argument of value to policy makers and analysts. Writing in the *American Prospect* shortly after the publication of the book, Elaine C. Kamarck noted that the new Barack Obama administration had already begun to restructure federal organizations into a more networked framework. "Kettl's book," concluded the reviewer, "has no single answer but at least points to the kind of leadership and methods of coordination that this new structure of government demands."

With Ronald J. Daniels and Howard Kunreuther, Kettl edited *On Risk and Disaster: Lessons from Hurricane*

Katrina. The book includes articles that address the failures of the Katrina response in particular, as well as more general issues of risk management. Kettl also edited *Unlocking the Power of Networks: Keys to High-Performance Government* with colleague Stephen Goldsmith, and with Steven Kelman he wrote *Reflections on 21st Century Government Management.*

BIOGRAPHICAL AND CRITICAL SOURCES:

BOOKS

Kettl, Donald F., *The Next Government of the United States: Why Our Institutions Fail Us and How to Fix Them,* W.W. Norton & Company (New York, NY), 2009.

PERIODICALS

American Historical Review, October, 1987, Elmus Wicker, review of *Leadership at the Fed,* p. 1051.

American Journal of Agricultural Economics, November, 2003, Darrell J. Bosch, review of *Environmental Governance: A Report on the Next Generation of Environmental Policy,* p. 1082.

American Political Science Review, September, 1981, review of *Managing Community Development in the New Federalism,* p. 774; March, 1985, review of *The Regulation of American Federalism,* p. 212; March, 1988, John T. Woolley, review of *Leadership at the Fed,* p. 292; June, 1989, J. Theodore Anagnoson, review of *Government by Proxy: (Mis?)Managing Federal Programs;* June, 1994, Gerald W. Johnson, review of *Sharing Power: Public Governance and Private Markets,* p. 477.

American Prospect, January 1, 2009, Elaine C. Kamarck, review of *The Next Government of the United States.*

American Review of Public Administration, December, 1993, Carol W. Lewis, review of *Agenda for Excellence: Public Service in America,* p. 422; December, 1998, James D. Carroll, review of *Inside the Reinvention Machine: Appraising Governmental Reform,* p. 402.

Annals of the American Academy of Political and Social Science, January, 1984, Frederick M. Finney, review of *Managing Community Development in the New Federalism,* p. 178; September, 1987, Arthur I. Bloomfield, review of *Leadership at the Fed,* p. 493.

Banker, November, 1986, Mark Gallagher, review of *Leadership at the Fed,* p. 154.

Bankers, July-August, 1987, Duane Kline, review of *Leadership at the Fed,* p. 74.

Booklist, November 15, 2008, Gilbert Taylor, review of *The Next Government of the United States,* p. 7.

Business History Review, summer, 1988, James Livingston, review of *Leadership at the Fed,* p. 335.

Choice: Current Reviews for Academic Libraries, December, 1980, review of *Managing Community Development in the New Federalism,* p. 592; April, 1984, review of *The Regulation of American Federalism,* p. 1196; January, 1987, review of *Leadership at the Fed,* p. 796; May, 1988, review of *Government by Proxy,* p. 1477; October, 1992, W.P. Browne, review of *Agenda for Excellence,* p. 381; November, 1993, J.S. Zacek, review of *Sharing Power,* p. 538; December, 1993, A.M. Khademian, review of *Improving Government Performance: An Owner's Manual,* p. 672; December, 1995, review of *Inside the Reinvention Machine,* p. 690; February, 1997, review of *The State of Public Management,* p. 1029; June, 2003, review of *The Transformation of Governance: Public Administration for Twenty-first Century America,* p. 1817.

Congress & the Presidency, spring, 1997, David T. Canon, review of *Civil Service Reform: Building a Government that Works,* p. 89.

Economic Books: Current Selections, June, 1987, review of *Leadership at the Fed,* p. 18.

Foreign Affairs Annual, 1986, review of *Leadership at the Fed,* p. 394; winter, 1986, William Diebold, Jr., review of *Leadership at the Fed,* p. 394.

Forum for Applied Research and Public Policy, winter, 1994, Victor S. Rezendes, review of *Sharing Power,* p. 137.

Government Finance Review, February, 1995, Timothy H. Riordan, review of *Sharing Power,* p. 50.

Journal of American History, June, 1987, Edward Montgomery, review of *Leadership at the Fed,* p. 150.

Journal of Economic History, June, 1987, review of *Leadership at the Fed,* p. 585.

Journal of Economic Literature, March, 1987, review of *Leadership at the Fed,* p. 205; March, 1997, review of *The State of Public Management,* p. 203.

Journal of Policy Analysis & Management, summer, 1989, Erwin C. Hargrove, review of *Government by Proxy,* p. 518; fall, 1994, William T. Gormley, Jr., review of *Sharing Power,* p. 790; spring, 1996, Eugene Bardach, review of *Inside the Reinvention Machine,* p. 295; summer, 1997, Fred D. Thompson, review of *The State of Public Management,* p. 484.

Journal of Politics, November, 1984, review of *The Regulation of American Federalism,* p. 1256; February, 1988, Raymond Tatalovich, review of *Leadership at the Fed,* p. 255; February, 1995, review of *Sharing Power,* p. 246.

Journal of Public Administration Research and Theory, April, 1994, John M. Bryson, review of *Sharing Power,* p. 267; July, 1997, Richard F. Callahan, review of *The State of Public Management,* p. 489.

Journal of the American Planning Association, autumn, 2007, Kenneth C. Topping, review of *On Risk and Disaster: Lessons from Hurricane Katrina,* p 475.

Kirkus Reviews, September 15, 1986, review of *Leadership at the Fed,* p. 1428; October 1, 2008, review of *The Next Government of the United States.*

Library Journal, June 15, 1993, Robert Logsdon, review of *Sharing Power,* p. 78.

Library Media Connection, May, 1988, review of *Government by Proxy,* p. 53.

Natural Resources & Environment, fall, 2002, JoAnne L. Dunec, review of *Environmental Governance,* p. 106.

New York Times Book Review, October 26, 1986, Lawrence A. Veit, review of *Leadership at the Fed,* p. 40.

Perspective, January, 1981, review of *Managing Community Development in the New Federalism,* p. 12; May, 1985, review of *The Regulation of American Federalism,* p. 70; September, 1987, review of *Leadership at the Fed,* p. 122.

Perspectives on Political Science, summer, 1994, review of *Sharing Power,* p. 145; spring, 1997, Norman Gill, review of *The State of Public Management,* p. 105.

Policy Studies Journal, December, 1994, Andrew Dunsire, review of *Agenda for Excellence,* p. 74; spring, 1996, review of *Inside the Reinvention Machine,* p. 161; winter, 1996, review of *Civil Service Reform* and *The State of Public Management,* p. 687; winter, 1997, review of *Civil Service Reform,* p. 651; winter, 2000, William B. Perkins, review of *The Global Public Management Revolution: A Report on the Transformation of Governance,* p. 879.

Political Science Quarterly, summer, 1981, review of *Managing Community Development in the New Federalism,* p. 345; spring, 1985, review of *The Regulation of American Federalism,* p. 169; spring, 1987, R.J. Saulnier, review of *Leadership at the Fed,* p. 160; fall, 1988, Donna Wilson Kirchheimer, review of *Government by Proxy,* p. 570.

Prairie Schooner, spring, 1987, review of *Leadership at the Fed,* p. 160; fall, 1988, review of *Government by Proxy,* p. 570.

Public Administration Review, July-August, 1991, Beryl Radin, review of *The Politics of the Administrative Process,* p. 368; September-October, 1992, Laurence E. Lynn, Jr., review of *Government by Proxy,* p. 520; November-December, 1993, Susan A. MacManus, review of *Sharing Power,* p. 577; March-April, 1994, Gerald E. Caiden, review of *Improving Government Performance,* pp. 123-128; May-June, 1994, Eugene B. McGregor, Jr., review of *Agenda for Excellence,* pp. 296-301; May-June, 1998, Gary Marshall, review of *The State of Public Management,* p. 274; November, 2000, review of *The Global Public Management Revolution,* p. 591; March-April, 2003, review of *The Transformation of Governance,* p. 248; September, 2003, review of *The Transformation of Governance,* p. 631.

Public Manager: The New Bureaucrat, spring, 1993, Gail Johnson, review of *Agenda for Excellence,* p. 63; fall, 2003, A.C. Hyde, review of *The Transformation of Governance,* p. 64; summer, 1995, Hyong Yi, review of *Fine Print: The Contract with America, Devolution, and the Administrative Realities of American Federalism,* p. 54; winter, 1996, Barry E. Shapiro, review of *Civil Service Reform,* p. 60.

Public Productivity and Management Review, summer, 1994, Ralph S. Hambrick, Jr., review of *Sharing Power,* p. 411; December, 1997, review of *The State of Public Management,* p. 222.

Public Studies Journal, winter, 1997, Winfield Rose and Charles E. Menifield, review of *Civil Service Reform,* p. 651.

Publishers Weekly, February 24, 2003, review of *Team Bush: Leadership Lessons from the Bush White House,* p. 67; September 15, 2008, review of *The Next Government of the United States,* p. 53.

Reference & Research Book News, September, 1993, review of *Sharing Power,* p. 20; September, 1995, review of *Inside the Reinvention Machine,* p. 39; February, 1997, review of *The State of Public Management,* p. 59; May, 2003, review of *The Transformation of Governance,* p 159; November 1, 2005, review of *The Politics of the Administrative Process,* 3rd edition; February 1, 2007, review of *System under Stress; Homeland Security and American Politics,* 2nd edition; May 1, 2009, review of *The Politics of the Administrative Process,* 4th edition.

Review of Policy Research, spring, 2002, Jeremy F. Plant, review of *The Global Public Management Revolution,* p. 238.

Washington Monthly, May, 1995, Timothy Noah, review of *Inside the Reinvention Machine,* p. 56.

Washington Post Book World, March 8, 1987, review of *Leadership at the Fed,* p. 6.

Wilson Quarterly, annual compilation, 1987, review of *Leadership at the Fed,* p. 146.

ONLINE

Brookings Institute Web site, http://www.brookings.edu/ (June 24, 2009), author profile.

University of Pennsylvania: Department of Political Science Web site, http://www.polisci.upenn.edu/ (June 24, 2009), faculty profile.

Washingtonpost.com (live online edition), http://washingtonpost.com/ (March 26, 2003), Stephen Barr, "Federal Diary Live," an author interview.*

*   *   *

KETTL, Donald Francis
See KETTL, Donald F.

*   *   *

KITTREDGE, William 1932-
(Owen Rountree, a joint pseudonym)

PERSONAL: Born August 14, 1932, in Portland, OR; son of Oscar Franklin (a rancher) and Josephine Kittredge; children: Karen Kittredge Zarosinski, Bradley. *Education:* Oregon State University, B.S., 1953; attended University of Oregon, 1968; University of Iowa, M.F.A., 1969.

ADDRESSES: Home—Missoula, MT. *Agent*—Amanda Urban, International Creative Management, 40 W. 57th St., New York, NY 10019.

CAREER: McRanch, Adel, OR, cattle rancher and ranch manager, 1957-67; University of Montana, Missoula, assistant professor, 1969-74, associate professor, 1974-80, professor of English, 1980-97. *Northwest Review,* Eugene, OR, assistant editor and consulting editor, 1968-70; *Rocky Mountain Magazine,* consulting editor, 1979-83; *Pacific Northwest Magazine,* consulting editor, 1979-86; *Outside,* consulting editor. *Puerto Del Sol,* advisory board member; *Montana: Magazine of Western History,* publication board member. Co-producer, *A River Runs Through It. Military service:* U.S. Air Force, 1954-57.

AWARDS, HONORS: University of Oregon Ernest Haycox Fiction prize, 1968; University of Montana summer grant, 1970, 1976, 1982, and Innovative Summer Program grant, 1977, 1978; Stegner fellow at Stanford University, 1973-74; grants from National Endowment for the Arts, 1974 and 1981; Montana Committee for the Humanities grant, 1979; PEN/NEA Syndicated Fiction Project award, 1983, 1988, and Fiction award, 1984; Neil Simon Award, 1984; Montana Governor's Award for the Arts, 1984; H.G. Merriam Award, 1988; Charles Frankel Prize, 1994; Robert Kirsch Award, *Los Angeles Times,* 2007.

WRITINGS:

The Van Gogh Field and Other Stories, University of Missouri Press (Columbia, MO), 1979.

We Are Not in This Together (short stories), edited and with a foreword by Raymond Carver, Graywolf Press (St. Paul, MN), 1982.

Owning It All: Essays, Graywolf Press (St. Paul, MN), 1987.

Phantom Silver (short stories), Kutenai Press (Missoula, MT), 1987.

Hole in the Sky: A Memoir, Knopf (New York, NY), 1992.

(Contributor) *Robert Helm, 1981-1993,* University of Houston (Houston, TX), 1994.

Who Owns the West?, Mercury House (San Francisco, CA), 1996.

Taking Care: Thoughts on Storytelling and Belief, Milkweed Editions (Minneapolis, MN), 1999.

The Nature of Generosity, Knopf (New York, NY), 2000.

Balancing Water: Restoring the Klamath Basin, photographs by Tupper Ansel Blake and Madeleine Graham Blake, University of California Press (Berkeley, CA), 2000.

Southwestern Homelands, National Geographic (Washington, DC), 2002.

The Best Short Stories of William Kittredge, Graywolf Press (St. Paul, MN), 2003.

(Author of introduction) Monte Hartman, *America's 100th Meridian: A Plains Journey,* Texas Tech University Press (Lubbock, TX), 2005.

The Willow Field (novel), Knopf (New York, NY), 2006.

The Next Rodeo: New and Selected Essays, Graywolf Press (Saint Paul, MN), 2007.

EDITOR

(And author of introduction) *Montana Spaces: Essays and Photographs in Celebration of Montana,* photographs by John Smart, Nick Lyons Books (New York, NY), 1988.

(With Annick Smith) *The Last Best Place: A Montana Anthology,* Montana Historical Society Press, 1988.

The Portable Western Reader, Penguin Books (New York, NY), 1997.

(With Allen Morris Jones) *The Best of Montana's Short Fiction,* Lyons Press (Guilford, CT), 2004.

EDITOR; WITH STEVEN M. KRAUZER

Great Action Stories, New American Library (New York, NY), 1977.

(And author of introduction) *The Great American Detective* (short stories), New American Library (New York, NY), 1978.

Stories into Film, Harper (New York, NY), 1979.

Also editor of *Contemporary Western Fiction TriQuarterly,* special edition, 1980.

"CORD" SERIES; WITH STEVEN M. KRAUZER; UNDER JOINT PSEUDONYM OWEN ROUNTREE

Cord, Ballantine (New York, NY), 1982.

The Nevada War, Ballantine (New York, NY), 1982.

Black Hills Gold, Ballantine (New York, NY), 1982.

Gunman Winter, Ballantine (New York, NY), 1983.

Hunt the Man Down, Ballantine (New York, NY), 1984.

King of Colorado, Ballantine (New York, NY), 1984.

Gunsmoke River, Ballantine (New York, NY), 1985.

Paradise Valley, Ballantine (New York, NY), 1986.

Brimstone Valley, Ballantine (New York, NY), 1986.

Contributor of stories and articles to periodicals, including *Atlantic Monthly, Harper's, Triquarterly, Iowa Review, Outside, Rolling Stone,* and *Paris Review.* Contributor to film script, *Heartland.*

SIDELIGHTS: English professor and former rancher William Kittredge draws upon his experience in these two seemingly disparate fields when creating his diverse works chronicling the American West. As Noel Perrin stated in the *Washington Post Book World,* Kittredge "is a man straight out of Western myth, who left the family ranch in mid-career and went to graduate school . . . [and who] looks back on the ranch with the cool eyes of a psychologically oriented intellectual." Peter Wild,

writing in *Twentieth-Century Western Writers,* discussed the similarities between Kittredge and his characters and suggested what those common bonds mean in his work. Wild observed that "his characters aren't necessarily versions of himself, but in the larger view the problems they contend with often are those Kittredge has struggled with, and in part resolved, over much of his life. This shakes down to basically one question: How should we live in the American West? The answer is not simple."

Montana Spaces: Essays and Photographs in Celebration of Montana, places Kittredge in an editorial role for this anthology of essays by over a dozen noted writers, accompanied by thirty-two black-and-white photos by John Smart. *Montana Spaces* is a literary and pictorial representation of life in the wilder areas of the state. In the nine-book "Cord" series of adventure novels, written with Steven M. Krauzer under the joint pseudonym Owen Rountree, Kittredge explores the Western milieu. Regarding one work, *King of Colorado,* Kristiana Gregory observed in the *Los Angeles Times Book Review* that the book displays "much color" and includes "interesting facts on miners, millionaires and other frontier fortunes."

Coedited by Annick Smith, *The Last Best Place: A Montana Anthology,* gathers in its 1,161 pages a wide sampling of prose and poems by Montanans about their state. Included is work by well-known writers such as novelists Norman Maclean, Dorothy Johnson, A.B. Guthrie Jr., and Thomas McGuane, stylist Wallace Stegner, critic Leslie Fiedler, poet Richard Hugo, and essayist David Quammen. The work also features accounts by explorers Lewis and Clark and other Caucasian settlers, balanced by tales, myth, and testimony from the Native American viewpoint. Ginny Merriam, reviewing *The Last Best Place* in Chicago *Tribune Books,* called the anthology "probably the most ambitious project of its type in U.S. history."

Kittredge's *Owning It All: Essays,* "is one of the quintessential books to read if you want to understand the ferment of the modern West," wrote *Nation* contributor Philip Connors. His first collection of essays, filled with autobiographical sketches and contemporary observations, critiques popular myths of the West that valorize conquest and private property. It calls for renewed respect for the land, and for policies that favor economic and environmental justice. Kittredge, as a writer for *Publishers Weekly* observed, "stands valiantly at the center of a fledgling regional literature emerging from shattered myths and discarded ideals."

Hole in the Sky: A Memoir chronicles a life gone sour and a man seeking atonement and redemption. Kittredge, despite a childhood which on the surface might appear the epitome of the rewards promised by the American Dream, lived a waking nightmare—his father's disinheritance by Kittredge's driven, unyielding grandfather, his own inability to communicate on an emotional level with family members, and later, two failed marriages and alcoholism. As John Schulian noted in the *Los Angeles Times Book Review,* things only began their change for the better after Kittredge married for the third time and his wife "wound up holding his hand until his dream of writing for a living became a reality." Kittredge, Schulian added, "needed to soften the lump of coal his heart had become, to recapture his youthful connection not only to mankind but to nature," and the book "should be trumpeted as an act of courage. For rare is the writer who is as unflinchingly honest as Kittredge about his hostilities and resentments, his regrets and shame." Writing in the *Tribune Books,* Jane Smiley declared: "*Hole in the Sky* is a valuable memoir that should be read with care, for it explores the first American dream, the dream of property that was written into the Declaration of Independence before anyone thought of 'the pursuit of happiness' and still stands, for many, as the real American dream. It is a dream that William Kittredge has found false and hollow. His voice should be a prophetic one."

A passionate elegy to a once-pristine American West and plea for the restoration of our last and most important natural resource, *Who Owns the West?* interweaves reminiscences from Kittredge's boyhood with more recent tales of his travels across ranchlands and plains, woods and towns, alone or with others, including his good friend, the writer Raymond Carver. According to a reviewer for *Publishers Weekly,* Kittredge is particularly good at depicting the lives of ordinary denizens of this landscape—ranchers, hunters, and others—who struggle to reclaim some personal autonomy and thereby "regain some piece of their horribly depleted lands." Comparing *Who Owns the West?* to the best work by Carver, the reviewer hailed the book as fitting reminder that the living world should not be taken for granted.

In *The Nature of Generosity,* Kittredge muses on art, nature, and culture as he travels to France, Alaska, and Peru. Throughout, he asks how and why various cultures have created social and political structures that degrade the environment and result in economic injustice; he argues that people should abandon such damaging habits and adopt instead what he calls "extreme long loop altruism," behavior that emphasizes sharing and generosity. Often inspired by art, Kittredge writes about his responses to the prehistoric cave paintings he saw in Europe as well as his viewing of Fra Angelico's early Renaissance frescoes and his love of Wordsworth's poetry. Donna Seaman, writing in *Booklist,* hailed Kittredge's writing as "provocative, imaginative, eloquent, and profoundly critical." A writer for *Publishers Weekly,* however, found the book's argument weakened by Kittredge's rushed prose and "jumbled summaries" of his thoughts and experiences.

Another volume inspired by travel, *Southwestern Homelands,* drew more consistently positive reviews. As described by *Nation* reviewer Philip Connors, the book contains "stories from thirty years of tooling the freeways and back roads of Nevada, Utah, Arizona and New Mexico," and Kittredge is "as fine a travel companion as a reader could hope for." The essays are unified by Kittredge's characteristic themes: modern ideas of progress, and its unacknowledged costs, and the need to imagine a way of life based on sharing. Kittredge recalls his encounter with a Hopi man who offered to explain his beliefs; the writer, mistrusting the man, turned away—to his lasting regret. The need to reach out to others, he comes to believe, is crucial to human life. As Connors noted, Kittredge "settles on a 'message' from the ancients: 'Be communal, join up, share your goods, and once in a while give your sweet time away, no charge, pro bono, and you'll be as close to home as you're likely to be.'"

Similar sentiments inform *The Next Rodeo: New and Selected Essays,* a collection of mostly autobiographical pieces, most of which had been previously published. As in all his work, the book confronts the problematic history of western expansion, as settlers sought—with often tragic results"to civilize the vast landscape into which they had inserted themselves. In the title piece, Kittredge imagines a new kid of rodeo in Montana in which attendees share a reverence for the land and a humility toward its generosity—an approach that, in Kittredge's view, offers a way forward after decades of exploitation of the land and its resources. Bill Ott, writing in *Booklist,* praised the book's "meditative, eloquent prose" and commented that Kittrege's fiction and nonfiction is "vital to our understanding of the American West." A writer for *Publishers Weekly* expressed similar reverence for *The Next Rodeo,* praising its sensitivity and "profound reflections."

Kittredge's first novel, *The Willow Field,* is a multigenerational saga set in the Bitterroot Mountains of Montana and in the desert of Nevada. The story begins in the 1930s, when Rossie Benasco decides to leave his family home in Reno "to be his own man with horses." He signs on with a big cattle drive that is moving 200 head from Nevada to Calgary, and soon meets the woman who will change his life, Eliza Stevenson. Their "transcendent" love, according to *Booklist* reviewer Bill Ott, is reminiscent of that between Rupert and Ursula in D.H. Lawrence's *Women in Love.* At the same time, the epic landscape of the American West is as much the heart of the book as is the love story itself. Kittredge, Ott concluded, "gets it exactly right" in this book. As the plot develops, Rossie marries and becomes a father; joins the Marines just after the attack on Pearl Harbor; and winds up in the treacherous field of local and state politics. Kittredge "moves Rossie along with a compelling confidence," observed a writer for *Publishers Weekly,* who described *The Willow Field* as a "memorable evocation of the American West."

In addition to his voluminous literary output, Kittredge served as co-producer, with his partner Annick Smith, of the film *A River Runs through It,* based on the novel by Norman Maclean. The critically-acclaimed book that became an immensely popular film recounts a boyhood spent in an around Missoula, Montana, in the early years of the twentieth century.

In 2007 the *Los Angeles Times* honored Kittredge with its Robert Kirsch Award for lifetime achievement. The award, according to a *Newswire* press release, honors an especially deserving living writer with a "substantial connection to the American West." Kittredge, the release went on to note, is a master storyteller, essayist and influential cultural voice" whose work communicates "an unflinching vision of the hardscrabble landscape of the West and the people who survive and die on it."

BIOGRAPHICAL AND CRITICAL SOURCES:

BOOKS

Kittredge, William, *Hole in the Sky: A Memoir,* Vintage Books (New York, NY), 1992.

Twentieth-Century Western Writers, 2nd edition, St. James Press (Detroit, MI), 1991.

PERIODICALS

American Libraries, June 1, 1987, review of *Owning It All: Essays,* p. 416; September 1, 1991, review of *Owning It All,* p. 824.

Apartment Life, December 1, 1980, Evelyn Renold, "Stories into Film," p. 115.

Booklist, February 15, 1996, Bill Ott, review of *Who Owns the West?,* p. 986; June 1, 1997, Brad Hooper, review of *The Portable Western Reader,* p. 1648; December 1, 2000, Donna Seaman, review of *The Nature of Generosity,* p. 691; June 1, 2002, Donna Seaman, review of *Southwestern Homelands,* p. 1673; October 15, 2004, Keir Graff, review of *The Best of Montana's Short Fiction,* p. 388; October 1, 2006, Bill Ott, review of *The Willow Field,* p. 37; January 1, 2008, Bill Ott, review of *The Next Rodeo: New and Selected Essays,* p. 34.

Christian Science Monitor, January 25, 2001, review of *The Nature of Generosity,* p. 20.

Film Quarterly, summer, 1981, Bill Desowitz, review of *Stories into Film.*

Humanities, September 1, 2001, "Outgrowing Myths," p. 4.

Internet Bookwatch, August 1, 2006, review of *America's 100th Meridian: A Plains Journey.*

Kirkus Reviews, September 1, 2007, review of *The Next Rodeo.*

Library Journal, August 1, 1987, Randy Dykhuis, review of *Owning It All,* p. 126; December 1, 1995, Randy Dykhuis, review of *Who Owns the West?,* p. 139; July 1, 1997, Charlotte L. Glover, review of *The Portable Western Reader,* p. 130; November 15, 1999, Cynde Bloom Lahey, review of *Taking Care: Thoughts on Storytelling and Belief,* p. 69; December 1, 2000, Nancy P. Shires, review of *The Nature of Generosity,* p. 132; July 1, 2003, Faye A. Chadwell, review of *The Best Short Stories of William Kittredge,* p. 127; October 1, 2006, Ken St. Andre, review of *The Willow Field,* p. 58.

Los Angeles Times, April 28, 2007, "Los Angeles Times Book Prize Winners."

Los Angeles Times Book Review, November 11, 1984, Kristiana Gregory, "Soft Cover," p. 12; July 5, 1992, John Schulian, "Regrets Like Rain," p. 1; February 11, 1996, Daniel Duane, "How the West Might Someday Be Won," p. 2.

Nation, September 30, 2002, Philip Connors, "Not So Pretty Horses, Too," p. 32.

New England Review and Bread Loaf Quarterly, winter, 1989, Christopher Merrill, review of *Owning It All.*

New York Times, June 8, 1992, Christopher Lehmann-Haupt, "A Decline and Fall in the Northwest," p. C16.

PR Newswire, March 2, 2007, "Los Angeles Times Book Prizes' Kirsch Award Honors William Kittredge."

Publishers Weekly, May 22, 1987, John Mutter, review of *Owning It All,* p. 71; December 18, 1995, review of *Who Owns the West?,* p. 45; December 18, 1995, review of *Who Owns the West?,* p. 45; June 2, 1997, review of *The Portable Western Reader,* p. 64; October 23, 2000, review of *The Nature of Generosity,* p. 64; August 14, 2006, review of *The Willow Field,* p. 178; August 6, 2007, review of *The Next Rodeo.*

Reference & Research Book News, May 1, 2001, review of *The Nature of Generosity,* p. 63.

Tribune Books (Chicago, IL), December 18, 1988, Ginny Merriam, "A Vast Collection of Writing from a Land That Writers Love," p. 4; July 12, 1992, Jane Smiley, "An American Family in the Landscape," p. 7.

UPI NewsTrack, April 28, 2007, "Los Angeles Times Book Prize Winners."

Washington Post Book World, May 31, 1992, Noel Perrin, "Back in the Saddle," p. 3; October 22, 2006, Ron Charles, "Wild, Wild West: A Young Cowboy Chases His Destiny," p. 7.

ONLINE

Internet Movie Database, http://www.imdb.com/ (July 30, 2008), Kittredge filmography.

Jesus Creed, http://www.jesuscreed.org/ (July 30, 2008), "William Kittredge: An Essayist from out West."*

* * *

KUGEL, James L. 1945-

PERSONAL: Born August 22, 1945, in New York, NY; son of John Hans and Adelaide Kugel; married Rachel B. Epstein, March 18, 1975; children: Jotham. *Education:* Yale University, B.A., 1968; Harvard University, graduate study, 1973-76; City University of New York, Ph.D., 1977. *Religion:* Jewish.

ADDRESSES: Home—Jerusalem, Israel. *Office*—Bible Department, Bar Ilan University, 42900 Ramat Gan, Israel. *E-mail*—jlk@jameskugel.com.

CAREER: U.S. Department of State, Washington, DC, interpreter, 1969; Dispatch News Service, Washington, DC, Boston correspondent, 1970-71; *Boston Phoenix,* Boston, MA, editor, 1971-72; *Harper's,* New York, NY, poetry editor, 1973-75; Harvard University, Cambridge, MA, Harry Starr professor of classical, modern Jewish, and Hebrew literature, 1982-2003; Bar Ilan University, Ramat Gan, Israel, professor of Bible and director of the Institute for the History of the Jewish Bible, 2003—.

MEMBER: Phi Beta Kappa.

AWARDS, HONORS: Woodrow Wilson, Danforth, and Fulbright fellowships; Grawemeyer Award in Religion, 2001, and National Book Critics Circle Award finalist, both for *The Bible as It Was.*

WRITINGS:

Issues of Educational Reform, privately printed, 1968.

The Techniques of Strangeness in Symbolist Poetry, Yale University Press (New Haven, CT), 1971.

The Idea of Biblical Poetry: Parallelism and Its History, Yale University Press (New Haven, CT), 1981.

(With Rowan A. Greer) *Early Biblical Interpretation,* Westminster Press (Philadelphia, PA), 1986.

In Potiphar's House: The Interpretive Life of Biblical Texts, HarperSanFrancisco (San Francisco, CA), 1990.

On Being a Jew: A Brief Presentation of Jewish Practices and Belief, HarperSanFrancisco (San Francisco, CA), 1990.

(Editor) *Poetry and Prophecy: The Beginnings of a Literary Tradition,* Cornell University Press (Ithaca, NY), 1990.

The Bible as It Was, Belknap Press of Harvard University Press (Cambridge, MA), 1997.

Traditions of the Bible: A Guide to the Bible as It Was at the Start of the Common Era, Harvard University Press (Cambridge, MA), 1998.

The Greatest Poems of the Bible: A Reader's Companion with New Translations, Free Press (New York, NY), 1999.

(Editor) *Studies in Ancient Midrash,* Harvard University Center for Jewish Studies (Cambridge, MA), 2000.

The God of Old: Inside the Lost World of the Bible, Free Press (New York, NY), 2003.

The Ladder of Jacob: Ancient Interpretations of the Biblical Story of Jacob and His Children, Princeton University Press (Princeton, NJ), 2006.

(Editor) *Prayers That Cite Scripture,* Harvard University Press (Cambridge, MA), 2006.

How to Read the Bible: A Guide to Scripture, Then and Now, Free Press (New York, NY), 2007.

Contributor to *Poetry, Harper's, Rolling Stone, New York Quarterly, Antioch Review, Midstream,* and *Response.*

SIDELIGHTS: James L. Kugel's *The Bible as It Was* examines how the first five books of the Bible—which make up the Pentateuch—were interpreted from about 200 B.C. to A.D. 100. He finds a large body of tradition behind the interpretations produced in this era and notes that there were similarities in how Jews and Christians explained these Scriptures. These readings of the Pentateuch, he contends, formed the basis for the way Jews and Christians in subsequent centuries thought about the Bible.

The early Biblical commentators took for granted that Scripture was the inspired and inerrant word of God, and that it carried messages that were pertinent to the lives and times of the interpreters, Kugel notes. They also assumed that these messages were often hidden. So they devoted themselves to finding the reasons behind God's preference for Abel over his brother Cain, God's selection of Abraham to be the father of the Israelites, and numerous other unexplained happenings detailed in the Bible.

"Using a staggering number of sources, Mr. Kugel evokes the manner in which the Bible was understood at the time of these interpreters; he also traces the origins of many of the explanations that have remained standard over the millennia," commented Richard Bernstein in the *New York Times,* adding that the book is a "fascinating piece of Biblical detective work." *Christian Century* contributor Mark Reasoner praised Kugel's ecumenical approach: "Kugel is refreshingly open, straightforward and undefensive about Christian interpretations—for example, that Melchizedek and his

bread and wine foreshadow Christ and the Eucharist, or that Abraham's offering of Isaac foreshadows the crucifixion of Jesus." Also, he noted, Kugel shows that in some cases New Testament writers picked up on common Jewish explanations of circumstances not made explicit in Biblical text: "For example, there is no evidence in the Old Testament that Abel was especially righteous, though the New Testament says he was."

Kugel's work may pave the way for scholarship concerning the interpretation of the rest of the Old Testament and the New Testament, asserted Fred L. Moriarty in *Theological Studies.* Moriarty expressed gratitude to Kugel for "the new avenues of research [he] has opened up" but voiced one reservation about the book: "There may be some exaggeration in K.'s chastening remarks about the price paid for the failure of modern scholarship to reckon sufficiently with the crucial role played by the ancient interpreter." Just the same, though, *The Bible as It Was* "compels us to look with fresh eyes" at ancient interpretations, Moriarty noted. *Commentary* critic Hillel Halkin remarked that Kugel has made clear the importance of these early readings of the Bible. "No matter how we rebel against received interpretation, we are also its creatures and heirs," Halkin states. "None of us has Adamic eyes; all are caught in tradition's web. *The Bible as It Was* guides us deftly through a web that turns out to be far more extensive and ecumenical than most of us would have thought."

In *The God of Old: Inside the Lost World of the Bible,* Kugel offers "a masterful survey of the way ancient Israelites understood God," observed a *Publishers Weekly* critic. The author contends that Biblical texts written around the time of late Judaism portray God as a remote and omniscient deity. "But a distinctly different God is discerned, Kugel says, in presumably early biblical passages in which human beings by turns imagine God as absent—so truly absent that he needs to be informed of what has gone on while he was away—and experience him as present, so truly present that he can be seen and touched as easily as the man he typically appears to be in such moments," observed *New York Times Book Review* contributor Jack Miles. Through an examination of those passages, Kugel asserts, readers "can glean new insights into the Israelites' earliest concepts of God and what he meant to them—and to us today," wrote *Library Journal* critic Charlie Murray. According to Walter Brueggemann, writing in

Interpretation, "Kugel's ultimate concern is not historical but contemporary. His book, in a rich variety of offerings, makes the case that the contemporary world, like the ancient world attested by the text, is indeed visited, haunted, and ultimately defined by the reality of God who is palpably, even if hiddenly, alive and effective in the world."

Kugel explores such texts as the Testament of Simeon, the Book of Jubilees, and the Book of Judith in *The Ladder of Jacob: Ancient Interpretations of the Biblical Story of Jacob and His Children.* Instead of relying on modern interpretations of the narratives, Kugel offers readings of the ancient sources, "explaining the way an ancient audience might have understood them," noted *Library Journal* reviewer Wesley A. Mills. In the words of a *Publishers Weekly* critic: "Kugel helpfully guides us through the marvelous world of ancient biblical interpretation." David Shasha, writing in *Tikkun,* hailed *The Ladder of Jacob* as a "vital and necessary" work that is "of momentous importance for the contemporary student because it places modern readers of the Bible in a tradition of reading that has been going on for thousands of years in many places and in different cultural contexts."

How to Read the Bible: A Guide to Scripture, Then and Now is, according to a *Publishers Weekly* reviewer, a "tour de force of biblical scholarship." The book explains how early interpreters of scripture read the Bible—as a divinely revealed, unified, but cryptic text that seeks to instruct and edify—and how current researchers approach it. Kugel argues that the first books of the Bible were not produced by a lone writer, but came from as many as four different writers. He questions the historical evidence for stories about the Flood, the exodus from Egypt, or even the fall of Jericho. What was important to the writers of Scripture, Kugel explains, was not the factual details of an occurrence; they wrote about stories like the sacrifice of Isaac because such tales provided wisdom about the workings of the world and of human nature.

Kugel also discusses the non-Israelite sources of Bible stories, including the Gilgamesh epic, from which the story of the Great Flood was taken. He writes that the story of the Ten Commandments may have come originally from ancient Hittite documents. And he suggests that the Israelites were probably ancient Canaanites who broke away from the main culture and, in time,

invented myths about their origins. In addition, Kugel disparages modern literalist interpretations of the Bible, explaining that this extreme approach is both relatively new and entirely against the grain of other Biblical readings through history.

Even though he accepts this scholarly reading of the Bible, Kugel also argues that Scripture should nevertheless be accepted in the spirit of the ancient interpreters. As *New York Times Book Review* critic David Plotz summarized, "Kugel seems to conclude that, scholarship be damned, there is some seed of divine inspiration in the Bible, even if he can't say exactly what it is."

In the opinion of the *Publishers Weekly* critic, the result is view of Scripture that is "fresh, even strange, and very rich." Plotz also noted the strange qualities of Kugel's argument, noting that the overall effect is one of awe. Abraham Socher, writing in *Commentary,* praised *How to Read the Bible* as a "wonderful book, one that lays bare the worlds both of modern biblical scholarship and of ancient biblical interpretation with wit and erudition." *Booklist* writer George Cohen expressed similar admiration, calling the book "an indispensable guide to a complex subject."

BIOGRAPHICAL AND CRITICAL SOURCES:

BOOKS

Najman, Hindy, and Judith H. Newman, editors, *The Idea of Biblical Interpretation: Essays in Honor of James L. Kugel,* Brill (Boston, MA), 2004.

PERIODICALS

Biblical Archaeology Review, January 1, 2008, "Ancient Biblical Interpreter."
Booklist, February 15, 2003, Ilene Cooper, review of *The God of Old: Inside the Lost World of the Bible,* p. 1021; August 1, 2007, George Cohen, review of *How to Read the Bible: A Guide to Scripture, Then and Now,* p. 11.
Choice: Current Reviews for Academic Libraries, March 1, 2007, G. Spinner, review of *The Ladder of Jacob: Ancient Interpretations of the Biblical*

Story of Jacob and His Children, p. 1184; May 1, 2007, R. Langer, review of *Prayers That Cite Scripture,* p. 1550.

Christian Century, April 22, 1998, Mark Reasoner, review of *The Bible as It Was,* p. 451.

Commentary, April, 1998, Hillel Halkin, review of *The Bible as It Was,* p. 54; January, 2000, Algis Valiuna, review of *The Greatest Poems of the Bible: A Reader's Companion with New Translations,* p. 68; December 1, 2007, Abraham Socher, "Book Sense," p. 77.

Commonweal, October 26, 2007, "Was Something Lost?," p. 35.

First Things: A Monthly Journal of Religion and Public Life, April 1, 2008, R.R. Reno, "The Bible inside and Out," p. 13.

Interpretation, January, 2005, Walter Brueggemann, review of *The God of Old,* p. 64; April 1, 2008, Ronald Hendel, review of *The Ladder of Jacob,* p. 182.

Library Journal, April 15, 2003, Charlie Murray, review of *The God of Old,* p. 93; March 15, 2006, Wesley A. Mills, review of *The Ladder of Jacob,* p. 76.

New York Times, December 8, 1997, Richard Bernstein, review of *The Bible as It Was;* September 15, 2007, Carolyn M. Craft, review of *How to Read the Bible,* p. 65.

New York Times Book Review, May 11, 2003, Jack Miles, "You Won't Believe Who I Just Saw!," review of *The God of Old,* p. 12; September 16, 2007, David Plotz, "Reading Is Believing, or Not," p. 12.

Publishers Weekly, January 27, 2003, review of *The God of Old,* p. 254; February 27, 2006, review of *The Ladder of Jacob,* p. 58; June 25, 2007, review of *How to Read the Bible,* p. 51 July 9, 2007, "The Bible According to Kugel," p. 26.

Reviewer's Bookwatch, April 1, 2008, Fred Reiss, review of *How to Read the Bible.*

Shofar, summer, 2004, Charlotte Fonrobert, review of *Studies in Ancient Midrash,* p. 159; fall, 2004, Serge Frolov, review of *The God of Old,* p. 166.

Theological Studies, March, 1998, Fred L. Moriarty, review of *The Bible as It Was,* p. 136; March, 2006, Stephen D. Ryan, review of *The Idea of Biblical Interpretation,* p. 178.

Tikkun, March 1, 2007, David Shasha, "Climbing the Ladder of Interpretation."

Times Literary Supplement, January 5, 2007, Sarah Gold, "And Israel Heard," p. 26.

ONLINE

BookPage, http://www.bookpage.com/ (July 30, 2008), Roger Bishop, "Great Poems of the Bible."

James Kugel Home Page, http://www.jameskugel.com (July 30, 2008).*

*   *   *

KUHFELD, Mary
See FERRIS, Monica

*   *   *

KUHFELD, Mary Pulver
See FERRIS, Monica

*   *   *

KUHLMAN, Evan

ADDRESSES: Home—OH. *E-mail*—e.l.kuhlman@gmail.com.

CAREER: Writer. Worked as a restaurant manager and a reporter.

AWARDS, HONORS: Winner of a short-story award for new writers; also received prizes for journalism.

WRITINGS:

Wolf Boy (novel), Shaye Areheart Books (New York, NY), 2006.

The Last Invisible Boy (novel), illustrated by J.P. Coovert, Atheneum Books for Young Readers (New York, NY), 2008.

Also author of a play, *The Bread Man.* Contributor to periodicals, including *Glimmer Train, Notre Dame Review, Salt Hill, Madison Review, Third Coast,* and *Vincent Brothers Review.*

SIDELIGHTS: Evan Kuhlman's *Wolf Boy* contains a graphic novel within a standard novel. The plot concerns a death within the Harrelson family and its aftermath. Francis Harrelson, the eldest child, is killed in a car accident on his way to an academic conference. His girlfriend, Jasmine, survives the crash, and she and the Harrelsons all enter a dark period of mourning. Despite the subject matter, Kuhlman manages to present his characters "with a deft combination of black humor and pathos that is always pulling itself up just short of bathetic sentimentality. . . . Light ironies save the riskiest passages from shameless tear-jerking, while Kuhlman generally seems quite sincere in drawing the emotional confusion" of this family, stated Madison Smartt Bell in the *Boston Globe.*

Francis's father, Gene, withdraws emotionally from his wife, Helen, and their two other children, Crispy and Stephen. Helen is haunted by guilt and lives in a state of numbness. Crispy tries to run away to join her favorite singer, and Stephen responds to his brother's death by developing a crush on Jasmine and writing a superhero comic called "The Adventures of Wolf Boy." He uses his drawings as a way to transfer the family's problems to another dimension where magical solutions might be possible. Kuhlman collaborated with graphic artists Brendan and Brian Fraim to draw the "Wolf Boy" sections of the novel.

Wolf Boy is "an impressive debut" that is "technically ambitious and emotionally sincere," commented Bell. A reviewer for *Rick Kleffel's Agony Column* judged the graphic-novel content of the book to be "strong enough that I wish there were more of it," and added: "Kuhlman also exceeded my expectations with the reality of his novel, the centeredness and density of his writing." Another recommendation was offered by M.L. Van Valkenburgh in the *Charleston City Paper Online:* "*Wolf Boy* is everything you could ask for from a story, and more. It is one of those rare books that reminds you of every beautifully poignant moment you've ever taken for granted, one that takes you back to your childhood— the real one, with pain and bitterness and confusion and joy and surprise all wrapped up in every day."

Kuhlman's second novel, *The Last Invisible Boy,* generated a similar critical response. Written for middle-school readers and also employing a story-within-a-story structure, the book focuses on Finn Garret, a twelve-year-old boy who believes that he is beginning

to disappear after the death of his beloved father. First he notices that his brown hair is turning white; then he sees that his once-ruddy skin is becoming pale. Each day, he fades a bit more. Worried that he will soon disappear completely, Finn decides to write a memoir before he becomes completely invisible. This memoir chronicles his happy memories of his father and family; his fantasies of space flight; and his friendship with Melanie. Finn also writes about his fascination with people's names and what they mean; he spends many hours tracing name derivations and meanings and judging their aptness in individual cases. But although Finn describes his encounters with the school psychologist, scheduled to help the boy grieve, he cannot bring himself to write about the day his father actually died. He does ask himself questions, though, and wonders if he's being erased as punishment for not having been able to save his father. Additionally, he wonders if his white hair is an indication of premature aging, and thus an attempt to grow closer to his dad. In time, however, Finn becomes able to understand more about his guilt and grief, and to open himself to the pain that his mother, brother, and grandfather also feel in their bereavement.

Despite its sad theme, the novel was described as both humorous and uplifting. *School Library Journal* reviewer Connie Tyrrell Burns noted that Kuhlman's style is "pitch-perfect [for] middle school," and said that the novel "is sure to have huge appeal." Similarly, *Booklist* contributor Thom Barthelmess enjoyed the "genuinely adolescent, funny, and moving" qualities of Finn's journal, which includes drawings, quizzes, log entries, mementos, and direct addresses to the reader. *BookPage* reviewer Andrea Tarr also noted Kuhlman's skill in capturing the voice of a young adolescent boy, stating that "Finn's memoirs reflect a wry innocence combined with the pain of loss, making this outing a sweet, sorrowful look at grieving and healing." Similarly, a writer for *Kirkus Reviews* described *The Last Invisible Boy* as a "poignant . . . quietly believable" story of a sensitive boy's mourning and maturation. Describing the book as "poignant, humorous and always insightful," Sarah Sawtelle, writing in *Kidsreads.com,* suggested that *The Last Invisible Boy* is "a novel that will stay with readers long after the last page has been turned."

Kuhlman's other writings include a play, *The Bread Man.* His short stories have appeared in numerous publications including *Glimmer Train* and *Third Coast.*

BIOGRAPHICAL AND CRITICAL SOURCES:

PERIODICALS

Booklist, November 1, 2008, Thom Barthelmess, review of *The Last Invisible Boy,* p. 40.

Boston Globe, July 16, 2006, Madison Smartt Bell, review of *Wolf Boy.*

Kirkus Reviews, February 1, 2006, review of *Wolf Boy,* p. 103; September 15, 2008, review of *The Last Invisible Boy.*

Publishers Weekly, January 16, 2006, review of *Wolf Boy,* p. 36; October 13, 2008, review of *The Last Invisible Boy,* p. 54.

School Library Journal, December 1, 2008, Connie Tyrrell Burns, review of *The Last Invisible Boy,* p. 130.

ONLINE

BookLoons, http://www.bookloons.com/ (September 26, 2006), Ricki Marking-Camuto, review of *Wolf Boy.*

BookPage, http://www.bookpage.com/ (June 25, 2009), Andrea Tarr, review of *The Last Invisible Boy.*

Charleston City Paper Online, http://www.charleston citypaper.com/ (July 5, 2006), M.L. Van Valkenburgh, review of *Wolf Boy.*

Evan Kuhlman Home Page, http://www.evankuhlman. com (June 25, 2009).

Flak, http://www.flakmag.com/ (September 25, 2006), review of *Wolf Boy.*

Kidsreads.com, http://www.kidsreads.com/ (June 25, 2009), Sarah Sawtelle, review of *The Last Invisible Boy.*

Miami University: Department of English Web site, http://www.units.muohio.edu/english/ (September 25, 2006), Steven Paul Lansky, interview with Evan Kuhlman.

Rick Kleffel's Agony Column, http://bookotron.com/ agony/ (May 3, 2006), review of *Wolf Boy.*

Wolf Boy Web site, http://www.wolfboynovel.com (September 25, 2006).*

L

LAKE, Robert
　　See RANDISI, Robert J.

　　　*　　*　　*

LAWRENCE-LIGHTFOOT, Sara 1944-

PERSONAL: Born August 2, 1944; daughter of Charles Radford (a sociologist) and Margaret (a child psychiatrist) Lawrence; divorced; children: two. *Education:* Swarthmore College, B.A., 1966; attended Bank Street College of Education, 1966-67; Harvard University, Ed. D., 1972.

ADDRESSES: Office—Department of Educational Administration, Harvard University, Cambridge, MA 02138.

CAREER: Harlem Hospital, New York, NY, research associate, 1966; Yeshiva University, Albert Einstein School of Medicine, Bronx, NY, research assistant in psychiatry, 1967-68; Educational Development Center, Cambridge, MA, research and evaluation consultant for social studies, 1971-72; Harvard University, Cambridge, assistant professor, 1972-76, associate professor, 1976-80, professor, 1980-98, Emily Hargroves Professor of Education, 1998—, member of executive board of Radcliffe Institute, 1974-76, faculty fellow of Bunting Institute, 1976-78, member of advisory board for W.E.B. DuBois Institute, 1974-75, 1991—. Center for the Advancement of Study in the Behavioral Sciences, Stanford, CA, research fellow, 1983-84. National Humanities Faculty, member of board of trustees, 1976-82; Swarthmore College, member of board of managers,

1981-89; Berklee College of Music, member of board of directors, 2005—. John D. and Catherine T. MacArthur Foundation, board member, 1991-2007, board chair, 2002-07; member of board of directors, Foundation for Child Development, 1978-91, Institute for Educational Leadership, 1980-83, International Study Center for Children and Families, 1982-89, Bright Horizons Family Solutions, 1993—, and Atlantic Philanthropies, 2006—. WGBH-Television, member of board of overseers, 1995-2000, member of board of trustees, 2000-09; member of board of directors or trustees, Reading Is Yours to Keep, 1975-78, Boston Young Women's Christian Association, 1976-79, and United South End Settlements, 1976-78; member of board of overseers, Boston Institute of Contemporary Art, 1991-99, and Boston Museum of Fine Arts, 1992-2000; consultant to National Urban League. *Boston Globe,* member of board of directors, beginning 1990; member of editorial board or board of editors, *Harvard Educational Review,* 1968-71, *Sociology of Education,* 1982-86, *Harvard Education Letter,* 1984-91, *Teaching and Teacher Education,* 1985-89, and *Journal of Youth and Adolescence,* 1987-92.

MEMBER: American Philosophical Society, American Educational Research Association, National Academy of Education (fellow).

AWARDS, HONORS: Candace Award, National Coalition of 100 Black Women; fellow, John D. and Catherine T. MacArthur Foundation, 1984; outstanding book award, American Educational Research Association, 1984, for *The Good High School: Portraits of Character and Culture;* Christopher Award, 1988, for *Balm in Gilead: Journey of a Healer;* George Ledlie prize, Harvard University, 1993, for research and discovery that benefits mankind; Meridian Award, Indianapolis Children's Museum, 1995; literary award in nonfiction, Black Caucus, American Library Association, 1995, for *I've Known Rivers: Lives of Loss and Liberation;* Spencer Foundation senior scholar, 1995; distinguished service medal, Teachers College, Columbia University, 1996; Sojourner Truth Award for Racial Justice, Young Women's Christian Association, Cambridge, MA, 1998; Crossing the River Jordan Award, Public Education Network, 2003; Ferguson Award for Service to Children and Families, National Louis University, 2004; Margaret Mead Award, American Academy of Political and Social Science, 2008; the Sara Lawrence-Lightfoot Chair was established in her honor at Swarthmore College; honorary degrees from Northeastern University, Boston College, Marymount Manhattan College, Hamilton College, Emerson College, Dartmouth College, University of Toronto, and numerous other institutions.

WRITINGS:

Worlds Apart: Relationships between Families and Schools, Basic Books (New York, NY), 1978.
(With Jean V. Carew) *Beyond Bias: Perspectives on Classrooms,* Harvard University Press (Cambridge, MA), 1979.
The Good High School: Portraits of Character and Culture, Basic Books (New York, NY), 1983.
Balm in Gilead: Journey of a Healer, Addison-Wesley (Reading, MA), 1988.
I've Known Rivers: Lives of Loss and Liberation, Penguin (New York, NY), 1994.
(With Jessica Hoffmann Davis) *The Art and Science of Portraiture,* Jossey-Bass (San Francisco, CA), 1997.
Respect: An Exploration, Perseus Books (Reading, MA), 1999.
The Essential Conversation: What Parents and Teachers Can Learn from Each Other, Random House (New York, NY), 2003.
The Third Chapter: Passion, Risk, and Adventure in the 25 Years after 50, Farrar, Straus & Giroux (New York, NY), 2009.

Author of several articles on American schools and education, including "A Question of Perspective: Toward a More Complex View of Classrooms," which was part of the Urban Diversity series published by Columbia University, 1978. Contributor to books, including *Another Voice: Feminist Perspectives on*

Social Life and Social Science, edited by Marcia Millman and Rosabeth Moss Kanter, Doubleday (New York, NY), 1975; *Educational Environments and Effects: Evaluation, Research, and Policy,* edited by Herbert Walberg, National Society for the Study of Education (Chicago, IL), 1978; *Shades of Brown: New Perspectives on School Desegregation,* edited by Derrick Bell, Teachers College Press (New York, NY), 1980; and *The World of Ideas: Conversations with Thoughtful Men and Women about American Life Today and the Ideas Shaping Our Future,* Doubleday, 1989. Contributor to periodicals, including *Journal of Research and Development in Education, Signs: Journal of Women in Culture and Society, Theory into Practice, Qualitative Inquiry, American Journal of Orthopsychiatry, Teachers College Record,* and *Daedalus: Journal of the Academy of Arts and Sciences.*

SIDELIGHTS: Sociologist Sara Lawrence-Lightfoot's writings examine issues of race and class and the experience of the American school system, focusing closely on that experience of education which is particular to minorities. With several extensive works published, Lightfoot has produced studies that one reviewer writing in *Choice,* described as "particularly insightful . . . analytic and descriptive."

In *Worlds Apart: Relationships between Families and Schools,* her first book, Lawrence-Lightfoot challenges the generally held notion that the competitive relationship between parents and teachers is a necessary and socially valuable one for the child. Criticizing this analysis, Lawrence-Lightfoot draws on her own observations as well as existing literature to reach conclusions about the negative impact of this struggle between family and school and to make recommendations for a more integrative, and therefore beneficial, approach to education. Lightfoot also places the relationship between family and school in a sociohistorical context, holding the lack of educational resources available to slave parents in America prior to emancipation responsible for the current negative feelings of black parents towards urban schools.

Lawrence-Lightfoot followed the negative appraisal offered in *Worlds Apart* with a look at the positive qualities of six schools in *The Good High School: Portraits of Character and Culture.* The book examines six high schools that, in the author's view, respond in a positive and creative way to the challenges they face. Included are portraits of two urban public schools, two suburban public schools, and two elite private schools. David Owen, writing in the *New Republic,* referred to the book as an occasionally "enlightening" attempt at "something grander" than mere sociology, "a kind of intimate portraiture." In this context, Lawrence-Lightfoot interviews teachers and examines such aspects of the six schools as the unique curriculum offered by some (John F. Kennedy High School in New York, for example, offers courses as diverse as yoga and roller disco), as well as the dedication of the various faculty members in these schools. Lawrence-Lightfoot concludes by offering *The Good High School* as a potential "catalyst for change within an institution," setting forth her examples of what aspects of education in America work in an attempt to add to the solutions offered previously in *Worlds Apart.*

The more personal work, *Balm in Gilead: Journey of a Healer,* is a biography of the author's mother, and has been viewed as an alternative perspective on the author's already-established preferred themes of race, class, and education. Margaret Morgan Lightfoot, a woman with a strong desire to fight injustice and improve the lives of African Americans, struggled against prejudice and racism to forge a career helping disturbed children. Having moved to Harlem from her native Mississippi to attend high school, Lightfoot was the only black undergraduate at Cornell University and, later, at Columbia Medical School. She became one of the first black child psychiatrists in the United States and spent most of her career at Harlem Hospital. Drawing on her mother's reminiscences of family, school, and work, Lawrence-Lightfoot creates a portrait of a pioneering woman supported by a strong network of extended family. The book, said *New York Times Book Review* contributor H. Jack Geiger, is also "full of interior pain, denial and rage repressed so deeply that it is never felt." The real subject of *Balm in Gilead,* noted Geiger, is "the wound within, the internalized racism that leads some victims, at unspeakable cost to their own sense of self, to embrace the values of their oppressors." This invisible wound remains unexamined in the book. Noting the affectionate and admiring approach that Lawrence-Lightfoot takes toward her mother in this book, the reviewer described *Balm in Gilead* as a work in which "critical judgment is . . . obscured by adulation" and "Margaret Lawrence's voice, unfiltered and undiluted," is not heard.

I've Known Rivers: Lives of Loss and Liberation, the title of which refers to a poem by Langston Hughes, presents portraits of six prominent African Americans, including lawyer Charles Ogletree, businesswoman Cheryle Wills, documentary filmmaker Orlando Bagwell, and theology professor Katie Cannon. Lawrence-Lightfoot was inspired to write the book to counter an argument by E. Franklin Frazier that, when blacks achieve middle-class education and status, they tend to become absorbed into mainstream society and turn away from their roots. Interviewing her subjects over a period of years, Lawrence-Lightfoot shows how their experiences of race and class shaped them from an early age and remained relevant forces in their later lives.

In a generally positive review, a contributor to *Publishers Weekly* observed that the author "has avoided some probing questions" of her subjects, such as their views on the challenges of interracial marriage. But *America* reviewer Valerie Babb gave *I've Known Rivers* a more positive assessment, concluding that Lawrence-Lightfoot "has critically and compassionately documented how individuals reconcile the contradictions that seem to be at the heart of existence: generational conflicts with a profound debt to forbearers; the way a privileged position separates them from the world of their less fortunate peers, and the optimism accomplishment fosters with the impotent rage felt when it cannot provide a shelter from racism."

In *Respect: An Exploration,* which *Cross Currents* reviewer Stephen J. Pope described as "a popular meditation on various virtues," Lawrence-Lightfoot rejects the idea that respect is an attribute of social power and status. Instead, she sees respect as essentially egalitarian. Respect, she writes, has six qualities: empowerment, healing, dialogue, curiosity, self-respect, and attention. Each of these qualities is illustrated in her book by the story of a notable individual whose life and work embodies it. Healing, for example, is illuminated in a chapter about pediatrician Dr. Johnye Ballenger, while self-respect is illustrated by a chapter on Episcopal priest Bill Wallace. Finding the book interesting and engaging, Pope nevertheless felt that it "offers nothing new concerning the notion of respect." While Lawrence-Lightfoot aims for "a kind of simplicity of theory," the reviewer went on to say,"she never shows philosophically what respect itself actually means [or] how its various 'qualities' are coherently related to one another." *Booklist* contributor Mary Carroll, however, mentioned that the book demonstrates "involving and provocative storytelling" that contributes to "a respectful dialogue with the reader."

Lawrence-Lightfoot returns to the subject of schooling in *The Essential Conversation: What Parents and*

Teachers Can Learn from Each Other. The book focuses on the topic of parent-teacher conferences, which, according to the author, are fraught with anxieties. Parents can feel awkward and unwelcome in this setting, and this discomfort is exacerbated when differences of language, ethnicity, and poverty are also present. For their part, teachers can feel defensive about challenges to their expertise and authority. Drawing from her own experience as a parent as well as from the stories of other parents and teachers, Lawrence-Lightfoot examines the dynamics between teachers and parents in wealthy suburban schools as well as struggling inner-city schools, showing how race and class contribute to misunderstandings and frustrations. She also offers advice for both teachers and parents on how to avoid these pitfalls and work more cooperatively to benefit their students and children. Vanessa Bush, writing in *Booklist,* considered *The Essential Conversation* to be "incredibly honest and insightful." Similarly, a writer for *Publishers Weekly* called the book a "significant and thoughtfully rendered exploration of a social ritual many adults commonly experience but seldom examine."

In *The Third Chapter: Passion, Risk, and Adventure in the 25 Years after 50* Lawrence-Lightfoot profiles forty Americans between the ages of fifty and seventy who have made significant life changes. She finds that people in this "third chapter" of their lives can discover deep new passions after leaving the demands of career. A retired newspaper executive, for example, enjoys playing jazz piano and writing fiction; a neurobiologist finds fulfillment working with AIDS patients in East Africa. As the author acknowledges, her subjects in this book are free of any financial constraints that might limit their choices, but their stories still convey a message applicable to anyone: that one's later years need not be ones of passivity and disappointment, and that learning should be a life-long process.

BIOGRAPHICAL AND CRITICAL SOURCES:

BOOKS

Lawrence-Lightfoot, Sara, *The Good High School: Portraits of Character and Culture,* Basic Books (New York, NY), 1983.

Lawrence-Lightfoot, Sara, *Balm in Gilead: Journey of a Healer,* Addison-Wesley (Reading, MA), 1988.

PERIODICALS

America, March 11, 1995, Valerie Babb, review of *I've Known Rivers: Lives of Loss and Liberation,* p. 34.

American Journal of Education, November, 1998, Elizabeth Vallance, review of *The Art and Science of Portraiture,* p. 66.

American Journal of Sociology, May, 1981, review of *Worlds Apart: Relationships between Families and Schools,* p. 1466.

Black Scholar, fall, 1994, review of *I've Known Rivers,* p. 61; summer, 1995, review of *Balm in Gilead* and *I've Known Rivers,* p. 71.

Booklist, September 15, 1978, review of *Worlds Apart,* p. 135; August, 1994, Mary Carroll, review of *I've Known Rivers,* p. 1987; March 1, 1999, Mary Carroll, review of *Respect: An Exploration,* p. 1102; September 15, 2003, Vanessa Bush, review of *The Essential Conversation: What Parents and Teachers Can Learn from Each Other,* p. 185.

Book Page, August, 2003, review of *The Essential Conversation,* p. 15.

Choice: Current Reviews for Academic Libraries, May, 1979, review of *Worlds Apart,* p. 431; February, 1995, R. Stewart, review of *I've Known Rivers,* p. 997; September, 1999, M.R. Rowlkes, review of *Respect,* p. 186.

Christian Century, April 4, 1979, Myron A. Marty, review of *Worlds Apart,* p. 382.

Christian Science Monitor, December 28, 1978, review of *Worlds Apart,* p. 18; January 23, 1989, Melinda M. Ponder, review of *Balm in Gilead,* p. 13.

Commentary, January, 1979, Rita Kramer, review of *Worlds Apart,* p. 77.

Commonweal, April 20, 1984, review of *The Good High School,* p. 245; June 2, 1989, Jane Redmont, review of *Balm in Gilead,* p. 345.

Contemporary Psychology, August, 1979, review of *Worlds Apart,* p. 642.

Contemporary Sociology, July, 1980, review of *Worlds Apart,* p. 541.

Cross Currents, fall, 2000, Stephen J. Pope, review of *Respect,* p. 415.

Education Digest, November, 1984, review of *The Good High School,* p. 70.

Essence, October, 1988, Paula Giddings, review of *Balm in Gilead,* p. 34; October, 1994, review of *I've Known Rivers,* p. 70.

Harvard Educational Review, May, 1980, review of *Worlds Apart,* p. 291; winter, 1999, review of *The Art and Science of Portraiture,* p. 489.

Journal of Marriage and the Family, August, 1979, review of *Worlds Apart,* p. 675.

Journal of Southern History, August, 1990, Any Thompson McCandless, review of *Balm in Gilead,* p. 559.

Kirkus Reviews, August 15, 1978, review of *Worlds Apart,* p. 931; July 1, 1994, review of *I've Known Rivers,* p. 906; February 15, 1999, review of *Respect,* p. 276; October 15, 2008, review of *The Third Chapter: Passion, Risk, and Adventure in the 25 Years after 50.*

Library Journal, September 1, 1978, review of *Worlds Apart,* p. 1632; July, 1979, review of *Beyond Bias: Perspectives on Classrooms,* p. 1450; September 1, 1994, Anita L. Cole, review of *I've Known Rivers,* p. 202; November 1, 1994, review of *I've Known Rivers,* p. 88; April 15, 1999, Lucille M. Boone, review of *Respect,* p. 128; September 1, 2003, Samuel T. Huang, review of *The Essential Conversation,* p. 180; February 1, 2009, Lisa Nussbaum, review of *The Third Chapter,* p. 84.

Los Angeles Times, July 28, 1985, Alex Raskin, review of *The Good High School,* p. 10.

Ms., September, 1994, review of *I've Known Rivers,* p. 77.

Nation, February 10, 1979, Benita Eisler, review of *Worlds Apart,* p. 150; March 20, 1989, Vanessa Northington, review of *Balm in Gilead,* p. 386.

New Republic, December 2, 1978, Joseph Featherstone, review of *Worlds Apart,* p. 41; January 23, 1984, David Owen, review of *The Good High School,* p. 40; March 27, 1989, Robert Coles, review of *Balm in Gilead,* p. 40.

New York Times, November 8, 1983, Fred M. Hechinger, review of *The Good High School,* p. C8.

New York Times Book Review, March 25, 1984, Judith K. Davison, review of *The Good High School,* p. 21; January 1, 1989, H. Jack Geiger, review of *Balm in Gilead,* p. 7; November 13, 1994, Mitchell Duneier, review of *I've Known Rivers,* p. 69; May 2, 1999, Ray Sawhill, review of *Respect,* p. 20.

Parnassus, spring, 1991, Suzanne Fox, review of *Balm in Gilead,* p. 132.

Phi Delta Kappan, March, 1979, Betty Jo Zander, review of *Worlds Apart,* p. 541; April, 1984, William W. Goetz, review of *The Good High School,* p. 571.

Publishers Weekly, July 24, 1978, review of *Worlds Apart,* p. 88; August 26, 1983, review of *The Good High School,* p. 375; September 16, 1988, review of *Balm in Gilead,* p. 71; July 11, 1994, review of *I've Known Rivers,* p. 69; February 22, 1999, review of *Respect,* p. 72; May 26, 2003, review of *The Essential Conversation,* p. 57; October 20, 2008, review of *The Third Chapter,* p. 45; December 1, 2008, Parul Sehgal, "PW Talks with Sarah Lawrence-Lightfoot: The Golden Age," p. 38.

Social Forces, June, 1979, review of *Worlds Apart,* p. 1423.

Social Work, May, 1980, review of *Worlds Apart,* p. 246.

Teachers College Record, spring, 1980, review of *Worlds Apart,* p. 395; September, 2003, Martin Bickman, review of *The Art and Science of Portraiture,* p. 1327.

Tribune Books (Chicago, IL), November 23, 2003, review of *The Essential Conversation,* p. 2.

Wall Street Journal, October 21, 1983, Grace Hechinger, review of *The Good High School,* p. 20.

Washington Post Book World, August 1, 1999, review of *Respect,* p. 8.

ONLINE

Harvard University: Graduate School of Education Web site, http://gse.harvard.edu/ (June 28, 2009), faculty profile.

Purpose Prize Web site, http://www.purposeprize.org/ (June 28, 2009), author profile.

Spirituality & Practice: Resources for Spiritual Journeys, http://www.spiritualityandpractice.com/ (June 28, 2009), Frederic and Mary Ann Brussat, review of *Respect.*

Thaindian News (Bangkok, Thailand), http://www.thaindian.com/ (June 28, 2009), "Sara Lawrence-Lightfoot Questions the Absence of Primal Questions."*

*   *   *

LEDD, Paul
    See RANDISI, Robert J.

*   *   *

LEIGH, Robert
    See RANDISI, Robert J.

*   *   *

LONG, Kate 1964-

PERSONAL: Born 1964; married, husband a government worker; children: two.

ADDRESSES: Home—Shropshire, England. *E-mail*—
simondalong@googlemail.com.

CAREER: Writer and educator. High school English
teacher, c. 1991-2003.

WRITINGS:

NOVELS

The Bad Mother's Handbook, Picador (London,
England), 2004.
Swallowing Grandma, Picador (London, England),
2005, published as *Family Sold Separately,* Ballan-
tine Books (New York, NY), 2008.
Queen Mum, Picador (London, England), 2006.
The Daughter Game, Picador (London, England), 2008.

SIDELIGHTS: Kate Long retired from teaching high
school after her first novel, *The Bad Mother's Handbook,* became a best seller in England. The novel
focuses on several women in the same British family
struggling to better themselves and make ends meet,
with the individual characters narrating their own
stories. In an interview with Stephen Moss for the
London *Guardian,* the author explained her choice of
characters: "I couldn't think of any female writers who
were writing about this kind of grey class that's just out
of the working class and is clinging by its fingertips to
middleclassness."

In the novel, the protagonist, Karen, is upset that her
seventeen-year-old daughter, Charlotte, has become
pregnant. Karen's concern is that her daughter is following in her own footsteps: she had Charlotte when
she was sixteen and knows firsthand how such an early
pregnancy can be a barrier to a better life and, in Charlotte's case, college. Karen's mother, Nan, is sick and
declining rapidly when Karen learns she is adopted.
She sets out to find her birth mother, thinking that possibly this may put her in touch with a better middle-
class existence. In a review of *The Bad Mother's Handbook* in *Booklist,* Joanne Wilkinson called the novel
"charming" and commended the author for her "saucy
humor." As a *Publishers Weekly* reviewer noted, "Long
tells the story . . . through shifting first-person sections
. . . moving wittily and gracefully toward an ending
that's happily realistic."

In 2008, Long published the novel *The Daughter Game.*
The story's heroine is a forty-something English teacher
named Anna, whose personal life is out of control. She
is unhappy with the relationship she has with her
husband, Jamie, who is an aspiring writer who does not
share Anna's strong desire to become a parent. Anna
bottles up her feelings and eventually starts an affair
with her husband's brother, Russ, in an attempt to get
pregnant. Meanwhile, at the private school where she
teaches, Anna takes troubled, sixteen-year-old poet Kali
under her wing, treating her as a surrogate daughter.
Overall, Long's novel was met with positive reviews by
readers and critics alike. Many critics cited the author's
sense of humor and satisfying character development as
highlights of the book. Long's "funny look at life and
love is compelling," wrote Eithne Farry in a review for
Marie Claire. Other reviewers lauded the author's writing style. *The Daughter Game* benefits from "direct,
pared-down prose," noted London *Independent* contributor Rachel Hore.

Long is also the author of *Swallowing Grandma,* a novel
about a teenage girl and her aging grandmother who is
the girl's only parent. The book was first published in
London, England, by Picador in 2005, then published
as *Family Sold Separately* in 2008 by Ballantine Books.

Long told *CA:* "I always loved English at school,
especially high school, and read voraciously as a young
child. But it was while I was a teacher that my writing
took off; my boss sent me on a course designed to
stimulate creativity in the classroom, and I began working on a story there which I carried on when I came
home. I'd caught the bug!"

Long states that the most surprising thing she has
learned as a writer is "the amazing stories that ordinary
people have to tell. Every time I do a public reading or
event, someone comes to me at the end and relates the
most astonishing tale of hardship, duplicity, or triumph
which happened to them or their families. We don't
have to look far for adventure or heroism: they're happening around us every day.

"I'm especially interested in family tensions, so almost
everything I see around me informs what I write. My
own experience of being adopted, of motherhood, of
marriage—all these experiences shape what I want to
say in my books. Though I should add that I never write
about people I know.

"I plan a lot before I start, drawing up timelines and
family trees and character studies and even cutting out
photographs I've printed from the internet to help me

off the starting line. When I know where I'm going, I begin writing and it all comes fairly fast after that. Every night, when my head seems to race with ideas, I make copious notes, and the next morning I type them up. The image of facing a blank piece of paper with nothing prepared fills me with dread.

"I hope very much my novels will make readers appreciate what they have in terms of friendships and family bonds. It's so important to tell people we care about them while they're still around."

BIOGRAPHICAL AND CRITICAL SOURCES:

PERIODICALS

Booklist, March 1, 2005, Joanne Wilkinson, review of *The Bad Mother's Handbook,* p. 1138.

Bookseller, February 29, 2008, review of *The Daughter Game,* p. 12.

Guardian (London, England), March 31, 2004, Stephen Moss, "G2: Portrait: The Tesco Triumph," p. 8.

Independent (London, England), April 6, 2008, Rachel Hore, review of *The Daughter Game.*

Kirkus Reviews, January 1, 2005, review of *The Bad Mother's Handbook,* p. 13.

Library Journal, March 15, 2005, Amy Brozio-Andrews, review of *The Bad Mother's Handbook,* p. 73.

Marie Claire, March 3, 2008, Eithne Farry, review of *The Daughter Game.*

Publishers Weekly, March 28, 2005, review of *The Bad Mother's Handbook,* p. 56; June 30, 2008, review of *Family Sold Separately,* p. 163.

ONLINE

Dunedin Public Libraries News & Reviews Blog, http://dunedinpubliclibraries.wordpress.com/ (July 31, 2008), review of *The Daughter Game.*

Kate Long Home Page, http://www.katelong.co.uk (June 10, 2009).

Mirror.co.uk, http://www.mirror.co.uk/ (March 14, 2008), Henry Sutton, review of *The Daughter Game.*

Trashionista, http://www.trashionista.com/ (June 10, 2009), interview with Kate Long; review of *The Daughter Game.*

LONGLEY, W.B.
   See RANDISI, Robert J.

*   *   *

LOWELL, Susan 1950-
   (Susan L. Humphreys)

PERSONAL: Born October 27, 1950, in Chihuahua, Mexico; daughter of J. David (a geologist) and Edith (a rancher) Lowell; married William Ross Humphreys (a management consultant), March 21, 1975; children: Anna, Mary. *Education:* Stanford University, A.B., 1972, A.M., 1974; Princeton University, M.A., Ph.D., 1979. *Hobbies and other interests:* Reading, cooking, hiking, horseback riding.

ADDRESSES: Home—Tucson, AZ. *Office*—Treasure Chest Books/Rio Nuevo Publishers, 451 N. Bonita Ave., Tucson, AZ 85745. *E-mail*—susanlowell@rionuevo.com.

CAREER: Writer, publisher, and rancher. Freelance writer, 1980—. University of Texas at Dallas, visiting assistant professor of English, 1979-80; University of Arizona, Tucson, adjunct lecturer of creative writing, 1989. Also worked as a journalist, editor, and publisher. Treasure Chest Books/Rio Nuevo Publishers (distributor and publisher), Tucson, AZ, co-owner with husband, Ross Humphreys.

MEMBER: Society of Children's Book Writers and Illustrators, Southern Arizona Society of Authors, Phi Beta Kappa.

AWARDS, HONORS: Milkweed National Fiction Award, Milkweed Editions, 1988, for *Ganado Red;* children's regional book award, Mountains and Plains Booksellers' Association, and Distinguished Children's Book citation, *Hungry Mind Review,* both 1993, both for *I Am Lavina Cumming;* Arizona Young Readers' Award for picture books, 1994, both for *The Three Little Javelinas;* named Arizona Children's Author of the Year, Arizona Library Association, 1994.

WRITINGS:

FOR CHILDREN

The Three Little Javelinas, illustrated by Jim Harris, Northland (Flagstaff, AZ), 1992, with audiotape, Scholastic (New York, NY), 1993.

I Am Lavina Cumming (novel), Milkweed Editions (Minneapolis, MN), 1993.

The Tortoise and the Jackrabbit, illustrated by Jim Harris, Northland (Flagstaff, AZ), 1994, bilingual edition, Rising Moon (Flagstaff, AZ), 2004.

The Boy with Paper Wings, Milkweed Editions (Minneapolis, MN), 1995.

Little Red Cowboy Hat, illustrated by Randy Cecil, Holt (New York, NY), 1997.

The Bootmaker and the Elves, illustrated by Tom Curry, Orchard Books (New York, NY), 1997.

Cindy Ellen: A Wild Western Cinderella, illustrated by Jane Manning, HarperCollins (New York, NY), 2000.

Dusty Locks and the Three Bears, illustrated by Randy Cecil, Holt (New York, NY), 2001.

(With Anna Humphreys) *Saguaro: The Desert Giant,* Rio Nuevo Publishers (Tucson, AZ), 2002.

Cactus Flowers, Rio Nuevo Publishers (Tucson, AZ), 2005.

Josefina Javelina: A Hairy Tale, illustrated by Bruce MacPherson, Rising Moon (Flagstaff, AZ), 2005.

The Elephant Quilt: Stitch by Stitch to California!, illustrated by Stacey Dressen-McQueen, Farrar, Straus (New York, NY), 2008.

OTHER

Ganado Red: A Novella and Stories, Milkweed Editions (Minneapolis, MN), 1988.

Clouds for Dessert: Sweet Treats from the Wild West, photographs by Robin Stancliff, Rio Nuevo Publishers (Tucson, AZ), 2002.

Navajo Rug Designs, photographs by Robin Stancliff, Rio Nuevo Publishers (Tucson, AZ), 2005.

Contributor, under name Susan L. Humphreys, of scholarly articles to literature journals.

SIDELIGHTS: Susan Lowell is known for creating original stories for young readers as well as for her retellings of traditional tales from a Southwestern point of view. Her books *The Three Little Javelinas, Cindy Ellen: A Wild Western Cinderella,* and *Dusty Locks and the Three Bears* each take a story familiar to most young children and give it a southwestern flair, while the novel *I Am Lavinia Cumming* is based on a story from Lowell's own family. In addition to her writing, Lowell is also a rancher and publisher who specializes in books focusing on her beloved Southwest.

Lowell patterned her first picture book, *The Three Little Javelinas,* after the familiar story of "The Three Little Pigs," but she recasts her version in a desert setting. The three javelinas, or peccaries, are pursed by the coyote, the traditional trickster in Southwestern lore. While the first little javelina builds his house out of tumbleweed, and the second builds his house out of the ribs of the saguaro tree, their sister is the one who provides an adequate shelter made of mud adobe bricks. The text is accompanied by explanatory notes. According to a critic for *Bloomsbury Review, The Three Little Javelinas* "is a funny and clever retelling of a familiar tale," and a *Publishers Weekly* reviewer called it "sprightly fun."

Readers who enjoyed the antics of the desert pigs in *The Three Little Javelinas* will root for the heroine in Lowell's *Josefina Javelina: A Hairy Tale.* Josefina is a frisky peccary with a dream of becoming a ballet dancer. Determined to make her dream a reality, she decides to travel to the big city, where she meets a tricky (and hungry) coyote that is posing as a talent agent named White E. Lamb. When the coyote forces the pig to take flight, she impresses all onlookers with her agility and lands a humorous role in a production of a classic holiday ballet. *Josefina Javelina* showcases Lowell's "originality and storytelling talents," asserted a *Children's Bookwatch* contributor, and in *School Library Journal* Polly L. Kotarba enjoyed the sophisticated text with its "swine and pig puns and tongue-in-cheek" humor.

Lowell again teams up with illustrator Jim Harris for a new take on the "Tortoise and the Hare" fable. Featuring a Southwestern theme, *The Tortoise and the Jackrabbit* finds a mature, white-gloved tortoise in a race against a flashy, bandana-topped jackrabbit. As the duo travel across the desert, Lowell introduces young readers to the unique and varied plant life there, identifying saguaro cacti and mesquite trees, as well as other vegetation native to the Southwest. Calling the book "a merry blend of play, allegory, and environmentalism," a *Publishers Weekly* reviewer wrote that "precise and punchy, Lowell's undated prose turns hip alongside Harris's comical characterizations." *School Library Journal* reviewer Donna L. Scanlon described the work as a "sprightly, fresh approach," while *Booklist* reviewer Ellen Mandel believed that Lowell's tale is "fetchingly told."

Little Red Riding Hood is transformed by Lowell into Little Red Cowboy Hat in a title of the same name. Here, Little Red dons a sheriff's badge and keeps an eye out for rattlesnakes in her dusty Southwest town. One day, however, a bigger threat appears in the form of a wolf who blocks her path. Raised to be polite, Little Red feels obliged to talk to the wolf who asks many questions. Later, she again encounters the wolf at her grandmother's house and thinks that the wolf has done something terrible to her granny. Instead of running off, Little Red tries to figure out what happened to Grandma who, as it turns out, was out chopping wood. When the missing relative finally rescues Little Red, the girl learns an important life lesson. Writing in *School Library Journal,* critic Ruth Semrau called *Little Red Cowboy Hat* "an amusing addition to the growing collection of fairy-tale spoofs."

Cinderella meets the Southwest in *Cindy Ellen.* Instead of keeping a house clean while her mean stepmother and stepsisters relax as in the traditional tale, Cindy Ellen must make repairs on the family's ranch, from fixing the fences to mucking out the corral. After she is forbidden to attend a neighbor's rodeo, Cindy Ellen receives a visit from her fairy godmother. Presenting her with a golden six-shooter, the fairy godmother insists that her magic is useless without a bit of Cindy Ellen's spunk. With that advice, the young girl sets out to win the rodeo and the heart of Joe Prince, her wealthy neighbor's son. "Lowell's savory slang adds punch to this tale," claimed a *Publishers Weekly* reviewer. Starr LaTronica, a contributor to *School Library Journal,* found that "an abundance of action combined with humor and high-spirited hyperbole make this a rip-roaring rendition" of the traditional Cinderella tale.

Goldilocks also receives the Wild West treatment, as Lowell sets her story about the young trespasser and the three bears in the American West. *Dusty Locks and the Three Bears* features a cowboy-boot wearing girl who comes across an empty cabin in the woods. Hungry for a good meal, Dusty Locks walks inside and tests the biggest bear's beans, much too spicy for her taste. Although Lowell has the young heroine follow the traditional storyline, breaking the cub's stool, falling asleep in his bed, and being woken by the bears, she adds a twist at the end when Dusty Locks's mother finally catches up with her. *School Library Journal* critic Adele Greenlee described the story as a "humorous and fresh retelling," while a *Publishers Weekly* reviewer predicted that "with its zippy lines and range of voices . . . this should be a read-aloud hit."

I Am Lavina Cumming was inspired by the life of her grandmother and is a novel infused with folktales. In the story, the widowed father of ten-year-old Lavina

decides that his daughter should learn ladylike behavior from her aunt and sends the girl from the Arizona Territory to Santa Cruz, California. While Lavina misses her family and has trouble coping with a younger girl, she begins to appreciate her aunt and the lessons she learns in her home. A reviewer for *Publishers Weekly* wrote that "Lavina is both likable and believable, her credibility enhanced by the author's skillful use of period details."

Also set during the mid-1800s, *The Elephant Quilt: Stitch by Stitch to California!* is based on the real-life experiences of settlers traveling by wagon from Missouri to California. Featuring illustrations by Stacey Dressen-McQueen, the story focuses on Lily Rose, who sews her impressions of the trip—including the hardships of the Santa Fe Trail, the birth of a baby sister, and meetings with Native Americans, trappers, and gold miners—into the colorful quilt top that her mother and grandmother are making. In her *School Library Journal* review of *The Elephant Quilt,* Shawn Brommer praised Lowell's "conversational style," and Linda Perkins dubbed Lily Rose an "exuberant" young heroine in her *Booklist* review. A *Kirkus Reviews* critic also enjoyed the story's up-beat perspective, concluding that *The Elephant Quilt* "kicks the energy level up a notch above" similar picture-book accounts of wagon-train travel.

Lowell once commented about her life in the southwest: "I was born in Chihuahua, Mexico. I have lived on both sides of the border since then, and in many other places, too, but my real home, and my family's home for five generations, is southern Arizona. A giant saguaro cactus is my favorite kind of tree, and I love to see sand-colored coyotes sneak through the desert outside my kitchen window. Sometimes we also see hairy, pig-like javelinas snuffling along, hungry for cactus (which they eat thorns and all).

"My husband and daughters and I own a small ranch at the base of a high mountain called Baboquivari, a sacred peak to the Tohono O'odham Nation, our neighbors on the other side of the mountain. For them, Baboquivari is the center of the universe. For me this is also true. My books, which I write for adults as well as children, have all grown from my lifelong experience of the West. Family stories, some handed down to me from pioneer days, fascinate me, and I am also particularly interested in the rich mixture of Native American, Mexican, and Anglo cultures in my region. Flying coyotes, lost treasures, bandit ghosts, tiny rubies in the sand—there are many stories here to tell, and I hope to keep on writing them down. Yet they are not necessarily all Southwestern stories. A center is not a limit. It's a beginning, a heart. The wide world lies open all around it."

BIOGRAPHICAL AND CRITICAL SOURCES:

PERIODICALS

Bloomsbury Review, October, 1992, review of *The Three Little Javelinas,* p. 25.

Booklist, January 15, 1995, Ellen Mandel, review of *The Tortoise and the Jackrabbit,* p. 937; April 15, 1997, Ilene Cooper, review of *Little Red Cowboy Hat,* p. 1436; September 15, 1997, Julie Corsaro, review of *The Bootmaker and the Elves,* p. 242; July, 2001, Hazel Rochman, review of *Dusty Locks and the Three Bears,* p. 2014; April 15, 2008, Linda Perkins, review of *The Elephant Quilt: Stitch by Stitch to California!,* p. 57.

Children's Bookwatch, February, 2006, review of *Josefina Javelina: A Hairy Tale.*

Horn Book, July, 2001, review of *Dusty Locks and the Three Bears,* p. 464.

Kirkus Reviews, March 1, 2008, review of *The Elephant Quilt.*

Los Angeles Times Book Review, September 11, 1988, Georgia Jones-Davis, review of *Ganado Red: A Novella and Stories,* p. 3.

Publishers Weekly, September 14, 1992, review of *The Three Little Javelinas,* p. 123; July 5, 1993, review of *I Am Lavina Cumming,* p. 74; November 7, 1994, review of *The Tortoise and the Jackrabbit,* p. 77; November 20, 1995, review of *The Boy with Paper Wings,* p. 78; March 3, 1997, review of *Little Red Cowboy Hat,* p. 75; September 22, 1997, review of *The Bootmaker and the Elves,* p. 80; June 19, 2000, review of *Cindy Ellen: A Wild Western Cinderella,* p. 78; May 21, 2001, review of *Dusty Locks and the Three Bears,* p. 107.

School Library Journal, February, 1995, Donna L. Scanlon, review of *The Tortoise and the Jackrabbit,* p. 76; May, 1997, Ruth Semrau, review of *Little Red Cowboy Hat,* pp. 104-105; June, 2000, Starr LaTronica, review of *Cindy Ellen,* p. 134; July, 2001, Adele Greenlee, review of *Dusty Locks and the Three Bears,* p. 96; May 31, 2004, review of *Clouds for Dessert: Sweet Treats from the Wild West,* p. 96; February, 2006, Polly L. Kotarba, review of *Josefina Javelina,* p. 106; July, 2008, Shawn Brommer, review of *The Elephant Quilt,* p. 77.

ONLINE

Susan Lowell Home Page, http://www.susanlowell.com (October 30, 2009).*

M

MACKALL, Joe 1958-

PERSONAL: Born 1958, in Cleveland, OH; son of Jim (a bricklayer and police detective) Mackall. *Education:* Cleveland State University, B.A.; University of Central Oklahoma, M.A.; Bowling Green State University, M.F.A.; Indiana University of Pennsylvania, Ph.D.

ADDRESSES: Home—West Salem, OH. *E-mail*—jmackall@ashland.edu.

CAREER: Washington Post, Washington, DC, former reporter; *Cleveland* magazine, Cleveland, OH, former editor; Ashland University, Ashland, OH, associate professor of English and journalism and director of creative writing program. Cofounding editor of *River Teeth: A Journal of Nonfiction Narrative.*

WRITINGS:

NONFICTION

Information Management, Ferguson (Chicago, IL), 1998, revised 2nd edition published as *Research and Information Management,* Ferguson (New York, NY), 2004.
The Last Street before Cleveland: An Accidental Pilgrimage (memoir), University of Nebraska Press (Lincoln, NE), 2006.
Plain Secrets: An Outsider among the Amish (memoir), Beacon Press (Boston, MA), 2007.

Contributor to periodicals, including the *Washington Post* and the *Cleveland Plain Dealer;* contributor of essays to *Morning Edition,* National Public Radio.

SIDELIGHTS: Joe Mackall details his working-class roots in Cleveland with his 2006 memoir, *The Last Street before Cleveland: An Accidental Pilgrimage.* Such a pilgrimage was indeed accidental for Mackall, for he returned to his roots when an old friend of his mysteriously died. The homecoming spurred thoughts of his youth and of Cleveland during the 1970s. Mackall's family became accidental residents of the city when a grandfather, an immigrant from Italy, decided to settle in the suburbs of Cleveland to stay one step ahead of gangsters. Despite having a police detective for a father, Mackall grew up with a penchant for trouble, vandalizing local businesses and even stealing communion wine to get drunk. In *The Last Street before Cleveland,* Mackall details his own bouts with depression, drugs, and alcohol abuse. He explains how a renewed sense of religion and spirituality helped him straighten out his life. With the help and support of his father, Mackall went to college, ultimately earning a doctorate in English. In a review for *Cleveland.com,* Karen R. Long stated that the "core of [*The Last Street before Cleveland*] is Mackall's struggles with Catholicism." A *Publishers Weekly* reviewer found the work to be a "focused but gloomy memoir," but added that "Mackall's elegy for the workers' world employs delightful language."

In 2007 Mackall published another memoir, titled *Plain Secrets: An Outsider among the Amish.* The book chronicles his time living next to the Swartzentruber Amish in Ohio for more than sixteen years. This group of Amish people is a conservative order, not using electricity or gasoline, and living without indoor plumbing. Mackall was neighbors with the Shetler family, and he slowly became acquainted with them over the years. *Plain Secrets,* portrays a complex and fascinating group of people who often deal with the same situations as their non-Amish counterparts. Mackall is straightforward in his writing, and he shares with readers the qualities he admires about his Amish friends, as well as the areas where he finds concern with their way of living, including the role of women in the Amish community.

Overall *Plain Secrets* was met with positive reviews by readers and critics. Many reviewers appreciated the author's balanced account of Amish life as well as the detailed information he provides on the day-to-day lifestyle of these people. In a review for *Booklist,* June Sawyers called the book "wonderful and enlightening." Many critics found the book to be a welcome addition to literature on the Amish people. A *Publishers Weekly* reviewer concluded that *Plain Secrets* is a "deeply respectful account" of the Amish community "that never veers toward sensationalism."

BIOGRAPHICAL AND CRITICAL SOURCES:

BOOKS

Mackall, Joe, *The Last Street before Cleveland: An Accidental Pilgrimage,* University of Nebraska Press (Lincoln, NE), 2006.

Mackall, Joe, *Plain Secrets: An Outsider among the Amish,* Beacon Press (Boston, MA), 2007.

PERIODICALS

Booklist, June 1, 2007, June Sawyers, review of *Plain Secrets,* p. 10.

Boston Globe, August 5, 2007, Tom Montgomery-Fate, review of *Plain Secrets.*

Christian Century, August 7, 2007, Levi Miller, review of *Plain Secrets,* p. 37.

Publishers Weekly, January 23, 2006, review of *The Last Street before Cleveland,* p. 197; April 9, 2007, review of *Plain Secrets,* p. 50; June 27, 2007, Andrea Useem, "Risking a Friendship to Tell a Story," review of *Plain Secrets.*

San Francisco Chronicle, July 16, 2007, David Ian Miller, review of *Plain Secrets.*

ONLINE

Ashland University Web site, http://www.ashland.edu/ (June 17, 2009), author biography.

Brevity, http://www.creativenonfiction.org/brevity/ (June 17, 2009), Todd Davis, review of *Plain Secrets.*

Cleveland.com, http://www.cleveland.com/ (April 11, 2006), Karen R. Long, review of *The Last Street before Cleveland.*

FaithfulReader.com, http://www.faithfulreader.com/ (June 17, 2009), Cindy Crosby, review of *Plain Secrets.*

GPBookBlog, http://gpbookblog.today.com/ (March 5, 2009), review of *Plain Secrets.*

Newton Reads, http://newtonreads.wordpress.com/ (August 22, 2007), review of *Plain Secrets.*

Plain Secrets Web site, http://www.plainsecrets.com (June 17, 2009), author biography.

Spirituality & Practice Web site, http://www.spirituality andpractice.com/ (June 17, 2009), Frederic and Mary Ann Brussat, review of *Plain Secrets.*

Times-Gazette.com (Ashland University), http://www. times-gazette.com/ (July 12, 2007), Jennifer Ditlevson, review of *Plain Secrets.**

*   *   *

MADDEN, Kerry 1961-
(Kerry Madden-Lunsford)

PERSONAL: Born November 22, 1961, in Daytona Beach, FL; married Kiffen Lunsford (a teacher); children: Flannery, Lucy, Norah. *Education:* University of Tennessee, B.A., M.F.A.

ADDRESSES: Home—Los Angeles, CA. *Agent*—Marianne Merola, Brandt & Hochman Literary Agents, 1501 Broadway, New York, NY 10036. *E-mail*—contactkerry@kerrymadden.com.

CAREER: Journalist, novelist, teacher, and playwright. Ningbo University, Ningbo, China, teacher of English, c. 1986; Los Angeles Unified School District, Los Angeles, CA, English as a Second Language teacher, 1989-95; University of California, Los Angeles, teacher of creative writing and fiction; host of writing workshops; freelance journalist.

AWARDS, HONORS: Walter Dakin fellow and Tennessee Williams scholar, Sewanee Writers Conference; New York Public Library Pick for Mature Teens, 1997, for

Offsides; New York Public Library 100 Books for Reading and Sharing, inclusion, and Chicago Public Library Best of the Best designation, both 2005, both for *Gentle's Holler.*

WRITINGS:

FOR CHILDREN

Offsides (novel), William Morrow (New York, NY), 1996.

Writing Smarts: A Girl's Guide to Writing Great Poetry, Stories, School Reports, and More!, illustrated by Tracy McGuinness, Pleasant Co. (Middleton, WI), 2002.

Gentle's Holler (novel), Viking (New York, NY), 2005.

Louisiana's Song (novel), Viking (New York, NY), 2007.

Jessie's Mountain, Viking (New York, NY), 2008.

Harper Lee, Viking Children's Books (New York, NY), 2009.

PLAYS

Blood and Marriage, produced in Los Angeles, CA, 1993.

The Goddess of My Heart, produced in Los Angeles, CA, 1994.

Chattanooga Flamenco, staged reading produced in Los Angeles, CA, 2003.

Contributor of essays, articles, and short fiction to periodicals, including *Shenandoah, L.A. Weekly, Tennessee Alumnus,* and *Los Angeles Times;* contributor to online publications, including *Salon.com, WebMD.com, Apira, Consumer Health Interactive, HipMama, Oxygen,* and *Homestore.com.*

SIDELIGHTS: Writing instructor and children's book author Kerry Madden is the author of the young-adult novel, *Offsides,* which is about the world of football, and *Gentle's Holler,* the story of a North Carolina family during the 1960s. *Gentle's Holler* is narrated by twelve-year-old Livy Two Weems and recounts the girl's ordeal in her seemingly dysfunctional family as well as her struggles with growing up in a small town. Dealing with her mixed emotions after her older brother runs away in hopes of finding a better job, Livy Two also must face the reality that her grandmother is mov-

ing in with the already-crowded family. Her frustrations over the inadequate care given to her younger sister, Gentle, who is blind, also perplex the girl, and her entire world is thrown into uncertainty after a sudden tragic accident places her father in a coma. Cindy Darling Codell wrote in *School Library Journal* that "Livy's narration rings true and is wonderfully voiced." Frances Bradburn, reviewing *Gentle's Holler* for *Booklist,* also enjoyed the book, stating that Madden's characters "form a strong unit that will help readers understand what it means to be a family."

Madden, whose family relocated throughout the Midwest and South during his childhood due to her father's job as a football coach, developed a talent for storytelling as a child. "I was . . . told to clean up the kitchen a lot when I was a kid," she explained on her Home Page. "I made up stories to escape in my head." During her college years, she attended the University of Tennessee and spent a year studying in England. Marrying Kiffen Lundsford after graduation, she joined him to teach English at Ningbo University in Ningbo, China. After returning to the United States, the couple raised three children, eventually settling in Los Angeles, California, where Madden has since worked as a journalist and teacher. Inspired by her memories of the Smokey Mountain region, *Gentle's Holler* was also influenced by her husband's stories about his large, colorful North Carolina family. "I think every child has stories to tell," Madden added on her Home Page. "It's why I love to do writing workshops to help kids find the stories they want to tell."

Madden followed up *Gentle's Holler* with the 2007 novel *Louisiana's Song.* This book again features Livy Two, who dreams of becoming a songwriter someday as she struggles with the difficult situation surrounding her father's condition after a major car accident. After eight months of rehabilitation, her father still has severe brain damage that makes him unable to provide for the large Weems family. Meanwhile, Livy Two's grandmother begins discussions of moving the Weems children to her house, a relocation that Livy Two and her siblings dread. Despite this turmoil, Livy Two finds solace in writing new songs, the lyrics appearing in the novel's text. Lauded by readers and critics, *Louisiana's Song* was called a fitting sequel to Madden's previous novel, demonstrating her strong character-building abilities. The book is a "warm, loving, and poignant saga," wrote Frances Bradburn in a review for *Booklist.* Many critics felt the book told a fitting story for Madden's young audience. *Louisiana's Song* is an "engaging sequel," noted a *Kirkus Reviews* contributor.

In 2008, Madden published her next novel, *Jessie's Mountain*. She revisits Livy Two's family one more time, where troubles still sully the young girl's hopes and dreams. Livy Two's father still has not recovered fully from his accident, and her grandmother again pushes for the family to move in with her, yet Livy Two's mother refuses to concede to her wishes. Money is tight for the family, and the children hatch a plan to pull their parents out of debt. After a failed attempt to sell their songs in Nashville, Tennessee, Livy Two and her sister set their sights on opening Jessie's Smoky Mountain Music Notes, a music hall, in order to raise money.

Jessie's Mountain was met with positive reviews by many critics upon its release. Many reviewers welcomed the novel as a fitting conclusion to the stories about the Weems family. The book is an "interesting character study," observed Nancy P. Reeder in a review for the *School Library Journal*. Other critics praised the author for her ability to connect with her readers. Madden has "created a heartwarming family story," wrote a *Kirkus Reviews* contributor.

In 2009, Madden published a different kind of children's book, a biography titled *Harper Lee*. The biography focuses on Alabama-born writer Harper Lee, who studied law in school and lived and worked in New York City before she sold her first novel. Best known for her Pulitzer Prize-winning novel *To Kill a Mockingbird*, which she published in 1960, Lee was overwhelmed at times at the vast amount of attention her book received. She eventually withdrew from the spotlight and refused to speak with biographers about her life. Nonetheless, Madden performed extensive research to write her biography and includes an extensive bibliography and acknowledgements section to substantiate her narrative. *Harper Lee* was generally lauded by critics and readers, many citing the book's fluid writing and well-formed chapters. The book is an "unusually readable biography," wrote Carolyn Phelan in a review for *Booklist*. Others offered praise for Madden and her shift to a different genre of writing. *Harper Lee* is a "straightforward, easy-to-read biography," noted *Horn Book* magazine contributor Betty Carter.

BIOGRAPHICAL AND CRITICAL SOURCES:

PERIODICALS

Booklist, March 1, 2005, Frances Bradburn, review of *Gentle's Holler,* p. 1197; June 1, 2007, Frances Bradburn, review of *Louisiana's Song,* p. 72; April 15, 2009, Carolyn Phelan, review of *Harper Lee,* p. 42.

Childhood Education, September 22, 2008, Caroline Cunningham, review of *Louisiana's Song,* p. 51.

Horn Book, March 1, 2009, Betty Carter, review of *Harper Lee,* p. 212.

Kirkus Reviews, February 15, 2005, review of *Gentle's Holler,* p. 232; May 15, 2007, review of *Louisiana's Song;* February 1, 2008, review of *Jessie's Mountain;* January 15, 2009, review of *Harper Lee.*

Library Journal, September 15, 1996, Kimberly G. Allen, review of *Offsides,* p. 97.

Publishers Weekly, August 20, 1996, review of *Offsides,* p. 77; March 28, 2005, review of *Gentle's Holler,* p. 80.

School Library Journal, June, 2005, Cindy Darling Codell, review of *Gentle's Holler,* p. 164; August 1, 2007, Catherine Threadgill, review of *Louisiana's Song,* p. 120; March 1, 2008, Nancy P. Reeder, review of *Jessie's Mountain,* p. 206.

Stone Soup, November 1, 2008, Anna West Ellis, review of *Louisiana's Song,* p. 12.

ONLINE

Armchair Interviews, http://reviews.armchairinterviews. com/ (June 19, 1009), Andrea Sisco, review of *Louisiana's Song.*

Brain Burps, http://authorkatiedavis.blogspot.com/ (April 22, 2009), author interview.

Favorite Pastimes, http://favoritepastimes.blogspot.com/ (January 2, 2008), review of *Louisiana's Song.*

Kerry Madden Home Page, http://www.kerrymadden. com (June 29, 2009).

Mediabistro.com, http://www.mediabistro.com/ (August 15, 2007), Kate Coe, "So What Do You Do, Kerry Madden, YA Author?"

Red Room, http://www.redroom.com/ (June 29, 2009), author biography.

Writers Net, http://www.writers.net/ (January 30, 2006), author profile.

Young Writers Guild Web site, http://www.youngpens. org/ (January 30, 2006), author profile.*

*   *   *

MADDEN-LUNSFORD, Kerry
See MADDEN, Kerry

MAGUIRE, Jesse
   See SMITH, Sherwood

*　　*　　*

MAITLAND, Barry

PERSONAL: Born in Scotland.

ADDRESSES: Home—New South Wales, Australia.

CAREER: Writer, architect, and educator. University of Newcastle, New South Wales, Australia, professor of architecture, 1984-2000.

AWARDS, HONORS: John Creasey Memorial Award shortlist, Crime Writers Association, for *The Marx Sisters;* Ned Kelly Award for Crime Writing, Crime Writers Association of Australia, 1996, for *The Malcontenta.*

WRITINGS:

(With David Gosling) *Design and Planning of Retail Systems,* Whitney Library of Design (New York, NY), 1976.
(With David Gosling) *Concepts of Urban Design,* St. Martin's Press (New York, NY), 1984.
Shopping Malls: Planning and Design, Nichols (New York, NY), 1985.
The Pender Index: A Guide to the Architectural Work of the Pender Practice of Maitland, N.S.W, 1863-1988, Faculty of Architecture, Building, and Design, University of Newcastle (Newcastle, New South Wales, Australia), 1999.

"BROCK & KOLLA" MYSTERY SERIES

The Marx Sisters, Hamish Hamilton (London, England), 1994, Arcade (New York, NY), 1999.
The Malcontenta, [England], 1995, Arcade (New York, NY), 2000.
All My Enemies, Hamish Hamilton (London, England), 1996, Minotaur Books (New York, NY), 2009.
The Chalon Heads, Allen & Unwin (St. Leonards, New South Wales, Australia), 1999, Arcade (New York, NY), 2001.

Silvermeadow, Orion (London, England), 2000, Arcade (New York, NY), 2002.
Babel, Orion (London, England), 2002, Arcade (New York, NY), 2003.
The Verge Practice, Arcade (New York, NY), 2003.
No Trace, St. Martin's Minotaur (New York, NY), 2006.
Spider Trap, St. Martin's Minotaur (New York, NY), 2007.
Dark Mirror, St. Martin's Minotaur (New York, NY), 2009.

SIDELIGHTS: A Cambridge-educated architect by profession, Barry Maitland is the author of the popular "Brock & Kolla" series of mysteries. Although born in Scotland, Maitland was raised in England, where he taught, practiced, and wrote about architecture. Among his architecture-related books are *Design and Planning of Retail Systems, Concepts of Urban Design,* and *Shopping Malls: Planning and Design.*

Maitland began writing while still a student, he told David Honeybone in an interview for *Crime Factory.* "It took me 30 years of writing before I had my first book published, *The Marx Sisters,* the first crime novel," Maitland said. *The Marx Sisters* introduces the Scotland Yard police detective team of Kathy Kolla, detective sergeant, and David Brock, chief inspector. The novel concerns three elderly sisters: Meredith Winterbottom, Peg Blythe, and Eleanor Harper, great-granddaughters of Karl Marx. When Meredith is discovered dead of unknown causes, her doctor suspects foul play; she was the sole dissenter in a plan to sell the sisters' home to land developers. Kolla and Brock begin an investigation and uncover a cast of suspicious characters, including a book dealer, the land developer, an American scholar, and Meredith's son. However, the investigation is abruptly cancelled by their superiors with little progress and no solution. Then, Eleanor also turns up murdered, a collection of books and manuscripts that may have been owned by Karl Marx takes on great importance, and Kolla and Brock are on the case again.

Rex E. Klett, writing in the *Library Journal,* remarked on the "good, solid prose" and called *The Marx Sisters* "fine work from an award-winning British mystery writer." Harriet Klausner, writing for *BookBrowser,* remarked that "the story line is crisp, filled with twists, and never lets up for a moment," declaring the book "must reading for fans of police procedurals." A *Publishers Weekly* critic commented on Maitland's "deft depiction of his idiosyncratic characters" and "clever use of Marxist theories and history." David Pitt, writing in *Booklist,* remarked that if upcoming "Brock & Kolla" books remain as "smartly constructed and as well written as this one, readers have a wonderful new series to look forward to."

Although Maitland moved to Australia in 1994 to teach architecture at the University of Newcastle, Kolla and Brock return in *The Malcontenta,* published in 1995. Temporarily reassigned to the Family and Juvenile Crime division, Kolla is eager to move on to more exciting duties. When a young physiotherapist is found dead at the Stanhope Naturopathic Clinic, an exclusive spa, she gladly takes on the investigation. The apparent suicide becomes more and more complicated and begins to look like a case of murder. However, Kolla is abruptly accused of making a mess of the investigation and is relieved of her duties before she can make any progress on the case. Baffled at her dismissal, she enlists Brock for help. Brock checks into Stanhope to look at things from the inside, and discovers there is much more to the case than a routine, if scandalous, suicide. A *Publishers Weekly* reviewer noted that the book is a "superb mystery," and that "Maitland is particularly good at describing old buildings and the drab English weather," a nod to his career in architecture and upbringing in London. "*The Malcontenta* is what the British mystery should be," wrote S.E. Warwick for *Over My Dead Body.*

All My Enemies is the third "Kolla and Brock" novel. Kolla investigates the brutal rape and murder of a young woman in South London, a case that begins to look more and more like the work of a serial killer. In the midst of the investigation, Kolla must deal with the sudden arrival of her Aunt Mary, an amateur thespian separated from her husband of fifty years. Kolla welcomes her aunt without complaint, but the amateur dramatic society Mary becomes involved with seems to have an unknown connection to the murder Kolla is investigating. "Maitland crafts a good story," wrote Sue Turnbull in the *Australian Book Review.* "He also excels at the evocation of place and space, which is hardly surprising given he supports his crime writing habit as a Professor of Architecture." Natasha Cooper, writing in the *Times Literary Supplement,* remarked that Kolla's pursuit of the killer "is both credible and interesting, as are her dealings with her colleagues and her reactions to the violence she has to confront." Cooper ultimately found the resolution of the novel "a little hard to swallow," but Turnbull remarked that Maitland's writing "continues to fascinate and intrigue."

Writing in the *Los Angeles Times Book Review,* Eugen Weber remarked that "Maitland is a master of mysteries, and his latest, *The Chalon Heads,* is a crafty and well-crafted showpiece of the genre." Stamp collecting is the theme of this 1999 novel. Eva, the wife of millionaire philatelist Sammy Starling, has been kidnapped. Ransom notes appear, affixed with once-valuable stamps called Chalon Heads, portraits of the young Queen Victoria created by artist Alfred Edward Chalon. The prized stamps are rendered worthless by being glued to the notes. The ransom demanded is a particularly rare stamp in exchange for Eva, who bears a strong resemblance to the young Queen depicted on the Chalon Heads. As the investigation unfolds, Starling's connection to an earlier investigation of police corruption becomes troublesome, a retired police officer turns up with a particular obsession with Sammy Starling, and Brock finds himself under investigation. Kolla, continuing the investigation alone, begins to wonder if Starling is a victim or a perpetrator. "This is a smart, suspenseful mystery, and fans of the series will be entirely satisfied," wrote Pitt, writing again in *Booklist.* Klett, in another article for *Library Journal,* declared the book to be "detailed, literate, satisfying." A *Publishers Weekly* critic noted that the plot is "so deviously complicated it's sometimes hard to follow," and that sections of the book seemed to have been written on several occasions and "stitched together with the seams showing." However, the same critic noted that the story "never fails to grip." George Easter, writing for *Deadly Pleasures,* remarked: "For me one of the elements that lifts a crime novel from being average to being extraordinary is the ability of the author to not only surprise me with a clever ending, but to surprise me several times over the course of the book. Maitland is just such an author."

Silvermeadow explores the darker side of people's obsession with shopping. Shortly after murderer and bank robber Gregory "Upper" North is seen on surveillance tape at Silvermeadow, a sprawling shopping mall in Essex, a young female mall employee is found crushed to death in an industrial box compactor. Brock and Kolla are called in to stake out the area in search of North, but their efforts are hindered by mall management, merchants, and employees who are worried about a murder investigation's effects on their reputation and livelihood. As the investigation unfolds, doubts emerge about North's involvement at Silvermeadow—and disturbing stories of more missing girls begin to surface. Pitt, again writing in *Booklist,* called *Silvermeadow* a "tense, surprising thriller." John Boyles, writing for *Tangled Web,* commented that the book "is well plotted and well written. Buy, beg or borrow it and look out for the previous Brock and Kolla mysteries. You will not be disappointed." A *Publishers Weekly* reviewer remarked that "Maitland fans surely will welcome this addition, with its fusion of commerce, detection and architecture, to his lively series."

The conclusion of *Silvermeadow* brought considerable trauma for Kolla, and in *Babel,* she is slowly recovering, but she is ready to seek less-stressful work. When Professor Springer, a noted philosopher, is killed on the steps of his London University office, Brock investigates. Despite initial resistance, Kolla becomes involved in the case when a reporter calls her with new information on Springer's murder. The professor's views may have angered an extremist Islamic group, but other factions criticized by Springer may also be to blame. Bob Cornwell, writing for *Tangled Web,* commented that "Maitland writes some of the most cunning and deliciously plotted crime novels around these days and this one is no exception."

The seventh title in Maitland's "Brock & Kolla" series, *The Verge Practice,* makes greater use of Maitland's experience as an architect along with the usual police and detective work for which the series is known. The story begins with the disappearance of architect Charles Verge and the murder of his wife. Not knowing the identity of the murderer or the location of Verge, Brock and Kolla investigate. Brock directs the investigation in London, while Kolla, battling with other obligations, sets out to investigate sightings of Verge. With an inventive and unpredictable ending, the novel further adds depth to the highly acclaimed "Brock & Kolla" series. Denise Wels praised the novel in an online review for *Reviewing the Evidence,* noting that "Maitland has, as usual, with his excellently written prose and wonderfully crafted plot, left the reader eager for more."

In *No Trace* Maitland once again portrays Brock and Kolla as they investigate a puzzling series of crimes. Two girls have been kidnapped, and after a third disappearance (the daughter of a famous artist), the crimes escalate into the murders of those in the artist's circle. Added to this are the eccentric actions of the artist, who, with the prompting of his agent, begins creating a series of works derived from his daughter's disappearance. In a review for *Booklist,* Pitt commented that *No Trace* "offers up a suspenseful story and a cast of engaging characters." A critic for *Publishers Weekly* also praised the novel, calling it a "haunting, unnerving work."

In *Spider Trap,* the ninth installment of the series, the bodies of two sixteen-year-old West Indian girls are discovered. They were known to be drug users and involved with criminal activities, and when they are found shot through their heads on Cockpit Lane in South London, it is suspected that they may have been killed by Jamaican drug dealers. In a separate incident a boy finds a human jawbone, and the investigation unearths the remains of three young men who were killed more than twenty years earlier during the Brixton race riots. Brock concentrates on the murders of the men, while Kolla is aided by Detective Inspector Tom Reeves of the Special Branch unit in investigating the murder of the young women. Brock is also feeling the guilt of not having convicted crime boss 'Spider" Roach and his sons decades ago, and now they may not be as respectable as they appear. Both Brock, in his fifties, and Kolla, in her thirties, are single loners, and in this story they begin to make strides toward possible relationships. "Both professionally and privately, they are bound together by subtle, unspoken loyalties and protectiveness," noted *Age Online* reviewer Rick Thompson. "Maitland is particularly skilful at what is not said."

Mostly Fiction contributor Eleanor Bukowsky concluded that the creator of Brock and Kolla "is not content merely to write an engrossing mystery, although he has certainly done that. He creates a richly detailed picture of socially and economically disadvantaged black immigrants being preyed upon by an entrenched white criminal syndicate; of power-hungry politicians stabbing one another in the back to achieve their dubious aims; of men who abuse their wives and rely on a code of silence to keep their activities hidden; and of people whose skeletons emerge from their closets at the most inopportune times." Pitt concluded his review by writing: "The series shows no signs of slowing down."

BIOGRAPHICAL AND CRITICAL SOURCES:

PERIODICALS

Australian Book Review, December, 1996-January, 1997, Sue Turnbull, review of *All My Enemies,* pp. 79-80; April, 2000, review of *Silvermeadow,* p. 46.
Booklist, May 15, 1999, David Pitt, review of *The Marx Sisters,* p. 1674; August, 2000, David Pitt, review of *The Malcontenta,* p. 2121; June 1, 2001, David Pitt, review of *The Chalon Heads,* p. 1852;

August, 2002, David Pitt, review of *Silvermeadow,* p. 1932; August, 2006, David Pitt, review of *No Trace,* p. 47; August, 2007, David Pitt, review of *Spider Trap,* p. 44.

Kirkus Reviews, August 1, 2000, review of *The Malcontenta,* p. 1078; July 15, 2002, review of *Silvermeadow,* pp. 996-997; June 1, 2004, review of *The Verge Practice,* p. 520; August 15, 2006, review of *No Trace,* p. 812; August 15, 2007, review of *Spider Trap.*

Law Institute Journal, March, 1995, J. Neville Turner, review of *The Marx Sisters,* p. 272.

Library Journal, June 1, 1999, Rex E. Klett, review of *The Marx Sisters,* p. 184; September 1, 1999, review of *The Marx Sisters,* p. 264; September 1, 2001, Rex E. Klett, review of *The Chalon Heads,* p. 238.

Los Angeles Times Book Review, November 18, 2001, Eugen Weber, review of *The Chalon Heads,* pp. 10-11.

Publishers Weekly, May 24, 1999, review of *The Marx Sisters,* p. 70; July 10, 2000, review of *The Malcontenta,* p. 48; July 16, 2001, review of *The Chalon Heads,* p. 161; July 29, 2002, review of *Silvermeadow,* p. 57; June 14, 2004, review of *The Verge Practice,* p. 47; July 24, 2006, review of *No Trace,* p. 39; July 23, 2007, review of *Spider Trap,* p. 46.

Times Literary Supplement, July 22, 1991, Julian Symons, review of *The Marx Sisters,* p. 21; October 25, 1996, Natasha Cooper, review of *All My Enemies,* p. 23.

ONLINE

ABC Melbourne Web site, http://www.abc.net.au/melbourne/ (December 5, 2002), Sian Prior, review of *Silvermeadow.*

Age Online, http://www.theage.com.au/ (December 24, 2004), Debi Enker, review of *No Trace;* (August 26, 2006) Rick Thompson, review of *Spider Trap.*

Aussie Reviews, http://www.aussiereviews.com/ (February 5, 2007), review of *The Verge Practice.*

Barry Maitland Home Page, http://www.barrymaitland.com (July 14, 2008).

BookBrowser, http://www.bookbrowser.com/ (December 5, 2002), Harriet Klausner, review of *The Marx Sisters.*

Crime Factory, http://www.crimefactory.net/ (December 5, 2002), David Honeybone, interview with Maitland.

Curled Up with a Good Book, http://www.curledup.com/ (July 14, 2008), Michael Leonard, review of *Spider Trap.*

Cybamuse, http://www.cybamuse.com/ (December 5, 2002), review of *Silvermeadow* and *All My Enemies.*

Deadly Pleasures, http://www.deadlypleasures.com/ (December 5, 2002), George Easter, review of *The Chalon Heads.*

Euro Crime, http://www.eurocrime.co.uk/ (July 14, 2008), Karen Chisholm, review of *Spider Trap.*

Mostly Fiction, http://www.mostlyfiction.com/ (November 15, 2007), Eleanor Bukowsky, review of *Spider Trap.*

Over My Dead Body, http://www.overmydeadbody.com/ (December 5, 2002), S.E. Warwick, review of *The Malcontenta.*

Reviewing the Evidence, http://www.reviewingtheevidence.com/ (December 5, 2007), Denise Wels, review of *The Verge Practice;* (July 14, 2008) Denise Pickles, review of *Spider Trap.*

Shots, http://www.shotsmag.co.uk/ (December 5, 2002), Angus Wells, review of *Babel.*

Tangled Web, http://www.twbooks.co.uk/ (February 5, 2007), John Boyles, review of *Silvermeadow;* Bob Cornwell, review of *Babel.*

Under the Covers, http://www.silcom/com/~manatee/utc/ (December 5, 2002), Harriet Klausner, review of *The Marx Sisters.**

*   *   *

MANGUEL, Alberto 1948-
(Alberto Adrian Manguel)

PERSONAL: Born March 13, 1948, in Buenos Aires, Argentina; immigrated to Canada, 1982, naturalized citizen, 1988; son of Pablo and Rosalia Manguel; married Pauline Ann Brewer (a teacher), 1975 (divorced, 1986); children: Alice Emily, Rachel Claire, Rupert Tobias. *Education:* Attended Universidad de Buenos Aires, 1967-68, and London University, 1976.

ADDRESSES: Home and office—Toronto, Ontario, Canada. *Agent*—Jeanne Fredericks, Jeanne Fredericks Literary Agency, Inc., 221 Benedict Hill Rd., New Canaan, CT 06849.

CAREER: Writer, editor, and translator. Worked as a member of editorial staffs of various publishing houses and periodicals and as a book and theater critic in the broadcast media.

MEMBER: International PEN, Writer's Union of Canada, Association of Canadian Television and Radio Artists, Literary Translators Association.

AWARDS, HONORS: Premio Literario, *La Nacion* (newspaper), 1971, for short story; (with Gianni Guadalupi) German critics prize, 1981, for *Von Atlantis bis Utopia* (translation of *The Dictionary of Imaginary Places*); McKitterick First Novel Award, British Society of Authors, 1992; Harbourfront Literary Award, 1992, for contribution to the arts; Canadian Authors' Association Award for Fiction, 1992; named officer, Order of Arts and Letters.

WRITINGS:

The Kipling Play (play), produced in Toronto, Ontario, Canada, 1983, excerpts published in *Descant,* fall, 1987.

(With Gianni Guadalupi) *The Dictionary of Imaginary Places,* Harcourt Brace Jovanovick (San Diego, CA), 1987.

News from a Foreign Country Came (novel), C.N. Potter (New York, NY), 1991.

A History of Reading, Viking (New York, NY), 1996.

Into the Looking-glass Wood: Essays on Books, Reading, and the World, Harcourt (San Diego, CA), 2000.

Reading Pictures: A History of Love and Hate, Random House (New York, NY), 2000.

Kipling: A Brief Biography for Young Adults, Bayeux Arts (Calgary, Alberta, Canada), 2001.

Stevenson under the Palm Trees (mystery), Thomas Allen Publishers (Toronto, Ontario, Canada), 2003.

A Reading Diary, Farrar, Straus & Giroux (New York, NY), 2004.

With Borges (nonfiction), Thomas Allen Publishers (Toronto, Ontario, Canada), 2004.

El regreso, Emece (Buenos Aires, Argentina), 2005.

Pinocchio & Robinson: pour une ethique de la lecture, translated from the English by Christine Le Buf and Charlotte Melancon, Escampette (Bordeaux, France), 2005.

The Library at Night, A.A. Knopf Canada (Toronto, Ontario, Canada), 2006, Yale University Press (New Haven, CT), 2008.

Magic Land of Toys, photography by Michel Pintado, Vendome Press (New York, NY), 2006.

The City of Words, House of Anansi Press (Toronto, Ontario, Canada), 2007.

Homer's The Iliad and The Odyssey: A Biography (*"Books That Changed the World"* series), Atlantic Monthly Press (New York, NY), 2007.

EDITOR

(And author of introduction) *Variaciones sobre un tema de durero,* Galerna (Buenos Aires, Argentina), 1968.

(And author of introduction) *Variaciones sobre un tema policial: cuentos,* Galerna (Buenos Aires, Argentina), 1968.

(And author of introduction) *Antologia de la literatura fantastica Argentina,* Kapelusz (Buenos Aires, Argentina), 1973.

(And author of introduction) *Black Water: The Anthology of Fantastic Literature,* Lester & Orpen Dennys (Toronto, Ontario, Canada), 1983, published as *Black Water: The Book of Fantastic Literature,* C.N. Potter (New York, NY), 1983.

(And author of introduction) *Dark Arrows: Chronicles of Revenge,* Penguin Books (Toronto, Ontario, Canada), 1985, published as *Dark Arrows: Great Stories of Revenge,* C.N. Potter (New York, NY), 1987.

(And author of introduction) *Other Fires: Short Fiction by Latin-American Women,* C.N. Potter (New York, NY), 1986.

(And author of introduction) *Evening Games: Chronicles of Parents and Children,* C.N. Potter (New York, NY), 1986.

(And author of introduction) *The Oxford Book of Canadian Ghost Stories,* Oxford University Press (Toronto, Ontario, Canada), 1990.

(And author of introduction) *Black Water II: More Fantastic Literature,* Lester & Orpen Dennys (Toronto, Ontario, Canada), 1990, published as *Black Water II: More Tales of the Fantastic,* C.N. Potter (New York, NY), 1990, published as *White Fire: Further Fantastic Literature,* Picador (London, England), 1991.

Seasons (anthology of children's poetry), paintings by Warabe Aska, Doubleday (New York, NY), 1990.

(And author of introduction) *Soho Square III* (anthology), Bloomsbury (London, England), 1990.

(And author of introduction) *Canadian Mystery Stories,* Oxford University Press (New York, NY), 1991.

(And author of introduction) *The Gates of Paradise: The Anthology of Erotic Short Fiction,* C.N. Potter (New York, NY), 1993.

(With Craig Stephenson; and author of introduction) *In Another Part of the Forest: An Anthology of Gay Short Fiction,* Crown Trade Paperbacks (New York, NY), 1994.

The Second Gates of Paradise: The Anthology of Erotic Short Fiction, Macfarlane Walter & Ross (Toronto, Ontario, Canada), 1994.

Fathers and Sons: An Anthology, Chronicle Books (San Francisco, CA), 1998.

Mothers and Daughters: An Anthology, Chronicle Books (San Francisco, CA), 1998.

By the Light of the Glow-worm Lamp, Plenum (New York, NY), 1999.

God's Spies: Stories in Defiance of Oppression, Macfarlane Walter & Ross (Toronto, Ontario, Canada), 1999.

The Ecco Book of Christmas Stories, Ecco (New York, NY), 2006.

TRANSLATOR

Marguerite Duras, *Two by Duras,* Coach House Press (Toronto, Ontario, Canada), 1993.

Marco Denev, *The Redemption of the Cannibal Woman; and Other Stories,* Coach House Press (Toronto, Ontario, Canada), 1993.

Philippe Sollers, *Watteau in Venice,* Scribner (New York, NY), 1994.

Marguerite Yourcenar, *A Blue Tale, and Other Stories,* University of Chicago Press (Chicago, IL), 1995.

Federico Andahazi, *The Anatomist,* Doubleday (New York, NY), 1998.

Amin Maalouf, *Ports of Call,* Harvill Press (London, England), 1999.

(Coauthor) Marguerite Yourcenar, *Mishima: A Vision of the Void,* University of Chicago Press (Chicago, IL), 2001.

Javier Sierra, *The Secret Supper,* Atria Books (New York, NY), 2006.

RADIO PLAYS

Faire un voyage, France Culture Radio (Paris, France), 1972.

Author of radio plays produced by the Canadian Broadcasting Corporation (CBC) for the *"Vanishing Point"* series, including *Death and the Compass* (adapted from the story of the same title by Jorge Luis Borges), 1984; *Secret Ceremony* (adapted from the story of the same title by Marco Denevi), 1984; *The Man Who Liked Dickens* (adapted from the story of the same title by Evelyn Waugh), 1986; *The Word for World Is Forest* (adapted from the novel of the same title by

Ursula K. Le Guinn), 1988; *The South* (adapted from the story of the same title by Jorge Luis Borges), 1989; *Five Stories by Julio Cortazar* (adaptation), 1990; and *Five Canadian Ghost Stories* (adapted from works by Antonine Maillet, Rohinton Mistry, Virgil Burnett, Ethel Wilson, and A.M. Klein), 1990. Author of radio plays produced by the CBC for the *"Morningside Drama"* series, including *The Alley Cat* (adapted from the novel of the same title by Yves Beauchemin), 1989, and *Five Stories by Bonnie Burnard* (adaptation), 1989.

Author of television plays produced by the CBC for the *"Inside Stories"* series, including *Reunion,* 1989, and, with Dany Laferriere, *Voodoo Taxi,* 1991.

Also author of short stories. Contributor to periodicals, including *Commonweal, New York Times, Saturday Night, Washington Post,* and *Village Voice.*

SIDELIGHTS: Alberto Manguel is considered an astute and original editor of anthologies. While reviewers have applauded his numerous works for their scholarship, they also cite Manguel's wide-ranging knowledge of the various genres in which he works. He has published and discussed fine examples of Latin American ghost stories, European classic tales, and American science fiction in such works as *The Dictionary of Imaginary Places, Black Water: The Book of Fantastic Literature,* and *Other Fires: Short Fiction by Latin-American Women.* He has exhibited an even greater range of expertise and an extraordinary passion for all things related to reading in *A History of Reading.*

The Dictionary of Imaginary Places, which Manguel wrote with Gianni Guadalupi, is a guidebook to more than twelve hundred fictional villages, kingdoms, continents, and countries devised by authors from classical Greece to the present day. Illustrated with maps and drawings, entries on such places as Camelot, Oz, Jonathan Swift's Brobdingnag, and Franz Kafka's Penal Colony, the author also provides a brief history of each region, a description of its inhabitants and topography, and a reading list in travel guide form. When visiting Dracula's Castle, for example, Manguel and Guadalupi advise bringing silver crosses and wooden stakes. "Presented with mock solemnity and written with grace and wit," as Peter S. Prescott wrote in *Newsweek, The Dictionary of Imaginary Places* "is a work of genuine scholarship that is also a pleasure to read."

Manguel collects seventy-two tales of horror from several centuries and five continents in *Black Water.* Writers such as Vladimir Nabokov, Nathaniel Hawthorne, Herman Hesse, Julio Cortazar, Max Beerbohm, Jorge Luis Borges, and H.G. Wells are represented in what *New York Times Book Review* contributor Jack Sullivan called "an uncommonly satisfying collection." Two years later Manguel edited *Dark Arrows: Chronicles of Revenge,* published in the United States as *Dark Arrows: Great Stories of Revenge,* a volume featuring tales of vengeance from writers as diverse as William Faulkner and Bram Stoker. This anthology also earned Manguel high praise. A *Washington Post Book World* contributor called him "an editor of real imagination," with an "expertise at discovering the unexpected."

In 1986 Manguel compiled *Other Fires,* possibly the first anthology dedicated to Latina writers. Comprised of stories from such prominent writers as Liliana Heker, Elena Poniatowska, and Rosario Castellanos, the collection exhibits a wide range of artistic styles—from fables to science fiction to magic realism—and subject matter, including depictions of betrayal and murder, loneliness and suicide, and male-female relationships in a society where women are subjugated by men. Commenting on the lack of anthologies devoted to Latin American women writers, *New York Times Book Review* contributor Mary Morris noted that, with the publication of *Other Fires,* "at last we can hear the voice that has been missing."

News from a Foreign Country Came, Manguel's first novel, recounts the story of an officer in the French army whose past comes back to haunt him and his family. As *Washington Post Book World* reviewer Richard Ryan stated: "It is clear that Manguel wanted to write a book about two of the most primitive aspects of human nature: violence and the family." Writing for *Spectator,* Celestria Noel observed that in the novel "brutality is not the exclusive property of regimes and torture has its roots in family life." While *Los Angeles Times Book Review* critic Richard Eder suggested that "any number of scenes are far-fetched and awkwardly handled," Ryan called *News from a Foreign Country Came* "a grim parable of considerable power," and noted: "This impressive first novel suggests that Manguel has both the intellect and the voice to speak to his readers on the highest levels of fiction."

Manguel once told *CA:* "I started compiling anthologies out of an urge to get my friends to read the stories I was crazy about, sometimes stories in other languages (which I had to translate), sometimes stories hidden in obscure collections. I see my anthologizing as a function of my reading—every reader is, in some measure, an anthologist, a collector of what he or she likes best.

"As a translator, I wish I had an extra life to devote to translating: there are so many authors I wish I had time to translate into English. Hector Bianciotti, Rodolfo Walsh, Liliana Heker, Juan Jose Hernandez, Salvador Garmedia, Amparo Davila . . . the list is endless.

"For the longest time, after having written a few forgotten short stories in Spanish, I decided I would not turn my hand to writing fiction because (using the oldest excuse in the book) I felt I would never be able to write as well as my favorite authors. But a story came to me, as these things will. I felt obliged to write it down in order to understand it. The result was *News from a Foreign Country Came.*"

Manguel's editorial work during the 1990s included the companion volumes *Fathers and Sons: An Anthology* and *Mothers and Daughters: An Anthology.* Like his earlier collections, these books have great depth. They include familiar and unfamiliar writers, stories representing many different cultures, and a time frame that begins with works by Edith Wharton and Steven Crane. The collections' women writers include Daphne Du Maurier, Sara Jeannette Duncan, Louise Erdrich, Frances Newman, Katherine Mansfield, and Anna Maria Ortese. Among the men are William Faulkner, Steven Crane, Richard Ford, Franz Kafka, Bruno Schultz, Kenzaburo Oe, Ben Okri, and John Edgar Wideman. Both books were reviewed in *Library Journal* by Nancy R. Ives, who valued them "for the insight they bring to the parent/child relationship and for the broad representation of writers included." Writing for *Booklist,* Mary Ellen Quinn noted the appeal of such a great range of writing styles and remarked: "There are many pleasures to be derived from reading these books."

In *By the Light of the Glow-worm Lamp,* Manguel expresses his concerns about the environmental damage being done by logging, mining, and other kinds of multinational operations by offering readers a collection of stories that touch upon the subject of the environment in direct and indirect ways. With extracts by Jean-Jacques Rousseau, Henry David Thoreau, Charles Dickens, Vladimir Nabokov, Rachel Carson, and Daniel Defoe, editor Manguel includes some writers who are unexpected in a book focusing on the environment. A reviewer in the *Economist* suggested that one "need not share Alberto Manguel's indignation or the views it presupposes to enjoy this collection of writings."

Manguel addresses a vast theme in *A History of Reading,* a scholarly yet idiosyncratic book. The lengthy and wide-ranging study includes personal commentary and autobiographical material in which the author's passion for reading is clearly present. The book's structure is also personalized; rather than using a chronological or otherwise formulaic organization, Manguel's chapters are based on unifying themes. As Michael Milburn explained in the *New York Times Book Review:* "Manguel probes his topic's logical and unpredictable roots, delivering concise histories of writing, memorization, bookmaking, vision, [and] eyeglasses," among other ideas. The book is filled with fascinating stories about famous readers and book collectors through the ages. It also concerns itself with the evolving form of books and includes a great number of reproductions of related items.

Critical response to *A History of Reading* was overwhelmingly positive. While Milburn expressed occasional dislike for the author's mode of expression, he noted: "Stylistic complaints aside, one feels . . . envious of his passion and grateful for this prodigious book; through it, his gift becomes our own." *New York Times* critic Michiko Kakutani called *A History of Reading* "a highly subjective and highly entertaining overview that leaves us with both a new appreciation of our own bibliomania and a deeper understanding of the role the written work has played throughout history." Writing for *American Scholar,* Jonathan Elukin considered the work to include "a dazzling range of subjects" and added that Manguel "leads us gently and naturally from one subject to another."

Manguel received praise for being informative and for exhibiting a love for books that was shared by critics, and he was also credited with a larger effect. Elukin saw *A History of Reading* as championing the individual reader: "One of the book's charms is how Manguel energizes different acts of reading. We all become heroic readers." Elukin also noted its bolstering of the reading public in general, writing that "Manguel's book helps assert the vitality of a culture of reading." *Maclean's* contributor Brian Bethune wrote: "One of Manguel's early priorities is a discussion of the science of how we

read." Bethune went on to note that "it is readers, not writers, who give the text meaning." Bethune further remarked that the author's "erudite, meandering and altogether beguiling study of an abiding human passion, proves his point—the history of reading is the history of each reader."

Manguel and coeditor Craig Stephenson present a variety of short stories featuring gay protagonists in *In Another Part of the Forest: An Anthology of Gay Short Fiction.* Unlike similar anthologies, this collection also features several noted writers usually not associated with gay fiction, such as William Faulkner, Theodore Sturgeon, and Daphne du Maurier. The editors also include short fiction by writers who are known for dealing with gay themes or for being gay themselves, including Truman Capote, Christopher Isherwood, and Tennessee Williams. Commenting on the eclectic selection of writers included in the collection, Ray Olson wrote in *Booklist* that the anthology "surveys another, albeit overlapping, part of the forest, indeed."

In his book *Into the Looking-glass Wood: Essays on Books, Reading, and the World* Manguel focuses primarily on literature and politics as he examines a broad range of writers and writings, including G.K. Chesterton, Cynthia Ozick, various poets, and the Old Testament Book of Jonah. The twenty-three essays include both personal and literary ruminations on topics such as Manguel's memories of his childhood and a homage to one of his early mentors. He also writes of Argentinean political issues, such as the idea of giving amnesty to war criminals, which the author opposes. "Although the book feels like a publisher's hotchpotch of academic essays (with footnotes), political articles and literary anecdotes, there is enough here to justify the venture," wrote James Hopkin in *New Statesman.* Hopkin also noted that the collection "makes up in wisdom what it lacks in warmth." Other reviewers were more enthusiastic about the volume. In her review in *Booklist,* Donna Seaman noted the author's "supple and unpredictable lines of reasoning." Writing in *Library Journal,* Nancy R. Ives commented that the author's "intricate knowledge of books shines through as do his humor and scholarship."

Manguel writes about art and artists in his collection of essays titled *Reading Pictures: A History of Love and Hate.* The author discusses works by artists such as Cezanne, Willem de Kooning, and Franz Kline. However, he also incorporates his interest in literature into the essays, introducing writings and thoughts about art by writers such as Ezra Pound and Samuel Becket, as well as the thoughts of noted psychologist and philosopher William James. Paul Trachtman, writing in the *Smithsonian,* commented that the author provides "a collection of essays so full of interesting information about pictures that the paintings themselves seem to pale in the light of his ruminations." In his review in *Library Journal,* Martin R. Kalfatovic called the book an "engaging and learned exploration of eleven works of art."

In *A Reading Diary* Manguel combines travels taken to various cities in 2002 and 2003 with the books he read on each journey. He visits his hometown of Buenos Aires, Paris, and London, as well as cities in Germany and Canada. The author comments on various social aspects of the areas he visits and ruminates on more philosophical questions, such as what does someone's "homeland" really mean to them. In addition, Manguel writes about family and friends, including fellow writers, and about other writers such as Rudyard Kipling, H.G. Wells, and Margaret Atwood. Calling the book "a gold mine," a *Publishers Weekly* contributor also commented that the author's "exquisitely distilled style and gentle humility are pure pleasure." Some critics noted the book's value to other writers. In a review in *Writer,* Erika Dreifus wrote: "For writers, Manguel's book offers the chance to study the craft by reading, assisted by an expert interpreter." Commenting on the long literary history of published diaries, Seaman wrote in *Booklist* that Manguel's "approach is unique in his selections, his perceptions, and his savoir faire."

Manguel uses his admiration of the work of Robert Louis Stevenson as a plot device in his mystery *Stevenson under the Palm Trees.* The story, partially based on actual letters by Stevenson, revolves around the classic author, who is suffering from tuberculosis in the South Sea island of Samoa. Following the rape and murder of a local woman, Stevenson begins to suspect that it may have something to do with his newfound acquaintance, Mr. Baker, a Scottish missionary. The book, which includes woodcut print attributed to Stevenson, features a story line that is a homage to Stevenson's *Dr. Jekyll and Mr. Hyde.* Referring to *Stevenson under the Palm Trees* as "a delectable little volume," Seaman also noted that the author "muses on the role of stories in culture." Other critics generally praised the short novel. A *Kirkus Reviews* contributor called it "a small but rich little

instant classic, as though Joseph Conrad had sent up a perfect new tale from the silence beyond the grave."

The author writes about one of his literary idols in *With Borges.* Manguel, who read to the noted author Jorge Luis Borges after Borges had gone blind, writes about the author's works, life, and his influence on Manguel. Malcolm Deas, writing in the *Spectator,* noted that Manguel "avoids the excessive reverence of which Borges in life and death has been a frequent victim" adding: "Manguel gives in his small compass a lot of facts."

In *The Library at Night,* Manguel takes his experience of designing and building his own home library and distills it into a meditation on how libraries represent the memories of not only individual people but entire cultures. Writing in *Biography,* Jessica Warner called *The Library at Night* "one of those great books" in that its entirety is not overshadowed by any specific essay or section. Chapters include "The Library as Order," "The Library as Shadow," "The Library as Mind," and "The Library as Survival." *Bookslut* Web site reviewer Sarah Burke noted: "Manguel is fascinated with the buildings, bookshelves, arrangement schemas, and human characters that dot the library landscape. Samuel Pepys built 'little high heels' so that all his books would stand at the same height. Jorge Luis Borges kept none of his own books. Manguel is particularly fond of Aby Warburg (1866-1929), who at age thirteen traded his right to run the family bank to his younger brother Max, with the understanding that Max would buy Aby every book he wanted for the rest of his life." "Endearingly discursive, *The Library at Night* celebrates the quixotic aspect of library love," wrote David Jays in *New Statesman.* "It charts a tension between order and chaos, glut and absence."

Reviewer's Bookwatch contributor Susan Bethany called *Magic Land of Toys* a "coffee table masterpiece." With text by Manguel and photography by Michel Pintado, the volume showcases hundreds of toys collected by the Musee des Arts Decoratifs in Paris, France. Included are trains, cars, and trucks, dolls and stuffed figures, miniature dishes, and wooden toys. The retrospective includes games from 1870 to contemporary video game consoles. *Library Journal* reviewer David McClelland noted that the toys, which are shown in very small size, are arranged into tableaux, appearing not as they might in a child's room, but as "psychosexual dramas more representative of the creators' thinking."

Spectator reviewer William Skidelsky wrote that *The City of Words* "is a book about storytelling—about mankind's age-old need to make sense of the world in words. Manguel wants to convince us that the storytelling impulse is not merely valuable, but is also, in some sense, at the root of our humanity. If we stop telling stories, his logic goes, we cease to be fully human (which is why societies that censor or persecute writers are so pernicious)." Manguel offers true instances of how stories and storytelling have helped people survive dark moments, as in the case of a concentration camp prisoner who forced herself to remember stories from the past.

Homer's The Iliad and The Odyssey: A Biography is Manguel's study of the two epics and a comparison of the various translations, including English, French, Spanish, German, and Arabic versions. Manguel suggests that Homer "was born not as a man but as a symbol." Bryce Christensen wrote in *Booklist* that this biography "is not the story of a mortal writer living in the world but, rather, of an immortal symbol transforming that world." A *Kirkus Reviews* contributor noted: "Perhaps too dense for casual readers, but lotus to lovers of Homer."

BIOGRAPHICAL AND CRITICAL SOURCES:

PERIODICALS

American Scholar, fall, 1997, Jonathan Elukin, review of *A History of Reading,* p. 614.

Biography, summer, 2003, Rene de Ceccatty, review of *With Borges,* p. 517; winter, 2007, Jessica Warner, review of *The Library at Night,* p. 145.

Booklist, May 15, 1994, Ray Olson, review of *In Another Part of the Forest: An Anthology of Gay Short Fiction,* p. 1664; October 1, 1995, Janet St. John, review of *A Blue Tale, and Other Stories,* p. 253; May 15, 1998, Mary Ellen Quinn, reviews of *Fathers and Sons: An Anthology* and *Mothers and Daughters: An Anthology,* p. 1595; December 1, 1998, Donna Seaman, review of *By the Light of the Glow-worm Lamp,* p. 627; November 15, 1999, Holly Cooley, review of *Ports of Call,* p. 604; August, 2000, Donna Seaman, review of *Into the Looking-glass Wood: Essays on Books, Reading, and the World,* p. 2098; September 15, 2001, Donna Seaman, review of *Reading Pictures: A His-*

tory of Love and Hate, p. 175; September 15, 2004, Donna Seaman, review of *A Reading Diary,* p. 194; September 15, 2004, Donna Seaman, review of *Stevenson under the Palm Trees,* p. 214; November 15, 2007, Bryce Christensen, review of *Homer's The Iliad and The Odyssey: A Biography,* p. 13.

Economist, February 13, 1999, review of *By the Light of the Glow-worm Lamp,* p. S8.

Financial Times, May 17, 2008, Lavinia Greenlaw, review of *The Library at Night,* p. 16.

First Things, May, 2007, Richard John Neuhaus, "Alberto Manguel, the Author of, among Other Books, *A History of Reading,* Was Serving as a Clerk in a Buenos Aires Bookstore When He Was Picked Up by Jorge Luis Borges," p. 68.

Historical Journal of Film, Radio and Television, March, 2000, Claire Fogg, review of *Bride of Frankenstein,* p. 129.

Kirkus Reviews, July 15, 2004, review of *A Reading Diary,* p. 675; September 1, 2004, review of *Stevenson under the Palm Trees,* p. 827; January 15, 2006, review of *The Secret Supper,* p. 60; October 1, 2007, review of *Homer's The Iliad and The Odyssey.*

Library Journal, June 1, 1998, Nancy R. Ives, reviews of *Fathers and Sons* and *Mothers and Daughters,* p. 164; August, 2000, Nancy R. Ives, review of *Into the Looking Glass Wood,* p. 103; September 1, 2001, Martin R. Kalfatovic, review of *Reading Pictures,* p. 175; September 1, 2004, Robert Kelly, review of *A Reading Diary,* p. 149; October 15, 2004, Susanne Wells, review of *Stevenson under the Palm Trees,* p. 55; February 1, 2006, Lisa O'Hara, review of *The Secret Supper,* p. 74; April 15, 2007, David McClelland, review of *Magic Land of Toys,* p. 87; December 1, 2007, T.L. Cooksey, review of *Homer's The Iliad and The Odyssey,* p. 118.

Los Angeles Times Book Review, April 7, 1991, Richard Eder, review of *News from a Foreign Country Came,* p. 3.

Maclean's, November 4, 1996, Brian Bethune, review of *A History of Reading,* p. 67.

New Statesman, April 26, 1999, James Hopkin, review of *Into the Looking-glass Wood,* p. 46; May 19, 2008, David Jays, review of *The Library at Night,* p. 55.

Newsweek, February 19, 1981, Peter S. Prescott, review of *The Dictionary of Imaginary Places,* p. 86.

New York Times, December 2, 1996, Michiko Kakutani, review of *A History of Reading,* p. B3.

New York Times Book Review, August 26, 1984, Jack Sullivan, review of *Black Water: The Book of Fantastic Literature,* p. 16; May 4, 1986, Mary Morris, review of *Other Fires: Short Fiction by Latin-American Women,* p. 35; November 17, 1996, Michael Milburn, review of *A History of Reading,* p. 37.

Publishers Weekly, June 7, 1993, review of *Soho Square III,* p. 66; September 20, 1993, review of *Two by Duras,* p. 66; October 18, 1993, review of *The Redemption of the Cannibal Woman; and Other Stories,* p. 68; June 13, 1994, review of *In Another Part of the Forest,* p. 62; July 31, 1995, review of *A Blue Tale, and Other Stories,* p. 66; June 19, 2000, review of *Into the Looking-glass Wood,* p. 65; July 2, 2001, review of *Reading Pictures,* p. 61; August 23, 2004, review of *Stevenson under the Palm Trees,* p. 40; August 1, 1994, review of *Watteau in Venice,* p. 73; June 28, 2004, review of *A Reading Diary,* p. 39; January 2, 2006, review of *The Secret Supper,* p. 33; October 1, 2007, review of *Homer's The Iliad and The Odyssey,* p. 48.

Reviewer's Bookwatch, July 15, 2008, Susan Bethany, review of *Magic Land of Toys.*

Review of Contemporary Fiction, spring, 1994, Steven Moore, review of *Two by Duras,* p. 233; spring, 1995, Alexander Theroux, review of *Watteau in Venice,* p. 163.

Smithsonian, March, 2002, Paul Trachtman, review of *Reading Pictures,* p. 110.

Spectator, March 23, 1991, Celestria Noel, review of *News from a Foreign Country Came,* p. 38; April 7, 2001, Jonathan Keates, review of *Reading Pictures,* p. 33; August 6, 2005, Jasper Griffin, review of *A Reading Diary,* p. 37; June 10, 2006, Malcolm Deas, review of *With Borges;* November 10, 2007, Tom Holland, review of *Homer's The Iliad and The Odyssey,* p. 54; March 22, 2008, William Skidelsky, review of *The City of Words,* p. 41.

USA Today, April 16, 2008, Bob Minzesheimer, review of *The Library at Night,* p. 3D.

Washington Post Book World, July 19, 1987, review of *Dark Arrows,* p. 12; May 5, 1991, Richard Ryan, review of *News from a Foreign Country Came,* p. 6.

Weekly Standard, March 3, 2008, David Wharton, review of *Homer's The Iliad and The Odyssey.*

Wilson Quarterly, spring, 2008, Matthew Battles, review of *The Library at Night,* p. 94.

Writer, June, 2005, Erika Dreifus, review of *A Reading Diary,* p. 48.

ONLINE

Bookslut, http://www.bookslut.com/ (August 8, 2008), Sarah Burke, review of *The Library at Night.*

Johnmiedema.ca, http://johnmiedema.ca/ (February 5, 2008), review of *The City of Words.*

WordFest, http://www.wordfest.com/ (April 11, 2007), brief profile of author.*

*   *   *

MANGUEL, Alberto Adrian
See MANGUEL, Alberto

*   *   *

MANKELL, Henning 1948-

PERSONAL: Born February 3, 1948, in Stockholm, Sweden; son of Ivan (a judge) and Birgitta (a librarian) Mankell; married and divorced three times; married fourth wife, Eva Bergman, 1998; children: Thomas, Marius, Morten, Jon.

ADDRESSES: Home—Skåne, Sweden; Maputo, Mozambique. *Office*—Leopard Publishing House, St. Paulsgatan 11, SE-118 45 Stockholm, Sweden.

CAREER: Theater director and manager, actor, and author. Worked as a merchant seaman and in the theater in Sweden; Teatro Avenida (a theater company), Maputo, Mozambique, director, 1987—; cofounder of Leopard Publishing House, Stockholm, Sweden, 2001—.

AWARDS, HONORS: Nils Holgersson Plaque, 1990, and Deutscher Jugendliteraurpreis, 1993, both for *The Dog that Ran Towards a Star;* Swedish Academy of Detective Stories Award and Scandinavian Criminal Society Award, both 1991, for *Faceless Killers;* Swedish Academy of Detective Stories Award, 1995, for *Sidetracked;* Listeners Prize, Swedish Radio Program I, 1996, for *Comedia Infantil;* Astrid Lindgren Award, 1996, and award from newspaper *Expressen,* 1997, both for *The Boy Who Slept with Snow in His Bed;* Children's Book Award, City of Berlin, 1997, for *The Secret of*

Fire; August Award, 1998, for *A Voyage to World's End;* Golden Paperback Award, 1999, for *Sidetracked* and *The Fifth Woman;* Macallan Golden Dagger Award, British Crime Writers Association, 2001, for *Sidetracked; Los Angeles Times* Book Award nomination, 2003, for *The Dogs of Riga,* and 2004, for *The Return of the Dancing Master;* Gumshoe Award for Best European Crime Novel, Mystery Ink, 2004; Tolerance Prize, Evangelische Akademie des Tutzing, 2004. Afrikas röst, a biennial Swedish award for notable African writers, was established in the author's name.

WRITINGS:

NOVELS

Daisy Sisters, Ordfront (Stockholm, Sweden), 1982.
Leopardens oega, Ordfront (Stockholm, Sweden), 1990, translated as *The Eye of the Leopard,* Harvill Secker (London, England), 2007, translated by Steven T. Murray, New Press (New York, NY), 2008.
Comedia infantil, Ordfront (Stockholm, Sweden), 1995, translation by Tiina Nunnally published as *Chronicler of the Winds,* The New Press (New York, NY), 2006.
Danslärarens återkomst, Ordfront (Stockholm, Sweden), 2000, translation by Laurie Thompson published as *The Return of the Dancing Master,* New Press (New York, NY), 2004.
Djup, Leopard (Stockholm, Sweden), 2005, translation by Laurie Thompson published as *Depths,* Harvill (London, England), 2006, New Press (New York, NY), 2007.
Kennedys hjärna, Leopard (Stockholm, Sweden), 2005, translation by Laurie Thompson published as *Kennedy's Brain,* Harvill (London, England), 2007, Vintage Books (New York, NY), 2008.
Italienska skor, Leopard (Stockholm, Sweden), 2006, translation by Laurie Thompson published as *Italian Shoes,* New Press (New York, NY), 2009.
When the Snow Fell, translated by Laurie Thompson, Delacorte Press (New York, NY), 2009.
Shadow of the Leopard, Annick Press (Toronto, Ontario, Canada), 2009.
The Fury in the Fire, Allen & Unwin (Sydney, New South Wales, Australia), 2009.

"KURT WALLANDER" SERIES; NOVELS

Moerdare utan ansikte, Ordfront (Stockholm, Sweden), 1991, translation by Steven T. Murray published as *Faceless Killers,* Vintage Books (New York, NY), 2003.

Hundarna i Riga, Ordfront (Stockholm, Sweden), 1991, translation by Laurie Thompson published as *The Dogs of Riga,* Vintage Books (New York, NY), 2004.
Den vita lejoninnan, Ordfront (Stockholm, Sweden), 1993, translation by Laurie Thompson published as *The White Lioness,* New Press (New York, NY), 1998.
Mannen som log, Ordfront (Stockholm, Sweden), 1994, translation by Laurie Thompson published as *The Man Who Smiled,* New Press (New York, NY), 2006.
Villospaar, Ordfront (Stockholm, Sweden), 1995, translation by Steven T. Murray published as *Sidetracked,* New Press (New York, NY), 1999.
Den femte kvinnan, Ordfront (Stockholm, Sweden), 1996, translation by Steven T. Murray published as *The Fifth Woman,* New Press (New York, NY), 2000.
Steget efter, Ordfront (Stockholm, Sweden), 1997, translation by Ebba Segerberg published as *One Step Behind,* Vintage Books (New York, NY), 2003.
Brandvaegg, Ordfront (Stockholm, Sweden), 1998, translation by Ebba Segerberg published as *Firewall,* New Press (New York, NY), 2002.
Pyramiden, 1999, translated as *The Pyramid,* Harvill Secker (London, England), 2008.
Innan frosten, Ordfront (Stockholm, Sweden), 2002, translation by Ebba Segerberg published as *Before the Frost,* New Press (New York, NY), 2005.
The Pyramid: And Four Other Kurt Wallander Mysteries, translation by Ebba Segerberg with Laurie Thompson, New Press (New York, NY), 2008.

JUVENILE NOVELS

Sandmaalaren (title means "The Sand Painter"), Foerfattarfoerlaget (Stockholm, Sweden), 1974.
Hunden som sprang mot en stjärna, Raben & Sjögren (Stockholm, Sweden), 1990, published as *A Bridge to the Stars,* Delacorte (New York, NY), 2007.
Skuggorna vaexer i skymningen, Raben & Sjögren (Stockholm, Sweden), 1991, translated by Laurie Thompson as *Shadows in the Twilight,* Delacorte (New York, NY), 2008.
Katten som aelskade regn, Ordfront (Stockholm, Sweden), 1992, translated as *The Cat Who Liked Rain,* Andersen Press (London, England), 2008.
Eldens hemlighet, Raben & Sjögren (Stockholm, Sweden), 1995, translation by Anne Connie Stuksrud published as *Secrets in the Fire,* Annick Press (Toronto, Ontario, Canada), 2003.

Pojken som sov med snoe i sin saeng (title means "The Boy Who Slept with Snow in His Bed"), Raben & Sjögren (Stockholm, Sweden), 1996.

Resan till vaerdens aende, Raben & Sjögren (Stockholm, Sweden), 1998, translated as *The Journey to the End of the World,* Andersen Press (London, England), 2008.

UNTRANSLATED NOVELS

Bergspraengaren (title means "The Rockblaster"), Foerfattarfoerlaget (Stockholm, Sweden), 1973.

Vettvillingen (title means "The Madman"), Foerfattarfoerlaget (Stockholm, Sweden), 1977.

Faangvaardskolonin som foersvann (title means "The Prison Camp that Disappeared"), Ordfront (Stockholm, Sweden), 1979.

Doedsbrickan (title means "The Badge of Death"), Ordfront (Stockholm, Sweden), 1981.

En seglares doed (title means "A Sailor's Death"), Ordfront (Stockholm, Sweden), 1981.

Sagan om Isidor (title means "The Tale of Isidor"), Ordfront (Stockholm, Sweden), 1984.

Beraettelse paa tidens strand (title means "Report from the Shore of Time"), Ordfront (Stockholm, Sweden), 1998.

Tea-bag, Leopard (Stockholm, Sweden), 2002.

OTHER

Apelsintraedet (play; title means "The Orange Tree"), Ordfront (Stockholm, Sweden), 1983.

Aelskade syster (play; title means "Dear Sister"), Ordfront (Stockholm, Sweden), 1983.

Eftertraedaren (screenplay), 1999.

Labyrinten (screenplay), 2000.

Jag dör, men minnet lever (nonfiction), Leopard (Stockholm, Sweden), 2003, translation by Laurie Thompson published as *I Die, but the Memory Lives On: A Personal Reflection on AIDS,* Harvill (London, England), 2004, New Press (New York, NY), 2005.

ADAPTATIONS: The novel *Comedia Infantil* was adapted into film under the same title, directed by Solveig Nordlund, 1998; the novels *Hundarna i Riga, Den Vita lejoninnan,* and *Kennedys hjärna* have also been adapted to film; more than a dozen films based on Mankell's novels featuring detective Kurt Wallander

have been produced in Sweden; Kurt Wallander was also the basis for a television series developed for the British Broadcasting Corporation.

SIDELIGHTS: Henning Mankell is a best selling Swedish author of adult and juvenile fiction who divides his time between Maputo, Mozambique and Skåne, Sweden. He is best known in the United States for his crime fiction series featuring police detective Kurt Wallander, including books such as *Faceless Killers, The Return of the Dancing Master,* and *The Man Who Smiled.* Mankell is also the author of *Secrets in the Fire* and other works for juvenile readers.

Wallander, Mankell's fictional detective, is a middle-aged chief inspector with a load of personal baggage: his wife has left him, his father is becoming senile, and he is estranged from his daughter. In the small town of Ystad, Sweden, he finds comfort in alcohol and opera. *Booklist* reviewer Bill Ott found in Wallander strains of other contemporary European detectives—John Harvey's Charlie Resnick and Donna Leon's Guido Brunetti: "Old World cops on the edge of being overwhelmed by the unremitting brutality of New World crime." Wallander's cases link Swedish crimes to the rest of the world; Ott wrote that Mankell combines "compelling procedural details with strong social consciousness." "I work in an old tradition that goes back to the ancient Greeks," Mankell told London *Guardian* contributor Ian Thomson. "You hold a mirror to crime to see what's happening in society. I could never write a crime story just for the sake of it, because I always want to talk about certain things in society."

In *Faceless Killers,* Wallander is faced with the double murder of a farm couple. Johannes Lovgren is found beaten and stabbed to death, and his wife, Maria, nearly dead, hangs from a noose around her neck. Before Marie dies, she utters the word "foreigner," which leads to anti-immigrant reaction and threats in the region. Wallander learns that the farmer had a secret life of which his wife was unaware. A *Publishers Weekly* reviewer called Mankell "skilled" and his characterization of Wallander "effective," but observed that Mankell "provides essential information only at the last minute, which makes the solution feel more like an appendix than a conclusion." A *Library Journal* reviewer called the first book in the series a "brilliant U.S. debut."

The White Lioness is set in 1990 and takes place in Sweden and South Africa. The body of a murdered Swedish homemaker is found in a well, and Wallander goes after a stalker, whose airtight alibi prevents Wallander from making an arrest. International intrigue builds, because the killer is a former KGB agent who is training an assassin for the murder of Nelson Mandela, planned by right-wing Afrikaaners. Wallander is caught up in race relations in South Africa as he tries to solve the murder in Sweden. A *Kirkus Reviews* critic noted the length of *The White Lioness* and called the "Kurt Wallander" series "a Viking-size saga. . . . Wallander personifies the charmingly melancholy Scandinavian of lore and tradition. But 560 pages of this would hobble the pace, and dim the charisma, of just about any protagonist." Ott wrote in *Booklist* that the plot is "a bit unwieldy, but the action is skillfully grounded in human rather than political concerns." A *Publishers Weekly* reviewer noted that because Mandela was not assassinated by the KGB or white terrorists, it makes Mankell's job "even harder." The same reviewer said Wallander continues to be "a solid character, whose strengths and weaknesses are utterly credible . . . Mankell . . . knows how to make the most of his virtues."

In *Sidetracked,* Wallander is faced with a series of murders in which the victims, all men, are killed with a hatchet, then scalped. The fact that there seems to be no connection between the victims makes the investigation difficult. The killer is actually a boy who is using the scalps in a ritual he hopes will revive his catatonic sister. *Booklist* reviewer Ott said: "Wallander slogs on, using the very tedium of the investigative process to insulate himself from the horrors he faces." Other critics also commented on Mankell's observations about contemporary society. "The author's treatment of modern themes such as juvenile killers and broken families adds richness to what is essentially a straightforward police procedural," wrote a *Publishers Weekly* reviewer. In a review for *Library Journal,* Rex E. Klett summarized that the book is "full of emotion, yet cleanly written."

In 2000 the English translation of *The Fifth Woman* was published. The crime novel "opens with the bloody killings of four nuns and a Swedish tourist (the fifth woman)," described Klett in *Library Journal.* This novel further highlighted the bleakness of Mankell's work. Ott noted in a *Booklist* review that "the European hard-boiled novel has taken the subgenre in a largely new direction: the heroes of this new breed of crime novel respond to the chaos of the modern world with sinking shoulders." A critic for *Publishers Weekly* wrote that "the narrative is so bleak and brooding that it certainly qualifies as the darkest of Swedish noir." Even if the atmosphere was bleak, the same critic noted that "Man-

kell is a talented writer." Klett also commented on "the intricate plotting, chilling psychological divination, and thrilling police procedural."

Wallander investigates the links between the murder of a cab driver and three other strange deaths in *Firewall.* A *Publishers Weekly* reviewer stated: "The recurring clues demonstrating the vulnerability of society in the electronic age remain just outside of the Luddite inspector's understanding." Other critics also noted the inspector's lack of technical savvy. "Wallender is a man reluctantly and slowly realising that he lives in a computer age, and there may be some advantages to this," noted Antonia Fraser in *Spectator.* "At the same time the villains, who naturally plan a hideous worldwide conspiracy, are well aware of the advantages to them and the disadvantages to everyone else."

In *One Step Behind,* Wallander battles exhaustion and illness as he investigates the bizarre murder of three college students whose bodies are found hidden weeks after their disappearance. When a colleague named Svedburg is gunned down in his own home, the detective suspects the two cases are connected. Wallander has an inkling that some of his colleagues are to blame, "voicing his constant fear that the department, like civilization itself, is 'coming apart at the seams,'" according to Marilyn Stasio in the *New York Times Book Review.* Other murders follow, and Wallander's suspicions come true: he is tracking a serial killer. Confronting "an adversary who becomes the personification of Wallander's worst fears," wrote *Booklist* contributor Ott, further noting that "the detective finds himself ironically reenergized in a kind of back-against-the-wall fight for the possibilities of life."

The Dogs of Riga, another Wallander novel published in English translation, "explores one man's struggle to find truth and justice in a society increasingly bereft of either," remarked a contributor in *Publishers Weekly.* A life raft carrying a pair of bodies washes ashore on the Swedish coast; the bullet-riddled corpses are identified as Latvian, with connections to the Russian mob. After a Latvian detective who assists the investigation is killed, Wallander journeys to Riga to help solve his murder, where he finds himself enmeshed in an increasingly complex and dangerous situation. "Wallander's introspection and self-doubt make him compellingly real," noted the *Publishers Weekly* critic, and Stasio remarked in the *New York Times Book Review* that the bleakness of *The Dogs of Riga* offers readers both a glimpse "of Wallander's state of mind and a comment on the greater darkness that he senses creeping over his country and his world."

Wallander teams with his daughter, Linda, a rookie police officer, to solve a grisly murder in *Before the Frost.* While Wallander investigates the ritualistic decapitation of a hiker, Linda searches for an old friend whose long-lost father has mysteriously reappeared after a decades-long absence. As the pair collect evidence, their cases begin to dovetail. "Despite the clumsiness of her professional techniques," remarked Stasio, "Linda is both smart and stubborn enough to follow the case on the twisted plot path that leads to an insidious religious subculture that threatens to undermine Sweden's famously tolerant social structure." In the novel, wrote *New Statesman* critic Joanna Kavenna, "Mankell stitches soapboxing, starkly poetic description and Scandinavian melancholy together into something racy and provocative."

Not all of the Wallander books have been published in English in the order they originally appeared in Swedish. First published in Sweden in 1994, *The Man Who Smiled,* Mankell's fourth Wallander mystery, was translated in 2006. On sick leave and contemplating retirement, Wallander returns to the force to investigate the death of an old friend that, on the surface, appears to be an accident. *Philadelphia Inquirer* critic Maxine Clarke said: "The heart of the book is the inner life and thoughts of this unromantic, fiftyish man, and how he doggedly convinces first himself and then his colleagues and superiors that there is a thread to follow, a thread that will lead to an answer."

In addition to his popular Wallander series, Mankell has published stand-alone mysteries and mainstream novels. *The Eye of the Leopard,* originally published in 1990 as *Leopardens oega,* is a coming-of-age story about Hans Olafsson, a young Swedish man who leaves his lonely childhood home and alcoholic father to try and find a more meaningful existence in the African nation of Zambia. Hans soon discovers the flaws of mankind are omnipresent as he arrives in a country torn by tribal warfare. The native people take over the lands settled by Europeans, including Hans's egg farm, thus destroying all his idyllic future dreams. Covering the transformative years in Zambia from the 1960s through the 1980s, the novel was praised by Jessica Moyer in *Booklist* for the author's "ability to evoke a sense of place" and for offering a "powerful exploration of the

stresses and challenges of freedom." Although a *Kirkus Reviews* writer felt that slow pacing results from occasional redundancy in the book, the reviewer asserted that this "impressive novel is intensely detailed and beautifully constructed." A *Publishers Weekly* contributor stated that Mankell adroitly captures the white settler's troubled relationship with Africa and that this is what makes "this disquieting novel so compelling."

Mankell introduces Detective Stefan Lindman in *The Return of the Dancing Master,* a stand-alone mystery. A middle-aged insomniac who was recently diagnosed with mouth cancer, Lindman chooses to forego some much needed rest to solve the brutal slaying of a retired colleague, Herbert Molin, in the remote village of Sveg. Thane Peterson, writing in *Business Week Online,* noted how Molin "was slowly whipped to death in the snowy yard of his isolated country house. Bloody footprints in his living room indicate that—before or after death—he had somehow been made to dance the fox-trot." "It's a case, a knotty one with tentacles reaching back to WWII and the Nazi monstrosity, that's just what Lindman needs," observed a *Kirkus Reviews* critic, while a *Publishers Weekly* contributor stated that "by the satisfying end readers with a taste for the unusual will find Lindman, and the mystery he solves, not in the least bit ordinary."

While Mankell's Wallander books have been considered grim by reviewers, they are leavened with a black sense of humor; this is not the case for the author's oppressively dark novel *Depths.* The story is about one man's evil side being suddenly released to cover an affair. Lars Tobiasson-Svartman was abused as a child and as an adult, he finds himself in a loveless marriage. Now a navy engineer at the beginning of World War I, he tries to find control in his life by conducting hydrographic surveys. Outwardly, Lars seems like a dull man, but one day he meets Sara Fredrika, a strange widow who lives by herself on a reef, surviving mostly by fishing. In Sara, Lars sees a more primitive force of nature that he finds compelling, and he begins an affair with her. His lies to her, telling Sara that his spouse died, as he conceals his affair from his now-pregnant wife. He also impregnates Sara, and Lars's worries that he will be found out cause him to become paranoid. This paranoia leads him to believe that several of his crew know what he is doing, and to hide his web of lies, he commits several brutal murders, completely without remorse. Eventually, Lars's actions cause him to lose everything dear in his life, including his job, family, and lover.

"Though *Depths* was a bestseller in Sweden," commented Thomson in a London *Guardian* review of the book, "critics disliked its graphic descriptions of violence, as German and Russian fleets blow each other up in the Baltic. At times, too, *Depths* is pretentious. . . . The sentences are self-consciously staccato and may strike some as affected. Even by Scandinavian standards, *Depths* is a fabulously gloomy book." Thomson added, however, that the setting is "beautifully evoked" and that the story "makes for powerful fiction. Mankell is, without doubt, one of the most impressive crime writers at work in Europe today." A *Publishers Weekly* contributor called it "bizarre and compelling" and felt that the character of Lars represents "a masterful portrait" in "a memorable and shocking psychological study." While some readers might miss the dry humor of Mankell's mysteries, *Depths* "shows us another dimension of his considerable talent," stated Keir Graff in *Booklist.*

Many critics have called *Kennedy's Brain* an odd mystery apparently inspired by the author's outrage over the AIDS crisis in Africa and those who have been exploiting it. When Louise Cantor discovers her son Henrik's body, she suspects that it was not suicide from sleeping pills, as the police believe. She resolves to unveil the mystery behind her son's death, tracing his footsteps over the years, which takes her to such lands as Austria and Africa. She learns that her son was obsessed with the mystery of what happened to part of John F. Kennedy's brain, which had been removed not long after his death, apparently to keep some secret from being discovered. The mystery of the missing piece of brain becomes a metaphor for the secrets of Henrik's life, according to a number of critics. The most disturbing part of the book occurs in Africa, where Louise discovers that authorities and organized criminals are exploiting the AIDS epidemic by controlling the supply of drugs needed to control the disease. Reviewers of *Kennedy's Brain* noted that the story seems to come apart somewhat as the heroine is overwhelmed by the insurmountable challenge of stopping the exploitation of Africa's AIDS victims, yet several also praised the character of Louise. "Louise is such a powerhouse that she almost salvages a plot too meandering to be persuasive," stated a *Kirkus Reviews* contributor. While a *Publishers Weekly* writer called Mankell "a deft and imaginative plotter and an insightful observer of the human condition," the writer added that the plot about the pharmaceutical industry "overshadows" the rest of the book. Fiona Walker, writing for *Euro Crime,* acknowledged that Mankell "was motivated by strong feeling, and has noble motives," adding that despite flaws in the novel, "Louise is fascinating, when removed from her sadness, and Mankell's crusading is powerful, as is his evocation of place and atmosphere."

Committed to the AIDS cause in more than just his fiction, Mankell works frequently with AIDS charities in Africa, where he is also director of the Teatro Avenida, a theater group, in Mozambique. His short work *I Die, but the Memory Lives On: A Personal Reflection on AIDS* is part of his "memory books" project, aimed at raising awareness of the crisis.

Published in English in 2009, *Italian Shoes* is another one of Mankell's stand-alone novels. The narrator of this novel is sixty-six-year-old Frederick Welin, an ex-surgeon who lost his surgical license after amputating the wrong arm of a woman with bone cancer. After this tragedy, Welin retired to a remote archipelago three miles from the Swedish mainland that he inherited from his grandparents. For twelve years he has lived in relative isolation—with only a dog, cat, and anthill as his only company. His life takes an unexpected turn with the unwanted arrival of Harriet Hornfeldt, an ex-lover Welin abandoned forty years ago. Harriet, who is terminally ill, demands that Welin take her to see the forest pool he described to her when they were together before she dies. He agrees, thus setting in motion a series of events that help Welin learn how to reconnect with humanity once again. "The tone throughout is elegiac—someone always seems to be dying, even as Welin is surging back to life—yet quietly hopeful, with each step forward a hard-won victory over winter's freeze," observed a *Kirkus Reviews* contributor. In a review for the London *Guardian*, Cathi Unsworth compared the book to *Depths*. She noted that they both take place on an island in the Swedish archipelago and that they have similar themes of isolation and estrangement. However, "there are no murders and little violence in *Italian Shoes,*" remarked Unsworth. She added: "A departure for a bestselling crime author best known for his creation of Inspector Wallander it may be, but Mankell's focus remains the same: this book is a voyage into the soul of a man." In a review for the *Bookbag* Web site, Sue Magee commented that the book "may well lack the technical brilliance of *Depths* but for me it's the best of Mankell's work. Difficult themes—aging and death—are dealt with sensitively and back lit by the bleak settings of the Stockholm archipelago and northern Sweden. The writing is elegant." Magee also praised the book for its "thought-provoking and intriguing story." "Mankell has always been an ambitious writer. Sometimes he takes on too much, straying into conspiracy theories or relying on over-dramatic plot devices," remarked London *Times* reviewer Joan Smith. "But this novel transcends the limits of his earlier work, suggesting that facing painful events has the power to unblock even the chilliest of human hearts," concluded Smith. In a review of the book for his Web log, Matt Beynon Rees noted: "This is a devastatingly honest and keenly personal novel." Rees also stated: "Mankell writes with a measured pace that's in tune with the frozen weather and the slow body of the aging Fredrik." *Booklist* reviewer Jessica Moyer also praised *Italian Shoes,* calling it a "short, beautiful, and ultimately life-affirming novel."

Discussing his approach to writing with Nicci Gerrard in the London *Observer,* Mankell stated: "Whatever I write, I have to begin with a question, something I don't know the answer to. Here, it is: what happens to people when they're thrown out on to the margins of society, who realise every day that they aren't needed? I always start with a question, an issue. Then the story comes." He added: "I came to the world to tell stories. The day I can't, I will die. The storytelling and the lifeline are the same."

BIOGRAPHICAL AND CRITICAL SOURCES:

PERIODICALS

Atlantic Monthly, October, 2006, review of *The Man Who Smiled,* p. 127.

Booklist, February 15, 1997, Bill Ott, review of *Faceless Killers,* p. 1008; August, 1998, Bill Ott, review of *The White Lioness,* p. 1976; April 15, 1999, Bill Ott, review of *Sidetracked,* p. 1482; July, 2000, Bill Ott, review of *The Fifth Woman,* p. 2013; February 15, 2002, Bill Ott, review of *One Step Behind,* p. 997; December 15, 2003, Hazel Rochman, review of *Secrets in the Fire,* p. 749; March 1, 2004, Bill Ott, review of *The Return of the Dancing Master,* p. 1142; January 1, 2005, Bill Ott, review of *Before the Frost,* p. 828; September 15, 2006, review of *The Man Who Smiled,* p. 6; April 1, 2007, Keir Graff, review of *Depths,* p. 28; September 1, 2007, Frank Sennett, review of *Kennedy's Brain,* p. 62; December 1, 2007, Michael Cart, review of *A Bridge to the Stars,* p. 45; March 15, 2008, Jessica Moyer, review of *The Eye of the Leopard,* p. 26; April 1, 2009, Jessica Moyer, review of *Italian Shoes,* p. 18.

Bookseller, November 17, 2006, Stephen Place, review of *Depths,* p. 11.

Christianity Today, January, 2008, John Wilson, review of *Kennedy's Brain,* p. 60.

Economist, October 2, 2004, "Know Your Limits; A Round-up of Thrillers," review of *Before the Frost,* p. 84.

Entertainment Weekly, April 6, 2007, Jeff Giles, review of *Depths,* p. 79.

Guardian (London, England), November 1, 2003, Ian Thomson, "True Crime," interview with Henning Mankell; November 11, 2006, Ian Thomson, "Beneath the Sea," review of *Depths*; April 18, 2009, Cathi Unsworth, review of *Italian Shoes.*

Horn Book, January-February, 2008, Lois Lowry, review of *A Bridge to the Stars,* p. 91.

Independent (London, England), August 31, 2007, Paul Binding, review of *Kennedy's Brain;* November 29, 2008, Gerard Gilbert, "Henning Mankell: Hot and Cold"; April 10, 2009, Anna Paterson, review of *Italian Shoes.*

Kirkus Reviews, July 1, 1998, review of *The White Lioness,* p. 935; January 1, 2002, review of *One Step Behind,* p. 19; September 1, 2002, review of *Firewall,* p. 1269; March 1, 2003, review of *The Dogs of Riga,* p. 349; January 15, 2004, review of *The Return of the Dancing Master,* p. 64; December 15, 2004, review of *Before the Frost,* p. 1168; April 1, 2006, review of *Chronicler of the Winds,* p. 317; July 15, 2006, review of *The Man Who Smiled,* p. 705; February 15, 2007, review of *Depths;* August 15, 2007, review of *Kennedy's Brain;* April 15, 2008, review of *The Eye of the Leopard*; March 1, 2009, review of *Italian Shoes.*

Kliatt, November, 2007, Paula Rohrlick, review of *A Bridge to the Stars,* p. 12.

Lancet, July 3, 2004, Alex Coutinho, review of *I Die, but the Memory Lives On: A Personal Reflection on AIDS,* p. 20.

Library Journal, December, 1996, review of *Faceless Killers,* p. 150; April 1, 1999, Rex E. Klett, review of *Sidetracked,* p. 132; November 15, 1999, Jo Ann Vicarel, review of *Sidetracked,* p. 132; June 1, 2000, Rex E. Klett, review of *The Fifth Woman,* p. 208; February 15, 2002, Francine Fialkoff, review of *One Step Behind,* p. 182; February 15, 2005, Wilda Williams, review of *Before the Frost,* p. 124; May 1, 2006, Rebecca Stuhr, review of *Chronicler of the Winds,* p. 82; March 15, 2007, Edward B. St. John, review of *Depths,* p. 61; September 1, 2007, Michele Leber, review of *Kennedy's Brain,* p. 129.

New Statesman, September 6, 2004, Joanna Kavenna, "The Swedish Morse," p. 54.

New York Times Book Review, June 13, 1999, Marilyn Stasio, "Crime," p. 26; March 3, 2002, Marilyn Stasio, review of *One Step Behind*; November 17, 2002, Marilyn Stasio, review of *Firewall;* May 4, 2003, Marilyn Stasio, review of *The Dogs of Riga;* March 28, 2004, Marilyn Stasio, review of *The*

Return of the Dancing Master; January 23, 2005, Marilyn Stasio, "Cult Status," review of *Before the Frost;* September 24, 2006, Marilyn Stasio, "Glumshoe," review of *The Man Who Smiled;* April 15, 2007, Lucy Ellman, "Under the Sea," review of *Depths.*

Observer, March 2, 2003, Nicci Gerrard, "Inspector Norse."

Philadelphia Inquirer, June 21, 2006, Carlin Romano, "Swede's Crime Stories Are Cerebral"; September 27, 2006, Maxine Clarke, review of *The Man Who Smiled.*

Publishers Weekly, December 16, 1996, review of *Faceless Killers,* p. 45; June 8, 1998, review of *The White Lioness,* p. 49; March 29, 1999, review of *Sidetracked,* p. 94; July 10, 2000, review of *The Fifth Woman,* p. 49; January 21, 2002, review of *One Step Behind,* p. 68; October 7, 2002, review of *Firewall,* p. 55; March 31, 2003, review of *The Dogs of Riga,* p. 46; March 1, 2004, review of *The Return of the Dancing Master,* p. 52; January 31, 2005, review of *Before the Frost,* p. 52; April 17, 2006, review of *Chronicler of the Winds,* p. 167; July 24, 2006, review of *The Man Who Smiled,* p. 39; February 12, 2007, review of *Depths,* p. 62; July 23, 2007, review of *Kennedy's Brain,* p. 42; December 17, 2007, review of *A Bridge to the Stars,* p. 52; March 10, 2008, review of *The Eye of the Leopard,* p. 57.

School Library Journal, May, 2004, Mary N. Oluonye, review of *Secrets in the Fire,* p. 152; January, 2008, D. Maria LaRocco, review of *A Bridge to the Stars,* p. 122.

South of Sweden, August-September, 2006, David Wiles, "Henning Mankell," pp. 34-37.

Spectator, April 3, 2004, Antonia Fraser, "Swedish Exercises in Crime," review of *Firewall,* p. 45; November 26, 2005, Harriet Waugh, "Recent Crime Novels," review of *The Man Who Smiled,* p. 49.

Swiss News, November, 2007, review of *Kennedy's Brain,* p. 60.

Time, June 7, 2004, Lev Grossman, "Murder Most Exotic," review of *The Return of the Dancing Master,* p. 121; October 23, 2006, Philip Elmer-DeWitt, "Five Novel Mysteries from Old Masters," review of *The Man Who Smiled,* p. 88.

Times (London, England), May 3, 2009, Joan Smith, review of *Italian Shoes.*

Wall Street Journal, March 28, 1997, Tom Nolan, review of *Faceless Killers,* p. A14.

ONLINE

Bookbag, http://www.thebookbag.co.uk/ (June 27, 2009), Sue Magee, review of *Italian Shoes.*

Business Week Online, http://www.businessweek.com/ (February 19, 2004), Thane Peterson, "Dark Knights of Sweden's Fragile Soul."

Euro Crime, http://www.eurocrime.co.uk/ (September 1, 2007), Fiona Walker, review of *Kennedy's Brain.*

Henning Mankell Home Page, http://www.henning mankell.com (June 21, 2009).

Matt Beynon Rees Web log, http://mattbeynonrees. blogspot.com/ (April 9, 2009), review of *Italian Shoes.*

Spiegel Online, http://www.spiegel.de/international/ (September 1, 2006), "Henning Mankell on AIDS in Africa."

Swedish Institute Web site, http://www.sweden.se/ (July 7, 2006), David Wiles, "On the Trail of Sweden's Most Famous Detective."*

*   *   *

MARTIN, Valerie 1948-

PERSONAL: Born March 14, 1948, in Sedalia, MO; daughter of John Roger (a sea captain) and Valerie Metcalf; married Robert M. Martin (an artist), December 10, 1970 (divorced, 1984); children: Adrienne. *Education:* University of New Orleans, B.A., 1970; University of Massachusetts, M.F.A., 1974.

ADDRESSES: Agent—Nikki Smith, Smith-Skolnik Literary Management, 303 Walnut St., Westfield, NJ 07090.

CAREER: Writer, educator. University of New Mexico, Las Cruces, visiting lecturer in creative writing, 1978-79; University of New Orleans, New Orleans, LA, assistant professor of English, 1980-84, 1985-86; University of Alabama, Tuscaloosa, writer in residence, 1984-85; Mt. Holyoke College, South Hadley, MA, lecturer in creative writing, 1986-89; University of Massachusetts—Amherst, associate professor of English, 1989-97; Loyola University, New Orleans, LA, visiting writer-in-residence, 1998-99; Sarah Lawrence College, Bronxville, NY, visiting writer, 1999, 2002.

MEMBER: Authors Guild, PEN.

AWARDS, HONORS: Louisiana Division of the Arts grant, 1982; grant, National Endowment for the Arts, 1990; Kafica Prize, University of Rochester, 1991; Orange Prize for Fiction, 2003, for *Property.*

WRITINGS:

Love: Short Stories, Lynx House Press (Amherst, MA), 1977, reprinted, Lost Horse Press (Sandpoint, ID), 1999.

Set in Motion (novel), Farrar, Straus (New York, NY), 1978.

Alexandra (novel), Farrar, Straus (New York, NY), 1979.

A Recent Martyr (novel), Houghton Mifflin (Boston, MA), 1987.

The Consolation of Nature, and Other Stories, Vintage (New York, NY), 1988.

Mary Reilly (novel), Doubleday (New York, NY), 1990.

The Great Divorce (novel), Doubleday (New York, NY), 1994.

Italian Fever (novel), Knopf (New York, NY), 1999.

Salvation: Scenes from the Life of St. Francis (nonfiction), Knopf (New York, NY), 2001.

Property (novel), Nan A. Talese/Doubleday (New York, NY), 2003.

The Unfinished Novel: And Other Stories, Vintage Contemporaries (New York, NY), 2006.

Trespass (novel), Nan A. Talese/Doubleday (New York, NY), 2007.

Confessions of Edward Day (novel), Nan A. Talese/Doubleday (New York, NY), 2009.

ADAPTATIONS: Mary Reilly was filmed by TriStar in 1996, starring Julia Roberts and John Malkovich.

SIDELIGHTS: Valerie Martin writes stories that "recall those by Edgar Allan Poe," according to *New York Times* columnist Michiko Kakutani. "It's not just the gothic subject matter or the tightly designed plots," Kakutani added. "It's [Martin's] ability to take that material and communicate extreme states of mind—to make it yield startling psychological truths that resonate in the mind." In the *Los Angeles Times Book Review,* Susan Slocum Hinerfeld described Martin's work as "neo-Gothic hyperbole of the New Orleans School. This is the literature of excess, swerving toward violence and despair. It's not easy to control such iridescent prose, such ardent imaginings." Martin's novels include *A Recent Martyr, The Great Divorce, Mary Reilly*—a version of Robert Louis Stevenson's *Dr. Jekyll and Mr. Hyde* told from the point of view of the doctor's housemaid, the Orange Prize-winning novel *Property,* and *Trespass.* Her collection *The Consolation of Nature, and Other Stories* has also received critical attention, as did her 2006 collection, *The Unfinished Novel: And Other Stories.*

A Recent Martyr, set in a plague-ridden New Orleans of the near future, depicts the sadomasochistic love affair between Emma Miller, who is unhappily married, and Pascal Toussaint. When Toussaint becomes obsessed with Claire, a postulant nun who works with Emma caring for the dying within the quarantine zone, their tangled relationship plays itself out amid the misery and fear of the suffering city. Geoffrey Stokes, writing in the *Village Voice,* claimed that Martin "can flat-out write. . . . In prose of liquid clarity, [she] applies pressure to her characters—a touch here, a prod there, a contusive thump in an out-of-the-way alley—and lets it flow, equally and undiminished, through every corner of their souls, every page of her remarkable book." Carolyn Banks, writing in the *New York Times Book Review,* found "much in *A Recent Martyr* that, in another author's hands, might be overwrought. . . . We are told these things, however, in Emma's voice, always steady, clear, elegant and direct."

A woman narrates *Mary Reilly* as well. Mary writes in her journal of the increasingly strange state of affairs around the Jekyll home, especially after the doctor supposedly hires an assistant named Edward Hyde. *Newsweek* contributor David Gates praised the author's memorable characters, especially "the utterly convincing Mary, with a housemaid's eye (rooms, to her, are furnished with things to be cleaned), a servant girl's rigorous sense of place—and a sufferer's hard-won dignity." In the *Los Angeles Times Book Review,* Judith Freeman also reflected on Mary as "a character of great kindness and goodness. Her perceptions of human nature ring with simple truth."

Abused by a drunken father, Mary tries hard to please the kindly Dr. Jekyll. "When Master is gay and kind to me," she writes in the journal she keeps, "then all the sadness I feel lifts as suddenly as a bird. . . . When he tells me he trusts me and shows he trusts me more than anyone else in this house, my heart leaps." According to Elizabeth Castor in the *Washington Post,* the story is "part psychological novel, part social history, part eerie horror tale . . . dark and moving and powerful—a fitting complement to the 19th-century original." Ellen Pall, writing in Chicago's *Tribune Books,* considered the novel "curiously lacking in . . . resonance for our time; despite the politically intriguing female-underclass point of view it adopts, it seems finally not to be about very much." But John Crowley offered a glowing review in the *New York Times Book Review.* Crowley stated that *Mary Reilly* "is an achievement—creativity skating exhilaratingly on thin ice." He concluded: "I think Valerie Martin's treatment of [Robert Louis Stevenson's] story actually succeeds in ways Stevenson himself could not have brought off and might well have admired." *Mary Reilly* was adapted for film by TriStar in 1996.

In the novel *The Great Divorce,* Martin weaves three stories concerning the relationship between humans and animals. One story tells of Ellen Clayton, a veterinarian for a New Orleans zoo, whose husband is leaving her for a younger woman at the same time the zoo is suffering from a viral outbreak. The second story concerns Camille, the zoo's keeper of big cats, who imagines herself as a leopard to escape from her intolerable private life. The third story tells of Elizabeth Schlaeger, nicknamed the catwoman of St. Francisville, a nineteenth-century woman who savagely murdered her husband. "In all three of its tales," wrote Emily Mitchell in *Time,* "*The Great Divorce* evocatively humanizes the wild nature that is just beneath the surface of us all." Francine Prose, in the *Los Angeles Times Book Review,* called *The Great Divorce* an "intellectually ambitious and readable new book" that "provides the immediate pleasures of a literary page-turner, but also has a more lasting influence."

Animals also play a prominent role in the stories gathered together in *The Consolation of Nature, and Other Stories.* In this ironically-titled collection, Martin spins tales of unease. "One comes away from these stories," explained Marianne Gingher in the *Washington Post Book World,* "feeling ambivalent about nature's role in human solace. Innocent lovers drown, a sea creature murderously castrates a fisherman, a hungry cat absurdly traps its face in a salmon can and dies, an enormous rat seizes a man by the throat." As Kakutani noted, Martin displays "a preoccupation with the dark underside of life, a taste for disturbing, even macabre imagery, and a tendency to use that imagery to delineate turning points in people's lives." Although Hinerfeld claimed that "what [the book] lacks—entirely—is humor," Gingher found *The Consolation of Nature, and Other Stories* to be "a curious, spooky, distinctive book."

Martin's *Italian Fever* is likewise animated by Gothic set pieces. The novel's young American heroine, Lucy Stark, travels to Italy to tidy up her employer's affairs and to search for a manuscript he was working on when he died under mysterious circumstances. "Lucy is a typical Martin heroine—alert but passive, capable and

interested but also reflective and full of doubts," observed Craig Seligman in the *New York Times Book Review.* Upon her arrival, Lucy tries to piece together what might have happened to her employer, searching the pages of his manuscript for clues—and experiencing both supernatural phenomena and a passionate affair with her Italian chauffeur. A *Publishers Weekly* correspondent declared: "With a few ghosts, several acts of love and numerous jibes at self-indulgent writers . . . the sophisticated romantic adventure is rendered with stylish flair. Martin controls the narrative momentum smoothly and recounts her tale with occasional wryness and engaging enthusiasm."

Seligman and other reviewers have admired *Italian Fever*'s nod to authors E.M. Forster and Henry James, both of whom wrote novels about young foreigners who become passionately enchanted during their trips to Italy. Seligman maintained, however, that Martin's Lucy "is neither as fresh nor as virginal as the young heroines Forster and James send to Italy for their confrontations with destiny—and, anyway, Martin doesn't believe in sudden, overwhelming alterations of consciousness or character." Seligman praised *Italian Fever* as the work of "a virtuoso," adding: "Valerie Martin's sureness of phrasing is one of the great pleasures of her recent fiction. In the two decades that she has been publishing novels and stories, her cool, remote voice has mellowed, and her competence has kindled into brilliance."

With her 2001 work, *Salvation: Scenes from the Life of St. Francis,* Martin turns her hand to fictionalized biography. Anna M. Donnelly, writing in *Library Journal,* described the book as "a series of thirty-one frescolike word panels on the radical popular stigmatist and founder of the Franciscan Order." Martin was inspired to write the life of St. Francis by the series of frescoes of his life created by various great Renaissance painters. According to Paul Lachance, writing in *Church History,* "[Martin's] procedure is to illuminate her story by focusing on some of the major scenes or themes from Francis's life, but reversing the sequence by beginning with his death and ending with his conversion." *School Library Journal* reviewer Lillian McAnally, thought that with *Salvation* "Martin has opened a window into the medieval world to present us with a vivid portrait of St. Francis." Similar praise came from *Christian Century* contributor Ellen L. Babinsky, who called the same work a "great narrative." A *Publishers Weekly* critic thought "Martin's scenes from Francis's life are exquisite and imaginative," and *Booklist* writer Margaret Flanagan noted that the author "portrays St. Francis as a man of his time and culture."

Returning to the novel in her 2003 *Property,* Martin tells a tale of sexual rivalry and a domestic power struggle set on an antebellum Louisiana plantation. Narrated by Manon Gaudet, the novel depicts a triangle between the infantile Manon, her cruel and dull husband, and the light-skinned female slave, Sarah, who has borne Manon's husband an illegitimate child. A *Kirkus Reviews* critic had high praise for this award-winning novel, terming it a "nimble, enlightening and horrific story about the morally corrosive effects of slavery and one childish soul, locked in a cycle of permanent bitterness." Writing on *Salon.com,* Laura Miller called *Property* a "ferociously honest book attacking a subject that has long been wrapped in what her heroine calls 'lies without end': race in America." A *Publishers Weekly* contributor also found the work "compelling," while *Library Journal* writer Andrea Kempf thought the novel "will resonate with readers long after it is finished."

"I'm really more interested in what power does to the person who has it than to the person who doesn't," Martin told *Publishers Weekly* interviewer Karen Holt, explaining why she chose to tell her story from the viewpoint of a slave owner—an extremely unsympathetic character. "I'm interested in what it does to a person's psychology to be someone who does terrible things." In Holt's assessment, the result is a novel distinguished by "restraint and unflinching exposure of moral flaws."

Martin's 2006 short story collection, *The Unfinished Novel,* gathers several tales dealing with artists' attempts to master their craft and gain public renown. The title story, for example, features a novelist, while "Blue Period" has a painter as the protagonist and "The Bower" has a college drama coach at its center. Troy Patterson, writing in *Entertainment Weekly,* praised Martin's "memorable depictions of artists' desires, jealousies, and ostrich-egg egos," while a *Publishers Weekly* contributor called the work a "suspenseful and piercingly acute collection," as well as "compulsively readable and impressively perceptive."

Political themes inform Martin's novel *Trespass.* The story concerns the love affair that develops between a young American man and a Croatian refugee. Toby Dale has lived a relatively sheltered life in rural New York until he falls for Salome, whose family has fled war-torn Croatia. Toby's mother, Chloe, strongly disapproves, thinking that Salome is trying to trap Toby into marriage by becoming pregnant. For Chloe, Salome embodies a threat to the comfortable and secure life that Chloe has built for her family. Several details emphasize this sense of impending violence: the country is preparing to go to war in Iraq; a poacher is roaming the Dales' property; Toby's father, a historian, is working on a book about the Crusades. Salome eventually discovers that her mother, thought killed in a Serbian attack on her village, is still alive, and she leaves the country to search for her. Salome's journey through the Balkans brings her through that region's recent history of atrocity and loss.

Writing in the London *Telegraph,* Jessica Mann noted the obvious parallels in the book, as Martin juxtaposes the experiences of Salome's family against the facile liberalism of the Dales. Though the reviewer observed that Martin writes well and that *Trespass* is "often moving and obviously heartfelt," Mann found the novel's anti-war message overstated, even for sympathetic readers. *Guardian* writer Aida Edemariam made a similar point, commenting that "we are never in any doubt as to the lessons we are meant to learn from this novel." Many critics, however, gave the novel praise. In *STL Today,* Shirley K. Murray described *Trespass* as a "sharp and perceptive look at conflict, personal and global, at poisonous relationships and mutual distrust, and at a never-ending circle of violence." London *Times* contributor Sarah Emily Miano wrote that Martin's "scrupulous attention to mood and atmosphere makes the story compelling," concluding that the novel is a "masterly tale of transgression, acceptance, diplomacy, war, class conflict, love, forgiveness and jealousy." And Lee Thomas, writing in *San Francisco Chronicle,* hailed *Trespass* as a "searing commentary on the human desire to set boundary lines against threats, perceived and real."

Martin once told *CA:* "For nearly thirty years, in life and literature, I have attempted to reconcile the contradictory attractions of a full blown, lyrical, pantheistic Romanticism with a terse, godless, and chilly Realism. My compass spins perpetually between these two poles, though lately Romanticism seems to exerting a powerful magnetism."

BIOGRAPHICAL AND CRITICAL SOURCES:

BOOKS

Martin, Valerie, *Mary Reilly,* Doubleday (New York, NY), 1990.

PERIODICALS

Belles Lettres, July, 1988, review of *The Consolation of Nature, and Other Stories,* p. 13; fall, 1991, review of *Mary Reilly,* p. 30.

Booklist, January 1, 1994, review of *The Great Divorce,* p. 787; March 15, 1999, review of *Italian Fever,* p. 1260; March 1, 2001, Margaret Flanagan, review of *Salvation: Scenes from the Life of St. Francis,* p. 1210; January 1, 2003, Kristine Huntley, review of *Property,* p. 848; July 1, 2007, Joanne Wilkinson, review of *Trespass,* p. 9.

Boston, July, 1990, review of *Mary Reilly,* p. 50.

Christian Century, August 1, 2001, Ellen L. Babinsky, review of *Salvation,* p. 33.

Church History, December, 2003, Paul Lachance, review of *Salvation,* p. 879.

Cosmopolitan, February, 1990, review of *Mary Reilly,* p. 36.

Dallas Morning News, November 21, 2007, Joy Tipping, review of *Trespass.*

Detroit Free Press, January 21, 1990, review of *Mary Reilly.*

Entertainment Weekly, April 8, 1994, review of *The Great Divorce,* p. 53; August 6, 1999, review of *Italian Fever,* p. 58; May 12, 2006, Troy Patterson, review of *The Unfinished Novel: And Other Stories,* p. 85; September 14, Jennifer Reese, 2007, "Mother's Nature," p. 152.

Financial Times, September 15, 2007, Anna Metcalfe, "Valerie Martin," p. 38.

Fort Worth Star-Telegram, October 3, 2007, Judy Wiley, "Intruders Wreak Havoc in 'Trespass'."

Glamour, February, 1990, review of *Mary Reilly,* p. 132.

Guardian (London, England), September 8, 2007, Aida Edemariam, review of *Trespass.*

Harper's Bazaar, March, 1994, review of *The Great Divorce,* p. 168.

Kirkus Reviews, November 15, 2002, review of *Property,* p. 1647; July 15, 2007, review of *Trespass.*

Library Journal, February 1, 1994, review of *The Great Divorce,* p. 113; May 1, 1999, review of *Italian Fever,* p. 111; February 15, 2001, Anna M. Donnelly, review of *Salvation,* p. 173; February 1, 2003, Andrea Kempf, review of *Property,* p. 118; August 1, 2007, Donna Bettencourt, review of *Trespass,* p. 71.

Los Angeles Times Book Review, July 12, 1987, review of *A Recent Martyr,* p. 4; February 7, 1988, Susan Slocum Hinerfeld, review of *The Consolation of Nature, and Other Stories,* p. 7; January 21, 1990, Judith Freeman, review of *Mary Reilly,* pp. 1, 10; March 27, 1994, Francine Prose, review of *The Great Divorce,* p. 2.

Mademoiselle, August, 1995, review of *The Great Divorce,* p. 109.

MS Best Books, June 4, 2003, "Winner of Orange Prize for Fiction Announced."

New Orleans, June, 1988, review of *The Consolation of Nature, and Other Stories,* p. 22.

New Statesman, September 24, 2007, Tadzio Koelb, "War Stories," p. 78.

New Statesman and Society, August 5, 1994, review of *The Great Divorce,* p. 37.

Newsweek, July 24, 1978, review of *Set in Motion,* p. 82; March 12, 1990, David Gates, review of *Mary Reilly,* p. 90.

New Yorker, July 30, 1979, review of *Alexandra,* pp. 88-89.

New York Times, June 23, 1978, review of *Set in Motion,* p. C23; June 21, 1979, review of *Alexandra;* January 13, 1988, Michiko Kakutani, review of *The Consolation of Nature, and Other Stories;* January 26, 1990, review of *Mary Reilly,* p. B4; February 18, 1994, review of *The Great Divorce,* p. C28.

New York Times Book Review, August 5, 1979, review of *Alexandra,* p. 10; June 7, 1987, Carolyn Banks, review of *A Recent Martyr;* January 31, 1988, review of *The Consolation of Nature, and Other Stories,* p. 22; February 4, 1990, John Crowley, review of *Mary Reilly,* p. 7; March 13, 1994, review of *The Great Divorce,* p. 7; August 1, 1999, Craig Seligman, review of *Italian Fever,* p. 9; March 2, 2003, review of *Property,* p. 26; May 21, 2006, Susann Cokal, "Casualties of Art," p. 25; September 16, 2007, Sue Halpern, "Love Croatian Style," p. 13.

People, March 5, 1990, review of *Mary Reilly,* p. 28; May 2, 1994, review of *The Great Divorce,* p. 33.

Publishers Weekly, April 10, 1978, review of *Set in Motion,* p. 68; May 21, 1979, review of *Alexandra,* pp. 56-57; February 9, 1990, review of *Mary Reilly,* pp. 41-42; January 3, 1994, review of *The Great Divorce,* p. 70; May 10, 1999, review of *Italian Fever,* p. 54; February 26, 2001, review of *Salvation,* p. 81; January 13, 2002, review of *Property,* p. 38; March 13, 2006, review of *The Unfinished Novel,* p. 38; May 29, 2006, Karen Holt, "Valerie Martin's Moves," p. 20; July 9, 2007, review of *Trespass,* p. 28.

Review of Contemporary Fiction, September 22, 2006, Irving Malin, review of *The Unfinished Novel,* p. 149.

San Francisco Chronicle, February 16, 2003, Alan Cheuse, review of *Property;* September 16, 2007, Lee Thomas, review of *Trespass.*

School Library Journal, August, 2002, Lillian McAnally, review of *Salvation,* p. S50.

Sewanee Review, October, 1978, review of *Set in Motion,* p. 609.

Southern Review, autumn, 1978, review of *Set in Motion,* p. 849; spring, 1988, review of *The Consolation of Nature, and Other Stories,* p. 445.

State, October 3, 2007, Claudia Smith Brinson, review of *Trespass.*

Time, February 19, 1990, review of *Mary Reilly,* p. 84; March 28, 1994, Emily Mitchell, review of *The Great Divorce,* p. 67.

Times (London, England), September 8, 2007, Sarah Emily Miano, review of *Trespass.*

Times Literary Supplement, October 28, 1988, review of *The Consolation of Nature, and Other Stories;* June 1, 1990, review of *Mary Reilly,* p. 586.

Tribune Books (Chicago, IL), February 4, 1990, Ellen Pall, review of *Mary Reilly,* p. 5; October 12, 2007, Carol Birch, "Awful Outsiders," p. 23; December 29, 2007, Laura Kiolkowski, "Worlds, Families Collide in New Novel," p. 4.

Village Voice, June 30, 1987, Geoffrey Stokes, review of *A Recent Martyr,* p. 55.

Vogue, June 1, 2006, Margaret Johnson, "True Colors," p. 128.

Voice Literary Supplement, October, 1987, review of *A Recent Martyr.*

Washington Post, January 17, 1990, review of *Mary Reilly,* p. D2; March 4, 1990, Elizabeth Castor, review of *Mary Reilly.*

Washington Post Book World, March 6, 1988, Marianne Gingher, review of *The Consolation of Nature, and Other Stories,* p. 9.

Women's Review of Books, July, 1990, review of *Mary Reilly,* p. 34.

ONLINE

AllReaders.com, http://www.allreaders.com/ (August 1, 2008), Althea Morin, synopsis of *Set in Motion.*

BookPage.com, http://www.bookpage.com/ (January 29, 2007), Becky Ohlsen, review of *Property;* (August 1, 2008) Alden Mudge, interview with Martin.

Curled Up with a Good Book, http://www.curledup.com/ (August 1, 2008), Luan Gaines, review of *Trespass.*

Guardian Unlimited, http://books.guardian.co.uk/ (June 4, 2003), John Ezard, "Turn-Up for the Books as Surprise Winner Takes Orange Fiction Prize"; (June 7, 2003) Valerie Martin, "Masters and Servants."

Mostly Fiction, http://mostlyfiction.com/ (August 1, 2008), profile of Martin.

Salon.com, http://www.salon.com/ (February 13, 2003), Laura Miller, review of *Property.*

STL Today, http://www.stltoday.com/ (August 1, 2008), Shirley K. Murray, review of *Trespass.**

*   *   *

MAYHEW, Margaret 1936-

PERSONAL: Born May 8, 1936, in London, England; married Philip Kaplan (a writer).

ADDRESSES: Home—Gloucestershire, England.

CAREER: Writer.

WRITINGS:

NOVELS

The Master of Aysgarth, Hamish Hamilton (London, England), 1976.

These Black Cormorants, Hale (London, England), 1976.

The Owlers, Hamish Hamilton (London, England), 1977.

The Railway King, Hamish Hamilton (London, England), 1979.

The Flame and the Furnace, Hamish Hamilton (London, England), 1981.

Bluebirds, Doubleday (London, England), 1993.

The Crew, Doubleday (London, England), 1997.

The Little Ship, Corgi (London, England), 1999.

Old Soldiers Never Die, Severn House (Sutton, England), 1999.

Our Yanks, Corgi (London, England), 2001, St. Martin's (New York, NY), 2002.

The Pathfinder, Severn House (Sutton, England), 2002.

Those in Peril, Corgi (London, England), 2003.

Rosebuds, Severn House (Sutton, England), 2004.

A Foreign Field, Severn House (Sutton, England), 2004.

Quadrille, Severn House (Sutton, England), 2005.

I'll Be Seeing You, Severn House (Sutton, England), 2007.

The Boat Girls, Bantam Press (New York, NY), 2007.

Three Silent Things, Severn House (Sutton, England), 2008.

The Other Side of Paradise, Bantam Press (New York, NY), 2009.

SIDELIGHTS: British author Margaret Mayhew has penned over a dozen novels since her first publication in 1976. Born May 8, 1936, in London, England, three years before the beginning of World War II, Mayhew formed vivid childhood memories of the bombing of the English capital by the Germans, and many of her novels deal with the events of that war and its aftermath. Mayhew's books often have romance and friendship at the center of their tales of men and women caught up in the turbulence and violence of wartime. In *The Little Ship,* for example, Mayhew presents a cast of young characters, English, Austrian, and German, who are friends and rivals before the war, and then in 1940 are tossed together again as the small boat they once sailed now becomes a lifeboat rescuing soldiers from Dunkirk. Reviewing the work in *Booklist,* Patty Engelmann noted that "Mayhew's gem of a book tells about childhood attachments and the upheaval of war."

Our Yanks was Mayhew's first book to be published in the United States. It tells the story of the confrontation of two uniquely different groups in England during World War II. When a U.S. Army Air Force fighter group is stationed near the small village of King's Thorpe, the stage is set for upheaval. The exuberant Americans affront many of the more reserved residents of this rural village, who have already experienced several years of war. However, there are also those on both sides who want to make this forced relationship work; romances and friendships develop between villagers and the American soldiers. "The process is often hilarious," noted Jeff Zaleski in *Publishers Weekly,* "despite the domestic dramas being played out against the grisly backdrop of war." Zaleski further praised Mayhew's "charming story" for presenting "poignant details of life in wartime England."

With *The Pathfinder* and *Rosebuds,* Mayhew focuses on the postwar world. In the former title, Michael Harrison is posted to Berlin, Germany, by the Royal Air Force in 1948 and is shocked by the destruction he finds there. Meeting a young German woman, he falls in love with her despite initial antagonisms on both sides. Yet the fact that she lives in the Russian sector does not make their romance any easier. Engelmann commended this "well-crafted" story in a *Booklist* review for providing "an insightful look at an overlooked facet of the post-World War II era." *Rosebuds* on the other hand, deals with postwar England through the lives of two best friends, Flora and Tally, who meet as ten year olds and come of age very differently during the 1950s. *Booklist* reviewer Emily Melton praised Mayhew's "realistic dialogue" and "appealing characters" in this "warm, engaging romance."

Mayhew offers another World War II romance in *Those in Peril,* a novel about the romance that develops between a French artist refugee from the Nazis and his new landlady, an attractive English widow. In a review for *Booklist,* Melton observed that Mayhew "writes winningly" about this era in a novel that is "a cut above the usual wartime romance saga." In *I'll Be Seeing You,* the action shifts to contemporary England, yet the war's shadow remains strong. Juliet Porter, mourning her mother's death as the novel begins, is shocked to discover a letter from her mother revealing that Juliet's father was really an American pilot stationed at an English air base. With no clues to the man's identity except a photograph, Juliet eventually goes to California to find her father. Melton, again writing in *Booklist,* deemed the novel "a charismatic combination of wartime drama, historical saga, and contemporary romance." Similarly well-received, *A Foreign Field* tells the story of an alcoholic journalist whose life is changed when he begins investigating claims that a Spitfire shot down during the war is still buried in rural Sussex.

Published in 2008, *Three Silent Things* brings back the character of "the colonel" from Mayhew's 1999 mystery novel *Old Soldiers Never Die.* He is still living in the Dorset village of Frog's End—where he retired to eleven years earlier after his wife, Laura, died. A year after the colonel moved to the village, he solved the murder of Lady Swynford and gained the respect of the villagers and the police. Now, he finds himself in the role of amateur sleuth again after he stumbles on the dead body of reclusive celebrity Lois Delaney while going door-to-door to collect money for the Save the Donkey fund. Although the police rule her death a suicide, the colonel is skeptical and sets out to uncover the real cause of her death. A *Kirkus Reviews* contributor was unsatisfied with *Three Silent Things,* noting that the author "has melded what might have been a classically cozy English whodunit with oddly dissonant bits of a mournful contemporary novel." Even so, *Booklist* reviewer Melton enjoyed the book, calling it "the best kind of village British cozy: warmhearted, gentle, and oh-so-English."

BIOGRAPHICAL AND CRITICAL SOURCES:

PERIODICALS

Booklist, March 1, 2003, Patty Engelmann, review of *The Pathfinder,* p. 1145; March 1, 2004, Patty Engelmann, review of *The Little Ship,* p. 1139; May 15, 2004, Emily Melton, review of *Rosebuds,* p. 1604; January 1, 2005, Emily Melton, review of *A Foreign Field,* p. 820; May 1, 2005, Emily Melton, review of *Quadrille,* p. 1574; April 1, 2006, Emily Melton, review of *I'll Be Seeing You,* p. 20; October 1, 2006, Emily Melton, review of *Those in Peril,* p. 44; November 15, 2008, Emily Melton, review of *Three Silent Things,* p. 22.

Kirkus Reviews, December 1, 2006, review of *Those in Peril,* p. 1193; October 1, 2008, review of *Three Silent Things.*

Publishers Weekly, January 14, 2002, Jeff Zaleski, review of *Our Yanks,* p. 40.

ONLINE

All about Romance Web site, http://www.likesbooks.com/ (July 1, 2004), Rachel Potter, review of *Our Yanks.**

*   *   *

McCARRICK, Chris Shea
   See GORMAN, Ed

*   *   *

McDEVITT, Jack 1935-
   (John Charles McDevitt)

PERSONAL: Born April 14, 1935, in Philadelphia, PA; son of John A. (a refinery worker) and Elizabeth (a homemaker) McDevitt; married Maureen McAdams (a teacher's aide), December 16, 1967; children: one daughter, two sons. *Education:* LaSalle College, B.A. 1957; Wesleyan University, M.A.L.S., 1971. *Hobbies and other interests:* Chess, astronomy.

ADDRESSES: Home and office—Brunswick, GA. *Agent*—Ralph Vicinanza, 303 W. 18th St., New York, NY 10011. *E-mail*—cryptic@gate.net.

CAREER: Writer, novelist, short-story writer, and educator. Woodrow Wilson High School, Levittown, PA, theater director and instructor in English and history, 1963-68; Mount St. Charles Academy, Woonsocket, RI, instructor in English, history, and theater, 1968-71; Newfound Memorial High School, Bristol, NH, English department chair, 1971-73; U.S. Customs Service, customs inspector in Pembina, ND, 1975-82, regional training officer in Chicago, IL, 1982-85, supervisor and management trainer specializing in motivational techniques and leadership at Federal Law Enforcement Training Center, Glynco, GA, 1985-95; full-time writer, 1995—. *Military service:* U.S. Navy, 1958-62; served in naval security group as a naval officer; earned commission.

MEMBER: U.S. Chess Federation, Science Fiction Writers of America, Military Officers Association of America.

AWARDS, HONORS: Locus Award, and Philip K. Dick Special Award, both 1987, both for *The Hercules Text;* Hugo Award nomination, 1988, for short story "The Fort Moxie Branch," and 1997, for novella "Time Travelers Never Die"; UPC Award, 1992, for novella "Ships in the Night," and 1994, for "Time Travellers Never Die"; Homer Award, 1997, for *Time Travellers Never Die;* John W. Campbell Award, 2004, for *Omega;* Nebula Award, 2007, for *Seeker;* thirteen additional Nebula nominations.

WRITINGS:

SCIENCE FICTION NOVELS

The Hercules Text (also see below), Ace Books (New York, NY), 1986.

A Talent for War (also see below), Ace Books (New York, NY), 1989.

The Engines of God, Ace Books (New York, NY), 1994.

Ancient Shores, HarperCollins (New York, NY), 1996.

Standard Candles (stories), Tachyon Publications (San Francisco, CA), 1996.

Eternity Road, HarperCollins (New York, NY), 1997.

Moonfall, HarperCollins (New York, NY), 1998.

Hello Out There (contains revision of *The Hercules Text* and *A Talent for War*), Meisha Merlin Atlantic (Stone Mountain, GA), 2000.

Infinity Beach, HarperCollins (New York, NY), 2000.

Deepsix, HarperCollins (New York, NY), 2001.

Chindi, Ace Books (New York, NY), 2002.

Omega, Ace Books (New York, NY), 2003.

Polaris, Ace Books (New York, NY), 2004.

Seeker, Ace Books (New York, NY), 2005.

Odyssey, Ace Books (New York, NY), 2006.

Outbound (collection of essays and fiction), Illinois Science Fiction in Chicago Press (Deerfield, IL), 2006.

Cauldron, Ace Books (New York, NY), 2007.

The Devil's Eye, Ace Books (New York, NY), 2008.

Time Travelers Never Die, Ace Books (New York, NY), 2009.

Contributor of short stories to magazines, including *Isaac Asimov's Science Fiction Magazine, Magazine of Fantasy and Science Fiction, Twilight Zone,* and *Full Spectrum.*

SIDELIGHTS: Although one of his childhood ambitions was to become a science fiction writer, Jack McDevitt did not realize his dream until he was in his forties. Prompted by his wife, Maureen, McDevitt wrote a short story, "The Emerson Effect," which was purchased by *Twilight Zone* magazine. Since then, McDevitt has produced numerous novels, as well as story contributions to periodicals; until 1995, McDevitt did this while working full-time for the U.S. Customs Service. In fact, his job in customs revived his interest in science fiction. While working the night shift as an inspector at his first post in Pembina, North Dakota, McDevitt stayed awake by reading science fiction novels. A town with a population of just six hundred, Pembina appears as Fort Moxie in several of McDevitt's short stories and in his novel *Ancient Shores.*

McDevitt is considered a "humanist" science fiction writer, as his stories typically place an ordinary person in unusual, sometimes threatening situations which often result from encounters with the unknown. As McDevitt once told *CA:* "I don't use antagonists (in the sense of villainous characters) in my writing. Each character thinks he/she is doing the right thing. The conflicts arise

from differences in perception." McDevitt also makes occasional use of religious themes in his fiction, exposing his characters to circumstances that challenge their belief systems. Said McDevitt: "I have no [religious] affiliation, but I enjoy creating situations in which characters must confront what they say they believe."

McDevitt's first novel, *The Hercules Text,* finds protagonist Harry Carmichael involved in a race with cold war Soviet scientists to decode information transmitted by extra-galactic aliens from a source in the Hercules constellation. Speculation that the transmission's data could have military applications has caused each government to scramble for the answers. Among the scientists assisting Carmichael in the processing of the information is a scientist and Catholic priest whose involvement with science may have cost him his faith. "The book," writes *Twentieth-Century Science Fiction Writers* contributor F. Brett Cox, "is a splendid example of what Algis Budrys has called the 'science-procedural novel,' concerning itself with the process of decoding the alien text and the power struggles that ensue as various scientific and governmental factions vie for control of the information contained in the transmission." Although the novel's emphasis "is on problem-solving," Cox states, "McDevitt does not neglect his characters, giving all the major figures believable lives whose individual quirks and problems are fully integrated into the central problem of the Hercules Text." McDevitt told *CA:* "In a revised version for the Meisha Merlin omnibus volume *Hello Out There,* the Cold War is gone, but the concerns with general release of technologically advanced information remain central to the action."

In McDevitt's second novel, *A Talent for War,* which is set thousands of years in the future, a young man named Alex Benedict quests for the truth about an adored war hero, whom he suspects was a fraud. "The bulk of the novel," Cox explains, "traces Benedict's journey from planet to planet as he investigates the problem; as he pieces the puzzle together, the most important people are not the soldiers who fought the war, as much as the historians and poets who witnessed the events and recorded them." The author's third book, *The Engines of God,* similarly revolves around a people's search for understanding of seemingly inexplicable events, this time the discovery of a mysterious formation on a moon orbiting a distant world.

The novel *Ancient Shores* is set in motion by an ordinary man's discovery of a quite remarkable artifact. In the story, a North Dakota wheat farmer, while clearing a field, unearths a sea vessel in perfect condition. Scientific tests reveal that the boat has a carbon number so high that its materials will never decompose. "Within weeks," wrote Carl Hays in *Booklist,* "the boat becomes a media sensation coveted by prospective buyers and scientists." In a very short time, "the national economy verges on collapse because the materials from which the artifacts are made seem to wear forever: obsolescence in goods made from the stuff will be obsolete," Hays concluded. "Right up to the climax," stated a *Publishers Weekly* critic, "McDevitt . . . tells his complex and suspenseful story with meticulous attention to detail, deft characterizations, and graceful prose."

Eternity Road is the story—set in a future world that has been decimated by a viral plague—of an expedition to recover some of the knowledge left behind by the people who built the great road system of North America. "McDevitt redeems the possible overfamiliarity of his quest plot," stated Roland Green in *Booklist,* "with a large cast of well-handled, original characters, starting with the principal protagonist, silversmith Chaka Milana." *Eternity Road,* Green concluded, "is eminently readable and a real credit to McDevitt."

"In *Infinity Beach,*" McDevitt explained, "humans have decided that either intelligent species are extremely rare, or that humanity is alone. But a mission that went out twenty years ago *may* have found something. If so, it's being kept quiet." In the novel, scientist Kim Brandywine is familiar with the ill-fated mission of the starship Hunter. She is suspicious that the explorers on the vessel found extraterrestrial life but the discovery is being suppressed for reasons unknown. She also suspects that the Hunter mission is somehow connected to the disappearance of her clone-sister, and that a strange presence appearing on the planet Greenway also has connections to the troubled starship. To answer the questions that haunt her, Brandywine must risk her life, her lover, and her reputation in her determined search for the truth. "Exquisitely timed revelations maximize suspense, and fine characterization and world building also hold the reader's interest," noted Green in a *Booklist* review. McDevitt has "created a future that is technologically sound and filled with hubristic, foolish people" whose choices are concerned more with image and the opinion of history rather than the actual benefit to society, commented a *Publishers Weekly* reviewer. "This is a wonderful mix of science-based fiction, mystery, and romance, with loads of action" and suspense, remarked *School Library Journal* reviewer Pam Johnson.

In *Deepsix,* the world of the year 2223 is about to be witness to a spectacular celestial event: the collision of planet Maleiva III, also known as Deepsix, with a rogue gas giant, Morgan's World. A collection of scientists, civilians, tourists, and reporters have gathered to observe the planetary impact. A previous mission to Deepsix, intended to search for intelligent life, was aborted when it was attacked by vicious birds. In the face of the impending collision and destruction, new findings suggest that not only life, but an established civilization exists on the surface of Deepsix. Starship pilot Priscilla "Hutch" Hutchins leads a mission to investigate the landmarks on Deepsix before its destruction. When an earthquake destroys the mission lander, the team is stranded on the world, and faces a harrowing trip across the surface of Deepsix to find a workable lander left by the previous expedition nearly two decades earlier. In the meantime, they must still do all they can to solve the mystery of the world's apparently vanished civilization. "McDevitt's captivating scenario plays out in a surprisingly relaxed, straightforward manner," remarked *Booklist* critic Bryan Baldus. "McDevitt puts his characters into predictable jeopardies while methodically solving the conundrum of the missing aliens," commented a *Publishers Weekly* contributor. Reviewer Paul Brink, writing in *School Library Journal,* noted that "the well-rounded characters grow through their adventures, without that growth seeming trite or inevitable." *Library Journal* critic Jackie Cassada commented favorably on McDevitt's "expert sense of pacing and a knack for cliffhanging suspense."

Chindi, the sequel to *Deepsix,* finds "Hutch" Hutchins on board for another mission. A brief transmission from the vicinity of a neutron star has attracted the attention of the Contact Society, which believes the broadcast must have come from an intelligent alien source. Hutch is selected to act as pilot and archaeologist for the mission. When the expedition arrives at the neutron star, they confirm the transmission but find no aliens. Instead, three hidden satellites are found to be sending data to an unknown source in a distant star system. As the story unfolds, more of these stealth satellites are discovered orbiting other worlds, including Earth. When a friend of Hutch's snags one of the satellites and takes it on board for inspection, the ship is destroyed by its explosion. Determined to uncover the mystery behind the satellites, Hutch and a group of colleagues set out on a mission where they find a world suffering from the aftermath of nuclear war. Inexplicably, in a far-flung star system, they explore a moon where they find a seemingly normal house containing objects, books, and a grave. Along with these strange findings, they also detect a huge, ominously silent alien spaceship refueling in the vicinity. "First contact is McDevitt's favorite theme, and he's also good at creating large and rather spectacular astronomical phenomena," observed a contributor to *Publishers Weekly*. Within the novel, "the puzzles wrapped in explanations within mysteries and cliffhanging resolution are well up to McDevitt's previous high standards," commented a *Kirkus Reviews* contributor. In his assessment of the novel, Green mused: "This one is really quite splendid." *Library Journal* reviewer Jackie Cassada called the novel "first-rate sf adventure" characterized by "smooth, well-plotted storytelling."

Omega, set in the same future universe as *Deepsix* and *Chindi,* brings Earth and other inhabited worlds into contact with the massively destructive "Omega cloud:" huge waves of energy with the power to destroy entire planets and devastate civilizations. An Omega cloud is discovered heading toward Earth, though its arrival is many years distant, giving scientists the opportunity to discover ways to divert it. Meanwhile, another cloud approaches a known populated world inhabited by the Korbikkan, a primitive but intelligent alien species. A desperate and daring expedition sets out from Earth in hopes of saving the endangered world, and also with the intention of finding out enough about the Omega effect to create a workable defense for Earth. McDevitt explores the ethical nature of altruism as the population of Earth wonders if it can spare the resources to save the Korbikkan in the face of its own impending peril. McDevitt "forges out of ethical dilemmas a plot as gripping as any action fan could want," commented Green in *Booklist*. McDevitt's characters "succeed in imposing their compassion on the void," observed a *Publishers Weekly* reviewer.

Polaris presents "another space mystery for antiquarian sleuths to resolve," noted a *Kirkus Reviews* contributor. The starship Polaris, populated with a group of scientists, celebrities, and other notables, has traveled to observe the spectacular cosmic event of an ordinary sun being torn apart by a dense neutron star. The ship is later reported to be returning home to Earth by pilot Maddy English, but it never arrives. Later, the Polaris is found adrift, its artificial intelligence systems shut off and all personnel gone. Six decades later, artifacts from the storied ship have turned up for sale. Antiquities dealer Alex Benedict buys a few, but the rest are destroyed in a suspicious explosion. Later, Alex's house is burglarized, with the thief managing to steal a blouse once owned by Maddy English. As the story progresses,

Alex realizes that someone has a great interest in artifacts from the Polaris, and is going to great lengths to find and recover them even while carefully concealing his or her identity. As Alex and assistant Chase Kolpath step up their investigation of the fate of the Polaris's passengers, they find their lives in danger. "This SF mystery's smooth and exciting surface makes it difficult to appreciate how exceptionally good it is at combining action and ideas," commented a *Publishers Weekly* reviewer. Cassada, in a *Library Journal* review, observed that the novel is characterized by "stellar plotting, engaging characters, and a mastery of storytelling."

In *Seeker,* Alex Benedict and Chase Kolpath encounter an ancient artifact that leads them to investigate the fate of a vanished, possibly legendary, colony of Earth people from nine millennia in the past. When Alex finds an unusual old cup inscribed with English characters, he believes it is from the Seeker, one of two transport ships that supposedly carried a group of 5,000 colonists away from Earth's religious dictatorship in the twenty-seventh century. Almost ninety centuries later, most believe the Seeker and the colonists' destination, the planet Margolia, to be a myth. However, Alex and Chase uncover information that leads them to believe that the Seeker exists and was discovered by two space survey employees, who concealed their discovery but died in an accident before they could take any further steps. Alex asks the assistance of the telepathic alien Mutes to recover the Seeker's original log. With determined effort, Alex and Chase manage to pinpoint the location of the Seeker, now an ancient derelict adrift with destroyed engines. More intriguing, however, is the fact that the star system where the Seeker drifts also contains a habitable world that may be the mysterious Margolia. "This novel delivers everything it promises—with a galactic wallop," remarked a *Publishers Weekly* reviewer.

Hutch returns in *Odyssey,* along with two new female characters. They are fifteen-year-old Amy Taylor, the fiery daughter of a senator, and pilot Valentina Kouros. Also returning is Gregory MacAllister, with whom Hutch has formed a friendship in spite of the fact that MacAllister has called for a decrease in the funding of space projects, as well as the dismantling of Hutch's department. He and Kouros face off on a talk show during which they debate these issues. Kouros also transports Amy, MacAllister, and Eric Samuel of the Academy through space in an attempt to prove the existence of the Moonriders. Steven H. Silver, writing for

SF Site online, noted: "While this could easily have turned into a laundry list of places, McDevitt successfully brings the wonder of the universe to the pages of Odyssey painting virtual Hubble images with his descriptions."

Silver also reviewed *Cauldron,* set in the year 2255, commenting that while it "does stand on its own quite well, knowledge of the five earlier novels will add depth and texture to the events McDevitt describes." The prologue that precedes the main part of the novel is set seven decades earlier. "One of the things which makes this such a depressing scenario is how closely it mirrors the current state of manned space exploration," wrote Silver. Hutch is now working a desk job as the interest in space travel wanes. Rudy Golombek, director of the Prometheus Foundation, wants to keep the dream alive, and at the urging of physicist Jon Silvestri, who claims to have produced a star drive that makes instantaneous travel possible, he arranges a journey involving two ships to prove the theory. Those involved include Golombek, Silvestri, Hutch, former pilot Matt Darwin, and science journalist Antonio Giannotti. The destination is the heart of the galaxy, with its stars, omega clouds, and the Cauldron, an enormous black hole. After a disappointment the trip goes forward. "Not peak McDevitt—slow to develop and not especially surprising—but workmanlike and brimming with the author's trademark low-key charms," concluded a *Kirkus Reviews* contributor. Silver wrote: "For all that Cauldron draws on McDevitt's earlier novels, everything a reader needs to know to enter his wonder-filled world is included in the book." Cassada noted in *Library Journal* that the novels of this series reflect McDevitt's "talent for character building and seamlessly blending hard science with sf action/adventure."

John Joseph Adams, who interviewed McDevitt on *Sci-Fi.com,* commented: "There's a Stephen King blurb on your books that says you are 'the logical heir to Isaac Asimov and Arthur C. Clarke.' Do you feel as though you're continuing in their tradition? And did you set out to do that?" McDevitt answered: "I set out, as I suspect most of us do, to write the kind of books and stories I liked to read. I can't make a judgment beyond that. That's for someone else to do. King paid me a substantial compliment and I'd like to think it's so. But however that may be, I'll take it and run."

In *The Devil's Eye,* antiquities dealer Alex Benedict receives a message from a famous writer, who presents him with an unusual challenge. Benedict accepts the challenge, but by the time he does the writer's memory has been erased, and she can recall nothing. Benedict soon finds himself on an adventure outside of the galaxy, uncovering secrets that someone is desperately trying to hide. A *Publishers Weekly* contributor commented: "McDevitt balances the two sides of his story well."

Commenting on the human and spiritual elements of his stories, McDevitt told a *Locus* interviewer: "Anything that's intelligent almost by definition is going to want to explain its existence. That gets you into the area of myth, into religious cycles. I would expect that if you could go back far enough with any intelligent species, assuming there are others, you'd find religious systems. The real question might be, what becomes of the religious systems, in time? Maybe you toss those over the side. If science is the new religion, science fiction is maybe the new mythology. I think science fiction is a more noble effort at resolving some of these issues than religion ever was anyhow." Summarizing his attraction to his chosen genre, McDevitt told *CA:* "I've always enjoyed a good mystery. Science fiction allows considerable space for this technique, not the classic whodunit, but rather a what-could-possibly-have-happened-here?

"I never knew a time when I wasn't thinking about writing. Somewhere around eight years old, I started *The Canals of Mars.* Fortunately, I got sidetracked."

On his influences, McDevitt commented: "Among novelists, probably John Dos Passos. Not sure how good the application is, but I learned a lot from reading *U.S.A.* Among SF writers, Ray Bradbury.

"[The] hardest part of the process, for me, is coming up with the initial concept. Once I have that, the novel pretty well writes itself. This is especially true if the base idea involves a mystery. E.g., three starships go out to watch a stellar collision. Two return. The third one announces 'departure imminent.' But it never arrives. A rescue unit finds the ship adrift with everyone missing. But the pressure suits are still on board. As is the lander. The local planetary system no longer has a sun. So there's no place to go. And no aliens in the area.

"The trick is to come up with a solution that makes sense, that doesn't draw on some sort of hyper technology. Something that, when the truth is revealed, the reader will say, 'Sure, I should have seen it coming.' This is the general approach for the Alex Benedict mysteries. The truth about the missing passengers, by the way, can be found in *Polaris.*

"Most of us are smarter than we think. We spend our early years being told what we have done wrong ('don't touch that you'll break it') and after a while we begin to believe it. To succeed as a writer, and pretty much as anything else, you have to get past that mindset.

"I just want people to enjoy reading [my books]. I'll settle for that. Readers periodically tell me they would never have become physicists or doctors or whatever had it not been for the fact that they got hooked on SF as kids. That's nice to hear. It's a bonus, but I'm pretty sure they'd have taken time to look past the rooftops anyhow."

BIOGRAPHICAL AND CRITICAL SOURCES:

BOOKS

Twentieth-Century Science Fiction Writers, 3rd edition, St. James Press (Chicago, IL), 1991.

PERIODICALS

Booklist, September 15, 1994, Carl Hayes, review of *The Engines of God,* p. 118; April 15, 1996, Carl Hays, review of *Ancient Shores,* p. 1425; May 15, 1997, Roland Green, review of *Eternity Road,* p. 1567; April, 1998, John Mort, review of *Moonfall,* p. 1307; January 1, 1999, p. 781; February 15, 2000, Roland Green, review of *Infinity Beach,* p. 1091; February 15, 2001, Bryan Baldus, review of *Deepsix,* p. 1122; July, 2002, Roland Green, review of *Chindi,* p. 1833; October 15, 2003, Roland Green, review of *Omega,* p. 399; November 1, 2004, Roland Green, review of *Polaris,* p. 472; November 1, 2005, Roland Green, review of *Seeker,* p. 32; October 1, 2006, Carl Hays, review of *Odyssey,* p. 45; November 1, 2007, Carl Hays, review of *Cauldron,* p. 33.

Kirkus Reviews, April 15, 2002, review of *Chindi,* p. 533; September 15, 2004, review of *Polaris,* p. 896; September 1, 2005, review of *Seeker,* p. 947; September 15, 2006, review of *Odyssey,* p. 934; September 15, 2007, review of *Cauldron.*

Library Journal, May 15, 1997, Susan Hamburger, review of *Eternity Road,* p. 106; April 15, 1998, Jackie Cassada, review of *Moonfall,* p. 118; February 15, 2000, Jackie Cassada, review of *Infinity Beach,* p. 201; March 15, 2001, Jackie Cassada, review of *Deepsix,* p. 110; January, 2002, Rex Klett, Jackie Cassada, and Kristin Ramsdell, review of *Deepsix,* p. 51; July, 2002, Jackie Cassada, review of *Chindi,* p. 127; November 15, 2003, Jackie Cassada, review of *Omega,* p. 101; November 15, 2004, Jackie Cassada, review of *Polaris,* p. 54; October 15, 2005, Jackie Cassada, review of *Seeker,* p. 50; October 15, 2006, Jackie Cassada, review of *Odyssey,* p. 54; January 1, 2007, Jackie Cassada, review of *Odyssey,* p. 50; November 15, 2007, Jackie Cassada, review of *Cauldron,* p. 53; November 15, 2008, Jackie Cassada, review of *The Devil's Eye,* p. 63.

Locus, February, 1995, interview with McDevitt, p. 4.

New York Times Book Review, March 7, 2004, Gerald Jonas, review of *Omega.*

Publishers Weekly, March 25, 1996, review of *Ancient Shores,* p. 67; April 21, 1997, review of *Eternity Road,* p. 65; February 23, 1998, review of *Moonfall,* p. 56; January 31, 2000, review of *Infinity Beach,* p. 86; February 26, 2001, review of *Deepsix;* June 24, 2002, review of *Chindi,* p. 44; October 13, 2003, review of *Omega,* p. 62; September 20, 2004, review of *Polaris,* p. 50; September 5, 2005, review of *Seeker,* p. 39; September 24, 2007, review of *Cauldron,* p. 49; September 22, 2008, review of *The Devil's Eye,* p. 42.

School Library Journal, July, 2000, Pam Johnson, review of *Infinity Beach,* p. 128; August, 2001, Paul Brink, review of *Deepsix,* p. 209.

ONLINE

Jack McDevitt Home Page, http://www.jackmcdevitt. com (March 10, 2007).

SciFi.com, http://www.scifi.com/ (January 1, 2007), John Joseph Adams, interview.

SF Site, http://www.sfsite.com/ (August 24, 2008), Steven H. Silver, reviews of *Odyssey* and *Cauldron.*

*   *   *

McDEVITT, John Charles
See McDEVITT, Jack

McNAMER, Deirdre 1950-

PERSONAL: Born October 17, 1950. *Education:* University of Montana, B.A., 1973, M.F.A., 1987; fellow at University of Michigan, Ann Arbor, 1982-83.

ADDRESSES: Home—Missoula, MT. *Office*—Department of English, LA 116, University of Montana, Missoula, MT 59812; fax: 406-243-4076. *E-mail*—deirdre. mcnamer@mso.umt.edu.

CAREER: University of Montana, Missoula, professor of creative writing. Instructor at University of Oregon, Cornell University, University of Alabama, Williams College, and Thurber House, Columbus, OH. Worked as a journalist.

AWARDS, HONORS: National Endowment for the Humanities fellowship for professional journalists.

WRITINGS:

Rima in the Weeds (novel), HarperCollins (New York, NY), 1991.
One Sweet Quarrel (historical novel), HarperCollins (New York, NY), 1994.
My Russian (novel), Houghton Mifflin (Boston, MA), 1999.
Red Rover (novel), Viking (New York, NY), 2007.

Contributor of short stories, articles, and reviews to the *New Yorker, New York Times Magazine, Outside, Ploughshares,* and *DoubleTake.*

SIDELIGHTS: Deirdre McNamer once commented that her "primary aim as an author is to leave the reader feeling amplified, entranced, wiser and wanting more." When writing she sees herself as her primary audience. She once wrote: "I try to make what I write interesting, musical, compelling to myself. Then I try to put myself in the place of astute readers—those who come fresh to the material and bring with them curiosity, a sense of humor, critical faculties, appreciation for a story well-told, and language that moves." Listing her primary influences as Alice Munro, Edna O'Brien, Eudora Welty, Louise Erdrich, and Flannery O'Connor, McNamer told *CA:* "What I admire most about them is their combination of boldness and precision, their shadowy humor, and the presence in their writing of a certain faith in the intangible."

McNamer's first three novels were well received by critics. Several reviewers commented on the way McNamer progresses in telling her story. "McNamer does lovely things with point of view—running through a scene, stopping, backing up, then playing it through again from a different angle of vision," observed Carol Anshaw in a Chicago *Tribune Book* assessment of McNamer's first novel, *Rima in the Weeds.* New York Times *Book Review* contributor Robert Houston also noted McNamer's non-chronological method of presenting the life-span of the Malone family in *One Sweet Quarrel,* commenting that McNamer "allow[s] those lives to come to us as our own memories do, in fragments, moments, rediscovered letters. Ms. McNamer fractures time at will by leaping from present tense to past to no tense at all—sometimes just giving us rapid, snapshot-like images. . . . As a result, history becomes what it truly is in our lives; not an orderly sequence of time, but a collection of times." Houston reported that, although for some this style might prove frustrating at times and her detailed descriptions may occasionally "overwhelm the story," McNamer succeeds by using "marvelous prose" to present a "vivid" portrait. Susan Bolotin, in her *New York Times Book Review* critique of McNamer's next novel, *My Russian,* similarly noted: "McNamer is a careful writer, a master of the small, telling observation, but her plotting slows things down."

My Russian is set in an unnamed Northwest college town and is the story of a misreported crime that involves issues of class. Bolotin further described the work as an "intimate" tale "of character played out against the largest of social backdrops." Unknown to her family, protagonist Francesca Woodbridge returns home early from her solo, identity-altering vacation. She remains in hiding while secretly observing her husband and son, and remembering and analyzing her life in order to gain a new perspective. "Her compulsion to see herself from the outside in doesn't feel like a falling apart; instead, it's more like a coming together—the need to meld self and identity that one usually associates with coming of age. And this is what I like most about *My Russian,*" wrote Bolotin. In addition to being "honest, straightforward, and clear," observed Michelle Kaske in *Booklist,* "Francesca's storytelling feels like a longtime friend confessing over coffee." Yvette Weller Olson also felt that Francesca is "a character to care about." Olson "highly recommended" *My Russian* in *Library Journal,* calling it "a bold, splendid novel . . . piercingly intuitive . . . provocative, compelling story." A *Publishers Weekly* reviewer concluded: "Other than a few moments of stilted dialogue, the narrative pulses and flows like good poetry—and its searing portrait of the consequences of choosing comfort over desire is memorable."

Red Rover is a fictional account of the death of McNamer's uncle. He joined the FBI and, during World War II, he was sent to Argentina on an undercover assignment. After the war ended, he was found dead in his apartment in Missoula, Montana. The coroner told the newspaper that his death by gunshot wound to the head was a suicide, but the death certificate cited it as being an accident. McNamer also noted the gunshot as being in a different location. The family was told it was a suicide, and only later learned that the FBI deemed the death an accident. The actual cause never became clear, and in this novel, McNamer creates a scenario of what might have happened.

The story opens in 1927, with Aidan Tierney and his brother Neil traveling on horseback to see Charles Lindbergh, who is touring the country and stopping in Montana. As Sven Birkerts noted in a *New York Times Book Review*, this is how McNamer introduces the "landscape of her storytelling—the closely observed Montana terrain, where so much of the novel's action will take place, and the untethered, almost speculative air space marked by history and vast ambition. From the moment of the sighting, she works with inventive narrative freedom, cutting sharply between various time periods, including sections in the near-present in which the surviving characters have grown old and are themselves subject to the time-bending torsions of memory." Aidan, the older brother, will die by gunshot, and Neil, who becomes a pilot, will live to old age, tormented by his brother's death. In between these two time periods, McNamer writes of both their lives and of Aidan's illness caused by a mysterious disease. Mary Ann Gwinn reviewed *Red Rover* for the *Seattle Times Online*, commenting that like McNamer's other books, this fourth novel "is lyrical, insightful and woven with vivid characterization and sense of place." Keir Graff concluded his *Booklist* review by writing: "Elegant and assured, with a joy in language that shows on every page."

BIOGRAPHICAL AND CRITICAL SOURCES:

BOOKS

Contemporary Literary Criticism, Volume 70: *Yearbook 1991,* Gale (Detroit, MI), 1992.

PERIODICALS

Booklist, January 15, 1991, review of *Rima in the Weeds,* p. 1007; February 1, 1994, Donna Seaman, review of *One Sweet Quarrel,* p. 994; September 1, 1997, review of *Rima in the Weeds,* p. 65; May 15, 1999, Michelle Kaske, review of *My Russian,* p. 1669; July 1, 2007, Keir Graff, review of *Red Rover,* p. 29.

Boston Phoenix, June, 1991, review of *Rima in the Weeds.*

Elle, June, 1991, review of *Rima in the Weeds,* p. 88.

Entertainment Weekly, August 24, 2007, Karen Valby, review of *Red Rover,* p. 137.

Kirkus Reviews, November 15, 1990, review of *Rima in the Weeds,* p. 1563; February 1, 1994, review of *One Sweet Quarrel,* p. 90.

Library Journal, January, 1991, Thomas Kilpatrick, review of *Rima in the Weeds,* p. 154; September 1, 1991, review of *Rima in the Weeds,* p. 268; February 15, 1994, Jane S. Bakerman, review of *One Sweet Quarrel,* p. 184; April 15, 1999, Yvette Weller Olson, review of *My Russian,* p. 144; June 1, 2007, Amy Ford, review of *Red Rover,* p. 110.

Los Angeles Times Book Review, February 8, 1991, review of *Rima in the Weeds,* p. E12; May 1, 1994, review of *One Sweet Quarrel,* p. 3.

Missoulian, March 8, 1991, review of *Rima in the Weeds,* p. E14.

New York Times Book Review, February 17, 1991, Ron Carlson, review of *Rima in the Weeds,* p. 9; February 2, 1992, review of *Rima in the Weeds,* p. 28; July 17, 1994, Robert Houston, review of *One Sweet Quarrel,* p. 9; December 4, 1994, review of *One Sweet Quarrel,* p. 71; April 2, 1995, review of *One Sweet Quarrel,* p. 24; July 11, 1999, Susan Bolotin, review of *My Russian,* p. 18; September 16, 2007, Sven Birkerts, review of *Red Rover.*

Publishers Weekly, December 14, 1990, review of *Rima in the Weeds,* p. 53; January 1, 1992, review of *Rima in the Weeds,* p. 53; February 28, 1994, review of *One Sweet Quarrel,* p. 74; April 12, 1999, review of *My Russian,* p. 52; May 14, 2007, review of *Red Rover,* p. 30.

San Diego Union, February 17, 1991, review of *Rima in the Weeds.*

San Francisco Review of Books, annual edition, 1994, review of *One Sweet Quarrel,* p. 10.

Tribune Books (Chicago, IL), February 24, 1991, Carol Anshaw, review of *Rima in the Weeds,* p. 1; February 16, 1992, review of *Rima in the Weeds,* p. 2.

Women's Review of Books, July, 1991, review of *Rima in the Weeds,* p. 40; July, 1994, Linda Niemann, review of *One Sweet Quarrel,* p. 47.

ONLINE

Los Angeles Times Online, http://www.latimes.com/ (May 12, 2008), Susan Reynolds, review of *Red Rover.*

New West, http://www.newwest.com/ (August 20, 2007), Jenny Shank, review of *Red Rover,* 'An Interview with Deirdre McNamer.''

Seattle Times Online, http://seattletimes.nwsource.com/ (August 10, 2007), Mary Ann Gwinn, review of *Red Rover.**

*   *   *

McWILLIAMS, James E. 1968-

PERSONAL: Born November 28, 1968. *Education:* Georgetown University, B.A., 1991; University of Texas, Austin, M.Ed., 1994; Harvard University, M.A., 1996; Johns Hopkins University, Ph.D., 2001.

ADDRESSES: Office—Texas State University, San Marcos, Department of History, San Marcos, TX 78666. *E-mail*—jm71@txstate.edu.

CAREER: Texas State University, San Marcos, assistant professor of history, 2003—; Yale University, New Haven, CT, associate fellow in the Agrarian Studies Program, 2007-08. Visiting assistant professor, Southwest Texas State University, 2000-03; scholar-in-residence, Peabody Essex Museum, Salem, MA, 2002.

AWARDS, HONORS: Fellowships from Johns Hopkins University, 1997-2001, Harvard Business School, 2000-01, and the University of Illinois at Urbana-Champaign, 2000-01; Walter Muir Whitehall Prize in Early American History, Colonial Society of Massachusetts, 2001; travel grant, International Association of Culinary Professionals Foundation, 2003; research grant, Harvard University; AltWeekly Award for arts criticism, Association of Alternative Newsweeklies, 2004.

WRITINGS:

A Revolution in Eating: How the Quest for Food Shaped America, Columbia University Press (New York, NY), 2005.

From the Ground Up: Internal Economic Development in the Seventeenth-century Massachusetts Bay Region, 1630-1700, University of Virginia Press (Charlottesville, VA), 2005.

Building the Bay Colony: Local Economy and Culture in Early Massachusetts, University of Virginia Press (Charlottesville, VA), 2007.

American Pests: The Losing War on Insects from Colonial Times to DDT, Columbia University Press (New York, NY), 2008.

Just Food: Where Locavores Get It Wrong and How We Can Truly Eat Responsibly, Little Brown and Company (New York, NY), 2009.

Contributor to books, including *Cultures and Identities in Colonial British America,* edited by Alan Tully and Robert Olwell, Johns Hopkins University Press, 2005, and *Recent Themes in Early American History: Historians in Conversation,* edited by Donald A. Yerxa, University of South Carolina Press, 2008. Contributor to periodicals, including *Texas Observer, Southwestern Historical Quarterly, Southwestern American Literature, Maryland Historical, Publishers Weekly, New England Quarterly, Maryland Historical, Journal of Interdisciplinary History, Austin-American Statesman, Los Angeles Times, Chronicle of Higher Education, Christian Science Monitor, San Antonio Express-News,* and *USA Today.*

SIDELIGHTS: Historian James E. McWilliams documents how settlers in North America adapted to one aspect of their new environment in *A Revolution in Eating: How the Quest for Food Shaped America,* a book described as "delicious from start to finish" by a *Kirkus Reviews* contributor. McWilliams writes that although they attempted to duplicate the gardens of their native England, settlers in the Massachusetts Bay Colony who were unable to grow wheat eventually accepted the corn grown by Native Americans, even though that grain was used only for feeding livestock in England. This was an embarrassment to those who wanted to continue the dietary mores of their homeland. Although colonists further south had the benefit of better weather and soils, it took them longer to become self-sufficient. No gardens were planted in Jamestown until three years after it was settled, and the residents made other choices to ward off starvation. Much of their energy went into planting tobacco, a highly valued cash crop. When the Virginians did begin to develop their agriculture, they cared less than their Northern neighbors about the perception that they were eating pig food (corn). They also tended to have other people do their work for them, beginning with Natives, then indentured white servants, and finally slaves. Grains grown for the production of alcohol became an important component of the agrarian society, which was a factor in the establishment of trade routes. *Library Journal* reviewer Courtney Greene wrote that *A Revolution in Eating* is "meticulously researched and packed with fascinating detail." *Building the Bay Colony: Local Economy and Culture in Early Massachusetts* is a history of how the Puritans of Massachusetts, who found it difficult to grow commercial crops, became merchants, a trade that they had viewed skeptically before they began to experience the considerable profits trans-Atlantic trade brought them.

American Pests: The Losing War on Insects from Colonial Times to DDT is McWilliams's study of pest management in the United States. He notes that early settlers not only had to deal with pests they brought with them but also with those with which they were totally unfamiliar. He provides a history of the spread of insects that feed on crops, caused to a great extent by the harvesting of timber, development, and monoculture. He notes that "the professional fight against insects" began in 1841 with the publication of a book written for farmers by self-taught entomologist Thaddeus William Harris. Some of the pests that plagued farmers included the hornworm (tobacco) and weevils (wheat), as well as the Colorado potato beetle and cinch bugs that were spread by trains and barges. The U.S. Department of Agricultural added an entomology division, but biological methods of control were soon discarded in favor of pesticide use. DDT, which was used effectively for the elimination of mosquitoes that carried malaria, was used more broadly and became the subject of Rachel Carson's *Silent Spring*, the early warning about the dangers of pesticides. Finally, McWilliams covers pest management today, emphasizing how government regulation has influenced current practices. *Library Journal* reviewer Marianne Stowell wrote that McWilliams "gives each event thorough coverage and enough facets to put the story on a human scale." A *Publishers Weekly* contributor concluded that the book is "well written" and "thorough and should appeal to readers interested in history as well as environmental issues."

BIOGRAPHICAL AND CRITICAL SOURCES:

BOOKS

McWilliams, James E., *American Pests: The Losing War on Insects from Colonial Times to DDT,* Columbia University Press (New York, NY), 2008.

PERIODICALS

Entertainment Weekly, August 12, 2005, Tina Jordan, review of *A Revolution in Eating: How the Quest for Food Shaped America,* p. 83.
Kirkus Reviews, May 1, 2005, review of *A Revolution in Eating,* p. 526.
Library Journal, May 15, 2005, Courtney Greene, review of *A Revolution in Eating,* p. 139; June 1, 2008, Marianne Stowell, review of *American Pests: The Losing War on Insects from Colonial Times to DDT,* p. 121.
Publishers Weekly, April 25, 2005, review of *A Revolution in Eating,* p. 45; May 19, 2008, review of *American Pests,* p. 48.
Reference & Research Book News, May, 2008, review of *Building the Bay Colony: Local Economy and Culture in Early Massachusetts.*
Washington Monthly, June, 2005, Alan Bjerga, review of *A Revolution in Eating,* p. 53.*

*   *   *

MEANEY, John 1957-

PERSONAL: Born 1957, in London, England; married. *Education:* Attended Birmingham University; graduated from Open University; Oxford University, postgraduate studies. *Hobbies and other interests:* Martial arts.

ADDRESSES: Home—Kent, England.

CAREER: Writer. Part-time instructor in the computer field teaching computer systems.

AWARDS, HONORS: Independent Publishers Book of the Year, SF/Fantasy category, for *Paradox.*

WRITINGS:

To Hold Infinity, Bantam/Transworld (London, England), 1998, Pyr (Amherst, NY), 2006.
Bone Song ("Donal Riordan" series), Gollancz (London, England), 2007, Bantam Books (New York, NY), 2008.
Dark Blood ("Donal Riordan" series), Gollancz (London, England), 2008, published as *Black Blood,* Bantam Books (New York, NY), 2009.

"NULAPEIRON SEQUENCE" SERIES

Paradox, Bantam/Transworld (London, England), 2000, Pyr (Amherst, NY), 2005.

Resolution, Bantam/Transworld (London, England), 2000, Pyr (Amherst, NY), 2006.

Context, Bantam/Transworld (London, England), 2002, Pyr (Amherst, NY), 2005.

Also author of short story "Sharp Tang"; work represented in anthologies, including *The Best of Interzone,* Voyager, 1997; *Year's Best SF #20,* edited by Gardner Dozois; and *Year's Best Short Novels 2004,* edited by Jonathan Strahan. Contributor of fiction to periodicals, including *Interzone;* maintains a blog.

SIDELIGHTS: John Meaney has gained renown as part of a new wave of important British science-fiction writers. In his novel *To Hold Infinity,* Meaney, who also works in the computer systems field, tells the story of a world where people's brains are augmented with computer technology. The book's success led to Meaney's "Nulapeiron Sequence," a trilogy that takes place in a far-future world where there is a strict dividing line between the rich and the poor, all of whom live on different subterranean levels—with the poor at the deeper levels. The world is ruled by the Logic Lords and Oracles who live mentally both in the past and the future and who can predict, or "truecast," the future. This ability is channeled by the Logic Lords to keep the poor in their place by declaring that everything is preordained and that there is no revolution in the future.

In *Paradox,* the first book in the "Nulapeiron Sequence" series, Meaney introduces readers to Tom Corcorigan, a poor boy who comes into possession of an info-crystal once the property of a member of the Pilots, a legendary race able to traverse the fractal universe known as "mu-space." When an Oracle abducts Tom's mother and Tom's father dies, Tom studies the crystal carefully and discovers that it contains not only a way for him to move up in society but also the key to his revenge. A *Publishers Weekly,* contributor commented that in *Paradox,* "Intriguing ruminations on the nature of time mesh well with Meaney's fine plotting and his excellent world building." Jackie Cassada, writing in *Library Journal,* called the book "a treat for those who enjoy logic puzzles, scientific paradoxes, and coming-of-age tales." A *Kirkus Reviews* contributor dubbed the first installment in the trilogy "a thoughtful, intricate" book and also noted that it is "fast-moving, distinctive, and sometimes spectacular."

In *Context* Tom turns from selfish revenge and begins searching for the woman he loves. He also deals with a force called the Blight, which causes humans to lose their individuality and become an insignificant part of a larger whole. In *Resolution,* the final book in the "Nulapeiron Sequence," series, Tom has become a revolutionary war hero. Through further study of the crystal he obtained in the first book, he learns more about the mysterious mu-space travelers known as the Pilots and also faces a new threat called the Anomaly, which is absorbing humans and aliens into itself.

Bone Song introduces protagonist Donal Riordan, a police lieutenant who works in a necropolis known as Tristopolis. The population consists of the living, the dead, and the undead, and the city is powered by incinerated corpses that produce the "necoflux" necessary to keep it running. In the opener a cult is killing talented artists and taking their bodies, through which they can view the world as the artist did. Riordan himself had this experience when he was once allowed to touch the bone of an artist whose work had substantially increased in value since his death. In a story that is heavy with death-related imagery, Riordan's task is to protect a visiting opera diva. He discovers during a performance that the attackers of the artist he is protecting are members of the audience, and that this has been the method used to kill others—through the programming of a group of minds. He also begins a relationship with Laura Steele, a beautiful blonde zombie who is in charge of a federal task force that is investigating the crimes.

In *Black Blood,* published in England as *Dark Blood,* Riordan and Laura are killed and her heart is transplanted to Riordan's body. Riordan, who is now a zombie, has also inherited all of Laura's wealth, but revenge against the Black Circle, not retirement, is his goal. Like all zombies, his cool, dark blood is being pumped by a heart that is recharged electrically. He also has greater control over his actions, increasing his ability to manipulate others, and can delve deeper into his own mind and access information in a way he could not when alive.

The Unity Party is encouraging the living, called "normals," to destroy the undead, who have the same rights of citizenship as the normals, and Riordan discovers that they are seeking a final solution, much like that of Hitler's Nazi Germany. The remaining members of Laura's team become more fully developed as characters as they are assigned to investigate a new telephone company that is installing lines made of human nerve fiber, and which have an effect on the people using them. Old people become younger and happier, and everyone becomes friendlier, but with a price. Except for the Bone Listeners and zombies, all who use them are becoming programmed to obey the Black Circle.

In reviewing *Black Blood* for *Genre Go Round Reviews,* Harriet Klausner concluded that as with the first book, this second novel "is a compelling tale that places a gothic horror inside a police procedural fantasy." Duncan Lawie wrote for *Strange Horizons* online: "Over the course of two books, Meaney has successfully integrated the tricks of horror with the techniques of crime and SF. The surface of this series is horror, but it is only skin deep. These books have the comfort of rationality. The flesh of *Dark Blood* is that of a detective novel. This can be difficult to manage convincingly in science fiction, but the hard work of building the universe in the first book is repaid here: we now have a conception of normality within the setting so we can seek clues ourselves and attempt to get ahead of Riordan."

BIOGRAPHICAL AND CRITICAL SOURCES:

PERIODICALS

Booklist, February 15, 2008, Carl Hays, review of *Bone Song,* p. 42.
Entertainment Weekly, March 11, 2005, Noah Robischon, review of *Paradox,* p. 108.
Kirkus Reviews, January 1, 2005, review of *Paradox,* p. 25.
Library Journal, February 15, 2005, Jackie Cassada, review of *Paradox,* p. 123; February 15, 2008, Jackie Cassada, review of *Bone Song,* p. 97; March 15, 2009, Jackie Cassada, review of *Black Blood,* p. 100.
Publishers Weekly, February 1, 2005, review of *Paradox,* p. 162; December 24, 2007, review of *Bone Song,* p. 33; January 26, 2009, review of *Black Blood,* p. 102.

ONLINE

Genre Go Round Reviews, http://genregoroundreviews. blogspot.com/ (January 19, 2009), Harriet Klausner, review of *Black Blood.*

Green Man Review, http://www.greenmanreview.com/ (June 16, 2009), Craig Clarke, reviews of *Bone Song* and *Black Blood.*
John Meaney Home Page, http://www.johnmeaney.com (June 16, 2009).
Science Fiction and Fantasy World, http://www. sffworld.com/ (April 16, 2007), Rob H. Bedford, review of *Bone Song.*
SF Reviews, http://www.sfreviews.com/ (June 1, 2003), review of *Paradox.*
SF Site, http://www.sfsite.com/ (June 16, 2009), Lou Anders, author interview.
Strange Horizons, http://www.strangehorizons.com/ (May 30, 2008), Duncan Lawie, review of *Dark Blood.**

*   *   *

MEEK, Joseph
See RANDISI, Robert J.

*   *   *

MEYER, Joyce 1943-

PERSONAL: Born June 4, 1943, in St. Louis, MO; married, 1961 (divorced, 1966); married David Benjamin Meyer, January 7, 1967; children: David, Laura Marie, Sandra Ellen, and Daniel. *Education:* Life Christian University, Tampa, FL, Ph.D.

ADDRESSES: Home—St. Louis, MO. *Office*—Joyce Meyer Ministries, P.O. Box 655, Fenton, MO 63026.

CAREER: Writer, evangelist, televangelist. Life Christian Center, minister, c. 1980s; Life in the Word, Inc., founder, 1985—, Life in the Word television ministry, founder, 1990—; Joyce Meyer Ministries, founder.

WRITINGS:

Beauty for Ashes: Receiving Emotional Healing, Harrison House (Tulsa, OK), 1994, revised and expanded edition, Warner Faith (New York, NY), 2003.
The Root of Rejection: Escape the Bondage of Rejection and Experience the Freedom of God's Acceptance, Harrison House (Tulsa, OK), 1994.

Battlefield of the Mind: How to Win in Your Mind, Harrison House (Tulsa, OK), 1995.

If Not for the Grace of God: Learning to Live Independently from Struggles and Frustrations, Harrison House (Tulsa, OK), 1995.

The Word, the Name, the Blood, Harrison House (Tulsa, OK), 1995.

Life without Strife, Creation House (Orlando, FL), 1995, revised edition, Creation House (Lake Mary, FL), 2000.

Enjoying Where You Are on the Way to Where You Are Going: Learning How to Live a Joyful Spirit-led Life, Harrison House (Tulsa, OK), 1996, Warner (New York, NY), 2002.

Life in the Word; Teachings, Quotes, Personal Insights, and Humor from One of Today's Leading Ministers, Harrison House (Tulsa, OK), 1997.

Managing Your Emotions: Instead of Your Emotions Managing You!, Harrison House (Tulsa, OK), 1997.

Me and My Big Mouth: Your Answer Is Right under Your Nose, Harrison House (Tulsa, OK), 1997.

Be Anxious for Nothing: The Art of Casting Your Cares and Resting in God, Harrison House (Tulsa, OK), 1998.

Help Me, I'm Afraid! Overcoming Emotional Battles with the Power of God's Word, Harrison House (Tulsa, OK), 1998.

Help Me, I'm Alone: Trusting God in Times of Loneliness and Grief, Harrison House (Tulsa, OK), 1998.

Help Me, I'm Stressed! Overcoming Emotional Battles with the Power of God's Word, Harrison House (Tulsa, OK), 1998.

Live in the Word Devotional, Harrison House (Tulsa, OK), 1998.

Weary Warriors, Fainting Saints: How You Can Outlast Every Attack of the Enemy, Harrison House (Tulsa, OK), 1998.

Eat and Stay Thin: Simple, Spiritual, Satisfying Weight Control, Harrison House (Tulsa, OK), 1999.

How to Succeed at Being Yourself: Finding the Confidence to Fulfill Your Destiny, Harrison House (Tulsa, OK), 1999.

Be Healed in Jesus' Name, Harrison House (Tulsa, OK), 2000.

Help Me, I'm Married!, Harrison House (Tulsa, OK), 2000.

Jesus, Name Above All Names: Releasing His Annointing in Your life, Harrison House (Tulsa, OK), 2000.

Reduce Me to Love: Unlocking the Secret to Lasting Joy, Harrison House (Tulsa, OK), 2000.

A Celebration of Simplicity: Loving God and Enjoying Life, Harrison House (Tulsa, OK), 2001.

Filled with the Spirit: Understanding God's Power in Your Life, Harrison House (Tulsa, OK), 2001.

Good Morning, This Is God! Teachings, Quotes, Personal Insights, and Humor from One of Today's Leading Ministers, Harrison House (Tulsa, OK), 2001.

The Joy of Believing Prayer: Deepen Your Friendship with God, Harrison House (Tulsa, OK), 2001.

A Leader in the Making: Essentials to Being a Leader after God's Own Heart, Harrison House (Tulsa, OK), 2001.

Secrets to Exceptional Living: Transforming Your Life through the Fruit of the Spirit, Warner Faith (New York, NY), 2002.

Teenagers Are People Too!, Harrison House (Tulsa, OK), 2002.

Never Lose Heart: Encouragement for the Journey, Warner Books (New York, NY), 2002.

The Battle Belongs to the Lord: Defeating Life's Struggles through Worship, Harrison House (Tulsa, OK), 2002, also published as *The Battle Belongs to the Lord: Overcoming Life's Struggles through Worship,* Warner Books (New York, NY), 2002.

(With Todd Hafer) *Battlefield of the Mind Study Guide,* Warner Books (New York, NY), 2002.

Being the Person God Made You to Be, Warner Books (New York, NY), 2002.

Celebration of Simplicity: Loving God and Enjoying Life, Warner Books (New York, NY), 2002.

Straight Talk on Stress: Overcoming Emotional Battles with the Power of God's Word, Warner Books (New York, NY), 2003.

Straight Talk on Worry: Overcoming Emotional Battles with the Power of God's Word, Warner Books (New York, NY), 2003.

Tell Them I Love Them: Receiving a Revelation of God's Love for You, Warner Books (New York, NY), 2003.

When, God? When: Learning to Trust in God's Timing, Warner Books (New York, NY), 2003.

Why, God, Why? How to Be Delivered from Confusion, Warner Books (New York, NY), 2003.

The Power of Being Positive: Enjoying God Forever, Warner Faith (New York, NY), 2003.

The Power of Determination: Looking to Jesus, Warner Faith (New York, NY), 2003.

The Power of Forgiveness: Keep Your Heart Free, Warner Faith (New York, NY), 2003.

Prepare to Prosper: Moving from the Land of Lack to the Land of Plenty, Warner Books (New York, NY), 2003.

The Secrets of Spiritual Power: Strength for Life's Battles, Warner Faith (New York, NY), 2003.

Starting Your Day Right: Devotions for Each Morning of the Year, Warner Faith (New York, NY), 2003.

Straight Talk on Depression: Overcoming Emotional Battles with the Power of God's Word!, Warner Books (New York, NY), 2003.

Straight Talk on Discouragement: Overcoming Emotional Battles with the Power of God's Word!, Warner Books (New York, NY), 2003.

Straight Talk on Fear: Overcoming Emotional Battles with the Power of God's Word!, Warner Books (New York, NY), 2003.

Straight Talk on Insecurity: Overcoming Emotional Battles with the Power of God's Word!, Warner Books (New York, NY), 2003.

Straight Talk on Loneliness: Overcoming Emotional Battles with the Power of God's Word!, Warner Books (New York, NY), 2003.

Do It Afraid: Obeying in the Face of Fear, Warner Books (New York, NY), 2003.

Don't Dread: Overcoming the Power of Dread with the Supernatural Power of God, Warner Books (New York, NY), 2003.

Eight Ways to Keep the Devil under Your Feet, Warner Faith (New York, NY), 2003.

Expect a Move of God . . . Suddenly!, Warner Books (New York, NY), 2003.

Healing the Brokenhearted Experience: Restoration through the Power of God's Word, Warner Books (New York, NY), 2003.

How to Hear from God: Learn to Know His Voice and Make Right Decisions, Warner Faith (New York, NY), 2003.

Knowing God Intimately: Being As Close to Him As You Want to Be, Warner Faith (New York, NY), 2003.

The Most Important Decision You Will Ever Make: A Complete and Thorough Understanding of What It Means to Be Born Again, Warner Books (New York, NY), 2003.

Peace, Warner Books (New York, NY), 2003.

Ending Your Day Right: Devotions for Every Evening of the Year, Warner Faith (New York, NY), 2004.

How to Hear from God: Learn to Hear His Voice and Make Right Decisions, Thorndike Press (Waterville, ME), 2004.

In Pursuit of Peace: 21 Ways to Conquer Anxiety, Fear, and Discontentment, Warner Faith (New York, NY), 2004.

Making Marriage Work: The Advice You Need for a Lifetime of Happiness, Warner Books (New York, NY), 2004.

The Secret Power of Speaking God's Word, Warner Books (New York, NY), 2004.

Seven Things that Steal Your Joy: Overcoming the Obstacles to Your Happiness, Warner Faith (New York, NY), 2004.

Approval Addiction: Overcoming the Need to Please Everyone, Warner Faith (New York, NY), 2005.

The Power of Simple Prayer: How to Talk to God about Everything, Warner Books (New York, NY), 2005.

Straight Talk: Overcoming Emotional Battles with the Power of God's Word, Warner Faith (New York, NY), 2005.

Battlefield of the Mind for Kids, Warner Faith (New York, NY), 2006.

Battlefield of the Mind for Teens: Winning the Battle in Your Mind, Warner Faith (New York, NY), 2006.

The Confident Woman: Start Today Living Boldly and without Fear, Warner Faith (New York, NY), 2006.

Look Great, Feel Great: 12 Keys to Enjoying a Healthy Life Now, Warner Faith (New York, NY), 2006.

A New Way of Living: Understanding What It Means to Be a Christian, Warner Faith (New York, NY), 2006.

The Everyday Life Bible: Containing the Amplified Old Testament and the Amplified New Testament, Warner Faith (New York, NY), 2006.

(With Deborah Bedford) *The Penny: A Novel,* Faith Words (New York, NY), 2007.

I Dare You: Embrace Life with Passion, Faith Words (New York, NY), 2007.

New Day, New You: 366 Devotions for Enjoying Everyday Life, Faith Words (New York, NY), 2007.

Woman to Woman: Candid Conversations from Me to You, Faith Words (New York, NY), 2007.

Conflict-free Living, Charisma House (Lake Mary, FL), 2008.

Never Give Up: Relentless Determination to Overcome Life's Challenges, Faith Words (New York, NY), 2008.

The Secret to True Happiness: Enjoy Today, Embrace Tomorrow, Faith Words (New York, NY), 2008.

Start Your New Life Today: An Exciting New Beginning with God, Faith Words (New York, NY), 2008.

(With Deborah Bedford) *Any Minute,* Faith Words (New York, NY), 2009.

ADAPTATIONS: A number of Meyer's books have been adapted for audio.

SIDELIGHTS: Joyce Meyer is a successful televangelist who launched the weekly *Life in the Word* television ministry in 1990. The author, who was picked by *Time* magazine as one of the twenty-five most influential evangelicals in the United States, has also written dozens of inspirational books focusing on life in relation to the Christian religion. Meyer distinguishes the difference between Christians who are just going through the motions and others who are truly connected to God in her book *Knowing God Intimately: Being As Close to Him As You Want to Be.* The author discusses her four levels of commitment that can lead to intimacy with God and how important this intimacy is in people's lives. "Charismatic readers and Meyer's legions of fans will appreciate this passionate discourse," wrote a *Publishers Weekly* contributor.

Meyer provides biblical accounts of the importance of joy in a person's life in *Seven Things that Steal Your Joy: Overcoming the Obstacles to Your Happiness.* In the process, she gives advice on how to keep problems in life from robbing a person of his or her joy, with the primary piece of advice being that people should surrender their lives to God. A *Publishers Weekly* contributor wrote that "her basic, straightforward discussion will appeal to many readers, walking them through some valuable self-examination." *How to Hear from God: Learn to Know His Voice and Make Right Decisions* focuses on the many ways that Meyer believes that God communicates his wishes to people, including dreams, visions, and even voices that people can hear. The author relates how important she thinks it is to listen to these communications in order to fulfill the plan that God has for their lives. She also recounts her own past resistance to listening to God and delves into the aspects of people's lives that can prevent them from hearing and heeding God's word. A *Publishers Weekly* contributor noted that "fans of Meyer's previous works will likely be delighted with this newest offering, and its back-to-basics approach will ensure new fans as well."

Meyer discusses what it means to live in peace with God, themselves, and others in her book *In Pursuit of Peace: 21 Ways to Conquer Anxiety, Fear, and Discontentment.* A *Publishers Weekly* contributor wrote that "there are many helpful principles" in the book. In *Approval Addiction: Overcoming the Need to Please Everyone,* the author emphasizes that there are many people who need to have the constant approval of all those around them. The author recounts her own past insecurities in this area as well as stories passed on by others. Meyer stresses that she and everyone else should live only for God's approval and outlines several steps people can take in their lives to achieve this goal. A *Publishers Weekly* contributor referred to the author's writing as "strong, pointed, no-nonsense and even pushy."

In the fourteen chapters of *The Power of Simple Prayer: How to Talk to God about Everything,* Meyer emphasizes the importance of balance in prayer, worship, thanksgiving, and petition making. She writes that while prayer is not complicated, it does require perseverance and persistence. A *Publishers Weekly* critic noted that Meyer contends that "effective prayer is characterized by a life of obedience, righteousness, continual petition and submission to divine authority."

Battlefield of the Mind for Kids and *Battlefield of the Mind for Teens: Winning the Battle in Your Mind* draw on the Bible to offer advice for kids and teens on how to live their lives. Graham Christian, writing in the *Library Journal,* commented that the books are "for collections where Meyer's readership is strong." Meyer turns her attention to physical appearance in *Look Great, Feel Great: 12 Keys to Enjoying a Healthy Life Now.* The author points out that the body is the temple for the spirit and, as a result, should be cared for appropriately. She offers a twelve-step program for staying fit and also addresses the issue of childhood obesity. A *Publishers Weekly* contributor commented that the author "blends self-help with Scripture in this peppy guide."

The Confident Woman: Start Today Living Boldly and without Fear focuses on how women can become more confident in all aspects of their lives. Meyer addresses what she believes to be God's view of women and how the Bible addresses women in the ministry. In addition to discussing how women can get rid of fear and the seven secrets of a confident woman, the author also examines specific passages in the Bible that are often difficult for modern women to understand and accept. "It's a vital message to be sure," wrote a *Publishers Weekly* contributor.

Meyer collaborated with inspirational fiction writer Deborah Bedford (*Remember Me*) in writing *The Penny: A Novel.* The story is set in the racially volatile St. Louis of the 1950s. Jenny Blake is an abused adolescent who finds a penny on the street that, through a series of events, leads to a job working for Miss Opal Shaw, who teaches her about forgiveness, love, and patience. "Meyer fans will easily recognize her themes of overcoming difficulties and shame through God's love and positive thinking," wrote a *Publishers Weekly* reviewer.

California Bookwatch reviewer Diane C. Donovan wrote that *The Everyday Life Bible: Containing the Amplified Old Testament and the Amplified New Testa-*

ment is "an easier route" to understanding the Bible. Meyer adds words to the original text to promote better understanding and prefaces each book of the Bible with an introduction.

In *I Dare You: Embrace Life with Passion,* Meyer includes her trademark straight-to-the-point instructions, such as: "If you really cannot stand your life, then do something about it; Make up your mind regarding what you believe, have God's words to back it up, and don't ever back down," and: "It's time to take action and make your life count." Her theme here is that passion for a purpose will enable a person to reach a particular goal. She notes the areas in which this can be most effective, including finances, emotions, and the mind and spirit. Her instructions include "I Dare You" sidebars to help readers through the suggested steps. A *Publishers Weekly* contributor concluded: "Meyer's message is sound, if unoriginal . . . and her method stern yet loving."

In *The Secret to True Happiness: Enjoy Today, Embrace Tomorrow,* Meyer advises the reader to be happy, not because of good health, wealth, or other circumstances, but for its own sake. She writes that happiness comes not only from within but from trusting in God. She suggests that by surrounding oneself with people who have positive attitudes and maintaining one, happiness will come more easily. Meyer begins each chapter with an anecdote and discusses subjects that include health, habits, discipline, simplicity, and creativity, and she distinguishes between being busy and being fruitful. She urges that readers be productive. A *Publishers Weekly* reviewer applauded Meyer's "can-do attitude."

BIOGRAPHICAL AND CRITICAL SOURCES:

BOOKS

Meyer, Joyce, *I Dare You: Embrace Life with Passion,* Faith Words (New York, NY), 2007.
Religious Leaders of America, Gale (Detroit, MI), 1999.

PERIODICALS

California Bookwatch, March, 2007, Diane C. Donovan, review of *The Everyday Life Bible: Containing the Amplified Old Testament and the Amplified New Testament.*

Christianity Today, March, 2004, Corrie Cutrer, "Joyce Meyer Ministry Flap: TV Preacher Agrees to 'Greatly Reduce' Her Pay in Wake of Controversy," p. 22.
Library Journal, July 1, 2006, Graham Christian, review of *Battlefield of the Mind for Teens: Winning the Battle in Your Mind,* p. 81; October 1, 2006, Graham Christian, review of *The Confident Woman: Start Today Living Boldly and without Fear,* p. 80.
Marriage Partnership, spring, 2006, Corrie Cutrer, "The Secret to Contentment: When Joyce Meyer Took a Risk to Love and Be Loved, She Discovered Something Deeper Than Happiness," p. 40.
Publishers Weekly, July 29, 2002, John F. Baker, "Big Warner Deal for Christian Author," p. 14; March 31, 2003, review of *Knowing God Intimately: Being As Close to Him As You Want to Be,* p. 59; July 14, 2003, review of *How to Hear from God: Learn to Know His Voice and Make Right Decisions,* p. 73; March 29, 2004, review of *Seven Things that Steal Your Joy: Overcoming the Obstacles to Your Happiness,* p. 59; August 16, 2004, review of *In Pursuit of Peace: 21 Ways to Conquer Anxiety, Fear, and Discontentment,* p. 61; March 28, 2005, review of *Approval Addiction: Overcoming the Need to Please Everyone,* p. 77; January 30, 2006, review of *Look Great, Feel Great: 12 Keys to Enjoying a Healthy Life Now,* p. 63; July 10, 2006, review of *The Confident Woman,* p. 72; August 28, 2006, review of *Battlefield of the Mind for Teens,* p. 59; February 12, 2007, review of *The Power of Simple Prayer: How to Talk to God about Everything,* p. 81; April 30, 2007, review of *The Penny: A Novel,* p. 139; July 9, 2007, review of *I Dare You: Embrace Life with Passion,* p. 50; March 10, 2008, review of *The Secret to True Happiness: Enjoy Today, Embrace Tomorrow,* p. 79.
St. Louis Journalism Review, May, 2005, Don Corrigan, "Joyce Meyer Attracts More Media Attention; Ministry's Financial Dealings Face Scrutiny," p. 14.
St. Louis Post-Dispatch, November 17, 2003, Carolyn Tuft and Bill Smith, "Money Pitch Is a Hit with Followers"; May 14, 2004, "Timeline of Joyce Meyer's Life"; April 30, 2005, Carolyn Tuft, "Meyer Received Millions, Records Show."

ONLINE

Beliefnet, http://www.beliefnet.com/ (June 16, 2009), Laura Sheahen, "'You're Responsible for Your Own Joy:' Interview with Joyce Meyer."

Joyce Meyer Ministries Web site, http://www.joyce meyer.org (June 16, 2009).

Let Us Reason Ministries, http://www.letusreason.org/ (June 16, 2009), "Joyce Meyer: Are You Paying Attention."*

*   *   *

MURPHY, Yannick 1962-

PERSONAL: Born 1962; married; children: three. *Education:* Attended Hampshire College and New York University.

ADDRESSES: Home—Reading, VT. *E-mail*—yannick@ hughes.net.

CAREER: Writer. Has taught at New York University, Oberlin College, University of Southern California, and University of California at Los Angeles.

AWARDS, HONORS: Whiting Writers' Award, Mrs. Giles Whiting Foundation, 1990, for *Stories in Another Language;* National Endowment for the Arts fellowship; MacDowell Artists' Colony fellowship, Chesterfield Screenwriting Fellowship (in conjunction with Amblin Studios); the story "In a Bear's Eye" was published in *The O. Henry Prize Stories 2007: The Best Stories of the Year,* 2007.

WRITINGS:

NOVELS

The Sea of Trees, Houghton Mifflin (Boston, MA), 1997.
Here They Come, McSweeney's (San Francisco, CA), 2006.
Signed, Mata Hari, Little, Brown (New York, NY), 2007.

OTHER

Stories in Another Language (short stories), Knopf (New York, NY), 1987.

Ahwoooooooo! (for children), illustrated by Claudio Munoz, Clarion Books (New York, NY), 2005.
In a Bear's Eye (short stories), Dzanc Books (Westland, MI), 2008.
Baby Polar, illustrated by Kristen Balouch, Clarion Books (New York, NY), 2009.

The short story "In a Bear's Eye" was published in *The O. Henry Prize Stories 2007: The Best Stories of the Year,* Anchor Books (New York, NY), 2007.

Contributor to periodicals, including *Antioch Review, McSweeney's, Agni Online,* and *Southwest Review.*

SIDELIGHTS: Yannick Murphy is the author of the award-winning short story collection *Stories in Another Language.* She was one of ten authors to receive the Whiting Writer's Award in 1990 from the Mrs. Giles Whiting Foundation, which at that time bestowed an award of thirty thousand dollars on each author in "recognition of the quality of current and past writing as well as the likelihood of outstanding future work." The seventeen stories in Murphy's collection—one of which is only a paragraph in length—involve young characters who experience adult-generated dangers. Murphy's subjects include grief, death, sexuality, violence, and incest. Her use of such serious themes involving child characters has drawn criticism at times.

Paul Stuewe, reviewing *Stories in Another Language* for *Quill & Quire,* called Murphy's stories "too coy and naive for their own good," but noted that "in a few cases the banality of her language and . . . her characters do coalesce into a telling whole." Although Mary Soete, reviewing the collection for *Library Journal,* found the stories "neither accessible nor comfortable in themes and style," she did note that events are "filtered through the transforming consciousness of children." Sybil Steinberg, in an appraisal for *Publishers Weekly,* considered the stories difficult reading but claimed that Murphy has a "keen eye for small, mundane details." Steinberg insisted that Murphy's fictional debut "evinces a deadpan voice that powerfully taps the interior world of emotions and thoughts."

Murphy's first novel, 1997's *The Sea of Trees,* centers on a young girl named Tian who is being held in a Japanese prison camp in Kontum, Indochina, in 1942. This is a "coming of age" saga that follows Tian's life from the age of twelve through the next two decades. The story's many settings include Kontum, Saigon, Shanghai (her former home), France, and New York. Along with her French mother, her Chinese father, and her "amah" (nanny), Tian faces dangers and hardships: war, imprisonment, separation, family illness, and hunger. A *Publishers Weekly* contributor commented on the novel's "spareness of style," saying it "lends a remote quality to the work that contrasts with its content." Emphasizing that the narrative of *The Sea of Trees* is one in which "torture, fear, murder, and hunger are constant realities," a *Kirkus Reviews* contributor called the work an "indefatigably forward-going" tale of "girlhood and family amid war, terror, loss—and sometimes luck." *Library Journal* contributor Francisca Goldsmith applauded Tian's character because she "remains authentic and caring" despite such hardships. Goldsmith stated that this "inspiring view of the unvanquished human soul belongs in all collections."

Murphy turns to writing for children with her picture book *Ahwooooooooo!* which is illustrated by Claudio Munoz. The story revolves around Little Wolf's efforts to learn how to howl at the moon. Unfortunately, Little Wolf is on his own, since his parents are too busy to teach him. After being taught by other animals how to hoot, croak, and sing like a Whippoorwill, Little Wolf's grandfather finally helps his grandson learn to be perhaps the most vocal member of the pack. "Themes of intergenerational bonding and childhood milestones lend substance to this agreeable picture book," wrote Jennifer Mattson in *Booklist*. A *Kirkus Reviews* contributor referred to *Ahwooooooooo!* as "a tender, sometimes humorous journey that evokes the yearning of childhood."

In her novel *Here They Come*, Murphy uses an unnamed thirteen-year-old narrator to tell the story of a struggling family in New York. The narrator, who can bend spoons with her mind, tells of her efforts to keep her family together. Her family members include her precocious sisters, her suicidal brother, her drunken grandmother, and her depressed mother, who is nevertheless full of resolve to make it. When their deadbeat father, who left the family to live with "the slut," disappears, the narrator's brother goes off to Spain to look for him while the rest of the family stays home to deal with their myriad problems. In a review of *Here They Come* in *Publishers Weekly*, a contributor wrote that the author "creates a world as magical and harrowing as the

struggle to come to grips with maturity." Michael Cart, writing in *Booklist*, commented: "This bizarre mixture of naturalism and surrealism is intriguing—and well written." A *Kirkus Reviews* contributor noted that Murphy has a "skill for lovely imagery." In his review in the *Library Journal*, Jim Coan remarked: "Not intended as a realistic portrait of troubled family life, this readable work is . . . at once funny and sad."

Murphy's next novel, *Signed, Mata Hari*, published in 2007, draws on the real-life experiences of the historical figure Margaretha Geertruida Zelle, more popularly known as Mata Hari. Zelle was a Dutch citizen who went on to become a well-known exotic dancer and courtesan to many wealthy and powerful men in Europe. She was also accused of being a spy during World War I, an allegation for which she was executed by firing squad in France in 1917. The novel opens with Zelle in a French prison awaiting her final appeal; it proceeds to alternate between stories from her past and her present ordeal in prison.

Many critics praised Murphy's third novel, among them *MostlyFiction* online reviewer Guy Savage, who called it "a marvelous creation that combines facts with legend, and legend with possibilities." Savage continued: "As a result, the novel's style mirrors its subject, and this is a delicately elusive tale that wisely leaves all judgment out of the narrative. Told at times in the third person, and at times in the first person, the novel weaves elements of Mata Hari's incredible story back and forth highlighting moments in her mysterious, exotic life while she languishes in the drab, dankness of Saint Lazare prison, and awaits her fate." "Murphy shows an uncanny technical mastery in her manipulation of these stories as she switches among first-, second-, and third-person perspectives to reconstruct" the life of Mata Hari, observed *A.V. Club* critic Ellen Wernecke. However, unlike many other critics, Julie Wheelwright, writing for the London *Independent*, felt that Murphy's intertwining of fact and fiction in this book was not a complete success: "Despite some sensual prose and a convincing character, the story creaks awkwardly where Murphy's invention clashes with historical facts. Such reinvention just adds another layer to the myth, obscuring rather than revealing the strange life" of Zelle.

In an interview with *Bookslut* contributor Donna Seaman, Murphy explains her approach to portraying a subject that has already been the focus of several other books and movies: "It was helpful to have a ready-made story, and when I read about the facts I thought, Oh my God, this poor woman. What she went through here, and how she overcame that and did this. At the same time, though, I knew that presenting her life would be much more interesting if I showed the things that no one could find out about. I was excited when I thought I would write this book because I said to myself, 'No one else is going to write this book the way I would.'"

Murphy's second collection of short stories is titled *In a Bear's Eye*. The twenty-four stories in this book touch on a number of themes, from aging, love, and death to motherhood and connections with animals. The title story, which captures the growing desperation of a mother whose son is in danger of falling prey to a bear by their home, was a 2007 O. Henry Prize winner. According to Melissa Albert in *Bookslut*, this "collection . . . is unlike any you have or will read." Albert went on to comment: "Seeded with fragmented conversation and gorgeous images—Moroccan linens at a street stand, sand drenched black by coconut milk, a floating toothbrush fallen from a shattered plane—they're enchanting without veering into whimsy or preciousness." The author's "tight, sharp sense of composition and tone renders these short takes more than mere formal exercises," stated a *Publishers Weekly* critic.

Murphy once told *CA:* "I hope [my books] whip people out of their sleep-state with their truth telling and their head-long passion, pressure and authority. I hope they will show the reader that I have tried to go beyond writing witty ruminations about motive and that the shape of my writing is driven by an idea of struggle. I hope they show that I have gone the distance by laboring for the rightness in my prose, and laying down my life to create a feeling of being overwhelmed. I hope my writing does not inform the reader, but that it transforms the reader and that my writing reveals that I have listened to my heart and provided against the horrors of regularity."

BIOGRAPHICAL AND CRITICAL SOURCES:

PERIODICALS

Austin Chronicle, March 17, 2006, Jess Sauer, review of *Here They Come.*

Booklist, February 1, 2006, Michael Cart, review of *Here They Come,* p. 30; August 1, 2006, Jennifer Mattson, review of *Ahwooooooooo!,* p. 92; September 1, 2007, Margaret Flanagan, review of *Signed, Mata Hari,* p. 56; February 1, 2008, Donna Seaman, review of *In a Bear's Eye,* p. 27.

Books, January 5, 2008, "Uncommon Spy: A Fictional Reimagining of the Life of Mata Hari," p. 11.

Boston Globe, December 3, 2007, Renée Graham, review of *Signed, Mata Hari.*

Dallas Morning News, December 12, 2007, review of *Signed, Mata Hari.*

Independent (London, England), September 19, 2007, Julie Wheelwright, review of *Signed, Mata Hari.*

Kirkus Reviews, March 1, 1997, review of *The Sea of Trees,* p. 329; January 1, 2006, review of *Here They Come,* p. 13; May 1, 2006, review of *Ahwooooooooo!,* p. 464; September 15, 2007, review of *Signed, Mata Hari.*

Library Journal, June 1, 1987, Mary Soete, review of *Stories in Another Language,* pp. 129-130; April 15, 1997, Francisca Goldsmith, review of *The Sea of Trees,* p. 118; April 1, 2006, Jim Coan, review of *Here They Come,* p. 85; August 1, 2007, Maureen Neville, review of *Signed, Mata Hari,* p. 72.

MBR Bookwatch, January 1, 2008, Olivera Baumgartner-Jackson, review of *Signed, Mata Hari.*

New York Times Book Review, June 7, 1987, Alida Becker, review of *Stories in Another Language,* p. 30; August 17, 1997, Catherine Bush, review of *The Sea of Trees,* p. 12; December 23, 2007, "Sleeping with the Enemy," p. 10.

Publishers Weekly, April 24, 1987, Sybil Steinberg, review of *Stories in Another Language,* p. 60; March 10, 1997, review of *The Sea of Trees,* p. 48; January 30, 2006, Craig Morgan Teicher, "A Wise Child," interview with author, p. 38, and review of *Here They Come,* p. 40; July 23, 2007, review of *Signed, Mata Hari,* p. 40; November 19, 2007, review of *In a Bear's Eye,* p. 33.

Quill & Quire, August, 1987, Paul Stuewe, review of *Stories in Another Language,* p. 34.

Record, December 16, 2007, Joy Tipping, review of *Signed, Mata Hari,* p. 9.

St. Petersburg Times, December 30, 2007, "Unveiling the Layers of Mata Hari," p. 9.

San Francisco Chronicle, November 11, 2007, Joan Frank, review of *Signed, Mata Hari,* p. M2.

School Library Journal, June, 2006, Marianne Saccardi, review of *Ahwooooooooo!,* p. 123.

Tampa Tribune, December 16, 2007, "Fictional Account Dances with Mata Hari's Appeal," p. 8.

Times (London, England), September 15, 2007, Peter Millar, review of *Signed, Mata Hari.*

ONLINE

All Things Girl, http://allthingsgirl.net/ (August 28, 2008), Deb Smouse, review of *Signed, Mata Hari.*

A.V. Club, http://www.avclub.com/ (November 21, 2007), Ellen Wernecke, review of *Signed, Mata Hari.*

Bookslut, http://www.bookslut.com/ (January 1, 2008), Donna Seaman, "An Interview with Yannick Murphy"; (January 1, 2008) Melissa Albert, review of *In a Bear's Eye.*

Curled Up with a Good Book, http://www.curledup.com/ (August 28, 2008), Michael Leonard, review of *Signed, Mata Hari.*

Emerging Writers Forum, http://www.breaktech.net/emergingwritersforum/ (February 9, 2007), "Interview with Yannick Murphy."

Hobart: Another Literary Journal, http://www.hobartpulp.com/ (July 1, 2008), Angela Jane Fountas, interview with Yannick Murphy.

LA Weekly, http://www.laweekly.com/ (March 8, 2006), Michelle Huneven, "Fatherless Manhattan," interview with author.

MostlyFiction, http://www.mostlyfiction.com/ (December 16, 2007), Guy Savage, review of *Signed, Mata Hari;* (August 28, 2008) biographical information on Yannick Murphy.

Reviews of Books, http://www.reviewsofbooks.com/ (August 28, 2008), W.R. Greer, review of *Signed, Mata Hari.*

Yannick Murphy Home Page, http://www.yannickmurphy.com (August 28, 2008).*

N

NAFTALI, Timothy

PERSONAL: Son of James D. and Marjorie Naftali. *Education:* Yale University, B.A. (magna cum laude); Johns Hopkins University, M.A.; Harvard University, M.A., Ph.D.

ADDRESSES: Home—Los Angeles, CA. *Agent*—Moses Cardona, John Hawkins & Associates, Inc., 71 W. 23rd St., Ste. 1600, New York, NY 10010.

CAREER: Historian. National Archives and Records Administration, Richard Nixon Presidential Library and Museum, Yorba Linda, CA, director-designate and director of the Nixon Presidential Materials Project, 2006—. Has worked variously at the University of Hawaii, department of history, assistant professor, 1993-97; Kennan Institute for Advanced Russian Studies, Woodrow Wilson International Center for Scholars, Washington, DC, research scholar; Charles Warren Center for Studies in American History, Harvard University, Cambridge, MA, visiting scholar; Yale University, New Haven, CT, visiting assistant professor of history and Olin Fellow, 1996-98; University of Virginia, Charlottesville, VA, Miller Center.

WRITINGS:

(With Aleksandr Fursenko) *One Hell of a Gamble: Khrushchev, Kennedy, Castro, and the Cuban Missile Crisis 1958-1964,* Norton (New York, NY), 1997.
(Editor, with Philip D. Zelikow and Ernest R. May) *The Presidential Recordings: John F. Kennedy, Volumes 1-3, The Great Crises,* Norton (New York, NY), 2001.

Blind Spot: The Secret History of American Counterterrorism, Basic Books (New York, NY), 2005.
(With Richard Breitman, Norman J.W. Goda, and Robert Wolfe) *U.S. Intelligence and the Nazis,* Cambridge University Press (New York, NY), 2005.
(With Aleksandr Fursenko) *Khrushchev's Cold War: The Inside Story of an American Adversary,* Norton (New York, NY), 2006.
George H.W. Bush, Times Books (New York, NY), 2007.

Contributor to the *New York Times, Wall Street Journal, Los Angeles Times,* and *Huffington Post* Web site.

SIDELIGHTS: Timothy Naftali is a professor and historian. Some thirty years after the Cuban Missile Crisis of October 1962, the end of the Cold War and the release of previously secret archival material by both the United States and the former Soviet Union allowed scholars to probe more deeply into the narrowly averted nuclear holocaust. Two scholars who benefited from the newly open information, and who have benefited the public in turn through their research, are Naftali and Aleksandr Fursenko, authors of 1997's *One Hell of a Gamble: Khrushchev, Kennedy, Castro, and the Cuban Missile Crisis 1958-1964.* Naftali is also a former student of Ernest R. May, coeditor of the best selling book *The Kennedy Tapes. Wall Street Journal* reviewer Richard J. Tofel, assessing both books in one article, observed that *One Hell of a Gamble* seemed to be "the perfect companion to *The Kennedy Tapes.*" Where May's *The Kennedy Tapes* present readers with previously secret tape recordings made in the Oval Office, *One Hell of a Gamble* offers previously secret Soviet archives.

As the dates in their book's subtitle imply, Naftali and Fursenko analyzed the background and the consequences of the missile crisis as well as the famous thirteen days of the crisis itself. *One Hell of a Gamble* shows how Cuban dictator Fidel Castro had been gradually pushed into the Soviet orbit by both Soviet and U.S. moves and by the communist beliefs of his brother Raul. It also outlines the history of U.S. attempts to topple the Castro regime and of Soviet maneuvers to strengthen its own foothold in the Caribbean, not only against American interests but against potential Chinese aggression as well.

As far as the October 1962 crisis itself, the book's authors present, as Robert Sam Anson put it in the *St. Petersburg Times,* numerous "shockers" about events behind the scenes, thus "producing one of those rare achievements: a book that takes our understanding of great events and stands it on its head." Among the micro-level shockers is the revelation that the Soviets were inadvertently warned about an imminent U.S. invasion of Cuba—which had not in fact been decided upon—when a Russian émigré bartender overheard two American reporters talking about their plans to cover such an invasion. Other revelations had to do with an unsettling willingness on both sides, at least during the speculative portions of secret conferences, to consider the possibility of nuclear attacks. Anson felt that the two authors had chipped away at the prevailing image of President John F. Kennedy as the cool-headed hero of the crisis, showing instead that Kennedy "chose the world-saving course . . . only because he had no other." The Russian and Cuban leaders, Anson declared, seemed no more statesmanlike in this chronicle, which was "chock-a-block with such lunacies, many freshly discovered and all grippingly portrayed."

Warren Bass, in an online review for *Slate,* called *One Hell of a Gamble* "important," "impressive," and "one of the best of a flood of new books about the Cold War." He also remarked that, in contrast to the thrills provided by spy fiction, this nonfiction diplomatic thriller, "while it will leave readers' knuckles white, is no fun at all to read, because the events it describes are so frightening." For Paul Roazen on the *Boston Book Review* Web site, *One Hell of a Gamble* is "diplomatic history at its best." Roazen commented: "Fursenko and Naftali have successfully recreated the high drama of the key few days back in October 1962. . . . Their reliance on Soviet sources means that *One Hell of a Gamble* has something to teach even the most conscientious students of foreign policy."

A reviewer for *Publishers Weekly,* mentioning that the authors "emphasize the ignorance and uncertainty that haunted all three countries," assessed *One Hell of a Gamble* thus: "If the writing is a little academic, the authors do illuminate and confirm past suppositions." *Library Journal* contributor Edward Goedeken praised the book, calling *One Hell of a Gamble* "a breathtaking view of the inner workings of the Soviet Politburo," and continued: "Seldom have scholars plumbed the depths of Soviet-American relations as deeply or effectively." For Goedeken, the previous standard for research on the Cuban Missile Crisis had been *Essence of Decision* (1971), by Graham Allison. The reviewer raved: "[Allison's] work has now been vastly improved upon by the investigations of Fursenko . . . and Naftali."

In *Blind Spot: The Secret History of American Counterterrorism,* Naftali turns his attention to the United States' ongoing war against terrorism, a battle that began in the 1940s and has continued into the modern, post-9/11 world. One of Naftali's primary points is that overall, much of the actions taken by the nation in the early part of the twenty-first century bear a striking resemblance to those actions taken decades ago. In the early 1960s, following a number of hijackings to Cuba, then-chief of the Federal Aviation Administration Najeeb Halaby suggested that flights would be safer with the inclusion of federal marshals, however the fear of accidental shootings or fire fights in midair ended the discussion. This is only one example of actions taken long before September 11, 2001, in an effort to prevent terrorism from endangering U.S. citizens. Writing for the *New York Times Book Review,* Eric Lichtblau observed that the book's "real punch . . . comes in Naftali's descriptions of the advances, retreats and inertia of presidential administrations and counterterrorism officials since World War II. And in an understated style, he points out the haunting similarities between the events surrounding 9/11 and the attacks and policy debates from previous generations." According to *Foreign Affairs* contributor Martha Crenshaw, the book "shows how a more complicated pattern—with some government officials stressing the dangers of terrorism and others then minimizing or ignoring them—has hampered Washington's ability to develop an effective counterterrorism strategy."

Naftali is one of several writers of the book *U.S. Intelligence and the Nazis,* an anthology that addresses various topics of World War II, including how much the United States knew about the activities of the Germans, particularly the use of concentration camps and postwar use of war criminals to gather further intelligence. Jurgen Matthaus, in a review for *American Jewish History*, noted that "if U.S. intelligence did perceive the true scope and unprecedented character of German crimes during the Second World War, few lessons were drawn from it at the time or later," going on to point out the events of later atrocities in world history where the United States failed to intervene. Rorin M. Platt, writing for *Canadian Journal of History*, commented that "the authors should have more critically examined presidential responsibility for the moral failure inherent in hiring war criminals."

Khrushchev's Cold War: The Inside Story of an American Adversary, which Naftali wrote with Aleksandr Fursenko, addresses the political strategies of former Soviet premier Nikita Khrushchev over the course of his time in office. Naftali looks at the various crises that Khrushchev was forced to handle and his policy of using aggression to maintain peace, a strategy based in his belief that the survival of the Soviet bloc relied on his ability to maintain the upper hand in all situations. Khrushchev believed in a strong military and used the threat of nuclear retaliation to gain ground against his enemies and with his allies. A contributor for *Kirkus Reviews* called *Khrushchev's Cold War* "sobering—[even] scary—and necessary reading for historians of the modern era." Mark Atwood Lawrence, writing for the *New York Times Book Review*, commented: "Fursenko and Naftali shrewdly point out that any success Khrushchev may have had came at an enormous cost. His risk-taking not only put the world through hair-raising crises but also played straight into the hands of American hawks, who demanded a major arms buildup and denounced any politician who dared advocate a relaxation of tensions."

In his next work, *George H.W. Bush,* Naftali offers readers a thorough profile of George Herbert Walker Bush, the first Bush to serve as president of the United States, following his tenure as vice president to Ronald Reagan. He follows Bush from his roots in New England, where he was born and raised, to Yale University and into the U.S. Navy, and finally through his move to Texas, where he first worked as an oilman and later spent his early days in politics. The bulk of the book, however, focuses on Bush's tenure in the White House, playing close attention to his foreign policy decisions and to the way he handled the end of the Cold War era and the beginning of relations between the United States and modern-day Russia, the reunification of Germany,

and the political tensions in the Middle East that eventually resulted in the first Gulf War. Naftali also addresses questions regarding Bush's management of domestic policies and how he dealt with some of the more serious events relating to the U.S. economy, such as the crisis regarding American savings and loan institutions. Bush also faced a difficult period relating to the Republican Party, which was beginning to show signs of significant policy divisions during Bush's tenure in office over issues such as abortion. With the perspective afforded by a number of years' distance, Naftali is able to portray Bush and his presidency in a positive light overall, illustrating just how many things he handled well, and the way that some of his less-polished dealings were often the result of longtime difficulties that had been building over the course of many years. Bush maintained a strong presidency and, despite a circle of opinionated advisors, was known to make his own decisions, proving himself willing to go against their counsel if he felt the situation warranted it. A contributor for *Kirkus Reviews* opined that "Naftali . . . offers a soft-pedaling, well-paced glimpse at the career highlights of a man whose presidency still remains murky and out-of-focus." A reviewer for *Publishers Weekly* remarked that "Naftali forthrightly dissects Bush's misdeeds . . . but he's less skeptical about the substance of Bush's policies, which he pointedly contrasts with Bush Jr.'s failures," noting the author's failure to connect the first Gulf War with the post-9/11 war in Iraq. Ray Olson, writing for *Booklist*, declared Naftali's work to be a "fine addition to the American Presidents series." *Library Journal* reviewer Thomas J. Baldino concluded that, "while informative, this book does not offer new insights or provide [a] satisfying . . . explanation for what motivated Bush." In contrast, however, *Foreign Affairs* contributor Walter Russell Mead found the book to be a "balanced and thoughtful survey of the life of the first President Bush."

BIOGRAPHICAL AND CRITICAL SOURCES:

PERIODICALS

American Jewish History, September 1, 2004, Jurgen Matthaus, review of *U.S. Intelligence and the Nazis,* p. 361.

Booklist, November 15, 2007, Ray Olson, review of *George H.W. Bush,* p. 16.

Canadian Journal of History, March 22, 2006, Rorin M. Platt, review of *U.S. Intelligence and the Nazis,* p. 163.

Foreign Affairs, July-August, 2005, Martha Crenshaw, review of *Blind Spot: The Secret History of American Counterterrorism,* p. 187; March-April, 2008, Walter Russell Mead, review of *George H.W. Bush,* p. 161.

Kirkus Reviews, August 15, 2006, review of *Khrushchev's Cold War: The Inside Story of an American Adversary,* p. 819; October 1, 1997, review of *George H.W. Bush.*

Library Journal, July 1, 1997, Edward Goedeken, review of *One Hell of a Gamble: Khrushchev, Kennedy, Castro, and the Cuban Missile Crisis 1958-1964,* p. 101; November 15, 2007, Thomas J. Baldino, review of *George H.W. Bush,* p. 65.

New York Times Book Review, July 10, 2005, Eric Lichtblau, "It Didn't Start on 9/11," review of *Blind Spot,* p. 28; December 17, 2006, Mark Atwood Lawrence, review of *Khrushchev's Cold War,* p. 15.

Publishers Weekly, May 19, 1997, review of *One Hell of a Gamble,* p. 60; October 1, 2007, review of *George H.W. Bush,* p. 48.

St. Petersburg Times, September 22-28, 1997, Robert Sam Anson, review of *One Hell of a Gamble.*

Wall Street Journal, September 23, 1997, Richard J. Tofel, review of *One Hell of a Gamble,* p. A20.

ONLINE

Boston Book Review, http://www.bookwire.com/bbr/bbr-home.html (March 3, 1998), Paul Roazen, review of *One Hell of a Gamble.*

Slate, http://www.slate.com/ (August 6, 1997), Warren Bass, "Cold War Follies," review of *One Hell of a Gamble.**

*　　*　　*

NELSON, Marilyn 1946-
(Marilyn Nelson Waniek)

PERSONAL: Born April 26, 1946, in Cleveland, OH; daughter of Melvin M. (in the U.S. Air Force) and Johnnie (a teacher) Nelson; married Erdmann F. Waniek, September, 1970 (divorced, 1979); married Roger R. Wilkenfeld, November 22, 1979 (divorced, 1998); children: (second marriage) Jacob, Dora. *Education:* University of California, Davis, B.A., 1968; University of Pennsylvania, M.A., 1970; University of Minnesota, Ph.D., 1978. *Politics:* "Yes." *Religion:* "Yes." *Hobbies and other interests:* Quilting, traveling.

ADDRESSES: Home—East Haddam, CT. *Office*—Department of English, University of Connecticut, Box U-4025, 215 Glenbrook Rd., Storrs, CT 06269-4025. *E-mail*—waniek@uconnvm.uconn.edu.

CAREER: Writer, poet, translator, and educator. National Lutheran Campus Ministry, lay associate, 1969-70; Lane Community College, Eugene, OR, assistant professor of English, 1970-72; Norre Nissum Seminarium, Norre Nissum, Denmark, English teacher, 1972-73; Saint Olaf College, Northfield, MN, instructor in English, 1973-78; University of Connecticut, Storrs, assistant professor, 1978-82, associate professor, 1982-88, professor of English, 1988-2002, professor emeritus, 2002—; University of Delaware, Newark, professor of English, 2002-04; Soul Mountain Retreat, East Haddam, CT, director, 2002—. Visiting assistant professor, Reed College, 1971-72, and Trinity College, 1982-83; visiting professor, University of Hamburg, spring, 1977, New York University, spring, 1988, spring, 1994, and Vermont College, spring, 1991; Elliston Professor, University of Cincinnati, spring, 1994; U.S. Military Academy, visiting faculty member, spring, 2000.

MEMBER: Society for the Study of Multi-Ethnic Literature of the United States, Society for Values in Higher Education, Modern Language Association, American Literary Translators Association, Poetry Society of America, Associated Writing Programs, Third World Villanelle Society, Phi Kappa Phi.

AWARDS, HONORS: Kent fellowship, 1976; National Endowment for the Arts fellowships, 1981 and 1990; Connecticut Arts Award, 1990; National Book Award finalist for poetry, 1991; Annisfield-Wolf Award, 1992; Fulbright teaching fellowship, 1995; National Book Award finalist for poetry, 1997; Poets' Prize, 1999, for *The Fields of Praise: New and Selected Poems;* Contemplative Practices fellowship, American Council of Learned Societies, 2000; named Poet Laureate for the State of Connecticut, Connecticut Commission on the Arts, 2001-06; J.S. Guggenheim Memorial Foundation fellowship, 2001; *Boston Globe/Horn Book* Award and National Book Award finalist in young people's literature category, both 2001, both for *Carver: A Life in Poems;* Coretta Scott King Honor Book, Flora Stieglitz Straus Award for Nonfiction, Newbery Honor, all 2002, for *Carver: A Life in Poems;* Coretta Scott King Book Award, 2005, for *Fortune's Bones: The Manumission Requiem;* two Pushcart Prizes; honor book, Michael L. Printz Award, honor book, Lee Bennett Hopkins Poetry Award, and Coretta Scott King Honor Award, all 2006, all for *A Wreath for Emmett Till*; Lifetime Achievement in Service to the Literary Community, Connecticut Book Awards, 2006.

WRITINGS:

The Fields of Praise: New and Selected Poems, Louisiana State University Press (Baton Rouge, LA), 1997.

Carver: A Life in Poems (young adult), Front Street (Asheville, NC), 2001.

Fortune's Bones: The Manumission Requiem (young adult), Front Street (Asheville, NC), 2004.

The Cachoeira Tales, and Other Poems, Louisiana State University Press (Baton Rouge, LA), 2005.

A Wreath for Emmett Till (young adult), illustrated by Philippe Lardy, Houghton Mifflin (Boston, MA), 2005.

The Freedom Business: Connecticut Landscapes through the Eyes of Venture Smith: Poems, Lyme Historical Society/Florence Griswold Museum (Old Lyme, CT), 2006.

(With Elizabeth Alexander) *Miss Crandall's School for Young Ladies and Little Misses of Color: Poems* (for young readers), illustrated by Floyd Cooper, Wordsong (Honesdale, PA), 2007.

The Freedom Business: Including a Narrative of the Life and Adventures of Venture, a Native of Africa (poems), art by Deborah Dancy, Wordsong (Honesdale, PA), 2008.

(With Tonya Hegamin) *Pemba's Song: A Ghost Story,* Scholastic Press (New York, NY), 2008.

Sweethearts of Rhythm: The Story of the Greatest All-girl Swing Band in the World, illustrated by Jerry Pinkney, Dial Books (New York, NY), 2009.

Beautiful Ballerina, photographs by Susan Kuklin, Scholastic Press (New York, NY), 2009.

AS MARILIYN NELSON WANIEK

For the Body (poems), Louisiana State University Press (Baton Rouge, LA), 1978.

(With Pamela Espeland) *The Cat Walked through the Casserole and Other Poems for Children,* Carolrhoda (Minneapolis, MN), 1984.

Mama's Promises (poems), Louisiana State University Press (Baton Rouge, LA), 1985.

The Homeplace (poems), Louisiana State University Press (Baton Rouge, LA), 1990.

Magnificat (poems), Louisiana State University Press (Baton Rouge, LA), 1994.

TRANSLATOR

(Translator) Pil Dahlerup, *Literary Sex Roles,* Minnesota Women in Higher Education (Minneapolis, MN), 1975.

(With Pamela Espeland) Halfdan Rasmussen, *Hundreds of Hens and Other Poems for Children,* Black Willow Press (Minneapolis, MN), 1982.

Inge Pederson, *The Thirteenth Month* (poems), Oberlin College Press, (Oberlin, OH), 2005.

Halfdan Rasmussen, *The Ladder* (for children), illustrated by Pierre Pratt, Candlewick (Cambridge, MA), 2006.

Contributor of poetry to numerous anthologies, including *A Formal Feeling Comes: Contemporary Women Formalist Poets,* 1993; and *The New Bread Loaf Anthology of Contemporary American Poetry,* 1999. Contributor to literary journals and periodicals, including the *Gettysburg Review, Obsidian II, Southern Review, MELUS, Minority Voices, Field,* and *Studies in Black Literature.* Manuscripts by Nelson and other archives relevant to her writing are held in the Kerlan Collection at the University of Minnesota and in the archives of the University of Connecticut.

SIDELIGHTS: Poet Marilyn Nelson, who has also published under her former married name of Waniek, writes in a variety of styles about many subjects, often dealing with topics involving the African Diaspora. She has also written verses for children and translated poetry from the Danish and German. A *Dictionary of Literary Biography* contributor called Nelson "one of the major voices of a younger generation of black poets." According to a news release for the *GlobalNewswire, Inc.* Web site, fellow poet Yusef Komunyakaa wrote of Nelson's work: "Rooted in the basic soil of redemptive imagination, the voices in Marilyn Nelson's poems seek a lyrical foothold in our daily lives. Her words teach us how to praise ourselves by praising each other."

Nelson's first poetry collection, *For the Body,* focuses on the relationships between individuals and the larger social groupings of family, extended family, and society. Using domestic settings and memories of her own childhood, Nelson fashions poetry that "sometimes sings, sometimes narrates," as the *Dictionary of Literary Biog-*

raphy contributor described it. In *Mama's Promises,* Nelson continues to experiment with poetic forms in verses about a woman's role in marriage and society, but she utilizes stanzaic division more than in her previous work. The poems in *Mama's Promises* also bear a cumulative theological weight, as the "Mama" named in each poem is revealed in the last poem to be God.

In *The Homeplace,* Nelson turns her attention to the history of her own family, telling their story from the time of her great-great-grandmother to the present in a series of interconnected poems ranging in style from traditional forms to colloquial free verse. Some reviewers praised the variety of poetic expression Nelson displays. "The sheer range of [Nelson's] voice," Christian Wiman wrote in *Shenandoah,* "is one of the book's greatest strengths, varying not only from poem to poem, but within individual poems as well." Suzanne Gardinier, reviewing the book for *Parnassus,* found that through her poems Nelson "reaches back through generations hemmed in on all sides by slavery and its antecedents; all along the way she finds sweetness, and humor, and more complicated truth than its disguises have revealed."

In her poetry for children, Nelson also writes of family situations, although in a more humorous manner. Her collection *The Cat Walked through the Casserole and Other Poems for Children,* written with Pamela Espeland, contains poems about domestic problems and pleasures. The title poem, for example, tells of the family dog and cat and the trouble they cause throughout the neighborhood. Such poems as "Grampa's Whiskers" and "When I Grow Up" also focus on family life in a lighthearted manner.

Although biblical allusions appear in her earliest poems, only with the collection *Magnificat* does Nelson write directly of spiritual subjects. Inspired by her friendship with a Benedictine monk, Nelson tells of her religious awakening to a more profound sense of Christian devotion. Writing in the *Multicultural Review,* Mary Walsh Meany found Nelson's voice—"humorous, earthy, tender, joyous, sorrowful, contemplative, speculative, attached, detached, sometimes silent"—to be what "makes the poems wonderful." A *Publishers Weekly* contributor noted that Nelson's "passion, sincerity and self-deprecating humor will engage even the most skeptical reader."

In *The Fields of Praise: New and Selected Poems,* Nelson's poems embrace numerous themes, including the changing nature of love, racism, motherhood, marriage, and domesticity. A *Publishers Weekly* contributor called the collection "stirring" and added: "Strongest is Section III; its poems, grappling with evil and filled with biblical and philosophical references, demonstrate a luminous power." Writing for *America,* Edward J. Ingebretsen commented that he was drawn to Nelson's humorous poems. "Nelson is at her best when she is wry and comic," Ingebretsen wrote. "Many of her narrative scenes are Swiftian indignities observed with compassion." Miller Williams, writing in the *African American Review,* called Nelson's voice "quietly lyrical" and her poems ones "of simple wisdom and straightforward, indelible stories."

The Cachoeira Tales, and Other Poems explores travel from an African American historical and social point of view. Nelson writes about an encounter with a cab driver, a trip to a Creole village, and a strange trip to Brazil's Bahia. A *Black Issues Book Review* contributor asserted: "Nelson's gift as a poet is her simple, fluid mastery of poetic forms."

In 2001, *Carver: A Life in Poems* was published to critical acclaim, notable nominations, and awards. Nelson provides a lyrical rendering through forty-four poems of the life of George Washington Carver, a renowned and revered African American botanist and inventor widely respected for his scholarly mind, hard work, and humility. As head of the agricultural department at the Tuskegee Institute, Carver specialized in crop research and was especially noted for his work with peanuts, including the development of peanut butter. Nelson's poems tell Carver's story within the political and cultural milieu of his time, and the book includes prose summaries of the events in Carver's life and numerous photographs. Ray Olson, writing a review of *Carver* in *Booklist,* noted that "Nelson beautifully and movingly revives his reputation." Cathryn M. Mercier commented in *Horn Book:* "As individual works, each poem stands as a finely wrought whole of such high caliber that one can hardly name a favorite, never mind the best." In the *School Library Journal,* Herman Sutter remarked: "The poems are simple, sincere, and sometimes so beautiful that they seem not works of artifice, but honest statements of pure, natural truths."

In *Fortune's Bones: The Manumission Requiem,* Nelson writes about the real-life Fortune, a slave whose master preserved his bones for anatomical research after Fortune died. The poems are based on information gathered by the Mattatuck Museum, which stored the bones. A *Kirkus Reviews* contributor called the collection of poems a "slim funeral mass, moving from grief to joy," adding that the author likens the slave's "death as his deliverance from slavery to the ultimate freedom." Hazel Rochman, writing for *Booklist,* commented: "Moved by the poetry and the history, readers will want to join the debate." *School Library Journal* contributor Nancy Palmer observed: "This volume sets history and poetry side by side and, combined with the author's personal note on inspirations, creates a unique amalgam."

Nelson writes about another notorious incident in her book *A Wreath for Emmett Till.* Till was a young African American from Chicago who was brutally beaten and murdered in Mississippi in 1955 for whistling at a white woman. A *Kirkus Reviews* contributor praised the author's ability to "take one of the most hideous events of the twentieth century and make of it something glorious." Cris Riedel, writing for the *School Library Journal,* referred to the book as "in the Homeric tradition of poet-as-historian." A *Publishers Weekly* contributor remarked: "For those readers who are ready to confront the evil and goodness of which human beings are capable, this wise book is both haunting and memorable."

Halfdan Rasmussen, a Danish poet who died in 2002, is among the poets whose works have been translated by Nelson for American audiences. His works *Hundreds of Hens and Other Poems for Children* and *The Ladder* feature rhyming couplets, the latter telling the story of an independently minded ladder which travels the countryside. "Not every translated rhyme is felicitous, but most are jaunty and light," wrote Abby Nolan of Nelson's translations in her review for *Booklist.* Nelson has also cowritten several books of poetry, including with Elizabeth Alexander, *Miss Crandall's School for Young Ladies and Little Misses of Color: Poems.*

Nelson served as the Poet Laureate for the State of Connecticut from 2001 through 2006. Also in 2006, Nelson received a Lifetime Achievement in Service to the Literary Community honor from Connecticut Book Awards. In her speech accepting the honor, she said she felt strange for receiving an award for something that came so naturally. "Poets are dreamers and live in the imagination," Nelson was recorded as having said by Carol Goldberg, reporting for the *Hartford Courant.* "My achievements are really blessings for being in the right place at the right time. It's odd to be honored for

being blessed." Along with continuing to write poetry, Nelson continues to teach her craft at the University of Connecticut and at Soul Mountain, a poet's retreat she helped to found. She has contributed as a writer and performer to the Poetry Foundation's podcasts, which introduce poetry as an oral tradition to students.

Nelson has continued to write and produce a variety of poetry and books. She is coauthor with Tonya Hegamin of *Pemba's Song: A Ghost Story.* Published in 2008, the supernatural tale is told through young Pemba's poetry and journal. Following her father's death, Pemba, an African American teen, and her mother move from Brooklyn to an old colonial house in Colchester, Connecticut. Missing her friends and life in the city, Pemba begins seeing someone else in her mirror. The apparition is an eighteenth-century slave girl named Phyllis who suffered a horrible fate that Pemba learns about during a series of blackouts, during which Phyllis's story is revealed. With the help of a strange old man named Abraham, Pemba learns about the history of the town and sets out to right the wrong that Phyllis experienced. Nelson presents the story in alternating chapters featuring Pemba's hip-hop poetry and journal entries.

"This is a great novel full of excitement and intrigue," noted *Common Sense Web* Web site contributor Terreece Clarke, adding that the "authors . . . weave a tale that takes the reader back and forth through time with the greatest of ease." Noting that African American teens are not usually featured in ghost stories, *School Library Journal* contributor Ginny Collier also wrote in the same review that "fewer still that are as well written and interesting as this one."

In her poetry collection *The Freedom Business: Including a Narrative of the Life and Adventures of Venture, a Native of Africa,* Nelson tells the story of Venture Smith, who was taken from his native Guinea at the age of six by slave traders and sold into slavery in the United States. The book features Smith's 1798 autobiography reproduced on the book's left-hand pages with poems by Nelson on the right-hand pages. "As in the book's title, the poems' elemental metaphor is the horror of people as 'business commodities,'" noted *Booklist* contributor Hazel Rochman. As told by Smith in his memoir, he eventually was able to purchase his freedom and then went on to work and earn enough money to purchase his pregnant wife. The author also includes a preface focusing on the history and significance of

Venture Smith, a longtime slave who not only gained his freedom but also went on to buy and sell slaves himself. The book includes twenty-five poems by Nelson, each inspired by a specific event in Venture Smith's life. The book includes illustrations by Deborah Dancy.

"An astonishing, heartbreaking cycle of poems," wrote a *Kirkus Reviews* contributor, who went on in the same review to call *The Freedom Business* "tragic, important, breathtaking." Nina Lindsay, writing for *School Library Journal*, commented that the author "adds to her unique body of work connecting youngsters to history through . . . primary-source material and verse."

BIOGRAPHICAL AND CRITICAL SOURCES:

BOOKS

Dictionary of Literary Biography, Volume 120: *American Poets since World War II, Third Series,* Gale (Detroit, MI), 1992.

PERIODICALS

African American Review, spring, 1999, Miller Williams, review of *The Fields of Praise: New and Selected Poems,* p. 179.

America, April 25, 1998, Edward J. Ingebretsen, review of *The Fields of Praise,* p. 27.

Black Issues Book Review, March-April, 2006, review of *The Cachoeira Tales, and Other Poems,* p. 18.

Booklinks, January-February, 2006, Chris Liska Carger and Mayra Carillo-Daniel, review of *A Wreath for Emmett Till,* p. 49.

Booklist, May 1, 2001, Ray Olson, review of *Carver: A Life in Poems,* p. 1658; November 15, 2004, Hazel Rochman, review of *Fortune's Bones: The Manumission Requiem,* p. 573; February 1, 2005, Gillian Engberg, review of *A Wreath for Emmett Till,* p. 970; January 1, 2006, review of *A Wreath for Emmett Till,* p. 12; June 1, 2006, Abby Nolan, review of *The Ladder,* p. 88; October 1, 2008, Hazel Rochman, review of *The Freedom Business: Connecticut Landscapes through the Eyes of Venture Smith: Poems,* p. 42; November 1, 2008, Gillian Engberg, review of *Pemba's Song: A Ghost Story,* p. 34.

Christian Century, December 14, 2004, review of *Fortune's Bones,* p. 24.

Christianity and Literature, summer, 1998, Anne West Ramirez, review of *The Fields of Praise,* p. 510.

Georgia Review, winter, 1997, Judith Kitchen, review of *The Fields of Praise,* p. 756.

Hartford Courant (Hartford, CT), December 4, 2006, Carole Goldberg, "Poet's 'Blessed' Life Honored at Connecticut Book Awards."

Horn Book, September, 2001, Cathryn M. Mercier, review of *Carver,* p. 606; January-February, 2002, Cathryn M. Mercier, review of *Carver,* p. 41; January-February, 2005, Sue Houchins, review of *Fortune's Bones,* p. 105; May-June, 2005, Betsy Hearne, review of *A Wreath for Emmett Till,* p. 339; January-February, 2006, review of *A Wreath for Emmett Till,* p. 22; March-April, 2006, "Coretta Scott King Author Award," p. 235, and "Michael L. Printz Award," p. 236; May-June, 2006, "Lee Bennett Hopkins Poetry Award," p. 365; November 1, 2008, Roger Sutton, review of *The Freedom Business.*

Hudson Review, spring, 1998, R.S. Gwynn, review of *The Fields of Praise,* p. 257; summer, 2005, David Mason, "The Passionate Pursuit of the Real," review of poetry books, pp. 319-328.

Internet Bookwatch, September 1, 2008, review of *The Freedom Business.*

Kirkus Reviews, October 15, 2004, review of *Fortune's Bones,* p. 1011; March 1, 2005, review of *A Wreath for Emmitt Till,* p. 292; August 15, 2008, review of *Pemba's Song;* September 15, 2008, review of *The Freedom Business.*

Multicultural Review, March, 1995, Mary Walsh Meany, review of *Magnificat.*

New York Times Book Review, July 15, 2001, review of *Carver,* p. 24.

Parnassus, Volume 17, number 1, 1992, Suzanne Gardinier, review of *The Homeplace,* pp. 65-78.

Poetry, May, 2006, D.H. Tracy, review of *The Cachoeira Tales, and Other Poems,* p. 159.

Publishers Weekly, November 16, 1990, review of *The Homeplace,* p. 52; August 29, 1994, review of *Magnificat,* p. 67; May 26, 1997, review of *The Fields of Praise,* p. 82; April 11, 2005, review of *A Wreath for Emmett Till,* p. 54.

Reading Today, December, 2005, David L. Richardson, review of *A Wreath for Emmett Till,* p. 34.

School Library Journal, July, 2001, Herman Sutter, review of *Carver,* p. 129; December, 2004, Nancy Palmer, review of *Fortune's Bones,* p. 166; April, 2005, Nina Lindsay, review of *Fortune's Bones,* p. 57; May, 2005, Cris Riedel, review of *A Wreath for Emmett Till,* p. 156; October, 2005, review of *A Wreath for Emmett Till,* p. S81; October, 2008, Nina Lindsay, review of *The Freedom Business,* p. 173; December, 2008, Ginny Collier, review of *Pemba's Song,* p. 124.

Shenandoah, winter, 1992, Christian Wiman, review of *The Homeplace.*

Women's Review of Books, May, 1998, Marilyn Hacker, review of *The Fields of Praise,* p. 17.

ONLINE

Academy of American Poets Web site, http://www.poets. org/ (June 21, 2009), profile of Marilyn Nelson.

African American Literature Book Club, http://aalbc. com/ (March 16, 2007), brief profile of Marilyn Nelson.

Blue Flower Arts, http://www.blueflowerarts.com/ (June 21, 2009), brief profile of author.

Common Sense Media, http://www.commonsensemedia. org/ (June 21, 2009), Terreece Clarke, review of *Pemba's Song.*

Connecticut State Poet Laureate Web site, http://vvv. state.ct.us/emblems/poet.htm (March 16, 2007), brief profile of Marilyn Nelson.

Global Newswire, Inc., http://primezone.com/news room/ (February 27, 2007), "Marygrove College Welcomes Marilyn Nelson as Nineteenth Contemporary American Author."

Poetry Foundation, http://www.poetryfoundation.org/ (March 16, 2007), brief profile of Marilyn Nelson.

Soul Mountain Retreat Web site, http://www.soul mountainretreat.org (June 21, 2009), brief profile of author.

University of Connecticut Web site, http://uconn.edu/ (June 21, 2009), faculty profile of Marilyn Nelson.*

*   *   *

NICHOLSON, Geoff 1953-

PERSONAL: Born March 4, 1953, in Sheffield, England; son of Geoffrey Howell (a carpenter) and Violet Theresa (a bookkeeper) Nicholson. *Education:* Gonville and Caius College, Cambridge, B.A., 1975, M.A., 1978; University of Essex, M.A., 1978.

ADDRESSES: Home—Los Angeles, CA. *Agent*—Derek Johns, A.P. Watt, 20 John St., London WC1N 2DR, England.

CAREER: Writer. Worked as chef, gardener, furniture sales representative, "dustman," and driving instructor.

AWARDS, HONORS: Winner of *Custom Car* short story competition, 1985, for "Boy-Raced from Oblivion"; finalist for Whitbread Prize, Booksellers Association of Great Britain and Ireland, for *Bleeding London.*

WRITINGS:

NOVELS

Street Sleeper, Quartet (London, England), 1987.

The Knot Garden, Hodder & Stoughton (London, England), 1989.

What We Did on Our Holidays, Hodder & Stoughton (London, England), 1990.

Hunters and Gatherers, Hodder & Stoughton (London, England), 1991, Overlook Press (Woodstock, NY), 1994.

The Food Chain, Hodder & Stoughton (London, England), 1992, Overlook Press (Woodstock, NY), 1993.

The Errol Flynn Novel, Sceptre (London, England), 1994.

Still Life with Volkswagens, Quartet (London, England), 1994, Overlook Press (Woodstock, NY), 1995.

Everything and More, Gollancz (London, England), 1994, St. Martin's Press (New York, NY), 1995.

Footsucker, Gollancz (London, England), 1995, Overlook Press (Woodstock, NY), 1996.

Bleeding London, Overlook Press (Woodstock, NY), 1997.

Flesh Guitar, Gollancz (London, England), 1998, Overlook Press (Woodstock, NY), 1999.

Female Ruins, Gollancz (London, England), 1999, Overlook Press (Woodstock, NY), 2000.

Bedlam Burning, Gollancz (London, England), 2000, Overlook Press (Woodstock, NY), 2002.

The Hollywood Dodo, Simon & Schuster (New York, NY), 2004.

OTHER

Sleeping Dogs (radio play), first broadcast by British Broadcasting Corp. (BBC), 1982.

Big Noises: Rock Guitar in the '90s, Quartet (London, England), 1991.

Day Trips to the Desert: A Sort of Travel Book, Hodder & Stoughton (London, England), 1992.

Andy Warhol: A Beginner's Guide, Hodder & Stoughton (London, England), 2002.

Frank Lloyd Wright: A Beginner's Guide, Hodder & Stoughton (London, England), 2002.

Sex Collectors: The Secret World of Consumers, Connoisseurs, Curators, Creators, Dealers, Bibliographers, and Accumulators of "Erotica," Simon & Schuster (New York, NY), 2006.

The Lost Art of Walking: The History, Science, Philosophy, and Literature of Pedestrianism, Riverhead Books (New York, NY), 2008.

Contributor of short stories to anthologies, including *Dark Terrors 4,* edited by Stephen Jones and David A. Sutton, Eclipse Books, 1998, and *The Mammoth Book of New Erotica,* Carroll & Graf, 1998. Contributor of articles and book reviews to periodicals, including *Wire, New York Times, Art Review and Modern Painters, Independent, Daily Telegraph, Financial Times,* and *Time Out.*

SIDELIGHTS: Geoff Nicholson aims to be "a serious comic writer," as he once told *CA.* His protagonists frequently take their interests to the point of obsession. The characters in *Hunters and Gatherers,* for instance, are consumed by collecting; a husband and wife collect cars and extramarital lovers, respectively, while another character, a writer, is obsessed with chronicling collectors. *New York Times Book Review* contributor Eric Kraft called the novel "a humorous but serious study of people who collect things, with ruminations on the psychological, sociological, and philosophical aspects of their obsession. It is also about people who tell stories, with ruminations on the nature of their obsession." Nicholson treats these subjects in a manner that is "clever, entertaining and intriguing . . . literate and rich, with references to culture high and low," Kraft noted, although he also wrote of Nicholson's characters: "Though they bump into one another now and then, they don't feel much when they do." To *Time* contributor John Skow, the book "is not so much a novel as a collection of loosely related fiction riffs, but it does not suffer at all from its lack of connective tissue." Nicholson's narrative, he added, is "always peculiar, frequently droll, and on several occasions funny."

In *Everything and More,* Nicholson turns a jaundiced eye on materialism, with a tale centering on a fictional London department store, Haden Brothers, which a

Publishers Weekly contributor described as "a combination of Harrod's, Kafka's Castle, and the Marx Brothers' *The Big Store.*" The primary characters are Vita Carlisle, a seemingly ideal salesperson who eventually tries to blow up the store; Charlie Mayhew, a would-be artist who takes a low-level job at Haden Brothers and falls in love with Vita; and Arnold Haden, the last of the brothers, who also longs for Vita. Quirky supporting players include a blind elevator operator who tells Charlie he smells right for the store and disgruntled workers who take their revenge on management by shoplifting. "The book bristles with energy, the plot moves quickly and there's a great sense of life and movement to all the characters," observed Susan Jeffreys in a review for *New Statesman and Society.* "There are also (a real bonus in a comic novel) some terrifically sensual passages, particularly when the store is being described." Jeffreys also wrote: "It is riddled with secret passages, underground chambers, and even a tomb." The *Publishers Weekly* contributor found *Everything and More* "a highly literate and bawdy assault on the principle that all things, including people, have exchange values."

In *Bleeding London,* the focus is again on obsessions, with one character, Mick Wilton, determined to avenge his girlfriend's rape; another, Stuart London, so obsessed with the city whose name he shares that he intends to walk every one of its streets; and a third, Judy Tanaka, driven to accumulate sexual partners. All use the same London city guide as an aid in their quests. "Nicholson constructs his plot lines to intersect like crossroads," noted J.D. Biersdorfer in the *New York Times Book Review,* adding that the result will "keep readers comfortably hooked." A *Publishers Weekly* commentator praised the novel's "delightfully cynical sense of humor" and many "vivid vignettes," finding fault only in the amount of time that it takes for the characters to meet. "Even so, getting there's most of the fun," the reviewer commented.

Flesh Guitar looks at a rock music fan's obsession with a guitarist named Jenny Slade, whose instrument appears to be made of human flesh. Slade is portrayed as an influence on many famed rockers, such as Frank Zappa, Jimi Hendrix, and Kurt Cobain. According to *New York Times Book Review* contributor Anthony Bourdain, the novel's concept is promising, but its execution is lacking; the novel, while "always clever, is seldom fun," he wrote. A *Publishers Weekly* contributor, however, deemed *Flesh Guitar* "a clever montage rife with signature black humor and ultrahip self-consciousness."

Nicholson mixes architectural theory with fiction in *Female Ruins.* Kelly Howell, daughter of the late English architect Christopher Howell, agrees to be a tour guide for American Jack Dexter. Dexter is actually an admirer of her father's, and wants to get close to Kelly in order to find out more about the man who was a great architect and a lousy father. Barbara Love, in a review for *Library Journal,* called *Female Ruins* an "entertaining read . . . enlivened by scattered riffs on architecture." A contributor to *Publishers Weekly* considered it "a complex, subtle story with equally intricate and modulated characters." Chris Jones wrote in a review for *Book* that *Female Ruins* "is a gripping tale with potent ideas that linger long in the mind."

In *Bedlam Burning,* narrator Mike Smith is both attractive and aimless. When his friend Gregory Collins enlists Mike to pose for the jacket photo for Gregory's first novel, Mike agrees. Gregory convinces Mike to stand in for him at an author reading as well, and soon Mike, posing as Gregory, finds himself accepting a writer-in-residence position at an insane asylum. The psychiatrists at the asylum first lock him up (the disorientation will help him identify with the patients). Once he is released, he steps into the role of writer-in-residence, and although he is not sure what to do with it, he eventually sets the inmates to writing their own pieces. In the meantime, he discovers that Kincaid's method for curing madness is to deprive his patients of visual images, and he beds psychiatrist Alicia Crowe, who is aroused by foul language. Nicholson "knows how to catch your interest from Page One," wrote Marcel Theroux in his review for the *New York Times Book Review,* continuing: "Mike is good company as a narrator: bright, engagingly straightforward, and yet virtually clueless about what's going on around him." A *Publishers Weekly* contributor wrote that *Bedlam Burning* "delightfully stretches sanity to its farcical breaking point."

The Hollywood Dodo is another story about obsession, or, more precisely, three stories in one. There is the story of aspiring film director Rick McCartney, who seems driven to acquire financing for his movie about the extinct dodo bird. There is the story of British physician Henry Cadwallader, who, while escorting his daughter Dorothy to Hollywood to seek fame and fortune on the silver screen, encounters McCartney and finds himself drawn ever deeper into the corruption and obsession that seem, in this novel at least, to define Tinseltown. Then there is the film story of seventeenth-century medical student William Draper and his obses-

sive quest to save the dodo from extinction by finding a mate for his own pet bird. The novel "seeks to be a Hollywood satire in the grand tradition," observed David L. Ulin in his *New York Times Book Review* article, masterfully weaving the three stories into a fabric both bizarre and provocative. Beyond the satire, Ulin suggested, "Nicholson means to make a point about artifice and actuality, illusion and truth, Hollywood and history," but ultimately misses his mark. He found *The Hollywood Dodo* to be not particularly convincing, albeit well written and very entertaining. *Salon.com* contributor Stephanie Zacharek commented similarly that the novel is less satisfying than hoped for, but nonetheless one of Nicholson's trademark "savory pleasures." She called *The Hollywood Dodo* "a journey of discovery, viewed not through prissy rose-colored glasses, but through some very dark, sexy ones."

In *Sex Collectors: The Secret World of Consumers, Connoisseurs, Curators, Creators, Dealers, Bibliographers, and Accumulators of "Erotica,"* Nicholson looks at a different form of obsession, one perhaps more voyeuristic than participatory. His characters are not the inventions of his creative mind, but real people who appear to be living their fantasies through the paraphernalia with which they surround themselves. His subjects range from a woman who collects plaster casts of the intimate body parts of rock musicians to a man who collects nude paintings of his own family members to Sigmund Freud, who collected archaeological artifacts which, though not overtly erotic on their own, reportedly reminded their owner of a link between collecting and a form of lust approaching the intensity of a biological urge. The subject matter, both the collections and their often-bizarre owners, provide a built-in trigger for Nicholson's sense of humor and appreciation of the absurd. According to *New York Times Book Review* contributor Emily Nussbaum, "Nicholson tries his best to find the nugget of humanity, the passion within the obsessiveness, in each of his subjects. He's such an appealing writer that you want him to succeed." In the end, however, the subject matter fails to live up to expectations. As Nussbaum pointed out, the art of collecting is not normally an erotic act, regardless of subject matter, and the act of writing about it is even less so, regardless of the author's talent. To *Los Angeles* magazine contributor Ariel Swartley, however, the success of *Sex Collectors* may depend more on the reader than the author. British readers, Swartley suggested, seem more likely to appreciate Nicholson's humor, satire, and wit for its own sake, while Americans "want him to get serious, take a stand." The reviewer reported that "*Sex Collectors* . . . offers the best of both worlds [in the form of] stimulation and satisfaction."

In his next nonfiction book, *The Lost Art of Walking: The History, Science, Philosophy, and Literature of Pedestrianism,* Nicholson examines the common act of walking as part of humankind's intellectual and cultural history. Writing in his book, the author notes: "Looked at a certain way, walking is the most ordinary, natural, ubiquitous activity. What could be more commonplace or lacking in eccentricity than the act of walking?" The author also writes that walking could be considered a "brainless activity," as evidenced by an Oxford scholar's experiment of taking a dead cat, removing its brain, and finding a way to make it walk, a feat duplicated with aborted human fetuses many years later.

Nevertheless, Nicholson goes on to reveal in his book that walking has a long history and its influence belies its simplicity or commonality. Writing for the *LA Weekly* Web site, Matthew Fleischer noted that the author reveals that "such a simple, apparently mindless, endeavor has provided creative fuel for some of the world's greatest artists, thinkers and mystics, from Lao Tzu and Thomas Jefferson to Dickens and Rousseau," whose final book was titled *Reveries of a Solitary Walker.*

In examining the intellectual aspects of walking, the author points to such phenomenon as the nineteenth-century Romantic movement's fostering of a cult that stressed the spiritual side of walking as a way to commune with nature and ultimately lead to a better understanding not only of nature's beauty but of truth as well. Nicholson also discusses "psychogeography," a theory developed by Guy Debord, which proposes that random walking is a work of art that produces a surrealistic sense of life as the walker makes random, chance encounters that ultimately lead to the recalling of old memories and the stirring of emotions. "If any single idea is central to Mr. Nicholson's ramble through the lore of pedestrianism, it's . . . [the] idea of walking as a method of discovery—both of the world and one's own thoughts about it," wrote David Propson in a review for the *Wall Street Journal Online.*

In addition to the intellectual side of walking, the author covers a wide range of topics, from pilgrimages to funny kinds of walking. He writes about walking songs and literature and even walking in films. For example, he discusses the movie about one-time heavyweight champion boxer Jim Corbett, played by Errol Flynn, in which Corbett is portrayed walking against pedestrian traffic on a busy sidewalk to gain better footwork in the ring. The author also writes of various famous mythical walkers, including the Wandering Jew. He discusses Neil Armstrong's walk on the moon and recounts the walking adventures of Captain Robert Barclay Allardice, a Scotsman who, during the nineteenth century, spent weeks on walking expeditions that were virtually non-stop except for an occasional hour break. In one expedition, he walked 1,000 miles in 1,000 hours, or twenty-four miles a day at a mile-per-hour, a feat that noted the captain's ability to fight sleep deprivation as much as anything. Discussing more recent walking exploits, the author writes about an ex-Marine who lost one hundred pounds from his 400-pound frame as he walked from San Diego to New York. He also details the exploits of Steve Gough, who twice took to walking naked from southwest England to the northern tip of Scotland, including one time with his naked girlfriend.

The author also features his own adventures in walking, including walking the cities of London, New York, and Los Angeles. Commenting on walking in New York, the author writes that it is "a risky activity, a form of combat, a struggle for dominance, sometimes a contact sport." On walking in London, the author notes that "London is, in every sense I can think of, well-trodden territory: a place of walkers, with a two-thousand-year-long history of pedestrianism." In Los Angeles, the author retraces some of the footsteps of Philip Marlowe, the famous detective in Raymond Chandler novels.

"This is a wonderful and strange book that, for all its exoticism and hardship, conveys the exhilaration and liberation of just plain walking," wrote Katherine A. Powers in a review for the *Boston Globe Online.* Noting that the author's "book is worth reading as a celebration of tangential and obsessive eccentricity," Lawrence Klepp, writing for the *Weekly Standard,* added: "His curiosity, standard equipment for walkers, is contagious and brings him to unexpected places as well as unexpected oddballs."

BIOGRAPHICAL AND CRITICAL SOURCES:

BOOKS

Nicholson, Geoff, *The Lost Art of Walking: The History, Science, Philosophy, and Literature of Pedestrianism,* Riverhead Books (New York, NY), 2008.

PERIODICALS

Book, September, 2000, Chris Jones, review of *Female Ruins,* p. 81.

Booklist, May 1, 2000, Brendan Dowling, review of *Female Ruins,* p. 1653; June 1, 2006, Mike Tribby, review of *Sex Collectors: The Secret World of Consumers, Connoisseurs, Curators, Creators, Dealers, Bibliographers, and Accumulators of "Erotica,"* p. 12; October 1, 2008, Colleen Mondor, review of *The Lost Art of Walking: The History, Science, and Literature of Pedestrianism,* p. 12.

Economist, November 29, 2008, "More than Just Gadding About; Walking," review of *The Lost Art of Walking,* p. 87.

Kirkus Reviews, September 15, 2008, review of *The Lost Art of Walking.*

Library Journal, May 1, 2000, Barbara Love, review of *Female Ruins,* p. 154; February 1, 2002, Barbara Love, review of *Bedlam Burning,* p. 132; October 15, 2008, Mary Grace Flaherty, review of *The Lost Art of Walking,* p. 84.

Los Angeles, July, 2006, Ariel Swartley, review of *Sex Collectors,* p. 121.

Magazine of Fantasy and Science Fiction, February, 2000, Charles De Lint, review of *Flesh Guitar,* p. 23.

New Statesman and Society, October 7, 1994, Susan Jeffreys, review of *Everything and More,* p. 47.

New York Times, February 27, 2002, Richard Eder, "When the Imposter Tries to Do the Job in Earnest," review of *Bedlam Burning,* p. B7.

New York Times Book Review, February 5, 1995, Eric Kraft, review of *Hunters and Gatherers;* January 4, 1998, J.D. Biersdorfer, review of *Bleeding London,* p. 16; March 14, 1999, Anthony Bourdain, review of *Flesh Guitar,* p. 23; July 23, 2000, Matthew Klam, "A Doll's House," review of *Female Ruins,* p. 11; February 10, 2002, Marcel Theroux, "Insanity Clauses," review of *Bedlam Burning,* p. 10; June 3, 2004, David L. Ulin, review of *The Hollywood Dodo;* June 18, 2006, Emily Nussbaum, review of *Sex Collectors;* December 14, 2008, D.T. Max, "Walk This Way," review of *The Lost Art of Walking,* p. 18.

Newsweek, December 15, 2008, Tony Dokoupil, "A Walk to Remember," review of *The Lost Art of Walking,* p. 14.

Publishers Weekly, September 6, 1993, review of *The Food Chain,* p. 83; May 1, 1995, review of *Everything and More,* p. 41; August 21, 1995, review of *Still Life with Volkswagens,* p. 46; August 12, 1996, review of *Footsucker,* p. 63; August 4, 1997, review of *Bleeding London,* p. 62; December 14, 1998, review of *Flesh Guitar,* p. 56; April 3, 2000, review of *Female Ruins,* p. 61; November 19, 2001, review of *Bedlam Burning,* p. 47; September 1, 2008, review of *The Lost Art of Walking,* p. 45.

Seattle Times, December 7, 2008, "The Everyday Wonders of Walking; Books and Authors," includes review of *The Lost Art of Walking,* p. 4.

Time, January 23, 1995, John Skow, review of *Hunters and Gatherers,* p. 59.

Washington Post, February 19, 2002, Chris Lehmann, "Into the Cuckoo's Nest," review of *Bedlam Burning,* p. C4.

Washington Post Book World, November 9, 2008, Jonathan Yardley, "A Pleasant Stroll through the History of Perambulation," review of *The Lost Art of Walking,* p. BW15.

Weekly Standard, September 29, 2008, Lawrence Klepp, "Happy Feet; the Joys of Walking, in Theory and Practice," review of *The Lost Art of Walking.*

ONLINE

Boston Globe Online, http://www.boston.com/ (November 30, 2008), Katherine A. Powers, "Pedestrian Pursuits," review of *The Lost Art of Walking.*

Geoff Nicholson Home Page, http://geoff-nicholson.tripod.com (June 21, 2009).

LA Weekly, http://www.laweekly.com/ (October 28, 2008), Matthew Fleischer, "Author Geoff Nicholson Gets Pedestrian," review of *The Lost Art of Walking.*

Los Angeles Times Online, http://www.latimes.com/ (November 16, 2008), Karla Starr, review of *The Lost Art of Walking.*

New York Observer Online, http://www.observer.com (November 4, 2008), "Fall Books: A Literary Leafpile," review of *The Lost Art of Walking.*

Paste, http://www.pastemagazine.com/ (December 1, 2008), Charles Bethea, review of *The Lost Art of Walkling.*

Pittsburgh Tribune-Review Online, http://www.pittsburghlive.com/ (December 9, 2008), Regis Behe, "Author Nicholson Finds Walking Is Anything but Mundane," interview with author.

Salon.com, http://www.salon.com/ (July 9, 2004), Stephanie Zacharek, review of *The Hollywood Dodo.*

Time Online, http://www.time.com/ (November 21, 2008), Gilbert Cruz, "A History of Walking," review of *The Lost Art of Walking.*

Wall Street Journal Online, http://online.wsj.com/ (November 21, 2008), David Propson, "Shoe-Leather Rhapsody," review of *The Lost Art of Walking.**

* * *

NORTH, Chris
See GORMAN, Ed

* * *

NUZUM, K.A.
(Kathy A. Nuzum)

PERSONAL: Born in CO; married; children: two sons. *Education:* Colorado University, B.A. (comparative religions), B.A., (environmental conservation), Vermont College, M.F.A., 2003.

ADDRESSES: Home—Eastern CO. *E-mail*—kanuzum@ earthlink.net.

CAREER: Writer, 2006—. Also worked as a ballroom dancer, a master gardener, and as a radio-show host.

WRITINGS:

A Small White Scar (novel), Joanna Cotler Books (New York, NY), 2006.
The Leanin' Dog (novel), Joanna Cotler Books (New York, NY), 2008.

ADAPTATIONS: The Leanin' Dog was adapted as an audiobook, Recorded Books, 2008.

SIDELIGHTS: K.A. Nuzum's *A Small White Scar,* set in 1940s Colorado, tells the coming-of-age story of Will, a young Colorado cowboy who dreams of competing in the professional rodeo circuit. Will, however, is held back by his devotion to his little brother Denny. Denny is afflicted with Down syndrome and Will, charged with his care, finds his brother a burden that interferes with his dreams. At the same time, he is deeply connected to Denny and is intensely protective of him. When Will flees his home in an attempt to follow his dream, Denny follows him into the wilderness and, eventually, to the rodeo circuit. "Although Will is the narrator," Wendy Smith-D'Arezzo explained in a review for *School Library Journal,* "readers also hear the voice of Denny through dialogue and through Will's projections of his brother's thoughts." In the end, stated *Kliatt* contributor Paula Rohrlick, "Will comes to understand how his caring for Denny has helped to make him a better person." "A confrontation with his father," declared a *Kirkus Reviews* contributor, "finally leads to some real communication and some solutions." "Part family tale, part adventure, part journey narrative," wrote Carolyn Phelan in *Booklist,* "this coming-of-age story has an emotional core that will touch . . . readers" who have never experienced a rodeo.

Nuzum's second novel, *The Leanin' Dog,* tells the story of the friendship between a young girl who fears leaving her family's small cabin and a stray dog equally afraid of small places. "A heavy snowstorm in the canyon lands of southeastern Colorado was half of my inspiration [for the book], and our fudge-colored dog, Moot, was the other half," the author noted in an interview on her Web site. The author went on to reveal that she was staying on a large cattle ranch and was sitting on a bed in an unheated room looking down at her dog Moot when it began to snow outside. She looked at her dog as the snow fell more rapidly. The author commented that "suddenly, a question popped into my head: What if there was a big, fudge-colored dog out in that storm? And I began to write."

In Nuzum's novel, which takes place in the 1930s, the eleven-year-old Dessa Dean has suffered a traumatic experience. One day, she and her mother went outside in the snow and wandered from their tiny, isolated, one-room cabin in Colorado. Before long they are lost and in dire straits. Her mother collapses, and Dessa tries to build a fire until someone comes to rescue them. However, their trail is covered by the heavily falling snow, and Dessa's mother dies in her arms. Now Dessa is a prisoner in her own home. Dessa no longer goes anywhere because she has developed agoraphobia, a fear of leaving the house. Meanwhile her father, a hunter and trapper, is dealing with his own sense of loss and grief and devoting much of his time to putting food on the table and gathering firewood to keep them warm through the harsh winter. One day during a cold winter shortly before Christmas, a nearly wild dog with a lame leg comes to the cabin's porch and Dessa sets out to befriend the animal. "This is a beautiful story in which friendship and the power of being needed trump despair," wrote Kim Dare in a review for *School Library Journal.*

Friendship with the dog, however, is not easily won. Ironically, the dog suffers from claustrophobia and Deanna has a hard time getting the dog to come into the tiny cabin. Eventually, when she does succeed in getting the dog to return and finally enter the cabin, she finds that she has to leave the door partially open, which causes Dessa to use up firewood quicker and leads to a major problem. The story culminates on Christmas Eve when the wild dog comes to Dessa's rescue, saves both his master and Christmas dinner, and earns a name for himself in the process. "*The Leanin' Dog* is written in spare language, which beautifully evokes the barebones world in which Dessa lives," wrote a contributor to the *Kinnelon Library Teen Blog*. Writing for the *BookPage* Web site, Angela Leeper noted that the author's "gifts to readers include her convincing regional dialogue and vivid descriptions of the Colorado wilderness and the range of emotions that sweep through the tiny cabin."

BIOGRAPHICAL AND CRITICAL SOURCES:

PERIODICALS

Booklist, August 1, 2006, Carolyn Phelan, review of *A Small White Scar,* p. 75; November 15, 2008, Carolyn Phelan, review of *The Leanin' Dog,* p. 43.

Kirkus Reviews, June 15, 2006, review of *A Small White Scar,* p. 636; September 15, 2008, review of *The Leanin' Dog.*

Kliatt, July, 2006, Paula Rohrlick, review of *A Small White Scar,* p. 12.

School Library Journal, August, 2006, Wendy Smith-D'Arezzo, review of *A Small White Scar,* p. 126; October, 2008, Kim Dare, review of *The Leanin' Dog,* p. 156.

ONLINE

Book Bits, http://westwoodchildrensdept.blogspot.com/ (December 4, 2008), Trudy Walsh, review of *The Leanin' Dog.*

BookPage, http://www.bookpage.com/ (June 21, 2009), Angela Leeper, review of *The Leanin' Dog.*

Eva's Book Addiction, http://evasbookaddiction.blog spot.com/ (March 26, 2009), review of *The Leanin' Dog.*

Ezine Articles, http://ezinearticles.com/ (June 21, 2009), Karen Haney, review of *The Leanin' Dog.*

K.A. Nuzum Home Page, http://www.kanuzum.com (June 21, 2009).

Kinnelon Library Teen Blog, http://kpl-teen-reads.livejournal.com/ (March 17, 2009), review of *The Leanin' Dog.*

Wausau Daily Herald Online, http://www.wausau dailyherald.com/ (March 31, 2009), Beth Martin, "Book Review: *Leanin' Dog* a Tale of Tragedy, Inspiration."*

*   *   *

NUZUM, Kathy A.
    See NUZUM, K.A.

O

O'CALLAGHAN, Joseph F. 1928-
  (Joseph Francis O'Callaghan)

PERSONAL: Born November 23, 1928, in Philadelphia, PA; son of William John (an administrator) and Helen O'Callaghan; married Anne Drummey (a director of religious education), June 15, 1957; children: William, Catherine, Anne, Joseph. *Education:* La Salle College, B.A., 1950; Marquette University, M.A., 1952; Fordham University, Ph.D., 1957.

ADDRESSES: Home—Norwalk, CT. *Office*—Department of History, Fordham University, Bronx, NY 10458.

CAREER: Historian, educator, and writer. Fordham University, Bronx, NY, instructor, 1954-59, assistant professor, 1959-63, associate professor, 1963-70, professor of history, 1970-94, retired, named professor emeritus of medieval history, also former director of the Center for Medieval Studies. Visiting assistant professor at Columbia University, New York, NY, 1963-64, and St. Joseph's Seminary, Yonkers, NY, beginning 1968.

MEMBER: American Catholic Historical Association (past-president), Mediaeval Academy of America, Academy of American Research Historians for Medieval Spain, Society to Advance the Retarded (Norwalk, CT), Norwalk Montessori Association.

AWARDS, HONORS: Institute of International Education fellowship for Spain, 1955-56; Fulbright fellowship for Spain, 1961-62; *consejero de honor* from Instituto de Estudios Manchegos, 1962; National Endowment for the Humanities fellowship, summer, 1971.

WRITINGS:

(Editor and contributor) *Studies in Medieval Cistercian History Presented to Professor Jeremiah F. O'Sullivan,* Cistercian Publications (Collegeville, MN), 1971.

(Translator) John C. Olin, editor, *The Autobiography of Saint Ignatius Loyola,* Harper (New York, NY), 1974.

A History of Medieval Spain, Cornell University Press (Ithaca, NY), 1975.

The Spanish Military Order of Calatrava and Its Affiliates, Variorum Reprints (London, England), 1975.

The Cortes of Castile-Leon, 1188-1350, University of Pennsylvania Press (Philadelphia, PA), 1989.

The Learned King: The Reign of Alfonso X of Castile, University of Pennsylvania Press (Philadelphia, PA), 1993.

Alfonso X and the Cantigas de Santa Maria: A Poetic Biography, Brill (Boston, MA), 1998.

Alfonso X, the Cortes, and Government in Medieval Spain, Ashgate (Brookfield, VT), 1998.

(Translator and author of introduction and notes) *The Latin Chronicle of the Kings of Castile,* Arizona Center for Medieval and Renaissance Studies (Tempe, AZ), 2001.

(Author of introduction), *Chronicle of Alfonso X,* translated by Shelby Thacker and José Escobar, University Press of Kentucky (Lexington, KY), 2002.

Reconquest and Crusade in Medieval Spain, University of Pennsylvania Press (Philadelphia, PA), 2003.

The O Callaghan Family of County Cork: A History, Irish Family Names (Dublin, Ireland), 2004.

Electing Our Bishops: How the Catholic Church Should Choose Its Leaders, Sheed & Ward (Lanham, MD), 2007.

Contributor to *Encyclopaedia Britannica, Encyclopedia Americana* and *New Catholic Encyclopedia.* Contributor of articles and reviews to history and hispanic studies journals, including the *American Historical Review, Catholic Historical Review, Speculum, Traditio, En la España Medieval, Hispania, Viator, Miscelánea de Estudios Medievales, Anuario de Historia del Derecho Español, Cuadernos de Historia de Espana, Concentus Libri, Medievalismo, Thought, Archivos Leoneses,* and *Analecta Sacri Ordinis Cisterciensis.*

SIDELIGHTS: Historian Joseph F. O'Callaghan, professor Emeritus of history at Fordham University, is primarily interested in the history of medieval kingship and parliaments and has a particular interest in medieval Spain. Among his many books on Spanish history are *The Learned King: The Reign of Alfonso X of Castile,* published in 1993, and *Reconquest and Crusade in Medieval Spain,* published in 2003.

The Learned King begins with an examination of the government administration of Alfonso X as well as the role of the Church during Alfonso's reign. The author also examines the thirteenth-century society and literature, as well as the economy of the era. In the book's second half, O'Callaghan focuses primarily on politics, including the relationship between Alfonso and other Christian states and his dealings with the Muslims. The author also examines Alfonso's attempt to gain an imperial title and subsequent opposition he faced from Castilian nobles. "The author's intention . . . is to provide as comprehensive a survey of Alfonso's reign as possible, and here he succeeds," noted A.J. Forey in a review for the *English Historical Review.* "The reader learns not only about the expected topics, but also about more esoteric matters, including astrology."

In *Reconquest and Crusade in Medieval Spain,* O'Callaghan examines the Christian military campaigns targeting Muslims in the Iberian Peninsula. The author draws from both Islamic and Christian sources to show that the hostilities between Christians and Muslims in the peninsula dated back to the eight century and by the twelfth century had been turned into a crusade by the papacy. Successive popes continued the crusade into the thirteenth century. The author pays special attention to the concept of the "reconquest," or *Reconquista,* of Spain, an idealized notion in the history of Spain that grew out of Christian propaganda that the war with Muslims in the Iberian Peninsula was an effort to take back territories that belonged to Christians. He also

discusses the long conflict within in the larger context of the Crusades and whether or not the "Reconquista" should be seen as part of this larger conflict between Muslims and Christians.

"In the light of recent events, the study of the long-lasting armed confrontation between Christianity and Islam can provide new clues for the understanding of the mechanisms of world power," wrote Ana Echevarria in a review for the *Institute of Historical Research Web site.* "Joseph O'Callaghan has provided an interesting approach to the phenomenon of religious wars, focused on such modern concerns as propaganda and economic foundations." Rowena Hernandez-Muzquiz, writing for the *Historian,* commented: "This is a solid work of scholarship and a much needed contribution to the field. It is also of great value to advanced students, demonstrating O'Callaghan's facility in articulating complex concepts and details in lucidly argued prose, which sets out logically each subtopic to be addressed, the evidence for his arguments, and the conclusions he has reached."

The author's 2007 book, *Electing Our Bishops: How the Catholic Church Should Choose Its Leaders,* focuses on a history of how bishops have been elected in the Catholic Church. The author also presents his argument that the church should return to the ancient tradition of bishops being elected by local clergy and people of the diocese instead of being appointed by Rome as they are now. According to the author, this reversion to the past approach will help renew the church's standing and popularity throughout the world. "O'Callaghan's provocative study encourages us to think hard about ways to change the system," wrote Lawrence S. Cunningham in a review for *Commonweal.*

O'Callaghan is also the translator of *The Latin Chronicle of the Kings of Castile* and author of the book's introduction and notes. "This annotated translation of a little-known chronicle of the thirteenth century was produced by Professor O'Callaghan to provide undergraduate students, effectively unable to read Latin, with a roughly contemporary account of the reigns of Kings Alfonso VIII (1158-1214) and Fernando III (1217-1252) of Castile," noted Bernard F. Reilly, writing for the *Catholic Historical Review.*

BIOGRAPHICAL AND CRITICAL SOURCES:

PERIODICALS

American Historical Review, June, 1976, review of *A History of Medieval Spain,* p. 569.

Americas, April, 1976, review of *A History of Medieval Spain,* p. 643.

Catholic Historical Review, July, 2003, Bernard F. Reilly, review of *The Latin Chronicle of the Kings of Castile,* p. 545; October, 2003, James William Brodman, review of *Reconquest and Crusade in Medieval Spain,* p. 753; July, 2008, Francis A. Sullivan, review of *Electing Our Bishops: How the Catholic Church Should Choose Its Leaders,* p. 523.

Choice, July, 1975, review of *A History Of Medieval Spain,* p. 738.

Commonweal, September 28, 2007, Lawrence S. Cunningham, review of *Electing Our Bishops.*

English Historical Review, September, 1996, A.J. Forey, review of *The Learned King: The Reign of Alfonso X of Castile,* p. 957.

Hispanic American Historical Review, February, 1974, review of *A History Of Medieval Spain,* p. 172.

Historian, spring, 2005, Rowena Hernandez-Muzquiz, review of *Reconquest and Crusade in Medieval Spain,* p. 159.

Reference & Research Book News, August, 2007, review of *Electing Our Bishops.*

Times Literary Supplement, July 7, 1975, review of *A History Of Medieval Spain,* p. 1339.

ONLINE

Institute of Historical Research Web site, http://www.history.ac.uk/ (June 21, 2009), Ana Echevarria, review of *Reconquest and Crusade in Medieval Spain.*

My Irish Books, http://myirishbooks.com/ (June 21, 2009), author discusses his career.

*   *   *

O'CALLAGHAN, Joseph Francis
    See O'CALLAGHAN, Joseph F.

*   *   *

ORR, Wendy 1953-
    (Sally George)

PERSONAL: Born November 19, 1953, in Edmonton, Alberta, Canada; daughter of Anthony M. (an air force pilot) and Elizabeth Ann (a teacher and homemaker) Burridge; married Thomas H. Orr (a farmer), January 11, 1975; children: James Anthony, Susan Elizabeth. *Education:* London School of Occupational Therapy, diploma, 1975; LaTrobe University, B.Sc., 1982. *Hobbies and other interests:* Animals, reading, gardening, people, travel, tai chi.

ADDRESSES: Home—Mornington Peninsula, Victoria, Australia. *Agent*—Debbie Golvan, Golvan Arts Management, P.O. Box 766, Kew, Victoria 3101, Australia; golvan@bigpond.net.au.

CAREER: Writer. Albury Community Health, Albury, Australia, occupational therapist, 1975-80; Language and Development Clinic, Shepparton, Australia, occupational therapist, 1982-91; author, 1986—. Also owner of a dairy farm in Victoria, Australia, for twenty years.

MEMBER: Australian Society of Authors, Australian Children's Book Council, Red Hill Readers.

AWARDS, HONORS: Shared first place award, Ashton Scholastic Picture Book Awards, 1987, for *Amanda's Dinosaur;* Book of the Year for Junior Readers shortlist, Children's Book Council of Australia (CBCA), 1993, for *Leaving It to You;* New South Wales Premier's Award shortlist, 1995, for *Yasou Nikki;* Book of the Year for Junior Readers, CBCA, 1995, for *Ark in the Park;* Australian Family Therapy Association Recommended designation, 1995, for *Ark in the Park,* and high commendation, 1997, for *Peeling the Onion;* Honor Book designation, CBCA, 1997, Best Books for Young Adults inclusion, American Library Association (ALA), Books for the Teen Age designation, New York Public Library, both 1998, and Best of the Best listee, ALA, all for *Peeling the Onion;* West Australian Young Readers' Book Award shortlist, 1998, for *Paradise Palace;* Honor Book designation, CBCA, 1999, for *Arabella;* BILBY Award shortlist, CBCA, 2000, for *Dirtbikes;* West Australian Young Readers' Book Award shortlist, and One Hundred Titles for Reading and Sharing inclusion, New York Public Library, both 2001, both for *Nim's Island;* West Australian Young Readers' Book Award shortlist, and Young Australian Readers' Award shortlist, both 2004, both for *Spook's Shack;* Community Relations Award and New South Wales Premier's Award shortlist, both for *Across the Dark Sea.*

WRITINGS:

Amanda's Dinosaur, illustrated by Gillian Campbell, Ashton Scholastic (Morningside, Queensland, Australia), 1988.

The Tin Can Puppy (picture book), illustrated by Brian Kogler, HarperCollins Australia/Angus & Robertson (Sydney, New South Wales, Australia), 1990.

Bad Martha, illustrated by Carol McLean Carr, Angus & Robertson (Sydney, New South Wales, Australia), 1991.

Aa-choo! (picture book), illustrated by Ruth Ohi, Annick Press (Toronto, Ontario, Canada), 1992.

Leaving It to You, Angus & Robertson (Sydney, New South Wales, Australia), 1992.

The Great Yackandandah Billy Cart Race, illustrated by Neil Curtis, HarperCollins Australia (Sydney, New South Wales, Australia), 1993.

Mindblowing! (middle-grade reader), illustrated by Ruth Ohi, Allen & Unwin Australia (St. Leonards, New South Wales, Australia), 1994, published as *A Light in Space,* Annick Press (Toronto, Ontario, Canada), 1994.

Ark in the Park, illustrated by Kerry Millard, Angus & Robertson (Sydney, New South Wales, Australia), 1994, Henry Holt (New York, NY), 1999.

The Laziest Boy in the World, illustrated by Farbio Nardo, HarperCollins Australia/Angus & Robertson (Sydney, New South Wales, Australia), 1994.

Yasou Nikki, illustrated by Kim Gamble, HarperCollins Australia (Sydney, New South Wales, Australia), 1995.

Dirtbikes, HarperCollins Australia (Sydney, New South Wales, Australia), 1995.

The Bully Biscuit Gang, HarperCollins Australia (Sydney, New South Wales, Australia), 1995.

Jessica Joan, illustrated by Ann James, Mammoth Australia (Port Melbourne, Victoria, Australia), 1995.

Grandfather Martin, illustrated by Kate Ellis, Houghton Mifflin (Boston, MA), 1996.

Alroy's Very Nearly Clean Bedroom, illustrated by Bettina Guthridge, Longman & Cheshire (Melbourne, Victoria, Australia), 1996, Sundance Publishing (Littleton, MA), 1997.

Peeling the Onion (young adult), Allen & Unwin Australia (St. Leonards, New South Wales, Australia), 1996, Holiday House (New York, NY), 1997.

Paradise Palace, illustrated by David Mackintosh, HarperCollins (Pymble, New South Wales, Australia), 1997.

Sally's Painting Room, illustrated by Janice Bowles, Koala Books (Redfern, New South Wales, Australia), 1997.

Arabella, illustrated by Kim Gamble, HarperCollins (Pymble, New South Wales, Australia), 1998.

Paradise Gold, illustrated by David Mackintosh, HarperCollins (Pymble, New South Wales, Australia), 1999.

Poppy's Path, illustrated by Ritva Voutila, Koala Books (Mascot, New South Wales, Australia), 2001.

The House at Evelyn's Pond (adult novel), Allen & Unwin Australia (St. Leonards, New South Wales, Australia), 2001.

Spook's Shack, illustrated by Kerry Millard, Allen & Unwin (St. Leonards, New South Wales, Australia), 2003.

Across the Dark Sea, illustrated by Donna Rawlins, National Museum of Australia Press (Canberra, Australian Capital Territory, Australia), 2006.

Too Much Stuff, illustrated by Kerry Millard, Penguin (Camberwell, Victoria, Australia), 2006.

Mokie and Bik, illustrated by Beth Norling, Allen & Unwin (Crows Nest, New South Wales, Australia), 2006, illustrated by Jonathan Bean, Henry Holt (New York, NY), 2007.

Mokie and Bik Go to Sea, illustrated by Jonathan Bean, Henry Holt (New York, NY), 2008.

"NIM" SERIES

Nim's Island, illustrated by Kerry Millard, Allen & Unwin (St. Leonards, New South Wales, Australia), 1999, Knopf (New York, NY), 2001.

Nim at Sea, illustrated by Kerry Millard, Allen & Unwin (Crows Nest, New South Wales, Australia), 2007, Knopf (New York, NY), 2007.

"MICKI AND DANIEL" PICTURE-BOOK SERIES

Pegasus and Ooloo Mooloo, illustrated by Ruth Ohi, Annick Press (Toronto, Ontario, Canada), 1993.

The Wedding, illustrated by Ruth Ohi, Annick Press (Toronto, Ontario, Canada), 1993.

The Train to the City, illustrated by Ruth Ohi, Annick Press (Toronto, Ontario, Canada), 1993.

Published in Australia as "Micki Moon and Daniel Day" series, illustrated by Mike Spoor, Allen & Unwin Australia (St. Leonards, New South Wales, Australia).

UNDER PSEUDONYM SALLY GEORGE

Bad Dog George, Thomas Nelson Australia (Melbourne, Victoria, Australia), 1994.

Breakfast in Bed, Thomas Nelson Australia (Melbourne, Victoria, Australia), 1994.

George at the Zoo, Thomas Nelson Australia (Melbourne, Victoria, Australia), 1994.

Orr's works have been translated into French, Japanese, Italian, German, Spanish, Basque, Korean, Thai, and Dutch.

ADAPTATIONS: Nim's Island was adapted as a major motion picture, Fox-Walden, 2008, and as an audio book, Blackstone Audio, 2008; *Nim's Island Movie Storybook,* adapted by Sonia Sander, Scholastic (New York, NY), 2008; *Nim's Friends,* a book by Danielle Denega, is based on characters created by Orr, Scholastic (New York, NY), 2008.

SIDELIGHTS: Australian author Wendy Orr has written books for children and young adults that are noted for their elements of fantasy and humor. She is widely known for her award-winning novel *Nim's Island,* which was adapted as a feature film, and its sequel, *Nim at Sea.* The inspiration for Orr's many works come from a variety of sources, she noted in an interview on her Web log: "Lots of ideas present themselves to you daily, and some stick around for a little while . . . but there are some that simply don't let you go. I presume those ones fulfill some psychic need, but I truly don't know. And sometimes I think there's enough magic in writing that it's best not to investigate too much and risk driving it away!"

Orr was fortunate to have a father who worked for the Royal Canadian Air Force. She spent her childhood in locations all across Canada, traveling to France, and living for a time in Colorado. Her broad experiences were put to good use later, when she began her career as a writer. "My parents instilled a love of language early," Orr once commented, "with books at bedtime and my father's stories of our dog's Great Great Great Grandfather, in the car. My own first 'book' was written when I was eight. 'Glossy the Horse' was a full four pages long and bore a striking resemblance to *Black Beauty,* which my mother had just read to us. Dramatic poems followed; how delighted my grandmother must have been to receive a 'Poem on Death' for her sixtieth birthday!

"On leaving high school," she added, "I spent a year studying animal care in Kingston, Ontario, went to England for a holiday, and stayed for three years to complete a diploma at the London School of Occupational Therapy. In my final year, 1975, I met and married an Australian farmer holidaying in the United Kingdom and returned to New South Wales with him after graduation.

"The business of growing up, and starting a career and family took over and except for an article on 'Living in Wheelchairs' when I was a student, my writing was limited to patient records and weekly epistles to my parents. At the end of 1982, however, when I had completed a bachelor of applied science and another post-graduate certificate, I decided that it was time to do what I had always wanted. In December 1986 I entered the Ashton Scholastic competition for a picture book manuscript. *Amanda's Dinosaur,* which shared the first place, was published in 1988 and subsequently had rights sold to Canada, New Zealand, and the United States."

Orr's "Micki and Daniel" picture-book series centers on the friendship between two young children and their pets, Pegasus, a miniature horse, and Ooloo Mooloo, a parrot. Although some critics have found these stories somewhat constrained by the author's attempt to be "politically correct," others have considered their adventures amusing and appealing to children. "It is refreshing to see stories of friendship featuring human children instead of the more usual animal quasi-adults," remarked Sarah Ellis in her *Quill & Quire* review of *The Wedding* and *The Train to the City.* In *Pegasus and Ooloo Mooloo,* Micki and Daniel find the animals that accompany them throughout the rest of the series. The four encounter evil circus-owners who want to steal Pegasus, the miniature horse, but Ooloo Mooloo the parrot saves the day when he makes a noise like a police siren and scares the bad guys away. Although some critics mentioned what they considered a lack of focus in the story, noting that the parrot rather than one of the children saves the day, others praised both the setup for the series and the intrinsic interest of the characters. *The Wedding,* the second book in the series, was found to be successful in its rendering of the story of a wedding ceremony in which Micki and Daniel are invited to take part, but their pets are not. Ooloo Mooloo and Pegasus insist on joining in nonetheless, "and it all adds up to a satisfying slapstick climax," according to Ellis.

Orr's science fiction adventure *Mindblowing!,* published outside Australia under the title *A Light in Space,* was widely praised as a fast-paced, compelling story of a boy who meets a being from outer space who, though friendly to him, intends to capture the earth's oxygen for her own planet. "This is top-quality science fiction," a reviewer for *Books in Canada* reported. Critics noted the skillful way in which the author contrasts the viewpoints of the human boy and the alien girl who intends to mine the earth's oxygen for her own planet, despite the deadly effect this would have on the earth's inhabitants. "The plot of this light book is entertaining and fast paced, while the characters are well drawn," remarked J.R. Wytenbroek in *Quill & Quire.* Although Wytenbroek faulted Orr for failing to dramatize the resolution to her story, Anne Connor, reviewing *A Light in Space* for *School Library Journal,* praised Orr's character development and suspenseful plot, dubbing the novel "unusual and fun."

After completing *A Light in Space,* Orr once explained: "I realized that despite being science fiction, it had also been influenced by my own life and concerns at the time of writing. It was actually started the week before [a car accident in 1991 that dramatically curtailed my mobility], and was written in the two years following—I am sure that some of the issues of control versus independence in the story must have been influenced by my own disabilities and fight to regain independence."

Peeling the Onion, a novel for young adults, centers on a similar theme. In this work, seventeen year-old protagonist Anna is tragically disabled in a car accident. While learning to make physical adjustments in order to function independently, Anna must also cope with the reactions of her family and friends, recognizing the inevitable strains that are put upon these relationships. According to *Booklist* critic Frances Bradburn, the novel "is superbly crafted. The physical pain Anna feels is palpable, and the fear that the doctors aren't quite on target, insidious." Reviewing *Peeling the Onion* for *Australian Bookseller & Publisher,* Olivia Craze wrote that Orr "mixes the spicy ingredients of authentic characters and relationships with a compelling plot to produce a novel full of power and honesty, touched with humour." Anne Briggs, writing in *Magpies,* reported that in *Peeling the Onion* Orr "displays yet again her precise observation of family relationships and her flair for creating original and richly individual characters of all ages."

Orr's picture books for preschoolers and first readers include *The Tin Can Puppy,* in which Dylan, who has been told he is too young to take care of the pet he so badly wants, finds a puppy in a tin can in the dump while he is looking for wheels for his cart. Dylan takes the puppy home and hides him, and when his parents discover the puppy, Dylan is allowed to keep him. This is "a slight story," according to Joyce Banks in a review for *School Librarian,* "but told in an amusing, percipient and economical way." Similarly, Orr's *Aa-choo!,* in which Megan wakes up one morning too sick to go to daycare, presents a common problem critics felt would be appreciated by the preschool audience for whom the book is intended. When no one can take the day off of work to stay home with her, Megan goes to work with her mother, camps out under her mother's desk during an important meeting, and has a few adventures while exploring the office looking for the bathroom. "The delicate dilemma of what to do when a young child is ill and parents have to work is treated gently and humorously," stated Theo Hersh in *Canadian Review of Materials.* Although Phyllis Simon found the story "rather contrived" in her review in *Quill & Quire,* Hersh called *Aa-choo!* "a book working parents will want to share with their children."

Ark in the Park, a chapter book for young readers, focuses on Sophie, a sensitive and lonely girl who lives in a high-rise apartment building with her family. Sophie has but two wishes: she wants cousins to visit her (though she has no extended family nearby) and she wants a pet to call her own. On her seventh birthday, Sophie convinces her parents to join her on a trip to The Noahs' Ark, a wondrous pet shop with a seemingly endless variety of animals. Mr. and Mrs. Noah, the shop's owners who wish for children of their own, take Sophie under their wing, and she soon proves herself a responsible and capable helper. By story's end, Catherine Andronik noted in *Booklist,* "all the wishes have come true, if not literally, then where it counts—in the heart."

"I tend to carry an idea for a story in my head for a year or so before I start writing," Orr once commented, "the characters develop further as I redraft and the plot usually changes considerably from my first ideas. Although much of my work verges on fantasy, it has also of course been influenced by my own life. My childhood in a French village gave me the emotional background for *Ark in the Park*—like Sophie, I not only longed for the normalcy of nearby grandparents, but was lucky enough to find some. Similarly, *Yasou Nikki* was loosely based on my own first day of school, when a little girl named Jacqueline took me under her wing, taught me to speak French, and remained a close friend ever after. And *Leaving It to You,* while not drawn on any particular situation, was of course influenced by my first job as a community based occupational therapist in Albury—both by my memories of the people that I met, and of myself, as an idealistic young therapist coming to terms with life."

Orr introduces a pair of rambunctious siblings in *Mokie and Bik,* an easy reader. Fraternal twins Mokie and Bik live on a houseboat with their mother, an artist, and Ruby, their nanny, while their father is away at sea. The energetic duo, who share a colorful and unusual vocabulary all their own, find no shortage of adventures around the harbor and spend their days helping a fisherman unload his catch, learning to swim with a rope tied around their waists, and doing battle with an enormous fish. "Orr has created a memorable tale with vivid characters," Carole Phillips remarked in *School Library Journal,* and a *Kirkus Reviews* contributor stated that the author's "rollicking, fancifully worded narrative" will appeal to "easy-reader graduates and read-aloud audiences in general." *Mokie and Bik Go to Sea* chronicles the further exploits of the title characters, who enjoy a clambake with their father, find themselves adrift in their houseboat, and rescue their dog, Waggles, when he falls overboard. A critic in *Kirkus Reviews* described the work as a "rollicking nautical slice of life," and Debbie Whitbeck, writing in *School Library Journal,* commented that the tale "packs so much energy that readers will be panting when they finish."

Orr's popular story *Nim's Island,* illustrated by Kerry Millard, centers on Nim, an intelligent and resourceful girl who lives on a remote tropical island with her scientist father, Jack. When Jack sets off on a three-day trip to collect plankton, Nim stays behind with a marine iguana, a sea turtle, and a sea lion to keep her company. After her father's boat is disabled, Nim must fend for herself, and she soon faces a series of crises, including a violent storm and a volcanic eruption. Fortunately, the youngster receives sound advice from Alex Rover, a novelist who had been corresponding via e-mail with Nim's father on his solar-panel-powered computer. Critics offered praise for the fantastical narrative of *Nim's Island.* "If readers can suspend belief long enough to accept this plot, they will have a great time with this modern survival/adventure story," Whitbeck wrote, and a *Publishers Weekly* contributor similarly noted that "the tale portrays the improbable so cleverly that readers will want to believe everything about the likable Nim and her idyllic isle."

In *Nim at Sea,* a sequel, Nim stows away aboard a cruise ship to chase an evil poacher who has kidnapped her beloved sea lion, Selkie. Meanwhile, Alex, who had since moved to the island, leaves abruptly after a misunderstanding, and Jack sets out aboard a raft to track down both his daughter and his girlfriend. Nim, Jack, and Alex eventually meet again in New York City, where they attempt to disrupt the poacher's plan to illegally sell exotic animals. According to Eva Mitnick in *School Library Journal,* Nim's "upbeat, unflappable affability is convincing enough to carry her through all manner of far-fetched scenarios and coincidences," and a *Kirkus Reviews* critic remarked that the tale ends in a "comically tumultuous climax, rescue and loving reunion."

Orr's books for preschoolers and young readers share a humorous approach to the common and uncommon dilemmas faced by her young heroes. Often employing elements of fantasy or science fiction, the author is noted for blending realistic human characters and their animal or alien counterparts in a way that illuminates the hearts and minds of each. While Orr is occasionally faulted for creating slim plots or both showing and telling readers about her characters, her most successful books are ones in which critics find a solid blend of character development, swift pacing, and humorous viewpoint.

BIOGRAPHICAL AND CRITICAL SOURCES:

PERIODICALS

Australian Bookseller & Publisher, July, 1996, Olivia Craze, review of *Peeling the Onion,* p. 78.

Booklist, April 1, 1997, Frances Bradburn, review of *Peeling the Onion,* p. 1322; September 15, 2000, Catherine Andronik, review of *Ark in the Park,* p. 243; June 1, 2001, Catherine Andronik, review of *Nim's Island,* p. 1883; June 1, 2007, Carolyn Phelan, review of *Mokie and Bik,* p. 82; March 1, 2008, Thom Barthelmess, review of *Nim at Sea,* p. 68; July 1, 2008, Carolyn Phelan, review of *Mokie and Bik Go to Sea,* p. 62.

Books in Canada, February, 1995, review of *A Light in Space,* p. 50.

Canadian Review of Materials, May, 1992, Theo Hersh, review of *Aa-choo!,* p. 161.

Kirkus Reviews, May 1, 2007, review of *Mokie and Bik;* March 1, 2008, review of *Nim at Sea;* May 1, 2008, review of *Mokie and Bik Go to Sea.*

Magpies, September, 1996, Anne Briggs, review of *Magpies,* p. 38.

Publishers Weekly, March 10, 1997, review of *Peeling the Onion,* p. 67; February 19, 2001, review of *Nim's Island,* p. 91; June 18, 2007, review of *Mokie and Bik,* p. 54.

Quill & Quire, March, 1992, Phyllis Simon, review of *Aa-choo!,* p. 66; July, 1993, Sarah Ellis, review of *The Wedding* and *The Train to the City,* pp. 55-56; December, 1994, J.R. Wytenbroek, review of *A Light in Space,* pp. 33-34.

School Librarian, November, 1993, Joyce Banks, review of *The Tin Can Puppy,* p. 156.

School Library Journal, February, 1995, Anne Connor, review of *A Light in Space,* p. 100; June, 2000, Kit Vaughan, review of *Ark in the Park,* p. 123; February, 2001, Debbie Whitbeck, review of *Nim's Island,* p. 104; July, 2007, Carole Phillips, review of *Mokie and Bik,* p. 82; May, 2008, Eva Mitnick, review of *Nim at Sea,* p. 105; July, 2008, Debbie Whitbeck, review of *Mokie and Bik Go to Sea,* p. 79.

ONLINE

Wendy Orr Home Page, http://www.wendyorr.com (October 10, 2009).

Wendy Orr Web log, http://wendyorrjournal.blogspot. com (October 10, 2009).*

P

PARKER, Robert B. 1932-
(Robert Brown Parker)

PERSONAL: Born September 17, 1932, in Springfield, MA; son of Carroll Snow (a telephone company executive) and Mary Pauline Parker; married Joan Hall (an education specialist), August 26, 1956; children: David F., Daniel T. *Education:* Colby College, B.A., 1954; Boston University, M.A., 1957, Ph.D., 1971; Northeastern University, LittD, 1987. *Hobbies and other interests:* Jogging, weightlifting.

ADDRESSES: Agent—Helen Brann Agency, 94 Curtis Rd., Bridgewater, CT 06752.

CAREER: Writer. Curtiss-Wright Co., Woodridge, NJ, management trainee, 1957; Raytheon, Co., Andover, MA, technical writer, 1957-59; Prudential Insurance Co., Boston, MA, advertising writer, 1959-62; Parker-Farman Co. (advertising agency), Boston, partner, 1960-62; film consultant to Arthur D. Little, 1962-64; Boston University, lecturer in English, 1962-64; Massachusetts State College at Lowell (now University of Lowell), instructor in English, 1964-66; Massachusetts State College at Bridgewater, instructor in English, 1966-68; Northeastern University, Boston, assistant professor, 1968-74, associate professor, 1974-76, professor of English, 1976-79. Lecturer, Suffolk University, 1965-66. *Military service:* U.S. Army, 1954-56.

MEMBER: Writers Guild, Writers League of America.

AWARDS, HONORS: Edgar Allan Poe Award from Mystery Writers of America, 1976, for *Promised Land;* Grand Master Award from Mystery Writers of America, 2002; Gumshoe Award for Lifetime Achievement, 2007.

WRITINGS:

(With others) *The Personal Response to Literature,* Houghton Mifflin (Boston, MA), 1970.

(With Peter L. Sandberg) *Order and Diversity: The Craft of Prose,* John Wiley (New York, NY), 1973.

(With John R. Marsh) *Sports Illustrated Weight Training: The Athlete's Free-weight Guide,* Lippincott (Philadelphia, PA), 1974.

(With wife, Joan Parker) *Three Weeks in Spring* (nonfiction), Houghton Mifflin (Boston, MA), 1978.

Wilderness (novel), Delacorte (New York, NY), 1979.

Love and Glory (novel), Delacorte (New York, NY), 1983.

The Private Eye in Hammett and Chandler, Lord John (Northridge, CA), 1984.

Parker on Writing, Lord John (Northridge, CA), 1985.

(With Raymond Chandler) *Poodle Springs,* Putnam (New York, NY), 1989.

(With Joan Parker) *A Year at the Races,* photographs by William Strode, Viking (New York, NY), 1990.

Perchance to Dream: Robert B. Parker's Sequel to Raymond Chandler's "The Big Sleep" (novel), Putnam (New York, NY), 1991.

All Our Yesterdays (novel), Delacorte (New York, NY), 1994.

Spenser's Boston, photographs by Kasho Kumagai, Otto Penzler (New York, NY), 1994.

Boston: History in the Making, Towery Publications (Memphis, TN), 1999.

Gunman's Rhapsody (novel), Putnam (New York, NY), 2001.

Double Play (novel), Putnam (New York, NY), 2004.

Appaloosa (novel), Putnam (New York, NY), 2005.

Edenville Owls (young adult novel), Philomel Books (New York, NY), 2007.

Resolution, Putnam (New York, NY), 2008.

The Boxer and the Spy (young adult novel), Philomel (New York, NY), 2008.

The Professional, Putnam (New York, NY), 2009.

Night and Day, Putnam (New York, NY), 2009.

Chasing the Bear: A Young Spenser Novel, Philomel (New York, NY), 2009.

Brimstone, Philomel (New York, NY), 2009.

"SPENSER" DETECTIVE SERIES

The Godwulf Manuscript (also see below), Houghton Mifflin (Boston, MA), 1974.

God Save the Child (also see below), Houghton Mifflin (Boston, MA), 1974.

Mortal Stakes (also see below), Houghton Mifflin (Boston, MA), 1975, reprinted, ImPress (Pleasantville, NY), 2002.

Promised Land (also see below), Houghton Mifflin (Boston, MA), 1976.

The Judas Goat, Houghton Mifflin (Boston, MA), 1978.

Looking for Rachel Wallace, Delacorte (New York, NY), 1980.

Early Autumn, Delacorte (New York, NY), 1981.

A Savage Place, Delacorte (New York, NY), 1981.

Surrogate: A Spenser Short Story, Lord John (Northridge, CA), 1982.

Ceremony, Delacorte (New York, NY), 1982.

The Widening Gyre, Delacorte (New York, NY), 1983.

Valediction, Delacorte (New York, NY), 1984.

A Catskill Eagle, Delacorte (New York, NY), 1985.

Taming a Sea-horse, Delacorte (New York, NY), 1986.

Pale Kings and Princes, Delacorte (New York, NY), 1987.

Crimson Joy, Delacorte (New York, NY), 1988.

Playmates, Putnam (New York, NY), 1989.

The Early Spenser: Three Complete Novels (contains *The Godwulf Manuscript, God Save the Child,* and *Mortal Stakes*), Delacorte (New York, NY), 1989.

Stardust, Putnam (New York, NY), 1990.

Pastime, Putnam (New York, NY), 1991.

Double Deuce, Putnam (New York, NY), 1992.

Paper Doll, Putnam (New York, NY), 1993.

Walking Shadow, Putnam (New York, NY), 1994.

Thin Air, Putnam (New York, NY), 1995.

Three Complete Novels (contains *The Godwulf Manuscript, Mortal Stakes,* and *Promised Land*), Wings Books (New York, NY), 1995.

Chance, Putnam (New York, NY), 1996.

Small Vices, Putnam (New York, NY), 1997.

Sudden Mischief, Putnam (New York, NY), 1998.

Hush Money, Putnam (New York, NY), 1999.

Potshot, Putnam (New York, NY), 2001.

Hugger Mugger, Putnam (New York, NY), 2001.

Widow's Walk, Putnam (New York, NY), 2002.

Back Story, Putnam (New York, NY), 2003.

Bad Business, Putnam (New York, NY), 2004.

Cold Service, Putnam (New York, NY), 2005.

School Days, Putnam (New York, NY), 2005.

A Triple Shot of Spenser, Berkley (New York, NY), 2005.

Hundred-dollar Baby, Putnam (New York, NY), 2006.

Now and Then, Putnam (New York, NY), 2007.

"JESSE STONE" DETECTIVE SERIES

Night Passage, Putnam (New York, NY), 1997.

Trouble in Paradise, Putnam (New York, NY), 1998.

Death in Paradise, Putnam (New York, NY), 2001.

Stone Cold, Putnam (New York, NY), 2003.

Sea Change, Putnam (New York, NY), 2006.

High Profile, Putnam (New York, NY), 2007.

"SUNNY RANDALL" DETECTIVE SERIES

Family Honor, Putnam (New York, NY), 1999.

Perish Twice, Putnam (New York, NY), 2000.

Shrink Rap, Putnam (New York, NY), 2002.

Melancholy Baby, Putnam (New York, NY), 2004.

Blue Screen, Putnam (New York, NY), 2006.

High Profile, Putnam (New York, NY), 2006.

Spare Change, Putnam (New York, NY), 2007.

Stranger in Paradise, Putnam (New York, NY), 2008.

Author of *Robert B. Parker Blog.*

Also author, sometimes with wife Joan Parker, of scripts for television series *Spencer: For Hire, A Man Called Hawk,* and *B.L. Stryker,* and for television movies based on *Spenser: For Hire* television series for A & E television network. Contributor to *Lock Haven Review* and *Revue des langues vivantes;* contributor of restaurant reviews to *Boston* magazine, 1976.

ADAPTATIONS: The American Broadcasting Corp. (ABC) television series *Spenser: For Hire,* 1985-88, was based on Parker's works; film rights have been sold to many "Spenser" series novels; *Family Honor* was optioned for a film starring actress Helen Hunt; *Appaloosa* was adapted for film by Robert Knott and Ed Harris and released by New Line Cinema, 2008.

SIDELIGHTS: Robert B. Parker's "Spenser" novel series follows the adventures of a Boston-based private detective whose first name has never been revealed. Through more than a quarter century of detective novels, Parker's Spenser has proven to be a popular and enduring sleuth, at once hard-boiled and sensitive, equally able to make wisecracks and literary allusions. Many elements have conspired to assure Spenser's success, among them Parker's writing style, a well-conceived Boston setting, and secondary characters who are far more than ornamentation for the hero. In a *Booklist* review of *Small Vices,* Parker's twenty-fifth "Spenser" novel, Bill Ott asked: "What is it about Spenser and his pals that makes it hard to stay away for long? . . . Spenser lives in the real world and deals with it the way we imagine we would if only we knew how."

Parker's career as a novelist began only after he spent years producing ad copy and technical writing for various companies. At his wife's urging, he completed his Ph.D. and entered the teaching profession to gain more time for his own writing projects. It took two and a half years of writing in his spare time for Parker to complete his first fiction manuscript, but only three weeks for it to be accepted for publication. Parker's doctoral thesis examined the classic detective fiction of Raymond Chandler and Dashiell Hammett, and his first novel, *The Godwulf Manuscript,* presents a detective in the tradition of the fictional Philip Marlowe and Sam Spade.

Parker followed *The Godwulf Manuscript* with *God Save the Child, Mortal Stakes, Promised Land,* and several other "Spenser" novels, and the series' success soon enabled him to quit his teaching post and devote himself to writing full-time. The author has estimated that it takes him three to five months to write a "Spenser" adventure. While some critics find the resulting works thinly plotted, Parker has been widely praised for his evocative descriptions and his sharp, witty dialogue, as well as for introducing a more human, emotional tone to the hard-boiled detective genre. In a review of *Pale Kings and Princes, Washington Post Book World* contributor Jean M. White wrote that Parker "writes some of the snappiest and sauciest dialogue in the business . . . lean and taut and crisply told with moments of genuine humor and genuine poignancy."

Sybil Steinberg, noting in a review for *Publishers Weekly* that Spenser "can still punch, sleuth and wisecrack with the best of them," found Parker's prose "as clean as a seabreeze."

Parker's "Spenser" series continues to be well received, both by fans and critics. In *Cold Service,* Parker offers readers a flip of the situation that featured in *Small Vices:* Hawk is shot in the back several times while trying to protect bookie Luther Gillespie from the Ukrainian mob that has been moving up from Brooklyn to Boston. Hawk and Spenser team up to go after the mobsters responsible after the local DA's office botches the investigation. A *Kirkus Reviews* writer remarked that "the testosterone-laced attitudinizing is sharp and often compelling." Writing for the *New York Times Book Review,* Marilyn Stasio commented: "The mob war is meticulously orchestrated, and the dialogue is precision-polished like a fine tool."

In *School Days,* Spenser is hired to prove that a seventeen-year-old boy was not a participant in a local school shooting, at the behest of the boy's well-to-do grandmother. However, the boy has confessed, and a friend of his has given a statement against him. Connie Fletcher, in a review for *Booklist,* found the book to be "one of the most psychologically astute and well-choreographed entries in the entire series." A critic for *Kirkus Reviews* considered the book to be the series' "most wide-ranging, deeply felt and penetrating case in years, one that will leave you wondering why . . . violence doesn't break out at schools more often."

Hundred-dollar Baby finds Spenser revisiting April Kyle, a woman he helped more than two decades earlier when she was a runaway teenager, providing her with the unlikely shelter of a brothel, run by successful madam Patricia Utley. April now runs her own brothel in the Back Bay area, and needs help to deal with a bully intent on worming his way into her business. This particular Spenser adventure was less well received, with a *Kirkus Reviews* contributor remarking of the book: "Spenser's detective chops are less in evidence than his messiah complex."

Now and Then takes Spencer into territory where he normally does not venture: the opportunity to express his feelings about his long-term relationship with Susan. Dennis Doherty approaches the detective with a request to find proof that his wife Jordan is cheating on him. Spencer comes up with the proof in the form of an explicit audio tape and, soon, Doherty, Jordan, and the man Spencer had trailing Jordan are all dead—victims of Jordan's lover, Perry Anderson. In the process of gathering evidence to convict Anderson, Spencer discovers that Doherty had been an FBI agent and that Jordan had been passing classified information about terrorist groups to Anderson. Soon Susan is drawn into the investigation in order to lure Anderson out. *Now and Then* gives "Spenser fans," wrote a *Publishers Weekly* reviewer, "exactly what they've come to expect from the reliable Parker—no-nonsense action and plenty of romantic give-and-take." "Spencer shows a vulnerable side to his personality that endears him further to his fans," stated Harriet Klausner on *Simegen.com.* "*Now and Then* is a great entry in this long-running saga." "Reading *Now and Then* is like listening to a great jazz performer at the top of his game on stage," concluded Tom Callahan on *Bookreporter.com.* "After it's over, you feel fortunate to have been in the room. We have been lucky to be able to read Robert B. Parker for all these years."

One of Parker's most notable departures from his detective novelist predecessors is Spenser's monogamous commitment to his psychologist lover, Susan Silverman. In his *Sons of Sam Spade, The Private-eye Novel in the Seventies* David Geherin stated his belief that the Spenser character has "grown significantly, especially in the area of self-knowledge, thanks in part to the frequent confrontations between his ever-deepening relationship with Susan. Even when she is absent . . . her presence is felt. . . . Parker's handling of Spenser's relationship with Susan effectively disproves Chandler's assertion that the love story and the detective story cannot exist in the same book. Not only do they coexist in Parker's novels, the love story adds an element of tension by serving as a poignant reminder of the vast distance that separates the mean streets from the quiet ones."

Noting Parker's influence on the detective genre, Geherin has stated that "with each novel Parker has exhibited growing independence from his predecessors, confidently developing his own themes, characters, and stylistic idiom. . . . However, despite his innovative efforts, he has remained faithful to the conventions of the genre, so effectively laid down by his predecessors." Geherin concluded: "He has thus earned for himself the right to be designated *the* legitimate heir to the Hammett-Chandler-Macdonald tradition, which, thanks to the efforts of writers like Parker, shows no signs of diminishing."

Parker is so clearly the heir of Chandler in particular that in 1988 the Chandler estate asked him to complete a thirty-page manuscript Chandler left uncompleted at his death. The result is *Poodle Springs,* a novel that carries both authors' names on its title page. Parker has also penned a sequel to Chandler's classic *The Big Sleep,* called *Perchance to Dream: Robert B. Parker's Sequel to Raymond Chandler's "The Big Sleep."* In the *New York Times Book Review,* Martin Amis criticized Chandler's portion of *Poodle Springs,* citing the master's stylistic lapses and his homophobia, but Amis was even less charitable to the contributions made by Parker. *Perchance to Dream,* the critic wrote, "is a chaos of tawdry shortcuts," and the "character of Marlowe collapses" into an "affable goon."

Another departure for Parker—or a harking back to his two mainstream novels, *Wilderness* and *Love and Glory*—is *All Our Yesterdays,* which *New York Times Book Review* contributor Walter Walker felt Parker wrote from a self-conscious desire to be taken seriously by the mainstream literary world. According to Walker, *All Our Yesterdays* "embraces two countries, two families, three generations, love, war, guilt, corruption, and angst." Despite some misgivings, Walker declared the novel to be "a most satisfying reading experience" in the same sense as the Spenser novels—that is, as "entertainment." In his review for the *Times Literary Supplement* Karl Miller concluded that *All Our Yesterdays* "is expertly plotted and tersely written" and that "Spenser fans, and a fair number of professors of English, may be unable to put it down."

Parker took an infrequent side trip away from his usual Boston locale in the 2001 novel *Gunman's Rhapsody,* a retelling of the famous gunfight at the O.K. Corral in Tombstone, Arizona. The shootout involved lawman Wyatt Earp, his brothers Virgil and Morgan, and their friend Doc Holliday, pitting these men against various outlaws roaming the area. Noting that Parker's characterization of Earp is "Spenser with spurs," *Booklist* contributor Wes Lukowsky remarked that every "Spenser" novel is in actuality standard Western fare: hard-edged men, prone to violence, in conflict over their code of honor. In *Gunman's Rhapsody* the author may be working familiar ground, but "no one does it better."

Parker mines the Western vein still further with the "Spenser" novel *Potshot.* In this book, the detective and his cohorts travel west to solve the murder of a local man who dared to resist an outlaw group that had terrorized his town for years. The result is "a real treat for fans of the long-running Spenser series: a sort of class reunion in which Spenser and all his favorite fellow tough guys get together to trade quips and bang a few heads," stated Bill Ott in *Booklist*. He further described the book as "a combination parody of and homage to" the classic western *The Magnificent Seven,* and Parker acknowledged the influence.

In *Appaloosa,* Parker returns to the stand-alone western novel. The book tells the story of two lawmen in the Old West, Virgil Cole, who has recently become marshal of the mining town of Appaloosa, and Everett Hitch, his deputy and the narrator of the novel. Randall Bragg is the villain of the tale, the rancher responsible for the deaths of the previous marshal and deputy. Cole and Hitch see that Bragg is arrested and tried, but before he can be executed, gunmen break him out of jail, resulting in a classic Western chase. A reviewer for *Publishers Weekly* remarked that "Parker manages to translate his signature themes (honor among men) from the mean streets to the wild west in one of his finest books to date." In a contribution for *Kirkus Reviews,* one writer commented that "the dialogue shines with a Western drawl in this admirably plotted change of pace from Parker." Lukowsky, again reviewing for *Booklist,* praised Parker for his reliably strong dialogue and action scenes, but noted that "it's the sense of melancholy and irrevocable sacrifice that will separate this fine novel from most of the author's recent work."

Resolution reunites Everett Hitch and Virgil Cole in what proves to be a confrontation between their employer, saloon-keeper Amos Wolfson, and the community of Resolution. Although Wolfson's forces win the battle, Hitch and Cole have to confront the morality of their boss and end up uniting with the opposing gunfighters, Cato Tillson and Frank Rose, to bring him down. "Virgil, Everitt, Cato and Rose are prepared to settle things the honorable way," declared a reviewer for *Publishers Weekly.* "Parker focuses on what he does best—ritualistically clipped dialogue and manly posturing," a *Kirkus Reviews* contributor stated, "and serves up a reminder of just how much hardboiled fiction owes the Western." "If he's disposed to take much more time away from Spenser et al.," concluded Ian Chipman in *Booklist,* "here's to hoping he'll linger awhile with Cole and Hitch."

Although the characters in a "Spenser" novel do not age as living people do, their creator has allowed them to grow somewhat older during the course of the series.

In *Small Vices* Spenser is nearly killed by an assassin, and spends much of the book recovering from the incident, ruminating on mortality and morality during the course of his painful rehabilitation. In her *New York Times Book Review* contribution, Marilyn Stasio declared that the mythic Spencer "has defied mortality altogether and become like some fertility god who lowers himself into the ground each winter and comes roaring back to life each spring. I say good luck to him." In *Booklist,* Lukowsky commented on the longevity of the series in a review of the novel *Chance,* concluding: "The Spenser series has had its ups and downs over more than twenty years, but this . . . entry finds the quick-witted sleuth and company to be in remarkably good health. Wonderfully entertaining reading."

Reviewers still waxed enthusiastic at Spenser's thirtieth appearance, *Back Story,* published in 2003. Inspired by the promise of a half-dozen Krispy Kreme doughnuts, Spenser takes up the investigation of a very old case involving a murder that took place in the 1970s, during a revolutionary raid on a Boston bank. *Back Story* "showcases the strengths of the series," commented *Booklist* writer Connie Fletcher, noting the novel's "well-developed characters, a deftly constructed plot, dialogue that is witty and crisp without sounding pretentious, evocative settings, and that Parker extra, a clearly defined and beautifully executed moral code." The book's climactic chase scenes and action sequences reveal a writer at the top of his form, opined Stasio in the *New York Times Book Review;* "it doesn't get any more immediate than Spenser's nimbly choreographed shootout with three triggermen in Harvard Stadium." *Back Story* is also notable for briefly teaming Spenser with Jesse Stone, the protagonist of another detective series written by Parker.

Stone is one of two new sleuths introduced by Parker in a novel series; Stone first appears in the book *Night Passage.* Alcoholic, depressed, and recently ditched by his wife, Stone has taken a job as chief of police in a Massachusetts town after being ousted from the Los Angeles police force. He has been hired by corrupt city officials who think he will not be effective, but he soon proves them wrong, uncovering a wealth of criminal activity and setting things right at no small peril to himself. In the *New York Times Book Review,* Stasio observed: "For all the obvious non-Spenserian Qualities that determine his character—his relative youth, the drinking thing, his lousy taste in women, an absence of humor, his raw isolation and social insecurities—it is this capacity to change his life and redeem his soul that really distinguishes the appealingly flawed Jesse from Spenser." In *Booklist,* Lukowsky contended that the "Stone" series "has a great deal going for it: an empathetic, painfully flawed protagonist; an atmospheric small-town setting rife with corruption; and a whole new set of fascinating secondary characters. Parker is a true craftsman."

Stone continued to get good reactions from reviewers in books that include *Death in Paradise* and *Stone Cold.* In the former, Stone finds the body of a murdered girl near his town's softball field. He must first figure out who she is, then unravel the puzzle of why she was killed. As the mystery plays out, readers also get more insight into Stone's personal life, including an ongoing relationship with his ex-wife. The sleuth's problems are "both interesting and completely believable," wrote Craig Shufelt in *Library Journal,* citing *Death in Paradise* as "another strong effort in what is already an impressive series." A *Publishers Weekly* writer called the novel "beautifully wrought," and added: "As usual with Parker these days . . . the book's ultimate pleasure lies in the words, suffused with a tough compassion won only through years of living, presented in prose whose impeccability speaks of decades of careful writing." Reviewing *Stone Cold* for *Entertainment Weekly,* Bruce Fretts went so far as to say that while Parker was most famous for Spenser, the author's "most rewardingly complicated shamus might be Jesse Stone."

Parker continues his "Jesse Stone" series with *Sea Change,* in which the body of an unidentified woman washes up in the cove near Paradise. Stone has no clues, and to make matters more complicated, the town is filled with tourists who plan to attend the local sailboat competition. Roland Person, in a review for the *Library Journal,* noted that "Parker is a master at creating . . . crime stories that are inevitably tied to social issues of some importance." Reviewing for *Booklist,* Connie Fletcher remarked that "Parker is dead-on here when it comes to police procedure and plotting." A critic for *Kirkus Reviews* found that "Jesse's fifth case . . . is strong enough to rank near his best."

In *Stranger in Paradise,* Jesse Stone encounters one of his most intriguing opponents—Wilson Cromartie, known as "Crow," an Apache warrior and occasional hit-man. "Crow has been hired by a Florida mobster to find his runaway 14-year-old daughter who disappeared with her drunken mother," explained Tom Callahan, writing on *Bookreporter.com.* "Crow visits Jesse to convince him to stay out of his way. As with any Par-

ker book, the writing is lean, tight and brilliant." "It turns out," Callahan continued, "that Crow likes women—really likes women." This causes a problem, the *Bookreporter.com* reviewer stated, when "the Florida mobster orders Crow to kill the mother and bring him the girl. Crow refuses and turns to Jesse for help in protecting the girl." "Crow steals the show with his odd but fascinating morality," stated reviewer Harriet Klausner on *Simegen.com.* "It allows him to double cross clients as he did ten years ago, kill men in cold blood, and steal from the dead, but not to harm a woman." "The plot ricochets through a classic double standoff," Fletcher declared in her *Booklist* review, "held together by the fate of the young woman Cromartie seeks." The two men "make an appealing odd couple," concluded a *Publishers Weekly* reviewer, "as they first warily size each other up then become grudging allies."

Parker's third fictional PI was created at the request of Academy Award-winning actress Helen Hunt, who asked Parker to write a novel with a female investigator Hunt could play in a feature film. Parker obliged, and the result was *Family Honor,* a story in which the heroine, Boston resident Sunny Randall, saves a teenage runaway. *Entertainment Weekly* correspondent Clarissa Cruz described the novel as "a breezy thriller that pits a petite blonde PI against shadowy mobster bruisers and a shady suburban couple. Accompanied by her mini bull terrier and gun-toting gay sidekick, Randall tries to stay a step ahead of the underworld heavies." A *Publishers Weekly* reviewer called Sunny "a female Spenser," adding: "How to live correctly is this novel's theme, as it is in the best Spenser novels." The reviewer concluded that *Family Honor* is "a bravura performance" that "launches what promises to be a series for the ages."

Sunny continues her career in the pages of *Perish Twice,* as she sorts through her friends' and relatives' relationship problems while also trying to protect a lesbian activist from a stalker. Tony Marcus, a gangster who challenges Spenser in other books, turns up to complicate the plot, and the novel evolves into "a wholly absorbing puzzle of confused motives and whodunits that Sunny picks at as doggedly as any PI going," advised a *Publishers Weekly* writer. "With its smooth blend of mystery, action and psychological probings," the reviewer added, *Perish Twice* ranks as "yet another first-rate, though not innovative, offering from a reliable old master." *Booklist* contributor Lukowsky also recommended *Perish Twice* as "vintage Parker: heart-racing action, stiletto-sharp dialogue, menacing tough guys, and very likable narrator/protagonist, and a moving romance." Sunny's third outing, *Shrink Rap,* was heralded as Parker's "strongest mystery in years" by a *Publishers Weekly* reviewer, and Fletcher, writing in *Booklist,* described it as "an intriguing look at the psychology of manipulation combined with a knockout plot that builds to a truly creepy, hair-raising climax."

Sunny returns in *Melancholy Baby.* College student Sarah Markham suspects she was adopted and hires Sunny to determine if the couple who raised her are actually her biological parents. In a cross-over of Parker's regular cast of characters, Dr. Susan Silverman, long-time love interest of Spenser, appears as Sunny's therapist. A reviewer for *Publishers Weekly* noted: "There's little here that Parker hasn't done before, . . . but he does it so well . . . fans will tremble with delight." Fletcher, writing in *Booklist,* found the book to be "very odd, almost teasing, but riveting nonetheless," having noted that Randall seems to be very much a female equivalent of Spenser.

Sunny teams up with police chief Jesse Stone in *Blue Screen.* Sunny gets hired to protect Erin Flint, an action star whose goal is to become the first female player for the Connecticut Nutmegs major league baseball team. Then Erin's sister, a member of her entourage, is murdered, and Jesse Stone becomes involved with the investigation, as the death occurs within his jurisdiction. Working together, Jesse and Sunny discover they have more in common than law enforcement, as both are recovering from recent divorces. A reviewer for *Publishers Weekly* commented on the "witty byplay between the principals," and Wes Lukowsky, reviewing for *Booklist,* agreed, remarking that "what makes this special is the dalliance between Stone and Randall."

Spare Change involves Sunny in her father's life. A couple of decades before, Phil Randall was charged with apprehending a serial killer who left three coins by the body of his victims. Someone has begun killing again, leaving the same three coins behind. Phil Randall returns to the force as a consultant, bringing with him his daughter Sunny—and Sunny, determined to impress her father, intends to find the murderer for him. Also, according to Harriet Klausner on *Simegen.com,* "Sunny works the case as a way of avoiding personal issues, such as her inability to live with or marry a man." Parker "never fails to entertain," concluded *Booklist* contributor Lukowsky, "with humor and recurring characters whom we welcome back into our lives like old friends."

In *Edenville Owls,* Parker takes another departure from her regular series work to look at a case of abuse in post-World War II Massachusetts. Eighth-grader Bobby

Anderson is in the process of helping his scratch basketball team, the Edenville Owls, make their way to the state tournament at Boston Gardens. At the same time, he is becoming more deeply involved with his friend Joanie Gibson and is trying to solve the mystery of the man who seems to be abusing his English teacher, Miss Delaney. Together Bobbie and his teammates "unravel the secret that Miss Delaney is hiding," declared a *Publishers Weekly* contributor, "and Bobby discovers a world of suburban white supremacy and neo-Nazism." "Bobby's questions of what it means to be honorable and to feel attraction to a female friend," Gillian Engberg stated in *Booklist,* "will draw readers as much as will the exciting mystery."

Assessing the novelist's achievement as a whole, Jeff Zaleski concluded in *Publishers Weekly:* "Parker's influence on the detective novel is, arguably, nearly as great as Poe's or Conan Doyle's. . . . Parker has modernized the American private-eye novel beyond its pulp roots, bringing to it psychological realism and sociopolitical awareness."

BIOGRAPHICAL AND CRITICAL SOURCES:

BOOKS

Contemporary Popular Writers, St. James Press (Detroit, MI), 1997.

Geherin, David, *Sons of Sam Spade: The Private-eye Novel in the Seventies,* Ungar Publishing Company (New York, NY), 1980.

St. James Guide to Crime and Mystery Writers, 4th edition, St. James Press (Detroit, MI), 1996.

Tallett, Dennis, *The Spenser Companion: "The Godwulf Manuscript" to "Small Vices": A Reader's Guide,* Companion Books (San Francisco, CA), 1997.

Winks, Robin W., *Mystery and Suspense Writers: The Literature of Crime, Detection, and Espionage,* Scribner (New York, NY), 1998.

PERIODICALS

Book, May, 2001, Randy Michael Signor, review of *Potshot,* p. 74; August, 2001, Connie Fletcher, review of *Death in Paradise,* p. 2052; September-October, 2002, "The Many Faces of Robert B. Parker," p. 21.

Booklist, March 1, 1996, Wes Lukowsky, review of *Chance,* p. 1077; January 1, 1997, Bill Ott, review of *Small Vices,* p. 779; July 19, 1997, Wes

Lukowsky, review of *Night Passage,* p. 1776; August 19, 1999, Emily Melton, review of *Family Honor,* p. 1988; February 15, 2000, Bill Ott, review of *Hugger Mugger,* p. 1052; August, 2000, Wes Lukowsky, review of *Perish Twice,* p. 2075; February 15, 2001, Bill Ott, review of *Potshot,* p. 1085; March 15, 2001, Wes Lukowsky, review of *Gunman's Rhapsody,* p. 1333; January 1, 2002, Bill Ott, review of *Widow's Walk,* p. 776; July, 2002, Connie Fletcher, review of *Shrink Rap,* p. 1798; January 1, 2003, Connie Fletcher, review of *Back Story,* p. 807; September 1, 2004, Connie Fletcher, review of *Melancholy Baby,* p. 6; April 1, 2005, Wes Lukowsky, review of *Appaloosa,* p. 1325; September 1, 2005, Connie Fletcher, review of *School Days,* p. 7; November 1, 2005, Connie Fletcher, review of *Sea Change,* p. 5; May 1, 2006, Wes Lukowsky, review of *Blue Screen,* p. 38; November 15, 2006, Wes Lukowsky, review of *High Profile,* p. 7; March 15, 2007, Wes Lukowsky, review of *Spare Change,* p. 5; May 1, 2007, Gillian Engberg, review of *Edenville Owls,* p. 45; July 1, 2007, Connie Fletcher, review of *Now and Then,* p. 9; November 15, 2007, Connie Fletcher, review of *Stranger in Paradise,* p. 6; March 15, 2008, Ian Chipman, review of *Resolution,* p. 6.

Boston Herald, February 11, 2003, Rosemary Herbert, review of *Back Story,* p. 44.

Bulletin of the Center for Children's Books, July 1, 2007, Elizabeth Bush, review of *Edenville Owls.*

Entertainment Weekly, September 10, 1999, Clarissa Cruz, "Mad about 'Spenser,'" p. 146; March 31, 2000, "Mass Murder: Juggling Three Book Series, including a New Spenser Novel, Robert B. Parker Is Boston's Peerless Man of Mystery," p. 62; October 3, 2003, Bruce Fretts, review of *Stone Cold,* p. 75; October 27, 2006, Paul Katz, review of *Hundred-dollar Baby,* p. 76; June 8, 2007, Bob Cannon, review of *Spare Change,* p. 84; October 26, 2007, Bob Cannon, review of *Now and Then,* p. 71.

Horn Book, July 1, 2007, Philip Charles Crawford, review of *Edenville Owls.*

Kirkus Reviews, January 1, 2005, review of *Cold Service,* p. 16; March 15, 2005, review of *Appaloosa,* p. 310; July 15, 2005, review of *School Days,* p. 761; December 1, 2005, review of *Sea Change,* p. 1259; August 1, 2006 review of *Hundred-dollar Baby,* p. 758; December 15, 2006, review of *High Profile,* p. 1246; March 15, 2007, review of *Edenville Owls;* March 15, 2007, review of *Spare Change;* August 15, 2007, review of *Now and Then;* December 1, 2007, review of *Stranger in Paradise;* April 1, 2008, review of *The Boxer and the Spy;* April 15, 2008, review of *Resolution.*

Kliatt, March 1, 2007, Paula Rohrlick, review of *Edenville Owls,* p. 17.

Library Journal, March 15, 2000, Patsy E. Gray, review of *Hugger Mugger,* p. 128; October 1, 2001, Craig Shufelt, review of *Death in Paradise,* p. 143; August, 2002, Ronnie H. Terpening, review of *Shrink Rap,* p. 144; September 15, 2003, Fred M. Gervat, review of *Stone Cold,* p. 96; January 1, 2006, Roland Person, review of *Sea Change,* p. 80.

New York Times Book Review, January 27, 1991, Martin Amis, review of *Perchance to Dream: Robert B. Parker's Sequel to Raymond Chandler's "The Big Sleep"* p. 9; February 12, 1995, Walter Walker, review of *All Our Yesterdays,* p. 32; April 13, 1997, Marilyn Stasio, review of *Small Vices,* p. 24; September 21, 1997, Marilyn Stasio, review of *Night Passage,* p. 36; May 7, 2000, Marilyn Stasio, review of *Hugger Mugger,* p. 30; October 8, 2000, Marilyn Stasio, review of *Perish Twice,* p. 32; March 25, 2001, Marilyn Stasio, review of *Potshot,* p. 16; October 14, 2001, Marilyn Stasio, review of *Death in Paradise,* p. 26; March 17, 2002, Marilyn Stasio, review of *Widow's Walk,* p. 20; September 22, 2002, Marilyn Stasio, review of *Shrink Rap,* p. 24; March 9, 2003, Marilyn Stasio, review of *Back Story,* p. 21; October 5, 2003, Marilyn Stasio, review of *Stone Cold,* p. 20; March 13, 2005, Marilyn Stasio, review of *Cold Service,* p. 28.

Orlando Sentinel, October 29, 2006, review of *Hundred-dollar Baby.*

People, April 1, 2002, Samantha Miller, review of *Widow's Walk,* p. 43.

Plain Dealer (Cleveland, OH), October 14, 2001, Michele Ross, review of *Potshot,* p. J13.

Publishers Weekly, April 24, 1987, Sybil Steinberg, review of *Pale Kings and Princes,* p. 63; August 16, 1999, review of *Family Honor,* p. 61; November 1, 1999, review of *Family Honor,* p. 48; March 13, 2000, review of *Hugger Mugger,* p. 65; August 14, 2000, review of *Perish Twice,* p. 331; February 26, 2001, review of *Potshot,* p. 62; July 23, 2001, review of *Death in Paradise,* p. 52; October 8, 2001, Jeff Zaleski, interview with Parker, p. 46; August 19, 2002, review of *Shrink Rap,* p. 70; September 30, 2002, Daisy Maryles, "Rap Artistry," p. 18; February 10, 2003, review of *Back Story,* p. 165; September 22, 2003, review of *Stone Cold,* p. 88; August 30, 2004, review of *Melancholy Baby,* p. 35; March 28, 2005, review of *Appaloosa,* p. 53; May 22, 2006, review of *Blue Screen,* p. 33; August 14, 2006, review of *Hundred-dollar Baby,* p. 179; December 4, 2006, review of *High Profile,* p. 33; April 9, 2007, review of *Spare Change,* p. 29; April 16, 2007, review of *Edenville*

Owls, p. 52; August 20, 2007, review of *Now and Then,* p. 43; August 27, 2007, review of *Spare Change,* p. 85; December 3, 2007, review of *Stranger in Paradise,* p. 48; March 31, 2008, review of *Resolution,* p. 35.

School Library Journal, July 1, 2007, Kim Dare, review of *Edenville Owls,* p. 108.

Telegraph, February 23, 2008, "Robert B. Parker: Hard-Boiled, Old School and Y'Know, a Bit Sloppy."

Times Literary Supplement, November 25, 1994, Karl Miller, review of *All Our Yesterdays,* p. 21.

Voice of Youth Advocates, June 1, 2007, Ed Goldberg, review of *Edenville Owls,* p. 150.

Washington Post Book World, June 21, 1987, Jean M. White, review of *Pale Kings and Princes,* p. 8.

Writer's Digest, October, 2000, Kelly Nickell, "Robert B. Parker's Boston," p. 16.

ONLINE

Bookreporter.com, http://www.bookreporter.com/ (June 3, 2008), Tom Callahan, reviews of *Stranger in Paradise, High Profile, Spare Change,* and *Now and Then.*

Books and Writers, http://www.kirjasto.sci.fi/ (June 3, 2008), "Robert B(rown) Parker (1932-)."

Genre Go Round Reviews, http://genregoroundreviews. blogspot.com/ (June 3, 2008), Harriet Klausner, review of *The Boxer and the Spy.*

Mystery Ink, http://www.mysteryinkonline.com/ (June 3, 2008), Gerald So, author profile.

Robert B. Parker Official Web site, http://www. robertbparker.net (June 3, 2008).

Simegen.com, http://www.simegen.com/ (June 3, 2008), Harriet Klausner, reviews of *High Profile, Spare Change, Stranger in Paradise,* and *Now and Then.**

*   *   *

PARKER, Robert Brown
See PARKER, Robert B.

*   *   *

PATCHETT, Ann 1963-

PERSONAL: Born December 2, 1963, in Los Angeles, CA; daughter of Frank (a police captain) and Jeanne Ray (a nurse) Patchett; second marriage to Karl VanDevender (an internist). *Education:* Sarah Lawrence College, B.A., 1984; University of Iowa, M.F.A., 1987. *Politics:* "Roosevelt Democrat."

ADDRESSES: Home—Nashville, TN. *Agent*—Lisa Bankoff, International Creative Management, 40 W. 57th St., New York, NY 10019.

CAREER: Ecco Press, editorial assistant, 1984; Allegheny College, Meadville, PA, writer-in-residence, 1989-90; Murray State University, Murray, KY, visiting assistant professor, 1992; University of the South, Nashville, TN, Tennessee Williams fellow in Creative Writing, 1997.

AWARDS, HONORS: Award for fiction, Trans-Atlantic Henfield Foundation, 1984; Editor's Choice Award for Fiction, *Iowa Journal of Literary Studies,* 1986, for "For Rita, Who Is Never Alice"; Editor's Choice Award for Fiction, *Columbia,* 1987, for "The Magician's Assistant's Dream"; residential fellow of Yaddo and Millay Colony for the Arts, both 1989; James A. Michener/ Copernicus Award, University of Iowa, 1989, for work on *Patron Saint of Liars;* residential fellow, Fine Arts Work Center, Provincetown, RI, 1990-91; Mary Ingrahm Bunting fellowship, 1993; Janet Heidinger Kafka Prize for best work of fiction, 1994, for *Taft;* Tennessee Writers Award of the Year, *Nashville Banner,* and Guggenheim fellowship, both 1994, both for *The Magician's Assistant;* National Book Critics Circle Award nomination in fiction category, 2001, and PEN/ Faulkner Award finalist, and Orange Prize for fiction, both 2002, all for *Bel Canto;* Alex Award, Margaret Alexander Edwards Trust and *Booklist,* 2005, for *Truth and Beauty: A Friendship.*

WRITINGS:

Truth and Beauty: A Friendship (memoir), HarperCollins (New York, NY), 2004.

(Editor, with series editor Katrina Kenison) *The Best American Short Stories 2006,* Houghton Mifflin (Boston, MA), 2006.

What Now?, HarperCollins Publishers (New York, NY), 2008.

NOVELS

The Patron Saint of Liars, Houghton Mifflin (Boston, MA), 1992.

Taft, Houghton Mifflin (Boston, MA), 1994.

The Magician's Assistant, Harcourt (New York, NY), 1997.

Bel Canto, HarperCollins (New York, NY), 2001.

Run, HarperCollins Publishers (New York, NY), 2007.

Work represented in anthologies, including *Twenty under Thirty,* edited by Debra Spark, Scribner (New York, NY), 1987; *Twenty for the Nineties,* edited by Monica Wood, J. Weston Walch (Portland, ME), 1992; and *The Anthology of the Fine Arts Work Center,* Sheepshead Press, 1993. Contributor of stories to periodicals, including *Columbia, Seventeen, Southern Review, Paris Review, New Madrid, Epoch,* and *Iowa Review.* Contributor of nonfiction to *GQ, Outside,* and *Vogue.* Editor, *Sarah Lawrence Review,* 1983-84; fiction editor, *Shankpainter,* 1990-91.

ADAPTATIONS: The story "All Little Colored Children Should Learn to Play Harmonica" was adapted as a play; *The Patron Saint of Liars* was filmed for television by CBS, 1997.

SIDELIGHTS: Author Ann Patchett has been hailed as one of the most interesting and unconventional writers of her generation. Patchett's power as a writer seems to derive from her unusual ability to make believable the voices of a sweeping array of characters. In 1984, on her twenty-first birthday, Patchett published her first story, "All Little Colored Children Should Learn to Play Harmonica," a narrative set in the 1940s about a black family with eight children. Patchett, a white woman from Nashville, Tennessee, had actually written the story two years earlier when she was a sophomore at New York's Sarah Lawrence College. "Because I was nineteen, I had the courage and confidence to approach such subject matter with authority," she told Elizabeth Bernstein in an interview for *Publishers Weekly.* Patchett described the origins of her diverse characters as occurring in moments of fantasy. "I never thought it was strange to pick these topics," she recounted to Bernstein. "I just really believe that using your imagination is the one time in your life you can really go anywhere."

The Patron Saint of Liars, Patchett's first novel, shows such imagination. It tells the story of a young pregnant woman who flees from a dull marriage, driving across the country to find a new, different, and unexpected sense of family at St. Elizabeth's, a Roman Catholic home for unwed mothers in Kentucky. Critics pointed out that the novel may strain belief at times, in particular because it provides no contextual sense of hotly debated social issues surrounding marriage and reproduction in the Catholic Church. However, as Alice McDermott,

reviewing the novel in the *New York Times Book Review,* pointed out, Patchett's project is to write "a made up story of an enchanted place." Comparing *The Patron Saint of Liars* to a fairy tale, McDermott explained that "the world of St. Elizabeth's, and of the novel itself, . . . retains some sense of the miraculous, of a genuine, if unanticipated, power to heal."

Patchett's next novel, *Taft,* also received critical praise, though reviewers' opinions differed as to whether or not this work exceeded Patchett's achievement in *The Patron Saint of Liars. Taft* 's action centers around a Memphis blues bar called Muddy's. The black, middle-aged bartender, Nickel, who narrates the story, becomes imaginatively and practically entangled in the life of a white working-class teenager, Fay Taft, and that of her family. Focusing on their relationship, Patchett weaves a multilayered narrative about unconventional kinds of love and improvisational familial ties.

In her critically acclaimed third novel, *The Magician's Assistant,* Patchett continues to explore the themes of unorthodox love, abandonment, and transcendence and the surprising places people go to feel at home. The protagonist and title character, Sabine, has long been in love with the gay magician she assists. As the narrative opens, Parsifal, the magician, who is afflicted with AIDS, dies suddenly from a stroke. Sabine and Parsifal had entered into an unusual marriage, and upon his death, she is embraced by his family, which she had not known existed. Sabine meets her estranged in-laws, and together they try to put together the pieces of Parsifal's past. As Sabine shares her grief, she finds a hint of redemption and a way to transform herself. Veronica Chambers, reviewing *The Magician's Assistant* for *Newsweek,* called it "a '90s love story wrought with all the grace and classic charm of a 19th-century novel."

By the time her fourth novel was released, Patchett had earned a reputation for quality fiction, and that reputation was sealed with the publication of *Bel Canto.* Loosely based on a real-life 1996 hostage crisis in Lima, Peru, *Bel Canto*—an opera term that means "fine singing"—takes place in an unnamed South American country where the vice presidential palace is the setting for a birthday reception honoring a prominent businessman, the chairman of a huge Japanese electronics concern. "The poor host country was throwing a birthday party of unreasonable expense, hoping that Hosokawa might help with training, trade, a factory—something that will make it look like the nation is moving away from drug trafficking," according to *Seattle Times* contributor Valerie Ryan. One of the star guests at this party is Roxane Cross, a revered American opera soprano who has agreed to perform for her biggest fan, Hosokawa. As the lights dim following her aria, the peace is shattered by the invasion of terrorists. The electronics tycoon, the diva, the vice president and sixty dignitaries are taken hostage. "In a marvelously loopy touch," noted David Kipen in the *San Francisco Chronicle,* "the president has begged off to watch his favorite telenovela." Negotiations reach a stalemate, but inside the mansion, hostages and guerillas are oblivious to the action. Instead, as the siege stretches to four-and-a-half months, hostages and terrorists form bonds of friendship and even love inside the mansion; "pretty soon, nobody wants to kill anybody," Kipen observed. However, some characters are not destined to survive.

Thematically, *Bel Canto* is "similar to my other works in that people are thrown together by circumstance," Patchett told David Podgurski in a *Milwaukee Journal Sentinel* interview. "But I wanted to write a truly omniscient third-person narrative, a 'Russian' novel." The author continued: "I wanted all of the drama as I saw it unfold on television—it seemed so operatic—and to have all that and yet keep it within a narrative that wasn't a potboiler."

Bel Canto received positive notices from many reviewers, among them *Salon.com*'s Laura Miller. "With this scenario, you'd expect [*Bel Canto*] to be populated by the kind of romantic figures found in books and movies like *Chocolat,* cartoonish outlines that invite the reader to stop inside and fancy herself the embodiment of, say, Joyous Sensuality or the Human Spirit. Instead, the characters Patchett has created are just that, characters; they're not empty enough to 'identify' with." *Guardian* contributor Alex Clark applauded Patchett's range. "With bravura confidence and inventiveness she varies her pace to encompass both lightning flashes of brutality and terror and long stretches of incarcerated ennui," he wrote. "The novel's sensibilities extend from the sly wit of observational humor to subtle, mournful insights into the nature of yearning and desire."

What was it about the real-life crisis that inspired Patchett's interest in a fictional retelling? In an essay on the *BookPage* Web site, she recalled her absorption in the unfolding events of 1996: "Very few disasters happen in slow motion: plane crashes, school shootings, earthquakes—by the time we hear about them, they're

usually over. But the story in Lima stretched on, one month, two, three." During that time, she added, "I couldn't stop thinking about these people. There is no such thing as a good kidnapping, but I heard the hostages played chess with their captors. I heard they played soccer. There were rumors of large pizza orders." To Patchett, the story had "all elements I was interested in: the construction of family, the displacement from home, a life that was at once dangerous and completely benign."

Following the death in 2002 of Lucy Grealy, Patchett's long-time friend and author of *Autobiography of a Face,* Patchett wrote the memoir *Truth and Beauty: A Friendship.* In an interview with *Publishers Weekly* contributor Elizabeth Millard, the author explained: "I give talks about my belief in fiction and the importance of the imagination, and I always say that one thing about my novels is that . . . I'm not a character in my books and I like that." Shortly after the death of her emotionally troubled friend, however, in an attempt to deal with her grief, Patchett wrote a piece for *New York* magazine and found herself wanting to write more; *Truth and Beauty* was the result. "When I look back now," she told Millard, "I think it really was a way to sit shiva for a year, to stay on her grave and be unwilling to get up and go on with my life." The author continued, noting that "going over the good times we had together, because things ended on a very bad note, I think it really gave me all the time I needed to feel terrible and to celebrate her. I feel it would be melodramatic to say the book saved my life, but it certainly put me in a better place." Jennifer Reese described *Truth and Beauty* in *Entertainment Weekly* as a "powerful . . . portrait of a fascinating, understandably tormented woman—and of a great friendship. . . . Patchett's voice—perfectly modulated, lucid, and steady . . . makes it both true and beautiful." Donna Seaman, writing for *Booklist,* called it "dazzling in its psychological interpretations, piquant in its wit, candid in its self-portraiture, and gracefully balanced between emotion and reason."

Patchett also served as guest editor of *The Best American Short Stories 2006.* The collection features twenty short stories from a wide range of American writers, from well-known popular writers such as Tobias Wolff, Ann Beattie, and Alice Munro to lesser-known writers such as Jack Livings, Aleksandar Hemon, and Katherine Bell. "Where a short-story collection by a single author tends to repeat patterns, rhythms and themes, there's a much greater sense of serendipity and surprise here," wrote a *Kirkus Reviews* contributor. Ellen Loughran, writing in *Booklist,* noted that the author's "introduction provides a graceful entry into the main event."

Most of Patchett's next novel, *Run* takes place over a weekend. It features protagonist Bernard Doyle, a widower whose wife, Bernadette, died of cancer sixteen years earlier, and the father of three sons, two of whom are adopted. Bernard's natural son, Sullivan, dragged Bernard into a scandal that cost him his political career, but Bernard continues to practice law in Boston. His adopted black sons are twenty-year-old Teddy, a dreamer who is leaning toward the priesthood, and Tip, one year older, who is studying at Harvard with the intention of becoming an ichthyologist. They are named for Massachusetts Democrats Ted Kennedy and Tip O'Neill.

As the novel begins it is snowing, and Bernard, who would like his sons to enter politics, has invited Tip and Teddy to a Jesse Jackson lecture. The reluctant brothers purposely arrive late, but Bernard wins out, as he lied about the start time of the event, saying that it was earlier than it actually is. Tip resents his father's efforts, and following the lecture, when Bernard asks them to attend the reception, he expresses his anger, steps off a curb, and is knocked to the ground by Tennessee Alice Moser, a black woman from the poor Roxbury neighborhood. Alice is hit by the SUV that threatened to collide with Tip, and she is rushed to the hospital with serious injuries. The Doyles accompany Tennessee's eleven-year-old daughter Kenya to the hospital, then take her home with them. As the story unfolds it becomes apparent that Tennessee has been connected to the family for many years, as has Kenya for her short life.

Central to the story is a wooden statue of the Virgin Mary, a family heirloom with a dark past from Ireland. Mary so closely resembles Bernadette that placed in the boys' room, she seemed to watch over them. *New York Times Book Review* contributor Leah Hager Cohen noted that themes include: "Absent mothers who are not entirely absent; present mothers who are not what they appear to be." Cohen noted the issues introduced from the beginning of the novel, including Boston's volatile political and racial history, interracial adoption and the closeness and divides that occur within families.

Cohen commented on a number of questions she felt are not answered by Patchett, including why a healthy and intelligent black mother would give up her sons for adoption. "What does it mean when a white politician adopts black sons in a city where many black constituents live in poverty? How has their upbringing informed Tip and Teddy's sense of themselves as black men? If Patchett had exhumed her characters' motivations more thoroughly, she might have persuaded readers of the circumstances that led to such a choice. And in so doing she might have elicited deeper sympathy and interest." An *Economist* reviewer wrote: "The novel is well plotted and Ms Patchett's universally sympathetic portraiture produces engaging characters. The writing is seamlessly smooth but never ostentatious, pushing story to the fore." *Publishers Weekly* contributor Andrew O'Hagan, wrote that the book "is lovely to read and is satisfyingly bold in its attempt to say something patient and true about family." Janet Maslin, also writing in the *New York Times Book Review,* wrote that *Run* "shimmers with its author's rarefied eloquence, and with the deep resonance of her insights."

BIOGRAPHICAL AND CRITICAL SOURCES:

BOOKS

American Women Writers, 2nd edition, St. James Press (Detroit, MI), 2000.
Patchett, Ann, *Truth and Beauty: A Friendship,* Harper-Collins (New York, NY), 2004.

PERIODICALS

Atlanta Journal-Constitution, August 26, 2001, Greg Changnon, review of *Bel Canto.*
Atlantic Monthly, November, 2007, review of *Run,* p. 154.
Booklist, June 12, 2001, Gilbert Taylor, review of *Bel Canto,* p. 1848; March 1, 2004, Donna Seaman, review of *Truth and Beauty: A Friendship,* p. 1098; April 1, 2005, Gillian Engberg, "The Alex Awards, 2005," p. 1355; October 15, 2006, Ellen Loughran, review of *The Best American Short Stories 2006,* p. 27.
Christian Science Monitor, October 9, 2007, Yvonne Zipp, review of *Run,* p. 13.
Daily News (Los Angeles, CA), July 29, 2001, David Kronke, "Singing Her Praises," p. L16.
Denver Post, June 10, 2001, Glenn Giffin, "Hostage Crisis a Study in Group Dynamics," p. L8.
Economist, September 15, 2007, review of *Run,* p. 103.

Entertainment Weekly, July 31, 1992, Annabel Davis-Goff, review of *The Patron Saint of Liars,* p. 57; October 10, 1997, p. 87; May 21, 2004, Jennifer Reese, review of *Truth and Beauty,* p. 82; September 28, 2007, Jennifer Reese, review of *Run,* p. 111.

Fort Worth Star-Telegram, June 30, 2004, Deborah King, review of *Truth and Beauty;* October 3, 2007, review of *Run.*

Gazette (Cedar Rapids, IA), February 10, 2008, Jessica Musil, review of *Run.*

Houston Chronicle, October 7, 2007, Nora Seton, review of *Run,* p. 22.

Kirkus Reviews, March 1, 2004, review of *Truth and Beauty,* p. 214; April 15, 2005, "Best Books for Reading Groups: Featuring Twenty-Five Titles Ideal for Discussion & Debate," p. S1; August 15, 2006, review of *The Best American Short Stories 2006,* p. 805; August 15, 2007, review of *Run.*

Lancet, January 1, 2005, Andy Brown, review of *Truth and Beauty,* p. 20.

Library Journal, August, 1997, Kimberly G. Allen, review of *The Magician's Assistant,* p. 134; May 15, 2004, Pam Kingsbury, review of *Truth and Beauty,* p. 85; July 1, 2007, Sarah Conrad Weisman, review of *Run,* p. 84.

Marie Claire, October, 2007, review of *Run,* p. 73.

Milwaukee Journal Sentinel, June 20, 2001, David Podgurski, "Novel Unfolds with the Expansiveness and Drama of Opera" (interview), p. 4; October 3, 2007, Whitney Gould, review of *Run.*

Newsweek, October 13, 1997, Veronica Chambers, review of *The Magician's Assistant,* p. 78; October 15, 2007, Barbara Kantrowitz, review of *Run,* p. 83.

New York Times, May 31, 2001, Janet Maslin, review of *Bel Canto,* p. E7; June 10, 2001, James Polk, review of *Bel Canto,* p. 37; May 13, 2004, Janet Maslin, review of *Truth and Beauty,* p. E7.

New York Times Book Review, July 26, 1992, Alice McDermott, review of *The Patron Saint of Liars,* p. 6; October 16, 1994, Diana Postlethwaite, review of *Taft,* p. 11; November 16, 1997, Suzanne Berne, review of *The Magician's Assistant,* p. 17; October 18, 1998, review of *The Magician's Assistant,* p. 36; September 20, 2007, Janet Maslin, review of *Run;* September 30, 2007, Leah Hager Cohen, review of *Run,* p. 7.

Observer (London, England), June 14, 1998, review of *The Magician's Assistant,* p. 18.

People, May 31, 2004, Laura Italiano, review of *Truth and Beauty,* p. 53; October 1, 2007, Sue Corbett, review of *Run,* p. 59.

Publishers Weekly, July 18, 1994, review of *Taft,* p. 233; July 14, 1997, review of *The Magician's Assistant,* p. 62; October 13, 1997, Elizabeth Bernstein, interview with Patchett, pp. 52-53; April 16, 2001, review of *Bel Canto,* p. 42; March 29, 2004, review of *Truth and Beauty,* p. 47, and Elizabeth Millard, review of *Truth and Beauty,* p. 148; July 16, 2007, Andrew O'Hagan, review of *Run,* p. 143.

San Francisco Chronicle, June 13, 2001, David Kipen, "Hostage Novel Ropes You In," review of *Bel Canto,* p. E1.

School Library Journal, September, 2004, Francisca Goldsmith, review of *Truth and Beauty,* p. 236.

Seattle Times, June 24, 2001, Valerie Ryan, review of *Bel Canto,* p. J10.

Star Telegram (Fort Worth, TX), October 3, 2007, Catherine Mallette, review of *Run.*

Star Tribune (Minneapolis, MN), October 7, 2007, "Setting Her Own Pace," interview, p. 1F.

Times Literary Supplement, February 6, 1998, review of *The Magician's Assistant,* p. 21; July 9, 1999, review of *Taft,* p. 21.

USA Today, September 27, 2007, Jocelyn McClurg, review of *Run,* p. 5; April 17, 2008, Carol Memmott, "5 Questions for Ann Patchett," interview, p. 6.

Washington Post Book World, January 18, 1998, review of *The Magician's Assistant,* p. 4.

Women's Review of Books, October, 2004, Mary Cappello, review of *Truth and Beauty,* p. 4.

WWD, September 25, 2007, Vanessa Lawrence, review of *Run,* p. 16.

ONLINE

Ann Patchett Home Page, http://www.annpatchett.com (July 6, 2008).

Blackbird, http://www.blackbird.vcu.edu/ (June 6, 2007), "An Interview with Elizabeth McCracken and Ann Patchett."

Blog Critics, http://blogcritics.com/ (September 25, 2007), Ted Gioia, review of *Run.*

BookBrowse.com, http://www.bookbrowse.com/ (August 11, 2004), "A Conversation with Ann Patchett."

BookPage, http://www.bookpage.com/ (August 11, 2004), Ann Patchett, "Turning a News Story into a Novel"; Laurie Parker, review of *The Magician's Assistant.*

Bookreporter.com, http://www.bookreporter.com/ (August 11, 2004), "On the Road with Ann Patchett, Week 1."

Guardian Unlimited, http://books.guardian.co.uk/ (August 11, 2004), Alex Clark, "Danger Arias."

Salon.com, http://www.salon.com/ (August 11, 2004), Laura Miller, "*Bel Canto* by Ann Patchett."*

*   *   *

PHILLIPS, Jayne Anne 1952-

PERSONAL: Born July 19, 1952, in Buckhannon, WV; daughter of Russell R. (a contractor) and Martha Jane (a teacher) Phillips; married; children: one son, two stepsons. *Education:* West Virginia University, B.A. (magna cum laude), 1974; University of Iowa, M.F.A., 1978.

ADDRESSES: Office—Department of English, Rutgers University, Newark Campus, Newark, NJ 07102-1801. *Agent*—Lynn Nesbit, Janklow & Nesbit, 445 Park Ave., 13th Fl., New York, NY 10022-2606. *E-mail*—ja shelter@aol.com; japhillips@andromeda.rutgers.edu.

CAREER: Writer, educator. Boston University, Boston, MA, adjunct associate professor of English, beginning 1982; Brandeis University, Waltham, MA, Fanny Howe Chair of Letters, 1986-87; Rutgers University, Newark, NJ, professor of English and director of program for M.F.A. in creative writing. Formerly taught at Harvard University, Humboldt State University, New York University, and Williams College; speaker at writers conferences throughout the United States.

MEMBER: Authors Guild, Authors League of America, PEN.

AWARDS, HONORS: Pushcart Prize, Pushcart Press, 1977, for *Sweethearts,* 1979, for short stories "Home" and "Lechery," and 1983, for short story "How Mickey Made It"; Fels Award in fiction, Coordinating Council of Literary Magazines, 1978, for *Sweethearts;* National Endowment for the Arts fellowships, 1978 and 1985; St. Lawrence Award for fiction, 1979, for *Counting;* Sue Kaufman Award for first fiction, American Academy and Institute of Arts and Letters, 1980, for *Black Tickets;* O. Henry Award, Doubleday and Co., 1980, for short story "Snow"; Bunting Institute fellowship, Radcliffe College, 1981; *New York Times* "best books" citation, 1984, and nomination for National Book Critics Circle

Award, both for *Machine Dreams;* Guggenheim fellowship, 1988; Academy Award in Literature, American Academy of Arts and Letters, 1997, for *Shelter.*

WRITINGS:

FICTION

Sweethearts (short stories), Truck Press (Carrboro, NC), 1976.

Counting, Vehicle Editions (New York, NY), 1978.

Black Tickets (short stories), Delacorte (New York, NY), 1979, Vintage Contemporaries (New York, NY), 2001.

How Mickey Made It (chapbook), Bookslinger (St. Paul, MN), 1981.

The Secret Country, Palaemon Press (Winston-Salem, NC), 1983.

Machine Dreams (novel), Dutton (New York, NY), 1984, Vintage Books (New York, NY), 1999.

Fast Lanes (short stories), Vehicle Editions (New York, NY), 1984.

Shelter (novel), Houghton Mifflin (Boston, MA), 1994.

MotherKind (novel), Knopf (New York, NY), 2000.

Lark and Termite (novel), Knopf (New York, NY), 2009.

OTHER

(Essayist) Jock Sturges, *The Last Day of Summer: Photographs,* Aperture (New York, NY), 1991.

Work represented in anthologies, including *Best American Short Stories,* 1979; *The O. Henry Awards,* 1980; *The Pushcart Prize Anthology,* Volumes 1, 2, 4; *Norton Anthology of Short Fiction,* 1999; and *Why I Write,* 1999. Contributor of short stories to magazines, including *Atlantic Monthly, Canto, Doubletake, Epoch, Esquire, Fiction, Granta, Grand Street, Harper's,* and *Rolling Stone.*

Recordings include *Jayne Anne Phillips Interview with Kay Bonetti,* American Audio Prose Library (Columbia, MO), 1991, and *Jayne Anne Phillips Reads Souvenir and Machine Dreams,* American Audio Prose Library, 1991.

Phillips's works have been translated into more than a dozen languages.

SIDELIGHTS: Jayne Anne Phillips "stepped out of the ranks of her generation as one of its most gifted writers," wrote Michiko Kakutani in the *New York Times.* "Her quick, piercing tales of love and loss [demonstrate] a keen love of language, and a rare talent of illuminating the secret core of ordinary lives with clearsighted unsentimentality," Kakutani continued.

The short stories in *Black Tickets,* Phillips's first collection for a commercial press, reportedly fall into three basic categories: very short stories, interior monologues by damaged misfits from the fringes of society, and longer stories about family life. In these stories, noted Michael Adams in the *Dictionary of Literary Biography Yearbook: 1980,* "Phillips explores the banality of horror and the horror of the banal through her examination of sex, violence, innocence, loneliness, illness, madness, various forms of love and lovelessness," and lack of communication. These stories were drawn, according to an article by James N. Baker in *Newsweek,* "from observations she made in her rootless days on the road," in the mid-1970s when she wandered from West Virginia to California and back again, "then developed in her imagination."

"Most of the stories in *Black Tickets,*" reported Thomas R. Edwards in the *New York Review of Books,* "examine the lives of people who are desperately poor, morally deadened, in some way denied comfort, beauty, and love." Stories of this genre in the collection include "Gemcrack," the monologue of a murderer driven by a voice in his head that he calls "Uncle," and "Lechery," the story of a disturbed teenage girl who propositions adolescents. These are "brittle episodes of despair, violence and sex," wrote *Harper's* reviewer Jeffrey Burke.

Other stories focus on less unique individuals. They are about "more or less ordinary people, in families, who are trying to love each other across a gap," according to Edwards. Stories such as "Home," "The Heavenly Animal," and "Souvenir" all deal with the problems of grownup children and their aging parents: a young woman's return home forces her divorced mother to come to terms with both her daughter's and her own sexuality; a father attempts to share his life—Catholic senior citizens meals, car repairs—with his daughter and fails; a mother slowly dying of cancer still has the courage to comfort her daughter. In them, Edwards stated: "Phillips wonderfully captures the tones and gestures in which familial love unexpectedly persists even after altered circumstances have made [that love] impossible to express directly."

While some reviewers—like Carol Rumens in the *Times Literary Supplement,* who called the dramatic monologues in *Black Tickets* "dazzling"—enjoyed Phillips's richly sensuous language, others commented that the author's best work is found in the more narrative stories concerning the sense of alienation felt by young people returning home. Stone called these stories "the most direct and honest of the longer works in the collection" and stated that "the language in these stories serves character and plot rather than the other way around." "The strength in these stories," wrote Mary Peterson in the *North American Review,* "is that even narrative gives way to necessity: honesty gets more time than forced technique; language is simple and essential, not flashy; and even the hard truth, the cruel one, gets telling."

Machine Dreams, Phillips's fifth book, was her first novel. According to John Irving, writing in the *New York Times Book Review,* the novel is the prose format in which Phillips excels. He observed that Phillips is at her best "when she sustains a narrative, manipulates a plot, and develops characters through more than one phase of their lives or behaviors." In *Machine Dreams,* the author uses the family in much the same way she has in some of the stories in *Black Tickets.* The sprawling novel tells the story of the Hampson family—Mitch, Jean, their daughter Danner and son Billy—focusing on the years between World War II and the Vietnam War, although it does show glimpses of an earlier, quieter time in Jean's and Mitch's reminiscences. It is the story of the family's collapse, told from the viewpoints of each family member.

In a larger sense, however, *Machine Dreams* is about disorientation in modern life. Mitch and Jean were raised in the days of the Depression, hard times, "but characterized by community, stability and even optimism. You could tell the good guys from the bad ones in the war Mitch fought," wrote Jonathan Yardley in the *Washington Post Book World. Machine Dreams* is, he concluded, "a story of possibility gradually turning into disappointment and disillusion," in which the Hampson family's dissolution mirrors "the simultaneous dissolution of the nation." Toronto *Globe and Mail* contributor Catherine Bush pointed out that the machine dreams of the title is "the belief in technology as perpetual onward-and-upward progress; the car as quintessential symbol of prosperity; the glamour of flight . . . become nightmares. Literally, the dream comes crashing down when Billy leaps out of a flaming helicopter in Vietnam." Bush noted that the Vietnam conflict itself, however, is not the cause of the dissolution; appropriately, she observed, Phillips "embeds the war in a larger process of breakdown." Part of this tragedy lies in the inability of the characters to understand or control what is happening to them. "This fundamental inexplicability to things," stated Nicholas Spice in the *London Review of Books,* "is compounded for Phillips's characters by their uncertainty about what it is exactly that needs explaining. Emerson's dictum 'Dream delivers us to dream, and there is no end to illusion' might aptly stand as the motto of the book."

Several reviewers acknowledged the strength and power of Phillips's prose in *Machine Dreams.* Phillips also rises to the technical challenge of using more than one point of view. John Skow observed in *Time* magazine that Phillips "expresses herself in all four [character] voices with clarity and grace." Geoffrey Stokes wrote in the *Voice Literary Supplement:* "That *Machine Dreams* would be among the year's best written novels was easy to predict," and Yardley called the novel "an elegiac, wistful, rueful book."

Like *Machine Dreams,* Phillips's next work—another collection of short stories—concerns itself with discontinuity and isolation from the past. *Fast Lanes* begins with "stories of youthful drift and confusion and gradually moves, with increasing authority, into the past and what we might call home," commented Jay McInerney in the *New York Times Book Review.* Many of the characters "are joined more by circumstances than by relationships;" they "lack purpose and authority," commented Pico Iyer in *Time.* "Their world is fluid, but they do not quite go under. They simply float."

In some reviewers' opinions, *Fast Lanes* suffers in comparison with *Machine Dreams.* David Remnick, writing for *Washington Post Book World,* found that the last two stories in the book—the ones most reminiscent of the novel—are "such strong stories that they erase any disappointment one might have felt in the other five. They are among the best work of one of our most fascinating and gritty writers, and there can be little disappointment in that." Chicago *Tribune Books* contributor Alan Cheuse similarly noted that in these stories "you can see [Phillips's] talent grow and flex its muscles and open its throat to reach notes in practice that few of us get to hit when trying our hardest at the height of our powers."

Some of Phillips's best writing, commented Marianne Wiggins in the *Times Literary Supplement,* concerns "the near-distant, fugitive past—life in the great USA

fifteen years ago," reflecting the unsettled aura of that period in American life. In some ways Phillips's writing returns to themes first expounded by the poets and novelists of the Beat generation. *Los Angeles Times Book Review* contributor Richard Eder called *Fast Lanes* "the closing of a cycle that began over three decades ago with Kerouac's *On the Road,*" the novel about the journey of the post-World War II generation in search of the ultimate experience. "It is the return trip," Eder concluded, "and Phillips gives it a full measure of pain, laced with tenderness." McInerney echoed this assessment, calling Phillips "a feminized Kerouac."

Unlike her expansive *Machine Dreams,* Phillips's second novel is "a tighter, smaller book, limited to a few voices and a few days; but what it lacks in scope, it gains in intensity," according to Andrew Delbanco, writing in the *New Republic.* In this novel Phillips once again examines human loss, this time the loss of childhood innocence. Set in 1963 in a West Virginia summer camp for girls, *Shelter,* like Phillips's earlier fiction, renders a full range of voices. As Delbanco noted, Phillips "writes in the idiom of the trailer-park Mama as comfortably as in that of the bookish dreamer." He added: "In *Shelter,* where each chapter amounts to an interior monologue belonging to a different consciousness, [Phillips's] virtuosity is on full display. The result is a novel that has the quality of an extended eavesdrop."

Shelter tells the connected stories of four of the campers—fifteen-year-old Lenny Swenson, her eleven-year-old sister Alma, Lenny's friend Cap Briarley, and Alma's friend Delia Campbell—as well as those of Buddy, the eight-year-old son of the camp's cook, and Carmody, his (ex-)convict stepfather. However, as Gail Caldwell stated in the *Boston Globe,* "it is Parson, a holy madman living on the fringes of the camp, who is Phillips's great creation." Parson has come to the camp ostensibly to lay pipe with a road crew, but actually in pursuit of Carmody, who he met in prison. "I wanted to think about evil," Phillips told Delbanco in explaining her motivation for writing *Shelter,* "about whether evil really exists or if it is just a function of damage, the fact that when people are damaged, they damage others."

The children in *Shelter,* Deb Schwartz explained in the *Nation,* are "confused, lonely, struggling to temper a barrage of information and emotions with only the crudest of skills. They are slightly grotesque, clumsily chasing their half-formed desires and attempting to outrun their fears." The four young girls have more than summer camp in common: Lenny and Alma's mother was in the midst of a love affair with Delia's father at the time he committed suicide. "Phillips," Schwartz wrote, "goes straight and true into their hearts and illuminates how children make sense of what they can."

Kakutani also noted Phillips's characterization: "In delineating the girls' relationships to one another and to their families, Ms. Phillips manages to conjure up the humid realm of adolescence: its inchoate yearnings, its alternately languid and hectic moods of expectation." Kakutani pointed out, too, the skillful way in which child molestation and incest are alluded to and "covered over with layers of emotional embroidery that transform the event even while setting it down in memory."

Though most reviews contained favorable responses to *Shelter,* R.Z. Sheppard found fault in a review for *Time.* Describing the novel as "overwritten and trendy," Sheppard noted that its treatment of sexual abuse will undoubtedly prove "a hot selling point." In contrast, though, Ann Hulbert wrote in the *New York Times Book Review:* "To be sure, Ms. Phillips plays skillfully with the rich metaphoric implications of violated children—the religious overtones of creatures being cast out, the mythic dimensions of generational rivalry and decay." Hulbert concluded that Phillips is "an astute chronicler of American preoccupations."

In her novel *MotherKind,* the author returns briefly to the Appalachian sites of *Machine Dreams* and *Shelter,* but places most of the action in the Boston suburbs where Kate, the protagonist of the story, now makes her home. Kate was born in West Virginia, and returns there to tell her mother, ill with cancer, that she is pregnant; her mother, whose death is expected within the year, agrees to move in with Kate in Boston. Katherine, Kate's mother, sacrifices all in order to be able to meet her new grandchild, and to live her last days close to a daughter with whom she has an extremely strong bond.

The novel, told from a third-person omniscient viewpoint that allows readers to hear the thoughts of all the major characters, dwells mostly on Kate's experience of new motherhood, and with her mother's decline into death. At the same time Kate celebrates this new life with her whole being, she must bear witness to her beloved mother's weakening state. But a new baby and a dying mother aren't Kate's only challenges: her son's father is also the father of two boys from a marriage he

is still trying to dissolve, and the older boys are not eager to join a reconstituted family with a new "mom" and half-brother. Kate must find a way to make a connection with these boys that doesn't threaten their tie to their own mother, or their burgeoning sense of identity and independence.

The title of the book comes from the agency Kate calls to help her care for her mother toward the end. On her Web site, Phillips herself described the relationship between the title and the novel in these words: "'MotherKind' is a term that refers to the human family women enter when they become mothers—a term that should be common usage. They enter a territory that is the other side of childhood and move from being someone's daughter, someone's lover, into the sudden fruition of passion and attachment that is labor, birth, and caring for an infant. . . . In *MotherKind,* birth and death happen as concurrent transformations, and the amazing strength of that relationship courses through and beyond both."

Critics' reactions to *MotherKind* were mixed. While a *Publishers Weekly* reviewer called the novel Phillips's "best so far," describing it as a "deeply felt, profoundly affecting" work, Eder in the *New York Times* complained that "there are many pages that the writing fails to bring to life." Like Eder, Michiko Kakutani, who also reviewed the book for the *New York Times,* compared the writing unfavorably to the domestic evocations of John Updike and Anne Tyler, stating that "the mundane routines of daily life do not fully engage her imagination." While the reviews of both Eder and Kakutani were lengthy and respectful of Phillips's gifts as a writer, both expressed disappointment in *MotherKind.* Other reviewers, however, found much to appreciate in the novel. *Chicago Tribune* reviewer Cheuse likened the novel to a Mary Cassatt portrait of mother and child, "beautifully composed and emotionally wrenching." "Even the most commonplace care . . . becomes lyrical—but never, never sentimental—in the enlivening embrace of Phillips's wonderful prose," he added. In *Booklist* Brad Hooper observed: "The story brims with vivid details of day-to-day family life, revealed largely through dialogue, which Phillips unerringly captures with consummate authenticity," an opinion that was also voiced by Judy Goldman in the *Washington Post Book World:* "Her latest novel is further proof of an extraordinary ability to reflect the texture of real life." In a review for the *Knight-Ridder/Tribune News Service* Marta Salij concluded: "Too few books touch on the ferocity of women's lives, the intense will it takes to shepherd births and deaths without shrinking. *Mother-Kind* is the rare one that tells that truth." *MotherKind* is "both technically impressive and deeply moving," asserted a *Sunday Telegraph* reviewer, who added that the novel "deserves to be widely read by both men and women."

In reviewing *Lark and Termite,* Kakutani wrote: "Jayne Anne Phillips's intricate, deeply felt new novel reverberates with echoes of Faulkner, Woolf, Kerouac, McCullers and Michael Herr's war reporting, and yet it fuses all these wildly disparate influences into something incandescent and utterly original."

The story moves back and forth through time, told by several narrators, the first, a young soldier named Robert Leavitt. Leavitt left his West Virginia town in peacetime, and he is now one of the first to serve in the Korean War. It is July of 1950, and as he is surrounded by friendly fire and dreaming of Lola, his pregnant wife, who is at that moment in labor. Writing in the *New York Times Book Review,* Kathryn Harrison wrote: "Most of Leavitt's sections are narrated from the shelter of a dark tunnel under a railway bridge, which becomes a birth canal as well as a tomb: Leavitt's 'spine opens like a star. He can feel Lola split apart, the baby fighting her, tearing his way.'" Through Robert, Phillips returns to a war that is often forgotten, and closely monitors Robert and the horrors of that war. The soldier rises in rank as those around him die, as does Robert while his son Termite is born.

The boy, severely disabled by hydrocephaly, is frail and nearly blind. At the age of nine, he can neither walk nor speak properly. He sometimes mimics the words of others. Lola has died, and Termite and his half-sister Lark are being cared for by their aunt Nonie. Lola knew Termite was extraordinary. Kathryn Harrison noted in the *New York Times Book Review:* "Phillips slips many hints of Termite's divinity into the narrative: the incorruptible sweetness of his nature; the distinctive insight granted by his acute hearing; the ability to summon generosity from almost everyone around him; the otherworldly pallor and light, curly hair that make him look angelic; the fair-haired gentleman with an 'almost luminous' face who provides assistance and appears 'related' to the boy, but whom no one else but Lark can see." Termite has acutely sensitive hearing, and he derives great joy from such things as the sound of a train clattering over its tracks. Sound had been important to Leavitt, a musician, and Termite can hear the gunfire

that surrounded his father through the sounds of the train. Leavitt died trying to save a Korean boy and his sister, and very much like Termite, the boy, who Phillips describes as insectlike, has cataracts and cannot see. "Jayne Anne Phillips renders what is realistically impossible with such authority that the reader never questions its truth," wrote Harrison.

Lark is eight years older than Termite, to whom she is devoted. She doesn't remember Lola and doesn't know that her father is actually Charlie, who owns the restaurant where Nonie works. Nonie and Charlie had been lovers, but he and Lola had also had a relationship. Lola gave Lark to Nonie when the girl was three. Nonie and Charlie resumed their relationship, but they never married. It was as a nightclub singer that Lola met Leavitt.

Sexually awakened Lark is dating motorcycle-riding Solly, the middle son of their neighbor Nick Tucci. Hoping to provide a life for Termite and herself, Lark she takes classes in secretarial skills. Nonie, who works tirelessly, relies on Lark to provide much of Termite's care. She continually fights representatives from "Social Services," who try to remove Termite from the home, and finally a sympathetic social worker, Robert Stamble, brings the boy a special child-size wheelchair. Stamble, a gentle albino, seems to understand the child and what can be done for him.

January reviewer Diane Leach wrote: "Weather is another character in the book: the July heat is its own stifling presence, one Lark and Termite actively escape, drawing in the cellar, hanging out in Charlie's air conditioned diner. Charlie adores the children; he has built a special seat at the counter for Termite, and prepares him ground-up foods that are easily swallowed." Termite enjoys being pulled in his wagon by Lark, who insists that he can understand more than he is given credit for. He has a small porcelain moon that he rubs in contentment for hours at a time and enjoys watching the blurred movement of a piece of blue plastic bag blowing in the wind. Termite's acute hearing enables him to hear the feral cat that is his constant companion, the rustling of grass, and the sounds between radio stations, and when a massive storm of biblical proportions approaches, he is able to hear the rising floodwaters. Although he cannot speak, he is capable of a form of communication that Lark and Nonie can interpret. Writing for the *Chicago Tribune,* Julia Keller commented that Phillips's "work is never still, rarely satisfied. Her words may seem quiet and docile on the page, but if you look a little closer, you'll realize that the story is actually jumping around in a frantic, fretful state, as restless as guilt. She has done in *Lark and Termite* what she did in previous novels . . . which is to take a relatively simple, straightforward tale and twist it into something luminous and haunting and singular." Kakutani concluded her review by writing that the characters of *Lark and Termite* "are so indelible, so intimately drawn, that they threaten to move in and take up permanent residence in the reader's mind."

BIOGRAPHICAL AND CRITICAL SOURCES:

BOOKS

Contemporary Literary Criticism, Gale (Detroit, MI), Volume 15, 1980, Volume 33, 1985.

Dictionary of Literary Biography Yearbook: 1980, Gale (Detroit, MI), 1981.

Robertson, Sarah, *The Secret Country: Decoding Jayne Anne Phillips's Cryptic Fiction,* Rodopi (New York, NY), 2007.

Short Story Criticism, Volume 16, Gale (Detroit, MI), 1994.

PERIODICALS

Booklist, April 5, 2000, Brad Hooper, review of *MotherKind,* p. 1525; October 15, 2008, Brad Hooper, review of *Lark and Termite,* p. 5.

Boston Globe, September 4, 1994, Gail Caldwell, review of *Shelter,* p. A12.

Chicago Tribune, May 14, 2000, Alan Cheuse, review of *MotherKind;* January 14, 2009, Julia Keller, review of *Lark and Termite.*

Christian Science Monitor, January 14, 2009, Yvonne Zip, review of *Lark and Termite,* p. 25.

Entertainment Weekly, January 16, 2009, Lisa Schwarzbaum, review of *Lark and Termite,* p. 71.

Globe and Mail (Toronto, Ontario, Canada), July 28, 1984, Catherine Bush, review of *Machine Dreams.*

Harper's, September, 1979, Jeffrey Burke, review of *Black Tickets.*

Kirkus Reviews, October 15, 2008, review of *Lark and Termite.*

Knight-Ridder/Tribune News Service, May 24, 2000, Marta Salij, review of *MotherKind.*

Library Journal, December 1, 2008, Starr E. Smith, review of *Lark and Termite,* p. 118.

London Review of Books, February 7, 1985, Nicholas Spice, review of *Machine Dreams,* p. 20.

Los Angeles Times Book Review, April 19, 1987, Richard Eder, review of *Fast Lanes,* p. 3.

Nation, November 14, 1994, Deb Schwartz, review of *Shelter,* pp. 585-588.

New Republic, December 26, 1994, Andrew Delbanco, review of *Shelter,* pp. 39-40.

New Statesman and Society, October 9, 2000, Justine Ettler, review of *MotherKind.*

Newsweek, October 22, 1979, James N. Baker, review of *Black Tickets.*

New Yorker, February 2, 2009, review of *Lark and Termite,* p. 67.

New York Review of Books, March 6, 1980, Thomas R. Edwards, review of *Black Tickets.*

New York Times, August 30, 1994, Michiko Kakutani, review of *Shelter,* p. C19; May 12, 2000, Michiko Kakutani, review of *MotherKind;* May 28, 2000, Richard Eder, review of *MotherKind;* January 6, 2009, Michiko Kakutani, review of *Lark and Termite,* p. C1.

New York Times Book Review, July 1, 1984, John Irving, review of *Machine Dreams;* May 3, 1987, Jay McInerney, review of *Fast Lanes,* p. 7; September 18, 1994, Ann Hulbert, review of *Shelter,* p. 7; January 18, 2009, Kathryn Harrison, review of *Lark and Termite,* p. 17.

North American Review, winter, 1979, Mary Peterson, review of *Black Tickets.*

Publishers Weekly, March 20, 2000, review of *MotherKind,* p. 72; October 27, 2008, review of *Lark and Termite,* p. 30.

Seattle Times, January 9, 2009, Wingate Packard, review of *Lark and Termite,* p. B9.

Sunday Telegraph (London, England), October 1, 2000, review of *Motherkind.*

Time, July 16, 1984, John Skow, review of *Machine Dreams;* June 1, 1987, Pico Iyer, review of *Fast Lanes,* p. 70; September 19, 1994, R.Z. Sheppard, review of *Shelter,* p. 82; May 15, 2000, Paul Gray, review of *MotherKind,* p. 84.

Times Literary Supplement, November 14, 1980, Carol Rumens, review of *Black Tickets;* September 11, 1987, Marianne Wiggins, review of *Fast Lanes,* p. 978.

Tribune Books (Chicago, IL), April 19, 1987, Alan Cheuse, review of *Fast Lanes,* p. 6.

USA Today, March 19, 2009, Olivia Barker, review of *Lark and Termite,* p. 5D.

Voice Literary Supplement, June, 1984, Geoffrey Stokes, review of *Machine Dreams.*

Washington Post Book World, June 24, 1984, Jonathan Yardley, review of *Machine Dreams;* April 26, 1987, David Remnick, review of *Fast Lanes;* May 14, 2000, Judy Goldman, review of *MotherKind.*

ONLINE

Independent Online (London, England), http://www.independent.co.uk/ (May 17, 2009), Lesley McDowell, review of *Lark and Termite.*

January, http://www.januarymagazine.com/ (June 18, 2009), Diane Leach, review of *Lark and Termite.*

Jayne Anne Phillips Home Page, http://www.jayneannephillips.com/ (June 18, 2009).

Los Angeles Times Online, http://www.latimes.com/ (January 11, 2009), Susan Salter Reynolds, review of *Lark and Termite,* and author interview.

Open Letters, http://openlettersmonthly.com/ (June 18, 2009), Sam Sacks, review of *Lark and Termite.*

Rutgers University: Newark Campus Web site, http://www.newark.rutgers.edu/ (July 13, 2009), author profile.

Telegraph Online (London, England), http://www.telegraph.co.uk/ (March 17, 2009), Michael Arditti, review of *Lark and Termite.**

*   *   *

POLLITT, Katha 1949-

PERSONAL: Born October 14, 1949, in New York, NY; daughter of Basil Riddiford and Leanora Pollitt. *Education:* Radcliffe College, B.A., 1972.

ADDRESSES: Home—CT. *Office*—The Nation, 33 Irving Place, New York, NY 10003. *E-mail*—info@kathapollitt.com.

CAREER: Writer, journalist, editor, poet, columnist, and commentator. *Nation,* New York, NY, literary editor, 1982-84, contributing editor, 1986-92, associate editor, 1992—. Guest on television networks and programs, including *McLaughlin Group, Dateline NBC,* and on Cable News Network (CNN) and British Broadcasting Corporation (BBC).

MEMBER: PEN.

AWARDS, HONORS: Poetry award, National Book Critics Circle, 1983, for *Antarctic Traveler;* National Endowment for the Arts grant, 1984; Peter I.B. Lavan Younger Poets Award, Academy of American Poets, 1984; Arvon Foundation Prize, *Observer,* 1986; grant, New York Foundation of the Arts, 1987; Guggenheim fellowship, 1987; National Magazine Award, 1992, for "Why We Read: Canon to the Right of Me . . ."; Whiting Foundation writing award, 1992; Maggie Award, Planned Parenthood Federation of America, 1993, for "Why Do We Romanticize the Fetus?"; "Freethought Heroine" Award, Freedom from Religion Foundation, 1995; Exceptional Merit Media Award, National Women's Political Caucus, 2001.

WRITINGS:

Antarctic Traveller (poetry), Knopf (New York, NY), 1982.

Reasonable Creatures: Essays on Women and Feminism, Knopf (New York, NY), 1994.

Subject to Debate: Sense and Dissents on Women, Politics, and Culture, Modern Library (New York, NY), 2001.

Virginity or Death! And Other Social and Political Issues of Our Time, Random House (New York, NY), 2006.

Learning to Drive: And Other Life Stories, Random House (New York, NY), 2007.

The Mind-body Problem: And Other Poems, Random House (New York, NY), 2009.

Author of regular column, "Subject to Debate," *Nation.*

Contributor to periodicals, including *Atlantic Monthly, Mother Jones, New Republic, New Yorker, New York Times Book Review, Harper's Mirabella, Glamour, Grant Street, Poetry, Antaeus,* and *Yale Review.*

SIDELIGHTS: Katha Pollitt is a poet as well as an acclaimed journalist, and as an associate editor for the liberal *Nation* magazine, she has been recognized for her commentary on political and cultural issues. Donna Seaman, commenting on Pollitt's talents as an editorial essayist, declared in *Booklist* that *Nation* readers "depend on their Pollitt fix to stay sane" as they peruse her "zestfully argued, blazingly commonsensical, . . . and morally precise columns."

Pollitt began her writing career in the mid 1970s when she published poetry in such magazines as the *Atlantic Monthly* and the *New Yorker.* When her poems were collected as *Antarctic Traveller,* she was quickly praised as a refreshing voice in contemporary poetry. Dana Gioia wrote in *Hudson Review* that Pollitt "has an extraordinarily good ear."

Critics have argued that one of Pollitt's most impressive skills as a poet is her ability to use visual imagery as a means of exploring human thought and emotion. Typically successful in this regard is "Five Poems From Japanese Paintings," in which largely descriptive verse conveys an appropriate sense of reflection or action. In the segment titled "Moon and Flowering Plum," for example, Pollitt employs a brief description of nature as a means for subtly addressing the implications of indecisiveness and commitment. "What Pollitt wants, what she creates," declared Richard Howard in *Nation,* "is the alternative life, unconditioned, eagerly espousing all that is unknown." Howard added that in "Five Poems from Japanese Paintings," the "decorous is the decisive moment, indulged only to be twitched away from us with a teasing laugh."

Critics note, however, that Pollitt's strengths are not exclusively visual. She is considered an insightful artist whose perspective encompasses both the personal and the universal. Her thematic interests are particularly evident in poems such as "Discussions of the Vicissitudes of History under a Pine Tree," where the vividness of nature leads to a commentary on human change; and "Thinking of the World as Idea," in which an observation of early morning harbor activities prompts a brief reflection on dreams, poetry, and the world. Even more modest efforts such as "Intimation," in which an old song sparks a mysterious memory, and "Sonnet," where the poet delineates a lover's perceptions, have been praised for the poignancy of their strictly personal contexts and offer stirring insights into behavior, perception, and even memory.

As a poet, Pollitt has often been compared to Wallace Stevens. Bruce Bennett, writing about *Antarctic Traveller* for the *New York Times Book Review,* noted that Pollitt seems preoccupied by the artistic process and the inevitabilities of existence. "Like Wallace Stevens," Bennett observed, "Pollitt contrasts life and art." Howard also found similarities between Pollitt and Stevens, but added that Pollitt is unique in avoiding obfuscation in her depictions and interpretations of people and nature. "What gives the distinction, the special twist of idiom we call style," Howard declared, "is the perception of delight in the world entertained on its own terms."

Antarctic Traveller enjoyed immense critical success upon publication in 1982. Gioia wrote that Pollitt "is a poet to watch" and commented: "Her lines are almost always exactly right, and there is a sense of finish and finality to her work one rarely sees in poets young or old—the diction clean and precise, the rhythms clear and effective." Pollitt had been getting positive reviews even before her book was published. In the 1981 volume *Bounds out of Bounds: A Compass for Recent American and British Poetry,* author Roberta Berke hailed Pollitt as "a miniaturist who captures elusive subjects with great delicacy and concision." Berke added that Pollitt's poems "are unabashedly intelligent and often metaphysical" and that Pollitt "combines her awareness of contraries and her intelligence with a vivid imagination that impels her best work toward that 'Supreme Fiction' which was Wallace Stevens's goal."

Not all critical comments, however, have been entirely free of objection. *New Republic* reviewer Jay Parini complained about Pollitt's use of the second person pronoun, a device that Parini called "an irritating mannerism passed around the various M.F.A. programs like the German measles." Both Gioia and *Georgia Review* critic Peter Stitt lamented Pollitt's occasional reluctance or inability to pursue the philosophical implications of some poems, but even Stitt, who was less enthusiastic than many reviewers, wrote that *Antarctic Traveller* signaled the continued existence of the "objective mode of lyric poetry." He added that Pollitt's "best poems have a spare delicacy reflective of a rigorous sense of decorum."

Despite her success as a poet, Pollitt is perhaps better known for her role as a leading social critic with essays written primarily for *Nation,* but also for periodicals such as the *New Yorker, Mother Jones,* and the *New York Times Book Review.* "A superb stylist, Pollitt can always be relied on for her wit and her keen sense of both the ridiculous and the sublime," observed a biographer on the *Nation* Web site. Pollitt describes herself as a liberal and a feminist, and she is particularly famous for her critiques of various facets of the feminist movement and its implications for female empowerment. Her commentary has been collected in two volumes, *Reasonable Creatures: Essays on Women and Feminism* and *Subject to Debate: Sense and Dissents on Women, Politics, and Culture.* In *Reasonable Creatures,* Pollitt deals with issues as diverse as abortion; arguments about the literary canon; "difference feminism"; and the rape trial involving William Kennedy Smith, during which journalists for the first time decided to expose the name of the alleged victim. Writing in the *Washington Post Book World,* Maureen Corrigan noted that to read these essays "is to be bombarded, gloriously, by the force of Pollitt's contempt for intellectual sloppiness." Similarly, *New Statesman & Society* reviewer Kirsty Milne called the essays "cheeringly argumentative and hearteningly accessible" and remarked that Pollitt "is living proof that journalism needn't be glib and feminism needn't be dull." Boyd Zenner, commenting in *Belles Lettres,* averred that *Reasonable Creatures* "will confirm [Pollitt's] standing as one of the most incisive, principled, and articulate cultural critics writing today." Zenner concluded: "Pollitt's graceful style and frequent flashes of real wit are reason enough for rejoicing, but even more impressive is the fact that they never obscure the power and urgency of what she has to say."

Subject to Debate earned similarly favorable reviews. The author "is out not only to criticize the left," Arianne Chernock suggested in the *New York Times Book Review,* "but also to reinvigorate it." A *Kirkus Reviews* contributor commended the work for its "clarity, logic, humor, and sensitivity," adding that the book would "perhaps challenge . . . the politically correct on the right or the left." A *Publishers Weekly* critic wrote: "Pollitt's . . . eye is steely, uncompromising, and sharp." The same critic concluded that Pollitt is "never tendentious and always witty."

Virginity or Death! And Other Social and Political Issues of Our Time assembles eighty-four of Pollitt's columns that appeared in the *Nation* from 2001 to 2006. "While it's become commonplace to describe journalism as a 'rough draft of history,' this collection of Pollitt's columns rises to the level of history itself," commented Jessica Clark in an *In These Times* Web site interview with Pollitt. The author "offers a running chronicle of the issues of the day," Clark noted, and "tackles each topic with humor and passion, always returning to the central role that women play in U.S. and international politics." Pollitt's work addresses a wide variety of social issues, foreign policy failures, political victories and defeats, scandals, and disasters that have dominated the news and national discourse in the half decade covered by her book. She considers the counterproductive and sometimes dangerous health advice given to women and argues that conservative antiabortion positions are often concealed under the guise of protection of women's health. She also discusses issues such as the privatization of Social Security, the sexual abuse scandals in the Catholic church, the difficulties with childcare availability in the United States, bogus research that undermines women's progress, and the continuing attempt by Republicans to overturn the landmark abortion case *Roe v. Wade.* Among the more notorious pieces is Pollitt's post-9/11 column in objection to unrestrained flag waving and uncontrolled American jingoism in the wake of the September terrorist attacks. A *Publishers Weekly* reviewer called Pollitt "one of the country's finest left commentators and feminist stalwarts," and found her essays to be "invariably witty, astute and relentlessly logical." *Library Journal* reviewer Erica J. Foley noted that Pollitt's "writings lean decidedly to the Left, but this collection deserves a place in any balanced political commentary section." This collection of "sharp, insightful columns," commented a *Kirkus Reviews* critic, "should be required reading for the left and the right: You may not agree with Pollitt, but you can't dismiss her."

Pollitt next wrote a collection of essays titled *Learning to Drive: And Other Life Stories.* The title, and opening essay, is a reflection on the difficulty of learning to drive at the age of fifty-two, which she was forced to do after her breakup with the philandering boyfriend who had been her driver. This essay and the second, "Webstalker," were previously published in the *New Yorker.* In "Webstalker," Pollitt recounts how she became addicted to searching online for information about her ex, and in "The Study Group" she describes how the man, a Marxist who formed study groups, padded the groups with past and present lovers. Pollitt reveals that although all the signs were there (she found another woman's panties in the laundry), she stayed for seven more years with a man who belittled her. In a review for *Salon. com,* Rebecca Traister noted that this revelation was hard to accept for some who had placed Pollitt at the top of the feminist pedestal. Traister wrote that "a number of Pollitt's essays are wise and very funny, and if not altogether pretty in content, then at least fine-boned in style. And in addition to being blood-and-guts revelations about her private devastations, they offer a view of the ways in which her political ideologies—the things we respect her for—have been woven throughout her romantic, social and familial life. In "After the Men are Dead," Pollitt wonders what life will be like if she outlives all the men who have found her desirable.

Other essays include "Memoir of a Shy Pornographer," in which Pollitt writes of job she held as a young copyeditor for which she proofread pornography. She writes of her alcoholic mother in "Mrs. Razzmatazz," and in

"Goodbye, Lenin," of her Communist father, whose FBI file was filled with errors. Pollitt, who lives in Connecticut, writes of the changing landscape in "End Of."

Frequent themes of these essays are love, marriage, sex, mothering, and growing older. A *Kirkus Reviews* contributor wrote: "A sardonic observer of human behavior, especially the relations between men and women, Pollitt leaves no doubt about her opinions." "Pollitt's observations are acute and her confessions tonic," wrote Seaman, who concluded: "Forget face-lifts; Pollitt's essays elevate the spirit."

In reviewing *Learning to Drive* for the *Guardian Online*, Linda Hall noted that Pollitt is featured on one page every two weeks in the *Nation*, but that the space doesn't reflect "her observations of 'a well-meaning, folk-art-decorated person'—a famous leftist writer—'who embarrasses herself for worthy causes.' . . . I find her more rewarding on these subjects than she is on *The First Wives Club* or why she didn't vote for Clinton the second time around. Don't get me wrong. I like Pollitt's column and use it to teach polemical writing. But she has deeper, more durable insights to offer as an essayist, a more complex view of both life and the left, and not only because she is not hostage to the topical."

BIOGRAPHICAL AND CRITICAL SOURCES:

BOOKS

Berke, Roberta, *Bounds out of Bounds: A Compass for Recent American and British Poetry,* Oxford University Press (Oxford, England), 1981.

Contemporary Literary Criticism, Volume 28, Gale (Detroit, MI), 1984.

PERIODICALS

Belles Lettres, spring, 1995, Boyd Zenner, review of *Reasonable Creatures: Essays on Women and Feminism,* p. 19.

Biography, winter, 2008, review of *Learning to Drive: And Other Life Stories,* p. 198.

Booklist, August, 1994, Mary Carroll, review of *Reasonable Creatures,* p. 2002; February 1, 2001, Donna Seaman, review of *Subject to Debate: Sense and Dissents on Women, Politics, and Culture,* p. 1034; June 1, 2006, Vanessa Bush, review of

Virginity or Death! And Other Social and Political Issues of Our Time, p. 22; September 15, 2007, Donna Seaman, review of *Learning to Drive,* p. 15.

Georgia Review, summer, 1982, Peter Stitt, review of *Antarctic Traveller.*

Hudson Review, winter, 1982-83, Dana Gioia, review of *Antarctic Traveller.*

Kirkus Reviews, January 1, 2001, review of *Subject to Debate,* p. 39; April 15, 2006, review of *Virginity or Death!,* p. 397; August 1, 2007, review of *Learning to Drive.*

Library Journal, May 15, 2006, Erica L. Foley, review of *Virginity or Death!,* p. 116; October 1, 2007, Stacy Russo, review of *Learning to Drive,* p. 72.

Ms., September-October, 1994, Mary Suh, review of *Reasonable Creatures,* p. 78.

Nation, March 20, 1982, Richard Howard, review of *Antarctic Traveller.*

National Review, January 27, 2007, "Their Moment," p. 16.

New Republic, April 14, 1982, Jay Parini, review of *Antarctic Traveller.*

New Statesman & Society, March 3, 1995, Kirsty Milne, review of *Reasonable Creatures,* p. 37.

New York, October 10, 1994, Walter Kirn, review of *Reasonable Creatures,* p. 78.

New Yorker, October 17, 1994, review of *Reasonable Creatures,* p. 121.

New York Times, September 23, 2007, "Questions for Katha Pollitt," interview, p. 17.

New York Times Book Review, March 14, 1982, Bruce Bennett, review of *Antarctic Traveller;* October 9, 1994, Susan Shapiro, review of *Reasonable Creatures,* p. 22; February 25, 2001, Arianne Chernock, review of *Subject to Debate,* p. 19; July 2, 2006, Ana Marie Cox, review of *Virginity or Death!,* p. 11.

Poetry, December, 1982, review of *Antarctic Traveller.*

Poets & Writers, March-April, 1997, Heather Stephenson, "Katha Pollitt," interview, p. 32.

Progressive, December, 1994, Ruth Conniff, "Katha Pollitt," p. 34.

Publishers Weekly, June 27, 1994, review of *Reasonable Creatures,* p. 64; March 12, 2001, review of *Subject to Debate,* p. 74; April 17, 2006, review of *Virginity or Death!,* p. 179; August 6, 2007, review of *Learning to Drive,* p. 185.

Washington Post Book World, September 25, 1994, Maureen Corrigan, review of *Reasonable Creatures,* p. 10.

Women's Review of Books, April, 1995, Rickie Solinger, review of *Reasonable Creatures,* p. 1; July, 2000, "Reasonable Doubts," p. 11; April, 2001, Kathryn

Abrams, "Refusing and Resisting," p. 1; March-April, 2007, Jaclyn Friedman, "Because Things are Worse, People are Paying Attention," interview.

ONLINE

Freethought Today, http://www.ffrf.org/fttoday/ (April 15, 2007), "Katha Pollitt: Freethought Heroine."

Guardian Online, http://www.guardian.co.uk/ (October 25, 2007), Ann Friedman, "Ann Friedman Asks Katha Pollitt about the Political Discussions of Her New Book of Personal Memoirs," interview, Linda Hall, "Mother, Daughter, Marxist (noncommittal), Human: Linda Hall Explains Why Her 80-Year Old Father Finds Katha Pollitt Such Excellent Company."

In These Times, http://www.inthesetimes.com/ (October 27, 2006), Jessica Clark, interview with Katha Pollitt; (October 9, 2007) Phoebe Connelly, review of *Learning to Drive.*

Katha Pollitt Home Page, http://kathapollitt.blogspot.com (August 15, 2008).

Lip Magazine, http://www.lipmagazine.org/ (April 15, 2007), Jessica Clark, "Beyond the Politics of Irony & Lip Gloss: An Interview with Feminist Writer Katha Pollitt."

Nation Online, http://www.thenation.com/ (April 15, 2007), biography of Katha Pollitt.

One-Minute Book Reviews, http://oneminutebookreviews.wordpress.com/ (October 16, 2007), Janice Harayda, review of *Learning to Drive.*

Salon.com, http://www.salon.com/ (September 26, 2007), Rebecca Traister, "The Feminist Who Made Me Blush."*

*   *   *

POYER, David 1949-

(David Andreissen, David C. Poyer, David Charles Poyer)

PERSONAL: Born November 26, 1949, in DuBois, PA; son of Charles and Margaret Poyer; married Lenore Elizabeth Hart (a novelist); children: Naia Elizabeth (daughter). *Education:* U.S. Naval Academy, B.S. (with merit), 1971; George Washington University, M.A.

ADDRESSES: Home—Nassawadox, VA.

CAREER: Writer, novelist, educator, lecturer, and Navy officer. U.S. Navy, 1971-2001, line officer on frigates and amphibious ships, 1971-77; transferred to U.S. Naval Reserve, 1977-2001, retired as captain after thirty years' service from his last duty assignment as senior policy advisor at Joint Forces Command. Instructor or lecturer at various educational institutions, including the U.S. Naval Academy, Flagler College, University of Pittsburgh, Old Dominion University, Armed Forces Staff College, University of North Florida, and Christopher Newport University. Guest on PBS's "Writer to Writer" series and on Voice of America. Founding member of Tidewater Writers Workshop; founding member of the *New Virginia Review.* Second distinguished visiting Writer at U.S. Naval Academy. Currently a member of the faculty in creative writing at Wilkes University. Board member of the Library of Virginia.

MEMBER: Authors Guild, U.S. Naval Institute, American Society of Naval Engineers, U.S. Naval Academy Alumni Association, SERVAS, Surface Navy Association.

WRITINGS:

NOVELS

White Continent (adventure novel), Jove (New York, NY), 1980.

The Shiloh Project (adventure novel), Avon (New York, NY), 1981.

(As David Andreissen) *Star Seed* (science fiction novel), Donning (Norfolk, VA), 1982.

The Return of Philo T. McGiffin (comic novel), St. Martin's Press (New York, NY), 1983.

Stepfather Bank (science fiction novel), St. Martin's Press (New York, NY), 1987.

The Only Thing to Fear, Forge (New York, NY), 1995.

"TALES OF THE MODERN NAVY/DAN LENSON" SERIES; NOVELS

The Med, St. Martin's Press (New York, NY), 1988.

The Gulf, St. Martin's Press (New York, NY), 1990.

The Circle, St. Martin's Press (New York, NY), 1993.

The Passage, St. Martin's Press (New York, NY), 1994.

Tomahawk, St. Martin's Press (New York, NY), 1998.

China Sea, St. Martin's Press (New York, NY), 2000.

Black Storm, St. Martin's Press (New York, NY), 2002.

The Command, St. Martin's Press (New York, NY), 2004.

The Threat, St. Martin's Press (New York, NY), 2006.

Korea Strait, St. Martin's Press (New York, NY), 2007.

The Weapon, St. Martin's Press (New York, NY), 2008.

The Crisis, St. Martin's Press (New York, NY), 2009.

"HEMLOCK COUNTY" SERIES

The Dead of Winter, Tor (New York, NY), 1988.

Winter in the Heart (also see below), Tor (New York, NY), 1993.

As the Wolf Loves Winter (also see below), Forge (New York, NY), 1996.

Thunder on the Mountain, Forge (New York, NY), 1999.

Winter Light (contains *Winter in the Heart* and *As the Wolf Loves Winter*), Forge (New York, NY), 2001.

"TILLER GALLOWAY" SERIES

Hatteras Blue, St. Martin's Press (New York, NY), 1989.

Bahamas Blue, St. Martin's Press (New York, NY), 1992.

Louisiana Blue, St. Martin's Press (New York, NY), 1994.

Down to a Sunless Sea, St. Martin's Press (New York, NY), 1996.

"CIVIL WAR AT SEA" SERIES

Fire on the Waters: A Novel of the Civil War at Sea, Simon & Schuster (New York, NY), 2001.

A Country of Our Own, Simon & Schuster (New York, NY), 2003.

That Anvil of Our Souls: A Novel of the Monitor and the Merrimack, Simon & Schuster (New York, NY), 2005.

OTHER

(Editor) *Command at Sea,* 4th edition, U.S. Naval Institute Press (Annapolis, MD), 1983.

Contributor of stories to periodicals, including *Analog, Galileo, Isaac Asimov's Science Fiction Magazine, Mike Shayne's Mystery,* and *Unearth.*

ADAPTATIONS: Film rights to *The Return of Philo T. McGiffin* were bought in 1991 by Universal.

SIDELIGHTS: David Poyer has won special praise for his books that exploit his knowledge of the sea and the world of sailors and divers. Speaking of Poyer's "Tales of the Modern Navy" series in *Booklist,* Roland Green called the books "one of the outstanding bodies of nautical fiction in English during the last half-century" and praised Poyer for balancing "hardware description and an extremely well-drawn cast of characters with enormous skill."

The "Tales of the Modern Navy" series features U.S. Navy officer Dan Lenson, an Annapolis graduate whose career leads him through many assignments and adventures. Reviewing *Tomahawk,* Green commented: "Poyer's Lenson novels are so character driven that calling them thrillers is misleading, and here Poyer includes a solid cast of secondary characters who are thoroughly individualized yet serve to raise the ethical questions Poyer always brings to the fore. This demanding, excellent novel is probably the best so far in a major contemporary seafaring saga."

China Sea finds Lenson ordered to deliver an outmoded frigate to the Pakistani government as part of a trade. On the voyage, he faces conflicts between the American and Pakistani crews, a serial killer stalking the ship, and an unexpected detour to battle a Chinese pirate organization. "Poyer displays a fine sense of pace and plot when the focus is on seagoing affairs, and the battle scenes are scintillating and satisfying," according to the critic for *Publishers Weekly.* Patrick J. Wall in *Library Journal* found that "Poyer's characters are as good as ever, and the action scenes are lively."

Lenson returns in *Black Storm,* set during the Gulf War of 1991. American intelligence has learned that Saddam Hussein has a secret weapon he plans to use against Israel; Lenson and a crew of special operations experts is sent to Baghdad to locate and destroy the weapon before it can be unleashed. Robert Conroy in *Library Journal* noted that "Poyer captures the technical and emotional feel of such a dangerous mission, which ranges across the bleak desert and through the claustrophobic sewers of Baghdad." Green labeled *Black Storm* "one of the strongest books in an outstanding series."

Lenson earns a promotion to commander in *The Command,* after which he takes charge of U.S.S. Thomas Horn, a helicopter-capable destroyer. On top of his new duties as the commanding officer of the Spruance-class Horn, Lenson is also charged with being the host ship for the Navy's initial experiments with integrating women into service aboard a warship. Much resentment and opposition simmers throughout the ranks of officers and enlisted, but Lenson sees the integration as a welcome and logical step in the evolution of the military. He even welcomes the presence of his new female executive officer. New female crew members clash with the old crew and a group of Navy SEALS recently assigned to the Horn. As the ship's mission is underway, considerable turmoil erupts, including a suspicious fire in the female barracks, an unexpected pregnancy, and a severed goat's head meant to intimidate. As the ship travels from the United States into foreign waters and the Persian Gulf, Navy criminal investigator Aisha Ar-Rahim follows an investigation of her own to the Horn, where the enormous destroyer makes a tempting target for local foes with destructive aspirations and nuclear capabilities. "Poyer packs story with both dense technical info and welcome local color," observed a *Kirkus Reviews* critic.

The Threat takes Lenson to unfamiliar territory in Washington, DC, where he joins the National Security Council and becomes the carrier of the "football," a case containing the vital codes to be used by the president in a nuclear conflict. Working with a president known for his womanizing, and who is detested by the military establishment, Lenson struggles to get used to the Washington bureaucracy while doing his best in a menial assignment with an anti-drug task force. Though he demonstrates great competence, even excellence, in dealing with the machinations of a Colombian drug lord, his superiors still look on him with suspicion and disdain. Abruptly, Lenson finds himself reassigned and in possession of the nuclear codes and closely aligned with a president whose handling of military matters is dubious at best. Making matters worse, his domestic life is in disarray as he experiences conflict with his higher-ranking wife, Blair, and realizes that she may be a target of the philandering president's affections. In the background, an assassination plot unfolds through the machinations of unknown parties. A *Kirkus Reviews* critic called the novel "a gloomy story, but Poyer remains the most thoughtful of the military-thriller set and a master of authentic detail." In assessing the novel, *Booklist* reviewer David Pitt named Poyer "a superior writer."

After foiling the assassination plot on his Commander in Chief in *The Threat,* the thirty-nine-year-old Lenson

finds himself in the unenviable position of being pushed toward retirement by his commanding officer. Lenson, however, has no intention of retiring, and thus is reassigned to a mission sure to make most men take early retirement: he is to command a Tactical Analysis Group and gather information from war games in the Korea Strait, being carried out jointly by South Korea, Australia, and Japan. Acting as an observer and stationed aboard the South Korean flagship, the Chung Nam, Lenson is also tasked with meeting with the South Koreans and escorting retired military and U.S. civilians at the war games. This seems a recipe for extreme boredom until, during the war games, the Chung Nam is attacked by unidentified submarines. Lenson quickly disobeys the order from the South Korean commander to leave the ship, and instead tries to help the commander, despite the fact that he has no authority to do so. Soon a typhoon adds to the troubles of the Chung Nam, and Lenson helps below decks to repair damage from the submarines. Finally, he must propose a startling maneuver in order to save the day.

This tenth installment in the "Tales of the Modern Navy" series won kudos from reviewers. *Mostly Fiction* contributor Kirstin Merrihew noted that "Poyer has a reputation as one of America's best military fiction authors," and went on to observe: "This thriller is highly engrossing in many respects besides the tautly told main plot of battle against uncertain foe and turbulent sea." For Merrihew, *Korea Strait* was "an expert tale of the modern Navy, authored by a real pro." Similar praise came from a *Publishers Weekly* reviewer who termed the novel "taut," adding that "Poyer's tech talk throughout is nicely turned, and Dan Lenson remains a winningly weary hero." A *Kirkus Reviews* critic also commended *Korea Strait,* concluding: "Well up to Poyer's excellent standards. No bluster, no dazzle, just real naval engagements that we may well see before long." *Library Journal* writer Robert Conroy pointed out that "fans of modern naval warfare will relish the details and sea action, as well as the insights into the Korean situation and the Korean people."

With *Fire on the Waters: A Novel of the Civil War at Sea,* Poyer began a new series of nautical adventures, this time set during the American Civil War. Elisha Eaker is a wealthy young man who has joined the navy to escape his domineering father and an unwanted marriage to his headstrong cousin. Assigned to protect the Union forces at Fort Sumter in South Carolina, Eaker finds that, as the South secedes from the Union, his position becomes more perilous. Along with a crew of varying loyalty to the besieged Union, he eventually battles not only Confederate forces but storms at sea before venturing to the Chesapeake Bay on a secret mission. A *Publishers Weekly* reviewer wrote that *Fire on the Waters* has "plenty of meat on the bones for Civil War and naval buffs." Margaret Flanagan, writing in *Booklist* called the novel "a solid introduction to a promising new series." Poyer's second novel in the series, *A Country of Our Own,* moves the spotlight to Confederate navy lieutenant Ken Custis Claiborne, a Virginian who goes south after Sumter, first defending his state on the banks of the Potomac, then commanding a sea-raider that attacks Yankee trade from Brazil to Boston.

That Anvil of Our Souls: A Novel of the Monitor and the Merrimack, the third of the "Civil War at Sea" series, provides a fictionalized account of the origins of ironclad warfare with the storied Civil War ships, the Monitor and the Merrimack. Poyer follows the basic true story of the two ships, covering the origins of the Merrimack, its capture and refitting as a southern ship named the Virginia, and the initial reactions to the smaller and seemingly ineffectual Monitor. On board the Virginia is Lieutenant Lomax Minter, brash perhaps to the point of being foolhardy, arrogant and handsome. Other crew members distrust Minter and fear that his attitude toward warfare will bring them and the ship to harm. Minter's counterpoint on the Monitor, Chief Engineer Theo Hubbard, is stalwart and duty-bound, determined and reliable in combat. Real Civil War figures and fictional characters interact as the story unfolds from the perspective of these two contrasting military men. A *Kirkus Reviews* contributor praised the novel as the "series best, and for those who see the Civil War as this country's defining drama, simply not to be missed." With his work, "Poyer makes readers see and feel the blockade and the men who tried to maintain it," observed a *Publishers Weekly* reviewer.

Several of Poyer's nautical novels feature deep-water diver Tiller Galloway, a maverick drifter who, although he is frequently depicted as self-centered and unlikable, is nonetheless "the perfect denizen of the undersea world: tough, stubborn, solitary, out of place on land," in the opinion of a *Publishers Weekly* writer. Reviewing *Louisiana Blue,* the critic noted that "the biggest thrills in this well-written and subtly plotted novel come from the way Poyer brings alive the dangerous, claustrophobia-inducing world of deep-sea diving." Tiller appeared again in *Down to a Sunless Sea,* rated "one of [Poyer's] best novels yet" by a *Publishers*

Weekly critic. Once again, the realistic descriptions of undersea escapades were singled out by the reviewer as "particularly memorable," especially the "extensive, harrowing" passages about "cave dives, which are riveting enough to terrify experienced divers and hydrophobes alike." Thomas Gaughan echoed this sentiment in *Booklist:* "The cave-diving scenes are riveting, claustrophobic, terrifying, and beautiful. And Tiller has grown into one of the most spectacularly flawed and failed characters ever to seek redemption in popular fiction. A ripping good read!"

Speaking of his nautical adventure novels in an interview posted on his Home Page, Poyer explained that his greatest problem in writing was how to use naval terminology so that the general reader would not be overwhelmed: "I start out defining my military terms in context; then, as the book goes on, I introduce more and more of them, especially in dialogue, because that's the really critical area. So by the end, the characters are speaking pretty unadulterated naval jargon, but you can understand it because you've been gradually introduced to it."

While Poyer's nautical books have proven to be popular, his land-based novels have also been praised as engrossing and thought-provoking works, particularly the "Hemlock County" series. These ecological thrillers feature an unlikely collection of heroes, including W.T. Halvorsen, an elderly, retired oil-driller, and his sidekick, high school student Phil Romanelli. In *Winter in the Heart,* Halvorsen becomes seriously ill after being splashed by contaminated snow. When he discovers that several other residents in his area have been similarly affected, he begins to investigate who is behind the illegal dumping of toxic waste. It turns out to be a bigger project than he expected, as everyone from the Mafia to the federal government struggles to cover up the crimes. A *Publishers Weekly* reviewer called *Winter in the Heart* an "absorbing tale" enlivened by "vividly imagined and deftly rendered characters, each one possessing real depth and a credible place in the story's richly evoked milieu." The sequel, *As the Wolf Loves Winter,* was praised by a *Publishers Weekly* critic for its "superb storytelling and characterization." *Thunder on the Mountain* is set in 1935, when young Bill Halvorsen finds himself entangled in unionizing efforts in the Pennsylvania oil fields. Violence erupts when ruthless communist organizers clash with corrupt businessmen, leading to sabotage, bribery, and death. *Thunder on the Mountain* is "violent, touching, and incredibly sad as the story careens to its explosive conclusion," Karen Anderson wrote in *Library Journal.* "Poyer's chilling look into the heart of the early union movement is dramatic and suspenseful, full of despair and hope," according to Melanie Duncan in *Booklist.* The critic for *Publishers Weekly* found the novel to be "a stunning period tale."

In *The Only Thing to Fear,* Poyer speculates on the wartime activities of a young John F. Kennedy as he embarks on a secret mission to protect President Franklin D. Roosevelt from assassination. The book follows this story line while constructing a comprehensive fictional portrait of Kennedy, including issues surrounding his health, his military service, and his role as the scion of a famous and prominent family. Roland Green, again writing in *Booklist,* remarked that Poyer's depiction of Kennedy is "one of the most fully realized presentations of JFK to appear in fiction."

Poyer once told *CA:* "I was born in a small town in northwestern Pennsylvania, in the hills, and named after David Copperfield. My sister, my brother, and I grew up in vicious poverty but always with books around, thanks to our mother. I knew I would write someday, but I needed to see something of the world first. With this in mind, I applied to the Naval Academy—a free education and certainly an opportunity to travel. Much to my surprise, I was accepted. I spent the next six years at sea, married, divorced, and finally asked for transfer to the Reserves. It was time to try for the dream.

"For five years after that, I did the garret-and-starvation routine in Norfolk, Virginia, trying to write. Times were rough at first, since my novels returned to my mailbox as surely and as rapidly as homing pigeons. I like to tell the story about raiding demolished buildings for the Civil Defense rations in the basements. A little moldy, but nutritious. . . . Eventually I found a steady market in regional magazines and began selling to mystery and science fiction magazines. I became a partner in a small guidebook publishing company. At that point, I began writing novels again. The seasoning helped, and *White Continent* and *Shiloh Project* sold.

"It is hard to see one's work from the outside; nevertheless I'll try. I admire strong stories with characters who must decide between good and evil—and situations where the choice is not as easy as it may sound. I value accurate backgrounds, believable characters, and realistic dialogue and dislike wordiness, schlock, and digression. My goal is very simple—to write a novel, someday, that will satisfy me."

Poyer added: "Since then, aside from brief periods as an engineer and consultant, I've worked as a novelist. Gradually success has come, in terms of sales and recognition. But even more heartening is the feeling that I'm still improving, still learning the craft (but with a long way to go yet). I love the profession of fiction. There's no other way I'd rather spend my life—relieved at intervals, of course, with some sailing."

BIOGRAPHICAL AND CRITICAL SOURCES:

PERIODICALS

Analog Science Fiction-Science Fact, February, 1983, Tom Easton, review of *Star Seed,* p. 164.

Booklist, March 15, 1992, Ray Olson, review of *The Circle,* p. 1316; December 15, 1994, Roland Green, review of *The Passage,* p. 736; April 15, 1995, Roland Green, review of *The Only Thing to Fear,* p. 1481; October 15, 1996, Thomas Gaughan, review of *Down to a Sunless Sea,* p. 407; April, 1998, Roland Green, review of *Tomahawk,* p. 1305; March 1, 1999, Melanie Duncan, review of *Thunder on the Mountain,* p. 1151; January 1, 2000, Roland Green, review of *China Sea,* p. 878; July, 2001, Margaret Flanagan, review of *Fire on the Waters: A Novel of the Civil War at Sea,* p. 1983; May 1, 2002, Roland Green, review of *Black Storm,* p. 1509; May 15, 2005, Jay Freeman, review of *That Anvil of Our Souls: A Novel of the Monitor and the Merrimack,* p. 1649; September 15, 2006, David Pitt, review of *The Threat,* p. 32; April 1, 2007, David Pitt, review of *The Threat,* p. 85.

Kirkus Reviews, May 1, 2004, review of *The Command,* p. 419; April 15, 2005, review of *That Anvil of Our Souls,* p. 445; August 15, 2006, review of *The Threat,* p. 806; September 15, 2007, review of *Korea Strait.*

Library Journal, November 15, 1982, review of *Star Seed,* p. 2192; May 1, 1983, A.J. Anderson, review of *The Return of Philo T. McGiffin,* p. 921; April 15, 1988, Edwin B. Burgess, review of *The Med,* p. 96; August 1, 1990, Elsa Pendleton, review of *The Gulf,* p. 145; May 1, 1992, Elsa Pendleton, review of *The Circle,* p. 119; April 1, 1995, Stacie Browne Chandler, review of *The Only Thing to Fear,* p. 125; March 15, 1999, Karen Anderson, review of *Thunder on the Mountain,* p. 110; February 1, 2000, Patrick J. Wall, review of *China Sea,* p. 118; May 15, 2001, Loretta Davis, review of

Fire on the Waters, p. 165; April 15, 2002, Robert Conroy, review of *Black Storm,* p. 126; September 15, 2007, Robert Conroy, review of *Korea Strait,* p. 53.

New York Times Book Review, September 23, 1990, Newgate Callendar, review of *The Gulf,* p. 16; July 26, 1992, Newgate Callendar, review of *The Circle,* p. 13.

Officer, June, 2005, David R. Bockel, review of *The Command,* p. 47.

Publishers Weekly, April 15, 1983, review of *The Return of Philo T. McGiffin,* p. 42; March 4, 1988, Sybil Steinberg, review of *The Med,* p. 95; June 23, 1989, review of *The Med,* p. 56; August 3, 1990, Sybil Steinberg, review of *The Gulf,* p. 64; March 16, 1992, review of *The Circle,* p. 66; May 3, 1993, review of *The Circle,* p. 303, and *Winter in the Heart,* p. 293; July 5, 1993, review of *The Circle,* p. 50; February 7, 1994, review of *Louisiana Blue,* p. 70; November 14, 1994, review of *The Passage,* p. 54; February 27, 1995, review of *The Only Thing to Fear,* p. 87; March 4, 1996, review of *As the Wolf Loves Winter,* p. 54; October 7, 1996, review of *Down to a Sunless Sea,* p. 63; February 16, 1998, review of *Tomahawk,* p. 202; February 1, 1999, review of *Thunder on the Mountain,* p. 77; January 31, 2000, review of *China Sea,* p. 83; June 18, 2001, review of *Fire on the Waters,* p. 56; May 6, 2002, review of *Black Storm,* p. 34; June 13, 2005, review of *That Anvil of Our Souls,* p. 32; September 18, 2006, review of *The Threat,* p. 34; September 24, 2007, review of *Korea Strait,* p. 43.

School Library Journal, September, 1983, review of *The Return of Philo T. McGiffin,* p. 143.

Tribune Books (Chicago, IL), April 3, 1988, review of *The Med,* p. 5.

Virginia Quarterly Review, autumn, 1995, review of *The Only Thing to Fear,* p. 131.

Voice of Youth Advocates, December, 1987, review of *Stepfather Bank,* p. 245; August 1, 1988, review of *The Dead of Winter,* p. 135.

ONLINE

Armchair Critic, http://thearmchaircritic.blogspot.com/ (December 13, 2006), review of *The Threat.*

David Poyer Home Page, http://www.poyer.com (June 10, 2007).

Mostly Fiction, http://www.mostlyfiction.com/ (January 10, 2008), Kirstin Merrihew, review of *Korea Strait.*

Mystery Gazette, http://themysterygazette.blogspot.com/ (November 30, 2007), Harriet Klausner, review of *Korea Strait.*

*   *   *

POYER, David C.
See POYER, David

*   *   *

POYER, David Charles
See POYER, David

*   *   *

PRIEST, Cherie 1975-

PERSONAL: Born July 30, 1975, in Tampa, FL; married, March, 2006; husband's name Aric. *Education:* Southern Adventist University, B.A., 1998; University of Tennessee, Chattanooga, M.A., 2001.

ADDRESSES: Home—Seattle, WA. *E-mail*—cherie.priest@gmail.com.

CAREER: Worked as a writer for an electronics company in Chattanooga, TN; Subterranean Press, Burton, MI, associate editor.

WRITINGS:

"EDEN MOORE" SERIES; NOVELS

Four and Twenty Blackbirds, Marietta Publishing (Marietta, GA), 2003, revised edition, Tor (New York, NY), 2005.

Wings to the Kingdom, Tor (New York, NY), 2006.

Not Flesh nor Feathers, Tor (New York, NY), 2007.

OTHER NOVELS

Dreadful Skin, Subterranean Press (Burton, MI), 2007.

Those Who Went Remain There Still, Subterranean Press (Burton, MI), 2008.

Fathom, Tor (New York, NY), 2008.

Boneshaker, Tor (New York, NY), 2009.

Writer for magazines and Web sites, and for role-playing projects, including *GhostOrb* and *Gnostica.* Maintains a blog.

SIDELIGHTS: Cherie Priest was born in Tampa, Florida, and lived in various places, including Chattanooga, Tennessee, where she graduated from the University of Tennessee. Her novels frequently feature Southern settings.

Priest created a modern Southern gothic in the classic tradition with her book *Four and Twenty Blackbirds.* In the story, a young woman named Eden Moore begins a search for her origins that eventually takes her on a journey across the South. She visits a swamp filled with the dead, the ruins of an old sanitarium, and other unsettling locations as she strives to discover the secret of her family's heritage. Eden experiences psychic visions, which seem to show her events from the past. Meanwhile, in the present she is the target of a stalker: a cousin whose mother is deeply involved in a cult of black magic practitioners. Events build to a "supernatural crescendo," according to a reviewer for *Publishers Weekly.* While offering the opinion that Priest adds "little new" to the world of gothic fiction, the reviewer stated that she crafts a story that will especially appeal to "postadolescent horror fans." *Four and Twenty Blackbirds* was originally published in a briefer form, then revised and expanded for publication by Tor Books. It became the first book of a trilogy that is continued in *Wings to the Kingdom,* and *Not Flesh nor Feathers,*

Eden's gift of being able to speak to the dead attracts people who want to communicate with their loved ones, and it is hard for her to refuse, living as she does in a small, Southern town that contains both Civil War and Native American burial grounds. A ghost is spotted at the historic Chickamauga battlefield, the first such specter to be seen in a century. The sighting begins Eden's search for clues to the past that brings her in contact with the Marshalls, ghost-busters who are called in when spiritual phenomena occur. While they are initially a nuisance to Eden, it is soon apparent that both Eden and the Marshalls have something great to

fear. Cara Chancellor noted in *Kliatt* that the adult language renders *Wings to the Kingdom* inappropriate for young readers, and wrote that it "is a spellbinding, spooky twist on traditional historical fiction, and it will be especially beloved by any reader with an interest in the Civil War."

In *Not Flesh nor Feathers,* Eden is about to move into a new apartment in Chattanooga when a storm destroys a dam that controls the Tennessee River, filling the streets of the city with water—and corpses. The undead become an army of zombies heading toward the Read House, and Eden looks for the connection to Caroline Read and a covered-up century-old atrocity. She meets "The White Lady," the spirit that has been haunting one of the rooms in the hotel, and also deals with her estranged brother, who has returned to patch up their relationship. "Priest's tale crackles with action and occult thrills," wrote a *Publishers Weekly* contributor.

A *Publishers Weekly* reviewer wrote that the novel *Dreadful Skin* raises "tantalizing philosophical questions about good and evil as well as the roles of hunter and prey." The story is offered in three sections titled "The Wreck of the Mary Byrd," "Halfway to Holiness," and "Our Lady of the Wasteland and the Hallelujah Chorus." Sister Eileen Callaghan is an Irish nun who keeps a revolver hidden beneath her skirts as she pursues werewolf John Gabert across post-Civil War America. He is an Englishman who was transformed in India, and who feasted on the blood of London prostitutes before coming to America. In the first section, Gabert picks off his victims as the boat the *Mary Byrd* is caught up in a storm on the Tennessee River between Chattanooga and Knoxville. The second section begins nine years later in Holiness, Texas, where Sister Eileen pursues rumors of a connection between deaths and a traveling ministry. The third section takes place two years later. Jack, who was thought to be drowned, is actually alive and about to become a father figure to Daniel, the son of the shape-shifting minister of the previous section. Sister Eileen is bitten in a struggle with Gabert, but, struggling to suppress her own blood cravings, she continues her mission. The final story is told through letters from Melissa Anderson, the only surviving woman of the ministry, to her friend, Leonard Dwyer. All the other women have been raped and killed, and the men have become a pack of werewolves. He relays the information to Sister Eileen, who meets him in Texas to save Melissa. Reviewing *Dread-*

ful Skin for the *Internet Review of Science Fiction*, Jason Erik Lundberg wrote: "The trio, along with McKenzie, the town's lawman, decide to make a stand against the revivalist pack on Mescalero's outskirts, in a brutal and bloody western shoot-out that would make Quentin Tarantino proud."

Those Who Went Remain There Still is a tale that begins with a message carved by Daniel Boone outside a Kentucky cave: "Cilled a thing heer." The thing he killed was a winged creature, but she did not die; she survived and generated offspring. The father of Heaster Wharton, Junior was with Boone when he fought the monster, and Heaster hides his will in the cave known as Witch's Pit, so that his descendants, the Manders and the Coys, will have to stop feuding and work together to locate it. When Heaster dies, they come together, including members who had escaped the brutality of their families. In reviewing the story for *SF Site* online, Tammy Moore noted that it is "more of a folk tale than a modern horror novel." Moore also commented that Priest's "narrative captured both the time period and the culture of the area, managing to be both unsentimental and affectionate about the people and their experiences."

In a *Library Journal* review, Jackie Cassada described *Fathom* as "part fairy tale, part work of modern gothic horror." The premise of the story is that when man was created, creatures and monsters known as myths were destroyed, except that a few survived to try to take back what had been theirs. Arahab is a water witch who wants her father, the ancient sea monster Leviathan, to destroy the human race, but he needs a human ally. Two humans, cousins Bernice and Nia, are vacationing on an island off the Florida coast. Nia witnesses Bernice's murder of her stepfather, who she claims abused her, and now, because she did see the crime committed, is afraid for her own life. Arahab chooses Bernice, who has achieved immortality, while earthly foes of Arahab protect Nia by encasing her in stone for years. When she emerges from her stone cocoon, Nia too is immortal and equal in power to her cousin Bernice. *Booklist* reviewer Carl Hays wrote that Priest's "creative vision is unlike anything else in contemporary fantasy."

BIOGRAPHICAL AND CRITICAL SOURCES:

PERIODICALS

Booklist, December 1, 2008, Carl Hays, review of *Fathom*, p. 37; December 15, 2008, Carl Hays, review of *Those Who Went Remain There Still*, p. 27.

Kirkus Reviews, July 15, 2005, review of *Four and Twenty Blackbirds*, p. 762; October 1, 2008, review of *Fathom*.

Kliatt, March, 2007, Cara Chancellor, review of *Wings to the Kingdom*, p. 28.

Library Journal, November 15, 2008, Jackie Cassada, review of *Fathom*, p. 63.

Publishers Weekly, August 15, 2005, review of *Four and Twenty Blackbirds*, p. 38; October 6, 2008, review of *Those Who Went Remain There Still*, p. 39; January 1, 2007, review of *Dreadful Skin*, p. 36; July 30, 2007, review of *Not Flesh nor Feathers*, p. 60; October 27, 2008, review of *Fathom*.

ONLINE

Blood of the Muse, http://www.bloodofthemuse.com/ (April 16, 2009), Paul Stotts, review of *Fathom*.

Bookslut, http://www.bookslut.com/ (June 20, 2009), Coleen Mondor, review of *Not Flesh nor Feathers*.

Cherie Priest Home Page, http://www.cheriepriest.com (June 20, 2009).

Defying Classification, http://www.pointy-stick.com/blog/ (December 10, 2007), Malcolm Tredinnick, review of "Eden Moore" series.

Green Man Review, http://www.greenmanreview.com/ (June 20, 2009), Kathleen Bartholomew, review of *Dreadful Skin*.

Internet Review of Science Fiction, http://www.irosf.com/ (March 1, 2007), Jason Erik Lundberg, review of *Dreadful Skin*.

Rick Kleffer's "The Agony Column" Online (blog related to the public radio program *The Agony Column*, KUSP-FM Central Coast Public Radio), http://bookotron.com/agony/ (June 20, 2009), review of *Four and Twenty Blackbirds*.

SF Site, http://www.sfsite.com/ (June 20, 2009), Tammy Moore, review of *Those Who Went Remain There Still*.

Strange Horizons, http://www.strangehorizons.com/ (March 13, 2007), J.C. Runolfson, review of *Dreadful Skin*; (April 22, 2009) Sara Polsky, review of *Fathom*.*

*   *   *

PULVER, Mary Monica
See FERRIS, Monica

R

RAMSLAND, Katherine 1953-

PERSONAL: Born January 2, 1953, in Ann Arbor, MI; daughter of Henry (an electrical engineer) and Barbara (a homemaker) Johnston; married Steven Ramsland (a mental health agency director), May 26, 1979. *Education:* Northern Arizona University, B.A., 1978; Duquesne University, M.A. (clinical psychology), 1979; Rutgers University, Ph.D., 1984. Received masters degree in forensic psychology from John Jay College of Criminal Justice.

ADDRESSES: Home—Upper Black Eddy, PA. *Office*—Department of Psychology, DeSales University, Center Valley, PA 18034. *E-mail*—indianni@aol.com; katherine.ramsland@desales.edu.

CAREER: Rutgers University, New Brunswick, NJ, professor of philosophy, 1980-95; DeSales University, Center Valley, PA, professor of psychology and forensic psychology, 2001—. Certified medical investigator, College of Forensic Examiners, 2003. Trial consultant, public speaker, and crisis counselor.

MEMBER: American Academy of Forensic Sciences, American Philosophical Practitioners Association, American Psychological Association, American Society of Trial Consultants, Horror Writers of America, Soren Kierkegaard Society.

WRITINGS:

NONFICTION

Engaging the Immediate: Applying Kiekegaard's Theory of Indirect Communication to the Practice of Psychotherapy, Bucknell University Press (Lewisburg, PA), 1988.

Prism of the Night: A Biography of Anne Rice, Dutton (New York, NY), 1991.

The Art of Learning: A Self-help Manual for Students, State University of New York Press (Albany, NY), 1992.

The Vampire Companion: The Official Guide to Anne Rice's Supernatural Universe, Ballantine (New York, NY), 1993.

The Witches' Companion: The Official Guide to Anne Rice's Lives of the Mayfair Witches, Ballantine (New York, NY), 1994.

The Anne Rice Trivia Book, Ballantine (New York, NY), 1994.

The Roquelaure Reader: A Companion to Anne Rice's Erotica, Plume (New York, NY), 1996.

Dean Koontz: A Writer's Biography, HarperPrism (New York, NY), 1997.

(With Steven Ramsland) *Quesadillas: Over 100 Fast, Fresh, and Festive Recipes,* Prima Publishing (New York, NY), 1997.

Piercing the Darkness: Undercover with Vampires in America Today, HarperPrism (New York, NY), 1998.

Bliss: Writing to Find Your True Self, Walking Stick (Cincinnati, OH), 2000.

The Forensic Science of C.S.I., Boulevard (New York, NY), 2001.

Cemetery Stories: Haunted Graveyards, Embalming Secrets, and the Life of a Corpse after Death, HarperEntertainment (New York, NY), 2001.

Ghost: Investigating the Other Side, Thomas Dunne Books/St. Martin's Press (New York, NY), 2001.

The Science of Vampires, Berkley Boulevard Books (New York, NY), 2002.

The Criminal Mind: A Writer's Guide to Forensic Psychology, Writer's Digest (Cincinnati, OH), 2002.

(With Gregg O. McCrary) *The Unknown Darkness: Profiling the Predators among Us,* Morrow (New York, NY), 2003.

The Science of Cold Case Files, Berkley Boulevard Books (New York, NY), 2004.

The Human Predator: A Historical Chronicle of Serial Murder and Forensic Investigation, Berkley Boulevard Books (New York, NY), 2005.

Inside the Minds of Mass Murderers: Why They Kill, Praeger (Westport, CT), 2005.

(With James E. Starrs) *A Voice for the Dead: A Forensic Investigator's Pursuit of the Truth in the Grave,* Putnam (New York, NY), 2005.

The C.S.I. Effect, Berkley Boulevard Books (New York, NY), 2006.

Beating the Devil's Game: A History of Forensic Science and Criminal Investigation, Berkley Boulevard Books (New York, NY), 2007.

Inside the Minds of Healthcare Serial Killers: Why They Kill, Praeger Publishers (Westport, CT), 2007.

Into the Devil's Den: How an FBI Agent Got inside the Aryan Nations and a Special Agent Got Him out Alive, Ballantine Books (New York, NY), 2008.

True Stories of C.S.I.: The Real Crimes behind the Best Episodes of the Popular TV Show, Berkley Boulevard (New York, NY), 2008.

(With Henry C. Lee and Elaine M. Pagliaro) *The Real World of a Forensic Scientist: Renowned Experts Reveal What it Takes to Solve Crimes,* Prometheus Books (Amherst, NY), 2009.

The Devil's Dozen: How Cutting-edge Forensics Took Down 12 Notorious Serial Killers, Berkley Books (New York, NY), 2009.

The Forensic Psychology of Criminal Minds, Berkley Books (New York, NY), 2009.

FICTION

(Editor) *The Anne Rice Reader,* Ballantine (New York, NY), 1997.

The Heat Seekers, Pinnacle Books (New York, NY), 2002.

The Blood Hunters, Kensington (New York, NY), 2004.

Also contributor of numerous articles on the subjects of serial killers, criminal investigation, and criminal psychology to periodicals. Contributor, *Philadelphia Inquirer.*

SIDELIGHTS: Katherine Ramsland has written many books that explore various aspects of forensic science and the darker side of criminal investigation. She teaches forensic psychology at DeSales University in Pennsylvania, concentrating on the ways in which psychologists and other mental health professionals can learn to diagnose and understand potential criminals. Certified as a medical investigator from the College of Forensic Examiners, Ramsland has appeared on popular media such as the *Today Show* and has been featured in documentaries on *A&E,* the *Learning Channel,* and *Discovery.* In the past, she has worked as a researcher for the FBI, contributing to the work of profiler John Douglas; her book *The Unknown Darkness: Profiling the Predators among Us* was written with another FBI profiler, Gregg McCrary. "She has also done courtroom research for forensic psychologist Dr. Barbara Kirwin, author of *The Mad, the Bad, and the Innocent,*" stated a contributor to the DeSales University Web site, "and has a part-time psychotherapy practice."

Ramsland is also the authorized biographer of "Vampire Chronicles" author Anne Rice, and an established expert on Rice's work, as well as on contemporary gothic subculture. After publishing *Prism of the Night: A Biography of Anne Rice,* Ramsland went on to pen several guides to Rice's writings, all with Rice's full cooperation. Ramsland has also published *Dean Koontz: A Writer's Biography,* about the famed horror writer. Though *Booklist* reviewer Ray Olson found Ramsland "mostly just synopsizes and biographically interprets [Koontz's] fiction," he appreciated the book's readability and popular appeal.

Ramsland's first book on true crime, *Piercing the Darkness: Undercover with Vampires in America Today,* was published in 1998. It is an account of her investigation into the disappearance of journalist Susan Walsh, who vanished while researching vampire cults in New York City. Trained in clinical psychology and philosophy, Ramsland brought what a *Publishers Weekly* reviewer described as "remarkable empathy" to this project, and which the contributor hailed as "immensely insightful and exciting" and a "model of engaged journalism." Reviewers for *Library Journal* and *Booklist* expressed similar enthusiasm for the book, which presents contemporary vampires as individuals who are sometimes disturbed and frightening, but who are also often misunderstood. Though Ramsland never solved the Walsh mystery, critics pointed out that her speculations as to the journalist's fate remain intriguing.

The subject matter was less dark in *Bliss: Writing to Find Your True Self.* In this book, Ramsland guides readers through exercises intended to develop greater personal fulfillment. Central to this approach is journal writing, through which readers can identify and clarify their thinking. A reviewer for *Publishers Weekly* considered it a "nurturing and pragmatic" work that provides a "solid foundation for understanding the concept of bliss," as well as an understanding of the developmental stages associated with its search.

In her 2001 collection, *Cemetery Stories: Haunted Graveyards, Embalming Secrets, and the Life of a Corpse after Death,* Ramsland offers readers "an amusing if grisly compendium of everything we never wished to know" about the dead and the social customs of funerals, according to a *Kirkus Reviews* writer. For this book of anecdotes, the author interviewed directors of funeral homes, looked into the history of funeral rituals, researched famous, well-preserved corpses—such as Vladimir Lenin's and Eva Peron's—and explored the special world of tagophiles, or people who are obsessed with gravestones. The *Kirkus Reviews* writer concluded that although there are no profound insights into the nature of death in *Cemetery Stories,* the book contains "shovelfuls of intriguing tidbits" about end-of-life matters.

Ramsland began working on *Ghost: Investigating the Other Side* while researching *Piercing the Darkness.* One of her "vampire" contacts had given her a ring that he claimed was possessed. Although Ramsland herself felt that there was nothing unusual about the object, others seemed to react very strongly to it, and the author began trying to unravel its secrets. Her initial skepticism toward the notion that the ring had inherent power gradually transformed to belief as her investigation progressed, and that transformation is made "all the more spinetingling" because of her initial resistance, stated a *Publishers Weekly* writer. Delving into the world of ghost hunters, psychics, and the like, *Ghost* is "credible, smart, sane and funny," according to the *Publishers Weekly* contributor.

Having written extensively about Anne Rice, the creator of a vampire novel series, and about the world of contemporary vampires, Ramsland turned to possible explanations of the vampire phenomenon in her book *The Science of Vampires.* Her study considers everything from fictional depictions of vampires, to contemporary subcultures who identify with the vampire image, to case studies of murderers who displayed vampiric traits in their crimes. A *Publishers Weekly* reviewer pointed out that despite its title, *The Science of Vampires* is "not a scholarly book aimed at the scientific community," but rather an interesting and useful collection of folklore and popular portrayals of vampires.

Ramsland collaborated with McCrary to write *The Unknown Darkness,* which details the investigative analysis of ten vicious crimes. The authors discuss the process of profiling, which involves collecting evidence, scientifically analyzing it, and using the information to develop a psychological profile of the perpetrator. "The book offers plenty of shockingly grisly and strange details to fascinate and horrify," advised a *Publishers Weekly* writer. It is "surprisingly lively," joked David Pitt in *Booklist.*

Ramsland focused on serial killers throughout history in *The Human Predator: A Historical Chronicle of Serial Murder and Forensic Investigation.* Discussing the psychological circumstances that lay the groundwork for the development of a killer's psyche, she gives readers concrete examples, proceeding chronologically from ancient Rome up to the present day. Her book "is a chilling reminder that the darkness that exists in human nature is not, as some might think, the product of modern society," commented a reviewer for *Forensic Examiner.*

Ramsland explored the realities and fallacies of forensic science as shown on popular television programs in her books *The Forensic Science of C.S.I., The C.S.I. Effect,* and *The Science of Cold Case Files.* In *The C.S.I. Effect,* she compares and contrasts the techniques shown on the program *C.S.I.: Crime Scene Investigation* with the ways the crimes probably would have been investigated in real life. In addition, she discusses the ways in which *C.S.I.* has had an effect on juries in real-life trials because of the ways it informs them, and misinforms them, about police procedures and evidence handling. The book is "a fascinating must-read for CSI fans and anyone interested in criminal justice," stated Kristine Huntley in *Booklist.*

BIOGRAPHICAL AND CRITICAL SOURCES:

PERIODICALS

American Scientist, January-February, 2003, James E. Starrs, review of *The Forensic Science of C.S.I.,* p. 84.

Booklist, February 15, 1997, Kathleen Hughes, review of *The Anne Rice Reader,* p. 994; November 15, 1997, Ray Olson, review of *Dean Koontz: A Writer's Biography,* p. 537; July, 1998, Mike Tribby, review of *Piercing the Darkness: Undercover with Vampires in America Today,* p. 1827; October 1, 2001, Margaret Flanagan, review of *Ghost: Investigating the Other Side,* p. 270; July, 2002, David Pitt, review of *The Criminal Mind: A Writer's Guide to Forensic Psychology,* p. 1815; July, 2003, David Pitt, review of *The Unknown Darkness: Profiling the Predators among Us,* p. 1851; February 1, 2005, Gilbert Taylor, review of *A Voice for the Dead: A Forensic Investigator's Pursuit of the Truth in the Grave,* p. 923; September 15, 2006, Kristine Huntley, review of *The C.S.I. Effect,* p. 11.

Forensic Examiner, May-June, 2002, review of *The Forensic Science of C.S.I.,* p. 46; summer, 2006, *The Human Predator: A Historical Chronicle of Serial Murder and Forensic Investigation,* p. 69.

Kirkus Reviews, August 15, 2001, review of *Cemetery Stories: Haunted Graveyards, Embalming Secrets, and the Life of a Corpse after Death,* p. 1197, and review of *Ghost,* p. 1198.

Law Enforcement Technology, October, 2006, review of *The C.S.I. Effect,* p. 193.

Library Journal, November 15, 1997, Ronald Ray Ratliff, review of *Dean Koontz,* p. 59; September 15, 1998, Christine A. Moesch, review of *Piercing the Darkness,* p. 97; November 1, 2001, Leroy Hommerding, review of *Ghost,* p. 120; July, 2003, Tim Delaney, review of *The Unknown Darkness,* p. 104; February 15, 2005, Tim Delaney, review of *A Voice for the Dead,* p. 146.

Publishers Weekly, August 17, 1998, review of *Piercing the Darkness,* p. 54; August 21, 2000, review of *Bliss: Writing to Find Your True Self,* p. 63; August 20, 2001, review of *Ghost,* p. 68; April 29, 2002, review of *The Criminal Mind,* p. 59; September 9, 2002, review of *The Science of Vampires,* p. 58; May 26, 2003, review of *The Unknown Darkness,* p. 60; January 31, 2005, John Silbersack, review of *A Voice for the Dead,* p. 60.

Reference & Research Book News, November, 2006, "Inside the Minds of Serial Killers."

ONLINE

DeSales University Web site, http://www.desales.edu/ (August 5, 2008), "Katherine Ramsland."

Katherine Ramsland Home Page, http://www.katherine ramsland.com (August 5, 2008).*

*　　　*　　　*

RANDALL, Joshua
　　See RANDISI, Robert J.

*　　　*　　　*

RANDISI, Robert J. 1951-
(Lew Baines, Nick Carter, a house pseudonym, Tom Cutter, Robert Lake, Paul Ledd, Robert Leigh, W.B. Longley, Joseph Meek, Joshua Randall, Robert Joseph Randisi, J.R. Roberts, Jon Sharpe, Cole Weston)

PERSONAL: Born August 24, 1951, in New York, NY; son of Joseph Francis and Rose Randisi; married Anna Y. Hom (a teacher), May 20, 1972; divorced; children: Christopher Robert, Matthew Joseph.

ADDRESSES: Home—St. Louis, MO.

CAREER: Writer, novelist, and editor. Mailroom boy, mailroom manager, and collection clerk, 1968-72; New York City Police Department, Brooklyn, NY, civilian police administrative aide, 1973-81. Cofounder and editor of *Mystery Scene* (magazine).

MEMBER: Private Eye Writers of America (founder and president), Western Writers of America, American Crime Writers' League (cofounder).

AWARDS, HONORS: Shamus Award nomination, Private Eye Writers of America, best private eye short story, 1982, for "The Snapdance," best paperback private eye novel, 1983, for *The Steinway Collection,* best private eye novel, 1984, for *Full Contact,* and best private eye short story, 1996, for "The Girl Who Talked to Horses"; Life Achievement Award, Southwest Mystery/Suspense Convention, 1993.

WRITINGS:

NOVELS

The Disappearance of Penny, Ace Books (New York, NY), 1980.

(With Warren Murphy) *Dangerous Games,* Pinnacle Books (New York, NY), 1980.

(With Warren Murphy) *Midnight Man,* Pinnacle Books (New York, NY), 1981.

(With Warren Murphy) *Total Recall,* Pinnacle Books (New York, NY), 1984.

The Ham Reporter (historical novel), Doubleday (New York, NY), 1986.

No Exit from Brooklyn (first novel in *"Nick Delvecchio"* series), St. Martin's Press (New York, NY), 1987.

Once upon a Murder, TSR (Lake Geneva, WI), 1987.

(With others) *Caribbean Blues,* Paperjacks (New York, NY), 1988.

(With others) *The Black Moon,* Lynx (New York, NY), 1989.

The Dead of Brooklyn (second novel in *"Nick Delvecchio"* series), St. Martin's Press (New York, NY), 1991.

Targett (western novel), M. Evans (New York, NY), 1991.

(Under pseudonym Robert Leigh) *The Turner Journals,* Walker & Co. (New York, NY), 1996.

(With Christine Matthews) *Murder Is the Deal of the Day,* St. Martin's Press (New York, NY), 1998.

The Ghost with Blue Eyes (western novel), Leisure (Norwalk, CT), 1999.

Delvecchio's Brooklyn (short stories), introduction by Max Allan Collins, Five Star (Unity, ME), 2001.

Miracle of the Jacal, Leisure Books (New York, NY), 2001.

(With Christine Matthews) *The Masks of Auntie Laveau,* Thomas Dunne Books/St. Martin's Minotaur (New York, NY), 2002.

Curtains of Blood (novel), Leisure Books (New York, NY), 2002.

The Offer, Five Star (Waterville, ME), 2003.

Lancaster's Orphans, Leisure Books (New York, NY), 2004.

(With Christine Matthews) *Same Time, Same Murder,* Thomas Dunne Books (New York, NY), 2005.

Cold Blooded, Leisure Books (New York, NY), 2005.

You're Nobody 'til Somebody Kills You, Minotaur Books (New York, NY), 2009.

"JOE KEOUGH" SERIES

Alone with the Dead, St. Martin's Press (New York, NY), 1995.

In the Shadow of the Arch, St. Martin's Press (New York, NY), 1997.

Fire under the Arch, St. Martin's Press (New York, NY), 2000.

Blood on the Arch, St. Martin's Press (New York, NY), 2000.

East of the Arch, Thomas Dunne Books/St. Martin's Minotaur (New York, NY), 2002.

Arch Angels, Thomas Dunne Books (New York, NY), 2004.

Blood of Angels, Leisure Books (New York, NY), 2004.

"WIDOWMAKER TRILOGY" SERIES

Invitation to a Hanging, Pocket Star Books (New York, NY), 2003.

Turnback Creek, Pocket Star Books (New York, NY), 2004.

"THE SONS OF DANIEL SHAYE" SERIES

The Sons of Daniel Shaye: Leaving Epitaph, HarperTorch (New York, NY), 2004.

Vengeance Creek, HarperTorch (New York, NY), 2005.

Pearl River Junction, HarperTorch (New York, NY), 2006.

"GAMBLERS'EM" SERIES

Butler's Wager, HarperCollins (New York, NY), 2007.

Denver Draw, HarperCollins (New York, NY), 2007.

Texas Bluff, HarperCollins (New York, NY), 2008.

"TEXAS HOLD'EM" SERIES; MYSTERY NOVELS

(With Vince Van Patten) *The Picasso Flop,* Mysterious Press (New York, NY), 2007.

"RAT PACK" SERIES; MYSTERY NOVELS

Everybody Kills Somebody Sometime, Thomas Dunne Books (New York, NY), 2006.

Luck Be a Lady, Don't Die, Thomas Dunne Books (New York, NY), 2007.

Hey There (You with the Gun in Your Hand), Minotaur Books (New York, NY), 2008.

"MILES JACOBY" SERIES; MYSTERY NOVELS

Eye in the Ring, Avon (New York, NY), 1982.
The Steinway Collection, Avon (New York, NY), 1983.
Full Contact, St. Martin's Press (New York, NY), 1984.
Separate Cases, Walker & Co. (New York, NY), 1990.
Hard Look, Walker & Co. (New York, NY), 1993.
Stand-up, Walker & Co. (New York, NY), 1994.

UNDER PSEUDONYM ROBERT LAKE

Lazarus Gun, Kensington (New York, NY), 1980.
Hanging Moon, Kensington (New York, NY), 1980.
Shelter the Bandit Queen, Kensington (New York, NY), 1981.
Lookout Mountain, Kensington (New York, NY), 1981.
Circus of Death, Kensington (New York, NY), 1981.
Ute Revenge, Kensington (New York, NY), 1981.
Apache Trail, Kensington (New York, NY), 1982.
Prisoner of Revenge, Kensington (New York, NY), 1983.
Chain Gang Kill, Kensington (New York, NY), 1983.
China Doll, Kensington (New York, NY), 1983.
Shelter No. 11: Rio Rampage, Kensington (New York, NY), 1983.
Shelter No. 13: Comanchero Blood, Kensington (New York, NY), 1983.
Shelter No. 14: The Golden Shaft, Kensington (New York, NY), 1983.
Wichita Gunman: Shelter Number Sixteen, Kensington (New York, NY), 1983.
Savage Night, Kensington (New York, NY), 1983.
Blood Mesa, Kensington (New York, NY), 1983.
The Naked Outpost: Shelter Number Seventeen, Kensington (New York, NY), 1984.
Taboo Territory, Kensington (New York, NY), 1984.
The Hard Men, Kensington (New York, NY), 1984.
Saddle Tramp, Kensington (New York, NY), 1984.
Shotgun Sugar, Kensington (New York, NY), 1985.
Fast-draw Filly, Kensington (New York, NY), 1985.
Wanted Woman, Kensington (New York, NY), 1985.
Tongue-tied Texan, Kensington (New York, NY), 1986.
The Slave Queen, Kensington (New York, NY), 1986.
Treasure Chest, Kensington (New York, NY), 1986.
Heavenly Hands, Kensington (New York, NY), 1987.
Lay of the Land, Kensington (New York, NY), 1987.
Bang-up Showdown, Kensington (New York, NY), 1987.
Whistlestop Wench, Kensington (New York, NY), 1988.
Hot and Spicy, Kensington (New York, NY), 1988.
Wyoming Wench, Kensington (New York, NY), 1989.

Tattle-tail, Kensington (New York, NY), 1989.
Backshooter, Kensington (New York, NY), 1990.
Texas Iron, Kensington (New York, NY), 1991.
Blood Trail to Kansas, Kensington (New York, NY), 1991.
Mountain Man's Vengeance, Kensington (New York, NY), 1993.

UNDER PSEUDONYM LEW BAINES

Cimarron 15: Cimarron Property, Signet (New York, NY), 1985.
Cimarron 17: Cimarron Coma, Signet (New York, NY), 1985.
Cimarron on the High Plains, Signet (New York, NY), 1985.
Cimarron 19: Cimarron Texas, Signet (New York, NY), 1986.

UNDER PSEUDONYM JACK HILD

The Barrabas Edge, Harlequin Books (Buffalo, NY), 1988.

MYSTERY NOVELS; UNDER HOUSE PSEUDONYM NICK CARTER

Run, Spy, Run, Award Books (New York, NY), 1964.
China Doll, Award Books (New York, NY), 1964.
Checkmate in Rio, Award Books (New York, NY), 1964.
Safari For Spies, Award Books (New York, NY), 1964.
Fraulein Spy, Award Books (New York, NY), 1964.
Saigon, Award Books (New York, NY), 1964.
A Bullet for Fidel, Award Books (New York, NY), 1965.
Thirteenth Spy, Tandem, 1965.
The Eyes of the Tiger, Award Books (New York, NY), 1965.
Istanbul, Award Books (New York, NY), 1965.
Web of Spies, Award Books (New York, NY), 1966.
Spy Castle, Award Books (New York, NY), 1966.
The Terrible Ones, Award Books (New York, NY), 1966.
Dragon Flame, Award Books (New York, NY), 1966.
Hanoi, Award Books (New York, NY), 1966.
Danger Key, Award Books (New York, NY), 1966.
Operation Starvation, Award Books (New York, NY), 1966.

The Mind Poisoners, Award Books (New York, NY), 1966.

The Weapon of Night, Mayflower, 1966.

The Golden Serpent, Award Books (New York, NY), 1967.

Mission to Venice, Award Books (New York, NY), 1967.

Double Identity, Award Books (New York, NY), 1967.

The Devil's Cockpit, Award Books (New York, NY), 1967.

The Chinese Paymaster, Award Books (New York, NY), 1967.

Seven Against Greece, Award Books (New York, NY), 1967.

A Korean Tiger, Award Books (New York, NY), 1967.

Assignment: Israel, Award Books (New York, NY), 1967.

The Red Guard, Award Books (New York, NY), 1967.

The Filthy Five, Award Books (New York, NY), 1967.

The Bright Blue Death, Tandem, 1967.

Macao, Award Books (New York, NY), 1968.

Operation Moon Rocket, Award Books (New York, NY), 1968.

The Judas Spy, Award Books (New York, NY), 1968.

Hood of Death, Award Books (New York, NY), 1968.

Amsterdam, Award Books (New York, NY), 1968.

Temple Of Fear, Award Books (New York, NY), 1968.

Fourteen Seconds to Hell, Tandem 1969.

The Defector, Tandem 1969.

Carnival for Killing, Tandem 1969.

Rhodesia, Tandem 1969.

Red Rays, Tandem 1969.

Peking-Tulip Affair, Tandem 1969.

The Amazon, Tandem 1969.

The Sea Trap, Tandem 1969.

Berlin, Tandem 1969.

The Human Time Bomb, Award Books (New York, NY), 1969.

The Cobra Kill, Award Books (New York, NY), 1969.

The Living Death, Award Books (New York, NY), 1969.

Operation Che Guevara, Award Books (New York, NY), 1969.

The Doomsday Formula, Award Books (New York, NY), 1970.

Operation Snake, Tandem, 1970.

The Casbah Killers, Tandem, 1970.

The Arab Plague, Award Books (New York, NY), 1970.

Red Rebellion, Tandem 1970.

The Executioners, Awards Books (New York, NY), 1970.

Black Death, Awards Books (New York, NY), 1970.

The Mind Killers, Ace Books (New York, NY), 1970.

Time Clock of Death, Awards Books (New York, NY), 1970.

Cambodia, Awards Books (New York, NY), 1970.

The Death Strain, Awards Books (New York, NY), 1970.

Jewel of Doom, Awards Books (New York, NY), 1970.

Moscow, Awards Books (New York, NY), 1970.

Slavemaster, Tandem, 1970.

Ice Bomb Zero, Awards Books (New York, NY), 1971.

Mark of Cosa Nostra, Awards Books (New York, NY), 1971.

Cairo, Tandem, 1972.

The Cairo Mafia, Awards Books (New York, NY), 1972.

Inca Death Squad, Tandem, 1972.

Assault on England, Awards Books (New York, NY), 1972.

The Omega Terror, Tandem 1972.

Code Name: Werewolf, Tandem 1973.

Strike Force Terror, Tandem 1973.

Target: Doomsday Island, Awards Books (New York, NY), 1973.

Night of the Avenger, Awards Books (New York, NY), 1973.

Assassination Brigade, Awards Books (New York, NY), 1973.

The Liquidator, Awards Books (New York, NY), 1973.

The Devil's Dozen, Awards Books (New York, NY), 1973.

The Code, Awards Books (New York, NY), 1973.

Agent Counter-agent, Awards Books (New York, NY), 1973.

Hour of the Wolf, Awards Books (New York, NY), 1973.

Our Agent in Rome is Missing, Awards Books (New York, NY), 1973.

The Kremlin File, Awards Books (New York, NY), 1973.

The Spanish Connection, Awards Books (New York, NY), 1973.

The Deaths Head Conspiracy, Awards Books (New York, NY), 1973.

The Peking Dossier, Awards Books (New York, NY), 1973.

The Stolen Pay Train, Arno Press (Victoria, British Columbia, Canada), 1974.

Butcher of Belgrade, Tandem, 1974.

Ice Trap Terror, Award Books (New York, NY), 1974.

Assassin: Code Name Vulture, Award Books (New York, NY), 1974.

Vatican Vendetta, Award Books (New York, NY), 1974.

Sign of the Cobra, Award Books (New York, NY), 1974.

The Man Who Sold Death, Award Books (New York, NY), 1974.

The N3 Conspiracy, Award Books (New York, NY), 1974.

Beirut Incident, Award Books (New York, NY), 1974.

Death of the Falcon, Award Books (New York, NY), 1974.

The Aztec Avenger, Award Books (New York, NY), 1974.

Massacre in Milan, Award Books (New York, NY), 1975.

The Jerusalem File, Award Books (New York, NY), 1975.

Counterfeit Agent, Award Books (New York, NY), 1975.

Dr. Death, Award Books (New York, NY), 1975.

The Z Document, Award Books (New York, NY), 1975.

The Ultimate Code, Award Books (New York, NY), 1975.

Assignment: Intercept, Award Books (New York, NY), 1976.

The Green Wolf Connection, Award Books (New York, NY), 1976.

The List, Award Books (New York, NY), 1976.

The Fanatics of Al Asad, Award Books (New York, NY), 1976.

The Snake Flag Conspiracy, Award Books (New York, NY), 1976.

The Turncoat, Award Books (New York, NY), 1976.

The Sign of the Prayer Shawl, Award Books (New York, NY), 1976.

The Vulcan Disaster, Award Books (New York, NY), 1976.

The Nichovev Plot, Award Books (New York, NY), 1976.

Triple Cross, Award Books (New York, NY), 1976.

The Gallagher Plot, Award Books (New York, NY), 1976.

Kathmandu Contract, Tandem, 1977.

Death Message: Oil 74-2, Award Books (New York, NY), 1978.

Six Bloody Summer Days, Tandem, 1978.

Revenge of the Generals, Tandem, 1978.

Under the Wall, Charter, 1978.

The Ebony Cross, Charter, 1978.

Deadly Doubles, Ace Books (New York, NY), 1978.

Race of Death, Ace Books (New York, NY), 1978.

Trouble in Paradise, Charter, 1978.

The Doomsday Spore, Ace Books (New York, NY), 1978.

The Asian Mantrap, Ace Books (New York, NY), 1979.

Thunderstrike in Syria, Ace Books (New York, NY), 1979.

The Redolmo Affair, Ace Books (New York, NY), 1979.

Jamaican Exchange, Ace Books (New York, NY), 1979.

Tropical Deathpact, Ace Books (New York, NY), 1979.

The Pemex Chart, Ace Books (New York, NY), 1979.

Hawaii, Charter, 1979.

Satan Trap, Ace Books (New York, NY), 1979.

Reich Four, Ace Books (New York, NY), 1979.

The Nowhere Weapon, Ace Books (New York, NY), 1979.

The Suicide Seat, Ace Books (New York, NY), 1980.

Cauldron of Hell, Ace Books (New York, NY), 1981.

The Coyote Connection, Grosset and Dunlap (New York, NY), 1981.

The Dubrovnik Massacre, Ace Books (New York, NY), 1981.

The G Man, Ace Books (New York, NY), 1981.

The Golden Bull, Ace Books (New York, NY), 1981.

The Ouster Conspiracy, Ace Books (New York, NY), 1981.

The Parisian Affair, Ace Books (New York, NY), 1981.

Solar Menace, Ace Books (New York, NY), 1981.

Strontium Code, Ace Books (New York, NY), 1981.

Pleasure Island, Ace Books (New York, NY), 1981.

Turkish Bloodbath, Ace Books (New York, NY), 1982.

Chessmaster, Ace Books (New York, NY), 1982.

The Mendoza Manuscript, Ace Books (New York, NY), 1982.

Appointment in Haiphong, Ace Books (New York, NY), 1982.

The Christmas Kill, Ace Books (New York, NY), 1982.

Damocles Threat, Ace Books (New York, NY), 1982.

The Death Star Affair, Ace Books (New York, NY), 1982.

Deathlight, Ace Books (New York, NY), 1982.

Dominican Affair, Ace Books (New York, NY), 1982.

Dr. DNA, Ace Books (New York, NY), 1982.

Earth Shaker, Ace Books (New York, NY), 1982.

The Hunter, Ace Books (New York, NY), 1982.

Israeli Connection, Ace Books (New York, NY), 1982.

The Last Samurai, Ace Books (New York, NY), 1982.

Norwegian Typhoon, Ace Books (New York, NY), 1982.

Operation: McMurdo Sound, Ace Books (New York, NY), 1982.

Puppet Master, Ace Books (New York, NY), 1982.

Retreat for Death, Ace Books (New York, NY), 1982.

Treason Game, Ace Books (New York, NY), 1982.

Typhoon Ray, Ace Books (New York, NY), 1982.

The Greek Summit, Ace Books (New York, NY), 1983.

The Death Dealer, Ace Books (New York, NY), 1983.

Hide and Go Die, Ace Books (New York, NY), 1983.

The Kali Death Cult, Ace Books (New York, NY), 1983.

Operation Vendetta, Ace Books (New York, NY), 1983.

The Outback Ghosts, Ace Books (New York, NY), 1983.

The Yukon Target, Ace Books (New York, NY), 1983.

The Istanbul Decision, Ace Books (New York, NY), 1983.

Earthfire North, Ace Books (New York, NY), 1983.

The Budapest Run, Ace Books (New York, NY), 1983.

The Decoy Hit, Ace Books (New York, NY), 1984.

The Caribbean Coup, Ace Books (New York, NY), 1984.

The Algarve Affair, Ace Books (New York, NY), 1984.

Zero-hour Strike Force, Ace Books (New York, NY), 1984.

Operation Sharkbite, Ace Books (New York, NY), 1984.

Death Island, Ace Books (New York, NY), 1984.

Night of the Warheads, Ace Books (New York, NY), 1984.

Day of the Mahdi, Ace Books (New York, NY), 1984.

Assignment: Rio, Ace Books (New York, NY), 1984.

Death Hand Play, Ace Books (New York, NY), 1984.

The Kremlin Kill, Ace Books (New York, NY), 1984.

The Mayan Connection, Ace Books (New York, NY), 1984.

San Juan Inferno, Ace Books (New York, NY), 1984.

Circle of Scorpions, Ace Books (New York, NY), 1985.

The Blue Ice Affair, Ace Books (New York, NY), 1985.

The Macao Massacre, Ace Books (New York, NY), 1985.

Pursuit of the Eagle, Ace Books (New York, NY), 1985.

The Vengeance Game, Ace Books (New York, NY), 1985.

Last Flight to Moscow, Diamond Books (New York, NY), 1985.

The Normandy Code, Diamond Books (New York, NY), 1985.

White Death, Ace Books (New York, NY), 1985.

The Assassin Convention, Ace Books (New York, NY), 1985.

Blood of the Scimitar, Ace Books (New York, NY), 1985.

The Execution Exchange, Diamond Books (New York, NY), 1985.

The Tarlov Cipher, Ace Books (New York, NY), 1985.

Target Red Star, Diamond Books (New York, NY), 1985.

The Killing Ground, Diamond Books (New York, NY), 1986.

The Berlin Target, Diamond Books (New York, NY), 1986.

Mercenary Mountain, Ace Books (New York, NY), 1986.

Blood Ultimatum, Ace Books (New York, NY), 1986.

The Cyclops Conspiracy, Ace Books (New York, NY), 1986.

Tunnel for Traitors, Diamond Books (New York, NY), 1986.

The Samurai Kill, Ace Books (New York, NY), 1986.

Terror Times Two, Ace Books (New York, NY), 1986.

Death Orbit, Ace Books (New York, NY), 1986.

Slaughter Day, Ace Books (New York, NY), 1986.

The Master Assassin, Ace Books (New York, NY), 1986.

Operation Petrograd, Ace Books (New York, NY), 1986.

Crossfire Red, Ace Books (New York, NY), 1987.

Blood of the Falcon, Ace Books (New York, NY), 1987.

Death Squad, Ace Books (New York, NY), 1987.

The Terror Code, Ace Books (New York, NY), 1987.

Holy War, Diamond Books (New York, NY), 1987.

Blood Raid, Diamond Books (New York, NY), 1987.

East of Hell, Jove (New York, NY), 1987.

Killing Games, Jove (New York, NY), 1987.

Terms of Vengeance, Jove (New York, NY), 1987.

Pressure Point, Jove (New York, NY), 1987.

Night of the Condor, Jove (New York, NY), 1987.

The Poseidon Target, Jove (New York, NY), 1987.

The Andropov File, Jove (New York, NY), 1988.

Dragonfire, Jove (New York, NY), 1988.

Bloodtrail to Mecca, Jove (New York, NY), 1988.

Deathstrike, Jove (New York, NY), 1988.

Lethal Prey, Jove (New York, NY), 1988.

Spykiller, Jove (New York, NY), 1988.

Bolivan Heat, Jove (New York, NY), 1988.

The Rangoon Man, Jove (New York, NY), 1988.

Code Name Cobra, Jove (New York, NY), 1988.

Afghan Intercept, Jove (New York, NY), 1988.

Countdown to Armageddon, Jove (New York, NY), 1988.

Black Sea Bloodbath, Jove (New York, NY), 1988.

The Deadly Diva, Jove (New York, NY), 1989.

Invitation to Death, Jove (New York, NY), 1989.

Day of the Assassin, Jove (New York, NY), 1989.

The Korean Kill, Jove (New York, NY), 1989.

Middle East Massacre, Jove (New York, NY), 1989.

Sanction to Slaughter, Jove (New York, NY), 1989.

Holiday in Hell, Jove (New York, NY), 1989.

Law of the Lion, Jove (New York, NY), 1989.

Hong Kong Hit, Jove (New York, NY), 1989.

Deep Sea Death, Jove (New York, NY), 1989.

Arms of Vengeance, Jove (New York, NY), 1989.
Hell-bound Express, Jove (New York, NY), 1989.
Isle of Blood, Jove (New York, NY), 1989.
Singapore Sling, Jove (New York, NY), 1990.
Ruby Red Death, Jove (New York, NY), 1990.
Arctic Abduction, Jove (New York, NY), 1990.
Dragon Slay, Jove (New York, NY), 1990.

WESTERN NOVELS; UNDER PSEUDONYM TOM CUTTER

The Winning Hand, Avon (New York, NY), 1983.
The Blue Cut Job, Avon (New York, NY), 1983.
Lincoln County, Avon (New York, NY), 1983.
Chinatown Chance, Avon (New York, NY), 1983.
The Oklahoma Score, Avon (New York, NY), 1985.
The Barbary Coast Tong, Avon (New York, NY), 1985.
Huntsville Breakout, Avon (New York, NY), 1985.

WESTERN NOVELS; UNDER PSEUDONYM W.B. LONGLEY

Angel Eyes: The Miracle of Revenge, Paperjacks (New York, NY), 1985.
Angel Eyes: Death's Angel, Paperjacks (New York, NY), 1985.
Wolf Pass, Paperjacks (New York, NY), 1985.
Angel Eyes: Chinatown Justice, Paperjacks (New York, NY), 1985.
Logan's Army, Paperjacks (New York, NY), 1986.
Bullets and Bad Times, Paperjacks (New York, NY), 1986.
Six Gun Angel, Paperjacks (New York, NY), 1986.
Avenging Angel, Paperjacks (New York, NY), 1986.
Angel for Hire, Paperjacks (New York, NY), 1987.

WESTERN NOVELS; UNDER PSEUDONYM JOSEPH MEEK

Mountain Jack Pike, Zebra Books (New York, NY), 1989.
Rocky Mountain Kill, Zebra Books (New York, NY), 1989.
Comanche Come-on (Mountain Jack Pike, No 3), Pinnacle Books (New York, NY), 1989.
Crow Bait, Zebra Books (New York, NY), 1989.
Green River Hunt, Zebra Books (New York, NY), 1990.
St. Louis Fire, Pinnacle Books (New York, NY), 1990.
Deep Canyon Kill, Pinnacle Books (New York, NY), 1992.
Bull's Eye Blood, Pinnacle Books (New York, NY), 1992.

Fire in the Hole, Pinnacle Books (New York, NY), 1993.
High Country Climax, Pinnacle Books (New York, NY), 1993.
Trail Heat (Mountain Jack Pike, No 14), Pinnacle Books (New York, NY), 1993.
Rough Trade (Mountain Jack Pike, No 15), Pinnacle Books (New York, NY), 1993.
Henry Lee Lucas (Mountain Jack Pike, No 9), Titan Books Ltd. (London, England), 1993.
Russian Bear (Mountain Jack Pike No 7), Kensington (New York, NY), 1994.
Hard for Justice (Mountain Jack Pike No 8), Kensington (New York, NY), 1994.

WESTERN NOVELS; UNDER PSEUDONYM JOSHUA RANDALL

Double the Bounty, Paperjacks (New York, NY), 1987.
Bounty on a Lawman, Paperjacks (New York, NY), 1987.
Beauty and the Bounty, Paperjacks (New York, NY), 1988.
Bounty on a Baron, Paperjacks (New York, NY), 1988.
Broadway Bounty, Paperjacks (New York, NY), 1988.

WESTERN NOVELS; UNDER PSEUDONYM J.R. ROBERTS

Apache Gold, Berkley (New York, NY), 1988.
The Mustang Hunters, Jove (New York, NY), 1988.
The Nevada Timber War, Jove (New York, NY), 1988.
Brothers of the Gun, Jove (New York, NY), 1989.
Six-gun Sideshow, Berkley (New York, NY), 1989.
Game of Death, Jove (New York, NY), 1991.
Ghost Town, Jove (New York, NY), 1992.
The Witness, Jove (New York, NY), 1992.
Gambler's Blood, Jove (New York, NY), 1993.
Samurai Hunt, Jove (New York, NY), 1993.
Vigilante Hunt, Jove (New York, NY), 1993.
Gillett's Rangers, Jove (New York, NY), 1994.
The Gambler, Jove (New York, NY), 1998.
The Gambler's Girl, Jove (New York, NY), 1999.
Legend of the Piasa Bird, Jove (New York, NY), 1999.
The Man from Peculiar, Jove (New York, NY), 1999.
Showdown at Daylight, Jove (New York, NY), 1999.
Safetown, Jove (New York, NY), 2000.
The Sioux City War, Jove (New York, NY), 2000.
Wanted: Clint Adams, Jove (New York, NY), 2000.
Ambush at Black Rock, Jove (New York, NY), 2000.
Barnum and Bullets, Jove (New York, NY), 2000.
Baron of Crime, Jove (New York, NY), 2000.

The Brothel Inspector, Jove (New York, NY), 2000.

The Cleveland Connection, Jove (New York, NY), 2000.

Dangerous Breed, Jove (New York, NY), 2000.

Dead Horse Canyon, Jove (New York, NY), 2000.

End of the Trail, Jove (New York, NY), 2000.

Justice in Rimfire, Jove (New York, NY), 2000.

The Lynched Man, Jove (New York, NY), 2000.

Stacked Deck, Jove (New York, NY), 2001.

Tales from the White Elephant Saloon, Jove (New York, NY), 2001.

Train Full of Trouble, Jove (New York, NY), 2001.

Bayou Ghosts, Jove (New York, NY), 2001.

Bullets for a Boy, Jove (New York, NY), 2001.

The Cherokee Strip, Jove (New York, NY), 2001.

Deadly Business, Jove (New York, NY), 2001.

High Card Dies, Jove (New York, NY), 2001.

The High Road, Jove (New York, NY), 2001.

The Killer Con, Jove (New York, NY), 2001.

Pay Dirt, Jove (New York, NY), 2001.

The Posse Men, Jove (New York, NY), 2001.

The Spirit Box, Jove (New York, NY), 2001.

Playing for Blood, Jove (New York, NY), 2002.

Random Gunfire, Jove (New York, NY), 2002.

The Shadow of the Gunsmith, Jove (New York, NY), 2002.

Dead and Buried, Jove (New York, NY), 2002.

Dead Man's Eyes, Jove (New York, NY), 2002.

Deadly Game, Jove (New York, NY), 2002.

The Doomsday Riders, Berkley (New York, NY), 2002.

Ghost Squadron, Jove (New York, NY), 2002.

The Making of a Bad Man, Jove (New York, NY), 2002.

A Man of the Gun, Jove (New York, NY), 2002.

The Marshal of Kingdom, Jove (New York, NY), 2002.

Next to Die, Jove (New York, NY), 2002.

Outlaw Luck, Jove (New York, NY), 2002.

Tangled Web, Jove (New York, NY), 2003.

Treasure Hunt, Jove (New York, NY), 2003.

Widow's Watch, Jove (New York, NY), 2003.

A Day in the Sun, Jove (New York, NY), 2003.

The Devil's Spark, Jove (New York, NY), 2003.

Empty Hand, Jove (New York, NY), 2003.

Faces of the Dead, Jove (New York, NY), 2003.

The Ghost of Billy the Kid, Jove (New York, NY), 2003.

Just Reward, Jove (New York, NY), 2003.

A Killer's Hands, Jove (New York, NY), 2003.

The Love of Money, Jove (New York, NY), 2003.

The Only Law, Jove (New York, NY), 2003.

No Turning Back, Jove (New York, NY), 2004.

The Red Queen, Jove (New York, NY), 2004.

Tricks of the Trade, Jove (New York, NY), 2004.

The Big Fork Game, Jove (New York, NY), 2004.

Big-sky Bandits, Jove (New York, NY), 2004.

The Canadian Job, Jove (New York, NY), 2004.

Dead End Pass, Jove (New York, NY), 2004.

Guilty as Charged, Jove (New York, NY), 2004.

The Hanging Tree, Jove (New York, NY), 2004.

In for a Pound, Jove (New York, NY), 2004.

Little Sureshot and the Wild West Show, Jove (New York, NY), 2004.

Long Way Down, Jove (New York, NY), 2004.

The Lucky Lady, Jove (New York, NY), 2004.

Rolling Thunder, Jove (New York, NY), 2005.

Scorpion's Tail, Jove (New York, NY), 2005.

Death in Denver, Jove (New York, NY), 2005.

The Ghost of Goliad, Jove (New York, NY), 2005.

The Hanging Judge, Jove (New York, NY), 2005.

Innocent Blood, Jove (New York, NY), 2005.

The Last Ride, Jove (New York, NY), 2005.

The Reapers, Jove (New York, NY), 2005.

The Reckoning, Jove (New York, NY), 2005.

Riding the Whirlwind, Jove (New York, NY), 2005.

Ring of Fire, Jove (New York, NY), 2005.

Dead Weight, Jove (New York, NY), 2005.

Amazon Gold (The Gunsmith, Book 289), Jove (New York, NY), 2005.

The Deadly and the Divine (The Gunsmith, Book 288), Jove (New York, NY), 2005.

Snakebite Creek, Jove (New York, NY), 2006.

The Road to Hell, Jove (New York, NY), 2006.

Loose Ends, Berkley (New York, NY), 2006.

The Long Arm of the Law, Jove (New York, NY), 2006.

The Imposter, Berkley (New York, NY), 2006.

Kira's Bounty, Jove (New York, NY), 2006.

Gunman's Crossing, Jove (New York, NY), 2006.

The Grand Prize, Jove (New York, NY), 2006.

Farewell Mountain, Jove (New York, NY), 2006.

Dangerous Cargo, Jove (New York, NY), 2006.

Alive or Nothing, Jove (New York, NY), 2006.

Gunsmith Giant 11: Red Mountain, Jove (New York, NY), 2006.

The Killing Blow, Berkley (New York, NY), 2007.

The Friends of Wild Bill Hickok, Jove (New York, NY), 2007.

One Man's Law, Berkley (New York, NY), 2007.

Red River Showdown, Berkley (New York, NY), 2007.

The Sapphire Gun, Berkley (New York, NY), 2007.

Shadow Walker, Berkley (New York, NY), 2007.

To Reap and to Sow, Jove (New York, NY), 2007.

Two for Trouble, Jove (New York, NY), 2007.

Under the Turquoise Sky, Jove (New York, NY), 2007.

Gunsmith Giant #12: The Knights of Misery, Jove (New York, NY), 2007.

Wildfire, Berkley (New York, NY), 2008.

Dying Wish, Berkley (New York, NY), 2008.

The Madame of Silver Junction, Jove (New York, NY), 2008.

Ace in the Hole, Jove (New York, NY), 2008.

The Valley of the Wendigo (The Gunsmith 317), Jove (New York, NY), 2008.

Five Points (The Gunsmith 318), Jove (New York, NY), 2008.

Out of the Past (The Gunsmith 319), Jove (New York, NY), 2008.

Straw Men (The Gunsmith 320), Jove (New York, NY), 2008.

The Greater Evil (The Gunsmith 321), Jove (New York, NY), 2008.

Louisiana Shoot-out (The Gunsmith 322), Jove (New York, NY), 2008.

A Daughter's Revenge (The Gunsmith 323), Jove (New York, NY), 2008.

Gunsmith Giant 13: The Marshal from Paris, Jove (New York, NY), 2008.

Ball and Chain (The Gunsmith 324), Jove (New York, NY), 2008.

Red Water (The Gunsmith 325), Jove (New York, NY), 2008.

"RYDER" SERIES; WRITING AS COLE WESTON

Buffalo Gal, Ivy Books (New York, NY), 1987.

Longhorn Sisters, Ivy Books (New York, NY), 1987.

Ryder's Army, Ivy Books (New York, NY), 1987.

Tong War, Ivy Books (New York, NY), 1987.

Flaming Arrows, Ivy Books (New York, NY), 1987.

Badlands Blood, Ivy Books (New York, NY), 1987.

Showdown, Ivy Books (New York, NY), 1987.

Blood Vengeance, Ivy Books (New York, NY), 1987.

Range War, Ivy Books (New York, NY), 1987.

"TRAILSMAN" SERIES; WRITING AS JON SHARPE

Condor Pass, Signet (New York, NY), 1982.

The Stalking Horse, New American Library (New York, NY), 1983.

Maverick Maiden, New American Library (New York, NY), 1983.

Calico Kill, New American Library (New York, NY), 1987.

Renegade Rebellion, New American Library (New York, NY), 1987.

Santa Fe Slaughter, New American Library (New York, NY), 1987.

Manitoba Marauders, Signet (New York, NY), 1987, 2000.

Smoky Hell Trail, New American Library (New York, NY), 1988.

White Hell, New American Library (New York, NY), 1988.

Call of the White Wolf, New American Library (New York, NY), 1988.

Devil's Den, Signet (New York, NY), 1988, 2004.

Brothel Bullets, New American Library (New York, NY), 1989.

Cave of Death, New American Library (New York, NY), 1989.

Death's Caravan, New American Library (New York, NY), 1989.

Mesabi Huntdown, New American Library (New York, NY), 1989.

Mexican Massacre, New American Library (New York, NY), 1989.

Target Conestoga, New American Library (New York, NY), 1989.

Texas Hell Country, New American Library (New York, NY), 1989.

Comstock Crazy, Signet (New York, NY), 1990.

King of Colorado, Signet (New York, NY), 1990.

Blood Prairie, Penguin Books (New York, NY), 1992.

Abilene Ambush, Signet (New York, NY), 1993.

Silver Fury, New American Library (New York, NY), 1993.

Texas Triggers, Signet (New York, NY), 1993.

Nebraska Nightmare, Signet (New York, NY), 1994.

Silver Hooves, Signet (New York, NY), 1998.

Flatwater Firebrand, Signet (New York, NY), 2000.

Navajo Revenge, New American Library (New York, NY), 2000.

Nebraska Slaying Ground, New American Library (New York, NY), 2000.

Wyoming War Cry, Signet (New York, NY), 2000.

Wyoming Whirlwind, Signet (New York, NY), 2001.

Apache Duel, New American Library (New York, NY), 2001.

Cherokee Justice, Signet (New York, NY), 2001.

Comanche Battle Cry, Signet (New York, NY), 2001.

Dakota Damnation, New American Library (New York, NY), 2001.

Denver City Gold, New American Library (New York, NY), 2001.

Flathead Fury, New American Library (New York, NY), 2001.

Frisco Filly, Signet (New York, NY), 2001.

Missouri Mayhem, New American Library (New York, NY), 2001.

Pacific Phantoms, New American Library (New York, NY), 2001.

Salt Lake Siren, New American Library (New York, NY), 2001.

Texas Blood Money, New American Library (New York, NY), 2001.

Woodland Warriors, Signet (New York, NY), 2001.

Arizona Ambush, New American Library (New York, NY), 2002.

Bloody Brazos, Signet (New York, NY), 2002.

Dead Man's Hand, Signet (New York, NY), 2002.

Nebraska Gunrunners, Signet (New York, NY), 2002.

Kansas City Swindle, Signet (New York, NY), 2002.

Pacific Polecats, Signet (New York, NY), 2002.

Seven Devils Slaughter, Signet (New York, NY), 2002.

Silver City Slayer, Signet (New York, NY), 2002.

Six-gun Justice, Signet (New York, NY), 2002.

Texas Death Storm, Signet (New York, NY), 2002.

Utah Uproar, Signet (New York, NY), 2002.

Colorado Cutthroats, Signet (New York, NY), 2002.

West Texas Uprising, New American Library (New York, NY), 2002.

Arkansas Assault, New American Library (New York, NY), 2003.

Badland Bloodbath, Signet (New York, NY), 2003.

Blood Wedding, Signet (New York, NY), 2003.

Casino Carnage, Signet (New York, NY), 2003.

Dakota Death Rattle, Signet (New York, NY), 2003.

Desert Death Trap, Signet (New York, NY), 2003.

High Country Horror, Signet (New York, NY), 2003.

Montana Madmen, Signet (New York, NY), 2003.

Six-gun Scholar, Signet (New York, NY), 2003.

Snake River Ruins, Signet (New York, NY), 2003.

Colorado Corpse, Signet (New York, NY), 2003.

St. Louis Sinners, Signet (New York, NY), 2004.

California Casualties, Signet (New York, NY), 2004.

Hell's Belles, New American Library (New York, NY), 2004.

Montana Massacre, Signet (New York, NY), 2004.

Mountain Manhunt, New American Library (New York, NY), 2004.

Nevada Nemesis, Signet (New York, NY), 2004.

New Mexico Nymph, Signet (New York, NY), 2004.

Ozarks Onslaught, Signet (New York, NY), 2004.

Skeleton Canyon, Signet (New York, NY), 2004.

California Camel Corps, Signet (New York, NY), 2005.

Colorado Claim Jumpers, Signet (New York, NY), 2005.

Dakota Prairie Pirates, Signet (New York, NY), 2005.

Gila River Dry-gulchers, Signet (New York, NY), 2005.

Kansas Weapon Wolves, Signet (New York, NY), 2005.

Mountain Mavericks, Signet (New York, NY), 2005.

Renegade Raiders, Signet (New York, NY), 2005.

Salt Lake Slaughter, Signet (New York, NY), 2005.

Texas Tart, Signet (New York, NY), 2005.

Texas Terror Trail, Signet (New York, NY), 2005.

South Texas Slaughter, Signet (New York, NY), 2006.

Backwoods Bloodbath, New American Library (New York, NY), 2006.

Black Rock Pass, Signet (New York, NY), 2006.

The Cutting Kind, Signet (New York, NY), 2006.

Dakota Danger, New American Library (New York, NY), 2006.

Dead Man's Bounty, Signet (New York, NY), 2006.

High Plains Grifters, New American Library (New York, NY), 2006.

Oasis of Blood, New American Library (New York, NY), 2006.

Oregon Outlaws, Signet (New York, NY), 2006.

Ozark Blood Feud, Signet (New York, NY), 2006.

San Francisco Showdown, Signet (New York, NY), 2006.

Six-gun Persuasion, Signet (New York, NY), 2006.

Alaskan Vengeance, Signet (New York, NY), 2007.

Border Bravados, New American Library (New York, NY), 2007.

California Carnage, New American Library (New York, NY), 2007.

Death Valley Demons, New American Library (New York, NY), 2007.

Montana Marauders, Signet (New York, NY), 2007.

Nebraska Night Riders, Signet (New York, NY), 2007.

Shanghaied Six-guns, Signet (New York, NY), 2007.

Terror Trackdown, Signet (New York, NY), 2007.

Wyoming Wipeout, Signet (New York, NY), 2007.

Beyond Squaw Creek, New American Library (New York, NY), 2008.

Mountain Mystery, Signet (New York, NY), 2008.

Nevada Nemesis, Signet (New York, NY), 2008.

Missouri Manhunt, Signet (New York, NY), 2008.

Louisiana Laydown, Signet (New York, NY), 2008.

Oregon Outrage, Signet (New York, NY), 2008.

Apache Ambush, Signet (New York, NY), 2008.

Wyoming Death Trap, Signet (New York, NY), 2008.

California Crackdown, Signet (New York, NY), 2008.

Seminole Showdown, Signet (New York, NY), 2008.

Silver Mountain Slaughter, Signet (New York, NY), 2008.

"GIANT TRAILSMAN" SERIES; WRITING AS JON SHARPE

Montana Maiden, Signet (New York, NY), 1982.

Spoon River Stud, Signet (New York, NY), 1983.

River Kill, Signet (New York, NY), 1987.

Desperate Dispatch, Signet (New York, NY), 1989.
Aztec Gold, Signet (New York, NY), 2000.
New Mexico Nightmare, Signet (New York, NY), 2003.
Menagerie of Malice, Signet (New York, NY), 2004.
Island Devils, New American Library (New York, NY), 2005.
Idaho Blood Spoor, New American Library (New York, NY), 2006.
Desert Duel, Signet (New York, NY), 2007.

"CANYON O'GRADY" SERIES

Dead Men's Trails, Signet (New York, NY), 1989.
Silver Slaughter, Signet (New York, NY), 1989.
Machine Gun Madness, Signet (New York, NY), 1989.
Shadow Guns, Signet (New York, NY), 1989.
The Lincoln Assignment, Signet (New York, NY), 1989.
Bleeding Kansas, Signet (New York, NY), 1990.
Counterfeit Madam, Signet (New York, NY), 1990.
The Great Land Swindle, Signet (New York, NY), 1990.
Soldier's Song, Signet (New York, NY), 1991.
Railroad Renegades, Signet (New York, NY), 1991.
Assassin's Trail, Signet (New York, NY), 1991.
Colonel Death, Signet (New York, NY), 1991.
Blood and Gold, Signet (New York, NY), 1991.
Death Ranch, Signet (New York, NY), 1991.
Killers Club, Signet (New York, NY), 1992.
Blood Bounty, Signet (New York, NY), 1992.
Rio Grande Ransom, Signet (New York, NY), 1992.
California Vengeance, Signet (New York, NY), 1992.
Wyoming Conspiracy, Signet (New York, NY), 1992.
Colorado Ambush, Signet (New York, NY), 1992.
Louisiana Gold Race, Signet (New York, NY), 1993.
Chicago Six-guns, Signet (New York, NY), 1993.
Rocky Mountain Feud, Signet (New York, NY), 1993.

EDITOR

The Eyes Have It: The First Annual PWA Anthology, Mysterious Press (New York, NY), 1984.
Mean Streets: The Second PWA Anthology, Mysterious Press (New York, NY), 1986.
An Eye for Justice: The Third PWA Anthology, Mysterious Press (New York, NY), 1988.
(With Edward Gorman) *Under the Gun,* New American Library (New York, NY), 1990.
Justice for Hire: The Fourth PWA Anthology, Mysterious Press (New York, NY), 1990.

(With Marilyn Wallace) *Deadly Allies: PWA/Sisters in Crime Collaborative Anthology,* Doubleday (New York, NY), 1992.
(With Susan Dunlap) *Deadly Allies II: PWA/Sisters in Crime Collaborative Anthology,* Doubleday (New York, NY), 1994.
The Eyes Still Have It: The Shamus Award-winning Stories, Dutton (New York, NY), 1995.
First Cases: First Appearances of Classic Private Eyes, Dutton (New York, NY), 1996.
(With Barbara Collins) *Lethal Ladies,* Berkley (New York, NY), 1996.
First Cases, Volume 2: First Appearances of Classic Amateur Detectives, Signet (New York, NY), 1997.
Writing the Private-eye Novel (nonfiction), Writer's Digest Books (Cincinnati, OH), 1997.
Lethal Ladies II, Prime Crime (New York, NY), 1998.
First Cases, Volume 3: New and Classic Tales of Detection, Signet (New York, NY), 1999.
Tin Star, Berkley (New York, NY), 2000.
The Shamus Game: Fourteen New Stories of Detective Fiction, Signet (New York, NY), 2000.
Mystery Street, Signet (New York, NY), 2001.
(With Christine Matthews) *Mayhem in the Midlands,* Hats Off (Tucson, AZ), 2001.
Most Wanted: A Lineup of Favorite Crime Stories, Signet (New York, NY), 2002.
First Cases, Volume 4: The Early Years of Famous Detection, Signet (New York, NY), 2002.
Boot Hill: An Anthology of the West, Forge Books (New York, NY), 2002.
Black Hats, Berkley (New York, NY), 2003.
High Stakes: Eight Sure-bet Stories of Gambling and Crime, New American Library (New York, NY), 2003.
Greatest Hits: Original Stories of Assassins, Hitmen, and Hired Guns, Carroll & Graf (New York, NY), 2006.
Hollywood and Crime: Original Crime Stories Set during the History of Hollywood, Pegasus Books (New York, NY), 2007.

Contributor to magazines, including *Armchair Detective* and *Poisoned Pen.*

SIDELIGHTS: Robert J. Randisi is a prolific writer of private eye and western novels who has sometimes turned out as many as sixteen novels a year. He is best known for his private eye mysteries and for championing the genre through the Private Eye Writers of America, which he founded. "My aim has been to elevate this field from a subgenre of mystery to a genre of its own," Randisi commented in the *St. James Guide to Crime and Mystery Writers.* It is clear from his writing that Randisi "loves the private eye," according to Gary Warren Niebuhr in the same volume.

Randisi is the creator of several series characters, including two who are private investigators and one series character who is a police detective. Miles Jacoby, a former prizefighter, and Nick Delvecchio, a one-time police officer, are the private eyes, while Joe Keough, a transplant from New York City to St. Louis, is the detective. Jacoby is a "prototypical everyman investigator," as Niebuhr put it, while Delvecchio is more complex. Keogh "maintains all the best attributes of the lone wolf P.I.," even though he is on a municipal payroll, according to Niebuhr. Private eye Henry Po, who specializes in probing gambling corruption, is the protagonist of Randisi's first novel, *The Disappearance of Penny,* and has made supporting appearances in the Jacoby series. Other authors' fictional private investigators have also made "guest appearances" in several of Randisi's novels.

Randisi's affection for the private eye genre does not keep him from bending its rules at times. In *The Steinway Collection,* for example, one of the mysteries remains unsolved; Jacoby finds the killer of his client, but not the magazine collection the client had hired him to find in the first place. "This is in direct violation of the 'private eye code' that says a P.I. has to finish what he starts no matter what," Randisi once told *CA.* "I was warned by a friend that I could not possibly do this, leave a mystery unsolved, but I went ahead and did it anyway."

Despite an occasional divergence from the genre's conventions, Randisi remains grounded in the tradition of the hard-boiled private eye story. For example, *Hard Look,* with Jacoby searching for a missing woman body builder in Florida, abounds in "sharp sleuth patter, hard luck, and cheap graft," according to a *Publishers Weekly* contributor. Writing private eye fiction is a challenge, noted Wes Lukowsky in a *Booklist* review of *Stand-up,* which finds Jacoby investigating the disappearance of a friend and the death of a comedian: "It's a balancing act in which you must simultaneously pay homage to past masters and make the song your own. [Raymond] Chandler and [Dashiell] Hammett would approve of the way Randisi bends his notes."

Randisi is also the creator of recurring series characters Claire and Gil Hunt, a husband-and-wife team of amateur detectives based in St. Louis, Missouri. Gil is the owner of a bookstore, while Claire hosts the St. Louis area's most popular home shopping show on television. In *Same Time, Same Murder,* Gil and Claire tell how they met at a mystery writers convention in Omaha, investigated a murder, and fell in love—in that order. When a dinner date goes sour, the two discover the body of the convention's guest of honor, Robin Westerly, who has been shot dead in his room. Police detectives seek out Gil's knowledge of the publishing world, hoping it will help in the investigation, while the authorities eye a nervous hotel maid as the killer. Bolstered by their own investigation, Gil and Claire are sure the killer is someone else. *Booklist* reviewer Sue O'Brien called the novel a "pleasant cozy with likable characters."

In *The Masks of Auntie Laveau,* Claire and Gil are dispatched to New Orleans to look for products Claire can feature on her home shopping show. In particular, they are on the lookout for a type of miniature Mardi Gras mask. Their first meeting with Auntie Laveau, the artist who makes the masks and claims direct lineage to famed voodoo queen Marie Laveau, raises their suspicions; later, when the real Auntie Laveau turns up dead, Claire and Gil realize that they were talking to an imposter. The Hunts tell the investigators all they know about Auntie Laveau and then return to St. Louis. Gil then finds himself thoroughly taken by the legends and concepts of voodoo, and when New Orleans police call for help in identifying a comatose woman they think the Hunts know, Gil immediately takes the opportunity to head south again. Gil confirms that the woman is the bogus Auntie Laveau, with whom he and Claire first met, but he cannot offer any insight into who she is or how she ended up in the hospital. As Gil becomes more and more involved in the case and deadly danger menaces him, he realizes that he seems unable to withdraw from the situation, causing him to wonder if he has been the victim of a voodoo spell. A *Publishers Weekly* reviewer commented: "Hexes, potions, and spells interweave with vivid settings, two delightful sleuths and credible supporting characters."

Randisi's "Joe Keough" series books are also set in St. Louis, and have distinctive titles that all refer in some way to the famed St. Louis Gateway Arch. *Arch Angels* "features a distinctive double plot and plenty of humanizing detail," commented a *Publishers Weekly* reviewer. Keough and his partner, Harriet Connors, are dispatched by the Federal Serial Killer Task Force to investigate two similar but geographically separated cases; one in Chicago in which three young girls are kidnapped and killed, and another in St. Louis, in which three young boys are similarly kidnapped and slain. In both locations, the detectives encounter resistance and resentment from local law enforcement, but they do their best to investigate despite their obstacles. As they analyze the evidence and build their case, Joe and Harriet begin to think that the killer is the same in both cases. This conclusion, however, defies the law of physics, requiring the killer to be in two places at the same time. If there are indeed two killers at work, the sleuths must learn what their connection is and why their methods are so uncannily similar. *Booklist* reviewer Lukowsky called Randisi's Keough stories "understated gems," adding: "An unsettling resolution adds just the right touch of uncertainty to this fine crime novel."

East of the Arch brings Joe Keough into contact with a brutal murderer who preys on pregnant women. In two cases in East St. Louis, Illinois, the battered bodies of pregnant women have been found with their unborn children viciously torn from their wombs. Joe's specialized knowledge of serial killers leads him to work on the case outside his normal jurisdiction, along with local partner, detective Marc Jeter. When the investigation slows and fails to produce any leads in a timely manner, the mayor of East St. Louis orders that a suspect be arrested, even though Keough is certain that the incarcerated man is not the killer. When the suspect is released from jail for lack of evidence, the detectives are blamed for botching the case, which infuriates Keough and fuels him with determination to solve the case, though the answers he finds are not at all what he expects. Emily Melton, writing in *Booklist,* called the novel "another exceptionally entertaining and riveting mystery from genre stalwart Randisi."

Some reviewers have found Randisi's detectives less than appealing. A *Publishers Weekly* critic, for one, was offended by intimations of Delvecchio's prejudiced attitudes in *No Exit from Brooklyn.* Randisi's plotting has received occasional negative comments as well; a *Publishers Weekly* reviewer described *No Exit*'s complicated story as an "unwieldy narrative." Other critics, however, have declared Randisi a solid practitioner of the private eye novel, a "no-nonsense" author whose work "doesn't waste a phrase or a plot turn," as another *Publishers Weekly* contributor put it. Niebuhr, assessing Randisi's body of work, maintained that the author "continues to write fine novels that contribute to the quality of the genre."

Randisi is also a prolific editor of anthologies in his selected genres of fiction. *Greatest Hits: Original*

Stories of Assassins, Hitmen, and Hired Guns contains original short mystery stories about contract killers by several of the genre's most notable names, including Lawrence Block, Ed Gorman, Max Allan Collins, and Jeffrey Deaver. Fans of hard-boiled mysteries "will be in seventh heaven," commented David Pitt in *Booklist.* A *Publishers Weekly* reviewer observed that "there isn't a bad story in the bunch, a notable accomplishment." *Boot Hill: An Anthology of the West,* contains fifteen short stories centered on the storied Western graveyard and how some of its inhabitants came to be buried there. Using the presence of an unnamed gravedigger as a framing device, Randisi assembles the diverse stories, "packed with vividly described gunplay," as the anonymous narrator heads toward a surprise ending, according to Charles C. Nash in *Library Journal.*

In 2008 Randisi published the third novel in the "Rat Pack" mystery series, *Hey There (You with the Gun in Your Hand).* Sands Casino pit boss Eddie Gianelli agrees to help Sammy Davis, Jr., who is being blackmailed for 50,000 dollars by a man who has an incriminating photo. Davis agrees to pay and asks Gianelli to complete the money/photo exchange. When a dead body turns up, however, the mob, FBI, local police, and local politicians, including the recently-elected JFK, begin manipulating the situation and making things difficult for everyone involved.

Harriet Klausner, writing on the *Merry Genre Go Round Reviews* Web site, remarked that the plot "is zany and a bit over the top, but no one will care as the Rat Pack steals the show." *Booklist* contributor Lukowsky opined that an additional political slant to the novel "adds a welcome seriousness to" the series, which is otherwise "breezy." Lukowsky concluded that "plot, dialogue, and characters are all up to veteran Randisi's high standards." A contributor writing in *Kirkus Reviews* was less supportive of the novel, calling it "a limp plot peopled by celebrities past their prime." A contributor writing in *Publishers Weekly* noted that "Randisi shows both respect and affection for his historical characters."

Through his work as an editor, and by founding the Private Eye Writers of America, which bestows the Shamus Award upon worthy authors, Randisi has done much to give "aid and comfort to his fellow writers," according to Niebuhr, who also credited the organization with aiding in the resurgence of the private eye story in the 1980s.

In addition to his detective fiction, Randisi has written numerous Western novels. His most enduring series is "The Gunsmith," which consists of well over two hundred titles. Randisi once told *CA* he "backed into" Western writing at the request of an editor. He has written almost all of his Westerns under pseudonyms so that his real name remains associated with the private eye genre.

BIOGRAPHICAL AND CRITICAL SOURCES:

BOOKS

St. James Guide to Crime and Mystery Writers, St. James Press (Detroit, MI), 1996.

PERIODICALS

Armchair Detective, winter, 1986, review of *Full Contact,* p. 21; spring, 1987, review of *Mean Streets: The Second PWA Anthology,* p. 192; spring, 1988, review of *No Exit from Brooklyn,* p. 148; winter, 1988, review of *The Eyes Have It: The First Annual PWA Anthology,* p. 108; spring, 1989, review of *An Eye for Justice: The Third PWA Anthology,* p. 216; winter, 1991, review of *Separate Cases,* p. 48; winter, 1995, review of *Deadly Allies II: PWA/Sisters in Crime Collaborative Anthology,* p. 100; spring, 1996, review of *First Cases: First Appearances of Classic Private Eyes,* p. 214; spring, 1996, review of *The Eyes Still Have It: The Shamus Award-winning Stories,* p. 214; fall, 1996, review of *The Turner Journals,* p. 503.

Booklist, June 15, 1983, review of *The Winning Hand,* p. 1325; October 15, 1984, review of *Full Contact,* p. 283; October 1, 1986, review of *Mean Streets,* p. 191; August, 1988, review of *An Eye for Justice,* p. 1892; August, 1990, review of *Justice for Hire: The Fourth PWA Anthology,* p. 2158; August, 1990, review of *Separate Cases,* p. 2160; July, 1991, review of *Targett,* p. 2030; March 15, 1992, Bill Ott, review of *Deadly Allies: PWA/Sisters in Crime Collaborative Anthology,* p. 1339; April 15, 1993, Wes Lukowsky, review of *Hard Look,* p. 1498; December 15, 1994, Wes Lukowsky, review of *Stand-up,* p. 739; January 1, 1996, Wes Lukowsky, review of *First Cases,* p. 795; June 1, 1996, George Needham, review of *The Turner Journals,* p. 1679; January 1, 1998, review of *In the Shadow of the Arch,* p. 784; January 1, 1999, Wes Lukowsky, review of *Murder Is the Deal of the Day,* p. 839; May 1, 2000, Wes Lukowsky, review of *Blood on the Arch,* p. 1624; December 15, 2000, Wes

Lukowsky, review of *Delvecchio's Brooklyn,* p. 792; December 15, 2001, Barbara Bibel, review of *The Masks of Auntie Laveau,* p. 707; September 1, 2002, Emily Melton, review of *East of the Arch,* p. 63; February 1, 2004, Wes Lukowsky, review of *Arch Angels,* p. 953; June 1, 2005, Sue O'Brien, review of *Same Time, Same Murder,* p. 1762; November 1, 2005, Keir Graff, review of *The Ham Reporter,* p. 29; November 15, 2005, David Pitt, review of *Greatest Hits: Original Stories of Assassins, Hitmen, and Hired Guns,* p. 29; August 1, 2006, Wes Lukowsky, review of *Everybody Kills Somebody Sometime,* p. 53; February 15, 2007, Frank Sennett, review of *The Picasso Flop,* p. 42; May 1, 2007, Wes Lukowsky, review of *Hollywood and Crime: Original Crime Stories Set during the History of Hollywood,* p. 28; November 15, 2007, Wes Lukowsky, review of *Luck Be a Lady, Don't Die,* p. 22; November 15, 2008, Wes Lukowsky, review of *Hey There (You with the Gun in Your Hand),* p. 20.

Chicago Tribune Books, April 5, 1992, review of *Deadly Allies,* p. 5; November 4, 2001, review of *Mystery Street,* p. 2.

Drood Review of Mystery, July, 2000, review of *The Shamus Game: Fourteen New Stories of Detective Fiction,* p. 24; November, 2000, review of *Delvecchio's Brooklyn,* p. 18.

Journal of the West, July, 1989, Joseph W. Snell, review of *The Ham Reporter,* p. 89.

Kirkus Reviews, October 1, 1984, review of *Full Contact,* p. 936; August 15, 1986, review of *Mean Streets,* p. 1253; May 15, 1987, review of *No Exit from Brooklyn,* p. 1759; June 15, 1988, review of *An Eye for Justice,* p. 863; June 15, 1990, review of *Separate Cases,* p. 840; July 15, 1990, review of *Justice for Hire,* p. 969; April 1, 1993, review of *Hard Look,* p. 414; January 15, 1996, review of *First Cases,* p. 104; April 1, 1996, review of *The Turner Journals,* p. 490; December 1, 1997, review of *In the Shadow of the Arch,* p. 1742; November 15, 1998, review of *Murder Is the Deal of the Day,* p. 1634; March 15, 2000, review of *Blood on the Arch,* p. 342; December 1, 2000, review of *Delvecchio's Brooklyn,* p. 1648; November 1, 2001, review of *The Masks of Auntie Laveau,* p. 1521; August 1, 2002, review of *East of the Arch,* p. 1082; December 1, 2003, review of *Arch Angels,* p. 1384; September 1, 2006, review of *Everybody Kills Somebody Sometime,* p. 880; April 15, 2007, review of *Hollywood and Crime,* p. 880; October 15, 2007, review of *Luck Be a Lady, Don't Die;* October 1, 2008, review of *Hey There (You with the Gun in Your Hand).*

Kliatt, January, 1988, review of *Mean Streets,* p. 28.

Library Journal, November 1, 1986, review of *Mean Streets,* p. 113; June 1, 1987, Jo Ann Vicarel, review of *No Exit from Brooklyn,* p. 132; July, 1991, Angela Washington-Blair, review of *Targett,* p. 137; March 1, 1992, Rex E. Klett, review of *Deadly Allies,* p. 123; May 1, 1993, Rex E. Klett, review of *Hard Look,* p. 121; June 1, 1996, Rex E. Klett, review of *The Turner Journals,* p. 156; May 15, 2002, Charles C. Nash, review of *Boot Hill: An Anthology of the West,* p. 128; January, 2003, Rex E. Klett, review of *The Offer,* p. 163.

Los Angeles Times, December 5, 1982, Don Strachan, review of *Eye in the Ring,* p. 13; January 8, 1984, Kristiana Gregory, review of *The Steinway Collection,* p. 4; January 27, 1984, review of *The Eyes Have It,* p. 10.

New York Law Journal, April 23, 1996, Cristi M. Shields, review of *First Cases,* p. 2.

New York Times Book Review, March 3, 1985, Newgate Callendar, review of *Full Contact,* p. 35.

Publishers Weekly, September 21, 1984, review of *Full Contact,* p. 91; June 27, 1986, review of *The Ham Reporter,* p. 75; May 1, 1987, Sybil Steinberg, review of *No Exit from Brooklyn,* p. 56; July 1, 1988, Sybil Steinberg, review of *An Eye for Justice,* p. 68; June 29, 1990, Sybil Steinberg, review of *Justice for Hire,* p. 88; June 7, 1991, review of *Targett,* p. 54; February 24, 1992, review of *Deadly Allies,* p. 46; March 15, 1993, review of *Hard Look,* p. 72; October 31, 1994, review of *Stand-up,* p. 46; September 18, 1995, review of *The Eyes Still Have It,* p. 116; February 5, 1996, review of *First Cases,* p. 79; April 29, 1996, review of *The Turner Journals,* p. 55; November 24, 1997, review of *In the Shadow of the Arch,* p. 56; November 30, 1997, review of *Murder Is the Deal of the Day,* p. 52; July 26, 1999, review of *The Ghost with Blue Eyes,* p. 88; March 20, 2000, review of *Blood on the Arch,* p. 74; December 18, 2000, review of *Delvecchio's Brooklyn,* p. 59; December 3, 2001, review of *The Masks of Auntie Laveau,* p. 43; May 20, 2002, review of *Boot Hill,* p. 49; September 2, 2002, review of *East of the Arch,* p. 57; December 2, 2002, review of *The Offer,* p. 37; February 23, 2004, review of *Arch Angels,* p. 55; September 26, 2005, review of *Cold Blooded,* p. 68; November 7, 2005, review of *Greatest Hits,* p. 56; August 14, 2006, review of *Everybody Kills Somebody Sometime,* p. 182; December 4, 2006, review of *The Picasso Flop,* p. 38; April 2, 2007, review of *Hollywood and Crime,* p. 41; October 8, 2007, review of *Luck Be a Lady, Don't Die,* p. 39;

September 8, 2008, review of *Hey There (You with the Gun in Your Hand),* p. 38.

Rapport: The Modern Guide to Books, Music, & More, 1993, review of *Hard Look,* p. 24.

Reference & Research Book News, February, 2000, review of *The Western,* p. 169.

Roundup Quarterly, spring, 1990, review of *Crow Bait,* p. 50; summer, 1991, review of *Russian Bear (Mountain Jack Pike No 7),* p. 51; fall, 1991, review of *Targett,* p. 65; December, 1999, review of *The Ghost with Blue Eyes,* p. 30; June, 2000, review of *The Western,* p. 41; February, 2002, review of *Miracle of the Jacal,* p. 30; August, 2002, review of *Boot Hill,* p. 26; December, 2002, review of *White Hats,* p. 28; February, 2005, review of *The Sons of Daniel Shaye: Leaving Epitaph,* p. 29; June, 2005, review of *Backshooter,* p. 50; February, 2008, review of *Blood Trail to Kansas,* p. 22; June, 2008, review of *Texas Iron,* p. 30.

Science Fiction Review, November, 1983, review of *Chinatown Chance,* p. 31.

Washington Post Book World, December 17, 2006, Kevin Allman, review of *Everybody Kills Somebody Sometime,* p. 13.

West Coast Review of Books, September, 1983, review of *The Winning Hand,* p. 52.

Wilson Library Bulletin, January, 1983, Jon Breen, review of *Eye in the Ring,* p. 420; March, 1984, Kathleen Maio, review of *The Steinway Collection,* p. 504.

ONLINE

American Western, http://www.readthewest.com/ (June 4, 2006), author interview.

Merry Genre Go Round Reviews, http://harstan.wordpress.com/ (October 11, 2008), Harriet Klausner, review of *Hey There (You with the Gun in Your Hand).*

Thrilling Detective, http://www.thrillingdetective.com/ (June 4, 2006), author profile.*

*   *   *

RANDISI, Robert Joseph
See RANDISI, Robert J.

*   *   *

RANSOM, Daniel
See GORMAN, Ed

RINELLA, Steven 1974(?)-

PERSONAL: Born c. 1974; son of Frank J. and Rosemary Rinella; stepson of Paul R. Johnson; married Catherine Parlette Finch, July 12, 2008. *Education:* Grand Valley State University, graduated; University of Montana, M.F.A.

ADDRESSES: Home—New York, NY; and AK. *E-mail*—americanbuffalo2008@gmail.com.

CAREER: Writer. *Outside* (magazine), correspondent.

WRITINGS:

The Scavenger's Guide to Haute Cuisine, Miramax Books (New York, NY), 2006.
American Buffalo: In Search of a Lost Icon, Spiegel & Grau (New York, NY), 2008.

Contributor to books, including the "Best American Travel Writing" series. Contributor to periodicals and Web sites, including *New York Times, New Yorker, Salon.com, Field and Stream, American Heritage, Bowhunter, Flyfisherman,* and *Nerve.com.*

SIDELIGHTS: Outdoor enthusiast Steven Rinella is a frequent contributor to magazines such as *Outdoor* and *Field and Stream.* His work, according to reviewers, often combines the sensory milieu of travel writing with the adventure and ruggedness of outdoor writing. In his first book, *The Scavenger's Guide to Haute Cuisine,* Rinella tells the story of what happened when a friend gave him a copy of *Le Guide Culinaire,* a hundred-year-old cookbook originally published in 1903 by master chef Auguste Escoffier. The cookbook included a number of exotic recipes for wildlife-based dishes, and the more Rinella perused the book, the more obsessed he became with it, "because of its assumption that any chef worth his salt kills his own antelope, catches his own trout and digs for his own oysters," related a *Kirkus Reviews* contributor. As an avid hunter and sportsman, Rinella was experienced at hunting and cooking his own food. Inspired by the book, by his own outdoor skills, and by Escoffier's example, Rinella undertook a year-long project to gather the ingredients, hunt the wildlife, and stockpile the supplies for a massive three-day, forty-five course wild game and natural food banquet for himself and his friends.

Throughout the book, Rinella describes the various hunting trips he took through the United States and Canada to acquire the necessary supplies of fish and game. He describes gathering plants and related ingredients and relates how he raised pigeons specifically for the feast. He tells how some types of foodstuffs, such as foie gras (the liver of deliberately fattened geese) and headcheese, are made, even though the descriptions could be considered repulsive to some of his readers. The story of the week-long frenzy of cooking and preparing the food, and worry over whether everything would be ready in time and even if some of the dishes would work, adds to the suspense. "Part food memoir, part hairy-chest hunting adventure, *The Scavenger's Guide to Haute Cuisine* turns out to be one of the most unlikely enjoyments of the literary season," observed David Abrams on the online periodical *January.* A *Publishers Weekly* reviewer noted that Rinella's "unusual memoir could serve as a tasty gift for sporting types." Maureen J. Delany-Lehman, writing in *Library Journal,* noted: "Readers of outdoor humorist Patrick McManus will find Rinella's airy style very similar and often as funny." Describing Rinella's work in a *NewWest.Net* review, Allen Jones wrote: "Crackling with enthusiasm and energy, alive with honest curiosity, here's a book that's an altogether unexpected kind of creature: Adventure writing ameliorated by cooking school and natural history, with maybe a soupcon of ethical philosophy thrown in for the salt."

In an interview by Thomas Scott McKenzie of *SlushPile.Net,* Rinella was asked which game dish was his favorite. He replied that he eats "normal" food like steak and burgers, and makes cured meats and sausages, as well as dishes using squirrel. Rinella said that if he had to choose one type of wild game dish, it would be a seven or eight inch piece "of loin (moose, buffalo, deer, elk, antelope, caribou, bear, you name it) and season it with coarse salt and crushed black pepper. Put on more pepper than you'd think you'd need. Then brown it on all sides in a combination of olive oil and butter over a burner set on high heat; get the surfaces nice and crispy. Then pop the loin, pan and all, into an oven at about 375 degrees. Cook it until the inside of the loin is 150 degrees. It's simple, and it really showcases the meat. I could eat that every day."

Rinella's interest in the American buffalo, or bison, began in 1999 when he found a buffalo skull in the Madison Range in southwest Montana that he had carbon-dated to the seventeenth century. In 2005, he was awarded one of the twenty-four permits given out through a lottery system by the State of Alaska for the Copper River buffalo hunt, taking place in the foothills of the Wrangell Mountains. This began a process that would lead to his documentation of that hunt and the knowledge he accumulated about the magnificent beast. His book, *American Buffalo: In Search of a Lost Icon,* is the result. Rinella was allowed to hunt between September and March on public lands and could not use a cell phone, all-terrain vehicle, laser gun-sight, or fully automatic weapon. "An engaging, sharp-eyed writer whose style fuses those of John McPhee and Hunter S. Thompson, Rinella chronicles the buffalo's transformation from Ice Age behemoth to American Indian food and shelter provider to modern-day theme-park sideshow," wrote Dennis Anderson in the Minneapolis *Star Tribune.* Jesse Barrett reviewed *American Buffalo* for the *San Francisco Chronicle Online,* writing: "At the start, these stories are appropriately shaggy and ruminative—Rinella loves these animals' cultural and historical odor as much as their reality, and his extended riff on 'buffalo-related facts' exudes loopy genius." Rinella writes of the controversy surrounding the Montana commemorative buffalo quarter, the origins of the buffalo, and the value of a buffalo hide in the middle of the nineteenth century. At that time, due to the actions of both whites and Native Americans, the buffalo was nearly extinct. The American Bison Society was founded in 1905 by a group of wealthy men, including Theodore Roosevelt, Frederic Remington, and Andrew Carnegie, who in 1907 sent fifteen animals to the newly established Wichita Bison Refuge in Oklahoma. By 1911, the group declared its work done, and they met for the last time in 1935.

Rinella tracks the history of the American buffalo, which is not native to the country, but is thought to be descended from Eurasian steppe bison that crossed over on the Bering land bridge to join other Paleolithic animals, including the woolly mammoth and American mastodon. The Alaska herd originated in Montana, taken from the descendants of a herd begun by a Native American named Sam Walking Coyote, who tamed six buffalo as atonement to the family of his first wife, because he had taken a second wife. He purchased his buffalo from Charles Allard and Michel Pablo. After Allard died, Pablo sold some of the herd to Canadian buyers, and other descendants of his animals were later released onto the National Bison Range. It was this course of events that probably saved the buffalo from extinction. The Alaskan buffalo herd was created by a group of hunters. Rinella notes that nearly all buffalo are now in private hands, including herds owned by celebrities such as Ted Turner. Buffalo from the private herd of singer-songwriter Neil Young (Buffalo Springfield) were used in the filming of Kevin Costner's film *Dancing with Wolves.*

The slaughter of buffalo by both Native Americans and whites is covered. Native tribes corralled herds using snow and deep water, and with buffalo jumps. Buffalo Jump State Park in Montana was created around a mile-long cliff over which buffalo were stampeded for more than 600 years. White hunters took the valuable hides and left carcasses to rot and bones to be collected in subsequent years. Rinella notes that Black Diamond, a buffalo born in captivity at the Bronx Zoo in New York, was the presumed model for the buffalo-head nickel.

Rinella describes the actual kill, why he is aiming for the lungs, how the buffalo falls, and his own feelings of thankfulness, appreciation, and guilt, "the curse of the human predator, I think." He describes cooking various parts of the animal, including tongue and marrow bones, wasting almost nothing. He also writes that he carried pieces of the butchered carcass, enough meat for nearly a year, down the mountain to a raft that he used to travel the four miles back to civilization.

In his review of *American Buffalo* in *High Country News,* Brian Kevin called it "natural history wrapped in the hide of a personal quest." Kevin wrote that "it's voices like Rinella's—hyperaware of the bison's symbolic value, yet clear-eyed in the face of fairly gruesome realities—that often seem to be missing in debates over bison in Yellowstone and elsewhere. Conservationists, ranchers, tribal leaders and wildlife managers could do worse than emulate Rinella's thoughtful and measured approach."

BIOGRAPHICAL AND CRITICAL SOURCES:

PERIODICALS

Booklist, November 1, 2008, Nancy Bent, review of *American Buffalo: In Search of a Lost Icon,* p. 8.
Christian Science Monitor, January 13, 2009, Larry Sears, review of *American Buffalo,* p. 25.
Economist, January 17, 2009, review of *American Buffalo,* p. 74.
Entertainment Weekly, Tina Jordan, review of *American Buffalo,* p. 67.
High Country News, January 19, 2009, Brian Kevin, review of *American Buffalo.*

Kirkus Reviews, January 15, 2006, review of *The Scavenger's Guide to Haute Cuisine,* p. 78.

Library Journal, February 1, 2006, Maureen J. Delaney-Lehman, review of *The Scavenger's Guide to Haute Cuisine,* p. 103.

Milwaukee Journal Sentinel, December 7, 2008, Jim Higgins, review of *American Buffalo.*

OnEarth, winter, 2009, Philip Connors, review of *American Buffalo,* p. 57.

Publishers Weekly, December 12, 2005, review of *The Scavenger's Guide to Haute Cuisine,* p. 51; September 8, 2008, review of *American Buffalo,* p. 41; September 22, 2008, Robert Anasi, author interview, p. 50.

Star Tribune (Minneapolis, MN), January 11, 2009, Dennis Anderson, review of *American Buffalo,* p. 13E.

ONLINE

Internet Review of Books, http://internetreviewofbooks. com/ (June 20, 2009), Gary Presley, review of *American Buffalo.*

January, http://www.januarymagazine.com/ (February, 2006), David Abrams, review of *The Scavenger's Guide to Haute Cuisine.*

Journal Advocate Online, http://www.journal-advocate. com/ (December 26, 2008), Terri Schlichenmeyer, review of *American Buffalo.*

Los Angeles Times Online, http://www.latimes.com/ (December 5, 2008), Jane Ciabattari, review of *American Buffalo.*

NewWest.Net, http://www.newwest.net/ (March 19, 2006), Allen Jones, review of *The Scavenger's Guide to Haute Cuisine.*

San Francisco Chronicle Online, http://www.sfgate. com/ (December 7, 2008), Jesse Barrett, review of *American Buffalo.*

Seattle Times Online, http://seattletimes.nwsource.com/ (December 11, 2008), Irene Wanner, review of *American Buffalo.*

SlushPile.net, http://www.slushpile.net/ (February 10, 2009), Thomas Scott McKenzie, author interview.

Steven Rinella Home Page, http://www.stevenrinella. com (September 29, 2006).

USA Today Online, http://www.usatoday.com/ (December 29, 2008), Don Oldenburg, review of *American Buffalo.**

*   *   *

ROBERTS, J.R.
See RANDISI, Robert J.

ROBERTS, Michèle 1949-
   (Michèle Brigitte Roberts)

PERSONAL: Born May 20, 1949, in Bushey, Hertfordshire, England; daughter of Reginald George (a businessman) and Monique Pauline Joseph (a teacher) Roberts; married Jim Latter (an artist). *Education:* Somerville College, Oxford, M.A. (with honors), 1970; University of London, library associate, 1972. *Politics:* "Socialist-feminist." *Religion:* "Unconventional." *Hobbies and other interests:* Cooking and eating, painting, mountain walking, dancing, swimming, traveling.

ADDRESSES: Home—London, England; Mayenne, France. *Agent*—Aitken & Stone, Ltd., 29 Fernshaw Rd., London SW1O 0TG, England. *E-mail*—micheroberts@ excite.co.uk.

CAREER: Educator, writer. Has worked as a librarian, cook, teacher, cleaner, pregnancy counselor, researcher, book reviewer, and broadcaster. British Council, Bangkok, Thailand, librarian, 1972-73; University of Essex, writer in residence, 1987-88; University of East Anglia, writer in residence, 1992, and visiting fellow in creative writing; Nottingham Trent University, visiting fellow, 1995-96, visiting professor, 1996—. Writer-in-residence, Lambeth Borough, London, England, 1981-82, and Bromley Borough, London, 1983-84; Feminist Writers Group, cofounder.

MEMBER: Writers Guild.

AWARDS, HONORS: Gay News literary award, 1978, for *A Piece of the Night;* Arts Council grant, 1978; Booker Prize shortlist, 1992, and W.H. Smith Literary Award, 1993, both for *Daughters of the House;* elected a fellow of the Royal Society of Literature, 1999; Chevalier de l'Ordre des Arts et des lettres (France), 2000.

WRITINGS:

POETRY

(Editor, with Michelene Wandor) *Cutlasses and Earrings,* Playbooks (London, England), 1977.
Licking the Bed Clean, [London, England], 1978.
Smile, Smile, Smile, Smile, [London, England], 1980.

(With Judith Karantris and Michelene Wandor) *Touch Papers,* Allison & Busby (London, England), 1982.

The Mirror of the Mother: Selected Poems, 1975-1985, Methuen (London, England), 1985.

All the Selves I Was: New and Selected Poems, Virago (London, England), 1995.

NOVELS

A Piece of the Night, Women's Press (London, England), 1978.

The Visitation, Women's Press (London, England), 1983.

The Wild Girl, Methuen (London, England), 1984, published as *The Secret Gospel of Mary Magdalene,* Pegasus (New York, NY), 2007.

The Book of Mrs. Noah, Methuen (London, England), 1987.

In the Red Kitchen, Methuen (London, England), 1990.

Psyche and the Hurricane, Methuen (London, England), 1991.

Daughters of the House, Morrow (New York, NY), 1992.

During Mother's Absence, Virago (London, England), 1993.

Flesh and Blood, Virago (London, England), 1994.

Impossible Saints, Little, Brown (Boston, MA), 1997.

Fair Exchange, Little, Brown (Boston, MA), 1999.

The Looking Glass, Little, Brown (Boston, MA), 2000.

The Mistressclass, Henry Holt (New York, NY), 2003.

Reader, I Married Him, Little, Brown (London, England), 2004, Pegasus (New York, NY), 2006.

Delusion, Pegasus (New York, NY), 2007.

SHORT STORIES

(With Alison Fell and others) *Tales I Tell My Mother,* Journeyman Press (London, England), 1978.

(With others) *More Tales I Tell My Mother,* Journeyman Press (London, England), 1987.

Playing Sardines, Virago (London, England), 2001.

NONFICTION

(Editor, with Sara Dunn and Blake Morrison) *Mind Readings: Writers' Journeys through Mental States,* Minerva (London, England), 1996.

Food, Sex and God: On Inspiration and Writing, Virago (London, England), 1998.

Paper Houses: A Memoir of the 70s and Beyond, Virago (London, England), 2007.

OTHER

The Journeywoman (play), produced in Colchester, England, 1988.

Author of screenplay *The Heavenly Twins.* Contributor to anthologies; author of introductions to books by others; contributor of nonfiction to *City Limits* and of poems to periodicals. Poetry editor of *Spare Rib,* 1975-77, and *City Limits,* 1981-83.

SIDELIGHTS: Michèle Roberts has received much acclaim for her fictional evocations of feminist themes. Born in England of a French Catholic mother and a British father, Roberts grew up speaking both languages and spending time in both countries. As a child, Roberts strongly identified with her mother's faith. She attended a convent school, and throughout her teenage years she wanted to be a nun. "She perceived the convent as a safe haven from a world in which women had no freedom of choice and had to submit to conflicting images of femininity," Genevieve Brassard explained in the *Dictionary of Literary Biography.*

However, Roberts decided to attend college before entering the convent. While at Somerville College, Oxford, Roberts discovered feminism. After graduation, she moved to London, joined a Marxist commune "in which rooms, possessions, and sexual partners were liberally shared," as Brassard described it, and abandoned her former commitment to Catholicism as petit-bourgeois spirituality. After a brief period of time working in Thailand, Roberts returned to London and became active as a feminist and as a writer.

Roberts writes of strong female characters who rebel against a male-dominated society. She sometimes employs Christian religious symbolism, as in the novels *The Wild Girl,* about the life of Mary Magdalene, and *The Book of Mrs. Noah,* in which Mrs. Noah and five other women journey in a metaphorical ark through history to examine the condition of women throughout the ages.

Roberts's first novel, *A Piece of the Night,* tells of a woman's journey to self-realization—from convent schoolgirl to wife and mother to feminist and lesbian.

Writing in the *New Statesman,* Valentine Cunningham described the novel as "a runaway chaos of inchoate bits, an incoherence that slumps well short of the better novel it might with more toil have become." "Much of *A Piece of the Night,*" according to Blake Morrison in the *Times Literary Supplement,* "gives the same impression of a book written under the stern eye of a women's workshop group, and not much interested in winning the hearts of those outside the charmed circle."

In *The Wild Girl,* Roberts writes of biblical figure Mary Magdalene and her life as a prostitute and as a follower of Christ. Because of its frank, fictionalized account of Mary Magdalene's life, *The Wild Girl* received harsh criticism. "A few people," according to Tracy Clark in *Feminist Writers,* "went so far as to seek formal accusation of Roberts for blasphemy." A reviewer for *Time Out* described this work as "a powerful attack on the law of the Father and a timely reminder that old myths do not just fade away." Writing in the *Times Literary Supplement,* Emma Fisher found that "Roberts is intelligent and passionate; by her rich use of symbols and metaphor she transforms feminist cliche into something alive and moving." Kate Fullbrook in *British Book News* admitted that "the sentiments that animate this novel are fine, even noble. But the fiction itself never comes alive. Mary Magdalene remains nothing but a committed feminist of the 1980s; Jesus becomes nothing but a simple archetype for the non-sexist male."

The reissuing of *The Wild Girl* in the United States under the title *The Secret Gospel of Mary Magdalene* sparked a series of reevaluations by critics who encountered Roberts's novel for the first time. "In Roberts' imagination, [Mary] is still a prostitute, but also a visionary given to mystical dreams, spontaneous songs and speeches, in a society in which women are second-class citizens," wrote a *Kirkus Reviews* contributor. Roberts herself emphasized the explicit feminism in the composition of the novel; she said in an interview published on her Home Page that "Catholicism . . . was a great treasure trove of stories which I could re-tell. I wanted to smash up the old stories, which I felt had damaged me, and make something new with them. Omniscient narrators such as God the Father and the Pope had snared me as an object in their stories; I needed to write women in as our own subjects." The extent to which she succeeded can be seen in the comments of reviewers like Ilene Cooper, who stated in *Booklist* that the character of Mary "radiates such strength and sensuality that even the earthly Jesus seems no match for her." *The Secret Gospel of Mary Magda-*

lene, declared Mary Cowper, writing for *MBR Bookwatch,* is a "moving chronicle of human faith that endures despite suffering and loss."

Religious concerns also figure in *The Visitation,* the story of Helen, who contacts female archetypal figures in her dreams. Roberts, wrote Laura Marcus in the *Times Literary Supplement,* blurs "the distinctions between reality and fantasy in a prose which is full, resonant and at times over-charged." Clark found that Roberts employs "lush physical description and enchanting mental imagery. Every once in a while, she also skillfully flashes back to Helen's younger days in order to give her readers a fuller perspective on the adult Helen's attitude toward conventional religion in general, and the Catholic church of her youth, specifically."

The Book of Mrs. Noah is, according to Helen Birch in the *New Statesman,* "Roberts' most ambitious and carefully conceived novel to date." Mrs. Noah, a librarian, imagines an ark filled with disenfranchised women from all periods in history, all of them wishing to write the story of womankind. "The ark becomes," Birch wrote, "Protean, a womb, the mother's body, containing the history and dreams of all the women." "The trouble," wrote Jennifer McKay in the *Listener,* "is that as a novel of ideas Mrs. Noah's ideas are not especially novel and they form too heavy a load for the fragile narrative."

Daughters of the House concerns Therese, a woman who is returning to her family after living for many years in a convent. "As is typical in Roberts's work," Clark wrote, "the novel is full of spiritual imagery: the convent, imagined concepts of heaven, and a favorite religious statue. Also present are numerous detailed physical descriptions: Therese's feeling too naked in street clothes because she is used to her thick, brown dress, for instance. This combination of highly styled description, heavy symbolism, and riveting plot was very well-received by critics." *Daughters of the House* was nominated for England's Booker Prize.

Religious themes also appear in *Impossible Saints,* a novel about ten people who would be saints, including Josephine, a nun who tries to seduce her father, fails, enters a convent, and successfully seduces a priest, yet still becomes a saint. As Jason Cowley of *New Statesman* commented, the writing of "*Impossible Saints* was [Roberts's] final attempt 'to exorcise' what Catholicism had done to her as a child." As Roberts explained to Linda Richards in an interview for *January* magazine:

"Because . . . the body is very scorned in Catholicism—particularly the female body—I wanted to rescue the body and cherish it and love it and touch it and smell it and make it into language." Roberts's women, who give into the pleasures of the body yet still become saints, show us "canonization as it might have been if the church were overseen by a matriarchy that celebrated human energy, weakness and desire," noted a *Publishers Weekly* reviewer.

In *The Looking Glass,* the story of an early twentieth-century French poet (partially inspired by Mallarme) and the four women who love him, Roberts again returns to her French and her feminist roots. *Library Journal* critic Rebecca Stuhr called the latter portions of the book "didactic and plodding," while *Booklist* reviewer Carol Haggas praised Roberts's "powerful prose and poetic imagery." Roberts was inspired to write a story set in France after her mother was forced to sell the cottage where they had spent summers when Roberts was a child. "My theory is that inspiration is born of loss," she explained to Richards. "I felt I proved that with this novel. It just began, 'It is the sea I miss most,' and that was my truth. And then I found that the voice talking wasn't my voice. . . . That's the interesting thing when you write in the first person. . . . You've been taken over and possessed by somebody else and you write to find out who it is."

The Mistressclass is Roberts's novel featuring two sets of sisters, the Brontes and the contemporary writer siblings, Catherine and Vinny, both in their fifties. Catherine is an English professor who, unknown to her novelist husband, Adam, writes erotic fiction under a pseudonym. Vinny, a poet who loved Adam first then lost him to her sister, continues to long for him from within an alcohol and drug-induced haze. Charlotte, meanwhile, communicates with a former teacher who commands her passion. Haggas described this novel as being a "sublimely emotive portrait of love and betrayal, attraction and rejection." Megan Harlan commented in the *New York Times Book Review* that "Roberts's sharp but sympathetic character studies give the love triangle uncommon depth."

"With a sassy cartoon sketch on the cover and a sparkly blurb about a woman who can't stop getting married, *Reader, I Married Him* is packaged as chick lit," wrote Kate Saunders in *New Statesman.* "Because it is by Michele Roberts, however, it amounts to more than a respected author's bid for a larger share of the popular

pound—she couldn't write a bad sentence no matter how hard she tried." Aurora, the narrator, is a thrice-married and widowed woman of fifty. Each of her marriages had been very different, and she now is looking for her true identity and attracted to the sexy Father Michael, a parish priest. She agrees to go on a retreat with her old friend Leonora, a feminist turned nun, and travels to Italy, hiding a gun Leonora has asked her to bring from customs. To Aurora's surprise Father Michael appears at a conference being hosted by Leonora, arriving with Aurora's domineering stepmother, Maude. Aurora also stays at the home of Frederico, an old friend she presumed to be gay and who now is sexually attracted to her. Haggas, in *Booklist,* wrote that the author "whimsically indulges her passion for favored themes of religion, sex, and food in this riotous and ribald tale."

Roberts explores the emergence of her personal feminism in *Paper Houses: A Memoir of the 70s and Beyond.* She explains in the book how a young girl from a conservative Anglo-French Catholic background found her way through the counterculture of the early 1970s. "Roberts roamed like a *flaneur* and took cheap rooms, sometimes in then far-flung parts where local youths regarded any woman walking alone as either lesbian or on the game," explained Chris Petit in the *Guardian.* "She lived in a Holloway collective where it was decided to hold everything in common—no more individual space or possessions—except the actual house, which remained owned by one of the 'collective.'" But her ambitions also met scorn from her fellow *communistas;* "Roberts's collective considered her as too wide-eyed and emotional," Petit stated, "and dismissed her writing ambitions as bourgeois individualism." Roberts's prose, wrote *Independent* reviewer Joan Smith, is "vivid and sardonic by turns, the period brought to life with accounts of clothes and meals, whose importance Roberts (unlike many other writers) has always understood." "Some episodes are described with startling candour, including two marriages, even though she has changed some names and censored some events: 'I don't want to bore you, and I don't want to hurt people, either. I have tried to be honest.'"

Delusion tells the tale of a nineteenth-century clairvoyant Flora Milk, who "aspires to achieve some means of success," said Beth Harrington on *Bookslut,* "by holding public séances in which she interacts with the spirits of the dead and possibly by allowing the scientific community to study her and monitor the veracity of her craft." Roberts's novel also examines how Flora's experiences affect the members of her family, the members of the family of the scientist who studies her, and even the spirits that she invokes in her trances. "I think I would have to read this book a second time in order to derive its full meaning," Harrington stated, but, she added, Roberts's "prose is enticing and evocative enough to make doing so a worthy task."

Roberts told *CA:* "My writing generally is fueled by the fact that I am a woman. I need to write in order to break through the silence imposed on women in this culture. The love of friends is central to my life."

BIOGRAPHICAL AND CRITICAL SOURCES:

BOOKS

Contemporary Literary Criticism, Volume 48, Gale (Detroit, MI), 1988.
Contemporary Novelists, 7th edition, St. James Press (Detroit, MI), 2001.
Feminist Writers, St. James Press (Detroit, MI), 1996.
Kenyon, Olga, *Women Writers Talk,* Carroll & Graf (New York, NY), 1990.
Moseley, Merritt, editor, *Dictionary of Literary Biography,* Volume 231: *British Novelists since 1960,* 4th series, Gale (Detroit, MI), 2000.

PERIODICALS

Booklist, July, 2001, Carol Haggas, review of *The Looking Glass,* p. 1983; August, 2003, Carol Haggas, review of *The Mistressclass,* p. 1958; February 1, 2006, Carol Haggas, review of *Reader, I Married Him,* p. 31; October 15, 2007, Ilene Cooper, review of *The Secret Gospel of Mary Magdalene,* p. 33.
Books Magazine, spring, 1999, review of *Fair Exchange,* p. 22.
British Book News, January, 1985, Kate Fullbrook, review of *The Wild Girl,* pp. 49-50.
Christian Science Monitor, July 2, 1998, review of *Impossible Saints,* p. B8.
Financial Times, January 8, 2005, Julia Sutherland, review of *Reader, I Married Him,* p. 32.
Globe and Mail (Toronto, Ontario, Canada), July 10, 1999, review of *Fair Exchange,* p. D12.
Guardian (London, England), July 21, 2007, Chris Petit, "Tales of the City."
Independent (London, England), June 22, 2007, Joan Smith, "The Luggage of Liberation."

Kirkus Reviews, April 15, 1998, review of *Impossible Saints,* p. 521; June 15, 2003, review of *The Mistressclass,* p. 830; February 15, 2006, review of *Reader, I Married Him,* p. 155; August 1, 2007, review of *The Secret Gospel of Mary Magdalene.*
Library Journal, March 1, 1998, review of *Impossible Saints,* p. 129; June 1, 2001, Rebecca Stuhr, review of *The Looking Glass,* p. 218; May 1, 2006, Christine Perkins, review of *Reader, I Married Him,* p. 83.
Listener, September 10, 1987, Jennifer McKay, review of *The Book of Mrs. Noah,* p. 23.
London Review of Books, October 2, 1997, review of *Impossible Saints,* p. 34.
MBR Bookwatch, February 1, 2008, Mary Cowper, review of *The Secret Gospel of Mary Magdalene.*
New Statesman, November 3, 1978, Valentine Cunningham, review of *A Piece of the Night,* p. 590; May 22, 1987, Helen Birch, review of *The Book of Mrs. Noah,* pp. 27-28; May 23, 1997, Jason Cowley, review of *Impossible Saints,* p. 49; July 4, 1997, Stephen Brasher, interview with Michèle Roberts, p. 21; January 24, 2005, Kate Saunders, review of *Reader, I Married Him,* p. 53.
New York Times Book Review, September 20, 1998, David Guy, review of *Impossible Saints,* p. 24; September 14, 2003, Megan Harlan, review of *The Mistressclass,* p. 25; June 25, 2006, Lauren Collins, review of *Reader, I Married Him,* p. 13.
Observer (London, England), January 17, 1999, review of *Fair Exchange,* p. 23.
People, August 20, 2001, review of *The Looking Glass,* p. 41.
Publishers Weekly, April 20, 1998, review of *Impossible Saints,* p. 49; July 21, 2003, review of *The Mistressclass,* p. 173.
Spectator, January 16, 1999, Andrew Barrow, review of *Fair Exchange,* p. 30.
Time Out, December, 1984, review of *The Wild Girl.*
Times Educational Supplement, August 28, 1998, review of *Food, Sex and God: On Inspiration and Writing,* p. 23.
Times Literary Supplement, December 1, 1978, Blake Morrison, review of *A Piece of the Night,* p. 1404; October 26, 1984, Emma Fisher, review of *The Wild Girl,* p. 1224; September 27, 1985, Laura Marcus, review of *The Visitation,* p. 1070; April 25, 1997, review of *Impossible Saints,* p. 24; October 16, 1998, review of *Food, Sex and God,* p. 32; January 15, 1999, review of *Fair Exchange,* p. 21.
Woman's Journal, January, 1999, review of *Fair Exchange,* p. 14.

ONLINE

Bookslut, http://www.bookslut.com/ (August 5, 2008), Beth Harrington, review of *Delusion.*

Cercles, http://www.cercles.com/ (January 31, 2007), Jenny Newman, "An Interview with Michèle Roberts."

Contemporary Writers in the UK, http://www. contemporarywriters.com/ (January 31, 2007), biography.

January, http://www.januarymagazine.com/ (March 7, 2007), Linda Richards, "January Talks to Michèle Roberts."

Michele Roberts Home Page, http://www.michele roberts.co.uk (August 5, 2008).*

*   *   *

ROBERTS, Michèle Brigitte
See ROBERTS, Michèle

*   *   *

ROMANO, Tony 1957-

PERSONAL: Born June 30, 1957; married; children: three daughters. *Education:* DePaul University, B.A.; Northeastern Illinois University, M.A.

ADDRESSES: Home—Glen Ellyn, IL. *Agent*—Marly Rusoff & Associates, Inc., P.O. Box 524, Bronxville, NY 10708.

CAREER: William Fremd High School, Palatine, IL, teacher of English and psychology. Producer of spoken-word CDs.

AWARDS, HONORS: Whetstone Prize; grants from the Illinois Arts Council; twice winner of the PEN Syndicated Fiction Project; two Pushcart Prize nominations; *Chicago Tribune* Best Books, and Midland Authors Finalist Prize, both 2007, both for *When the World Was Young; Chicago Tribune* Best Books, and Midland Authors Finalist Prize, both 2008, both for *If You Eat, You Never Die: Chicago Tales.*

WRITINGS:

(With Frank B. McMahon and Judith W. McMahon) *Psychology and You* (high school textbook), West Publishing (St. Paul, MN), 1990, 2nd edition, 1995.

When the World Was Young (novel), HarperCollins (New York, NY), 2007.
(With Gary Anderson) *Expository Composition: Discovering Your Voice,* foreword by Naomi Shihab Nye, EMC Publishing (St. Paul, MN), 2008.
If You Eat, You Never Die: Chicago Tales, Harper Perennial (New York, NY), 2009.

Contributor to periodicals, including the *Chicago Tribune, Whetstone, Sou'wester, Bluff City,* and *VIA: Voices in Italian Americana.*

ADAPTATIONS: Romano's fiction has been produced for National Public Radio.

SIDELIGHTS: Tony Romano has spent many years teaching psychology and English at William Fremd High School in Palatine, Illinois. He is the author of two nonfiction books: the high school textbook *Psychology and You,* with Frank B. McMahon and Judith W. McMahon, and *Expository Composition: Discovering Your Voice,* with Gary Anderson. Romano is a writer of short stories and has received two Pushcart Prize nominations, and he has also twice won the PEN Syndicated Fiction Project. He is also the author of a first novel, *When the World Was Young.* Set in 1950s Chicago, it is the story of the Italian American Peccatori family. Agostino and Angela Rosa are immigrants who miss their Italian hometown but who are kept busy raising their five children. Agostino and his brother Vincenzo own a neighborhood tavern in a building that was formerly a funeral home. His work exposes him to temptations that he does not resist. Angela is happier at home in the unfamiliar culture and spends most of her time cooking and cleaning while her husband is at the bar. Her marriage is now passionless, and she silently tolerates her husband's infidelities. Santo, their eldest, has recently graduated from high school and is looking for girls and independence, while attempting to emulate the ease with which his father handles life. Sixteen-year-old Victoria breaks the rules and flirts with local hood Eddie Milano, and Santo tries to intervene. He is also curious about an attack on his father by an older Italian woman and becomes increasingly aware of his father's indiscretions.

The story takes a turn when their two-year-old Benito becomes ill and dies of a high fever. Angela grieves for him while feeling she could have somehow prevented his death, while Agostino thinks his child's death is punishment for his adultery. A *Kirkus Reviews* contributor praised the story and the characters Victoria and Santo as "especially well-drawn figures among the young generation." A *Publishers Weekly* critic wrote of the "rich vein of material in a place and time buffeted by changing mores, insularity and tenuous ties." *Booklist* reviewer Joanne Wilkinson was impressed by Romano's depiction of the Chicago neighborhood, with its shops and magnificent Catholic church. Wilkinson noted that Romano "describes the mourning process in heart-wrenching passages even as he relays the love and the secrets."

Romano's next work of fiction is a book of connected or linked short stories titled *If You Eat, You Never Die: Chicago Tales.* The book was written before Romano's novel but was published afterward. The stories follow the Cummings family, the descendants of Italian immigrants whose name was Americanized from the original Comingo surname. Three generations of the family are portrayed in the collection's various stories, with Romano covering such topics as tense marriages and adolescence. Much of the action is set in Chicago, and the central character is Jimmy Cummings (originally named Giacomo Comingo). Praising the volume in *Time Out Chicago,* reviewer Robert Duffer observed that the story portrays "two continents of the Comingos—from Lucia's arranged marriage in Italy to the domestic Americanized households of her grandchildren." He added that the book "is less about grand events than the intimate private moments that are the essence of family. Marriages strain and sons grow out of the awkwardness of adolescence into the regret of adulthood."

Most critics found that the book is an expertly written and poignant exploration of family dynamics. A contributor to the online *Novel World* remarked that *If You Eat, You Never Die* is "a quick read full of insights into life and relationships. . . . [and] a good way to realize that everyone has a story to tell." Lynna Williams, writing in the *Chicago Tribune,* was also impressed, finding that "family history, collective and personal . . . is at the heart of" the collection. Williams added that "the structure of the book supports a kind of kaleidoscope: parts that, put together, influence the whole. The result is an evocation of time, place and immigrant experience that comes alive with strong detail." A *Publishers Weekly* contributor stated that *If You Eat, You Never Die* is a "moving collection of tales that will stay with the reader long after the book is shut." Offering praise in *Booklist,* Donna Seaman noted that Romano shows a "deep understanding of how helpless we are when emotions and actions betray reason." A *Kirkus*

Reviews writer opined that the stories are "a spirited evocation of a complex immigrant culture, willing to show the scars its characters bear." Megan Hodge, writing in *Library Journal,* gave a similar assessment, declaring that "Romano deftly and sensitively guides readers through lives that are both pedestrian and profound."

Once, when asked how he first became interested in writing, Romano told *CA:* "Swimming. Or lack thereof. For some reason, many Italian immigrants, though they were surrounded by water nearly their entire lives, never learned to swim and never tried to enroll their children in swim classes. They simply didn't think of it, worrying instead about how they'd get in enough hours at the factory so they could feed their children. This was my world, at least. We lived about ten minutes away from Lake Michigan (every distance in Chicago is measured in minutes rather than miles), so my friends would take the Chicago Transit Authority bus every so often to the lake and dive in. Because I feared they'd throw me in, and I wouldn't blame them, I stayed behind and amused myself by reading comic books. Soon I became enthralled and obsessed and began scrounging the neighborhood for discarded pop bottles that I could cash in for two cents each at Bruno's, where I trekked each Thursday morning to see the latest installments of *Superman* and *Batman.* Some of my fondest memories are of sitting on the stoop, immersed in this other, more colorful world. In other words, an interest in writing always begins with an interest in reading, and this was my start.

"On my stoop, I'd read not only comic books, but also books by the authors H.P. Lovecraft, Harlan Ellison, Arthur Conan Doyle, and Edgar Allan Poe. A little later I read Philip Roth. Now I read and am inspired by Richard Russo, Geraldine Brooks, Don DeLillo, as well as many others.

"In terms of ideas, I'm mainly influenced by the dynamics of family. I'd like to think that I'm writing about universal issues, but I don't know any other way of approaching those issues other than through the screen door and the kitchen and the living room.

"I still haven't found a solid writing routine over the years. At times, I write in a bound notebook (not one with rings because I'm a lefty and the world of notebooks is unfriendly to lefties), skipping lines, pushing forward each day, weaving in ideas from the previous day's work. If I feel stuck, I'll move to the computer. Lately, I've holed myself away in our storage room, a place where no one needs access. I have a CD player and a dictionary and a laptop, and I wish I had hid myself away sooner because I'm being fairly productive. To have a place where you can write undisturbed for a few hours is key since this allows you to enter a waking dream state. When people ask me, 'Where do you get your ideas?' I sometimes ask, 'Where do you get your dreams?' I don't expect an answer, but what I mean is that the writing ideas are just as elusive in origin. I don't want to know where I get my ideas from, as long as they keep coming. And it's not a mystical process. Anyone disciplined enough to sit and wait and listen will have ideas worth writing about.

"I've always viewed writing as a solitary activity, but true writing brings people together. I help coordinate an event at my school we call Writers Week, during which writers from around the country converge on our campus to read and discuss their work. Students and faculty take to the stage as well. I am inspired anew by the risks writers take in sharing their work, especially student writers. And the audience recognizes the inherent risks in sharing one's work. As a result, a sense of community develops. It's one of the things I do that I'm most proud of."

When asked which of his books is his favorite, Romano responded: "I think most writers say this: my favorite book is the one I'm currently working on. It's the most important because it's the only way I can continue to call myself a writer. I do have a special fondness for my first book, *When the World Was Young,* because before it was published, after being rejected for about five years, I seriously questioned whether I'd keep sending work out. I almost gave in to the rejections and began to believe that the rejections were a reflection of the work. I'm glad I didn't listen."

BIOGRAPHICAL AND CRITICAL SOURCES:

PERIODICALS

Booklist, April 15, 2007, Joanne Wilkinson, review of *When the World Was Young,* p. 35; December 15, 2008, Donna Seaman, review of *If You Eat, You Never Die: Chicago Tales,* p. 23.

Chicago Sun-Times, May 19, 2007, review of *When the World Was Young.*

Chicago Tribune, December 20, 2008, Lynna Williams, review of *If You Eat, You Never Die.*

Kirkus Reviews, April 15, 2007, review of *When the World Was Young;* October 15, 2008, review of *If You Eat, You Never Die.*

Library Journal, May 15, 2007, Joshua Cohen, review of *When the World Was Young,* p. 84; January 1, 2009, Megan Hodge, review of *If You Eat, You Never Die,* p. 86.

Philadelphia Enquirer, August 5, 2007, review of *When the World Was Young.*

Publishers Weekly, April 16, 2007, review of *When the World Was Young,* p. 30; October 20, 2008, review of *If You Eat, You Never Die,* p. 33.

Time Out Chicago, January 1-7, 2009, Robert Duffer, review of *If You Eat, You Never Die.*

Tribune Books (Chicago, IL), May 19, 2007, Kristin Kloberdanz, "Preserving a More-Innocent Past," p. 5; May 19, 2007, Jessica Treadway, review of *When the World Was Young,* p. 5; June 2, 2007, Kristin Kloberdanz, review of *When the World Was Young,* p. 7.

ONLINE

Novel World, http://thenovelworld.com/ (December 23, 2008), review of *If You Eat, You Never Die.**

*   *   *

ROSOFF, Meg 1956-

PERSONAL: Born 1956, in Boston, MA; daughter of Chester (a surgeon) and Lois (a psychiatric social worker) Rosoff; married Paul Hamlyn (a painter); children: Gloria. *Education:* Attended Harvard University; attended St. Martin's College of Art (London, England); completed B.A. degree in the United States.

ADDRESSES: Home—Highbury, North London, England.

CAREER: Writer. Worked previously in publishing and advertising.

AWARDS, HONORS: Guardian Children's Fiction Prize, 2004, Whitbread Award shortlist, 2004, Branford Boase Award, 2005, Julia Ward Howe Award for Young Readers, 2005, and Michael L. Printz Award, 2005, all for *How I Live Now.*

WRITINGS:

(With Caren Acker) *London Guide,* Open Road (New York, NY), 1995, 2nd edition, 1998.

How I Live Now (young adult novel), Wendy Lamb Books (New York, NY), 2004.

Meet Wild Boars (picture book), illustrated by Sophie Blackall, Henry Holt (New York, NY), 2005.

Just in Case (young adult novel), Wendy Lamb Books (New York, NY), 2006.

What I Was (young adult novel), Penguin (New York, NY), 2007.

Jumpy Jack and Googily (picture book), illustrated by Sophie Blackall, Henry Holt (New York, NY), 2008.

The Bride's Farewell, Viking (New York, NY), 2009.

Also author of screenplay adaptation of *How I Live Now.* Contributor to *The Brighton Book,* Myriad Editions (Brighton, England), 2005.

SIDELIGHTS: When Meg Rosoff's youngest sister died of breast cancer, Rosoff decided that life was too short not to make an attempt to follow her own dream of being a writer. She left her job in advertising and began writing a novel, and the result was *How I Live Now.* Ironically, the book was published just after Rosoff herself was diagnosed with breast cancer. "I was in the hospital for my first operation when the book was released and all these flowers started arriving," Rosoff recalled to *Publishers Weekly.* "Half of the cards said 'Congratulations,' the other half said, 'We're so sorry.'" In spite of the diagnosis, Rosoff has remained upbeat, and *How I Live Now* has received critical acclaim, having been shortlisted for the Whitbread Award and received the *Guardian* Children's Fiction Prize.

How I Live Now tells the story of sassy New York native Daisy, who is spending her summer in England with relatives. She is relieved to get away from her father and "wicked" stepmother, and when she arrives in England she falls in love both with the farm where she is staying and with her first cousin, Edward. When her aunt goes out of town for a conference, it seems that the world belongs to Daisy and her cousins, but war erupts and shatters their adult-free world. Soldiers seize the farm and separate the cousins, placing Daisy with her much younger female cousin while the boys are taken elsewhere. Unwilling to be separated for long, Daisy and her cousin trek across the country to recon-

nect, only to face the violent results of the war before finally being reunited with each other. A reviewer for *Christian Century* hailed the book as "an astonishing work of speculative fiction," while Deirdre F. Baker, writing in *Horn Book,* considered the story "a winning combination of acerbic commentary, innocence, and sober vision." Though some critics, including Jennifer Mattson, writing in *Booklist,* noted the discomfort in the incestuous romance between Daisy and Edmond, Mattson concluded: "More central to the potency of Rosoff's debut . . . is the ominous prognostication of what a third world war might look like." "A strength in the novel is the voice of Daisy—funny, spiky, and vulnerable," commented Benedicte Page in *Bookseller,* "and it is difficult not to see a likeness to the author herself, a self-confessed 'bigmouth' . . . who says there is one line Daisy speaks in the novel which she herself thoroughly relates to: 'I don't get nearly enough credit in life for the things I manage not to say.'" Other reviewers also fell in love with Daisy's narration; Claire Rosser called the character "an unforgettable heroine— vulnerable and flawed, yes, but fiercely loving and tough as well." A critic for *Kirkus Reviews* wrote that the story is "told in honest, raw first-person and filled with humor, love, pathos, and carnage." A *Publishers Weekly* reviewer concluded: "Like the heroine, readers will emerge from the rubble much shaken, a little wiser, and with perhaps a greater sense of humanity."

Rosoff next published a critically acclaimed picture book titled *Meet Wild Boars,* illustrated by Sophie Blackall. Deemed a "silly cautionary tale" by *School Library Journal* contributor Mary Elam, the work concerns four outrageously impudent boars who revel in creating mayhem, such as devouring stuffed toys or bathing in the toilet. "There's not a bad habit, predilection, or odor that isn't described or drawn," noted Ilene Cooper in *Booklist.* According to a critic in *Publishers Weekly,* young readers will "relish rut-rutting such an uncouth crew, while secretly delighting in the boars' unmitigated chutzpah."

In Rosoff's second young adult novel, *Just in Case,* the author "examines the idea of fate through minutely observed, concatenated catastrophes and the intersection of exquisitely drawn characters," observed a contributor in *Kirkus Reviews.* After rescuing his little brother from falling out of an open window, fifteen-year-old David Case concludes that tragedy lurks around every corner, and he attempts to cheat Fate by adopting a new identity, that of Justin Case. While shopping for a new wardrobe at a thrift store, David meets Agnes, an edgy fashion photographer with whom he falls in love, though she uses the teen to propel her own career forward, going so far as to photograph him in the aftermath of a horrific plane crash. *Just in Case* garnered strong reviews. Writing in *Booklist,* Gillian Engberg praised Rosoff's "often poetic plunge into subjects of cosmic proportion, such as faith, time, free will, illusions, and the boundaries of love and sex," and *School Library Journal* critic Francisca Goldsmith observed that the author "writes of these characters and Justin's interior and exterior adventures with beautiful grace and wit."

What I Was is a story that has appeal for mature teens and adults "who will appreciate Rosoff's questions about the nature of time, memory, and the events that become, over a life's arc, the defining moments," noted Engberg in *Booklist.* The protagonist is a one hundred-year-old man recalling his schoolboy crush in 1962. As a sixteen-year-old boy whose name is unmentioned until the end of the book, he has little going for him. His grades are substandard, as are his looks and athletic abilities. He is, therefore, placed by his parents in St. Oswald's, a mediocre boarding school on the coast of East Anglia. Having failed at other schools, the boy hopes to do better, but he has a great distaste for the regimentation of school life and the prospect of growing up to become an adult with a "minor job, minor wife, minor life." While taking a mandatory run along the beach, the boy meets Finn, about his age, who has somehow managed to evade the authorities who see to the well-being of children. Finn lives alone in a shack, eating the crabs and herring he catches offshore in his kayak and trading his excess in town for the other things he needs. The protagonist sees Finn as a warrior, like St. Oswald for whom his school was named, and "a purer, bolder, more compelling version of myself." He breaks school rules to spend more and more time with Finn, but this coming-of-age story ends with tragedy. In reviewing the book for the *Los Angeles Times Online,* Donna Rifkind noted that Rosoff's earlier young adult novels were "weighed down by an anxious-to-please sensationalism: anorexia, World War III, airport disasters, flying body parts, regrettable sexual impulsiveness. *What I Was* shows us a more confident author whose poetry lies in her elegant, straightforward descriptions of human activity—cooking crabs, climbing a chalk cliff, learning to sail—instead of lurid embellishment. The result is a beautifully crafted tale that seems, like its protagonist, both enduringly old and fluently new." "The reader is in for an intriguing read," concluded Robin Nesbitt in *Library Journal.*

Rosoff and Blackall again collaborated for *Jumpy Jack and Googily,* a story featuring a snail (Jumpy Jack), who has a fear of daytime monsters, and who looks for protection and reassurance from Googily, who is himself a blue, toothy, tentacled, and kindly monster. A *Publishers Weekly* contributor concluded: "For all Jumpy Jack's na'ivete and Googily's weirdness, they make a winsome pair." Reviewing the picture book in the *School Library Journal,* Rachael Vilmar wrote that the "muted palette, along with the friendly expressiveness of the protagonists' faces, sends the subtle message that there is truly nothing here to fear."

"I like writing for and about teens because it's a very extreme time of life, and that makes for intense transformations, intense possibilities for growth," Rosoff reported in an interview for *Bookbrowse.com.* "I think many people find their teens a difficult and disturbing time, but also a time of great excitement and intensity. As a writer, you can't ask for a better set-up than that."

BIOGRAPHICAL AND CRITICAL SOURCES:

PERIODICALS

Booklist, September 1, 2004, Jennifer Mattson, review of *How I Live Now,* p. 123; March 15, 2005, Ilene Cooper, review of *Meet Wild Boars,* p. 1287, and Ilene Cooper, "Meg Rosoff: The *Booklist* Interview," p. 1289; June 1, 2006, Gillian Engberg, review of *Just in Case,* p. 64; December 1, 2007, Gillian Engberg, review of *What I Was,* p. 23; March 15, 2008, Ilene Cooper, review of *Jumpy Jack and Googily,* p. 56.

Bookseller, June 4, 2004, Benedicte Page, "Living through Wartime," p. 28; August 25, 2006, Lauren Ace, review of *Just in Case,* p. 11.

Children's Bookwatch, June, 2005, review of *Meet Wild Boars;* October, 2006, review of *Just in Case.*

Christian Century, December 14, 2004, review of *How I Live Now,* p. 24.

Daily Mail (London, England), July 1, 2005, Angela Levin, interview with Meg Rosoff, p. 18.

English Journal, September, 2005, review of *How I Live Now,* p. 106.

Entertainment Weekly, February 1, 2008, Jennifer Reese, review of *What I Was,* p. 79.

Evening Standard (London, England), August 2, 2004, David Sexton, review of *How I Live Now,* p. 65.

Globe & Mail (Toronto, Ontario, Canada), July 30, 2005, Susan Perren, review of *How I Live Now,* p. D13.

Guardian (London, England), October 9, 2004, Julia Eccleshare, "Love, Loss, and Loyalty"; November 20, 2004, Meg Rosoff, "How I Jumped Out of the Sack Race," p. 7; July 23, 2005, Catherine Taylor, review of *How I Live Now*, p. 26; July 30, 2006, Kate Kellaway, "Don't Call Me Lucky," interview with Meg Rosoff.

Horn Book, September-October, 2004, Deirdre F. Baker, review of *How I Live Now*, p. 597; September-October, 2006, Christine M. Heppermann, review of *Just in Case*, p. 597.

Independent (London, England), July 8, 2005, Emma Hagestadt, review of *How I Live Now*, p. 27.

Journal of Adolescent & Adult Literacy, March, 2005, Laura McAndrews, review of *How I Live Now*, p. 528.

Kirkus Reviews, July 15, 2004, review of *How I Live Now*, p. 693; April 15, 2005, review of *Meet Wild Boars*, p. 481; July 15, 2006, review of *Just in Case*, p. 729; December 1, 2006, "Best Children's Books of 2006," review of *Just in Case*, p. S1; April 15, 2008, review of *Jumpy Jack and Googily*.

Kliatt, July, 2004, Claire Rosser, review of *How I Live Now*, p. 12; March, 2005, Meg Rosoff, "My Unbrilliant Career (or How I Wrote My First Novel in Just 26 Years)," pp. 3-4; July, 2006, Claire Rosser, review of *Just in Case*, p. 14.

Library Journal, October 15, 2007, Robin Nesbitt, review of *What I Was*, p. 57.

Magpies, March, 2005, Jo Goodman, review of *How I Live Now*, p. 43; August 14, 2006, Liza Nelson, review of *Just in Case*, p. 51.

New York Times Book Review, March 15, 2005, review of *How I Live Now*, p. 21.

Observer (London, England), July 25, 2004, Geraldine Bedell, review of *How I Live Now*, p. 16.

Publishers Weekly, July 5, 2004, review of *How I Live Now*, p. 56; December 20, 2004, Sue Corbett, "Flying Starts: Five Acclaimed Fall Children's Book Debuts," p. 30; March 28, 2005, review of *Meet Wild Boars*, p. 78; July 24, 2006, review of *Just in Case*, p. 59; May 26, 2008, review of *Jumpy Jack and Googily*, p. 65; October 15, 2007, review of *What I Was*, p. 38.

School Library Journal, September, 2004, Douglas P. Davey, review of *How I Live Now*, p. 216; March, 2005, Meg McCaffrey, "Answering the Call," pp. 46-48; July, 2005, Mary Elam, review of *Meet Wild Boars*, p. 82; September, 2006, Francisca Goldsmith, review of *Just in Case*, p. 217; May, 2008, Rachael Vilmar, review of *Jumpy Jack and Googily*, p. 107.

Sun (London, England), July 15, 2005, Sam Wostear, review of *How I Live Now*, p. 59.

Sunday Herald (Glasgow, Scotland), January 23, 2005, interview with Meg Rosoff, p. 11.

Sunday Times (London, England), November 14, 2004, Amanda Craig, interview with Meg Rosoff, p. 5.

Times (London, England), July 30, 2005, Alyson Rudd, review of *How I Live Now*, p. 11.

Virginian Pilot, December 24, 2004, Tonet Mariano, review of *How I Live Now*, p. E4.

Voice of Youth Advocates, April, 2005, review of *How I Live Now*, p. 13.

ONLINE

Bookbrowse.com, http://wwwbookbrowse.com/ (January 1, 2007), "Author Biography: Meg Rosoff."

Bookslut, http://www.bookslut.com/ (July 19, 2008), Benjamin Jacob Hollars, review of *What I Was*.

British Book Trust, http://www.booktrusted.co.uk/ (February 1, 2006), Madelyne Travis, "Living in Dangerous Times," interview with Meg Rosoff.

Canadian Broadcasting Centre, http://www.cbc.ca/ (February 26, 2008), Rachel Giese, "Eternal Youth" (interview).

Los Angeles Times Online, http://www.latimes.com/ (February 3, 2008), Donna Rifkind, review of *What I Was*.

Meg Rosoff Home Page, http://www.megrosoff.co.uk (July 19, 2008).

Penguin UK Web site, http://www.penguin.co.uk/ (August 27, 2005), "Author of the Month," interview with Meg Rosoff.

Random House Web site, http://www.randomhouse.com/ (February 1, 2006), "Author Spotlight: Meg Rosoff."

Times Online (London, England), http://entertainment.timesonline.co.uk/ (August 11, 2007), Amanda Craig, review of *What I Was*. *

* * *

ROUNTREE, Owen
See KITTREDGE, William

* * *

ROWLAND, Laura Joh 1953-

PERSONAL: Born 1953, in Harper Woods, MI; married, husband's name Marty (an environmental engineer). *Education:* University of Michigan, B.S., M.P.H.

ADDRESSES: Home—New Orleans, LA. *Agent*—Pamela Ahearn, Ahearn Agency Inc., 2021 Pine St., New Orleans, LA 70118.

CAREER: Novelist. Worked as a chemist, a microbiologist, and a sanitary inspector; Martin Marietta, New Orleans, LA, senior quality control engineer, for fourteen years.

WRITINGS:

The Secret Adventures of Charlotte Brontë (historical mystery novel), Overlook (New York, NY), 2008.

"SANO ICHIRO" MYSTERY SERIES

Shinju, Random House (New York, NY), 1994.
Bundori, Villard (New York, NY), 1996.
The Way of the Traitor, Villard (New York, NY), 1997.
The Concubine's Tattoo, St. Martin's Press (New York, NY), 1998.
The Samurai's Wife, St. Martin's Press (New York, NY), 2000.
Black Lotus, St. Martin's Minotaur (New York, NY), 2001.
The Pillow Book of Lady Wisteria, St. Martin's Minotaur (New York, NY), 2002.
The Dragon King's Palace, St. Martin's Minotaur (New York, NY), 2003.
The Perfumed Sleeve, St. Martin's Minotaur (New York, NY), 2004.
The Assassin's Touch, St. Martin's Minotaur (New York, NY), 2005.
Red Chrysanthemum, St. Martin's Minotaur (New York, NY), 2006.
The Snow Empress, St. Martin's Minotaur (New York, NY), 2007.
The Fire Kimono, St. Martin's Minotaur (New York, NY), 2008.
The Cloud Pavillion, St. Martin's Minotaur (New York, NY), 2009.

SIDELIGHTS: Before becoming a published author, Laura Joh Rowland worked as a quality control engineer at an aerospace company, using her lunch hours and weekends to pursue her dream of becoming a novelist. Her first two novels were repeatedly rejected for publication, but the undaunted Rowland wrote a third, *Shinju,* which she presented to a Random House editor at a writers' conference. Rowland's agent, meanwhile, sent the book to several other publishers. Three publishers auctioned for the rights to *Shinju* and its sequel, with Random House winning at a cost of one hundred thousand dollars.

Shinju, the Japanese term for "double love suicide," is set in seventeenth-century Tokyo, where police are investigating the apparent shinju of a peasant and the daughter of a prominent citizen. Although the investigating officer, Sano Ichiro, is instructed to close the case because it looks like a suicide, he strongly suspects it to be a murder. Sano subsequently launches his own investigation, which leads him to confront corrupt and deceitful elements in the upper echelon of Japanese society. F.G. Notehelfer wrote in his *New York Times Book Review* assessment of *Shinju:* "An interesting and even exciting tale, Ms. Rowland's novel introduces us to a new detective who, I suspect, will appear in further adventures." While Notehelfer indicated flaws in Rowland's historical research, he nevertheless concluded: "I trust that her considerable talent for historical fiction will not be undermined by a crotchety historian's own concerns for the truth." *Shinju* was also applauded by a *Publishers Weekly* critic: "Rowland crafts a competent mystery her first time out, shows sure command of her background material and demonstrates that she is a writer of depth and potential."

In a contribution to the *Laura Joh Rowland Home Page,* Rowland, who is of Korean and Chinese ancestry, commented on the unique historical setting of her mystery. "I wanted to explore a time, place, and characters that didn't appear in other books I'd read," the author remarked. "I wanted to experience a world other than my own." Rowland added that seventeenth-century Japan "was a police state, filled with simmering tensions, political corruption, sex, and violence. Arts, entertainment, and religion flourished. This was an environment that had great potential for interesting crime."

Sano Ichiro returns in *Bundori,* the story of a series of particularly gruesome murders in 1690s Tokyo, in which the killer leaves his victims' severed heads in public places. All of the victims are descendants of warriors involved a century earlier in the murder of a Japanese warlord. Sano's investigation leads him to members of Tokyo's ruling elite who have revenge in mind. According to the critic in *Publishers Weekly:* "The novel reads smoothly and positively smokes with historical atmospherics."

The Way of the Traitor finds Sano trying to locate a missing Dutch trade director in the city of Nagasaki. When the missing man is found murdered, the Dutch demand a quick accounting of the facts by training their warships' heavy guns on the city. Amid the international tension caused by the death, Sano must confront powerful government officials in unraveling the case. Rex E. Klett, writing in *Library Journal,* called the novel "exciting, exotic entertainment," while David Pitt in *Booklist* labeled the mystery "well constructed, superbly written, and very entertaining . . . an excellent whodunit."

Sano is marrying the Lady Ueda Reiko at the opening of *The Concubine's Tattoo,* but he is called away unexpectedly by the death of a concubine employed by the local shogun. The concubine has been poisoned by ink she used in a tattoo. Sano's investigation must be successful or the shogun will put him to death. His new bride insists on involving herself in the dangerous case as well. "Rowland's understanding of the society she depicts," wrote the critic for *Publishers Weekly,* "shines through, and she succeeds in presenting Sano as an intriguing combination of wiliness and decency, making this a good bet for fans of historicals as well as of mysteries past."

Sano and Reiko combine their skills to unravel the mystery surrounding the murder of an imperial minister in *The Samurai's Wife.* The dead man was a spy with many valuable secrets, and was killed with a rare martial art technique. Sano learns that the dead man had also uncovered a plot against the shogun. Civil war is a possibility if the assassin is not found. Rowland portrays the "class distinctions of her characters with subtlety and pulls together the strands of her multifaceted plot with enviable grace," commented a *Publishers Weekly* writer. The author's "fascinating insights" into life in seventeenth-century Japan were also praised by George Needham in *Booklist.*

The husband-and-wife crime-solving team are pitted against each other in *Black Lotus,* in which a teenage girl is accused of arson and murder. Sano feels the girl is guilty, but Reiko does not. As they take different tacks in investigating the crime, their dogged pursuit "for the truth threatens the fabric of their marriage," observed a *Publishers Weekly* writer. The same writer added: "The question of religious cults and the abuse of their influence gives this story contemporary resonance."

The Pillow Book of Lady Wisteria exposes the more bizarre sexual practices of old Japan in another tale of court intrigue. When the shogun's heir is found dead in an opulent brothel, everyone in Japan hopes to find the killer and thus win the favor of the shogun, but rivalries and loves among those who seek to solve the crime complicate the issue. Readers must decide for themselves if the "salacious details spice or undercut Sano's struggle to remain honorable in a dishonorable world," advised a *Kirkus Reviews* contributor. A *Publishers Weekly* writer found that "all the animosity and fear in this seamless work is put forth in demure language that perfectly suits the culture Rowland portrays."

The Dragon King's Palace, Rowland's eighth "Sano Ichiro" mystery, is "a lively dissection of the samurai code of honor, sexual dishonor, palace infighting, and ancient Japanese mores," observed a critic in *Kirkus Reviews.* While traveling to Mount Fiji, Reiko is abducted along with Midori, her best friend, Lady Keisho-in, the shogun's mother, and Lady Yanagisawa, the demented wife of Chamberlain Yanagisawa. The four are imprisoned by the enigmatic Dragon King, who declares that he will free the captives if the shogun assassinates Police Commissioner Hoshina. At the request of the shogun, Sano must work with his political archrivals, Yanagisawa and Hoshina, to rescue the women. "Rowland's masterful evocation of the period enables the reader to identify with the universal human emotions and drives that propel her characters," a *Publishers Weekly* reviewer noted.

In *The Perfumed Sleeve,* Sano investigates the suspicious death of Makino Narasada, a senior elder and a trusted advisor to the shogun. Though it first appears Makino died of natural causes, Sano finds a clue pointing to murder: a perfumed sleeve that was torn from a kimono. The investigator's work comes under close scrutiny from the shogun's cousin, Lord Matsudaira, and Chamberlain Yanagisawa, both of whom wish to succeed the shogun and accuse the other of Makino's death. A contributor to *Kirkus Reviews* stated that the author "pushes aside the mystery altogether to stir up a stew of sexual and political intrigue, above which Sano stoically rises."

Sano and Reiko look into a pair of seemingly unrelated mysteries in *The Assassin's Touch.* When a high-ranking intelligence officer dies suddenly during a horse race, Sano, now the shogun's chamberlain, learns that the official was assassinated by a martial arts master. Reiko, meanwhile, pursues a sensitive case involving an outcast young woman who is accused of murdering her parents and sister. During their investigations, Sano and Reiko uncover a secret group intent on overthrowing the regime. A critic in *Publishers Weekly* noted that "the compelling story line, evocative detail and suspense should engage newcomers and satisfy longtime fans alike."

In *Red Chrysanthemum,* Sano probes the gruesome murder of a treasonous nobleman. The chief suspect is Sano's pregnant wife, Reiko, who was found, naked and bloody, next to the mutilated corpse of Lord Mori. When Reiko cannot explain what transpired, Sano begins to doubt his spouse's innocence. *Library Journal* reviewer Jo Ann Vicarel called *Red Chrysanthemum* "a gem of exquisite plotting and characterization."

In *The Snow Empress,* Sano and Reiko trek to the island province of Ezogashima in search of their eight-year-old son, Masahiro, who has been kidnapped by one of Sano's chief adversaries. Once there, they find the island under siege by Lord Matsumae, who is extremely distressed over the recent murder of his mistress. He is keeping the citizens of his province prisoner until someone admits to murdering her. In hopes of recovering his son and bringing peace again to Ezogashima, Sano agrees to track down the killer of Lord Matsumae's mistress. Many critics had positive feedback for this twelfth installment of the Sano Ichiro mystery series. A *Kirkus Reviews* critic noted that the story "threatens to become overheated and overplotted, but abundant historical color and an elegant, controlled style keep it nicely grounded." David Pitt, in his review of *The Snow Empress* for *Booklist,* remarked that the book is "a seamless blending of historical research and old-fashioned crime solving." "Compelling pacing and well-rounded characters enhance the intriguing plot" exclaimed a *Publishers Weekly* critic.

In 2008, Rowland published her first book outside the Sano Ichiro mystery series. Titled *The Secret Adventures of Charlotte Brontë,* the novel is a historical mystery that transforms Charlotte Brontë, the author of *Jane Eyre,* and her sisters, Emily and Anne Brontë into nineteenth-century sleuths. The book opens with Charlotte and her sister Anne setting out to London, England, by train after Charlotte receives a letter from her publisher, George Smith, accusing her of breach of contract. On the train to London they encounter Isabel White, a young governess, who is later stabbed to death in London. After witnessing the murder, Charlotte teams up with Mr. Slade, a spy for Her Majesty's Foreign Office, in order to capture White's murderer. Several critics were impressed with Rowland's new mystery, although a few complained about the plot's implausible nature. "Brontë aficionados will enjoy the frequent biographical touches, but the plot becomes too far-fetched," remarked a *Christian Science Monitor* critic. A *Library Journal* critic had the same criticism: "Rowland tells a thrilling story, but the details are too far-fetched to be believed." However, the novel's improbable plot did not seem to faze *Star Tribune* reviewer Katherine Bailey: "Rowland's impressive, detailed descriptions of the sites and phenomena of Victorian England, particularly of London, give the narrative depth and compensate, perhaps, for some unlikely plot twists. Never mind plausibility, Rowland simply refuses to let readers lift their eyes from the page." "A very Victorian murder, the evils of British imperialism and a beloved novelist unite in this appealing literary mystery," asserted a *Kirkus Reviews* critic.

When asked by a *Publishers Weekly* contributor what inspired her to write a novel that involved the real-life author Charlotte Brontë, Rowland replied: "This is my tribute to her and my love of Victorian literature." She added: "It may be the start of a new series; I'm waiting to see how well this one does."

Also in 2008, Rowland authored *The Fire Kimono,* her next installment in the "Sano Ichiro" series. This time, Sano's mother is accused of murder, and he must use his detective skills to clear her name. Sano is preparing to attack Lord Matsudaira, as each man battles for supremacy in order to take the ineffective shogun's place. However, a skeleton is unearthed and the body is somehow connected to Sano's mother. Critics applauded the book as one of the stronger works in the series. As usual, they also noted Rowland's skillful portrayal of seventeenth-century Japan. Patrick Anderson, writing in *Washington Post Book World,* called *The Fire Kimono* "an exercise in pure entertainment. It's not deep or profound, but it takes us to an exotic time and place and overwhelms us with intrigue, romance, adventure and frequent bloodshed." Anderson also stated: "Rowland writes gracefully, and much of the pleasure of the book lies in her portrait of a society largely unknown to most of us," adding that the author "does a good job of capturing the beauty and barbarism of Japan at a certain moment in its history." A reviewer for the online *Book Bird Dog* declared: "I loved the unfolding of the plot and how relationships are developed and tested during the novel." A reviewer for the online *Book Blogger's Diary* was also impressed with the work, calling the story "thrilling" and "expertly crafted." The same reviewer noted that "it's filled to the brim, indeed overflowing, with the palace intrigue, political and military maneuvering that fans of this series have come to love and expect." Connie Williams, writing in *School Library Journal,* was also pleased with the story, remarking that "Rowland brings Sano, his wife, a cast of supporting characters, and 18th-century Japan to life with a sweet, simple writing style." Commending *The Fire Kimono* in *Kirkus Reviews,* a contributor observed that "Sano's frantic sleuthing runs constantly up against the machinations of an old and exiled enemy." The same contributor commented that "far from being distracting, the historic setting is mesmerizing," making for "great escape fiction." Pitt, again writing for *Booklist,* applauded "Rowland's gifts for seamlessly incorporating period detail and historical information into the traditional mystery format." Offering praise in *Publishers Weekly,* a reviewer concluded that the author "has given her hero his greatest challenge yet in this suspenseful look at feudal Japan."

BIOGRAPHICAL AND CRITICAL SOURCES:

PERIODICALS

AB Bookman's Weekly, September 20, 1999, review of *The Concubine's Tattoo,* p. 380.

Booklist, April 15, 1997, David Pitt, review of *The Way of the Traitor,* p. 1412; March 1, 2000, George Needham, review of *The Samurai's Wife,* p. 1199; February 15, 2003, David Pitt, review of *The Dragon King's Palace,* p. 1055; July 1, 2005, David Pitt, review of *The Assassin's Touch,* p. 1906; October 1, 2006, David Pitt, review of *Red Chrysanthemum,* p. 42; October 1, 2007, David Pitt, review of *The Snow Empress,* p. 37; October 1, 2008, David Pitt, review of *The Fire Kimono,* p. 27.

Christian Science Monitor, April 11, 2008, review of *The Secret Adventures of Charlotte Brontë,* p. 14.

Drood Review of Mystery, January, 2001, reviews of *The Samurai's Wife* and *Black Lotus,* p. 23.

Entertainment Weekly, November 24, 2006, Adam B. Vary, review of *Red Chrysanthemum,* p. 113; March 21, 2008, Tina Jordan, review of *The Secret Adventures of Charlotte Brontë,* p. 63.

Kirkus Reviews, February 15, 2002, review of *The Pillow Book of Lady Wisteria,* p. 226; February 1, 2003, review of *The Dragon King's Palace,* p. 192; March 15, 2004, review of *The Perfumed Sleeve,* p. 252; July 1, 2005, review of *The Assassin's Touch,* p. 711; September 15, 2006, review of *Red Chrysanthemum,* p. 932; August 15, 2007, review of *The Snow Empress;* February 1, 2008, review of *The Secret Adventures of Charlotte Brontë;* September 15, 2008, review of *The Fire Kimono.*

Library Journal, May 1, 1997, Rex E. Klett, review of *The Way of the Traitor,* p. 143; March 1, 2001, Rex E. Klett, review of *Black Lotus,* p. 133; March 1, 2003, Rex E. Klett, review of *The Dragon King's Palace,* p. 123; April 1, 2004, Rex E. Klett, review of *The Perfumed Sleeve,* p. 128; August 1, 2005, Rex E. Klett, review of *The Assassin's Touch,* p. 59; November 1, 2006, Jo Ann Vicarel, "Mystery," review of *Red Chrysanthemum,* p. 54; November 15, 2007, Anna M. Nelson, review of *The Secret Adventures of Charlotte Brontë,* p. 54.

New York Times Book Review, October 9, 1994, F.G. Notehelfer, review of *Shinju,* p. 11.

Publishers Weekly, August 8, 1994, review of *Shinju,* p. 368; January 15, 1996, review of *Bundori,* p. 443; May 12, 1997, review of *The Way of the Traitor,* p. 62; September 21, 1998, review of *The Concubine's Tattoo,* p. 77; March 6, 2000, review of *The Samurai's Wife,* p. 86; January 29, 2001, review of *Black Lotus,* p. 68; March 11, 2002, review of *The Pillow Book of Lady Wisteria,* p. 54; February 3, 2003, review of *The Dragon King's Palace,* p. 57; March 1, 2004, review of *The Perfumed Sleeve,* p. 53; June 6, 2005, review of *The Assassin's Touch,* p. 43; August 28, 2006, review of *Red Chrysanthemum,* p. 34; September 10, 2007, review of *The Snow Empress,* p. 43; September 24, 2007, "PW Talks with Laura Joh Rowland: A Samurai Sleuth: Laura Joh Rowland Is the Author of the Snow Empress, Her 12th Mystery Set in 17th-century Japan to Feature Sano Ichiro, a High Official in the Shogun Court," p. 47; December 24, 2007, review of *The Secret Adventures of Charlotte Brontë,* p. 26; September 1, 2008, review of *The Fire Kimono,* p. 38.

School Library Journal, November 1, 2008, Connie Williams, review of *The Fire Kimono,* p. 157.

Star Tribune (Minneapolis-St. Paul, MN), March 7, 2008, Katherine Bailey, review of *The Secret Adventures of Charlotte Brontë.*

Tribune Books (Chicago, IL), April 1, 2001, review of *Black Lotus,* p. 2.

Washington Post Book World, December 22, 2008, Patrick Anderson, review of *The Fire Kimono,* p. 2.

ONLINE

Book Bird Dog, http://bookbirddog.blogspot.com/ (March 22, 2009), review of *The Fire Kimono.*

Book Blogger's Diary, http://abookbloggersdiary.blog spot.com/ (March 22, 2009), review of *The Fire Kimono.*

BookBrowse, http://www.bookbrowse.com/ (October 1, 2002), author profile.

BookReporter.com, http://www.bookreporter.com/ (May 1, 2002), Michelle Calabro Hubbard, review of *The Samurai's Wife.*

Laura Joh Rowland Home Page, http://www.laurajoh rowland.com (June 24, 2009).

Mystery Reader, http://www.themysteryreader.com/ (May 1, 2002), Lesley Dunlap, review of *Black Lotus.**

S

SANTOPIETRO, Tom

PERSONAL: Born in Waterbury, CT. *Education:* Graduated from the University of Connecticut School of Law.

CAREER: Writer, biographer, lawyer, and Broadway stage manager. Manager of Broadway shows and performances, including *A Few Good Men, A Doll's House, Master Class, The Iceman Cometh, Tru,* and *Noises Off.* Former professional tennis player.

WRITINGS:

BIOGRAPHIES

The Importance of Being Barbra, Thomas Dunne Books (New York, NY), 2006.
Considering Doris Day, Thomas Dunne Books (New York, NY), 2007.
Sinatra in Hollywood, Thomas Dunne Books (New York, NY), 2008.

SIDELIGHTS: A writer, biographer, and nonpracticing lawyer, Tom Santopietro is a stage manager on Broadway in New York, where he has worked for more than twenty years. In his first book, *The Importance of Being Barbra,* Santopietro takes a careful, critical look at the career and music of diva Barbra Streisand. Santopietro "evaluates Streisand's professional, not personal, life," noted a *Kirkus Reviews* critic, and added that private particulars are noted "only as they may have shaped her work." The author divides Streisand's work into distinct categories, including musical recordings, films, tele-

vision specials, and concerts, and offers background information, accounts of contemporary events, and critiques of the material under survey. The book emerges as an "opinionated analysis of the Streisand canon, with distinctive views on her many career highs and those more-than-a-few career missteps," noted Phil Hall on the *EDGE Boston* Web site. In addition, "Santopietro astutely embeds his subject in cultural context to underscore her zeitgeist appeal," observed a *Publishers Weekly* critic, exploring her brash personality, her unabashed ethnicity, and her strong appeal to alternative audiences, including feminists and gays. Rob Lester, on *EDGE Boston,* commented that for Streisand's many and varied fans, Santopietro's work is "a treasure of information and does go through her many achievements without being distracted very much by her personal life. This is not the book for dish and gossip, but it's chatty and informal at times, while taking the work quite seriously." Santopietro "holds strong opinions on all things Streisand that are usually right on," observed Rosellen Brewer in *Library Journal.* The *Kirkus Reviews* writer noted that Santopietro's "individual critiques are vivid and perceptive," while the *Publishers Weekly* contributor commented favorably on the author's "discerning, nuanced critiques of Streisand's works."

In 2007, Santopietro published a second work, *Considering Doris Day.* The book is biography of singer and actress Doris Day and is written with a similar approach to that used in *The Importance of Being Barbra.* Discussing the volume in an interview for the *Discovering Doris* Web site, Santopietro stated that his book "is my attempt to grant Doris Day her rightful place as a great American artist, placing her career and persona within the context of American society in the second half of the twentieth century." He added: "It is not a standard biography, but rather, a critical analysis of the extraordinary body of work which constitutes Doris Day's career. I examine of all of her films, most of her 600 recordings, and all five seasons of [her] CBS sitcom. It's an examination of why her work continues to resonate today, even though she has not worked as a performer in over twenty years, and how she came to be a genuine, worldwide icon." Furthermore, Santopietro noted that "this makes the book all sound very serious, like a textbook, and it's not—I treat Doris Day very seriously, as any true artist should be treated, but I deliberate wanted to make the book conversational in tone so that it is a fun read for people. Hopefully I have achieved that goal."

Reviewers remarked that Santopietro has accomplished what he set out to do. A *Publishers Weekly* writer found that "there is enough biographical detail as it concerns her career choices to create a vibrant portrait of the artist." Although David Finkle in *Back Stage East* stated that "my wish is [Sanpietro] hadn't spoken up so hyper-comprehensively," he nevertheless acknowledged "gratitude that Santopietro has spoken up" at all. June Sawyers, writing in *Booklist,* was also impressed. "Santopietro reveals a complex human being behind the pitch-perfect persona," she found. A *Kirkus Reviews* writer stated that although "the author's writing is rough . . . his perceptions will send readers to Day's CDs and DVDs for an overdue re-take." Proffering more straightforward praise in the *New York Times Book Review,* Nellie McKay remarked that the book "includes a comprehensive filmography, a selected discography and many photographs, and covers ground less traveled by traditional biographies." She added: "It's an easy read, at times illuminating."

In yet another biography, *Sinatra in Hollywood,* Santopietro addresses the career of Frank Sinatra. Rather than take a comprehensive look at Sinatra's career, however, Santopietro devotes his attention to Sinatra's acting roles and his life in Hollywood, California. The author notes that Sinatra was as talented an actor as he was a singer, an opinion that is seldom espoused. The author also discusses Santopietro's failed marriages to the actresses Ava Gardner and Mia Farrow, and he examines the rumors that Sinatra's career was subsidized by the mob. Like its predecessors, the book met with critical approbation. A *Kirkus Reviews* writer called it "a terrifically lucid and entertaining look at an undervalued area of Sinatra's achievement." Gordon Flagg, writing in *Booklist,* was also impressed, finding that "Santopietro makes a compelling argument for Sinatra's

status as a great actor too often saddled with subpar" movies and roles. A *Publishers Weekly* reviewer proffered further praise, noting that the biography is "filled with forgotten facts" and "is certain to satisfy Sinatra's legions of fans." A contributor to the *Turner Classic Movies* Web site observed that "Santopietro writes vividly about Sinatra's sixty-year career and over 60 films. Drawing on the observations of Sinatra's contemporaries and the actor's own self-criticism, he constructs the history of Sinatra's films, including the musicals."

BIOGRAPHICAL AND CRITICAL SOURCES:

PERIODICALS

Back Stage East, September 20, 2007, David Finkle, review of *Considering Doris Day,* p. 11.
Biography, June 22, 2007, Keith Garebian, review of *Considering Doris Day,* p. 421.
Booklist, February 15, 2007, June Sawyers, review of *Considering Doris Day,* p. 32; October 15, 2008, Gordon Flagg, review of *Sinatra in Hollywood,* p. 12.
California Bookwatch, September, 2006, review of *The Importance of Being Barbra.*
Kirkus Reviews, April 1, 2006, review of *The Importance of Being Barbra,* p. 339; December 1, 2006, review of *Considering Doris Day,* p. 1213; September 15, 2008, review of *Sinatra in Hollywood.*
Library Journal, May 15, 2006, Rosellen Brewer, review of *The Importance of Being Barbra,* p. 103; February 1, 2007, Rosellen Brewer, review of *Considering Doris Day,* p. 75; October 1, 2008, Peter Thornell, review of *Sinatra in Hollywood,* p. 72.
New York Times Book Review, June 3, 2007, Nellie McKay, "Eternal Sunshine," p. 50.
Publishers Weekly, March 20, 2006, review of *The Importance of Being Barbra,* p. 46; November 27, 2006, review of *Considering Doris Day,* p. 39; September 22, 2008, review of *Sinatra in Hollywood,* p. 49.
San Diego Union-Tribune, July 14, 2006, Howard Cohen, "A High Road, a Low Road on Streisand," review of *The Importance of Being Barbra.*

ONLINE

Discovering Doris Web site, http://www.dorisdaytribute.com/ (June 25, 2009), author interview.

EDGE Boston, http://www.edgeboston.com/ (July 1, 2006), Rob Lester, review of *The Importance of Being Barbra;* (July 12, 2006) Phil Hall, review of *The Importance of Being Barbra.*

Tom Santopietro Home Page, http://www.tom santopietro.com (June 25, 2009).

Turner Classic Movies Web site, http://www.tcm.com/ (June 25, 2009), review of *Sinatra in Hollywood.*

WTNH.com, http://www.wtnh.com/ (August 31, 2006), author biography.*

*   *   *

SCHLESIER, Karl H. 1927-

PERSONAL: Born July 31, 1927, in Germany; immigrated to United States.

ADDRESSES: Home—Corrales, NM.

CAREER: Anthropologist, educator, and novelist. Wichita State University, Wichita, KS, professor of anthropology, then professor emeritus. *Military service:* Served in German Army, 1945.

WRITINGS:

The Archeology of Sedna Creek, Wichita State University (Wichita, KS), 1971.

The Wolves of Heaven: Cheyenne Shamanism, Ceremonies, and Prehistoric Origins, University of Oklahoma Press (Norman, OK), 1987.

(Editor and contributor) *Plains Indians, A.D. 500-1500: The Archaeological Past of Historic Groups,* University of Oklahoma Press (Norman, OK), 1994.

NOVELS

Josanie's War: A Chiricahua Apache Novel, University of Oklahoma Press (Norman, OK), 1998.

Trail of the Red Butterfly, Texas Tech University Press (Lubbock, TX), 2007.

Aurora Crossing: A Novel of the Nez Perces, Texas Tech University Press (Lubbock, TX), 2008.

Also contributor to scholarly and literary journals of ten countries, including the *Wichita State University Bulletin* and *Annali Lateranensi.*

SIDELIGHTS: Karl H. Schlesier, a professor emeritus of anthropology at Wichita State University, and is best known for his anthropological study of Native American tribes. Prompted in his interest by witnessing, as a teen, an act of bravery on the part of a Native American on the battlefield of World War II, Schlesier has become a "proponent of Action Anthropology which promotes the idea that anthropologists should not only be scientists and scholars, but should openly advocate the cultural and political causes of native peoples," explained John H. Moore in *American Anthropologist.* Schlesier's advocacy is demonstrated in *The Wolves of Heaven: Cheyenne Shamanism, Ceremonies, and Prehistoric Origins,* in which he interprets literal truths from oral and historical data to present a cultural reconstruction of the Cheyenne people and their religious traditions.

In *The Wolves of Heaven* Schlesier puts forth the theory, based on the archaeological remains of the Cheyenne people, that a Cheyenne presence existed on the plains of America beginning from 500 BCE. A comparison between Cheyenne shamanism and Siberian shamanism places the Cheyenne people in the same pedigree as all Algonquian tribes. Schlesier presents his argument based on comparisons between rituals of the Cheyenne and other Algonquian tribes, such as the Yuroks of California, the Mahicans of New England, and the Evenks of Siberia. However, the Cheyenne tribe emerged as a distinct people with their creation of the Massaum, a ceremony of earth-giving. According to Schlesier, the Massaum was an elaborate ceremony of world revitalization, ritual theater, and performances of magic. Peter Nabokov, writing in the *Journal of Religion,* stated that "Schlesier is trying to conjure up a nonstatic American Indian world in which peoples and ideas circulate, constellate, and periodically achieve new plateaus of religious-social integration."

Schlesier again attempts to correlate prehistory with archaeological evidence of historic Indian tribes in his editing of *Plains Indians, A.D. 500-1500: The Archaeological Past of Historic Groups.* This 1994 book consists of a collection of thirteen essays, each representing a different subcultural or archaeological region of the Great Plains. The object of each chapter is to identify historic ethnic groups with ancestral prehistoric populations by using incomplete archaeological records and findings. Even with evidence of tribal migration, population decimations, and cultural borrowing of implements, Schlesier bridges the distant prehistoric past with the dynamic Plains groups. With the same evidence, he addresses particular tribal behavior based on aspects of environment, climate changes, migrations, and human composition. "Overall, this volume succeeds rather well in its intention, and without question makes an important contribution to Great Plains archeology," commented Jeffrey R. Hanson in a review for the *Journal of Interdisciplinary History.*

Utilizing historical data, Schlesier makes his fictional debut with *Josanie's War: A Chiricahua Apache Novel.* Five bands of Chiricahua Apaches flee their reservation on Turkey Creek in Arizona on May 17, 1885, hoping to find a new homeland in Mexico outside the jurisdiction of the U.S. government. The story focuses on one of the bands led by the infamous warrior Chihuahua and his older brother, Josanie, in a detailed account of the last great Apache war as the band fights against the combined military forces of both the United States and Mexico. Combining historical documents, such as military records and newspaper reports, with fictitious action and events, Schlesier illustrates the Apaches' resourcefulness, spirituality, and humanity as they fight to the death in a last effort to obtain a Chiricahua homeland. Emphasizing Schlesier's in-depth knowledge of his subject, Peter Bricklebank noted of the novel in his *New York Times Book Review* appraisal that *Josanie's War* "takes us into a harsh world, showing how injustice and prejudice proved despicably, needlessly destructive."

In Schlesier's second novel, *Trail of the Red Butterfly,* Jean Valle is living and trading with Cheyenne Indians. The novel is set in 1804 and Valle tells tales of horse raids on Spanish colonies as well as stories of Lewis and Clark. Praising the novel on the online *Curled Up with a Good Book,* Benet Exton called it "a delight to read, its story based on what life was like in the Southwest and northern Mexico as Native Americans came into contact with the Spanish." Exton went on to note that "Schlesier shows what it probably was like for Indians from the Great Plains to discover cities, churches, various peoples, and languages," adding that "this book is highly recommended." An *Internet Bookwatch* writer echoed these sentiments, finding that *Trail of the Red Butterfly* is "highly recommended as an original jewel of Western Fiction."

Aurora Crossing: A Novel of the Nez Perces, Schlesier's third work of fiction, was released in 2008. The book

again draws on the author's extensive Native American expertise, and it tells the tale of the Nez Perce Indian's flight from U.S. troops. The tribe attempted to make it to the Canadian border to escape persecution. The protagonist, John Seton, is the child of a Nez Perce mother and a Caucasian father, but he was abandoned by his father when he was eight. Raised by his mother, John, now eighteen years old, joins the Lamtama, a non treaty group that is resisting being forced onto reservation land. In addition, John is mourning his mother's recent death. He and the Lamtama, along with four other such groups, are migrating to the plains country. They make up a group of 810 Native Americans. The bands of Indians are also herding over four thousand horses on their journey, creating a caravan that stretches out over a distance of four miles. Like *Josanie's War* and *Trail of the Red Butterfly, Aurora Crossing* was predominantly well received by critics. An *Internet Bookwatch* contributor stated that the novel is "recommended . . . for anyone intrigued by native American culture." Deborah Donovan, writing in *Booklist,* was also impressed with the work, stating that the book "incorporates precise details of traditional ceremonies . . . and brings this moment in Nez Perce history vividly to life." A *Kirkus Reviews* writer called *Aurora Crossing* "a satisfying, ethnographically detailed coming-of-age novel" and noted that "without falling into traps of didacticism, Schlesier guides Seton toward a decision that turns on visions, signs and portents."

BIOGRAPHICAL AND CRITICAL SOURCES:

PERIODICALS

American Anthropologist, June, 1988, John H. Moore, review of *The Wolves of Heaven: Cheyenne Shamanism, Ceremonies, and Prehistoric Origins,* p. 450.

American Historical Review, February, 1989, William K. Powers, review of *The Wolves of Heaven,* p. 201.

Booklist, October 15, 2008, Deborah Donovan, review of *Aurora Crossing: A Novel of the Nez Perces,* p. 22.

California Bookwatch, January 1, 2009, review of *Aurora Crossing.*

Choice: Current Reviews for Academic Libraries, January, 1988, D.R. Parks, review of *The Wolves of Heaven,* p. 806; June, 1995, T.A. Foor, review of *Plains Indians, A.D. 500-1500: The Archaeological Past of Historic Groups,* pp. 1662-1663.

Internet Bookwatch, March 1, 2008, review of *Trail of the Red Butterfly;* January 1, 2009, review of *Aurora Crossing.*

Journal of American History, September, 1995, R. Douglas Hurt, review of *Plains Indians, A.D. 500-1500,* p. 678.

Journal of Interdisciplinary History, summer, 1996, Jeffrey R. Hanson, review of *Plains Indians, A.D. 500-1500,* pp. 147-148.

Journal of Religion, October, 1989, Peter Nabokov, review of *The Wolves of Heaven,* pp. 593-594.

Kirkus Reviews, September 15, 2008, review of *Aurora Crossing.*

New York Times Book Review, November 15, 1998, Peter Bricklebank, review of *Josanie's War: A Chiricahua Apache Novel,* p. 63.

Publishers Weekly, August 17, 1998, review of *Josanie's War,* p. 50.

ONLINE

Curled Up with a Good Book, http://www.curledup.com/ (June 24, 2009), Benet Exton, review of *Trail of the Red Butterfly.*

* * *

SCHRAG, Peter 1931-

PERSONAL: Born July 24, 1931, in Karlsruhe, Germany; son of Otto (a businessman) and Judith Schrag; married Jane Mowrer, June 9, 1953 (divorced, 1969); married Diane Divoky (a writer), May 24, 1969; children: (first marriage) Mitzi, Erin Andrew; (second marriage) David, Benaiah. *Education:* Amherst College, B.A., 1953; graduate study at Amherst College and University of Massachusetts, 1957-59. *Hobbies and other interests:* Travel and sailing.

ADDRESSES: Home—Sacramento, CA.

CAREER: El Paso Herald Post, El Paso, TX, reporter, 1953-55; Amherst College, Amherst, MA, assistant secretary, 1955-66, instructor in American studies, 1960-64; *Saturday Review,* New York, NY, associate education editor, 1966-68, executive editor, 1968-69, contributing editor, 1970-73; *Change* magazine, New York, NY, editor, 1969-70; full-time writer, 1970-78; *Sacramento Bee,* Sacramento, CA, editorial page editor,

beginning 1978. Lecturer at University of Massachusetts, 1970-72, and University of California, Berkeley, 1974-78. Member, Committee on the Study of History. Consultant to Science Research Associates, 1960-61, U.S. Office of Education, and U.S. Information Service.

AWARDS, HONORS: Guggenheim fellow, 1971-72; professional journalism fellow, Stanford University, 1973-74.

WRITINGS:

(Editor) *The Ratification of the Constitution and the Bill of Rights,* D.C. Heath (Boston, MA), 1964.

Voices in the Classroom: Public Schools and Public Attitudes, Beacon (Boston, MA), 1965.

(Editor) *The European Mind and the Discovery of a New World,* D.C. Heath (Boston, MA), 1965.

Village School Downtown, Beacon (Boston, MA), 1967.

Out of Place in America, Random House (New York, NY), 1970.

Decline of the WASP, Simon & Schuster (New York, NY), 1972.

The End of the American Future, Simon & Schuster (New York, NY), 1973.

Test of Loyalty, Simon & Schuster (New York, NY), 1974.

(With wife, Diane Divoky) *Myth of the Hyperactive Child,* Pantheon (New York, NY), 1975.

Mind Control, Pantheon (New York, NY), 1978.

Paradise Lost: California's Experience, America's Future, New Press (New York, NY), 1998.

Final Test: The Battle for Adequacy in America's Schools, New Press (New York, NY), 2004.

California: America's High-stakes Experiment, University of California Press (Berkeley, CA), 2006.

Contributor to periodicals, including *Saturday Review, New Republic, Commonweal, Progressive, College Board Review, Playboy, New West, New York Review, Atlantic, New York Times Education Supplement, Nation,* and *Harper's.*

SIDELIGHTS: Peter Schrag is a journalist and author or editor of several books of nonfiction. In 1964 and 1965, respectively, he edited *The Ratification of the Constitution and the Bill of Rights* and *The European Mind and the Discovery of a New World.* He is also the author of the 1967 book *Village School Downtown* and the 1970 volume *Out of Place in America.* Some of Schrag's other works include the 1975 *Myth of the Hyperactive Child* (written with his wife, Diane Divoky), and the 1978 book *Mind Control.* Next, following a twenty-year break in his publication schedule, Schrag authored *Paradise Lost: California's Experience, America's Future.* The book is a critique of California's voting laws and economic processes. As *Reason* contributor Nick Gillespie explained, "for Schrag, California's demise is identical to what he considers the ruin of its public sector." Gillespie also noted that Schrag writes that "the underfunded public schools are no good anymore; the freeways are in disrepair; public libraries have shortened their hours if not shut their doors altogether." In fact, "the snake in the grass of Schrag's paradise is the ballot initiative process. This is no easy admission for the author, who, as a professed admirer of populist reformers, notes in passing that California's initiative law, passed in 1911, is itself 'a Progressive Era instrument whereby 'the people' could from time to time check the excesses of a state government.'"

Reviewers largely praised *Paradise Lost,* and *Booklist* reviewer Alice Joyce called it "enormously thought provoking," adding that "Schrag's book merits study." A *Publishers Weekly* writer was also impressed, noting that "Schrag's 'urgent cautionary tale' is, if not dispassionate, astonishingly clear in its explanation of how California arrived at its present situation." Jill Ortner, writing in *Library Journal,* also applauded the book. She called the book "a well-documented text," and went on to note that it "can be appreciated by both scholars and lay readers."

In his 2006 book, *California: America's High-stakes Experiment,* Schrag returns to the subject of California and its political and economic travails. *Antioch Review* writer George Judson stated that the book is "a curiously parochial tale. . . . But by the end one can't help feeling that Schrag is not perplexed by his state's behavior so much as embarrassed." A *Publishers Weekly* critic found that "Schrag offers one of the best analyses yet of the California train wreck and its troubling implications for America's future."

BIOGRAPHICAL AND CRITICAL SOURCES:

PERIODICALS

Antioch Review, January 1, 2007, George Judson, review of *California: America's High-stakes Experiment,* p. 193.

Booklist, February 15, 1998, Alice Joyce, review of *Paradise Lost: California's Experience, America's Future,* p. 956.
California Bookwatch, August 1, 2006, review of *California.*
Library Journal, January 1, 1998, Jill Ortner, review of *Paradise Lost,* p. 121.
Publishers Weekly, January 19, 1998, review of *Paradise Lost,* p. 360; February 20, 2006, review of *California,* p. 149.
Reason, December 1, 1998, Nick Gillespie, review of *Paradise Lost.**

*   *   *

SEFTON, Maggie

PERSONAL: Born in Richmond, VA; married; children: four daughters. *Education:* Holds B.A. degrees in English literature and journalism.

ADDRESSES: Home—CO. *E-mail*—maggie@maggiesefton.com.

CAREER: Certified public accountant, real estate agent, and novelist.

WRITINGS:

Abilene Gamble (western historical novel), Berkley (New York, NY), 1995.
Dying to Sell (mystery novel), Five Star (Waterville, ME), 2005.

"KNITTING MYSTERY" NOVELS

Knit One, Kill Two, Berkley Prime Crime (New York, NY), 2005.
Needled to Death, Berkley Prime Crime (New York, NY), 2005.
A Deadly Yarn, Berkley Prime Crime (New York, NY), 2006.
A Killer Stitch, Berkley Prime Crime (New York, NY), 2007.
Dyer Consequences, Berkley Prime Crime (New York, NY), 2008.

Fleece Navidad, Berkley Prime Crime (New York, NY), 2008.

Dropped Dead Stitch, Berkley Prime Crime (New York, NY), 2009.

Author maintains a blog.

SIDELIGHTS: Mystery novelist Maggie Sefton notes on her Home Page: "If I were being completely honest, I'd have to admit that I always knew I was a born to be a writer. I spent my childhood with my nose in a book and loved writing." Still, as she grew older, the responsibilities of raising her family and continuing her education prevented her from expending effort on her interest in writing. Despite her diverted attention, however, the characters kept coming, and ideas for stories continued to form in her mind. Eventually, she noted, these characters demanded that she write their stories, and she delved into creating numerous historical stories and scenarios. She also focused her attention on what she calls her "apprenticeship in the craft," consisting of actions such as attending writers' conferences, getting and giving critiques, and studying the markets. Sefton eventually realized that her stories always included a mystery and copious murder, an insight that prompted her to devote her writing efforts to the mystery genre.

Coinciding with a career change into real estate, Sefton's debut novel combines mystery and her vocation. *Dying to Sell* revolves around recently divorced realtor Katie Doyle, who is charged with the painful task of selling the home of Mark and Amanda Shuster, two longtime friends struggling through a difficult divorce. While the divorce lawyers battle, Amanda uncovers mounting evidence that the philandering Mark is hiding the couple's assets. When Katie finds Mark stabbed to death in the couple's for-sale home, Amanda is immediately suspected as the murderer. Stonewalled by police detective Bill Levitz, who also happens to be her brother-in-law, Katie takes it upon herself to find the evidence to exonerate Amanda and locate Mark's killer. A *Kirkus Reviews* critic called the novel "a bustling, formulaic debut soothing as warm milk despite the casualties." Rex E. Klett, writing in *Library Journal,* called Katie a "believable and sympathetic" protagonist.

Knit One, Kill Two intertwines mystery and knitting when the aunt of accountant Kelly Flynn is murdered the day she cashes a hefty mortgage check. The ladies of a local knitting group all knew and liked Kelly's aunt. When the Flynn family quilt comes up missing, the knitting ladies and Kelly are convinced that the police have arrested the wrong man. Aided by the knitting group and a retired police detective, Kelly begins finding clues to the real murderer's identity. In his *Library Journal* review, Klett remarked that this first book in a projected series "exhibits all the trappings of an enticing cozy."

Knit One, Kill Two became the first book in Sefton's emerging "Knitting Mystery" series. The second installment in the series, *Needled to Death,* was published in 2005. The book finds Kelly enjoying her new life in Fort Conner, Colorado. Kelly also finds herself investigating the untimely death of Vicki, who appears to have been murdered by her estranged husband, Bob. Bob now stands to inherit all of Vicki's assets, including the successful family business. The book received praise from critics, who noted that it is an entertaining read. Tara Gelsomino, writing on the *Romantic Times Online,* found that "nonknitters and fiber fanatics alike will enjoy the yarn-shop setting." Jennifer Monahan Winberry, reviewing the book for the *Mystery Reader* Web site, was also impressed. She called the book "a solid addition to a fledgling series" and found that "as Kelly's new life begins to take shape, she becomes more interesting and more enjoyable." Winberry called *Needled to Death* "a fun, quick read, especially for those caught up in the current knitting craze." Proffering further praise on the *Best Reviews* Web site, Harriet Klausner found that the novel is "a fine yarn that has cozy fans trying to unravel the threads of who-done-it along side of the heroine."

Kelly continues her sleuthing in *A Deadly Yarn,* as well as in *A Killer Stitch.* In the latter installment, Kelly is preparing for the Christmas holiday, busily knitting the gifts she intends to give. She is pulled away from her projects by the murder of Derek Cooper, an alpaca farmer known for dating several women at once. Like the previous books in the "Knitting Mystery" series, *A Killer Stitch* was well received by critics. Stephanie Schneider, writing on the *Romantic Times Online,* observed that although the novel is "not a page-turner," it is nevertheless "a pleasant afternoon read." Klausner, again writing in the online *Best Reviews,* observed with interest that "the amateur sleuthing reads smoother than the kiss and tell locker room chatter amidst the knitters." In a more positive assessment, a *Publishers Weekly* writer remarked that "knitting devotees will enjoy this crafty cozy." Ilene Cooper, writing in *Booklist,* observed that "knitters will be pleased to add Sefton's series . . . to their knitting-related fiction shelf."

In the 2008 installment *Dyer Consequences,* Kelly has just purchased an alpaca farm of her own. However, a recent spate of vandalism nearby troubles her. Soon, a murder is committed at the House of Lambspun store, and Kelly must find the murderer. The book, according to a *Publishers Weekly* writer, is "a volume sure to please series fans." *Fleece Navidad,* also published in 2008, once again finds Kelly in the midst of a Christmas season murder mystery. Shortly after Thanksgiving, tragedy strikes when the town's librarian, Juliet, is run over by a car. Even worse, what at first appears to have been an accident may have been intentional. Although Kelly's knitting cohorts suspect that the newcomer in their midst may be the culprit, Kelly is not convinced. Applauding the novel on the *Romantic Times Online,* Barb Anderson noted that "the characters are well-developed and likable." She also found that Sefton presents a "well-rounded story with a bit of romance." Klausner, this time writing on the online *Genre Go Round Reviews,* commented that *Fleece Navidad* is "a charming Colorado cozy with an eccentric cast [whose] off beat humor has the audience chuckling." She added that "fall in the Rockies sounds like fun when Ms. Sefton is the hostess." Mary Jo Doig, a contributor to the *Story Circle Book Reviews* Web site, was also impressed, stating that "in addition to the sparkles of the Christmas season inside the House of Lambspun and the vivid yarn descriptions that allow the reader to both see and feel them, *Fleece Navidad* is a bountiful haven of sights, tastes, and smells." A reviewer for the *Booknotes by Lisa* Web site thought the plot was somewhat thin, but nevertheless stated that "one thing I did like about this one is that it contained more than the usual one recipe and one knitting pattern. Instead, it contained five knitting patterns and seven recipes."

Kelly returns in *Dropped Dead Stitch.* Cal Everett, the owner of a nearby ranch, is hosting a retreat for the survivors of assault. Kelly's friend Jennifer is attending the retreat, but she is raped by Cal during the event. Cal is killed soon after, and Kelly takes up the case. Although reviewers felt that the cast of characters was too large, they nevertheless praised the story. They also applauded the inclusion of knitting patterns and recipes in the book, a practice that has become a favorite hallmark of the series. Commending *Dropped Dead Stitch* in *Publishers Weekly,* an anonymous contributor noted that "Sefton skillfully handles a sensitive topic."

BIOGRAPHICAL AND CRITICAL SOURCES:

PERIODICALS

Booklist, May 1, 2007, Ilene Cooper, review of *A Killer Stitch,* p. 40; May 1, 2008, Cooper, review of *Dyer Consequences,* p. 44; October 15, 2008, Judy Coon, review of *Fleece Navidad,* p. 25; May 1, 2009, Cooper, review of *Dropped Dead Stitch,* p. 22.

Kirkus Reviews, August 15, 2005, review of *Dying to Sell,* p. 887.

Library Journal, June 1, 2005, Rex E. Klett, review of *Knit One, Kill Two,* p. 107; October 1, 2005, Klett, review of *Dying to Sell,* p. 62.

Publishers Weekly, March 5, 2007, review of *A Killer Stitch,* p. 43; April 28, 2008, review of *Dyer Consequences,* p. 116; April 20, 2009, review of *Dropped Dead Stitch,* p. 34.

ONLINE

Best Reviews, http://thebestreviews.com/ (June 26, 2009), Harriet Klausner, reviews of *Needled to Death* and *A Killer Stitch.*

Booknotes by Lisa, http://booknotesbylisa.blogspot.com/ (December 17, 2008), review of *Fleece Navidad.*

Genre Go Round Reviews, http://genregoroundreviews. blogspot.com/ (August 5, 2008), Harriet Klausner, review of *Fleece Navidad.*

Maggie Sefton Home Page, http://www.maggiesefton. com (June 26, 2009).

Mystery Reader, http://www.themysteryreader.com/ (June 26, 2009), Jennifer Monahan Winberry, review of *Needled to Death.*

Romantic Times Online, http://www.romantictimes.com/ (June 26, 2009), Tara Gelsomino, review of *Needled to Death;* (June 26, 2009) Stephanie Schneider, review of *A Killer Stitch;* (June 26, 2009) Barb Anderson, review of *Fleece Navidad.*

Story Circle Book Reviews, http://www.storycirclebook reviews.org/ (November 9, 2008), Mary Jo Doig, review of *Fleece Navidad.**

*   *   *

SHANNON, Harry 1948-

PERSONAL: Born 1948, in NV; married Suzanne Klee (divorced); married Wendy Kramer; children: Paige (daughter; second marriage).

ADDRESSES: E-mail—halsbaby2@aol.com; ghoulish guy@aol.com.

CAREER: Author and therapist. Carolco Pictures, vice president of music, 1988-93. Counselor in private practice, beginning 1988. Has worked as an actor, singer, songwriter, music publisher, film studio executive, and motion picture music supervisor.

MEMBER: Horror Writers Association, Mystery Writers of America.

AWARDS, HONORS: Emmy nomination for songwriting, 1982, for "The Gift of Life"; two awards for country-music songwriting from American Society of Composers, Authors, and Publishers; Tombstone Award for best novel of 2003, for Night of the Werewolf.

WRITINGS:

NOVELS; EXCEPT WHERE NOTED

Bad Seed (stories), River City Books, LLC (Tualatin, OR), 2001.
Night of the Beast, Medium Rare Books Publishing (Anaheim, CA), 2002.
Night of the Werewolf, Medium Rare Books Publishing (Anaheim, CA), 2003.
Night of the Daemon, Delirium Books (Webster, IN), 2005.
The Pressure of Darkness: A Thriller, Five Star (Waterville, ME), 2006.
Daemon, Delirium Books (Webster, IN), 2008.
Dead and Gone, Delirium Books (Webster, IN), 2008.

"MICK CALLAHAN" SERIES

Memorial Day, Five Star (Waterville, ME), 2004.
Eye of the Burning Man, Five Star (Waterville, ME), 2004.
One of the Wicked, Five Star (Waterville, ME), 2008.

Also author of the Dead and Gone screenplay. Contributor to anthologies, including Brimstone Turnpike, Small Bites, Tales from the Gorezone, The Fear Within, and Deadly Ground. Contributor of short fiction to magazines, including Cemetery Dance, City Slab, Futures, Crime Spree, Crimestalker Casebook, Twilight Showcase, and Horror World.

SIDELIGHTS: Novelist and short-story writer Harry Shannon writes within the horror and mystery genres, but his multifaceted career has taken him to other creative venues as well. He has been a country music songwriter who earned a pair of awards from the American Society of Composers, Authors, and Publishers (ASCAP) for his efforts. His songwriting has also garnered him an Emmy Award nomination. "Back in the 1970s I had a string of 'country music' hits for the likes of Eddy Arnold, Kathy Mattea, and Reba McIntire, some movie title songs and pop chart singles, but I burned out on all of that as well," Shannon related in a interview with Scott Nicholson on the Haunted Computer Web site.

"After sobering up in 1986, I went back to school to study counseling," Shannon told Nicholson. He opened a private counseling practice in 1988, while simultaneously working as a vice president of music for Carolco Pictures on films such as Terminator Two, The Doors, and the "Rambo" movies First Blood, Rambo: First Blood Part II, and Rambo III. He also worked as a music supervisor in the motion-picture industry on films such as Universal Soldier and Basic Instinct. "I have a pretty eclectic background," Shannon told Nicholson. "That helps a great deal when one is dreaming up characters and situations and trying to harness melodrama for the sake of a story."

Shannon's detours into acting and music temporarily sidelined an early interest in writing, but he returned to fiction in 1999, he related in the interview with Nicholson. Shannon has contributed short fiction to a variety of genre publications and anthologies, including Crime Spree, Cemetery Dance, and Gothic.net. His debut horror and noir collection Bad Seed was published in 2001. He has also written several horror novels, including Night of the Beast, Night of the Werewolf, and Night of the Daemon. He earned a Tombstone Award in 2003 for Night of the Werewolf.

Mick Callahan, the protagonist of Shannon's novel Memorial Day, had once been a famous pop psychologist, a television star who enjoyed every fringe benefit that being a media celebrity could bring. But an overinflated ego and copious amounts of drugs and alcohol finally brought Callahan down. Recovering from alcoholism, Callahan returns to familiar territory, the Nevada town of Dry Wells, where he makes guest appearances on call-in radio and keeps working on sorting out his life. Callahan's career options start looking up again when he lands an interview that could put him back on television. His resurrection is delayed, however, when a pair of murders occurs. One of the victims, dubbed "Ophelia," was a regular caller to his radio show. Still haunted by his failure to help a needy client years earlier, Callahan is determined not to let Ophelia's murder go unpunished. With technical assistance from a computer-expert friend, and an investigation sure to rile the area's most prominent family, Callahan dives in to solve the murders before scandal again taints his career. "Mick's road to redemption is wry, bittersweet, and altogether touching in this notable and brilliant new addition to the mystery genre," commented an interviewer for the *New Mystery Reader* Web site. "The crisply detailed small-town desert setting adds to the novel's sense of freshness," commented David Pitt in *Booklist,* while *Library Journal* reviewer Rex E. Klett called *Memorial Day* "a most promising first mystery."

"I've known guys like Mick all my life," Shannon told the *New Mystery Reader* Web site interviewer. "He's a redneck at heart, but way too intelligent to be comfortable in the high desert culture that he came from—yet he is still too 'country' for the city. As a result, he tries all kinds of professions and pursues his varied interests, yet never feels like he belongs anywhere." His main character is "a mass of contradictions, as are most people I find truly interesting." Although Callahan is not Shannon's fictional alter-ego, he admitted in his interview: "I put enough of myself in Mick to make me cringe a bit at times."

Mick returns in *Eye of the Burning Man.* The story finds Shannon's protagonist attempting to stay sober while working full-time as a psychologist on a local radio talk show. Mick struggles with his violent rages, but puts them to good use when his maid's nephew is abducted by child pornographers. However, the case may not be so clear cut, and it is possible that Mick's good intentions are being manipulated for more nefarious ends. The large cast of characters includes a pornographer, two police officers, a bizarre U.S. Federal Bureau of Investigation agent, and an alcoholic computer technician. The title of the story is taken from the Burning Man Festival, where Mick finds himself in pursuit of the kidnappers. Although reviewers praised the protagonist, they also found that the other characters fell somewhat flat. For instance, a *Publishers Weekly* reviewer found that while "the other characters are forgettable," Mick is nevertheless "convincingly righteous, vengeful and wisecracking in this second outing." *Booklist* writer Jenny McLarin also praised the book's protagonist, finding that he is "the type of flawed hero readers—and several of the female characters—love to embrace." A *Kirkus Reviews* contributor was also impressed with the work, noting that "Mick is sensitive, studly, good with his hands and well-armed to boot." *Library Journal* reviewer Rex E. Klett called *Eye of the Burning Man* "a high-energy read."

Mick next appears in *One of the Wicked.* He is still working at the radio station and successfully staying sober. His friend and former military cohort, Bud Stone, owes money to mobster Big Paul Pesci, and he is also concerned about the safety of his ex-girlfriend, Brandi. Mick acts as a bodyguard for her, but things go from bad to worse when Bud robs a drug dealer in a desperate attempt to clear his debt with Pesci. Reviewers noted that *One of the Wicked* is the strongest book thus far in the "Mick Callahan" series. Pitt, again writing in *Booklist,* noted that "with any luck this is still early days for this increasingly addictive series." A *Kirkus Reviews* contributor was also impressed, finding that "in spite of, or maybe because of, some wacky shifts in point of view, the action keeps on coming in Mick's third case." Praising the work in the online *Genre Go Round Reviews,* Harriet Klausner called *One of the Wicked* "an exhilarating tale that grips readers from the moment that Stone visits Mick and never slows down as the hero and his team try to protect Brandi."

BIOGRAPHICAL AND CRITICAL SOURCES:

PERIODICALS

Booklist, May 1, 2004, David Pitt, review of *Memorial Day,* p. 1519; November 1, 2005, Jenny McLarin, review of *Eye of the Burning Man,* p. 29; October 1, 2008, David Pitt, review of *One of the Wicked,* p. 30.
Kirkus Reviews, October 1, 2005, review of *Eye of the Burning Man,* p. 1056; September 15, 2008, review of *One of the Wicked.*
Library Journal, May 1, 2004, Rex E. Klett, review of *Memorial Day,* p. 144; November 1, 2005, Rex E. Klett, review of *Eye of the Burning Man,* p. 56.
Publishers Weekly, April 12, 2004, review of *Memorial Day,* p. 43; October 10, 2005, review of *Eye of the Burning Man,* p. 36.

ONLINE

AllReaders.com, http://www.allreaders.com/ (November 18, 2004), Harriet Klausner, review of *Memorial Day.*
AuthorsDen.com, http://www.authorsden.com/ (November 18, 2004), "Harry Shannon."
Genre Go Round Reviews, http://genregoroundreviews. blogspot.com/ (October 6, 2008), Harriet Klausner, review of *One of the Wicked.*

Harry Shannon Home Page, http://www.harryshannon. com (June 25, 2009).

Harry Shannon MySpace Profile, http://www.myspace. com/harryshannon (June 25, 2009).

Haunted Computer, http://www.hauntedcomputer.com/ (November 18, 2004), Scott Nicholson, "Ghost-writer," author interview.

New Mystery Reader, http://www.newmysteryreader. com/ (November 18, 2004), author interview.

SFFWorld.com, http://www.sffworld.com/ (December 17, 2004), Steve Savile, review of *Night of the Beast.*

*　　*　　*

SHARPE, Jon
See RANDISI, Robert J.

*　　*　　*

SHAW, June

PERSONAL: Married (husband deceased); children: five. *Education:* B.A. *Hobbies and other interests:* Swimming, fishing, dancing, flower gardening.

ADDRESSES: Home—LA.

CAREER: Writer. Former teacher.

MEMBER: Mystery Writers of America, Romance Writers of America, Sisters in Crime.

AWARDS, HONORS: Grants from Louisiana Division of the Arts; David Award for Best Mystery of the Year, Five Star, for *Relative Danger.*

WRITINGS:

NOVELS; EXCEPT WHERE NOTED

Essential Italy (nonfiction), Passport Books (Lincoln-wood, IL), 1998.

Approaching Danger, Romance Foretold, 2001.

Relative Danger (mystery novel), Five Star (Waterville, ME), 2006.

Killer Cousins, Five Star (Waterville, ME), 2009.

Also author of one-act plays produced Off-Off-Broadway. Author of *Attacked,* a screenplay. Contributor to periodicals.

SIDELIGHTS: June Shaw is the author of the mystery novel *Relative Danger,* featuring widowed business owner Cealie Gunther. Shaw, who raised five children, earned a college degree, and became a teacher after her husband passed away, has published a number of short stories, completed a screenplay, and had two plays produced Off-Off-Broadway.

In *Relative Danger,* Cealie arrives in the suburbs of Chicago, Illinois, to visit her granddaughter, Kat, an honor student who is about to graduate from high school. A dark cloud falls over the upcoming ceremony when a school custodian, Mr. Labruzzo, is found dead in the auditorium, having fallen from a balcony. Police soon rule the death a murder, however, and one of Kat's favorite teachers, Miss Hernandez, who has become a mother figure to the motherless girl, becomes the chief suspect. A distraught Kat refuses to go back to class, though it means she will miss final exams and graduation. In an effort to solve the crime and get Kat back in class, Cealie takes a job as a substitute teacher at the school, where she encounters unruly students and eccentric colleagues. Shaw's debut novel received generally strong reviews. "*Relative Danger* has lots going for it: a likeable heroine, a bit of romance and a sense of humor," noted a contributor to the *Cozy Library* Web site. A *Publishers Weekly* critic observed that "humorous dialogue, a suspenseful climax and good character development should please . . . fans."

Cealie is also the protagonist in Shaw's next novel, *Killer Cousins.* Discussing the book in an online *Poe's Deadly Daughters* interview with Lonnie Cruse, Shaw noted that it is dedicated to her mother. Shaw stated that *Killer Cousins* "came out at the end of January, the day before she died, so we were able to read the dedication to her. We were so blessed. She was 102 and still coming to line dance classes with me." Shaw added that "although my main character, Cealie, is nowhere near Mom's age, she has Mom's spunk. Cealie is who I want to be." The author reiterated this exact statement to Jean Henry Mead in an interview for the *Mysterious People* Web site: "Cealie is who I want to be, . . . she will do and say anything without considering the consequences or worrying about what anyone thinks. Lots of readers tell me they want to be Cealie."

As *Killer Cousins* opens, Cealie is happily running her business and finding herself in the wake of her husband's death. She travels to Tennessee to visit her cousin Stevie. When she arrives, she finds a body in Stevie's backyard. Yet more surprises await her, as her once charming and happy cousin is now belligerent and obese. She is also attempting to quit smoking, and the dead man in Stevie's backyard was part of her support group. Cealie begins to investigate and must also deal with pressure from her boyfriend, Gil, who wants her to commit to him. Meanwhile, Gil has just opened a new chain of Cajun restaurants, one of which is in Tennessee. While Cealie and Stevie are eating there, another of Stevie's support group friends dies in front of them. Cealie questions the group leader, who has never been a smoker. Another member of the group, a priest, is also suspicious, as he is known to associate with prostitutes, even bringing them with him to the support group's meetings. According to online *Armchair Interviews* writer Nikki Young, the novel "feels more like chick lit. The mystery is there but it really takes a back seat to the other issues the characters are dealing with. With that said I would still recommend this book." A *Publishers Weekly* reviewer noted that Cealie and Stevie "become more likable as they unite in their fight against smoking and flab," while a *Kirkus Reviews* critic found that "Shaw amplifies Cealie's character" in her second appearance.

Shaw once told *CA:* "I'm thrilled to be included in *Contemporary Authors,* first of all because it affirms that I've fulfilled my childhood dream of becoming an author! I'm also excited because as a student, I often did research for school reports in *Contemporary Authors.*

"My dream started in ninth grade. My English teacher told me to write a paragraph about a splinter to practice writing for an upcoming literary rally. I described a sliver of wood and he said, 'No, like this.' And then he wrote 'Ouch!' He told me to take it from the splinter's point of view. Someone just sat on him. That was it—my inspiration for becoming a writer. Before that I thought all authors were old men who'd died in Europe. I had no idea that a writer could create a thing or person who did and said what the author wanted the character to do.

"I was busy in school and soon afterward, with getting married and having five children close together. My husband died while they were young. Besides the emotional turmoil, I knew I had to earn a living. I wanted to write—but my silly children wanted to wear shoes and eat. I finished college and then taught English to teenagers while I raised my own and sold a few short pieces to periodicals. I've retired now, and my sweet children have given me eight terrific grandkids. And I sold my debut novel!

"I enjoy numerous authors, especially the humor and pace of the 'Stephanie Plum' books by Janet Evanovitch. I feel truly honored to have some readers compare my work to hers.

"I also feel successful because many readers tell me *Relative Danger* made them fear, laugh, and cry. Their feedback makes believe I've done my job of being entertaining. I hope I'll be able to entertain readers for many more years."

BIOGRAPHICAL AND CRITICAL SOURCES:

PERIODICALS

Kirkus Reviews, October 1, 2006, review of *Relative Danger,* p. 993; October 15, 2008, review of *Killer Cousins.*

Publishers Weekly, October 30, 2006, review of *Relative Danger,* p. 41; November 10, 2008, review of *Killer Cousins,* p. 35.

ONLINE

Armchair Interviews, http://reviews.armchairinterviews. com/ (June 25, 2009), Nikki Young, review of *Killer Cousins.*

Cozy Library, http://www.cozylibrary.com/ (September 13, 2006), review of *Relative Danger.*

June Shaw Home Page, http://www.juneshaw.com (June 25, 2009).

Mysterious People, http://mysteriouspeople.blogspot. com/ (April 5, 2009), Jean Henry Mead, author interview.

Poe's Deadly Daughters, http://poesdeadlydaughters. blogspot.com/ (March 20, 2009), Lonnie Cruse, author interview.

Spinetingler, http://www.spinetinglermag.com/ (January 2, 2007), Dawn Dowdle, review of *Relative Danger.**

SINGER, Nathan 1976-
(Nathan Michael Singer)

PERSONAL: Born March 6, 1976, in Cincinnati, OH. *Education:* Northern Kentucky University, B.A., 2000; Antioch University McGregor, M.A., 2002.

ADDRESSES: Home—Cincinnati, OH. *Office*—Raymond Walters College, University of Cincinnati, 9555 Plainfield Rd., Blue Ash, OH 45236-1096. *E-mail*—nathan.singer@uc.edu.

CAREER: Musician, performance artist, and author. University of Cincinnati, Blue Ash, OH, writing instructor; Northern Kentucky University, Highland Heights, former writing instructor.

WRITINGS:

NOVELS

A Prayer for Dawn, Bleak House Books (Madison, WI), 2004.
Chasing the Wolf, Bleak House Books (Madison, WI), 2006.
In the Light of You, Bleak House Books (Madison, WI), 2008.

SIDELIGHTS: Nathan Singer is a multitalented artist who has found success as a university instructor, composer, singer, guitarist, and experimental performance artist. After cold-mailing the manuscript of his novel *A Prayer for Dawn* to numerous publishers, he finally added "published author" to his list of creative accomplishments. *A Prayer for Dawn* follows a group of Cincinnatians—a publicist, a prisoner, an artist, a drug-addicted runaway, and a writer—as their chaotic lives swirl around the central character in the story: an eight-year-old girl. The book was described as "a crackling, darkly comic debut" and "a raging, rollicking ride through the underbelly of American society" by a *Publishers Weekly* reviewer. Brandon Brady, a contributor to *CityBeat,* called the book "a thrash novel that's in-your-face, edgy and fast. Every word, Singer says, is exactly how he wants it: fractured sentences, nonsense verse and all."

Chasing the Wolf was Singer's first novel, but it remained unpublished until 2006. It tells the story of Eli, a New York City artist who suffers a mental breakdown after the death of his wife. He is subsequently transported back sixty years in time to the blues-infused world of Mississippi. Eli's life becomes more complicated by a burgeoning interracial relationship and the appearance of a "time walker" who knows the secret to sending Eli home. A contributor to the *Herald Standard* of Uniontown, Pennsylvania, wrote that the novel has "so many levels of subtle action that you will want to savor each one. . . . *Chasing the Wolf* is a book worth chasing down." A *Publishers Weekly* reviewer also noted how "Singer's freewheeling prose style moves the story at a brisk pace."

Singer's third novel, *In the Light of You,* features Mikal Fanon, a sixteen-year-old loner. He becomes fascinated with the white power movement and finds his niche within their subculture. When Mikal and his family move, his new high school is fraught with racial tension. Without any friends at the school to aid him, Mikal is constantly picked on by a group of African American students. Mikal then meets Richard Lovecraft, a man who heads a neo-Nazi skinhead gang. After Mikal joins the gang, he finally feels the acceptance he's been craving. Before long, he is participating in violent activities, attacking African Americans and homosexuals with his fellow gang members. The gang even begins fighting with another, more violent gang. Several reviewers favored *In the Light of You,* noting that it is an edifying exploration of racist subcultures in the twenty-first-century United States. A *Publishers Weekly* writer noted that "readers will find Mikal's erratic passage through a rough adolescence both vivid and compelling." Joanne Wilkinson wrote in *Booklist* that, in the end, "Singer's percussive prose will have worked its magic" on readers. Wilkinson also called the book a "chilling yet riveting portrait."

BIOGRAPHICAL AND CRITICAL SOURCES:

PERIODICALS

Booklist, May 1, 2008, Joanne Wilkinson, review of *In the Light of You,* p. 71.
Herald Standard (Uniontown, PA), May 15, 2006, review of *Chasing the Wolf.*
Publishers Weekly, May 23, 2005, review of *A Prayer for Dawn,* p. 58; January 9, 2006, review of *Chasing the Wolf,* p. 34; April 14, 2008, review of *In the Light of You,* p. 38.

ONLINE

CityBeat, http://www.citybeat.com/ (July 7, 2004), Brandon Brady, "Dawn Patrol: Cincinnati Novelist Is a Creative Multi-Tasker."

Nathan Singer Home Page, http://www.nathansinger.net (June 23, 2009).*

* * *

SINGER, Nathan Michael
See SINGER, Nathan

* * *

SMITH, Sherwood 1951-
(Nicholas Adams, Jesse Maguire, Robyn Tallis, a house pseudonym)

PERSONAL: Born May 28, 1951, in Glendale, CA. *Education:* University of Southern California, B.A., 1973; University of California, Santa Barbara, M.A., 1977. *Hobbies and other interests:* Music, animals, children, nature, good tea, cozy firesides, stimulating conversation.

ADDRESSES: Agent—Valerie Smith, 1746 Rte. 44-55, Modena, NY 12548. *E-mail*—sherwood-smith@world net.att.net.

CAREER: Writer. Taught elementary and high school for ten years. Has also tutored children with learning disabilities, run online workshops, and evaluated manuscripts for writers.

MEMBER: Science Fiction Writers of America, Mythopoeic Society, RWA, NINC.

AWARDS, HONORS: Best Books for Young Adult Readers citation, New York Public Library, 1993, for *Wren's Quest; Booklist* Editor's Choice, New York Public Library Best Books for Teen Age, and finalist for Mythopoeic Fantasy Award for Children's Literature, all 1995, and Anne Lindbergh Honor Book, 1996, all for *Wren's War;* New York Public Library Best Books for Teen Age for *Crown Duel* and *Court Duel;* Nebula Award finalist, 2001, for "Mom and Dad at the Home Front."

WRITINGS:

FANTASY FOR YOUNG ADULTS

Wren to the Rescue, Harcourt (San Diego, CA), 1990.
Wren's Quest, Harcourt (San Diego, CA), 1993.

Wren's War, Harcourt (San Diego, CA), 1995.
The Borrowers (novelization of the screenplay by Scott and John Kamps), Harcourt (San Diego, CA), 1997.
Crown Duel (also see below), Harcourt (San Diego, CA), 1997.
Court Duel (also see below), Harcourt (San Diego, CA), 1998.
Journey to Otherwhere, Random House (New York, NY), 2000.
A Posse of Princesses, Norilana (Winnetka, CA), 2008.

SARTORIAS-DELES NOVELS

Crown Duel (revised edition of previously published novels *Crown Duel* and *Court Duel*), Firebird (New York, NY), 2002.
Inda (for adults), DAW (New York, NY), 2006.
Senrid, Norilana (Winnetka, CA), 2007.
The Fox (for adults), DAW (New York, NY), 2007.
Over the Sea: CJ's First Notebook, Norilana (Winnetka, CA), 2007.
The King's Shield (for adults), DAW (New York, NY), 2008.
The Trouble with Kings, Samhain (Macon, GA), 2008.
A Stranger to Command, Norilana (Winnetka, CA), 2008.
Mearsies Heili Bounces Back, Norilana (Winnetka, CA), 2008.
Once a Princess, Samhain (Macon, GA), 2009.
Twice a Prince, Samhain (Macon, GA), 2009.
Treason's Shore (for adults), DAW (New York, NY), 2009.

FANTASY FOR YOUNG ADULTS; WITH ANDR&EACUTE; NORTON

Derelict for Trade, Tor (New York, NY), 1997.
A Mind for Trade, Tor (New York, NY), 1999.
Echoes in Time, Tor (New York, NY), 1999.
Atlantis Endgame, Tor (New York, NY), 2000.

"EXORDIUM" SERIES; WITH DAVE TROWBRIDGE

The Phoenix in Flight, Tor (New York, NY), 1993.
Ruler of Naught, Tor (New York, NY), 1993.
A Prison Unsought, Tor (New York, NY), 1994.
The Rifter's Covenant, Tor (New York, NY), 1995.
The Thrones of Kronos, Tor (New York, NY), 1996.

"PLANET BUILDERS" SERIES; UNDER PSEUDONYM ROBYN TALLIS; YOUNG ADULT SCIENCE FICTION

Rebel from Alphorion (book 3), Ivy Books (New York, NY), 1989.

Visions from the Sea (book 4), Ivy Books (New York, NY), 1989.

The Giants of Elenna (book 9), Ivy Books (New York, NY), 1989.

Fire in the Sky (book 10), Ivy Books (New York, NY), 1989.

"NOWHERE HIGH" SERIES; UNDER HOUSE PSEUDONYM JESSE MAGUIRE; YOUNG ADULT

The Beginning (book 1), Ivy Books (New York, NY), 1989.

Crossing Over (book 3), Ivy Books (New York, NY), 1990.

Getting It Right (book 5), Ivy Books (New York, NY), 1991.

Breaking the Rules (book 6), Ivy Books (New York, NY), 1992.

OTHER

(Under pseudonym Nicholas Adams) *Final Curtain: Horror High #8* (for young adults), Harper (New York, NY), 1991.

Gene Roddenberry's Earth: Final Conflict—Augur's Teacher, Tor (New York, NY), 2001.

Gene Roddenberry's Andromeda: Paradise Drift, Tor (New York, NY), 2005.

The Emerald Wand of Oz, HarperCollins (New York, NY), 2005.

Trouble under Oz, HarperCollins (New York, NY), 2006.

Author of short stories collected in anthologies, including "Ghost Dancers" in *Things That Go Bump in the Night,* "Beauty" in *Firebirds,* and "Curing the Bozos" in *Bruce Coville's Book of Aliens.* Smith's works have been translated into Danish.

SIDELIGHTS: Fantasy writer Sherwood Smith became known in the mid-1990s for her strong heroines and girl-oriented adventures. Since then, she has published a number of novels for children, young adults, and adults set in her sweeping Sartorias-Deles setting. Rang-ing from the adventures of girls from different worlds as they secure a kingdom for a child queen, to the epic of a boy who becomes the greatest military strategist in the world's history, the "Sartorias-Deles" tales show "the depths of Smith's world-building," wrote a *Publishers Weekly* critic in a review of *The Fox.* Orson Scott Card, reviewing *Inda* on his blog, felt the novel "seriously threatens to move her into the lofty ranks of 'major writers of fantasy.'" *Voice of Youth Advocates* contributor Lesa M. Holstine, reviewing Smith's earlier novels, felt that the "author is a welcome addition to the fantasy field."

Smith's first series stars a young adventure-craving heroine named Wren, who has a knack for magic. *Wren to the Rescue* introduces the title character, a twelve-year-old orphan whose best friend, Tess, is revealed to be a princess in hiding. Over the course of the book, Wren befriends two stalwart companions: Tyron, a magician's apprentice, and Prince Connor, Tess's cousin. The novel opens in an orphanage, where the two girls live until the day Tess's identity is revealed and she, accompanied by Wren, goes to live in the palace. Soon thereafter, however, Tess is kidnapped by her evil uncle, and Wren, eventually joined by Tyron and Prince Connor, goes in search of her friend. *School Library Journal* contributor Carol A. Edwards praised the fantasy world described in these children's adventures as "solidly constructed and divertingly revealed." Edwards, like some other reviewers, predicted a sequel to *Wren to the Rescue* and expressed the hope that subsequent titles would bring further character development as well as the answer to some of the many questions raised in the first volume. "Young fantasy lovers will enjoy the spunky heroine, the suspenseful plot, and some inventive magic," concluded *Horn Book* critic Ann A. Flowers.

Smith's sequel, *Wren's Quest,* employs many of the same elements reviewers appreciated in *Wren to the Rescue,* including an action-packed plot set in a well-realized fantasy world populated by interesting characters. In this story, Wren seeks clues to the identity of her parents and begins learning more about her magical powers with the help of Tyron, while Princess Tess becomes involved in the mysterious troubles that have been plaguing the palace court. In *Voice of Youth Advocates,* reviewer Lucinda Deatsman noted Smith's effective inclusion of magical elements, including commentary on the ethics of its use, and predicted that young readers would identify with Smith's characters, whom she described as "typical teenagers." Deatsman concluded by suggesting that both *Wren to the Rescue* and *Wren's Quest* would "be popular with students and adults." *Wren's War,* the third volume in the series, begins with the murder of Tess's parents. Tess must take on the role of the ruler of her nation, and she relies on Wren, Tyron, and Connor to keep their enemies at bay. "Readers will enjoy the fast-paced plot, but the novel's greatest strength is the subtle portrayal of its characters," wrote *Booklist* contributor Carolyn Phelan. Peter D. Sieruta, writing for *Horn Book,* complimented Smith's "richly worded descriptions."

Smith's next novels, *Crown Duel* and *Court Duel,* originally appeared in the same setting as the "Wren" books. However, they were intended as a part of the larger setting of the Sartorias-Deles world. In 2002, the books were republished with added scenes in a single volume, *Crown Duel,* and were placed in the Sartorias-Deles setting. The heroine of the novels is Meliara Astair, the young and prickly countess of Tlanth, who is "one tough cookie in a land where women and girls fight, spy, run companies of military guards, and battle with short swords," according to a *Publishers Weekly* reviewer. The story begins with "Mel" and her brother Bran leading a revolution against an unjust ruler. When Mel is captured, she finds herself at the hands of a man she believes to be an enemy, Vidanric, Marquis of Shevraeth, who is leading the corrupt king's forces. But there is more to Shevraeth than meets the eye, and more political maneuverings than Mel and Bran had realized were in the works. Carolyn Phelan noted in *Booklist* that the plot relies "less on magical elements than in the 'Wren' trilogy." As the story continues, Mel navigates the dangers of the royal court, and finds them more treacherous than the battlefield. She is "constantly trying to tell friends from enemies as she endeavors to learn the subtle language of [her] courtiers," Phelan wrote in *Booklist.* Rich Horton reviewed the originally published pair for *SF Site,* writing: "Both these books are, first of all, great reads. . . . They are nice formal contrasts: the first almost all action and war, the second more magic and formal court life."

After a gap in years, Smith's first adult novel in Sartorias-Deles, *Inda,* was published. Inda, who is the second son of a noble family in Marloven Hess, is summoned to military training, which had previously been reserved for the eldest sons, who are responsible for teaching their younger siblings. The heir prince has been unwilling to train his younger brother, however, so Inda and his peers become the first class of second sons to train in the royal capital. There Inda learns that the war games at which he has always excelled do not always follow the rules of honor, and he is betrayed, then exiled, forced to live away from his homeland. Orson Scott Card, writing in his blog, commented on the depths of Smith's characters. "What makes the characters complex is that Sherwood Smith is not content to have good guys and bad guys," he wrote. "Indeed, just when we think it's safe to hate somebody, she throws us a curve and makes the bad guy's motives complicated and at least somewhat understandable." Roxy of *Book Spot* felt that *Inda* was "written in both broad sweeps of the pen and behind-the-scene details, bringing this world into three dimensional relief."

The Fox picks up where *Inda* left off: Inda and his friends in exile have been captured by pirates and must find a way to escape. He discovers two other Marlovens among the crew, Barend, the prince's cousin, and Fox, scion of an exiled noble house. The three plot together to overthrow the pirate who has captured them, and after taking his ship, they turn their attentions to hunting the pirates that still plague the coasts. Their actions earn them the attention of some very powerful potential allies, including a mage who warns them of a great threat against Marloven Hess from the dark land of Norsunder. "*The Fox,* second in a brilliant, multi-layered series, is filled with thrilling action on land and at sea, captures and escapes, betrayals and treachery, and even some romance for its beleaguered leads," wrote Hilary Williamson in her *BookLoons* review. Orson Scott Card, reviewing the novel on his blog, wrote: "The achievement of this writer is only getting more remarkable. . . . Smith handles the relationships and machinations among [nations] so deftly that you don't realize you're being given a course in politics." Inda's story continues in *The King's Shield* and *Treason's Shore.*

The young adult novel *Senrid* features the same nation that is the setting for the "Inda" books, but takes place many years later, when the boy king Senrid of Marloven Hess seeks to conquer an adjoining kingdom in order to wrest control of his nation from his uncle. Bridging the story between *Senrid* and *Crown Duel, A Stranger to Command* is the story of Vidanric of Shevraeth's training at the court of Marloven Hess. Sent away from home secretly to avoid alerting the king to Shevraeth's true intentions, Shevraeth studies the art of war so that one day, he and his family can challenge the corrupt king. But Marloven Hess is not itself at peace; the young ruler Senrid knows that the land of Norsunder threatens his kingdom with powerful, dark magic. *BookLoons* critic Hilary Williamson called *A Stranger to*

Command "an engaging prequel to Sherwood Smith's excellent and fast-paced *Crown Duel*."

Smith has also continued to write in Wren's world. *A Posse of Princesses* is the story of teenage Princess Rhis, who, along with the other young princes and princesses in her part of the world, is invited to the coming-of-age celebration for the Crown Prince Lios. When one of the other princesses is kidnapped, Rhis is determined to bring her back, and several of the other princesses join her. Along the way, Rhis discovers that she is attracted not to a prince, but to Lios's scribe. "Smith's humorous narrative, colorful descriptions of palace life, and fully realized characters will appeal to romance and fantasy buffs alike," wrote *School Library Journal* contributor Leah J. Sparks.

Along with her independent novels, Smith has also teamed up with other authors and contributed to ongoing series based on television shows. With André Norton, she wrote the "Solar Queen" and "Time Traders" novels, continuations of a series of books that stretch back to the 1950s. One entry, *A Mind for Trade*, was hailed by a *Publishers Weekly* reviewer as a worthy successor to the classic older tales, with the two authors merging "their styles seamlessly." Smith contributed two novels as tie-ins to television series created by Gene Roddenberry. In *Gene Roddenberry's Andromeda: Paradise Drift*, a *Kirkus Reviews* contributor felt that "one can practically hear Kevin Sorbo's voice when reading Hunt's dialogue." Smith has also written two novels continuing L. Frank Baum's "Oz" series. Elizabeth Bird of *School Library Journal*, in a review of *Trouble under Oz*, wrote: "The book's tone and content are faithful to L. Frank Baum's vision."

BIOGRAPHICAL AND CRITICAL SOURCES:

PERIODICALS

Analog Science Fiction & Fact, April, 2000, Tom Easton, review of *Echoes in Time*, p. 135.

Booklist, March 1, 1995, Carolyn Phelan, review of *Wren's War*, p. 1241; February 1, 1997, Roland Green, review of *Derelict for Trade*, p. 929; April 15, 1997, Carolyn Phelan, review of *Crown Duel*, p. 1430; October 1, 1997, Roland Green, review of *A Mind for Trade*, p. 312; March 1, 1998, Carolyn Phelan, review of *Court Duel*, p. 136; November 15, 1999, Roland Green, review of *Echoes in Time*,

p. 609; September 15, 2001, Regina Schroeder, review of *Gene Roddenberry's Earth: Final Conflict—Augur's Teacher*, p. 201; December 15, 2002, Roland Green, review of *Atlantis Endgame*, p. 740; November 15, 2005, review of *Gene Roddenberry's Andromeda: Paradise Drift*, p. 34.

Horn Book, March-April, 1991, Ann A. Flowers, review of *Wren to the Rescue*, p. 202; May-June, 1993, review of *Wren's Quest*, p. 348; September-October, 1995, review of *Wren's War*, p. 627.

Kirkus Reviews, August 1, 1990, review of *Wren to the Rescue*, p. 1092; November 15, 2002, review of *Atlantis Endgame*, p. 1664; September 15, 2005, review of *Gene Roddenberry's Andromeda*, p. 1006.

Library Journal, December, 1996, Susan Hamburger, review of *Derelict for Trade*, p. 152; October 15, 1997, Susan Hamburger, review of *A Mind for Trade*, p. 98; December, 1999, Jackie Cassada, review of *Echoes in Time*, p. 193; January, 2003, Jackie Cassada, review of *Atlantis Endgame*, p. 165.

New York Review of Science Fiction, February, 2002, review of *Gene Roddenberry's Earth*.

Publishers Weekly, January 27, 1997, review of *Derelict for Trade*, p. 82; March 10, 1997, review of *Crown Duel*, p. 67; September 29, 1997, review of *A Mind for Trade*, p. 71; October 25, 1999, review of *Echoes in Time*, p. 56; October 8, 2001, review of *Gene Roddenberry's Earth*, p. 49; December 2, 2002, review of *Atlantis Endgame*, p. 38; July 16, 2007, review of *The Fox*, p. 151.

School Library Journal, November, 1990, Carol A. Edwards, review of *Wren to the Rescue*, p. 140; June, 1993, Patricia A. Dollisch, review of *Wren's Quest*, pp. 110, 112; August, 1997, Patricia Lothrop-Green, review of *Crown Duel*, p. 158; April, 1998, Eva Mitnick, review of *Court Duel*, p. 138; December, 2006, Elizabeth Bird, review of *Trouble under Oz*, p. 155; April, 2008, Leah J. Sparks, review of *A Posse of Princesses*, p. 148.

Voice of Youth Advocates, December, 1990, Lesa M. Holstine, review of *Wren to the Rescue*, p. 302; June, 1993, Lucinda Deatsman, review of *Wren's Quest*, p. 105; April, 1996, review of *Wren's War*, p. 23.

ONLINE

BookLoons, http://www.bookloons.com/ (March 2, 2009), Hilary Williamson, reviews of *A Stranger to Command* and *The Fox*.

Book Spot, http://www.bookspotcentral.com/ (November 13, 2007), Roxy, review of *Inda.*

Good Reads, http://www.goodreads.com/ (March 2, 2009), profile of Smith.

Internet Speculative Fiction Database, http://www.isfdb.org/ (March 6, 2009), profile of Smith.

Orson Scott Card's Home Page, http://www.hatrack.com/ (March 2, 2009), Orson Scott Card, reviews of *Inda* and *The Fox.*

SF Site, http://www.sfsite.com/ (March 2, 2009), Rich Horton, review of *Crown Duel* and *Court Duel*; George T. Dodd, review of *A Posse of Princesses.*

Sherwood Smith's Home Page, http://www.sherwoodsmith.net (March 6, 2009).

*   *   *

SOULJAH, Sister 1963-
(Lisa Williamson)

PERSONAL: Born July 25, 1963, in Bronx, NY; married; children: one son. *Education:* Graduated from Rutgers University; attended Cornell University and the University of Salamanca.

ADDRESSES: Agent—Vernon J. Brown, V. Brown and Co., Inc., 10 Bank St., 8th Fl., White Plains, NY 10606. *E-mail*—souljahbiz@gmail.com.

CAREER: Community activist, singer, and writer. Affiliated with Commission for Racial Justice, United Church of Christ; African Youth Survival Camp, Enfield, NC (summer camp for homeless children), founder; member of rap group Public Enemy; released solo album, *360 Degrees of Power,* Epic Records, 1992; featured in the films *The Hate That Hate Produced,* directed by Lionel C. Martin, 1991, and *Lauren Hutton and . . . Sister Souljah,* directed by Luca Babini, 1995; Daddy's House Social Programs, Bad Boy Entertainment, executive director, 1995-2007.

WRITINGS:

No Disrespect (autobiography), Times Books (New York, NY), 1994.

The Coldest Winter Ever (novel), Pocket Books (New York, NY), 1999.

Midnight: A Gangster Love Story, Atria (New York, NY), 2008.

SIDELIGHTS: Community activist, rap singer, and outspoken public figure Sister Souljah wrote her autobiography, *No Disrespect,* to credit the people who had influenced her life and career, and to provide guidance to other African Americans growing up in similarly disadvantaged circumstances. The book, published in 1994, also attempts to shed light on relationships between African American men and women, offering both critiques and suggestions for improvement.

Souljah, born Lisa Williamson, grew up in public housing projects and witnessed first-hand the effects that economic hardship and subtle discrimination had on her urban community. In *No Disrespect,* she writes of the unstable family life she experienced, and of her own determination to escape those circumstances. Souljah's mother encouraged her to read as a child, and her studiousness as a teen earned her scholarships that led to a university education. In her book, she discusses the environmental roadblocks that confront young African American women.

After beginning her college career at Cornell University, Souljah transferred to New Jersey's Rutgers University to study history. During these years, she became a student activist. As she related to Kim Neely in *Rolling Stone,* Souljah made an important discovery while marching with other students through the predominantly African American city of Newark as part of an anti-apartheid demonstration. Observing the poverty in the community around her, Souljah realized: "These people can't free South Africa—they haven't even freed themselves!"

As she recalls in *No Disrespect,* Souljah's activism soon became more focused on concerns closer to home. She founded the African Youth Survival Camp, a retreat for homeless youngsters in North Carolina. Proceeds from a series of rap concerts provided money for the camp. Souljah also worked for the United Church of Christ's Commission for Racial Justice, a civil-rights organization run by Benjamin Chavis, future leader of the National Association for the Advancement of Colored People. Souljah's book chronicles how this community activism, combined with musical leanings, attracted the attention of the rap group Public Enemy, one of the most outspoken acts of the genre.

Souljah's work with Public Enemy eventually led to her own recording contract and 1992's *360 Degrees of Power,* a solo effort whose message *Rolling Stone* writer

Neely described as "a call for black unity and empowerment, stressing education and economic self-sufficiency." Although Souljah discusses little of the album in her book, much of the same message unites the themes of *No Disrespect.* By this time in the author's life her increasing public presence—and outspokenness—was drawing some criticism, especially in the aftermath of the 1992 Los Angeles riots—riots that followed the acquittal of the white police officers who had beaten African American Rodney King. In the wake of these polarizing events, Souljah's sometimes inflammatory comments on race relations in the United States were often taken at face value and out of context by the media.

Souljah's pronouncements attracted the ire of then-President George Bush and Presidential hopeful Bill Clinton, who roundly denounced them. Though she includes little of this controversy in *No Disrespect,* her autobiography does include frank views on the virulent interracial disunity in America, and she offers her opinion on why this situation has deteriorated in the 1990s. A reliance on welfare, as well as the long after-effects of slavery, are some of the themes of the activist's platform. Souljah concludes *No Disrespect* with a chapter titled "Listen Up! (Straighten It Out)," in which she offers a series of guidelines for the betterment of the African American community. "Remember: No one will save us but ourselves," she writes. *Los Angeles Times Book Review* writer Heidi Siegmund called Souljah's autobiography "a queer duck. The book isn't filled with the revolutionary musings one might have expected. . . . Rather, it aims to be a discourse on troubled relations between black men and women in America. Unfortunately, Souljah keeps getting sidetracked by ego-gratifying tangents."

Five years after the release of her autobiography, Souljah published her first novel, *The Coldest Winter Ever.* The book portrays young Winter, the spoiled daughter of Brooklyn gang leader Santiaga. However, when Winter's father falls from power, she must adjust to her family's suddenly reduced circumstances. Souljah appears as a character in her story, one who works as a community activist. In the book, Winter and her family learn from Souljah's example. Although several reviewers felt the book was not well-written, they applauded the plot and its message. According to Sean Elder, writing on *Salon.com,* "most of the characters are one dimensional, and the occasional bits of speechifying, while impassioned, complement this crime novel about as well as spinach goes with cherry pie." Yet, he went

on to note that Winter is "a deadpan narrator in the Huck Finn mode," adding that "even in the best-intentioned work, wit plays better than wisdom." *Celebrity Cafe* contributor Stephanie DeLuca was far more impressed, declaring: "I love how the author accurately describes the ghetto culture and even includes herself as one of the characters to teach Winter a lesson." *Black Issues Book Review* writer Arin M. Lawrence remarked that "often noted as the spark that set the fire, *The Coldest Winter Ever* can easily be classified as consummate 'Mother' of the genre now known as 'urban-lit.'" Indeed, "when it was first published, the story opened the door to a very well-known world that few had the gall or desire to write about," Lawrence observed. However, *Booklist* reviewer Lillian Lewis was ambivalent in her assessment. Readers "will find the language real and raw, yet the story could have been told with less obscenities and vulgarity," she found. A *Publishers Weekly* critic held a similar, but more positive, opinion: "Souljah peppers her raunchy and potentially offensive prose with epithets and street lingo, investing her narrative with honesty albeit often at the expense of disciplined writing." Nancy Pearl, writing in *Library Journal,* found that "the trials and tribulations of young Winter Santiaga are described in gritty detail"

Nearly ten years after writing *The Coldest Winter Ever,* Souljah wrote her second novel, *Midnight: A Gangster Love Story.* The book is actually a prequel to *The Coldest Winter Ever.* It, too, is a coming-of-age novel, following seven-year-old Midnight and his mother, Umma, who is pregnant. The family was exiled from Sudan, where they lived in the upper class, but they now live hand-to-mouth in Brooklyn. The story follows Midnight as he grows up there. Eventually, he falls in love, and he must navigate his increasingly complicated life. According to an *Azizi Books* reviewer, "while *Midnight* overall is a good read, Urban fiction fans, who have waited so long for more insight into Winter's story, may be ultimately let down." However, *Fresh Fiction* contributor Patricia Woodside declared: "I don't know whether I've ever read a more poignant coming of age or more tender urban love story." A *Kirkus Reviews* contributor noted that "in spite of its interesting point of view, [the novel] reads more like a setup for future volumes than a freestanding cohesive story." A *Publishers Weekly* critic was more impressed, finding that "Souljah has obvious talent and sincere motives, making her a street-lit sophomore worth watching." More praise was proffered by Vanessa Bush in *Booklist,* who stated that "master storyteller Souljah offers biting social critique on contemporary urban culture tucked inside a love story."

BIOGRAPHICAL AND CRITICAL SOURCES:

BOOKS

Souljah, Sister, *No Disrespect,* Times Books (New York, NY), 1994.

PERIODICALS

Black Issues Book Review, March 1, 2005, Arin M. Lawrence, "After a Season: The Book Credited with Igniting the Urban Genre, Sister Souljah's the Coldest Winter Ever, Is Back in a Collector's Edition."

Booklist, February 15, 1999, Lillian Lewis, review of *The Coldest Winter Ever,* p. 1043; October 1, 2008, Vanessa Bush, review of *Midnight: A Gangster Love Story,* p. 24.

Essence, November 1, 2008, "In the Midnight Hour: Nine Years after the Release of the Coldest Winter Ever, Sister Souljah Returns to Bookstores with a Bang," p. 79.

Kirkus Reviews, September 15, 2008, review of *Midnight.*

Library Journal, April 15, 1999, Nancy Pearl, review of *The Coldest Winter Ever,* p. 146.

Los Angeles Times Book Review, March 19, 1995, Heidi Siegmund, review of *No Disrespect,* p. 10.

Publishers Weekly, December 5, 1994, review of *No Disrespect,* p. 60; February 22, 1999, review of *The Coldest Winter Ever,* p. 63; August 25, 2008, review of *Midnight,* p. 52.

Rolling Stone, August 6, 1992, Kim Neely, author profile and interview, p. 15.

ONLINE

Azizi Books, http://azizibooks.blogspot.com/ (June 24, 2009), review of *Midnight.*

Celebrity Cafe, http://thecelebritycafe.com/ (June 24, 2009), Stephanie DeLuca, review of *The Coldest Winter Ever.*

Fresh Fiction, http://freshfiction.com/ (June 24, 2009), Patricia Woodside, review of *Midnight.*

Salon.com, http://www.salon.com/ (June 24, 2009), Sean Elder, review of *The Coldest Winter Ever.*

Sister Souljah Home Page, http://www.sistersouljah.com (June 23, 2009).*

SQUIRE, Susan 1950-

PERSONAL: Born October 17, 1950, in Stamford, CT; married David Hirshey (a publishing executive); children: Emily Hirshey. *Education:* Pomona College, B.A., 1972.

ADDRESSES: Home—New York, NY. *Agent*—Kris Dahl, International Creative Management, 825 8th Ave., 26th Fl., New York, NY 10019. *E-mail*—winphobe@gmail.com.

CAREER: Los Angeles Herald Examiner, Los Angeles, CA, lifestyle editor, 1976-77; *Los Angeles* magazine, Los Angeles, articles editor, 1977-83, special features editor, 1983—.

WRITINGS:

NONFICTION

The Slender Balance: Causes and Cures for Bulimia, Anorexia, and the Weight-loss/Weight-gain Seesaw, Putnam (New York, NY), 1983.

(Editor and contributor) Henri Gault and Christian Millau, *The Best of Los Angeles,* Crown (New York, NY), 1984.

For Better, for Worse: A Candid Chronicle of Five Couples Adjusting to Parenthood, Doubleday (New York, NY), 1993.

I Don't: A Contrarian History of Marriage, Bloomsbury USA (New York, NY), 2008.

Contributor to books, including *The Bitch in the House: 26 Women Tell the Truth about Sex, Solitude, Work, Motherhood, and Marriage,* edited by Cathi Hanauer, William Morrow, 2002.

Contributor to magazines, including *Redbook, Glamour, Travel and Leisure, New York Times* magazine, *Conde Nast Traveler, Washington Post, GQ, Elle,* and *Harpers Bazaar.*

SIDELIGHTS: Susan Squire is a journalist and the author of several nonfiction books. Describing her decision to become a career writer, she told *CA:* "Accident prompted me to become a journalist. I thought I would go to graduate school in English literature and become a college professor, but I decided to take some time off from school when I earned my undergraduate degree. I got a job as an editorial assistant at a magazine in Los Angeles and found the professional world of publishing and the internal world of writing to be more interesting than academics."

Squire's first book, *The Slender Balance: Causes and Cures for Bulimia, Anorexia, and the Weight-loss/ Weight-gain Seesaw,* was published in 1983. Regarding her book, she told *CA:* "*The Slender Balance* is a nonfiction study of food addiction in America affecting men, women, and adolescents. It addresses a secret population of basically normal-weight, normally functioning citizens who use food, as others might use alcohol or drugs or poker games, to avoid dealing with their emotional needs and voids. The book was developed from two magazine pieces I wrote for *Glamour,* which were in turn based on diaries I kept during my own struggles with food addiction as a 105-pound perfectionist college student years ago. The subject of food addiction and the underlying psychological issues allowed me to spend a year writing about human behavior and the forces that drive it, which I find endlessly fascinating."

Squire has contributed articles to a number of magazines, including *Redbook, Glamour, Travel and Leisure, New York Times* magazine, *Cuisine,* and *National Wildlife.* She was a contributing editor for *The Best of Los Angeles,* a 1984 guidebook in the travel series edited by Henri Gault and Christian Millau. In 1993 she published her second book, *For Better, for Worse: A Candid Chronicle of Five Couples Adjusting to Parenthood.*

In 2008 Squire returned to the topic of marriage with *I Don't: A Contrarian History of Marriage.* Discussing the history of marriage and its possible future in a *Salon. com* interview with Katharine Mieszkowski, Squire remarked: "Progress is not linear. Changes in the idea of marriage have come up, and then been pushed back, because [change] is too threatening. It's very threatening even if it seems promising." Regarding the cyclical nature of changing views toward marriage, the author added: "If anything is going to shock us, it might be that in 200 years, we'll be looking at traditional marriage again, where women just kind of go back into their maternal roles, and men lead the public lives, because maybe the family operates better that way. Maybe it helps to have a chief. I mean, I would hate it, but I would say that's more likely than some radical change." Yet Squire also acknowledged the possibility

that "maybe we'll just keep lurching forward into this brave new world of equal partnership, and it will become old hat for a woman to be president."

Squire pointed out in a *Huffington Post Online* interview with Cynthia Kling that the idea of love being an aspect of marriage is itself a relatively new concept. Although the institution of marriage has existed for several millennia, the view that love and marriage are inextricably bound did not emerge until the sixteenth century. She told Kling that "the Greeks considered heterosexual love, inside or outside marriage, as demeaning to men; the Christian church said that men who 'loved' (read: desired) their wives too much were no better than adulterers; the medieval aristocracy's code of courtly love was all about adultery. Martin Luther placed love high on the marital-priority list, a refreshing change— but in his vision, married love was something that developed over time and was rooted in mutual affection and respect." Due to thought-provoking revelations like these, reviewers praised *I Don't.* In the *New York Times Book Review,* Dahlia Lithwick called the volume "a charming book and a wonderful resource."

BIOGRAPHICAL AND CRITICAL SOURCES:

PERIODICALS

Kirkus Reviews, June 15, 2008, review of *I Don't: A Contrarian History of Marriage.*

New York Times Book Review, September 7, 2008, Dahlia Lithwick, "I Now Pronounce You Totally Confused," p. 19.

O, August, 2008, "The True History of Marriage," review of *I Don't.*

People Weekly, May 10, 1993, Lisa Shea, review of *For Better, for Worse: A Candid Chronicle of Five Couples Adjusting to Parenthood,* p. 29.

Publishers Weekly, March 1, 1993, review of *For Better, for Worse,* p. 47; June 23, 2008, review of *I Don't,* p. 50.

ONLINE

Huffington Post Online, http://www.huffingtonpost.com/ (August 5, 2008), Cynthia Kling, author interview.

Salon.com, http://www.salon.com/ (August 9, 2008), Katharine Mieszkowski, author interview.

Susan Squire Home Page, http://www.susansquire.net (June 23, 2009).

Zulkey: A Web Site, http://www.zulkey.net/ (September 11, 2008), "The Susan Squire Interview."

T

TALLIS, Robyn
See SMITH, Sherwood

*   *   *

TAPPLY, William G. 1940-
(William George Tapply)

PERSONAL: Born July 16, 1940, in Waltham, MA; son of H.G. (a writer) and Muriel (a registered nurse) Tapply; married Alice Sandra Knight, 1962 (divorced, 1966); married Cynthia Ehrgott (a secretary), March 7, 1970 (divorced, 1995); married Vicki Stiefel, May 7, 2004; children: Michael, Melissa, Sarah, Blake, Ben. *Ethnicity:* "Caucasian." *Education:* Amherst College, B.A., 1962; Harvard University, M.A.T., 1963; Tufts University, postgraduate study, 1966-68.

ADDRESSES: Home—Hancock, NH. *Agent*—Fred Morris, The Jed Mattes Agency, 2095 Broadway, Ste. 302, New York, NY 10023.

CAREER: Lexington High School, Lexington, MA, history teacher, 1963-66; Tufts University, Medford, MA, director of economic studies, 1968-69; Lexington High School, housemaster and teacher, 1972-90; Writer's Digest School, editorial associate, 1992—; Clark University, Worcester, MA, and Emerson College, Boston, MA, writing instructor, 1995-2003; Clark University, writer-in-residence, 1995—; *The Writer,* editorial board, 2006—. Cofounder of The Writers Studio at Chickadee Farm, Hanover, NH.

MEMBER: Mystery Writers of America, Authors Guild, Authors League of America, Private Eye Writers of America.

AWARDS, HONORS: Scribner Crime Novel award, 1984, for *Death at Charity's Point.*

WRITINGS:

"*BRADY COYNE*" *MYSTERY SERIES*

Death at Charity's Point, Scribner (New York, NY), 1984.
The Dutch Blue Error, Scribner (New York, NY), 1985.
Follow the Sharks, Scribner (New York, NY), 1985.
The Marine Corpse, Scribner (New York, NY), 1986.
Dead Meat, Scribner (New York, NY), 1987.
The Vulgar Boatman, Scribner (New York, NY), 1987.
A Void in Hearts, Scribner (New York, NY), 1988.
Dead Winter, Delacorte (New York, NY), 1989.
Client Privilege, Delacorte (New York, NY), 1989.
The Spotted Cats, Delacorte (New York, NY), 1991.
Tight Lines, Delacorte (New York, NY), 1992.
The Snake Eater, Otto Penzler (New York, NY), 1993.
The Seventh Enemy, Otto Penzler (New York, NY), 1995.
Close to the Bone, St. Martin's Press (New York, NY), 1996.
Cutter's Run, St. Martin's Press (New York, NY), 1998.
Muscle Memory, St. Martin's Press (New York, NY), 1999.
Scar Tissue, St. Martin's Press (New York, NY), 2000.
A Brady Coyne Omnibus, St. Martin's Press (New York, NY), 2000.
Past Tense, St. Martin's Press (New York, NY), 2001.
(With Philip R. Craig) *First Light,* St. Martin's Press (New York, NY), 2001.
A Fine Line, St. Martin's Press (New York, NY), 2002.

Shadow of Death, St. Martin's Press (New York, NY), 2003.

(With Philip R. Craig) *Second Sight,* Scribner (New York, NY), 2005.

Nervous Water, St. Martin's Minotaur (New York, NY), 2005.

Out Cold, St. Martin's Minotaur (New York, NY), 2006.

(With Philip R. Craig) *Third Strike,* Scribner (New York, NY), 2007.

One-way Ticket, St. Martin's Minotaur (New York, NY), 2007.

Hell Bent, St. Martin's Minotaur (New York, NY), 2008.

Dark Tiger, St. Martin's Minotaur (New York, NY), 2009.

OTHER FICTION

(With Linda Barlow) *Thicker Than Water* (suspense novel), Signet (New York, NY), 1995.

Bitch Creek ("Stoney Calhoun" mystery series), Lyons Press (Guilford, CT), 2004.

Gray Ghost ("Stoney Calhoun" mystery series), St. Martin's Minotaur (New York, NY), 2007.

NONFICTION

Those Hours Spent Outdoors, Scribner (New York, NY), 1988.

Opening Day and Other Neuroses, Lyons & Burford (New York, NY), 1990.

Home Water Near and Far, Lyons & Burford (New York, NY), 1992.

Sportsman's Legacy, Lyons & Burford (New York, NY), 1993.

The Elements of Mystery Fiction, Writer, Inc. (Boston, MA), 1995.

A Fly-fishing Life, Lyons & Burford (New York, NY), 1997.

Bass Bug Fishing, Lyons Press (New York, NY), 1999.

Upland Days, Lyons Press (New York, NY), 2000.

Pocket Water: Favorite Streams, Favorite Fish, Lyons Press (New York, NY), 2001.

The Orvis Pocket Guide to Fly Fishing for Bass, Lyons Press (Guilford, CT), 2002.

Gone Fishin': Ruminations on Fly Fishing, Lyons Press (Guilford, CT), 2004.

Trout Eyes, Skyhorse Publishers (New York, NY), 2007.

Contributor to periodicals, including *Sports Illustrated, Better Homes and Gardens, Organic Gardening, Scholastic Coach, Drummer, Writer, Fins and Feathers, Worcester,* and *Outdoor Life;* contributing editor to *Field and Stream* and *Upland Journal;* special correspondent, *American Angler.*

SIDELIGHTS: William G. Tapply is the author of a number of mystery novels featuring Brady Coyne, a Boston attorney serving a wealthy clientele. In an essay for the *St. James Guide to Crime and Mystery Writers,* Jim Huang called Coyne "a skillful blend of amateur versus professional, serious versus frivolous, and intellectual versus physical." Coyne selects interesting clients to make his otherwise boring legal practice bearable. He also sees his career as a means to finance his avocation, fishing, which is Tapply's own great love and the subject of several of the author's nonfiction works.

Over the course of the series, Coyne has dealt with a variety of cases. A murder takes place on what is believed to be sacred Native American land in *Dead Meat;* an author dies under mysterious circumstances in *The Marine Corpse;* a Vietnam veteran's memoirs cause trouble for many people in *The Snake Eater;* and the controversy over gun control is a key plot element in *The Seventh Enemy.* The "Brady Coyne" series has won Tapply plaudits for his narrative skills. Lauding Tapply for writing "quietly and perceptively" in *Death at Charity's Point,* the story of Coyne's investigation of an apparent suicide, London *Times* contributor Marcel Berlins declared the book a "superior" thriller. Marilyn Stasio, critiquing *The Seventh Enemy* for the *New York Times Book Review,* called Tapply "a smooth stylist;" in a review of *The Snake Eater* for the same publication, she noted that "there's never a break in that practiced, flowing style he has mastered over a dozen books." Huang asserted that "Tapply is among the smoothest storytellers around—his books glide along quickly and effortlessly—but the plots tend towards the straightforward and they're not necessarily fair. He will introduce new elements in the closing chapters in order to facilitate a resolution. . . . But only rarely do Tapply's stories really disappoint."

While praising the author's portrayal of Coyne's eccentric clients, Huang commented: "If Tapply has a significant flaw, it's in Brady Coyne's peculiar reticence about his own life and feelings. . . . The adventures leave no mark on Coyne." For instance, Huang observed, Coyne remains unperturbed after being nearly blown to bits in *Dead Meat,* and he is largely unaffected by pleas to help the homeless in *The Marine Corpse.* Stasio found *The Snake Eater* to be an exception to Coyne's usual stoicism. "Tapply wrings some rare passion from Brady Coyne," she remarked, adding: "This time his theme of friendship has jagged edges of anger and pain that cut through Coyne's reserve and draw blood." Huang granted that the character's customary restraint has its uses in the series: "Brady Coyne's wry, good-humored narration reminds us not to take it all too seriously." Tapply explained to Peter Cannon in *Publishers Weekly* that "Brady is a Yankee, and I suppose we Yankees tend to be reticent about our feelings. Books I read where the first-person narrators are terribly forthcoming about their feelings don't ring true to me. My writing philosophy is show don't tell."

Tapply's approach has clearly worked for the "Brady Coyne" series, and the author continues to add installments. In *A Fine Line* Coyne takes a packet of rare letters to a book dealer for authentication on behalf of his friend, Walt Duffy, a nature photographer who has been paralyzed in a recent accident. When Duffy is killed during yet another accident, and his son Ethan goes missing, Coyne finds himself in the midst of a murder investigation. A reviewer for *Publishers Weekly* remarked that "the low-key, fly-fishing Boston lawyer with an overly developed need for self-reliance has never been in better form." *Nervous Water* sees Coyne involved in a family mystery, when his Uncle Moze seeks his help in locating his missing daughter, Cassie. Bill Ott, writing for *Booklist,* called this novel "another winner in an always-satisfying series." In a review for *Publishers Weekly,* a contributor felt that the "series remains fresh and Tapply underrated as one of today's finest regional mystery writers."

In *First Light* Tapply teams up his hero with mystery writer Philip R. Craig's character J.W. Jackson. Jackson is an ex-cop who lives in Martha's Vineyard with his wife and two small children. In alternating chapters told from the viewpoints of their respective characters, Tapply and Craig weave a story involving two missing women, clashes between real estate developers and environmentalists, and unexpected violence. A reviewer for *Publishers Weekly* called *First Light* an "ultimately satisfying crime drama" that offers "an intriguing and evocative picture of this high-profile vacation spot." *Library Journal* critic Rex Klett described *First Light* as "a most captivating read."

The success of *First Light* led Tapply and Craig to continue the association of their characters in other col-

laborations. In the follow up *Second Sight,* Brady Coyne tracks a runaway to Martha's Vineyard, where Jackson is currently a chauffeur and head of security for a famous singer. When the singer's bodyguard is killed, both Coyne and Jackson find their investigations leading them to a local spiritual retreat that has cultish overtones. A reviewer for *Publishers Weekly* remarked that, while "the plot is a bit far-fetched, with most of the page-turning action bottlenecked at the end," fans of both writers were likely to enjoy the mystery. Wes Lukowsky, in a review for *Booklist,* commented: "Collaborations . . . are often awkward, but this one . . . is an entertaining exception."

The final book by Tapply and Craig, *Third Strike,* finds Coyne responding to a plea from a client who lives on the Vineyard, and who fears for his safety after seeing armed men loading what appeared to be suspicious cargo onto a boat. Because a strike of ferryboat operators is in progress, Coyne calls on Jackson to help him reach the island.

Jackson is involved in the case of a striking worker's death as the result of an explosion on one of the ferries. The protagonists who, like their creators, enjoy a special friendship, work individually and together as the strike, and a murder, cause tensions to grow. A *Publishers Weekly* contributor concluded that his final volume "marks the highly enjoyable and poignant end to a short, sweet series." Craig died shortly after the publication of this book. Lukowsky called the collaboration "a fine partnership."

In 2004, Tapply began a new mystery series set in rural Maine. It features Stoney Calhoun, who lost his memory in a lightning strike five years prior to his introduction in the first volume of the series, *Bitch Creek.* After recovering from his accident, Stoney moved to Maine with his insurance money and began working at Kate Balaban's bait and tackle shop. It is while attending his duties at the shop one day that he encourages local college student Lyle McMaban to act as guide for a customer who is planning a wilderness trip. When Stoney later finds Lyle's body, guilt sets him off on the trail of the customer whom he assumes to be the killer. In a review for *Publishers Weekly,* one contributor believed that "a far-fetched and excessively violent resolution spoils the rustic mood" of the descriptions of rural Maine. Again reviewing for *Booklist,* Lukowsky found that Tapply's effort "mixes crisp plotting and character development with a subtle sense of time and place."

Tapply continues the Stoney Calhoun series with *Gray Ghost*. In this volume readers continue to receive clues to Stoney's past life as he learns that he has mysterious abilities that seem to manifest themselves as he assists the local sheriff in yet another murder investigation. Serving as guide for historian Paul Vecchio, Stoney comes across another dead body, one that has obviously been tortured and then set on fire. Although Stoney is reluctant to play detective again, a series of events, including the shooting of Vecchio as he sits on Stoney's porch, push him into helping with the case. Lukowsky wrote that the author "presents a complex plot with wonderful characters while teasing readers with small hints about his protagonist's murky past."

Next in the series featuring Brady Coyne is *Out Cold*, in which the attorney finds the body of a teenage girl in the snow in the yard of his Beacon Hill home. The girl, who had Coyne's address in her pocket, died of blood loss and hypothermia. Coyne attempts to learn her identity from teens who live on the streets of Boston, and some of these are then also found dead. Someone is attempting to block Coyne's investigation, which leads him to a scientist living in a secluded New Hampshire farmhouse. A *Publishers Weekly* contributor commented: "Longtime series fans will be most rewarded."

In *One-way Ticket*, Coyne is contacted by Robert Lancaster, son of his friend Dalton, a Boston restaurateur who was once gripped by a gambling addiction. Dalton has been beaten by thugs over a gambling debt, which was actually run up by Robert, who has his own gambling addiction. What the mob wants, however, is special treatment by Dalton's mother, who is scheduled to hear a case involving the interests of the Russo family, headed by Vincent, whose son Paulie was responsible for Dalton's beating. Coyne explains the situation to the judge, who recuses herself, but who then is sent a CD of Robert bound and with a note attached to him demanding that cash be given to Coyne. The family, dreading the adverse publicity, hesitates to involve law enforcement. In a review of the novel, Lukowsky commented that this installment contains all of the elements fans of the series would expect, including "excellent plotting; conversational, friendly narration; and a compelling secondary story line."

A former girlfriend seeks Coyne's help in *Hell Bent*. Alex Sinclair's brother, Augustine, was a happily married photojournalist whose life and marriage fell apart when he returned from Iraq missing a hand. Alex wants

Coyne to handle her brother's divorce, but Augustine is found dead in his apartment, apparently a suicide. Coyne concludes, however, that it was staged, that someone wanted the journalist silenced.

Tapply once told *CA* that he is reluctant to call his books mystery novels. "I write novels that, like most worthwhile novels, contain mysteries," he said. "I try to avoid formulas, although I suppose with a series character like my attorney Brady Coyne I have conceded that much. I place great emphasis in my writing on characterization, motivation, suspense, and humor—all of which seem to me important in all fiction. I try to tell stories rather than truths, but I think my stories convey some small truths now and then. I have been asked on occasion when I intend to write a 'real novel.' I reply, of course, that I already have."

More recently, Tapply told *CA:* "My father wrote a monthly column for *Field & Stream* for thirty-five years. I watched him work, absorbed his perfectionism, understood how hard writing was. This postponed my itch to write until I was in my thirties. When I began writing, I was fully prepared for the difficulty and frustrations. This, more than any writing lesson, has enabled me to stick to it.

"I've learned some things about the business of writing. We have to be businessmen as well as artists. I never anticipated any of that."

When asked which book was his favorite, Tapply answered: "My current book is always my favorite, because it's the only one I really think about. Still, I am fond of *Sportsman's Legacy*. . . . It's about my relationship with my father, and was the hardest piece of writing I ever had to do." When asked what effect he hoped his books would have, Tapply said: "I hope they will keep people up all night turning the pages."

BIOGRAPHICAL AND CRITICAL SOURCES:

BOOKS

St. James Guide to Crime and Mystery Writers, 4th edition, St. James Press (Detroit, MI), 1996.

PERIODICALS

Booklist, September 15, 1996, Bill Ott, review of *Close to the Bone,* p. 225; August, 1997, John Rowen, review of *A Fly-fishing Life,* p. 1868; June 1, 1998,

Wes Lukowsky, review of *Cutter's Run,* p. 1735; August, 1999, Wes Lukowsky, review of *Muscle Memory,* p. 2036; August, 2000, Bill Ott, review of *Scar Tissue,* p. 2123; September 1, 2001, Bill Ott, review of *Past Tense,* p. 57; November 15, 2001, John Rowen, review of *Pocket Water: Favorite Streams, Favorite Fish,* p. 540; December 1, 2001, GraceAnne A. DeCandido, review of *First Light,* p. 632; October 15, 2002, Frank Sennett, review of *A Fine Line,* p. 393; September 15, 2004, Wes Lukowsky, review of *Bitch Creek,* p. 214; January 1, 2005, Wes Lukowsky, review of *Second Sight,* p. 825; July, 2005, Bill Ott, review of *Nervous Water,* p. 1907; September 1, 2006, Bill Ott, review of *Out Cold,* p. 64; February 1, 2007, Wes Lukowsky, review of *Gray Ghost,* p. 36; July 1, 2007, Wes Lukowsky, review of *One-way Ticket,* p. 35; December 1, 2007, Wes Lukowsky, review of *Third Strike,* p. 28.

Kirkus Reviews, August 15, 2001, review of *Past Tense,* p. 1174; November 1, 2001, review of *First Light,* p. 1517; October 1, 2002, review of *A Fine Line,* p. 1432; July 15, 2004, review of *Bitch Creek,* p. 664; August 1, 2006, review of *Out Cold,* p. 759; January 15, 2007, review of *Gray Ghost,* p. 55; July 15, 2007, review of *One-way Ticket.*

Library Journal, February 1, 1998, M. Anna Falbo, review of *Close to the Bone,* p. 130; July, 1999, Rex Klett, review of *Muscle Memory,* p. 141; September 1, 2001, Rex Klett, review of *Past Tense,* p. 239; January, 2002, Rex Klett, review of *First Light,* p. 158.

New York Times Book Review, December 26, 1993, Marilyn Stasio, review of *The Snake Eater;* January 22, 1995, Marilyn Stasio, review of *The Seventh Enemy;* November 5, 2000, Marilyn Stasio, review of *Scar Tissue,* p. 32.

Publishers Weekly, July 7, 1997, review of *A Fly-Fishing Life,* p. 58; June 28, 1999, review of *Muscle Memory,* p. 57; September 11, 2000, Peter Cannon, "*PW* Talks to William G. Tapply," p. 72, and review of *Scar Tissue,* p. 72; December 10, 2001, review of *First Light,* p. 54; October 28, 2002, review of *A Fine Line,* p. 55; August 16, 2004, review of *Bitch Creek,* p. 46; December 6, 2004, review of *Second Sight,* p. 46; August 1, 2005, review of *Nervous Water,* p. 48; August 7, 2006, review of *Out Cold,* p. 36; July 16, 2007, review of *One-way Ticket,* p. 148; October 22, 2007, review of *Third Strike,* p. 38.

Times (London, England), January 31, 1985, Marcel Berlins, review of *Death at Charity's Point.*

ONLINE

Mysterious Reviews, http://www.mysteriousreviews. com/ (June 25, 2008), review of *Out Cold.*
William G. Tapply Home Page, http://www.williamg tapply.com (June 25, 2008).*

*   *   *

TAPPLY, William George
See TAPPLY, William G.

*   *   *

TAYLOR, Charles 1931-
(Charles Margrave Taylor)

PERSONAL: Born November 5, 1931, in Montreal, Quebec, Canada; son of Walter Margrave (an industrialist) and Simone (a fashion designer) Taylor; married Alba Romer (an artist), April 2, 1956; children: Karen, Miriam, Wanda, Gabriella, Gretta. *Education:* McGill University, B.A., 1952; Oxford University, B.A., 1955, M.A., 1960, D.Phil., 1961.

ADDRESSES: Office—Law School, Northwestern University, 633 Clark St., Evanston, IL 60208. *E-mail*—charles-taylor@law.northwestern.edu.

CAREER: McGill University, Montreal, Quebec, Canada, began as assistant professor, 1961—, became professor of philosophy and political science, professor emeritus, 1998—; University of Montreal, professor of philosophy, 1962-71. Chichele Professor of Social and Political Theory, Oxford University, 1976; Northwestern University, Evanston, IL, Board of Trustees professor of law and philosophy, 2002—. Vice-president of New Democrat Party of Canada, 1965-73; guest lecturer at various universities, including University of California, Berkeley, University of Frankfurt, Centre for the Study of Developing Societies, Delhi, India, Queen's University, Carleton University, University of Oxford, Hebrew University of Jerusalem, Stanford University, and Yale University.

MEMBER: Canadian Philosophical Association, Canadian Political Science Association, Royal Society of Canada, Ligue des Droits de l'Homme.

AWARDS, HONORS: Companion of the Order of Canada, 1995; named a grand officer de l'Ordre National du Quebec, 2000; Prix Léon-Gérin, Quebec provincial government, 2002, for contribution to Quebec intellectual life; Templeton Prize, John Templeton Foundation, 2007, for progress toward research or discoveries about spiritual realities.

WRITINGS:

NONFICTION

The Explanation of Behaviour, Humanities Press (New York, NY), 1964.

Pattern of Politics, McClelland & Stewart (Toronto, Ontario, Canada), 1970.

Hegel, Cambridge University Press (New York, NY), 1975.

Hegel and Modern Society, Cambridge University Press (New York, NY), 1979.

Social Theory as Practice, Oxford University Press (New York, NY), 1983.

Human Agency and Language, Cambridge University Press (New York, NY), 1985.

Philosophy and the Human Sciences, Cambridge University Press (New York, NY), 1985.

Sources of the Self: The Making of the Modern Identity, Harvard University Press (Cambridge, MA), 1989.

The Malaise of Modernity, Anansi (Concord, Ontario, Canada), 1991, published as *The Ethics of Authenticity,* Harvard University Press (Cambridge, MA), 1992.

Multiculturalism and "The Politics of Recognition": An Essay, Princeton University Press (Princeton, NJ), 1992.

Reconciling the Solitudes: Essays on Canadian Federalism and Nationalism, edited by Guy Laforest, McGill-Queen's University Press (Montreal, Quebec, Canada), 1993.

Philosophy in an Age of Pluralism: The Philosophy of Charles Taylor in Question, edited by James Tully, Cambridge University Press (New York, NY), 1994.

Philosophical Arguments, Harvard University Press (Cambridge, MA), 1995.

Charles Taylor Et L'interprétation de l'Identityé Moderne, Presses de l'Université Laval (Sainte-Foy, Quebec, Canada), 1998.

A Catholic Modernity? Charles Taylor's Mirianist Award Lecture, with Responses by William M. Shea, Rosemary Luling Haughton, George Marsden, and Jean Bethke Elshtain, Oxford University Press (New York, NY), 1999.

Varieties of Religion Today: William James Revisited, Harvard University Press (Cambridge, MA), 2002.

Etica e Umanita, Vita e Pensiero (Milan, Italy), 2004.

Modern Social Imaginaries, Duke University Press (Durham, NC), 2004.

A Secular Age, Belknap Press (Cambridge, MA), 2007.

Contributor of articles to political and philosophical journals. Founder and former editor, *New Left Review.*

SIDELIGHTS: Charles Taylor is an internationally renowned philosopher. Taylor once told *CA:* "I am interested in philosophical anthropology, the theory of human nature; I am dissatisfied with widespread mechanistic accounts, more drawn to views defended in other philosophical traditions, e.g., Hegel, Humboldt, Heidegger; but believe these must be reformulated. No one philosophical school has the resources for this reformulation alone."

Upon graduating from Oxford University with his Ph.D. in 1961, Taylor began lecturing at McGill University in Montreal. Although he accepted a number of visiting and adjunct professorships at universities and institutes around the world, he remained affiliated with McGill through acquiring professor emeritus status in 1998. In addition to academia, Taylor was also active in Canadian politics in the 1960s. He ran for a seat in the Canadian House of Commons four times for the New Democratic Party in Quebec. His service to Quebec life and intellectual notoriety earned him provincial honors, including being named a grand officer de l'Ordre National du Quebec in 2000 and winning the Prix Léon-Gérin in 2002. Taylor was recognized as a Companion of the Order of Canada in 1995. Internationally, he received the Templeton Prize in 2007 for progress toward research about spiritual realities.

Throughout his career Taylor has supported his philosophical studies by analyzing a wide array of philosophers. Taylor also told *CA:* "I am very interested in French and German, as well as Anglo-Saxon philosophy. Being from Montreal, I grew up bi-lingual; and have since also learned German, Spanish, some Italian and Polish, and of course, Latin and Greek."

Modern Social Imaginaries is a continuation of Taylor's study of multiple modernities. In examining these differences, he presents the concept of the social imaginary, a way in which a group of people perceive their social life. Taylor prioritizes three main factors in this self-understanding of one within society: the public sphere, the economy, and the actual practice of democratic self-rule. Jeffery L. Nicholas reviewed the book in the *Review of Metaphysics,* describing it as "important for its attempt to continue a project which has engaged Taylor for some years now: to investigate the foundations of modernity and to uncover the good and the bad. This book is worth reading for those concerned with ethics, politics, and modernity and rises to the top of Taylor's more recent work."

Varieties of Religion Today: William James Revisited, covers the philosophies of William James and his view of religion in modern times along with Taylor's own views and comments on James's texts. The volume is based on lectures Taylor gave at the Institute for Human Sciences in Vienna, Austria, in 2000; the book was published one hundred years after James delivered his lectures that became *The Varieties of Religious Experience.* The four sections of Taylor's book are "James: Varieties, The 'Twice-Born,' Religion Today," and "So Was James Right?" Taylor revisits the questions posed in James's text in an examination of contemporary religion and of James's work in historical and cultural contexts. In reviewing the volume for *Notre Dame Philosophical Review Online,* Philip L. Quinn wrote: "Taylor is convinced that a profound alteration in the social conditions of religious belief has taken place in the past half-century. As he sees it, the consumer revolution and the rise of youth culture are external manifestations of this change. The spread of expressivist individualism and the culture of authenticity downward from an intellectual elite, which is a legacy of Romanticism, reflects this transformation at the level of cultural self-understanding." Quinn further wrote: "According to Taylor, 'in the new expressivist dispensation, there is no necessary embedding of our link to the sacred in any particular broader framework, whether "church" or state' (95). Religiously speaking, society now leaves each of us on our own, at liberty to do our own thing spiritually. For Taylor, this is the state of affairs brilliantly foreshadowed by the individualistic experientialism advocated by James."

In *A Secular Age,* Taylor disputes the idea that, with the advancement of science and democracy, less time and effort is spent on godly and spiritual pursuits. He contends rather that, although we have more choices when it comes to our faith in "Western Christendom," belief in God continues in an environment of spirituality that continues to evolve. "Taylor has translated complex philosophical theories into language that any educated reader will be able to follow, yet he has not sacrificed an iota of sophistication or nuance," commented a *Kirkus Reviews* contributor. John Patrick Diggins reviewed the volume in the *New York Times Book Review,* writing: "Taylor's deconstruction of the death-of-God thesis rests on his conviction that 'the arguments from natural science to Godlessness are not all that convincing.' He has no patience with atheists like Richard Dawkins and Daniel Dennett, who argue that science, particularly the theory of evolution, has consigned religion to the ash heap of history. Taylor, in contrast, sees science as reinforcing religion, since God is implicated in a social existence where the contemplation of meaning and order suggests 'something divine in us.' For Taylor, belief is not what science finds but what religion hopes for."

BIOGRAPHICAL AND CRITICAL SOURCES:

PERIODICALS

Amerasia Journal, January, 1995, review of *Multiculturalism and "The Politics of Recognition": An Essay,* p. 233.

America, October 22, 2007, Dennis O'Brien, review of *A Secular Age,* p. 24.

American Political Science Review, June, 1993, review of *Multiculturalism and "The Politics of Recognition,"* p. 482.

Antioch Review, spring, 1993, review of *Sources of the Self: The Making of the Modern Identity.*

Change, March, 1993, review of *Multiculturalism and "The Politics of Recognition,"* p. 54.

Choice, February, 1993, review of *Multiculturalism and "The Politics of Recognition,"* p. 1027; October, 1993, review of *Reconciling the Solitudes: Essays on Canadian Federalism and Nationalism,* p. 362; November, 1995, review of *Sources of the Self,* p. 411.

Christian Century, December 2, 1992, review of *The Ethics of Authenticity,* p. 1115.

Commonweal, July 16, 2004, Mark Sargent, review of *Modern Social Imaginaries,* p. 30.

Ethics, October, 1993, review of *The Ethics of Authenticity,* p. 192; January, 1994, review of *Multiculturalism and "The Politics of Recognition,"* p. 384.

First Things, May 7, 2007, review of *Modern Social Imaginaries,* p. 63.

Foreign Affairs, January, 1993, review of *Reconciling the Solitudes,* p. 173.

Hastings Center Report, September, 1994, review of *Multiculturalism and "The Politics of Recognition,"* p. 44.

Journal of the History of Ideas, January, 1993, review of *The Ethics of Authenticity,* p. 174.

Kirkus Reviews, June 15, 2007, review of *A Secular Age.*

Library Journal, August 1, 2007, John Jaeger, review of *A Secular Age,* p. 94.

New York Times Book Review, December 16, 2007, John Patrick Diggins, review of *A Secular Age.*

Publishers Weekly, June 11, 2007, review of *A Secular Age,* p. 54.

Review of Metaphysics, December, 2005, Jeffery L. Nicholas, review of *Modern Social Imaginaries,* p. 454.

Spectator, October 13, 2007, Edward Norman, review of *A Secular Age,* p. 52.

Theological Studies, December, 2004, Philip Rossi, review of *Modern Social Imaginaries,* p. 907.

Times Literary Supplement, January 29, 1993, review of *Multiculturalism and "The Politics of Recognition,"* p. 5.

Wilson Quarterly, winter, 2008, Jay Tolson, review of *A Secular Age,* p. 107.

ONLINE

Notre Dame Philosophical Review Online, http://ndpr.nd.edu/ (April 4, 2003), Philip L. Quinn, review of *Varieties of Religion Today: William James Revisited.*

Templeton Prize, http://www.templetonprize.org/ (June 3, 2007), author profile.*

*   *   *

TAYLOR, Charles Margrave
See TAYLOR, Charles

*   *   *

TRACY, John Nicholas
See TRACY, Nicholas

TRACY, Nicholas 1944-
    (John Nicholas Tracy)

PERSONAL: Born July 21, 1944, in Edmonton, Alberta, Canada; son of Clarence and Minerva Tracy; married Antoinette Huth, 1968 (died, 1977). *Education:* University of Saskatchewan, B.A. (with honors), 1966; University of Southampton, M.Phil., 1968, Ph.D., 1972.

ADDRESSES: Home—Fredericton, New Brunswick, Canada.

CAREER: Acadia University, Wolfville, Nova Scotia, research associate in political science, 1973; Dalhousie University, Halifax, Nova Scotia, research associate in political science, 1974-79; University of New Brunswick, Fredericton, assistant professor of history, 1981; St. Thomas University, Fredericton, assistant professor of history, 1982; University of New Brunswick, assistant professor of history, 1983; National University of Singapore, Kent Ridge, associate professor and senior visiting fellow, 1984-86; freelance researcher and writer, 1987—. University of New Brunswick, adjunct professor, 1993—. *Military service:* Royal Canadian Naval Reserve, retired, 1965; became sub-lieutenant.

MEMBER: International Institute for Strategic Studies, Royal Historical Society (associate), Navy Records Society, Society for Nautical Research.

AWARDS, HONORS: Fellow of Social Sciences and Humanities Research Council of Canada, 1986-87; grants from Social Science Federation of Canada, Canadian Institute for International Peace and Security, and Canadian Department of External Affairs.

WRITINGS:

Navies, Deterrence, and American Independence, University of British Columbia Press (Vancouver, British Columbia, Canada), 1988.

(Editor) Brian Tunstall, *Naval Warfare in the Age of Sail: The Evolution of Fighting Tactics, 1680-1815,* Conway Maritime Press (London, England), 1990.

Attack on Maritime Trade, University of Toronto Press (Toronto, Ontario, Canada), 1991.

A Cruising Guide to the Bay of Fundy and the St. John River, Including Passamoquoddy Bay and the Southwestern Shore of Nova Scotia, Goose Lane Press (Fredericton, New Brunswick, Canada), 1992.

Manila Ransomed: The British Assault on Manila in the Seven Years War. University of Exeter Press (Exeter, England), 1995.

Nelson's Battles: The Art of Victory in the Age of Sail, Naval Institute Press (Annapolis, MD), 1996, revised edition published as *Nelson's Battles: The Triumph of British Seapower,* 2008.

Rastafari: A Way of Life, Frontline Distribution International (Chicago, IL), 1996.

The Collective Naval Defense of the Empire, 1900-1940, Ashgate (Brookfield, VT), 1997.

(Editor) *Sea Power and the Control of Trade: Belligerent Rights from the Russian War to the Beira Patrol; 1854-1970,* Ashgate (Burlington, VT), 2005.

Who's Who in Nelson's Navy: 200 Naval Heroes, Chatham Publishing (London, England), 2006.

Britannia's Palette: The Arts of Naval Victory, McGill-Queen's University Press (Montreal, Quebec, Canada), 2007.

The Miracle of the Kent: A Tale of Courage, Faith, and Fire, Westholme Publishing (Yardley, PA), 2008.

Work represented in anthologies, including *Northern Waters, Security, and Resource Issues,* edited by Clive Archer and David Scrivener, (London, England), 1986; contributor to periodicals, including *English Historical Review, Eighteenth-Century Studies, Historical Journal, Mariners's Mirror,* and *International Journal.*

SIDELIGHTS: Historian and educator Nicholas Tracy is the author of a number of volumes, including *Nelson's Battles: The Art of Victory in the Age of Sail,* a revised edition of which was published as *Nelson's Battles: The Triumph of British Seapower.* Tracy offers a history of British naval hero Vice Admiral Horatio Lord Nelson over the course of his career, beginning with his 1798 battle of the Nile Napoleonic War victory to his death at the battle of Trafalgar in 1805. Tracy discusses Nelson's tactics and legacy and provides a brief biography, indexes, and maps and illustrations of important battles.

Tracy is editor of *Sea Power and the Control of Trade: Belligerent Rights from the Russian War to the Beira Patrol; 1854-1970,* a volume that studies the rights of ships of countries involved in a conflict and those of neutral nations who wish to continue engaging in free trade that are not. In both cases, concessions had to be made, as they did for humanitarian efforts. The primary documents of this collection cover the Russian War, the Declaration of Paris, the United States Civil War, the period of the nineteenth century, the Hague Conference, the Declaration of London (1899 to 1916), and the periods from 1918 to 1930, and 1937 to 1970. Included are a chronology and index of ships.

Tracy tells a story of a rescue that took place in 1825 in *The Miracle of the Kent: A Tale of Courage, Faith, and Fire.* "Tracy's satisfying narrative constitutes the first modern account," noted a *Kirkus Reviews* contributor. The East India Company's ship *Kent* set sail from England loaded with cargo, crew, and six hundred passengers, many of them the soldiers of the Thirty-first Regiment, and their families. During the trip to India, they encountered a violent storm in the Bay of Biscay. A soldier who went below into the hold, where alcohol or kerosene had spilled from their casks, accidentally ignited a fire with his lantern. It quickly spread out of control and raced toward that part of the ship where gunpowder was stored.

The *Cambria,* a small vessel carrying a crew and twenty Cornish miners on their way to Mexico, saw the blaze and initiated a rescue. Over the course of a day and part of a night, as the storm continued unrelenting, the crews of both ships transferred nearly all of the passengers of the *Kent* to the *Cambria* by tiny lifeboats. Of the seventy who were left, fourteen were later retrieved by another small vessel. The rest perished. Tracy relied on firsthand accounts in documenting this "miracle," including that of survivor Duncan MacGregor. A *Publishers Weekly* reviewer noted that through his account, Tracy also examines Victorian values as the passengers were torn between self-preservation and the codes of propriety of the time. The reviewer wrote: "The result is a naturally gripping adventure tale that sets its heroics in an insightful historical context." "The story of [the] Kent is both powerful and intensely focused," concluded George Cohen in *Booklist.*

Nicholas Tracy once told *CA:* "My historical writing is primarily conceived of as the basis for the development of public policy in international relations. My present work, which is supported by the Department of External Affairs, seeks to apply my study of five centuries of economic warfare to the problem of making economic sanctions a more useful tool of the United Nations."

BIOGRAPHICAL AND CRITICAL SOURCES:

PERIODICALS

Booklist, October 15, 2008, George Cohen, review of *The Miracle of the Kent: A Tale of Courage, Faith, and Fire,* p. 7.

Kirkus Reviews, September 15, 2008, review of *The Miracle of the Kent.*

Publishers Weekly, September 1, 2008, review of *The Miracle of the Kent,* p. 49.

Reference & Research Book News, May, 2006, review of *Sea Power and the Control of Trade: Belligerent Rights from the Russian War to the Beira Patrol; 1854-1970;* May, 2009, review of *Nelson's Battles: The Triumph of British Seapower.**

*　　*　　*

TROPPER, Jonathan 1970-

PERSONAL: Born February 19, 1970, in New York, NY; son of David (a businessman) and Ina Tropper; married Elizabeth Parker, June 2, 1996; children: Spencer Louis. *Education:* Yeshiva University, B.A., 1991; New York University, M.A., 1993. *Religion:* Jewish. *Hobbies and other interests:* Piano, martial arts.

ADDRESSES: Home—Westchester, NY. *Agent*—Simon Lipskar, Writers House, 21 W. 26th St., New York, NY 10010. *E-mail*—jtropper@msn.com.

CAREER: Writer, novelist, and educator. Manhattanville College, instructor.

WRITINGS:

NOVELS

Plan B, St. Martin's Press (New York, NY), 2000.

The Book of Joe, Delacorte Press (New York, NY), 2004.

Everything Changes, Delacorte Press (New York, NY), 2005.

How to Talk to a Widower, Bantam Dell (New York, NY), 2007.

This Is Where I Leave You, Dutton (New York, NY), 2009.

Contributor to periodicals, including the *New York Times.*

ADAPTATIONS: Everything Changes is in development as a feature film for Sony Pictures; *The Book of Joe* is in development as a feature film for Warner Brothers.

SIDELIGHTS: Jonathan Tropper is best known for writing novels that exhibit his razor-sharp wit and intelligence while depicting family life and the ups and downs of relationships. Tropper told *CA:* "When I write, I enjoy using fiction to illustrate my observations and insights into the quirkier, more abstract facets of human nature. . . . I like to write about people who are self-aware enough to be unsatisfied with aspects of their personalities, and then place them in situations that will force those foibles to the forefront, to be dealt with along with the extenuating circumstances. It provides for me, as well as the reader, a sense of catharsis and closure that real life seldom provides."

Tropper's first novel, *Plan B,* addresses how five college friends, upon reaching the age of thirty, deal with adulthood and the main issues in their lives. They grapple with divorce, job frustration, failed relationships, and particularly drug abuse, as four members of the group attempt to slow the fifth member's downward spiral. When plan A, a standard intervention, fails, they resort to the plan B of the title: kidnapping the protagonist and holding him in a cabin in the woods until he has gone through withdrawal. In a review for *Booklist,* Carolyn Kubisz called the plan an excuse for the author "to explore the group's personal demons, failings, and relationships." A contributor for *Publishers Weekly* remarked that "the picaresque plot is diverting in a sitcom kind of way."

In his follow-up effort, *The Book of Joe,* Tropper again looks at turning points in a person's life. Joe Goffman, a writer who returns to his small hometown in Connecticut after his autobiographical novel becomes a best seller, must face the anger of friends and family at the truths he has revealed. A reviewer for *Publishers Weekly* remarked: "Despite its charms, . . . this boy-who-won't-grow-up novel relies too heavily on canned lines . . . and easy melodrama." On the other hand, *Booklist* contributor John Green found it "a first-rate tale of a thirtysomething's belated coming-of-age." Joe is forced to address people's issues with him on an adult level. In an interview for *Bookreporter.com,* Tropper discussed his protagonist's experience: "Joe goes from being a sullen, selfish loner . . . to suddenly seeing the value in caring for others. We all carry around a certain degree of anger or resentment toward members of our family, and letting go of it is never easy, but infinitely rewarding."

Everything Changes tells the story of Zack King, a man in his early thirties who is restless and discontented, despite the fact that his life is ostensibly on course.

Tropper once again shows how easily change can come into the most settled of lives, as Zack's long-absent father returns looking for absolution and Zack suffers a health scare. A *Publishers Weekly* critic remarked that "pithy observations on love, marriage and corporate life give the book a graceful charm." Kristine Huntley, in a review for *Booklist,* called the book "by turns funny and moving."

The protagonist of Tropper's novel *How to Talk to a Widower* is twenty-nine-year-old magazine columnist Doug Parker, whose wife Hailey was killed in a plane crash the previous year. Hailey was beautiful and several years older than Doug, who considered her to be out of his league. Yet their two years of married life were very happy, and in her absence, Doug is often inconsolable in his ongoing bereavement; he refuses to come to terms with Hailey's death and move on with his life. Living in Hailey's house and benefitting from a settlement with the airline involved in the plane crash, Doug does not have to work. Instead, he mopes around, drinks, and regularly muses on his predicament in his column, "How to Talk to a Widower," which he writes for *M* magazine. The column, to his dismay, makes him a bit of a celebrity. Doug eventually finds himself surrounded by people who care for him and work to break him out of his emotional shell. "Doug's flawed new life is a series of hits and mostly misses, but you get the feeling he just might learn to love life—and women—again," observed *USA Today* reviewer Carol Memmott. "Alternately flippant and sad, Tropper's book is a smart comedy of inappropriate behavior at an inopportune time," commented a *Publishers Weekly* reviewer. Tropper's "prose is funny and insightful, his characters quirky and just a bit off-balance but decent enough to take to our hearts," observed Bette-Lee Fox, writing in *Library Journal.* A *Kirkus Reviews* critic called the novel a "resigned yet hopeful examination of grief with a side of human absurdity."

Tropper's novel *This Is Where I Leave You* follows a Jewish family on a seven-day ritual, shiva. The book explores the theme of family and Bette-Lee Fox, writing in *Library Journal,* warned that fans will"rejoice at the opportunity to indulge"

BIOGRAPHICAL AND CRITICAL SOURCES:

PERIODICALS

Booklist, January 1, 2000, Carolyn Kubisz, review of *Plan B,* p. 881; March 15, 2004, John Green, review of *The Book of Joe,* p. 1268; March 15,

2005, Kristine Huntley, review of *Everything Changes,* p. 1268; May 15, 2007, Joanne Wilkinson, review of *How to Talk to a Widower,* p. 20.

Bookseller, May 12, 2006, "Orion Learns Language of Lost Love," p. 15.

Entertainment Weekly, July 20, 2007, Tim Stack, review of *How to Talk to a Widower,* p. 79.

Kirkus Reviews, January 15, 2004, review of *The Book of Joe,* p. 59; May 1, 2007, review of *How to Talk to a Widower.*

Library Journal, May 1, 2007, Bette-Lee Fox, review of *How to Talk to a Widower,* p. 76; June 1, 2009, Bette-Lee Fox, review of *This is Where I Leave You,* p. 94.

Publishers Weekly, January 31, 2000, review of *Plan B,* p. 84; December 1, 2003, review of *The Book of Joe,* p. 38; February 21, 2005, review of *Everything Changes,* p. 156; April 16, 2007, review of *How to Talk to a Widower,* p. 27; June 1, 2009, Eleanor Brown, interview with Tropper.June 1, 2009, review of *This is Where I Leave You,* p. 31.

USA Today, July 16, 2007, Carol Memmott, "'Widower' Wallows in Grief, Finds Fresh Start," review of *How to Talk to a Widower,* p. 1D.

ONLINE

BookPage, http://www.bookpage.com/ (May 25, 2008), Ian Schwartz, "No Place Like Home," review of *The Book of Joe.*

Bookreporter.com, http://www.bookreporter.com/ (May 25, 2008), Carol Fitzgerald, Wiley Saichek, Brandon M. Stickney, interview with Jonathan Tropper; Alexis Burling, review of *How to Talk to a Widower.*

January, http://www.januarymagazine.com/ (May 25, 2008), Chris Gsell, "Small Town Evisceration," review of *The Book of Joe.*

Jonathan Tropper Home Page, http://www.jonathan tropper.com (April 15, 2007).

Mostly Fiction, http://mostlyfiction.com/ (August 2, 2007), Eleanor Bukowsky, review of *How to Talk to a Widower.**

*   *   *

TUCKER, Todd 1968-

PERSONAL: Born March 14, 1968. *Education:* University of Notre Dame, B.A., 1990.

ADDRESSES: Home—Valparaiso, IN.

CAREER: Writer. *Military service:* U.S. Navy, 1990-95, including service on U.S.S. Alabama.

WRITINGS:

Notre Dame Game Day: Getting There, Getting In, and Getting in the Spirit, Diamond Communications (South Bend, IN), 2000.

Notre Dame vs. the Klan: How the Fighting Irish Defeated the Ku Klux Klan, Loyola Press (Chicago, IL), 2004.

The Great Starvation Experiment: The Heroic Men Who Starved So That Millions Could Live, Free Press (New York, NY), 2006.

Over and Under (novel), Thomas Dunne Books (New York, NY), 2008.

Atomic America: How a Deadly Explosion and a Feared Admiral Changed the Course of Nuclear History, Free Press (New York, NY), 2009.

Contributor to periodicals, including *Rotarian, TWA Ambassador, Inside Sports,* and *Historic Traveler.*

SIDELIGHTS: Todd Tucker is a graduate of the University of Notre Dame and a veteran of the Nuclear Propulsion Program of the U.S. Navy. He has written several books, focusing on both history and his love for his alma mater. His first book, *Notre Dame Game Day: Getting There, Getting In, and Getting in the Spirit,* is a travel guide for the sports fan who wants to enjoy football at Notre Dame. His next book, however, *Notre Dame vs. the Klan: How the Fighting Irish Defeated the Ku Klux Klan,* explores a more serious side of the university. The book recounts an incident in May of 1924, when a group of students from the school battled against a number of sheriff's deputies who were connected to the local Klan chapter. R.C. Cottrell, in a review for *Library Journal,* called the book "an intriguing tale."

Tucker's next book, *The Great Starvation Experiment: The Heroic Men Who Starved So That Millions Could Live,* tells the story of a group of men—conscientious objectors—who volunteered to starve as part of an experiment during World War II, the premise being that scientists would be better prepared to deal with the possible effects of postwar starvation if they could observe the process in a controlled environment ahead of time. A reviewer for *Publishers Weekly* reported: "Tucker tells the story with verve and economy." A contributor

to *Kirkus Reviews* stated that the book "sheds welcome light on a little-known historical event and on the role of conscientious objectors in WWII."

In *Atomic America: How a Deadly Explosion and a Feared Admiral Changed the Course of Nuclear History* Tucker tells the story of a significant but little-known chapter in the history of the U.S. nuclear program. On January 3, 1961, an accidental explosion at the National Reactor Testing Station in Idaho Falls, Idaho killed all three men working on the project. Tucker investigates the rumor that two of the men had been rivals in a love triangle, which prompted speculations about their competence to adhere to safety protocols, but concludes that the accident resulted from more mundane conditions: faulty maintenance, inadequate training, and negligence. Admiral Hyman Rickover, who fought strenuously to rehabilitate the nuclear program after this accident and who insisted on cutting-edge technologies and impeccable training, figures prominently in the book as the author traces the development of the U.S. nuclear program in the decades following the accident. Tucker is critical of Rickover, whom he blames for single-mindedly squelching any dissent about the future of nuclear propulsion by U.S. military forces. Tucker also exposes the careless approach to nuclear safety demonstrated by the Army in the 1950s. Describing *Atomic America* as an "eye-opening" work, *Washington Post Book World* reviewer Seth Shulman nevertheless found its focus overly broad and its central message "muddled." Observing that Tucker presents his story as "a morality tale," a contributor to *Kirkus Reviews* described the book as "interesting though blandly told." A *Publishers Weekly* reviewer, noting the pressure to build more nuclear energy plants to meet energy needs without burning fossil fuels, called *Atomic America* "vitally relevant."

Tucker's first novel, *Over and Under,* is set in a small town in southern Indiana in 1979. The book tells the story of Tom and Andy, fourteen-year-old best friends who begin to face some of the complexities of the adult world when workers at the local Borden Casket Company go on strike. Andy's dad is a manager at the factory while Tom's is a laborer, and this fact forces the boys to think more deeply about family loyalty and the bonds of friendship. Matters grow more difficult after an explosion at the factory kills the company president. Subplots include a mysterious secret between Andy's mother and the town sheriff and the escape of two fugitives. Writing in *Booklist,* Michael Cart described the novel as a "nostalgic adolescent adventure" with all the hallmarks of a coming-of-age classic. Particularly notable, said the reviewer, are the "gracefully realized" setting and sympathetic main characters. Describing the book as a "haunting" story, a writer for *Publishers Weekly* observed that *Over and Under* is a "poignant and memorable tale of lost innocence."

BIOGRAPHICAL AND CRITICAL SOURCES:

PERIODICALS

American Enterprise, July-August, 2005, Naomi Schaefer Riley, "Shamrocks against Sheets," p. 56.

Booklist, March 15, 2006, George Cohen, review of *The Great Starvation Experiment: The Heroic Men Who Starved So That Millions Could Live,* p. 21; June 1, 2008, Michael Cart, review of *Over and Under,* p. 45; February 15, 2009, Gilbert Taylor, review of *Atomic America: How a Deadly Explosion and a Feared Admiral Changed the Course of Nuclear History,* p. 8.

Kirkus Reviews, March 15, 2006, review of *The Great Starvation Experiment,* p. 282; January 15, 2009, review of *Atomic America.*

Library Journal, October 1, 2004, R.C. Cottrell, review of *Notre Dame vs. the Klan: How the Fighting Irish Defeated the Ku Klux Klan,* p. 97; April 15, 2006, Edwin B. Burgess, review of *The Great Starvation Experiment,* p. 131; January 1, 2009, Dan Blewett, review of *Atomic America,* p. 107.

Publishers Weekly, March 6, 2006, review of *The Great Starvation Experiment,* p. 253; May 26, 2008, review of *Over and Under,* p. 39; January 5, 2009, review of *Atomic America,* p. 41.

Voice of Youth Advocates, October, 2008, Thomas C. Reed and Danny B. Stillman, review of *Atomic America,* p. 344.

Washington City Paper, April 30, 2009, Mike Kanin, review of *Atomic America.*

Washington Post Book World, April 19, 2009, Seth Shulman, review of *Atomic America.*

ONLINE

Simon & Schuster Web site, http://authors.simonand schuster.com/ (June 22, 2009), author profile.*

W

WANIEK, Marilyn Nelson
See NELSON, Marilyn

*   *   *

WATKINS, Stephen
See WATKINS, Steve

*   *   *

WATKINS, Stephen H.
See WATKINS, Steve

*   *   *

WATKINS, Stephen Hulme
See WATKINS, Steve

*   *   *

WATKINS, Steve 1954-
(Stephen Watkins, Stephen H. Watkins, Stephen Hulme Watkins)

PERSONAL: Born October 9, 1954, in Alexandria, VA; son of Shirley Clyde (a planning and reclamation engineer for phosphate and coal mines) and Nora Lea (a preschool teacher and a director and trainer for nonprofit centers) Watkins; married Laurie Louise Wilson (an artist and massage therapist), February 29, 1984 (divorced July, 2000); married Janet Marshall Watkins, June, 2001; children: Margaret Lea, Eva Jane, Claire, Lili. *Education:* Attended North Carolina Wesleyan College, 1973, and University of North Carolina at Wilmington, 1973-75; Florida State University, B.A. (magna cum laude), 1977, M.A., 1985, Ph.D., 1990. *Hobbies and other interests:* Practicing and teaching Ashtanga yoga, swimming, running.

ADDRESSES: Home—Fredericksburg, VA. *Office*—Department of English, Linguistics, and Speech, Mary Washington College, Fredericksburg, VA 22401. *Agent*—Kelly Sonnack, Sandra Dijkstra Literary Agency, 1155 Camino Del Mar, Del Mar, CA 92104. *E-mail*—swatkins@umw.edu.

CAREER: Pelouze Scale Co., Evanston, IL, assembly line worker, 1972; New Hanover Memorial Hospital, Wilmington, NC, nurse's aide, 1974-75; *Florida Flambeau,* Tallahassee, writer, 1975-76, associate editor, 1977-78, editor, 1978-80; teacher at a child care center in Leon County, FL, 1981; *Tallahassee Democrat,* Tallahassee, assistant news editor, 1981-82, assistant features editor, 1982-83, arts and features writer, 1983; Therapeutic Concepts Inc., Tallahassee, writer and editor, 1988; Red Letter Editorial Consultants, Tallahassee, writer and editor, 1988; Mary Washington College, Fredericksburg, VA, assistant professor, 1990-96, associate professor of English, 1996—. Court Appointed Special Advocates, volunteer.

AWARDS, HONORS: Silver award for feature writing and Charlie Award for best written magazine, both Florida Magazine Association, 1988; grant from Florida Arts Council, 1990; winner of short fiction contest, *Snake Nation Review,* 1991, for "Kafka's Sister"; Pushcart Prize, best of the small presses, 1992, for short story "Critterworld"; Golden Kite Award, Society of Children's Book Writers and Illustrators, 2009, for *Down Sand Mountain.*

WRITINGS:

The Black O: Racism and Redemption in an American Corporate Empire, University of Georgia Press (Athens, GA), 1997.
My Chaos Theory: Stories, Southern Methodist University Press (Dallas, TX), 2006.
Down Sand Mountain (young adult novel), Candlewick Press (Cambridge, MA), 2008.

Work represented in anthologies, including *North of Wakulla: An Anhinga Anthology,* edited by Mary Jane Ryals and Donna Decker, Anhinga Press (Tallahassee, FL), 1989; and *Pushcart Prize Anthology: Best of the Small Presses, 1992-93,* edited by Bill Henderson, Pushcart Press (Winscott, NY), 1992. Contributor of articles, short fiction, poetry, and reviews to journals including *Mississippi Review, New Virginia Review, Fiction and Drama, Poets and Writers, Witness, Nation, Snake Nation Review, Apalachee Quarterly, Sequoia,* and *Denver Quarterly.*

SIDELIGHTS: Steve Watkins once told *CA:* "I began researching my book in 1990, shortly after completing my doctorate in English. Over the next seven years I continued my research, following the development of the largest racial class-action job discrimination lawsuit in United States history, Haynes v. Shoney's, Inc., which was settled in 1993."

With his book *The Black O: Racism and Redemption in an American Corporate Empire,* Watkins contributed a chapter to the ongoing story of racial discrimination in the United States. *The Black O* chronicles the employment discrimination case filed against the Shoney's Corporation (the parent company of Shoney's restaurants) on behalf of 20,909 claimants. After five years of litigation, the plaintiffs received a 132.5 million-dollar settlement and the Shoney's Corporation altered its hiring practices. The black "O" of Watkins's title refers to the common practice of blackening the letter "o" in the name Shoney's on any application submitted by an African American.

Officials of Shoney's fired the white restaurant managers Billie and Henry Elliott for *not* firing African American employees. The Elliotts visited Tommy Warren's law office in Tallahassee, Florida, in 1988 to initiate legal action against their former employer, and Warren eventually became one of the lead attorneys for thousands of plaintiffs. The book describes how Warren gathered support for his case by taking colleagues who had never been to a Shoney's restaurant to one of the restaurants for lunch. Before they arrived, Warren gave his lunch companions a preview of what they would encounter at the restaurant: the hostess, the manager at the cash register, and the waiters would be almost exclusively white. Kitchen workers (glimpsed from behind a swinging door), bus persons, and salad bar stockers would be almost exclusively black. As Watkins recounts: "When the three men sit down at the Fernandina Beach, Florida Shoney's, the tableau unfolds exactly as Warren predicted it would." Warren's predictions convinced another attorney and his firm to support the suit. That support would eventually cost the other firm 700,000 dollars, a big risk for what would inevitably be a complicated case against a highly trained and generously paid legal defense team.

The Elliotts' discrimination claims were bolstered by the 270 complaints about unfair labor practices at Shoney's that were filed with the Equal Employment Opportunity Commission from 1985 to 1990, when Clarence Thomas led the agency before being appointed to the U.S. Supreme Court. A telling incident in the book, cited by John Greenya in the *Washington Post Book World,* occurred when Shoney's founder Ray Danner arrived at a meeting at corporate headquarters with an Igloo cooler in which he had placed a smaller-than-normal piece of fish. According to Greenya, Danner had been served this fish "in the only one of his Captain D's restaurants (also owned by Shoney's) in Murfreesboro, Tennessee, to have a black manager." Flinging the piece of fish against a wall, Danner exclaimed: "That is a prime example of black management in our company," writes Watkins. After courts found the Shoney's hiring practices discriminatory, Danner himself was personally required to pay approximately one-half of the 132.5 million-dollar settlement.

The Black O received positive reviews. Greenya called it "a very readable book about a landmark legal battle." Raye Snover, writing in the *New York Times Book Review,* called the book "a meticulously documented account of the work of Warren and his co-counsel Barry Goldstein."

Watkins once told *CA:* "*The Black O* was originally under contract with Longstreet Press, but on the eve of publication, Longstreet cancelled the contract, though the book had been the lead work in their fall, 1995 catalog, and was already being heavily promoted by the Press. The reason: fear of legal reprisal from Shoney's and its executives, past and present. The University of Georgia Press bought the book almost immediately, and brought it out in the fall of 1997."

Watkins's first collection of short fiction, *My Chaos Theory: Stories,* represents a departure from the journalistic tone of his first book. The stories in the collection "explore the male psyche," Roberto Ontiveros reported in the *Texas Observer,* "under a haze of obligations toward women: mothers, daughters, stepdaughters, wives deceased or just divorced from their men." In one story, for instance, Uma Thurman appears to instruct a beachcomber on how to fold the corpse of a drowned man into a yoga position called, appropriately enough, "the corpse." In another, three boys plot to kill a circus elephant only to have it expire—and collapse on a nearby car, trapping a little girl inside—before they can carry out their plan. "Disaster is the rule," wrote a *Kirkus Reviews* contributor, "in this aptly titled, darkly comic debut collection."

Down Sand Mountain is Watkins's first novel for young adults. The novel is set in 1966 in a small, segregated town in Florida. It is the story of twelve-year-old Dewey, a white boy and son of one of the local miners, as he comes to understand the various effects of prejudice and racism, and how they are not as clear-cut as the division between blacks and whites. Like most boys his age, Dewey wants to fit in with his community, where people know one another within the confines of their own side of town. However, his father has been running for town council, something he does each election, though he never wins. His campaign promise to help improve the quality of living on the black side of town not only guarantees his repeated losses, but also reflects on Dewey, who finds himself in the shadow of his father's reputation. The situation worsens when Dewey, in order to perform in the local minstrel show, darkens his skin with black shoe polish and attracts unwanted attention from local bullies. Dewey then befriends a girl who also finds herself on the fringe of acceptability, and he slowly becomes aware of the true level of racism in the town. Hazel Rochman, in a review for *Booklist,* commented that "the simple, beautiful prose remains totally true to the child's bewildered viewpoint." Joel Shoemaker, writing for *School Library Journal,* remarked that "readers will understand that Dewey's innocence dims his understanding of the politics of hate, but will easily identify with his deeply felt fears."

BIOGRAPHICAL AND CRITICAL SOURCES:

BOOKS

Watkins, Steve, *The Black O: Racism and Redemption in an American Corporate Empire,* University of Georgia Press (Athens, GA), 1997.

PERIODICALS

Booklist, August 1, 2008, Hazel Rochman, review of *Down Sand Mountain,* p. 68.
Kirkus Reviews, September 1, 2006, review of *My Chaos Theory: Stories,* p. 875; September 15, 2008, review of *Down Sand Mountain.*
Library Journal, November 15, 1997, Steven Anderson, *The Black O,* p. 66.
New York Times Book Review, April 26, 1998, Raye Snover, *The Black O,* p. 23.
School Library Journal, December 1, 2008, Joel Shoemaker, review of *Down Sand Mountain,* p. 142.
Texas Observer, January 12, 2007, Roberto Ontiveros, "Voice-Over Lightly."
Voice of Youth Advocates, December, 2008, Ann T. Reddy-Damon, review of *Down Sand Mountain,* p. 442.
Washington Post Book World, October 12, 1997, John Greenya, review of *The Black O.*

ONLINE

University of Mary Washington, http://www.umw.edu/ (July 9, 2007), "Watkins, Stephen H.," author profile.

*   *   *

WELLINGTON, David 1971-

PERSONAL: Born April 23, 1971 in Pittsburgh, PA; married; wife's name Elizabeth. *Education:* Pennsylvania State University, M.F.A.; Pratt Institute, M.L.A.

ADDRESSES: Home—New York, NY. *E-mail*—contact monster@hotmail.com.

CAREER: Writer. United Nations, New York, NY, librarian and archivist.

WRITINGS:

23 Hours: A Vengeful Vampire Tale, Three Rivers Press (New York, NY), 2009.
Frostbite: A Werewolf Tale, Three Rivers Press (New York, NY), 2009.

ZOMBIE TRILOGY

Monster Island: A Zombie Novel, Thunder's Mouth Press (New York, NY), 2006.
Monster Nation: A Zombie Novel, Thunder's Mouth Press (New York, NY), 2006.
Monster Planet: A Zombie Novel, Thunder's Mouth Press (New York, NY), 2007.

"LAURA CAXTON" SERIES

13 Bullets: A Vampire Tale, Three Rivers Press (New York, NY), 2007.
99 Coffins: A Historical Vampire Tale, Three Rivers Press (New York, NY), 2007.
Vampire Zero: A Gruesome Vampire Tale, Three Rivers Press (New York, NY), 2008.

Contributor to anthologies, including *The Undead: Zombie Anthology,* Permuted Press, 2005, and *The Undead: Skin and Bones,* Permuted Press, 2007.

SIDELIGHTS: David Wellington was born in Pittsburgh, Pennsylvania, where George Romero shot his classic zombie films, including *Night of the Living Dead.* Wellington has created his own zombie trilogy, beginning with *Monster Island: A Zombie Novel,* which was first published serially and posted on a blog before being published by Thunder's Mouth Press. His novel *Frostbite: A Werewolf Tale* was also posted on a blog prior to print publication.

Monster Island is set in Manhattan, Wellington's home when he wrote the novel, and it is the island of the title. Animated corpses have overrun the city. When a contingent from Africa arrives in town seeking medicine, the delegates unexpectedly find themselves in the midst of a gory zombie battle. Luckily, the group

includes DeKalb, a former United Nations weapons inspector, and soldiers who are all well-armed teenage girls. In the story, a New York doctor-turned-zombie named Gary Fleck learns that he can retain his mental faculties by oxygenating his body, overcoming the lack of oxygen that normally destroys zombie brains. With this extra power, he becomes the most dangerous zombie of them all. *Booklist* contributor Regina Schroeder described this debut as "a fantastic zombie novel." A *Publishers Weekly* reviewer observed that this novel contains "provocative thoughts about the purpose of life and death underlaid with some ultra-dark humor." In reviewing the first book of the trilogy for *SciFi.com,* Paul Witcover wrote: "Wellington's idea of how to make a smart zombie is truly inspired, as is his notion of zombie mummies. . . . It's a stroke of genius. These may be the most noticeable of Wellington's innovations, but they are far from the only ones."

Monster Nation: A Zombie Novel tells the story of Nilla, a California zombie woman who, like Gary, has learned the secret to retaining her mental capabilities. As the story progresses, Nilla also becomes aware that she possesses psychic powers, including a special golden energy that enables the zombies to bear their miserable, undead state of being. Witcover wrote in his *SciFi.com* review that, like its predecessor, *Monster Nation* "retains all the addictive and propulsive narrative energy of serial publication at its best."

Wellington concludes his zombie series with *Monster Planet: A Zombie Novel.* In this book, set twelve years after the events of the earlier novels, one of the few surviving human beings in the wake of the zombie epidemic is a teenaged girl named Sarah. Sarah sets out to rescue Ayaan, who had formerly protected her, but has now been captured by the zombies himself. Her efforts find her journeying all the way from Egypt to the coast of New York City, and Governor's Island, where the final battle for the fate of the future between the zombies and the remaining humans takes place. A reviewer for *Publishers Weekly* suggested that "fans will relish the monster mash finale." Regina Schroeder, in a review for *Booklist,* dubbed the trilogy "horrifyingly entertaining," and concluded that "Wellington handles the zombie matter with just the right balancing of tension and humor."

In *13 Bullets: A Vampire Tale,* Wellington begins a new series. This one, also focused on vampires, features a young state trooper named Laura Caxton, and a much older U.S. marshal named Jameson Arkeley. In Wellington's fictional world, vampires have existed far back into history, and people have long been aware of their existence. Humans have been fighting vampires for centuries, continuously improving their means of revealing and killing them and relying on the larger human population to give themselves a strategic advantage. By the 1980s, the vampire population declined to the point where humans assumed they had become extinct. Set in the twenty-first century, *13 Bullets* reveals new evidence to the contrary. A group of violent and brazen vampires in Pennsylvania are killing humans there at a steady rate. Caxton and Arkeley are called upon to protect the public. Caxton is a fairly new member of the highway patrol, who has not yet fired her gun in the line of duty. Arkeley is a seasoned professional with retirement on his mind, but he is also the last living vampire hunter. Arkeley knows that vampires are not really extinct; he has spent the past twenty years on vampire research. Arkeley teaches Caxton how to hunt and kill vampires. A *Publishers Weekly* reviewer found the book to be "minimally plotted and driven by nonstop action." Patricia Altner commented in *Library Journal* that "there is plenty of gripping, fast-paced action and enough carnage here to delight the hearts of horror buffs."

99 Coffins: A Historical Vampire Tale is a sequel to *13 Bullets*. A student-run archaeological dig unearths a large number of coffins dating back to the Civil War era. Each coffin houses a corpse from which the heart was removed, and Arkeley decided they were the corpses of Union vampire soldiers. By the time Caxton joins his investigation, someone has revived one of these vampire soldiers, and soon a new, undead version of the Battle of Gettysburg begins. A reviewer for *Publishers Weekly* reported that "the taut narrative never slackens, providing thrilling entertainment for readers."

In *Vampire Zero: A Gruesome Vampire Tale,* the third volume in the series, Laura Caxton faces her most daunting challenge to date. In the previous novel, Arkeley allowed himself to be turned into a vampire in order to save Caxton's life, and now it is up to Caxton to hunt him down. Craig Young, reviewing for the *GayNZ* Web site, commented that "Laura's a tough, flawed but highly professional lesbian protagonist, and this is an excellent series."

BIOGRAPHICAL AND CRITICAL SOURCES:

PERIODICALS

Booklist, March 15, 2006, Regina Schroeder, review of *Monster Island: A Zombie Novel,* p. 36; July 1, 2007, Regina Schroeder, review of *Monster Planet: A Zombie Novel,* p. 42.

Library Journal, May 15, 2006, Jackie Cassada, review of *Monster Island,* p. 92; April 15, 2007, Patricia Altner, review of *13 Bullets: A Vampire Tale,* p. 79; July 1, 2007, Karl G. Siewert, review of *Monster Planet,* p. 82.
Publishers Weekly, March 13, 2006, review of *Monster Island,* p. 47; March 12, 2007, review of *13 Bullets,* p. 42; June 4, 2007, review of *Monster Planet,* p. 33; November 19, 2007, review of *99 Coffins: A Historical Vampire Tale,* p. 43.

ONLINE

Conversations with Writers, http://conversationswith writers.blogspot.com/ (October 7, 2008), author interview.
Curled Up with a Good Book, http://www.curledup. com/ (June 22, 2009), Lance Eaton, review of *Monster Nation,* and Douglas R. Cobb, review of *99 Coffins.*
Dark Party Review, http://darkpartyreview.blogspot. com/ (May 11, 2008), author interview.
David Wellington Home Page, http://www.brokentype. com/davidwellington (June 22, 2009).
Fatally Yours, http://www.fatally-yours.com/ (June 22, 2009), author interview.
Flames Rising, http://www.flamesrising.com/ (October 29, 2008), Matt M. McElroy, author interview.
GayNZ Web site, http://gaynz.com/ (January 26, 2009), Craig Young, review of *Vampire Zero: A Gruesome Vampire Tale.*
My Book, the Movie, http://mybookthemovie.blogspot. com/ (November 25, 2007), Marshal Zeringue, author interview.
SciFi.com, http://www.scifi.com/ (May 17, 2006), Paul Witcover, review of *Monster Island;* (September 27, 2006) Paul Witcover, review of *Monster Nation: A Zombie Novel.**

*   *   *

**WESTON, Cole
See RANDISI, Robert J.**

*   *   *

**WHYTE, Jack 1940-
(John D. Whyte)**

PERSONAL: Born March 15, 1940, in Johnstone, Scotland; immigrated to Canada, 1967; son of Francis and Sarah Keenan Whyte; married Beverley Ann

Mitchell, May 6, 1970; children: five. *Education:* University de Poiltiers, Diplôme d'Études Françaises, 1962; attended Strawberry Hill Teacher Training College (England), 1963. *Hobbies and other interests:* Music, reading, golf.

ADDRESSES: Home—Kelowna, British Columbia, Canada. *Agent*—Dean Cooke, The Cooke Agency, 278 Bloor St. E, Ste. 305, Toronto, Ontario M4W 3M4, Canada.

CAREER: Writer, novelist, copywriter, educator, and playwright. Taught English and French, 1963-68; professional musician, entertainer, performer, 1968-78; wrote for CBC national television; copy chief and creative director for advertising agencies, 1978-80; in corporate communications, 1980-96. Simon Fraser University, part-time instructor.

MEMBER: Burns Club of Calgary (past president and honorary life member).

AWARDS, HONORS: Honorary Regimental Bard, 1975; two Gold Medals, environmental category, for best writing and best narration, New York International Film Festival, 1992; Chieftain, Order of Gallant Canadians, Calgary Highlanders Regiment, 1994.

WRITINGS:

Jack Whyte: Forty Years in Canada, Heritage House (Custer, WA), 2007.

"A DREAM OF EAGLES"/"CAMULOD CHRONICLES" SERIES

The Skystone, Viking Canada (Toronto, Ontario, Canada), 1992, Forge Books (New York, NY), 1996.
The Singing Sword, Viking Canada (Toronto, Ontario, Canada), 1992, Forge Books (New York, NY), 1996.
The Eagles' Brood, Viking Canada (Toronto, Ontario, Canada), 1994, Forge Books (New York, NY), 1997.
The Saxon Shore, Viking Canada (Toronto, Ontario, Canada), 1995, Forge Books (New York, NY), 1998.

The Sorcerer, Book I: The Fort at River's Bend, Viking Canada (Toronto, Ontario, Canada), 1997, Forge Books (New York, NY), 1999.
The Sorcerer, Book II: Metamorphosis, Viking Canada (Toronto, Ontario, Canada), 1997, Forge Books (New York, NY), 1999.
Uther, Viking Canada (Toronto, Ontario, Canada), 2000, Forge Books (New York, NY), 2001.
Clothar the Frank, Viking Canada (Toronto, Ontario, Canada), 2003, published as *The Lance Thrower,* Forge Books (New York, NY), 2004.
The Eagle, Viking Canada (Toronto, Ontario, Canada), 2005, Forge (New York, NY), 2007.

"TEMPLAR" TRILOGY

Knights of the Black and White, Penguin (New York, NY), 2006.
Standard of Honor, G.P. Putnam's Sons (New York, NY), 2007.
Order in Chaos, G.P. Putnam's Sons (New York, NY), 2009.

Also author of *Rantin' Rovin' Robin* (one-man show based on the life of Robert Burns), performed by Whyte in Canada, 1974-78, and *Canada, Our Adopted Land* (narrative poem), 1984. Author's works have been translated into numerous languages.

SIDELIGHTS: Jack Whyte is a novelist, advertising copywriter, playwright, and educator. He has written a popular series based on the tale of King Arthur. First called "A Dream of Eagles," the series name was changed to the "Camulod Chronicles" for its U.S. editions. Whyte was born and raised in Scotland and moved to Canada in 1967. He taught high school in Canada for one year, then changed careers to become a singer, actor, musician, and entertainer. He wrote and performed in a one-man play based on the life of Scotland's national poet, Robert Burns, and took the show on the road. Whyte wrote for Canadian television, embarked on another career in advertising, and acted as communications director for a number of public and private companies before becoming a full-time writer in 1996.

Whyte was classically educated and has a strong interest in fifth-century history and the Roman occupation of Britain. That interest, along with his preoccupation with the legend of King Arthur, led him to develop the series of books in which he places Arthur in a historical context. In the debut book in the series, *The Skystone,* the detailed history of the final years of the Roman Empire is provided by narrator Gaius Publius Varrus, a Roman who fought under the command of his friend Caius Brittanicus until they joined with King Pendragon to create a free Britain. The story begins in the year A.D. 365, before the combined attack of the Scots from Hibernia (now Ireland), the Picts from Caledonia (now Scotland), and the Saxons from Germania (now Germany), and goes forward eighty years. Whyte uses the Christian dating system (not developed for another 200 years) for the benefit of modern readers. *Quill & Quire* contributor Deirdre Kelly described Varrus as "a good-natured, morally upright yet naive man whose fatal flaw is acting on compulsion, particularly to vent his anger," and added that because Varrus is a professional soldier, "the concentration on military life is appropriate." *Books in Canada* reviewer Douglas Hill stated that in Whyte's military history, "the canvas is broad, the action is exciting." Whyte includes an appendix that explains the structure of the Roman army, Roman place names, pronunciations, equivalents, and a map of Roman Britain.

Varrus leaves soldiering because of an injured leg and takes up his grandfather's profession, swordmaking. The stone of the title refers to meteorites, which provide the most long-lasting material from which to craft swords, and these are the stones Varrus seeks out to create his masterpieces. In evaluating the book for younger readers in *Kliatt,* Jerome V. Reel, Jr., noted that it does contain some sex and violence, but he added that "the strength of the story, with its curious twists that lead the reader towards Arthur's Britain, makes this a worthwhile book." A *Publishers Weekly* contributor felt that while Whyte's interpretation of the legend of Arthur is presented in its "least mystical form, his finely wrought background makes the tale more dazzling than any fantastic setting possibly could."

A *Publishers Weekly* reviewer wrote that in *The Singing Sword* Whyte "focuses even more strongly on a sense of place . . . making this series more realistic and believable than nearly any other Arthurian epic." Varrus and Britannicus, who are the grandfathers of Arthur, fight for their adopted land Camulod (Camelot), the thriving colony populated by Romans and Britons in southwestern England that will become the base in fighting the barbarians from the north. In this book, Caius Merlyn Britannicus, soon to be known as Merlin the magician, is born, the beginnings of the Round Table

are developed, and the sword Excalibur is forged. In a *Quill & Quire* review, Michelle Sagara commented that the book lacks "the sense of legend, of myth, of greatness, that has always accompanied Arthurian legend," but went on to say that Whyte has "added a distinct twist and interpretation to what has become familiar ground." A contributor in *Virginia Quarterly Review* called this second book in the series "story-telling on a grand scale."

In *The Eagles' Brood* the narrator is Merlyn, typically portrayed as the sorcerer but, noted a *Kirkus Reviews* contributor, "sanitized here to the most high-minded of soldiers who survives wars, betrayal, and a tragic love affair." Merlyn is commander of Camulod and rules with his cousin, Uther Pendragon, a warrior with a terrible temper. Reel noted that "while few of the major characters are historical, the background is full of documentable folk such as Vortigern, Ambrosius Aurelianus, and Germanus of Auxerre. The story is replete with the intrigues of a decaying culture and with major issues such as the Pelagian controversy."

The bond of friendship and blood is broken when Merlyn suspects that Uther has beaten the deaf girl, whom Merlyn later named Cassandra, after she resisted Uther's sexual advances. After she is healed, Cassandra becomes Merlyn's wife, but she ultimately dies a horrible death. The struggle to establish a Christian church and explanations regarding Excalibur and the Lady of the Lake appear in this third book, which Eric Robbins described in *Booklist* as being "chock-full of sexual dalliances and bloody battlefield conflicts." At the end Uther and King Lot die, and Merlyn holds the orphaned baby Arthur, the bastard son of Uther and Lot's wife, Ygraine, now also dead. He looks into the baby's golden eyes and sees him as king, wielding Excalibur. A *Publishers Weekly* contributor wrote that "this isn't the usual Arthurian tale with a fantasy gloss; in graphic realism lies its fascination, and its power."

Merlyn, now in his thirties, narrates *The Saxon Shore.* Frances Reiher wrote in *School Library Journal:* "Much that is new and intriguing brightens a legend that in many forms has always been enchanting." Merlyn is now responsible for the protection of his young cousin, Arthur, born of Roman and Hibernian and Celtic royal blood, and now heir to Camulod. The guardian must prepare the young man for the unification of the clans and the guardianship of the sword crafted by his great uncle, Publius Varrus. Merlyn develops a relationship with Connor, son of the High King of the Scots of Eire, who takes the baby Arthur with him to Eireland. With the help of the Scots and their war horses, Merlyn returns to England to continue building the fortressed community with plans of sheltering Arthur until he is ready to reign over Camulod. A *Publishers Weekly* reviewer wrote that "Whyte's descriptions, astonishingly vivid, of this ancient and mystical area ring true, as do his characters, who include a number of strong women."

The fifth and sixth books of the series are linked. In the former, an attempt is made on Arthur's life, and Merlyn takes him, with three young companions, to an abandoned Roman fort where he continues to train the young king. Merlyn's absence from Camulod renders it vulnerable to those who would take it, including Peter Ironhair and his friend, Carthac, and Merlyn must decide whether to risk returning and, in doing so, also risking the life of his charge. This book contains a great deal of information about the military skills Arthur must master, as well as the process of rebuilding the old fort. A *Publishers Weekly* reviewer deemed young Arthur "less absorbing a character than many of the others presented . . . but readers will revel in the impressively researched facts and in how Whyte makes the period come alive." Whyte "has a grand time bolting his story together," stated a *Kirkus Reviews* contributor. "Not as bloody as some of its predecessors in this series, Whyte's latest continues to bring the myth convincingly to life," wrote Melanie Duncan in *Booklist*.

Arthur becomes a man in *The Sorcerer, Book II: Metamorphosis*. Merlyn has Tressa, a new love, and his black horse, Germanicus, but life is not all bliss. Tressa dies, Merlyn must face Ironhair and Carthac, and he makes the decision to have Arthur take his place as king of Camulod. Merlyn takes two years to recover from a brush with death, and Arthur faces their enemies in battle, carrying a sword that is, unknown to him, a substitute for Excalibur. Arthur draws the real Excalibur from an altar stone at the end, in time to meet a new onslaught of enemies. A *Kirkus Reviews* writer noted that "the slow pace is necessary in creating the dense experience Whyte intends. Jump in here, now that Arthur's in motion, and you can always go back to earlier volumes if this look at the legend's subtext grabs you." *Library Journal* reviewer Jackie Cassada wrote that this installment is "compellingly told."

With *Uther*, Whyte provides a broader perspective on the life of Arthur's father. In this telling, the affair of Uther and Ygraine is actually a conspiracy in which they plan to overthrow Ygraine's husband Lot and unite Britain under Uther. *Quill & Quire* reviewer Meredith Renwick felt "those who prefer sorcery over swordplay will be disappointed. But history buffs should enjoy the richly detailed descriptions of military strategy, weaponry, political intrigues, and the day-to-day life of post-Roman Britain." Cassada commented that *Uther* is "able to stand on its own merits as a tale of a life lived boldly and with passion." *Booklist* reviewer Brad Hooper concluded: "As Whyte waves off the fog of fantasy and legend surrounding the Arthurian story, he renders characters and events real and plausible."

In *Clothar the Frank* (also published as *The Lance Thrower*), Whyte focuses on the story of Clothar, who will later be known as Lancelot, and his role in the founding and evolution of Arthur's magnificent reign. The son of a Frankish lord, Clothar is sent as a young man to one of the few remaining schools in Britain, where he is educated in logic and rhetoric as well as the military arts. Barbarism is rampant throughout the lands of ancient Britain, and those with the sharpest swords and most vicious attitudes dominate. The few remaining elements of organized civilization are threatened by the crumbling of order throughout the land. As Clothar matures, he becomes dedicated to the concepts of righteousness and justice. When his family is brutally killed, his resolve is tested and revenge is large in his mind. Instead, however, his mentor convinces him to join forces with the young Arthur Pendragon. There, Lancelot swears fealty to Arthur and helps forge the legend of Camelot and the Round Table. The bond of oath and friendship will be tested, however, through the love he and Arthur share for Queen Guinevere.

The final book of the "Camulod Chronicles" series is *The Eagle*. Narrated by Clothar (Lancelot), the story covers Arthur's attempts to unite Britain in the face of fighting local rulers and Saxon invaders. Two local kings, however, have different ideas. Symmachus and Connlyn join forces to thwart Arthur's noble goals. In the shadow of the main story, Clothar also tells about his affair with a woman engaged to another man. He details the paternity of Arthur's inadvertent son Mordred, the product of an unintentional liaison with his half-sister, Morgana. He also relates a seven-year mission in Gaul to train a cavalry force and to save his cousin's kingdom from the Huns. When he returns to Britain, he finds that danger looms everywhere, and a final confrontation between Camulod and its many enemies is inevitable, and approaching quickly. A *Publishers Weekly* contributor noted that "fans of Whyte's exhaustive retelling of the Camelot legend will welcome this final chapter." *Library Journal* reviewer Jackie Cassada called the novel "a welcome addition to the many retellings of a classic tale."

Whyte inaugurates a new trilogy with *Knights of the Black and White,* a novel about the history of the embattled Knights Templar. Hugh de Payens is a young knight in the year 1088, and when he is initiated into a secret organization called the Order of the Rebirth of Sion, he becomes an adversary of the Christian Church. Among the Order's beliefs are the conviction that the truth about Jesus and the founding of Christianity is secreted beneath the Temple Mount in Jerusalem. Soon, Sir Hugh finds himself part of a group summoned by Pope Urban to undertake a Holy Crusade against the Muslims to liberate Jerusalem from their control. Sir Hugh's experiences during the bloody and violent First Crusade are so traumatic that he decides to retire from warfare and spend the rest of his life in religious observance. However, his goals are derailed after the fall of Jerusalem, when he becomes the founder of a new order of battle-trained monks, and the search intensifies for the treasure alleged to be buried under the Temple Mount. Whyte draws the reader into the story of Sir Hugh and the early Templars "with his usual deft combination of historical drama and old-fashioned adventure," commented David Pitt, writing in *Booklist.*

Standard of Honor is the sequel to Whyte's *Knights of the Black and White.* The novel, set in the twelfth century, finds Alexander Sinclair, a Knight Templar, hiding out in the Holy Land, trying to give his wounds time to heal in the wake of the Battle of Hattin. At this time and in this place, the Knights of the Templar order are in grave danger, despised by many of those in power, and many of the other survivors of the battle have been executed simply for their affiliation to that order. Because of this, Sinclair carefully keeps his relationship to the Knights Templar a secret. However, only two years later, everything spills into the foreground when Sir Henry St. Clair, uncle to Alexander and father to his cousin Andre, is asked by Richard the Lionheart himself to join him on his most recent crusade as his right-hand man. Henry's acceptance drives a wedge into the family, as Andre is a Templar as well, is rising rapidly through their ranks, and holds a strong loyalty to his cousin Alexander as well as to the order. David Pitt, in a review for *Booklist,* cited the recent increase in books and films relating in some way to the Knights Templar and dubbed Whyte's book "a must for both historical adventure fans and anyone whose interest in the Templars has been sparked."

BIOGRAPHICAL AND CRITICAL SOURCES:

PERIODICALS

Booklist, September 1, 1997, Eric Robbins, review of *The Eagles' Brood,* p. 61; June 1, 1998, Grace Lee, review of *The Saxon Shore,* p. 1722; April 1, 1999, Melanie Duncan, review of *The Fort at River's Bend,* p. 1391; April 1, 2001, Brad Hooper, review of *Uther,* p. 1454; July 1, 2006, David Pitt, review of *Knights of the Black and White,* p. 34; December 15, 2006, Margaret Flanagan, review of *The Eagle,* p. 24.

Books in Canada, December, 1992, Douglas Hill, "First Novels: Difficult Loves," p. 55; October 15, 2007, David Pitt, review of *Standard of Honor,* p. 37.

Canadian Book Review Annual, 1998, Carol U. Merriam, review of *The Fort at River's Bend* and *The Sorcerer, Book II: Metamorphosis,* p. 202.

Kirkus Reviews, August 1, 1997, review of *The Eagles' Brood,* p. 1152; May 1, 1998, review of *The Saxon Shore,* p. 617; February 15, 1999, review of *The Fort at River's Bend,* p. 256; May 15, 1999, review of *The Sorcerer, Book II,* p. 755.

Kliatt, March, 1997, Jerome V. Reel, Jr., review of *The Skystone,* p. 14; September, 1998, Jerome V. Reel, Jr., review of *The Eagles' Brood,* p. 24.

Library Journal, December, 1995, Jackie Cassada, review of *The Skystone,* p. 163; July, 1999, Jackie Cassada, review of *The Sorcerer, Book II,* p. 143; April 15, 2001, Jackie Cassada, review of *Uther,* p. 135; December 1, 2006, Jackie Cassada, review of *The Eagle,* p. 115.

Magazine of Fantasy and Science Fiction, October, 1997, Robert K.J. Killheffer, review of *The Eagles' Brood,* p. 44.

Publishers Weekly, January 29, 1996, review of *The Skystone,* p. 88; September 23, 1996, review of *The Singing Sword,* p. 61; August 4, 1997, review of *The Eagles' Brood,* p. 67; May 25, 1998, review of *The Saxon Shore,* p. 66; March 8, 1999, review of *The Fort at River's Bend,* p. 52; March 19, 2001, review of *Uther,* p. 78; May 8, 2006, review of *Knights of the Black and White,* p. 46; September 11, 2006, review of *The Eagle,* p. 32.

Quill & Quire, November, 1992, Deirdre Kelly, review of *The Skystone,* p. 24; June, 1993, Michelle Sagara, review of *The Singing Sword,* p. 27; December, 2000, Meredith Renwick, review of *Uther,* pp. 25-26.

School Library Journal, April, 1999, Frances Reiher, review of *The Saxon Shore,* p. 162.

Virginia Quarterly Review, spring, 1997, review of *The Singing Sword,* p. 57.

ONLINE

Barnes & Noble Web site, http://www.barnesandnoble.com/ (May 16, 2007), Harriet Klausner, review of *Uther.*

Jack Whyte Home Page, http://www.camulod.com (May 16, 2007).

Twisted Kingdom Web log, http://twisted-kingdom.blogspot.com/ (May 16, 2007).*

*   *   *

WHYTE, John D.
  See WHYTE, Jack

*   *   *

WICKER, Christine 1953-

PERSONAL: Born July 6, 1953; married Philip Seib.

ADDRESSES: Agent—Jandy Nelson, Manus and Associates Literary Agency, 425 Sherman Ave., Ste. 200, Palo Alto, CA 94306. *E-mail*—christine@christinewicker.com.

CAREER: Dallas Morning News, Dallas, TX, worked seventeen years as a feature writer, columnist, and religion reporter.

AWARDS, HONORS: Numerous awards include Clarion Award, Association for Women in Communications; Wilbur Award, Religion Communicators Council; first place award for feature writing, Sunday Magazine Editors Association; and seven first prizes from Dallas Press Club.

WRITINGS:

(With John Matthews) *The Eyeball Killer* (nonfiction), Pinnacle Books (New York, NY), 1996.

God Knows My Heart (autobiography), St. Martin's Press (New York, NY), 1999.

Lily Dale: The True Story of the Town that Talks to the Dead, HarperSanFrancisco (San Francisco, CA), 2003.

Not in Kansas Anymore: A Curious Tale of How Magic Is Transforming America, HarperOne (New York, NY), 2005.

The Fall of the Evangelical Nation: The Surprising Crisis inside the Church, HarperOne (New York, NY), 2008.

SIDELIGHTS: Christine Wicker was raised primarily in the American South, including Oklahoma and Texas. The great-granddaughter of a Baptist preacher and the granddaughter of a coal miner, she was the first in her family to become a journalist. Her work took her away from her roots and exposed her to travel, politics, and cultures vastly different from what she experienced in childhood. As a reporter for the *Dallas Morning News,* Wicker found herself covering demonstrations in Nairobi, Pope John II's trip to Cuba, and Lady Diana Spencer's funeral in London, among other important events. Her first book, *The Eyeball Killer,* which she wrote with Dallas police officer John Matthews, is a true-crime story about a serial murderer who removed the eyes of his prostitute victims. Matthews and his partner were able to break the case because they were willing to talk to other prostitutes and listen to their stories, details that Wicker describes in the book.

God Knows My Heart, Wicker's next book, addresses a very different subject. Here she examines her relationship with religion, from her upbringing as a Southern Baptist to her estrangement from the church of her childhood, to her search for a way to combine faith with her adult viewpoint of the world. Several critics found the book moving. A reviewer for *Publishers Weekly* called it "a record of a spiritual search that is by turns both painful and exhilarating," while Sandra Collins observed in *Library Journal* that "as a catalog of religion in the world, Wicker's insights prove intriguing."

Lily Dale: The True Story of the Town that Talks to the Dead examines the way of life in a small town in upstate New York that was settled by Spiritualists—sometimes known as mediums. Wicker recounts the history of the town, but she also uses it as a focus to discuss various types of faith and the motivations behind a person's need to communicate with those who have passed away. "Wicker's jaunty pacing and humor keep the work from growing too dark and leave the reader with a feeling of tenderness, rather than pity, toward her subjects," observed a *Publishers Weekly* critic.

In her next work, *Not in Kansas Anymore: A Curious Tale of How Magic Is Transforming America,* Wicker continues to deal with other-worldly subjects. Included here are stories and theories that Wicker collected as she traveled across the country in search of all things related to magic. She covers witchcraft, vampirism, and numerous other occult practices and beliefs, and she reflects on the many ways in which members of various faiths have resisted scientific reasoning. Some reviewers deemed the work intriguing. A contributor to *Kirkus Reviews* referred to Wicker's book as a collection of "entertaining adventures in esoterica, with some serious side effects." *Library Journal* correspondent Heather McCormack described the book as "more a spiritual memoir than a journalistic study, wherein Wicker reaffirms her right to find meaning in everyday life."

The Fall of the Evangelical Nation: The Surprising Crisis inside the Church covers another topic related to spiritualism and religious faith. In the late twentieth and early twenty-first centuries, evangelical Christians gained a reputation as a powerful force in U.S. culture and politics, especially as a reliable source of votes for conservative political candidates. Wicker makes a case, however, that the numbers and influence of evangelicals are less substantial than generally believed. She defines "evangelical" in terms of adherence to certain fundamental beliefs, such as Biblical inerrancy and salvation only through faith in Jesus Christ, and finds that only seven percent of American adults can be classified as such, compared with the twenty-five-percent figure often cited by pollsters. This seven percent has been "scaring the bejesus out of the rest of America," she writes in her book, and has received disproportionate media coverage "despite the fact that other Christians outnumber them by 5 or 6 to one," she told Hemant Mehta in an interview for his blog *Friendly Atheist.* The idea of evangelical power, she wrote in an opinion piece for the *Dallas Morning News* Web site, is "hype" from "a relatively small group of dedicated, focused, political power-seekers."

She also sees the role of evangelicals waning; she predicts that their population will decline as pastors of "mega-churches" age and retire, and as younger members of such congregations adopt more liberal social beliefs, including support for gay rights, acceptance of sex outside marriage, and respect for practitioners of other faiths. "When I was a kid," Wicker told *Dallas Morning News* interviewer Jeffrey Weiss, "there may have been people who didn't want to think we [Christians] were the only ones who were saved. But there weren't many of them. It didn't gag people. It does now."

Several critics found Wicker's work captivating, even if some did not agree with her conclusions. *Booklist* contributor Ray Olson, noting that Wicker "scrutinizes received wisdom," called the book "most enlightening." Even while skeptical of evangelical beliefs and the power of this group, she remains sympathetic toward many evangelicals, he added. To *Library Journal* reviewer James A. Overbeck, *The Fall of the Evangelical Nation* was "very readable," enhanced by Wicker's discussion of her own religious experiences as well as "much entertaining anecdotal description of evangelical ministries." A *Publishers Weekly* commentator, though, found the book to be "tendentious" and "confused." Wicker needs to support her claims, the critic wrote, with "more rigorous research and source citation." A contributor to the Web site *Peace Theology* also called for "more solid research and careful writing on this topic." "Wicker does give us some strong evidence" that evangelicals' influence has been overestimated, the reviewer noted, while also observing that her "breezy style and lack of precision . . . foster a bit of a sense of skepticism." *Mark of Ashen Wings* blogger Dru Pagliasotti found Wicker's book to be convincing, for the most part, writing: "Her analysis is as scrupulous and careful as she can make it, calling on evangelicals' own data and spokespeople as she describes the problems evangelicals are having." Wicker's Southern Baptist background, the blogger added, has helped her produce a "nuanced" work that "is of equal interest to both evangelicals and non-evangelicals."

BIOGRAPHICAL AND CRITICAL SOURCES:

BOOKS

Wicker, Christine, *God Knows My Heart,* St. Martin's Press (New York, NY), 1999.

PERIODICALS

Booklist, October 15, 2005, Patricia Monaghan, review of *Not in Kansas Anymore: A Curious Tale of How Magic Is Transforming America,* p. 7; April 15,

2008, Ray Olson, review of *The Fall of the Evangelical Nation: The Surprising Crisis inside the Church*, p. 8.

Book News, February, 2006, review of *Not in Kansas Anymore.*

Christianity Today, April, 2008, "Yes, Nominal Evangelicals Exist."

Dallas Morning News, May 10, 2008, Jeffrey Weiss, "New Book Says Evangelicals' Numbers Are Dwindling," p. B14.

Detroit Free Press, March 23, 2003, review of *Lily Dale,* p. 4E.

Kirkus Reviews, March 15, 1999, review of *God Knows My Heart,* p. 441; August 1, 2005, review of *Not in Kansas Anymore,* p. 840.

Library Journal, March 1, 1999, Sandra Collins, review of *God Knows My Heart,* p. 90; January, 2003, May Prokop, review of *Lily Dale,* p. 120; September 1, 2005, Heather McCormack, review of *Not in Kansas Anymore,* p. 149; May 1, 2008, James A. Overbeck, review of *The Fall of the Evangelical Nation,* p. 72.

Mother Jones, December, 2005, April Dembosky, review of *Not in Kansas Anymore,* p. 73.

Publishers Weekly, February 22, 1999, review of *God Knows My Heart,* p. 84; January 20, 2003, review of *Lily Dale,* p. 69; September 8, 2003, John F. Baker, "A Magical Mystery Tour," p. 14; July 25, 2005, review of *Not in Kansas Anymore,* p. 71; August 29, 2005, Heather Grennan Gary, "In Profile: Journalists Tackle Religion's Connects and Disconnects," p. S14; March 10, 2008, review of *The Fall of the Evangelical Nation,* p. 78.

Washington Post Book World, March 28, 1999, Colman McCarthy, review of *God Knows My Heart,* p. 6.

ONLINE

Australian Broadcasting Corporation Web site, http://www.abc.net.au/ (June 30, 2008), transcript of interview conducted by Paul Comrie-Thomson on the program *Counterpoint.*

BookPage, http://bookpage.com/ (March, 2003), review of *Lily Dale: The True Story of the Town that Talks to the Dead,* p. 6.

Christine Wicker Home Page, http://www.christine wicker.com (June 30, 2009).

Conversation at the Edge, http://conversationattheedge. com/ (May 4, 2008), author interview.

Dallas Morning News Web site, http://www.dallasnews. com/ (June 1, 2008), Christine Wicker, "The Great Evangelical Decline."

Friendly Atheist, http://friendlyatheist.com/ (June 4, 2008), Hemant Mehta, author interview.

HarperCollins Web site, http://www.harpercollins.com/ (June 30, 2009), author profile.

Mark of Ashen Wings, http://ashenwings.com/ (January 7, 2009), Dru Pagliasotti, review of *The Fall of the Evangelical Nation.*

On the Media Web site, http://www.onthemedia.org/ (July 4, 2008), transcript of author interview on the National Public Radio program *On the Media,* conducted by program host Bob Garfield.

Peace Theology, http://peacetheology.net/ (January 26, 2009), review of *The Fall of the Evangelical Nation.**

*　　*　　*

WILLIAMSON, Lisa
See SOULJAH, Sister

*　　*　　*

WOODWORTH, Steven E. 1961-
(Steven Edward Woodworth)

PERSONAL: Born January 28, 1961, in Akron, OH; son of Ralph Leon (a pastor and educator) and Erma Jean (a homemaker) Woodworth; married Leah Dawn Bunke (a homemaker), August 13, 1983; children: Nathan William, Jonathan Steven, David Eric, Daniel Timothy, Anna Constance, Elizabeth Grace. *Education:* Southern Illinois University at Carbondale, B.A. (with high honors), 1982; attended University of Hamburg, 1982-83; Rice University, Ph.D., 1987.

ADDRESSES: Office—Department of History, Texas Christian University, P.O. Box 297260, Fort Worth, TX 76129. *E-mail*—s.woodworth@tcu.edu.

CAREER: Writer, historian, and educator. Teacher at Baptist schools in Houston, TX, 1984-86; Houston Community College, adjunct instructor, 1984-87; Bartlesville Wesleyan College, Bartlesville, OK, instructor in history, 1987-89; Toccoa Falls College, Toccoa Falls, GA, assistant professor, 1989-94, associate professor of history, 1994-97; Texas Christian University, Fort Worth, began as assistant professor, became professor of history, 1997—.

MEMBER: American Historical Association, Organization of American Historians, Southern Historical Association.

AWARDS, HONORS: Fletcher Pratt Award, 1991, for *Jefferson Davis and His Generals: The Failure of Confederate Command in the West,* and 1996, for *Davis and Lee at War.*

WRITINGS:

Jefferson Davis and His Generals: The Failure of Confederate Command in the West, University Press of Kansas (Lawrence, KS), 1990.

The Essentials of United States History, 1841 to 1877: Westward Expansion and the Civil War, Research & Education Association (Piscataway, NJ), 1990, revised version edited by Max Fogiel, 2001.

The Essentials of United States History, 1500 to 1789: From Colony to Republic, Research & Education Association (Piscataway, NJ), 1990.

Davis and Lee at War, University Press of Kansas (Lawrence, KS), 1995.

(With Grady McWhiney) *A Deep Steady Thunder: The Battle of Chickamauga,* Ryan Place Publishers (Fort Worth, TX), 1996.

Six Armies in Tennessee: The Chickamauga and Chattanooga Campaigns, University of Nebraska Press (Lincoln, NE), 1998.

No Band of Brothers: Problems in the Rebel High Command, University of Missouri Press (Columbia, MO), 1999.

Cultures in Conflict: The American Civil War, Greenwood Press (Westport, CT), 2000.

While God Is Marching On: The Religious World of Civil War Soldiers, University Press of Kansas (Lawrence, KS), 2001.

(With Warren Wilkinson) *A Scythe of Fire: The Civil War Story of the Eighth Georgia Infantry Regiment,* W. Morrow (New York, NY), 2002.

The Loyal, True, and Brave: America's Civil War Soldiers, edited by Steven E. Woodworth, SR Books (Wilmington, DE), 2002.

Beneath a Northern Sky: A Short History of the Gettysburg Campaign, SR Books (Wilmington, DE), 2003, 2nd edition, Rowman & Littlefield (Lanham, MD), 2008.

(With Kenneth J. Winkle) *Oxford Atlas of the Civil War,* foreword by James M. McPherson, Oxford University Press (New York, NY), 2004.

(Author of introduction) *Southern Sons, Northern Soldiers: The Civil War Letters of the Remley Brothers, Twenty-second Iowa Infantry,* edited by Julie Holcomb, Northern Illinois University Press (DeKalb, IL), 2004.

Nothing but Victory: The Army of the Tennessee, 1861-1865, Alfred A. Knopf (New York, NY), 2005.

(With Mark Grimsley) *Shiloh: A Battlefield Guide,* University of Nebraska Press (Lincoln, NE), 2006.

Decision in the Heartland: The Civil War in the West, Praeger (Westport, CT), 2008.

Sherman, Palgrave Macmillan (New York, NY), 2009.

WITH JEROME MCDUFFIE AND GARY PIGGREM

The Advanced Placement Examination in United States History, Research & Education Association (Piscataway, NJ), 1990.

The Best Test Preparation for the Advanced Placement Examination, United States History, with CD-ROM, Research & Education Association (Piscataway, NJ), 2000, revised version edited by Max Fogiel, 2001.

United States History, edited by Paul R. Babbitt, Research & Education Association (Piscataway, NJ), 2005.

EDITOR

Leadership and Command in the American Civil War, Savas Woodbury (Campbell, CA), 1995.

The American Civil War: A Handbook of Literature and Research, Greenwood Press (Westport, CT), 1996.

The Musick of the Mocking Birds, the Roar of the Cannon: The Civil War Diary and Letters of William Winters, University of Nebraska Press (Lincoln, NE), 1998.

The Art of Command in the Civil War, University of Nebraska Press (Lincoln, NE), 1998.

Civil War Generals in Defeat, University Press of Kansas (Lawrence, KS), 1999.

Chickamauga: A Battlefield Guide with a Section on Chattanooga, cartography by Marcia McLean, University of Nebraska Press (Lincoln, NE), 1999.

The Human Tradition in the Civil War and Reconstruction, SR Books (Wilmington, DE), 2000.

Grant's Lieutenants: From Cairo to Vicksburg, University Press of Kansas (Lawrence, KS), 2001.

American Civil War, Gale (Detroit, MI), 2008.

Grant's Lieutenants: From Chattanooga to Appomattox, University Press of Kansas (Lawrence, KS), 2008.

The Shiloh Campaign, Southern Illinois University Press (Carbondale, IL), 2009.

Also author (with Gary Piggrem, N.R. Holt, and W.T. Walker) of *The Graduate Record Examination in History,* 1993. Work represented in anthologies, including *The Confederate General,* edited by William C. Davis, Cowles Magazines. Contributor of articles and reviews to history and education journals.

SIDELIGHTS: Writer, educator, and Civil War historian Steven E. Woodworth is a professor of history at Texas Christian University. He is the author or editor of more than two dozen books, most of which concern topics related to the American Civil War. His books cover specific regiments, individual generals and campaigns, and overall concepts such as religion as it was practiced by Civil War soldiers. In *Davis and Lee at War,* Woodworth analyzes the strategies two of the Civil War South's most prominent military figures, Jefferson Davis and Robert E. Lee. Woodworth explores how Davis's strategy was not aggressive but employed endurance and persistence in an attempt to win the war simply by not losing it. Davis believed that Lee would exhaust himself and pave the way for a Northern win. Lee, in contrast, was a bold and aggressive strategist, preferring to fight hard and let his victories accumulate. A succession of quick, decisive victories, Lee believed, would convince the North to give up the war. Woodworth notes that both approaches had merit, but neither was applied consistently, eroding their effectiveness. It was Lee and Davis's professional relationship, Woodworth argues, that prevented a decision on which strategy to use. Without a strong and consistent strategy, the Confederacy eventually lost. A *Publishers Weekly* contributor called Woodworth's book an "engaging, well-written account" of Davis's and Lee's approaches to war. "Woodworth has produced a lively and readable narrative account of a topic in need of exploration," commented Kenneth H. Williams in *Civil War History,* though Williams also expressed a desire to see more corroborating evidence. Chris Patsilelis, writing in the *New York Times,* concluded: "This well-written and highly illuminating work is not only an incisive study of military command but a penetrating psychological analysis of Davis, Lee," and other prominent personalities of the Confederacy.

A Scythe of Fire: The Civil War Story of the Eighth Georgia Infantry Regiment contains a ground-level history of the Eighth Georgia, a regiment that participated in some of the major battles of the Civil War, including Gettysburg, numerous Shenandoah Valley campaigns, and Appomattox. Woodworth derives his history from a number of primary source documents, such as letters, diaries, newspaper accounts, and other written materials. Woodworth notes that few of the soldiers even mention slavery, nor do they seem to have made any personal decision as to its morality. The narrative demonstrates a strong loyalty among the Eighth's soldiers, both to each other and to the regiment itself. Woodworth relates stories of common experiences, daily hardships, and individual victories, as well as harrowing battle stories. He tells of how even the valiant Eighth Georgia eventually dissolved under the stress of combat and starvation. Jay Freeman, writing in *Booklist,* observed that Woodworth's book illustrated "what war is like at ground level as experienced by common foot soldiers." Woodworth "brings an intensely human face to this unit, detailing the casualties and human suffering the Civil War entailed," remarked a *Publishers Weekly* reviewer. Woodworth's account chronicles the transformation of the soldiers of the Eight Georgia from "enthusiastic, patriotic boys to war-hardened, weary men who pray for an end to the fighting," noted Robert Flatley in *Library Journal.*

With *While God Is Marching On: The Religious World of Civil War Soldiers,* Woodworth addresses a topic that is often overlooked, downplayed, or ignored in Civil War scholarship: the ways in which Civil War soldiers on both sides of the conflict practiced their religion and managed to reconcile their religious beliefs with the war they were fighting. Again relying on important primary documents such as diaries and letters, Woodworth describes how most Civil War soldiers, Union and Confederate alike, were Christians, both praying to the same God for guidance and protection, both believing in the righteousness of their struggle and that God would ultimately deliver victory to them. Many of the soldiers found victories in battle to be evidence of God's favor, while defeats were seen as testing and purifying the soldiers. Woodworth explores issues related to the soldiers' views on personal salvation and how both Union and Confederate sides were swept by a "Great Revival" that kept religious observance consistently in the minds of the faithful. Regular prayer meetings and religious services also helped soldiers resist the sins and temptations common to military life. Others, Woodworth notes, believed that their Christianity helped prevent even greater carnage, widespread looting, and violation of the enemy. Soldiers of the Civil War, Woodworth concludes, had a thorough understanding of fundamental Christian concepts and doctrine, and these soldiers continued to practice their religion even in the most difficult periods of the war. In looking at the importance of religion during the Civil War itself, Woodworth "contributes something important to the study of American religious history," commented a *Publishers Weekly* critic. Kathleen M. Conley, writing in *Library Journal,* called Woodworth's book a "much-needed addition to Civil War scholarship." The author "has a fine ear for the telling anecdote, and his narration will satisfy Civil War buffs and American religious historians alike," concluded Dan McKanan in the *Journal of Religion.*

Beneath a Northern Sky: A Short History of the Gettysburg Campaign contains a concise history of what may be the Civil War's best-known battle. In the face of many volumes of academic and popular scholarship on Gettysburg and the Civil War, noted David Dixon in the *Journal of Southern History,* "this book is designed to synthesize the voluminous body of literature currently available on the topic into a compelling and concise narrative that will satisfy both novice and logician." Woodworth assembles modern scholarship from notable researchers such as Earl J. Hess, David G. Martin, and Richard S. Shue. He "does a masterful job of weaving these complex modern interpretations into a seamless overview" of Gettysburg and the war, Dixon remarked. Woodworth also brings to bear earlier classics and other works. The book includes photographs of the Gettysburg battlefield and portraits of significant leaders.

Because *Beneath a Northern Sky* deals with the most significant battle of one of the most written-about wars in the history of the world, it reworks some very familiar material. However, the volume shows "the most recent scholarship on the battle," according to a *Reference & Research Book News* reviewer, "in a comprehensive and accessible format." *H-Net Reviews* contributor Jeffrey C. Hall wrote: "Woodworth does more than provide a strong narrative line. The author pauses frequently to supply interpretations of the events and evaluations of actions performed by major members of the cast of characters." "Those who research Gettysburg then write endlessly about it are analyzing this military event into oblivion," Hall continued; however, "the author being considered at the moment at least avoids a pure recycling of the usual and global negativity about the performance of the Confederate high command." In Hall's view, "Woodworth's forays into Gettysburg analysis are more than enough to keep the mind alert as one works his way through this version of the story."

"Woodworth's work," Hall concluded, "strikes a fine balance between too superficial and overly dry, on the one hand, and a case of 'more and more about less and less,' on the other."

Woodworth and Kenneth J. Winkle offer a detailed visual resource covering important Civil War places and concepts in the *Oxford Atlas of the Civil War.* The book includes "narrative sketches, illustrations, and annotated maps of the major events and battles of the Civil War era," noted Willard Carl Klunder in *History: Review of New Books.* The major portion of the book is divided into five chapters, each of which covers events and activities during a single year from 1861 to 1865. The authors present antebellum topics related to such areas as the spread of slavery, industrial expansion, immigration, and territorial growth. They also provide visual references for postwar subjects such as reconstruction, the spread of Jim Crow legislation, homesteading, sharecropping, and presidential elections to 1892. Maps and illustrations depict not just war-related information, but other data relevant to the world surrounding the war, such as the price of farmland, the spread of railroads, population, and cultural aspects of the Civil War years. Woodworth and Winkle also include a chronology of the war and a glossary of terms and concepts. Klunder concluded that the book "provides the general reader with a handy reference guide to the Civil War era."

In *Nothing but Victory: The Army of the Tennessee, 1861-1865,* Woodworth examines a largely ignored military division of the North that boasted an impressive string of victories over opponents at Shiloh and elsewhere, that played important roles in decisive battles such as Vicksburg and Atlanta, and that served as a proving ground for many of the Civil War's best generals. The Army of the Tennessee, Woodworth notes, has been neglected while greater attention was paid to hard-fighting units such as the Army of the Potomac and the Army of the Cumberland. He delves into the history and accomplishments of the Army of the Tennessee to show that this unit was just as important as its better-known counterparts, that it served with distinction as great as any other Civil War unit, and that its victories were had through skill and finesse rather than blunt force. He describes how the unit was assembled from volunteers from Illinois, Wisconsin, and Iowa, and how its character and abilities were shaped by commanders such as Ulysses S. Grant and William Sherman. Woodworth notes how the pride of excellence extended through lower-ranked field commanders, company officers, and civilian corps commanders. Woodworth's history of the Army of the Tennessee is "arguably the best one-volume history written to date of a Civil War field army," remarked a *Publishers Weekly* reviewer. "Balanced and readable, Woodworth's work is an exemplary army-level unit history," concluded *Booklist* reviewer Gilbert Taylor.

Woodworth's *American Civil War: A Handbook of Literature and Research* forms a part of the "Gale Library of Daily Life" series and tries to "connect to Civil War history on a more human level than is normally done in reference works," wrote *Booklist* contributor Michael Tasko. "What was it like to live during this time?" In two hundred separate essays, the contributors to *American Civil War* describe how soldiers and civilians dealt with the vagaries of their lives—sometimes in their own words, through excerpts from letters and diaries. "Breadth is this title's strong point," stated Daniel Sifton in *Library Journal*, "as the essays explor[e] African American soldiers, Native American soldiers, women on the battlefield, sanitation, [and] food." "There are, of course, numerous works on the topic of the American Civil War," Jamie Seeholzer said in a *Reference & User Services Quarterly* review, "but, as the editor states, no other Civil War work focuses so completely on components of daily life." This work, declared a *Reference & Research Book News* reviewer, is an "academic text [that] provides a solid reference for students, general readers, historians, and researchers."

Woodworth's *Sherman* forms a part of Palgrave Macmillan's "Great Generals" series and concentrates on Sherman's career in the Union army. "Woodworth neatly lays out Sherman's Civil War service," Frieda Murray wrote in *Booklist*, "from appointment as a colonel in May 1861" to the surrender of Joe Johnson's army at the end of the war. Despite having graduated from West Point and having seen service in the Mexican War (in California), Sherman's greatest moments came between 1861 and 1865, when he served as "Grant's most trusted, effective subordinate," declared a *Kirkus Reviews* contributor. The result, the reviewer concluded, is "a crisp assessment of a warrior who perfected the doctrine of striking at the enemy's economic resources and will to resist."

Woodworth told *CA:* "If I write books, even on topics that are not explicitly Christian, it is for the glory of God. I hope someday to be able to do some writing that will be more explicit in relating history and the Christian world-view."

BIOGRAPHICAL AND CRITICAL SOURCES:

PERIODICALS

American Historical Review, October, 1991, Michael B. Ballard, review of *Jefferson Davis and His Generals: The Failure of Confederate Command in the West,* p. 1296; April, 1997, Richard E. Beringer, review of *Davis and Lee at War,* p. 525.

Booklist, November 15, 1996, review of *The American Civil War: A Handbook of Literature and Research,* p. 607; February 15, 2002, Jay Freeman, review of *A Scythe of Fire: The Civil War Story of the Eighth Georgia Infantry Regiment,* p. 989; July, 2005, Abbie Landry, review of *Oxford Atlas of the Civil War,* p. 1938; October 1, 2005, Gilbert Taylor, review of *Nothing but Victory: The Army of the Tennessee, 1861-1865,* p. 21; September 15, 2008, Michael Tasko, review of *American Civil War,* p. 75; January 1, 2009, Frieda Murray, review of *Sherman,* p. 29.

Books & Culture, July-August, 2003, David Rolfs, "When Thou Goest out to Battle: The Religious World of Civil War Soldiers," review of *While God Is Marching On: The Religious World of Civil War Soldiers,* p. 19.

Choice, January, 2000, L.E. Babits, review of *Chickamauga: A Battlefield Guide with a Section on Chattanooga,* p. 1000.

Chronicle of Higher Education, October 5, 2001, Nina C. Ayoub, review of *While God Is Marching On.*

Civil War History, March, 1997, Kenneth H. Williams, review of *Davis and Lee at War,* p. 75; December, 1997, Lesley Gordon, review of *The American Civil War,* p. 335.

First Things: A Monthly Journal of Religion and Public Life, December, 2001, George McKenna, review of *While God Is Marching On,* p. 50.

Historian, spring, 2001, Mark A. Weitz, review of *No Band of Brothers: Problems in the Rebel High Command,* p. 659.

History: Review of New Books, summer, 2005, Willard Carl Klunder, review of *Oxford Atlas of the Civil War,* p. 141.

Journal of American History, December, 1996, Craig L. Symonds, review of *Davis and Lee at War,* p. 1022; September, 1997, Edward Hagerman, review of *The American Civil War,* p. 666.

Journal of Military History, January, 1999, Judith Lee Hallock, review of *Six Armies in Tennessee: The Chickamauga and Chattanooga Campaigns,* p. 190;

April, 2000, Sharon S. MacDonald, review of *No Band of Brothers,* p. 538; July, 2000, Richard M. McMurry, review of *Civil War Generals in Defeat,* p. 846; October, 2001, Herman Hattaway, review of *The Art of Command in the Civil War,* p. 1098; July, 2002, Symonds, review of *Grant's Lieutenants: From Cairo to Vicksburg,* p. 853.

Journal of Religion, July, 2002, Dan McKanan, review of *While God Is Marching On,* p. 450.

Journal of Southern History, August, 1999, Kenneth W. Noe, review of *Six Armies in Tennessee,* p. 638; August, 2000, Edward J. Hagerty, review of *The Art of Command in the Civil War,* p. 640; November, 2000, Edward Hagerman, review of *Civil War Generals in Defeat,* p. 877; November, 2001, James M. Beeby, review of *The Human Tradition in the Civil War and Reconstruction,* p. 877; February, 2002, Peter S. Carmichael, review of *Cultures in Conflict: The American Civil War,* p. 193; May, 2003, Anne C. Rose, review of *While God Is Marching On,* p. 441; November, 2003, Dan R. Frost, review of *The Loyal, True, and Brave: America's Civil War Soldiers,* p. 918; November, 2004, David Dixon, review of *Beneath a Northern Sky: A Short History of the Gettysburg Campaign,* p. 934.

Kirkus Reviews, October 1, 2008, review of *Sherman.*

Library Journal, March 15, 1999, John Carver Edwards, review of *Civil War Generals in Defeat,* p. 90; August, 2001, Kathleen M. Conley, review of *While God Is Marching On,* p. 134; January, 2002, Robert Flatley, review of *A Scythe of Fire,* p. 126; August 1, 2008, Daniel Sifton, review of *American Civil War,* p. 112.

Mississippi Quarterly, winter, 1992, William Alan Blair, review of *Jefferson Davis and His Generals,* p. 156.

New York Times, January 28, 1996, Chris Patsilelis, review of *Davis and Lee at War.*

Publishers Weekly, September 25, 1995, review of *Davis and Lee at War,* p. 37; July 23, 2001, review of *While God Is Marching On,* p. 74; January 21, 2002, review of *A Scythe of Fire,* p. 75; September 5, 2005, review of *Nothing but Victory,* p. 46.

Reference & Research Book News, May 1, 2008, review of *Decision in the Heartland: The Civil War in the West;* August 1, 2008, review of *Beneath a Northern Sky;* November 1, 2008, review of *American Civil War.*

Reference & User Services Quarterly, summer, 1998, Hope Yelich, review of *The American Civil War,* p. 307; March 22, 2009, Jamie Seeholzer, review of *American Civil War,* p. 303.

Reviews in American History, March, 1994, Brooks D. Simpson, review of *Jefferson Davis and His Generals,* p. 73.

School Library Journal, June, 2005, Patricia Ann Owens, review of *Oxford Atlas of the Civil War,* p. 94; October, 2005, review of *Oxford Atlas of the Civil War,* p. S68.

Teaching History: A Journal of Methods, spring, 2004, Michael E. Long, review of *The Loyal, True, and Brave,* p. 53.*

ONLINE

History Department, Texas Christian University Web site, http://www.his.tcu.edu/ (June 30, 2009), author profile.

H-Net Reviews, http://www.h-net.org/ (June 30, 2009), Jeffrey C. Hall, review of *Beneath a Northern Sky.**

*   *   *

WOODWORTH, Steven Edward
See WOODWORTH, Steven E.

Y

YELLIN, Tamar 1963-

PERSONAL: Born 1963, in Leeds, England; married Bob Tasker. *Education:* Graduated from Oxford University.

ADDRESSES: Home—Yorkshire, England. *E-mail*—tamar@tamaryellin.com.

CAREER: Writer. Worked variously as a supermarket clerk, primary school teacher, college lecturer in Judaism, and Jewish faith advisor to schools.

AWARDS, HONORS: Pusey and Ellerton Prize for Biblical Hebrew, Oxford University; Sami Rohr Prize and Ribalow Prize, both for *The Genizah at the House of Shepher;* Reform Judaism Prize for *Kafka in Brontëland and Other Stories.*

WRITINGS:

The Genizah at the House of Shepher (novel), Toby Press (New York, NY), 2005.
Kafka in Brontëland and Other Stories, Toby Press (New Milford, CT), 2006.
Tales of the Ten Lost Tribes (short stories), St. Martin's Griffin (New York, NY), 2009.

Contributor to periodicals, including *London, Stand, Jewish Quarterly, Panurge, Writing Women, Metropolitan, Leviathan Quarterly, Iron, Third Alternative, Big Issue, Staple,* and *Nemonymous.* Contributor to anthologies, including *Slow Mirror and Other Stories: New Fiction by Jewish Writers,* edited by Sonja Lyndon and Sylvia Paskin, Five Leaves (Nottingham, England), 1996; *Leviathan 3,* edited by Jeff Vandermeer, Prime Books (Holicong, PA), 2002; *Mordecai's First Brush with Love: New Stories by Jewish Women in Britain,* edited by Laura Phillips and Marion Baraitser, Loki Press (London, England), 2004; and *Best Short Stories.*

SIDELIGHTS: Author Tamar Yellin studied Hebrew at Oxford University and began publishing short stories in respected literary journals at age thirty. Her first novel, however, was fifteen years in the making. The story behind *The Genizah at the House of Shepher* began in 1987, when Yellin, then age twenty-four, traveled from her native England to her grandparents' Jerusalem home for a final visit before the building's scheduled demolition. Hidden in the attic among an impressive collection of historical papers was a notebook, missing since 1915, that proved to be of vital importance in recreating an ancient Biblical text lost in a 1947 fire. Yellin soon began work on a fictional narrative based on nearly 150 years of her family's history, a project that took until 2005 to complete and publish. In an interview with *Yorkshire Post Today* reporter Sheena Hastings, Yellin remarked: "I wish the book hadn't taken up so much of my life, but nor was I ever going to give up on it."

In a review for *Booklist,* Debi Lewis called Yellin's debut novel "impossible to put down," adding that the book's story is infused with "beauty, deep love, and a timelessness that will likely make it a classic." A contributor to *Publishers Weekly* called the work "warm and engrossing, rich with historical detail and unmet yearning." *Library Journal* reviewer Molly Abramowitz remarked, "Filled with myth, mystery, and history, this novel gives the flavor of Jerusalem neighborhoods through the modern era." A *Kirkus Reviews* contributor described the book as "a warmly portrayed, densely researched fictional history of a scattered Jewish clan migrated to Jerusalem" and "a fascinating, labyrinthine journey."

Kafka in Brontëland and Other Stories, Yellin's first short story collection, continued the award-winning pattern established by her first novel; the volume received the Reform Judaism Prize, was longlisted for the Frank O'Connor International Short Story Award, and was a finalist for the Edge Hill Prize. "*Kafka in Brontëland and Other Stories* is a collection of thirteen pieces that address the universal themes of identity and displacement, belonging and not belonging, through the lens of contemporary Jewish experience," explained a contributor to the Union for Reform Judaism Web site, continuing, "the stories are informed by Yellin's own experience growing up in the North of England."

Yellin confided to interviewer Zoran Zivkovic that the Brontë sisters—also residents of the north of England—were a primary influence on her work. "I was a very strange young writer: I hardly read at all," she explained. "Until the age of about fifteen, though I wrote prolifically, it was only with the greatest of effort that I could be induced to read a book." "However, there was one significant exception to the rule," she told Zivkovic: "I would read anything by or about the Brontë sisters. So I can honestly say that almost my whole literary education, at that crucial early stage, was conducted by the Brontës and their biographers. Fortunately, they were good teachers. I acquired an extremely wide vocabulary just from reading their books."

Although *Kafka in Brontëland and Other Stories* was published after *The Genizah at the House of Shepher,* some of the stories in it date from before Yellin completed the novel. "The stories in *Kafka,*" the author stated in an interview with Vanda Ivanovic published on the *Infinity Plus* Web site, "were written over a long period of time—the earliest in 1989 and the most recent only two or three years ago, during which I must have produced several dozen others, both published and unpublished. I was never in much doubt as to which to select for the collection, though. They were those which I felt able to shape into a kind of narrative arc, running from childhood through maturity and into old age, and

a thematic arc touching on those ever-present questions of identity, exile and belonging." "Roughly speaking," she explained in an interview in the *Short Review* Web site, "the stories follow a progression from childhood to adulthood and old age. From home and out into the world. The second, title story, and the last, act as a sort of frame—both refer to Kafka but in very different ways."

Yellin's second short story collection, *Tales of the Ten Lost Tribes,* "is about lost people living among us," wrote *Bookslut* contributor Sarah Burke, "and once again Yellin examines the place of an individual in the world. Certain images recur from *Genizah:* a solitary woman who lives in a room at the top of a tall house, an old man who carries a small radio with him from room to room so that he never misses any news. Books recur as powerful objects as well: one story examines an antiquarian book-dealer and his relationship with the narrator's father, who can never find the perfect book that will end his feverish collecting." "The narrator encounters all kinds of people in these fictional stories, each involving some kind of traveling or journeying. And each story ends with an unsettled feeling, a bizarre open-endedness, leaving the reader with questions, and a thirst to find some answers," declared Temima Shulman in *Intermountain Jewish News Online.* "But even if one can find contentment in any of the short stories' endings, Yellin makes sure to introduce the next tribe, or story, by quoting passages from anthropological works, or the Torah, forcing the enigma of identity to settle permanently in the reader's mind." In a *Library Journal* review, Abramowitz wrote that "Yellin brilliantly captures mood in time and place; her stories are true gems." "Each mournful, startling portrait," concluded a *Publishers Weekly* reviewer, "proves that award-winning Yellin . . . is a stylist to watch."

BIOGRAPHICAL AND CRITICAL SOURCES:

PERIODICALS

Booklist, March 1, 2005, Debi Lewis, review of *The Genizah at the House of Shepher,* p. 1143; February 1, 2006, Regina Schroeder, review of *Kafka in Brontëland and Other Stories,* p. 32.

Guardian (London, England), April 22, 2006, Stevie Davies, "Jerusalem Comes to Yorkshire," review of *Kafka in Brontëland and Other Stories.*

Kirkus Reviews, January 15, 2005, review of *The Genizah at the House of Shepher,* p. 82.

Library Journal, March 1, 2005, Molly Abramowitz, review of *The Genizah at the House of Shepher,* p. 81; March 15, 2006, Leora Bersohn, review of *Kafka in Brontëland and Other Stories,* p. 67; September 1, 2008, Abramowitz, review of *Tales of the Ten Lost Tribes,* p. 124.

Publishers Weekly, February 7, 2005, review of *The Genizah at the House of Shepher,* p. 38; June 30, 2008, review of *Tales of the Ten Lost Tribes,* p. 160.

ONLINE

Bella Online, http://www.bellaonline.com/ (June 30, 2009), M.E. Wood, "Tamar Yellin—Author Interview."

Bookslut, http://www.bookslut.com/ (June 30, 2009), Sarah Burke, "Identity Crisis: Tamar Yellin's Tales of the Ten Lost Tribes."

Fantastic Metropolis, http://www.fantasticmetropolis. com/ (June 30, 2009), author interview.

HorrorScope, http://ozhorrorscope.blogspot.com/ (June 30, 2009), review of *Kafka in Brontëland and Other Stories.*

Infinity Plus, http://www.infinityplus.co.uk/ (June 20, 2009), Vanda Ivanovic, "An Interview with Tamar Yellin."

Intermountain Jewish News Online (Denver, CO), http://www.ijn.com/ (June 30, 2009), Temima Shulman, "A Question of Identity: A Tribal Lens," review of *Tales of the Ten Lost Tribes.*

Jewish Week (New York, NY), http://www.thejewish week.com/ (June 30, 2009), Sandee Brawarsky, "Wandering Jews," review of *Tales of the Ten Lost Tribes.*

Short Review, http://www.theshortreview.com/ (June 30, 2009), author interview; Tania Hershman, review of *Kafka in Brontëland and Other Stories.*

Strange Horizons, http://www.strangehorizons.com/ (June 30, 2009), Paul Kincaid, review of *Kafka in Brontëland and Other Stories.*

Tamar Yellin Home Page, http://www.tamaryellin.com (June 30, 2009), author profile; Zoran Zivkovic, author interview.

Union for Reform Judaism Web site, http://urj.org/ (June 30, 2009), "Tamar Yellin Wins Reform Judaism Prize for Jewish Fiction."

Yorkshire Post Today Online, http://www.yorkshire today.co.uk/ (May 4, 2005), Sheena Hastings, "A Secret in the Attic and a Mystery That Spans the Years," review of *The Genizah at the House of Shepher.*

Zeek, http://www.zeek.net/ (June 30, 2009), Dan Friedman, "A World Written: In Conversation with Tamar Yellin."*

*   *   *

YORK, Alissa 1970-

PERSONAL: Born 1970, in Athabasca, Alberta, Canada; daughter of a high-school English teacher and an elementary school teacher; married Clive Holden (a writer and filmmaker). *Education:* Attended McGill University.

ADDRESSES: Home—Toronto, Ontario, Canada. *Agent*—Denise Bukowski, The Bukowski Agency, 14 Prince Arthur Ave., Ste. 202, Toronto, Ontario M5R 1A9, Canada. *E-mail*—mail@alissayork.com.

CAREER: Short story writer and novelist.

AWARDS, HONORS: Bronwen Wallace Award, 1997, for "Stitches"; Journey Prize, 1999, for "The Back of the Bear's Mouth"; Mary Scorer Award for Best Book by a Manitoba Publisher, 2000, for *Any Given Power*; John Hirsch Award for Most Promising Manitoba Writer, 2001; Giller Prize shortlist, for *Effigy.*

WRITINGS:

Any Given Power (short stories), Arbeiter Ring Publishing (Winnipeg, Manitoba, Canada), 1999.

Mercy (novel), Random House Canada (Toronto, Ontario, Canada), 2003.

Effigy (novel), Thomas Dunne Books (New York, NY), 2008.

SIDELIGHTS: Award-winning short-story writer Alissa York received acclaim for her first story collection, *Any Given Power,* in which families struggle with poverty and racism in small towns and cities across Canada.

One story in particular, "The Back of the Bear's Mouth," has received numerous awards for promising Canadian fiction. Writing in the *Vancouver Sun,* Robert Wiersema found the collection as a whole "an overlooked gem, a powerful, exciting collection beloved by critics (and by those readers fortunate enough to discover it)."

A few years later, York followed up with a full-length novel, *Mercy.* "Lust and sin grapple with religious piety in this moving, occasionally overwrought novel," wrote a *Publishers Weekly* reviewer. The story opens with a young priest, August Day, traveling to the isolated community of Mercy, Manitoba, Canada, in 1948. Brought in to assist the aged parish priest, Father August discovers on his arrival that the old priest has died, and almost immediately he has to preside over a wedding. Inconvenience gradually turns into disaster after the inexperienced priest beholds the beautiful, lively bride, Matilda. When Matilda comes to confess that she lied to her good-natured but dull husband on their wedding night in order to avoid sleeping with him, Father August finds himself overwhelmed with lust. The two engage in a brief, furtive fling, but guilt drives them apart. Unfortunately, Matilda is pregnant by then, which sets the scene for a tragic climax on the edge of town. As a *Kirkus Reviews* contributor noted that "the fallen priest is an old story, but newcomer York's searing images mark her as a talent to watch."

The novel's second part, set over fifty years later, describes generations blighted by Matilda and Father Day's guilty secret. This section of the novel centers on Mary, their daughter, who was adopted by a visionary hermit who plays a key role in the previous events. Living in her father's hut on the bog at the edge of town, Mary has a strange encounter with another clergyman, an evangelical preacher who has none of Father August's embarrassment or regret about his lusts and his conquests. He has come to pave over the bog itself, and the two find themselves in a curious war of wills between logic and guilt-free impulses and the allure of darker mysteries. "As much as I admired the last third of this book and its lecherous priest trapped in the shack of a bog-woman whose swamp he aims to pave over, I couldn't help but feel that I was in a different novel," commented *This* magazine contributor Hal Niedzviecki. More favorably, *Library Journal* contributor Eleanor J. Bader found the events in this section "poignantly rendered." Wiersema dubbed the novel, as a whole,

"compulsively readable, a triumph of York's storytelling prowess," adding: "It would be an impressive novel from an established author; from a debut novelist, it is a small miracle, graceful and unflinching, violent and beautiful, heartfelt and haunting."

In *Effigy,* York takes up the historical story of the 1857 attack on a group of migrants passing through Utah territory on its way to California. "The incident," wrote a reviewer for the *Prairie Mary* Web site, "involves Indians and Mormons disguised as Indians attacking an emigrant wagon trail, murdering all but the small children, and looting the belongings." The Mormons held the group, which included many people from Arkansas, responsible for the murder of one of their number in that state. York's story, however, "is not a history story (that's been done): rather it is a reflection, a flight of fancy, and an occasion for poetic language describing intense scenes," explained the *Prairie Mary* reviewer. "The central character is a little girl who is rescued (though the rescue is not a particularly benign one in such a harsh world) and who grows up to be a taxidermist, thus producing the 'effigies' of the title."

Ten years after the massacre, Dorrie (only fourteen years old) has become the fourth wife of Erastus Hammer, "a nasty piece of work," according to Cherie Thiessen, writing in *January,* "and although he did not participate in that slaughter, it's clear that he would not have hesitated had he been invited to the bloodbath. He has unhesitatingly and sanctimoniously killed others, and the enjoyment he gets out of squandering so many hours in the killing of animals and in the taking of trophies . . . shows his brutal streak." The tension spreads throughout his family, including the senior wife Ursula (who runs the household and raises the children), Ruth (who bears children but is more interested in the silkworms she cultivates), Thankful (a former actress who entertains Erastus with sex games), and Lal, Ursula's only child, who at nineteen is rapidly becoming frustrated with his subordinate role in the household. "*Effigy* is written in convincing, image-rich prose," Jenny Shank wrote in the *New West,* "and features a singular cast of characters who interact in complex and surprising ways." "At its core," declared Gwen Dawson in *Literary License,* "*Effigy* explores the link between actions and their consequences, hinting at a greater power that metes out deserved outcomes based on prior decisions." *Ampersand* reviewer Mark Medley commented that "the rhythm York creates in her writing captures perfectly the rhythm of life as one might imagine it to be on an 1857 Mormon Ranch in Utah." "*Effigy* fulfills John Gardner's prescription that a great work of fiction should be like a 'vivid and continuous dream,'" Shank wrote, continuing: "Besides telling a great story, *Effigy* is doubly satisfying for those with an interest in the pioneer history of the Western United States, which York animates with surpassing skill." In a *Library Journal* review, Christine DeZelar-Tiedman concluded: "This is historical fiction at its best."

BIOGRAPHICAL AND CRITICAL SOURCES:

PERIODICALS

Booklist, September 15, 2004, Misha Stone, review of *Mercy*, p. 211; September 1, 2008, Michael Cart, review of *Effigy*, p. 44.

Chatelaine, March, 2003, Bonnie Schiedel, review of *Mercy*, p. 24.

Herizons, winter, 2004, Cheryl Gudz, review of *Mercy*, p. 33.

Kirkus Review, August 15, 2004, review of *Mercy*, p. 777.

Library Journal, September 1, 2004, Eleanor J. Bader, review of *Mercy*, p. 144; September 1, 2008, Christine DeZelar-Tiedman, review of *Effigy*, p. 124.

Publishers Weekly, October 4, 2004, review of *Mercy*, p. 67; July 14, 2008, review of *Effigy*, p. 44.

Quill & Quire, April, 2007, Maureen Garvie, review of *Effigy*.

This, July-August, 2003, Hal Niedzviecki, review of *Mercy*, p. 14.

Vancouver Sun, February 1, 2003, Robert Wiersema, "The Quality of Mercy," review of *Mercy*.

ONLINE

Alissa York Home Page, http://www.alissayork.com (June 30, 2009).

Ampersand, http://network.nationalpost.com/ (June 30, 2009), Mark Medley, review of *Effigy*.

BookLounge, http://www.booklounge.ca/ (June 30, 2009), author profile.

January, http://www.januarymagazine.com/ (June 30, 2009), Cherie Thiessen, review of *Effigy*.

Literary License, http://litlicense.blogspot.com/ (June 30, 2009), Gwen Dawson, review of *Effigy*.

New West, http://www.newwest.net/ (June 30, 2009), Jenny Shank, "Mormons & Taxidermy: Alissa York's 'Effigy.'"

Now (Toronto, Ontario, Canada), http://www.nowtoronto.com/ (June 30, 2009), Susan G. Cole, "Effigy Burns," review of *Effigy*.

Prairie Mary, http://prairiemary.blogspot.com/ (June 30, 2009), review of *Effigy*.*